Alternative Dispute Resolution

KANOWITZ' CASES AND MATERIALS ON ALTERNATIVE DISPUTE RESOLUTION, 1024 pages, 1986. Teacher's Manual available. (Casebook) 1990 Supplement.

RISKIN AND WESTBROOK'S DISPUTE RESOLUTION AND LAWYERS, 468 pages, 1987. Teacher's Manual available. (Casebook)

RISKIN AND WESTBROOK'S DISPUTE RESOLUTION AND LAWYERS, Abridged Edition, 223 pages, 1987. Softcover. Teacher's Manual available. (Casebook)

American Indian Law

CANBY'S AMERICAN INDIAN LAW IN A NUTSHELL, Second Edition, 336 pages, 1988. Softcover. (Text)

GETCHES AND WILKINSON'S CASES AND MATERIALS ON FEDERAL INDIAN LAW, Second Edition, 880 pages, 1986. (Casebook)

Antitrust—see also Regulated Industries, Trade Regulation

FOX AND SULLIVAN'S CASES AND MATERIALS ON ANTITRUST, 935 pages, 1989. Teacher's Manual available. (Casebook)

GELLHORN'S ANTITRUST LAW AND ECONOMICS IN A NUTSHELL, Third Edition, 472 pages, 1986. Softcover. (Text)

HOVENKAMP'S BLACK LETTER ON ANTITRUST, 323 pages, 1986. Softcover. (Review)

HOVENKAMP'S HORNBOOK ON ECONOMICS AND FEDERAL ANTITRUST LAW, Student Edition, 414 pages, 1985. (Text)

OPPENHEIM, WESTON AND MCCARTHY'S CASES AND COMMENTS ON FEDERAL ANTITRUST LAWS, Fourth Edition, 1168 pages, 1981. (Casebook) 1985 Supplement.

POSNER AND EASTERBROOK'S CASES AND ECONOMIC NOTES ON ANTITRUST, Second Edition, 1077 pages, 1981. (Casebook) 1984–85 Supplement.

SULLIVAN'S HORNBOOK OF THE LAW OF ANTITRUST, 886 pages, 1977. (Text)

Appellate Advocacy—see Trial and Appellate Advocacy

Architecture and Engineering Law

SWEET'S LEGAL ASPECTS OF ARCHITECTURE, ENGINEERING AND THE CONSTRUCTION PROCESS, Fourth Edition, 889 pages, 1989. Teacher's Manual available. (Casebook)

Art Law

DUBOFF'S ART LAW IN A NUTSHELL, 335 pages, 1984. Softcover. (Text)

Banking Law

BANKING LAW: SELECTED STATUTES AND REGULATIONS. Softcover. Approximately 265 pages, 1991.

LOVETT'S BANKING AND FINANCIAL INSTITUTIONS LAW IN A NUTSHELL, Second Edition, 464 pages, 1988. Softcover. (Text)

SYMONS AND WHITE'S BANKING LAW: TEACHING MATERIALS, Third Edition, approximately 775 pages, 1991. Teacher's Manual available. (Casebook)

  Statutory Supplement. *See Banking Law: Selected Statutes*

Business Planning—see also Corporate Finance

PAINTER'S PROBLEMS AND MATERIALS IN BUSINESS PLANNING, Second Edition, 1008 pages, 1984. (Casebook) 1990 Supplement.

  Statutory Supplement. *See Selected Corporation and Partnership*

Civil Procedure—see also Federal Jurisdiction and Procedure

AMERICAN BAR ASSOCIATION SECTION OF LITIGATION—READINGS ON ADVERSARIAL JUSTICE: THE AMERICAN APPROACH TO ADJUDICATION, 217 pages, 1988. Softcover. (Coursebook)

CLERMONT'S BLACK LETTER ON CIVIL PROCEDURE, Second Edition, 332 pages, 1988. Softcover. (Review)

COUND, FRIEDENTHAL, MILLER AND SEXTON'S CASES AND MATERIALS ON CIVIL PROCEDURE, Fifth Edition, 1284 pages, 1989. Teacher's Manual available. (Casebook)

COUND, FRIEDENTHAL, MILLER AND SEXTON'S CIVIL PROCEDURE SUPPLEMENT. 460 pages, 1990. Softcover. (Casebook Supplement)

FEDERAL RULES OF CIVIL PROCEDURE—EDUCATIONAL EDITION. Softcover. 632 pages, 1990.

FRIEDENTHAL, KANE AND MILLER'S HORNBOOK ON CIVIL PROCEDURE, 876 pages, 1985.

American Casebook Series
Hornbook Series and Basic Legal Texts
Black Letter Series and Nutshell Series

of

WEST PUBLISHING COMPANY
P.O. Box 64526
St. Paul, Minnesota 55164–0526

Accounting

FARIS' ACCOUNTING AND LAW IN A NUTSHELL, 377 pages, 1984. Softcover. (Text)

FIFLIS' ACCOUNTING ISSUES FOR LAWYERS, TEACHING MATERIALS, , approximately 750 pages, July, 1991 Pub. (Casebook)

SIEGEL AND SIEGEL'S ACCOUNTING AND FINANCIAL DISCLOSURE: A GUIDE TO BASIC CONCEPTS, 259 pages, 1983. Softcover. (Text)

Administrative Law

BONFIELD AND ASIMOW'S STATE AND FEDERAL ADMINISTRATIVE LAW, 826 pages, 1989. Teacher's Manual available. (Casebook)

GELLHORN AND LEVIN'S ADMINISTRATIVE LAW AND PROCESS IN A NUTSHELL, Third Edition, 479 pages, 1990. Softcover. (Text)

MASHAW AND MERRILL'S CASES AND MATERIALS ON ADMINISTRATIVE LAW—THE AMERICAN PUBLIC LAW SYSTEM, Second Edition, 976 pages, 1985. (Casebook) 1989 Supplement.

ROBINSON, GELLHORN AND BRUFF'S THE ADMINISTRATIVE PROCESS, Third Edition, 978 pages, 1986. (Casebook)

Admiralty

HEALY AND SHARPE'S CASES AND MATERIALS ON ADMIRALTY, Second Edition, 876 pages, 1986. (Casebook)

MARAIST'S ADMIRALTY IN A NUTSHELL, Second Edition, 379 pages, 1988. Softcover. (Text)

SCHOENBAUM'S HORNBOOK ON ADMIRALTY AND MARITIME LAW, Student Edition, 692 pages, 1987 with 1989 pocket part. (Text)

Agency—Partnership

DEMOTT'S FIDUCIARY OBLIGATION, AGENCY AND PARTNERSHIP: DUTIES IN ONGOING BUSINESS RELATIONSHIPS, 740 pages, 1991. Teacher's Manual available. (Casebook)

FESSLER'S ALTERNATIVES TO INCORPORATION FOR PERSONS IN QUEST OF PROFIT, Third Edition, approximately 340 pages, 1991. Softcover. Teacher's Manual available. (Casebook)

HENN'S CASES AND MATERIALS ON AGENCY, PARTNERSHIP AND OTHER UNINCORPORATED BUSINESS ENTERPRISES, Second Edition, 733 pages, 1985. Teacher's Manual available. (Casebook)

REUSCHLEIN AND GREGORY'S HORNBOOK ON THE LAW OF AGENCY AND PARTNERSHIP, Second Edition, 683 pages, 1990. (Text)

SELECTED CORPORATION AND PARTNERSHIP STATUTES, RULES AND FORMS. Softcover. 727 pages, 1989.

STEFFEN AND KERR'S CASES ON AGENCY-PARTNERSHIP, Fourth Edition, 859 pages, 1980. (Casebook)

STEFFEN'S AGENCY-PARTNERSHIP IN A NUTSHELL, 364 pages, 1977. Softcover. (Text)

Agricultural Law

MEYER, PEDERSEN, THORSON AND DAVIDSON'S AGRICULTURAL LAW: CASES AND MATERIALS, 931 pages, 1985. Teacher's Manual available. (Casebook)

List current as of March, 1991

Civil Procedure—Cont'd
(Text)

KANE AND LEVINE'S CIVIL PROCEDURE IN CALIFORNIA: STATE AND FEDERAL Approximately 600 pages, July, 1991 Pub. Softcover. (Casebook Supplement)

KANE'S CIVIL PROCEDURE IN A NUTSHELL, Third Edition, approximately 290 pages, 1991. Softcover. (Text)

KOFFLER AND REPPY'S HORNBOOK ON COMMON LAW PLEADING, 663 pages, 1969. (Text)

LEVINE, SLOMANSON AND WINGATE'S CALIFORNIA CIVIL PROCEDURE, CASES AND MATERIALS, . Approximately 550 pages, June, 1991 Pub. (Casebook)

MARCUS, REDISH AND SHERMAN'S CIVIL PROCEDURE: A MODERN APPROACH, 1027 pages, 1989. Teacher's Manual available. (Casebook)

MARCUS AND SHERMAN'S COMPLEX LITIGATION–CASES AND MATERIALS ON ADVANCED CIVIL PROCEDURE, 846 pages, 1985. Teacher's Manual available. (Casebook) 1989 Supplement.

PARK AND MCFARLAND'S COMPUTER-AIDED EXERCISES ON CIVIL PROCEDURE, Third Edition, approximately 300 pages, July, 1991 Pub. Softcover. (Coursebook)

SIEGEL'S HORNBOOK ON NEW YORK PRACTICE, Second Edition, Student Edition, 1068 pages, 1991. Softcover. (Text)

Commercial Law

BAILEY AND HAGEDORN'S SECURED TRANSACTIONS IN A NUTSHELL, Third Edition, 390 pages, 1988. Softcover. (Text)

EPSTEIN, MARTIN, HENNING AND NICKLES' BASIC UNIFORM COMMERCIAL CODE TEACHING MATERIALS, Third Edition, 704 pages, 1988. Teacher's Manual available. (Casebook)

HENSON'S HORNBOOK ON SECURED TRANSACTIONS UNDER THE U.C.C., Second Edition, 504 pages, 1979, with 1979 pocket part. (Text)

MURRAY'S COMMERCIAL LAW, PROBLEMS AND MATERIALS, 366 pages, 1975. Teacher's Manual available. Softcover. (Coursebook)

NICKLES' BLACK LETTER ON COMMERCIAL PAPER, 450 pages, 1988. Softcover. (Review)

NICKLES, MATHESON AND DOLAN'S MATERIALS FOR UNDERSTANDING CREDIT AND PAYMENT SYSTEMS, 923 pages, 1987. Teacher's Manual available. (Casebook)

NORDSTROM, MURRAY AND CLOVIS' PROBLEMS AND MATERIALS ON SALES, 515 pages, 1982. (Casebook)

NORDSTROM, MURRAY AND CLOVIS' PROBLEMS AND MATERIALS ON SECURED TRANSACTIONS, 594 pages, 1987. (Casebook)

RUBIN AND COOTER'S THE PAYMENT SYSTEM: CASES, MATERIALS AND ISSUES, 885 pages, 1989. Teacher's Manual Available. (Casebook)

SELECTED COMMERCIAL STATUTES. Softcover. 1776 pages, 1990.

SPEIDEL'S BLACK LETTER ON SALES AND SALES FINANCING, 363 pages, 1984. Softcover. (Review)

SPEIDEL, SUMMERS AND WHITE'S COMMERCIAL LAW: TEACHING MATERIALS, Fourth Edition, 1448 pages, 1987. Teacher's Manual available. (Casebook)

SPEIDEL, SUMMERS AND WHITE'S COMMERCIAL PAPER: TEACHING MATERIALS, Fourth Edition, 578 pages, 1987. Reprint from Speidel et al., Commercial Law, Fourth Edition. Teacher's Manual available. (Casebook)

SPEIDEL, SUMMERS AND WHITE'S SALES: TEACHING MATERIALS, Fourth Edition, 804 pages, 1987. Reprint from Speidel et al., Commercial Law, Fourth Edition. Teacher's Manual available. (Casebook)

SPEIDEL, SUMMERS AND WHITE'S SECURED TRANSACTIONS: TEACHING MATERIALS, Fourth Edition, 485 pages, 1987. Reprint from Speidel et al., Commercial Law, Fourth Edition. Teacher's Manual available. (Casebook)

STOCKTON'S SALES IN A NUTSHELL, Second Edition, 370 pages, 1981. Softcover. (Text)

STONE'S UNIFORM COMMERCIAL CODE IN A NUTSHELL, Third Edition, 580 pages, 1989. Softcover. (Text)

WEBER AND SPEIDEL'S COMMERCIAL PAPER IN

Commercial Law—Cont'd

A NUTSHELL, Third Edition, 404 pages, 1982. Softcover. (Text)

WHITE AND SUMMERS' HORNBOOK ON THE UNIFORM COMMERCIAL CODE, Third Edition, Student Edition, 1386 pages, 1988. (Text)

Community Property

MENNELL AND BOYKOFF'S COMMUNITY PROPERTY IN A NUTSHELL, Second Edition, 432 pages, 1988. Softcover. (Text)

VERRALL AND BIRD'S CASES AND MATERIALS ON CALIFORNIA COMMUNITY PROPERTY, Fifth Edition, 604 pages, 1988. (Casebook)

Comparative Law

BARTON, GIBBS, LI AND MERRYMAN'S LAW IN RADICALLY DIFFERENT CULTURES, 960 pages, 1983. (Casebook)

GLENDON, GORDON AND OSAKWE'S COMPARATIVE LEGAL TRADITIONS: TEXT, MATERIALS AND CASES ON THE CIVIL LAW, COMMON LAW AND SOCIALIST LAW TRADITIONS, 1091 pages, 1985. (Casebook)

GLENDON, GORDON AND OSAKWE'S COMPARATIVE LEGAL TRADITIONS IN A NUTSHELL. 402 pages, 1982. Softcover. (Text)

LANGBEIN'S COMPARATIVE CRIMINAL PROCEDURE: GERMANY, 172 pages, 1977. Softcover. (Casebook)

Computers and Law

MAGGS AND SPROWL'S COMPUTER APPLICATIONS IN THE LAW, 316 pages, 1987. (Coursebook)

MASON'S USING COMPUTERS IN THE LAW: AN INTRODUCTION AND PRACTICAL GUIDE, Second Edition, 288 pages, 1988. Softcover. (Coursebook)

Conflict of Laws

CRAMTON, CURRIE AND KAY'S CASES–COMMENTS–QUESTIONS ON CONFLICT OF LAWS, Fourth Edition, 876 pages, 1987. (Casebook)

HAY'S BLACK LETTER ON CONFLICT OF LAWS, 330 pages, 1989. Softcover. (Review)

SCOLES AND HAY'S HORNBOOK ON CONFLICT OF LAWS, Student Edition, 1085 pages, 1982, with 1988–89 pocket part. (Text)

SIEGEL'S CONFLICTS IN A NUTSHELL, 470 pages, 1982. Softcover. (Text)

Constitutional Law—Civil Rights—see also First Amendment and Foreign Relations and National Security Law

ABERNATHY'S CASES AND MATERIALS ON CIVIL RIGHTS, 660 pages, 1980. (Casebook)

BARRON AND DIENES' BLACK LETTER ON CONSTITUTIONAL LAW, Third Edition, approximately 400 pages, 1991. Softcover. (Review)

BARRON AND DIENES' CONSTITUTIONAL LAW IN A NUTSHELL, Second Edition, approximately 475 pages, 1991. Softcover. (Text)

ENGDAHL'S CONSTITUTIONAL FEDERALISM IN A NUTSHELL, Second Edition, 411 pages, 1987. Softcover. (Text)

FARBER AND SHERRY'S HISTORY OF THE AMERICAN CONSTITUTION, 458 pages, 1990. Softcover. Teacher's Manual available. (Text)

GARVEY AND ALEINIKOFF'S MODERN CONSTITUTIONAL THEORY: A READER, Second Edition, approximately 575 pages, August, 1991 Pub. Softcover. (Reader)

LOCKHART, KAMISAR, CHOPER AND SHIFFRIN'S CONSTITUTIONAL LAW: CASES–COMMENTS–QUESTIONS, Seventh Edition, approximately 1600 pages, 1991. (Casebook) 1991 Supplement.

LOCKHART, KAMISAR, CHOPER AND SHIFFRIN'S THE AMERICAN CONSTITUTION: CASES AND MATERIALS, Seventh Edition, approximately 1250 pages, September, 1991 Pub. Abridged version of Lockhart, et al., Constitutional Law: Cases–Comments–Questions, Seventh Edition. (Casebook) 1991 Supplement.

LOCKHART, KAMISAR, CHOPER AND SHIFFRIN'S CONSTITUTIONAL RIGHTS AND LIBERTIES: CASES AND MATERIALS, Seventh Edition, approximately 1250 pages, September, 1991 Pub. Reprint from Lockhart, et al., Constitutional Law: Cases–Comments–Questions, Seventh Edition. (Casebook) 1991 Supplement.

MARKS AND COOPER'S STATE CONSTITUTIONAL LAW IN A NUTSHELL, 329 pages, 1988. Softcover. (Text)

NOWAK AND ROTUNDA'S HORNBOOK ON CON-

Constitutional Law—Civil Rights—Cont'd

STITUTIONAL LAW, Fourth Edition, approximately 1200 pages, August, 1991 Pub. (Text)

ROTUNDA'S MODERN CONSTITUTIONAL LAW: CASES AND NOTES, Third Edition, 1085 pages, 1989. (Casebook) 1990 Supplement.

VIEIRA'S CONSTITUTIONAL CIVIL RIGHTS IN A NUTSHELL, Second Edition, 322 pages, 1990. Softcover. (Text)

WILLIAMS' CONSTITUTIONAL ANALYSIS IN A NUTSHELL, 388 pages, 1979. Softcover. (Text)

Consumer Law—see also Commercial Law

EPSTEIN AND NICKLES' CONSUMER LAW IN A NUTSHELL, Second Edition, 418 pages, 1981. Softcover. (Text)

SELECTED COMMERCIAL STATUTES. Softcover. 1776 pages, 1990.

SPANOGLE, ROHNER, PRIDGEN AND RASOR'S CASES AND MATERIALS ON CONSUMER LAW, Second Edition, approximately 900 pages, 1991. (Casebook)

Contracts

CALAMARI AND PERILLO'S BLACK LETTER ON CONTRACTS, Second Edition, 462 pages, 1990. Softcover. (Review)

CALAMARI AND PERILLO'S HORNBOOK ON CONTRACTS, Third Edition, 1049 pages, 1987. (Text)

CALAMARI, PERILLO AND BENDER'S CASES AND PROBLEMS ON CONTRACTS, Second Edition, 905 pages, 1989. Teacher's Manual Available. (Casebook)

CORBIN'S TEXT ON CONTRACTS, One Volume Student Edition, 1224 pages, 1952. (Text)

FESSLER AND LOISEAUX'S CASES AND MATERIALS ON CONTRACTS—MORALITY, ECONOMICS AND THE MARKET PLACE, 837 pages, 1982. Teacher's Manual available. (Casebook)

FRIEDMAN'S CONTRACT REMEDIES IN A NUTSHELL, 323 pages, 1981. Softcover. (Text)

FULLER AND EISENBERG'S CASES ON BASIC CONTRACT LAW, Fifth Edition, 1037 pages, 1990. (Casebook)

HAMILTON, RAU AND WEINTRAUB'S CASES AND MATERIALS ON CONTRACTS, 830 pages, 1984. (Casebook)

JACKSON AND BOLLINGER'S CASES ON CONTRACT LAW IN MODERN SOCIETY, Second Edition, 1329 pages, 1980. Teacher's Manual available. (Casebook)

KEYES' GOVERNMENT CONTRACTS IN A NUTSHELL, Second Edition, 557 pages, 1990. Softcover. (Text)

SCHABER AND ROHWER'S CONTRACTS IN A NUTSHELL, Third Edition, 457 pages, 1990. Softcover. (Text)

SUMMERS AND HILLMAN'S CONTRACT AND RELATED OBLIGATION: THEORY, DOCTRINE AND PRACTICE, 1074 pages, 1987. Teacher's Manual available. (Casebook)

Copyright—see Patent and Copyright Law

Corporate Finance—see also Business Planning

HAMILTON'S CASES AND MATERIALS ON CORPORATION FINANCE, Second Edition, 1221 pages, 1989. (Casebook)

OESTERLE'S THE LAW OF MERGERS, ACQUISITIONS AND REORGANIZATIONS, Approximately 1100 pages, June, 1991 Pub. (Casebook)

Corporations

HAMILTON'S BLACK LETTER ON CORPORATIONS, Second Edition, 513 pages, 1986. Softcover. (Review)

HAMILTON'S CASES AND MATERIALS ON CORPORATIONS—INCLUDING PARTNERSHIPS AND LIMITED PARTNERSHIPS, Fourth Edition, 1248 pages, 1990. Teacher's Manual available. (Casebook) 1990 Statutory Supplement.

HAMILTON'S THE LAW OF CORPORATIONS IN A NUTSHELL, Third Edition, approximately 500 pages, 1991. Softcover. (Text)

HENN'S TEACHING MATERIALS ON THE LAW OF CORPORATIONS, Second Edition, 1204 pages, 1986. Teacher's Manual available. (Casebook)

Statutory Supplement. *See Selected Corporation and Partnership*

HENN AND ALEXANDER'S HORNBOOK ON LAWS OF CORPORATIONS, Third Edition, Student Edition, 1371 pages, 1983, with 1986 pocket part. (Text)

Corporations—Cont'd

SELECTED CORPORATION AND PARTNERSHIP STATUTES, RULES AND FORMS. Softcover. 727 pages, 1989.

SOLOMON, SCHWARTZ AND BAUMAN'S MATERIALS AND PROBLEMS ON CORPORATIONS: LAW AND POLICY, Second Edition, 1391 pages, 1988. Teacher's Manual available. (Casebook) 1990 Supplement.

> Statutory Supplement. *See Selected Corporation and Partnership*

Corrections

KRANTZ' THE LAW OF CORRECTIONS AND PRISONERS' RIGHTS IN A NUTSHELL, Third Edition, 407 pages, 1988. Softcover. (Text)

KRANTZ AND BRANHAM'S CASES AND MATERIALS ON THE LAW OF SENTENCING, CORRECTIONS AND PRISONERS' RIGHTS, Fourth Edition, approximately 625 pages, 1991. (Casebook)

ROBBINS' CASES AND MATERIALS ON POST-CONVICTION REMEDIES, 506 pages, 1982. (Casebook)

Creditors' Rights

BANKRUPTCY CODE, RULES AND OFFICIAL FORMS, LAW SCHOOL EDITION. 909 pages, 1991. Softcover.

EPSTEIN'S DEBTOR-CREDITOR LAW IN A NUTSHELL, Fourth Edition, approximately 400 pages, 1991. Softcover. (Text)

EPSTEIN, LANDERS AND NICKLES' CASES AND MATERIALS ON DEBTORS AND CREDITORS, Third Edition, 1059 pages, 1987. Teacher's Manual available. (Casebook)

LoPUCKI'S PLAYER'S MANUAL FOR THE DEBTOR-CREDITOR GAME, 123 pages, 1985. Softcover. (Coursebook)

NICKLES AND EPSTEIN'S BLACK LETTER ON CREDITORS' RIGHTS AND BANKRUPTCY, 576 pages, 1989. (Review)

RIESENFELD'S CASES AND MATERIALS ON CREDITORS' REMEDIES AND DEBTORS' PROTECTION, Fourth Edition, 914 pages, 1987. (Casebook) 1990 Supplement.

WHITE'S CASES AND MATERIALS ON BANKRUPTCY AND CREDITORS' RIGHTS, 812 pages, 1985. Teacher's Manual available. (Casebook) 1987 Supplement.

Criminal Law and Criminal Procedure—see also Corrections, Juvenile Justice

ABRAMS' FEDERAL CRIMINAL LAW AND ITS ENFORCEMENT, 866 pages, 1986. (Casebook) 1988 Supplement.

AMERICAN CRIMINAL JUSTICE PROCESS: SELECTED RULES, STATUTES AND GUIDELINES. 723 pages, 1989. Softcover.

CARLSON'S ADJUDICATION OF CRIMINAL JUSTICE: PROBLEMS AND REFERENCES, 130 pages, 1986. Softcover. (Casebook)

DIX AND SHARLOT'S CASES AND MATERIALS ON CRIMINAL LAW, Third Edition, 846 pages, 1987. (Casebook)

GRANO'S PROBLEMS IN CRIMINAL PROCEDURE, Second Edition, 176 pages, 1981. Teacher's Manual available. Softcover. (Coursebook)

HEYMANN AND KENETY'S THE MURDER TRIAL OF WILBUR JACKSON: A HOMICIDE IN THE FAMILY, Second Edition, 347 pages, 1985. (Coursebook)

ISRAEL, KAMISAR AND LaFAVE'S CRIMINAL PROCEDURE AND THE CONSTITUTION: LEADING SUPREME COURT CASES AND INTRODUCTORY TEXT. 747 pages, 1990 Edition. Softcover. (Casebook)

ISRAEL AND LaFAVE'S CRIMINAL PROCEDURE—CONSTITUTIONAL LIMITATIONS IN A NUTSHELL, Fourth Edition, 461 pages, 1988. Softcover. (Text)

JOHNSON'S CASES, MATERIALS AND TEXT ON CRIMINAL LAW, Fourth Edition, 759 pages, 1990. Teacher's Manual available. (Casebook)

JOHNSON'S CASES AND MATERIALS ON CRIMINAL PROCEDURE, 859 pages, 1988. (Casebook) 1990 Supplement.

KAMISAR, LaFAVE AND ISRAEL'S MODERN CRIMINAL PROCEDURE: CASES, COMMENTS AND QUESTIONS, Seventh Edition, 1593 pages, 1990. (Casebook) 1990 Supplement.

KAMISAR, LaFAVE AND ISRAEL'S BASIC CRIMINAL PROCEDURE: CASES, COMMENTS AND QUESTIONS, Seventh Edition, 792 pages, 1990. Softcover reprint from Kamisar, et al., Modern Criminal Procedure: Cases, Comments and Questions, Seventh Edi-

Criminal Law and Criminal Procedure—Cont'd

tion. (Casebook) 1990 Supplement.

LaFave's Modern Criminal Law: Cases, Comments and Questions, Second Edition, 903 pages, 1988. (Casebook)

LaFave and Israel's Hornbook on Criminal Procedure, Second Edition, Student Edition, approximately 1200 pages, December, 1991 Pub. (Text)

LaFave and Scott's Hornbook on Criminal Law, Second Edition, 918 pages, 1986. (Text)

Langbein's Comparative Criminal Procedure: Germany, 172 pages, 1977. Softcover. (Casebook)

Loewy's Criminal Law in a Nutshell, Second Edition, 321 pages, 1987. Softcover. (Text)

Low's Black Letter on Criminal Law, Revised First Edition, 443 pages, 1990. Softcover. (Review)

Saltzburg's Cases and Commentary on American Criminal Procedure, Third Edition, 1302 pages, 1988. Teacher's Manual available. (Casebook) 1990 Supplement.

Uviller's The Processes of Criminal Justice: Investigation and Adjudication, Second Edition, 1384 pages, 1979. (Casebook) 1979 Statutory Supplement. 1986 Update.

Vorenberg's Cases on Criminal Law and Procedure, Second Edition, 1088 pages, 1981. Teacher's Manual available. (Casebook) 1990 Supplement.

Decedents' Estates—see Trusts and Estates

Domestic Relations

Clark's Hornbook on Domestic Relations, Second Edition, Student Edition, 1050 pages, 1988. (Text)

Clark and Glowinsky's Cases and Problems on Domestic Relations, Fourth Edition. 1150 pages, 1990. Teacher's Manual available. (Casebook)

Krause's Black Letter on Family Law, 314 pages, 1988. Softcover. (Review)

Krause's Cases, Comments and Questions on Family Law, Third Edition, 1433 pages, 1990. (Casebook)

Krause's Family Law in a Nutshell, Second Edition, 444 pages, 1986. Softcover. (Text)

Krauskopf's Cases on Property Division at Marriage Dissolution, 250 pages, 1984. Softcover. (Casebook)

Economics, Law and—see also Antitrust, Regulated Industries

Goetz' Cases and Materials on Law and Economics, 547 pages, 1984. (Casebook)

Malloy's Law and Economics: A Comparative Approach to Theory and Practice, 166 pages, 1990. Softcover. (Text)

Education Law

Alexander and Alexander's The Law of Schools, Students and Teachers in a Nutshell, 409 pages, 1984. Softcover. (Text)

Yudof, Kirp and Levin's Educational Policy and the Law, Third Edition, approximately 975 pages, April, 1991 Pub. (Casebook)

Employment Discrimination—see also Women and the Law

Estreicher and Harper's Cases and Materials on the Law Governing the Employment Relationship, 962 pages, 1990. Teacher's Manual available. (Casebook) Statutory Supplement.

Jones, Murphy and Belton's Cases and Materials on Discrimination in Employment, (The Labor Law Group). Fifth Edition, 1116 pages, 1987. (Casebook) 1990 Supplement.

Player's Federal Law of Employment Discrimination in a Nutshell, Second Edition, 402 pages, 1981. Softcover. (Text)

Player's Hornbook on Employment Discrimination Law, Student Edition, 708 pages, 1988. (Text)

Player, Shoben and Lieberwitz' Cases and Materials on Employment Discrimination Law, 827 pages, 1990. Teacher's Manual available. (Casebook)

Energy and Natural Resources Law—see also Oil and Gas

Laitos' Cases and Materials on Natural

LAW SCHOOL PUBLICATIONS—Continued

Energy and Natural Resources Law—Cont'd
RESOURCES LAW, 938 pages, 1985. Teacher's Manual available. (Casebook)

SELECTED ENVIRONMENTAL LAW STATUTES—EDUCATIONAL EDITION. Softcover. 1020 pages, 1990.

Environmental Law—see also Energy and Natural Resources Law; Sea, Law of

BONINE AND MCGARITY'S THE LAW OF ENVIRONMENTAL PROTECTION: CASES—LEGISLATION—POLICIES, 1076 pages, 1984. Teacher's Manual available. (Casebook)

FINDLEY AND FARBER'S CASES AND MATERIALS ON ENVIRONMENTAL LAW, Third Edition, approximately 750 pages, 1991. (Casebook)

FINDLEY AND FARBER'S ENVIRONMENTAL LAW IN A NUTSHELL, Second Edition, 367 pages, 1988. Softcover. (Text)

RODGERS' HORNBOOK ON ENVIRONMENTAL LAW, 956 pages, 1977, with 1984 pocket part. (Text)

SELECTED ENVIRONMENTAL LAW STATUTES—EDUCATIONAL EDITION. Softcover. 1020 pages, 1990.

Equity—see Remedies

Estate Planning—see also Trusts and Estates; Taxation—Estate and Gift

LYNN'S AN INTRODUCTION TO ESTATE PLANNING IN A NUTSHELL, Third Edition, 370 pages, 1983. Softcover. (Text)

Evidence

BROUN AND BLAKEY'S BLACK LETTER ON EVIDENCE, 269 pages, 1984. Softcover. (Review)

BROUN, MEISENHOLDER, STRONG AND MOSTELLER'S PROBLEMS IN EVIDENCE, Third Edition, 238 pages, 1988. Teacher's Manual available. Softcover. (Coursebook)

CLEARY, STRONG, BROUN AND MOSTELLER'S CASES AND MATERIALS ON EVIDENCE, Fourth Edition, 1060 pages, 1988. (Casebook)

FEDERAL RULES OF EVIDENCE FOR UNITED STATES COURTS AND MAGISTRATES. Softcover. 381 pages, 1990.

FRIEDMAN'S THE ELEMENTS OF EVIDENCE, 310 pages, 1991. Teacher's Manual available. (Coursebook)

GRAHAM'S FEDERAL RULES OF EVIDENCE IN A NUTSHELL, Second Edition, 473 pages, 1987. Softcover. (Text)

LEMPERT AND SALTZBURG'S A MODERN APPROACH TO EVIDENCE: TEXT, PROBLEMS, TRANSCRIPTS AND CASES, Second Edition, 1232 pages, 1983. Teacher's Manual available. (Casebook)

LILLY'S AN INTRODUCTION TO THE LAW OF EVIDENCE, Second Edition, 585 pages, 1987. (Text)

MCCORMICK, SUTTON AND WELLBORN'S CASES AND MATERIALS ON EVIDENCE, Sixth Edition, 1067 pages, 1987. (Casebook)

MCCORMICK'S HORNBOOK ON EVIDENCE, Third Edition, Student Edition, 1156 pages, 1984, with 1987 pocket part. (Text)

ROTHSTEIN'S EVIDENCE IN A NUTSHELL: STATE AND FEDERAL RULES, Second Edition, 514 pages, 1981. Softcover. (Text)

Federal Jurisdiction and Procedure

CURRIE'S CASES AND MATERIALS ON FEDERAL COURTS, Fourth Edition, 783 pages, 1990. (Casebook)

CURRIE'S FEDERAL JURISDICTION IN A NUTSHELL, Third Edition, 242 pages, 1990. Softcover. (Text)

FEDERAL RULES OF CIVIL PROCEDURE—EDUCATIONAL EDITION. Softcover. 632 pages, 1990.

REDISH'S BLACK LETTER ON FEDERAL JURISDICTION, Second Edition, approximately 230 pages, 1991. Softcover. (Review)

REDISH'S CASES, COMMENTS AND QUESTIONS ON FEDERAL COURTS, Second Edition, 1122 pages, 1989. (Casebook) 1990 Supplement.

VETRI AND MERRILL'S FEDERAL COURTS PROBLEMS AND MATERIALS, Second Edition, 232 pages, 1984. Softcover. (Coursebook)

WRIGHT'S HORNBOOK ON FEDERAL COURTS, Fourth Edition, Student Edition, 870 pages, 1983. (Text)

First Amendment

SHIFFRIN AND CHOPER'S FIRST AMENDMENT, CASES—COMMENTS—QUESTIONS, Approximately 700 pages, 1991. Softcover. (Casebook)

Foreign Relations and National Security Law

FRANCK AND GLENNON'S FOREIGN RELATIONS AND NATIONAL SECURITY LAW, 941 pages, 1987. (Casebook)

Future Interests—see Trusts and Estates

Health Law—see Medicine, Law and

Human Rights—see International Law

Immigration Law

ALEINIKOFF AND MARTIN'S IMMIGRATION: PROCESS AND POLICY, Interim Second Edition, approximately 1075 pages, 1991. (Casebook)

Statutory Supplement. *See Immigration and Nationality Laws*

IMMIGRATION AND NATIONALITY LAWS OF THE UNITED STATES: SELECTED STATUTES, REGULATIONS AND FORMS. Softcover. 400 pages, 1990.

WEISSBRODT'S IMMIGRATION LAW AND PROCEDURE IN A NUTSHELL, Second Edition, 438 pages, 1989, Softcover. (Text)

Indian Law—see American Indian Law

Insurance Law

DEVINE AND TERRY'S PROBLEMS IN INSURANCE LAW, 240 pages, 1989. Softcover. Teacher's Manual available. (Coursebook)

DOBBYN'S INSURANCE LAW IN A NUTSHELL, Second Edition, 316 pages, 1989. Softcover. (Text)

KEETON'S CASES ON BASIC INSURANCE LAW, Second Edition, 1086 pages, 1977. Teacher's Manual available. (Casebook)

KEETON'S COMPUTER-AIDED AND WORKBOOK EXERCISES ON INSURANCE LAW, 255 pages, 1990. Softcover. (Coursebook)

KEETON AND WIDISS' INSURANCE LAW, Student Edition, 1359 pages, 1988. (Text)

WIDISS AND KEETON'S COURSE SUPPLEMENT TO KEETON AND WIDISS' INSURANCE LAW, 502 pages, 1988. Softcover. Teacher's Manual available. (Casebook)

WIDISS' INSURANCE: MATERIALS ON FUNDAMENTAL PRINCIPLES, LEGAL DOCTRINES AND REGULATORY ACTS, 1186 pages, 1989. Teacher's Manual available. (Casebook)

YORK AND WHELAN'S CASES, MATERIALS AND PROBLEMS ON GENERAL PRACTICE INSURANCE LAW, Second Edition, 787 pages, 1988. Teacher's Manual available. (Casebook)

International Law—see also Sea, Law of

BUERGENTHAL'S INTERNATIONAL HUMAN RIGHTS IN A NUTSHELL, 283 pages, 1988. Softcover. (Text)

BUERGENTHAL AND MAIER'S PUBLIC INTERNATIONAL LAW IN A NUTSHELL, Second Edition, 275 pages, 1990. Softcover. (Text)

FOLSOM, GORDON AND SPANOGLE'S INTERNATIONAL BUSINESS TRANSACTIONS—A PROBLEM-ORIENTED COURSEBOOK, Second Edition, approximately 1150 pages, 1991. Teacher's Manual available. (Casebook) 1991 Documents Supplement.

FOLSOM, GORDON AND SPANOGLE'S INTERNATIONAL BUSINESS TRANSACTIONS IN A NUTSHELL, Third Edition, 509 pages, 1988. Softcover. (Text)

HENKIN, PUGH, SCHACHTER AND SMIT'S CASES AND MATERIALS ON INTERNATIONAL LAW, Second Edition, 1517 pages, 1987. (Casebook) Documents Supplement.

JACKSON AND DAVEY'S CASES, MATERIALS AND TEXT ON LEGAL PROBLEMS OF INTERNATIONAL ECONOMIC RELATIONS, Second Edition, 1269 pages, 1986. (Casebook) 1989 Documents Supplement.

KIRGIS' INTERNATIONAL ORGANIZATIONS IN THEIR LEGAL SETTING, 1016 pages, 1977. Teacher's Manual available. (Casebook) 1981 Supplement.

WESTON, FALK AND D'AMATO'S INTERNATIONAL LAW AND WORLD ORDER—A PROBLEM-ORIENTED COURSEBOOK, Second Edition, 1335 pages, 1990. Teacher's Manual available. (Casebook) Documents Supplement.

Interviewing and Counseling

BINDER AND PRICE'S LEGAL INTERVIEWING AND COUNSELING, 232 pages, 1977. Teacher's Manual available. Softcover. (Coursebook)

BINDER, BERGMAN AND PRICE'S LAWYERS AS COUNSELORS: A CLIENT–CENTERED APPROACH, Approximately 425 pages, 1991. Softcover. (Coursebook)

LAW SCHOOL PUBLICATIONS—Continued

Interviewing and Counseling—Cont'd

SHAFFER AND ELKINS' LEGAL INTERVIEWING AND COUNSELING IN A NUTSHELL, Second Edition, 487 pages, 1987. Softcover. (Text)

Introduction to Law—see Legal Method and Legal System

Introduction to Law Study

HEGLAND'S INTRODUCTION TO THE STUDY AND PRACTICE OF LAW IN A NUTSHELL, 418 pages, 1983. Softcover. (Text)

KINYON'S INTRODUCTION TO LAW STUDY AND LAW EXAMINATIONS IN A NUTSHELL, 389 pages, 1971. Softcover. (Text)

Judicial Process—see Legal Method and Legal System

Jurisprudence

CHRISTIE'S JURISPRUDENCE—TEXT AND READINGS ON THE PHILOSOPHY OF LAW, 1056 pages, 1973. (Casebook)

Juvenile Justice

FOX'S CASES AND MATERIALS ON MODERN JUVENILE JUSTICE, Second Edition, 960 pages, 1981. (Casebook)

FOX'S JUVENILE COURTS IN A NUTSHELL, Third Edition, 291 pages, 1984. Softcover. (Text)

Labor and Employment Law—see also Employment Discrimination, Social Legislation

FINKIN, GOLDMAN AND SUMMERS' LEGAL PROTECTION OF INDIVIDUAL EMPLOYEES, (The Labor Law Group). 1164 pages, 1989. (Casebook)

GORMAN'S BASIC TEXT ON LABOR LAW—UNIONIZATION AND COLLECTIVE BARGAINING, 914 pages, 1976. (Text)

LESLIE'S LABOR LAW IN A NUTSHELL, Second Edition, 397 pages, 1986. Softcover. (Text)

NOLAN'S LABOR ARBITRATION LAW AND PRACTICE IN A NUTSHELL, 358 pages, 1979. Softcover. (Text)

OBERER, HANSLOWE, ANDERSEN AND HEINSZ' CASES AND MATERIALS ON LABOR LAW—COLLECTIVE BARGAINING IN A FREE SOCIETY, Third Edition, 1163 pages, 1986. Teacher's Manual available. (Casebook) Statutory Supplement.

RABIN, SILVERSTEIN AND SCHATZKI'S LABOR AND EMPLOYMENT LAW: PROBLEMS, CASES AND MATERIALS IN THE LAW OF WORK, (The Labor Law Group). 1014 pages, 1988. Teacher's Manual available. (Casebook) 1988 Statutory Supplement.

Land Finance—Property Security—see Real Estate Transactions

Land Use

CALLIES AND FREILICH'S CASES AND MATERIALS ON LAND USE, 1233 pages, 1986. (Casebook) 1988 Supplement.

HAGMAN AND JUERGENSMEYER'S HORNBOOK ON URBAN PLANNING AND LAND DEVELOPMENT CONTROL LAW, Second Edition, Student Edition, 680 pages, 1986. (Text)

WRIGHT AND GITELMAN'S CASES AND MATERIALS ON LAND USE, Fourth Edition, approximately 1225 pages, 1991. Teacher's Manual available. (Casebook)

WRIGHT AND WRIGHT'S LAND USE IN A NUTSHELL, Second Edition, 356 pages, 1985. Softcover. (Text)

Legal History—see also Legal Method and Legal System

PRESSER AND ZAINALDIN'S CASES AND MATERIALS ON LAW AND JURISPRUDENCE IN AMERICAN HISTORY, Second Edition, 1092 pages, 1989. Teacher's Manual available. (Casebook)

Legal Method and Legal System—see also Legal Research, Legal Writing

ALDISERT'S READINGS, MATERIALS AND CASES IN THE JUDICIAL PROCESS, 948 pages, 1976. (Casebook)

BERCH AND BERCH'S INTRODUCTION TO LEGAL METHOD AND PROCESS, 550 pages, 1985. Teacher's Manual available. (Casebook)

BODENHEIMER, OAKLEY AND LOVE'S READINGS AND CASES ON AN INTRODUCTION TO THE ANGLO-AMERICAN LEGAL SYSTEM, Second Edition, 166 pages, 1988. Softcover. (Casebook)

DAVIES AND LAWRY'S INSTITUTIONS AND METHODS OF THE LAW—INTRODUCTORY

Legal Method and Legal System—Cont'd

TEACHING MATERIALS, 547 pages, 1982. Teacher's Manual available. (Casebook)

DVORKIN, HIMMELSTEIN AND LESNICK'S BECOMING A LAWYER: A HUMANISTIC PERSPECTIVE ON LEGAL EDUCATION AND PROFESSIONALISM, 211 pages, 1981. Softcover. (Text)

KEETON'S JUDGING, 842 pages, 1990. Softcover. (Coursebook)

KELSO AND KELSO'S STUDYING LAW: AN INTRODUCTION, 587 pages, 1984. (Coursebook)

KEMPIN'S HISTORICAL INTRODUCTION TO ANGLO-AMERICAN LAW IN A NUTSHELL, Third Edition, 323 pages, 1990. Softcover. (Text)

MEADOR'S AMERICAN COURTS, Approximately 121 pages, 1991. Softcover. (Text)

REYNOLDS' JUDICIAL PROCESS IN A NUTSHELL, Second Edition, approximately 310 pages, 1991. Softcover. (Text)

Legal Research

COHEN'S LEGAL RESEARCH IN A NUTSHELL, Fourth Edition, 452 pages, 1985. Softcover. (Text)

COHEN, BERRING AND OLSON'S HOW TO FIND THE LAW, Ninth Edition, 716 pages, 1989. (Text)

COHEN, BERRING AND OLSON'S FINDING THE LAW, 570 pages, 1989. Softcover reprint from Cohen, Berring and Olson's How to Find the Law, Ninth Edition. (Coursebook)

  Legal Research Exercises, 3rd Ed., for use with Cohen, Berring and Olson, 229 pages, 1989. Teacher's Manual available.

ROMBAUER'S LEGAL PROBLEM SOLVING—ANALYSIS, RESEARCH AND WRITING, Fifth Edition, approximately 520 pages, 1991. Teacher's Manual with problems available. (Coursebook)

STATSKY'S LEGAL RESEARCH AND WRITING, Third Edition, 257 pages, 1986. Softcover. (Coursebook)

TEPLY'S LEGAL RESEARCH AND CITATION, Third Edition, 472 pages, 1989. Softcover. (Coursebook)

  Student Library Exercises, 3rd ed., 391 pages, 1989. Answer Key available.

Legal Writing

CHILD'S DRAFTING LEGAL DOCUMENTS: MATERIALS AND PROBLEMS, 286 pages, 1988. Softcover. Teacher's Manual available. (Coursebook)

DICKERSON'S MATERIALS ON LEGAL DRAFTING, 425 pages, 1981. Teacher's Manual available. (Coursebook)

FELSENFELD AND SIEGEL'S WRITING CONTRACTS IN PLAIN ENGLISH, 290 pages, 1981. Softcover. (Text)

GOPEN'S WRITING FROM A LEGAL PERSPECTIVE, 225 pages, 1981. (Text)

MELLINKOFF'S LEGAL WRITING—SENSE AND NONSENSE, 242 pages, 1982. Softcover. Teacher's Manual available. (Text)

PRATT'S LEGAL WRITING: A SYSTEMATIC APPROACH, 468 pages, 1990. Teacher's Manual available. (Coursebook)

RAY AND COX'S BEYOND THE BASICS: A TEXT FOR ADVANCED LEGAL WRITING, Approximately 425 pages, 1991. Softcover. (Text)

RAY AND RAMSFIELD'S LEGAL WRITING: GETTING IT RIGHT AND GETTING IT WRITTEN, 250 pages, 1987. Softcover. (Text)

SQUIRES AND ROMBAUER'S LEGAL WRITING IN A NUTSHELL, 294 pages, 1982. Softcover. (Text)

STATSKY AND WERNET'S CASE ANALYSIS AND FUNDAMENTALS OF LEGAL WRITING, Third Edition, 424 pages, 1989. Teacher's Manual available. (Text)

TEPLY'S LEGAL WRITING, ANALYSIS AND ORAL ARGUMENT, 576 pages, 1990. Softcover. Teacher's Manual available. (Coursebook)

WEIHOFEN'S LEGAL WRITING STYLE, Second Edition, 332 pages, 1980. (Text)

Legislation

DAVIES' LEGISLATIVE LAW AND PROCESS IN A NUTSHELL, Second Edition, 346 pages, 1986. Softcover. (Text)

ESKRIDGE AND FRICKEY'S CASES AND MATERIALS ON LEGISLATION: STATUTES AND THE CREATION OF PUBLIC POLICY, 937 pages, 1988. Teacher's Manual available. (Casebook) 1990 Supplement.

Legislation—Cont'd

NUTTING AND DICKERSON'S CASES AND MATERIALS ON LEGISLATION, Fifth Edition, 744 pages, 1978. (Casebook)

STATSKY'S LEGISLATIVE ANALYSIS AND DRAFTING, Second Edition, 217 pages, 1984. Teacher's Manual available. (Text)

Local Government

FRUG'S CASES AND MATERIALS ON LOCAL GOVERNMENT LAW, 1005 pages, 1988. (Casebook)

MCCARTHY'S LOCAL GOVERNMENT LAW IN A NUTSHELL, Third Edition, 435 pages, 1990. Softcover. (Text)

REYNOLDS' HORNBOOK ON LOCAL GOVERNMENT LAW, 860 pages, 1982, with 1990 pocket part. (Text)

VALENTE'S CASES AND MATERIALS ON LOCAL GOVERNMENT LAW, Third Edition, 1010 pages, 1987. Teacher's Manual available. (Casebook) 1989 Supplement.

Mass Communication Law

GILLMOR, BARRON, SIMON AND TERRY'S CASES AND COMMENT ON MASS COMMUNICATION LAW, Fifth Edition, 947 pages, 1990. (Casebook)

GINSBURG, BOTEIN AND DIRECTOR'S REGULATION OF THE ELECTRONIC MASS MEDIA: LAW AND POLICY FOR RADIO, TELEVISION, CABLE AND THE NEW VIDEO TECHNOLOGIES, Second Edition, approximately 650 pages, 1991. (Casebook) 1991 Statutory Supplement.

ZUCKMAN, GAYNES, CARTER AND DEE'S MASS COMMUNICATIONS LAW IN A NUTSHELL, Third Edition, 538 pages, 1988. Softcover. (Text)

Medicine, Law and

FISCINA, BOUMIL, SHARPE AND HEAD'S MEDICAL LIABILITY, 487 pages, 1991. Teacher's Manual available. (Casebook)

FURROW, JOHNSON, JOST AND SCHWARTZ' HEALTH LAW: CASES, MATERIALS AND PROBLEMS, Second Edition, approximately 1200 pages, June, 1991 Pub. Teacher's Manual available. (Casebook)

HALL AND ELLMAN'S HEALTH CARE LAW AND ETHICS IN A NUTSHELL, 401 pages, 1990. Softcover (Text)

JARVIS, CLOSEN, HERMANN AND LEONARD'S AIDS LAW IN A NUTSHELL, Approximately 350 pages, 1991. Softcover. (Text)

KING'S THE LAW OF MEDICAL MALPRACTICE IN A NUTSHELL, Second Edition, 342 pages, 1986. Softcover. (Text)

SHAPIRO AND SPECE'S CASES, MATERIALS AND PROBLEMS ON BIOETHICS AND LAW, 892 pages, 1981. (Casebook)

Military Law

SHANOR AND TERRELL'S MILITARY LAW IN A NUTSHELL, 378 pages, 1980. Softcover. (Text)

Mortgages—see Real Estate Transactions

Natural Resources Law—see Energy and Natural Resources Law, Environmental Law

Negotiation

GIFFORD'S LEGAL NEGOTIATION: THEORY AND APPLICATIONS, 225 pages, 1989. Softcover. (Text)

WILLIAMS' LEGAL NEGOTIATION AND SETTLEMENT, 207 pages, 1983. Softcover. Teacher's Manual available. (Coursebook)

Office Practice—see also Computers and Law, Interviewing and Counseling, Negotiation

HEGLAND'S TRIAL AND PRACTICE SKILLS IN A NUTSHELL, 346 pages, 1978. Softcover (Text)

MUNNEKE'S LAW PRACTICE MANAGEMENT, COURSE MATERIALS, Approximately 630 pages, 1991. (Casebook)

STRONG AND CLARK'S LAW OFFICE MANAGEMENT, 424 pages, 1974. (Casebook)

Oil and Gas—see also Energy and Natural Resources Law

HEMINGWAY'S HORNBOOK ON THE LAW OF OIL AND GAS, Third Edition, Student Edition, approximately 700 pages, Aug., 1991 Pub. (Text)

KUNTZ, LOWE, ANDERSON AND SMITH'S CASES AND MATERIALS ON OIL AND GAS LAW, 857 pages, 1986. Teacher's Manual available. (Casebook) Forms Manual. Revised.

LOWE'S OIL AND GAS LAW IN A NUTSHELL,

Oil and Gas—Cont'd

Second Edition, 465 pages, 1988. Softcover. (Text)

Partnership—see Agency—Partnership

Patent and Copyright Law

CHOATE, FRANCIS AND COLLINS' CASES AND MATERIALS ON PATENT LAW, INCLUDING TRADE SECRETS, COPYRIGHTS, TRADEMARKS, Third Edition, 1009 pages, 1987. (Casebook)

MILLER AND DAVIS' INTELLECTUAL PROPERTY—PATENTS, TRADEMARKS AND COPYRIGHT IN A NUTSHELL, Second Edition, 437 pages, 1990. Softcover. (Text)

NIMMER, MARCUS, MYERS AND NIMMER'S CASES AND MATERIALS ON COPYRIGHT AND OTHER ASPECTS OF ENTERTAINMENT LITIGATION ILLUSTRATED—INCLUDING UNFAIR COMPETITION, DEFAMATION AND PRIVACY, Fourth Edition, Approximately 1175 pages, 1991. (Casebook)

Products Liability

FISCHER AND POWERS' CASES AND MATERIALS ON PRODUCTS LIABILITY, 685 pages, 1988. Teacher's Manual available. (Casebook)

NOEL AND PHILLIPS' CASES ON PRODUCTS LIABILITY, Second Edition, 821 pages, 1982. (Casebook)

PHILLIPS' PRODUCTS LIABILITY IN A NUTSHELL, Third Edition, 307 pages, 1988. Softcover. (Text)

Professional Responsibility

ARONSON, DEVINE AND FISCH'S PROBLEMS, CASES AND MATERIALS IN PROFESSIONAL RESPONSIBILITY, 745 pages, 1985. Teacher's Manual available. (Casebook)

ARONSON AND WECKSTEIN'S PROFESSIONAL RESPONSIBILITY IN A NUTSHELL, Second Edition, approximately 500 pages, 1991. Softcover. (Text)

MELLINKOFF'S THE CONSCIENCE OF A LAWYER, 304 pages, 1973. (Text)

PIRSIG AND KIRWIN'S CASES AND MATERIALS ON PROFESSIONAL RESPONSIBILITY, Fourth Edition, 603 pages, 1984. Teacher's Manual available. (Casebook)

ROTUNDA'S BLACK LETTER ON PROFESSIONAL RESPONSIBILITY, Second Edition, 414 pages, 1988. Softcover. (Review)

SCHWARTZ AND WYDICK'S PROBLEMS IN LEGAL ETHICS, Second Edition, 341 pages, 1988. (Coursebook)

SELECTED STATUTES, RULES AND STANDARDS ON THE LEGAL PROFESSION. Softcover. 678 pages, 1990.

SMITH AND MALLEN'S PREVENTING LEGAL MALPRACTICE, 264 pages, 1989. Reprint from Mallen and Smith's Legal Malpractice, Third Edition. (Text)

SUTTON AND DZIENKOWSKI'S CASES AND MATERIALS ON PROFESSIONAL RESPONSIBILITY FOR LAWYERS, 839 pages, 1989. Teacher's Manual available. (Casebook)

WOLFRAM'S HORNBOOK ON MODERN LEGAL ETHICS, Student Edition, 1120 pages, 1986. (Text)

Property—see also Real Estate Transactions, Land Use, Trusts and Estates

BERNHARDT'S BLACK LETTER ON PROPERTY, Second Edition, approximately 375 pages, June, 1991 Pub. Softcover. (Review)

BERNHARDT'S REAL PROPERTY IN A NUTSHELL, Second Edition, 448 pages, 1981. Softcover. (Text)

BOYER, HOVENKAMP AND KURTZ' THE LAW OF PROPERTY, AN INTRODUCTORY SURVEY, Fourth Edition, approximately 660 pages, 1991. (Text)

BROWDER, CUNNINGHAM, NELSON, STOEBUCK AND WHITMAN'S CASES ON BASIC PROPERTY LAW, Fifth Edition, 1386 pages, 1989. Teacher's Manual available. (Casebook)

BRUCE, ELY AND BOSTICK'S CASES AND MATERIALS ON MODERN PROPERTY LAW, Second Edition, 953 pages, 1989. Teacher's Manual available. (Casebook)

BURKE'S PERSONAL PROPERTY IN A NUTSHELL, 322 pages, 1983. Softcover. (Text)

CUNNINGHAM, STOEBUCK AND WHITMAN'S HORNBOOK ON THE LAW OF PROPERTY, Student Edition, 916 pages, 1984, with 1987 pocket part. (Text)

DONAHUE, KAUPER AND MARTIN'S CASES ON PROPERTY, Second Edition, 1362 pages, 1983. Teacher's Manual available. (Case-

Property—Cont'd
book)

HILL'S LANDLORD AND TENANT LAW IN A NUTSHELL, Second Edition, 311 pages, 1986. Softcover. (Text)

KURTZ AND HOVENKAMP'S CASES AND MATERIALS ON AMERICAN PROPERTY LAW, 1296 pages, 1987. Teacher's Manual available. (Casebook) 1988 Supplement.

MOYNIHAN'S INTRODUCTION TO REAL PROPERTY, Second Edition, 239 pages, 1988. (Text)

Psychiatry, Law and

REISNER AND SLOBOGIN'S LAW AND THE MENTAL HEALTH SYSTEM, CIVIL AND CRIMINAL ASPECTS, Second Edition, 1117 pages, 1990. (Casebook)

Real Estate Transactions

BRUCE'S REAL ESTATE FINANCE IN A NUTSHELL, Third Edition, approximately 270 pages, 1991. Softcover. (Text)

MAXWELL, RIESENFELD, HETLAND AND WARREN'S CASES ON CALIFORNIA SECURITY TRANSACTIONS IN LAND, Third Edition, 728 pages, 1984. (Casebook)

NELSON AND WHITMAN'S BLACK LETTER ON LAND TRANSACTIONS AND FINANCE, Second Edition, 466 pages, 1988. Softcover. (Review)

NELSON AND WHITMAN'S CASES ON REAL ESTATE TRANSFER, FINANCE AND DEVELOPMENT, Third Edition, 1184 pages, 1987. (Casebook)

NELSON AND WHITMAN'S HORNBOOK ON REAL ESTATE FINANCE LAW, Second Edition, 941 pages, 1985 with 1989 pocket part. (Text)

Regulated Industries—see also Mass Communication Law, Banking Law

GELLHORN AND PIERCE'S REGULATED INDUSTRIES IN A NUTSHELL, Second Edition, 389 pages, 1987. Softcover. (Text)

MORGAN, HARRISON AND VERKUIL'S CASES AND MATERIALS ON ECONOMIC REGULATION OF BUSINESS, Second Edition, 666 pages, 1985. (Casebook)

Remedies

DOBBS' HORNBOOK ON REMEDIES, 1067 pages, 1973. (Text)

DOBBS' PROBLEMS IN REMEDIES. 137 pages, 1974. Teacher's Manual available. Softcover. (Coursebook)

DOBBYN'S INJUNCTIONS IN A NUTSHELL, 264 pages, 1974. Softcover. (Text)

FRIEDMAN'S CONTRACT REMEDIES IN A NUTSHELL, 323 pages, 1981. Softcover. (Text)

LEAVELL, LOVE AND NELSON'S CASES AND MATERIALS ON EQUITABLE REMEDIES, RESTITUTION AND DAMAGES, Fourth Edition, 1111 pages, 1986. Teacher's Manual available. (Casebook)

McCORMICK'S HORNBOOK ON DAMAGES, 811 pages, 1935. (Text)

O'CONNELL'S REMEDIES IN A NUTSHELL, Second Edition, 320 pages, 1985. Softcover. (Text)

SCHOENBROD, MACBETH, LEVINE AND JUNG'S CASES AND MATERIALS ON REMEDIES: PUBLIC AND PRIVATE, 848 pages, 1990. Teacher's Manual available. (Casebook)

YORK, BAUMAN AND RENDLEMAN'S CASES AND MATERIALS ON REMEDIES, Fifth Edition, approximately 1050 pages, September, 1991 Pub. Teacher's Manual available. (Casebook)

Sea, Law of

SOHN AND GUSTAFSON'S THE LAW OF THE SEA IN A NUTSHELL, 264 pages, 1984. Softcover. (Text)

Securities Regulation

HAZEN'S HORNBOOK ON THE LAW OF SECURITIES REGULATION, Second Edition, Student Edition, 1082 pages, 1990. (Text)

RATNER'S SECURITIES REGULATION IN A NUTSHELL, Third Edition, 316 pages, 1988. Softcover. (Text)

RATNER AND HAZEN'S SECURITIES REGULATION: CASES AND MATERIALS, Fourth Edition, approximately 1,075 pages, 1991. (Casebook) Problems and Sample Documents Supplement.

Statutory Supplement. *See Securities Regulation, Selected Statutes*

SECURITIES REGULATION, SELECTED STATUTES, RULES, AND FORMS. Softcover. Approximately 1,300 pages, 1991.

Social Legislation—see Workers' Compensation

Sports Law
SCHUBERT, SMITH AND TRENTADUE'S SPORTS LAW, 395 pages, 1986. (Text)

Tax Practice and Procedure
GARBIS, STRUNTZ AND RUBIN'S CASES AND MATERIALS ON TAX PROCEDURE AND TAX FRAUD, Second Edition, 687 pages, 1987. (Casebook)

MORGAN'S TAX PROCEDURE AND TAX FRAUD IN A NUTSHELL, 400 pages, 1990. Softcover. (Text)

Taxation—Corporate
KAHN AND GANN'S CORPORATE TAXATION, Third Edition, 980 pages, 1989. Teacher's Manual available. (Casebook)

SCHWARZ AND LATHROPE'S BLACK LETTER ON CORPORATE AND PARTNERSHIP TAXATION, Approximately 500 pages, September, 1991 Pub. Softcover. (Review)

WEIDENBRUCH AND BURKE'S FEDERAL INCOME TAXATION OF CORPORATIONS AND STOCKHOLDERS IN A NUTSHELL, Third Edition, 309 pages, 1989. Softcover. (Text)

Taxation—Estate & Gift—see also Estate Planning, Trusts and Estates
McNULTY'S FEDERAL ESTATE AND GIFT TAXATION IN A NUTSHELL, Fourth Edition, 496 pages, 1989. Softcover. (Text)

PENNELL'S CASES AND MATERIALS ON INCOME TAXATION OF TRUSTS, ESTATES, GRANTORS AND BENEFICIARIES, 460 pages, 1987. Teacher's Manual available. (Casebook)

Taxation—Individual
DODGE'S THE LOGIC OF TAX, 343 pages, 1989. Softcover. (Text)

GUNN AND WARD'S CASES, TEXT AND PROBLEMS ON FEDERAL INCOME TAXATION, Second Edition, 835 pages, 1988. Teacher's Manual available. (Casebook) 1990 Supplement.

HUDSON AND LIND'S BLACK LETTER ON FEDERAL INCOME TAXATION, Third Edition, 406 pages, 1990. Softcover. (Review)

KRAGEN AND McNULTY'S CASES AND MATERIALS ON FEDERAL INCOME TAXATION—INDIVIDUALS, CORPORATIONS, PARTNERSHIPS, Fourth Edition, 1287 pages, 1985. (Casebook)

McNULTY'S FEDERAL INCOME TAXATION OF INDIVIDUALS IN A NUTSHELL, Fourth Edition, 503 pages, 1988. Softcover. (Text)

POSIN'S HORNBOOK ON FEDERAL INCOME TAXATION, Student Edition, 491 pages, 1983, with 1989 pocket part. (Text)

ROSE AND CHOMMIE'S HORNBOOK ON FEDERAL INCOME TAXATION, Third Edition, 923 pages, 1988, with 1989 pocket part. (Text)

SELECTED FEDERAL TAXATION STATUTES AND REGULATIONS. Softcover. Approximately 1560 pages, 1992.

SOLOMON AND HESCH'S PROBLEMS, CASES AND MATERIALS ON FEDERAL INCOME TAXATION OF INDIVIDUALS, 1068 pages, 1987. Teacher's Manual available. (Casebook)

Taxation—International
DOERNBERG'S INTERNATIONAL TAXATION IN A NUTSHELL, 325 pages, 1989. Softcover. (Text)

KAPLAN'S FEDERAL TAXATION OF INTERNATIONAL TRANSACTIONS: PRINCIPLES, PLANNING AND POLICY, 635 pages, 1988. (Casebook)

Taxation—Partnership
BERGER AND WIEDENBECK'S CASES AND MATERIALS ON PARTNERSHIP TAXATION, 788 pages, 1989. Teacher's Manual available. (Casebook)

BISHOP AND BROOKS' FEDERAL PARTNERSHIP TAXATION: A GUIDE TO THE LEADING CASES, STATUTES, AND REGULATIONS, 545 pages, 1990. Softcover. (Text)

SCHWARZ AND LATHROPE'S BLACK LETTER ON CORPORATE AND PARTNERSHIP TAXATION, Approximately 500 pages, September, 1991 Pub. Softcover. (Review)

Taxation—State & Local
GELFAND AND SALSICH'S STATE AND LOCAL TAXATION AND FINANCE IN A NUTSHELL, 309 pages, 1986. Softcover. (Text)

HELLERSTEIN AND HELLERSTEIN'S CASES AND MATERIALS ON STATE AND LOCAL TAXATION, Fifth Edition, 1071 pages, 1988. (Casebook)

LAW SCHOOL PUBLICATIONS—Continued

Torts—see also Products Liability

CHRISTIE AND MEEKS' CASES AND MATERIALS ON THE LAW OF TORTS, Second Edition, 1264 pages, 1990. (Casebook)

DOBBS' TORTS AND COMPENSATION—PERSONAL ACCOUNTABILITY AND SOCIAL RESPONSIBILITY FOR INJURY, 955 pages, 1985. Teacher's Manual available. (Casebook) 1990 Supplement.

KEETON, KEETON, SARGENTICH AND STEINER'S CASES AND MATERIALS ON TORT AND ACCIDENT LAW, Second Edition, 1318 pages, 1989. (Casebook)

KIONKA'S BLACK LETTER ON TORTS, 339 pages, 1988. Softcover. (Review)

KIONKA'S TORTS IN A NUTSHELL: INJURIES TO PERSONS AND PROPERTY, 434 pages, 1977. Softcover. (Text)

MALONE'S TORTS IN A NUTSHELL: INJURIES TO FAMILY, SOCIAL AND TRADE RELATIONS, 358 pages, 1979. Softcover. (Text)

PROSSER AND KEETON'S HORNBOOK ON TORTS, Fifth Edition, Student Edition, 1286 pages, 1984 with 1988 pocket part. (Text)

ROBERTSON, POWERS AND ANDERSON'S CASES AND MATERIALS ON TORTS, 932 pages, 1989. Teacher's Manual available. (Casebook)

Trade Regulation—see also Antitrust, Regulated Industries

McMANIS' UNFAIR TRADE PRACTICES IN A NUTSHELL, Second Edition, 464 pages, 1988. Softcover. (Text)

OPPENHEIM, WESTON, MAGGS AND SCHECHTER'S CASES AND MATERIALS ON UNFAIR TRADE PRACTICES AND CONSUMER PROTECTION, Fourth Edition, 1038 pages, 1983. Teacher's Manual available. (Casebook) 1986 Supplement.

SCHECHTER'S BLACK LETTER ON UNFAIR TRADE PRACTICES, 272 pages, 1986. Softcover. (Review)

Trial and Appellate Advocacy—see also Civil Procedure

APPELLATE ADVOCACY, HANDBOOK OF, Second Edition, 182 pages, 1986. Softcover. (Text)

BERGMAN'S TRIAL ADVOCACY IN A NUTSHELL, Second Edition, 354 pages, 1989. Softcover. (Text)

BINDER AND BERGMAN'S FACT INVESTIGATION: FROM HYPOTHESIS TO PROOF, 354 pages, 1984. Teacher's Manual available. (Coursebook)

CARLSON AND IMWINKELRIED'S DYNAMICS OF TRIAL PRACTICE: PROBLEMS AND MATERIALS, 414 pages, 1989. Teacher's Manual available. (Coursebook) 1990 Supplement.

DESSEM'S PRETRIAL LITIGATION: LAW, POLICY AND PRACTICE, Approximately 615 pages, 1991. Softcover. (Coursebook)

DEVINE'S NON-JURY CASE FILES FOR TRIAL ADVOCACY, Approximately 265 pages, 1991. (Coursebook)

GOLDBERG'S THE FIRST TRIAL (WHERE DO I SIT? WHAT DO I SAY?) IN A NUTSHELL, 396 pages, 1982. Softcover. (Text)

HAYDOCK, HERR, AND STEMPEL'S FUNDAMENTALS OF PRE-TRIAL LITIGATION, 768 pages, 1985. Softcover. Teacher's Manual available. (Coursebook)

HAYDOCK AND SONSTENG'S TRIAL: THEORIES, TACTICS, TECHNIQUES, 711 pages, 1991. Softcover. (Text)

HEGLAND'S TRIAL AND PRACTICE SKILLS IN A NUTSHELL, 346 pages, 1978. Softcover. (Text)

HORNSTEIN'S APPELLATE ADVOCACY IN A NUTSHELL, 325 pages, 1984. Softcover. (Text)

JEANS' HANDBOOK ON TRIAL ADVOCACY, Student Edition, 473 pages, 1975. Softcover. (Text)

LISNEK AND KAUFMAN'S DEPOSITIONS: PROCEDURE, STRATEGY AND TECHNIQUE, Law School and CLE Edition. 250 pages, 1990. Softcover. (Text)

MARTINEAU'S CASES AND MATERIALS ON APPELLATE PRACTICE AND PROCEDURE, 565 pages, 1987. (Casebook)

NOLAN'S CASES AND MATERIALS ON TRIAL PRACTICE, 518 pages, 1981. (Casebook)

SONSTENG, HAYDOCK AND BOYD'S THE TRIALBOOK: A TOTAL SYSTEM FOR PREPARATION AND PRESENTATION OF A CASE, 404 pages, 1984. Softcover. (Coursebook)

WHARTON, HAYDOCK AND SONSTENG'S CALI-

LAW SCHOOL PUBLICATIONS—Continued

Trial and Appellate Advocacy—Cont'd
FORNIA CIVIL TRIALBOOK, Law School and CLE Edition. 148 pages, 1990. Softcover. (Text)

Trusts and Estates
ATKINSON'S HORNBOOK ON WILLS, Second Edition, 975 pages, 1953. (Text)

AVERILL'S UNIFORM PROBATE CODE IN A NUTSHELL, Second Edition, 454 pages, 1987. Softcover. (Text)

BOGERT'S HORNBOOK ON TRUSTS, Sixth Edition, Student Edition, 794 pages, 1987. (Text)

CLARK, LUSKY AND MURPHY'S CASES AND MATERIALS ON GRATUITOUS TRANSFERS, Third Edition, 970 pages, 1985. (Casebook)

DODGE'S WILLS, TRUSTS AND ESTATE PLANNING–LAW AND TAXATION, CASES AND MATERIALS, 665 pages, 1988. (Casebook)

KURTZ' PROBLEMS, CASES AND OTHER MATERIALS ON FAMILY ESTATE PLANNING, 853 pages, 1983. Teacher's Manual available. (Casebook)

MCGOVERN'S CASES AND MATERIALS ON WILLS, TRUSTS AND FUTURE INTERESTS: AN INTRODUCTION TO ESTATE PLANNING, 750 pages, 1983. (Casebook)

MCGOVERN, KURTZ AND REIN'S HORNBOOK ON WILLS, TRUSTS AND ESTATES–INCLUDING TAXATION AND FUTURE INTERESTS, 996 pages, 1988. (Text)

MENNELL'S WILLS AND TRUSTS IN A NUTSHELL, 392 pages, 1979. Softcover. (Text)

SIMES' HORNBOOK ON FUTURE INTERESTS, Second Edition, 355 pages, 1966. (Text)

TURANO AND RADIGAN'S HORNBOOK ON NEW YORK ESTATE ADMINISTRATION, 676 pages, 1986. (Text)

UNIFORM PROBATE CODE, OFFICIAL TEXT WITH COMMENTS. 615 pages, 1989. Softcover.

WAGGONER'S FUTURE INTERESTS IN A NUTSHELL, 361 pages, 1981. Softcover. (Text)

WATERBURY'S MATERIALS ON TRUSTS AND ESTATES, 1039 pages, 1986. Teacher's Manual available. (Casebook)

Water Law—see also Energy and Natural Resources Law, Environmental Law
GETCHES' WATER LAW IN A NUTSHELL, Second Edition, 459 pages, 1990. Softcover. (Text)

SAX, ABRAMS AND THOMPSON'S LEGAL CONTROL OF WATER RESOURCES: CASES AND MATERIALS, Approximately 1030 pages, July, 1991 Pub. (Casebook)

TRELEASE AND GOULD'S CASES AND MATERIALS ON WATER LAW, Fourth Edition, 816 pages, 1986. (Casebook)

Wills—see Trusts and Estates

Women and the Law—see also Employment Discrimination
KAY'S TEXT, CASES AND MATERIALS ON SEX–BASED DISCRIMINATION, Third Edition, 1001 pages, 1988. (Casebook) 1990 Supplement.

THOMAS' SEX DISCRIMINATION IN A NUTSHELL, 399 pages, 1982. Softcover. (Text)

Workers' Compensation
HOOD, HARDY AND LEWIS' WORKERS' COMPENSATION AND EMPLOYEE PROTECTION LAWS IN A NUTSHELL, Second Edition, 361 pages, 1990. Softcover. (Text)

MALONE, PLANT AND LITTLE'S CASES ON WORKERS' COMPENSATION AND EMPLOYMENT RIGHTS, Second Edition, 951 pages, 1980. Teacher's Manual available. (Casebook)

WEST'S LAW SCHOOL ADVISORY BOARD

JOHN A. BAUMAN
Professor of Law, University of California, Los Angeles

CURTIS J. BERGER
Professor of Law, Columbia University

JESSE H. CHOPER
Dean and Professor of Law,
University of California, Berkeley

DAVID P. CURRIE
Professor of Law, University of Chicago

YALE KAMISAR
Professor of Law, University of Michigan

MARY KAY KANE
Professor of Law, University of California,
Hastings College of the Law

WAYNE R. LaFAVE
Professor of Law, University of Illinois

RICHARD C. MAXWELL
Professor of Law, Duke University

ARTHUR R. MILLER
Professor of Law, Harvard University

ROBERT A. STEIN
Dean and Professor of Law, University of Minnesota

JAMES J. WHITE
Professor of Law, University of Michigan

CHARLES ALAN WRIGHT
Professor of Law, University of Texas

THE LAW OF MERGERS, ACQUISITIONS, AND REORGANIZATIONS

By

Dale A. Oesterle
*Professor of Law
Cornell Law School*

AMERICAN CASEBOOK SERIES®

WEST PUBLISHING CO.
ST. PAUL, MINN., 1991

American Casebook Series, the key number appearing on the front cover and the WP symbol are registered trademarks of West Publishing Co. Registered in U.S. Patent and Trademark Office.

COPYRIGHT © 1991 By WEST PUBLISHING CO.
50 West Kellogg Boulevard
P.O. Box 64526
St. Paul, MN 55164–0526
All rights reserved
Printed in the United States of America

Library of Congress Cataloging-in-Publication Data

Oesterle, Dale A., 1950–
  The law of mergers, acquisitions, and reorganizations / by Dale A. Oesterle.
    p.   cm. — (American casebook series)
  Includes index.
  ISBN 0–314–85043–0
  1. Consolidation and merger of corporations—United States—Cases.
2. Corporate reorganizations—United States—Cases. I. Title.
II. Series.
KF1477.A7033 1991
346.73'06626—dc20
[347.3066626]
                                                       91–11315
                                                          CIP

ISBN 0–314–85043–0

Oesterle, Law of Mergers ACB

To Pat

*

Preface

The acquisition and reorganization boom of the 80s has transformed our thinking about business entities and financial markets forever. We have discovered that firms are themselves liquid. Sophisticated methods of raising large amounts of cash have led to transactions of startling size. We are also convinced that this development has profound implications for our system of corporate regulation, but we are unable to agree on what the implications are. The boom has thus generated a pattern of lurching change in corporate codes, state caselaw on fiduciary duty, federal securities law, antitrust law, tax law, accounting, and bankruptcy law. The transactions also have effected modifications in environmental law, tort law, and law on pensions. Acquisitions and reorganizations are, without doubt, the most regulated discrete events in United States jurisprudence. I have gathered these materials to chronicle our unsteady movements in these areas and to allow us to reassess, if possible, whether we are at present ahead or behind in the game.

I have found, in teaching the materials in preliminary editions, that the course offers law students other benefits. First, the course builds on the concepts that students have learned in their other basic courses—it is, if you will, a modern version of the old corporate planning course. In this regard my attempt to cover basic ground thoroughly as a platform for more sophisticated analysis leads to minor overlap with some materials in other courses. Second, the course attracts students from other university schools (my course is, for example also listed in the business school), and the mixture of law students and students from these other schools provides a rare and special moment in their education. Students engage each other readily in heartfelt debate on the many issues in the materials. Third, and perhaps most significant, the course asks students to integrate material from several legal disciplines for application to one business event. Our curriculum is highly specialized, reflecting that the practice of law is highly specialized, but there is special value accorded the lawyer who can provide integrated advice for a client faced with a concrete problem that transcends individual specialties. Consider, for example, the legal knowledge a lawyer must have to answer the client who asks only "How should I structure my acquisition?"

To go through all the materials in the volume at a reasonable pace would require more than the three hours per week a school will normally allot to the course. Since each instructor will necessarily have a view as to which topics his or her course ought to cover, I have sought to give instructors a maximum range of choice. An instructor may want to omit entire sections—the materials on the Clayton Act in Chapter Eight, for example, could be left to a school's antitrust course—or omit some materials within a section—the *Edgar v. Mite* opinion could be omitted in Chapter Four, for example. In any event, I encourage an instructor to cover what he or she believes to be fun; there are bottomless issues aplenty in each Chapter.

Finally, let me say a word about my editing policies. The text of most of the statutes and many of the rules referenced in the text is contained in West Publishing Company's basic statutory supplement, *Selected Corporation and Partnership Statutes, Rules and Forms*. I place heavy reliance on a careful reading of the primary sources of law in the belief that students ought to begin to develop professional habits in law school and that a continuously updated personal acquaintance with first hand legal sources are essential to good lawyering. In editing cases on acquisitions, which tend to be quite long, I have, as much as possible, left in the facts that describe the sophisticated transactions in issue. An understanding of the principal parties and their motivations, financial and otherwise, is an important byproduct of the materials. By reading the facts of the important transactions of the last decade, students gain a leg-up on experience.

DALE A. OESTERLE

April, 1991

Acknowledgments

The editor wishes to thank the law library staff and the secretarial staff at the Cornell Law School, particularly Jackie L. and Jeffery L. Glezen and Jyland M. Diles. Many Cornell Law students aided in various stages of the preparation of these materials and the editor expresses his thanks to them all, with special thanks to Gregory Husisian and Anita Singh, Class of 1990, Jill L. Miller and Kenneth A. Remfry, Jr., Class of 1991, and Teri Weaver and Michael Overman, Class of 1992. The editor also wishes to thank Professors Robert A. Green, Russell K. Osgood, and Alan R. Palmiter for their help on selected portions of the book and Lynn Colvin for her editorial assistance. The editor is grateful for the financial support of Dean Russell K. Osgood from the Milton & Eleanor Gould fund at the Cornell Law School.

The editor also wishes to thank the authors and publishers of the following for permitting me to include excerpts from their works:

Allen, Independent Directors in MBO Transactions: Are They Fact or Fantasy, 45 Business Lawyer, p. 2055 (August 1990). Reprinted with permission from William T. Allen, 1020 North King Street, Wilmington, DE 19801.

American Law Institute, Federal Income Tax Project, Subchapter C — Proposals of The American Law Institute on Corporate Acquisitions and Dispositions, pp. 30–33 (1982). Copyright © 1982 by The American Law Institute. Reprinted with the permission of The American Law Institute, 4025 Chestnut Street, Philadelphia, PA 19104.

Anderson, Chapter 11 Reorganizations, Chapter 11 Reorganizations 1-1 to 1-3 (1983). Reprinted from *Chapter 11 Reorganizations*, by John C. Anderson, copyright © 1983 by McGraw-Hill, Inc. Reprinted by permission of Shepard's/McGraw-Hill, Inc. Further reproduction is strictly prohibited.

Brodsky & Zweibel, Chapter 11 Acquisitions: Payoffs for Patience, Mergers & Acquisitions 47 (Sept./Oct. 1990). Reprinted with permission from MLR Publishing Company, 229 South 18th Street, Philadelphia, PA 19103.

Burak & Brown, EPA's Policy on Corporate Successor Liability Under Superfund, Chemical & Radioactive Waste Litigation Reporter, pp. 649, 651–52 (1981). Copyright © 1981 Chemical & Radiation Waste Litigation Reporter. Reprinted by Permission, Suite 200, 1519 Connecticut Avenue N.W., Washington, D.C. 20036.

Burrough & Helyar, Barbarians At the Gate, pp. 512–514 (1990). Copyright © 1990 by Brian and John Helyar. Reprinted by permission of Harper Collins Publishers, 10 East 53rd St., New York, NY 10022.

Cieri, Heiman, Henze, Jenks, Kirschner, Riley, & Sullivan, An Introduction to Legal and Practical Considerations in the Restructuring of Troubled Leveraged Buyouts, 45 Business Lawyer, pp. 333, 337–347, 385–389 (Nov. 1989). Reprinted with permission from Richard M. Cieri on behalf of all authors, I/C Jones, Day, Reavis, & Pogue, North Point, 901 Lakeside Ave., Cleveland, OH 44114.

Coffee, Unstable Coalitions: Corporate Governance As a Multi-Player Game, 78 Georgetown Law Journal, pp. 1495, 1519–20, 1523–25 (1990). Reprinted with permission from Professor John C. Coffee, Jr., Columbia University School of Law, 435 West 116th Street, New York, NY 10027.

Conard, Amendments of Model Business Corporation Act Affecting Dissenters' Rights. 33 Business Lawyer 2587 at 2595–96 (July 1978). Reprinted with permission from American Bar Association, 750 North Lake Shore Drive, Chicago, IL 60611. Reprinted with permission from Professor Alfred F. Conard, University of Michigan Law School, Ann Arbor, MI 48109.

Corso & Silfen, Disclosure of Financial Information in Contested Proxy Solicitations, M & A and Corporate Governance Law Reporter 468 (Nov. 1990). Reprinted with permission from M & A and Corporate Governance Law Reporter, Suite 200, 1519 Connecticut Avenue N.W., Washington, D.C. 20036. Reprinted with permission from Gregg W. Corso, Securities and Exchange Commission, 450 5th Street, N.W., Washington, D.C. 20549. Reprinted with permission from Richard A. Silfen, Carlton, Fields, Ward, Emmanuel, Smith & Cutler, P.A., P.O. Box 3239, Tampa, FL 33601. The Commission, as a matter of policy, disclaims responsibility for any private publication or statement by any of its employees. The views expressed herein are those of the authors and do not necessarily reflect the views of the Commission or of the authors' colleagues on the staff of the Commission.

9 Cowan, New Play "Tin Parachutes", New York Times, March 19, 1987 at D1. Copyright © 1987 by The New York Times Company, 229 W. 43rd St., New York, NY 10036. Reprinted by permission.

Easterbrook & Fischel, Mandatory Disclosure and The Protection of Investors, 70 Virginia Law Review, pp. 669, 670, 680–687, 689–90 (1984). Reprinted with permission from Virginia Law Review, Association, published and copyrighted © by Virginia Law Review Association, University of Virginia School of Law, Charlottesville, VA 22901. Reprinted with permission from Fred B. Rothman & Co., 10368 W. Centennial Rd., Littleton, CO 80127.

Easterbrook & Fischel, The Corporate Contract, 89 Columbia Law Review, pp. 1416, 1419, 1430, 1442–1445 (1989). Copyright © 1989 by the Directors of the Columbia Law Review Association, Inc. All Rights Reserved. Reprinted by permission from Columbia Law Review, 435 West 116th Street, New York, NY 10027.

Eisenberg, The Structure of the Corporation, pp. 231–32, 250–51 (1976). Reprinted with permission by Little, Brown and Company, published and copyrighted © by Little, Brown, and Company, Publishers, 34 Beacon Street, Boston, MA 02108.

Faber, New York State Antitakeover Bill: First Step Down a Rocky Road, Tax Notes vol. 43 nos. 1–13, pp. 1263–72 (June 5, 1989). Reprinted with permission from Tax Analysts, Tax Notes, 6830 Fairfax Dr., Arlington, VA 22213. Reprinted with permission from Peter L. Faber, Law Firm of Kaye, Scholer, Fierman, Hays & Handler, 425 Park Ave., New York, NY 10022.

Ferrara, Brown, Hall, Takeovers, Butterworth Legal Publishers, pp. 337–343, 355–56 (1987). Reprinted by permission of Butterworth Legal Publishers, 90 Stiles Road, Salem, NH 03079. Copyright © 1987.

Frauman & Blauner, Bankrupt Entities Targeted: Trading Claim Can Serve as the Basis of a Takeover, New York Law Journal, p. 5, col. 2 (June 4, 1990). Reprinted with the permission of the New York Law Journal, Copyright © 1990. The New York Law Publishing Company, 111 Eighth Avenue, New York, NY 10011. Reprinted with permission from Steven Blauner, the authors and partners in the Bankruptcy/Business Reorganization Department of Milbank, Tweed, Hadley, & McCloy, 1 Chase Manhattan Plaza, New York, NY 10005. Reprinted with permission from Mr. David Frauman, Milbank, Tweed, Hadley, & McCloy, 515 South Figueroa Street, Suite 1800, Los Angeles, CA 90071.

Ginsburg, M. & Levin, J., Mergers, Acquisitions and Leveraged Buyouts—Transactional Analysis 626–628 (CCH Bound Series, 1-1-91). Reprinted with permission from Commerce Clearing House, 4025 West Peterson, Chicago, IL 60646.

Gordon, The Mandatory Structure of Corporate Law, 89 Columbia Law Review, pp. 1549, 1575–77, 1580 (1989). Copyright © 1989 by the Directors of the Columbia Law Review Association, Inc. All Rights Reserved.

Gorman, How Accounting Rules Shook Up LBO Dealmaking, Mergers & Acquisitions 45, 46, 48, 50 (July/Aug. 1990). Reprinted with permission from Mergers & Acquisitions, 229 S. 18th Street, Philadelphia, PA 19103.

Green, Successor Liability: The Superiority of Statutory Reform to Protect Products Liability Claimants, 72 Cornell Law Review, pp. 17, 49–55, 57 (1986). Copyright © 1986 by Cornell University, Cornell Law Review, Cornell Law School, Myron Taylor Hall,

Ithaca, NY 14853. Copyright © 1986 by Paul A. Rothman, President, Fred B. Rothman & Co., 10368 W. Centennial Rd., Littleton, CO 80127. All Rights Reserved. Reprinted with permission from Professor Michael Green, University of Iowa, College of Law, Iowa City, IA 52242.

Hansmann, When Does Worker Ownership Work? ESOPs, Law Firms, Codetermination and Economic Democracy, 99 Yale Law Journal, pp. 1749, 1811–12 (1990). Reprinted by permission of The Yale Law Journal Company and Fred B. Rothman & Company; reprinted with permission from Professor Henry Hansmann, Yale Law School, Drawer 401A Yale Station, New Haven, CT 06520.

Herz & Abahoonie, Innovations to Minimize Acquisition Goodwill, Mergers & Acquisitions 35, 36, 38 (March/April 1990). Reprinted with permission from Mergers & Acquisitions, 229 S. 18th Street, Philadelphia, PA 19103.

Jensen, Eclipse of the Public Corporation, 67 Harvard Business Review, pp. 61–74 (Sept.—Oct. 1989). Reprinted by permission of Harvard Business Review. An excerpt from Eclipse of the Public Corporation by Michael C. Jensen, issue (67 Harvard Business Review, pp. 61–74 Sept.—Oct. 1989). Copyright © 1989 by the President and Fellows of Harvard College; all rights reserved. Reprinted with permission from Professor Michael C. Jensen, Harvard Business School, Soldiers Field Rd., SFP 221, Boston, MA 02163.

Jensen, Kaplan, & Stiglin, Effects of LBOs On Tax Revenues of The U.S. Treasury, Tax Notes vol. 42 nos. 1–6, pp. 727–33 (Feb. 6, 1989). Reprinted with permission from Tax Analysts, Tax Notes, 6830 Fairfax Dr., Arlington, VA 22213. Reprinted with permission from Professor Michael C. Jensen, Harvard Business School, Soldiers Field Rd., SFP 221, Boston, MA 02163. Reprinted with permission from Professor Steven Kaplan, University of Chicago, 1101 East 58th Street, Room 419, Chicago, IL 60637. Reprinted with permission from Laura E. Stiglin, Analysis Group, Inc., 18 Moore Street, Belmont, MA 02178. Laura Stiglin is a Principal of Analysis Group, Inc.

Kahn & Gann, Corporate Taxation, West Publishing, pp. 674–75 (3rd ed. 1989). Reprinted with permission from West Publishing Co., 50 W. Kellogg Blvd., St. Paul, MN 55102.

Kale, Noe & Gay, Share Repurchase Through Transferable Put Rights, Journal Financial Economics 25 (1989) pp. 141–160, North Holland. Reprinted with permission from Elsevier Sequoia S.A., P.O. Box 564, 1001 Lausanne 1, Switzerland.

Kanda and Levmore, The Appraisal Remedy & The Goals of Corporate Law, 32 U.C.L.A. Law Review, pp. 431, 434–37, 463–65 (1985). Reprinted with permission from Professor Saul Levmore, Langdell 362, Harvard Law School, 1563 Massachusetts Avenue, Cambridge, MA 02138. Reprinted with permission from UCLA Law Review,

School of Law, 405 Hilgard Avenue, Los Angeles, CA 90024–1476. Reprinted with permission from Fred B. Rothman & Co., 10368 W. Centennial Rd., Littleton, CO 80127. All Rights Reserved. Reprinted with permission from Professor Hideki Kanda, The University of Tokyo, Faculty of Law, Hongo, Bunkyo-ku, Tokyo, 113, Japan.

Kornhauser, The Nexus of Contracts Approach to Corporations, 89 Columbia Law Review, pp. 1449, 1456–1457 (1989). Reprinted with permission from Professor Lewis Kornhauser, New York University School of Law, 40 Washington Square South, New York, NY 10012.

Levin, Cleaning Up The Mess: The Need for Bankruptcy Reform, Investment Dealers' Digest 18 (April 16, 1990). Reprinted with permission of Investment Dealers' Digest, Inc., Copyright © 1990, Investment Dealers' Digest, Inc., 2 World Trade Center, New York, NY 10048.

Manning & Hanks, A Concise Textbook on Legal Capital, pp. 13–16, 63–64 (3rd ed. 1990). Reprinted with permission from The Foundation Press, 615 Merrick Ave., Westbury, NY 11590.

New York Stock Exchange Listed Company. Manual Sections 202.01, 202.03, 202.04, and 202.05. Reprinted with permission from New York Stock Exchange, 11 Wall Street, New York, NY 10005.

NOTE, Corporate Life After Death: CERCLA Preemption of State Corporate Dissolution Law, 88 Michigan Law Review, pp. 131, 149–155 (1989). Reprinted with permission from Michigan Law Review Association, Hutchins Hall, University of Michigan, Ann Arbor, MI 48109.

Pfunder, Boudin, Clark, Nanni, Merger Enforcement at the Antitrust Division, 58 Antitrust Law Journal, pp. 329, 330–33, 338–42 (1989). Reprinted with permission from Malcolm R. Pfunder, 888 16th St., N.W., Washington, D.C. 20006. Reprinted with permission from John W. Clark, Antitrust Division, U.S. Department of Justice, Washington, D.C. 20530. Reprinted with permission from Anthony V. Nanni, Antitrust Division, U.S. Department of Justice, Washington, D.C. 20530.

Shleifer & Vishny, The Takeover Wave of the 1980s, Vol. 249 Science, p. 745 (Aug. 17, 1990). Copyright © 1990 by the American Association for the Advantagement of Science, 1333 H Street, N.W., Washington, D.C. 20005. Reprinted with permission on behalf of all authors from Professor Andrei Shleifer, Department of Economics, Harvard University, Littauer Center, Cambridge, MA 02138.

Short & Welsch, Fundamentals of Financial Accounting, Fundamentals of Financial Accounting, p. 683 (6th ed. 1990). Reprinted with permission from Daniel G. Short, Glenn A. Welsch and Richard D. Irwin, Inc., 1818 Ridge Road, Homewood, IL 60430.

Smith, Green & Bernstein, Risk Management: The Dangers for Buyers Who Inherit Flawed Products, Mergers & Acquisitions, July/August 1989 at 48–53. Reprinted with permission from MLR Publishing Co., 229 S. 18th St., Philadelphia, PA 19103.

Spiegel & Berg, The National Security Test For Foreign Acquisitions, Mergers & Acquisitions 32, 34, 36–37 (Nov./Dec. 1989). Reprinted with permission from Mergers & Acquisitions, 229 S. 18th Street, Philadelphia, PA 19103.

Stout, Are Takeover Premiums Really Premiums? Market Price, Fair Value and Corporate Law, 99 Yale Law Journal, pp. 1235, 1287, 1289–1292. Reprinted by permission of The Yale Law Journal Company and Fred B. Rothman & Company from *The Yale Law Journal,* Vol. 99, pp. 1235–1296. Reprinted with permission from Associate Professor Lynn Stout, Georgetown University Law Center, 600 New Jersey Avenue N.W., Washington, D.C. 20001.

Tauke, Should Bonds Have More Fun? A Reexamination of the Debate Over Corporate Bondholders Rights, 1989 Col.Bus.L.Rev., pp. 1, 53–67, 131–132. Reprinted with permission from Columbia Business Law Review, Box B–26, Columbia University School of Law, 435 W. 116th St., New York, NY 10027.

Vlahakis, Deleveraging: A Search for Rules in a Financial Free-for-All, 5 M & A and Corporate Governance Law Reporter 290 (1990). Reprinted with permission from M & A and Corporate Governance Law Reporter, Suite 200, 1519 Connecticut Avenue N.W., Washington, D.C. 20036. Reprinted with permission from Patricia Vlahakis, I/C Wachtell, Lipton, Rosen & Katz, 299 Park Avenue, New York, NY 10171.

Warren, Recent Corporate Restructuring and The Corporate Tax System, Tax Notes Vol. 42 nos. 1–6, pp. 715–20 (Feb. 6, 1989). Reprinted with permission from Tax Analysts, Tax Notes, 6830 Fairfax Dr., Arlington, VA 22213. Reprinted with permission from Professor Alvin C. Warren, Jr., Harvard University Law School, Cambridge, MA 02138.

Yamin, The Achilles Heel of the Takeover: Nature and Scope of Successor Corporation, Products Liability in Asset Acquisitions, 7 Harvard Journal of Law & Public Policy, pp. 187, 248–256 (1984). Reprinted with permission from Harvard Society for Law & Public Policy, Harvard Law School, Cambridge, MA 02138.

Summary of Contents

	Page
PREFACE	xxiii
ACKNOWLEDGMENTS	xxv
TABLE OF CASES	li

Chapter One. An Introduction to Acquisitions 1

Subchapter

A. An Introduction to Events and Social Issues 1

B. The Various Topologies of Mergers, Acquisitions, and Reorganizations 35

Chapter Two. Shareholder Voting and Appraisal Rights 41

A. State Corporate Codes 41

Section

1. Introduction 41
2. The Basic Structure of the Codes 42
3. The Dissenting Shareholders' Appraisal Remedy 52
4. Transactions Structured to Circumvent Statutory Requirements 86
5. Maverick Attempts to Treat Equivalent Transactions Alike 111
6. Should Shareholders Have the Power to Vote Not to Vote? Form and Substance in State Corporate Codes 117

B. Federal Proxy Regulations 132

1. The Basics of Proxy Solicitation Disclosure Requirements in Acquisitions 133
2. Can Managers "Sell the Deal" to Their Shareholders in the Proxy Materials? 134
3. The Mandatory Disclosure Debate 148

Chapter Three. Successor Liability: The Effect of an Acquisition on Bondholders, Patent Licensors, Lessors, Labor Union Members, Pensioners, and Contingent Product, Environmental, and Civil Rights Claimants 155

Subchapter

A. Introduction to the Problems of Externalities and Opportunistic Behavior in Acquisitions 155

Subchapter	Page
B. The Effect of Transactions on Debt Obligations, Real and Intellectual Property Rights, and Other Contract Rights	162

Section
1. The Basic Distinctions 162
2. The Special Problems of Protecting Preexisting Bondholders in Leveraged Buyouts and Leveraged Recapitalizations 183

C. Employee Contracts: Collective Bargaining Agreements and Pension Plans 223

Section
1. Collective Bargaining Agreements 223
2. Federal Regulation of Pension Plans 264

D. Successor Firm and Acquisition Lender Liability for Product Liability, Employment Discrimination, and Environmental Claims 276

Section
1. Liability of the Buyer in Asset Acquisitions 277
2. Parent Liability for Claims Against a Subsidiary 318
3. Lender Liability 329

Chapter Four. Introduction to Stock Acquisitions: The Williams Act and State Antitakeover Statutes 335

Subchapter

A. Federal Regulation: The Williams Act 335

Section
1. 13(d): Disclosure of a 5 Percent Acquisition 335
2. Third–Party Tender Offers 351
3. Issuer Repurchases of Its Own Stock or Debt: Buybacks and Buyouts 392

B. State Regulation of Stock Acquisitions: Antitakeover Statutes 414

Chapter Five. the Power and Fiduciary Responsibility of Boards of Directors Attempting, Defending Against, or Agreeing to Takeovers 461

Subchapter

A. The Power of Boards of Directors to Erect Takeover Defenses 462

Section
1. Introduction to Firm–Specific Takeover Defenses 462
2. Shark Repellent Amendments: When Is An Affirmative Vote Not Enough? 469
3. Poison Pill Plans: The Power of the Board to Adopt Takeover Defenses Without Resort to Shareholder Ratification 485

B. Fiduciary Duties of Controlling Officials and Shareholders .. 529

Section
1. The Decision to Sell: Must the Target Board Publicly Auction Off the Firm? 529

Subchapter

B. Fiduciary Duties of Controlling Officials and Shareholders—Continued
   Section
   2. Defensive Reorganizations: The Target Board's Decision Not to Sell 612
   3. Buying Out the Unwanted Bidder: Greenmail Payments 660
   4. Rights of a Frustrated Buyer Under a Broken Acquisition Agreement 668

C. The Obligation of Shareholders Selling a Controlling Block of Stock 687

D. Fiduciary Duties of the Managers of an Acquiring Firm 702
   Section
   1. Duties to Acquiring-Firm Shareholders 702
   2. Duties to Target-Firm Shareholders 705

Chapter Six. the Registration and Disclosure Requirements of the Federal Securities Act 728

Subchapter

A. Registration Under the Federal Securities Act of 1933: Exchange Transactions 728

B. The General Antifraud Provisions of the Federal Securities Laws as They Apply to Acquisitions 742
   Section
   1. A Federal Common Law of Fiduciary Duty? 743
   2. Specific Disclosure Questions 765

C. Insider Trading in Advance of Acquisitions 866

D. The Short Swing Profits Prohibition: A Trap for the Unwary 877

Chapter Seven. Accounting and Tax Issues in Mergers and Acquisitions 891

Subchapter

A. Accounting for Mergers and Acquisitions 892
   Section
   1. Cost Method: Acquisitions of Less Than 20 Percent of Target's Outstanding Common Stock 895
   2. Equity Method: Acquisitions of 20 Percent to 50 Percent of Target's Outstanding Stock 897
   3. Purchase and Pooling Consolidations: One Company Acquires Over 50 Percent of the Stock of Another 900

B. Tax Treatment of Mergers, Acquisitions, and Reorganizations 921
   Section
   1. Tax-Free Reorganizations 922
   2. Are Acquisitions Driven By Taxes? 941
   3. Miscellaneous Tax Provisions Relevant to Acquisitions: Golden Parachutes, Greenmail, Poison Pills, and Acquisition Expenses 968

Chapter Eight. Protecting Consumer and National Security Interests in Mergers and Acquisitions 979

Subchapter
A. Consumer Protection: Antitrust Laws 979
   Section
   1. The Clayton Act 980
   2. Premerger Notification: The Hart–Scott–Rodino Antitrust Improvements Act of 1976 997
   3. Collusion Between Bidders in Tender Offers 1012
B. Foreign Acquisitions of United States Corporations That "Impair National Security"—The Exon–Florio Amendment 1017

Chapter Nine. Deleveraging: Workouts and Bankruptcy Reorganizations 1024

Subchapter
A. Workouts 1027
B. Chapter 11 Reorganizations 1044
   Section
   1. Who Runs a Firm in Chapter 11? 1049
   2. The Bargaining Position of Equity Holders in Chapter 11 Proceedings 1057
   3. The Application of State Corporate Codes and Federal Securities Laws in a Bankruptcy Proceeding 1067
   4. Chapter 11 Acquisitions: "Vulture Takeovers" 1080

INDEX 1091

Table of Contents

	Page
PREFACE	xxiii
ACKNOWLEDGMENTS	xxv
TABLE OF CASES	li

Chapter One. An Introduction to Acquisitions — 1

Subchapter A. An Introduction to Events and Social Issues — 1
- Shleifer & Vishny, The Takeover Wave of the 1980s — 1
- Jensen, Eclipse of the Public Corporation — 12
- Takeovers in the Nineties — 28
- The Policy Debate — 29
  - Questions — 33

Subchapter B. The Various Topologies of Mergers, Acquisitions, and Reorganizations — 35
- Questions — 40

Chapter Two. Shareholder Voting and Appraisal Rights — 41

Subchapter A. State Corporate Codes — 41

Section
1. Introduction — 41
2. The Basic Structure of the Codes — 42
   a. State Statutes on Mergers and Acquisitions — 42
      - "Substantially All" — 42
      - State Legislation Restraining Stock Acquisition ("Antitakeover Statutes") — 43
        - Questions — 43
        - Problem — 45
      - Corporate Codes in Other States — 45
      - *Shidler v. All American Life & Financial Corp.* — 46
      - The Extraterritorial Effect of Some State Corporate Codes — 49
   b. Single–Firm Capital Reorganizations — 50
      - Questions — 50
3. The Dissenting Shareholders' Appraisal Remedy — 52
   a. State Corporate Codes — 52
      - Questions — 52
      - Other Jurisdictions — 53
      - Conard, Amendments of Model Business Corporation Act Affecting Dissenter's Rights (Sections 73, 74, and 80) — 53
      - Kanda & Levmore, The Appraisal Remedy and the Goals of Corporate Law — 54
      - Appraisal Procedure — 57
        - Questions — 58

Section		Page
3.	The Dissenting Shareholders' Appraisal Remedy—Continued	
	b. Case Law on Fair Value in Appraisal Proceedings	59
	Beerly v. Department of the Treasury	60
	Weinberger v. UOP, Inc.	64
	In re Valuation of Common Stock of Libby, McNeill & Libby	67
	Stout, Are Takeover Premiums Really Premiums? Market Price, Fair Value and Corporate Law	71
	Questions	74
	c. The Exclusivity of the Appraisal Remedy	75
	Delaware's Wandering Journey	75
	Rabkin v. Philip A. Hunt Chemical Corp.	76
	Cede & Co. v. Technicolor, Inc.	77
	Cavalier Oil Corp. v. Harnett	78
	Question	83
	Other Jurisdictions	83
	Steinberg v. Amplica, Inc.	83
	Questions	85
4.	Transactions Structured to Circumvent Statutory Requirements	86
	a. Asset Sales and Reverse Asset Sales	86
	Hariton v. Arco Electronics, Inc.	86
	Rath v. Rath Packing Co.	88
	Legislative Responses to the De Facto Merger Doctrine	91
	b. Exchange Tender Offers	92
	Irving Bank Corp. v. Bank of New York Co.	92
	c. Triangular Mergers	94
	Equity Group Holdings v. DMG, Inc.	94
	Rauch v. RCA Corp.	98
	d. Mergers as Single–Firm Reorganizations of Capital Structure	102
	Warner Communications v. Chris–Craft Ind.	102
	e. Partnerships and Long–Term Supply Contracts	109
	Pratt v. Ballman–Cummings Furniture Co.	109
	Good v. Lackawanna Leather Co.	110
5.	Maverick Attempts to Treat Equivalent Transactions Alike	111
	a. The California Corporations Code	111
	M. Eisenberg, the Structure of the Corporation	112
	Questions	113
	Problem	114
	b. Listing Requirements on the New York Stock Exchange Relevant to Shareholder Voting	114
	New York Stock Exchange Listed Company Manual	114
	Questions	116
	Easterbrook & Fischel, Mandatory Disclosure and the Protection of Investors	116
	The "Race to Laxity" Debate	117

Section	Page
6. Should Shareholders Have the Power to Vote Not to Vote? Form and Substance in State Corporate Codes	117
Easterbrook & Fischel, The Corporate Contract	121
Kornhauser, The Nexus of Contracts Approach to Corporations: A Comment on Easterbrook and Fischel	123
Easterbrook & Fischel, The Corporate Contract	124
Questions	126
Gordon, The Mandatory Structure of Corporate Law	128

Subchapter B. Federal Proxy Regulations	132

Section	
1. The Basics of Proxy Solicitation Disclosure Requirements in Acquisitions	133
2. Can Managers "Sell the Deal" to Their Shareholders in the Proxy Materials?	134
South Coast Services, Inc. v. Santa Ana Valley Irrigation Co.	138
Problem	148
3. The Mandatory Disclosure Debate	148
Easterbrook & Fischel, Mandatory Disclosure and the Protection of Investors	149

Chapter Three. Successor Liability: The Effect of an Acquisition on Bondholders, Patent Licensors, Lessors, Labor Union Members, Pensioners, and Contingent Product, Environmental, and Civil Rights Claimants 155

Subchapter A. Introduction to the Problems of Externalities and Opportunistic Behavior in Acquisitions	155
Bargaining Theory	160
Questions	162

Subchapter B. The Effect of Transactions on Debt Obligations, Real and Intellectual Property Rights, and Other Contract Rights	162

Section	
1. The Basic Distinctions	162
Statutory Mergers	162
PPG Industries Inc. v. Guardian Industries Corp.	163
Questions	168
Mesa Partners v. Phillips Petroleum Co.	169
Asset Acquisitions	175
Bud Antle, Inc. v. Eastern Foods, Inc.	175
Questions	180
Stock Acquisitions	181
Branmar Theatre Co. v. Branmar, Inc.	181
Questions	183

Section	Page
2. The Special Problems of Protecting Preexisting Bondholders in Leveraged Buyouts and Leveraged Recapitalizations	183
a. Fiduciary Duty for Bondholders?	183
Metropolitan Life Ins. Co. v. RJR Nabisco, Inc.	183
Questions	190
Leveraged Recaps	192
The Empirical Evidence	192
The Market Response	192
Coffee, Unstable Coalitions: Corporate Governance as a Multi–Player Game	193
Taulce, Should Bonds Have More Fun? A Reexamination of the Debate Over Corporate Bondholders Rights	194
Insolvency Standards for Corporate Distributions	197
b. State Corporate Code Provisions Restricting Dividends and Redemptions	197
B. Manning & J. Hanks, a Concise Textbook on Legal Capital	197
Questions	200
c. Fraudulent Conveyance Acts and Leveraged Buyouts	201
United States of America v. Tabor Court Realty Corp.	201
Questions	207
Kupetz v. Wolf	209
Questions	216
Post–LBO Creditors	216
d. Bulk Sales Acts	217
National Conference of Commissioners on Uniform State Laws, Prefatory Note and Official Comment to Section 6–101 on Revising Discussion Draft	219
Questions	222
Problem	223
Subchapter C. Employee Contracts: Collective Bargaining Agreements and Pension Plans	223
Section	
1. Collective Bargaining Agreements	223
a. Control Change Clauses in Collective Bargaining Agreements	224
Pittsburgh and Lake Erie R.R. Co. v. Railway Labor Executives' Ass'n	224
Questions	233
Air Line Pilots Ass'n Intern. v. UAL Corp., Intern. Ass'n of Machinists & Aerospace Workers	233
Air Line Pilots Ass'n Intern. v. UAL Corp., Intern. Ass'n of Machinists & Aerospace Workers	238
The History of the UAL Buyout	239
Coffee, Unstable Coalitions: Corporate Governance as a Multi–Player Game	239
Questions	241
New Ploy: "Tin Parachutes"	242

Section	Page
1. Collective Bargaining Agreements—Continued	
b. Must the Buyer Adopt the Seller's Labor Contracts or Bargain with the Seller's Union?	243
John Wiley & Sons, Inc. v. Livingston	243
NLRB v. Burns Intern. Sec. Services, Inc.	246
Howard Johnson Co. v. Detroit Local Joint Executive Bd., AFL–CIO	249
Fall River Dyeing & Finishing Corp. v. NLRB	253
Questions	258
c. New State Legislation Protecting Employees in Acquisitions	259
Federal Plant Closing Statute	260
Worker Adjustment and Retraining Act	260
Questions	262
Union Strategy in Seeking Protections Through Legislation Rather Than Collective Bargaining	263
2. Federal Regulation of Pension Plans	264
Buying–Firm Liability for Selling–Firm Terminations	265
Employee's Retirement Income Security Act, Sec. 1369	266
Selling–Firm Liability When Buying Firm Assumes and Terminates a Plan	267
Employee's Retirement Income Security Act, § 1384(a)	267
Buyer Termination of Overfunded Target Plans for Acquisition Financing	269
Questions	271
Ryan v. Chromalloy American Corp.	271
Questions	276
Subchapter D. Successor Firm and Acquisition Lender Liability for Product Liability, Employment Discrimination, and Environmental Claims	276
Section	
1. Liability of the Buyer in Asset Acquisitions	277
a. Basic Standards	277
Keller v. Clark Equipment Co.	277
Questions	281
Rights of Contingent Claimants Against a Dissolved Corporation	282
Corporate Life After Death: CERCLA Preemption of State Corporate Dissolution Law	282
Questions	284
Problem	285
Green, Successor Liability: The Superiority of Statutory Reform to Protect Products Liability Claimants	285
Questions	287
b. Product Liability Claims	287
Niccum v. Hydra Tool Corp.	287
Questions	290

Section	Page
1. Liability of the Buyer in Asset Acquisitions—Continued	
Smith, Green, and Bernstein, Risk Management: The Dangers for Buyers Who Inherit Flawed Products	291
Yamin, The Achilles Heel of the Takeover: Nature and Scope of Successor Corporation Products Liability in Asset Acquisitions	294
c. Employee Discrimination Claims	298
EEOC v. Vucitech	298
Golden State Bottling Co. v. NLRB	302
Questions	303
d. Environmental Law Claims	304
Department of Transp. v. PSC Resources, Inc.	304
Questions	309
CERCLA	310
Smith Land & Improvement Corp. v. Celotex Corp.	312
Burak & Brown, EPA's Policy on Corporate Successor Liability Under Superfund	314
Problem	317
2. Parent Liability for Claims Against a Subsidiary	318
United States v. Kayser–Roth Corp.	318
U.S. v. Kayser–Roth Corp.	321
Restructurings After an LBO	322
Schmoll v. Acands, Inc.	323
3. Lender Liability	329
In re Bergsoe Metal Corp.	329
Question	334

Chapter Four. Introduction to Stock Acquisitions: The Williams Act and State Antitakeover Statutes — 335

Section	Page
Subchapter A. Federal Regulation: The Williams Act	335
1. 13(d): Disclosure of a 5 Percent Acquisition	335
Proposed Rules Under Section 13(d)	335
Questions	336
The Effect of Section 13(d)	338
Relief for Section 13(d) Violations	339
Rondeau v. Mosinee Paper Corp.	340
Questions	342
Chromalloy American Corp. v. Sun Chemical Corp.	343
Questions	347
Dan River, Inc. v. Icahn	347
The SEC as Plaintiff	349
SEC v. First City Financial Corp.	349
Question	351
2. Third–Party Tender Offers	351
The Form and Disclosure Requirements for a Bidder	352
Questions	352

Section	Page
2. Third–Party Tender Offers—Continued	
Tender Offer Conditions: The Role of Contract Law	354
Gilbert v. El Paso Co.	354
The Effect of the Williams Act	357
Equal Treatment of Shareholders in Tender Offers	358
Oesterle, The Rise and Fall of Street Sweep Takeovers	358
Question	361
The Definition of a "Tender Offer": When is a "Street Sweep" Included?	361
Hanson Trust PLC v. SCM Corp.	361
Field v. Trump	371
Street Sweeps	374
Oesterle, The Rise and Fall of Street Sweep Takeovers	374
The Definition of "Bidder" in Rule 14d–1(b)(1)	379
MAI Basic Four, Inc. v. Prime Computer, Inc.	379
Questions	385
The Obligations of a Target Subject to a Third–Party Tender Offer	385
Questions	385
An Introduction to Bidder–Target Tactical Litigation Over Disclosure Requirements	386
Koppers Co., Inc. v. American Express Co.	386
3. Issuer Repurchases of Its Own Stock or Debt: Buybacks and Buyouts	392
Self–Tender Offers	393
Questions	393
Transferable Put Rights (TPRs)	393
Kale, Noe, & Gay, Share Repurchase Through Transferable Put Rights	393
Going–Private Stock Repurchases	396
Kaufmann v. Lawrence	396
Questions	399
Comparing the Regulation of Issuer Buybacks and Leveraged Buyouts	401
Oesterle & Norberg, Management Buyouts: Creating or Appropriating Shareholder Wealth	401
Questions	403
The Puzzle of the Large Premiums in Stock Buybacks	404
Oesterle & Norberg, Management Buyouts: Creating or Appropriating Shareholder Wealth?	405
Reverse LBOs: Buying Back Debt	408
Katz v. Oak Industries, Inc.	409
Questions	414
Subchapter B. State Regulation of Stock Acquisitions: Antitakeover Statutes	414
The Frequency of the Statutes	415
Edgar v. Mite Corp.	416

TABLE OF CONTENTS

Page

Subchapter B. State Regulation of Stock Acquisitions: Antitakeover Statutes—Continued

Control Share Acts	423
Questions	423
Fair Price Statutes	424
Questions	424
CTS Corp. v. Dynamics Corp. of America	425
Can a State Constitutionally Protect Nonshareholder Constituencies Through Antitakeover Legislation?	435
Oesterle, Delaware's Takeover Statutes: Of Chills, Pills, Standstills and Who Gets Iced	435
Questions	438
Business Combination (Freeze–Out) Acts	439
New York's Act	439
Questions	440
Arguments Against, For, and Neutral on the Value of Business Combination Statutes to Shareholders	443
Redemption or Appraisal Statutes	446
Amanda Acquisition Corp. v. Universal Foods Corp.	447
Questions	455
Will States Eventually Repeal Antitakeover Statutes?	455
The Pennsylvania Disgorgement Statute	458
Questions	458
The Effect of the State Statutes on Share Prices	459

Chapter Five. The Power and Fiduciary Responsibility of Boards of Directors Attempting, Defending Against, or Agreeing to Takeovers 461

Subchapter A. The Power of Boards of Directors to Erect Takeover Defenses 462

Section

1. Introduction to Firm–Specific Takeover Defenses 462
    Empirical Data on the Use and Effect of the Takeover Defenses 465
2. Shark Repellent Amendments: When Is an Affirmative Vote Not Enough? 469
    a. State Corporate Codes 469
        Georgia–Pacific Corp. v. Great Northern Nekoosa Corp. 469
        Questions 472
        Stahl v. Apple Bancorp. Inc. 473
    b. NYSE Restrictions on Charter Amendments that Restrict the Voting Rights of Outstanding Stock 478
        Exchange Act Release Nos. 25,891 & 25,891a, July 7 and 13, 1988 479
        Questions 484
3. Poison Pill Plans: The Power of the Board to Adopt Takeover Defenses Without Resort to Shareholder Ratification 485
    Moran v. Household International, Inc. 485
    Poison Pill Plan Typology 493

Section	Page
3. Poison Pill Plans: The Power of the Board to Adopt Takeover Defenses Without Resort to Shareholder Ratification—Continued	
R. Ferrara, M. Brown & J. Hall, Takeovers	493
Questions	498
Dynamics Corp. of America v. CTS Corp.	498
Questions	510
Early Court Defeats for Discriminatory Plans and Curative State Legislation	510
Minstar Acquiring Corp. v. AMF, Inc.	510
Questions	513
The Bank of New York Co. v. Irving Bank Corp.	515
Questions	518
Stahl v. Apple Bancorp., Inc.	519
Question	523
Supervoting Poison Pill Plans	523
Unilever Acquisition Corp. v. Richardson–Vicks, Inc.	524
Questions	526
Shareholder Resolutions Under Rule 14a–8 Attacking Management Conduct in Takeovers	527
Subchapter B. Fiduciary Duties of Controlling Officials and Shareholders	529

Section	Page
1. The Decision to Sell: Must the Target Board Publicly Auction Off the Firm?	529
Smith v. Van Gorkom	529
The Effect of *Van Gorkom* on D & O Insurance	544
Revlon, Inc. v. MacAndrews & Forbes Holdings, Inc.	545
Mills Acquisition Co. v. MacMillan, Inc.	553
The Special Problems of LBOs	573
Allen, Independent Directors in MBO Transactions: Are They Fact or Fantasy?	573
Barkan v. Amsted Industries, Inc.	578
Citron v. Fairchild Camera and Instrument Corp.	583
Gilbert v. The El Paso Company	588
Questions	590
The High–Water Mark of LBOs?	591
In Re RJR Nabisco	591
Questions	604
B. Burrough & J. Helyar, Barbarians at the Gate	604
Statutes Empowering Firms to Waive Director Liability in Acquisitions	606
Questions	606
Liability of Investment Bankers in LBOs	607
Wells v. Shearson Lehman/American Exp., Inc.	607
Schneider v. Lazard Freres & Co.	609
Questions	611

Section	Page
2. Defensive Reorganizations: The Target Board's Decision Not to Sell	612
Ivanhoe Partners v. Newmont Mining Corp.	613
Question	620
Shamrock Holdings, Inc. v. Polaroid Corp.	621
Tax Advantages of ESOPs	631
Federal Income Tax Aspects of Corporate Financial Structures, Staff Report	631
Empirical Data on ESOPs	635
Hansmann, When Does Worker Ownership Work? ESOPs, Law Firms, Codetermination and Economic Democracy	635
Questions	636
The Fiduciary Duty of ESOP or ERISA Trustees Responding to a Tender Offer	636
Labor Department Opinion Letter on Tender Offers	636
Donovan v. Bierwirth	638
Joint Department of Labor/Department of Treasury Statement of Pension Investments	645
Paramount Communications, Inc. v. Time Inc.	646
Questions	655
The Frustrated Bidder's Standing to Sue the Target for Breach of Fiduciary Duty	657
City Capital Associates Ltd. Partnership v. Interco, Inc.	657
Question	658
State Constituency Statutes	658
Questions	659
3. Buying Out the Unwanted Bidder: Greenmail Payments	660
Cheff v. Mathes	660
Questions	664
Tomczak v. Morton Thiokol, Inc.	664
4. Rights of a Frustrated Buyer Under a Broken Acquisition Agreement	668
Jewel Cos. Inc. v. Pay Less Drug Stores Northwest, Inc.	669
NBT Bancorp, Inc. v. Fleet/Norstar Financial Group, Inc.	675
Texaco, Inc. v. Pennzoil, Co.	679
Questions	686
Subchapter C. The Obligation of Shareholders Selling a Controlling Block of Stock	687
Selling to a "Looter"	687
Debaun v. First Western Bank and Trust Co.	687
Questions	693
Selling an Office	693
Essex Universal Corp. v. Yates	693
Questions	698
Sharing the Proceeds From the Sale	699
Zetlin v. Hanson Holdings, Inc.	699
Questions	700

TABLE OF CONTENTS

Subchapter C. The Obligation of Shareholders Selling a Controlling Block of Stock—Continued
Corporate Opportunity 700
David J. Greene & Co. v. Dunhill Intern., Inc. (Part I) 700
   Questions 702

Subchapter D. Fiduciary Duties of the Managers of an Acquiring Firm 702

Section
1. Duties to Acquiring–Firm Shareholders 702
   Muschel v. Western Union Corp. 703
   Questions 705
2. Duties to Target–Firm Shareholders 705
   "Frozen-In" Minority Shareholders 706
   Summa Corp. v. Trans World Airlines, Inc. 706
   "Frozen–Out" Minority Shareholders 708
   Weinberger v. UOP, Inc. 708
   Rosenblatt v. Getty Oil Co. 715
   Coggins v. New England Patriots Football Club, Inc. 722
   Questions 725
   Fair Value in Squeeze–Out Mergers 726

Chapter Six. The Registration and Disclosure Requirements of the Federal Securities Act 728

Subchapter A. Registration Under the Federal Securities Act of 1933: Exchange Transactions 728
Effect of the Act on Exchange Tender Offers 728
Piper v. Chris–Craft Industries, Inc. 732
Effect of the Act on Statutory Mergers and Asset Sales 735
Securities Act Release No. 5316 735
Securities Act of 1933, SEC Release No. 5463 736
   Problem 739
The Effect of the Action Exchange Reorganizations 739
SEC Division of Corp. Finance, No Action Letter, Time, Inc. ... 740
   Questions 741

Subchapter B. The General Antifraud Provisions of the Federal Securities Laws as They Apply to Acquisitions ... 742

Section
1. A Federal Common Law of Fiduciary Duty? 743
   Santa Fe Industries, Inc. v. Green 744
   Goldberg v. Meridor 748
   Questions 751
   Schreiber v. Burlington Northern, Inc. 751
   Questions 754
   Panter v. Marshall Field & Co. 755
   Kramer v. Time Warner, Inc. 756
   The Frustrated Bidder's Standing to Sue Under Section 14(e) ... 760

Section	Page
1. A Federal Common Law of Fiduciary Duty?—Continued	
Piper v. Chris–Craft Industries, Inc.	760
Mobil Corp. v. Marathon Oil Co.	763
2. Specific Disclosure Questions	765
a. General Principles—Materiality and the Duty to Disclose	765
TSC Industries, Inc. v. Northway, Inc.	765
Questions	772
"Qualitative" Information	774
GAF Corp. v. Heyman	774
United States v. Matthews	781
The Duty to Disclose	784
Roeder v. Alpha Industries, Inc.	784
State Law	786
Roberts v. General Instrument Corp.	786
b. Preliminary Merger Negotiations	788
In The Matter of Carnation Company Exchange Act Release No. 22,214	788
Basic Inc. v. Levinson	791
Taylor v. First Union Corp.	796
More on the Duty to Disclose	799
SEC Release (May 18, 1989)—Section III F 4. Sea, Release No. 33–6835; 34–26831	799
In re Revlon	801
In re Kern	808
Questions	825
c. Projections of Postacquisition Performance	825
Panter v. Marshall Field & Co.	826
Walker v. Action Industries, Inc.	831
Isquith v. Middle South Utilities, Inc.	836
In re Genentech, Inc.	839
d. Backdoor Protection for Bondholders?	848
McMahan & Company v. Wherehouse Entertainment, Inc.	848
Corso and Silfen, Disclosure of Financial Information in Contested Proxy Solicitations, M & A and Corp. Governance Rep. 468	853
e. A Bidder's Public Promises	859
In re Phillips Petroleum Securities Litigation	859
Question	865
Subchapter C. Insider Trading in Advance of Acquisitions	866
SEC, Report From the Office of Chief Economist, Stock Trading Before the Announcement of Tender Offers: Insider Trading or Market Anticipation?	866
Chiarella v. United States	871
United States of America v. Chestman	874
Carpenter v. United States	875

	Page
Subchapter D. The Short Swing Profits Prohibition: A Trap for the Unwary	877
Kern County Land Co. v. Occidental Corp.	877
Texas International Airlines v. National Airlines, Inc.	884
Sterman v. Ferro Corp.	887
Questions	890

Chapter Seven. Accounting and Tax Issues in Mergers and Acquisitions 891

Subchapter A. Accounting for Mergers and Acquisitions	892
Introduction to Financial Statements	892
Introduction to Accounting Issues in Intercompany Ownership	893

Section

1. Cost Method: Acquisitions of Less Than 20 Percent of Target's Outstanding Common Stock 895
2. Equity Method: Acquisitions of 20 Percent to 50 Percent of Target's Outstanding Stock 897
3. Purchase and Pooling Consolidations: One Company Acquires Over 50 Percent of the Stock of Another 900

The Accounting Rules in Practice	909
The Test for Pooling	912
M. Ginsburg & J. Levin, Mergers, Acquisitions and Leveraged Buyouts	913
Minimizing Goodwill in Purchase Transactions	916
Herz & Abahoonie, Innovations to Minimize Acquisition Goodwill	916
Accounting for LBOs	917
Gorman, How Accounting Rules Shook Up LBO Deal Making	918
Subchapter B. Tax Treatment of Mergers, Acquisitions, and Reorganizations	921
Introduction	921

Section

1. Tax–Free Reorganizations 922

I.R.C. Section 368	923
Treas. Reg. § 1.368–1	926
Treas. Reg. § 1.368–2	927
Questions	931
American Law Institute, Proposals on Corporate Acquisitions and Dispositions	934
The Mechanics of Tax–Free Treatment	938
D. Kahn & P. Gann, Corporate Taxation	938
Tax Attribute Provisions	940
A Taxable Exchange Compared	940

2. Are Acquisitions Driven by Taxes? 941

Introduction	941
a. Survival of Tax Attributes in an Acquisition	942
Tax Reform Act of 1986	943
Revenue Reconciliation Act of 1989	945

Section	Page
2. Are Acquisitions Driven by Taxes?—Continued	
b. Leverage and the Corporate Tax System	947
Staff Report, Federal Income Tax Aspects of Corporate Financial Structures	947
The Debt–Equity Distinction: Section 385	957
Problem	958
Original Issue Discount Instruments: Section 163(e)(5) and (i)	959
Revenue Reconciliation Act of 1989	959
General Limits on Acquisition Indebtedness: Section 279	960
State Tax Law	961
Faber, New York State Antitakeover Bill: First Step Down a Rocky Road	961
The Policy Debate	962
Warren, Recent Corporate Restructuring and the Corporate Tax System	962
Jensen, Kaplan, Effects of LBOs on Tax Revenues of the U.S. Treasury	966
3. Miscellaneous Tax Provisions Relevant to Acquisitions: Golden Parachutes, Greenmail, Poison Pills, and Acquisition Expenses	968
Golden Parachutes: Sections 280G and 4999	969
IRS Proposed Regulations (PS–217–84)	969
Popularity of Golden and Tin Parachutes	971
Greenmail: Section 5881	972
Revenue Act of 1987	972
Poison Pill Plans	973
IRS Rev.Rul. 90–11	973
Deductibility of Acquisition Fees and Expenses	973
National Starch & Chemical Corp. v. C.I.R.	973

Chapter Eight. Protecting Consumer and National Security Interests in Mergers and Acquisitions   979

Subchapter A. Consumer Protection: Antitrust Laws	979

Section	
1. The Clayton Act	980
The Clayton Act, § 7	980
U.S. Dept. of Justice 1987 Merger Guidelines	981
Nanni, Merger Enforcement at the Antitrust Division	988
United States v. Waste Management, Inc.	990
Questions	996
2. Premerger Notification: The Hart–Scott–Rodino Antitrust Improvements Act of 1976	997
15 U.S.C.A. § 7A	997
Rules, Regulations, Statements and Interpretations Under the Hart–Scott–Rodino Antitrust Improvements Act of 1976	1000
The HSR Waiting Period and the Confidentiality of HSR Filings	1005
Clark, Merger Enforcement at the Antitrust Division	1008

Section	Page
2. Premerger Notification: The Hart–Scott–Rodino Antitrust Improvements Act of 1976—Continued	
Question	1009
California v. American Stores Co.	1009
Questions	1012
3. Collusion Between Bidders in Tender Offers	1012
Finnegan v. Campeau Corp.	1012
Question	1017
Subchapter B. Foreign Acquisitions of United States Corporations That "Impair National Security"—The Exon–Florio Amendment	1017
Omnibus Trade and Competitiveness Act of 1988	1017
Spiegel & Berg, The National Security Test for Foreign Acquisitions, Mergers and Acquisitions	1019
Questions	1022
Congressional Inadvertence?	1023

Chapter Nine. Deleveraging: Workouts and Bankruptcy Reorganizations 1024

Introduction 1024
J. Anderson, Chapter 11 Reorganizations 1–1 to 1–3 1025

Subchapter A. Workouts 1027
　The Participants in the Renegotiation 1027
　Cieri, Heiman, Henze, Jenks, Kirschner, Riley, & Sullivan, An Introduction to Legal and Practical Considerations in the Restructuring of Troubled Leveraged Buyouts 1027
　Contract Rights 1035
　Vlahakis, Deleveraging: A Search for Rules in a Financial Free-for-All 1035
　State Law 1037
　Federal Securities Law 1038
　SEC No-Action Letter, Seaman Furniture 1038

Subchapter B. Chapter 11 Reorganizations 1044
　Cieri, Heiman, Henze, Jenks, Kirschner, Riley & Sullivan, An Introduction to Legal and Practical Considerations in the Restructuring of Troubled Leveraged Buyouts 1046
　Levin, Cleaning Up the Mess: The Need for Bankruptcy Reform 1048

Section	
1. Who Runs a Firm in Chapter 11?	1049
In re Sharon Steel Corp.	1050
Committee of Dalkon Shield Claimants v. A.H. Robins Co., Inc.	1055
Question	1056
2. The Bargaining Position of Equity Holders in Chapter 11 Proceedings	1057
In re Genesee Cement, Inc.	1057
In re Future Energy Corp.	1059

TABLE OF CONTENTS

Section	Page
2. The Bargaining Position of Equity Holders in Chapter 11 Proceedings—Continued	
Questions	1064
Norwest Bank Worthington v. Ahlers	1065
3. The Application of State Corporate Codes and Federal Securities Laws in a Bankruptcy Proceeding	1067
a. State Corporation Laws	1067
In re White Motor Credit Corp.	1067
Question	1071
In re Johns–Manville Corp.	1071
Question	1075
b. Federal Securities Laws	1076
SEC Ruling on SEC Role in Bankruptcy Reorganization	1076
4. Chapter 11 Acquisitions: "Vulture Takeovers"	1080
Frauman & Blauner, Bankrupt Entities Targeted: Trading Claims Can Serve as the Basis of a Takeover	1080
Brodsky & Zweibel, Chapter 11 Acquisitions: Payoffs for Patience	1083
Question	1090
INDEX	1091

Table of Cases

The principal cases are in bold type. Cases cited or discussed in the text are roman type. References are to pages. Cases cited in principal cases and within other quoted materials are not included.

Adams v. Standard Knitting Mills, Inc., 751
Air Line Pilots Ass'n, Intern. v. UAL Corp., 238, 241, 242, 263
Air Line Pilots Ass'n, Intern. v. UAL Corp., Intern. Ass'n of Machinists & Aerospace Workers, 233
Alamo Bank of Texas, United States v., 168
Amalgamated Sugar Co. v. NL Industries, Inc., 446, 513, 514
Amanda Acquisition Corp. v. Universal Foods Corp., 447, 455, 498
Anderson Industries, Inc., In re, 208
Applestein v. United Board & Carton Corp., 92
Asarco, Inc. v. Court, 513, 526

Bank Leumi–Le–Israel, B. M., Philadelphia Branch v. Sunbelt Industries, Inc., 1037
Bank of New York Co., Inc. v. Irving Bank Corp., 446, 515, 518, 523
Barkan v. Amsted Industries, Inc., 578, 591
Basic, Inc. v. Levinson, 791, 799, 826, 1044
Beerly v. Department of Treasury, 60
Bergsoe Metal Corp., In re, 329, 334
Branmar Theatre Co. v. Branmar, Inc., 181
Brown v. Halbert, 702
Bud Antle, Inc. v. Eastern Foods, Inc., 175, 180

California v. American Stores Co., 1008, 1009
Cargill, Inc. v. Monfort of Colorado, Inc., 1012
Carnation Co., Matter of, 788
Carpenter v. United States, 875
Cavalier Oil Corp. v. Harnett, 59, 75, 78, 83
Cede & Co. v. Technicolor, Inc., 77
Champion Parts Rebuilders, Inc. v. Cormier Corp., 336
Cheff v. Mathes, 660
Chestman, United States v., 874
Chiarella v. United States, 871
Chromalloy American Corp. v. Sun Chemical Corp., 343

Citron v. Fairchild Camera and Instrument Corp., 583, 591
City Capital Associates Ltd. Partnership v. Interco Inc., 657
City of (see name of city)
Cleary v. American Airlines, Inc., 259
Coggins v. New England Patriots Football Club, Inc., 722, 726
Committee of Dalkon Shield Claimants v. A.H. Robins Co., Inc., 1055
Condec Corp. v. Lunkenheimer Co., 463
Crane Co. v. Harsco Corp., 658
Credit Managers Ass'n of Southern California v. Federal Co., 207
CRTF Corp. v. Federated Dept. Stores, Inc., 353
CTS Corp. v. Dynamics Corp. of America, 50, 424, 425, 457

Dan River, Inc. v. Icahn, 337, 347
David J. Greene & Co. v. Dunhill Intern., Inc., 700
Davis Acquistion, Inc. v. NWA, Inc., 519
DeBaun v. First Western Bank & Trust Co., 687, 693
Department of Transp. v. PSC Resources, Inc., 304, 310
Donovan v. Bierwirth, 638
Dynamics Corp. of America v. CTS Corp., 805 F.2d 705, p. 498, 658
Dynamics Corp. of America v. CTS Corp., 637 F.Supp. 406, p. 513

Edgar v. MITE Corp., 414, 415, 416
E.E.O.C. v. Vucitech, 298, 303
Equity Group Holdings v. DMG, Inc., 94, 116, 120
Essex Universal Corp. v. Yates, 693, 699

Fall River Dyeing & Finishing Corp. v. N.L.R.B., 253, 258
Farris v. Glen Alden Corp., 91
Field v. Trump, 371
Finnegan v. Campeau Corp., 1012
Fleet Aerospace Corp. v. Holderman, 424
Fleet Factors Corp., United States v., 329
Florida Commercial Banks v. Culverhouse, 339
Flynn v. Bass Bros. Enterprises, Inc., 353

li

TABLE OF CASES

Ford v. Bierwirth, 644
Foremost–McKesson, Inc. v. Provident Securities Co., 890
Future Energy Corp., In re, 1059

GAF Corp. v. Heyman, 774
GAF Corp. v. Milstein, 336
Gearhart Industries, Inc. v. Smith Intern., Inc., 741 F.2d 707, p. 339
Gearhart Industries, Inc. v. Smith Intern., Inc., 592 F.Supp. 203, p. 191
Gelco Corp. v. Coniston Partners, 513
Genentech, Inc. Shareholders Litigation, In re, 839
Genesee Cement, Inc., In re, 1057, 1076
Georgia–Pacific Corp. v. Great Northern Nekoosa Corp., 469, 510, 515
Gerstle v. Gamble–Skogmo, Inc., 134
Gilbert v. El Paso Co., 354, 588, 591, 754
Gimbel v. Signal Companies, Inc., 42
Glass, Molders, Pottery, Plastics and Allied Workers Intern. Union, AFL–CIO v. Wickes Companies, Inc., 678
Gleneagles Inv. Co., Inc., United States v., 584 F.Supp. 671, p. 201
Gleneagles Inv. Co., Inc., United States v., 571 F.Supp. 935, p. 201
Gleneagles Inv. Co., Inc., United States v., 565 F.Supp. 556, p. 201
Goldberg v. Meridor, 748, 751, 755
Golden State Bottling Co., Inc. v. N. L. R. B., 302
Good v. Lackawanna Leather Co., 110
Gould v. American–Hawaiian S. S. Co., 751
Graphic Arts Intern. Union Local 1B, Twin Cities v. Martin Podany Associates, Inc., 258

Hanson Trust PLC v. SCM Corp., 361
Hariton v. Arco Electronics, Inc, 86
Harvard Industries, Inc. v. Tyson, 513
Heublein, Inc. v. F. T. C., 1005
Howard Johnson Co., Inc. v. Detroit Local Joint Executive Bd., 249, 258

Icahn v. Blunt, 424
In re (see name of party)
International Ass'n of Machinists & Aerospace Workers v. United States Can Co., 208
Irving Bank Corp. v. Bank of New York Co., Inc., 92
Isquith for and on Behalf of Isquith v. Middle South Utilities, Inc., 836
Ivanhoe Partners v. Newmont Min. Corp., 613, 620, 655

Jefferson Indus. Bank v. First Golden Bancorporation, 50
Jewel Companies, Inc. v. Pay Less Drug Stores Northwest, Inc., 669, 686
John Hancock Capital Growth Management, Inc. v. Aris Corp., 607
John Wiley & Sons, Inc. v. Livingston, 243, 258
Johns–Manville Corp., In re, 1071

Katz v. Bregman, 43
Katz v. Oak Industries Inc., 409
Kaufmann v. Lawrence, 396, 399, 403
Kayser–Roth Corp., United States v., 910 F.2d 24, p. 318
Kayser–Roth Corp., United States v., 724 F.Supp. 15, p. 321
Keller v. Clark Equipment Co., 277, 282, 287
Kern, In re, 808
Kern County Land Co. v. Occidental Petroleum Corp., 877
Koons v. Walker, 291
Koppers Co., Inc. v. American Exp. Co., 386
Kramer v. Time Warner, Inc., 756
Kupetz v. Wolf, 209, 216, 217

Liberty Nat. Ins. Holding Co. v. Charter Co., 339
Lieberman v. F.T.C., 1006

MAI Basic Four, Inc. v. Prime Computer, Inc., 379, 385
Matter of (see name of party)
Matthews, United States v., 781
McMahan & Co. v. Wherehouse Entertainment, Inc., 848
Mesa Partners v. Phillips Petroleum Co., 168, 169
Metropolitan Life Ins. Co. v. RJR Nabisco, Inc., 183, 191
Meyers v. Moody, 1037
Mills Acquisition Co. v. Macmillan, Inc., 529, 553, 590, 591, 604, 607, 620
Minstar Acquiring Corp. v. AMF, Inc., 510, 513, 514, 527
Mobil Corp. v. Marathon Oil Co., 763
Moran v. Household Intern., Inc., 485, 498, 510, 527
Morse Tool, Inc., In re, 216, 217
Muschel v. Western Union Corp., 703

National Intergroup, Inc. Rights Plan Litigation, In re, 528
National Starch and Chemical Corp. v. C.I.R., 973
NBT Bancorp, Inc. v. Fleet/Norstar Financial Group Inc., 675
Nelson v. All American Life & Financial Corp., 85
Newmont Min. Corp. v. Pickens, 353
Niccum v. Hydra Tool Corp., 287, 290
Nixon v. Celotex Corp., 323
N. L. R. B. v. Burns Intern. Sec. Services, Inc., 246, 258
Norwest Bank Worthington v. Ahlers, 1065

Ohio Corrugating Co., In re, 216, 217

Panter v. Marshall Field & Co., 755, 826
Paramount Communications, Inc. v. Time Inc., 646, 655, 656, 657
Pension Ben. Guar. Corp. v. LTV Corp., 645

TABLE OF CASES

Pepper v. Litton, 1037
Phillips Petroleum Securities Litigation, In re, 859
Piper v. Chris–Craft Industries, Inc., 732, 760
Pittsburgh, City of v. May Dept. Stores Co., Inc., 1012
Pittsburgh & Lake Erie R. Co. v. Railway Labor Executives' Ass'n, 224
PPG Industries, Inc. v. Guardian Industries Corp., 163, 168
Pratt v. Ballman–Cummings Furniture Co., 109
Public Service Co. of New Hampshire v. Consolidated Utilities and Communications, Inc., 1076

Rabkin v. Philip A. Hunt Chemical Corp., 76, 77
Radol v. Thomas, 352
Rath v. Rath Packing Co., 88, 91
Rauch v. RCA Corp., 46, 98
R.D. Smith & Co., Inc. v. Preway Inc., 526
Revco D.S., Inc., In re, 208
Revlon, In re, 801
Revlon, Inc. v. MacAndrews & Forbes Holdings, Inc., 513, 527, 545, 590, 591, 607, 612, 620, 655, 657, 659
RJR Nabisco, Inc. Shareholders Litigation, In re, 576 A.2d 654, p. 611, 612
RJR Nabisco, Inc. Shareholders Litigation, In re, Fed.Sec.L.Rep. (CCH) ¶ 94,194, p. 591, 604
Robert M. Bass Group, Inc. v. Evans, 485
Roberts v. General Instrument Corp., 786
Roeder v. Alpha Industries, Inc., 784
Rondeau v. Mosinee Paper Corp., 340, 342, 343, 357
Rosenblatt v. Getty Oil Co., 715
Ryan v. Chromalloy American Corp., 271

Sante Fe Industries, Inc. v. Green, 744, 751
Schmoll v. ACandS, Inc., 323
Schneider v. Lazard Freres & Co., 609, 611
Schreiber v. Burlington Northern, Inc., 751, 754
S.E.C. v. First City Financial Corp., Ltd., 890 F.2d 1215, p. 349
S.E.C. v. First City Financial Corp., Ltd., 688 F.Supp. 705, p. 337
Shamrock Holdings, Inc. v. Polaroid Corp., 620, 636, 656
Sharon Steel Corp., In re, 1050
Shidler v. All American Life & Financial Corp., 775 F.2d 917, p. 84, 85
Shidler v. All American Life & Financial Corp., 298 N.W.2d 318, p. 46
Smith v. Van Gorkom, 529, 544, 590, 591, 607, 655, 659, 668

Smith Land & Imp. Corp. v. Celotex Corp., 312
South Coast Services Corp. v. Santa Ana Valley Irr. Co., 137, 138
Spinner Corp. v. Princeville Development Corp., 526
Stahl v. Apple Bancorp, Inc., Fed.Sec.L. Rep. ¶ 95,412, p. 519
Stahl v. Apple Bancorp, Inc., 579 A.2d 1115, p. 473
Steinberg v. Amplica, Inc., 83
Stepak v. Schey, 85
Sterling v. Mayflower Hotel Corporation, 726
Sterman v. Ferro Corp., 887
Summa Corp. v. Trans World Airlines, Inc., 706
Syenergy Methods, Inc. v. Kelly Energy Systems, Inc., 180

Tabor Court Realty Corp., United States v., 201, 207, 216
Tate & Lyle PLC v. Staley Continental, Inc., 658
Taylor v. First Union Corp. of South Carolina, 796
Tengelmann Warenhandelsgesellschaft, United States v., 1007
Texaco, Inc. v. Pennzoil, Co., 679, 686
Texas Intern. Airlines v. National Airlines, Inc., 884
TLX Acquisition Corp. v. Telex Corp., 438
Tomczak v. Morton Thiokol, Inc., 656, 664
Trump, United States v., 1007
TSC Industries, Inc. v. Northway, Inc., 765

Unilever Acquisition Corp. v. Richardson–Vicks, Inc., 485, 523, 524, 527
United States v. ____ (see opposing party)
Unocal Corp. v. Mesa Petroleum Co., 241, 469, 529, 590, 606, 659

Valuation of Common Stock of Libby, McNeill & Libby, In re, 67, 75

Walker v. Action Industries, Inc., 831
Warner Communications Inc. v. Chris–Craft Industries, Inc., 102, 118
Waste Management, Inc., United States v., 990
Weinberger v. UOP, Inc., 59, 64, 75, **708,** 725, 726
Wells v. Shearson Lehman/American Exp., Inc., 208, 607, 611, 612
White Motor Credit Corp., In re, 1067

Zetlin v. Hanson Holdings, Inc., 699

THE LAW OF MERGERS, ACQUISITIONS, AND REORGANIZATIONS

Chapter One

AN INTRODUCTION TO ACQUISITIONS

Corporate merger, acquisition, and reorganization transactions are perhaps the most heavily regulated events in all of American law. Five major bodies of rules—tax law, accounting standards, state corporate law, federal securities regulation, and antitrust law—play lead roles in these corporate transactions. Several other areas of the law—labor law, rules governing pension plans, environmental law, products liability law, debtor-creditor law, basic contract law, law of various regulated industries (banking law, utilities law, insurance law, and casino law, for example)—also play minor roles and can assume a lead role in any given transaction. A study of the law governing corporate acquisitions then is an integration and application of these various systems of rules. The opening materials of the book are designed to suggest the richness of this interwoven texture and introduce the later materials that focus on the relevant legal doctrines one at a time.

SUBCHAPTER A. AN INTRODUCTION TO EVENTS AND SOCIAL ISSUES

SHLEIFER & VISHNY, THE TAKEOVER WAVE OF THE 1980s
249 Science 745 (Aug. 17, 1990).

Takeovers dramatically altered the U.S. economy in the 1980s. The total value of assets changing hands in this period was $1.3 trillion. Of the 500 largest industrial corporations in the United States in 1980 (Fortune 500), at least 143 or 28% had been acquired by 1989. The majority of takeovers have been friendly, carried out with the consent of the management of the target firm. But in many other so-called "hostile" takeovers, the target firm's management fought the bid. The period also saw the rise of management buyouts, in which managers used borrowed funds to buy the company they run.

Hostile takeovers and management buyouts have sparked enormous public controversy as well as calls for and enactment of antitakeover laws. Takeovers are blamed for layoffs, decimation of communities, cuts in investment and R & D, short horizons of U.S. managers, increased instability resulting from higher debt, as well as the decline of U.S. competitiveness. Many new state laws all but ban hostile takeovers, and Congress periodically considers federal antitakeover legislation. In 1988, a presidential candidate promised that his Justice Department would block mergers between large firms in the same industry to protect consumers from monopoly.

In this article, we summarize what we and others have learned about the 1980s takeover wave. The evidence suggests that takeovers in the 1980s represent a comeback to specialized, focused firms after years of diversification. In the 1980s, most acquirers bought other firms in their own lines of business. In addition, many diversified firms (conglomerates) were taken over, and their various business lines were sold off to different buyers in the same line of business. To a significant extent, takeovers in the 1980s reflect the deconglomeration of American business. Hostile takeovers and leveraged buyouts, which have attracted much public scrutiny, facilitated this process of deconglomeration. We show below that some of the common objections to takeovers, such as reduction of competition, cuts in employment, investment, and R & D, are not supported by the data. Although there is no evidence on the longrun post takeover performance of the 1980s acquisitions, the past failures of conglomerates suggest that performance is likely to improve.

We begin with a historical perspective on the 1980s takeover wave, then address some common concerns about takeovers, and finally discuss public policy.

Takeovers in the 1980s in Historical Perspective

There have been four takeover waves in the 20th century. The largest of them occurred around the turn of the century. The Sherman Antitrust Act of 1890 precluded collusive agreements between firms but allowed the creation of near monopolies with 50 to 90% market shares. In response to this law and with the help of new stock issues during the booming market, many industries merged into near monopolies overnight [1]. The U.S. Steel Corporation was formed in this period and controlled 65% of steel-making capacity. American Tobacco had a 90% market share. (However, General Motors could not find financing to buy Ford for $3 million!) The wave ended in 1904 when the Northern Securities decision of the Supreme Court greatly expanded the interpretation of the Sherman Act. Congress firmed up this case law by prohibiting monopolization through merger in the Clayton Antitrust Act of 1914.

The second merger wave came in the late 1920s, again coincident with a buoyant stock market receptive to new securities issued to finance the takeovers. As in the first wave, most deals were mergers of

---

1. G.S. Stigler, *Am.Econ.Rev.* 40, 23 (1950).

firms in the same industry. Now the courts did not allow monopoly, but still permitted formation of oligopolies—concentrated industries dominated by a few firms. Allied Chemical and Bethlehem Steel are products of this wave. This merger wave was stopped by the Great Depression and the collapse of the stock market, rather than by regulation.

The third wave is the conglomerate mergers of the late 1960s. Like the previous waves, it came during a stock market boom, which enabled buyers whom the stock market rewarded with high price/earnings ratios to finance their acquisitions with equity at attractive terms. Unlike those in the previous merger waves, a typical 1960s merger brought together two firms from completely different industries, leading to the formation of the so-called conglomerates. ITT and Teledyne are famous products of this era. The most likely reason for diversification was the antitrust policy which turned fiercely against mergers between firms in the same industry when the Celler–Kefauver Act passed in 1950. Unable to acquire businesses related to their own, flush with cash, and facing a favorable market for equity issues, acquirers bought companies outside their industries.

At the time conglomerates were formed, several theories were advanced to explain how they would improve the efficiency of U.S. businesses. One idea was that control of businesses changed from self-taught, unsophisticated entrepreneurs who started their own firms to experienced professional managers of conglomerates. Another idea was that conglomerates were an efficient way to monitor individual businesses by subjecting them to regular quantitative evaluations by the central office. Perhaps the most widely accepted rationale for conglomerates was the view that the central office reallocated investment funds from slowly growing subsidiaries, which generated cash, such as insurance and finance, to fast growing high technology businesses, which required investment funds. In this way, each conglomerate created an internal capital market, which could allocate investment funds more cheaply and efficiently than the banks or the stock and the bond markets.

The alleged superior efficiency of conglomerates is probably not what drove their creation. As in all other waves, it was more likely the case that firms wanted to grow and had access to cheap internal and external funds. But they could not continue to grow in their own lines of business because of aggressive antitrust enforcement. As a second best alternative from the point of view of growth-oriented managers, firms diversified. From the point of view of the shareholders, it might well have been best just to pay out the 1960s profits as dividends.

Recent evidence shows that conglomerate acquisitions typically failed. Although the buyers paid a premium to acquire the businesses, earnings of these businesses did not rise when they were acquired by conglomerates. In fact, some studies find that their earnings performance deteriorated[2]. Equally telling are the massive divestitures of assets acquired by conglomerates during the 1960s and 1970s. According to one estimate, 60% of the unrelated acquisitions taking place between 1970 and 1982 had been divested by 1989[3].

Why have conglomerates failed, despite all the efficiency arguments advanced in their favor? Perhaps the most important reason is that conglomerate builders ignored Adam Smith's principle that specialization raises productivity. In conglomerates, managers running central offices often knew little about the operations of the subsidiaries and could not allocate funds nearly as well as experts could. Nor could they rely on the managers of the subsidiaries to give them honest and accurate information, since each manager lobbied for his own business, and had little incentive to give up resources for the benefit of the other parts of the conglomerate. As a result, the crucial business decisions were made by nonspecialists with only limited information who had to divide their attention and resources between multiple businesses. Some divisions were neglected; others were probably overfed. For example, the Eveready battery division of Kraft is alleged to have been ignored as cheese took priority, and the cosmetics business of Revlon suffered as the company dedicated its scarce capital to expanding its health care subsidiaries. In addition, conglomerates lost many divisional top managers, who left to run their own shows at smaller specialized firms. The inefficiency of decision-making by nonspecialists offset the potential benefits of conglomerates.

In their attempt to monitor the divisions, conglomerates developed large and expensive central offices. But these central office controls often proved much less effective than the market discipline that stand-alone businesses are subjected to. Such businesses face competition in product markets, competition for capital in capital markets, and managerial competition. To a large extent, divisions of conglomerates are insulated from these forces, because they can afford to lose money and can be subsidized by other divisions, do not have to raise external capital, and face weaker managerial competition. In some respects, conglomerates resembled state ministries in centrally planned economies, where centralized control and transfer pricing replaced market forces. As this happened, many divisions of conglomerates became weaker competitors and often performed very poorly—as measured by low earnings and the high rate of divestitures. Below we argue that the takeover wave of the 1980s was to a large extent a response to the disappointment with conglomerates.

2. D.C. Mueller's "The Effects of Conglomerate Mergers" [*J.Bank.Financ.* 1, 315 (1977)] is a survey of these studies. D.J. Ravenscraft and F.M. Scherer's *Mergers, Sell–Offs, and Economic Efficiency* (Brookings Institution, Washington, DC, 1987) is the most recent and detailed study.

3. S.N. Kaplan and M. Weisbach, "Acquisitions and Divestitures: What Is Divested and How Much Does the Market Anticipate?" University of Chicago, mimeo, 1990.

As did all merger waves, the 1980s saw rising stock prices and rising corporate cash reserves stimulating the usual demand for expansion through acquisitions. However, in the 1980s the Reagan Administration consciously eased up on antitrust enforcement in an effort to leave the market alone. As a consequence, intraindustry acquisitions became possible on a large scale for the first time in 30 years. The easy availability of internal and external funds for investment coupled with the negative experience with the diversification of the 1960s and the first laissez-faire antitrust policy in decades shaped the takeover wave of the 1980s.

The return to expansion in core businesses is evident in the prevalence of two types of deals in the 1980s. In the first type, a large firm with most of its assets in a particular industry bought another large firm in the same industry. Some peripheral businesses were divested, but most of the acquired assets were kept. Such deals were common in gas pipelines, food, banking, airlines, and oil. In the second type of deal, a "bustup," the acquired firm was typically a conglomerate. Placing its assets in specialists' hands required a sale of many divisions to separate buyers. Our data indicate that in 62 hostile takeover contests between 1984 and 1986, 30% of the assets were on average sold off within 3 years [4]. In 17 cases more than half the assets were sold. Roughly 70% of the selloffs were to buyers in the same line of business.

In the face of the hostile pressure to divest, some managers realized that they themselves could profit from bustups, by taking the company private and then selling peripheral business to specialized acquirers. This realization explains a significant number of leveraged buyouts of the 1980s followed by large-scale divestitures. For leveraged buyouts in our 1984 to 1986 sample, selloffs are even higher than for takeovers as a whole, amounting to 44% of total assets.

In the 1980s takeover wave, the so-called "corporate raiders" and many leveraged buyout (LBO) specialists played the critical role of brokers. They acquired conglomerates, busted them up, and sold off most business segments to large corporations in the same businesses. Michael Jensen has argued that takeovers by raiders and by leveraged buyout funds move us toward a new incentive-infused organizational form that will permanently deliver shareholders from the wasteful ways of public corporations [5]. The evidence does not support his view. First, most takeovers do not involve raiders or LBO funds. Second, many raider and LBO-controlled firms are temporary organizations designed to last only as long as it takes to sell off the pieces of the acquired firm to other public corporations. The remaining pieces are often reoffered to the public, especially when their value has been enhanced by some operating changes.

---

4. S. Bhagat, A. Shleifer, R.W. Vishny, "Hostile Takeovers in the 1980s: The Return to Corporate Specialization," *Brookings Pap.Econ.Act.Microecon.* (1990), p. 1.

5. M.C. Jensen, *Har.Bus.Rev.* 67, 61 (1989).

A takeover that illustrates some of the features of the 1980s wave is the acquisition of cosmetics giant Revlon by the raider Ronald Perelman. This fiercely hostile takeover took place in 1985, at the price of $2.3 billion. Before the takeover, Revlon acquired many businesses outside cosmetics, particularly in health care. The top management of Revlon thought that health care offered better growth opportunities than cosmetics, and so reduced the investment and advertising budget of cosmetics to support the growth of the health care business. After the takeover, Perelman sold off $2.06 billion of Revlon's health care and other noncosmetics businesses. Perelman had an offer to sell the cosmetics business for $905 million (which, combined with $2.06 billion, shows how profitable this bustup was), but turned it down. About 60% of asset selloffs were to other companies in the health care field, but some were to management buyout groups. After the selloffs, Revlon substantially revamped the cosmetics business and tripled its advertising budget. ("Some of the most beautiful women in the world wear Revlon.") Headquarters staff was also reduced, although there is no evidence of blue-collar layoffs or of investment cuts. Revlon's profits increased substantially.

Table 1 summarizes more systematically the eventual allocation of assets induced by the hostile takeovers of 1984 to 1986. Combining direct acquisition of related assets with acquisitions of divested assets, we find that 72% of all assets that changed hands as a result of hostile takeovers were sold to public corporations in closely related businesses within 3 years. Only 15% of the assets ended up in private firms, such as those formed when management and leveraged buyout specialists take divisions private (MBOs). And only 4.5% of the assets was bought by public corporations acquiring outside of their core businesses. This last number clearly illustrates the move away from conglomerates.

Table 1. The movement of assets, 1984 to 1986.

Type of asset	Millions of dollars	Percent
Assets that changed hands	68,743	100
Assets that went to strategic buyers	49,660	72
Strategic acquisitions net of selloffs	26,010	38
Selloffs to strategic buyers	23,650	34
Assets that went to MBOs	10,234	15
Direct MBOs net of selloffs	4,834	7
Selloffs to MBOs	5,400	8
Assets that stayed with initial nonstrategic bidders	3,810	5.5
Assets that went to unrelated acquisitions	3,154	4.5
Direct unrelated bidders	373	0.5
Selloffs to unrelated bidders	2,781	4
Selloffs of headquarters, stocks	667	1
Not identified selloffs	1,219	2

Type of asset	Millions of dollars	Percent
Assets that did not change hands (nondivested assets of targets remaining independent)	39,716	
Total value of offers in the sample	108,459	

Has deconglomeration and expansion in core businesses raised efficiency and U.S. competitiveness? Some economists have taken the increase in stock prices of the acquired firms—which is not nearly offset by the modest stock price declines of acquiring firms—to be by itself incontrovertible evidence that efficiency must have improved. We do not take this position, since much evidence shows that the stock market can make large valuation mistakes [6]. The possibility that the stock market is overly enthusiastic about the takeovers of the 1980s should not be dismissed. After all, the market greeted the conglomerate mergers of the 1960s with share price increases, and most of these mergers failed. Nonetheless, there are reasons to expect the takeovers of the 1980s to raise long-term efficiency.

The fact that many takeovers dismantle conglomerates and allocate divisions to specialists creates a presumption that performance should improve. There is, in fact, evidence that divisions are more productive when they are part of less diversified companies, although this evidence does not establish the link specifically for divested divisions [7]. There is also evidence that acquired firms are less profitable than the firms buying them [8]. This suggests that more assets in an industry are being allocated to the organizations that can better manage them. Overall, the evidence recommends cautious optimism about the efficiency of takeovers in the 1980s.

SOME OBJECTIONS TO TAKEOVERS

The takeover wave of the 1980s aroused much public concern about reduced competition, employment cuts, and reductions in investment, especially in research and development. These concerns are largely unsupported by the data.

Since most of the mergers in the 1980s have been between firms that compete in product markets, the obvious question is whether these takeovers decrease competition and lead to price increases. After all, mergers from the first two waves of this century had the explicit goal of raising prices. Some takeovers in the 1980s could potentially reduce competition and raise prices, particularly among airlines, gas pipelines, and supermarkets where markets are regional rather than national, and so, easier to dominate. However, gaining significant market power through takeovers in the 1980s seems to be the exception rather than

6. For a review of this evidence, see A. Shleifer and L.H. Summers, "The Noise Trader Approach to Finance" [*J.Econ.Perspect.* 4, 19 (1990)].

7. F.R. Lichtenberg, "Industrial De-Diversification and Its Consequences for Productivity," Columbia University, manuscript, 1990.

8. H. Servaes, "Tobin's Q, Agency Costs, and Corporate Control," University of Chicago, mimeo, 1989.

the rule. First, in most cases the market share of the combined companies remains too small for effective market dominance: much smaller than that of 1920s oligopolies let alone the turn of the century trusts. Second, the share price behavior of nonmerging firms in the industry suggests that large profits from decreased competition are not the driving force behind most mergers. Oligopoly theory predicts that when an anticompetitive merger takes place, all firms in the industry should experience a rise in their profits and share prices since they all benefit from industry price increases. Conversely, when an anticompetitive merger is blocked by the antitrust authorities the share prices of all firms in the industry should decline along with those of the merging firms. The evidence, in contrast, shows that share prices of most nonmerging firms in an industry actually rise when a merger is challenged, inconsistent with the importance of decreased competition [9]. While the evidence is not conclusive, decreased competition and higher consumer prices from takeovers are probably not important in the 1980s.

The second major concern is the effect of hostile takeovers on employment. It has been argued that hostile takeovers represent a breach of employees' trust and transfer wealth from employees to shareholders through wage reductions and employment cuts [10]. Recent research sheds substantial light on this issue. First, except in isolated episodes, there is no evidence of substantial wage cuts following hostile takeovers [11]. Second, removal of excess pension assets from pension plans does accelerate after takeovers, which probably means a reduction in expected pensions. On average, however, these removals are small [12]. Third, layoffs rise after hostile takeovers. Among the 62 targets of hostile takeovers between 1984 and 1986, the total post takeover layoffs were about 26,000 people, which amounts to about 2.5% of the labor force of an average target firm. These layoffs are noticeable for the target firm, but small in the context of the national economy. By comparison, General Electric cut its work force by over 100,000 between 1981 and 1987.

Post takeover layoffs are disproportionately targeted at high-level white collar workers as hostile takeovers lead to reduction of headquarters employment, consolidation of headquarters, and other corporate staff reductions (4). When incumbent managers are reluctant to lay off redundant headquarters employees without external pressure, hostile acquirers do the dirty job for them. It is hard to worry too

---

9. R. Stillman, *J.Finan.Econ.* 11, 225 (1983).

10. A. Shleifer and L.H. Summers, "Breach of Trust in Hostile Takeovers," in *Corporate Takeovers: Causes and Consequences,* A.J. Auerbach, Ed. (Univ. of Chicago Press, Chicago, 1988), pp. 33–68.

11. J. Rosett, "Do Union Wealth Concessions Explain Takeover Premiums? The Evidence on Contract Wages" (NBER Working Paper 3187, National Bureau of Economic Research, Cambridge, MA, November, 1989).

12. J. Pontiff, A. Shleifer, M. Weisbach, "Excess Pension Fund Reversions After Takeovers," University of Rochester, mimeo, 1989.

much about these layoffs, since unemployment among educated white collar workers barely exists in the United States.

In sum, transfers from employees clearly do take place after hostile takeovers, but their magnitude is small relative to the wealth gains of the shareholders.

Perhaps the greatest public concern about takeovers is that they reduce investment in physical capital and particularly in R & D. Insufficient investment in physical capital and in R & D is often held responsible for declining U.S. competitiveness, as outdated products come out of outdated plants. An opposing view holds that the trouble with U.S. industry is excessive investment in businesses and technologies that should rationally be abandoned to lower cost foreign rivals [13]. Such investment only sucks up capital from high-tech industries and high-tech manufacturing where the United States should take the lead. This view makes investment cuts in basic industries a primary source of post takeover efficiency gains. Takeovers are needed because managers in declining industries are reluctant to shrink operations and distribute cash to shareholders.

Investment cuts that follow hostile takeovers have been large in some basic industries, especially the oil industry, where exploration was arguably excessive in the early and mid-1980s. One can also point to sporadic examples of investment cuts in other industries. On the other hand, our own evidence on hostile takeovers 1984 to 1986 suggests that investment cuts are neither the reason for, nor an important consequence of, most hostile takeovers. Of the 62 takeover contests that we study, investment cuts play a central role in at most 12 cases.

Investment is more often reduced after highly leveraged acquisitions, such as leveraged buyouts. In the struggle to meet interest payments after a buyout, good projects as well as bad ones may be abandoned. But these deals represent at most 15 to 20% of the takeover activity during this period [14]. Not having yet seen a post takeover recession, it is difficult to evaluate the difficulties that these highly leveraged deals will experience. It is important to notice, however, that selloffs usually enable firms to pay off a substantial share of their debt within a few years. In fact, many debt contracts have provisions requiring firms to sell off assets and reduce the debt. On the whole, with the exception of highly leveraged acquisitions there is not much evidence that takeovers result in large capital spending cuts.

With respect to R & D cuts, the evidence is clear. Targets of takeovers are not R & D-intensive companies [15]. On the contrary, they

---

13. M.C. Jensen, *Am.Econ.Rev.* 76, 323 (1986).

14. S.N. Kaplan, "The Effects of Management Buyouts on Operating Performance and Value," *J.Finan.Econ.* 24, 217 (1989).

15. B.H. Hall, "The Impact of Corporate Restructuring on Industrial Research and Development," *Brookings Pap.Econ. Act.Microecon.*, p. 85 (1990).

tend to be companies in mature, capital-intensive industries that are performing poorly and are not at the cutting edge of technology. Because takeover targets do little R & D to begin with, there are no noticeable R & D cuts after takeovers. It is a mistake to believe that R & D cuts are an important motive for or even an important consequence of takeovers.

The concern over debt and over R & D and investment cuts are part of the broader concern, which does not pertain to takeovers alone, that managers of U.S. corporations have short horizons. This concern has been expressed in particular in an influential MIT study, which argues that the economy of the United States is losing its competitiveness because the pressures of debt and of financial markets prevent managers from undertaking long-term projects [16].

Although there may be important differences between the United States and Japan in terms of planning horizon and willingness to invest, these differences are only marginally affected by takeovers. The differences appear to run much deeper. Part of the difference may stem from higher savings rates in Japan and more bullish stock market investors, and the rest may be due to a relatively greater emphasis by Japanese managers on growth and market share than on profitability. Takeovers are a minor factor by comparison to these considerations.

In sum, the evidence suggests that the three common concerns about hostile takeovers are exaggerated. The fact that takeovers of the 1980s have helped move assets out of conglomerates and toward more specialized users creates a presumption in their favor.

Public Policy Toward Takeovers

Public policy toward takeovers has taken several forms, including antitrust enforcement, state antitakeover legislation, and changes in tax policy particularly with respect to tax deductibility of interest payments on debt. We consider these policies briefly.

Federal antitrust policy has been quite important for takeovers. The hands off policy in the 1980s permitted the wave of related acquisitions. In a few cases, such as airlines, enforcement should probably have been tighter. However, a return to the antitrust stringency of the 1950s and 1960s, where an acquisition that raised a firm's market share from 5 to 7% could be disallowed, would be a mistake. The failed conglomerate wave was a direct consequence of this policy. In many cases, it might well be best if the firm did not make any acquisitions at all, and simply returned its excess earnings to shareholders. But as long as corporations are committed to survival and growth, and so continue to make acquisitions, the bias toward diversification induced by aggressive antitrust is damaging. For this reason, we would like to see antitrust policy remain largely as it is.

16. M.L. Dertouzos, R.K. Lester, R.M. Solow, *Made in America* (MIT Press, Cambridge, MA, 1989).

Much more damaging interventions are currently coming from state antitakeover laws, which aim to completely stop hostile takeovers. The usual justification of such laws is that, first, they enable managers to focus on the long term without the pressure of takeovers and, second, they prevent large-scale layoffs. These arguments, although theoretically appealing, do not have a large amount of empirical support; there is certainly little support for the view that large cuts in employment take place. The real reason for the state laws probably has little to do with these two arguments. Rather, these laws reflect the desire of target firms' managers to keep their jobs and their ability to influence legislators. The politics of the state laws are simple: managers and employees are voters as well as contributors, whereas shareholders typically reside out of state and are therefore neither.

State antitakeover laws entrench managers and allow conglomerates to survive. The best alternative to these laws is probably a federal law that subsumes them.

Last, tax policy has had a large effect on takeovers. Of the tax provisions that subsidize takeovers, the most important is tax deductibility of interest payments. If a company pays out $1 of its profit as interest, it can reduce its corporate profits tax base, whereas if it pays out the same $1 as dividends, it cannot have the deduction. This asymmetry allows firms to raise their values through increased use of debt. In this way, tax law subsidizes debt-financed acquisitions.

The extent of this subsidy is not as great as one might think, for several reasons. First, the target firm can itself borrow and buy back its own shares and so keep the gains from increased debt from accruing to the acquirer. Presumably, the acquiring firm can only profit to the extent that it can tolerate more debt, perhaps because it can cut some of the spending or divest divisions. Second, much of the debt is temporary, which greatly limits the value of the tax shield. As we pointed out earlier, divestitures usually lead to rapid reductions in debt.

Despite these limits on the value of the debt subsidy, there is no reason to subsidize debt at all. Accordingly, a limitation on tax deductibility of interest, or alternatively making dividend payments tax deductible as well, would reduce the distortion. An increase in the basic tax rate on corporate profits could keep the latter reform from increasing the budget deficit.

Conclusion

The takeovers of the 1980s, like those of the previous merger waves, partly reflect the desired expansion of large corporations in times of easy access to funds. With the current antitrust stance, this expansion has taken place within the areas of expertise of the acquiring firms and has made corporations more focused. Although the jury is still out on this takeover wave, the disappointing experience with conglomerates suggests that these takeovers are likely to raise efficiency as corporations realize the gains from specialization.

JENSEN, ECLIPSE OF THE PUBLIC CORPORATION
Harv.Bus.Rev. 61 (Sept.–Oct. 1989).

New organizations are emerging in its place—organizations that are corporate in form but have no public shareholders and are not listed or traded on organized exchanges. These organizations use public and private debt, rather than public equity, as their major source of capital. Their primary owners are not households but large institutions and entrepreneurs that designate agents to manage and monitor on their behalf and bind those agents with large equity interests and contracts governing the use and distribution of cash.

Takeovers, corporate breakups, divisional spinoffs, leveraged buyouts, and going-private transactions are the most visible manifestations of a massive organizational change in the economy. These transactions have inspired criticism, even outrage, among many business leaders and government officials, who have called for regulatory and legislative restrictions. The backlash is understandable. Change is threatening; in this case, the threat is aimed at the senior executives of many of our largest companies.

Despite the protests, this organizational innovation should be encouraged. By resolving the central weakness of the public corporation—the conflict between owners and managers over the control and use of corporate resources—these new organizations are making remarkable gains in operating efficiency, employee productivity, and shareholder value. Over the long term, they will enhance U.S. economic performance relative to our most formidable international competitor, Japan, whose companies are moving in the opposite direction. The governance and financial structures of Japan's public companies increasingly resemble U.S. companies of the mid–1960s and early 1970s—an era of gross corporate waste and mismanagement that triggered the organizational transformation now under way in the United States.

Consider these developments in the 1980s:

The capital markets are in transition. The total market value of equity in publicly held companies has tripled over the past decade—from $1 trillion in 1979 to more than $3 trillion in 1989. But newly acquired capital comes increasingly from private placements, which have expanded more than ten times since 1980, to a rate of $200 billion in 1988. Private placements of debt and equity now account for more than 40% of annual corporate financings. Meanwhile, in every year since 1983, at least 5% of the outstanding value of corporate equity has disappeared through stock repurchases, takeovers, and going-private transactions. Finally, households are sharply reducing their stock holdings.

The most widespread going-private transaction, the leveraged buyout, is becoming larger and more frequent. In 1988, the total value of the 214 public-company and divisional buyouts exceeded $77 billion—nearly one-third of the value of all mergers and acquisitions. The total value of the 75 buyouts in 1979 was only $1.3 billion (in constant 1988 dollars), while the 175 buyouts completed in 1983 had a total value of $16.6 billion. This process is just getting started; the $77 billion of LBOs in 1988 represented only 2.5% of outstanding public-company equity.

Entire industries are being reshaped. Just five years ago, the leading U.S. truck and automobile tire manufacturers were independent and diversified public companies. Today each is a vastly different enterprise. Uniroyal went private in 1985 and later merged its tire-making operations with those of B.F. Goodrich to form a new private company called Uniroyal Goodrich. In late 1986, Goodyear borrowed $2.6 billion and repurchased nearly half its outstanding shares to fend off a hostile tender offer by Sir James Goldsmith. It retained its core tire and rubber business while moving to divest an array of unrelated operations, including its Celeron oil and gas subsidiary, California-to-Texas oil pipeline, aerospace operation, and Arizona resort hotel. In 1987, GenCorp issued $1.75 billion of debt to repurchase more than half its outstanding shares. It divested several operations, including its General Tire subsidiary, to pay down the debt and focus on aerospace and defense. Last year, Firestone was sold to Bridgestone, Japan's largest tiremaker, for $2.6 billion, a transaction that created shareholder gains of $1.6 billion.

Developments as striking as the restructuring of our financial markets and major industries reflect underlying economic forces more fundamental and powerful than financial manipulation, management greed, reckless speculation, and the other colorful epithets used by defenders of the corporate status quo. The forces behind the decline of the public corporation differ from industry to industry. But its decline is real, enduring, and highly productive. It is not merely a function of the tax deductibility of interest. Nor does it reflect a transitory LBO phase through which companies pass before investment bankers and managers cash out by taking them public again. Nor, finally, is it premised on a systematic fleecing of shareholders and bondholders by managers and other insiders with superior information about the true value of corporate assets.

The current trends do not imply that the public corporation has no future. The conventional twentieth-century model of corporate governance—dispersed public ownership, professional managers without substantial equity holdings, a board of directors dominated by management-appointed outsiders—remains a viable option in some areas of the economy, particularly for growth companies whose profitable investment opportunities exceed the cash they generate internally. Such companies can be found in industries like computers and electronics, biotechnology, pharmaceuticals, and financial services. Companies choosing among a surplus of profitable projects are unlikely to invest systematically in unprofitable ones, especially when they must regularly turn to the capital markets to raise investment funds.

The public corporation is not suitable in industries where long-term growth is slow, where internally generated funds outstrip the opportunities to invest them profitably, or where downsizing is the most productive long-term strategy. In the tire industry, the shift to radials, which last three times longer than bias-ply tires, meant that manufacturers needed less capacity to meet world demand. Overcapacity inevitably forced a restructuring. The tenfold increase in oil prices from 1973 to 1981, which triggered world-wide conservation measures, forced oil producers into a similar retrenchment.

Industries under similar pressure today include steel, chemicals, brewing, tobacco, television and radio broadcasting, wood and paper products. In these and other cash-rich, low-growth or declining sectors, the pressures on management to waste cash flow through organizational slack or investments in unsound projects is often irresistible. It is in precisely these sectors that the publicly held corporation has declined most rapidly. Barring regulatory interference, the public corporation is also likely to decline in industries such as aerospace, automobiles and auto parts, banking, electric power generation, food processing, industrial and farm implements, and transportation equipment.

The public corporation is a social invention of vast historical importance. Its genius is rooted in its capacity to spread financial risk over the diversified portfolios of millions of individuals and institutions and to allow investors to customize risk to their unique circumstances and predilections. By diversifying risks that would otherwise be borne by owner-entrepreneurs and by facilitating the creation of a liquid market for exchanging risk, the public corporation lowered the cost of capital. These tradable claims on corporate ownership (common stock) also allowed risk to be borne by investors best able to bear it, without requiring them to manage the corporations they owned.

From the beginning, though, these risk-bearing benefits came at a cost. Tradable ownership claims create fundamental conflicts of interest between those who bear risk (the shareholders) and those who manage risk (the executives). The genius of the new organizations is that they eliminate much of the loss created by conflicts between owners and managers, without eliminating the vital functions of risk diversification and liquidity once performed exclusively by the public equity markets.

In theory, these new organizations should not be necessary. Three major forces are said to control management in the public corporation: the product markets, internal control systems led by the board of directors, and the capital markets. But product markets often have not played a disciplining role. For most of the last 60 years, a large and vibrant domestic market created for U.S. companies economies of scale and significant cost advantages over foreign rivals. Recent reversals at the hands of the Japanese and others have not been severe enough to sap most companies of their financial independence. The idea that outside directors with little or no equity stake in the company could effectively monitor and discipline the managers who selected them has proven hollow at best. In practice, only the capital markets have played much of a control function—and for a long time they were hampered by legal constraints.

Indeed, the fact that takeover and LBO premiums average 50% above market price illustrates how much value public-company managers can destroy before they face a serious threat of disturbance. Takeovers and buyouts both create new value and unlock value destroyed by management through misguided policies. I estimate that transactions associated with the market for corporate control unlocked shareholder gains (in target companies alone) of more than $500 billion between 1977 and 1988—more than 50% of the cash dividends paid by the entire corporate sector over this same period.

The widespread waste and inefficiency of the public corporation and its inability to adapt to changing economic circumstances have generated a wave of organizational innovation over the last 15 years—innovation driven by the rebirth of "active investors." By active investors I mean investors who hold large equity or debt positions, sit on boards of directors, monitor and sometimes dismiss management, are involved with the long-term strategic direction of the companies they invest in, and sometimes manage the companies themselves.

Active investors are creating a new model of general management. These investors include LBO partnerships such as Kohlberg Kravis Roberts and Clayton & Dubilier; entrepreneurs such as Carl Icahn, Ronald Perelman, Laurence Tisch, Robert Bass, William Simon, Irwin Jacobs, and Warren Buffett; the merchant banking arms of Wall Street houses such as Morgan Stanley, Lazard Frères, and Merrill Lynch; and family funds such as those controlled by the Pritzkers and the Bronfmans. Their model is built around highly leveraged financial structures, pay-for-performance compensation systems, substantial equity ownership by managers and directors, and contracts with owners and creditors that limit both cross-subsidization among business units and the waste of free cash flow. Consistent with modern finance theory, these organizations are not managed to maximize earnings per share but rather to maximize *value*, with a strong emphasis on cash flow.

More than any other factor, these organizations' resolution of the owner-manager conflict explains how they can motivate the same people, managing the same resources, to perform so much more effectively under private ownership than in the publicly held corporate form.

In effect, LBO partnerships and the merchant banks are rediscovering the role played by active investors prior to 1940, when Wall Street banks such as J.P. Morgan & Company were directly involved in the strategy and governance of the public companies they helped create. At the height of his prominence, Morgan and his small group of partners served on the boards of U.S. Steel, International Harvester,

First National Bank of New York, and a host of railroads, and were a powerful management force in these and other companies.

Morgan's model of investor activism disappeared largely as a result of populist laws and regulations approved in the wake of the Great Depression. These laws and regulations—including the Glass–Steagall Banking Act of 1933, the Securities Act of 1933, the Securities Exchange Act of 1934, the Chandler Bankruptcy Revision Act of 1938, and the Investment Company Act of 1940—may have once had their place. But they also created an intricate web of restrictions on company "insiders" (corporate officers, directors, or investors with more than a 10% ownership interest), restrictions on bank involvement in corporate reorganizations, court precedents, and business practices that raised the cost of being an active investor. Their long-term effect has been to insulate management from effective monitoring and to set the stage for the eclipse of the public corporation.

Indeed, the high cost of being an active investor has left financial institutions and money management firms, which control more than 40% of all corporate equity in the United States, almost completely uninvolved in the major decisions and long-term strategies of the companies their clients own. They are almost never represented on corporate boards. They use the proxy mechanism rarely and usually ineffectively, notwithstanding recent efforts by the Council of Institutional Investors and other shareholder activists to gain a larger voice in corporate affairs.

All told, institutional investors are remarkably powerless; they have few options to express dissatisfaction with management other than to sell their shares and vote with their feet. Corporate managers criticize institutional sell-offs as examples of portfolio churning and short-term investor horizons. One guesses these same managers much prefer churning to a system in which large investors on the boards of their companies have direct power to monitor and correct mistakes. Managers really want passive investors who can't sell their shares.

The absence of effective monitoring led to such large inefficiencies that the new generation of active investors arose to recapture the lost value. These investors overcome the costs of the outmoded legal constraints by purchasing entire companies—and using debt and high equity ownership to force effective self-monitoring.

A central weakness and source of waste in the public corporation is the conflict between shareholders and managers over the payout of free cash flow—that is, cash flow in excess of that required to fund all investment projects with positive net present values when discounted at the relevant cost of capital. For a company to operate efficiently and maximize value, free cash flow must be distributed to shareholders rather than retained. But this happens infrequently; senior management has few incentives to distribute the funds, and there exist few mechanisms to compel distribution.

A vivid example is the senior management of Ford Motor Company, which sits on nearly $15 billion in cash and marketable securities in an industry with excess capacity. Ford's management has been deliberating about acquiring financial service companies, aerospace companies, or making some other multibillion-dollar diversification move—rather than deliberating about effectively distributing Ford's excess cash to its owners so they can decide how to reinvest it.

Ford is not alone. Corporate managers generally don't disgorge cash unless they are forced to do so. In 1988, the 1,000 largest public companies (by sales) generated total funds of $1.6 trillion. Yet they distributed only $108 billion as dividends and another $51 billion through share repurchases.

Managers have incentives to retain cash in part because cash reserves increase their autonomy vis-à-vis the capital markets. Large cash balances (and independence from the capital markets) can serve a competitive purpose, but they often lead to waste and inefficiency. Consider a hypothetical world in which companies distribute excess cash to shareholders and then must convince the capital markets to supply funds as sound economic projects arise. Shareholders are at a great advantage in this world, where management's plans are subject to enhanced monitoring by the capital markets. Wall Street's analytical, due diligence, and pricing disciplines give shareholders more power to quash wasteful projects.

Managers also resist distributing cash to shareholders because retaining cash increases the size of the companies they run—and managers have many incentives to expand company size beyond that which maximizes shareholder wealth. Compensation is one of the most important incentives. Many studies document that increases in executive pay are strongly related to increases in corporate size rather than value.

The tendency of companies to reward middle managers through promotions rather than annual performance bonuses also creates a cultural bias toward growth. Organizations must grow in order to generate new positions to feed their promotion-based reward systems.

Finally, corporate growth enhances the social prominence, public prestige, and political power of senior executives. Rare is the CEO who wants to be remembered as presiding over an enterprise that makes fewer products in fewer plants in fewer countries than when he or she took office—even when such a course increases productivity and adds hundreds of millions of dollars of shareholder value. The perquisites of the executive suite can be substantial, and they usually increase with company size.

The struggle over free cash flow is at the heart of the role of debt in the decline of the public corporation. Bank loans, mezzanine securities, and high-yield bonds have fueled the wave of takeovers, restructurings, and going-private transactions. The combined borrowings of all nonfinancial corporations in the United States approached $2 trillion in

1988, up from $835 billion in 1979. The interest charges on these borrowings represent more than 20% of corporate cash flows, high by historical standards.

This perceived "leveraging of corporate America" is perhaps the central source of anxiety among defenders of the public corporation and critics of the new organizational forms. But most critics miss three important points. First, the trebling of the market value of public-company equity over the last decade means that corporate borrowing had to increase to avoid a major *de*leveraging.

Second, debt creation *without retention of the proceeds of the issue* helps limit the waste of free cash flow by compelling managers to pay out funds they would otherwise retain. Debt is in effect a substitute for dividends—a mechanism to force managers to disgorge cash rather than spend it on empire-building projects with low or negative returns, bloated staffs, indulgent perquisites, and organizational inefficiencies.

By issuing debt in exchange for stock, companies bond their managers' promise to pay out future cash flows in a way that simple dividend increases do not. "Permanent" dividend increases or multiyear share repurchase programs (two ways public companies can distribute excess cash to shareholders) involve no contractual commitments by managers to owners. It's easy for managers to cut dividends or scale back share repurchases.

Take the case of General Motors. On March 3, 1987, several months after the departure of GM's only active investor, H. Ross Perot, the company announced a program to repurchase up to 20% of its common stock by the end of 1990. As of mid–1989, GM had purchased only 5% of its outstanding common shares, even though its $6.8 billion cash balance was more than enough to complete the program. Given management's poor performance over the past decade, shareholders would be better off making their own investment decisions with the cash GM is retaining. From 1977 to 1987, the company made capital expenditures of $77.5 billion while its U.S. market share declined by 10 points.

Borrowing allows for no such managerial discretion. Companies whose managers fail to make promised interest and principal payments can be declared insolvent and possibly hauled into bankruptcy court.

In the imagery of G. Bennett Stewart and David M. Glassman, "Equity is soft, debt hard. Equity is forgiving, debt insistent. Equity is a pillow, debt a sword." Some may find it curious that a company's creditors wield far more power over managers than its public shareholders, but it is also undeniable.

Third, debt is a powerful agent for change. For all the deeply felt anxiety about excessive borrowing, "overleveraging" can be desirable and effective when it makes economic sense to break up a company, sell off parts of the business, and refocus its energies on a few core operations. Companies that assume so much debt they cannot meet the debt service payments out of operating cash flow force themselves to rethink their entire strategy and structure. Overleveraging creates the crisis atmosphere managers require to slash unsound investment programs, shrink overhead, and dispose of assets that are more valuable outside the company. The proceeds generated by these overdue restructurings can then be used to reduce debt to more sustainable levels, creating a leaner, more efficient and competitive organization.

In other circumstances, the violation of debt covenants creates a board-level crisis that brings new actors onto the scene, motivates a fresh review of top management and strategy, and accelerates response. The case of Revco D.S., Inc., one of the handful of leveraged buyouts to reach formal bankruptcy, makes the point well.

Critics cite Revco's bankruptcy petition, filed in July 1988, as an example of the financial perils associated with LBO debt. I take a different view. The $1.25 billion buyout, announced in December 1986, did dramatically increase Revco's annual interest charges. But several other factors contributed to its troubles, including management's decision to overhaul pricing, stocking, and merchandise layout in the company's drugstore chain. This mistaken strategic redirection left customers confused and dissatisfied, and Revco's performance suffered. Before the buyout, and without the burden of interest payments, management could have pursued these policies for a long period of time, destroying much of the company's value in the process. Within six months, however, debt served as a brake on management's mistakes, motivating the board and creditors to reorganize the company before even more value was lost.

Developments at Goodyear also illustrate how debt can force managers to adopt value-creating policies they would otherwise resist. Soon after his company warded off Sir James Goldsmith's tender offer, Goodyear chairman Robert Mercer offered his version of the raiders' creed: "Give me your undervalued assets, your plants, your expenditures for technology, research and development, the hopes and aspirations of your people, your stake with your customers, your pension funds, and I will enhance myself and the dealmakers."

What Mr. Mercer failed to note is that Goodyear's forced restructuring dramatically increased the company's value to shareholders by compelling him to disgorge cash and shed unproductive assets. Two years after this bitter complaint, Tom Barrett, who succeeded Mercer as Goodyear's CEO, was asked whether the company's restructuring had hurt the quality of its tires or the efficiency of its plants. "No," he replied. "We've been able to invest and continue to invest and do the things we've needed to do to be competitive."

Robert Mercer's harsh words are characteristic of the business establishment's response to the eclipse of the public corporation. What explains such vehement opposition to a trend that clearly benefits shareholders and the economy? One important factor, as my Harvard Business School colleague Amar Bhide suggests, is that Wall Street now competes directly with senior management as a steward of shareholder wealth. With its vast increases in data, talent, and technology, Wall Street can allocate capital among competing businesses and monitor and discipline management more effectively than the CEO and headquarters staff of the typical diversified company. KKR's New York offices and Irwin Jacobs' Minneapolis base are direct substitutes for corporate headquarters in Akron or Peoria. CEOs worry that they and their staffs will lose lucrative jobs in favor of competing organizations. Many are right to worry; the performance of active investors versus the public corporation leaves little doubt as to which is superior.

Active investors are creating new models of general management, the most widespread of which I call the LBO Association. A typical LBO Association consists of three main constituencies: an LBO partnership that sponsors going-private transactions and counsels and monitors management in an ongoing cooperative relationship; company managers who hold substantial equity stakes in an LBO division and stay on after the buyout; and institutional investors (insurance companies, pension funds, and money management firms) that fund the limited partnerships that purchase equity and lend money (along with banks) to finance the transactions.

Much like a traditional conglomerate, LBO Associations have many divisions or business units, companies they have taken private at different points in time. KKR, for example, controls a diverse collection of 19 businesses including all or part of Beatrice, Duracell, Motel 6, Owens–Illinois, RJR Nabisco, and Safeway. But LBO Associations differ from publicly held conglomerates in at least four important respects. (See the illustration, "Public Company vs. LBO Association.")

Management incentives are built around a strong relationship between pay and performance. Compensation systems in LBO Associations usually have higher upper bounds than do public companies (or no upper bounds at all), tie bonuses much more closely to cash flow and debt retirement than to accounting earnings, and otherwise closely link management pay to divisional performance. Unfortunately, because these companies are private, little data are available on salaries and bonuses.

Public data are available on stock ownership, however, and equity holdings are a vital part of the reward system in LBO Associations. The University of Chicago's Steven Kaplan studied all public-company buyouts from 1979 through 1985 with a purchase price of at least $50 million. Business-unit chiefs hold a median equity position of 6.4% in their unit. Even without considering bonus and incentive plans, a $1,000 increase in shareholder value triggers a $64 increase in the personal wealth of business-unit chiefs. The median public-company CEO holds only .25% of the company's equity. Counting *all* sources of compensation—including salary, bonus, deferred compensation, stock options, and dismissal penalties—the personal wealth of the median public-company CEO increases by only $3.25 for a $1,000 increase in shareholder value.

Thus the salary of the typical LBO business-unit manager is almost 20 times more sensitive to performance than that of the typical public-company manager. This comparison understates the true differences in compensation. The personal wealth of managing partners in an LBO partnership (in effect, the CEOs of the LBO Associations) is tied almost exclusively to the performance of the companies they control. The general partners in an LBO Association typically receive (through overrides and direct equity holdings) 20% or more of the gains in the value of the divisions they help manage. This implies a pay-for-performance sensitivity of $200 for every $1,000 in added shareholder value. It's not hard to understand why an executive who receives $200 for every $1,000 increase in shareholder value will unlock more value than an executive who receives $3.25.

LBO Associations are more decentralized than publicly held conglomerates. The LBO Association substitutes compensation incentives and ownership for direct monitoring by headquarters. The headquarters of KKR, the world's largest LBO partnership, has only 16 professionals and 44 additional employees. In contrast, the Atlanta headquarters of RJR Nabisco employed 470 people when KKR took it private last year in a $25 billion transaction. At the time of the Goldsmith tender offer for Goodyear, the company's Akron headquarters had more than 5,000 people on its salaried payroll.

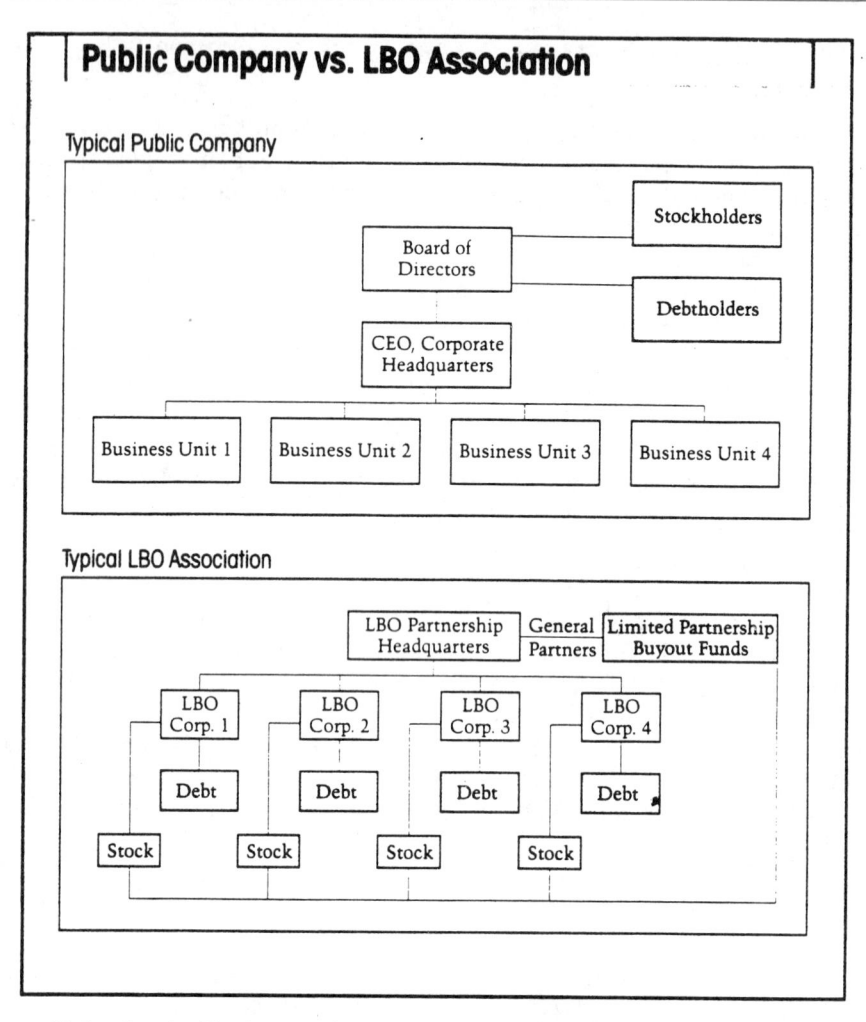

Public Company vs. LBO Association

Typical Public Company

```
                              Board of ─────── Stockholders
                              Directors
                                 │  └──────── Debtholders
                              CEO, Corporate
                              Headquarters
          ┌──────────────┬──────────┴──────────┬──────────────┐
    Business Unit 1  Business Unit 2    Business Unit 3   Business Unit 4
```

Typical LBO Association

```
                     LBO Partnership   General   Limited Partnership
                     Headquarters      Partners  Buyout Funds
            ┌──────────┬──────────────┬──────────────┐
         LBO        LBO            LBO            LBO
         Corp. 1    Corp. 2        Corp. 3        Corp. 4
           │          │              │              │
         Debt       Debt           Debt           Debt

    Stock      Stock          Stock          Stock
```

    It is physically impossible for KKR and other LBO partnerships to become intimately involved in the day-to-day decisions of their operating units. They rely instead on stock ownership, incentive pay that rewards cash flow, and other compensation techniques to motivate managers to maximize value without bureaucratic oversight. My survey of 7 LBO partnerships found an average headquarters staff of 13 professionals and 19 nonprofessionals that oversees almost 24 business units with total annual sales of more than $11 billion.

    LBO Associations rely heavily on leverage. The average debt ratio (long-term debt as a percentage of debt plus equity) for public companies prior to a buyout is about 20%. The Kaplan study shows the average debt ratio for an LBO is 85% on completion of the buyout.

    Intensive use of debt dramatically shrinks the amount of equity in a company. This allows the LBO general partners and divisional managers to control a large fraction of the total ownership without requiring huge investments they would be unable to make or large grants of free equity. For example, in a company with $1 billion in assets and a debt ratio of 20%, management would have to raise $80 million to buy 10% of the equity. If that same company had a debt ratio of 90%, management would have to raise only $10 million to control a 10% stake. By concentrating equity holdings among managers and LBO partners, debt intensifies the ownership incentives that are so important to efficiency.

High debt also allows LBO Associations and other private organizations to tap the benefits of risk diversification once provided only by the public equity market. Intensive use of debt means much of it must be in the form of public, high-yield, noninvestment-grade securities, better known as junk bonds. This debt, which was pioneered by Drexel Burnham Lambert, reflects more of the risk borne by shareholders in the typical public company. Placing this public debt in the well-diversified portfolios of large financial institutions spreads equitylike risk among millions of investors, who are the ultimate beneficiaries of mutual funds and pension funds—without requiring those risks to be held as equity. Indeed, high-yield debt is probably the most important and productive capital market innovation in the last 40 years.

LBO Associations have well-defined obligations to their creditors and residual claimants. Most buyout funds are organized as limited partnerships in which the partners of the sponsoring LBO firm serve as general partners. The buyout fund purchases most of the equity and sometimes provides debt financing. The limited partnership agreement denies the general partner the right to transfer cash or other resources from one LBO division to another. That is, all returns from a business must be distributed to the limited partners and other equity holders of that business. Such binding agreements reduce the risk of unproductive reinvestment by prohibiting cross-subsidization among LBO units. In effect, the LBO sponsor must ask its institutional investors for permission to reinvest funds, a striking difference from the power of public-company managers to freely shift resources among business units.

The management, compensation, and financial structures of the LBO Association square neatly with the rebirth of active investors. Institutional investors delegate the job of being active monitors to agents best qualified to play the role. The LBO partnerships bond their performance by investing their own resources and reputations in the transaction and taking the bulk of their compensation as a share in the companies' increased value.

To be sure, this delegation is not without its tensions. The fact that LBO partnerships and divisional managers control the LBO Associations' small equity base but hold little of the debt creates incentives for them to take high-risk management gambles. If their gambles succeed, they reap large rewards by increasing their equity value; if their gambles fail, creditors bear much of the cost. But the reputational consequences of such reckless behavior can be large. As long as creditors behave rationally, an LBO partnership that tries to profit at the expense of its creditors or walks away from a deal gone sour will not be able to raise funds for future investments.

To date, the performance of LBO Associations has been remarkable. Indeed, it is difficult to find any systematic losers in these transactions, and almost all of the gains appear to come from real increases in productivity. The best studies of LBO performance reach the following conclusions:

LBOs create large gains for shareholders. Studies estimate that the average total premium to public shareholders ranges from 40% to 56%. Kaplan finds that in buyouts that go public again or are otherwise sold (which occurs on average 2.7 years after the original transaction), total shareholder value increases by an average of 235%, or nearly 100% above market-adjusted returns over the same period. These returns are distributed about equally between prebuyout shareholders and the suppliers of debt and equity to the transaction. Prebuyout shareholders earn average market-adjusted premiums of 38%, while the total return to capital (debt plus equity) for buyout investors is 42%. This return to buyout investors is measured on the total purchase price of the LBO, not the buyout equity. Because equity returns are almost a pure risk premium, and therefore independent of the amount invested, they are very high. The median market-adjusted return on buyout equity is 785%, or 125% per year.

Value gains do not come at the expense of other financial constituencies. Some critics argue that buyout investors, especially managers, earn excessive returns by using inside information to exploit public shareholders. Managers do face severe conflicts of interest in these transactions; they cannot simultaneously act as buyer and agent for the seller. But equity-owning managers who are not part of post-buyout management teams systematically sell their shares into LBOs. This would be foolish if the buyout were significantly underpriced in light of inside information, assuming that these nonparticipating insiders have the same inside information as the continuing management team. Moreover, LBO auctions are becoming common; underpriced buyout proposals (including those initiated by management) quickly generate competing bids.

No doubt some bondholders have lost value through going-private transactions. By my estimate, RJR Nabisco's prebuyout bondholders lost almost $300 million through the downgrading of their claims on the newly leveraged company. This is a small sum in comparison to the $12 billion in total gains the transaction produced. As yet, there is no evidence that bondholders lose on average from LBOs. Evidence on LBOs completed through 1986 does show that holders of convertible bonds and preferred stock gain a statistically significant amount and that straight bondholders suffer no significant gains or losses.

New data may document losses for bondholders in recent transactions. But the expropriation of wealth from bondholders should not be a continuing problem. The financial community is perfecting many techniques, including poison puts and repurchase provisions, to protect bondholders in the event of substantial restructurings. In fact, versions of these loss-prevention techniques have been available for some time. In the past, bondholders such as Metropolitan Life, which sued RJR Nabisco over the declining value of the company's bonds, chose not to pay the premium for protection.

LBOs increase operating efficiency without massive layoffs or big cuts in research and development. Kaplan finds that average operating earnings increase by 42% from the year prior to the buyout to the third year after the buyout. Cash flows increase by 96% over this same period. Other studies document significant improvements in profit margins, sales per employee, working capital, inventories, and receivables. Those who doubt these findings might take a moment to scan the business press, which has chronicled the impressive postbuyout performance of companies such as Levi Strauss, A.O. Scott, Safeway, and Weirton Steel.

Importantly, employment does not fall systematically after buyouts, although it does not grow as quickly as in comparable companies. Median employment for all companies in the Kaplan study, including those engaged in substantial divestitures, increased by nearly 1%. Companies without significant divestitures increased employment by 5%.

Moreover, the great concern about the effect of buyouts on R & D and capital investment is unwarranted. The low-growth companies that make the best candidates for LBOs don't invest heavily in R & D to begin with. Of the 76 companies in the Kaplan study, only 7 spent more than 1% of sales on R & D before the buyout. Another recent study shows that R & D as a fraction of sales grows at the same rate in LBOs as in comparable public companies. According to Kaplan's study, capital expenditures are 20% lower in LBOs than in comparable non-LBO companies. Because these cuts are taking place in low-growth or declining industries and are accompanied by a doubling of market-adjusted value, they appear to be coming from reductions in low-return projects rather than productive investments.

Taxpayers do not subsidize going-private transactions. Much has been made of the charge that large increases in debt virtually eliminate the tax obligations of an LBO. This argument overlooks five sources of additional tax revenues generated by buyouts: capital gains taxes paid by prebuyout shareholders; capital gains taxes paid on postbuyout asset sales; tax payments on the large increases in operating earnings generated by efficiency gains; tax payments by creditors who receive interest payments on the LBO debt; and taxes generated by more efficient use of the company's total capital.

Overall, the U.S. Treasury collects an estimated 230% more revenues in the year after a buyout than it would have otherwise and 61% more in long-term present value. The $12 billion gain associated with the RJR Nabisco buyout will generate net tax revenues of $3.3 billion in the first year of the buyout; the company paid $370 million in federal taxes in the year before the buyout. In the long term, the transaction will generate total taxes with an estimated present value of $3.8 billion.

LBO sponsors do not have to take their companies public for them to succeed. Most LBO transactions are completed with a goal of returning the reconfigured company to the public market within three to five years. But recent evidence indicates that LBO sponsors are keeping their companies under private ownership. Huge efficiency gains and high-return asset sales produce enough cash to pay down debt and allow LBOs to generate handsome returns as going concerns. The very proliferation of these transactions has helped create a more efficient infrastructure and liquid market for buying and selling divisions and companies. Thus LBO investors can "cash out" in a secondary LBO or private sale without recourse to a public offering. One recent study finds that only 5% of the more than 1,300 LBOs between 1981 and 1986 have gone public again.

Public companies can learn from LBO Associations and emulate many of their characteristics. But this requires major changes in corporate structure, philosophy, and focus. They can reduce the waste of free cash flow by borrowing to repurchase stock or pay large dividends. They can alter their charters to encourage large investors or experiment with alliances with active investors such as Lazard Frères' Corporate Partners fund. They can increase equity ownership by directors, managers, and employees. They can enhance incentives through pay-for-performance systems based on cash flow and value rather than accounting earnings. They can decentralize management by rethinking the role of corporate headquarters and shrinking their staffs.

Some corporations are experimenting with such changes—FMC, Holiday, and Owens–Corning—and the results have been impressive. But only a coordinated attack on the status quo will halt the eclipse of the public company. It is unlikely such an attack will proceed fast enough or go far enough.

Who can argue with a new model of enterprise that aligns the interests of owners and managers, improves efficiency and productivity, and unlocks hundreds of billions of dollars of shareholder value? Many people, it seems, mainly because these organizations rely so heavily on debt. As I've discussed, debt is crucial to management discipline and resolving the conflict over free cash flow. But critics, even some who concede the control function of debt, argue that the costs of leverage outweigh the benefits.

Wall Street economist Henry Kaufman, a prominent critic of the going-private trend, issued a typical warning earlier this year: "Any severe shock—a sharp increase in interest rates in response to Federal Reserve credit restraint, or an outright recession that makes the whole stock market vulnerable, or some breakdown in the ability of foreign firms to bid for pieces of U.S. companies—will drive debt-burdened companies to the government's doorstep to plead for special assistance."

The relationship between debt and insolvency is perhaps the least understood aspect of this entire organizational evolution. New hedging techniques mean the risk associated with a given level of corporate debt is lower today than it was five years ago. Much of the bank debt associated with LBOs (which typically represents about half of the total debt) is done through floating-rate instruments. But few LBOs accept unlimited exposure to interest rate fluctuations. They purchase caps to set a ceiling on interest charges or use swaps to convert floating-rate debt into fixed-rate debt. In fact, most banks require such risk management techniques as a condition of lending.

Critics of leverage also fail to appreciate that insolvency in and of itself is not always something to avoid—and that the costs of becoming insolvent are likely to be much smaller in the new world of high leverage than in the old world of equity-dominated balance sheets. The proliferation of takeovers, LBOs, and other going-private transactions have inspired innovations in the reorganization and workout process. I refer to these innovations as "the privatization of bankruptcy." LBOs do get in financial trouble more frequently than public companies do. But few LBOs ever enter formal bankruptcy. They are reorganized quickly (a few months is common), often under new management, and at much lower costs than under a court-supervised process.

How can insolvency be less costly in a world of high leverage? Consider an oversimplified example. Companies A and B are identical in every respect except for their financial structures. Each has a going-concern value of $100 million (the discounted value of its expected future cash flows) and a liquidation or salvage value of $10 million. Company A has an equity-dominated balance sheet with a debt ratio of 20%, common for large public companies. Highly leveraged Company B has a debt ratio of 85%, common for LBOs.

Now both companies experience business reversals. What happens? Company B will get in trouble with its creditors much sooner than Company A. After all, Company B's going-concern value doesn't have to shrink very much for it to be unable to meet its payments on $85 million of debt. But when it does run into trouble, its going-concern value will be nowhere near its liquidation value. If the going-concern value shrinks to $80 million, there remains $70 million of value to preserve by avoiding liquidation. So Company B's creditors have strong incentives to preserve the remaining value by quickly and efficiently reorganizing their claims outside the courtroom.

No such incentives operate on Company A. Its going-concern value can fall dramatically before creditors worry about their $20 million of debt. By the time creditors do intervene, Company A's going-concern value will have plummeted. And if Company A's value falls to under $20 million, it is much more likely than Company B to be worth less than its $10 million salvage value. Liquidation in this situation is the likely and rational outcome, with all its attendant conflicts, dislocations, and costs.

There are already some worrisome structural issues. I look with discomfort on the dangerous tendency of LBO partnerships, bolstered by their success, to take more of their compensation in front-end fees rather than in back-end profits earned through increased equity value. As management fees and the fees for completing deals get larger, the incentives to do deals, rather than good deals, also increases. Institutional investors (and the economy as a whole) are best served when the LBO partnership is the last member of the LBO Association to get paid and when the LBO partnership gets paid as a fraction of the back-end value of the deals, including losses.

Moreover, we have yet to fully understand the limitations on the size of this new organizational form. LBO partnerships are understandably tempted to increase the reach of their talented monitors by reconfiguring divisions as acquisition vehicles. This will be difficult to accomplish successfully. It is likely to require bigger staffs, greater centralization of decision rights, and dilution of the high pay-for-performance sensitivity that is so crucial to success. As LBO Associations expand, they run the risk of recreating the bureaucratic waste of the diversified public corporation.

These and other problems should not cloud the remarkable benefits associated with the eclipse of the large public corporation. What surprises me is how few mistakes have occurred thus far in an organizational change as profound as any since World War II.

Note

Takeovers in the Nineties

As this book goes to press, there have been three significant developments in mergers and acquisitions not covered by the Shleifer & Vishny article.

First, acquirers have found it much more difficult and expensive to secure financing for takeovers. Several large takeovers have put the acquiring company into extreme financial difficulty. Large lenders such as Japanese commercial banks have become much more cautious, and junk bonds have fallen in value, driving up the yields that must be paid on new offerings. Moreover, the collapse of an investment bank, Drexel, Burnham & Lambert, which was the principal market maker in junk bonds, has left the junk bond market in disarray. Consequently in early 1990 takeover activity was down 50 percent from 1989. The financial pinch is felt most strongly by erstwhile participants in large leveraged deals, which have all but disappeared. The frequency of middle-market acquisitions, acquisitions by ongoing firms of other medium-sized firms, has not been affected significantly, however, although there is significantly less debt financing (more equity) in the acquisitions. Moreover, more American firms and investors have been turning their attention abroad, giving increasing attention to international acquisitions.

Second, state antitakeover statutes and firm-specific defenses have all but stopped hostile stock acquisitions. An acquirer must have target board approval to purchase a controlling block of target stock. This has caused hostile bidders to resort to an old tactic with a new twist: proxy fights. The new battering ram is a takeover bid coupled with a proxy fight. The hostile bidder makes a tender offer for target shares at a healthy premium over market price conditioned on approval by the target board (to avoid state legislation and firm defenses), knowing that the target board will refuse. The bidder then uses the refusal to mount a proxy contest to oust the board, arguing in the proxy statement that the existing board is denying its shareholders the tender offer premium. The threat of losing the proxy contest is often enough to get the board to capitulate. In early 1990 four companies agreed to be acquired or auctioned after proxy challenges by bidders. See Smith, Barracudas Barrage Firms' Barricades: Takeover Defenses Prove to Be Flimsy, Wall St.J., C1, col. 2, May 10, 1990. Firms and state legislatures are now turning their attention to whether they can curtail proxy contests. See chapter 4 infra.

Third, a growing number of investors are turning their attention to bankrupt companies. Wall St.J., C1, April 16, 1990. Instead of purchasing equity securities, which are worthless, they purchase debt securities and other claims against the bankrupt entity held by a variety of lenders such as banks and trade creditors. For example, in early 1990 Japonica Partners purchased nearly $70 million bank claims against Allegheny International and became the firm's largest creditor. Japonica subsequently voted against Allegheny's bankruptcy reorganization plan and initiated a hostile takeover of the company. See chapter 9 infra.

Note

The Policy Debate

The striking phenomenon of takeovers is the extraordinarily high premiums that bidders have been willing to pay for the stock of target corporations. Bidders pay, on average, roughly 150 percent of preacquisition market price for target shares.[1] If target shares trade in a liquid secondary market, the market price reflects the educated consensus of a large number of investors on the value of the stock. Why are individual bidders willing to invest large amounts based on extreme valuations of a target firm's worth? A claim that there are two different markets at work, a market for individual shares and a market for control of a firm, is not a full answer. At issue is an explanation of why control of a firm is so much more valuable than the aggregated value of individually traded shares of stock in a liquid market.

There are several possible explanations. Some of the explanations support claims that takeovers are socially beneficial, and some explana-

---

1. See Black, Bidder Overpayment in Takeovers, 41 Stan.L.Rev. 597, 601 (1989). The average premiums paid vary dramatically, depending on the characteristics of the takeover. For example, the average premium for partial tender offer of less than 50 percent is much lower than for any-and-all tender offers.

tions support claims that takeovers are socially harmful. A scorecard of which explanations most often describe accurately the motivation for takeovers is, of course, directly relevant to the debate in Congress and in state legislatures over whether to pass takeover restrictions or to enact prohibitions on takeover defenses. We shall see these explanations pop up throughout the material in this book, and it is best to get them all on the table in a systematic fashion early in the materials. In later chapters we will more thoroughly investigate individual components of the claims, with emphasis on existing empirical studies. There are six basic arguments.

First, and the favorite of neoclassical economists and raiders, the bidder pays a premium over market price because it believes that the target's assets have not been optimally used by the existing managers and that under superior management the assets could earn a higher return. See, e.g., Easterbrook & Fischel, The Proper Role of Target's Management in Responding to a Tender Offer, 94 Harv.L.Rev. 1161 (1981); Jensen, Eclipse of the Public Corporation, Harv.Bus.Rev. 61 (Sept.–Oct. 1989). The higher the premium, the greater the degree of mismanagement that the bidder perceives. So viewed, the tender offer is socially desirable, benefiting both the bidder and the target shareholders, who divide among themselves the value that the incumbent managers had left on the table. This underutilization of assets can take a wide variety of forms. The mismanagement of a firm's physical assets is the most obvious. The mismanagement of a firm's capital structure, its use and retention of cash, and its failure to use untapped debt capacity, among other things, are less obvious to laypeople but may lie behind many acquisitions.[1] Professors Shleifer and Vishny argue in the *Science* article above that several of the takeovers of the 1980s represent a necessary correction of ill-advised conglomerate mergers in the late 1960s.

Second, and the favorite of blue-chip acquirers, the premium is justified not by the suboptimal performance of the target but by the unique fit of bidders' and targets' operations. The value of the combined enterprise is greater than the added value of the separate companies. This "synergy" can come from a variety of factors. The bidder and target, for example, could combine separate distribution networks for their complementary products, eliminating excess facilities and staff. Or a firm with a widespread distribution network and fading products could merge with a firm with no distribution network and advanced products. The problem is that synergy is very hard to quantify and can generate some very optimistic projections. In the conglomerate merger wave of the late 1960s purchasers seem to have vastly overestimated the benefits of synergy in financial structure ("We can better move capital among divisions") and underestimated the losses due to the absence of specialization of function. In short,

---

1. I have omitted from the list of possible explanations one often found in the literature—the "P/E game." See P. Steiner, *Mergers: Motives, Effects, Policies* 103–19 (1975). A firm with a high P/E ratio buys, using its stock, all the stock of a firm with a low P/E ratio. After the acquisition the bidder's P/E ratio attaches to the earnings of the now-absorbed target assets. This magic either assumes a very dumb pool of investors who ought to, but do not, use a weighted P/E ratio to calculate the value of the bidder's stock after the merger, an assumption I am not willing to make. The bidder's managers replace the target's managers and better use the assets.

if a CEO has a proclivity toward firm expansion, he can hypothecate, with a stack of supporting documents, synergy gains.

Third, and the favorite of the more cynical observers of the American economic system, the bidder may be a sucker and simply have overpaid target shareholders. See, e.g., Black, Bidder Overpayment in Takeovers, 41 Stan.L.Rev. 597 (1989). There are two versions of this thesis, resting on one's views about whether the managers of a specific acquirer are gullible or devious. The managers of the bidders may hold, quite innocently, exaggerated views on their ability to better manage the target assets or exaggerated views on the synergy gains available from an acquisition. Sometimes referred to as the "winner's curse" in an auction contest, the successful bidder may be the one market participant who misvalued the target, paying above market value. On the other hand, target managers may also knowingly and willingly have overpaid to build a personal empire at the expense of their own shareholders. Greater size of a firm corresponds to higher compensation and enhanced prestige for managers.

An important corollary of the third explanation is the argument that investment banker and lawyer fees drive the acquisitions. See, e.g., J. Brooks, *The Takeover Game* 251–55 (1987). Executives suffer such fees either because they are duped innocents or empire building at the expense of their firms. Executives pursue deals at the behest of investment bankers and lawyers motivated by the prospect of very high fees. By tradition, fees for investment bankers are based on a sliding percentage of the amount of the transaction. A common fee system in the mid-eighties was a basic charge of one percent for a $100 million transaction, .5 percent for one of $500 million, .4 percent for one of $1 billion, and .23 percent for one of $4 billion. And, of course, each side pays its bankers and lawyers. In the 1985 Philip Morris–General Foods merger, for example, First Boston collected $10.1 million from Philip Morris, and Goldman Sachs and Shearson Lehman collected $7.1 million each from General Foods. The argument rests on dubious assumptions: Either corporate heads are indifferent to fees or there is very limited price competition among investment banks.

Fourth, and a favorite of executives who fear or condemn takeovers, the bidder is an opportunist and has exploited temporary depressions (discounts) in the target's stock price to seize a firm in a bargain purchase. See, e.g., Kraakman, Taking Discounts Seriously: The Implications of "Discounted" Share Prices as an Acquisition Motive, 88 Colum.L.Rev. 891 (1988). The argument is usually coupled with a corollary: Bidders often do not know how to, or do not care to, run businesses they purchase; they are financial wizards intent on making a fast buck. Economists sharply question this view, but it has many adherents in the business community who see the stock market either dominated by pessimism or preoccupied with short-term trading profits. Both phenomena, it is argued, cause swings in stock prices that are unrelated to the fundamental underlying value of the firm. Takeovers then give managers a Hobson's choice: Managers must either suffer losing their positions whenever a "bargain" price appears in the stock market or worry incessantly about keeping their stock prices up with short-term operating strategies, sacrificing long-term firm health to generate immediate earnings.

Fifth, and the favorite of bond holders, labor unions, and state politicians, the bidder pays a premium to loot the firm, exploiting minority target shareholders who are left after the acquisition or exploiting non-shareholder constituencies in the target firm. See, e.g., Coffee, Shareholders Versus Managers: The Strain in the Corporate Web, 85 Mich.L.Rev. 1 (1986); McDaniel, Bondholders and Stockholders, 135 J.Corp.Law 205 (1988). The latter argument seems to get the most play. The bidder, it is argued, leverages the firm to take value from preexisting creditors (who see the value of their debt securities drop), fires middle managers and employees who have implicit or explicit long-term employment contracts, raids pension plans, and squeezes local political units for tax breaks with threats to close local facilities.

Sixth, takeover premiums are explained by simple price pressure. A bidder is purchasing large amounts of a limited resource in a very short time period. See Levmore, A Primer on the Sale of Corporate Control, 65 Tex.L.Rev.1961 (1987); Stout, Are Takeover Premiums Really Premiums? Market Price, Fair Value, and Corporate Law, 99 Yale L.J. 1235 (1990). Bidders must offer above-market prices to induce enough shareholders to sell, because some of them value their stock more than the preacquisition market price. The premium price is necessary to persuade the more optimistic shareholders with higher reservation prices to sell the final shares the bidder must purchase to gain effective control. The price is not a "premium" for these last grudging holdout sellers, but rather only a premium for those more pessimistic shareholders that get the benefit of the higher price dictated by the holdouts in, say, an any-and-all tender offer. The pessimistic shareholders would have eagerly sold their shares for much less than the tender offer price. The position, of course, does not explain why bidders, as individual players in the market, are themselves willing to meet the price demands of the more optimistic shareholders.

The sixth theory must explain why the bidder is the only investor who acts on a belief that a particular stock is valued more highly than its market price. Why do all such optimistic investors not buy until they bid the stock up to their optimistic valuations? In other words, if some investors hold stock at, say, a present value of $150 a share when market price is at $100 a share, why do they value shares they do not hold at a present value of less than $100? Resource limitations must be the answer. But do investors' resource and credit limitations explain the full differential? There is clearly some variation in subjective evaluation of the worth of a stock at any point in time, but the theory seems to overstate the number and size of the deviations from market price neutral of any bid.

If the average tender offer premium of 50 percent is explained solely by heterogeneous beliefs about the price of the stock, there must be a significant number of people who value their stock, *in present value terms,* at 150 percent of market price. The existence of such extreme deviations from market price in a large number of investors in a liquid market stretches credibility. It seems more plausible to argue that most of the takeover premium is due to new value in the target stock created by the bid itself. See Carney, Shareholder Coordination Costs, Shark Repellents, and Takeout Mergers: The Case against Fiduciary Duties, 1983 A.B.F.Res.J. 341, 347. The bid gives information to target shareholders that causes them to revalue their stock and, perhaps, increase their disagreements over what the new value ought to be. Even so, it is the bid that generates the new optimism.

The policy debate is complicated by imperfect attacks on acquisitions as causing problems that are not necessarily linked to acquisitions but to other, broader regulatory glitches. For example, it is popular to condemn leveraged buyouts (LBOs) and other forms of leveraged acquisitions for adding excessive debt to a firm's capital structure. Assuming for a moment that the amounts of debt used in such acquisitions are excessive, we ought to note that firms can and do, on their own, float similar amounts of debt in single-firm recapitalizations. What causes "excess debt"? Perhaps the tax code (Does it favor debt financing?) or bankruptcy law (Has it reduced the costs of defaulting on interest payments?) is the culprit. Perhaps bidders are doing through acquisitions what target managers ought to do on their own—taking advantage of tax law quirks—to maximize firm share value. If so, this may be a version of the first explanation noted above. And acquisitions may be only a symptom of a deeper policy problem, an imbalance in the tax code, for example.

How do these six explanations relate to the basic question of whether takeovers are socially beneficial or harmful? Explanations one and two support a positive view. Explanations three, four, and five support a negative view. And explanation six is neutral on the merits but important in that it argues against a commonly stated inference: Takeovers are socially useful because the added value of the stock of the acquirer and the target before the acquisition is less than the value of the stock of the surviving firm after the acquisition plus the value of the nonstock consideration received by the target-firm shareholders in the acquisition.

Questions

1. What kind of substantial conduct by target managers stimulates a takeover? Once the valuables are stolen, does it make sense to buy the empty safe?

2. Are all synergy gains from acquisitions socially beneficial? Are combinations motivated by a desire to acquire market power socially beneficial?

3. Does the threat of takeovers acting on managers of bidding firms have a curative effect on the bidder overpayment problem? If a bidder overpays for a target, is not the bidder itself ripe for a takeover? Are socially harmful acquisitions the necessary product of investment banker "sales pitches"? Could investment bankers be providing an information search service of value to firms? Could investment bankers be providing such services at a cheaper cost than if the firms performed such functions internally?

4. "A bargain that stays a bargain is not a bargain." Why can the chief executive officer of a single bidder, or for that matter the CEO of a target, predict more accurately that a target stock will soon rise to its "true value" than the thousands of professional investors who participate routinely in the stock markets? Do managers have a natural human tendency

to view the market price of a share of stock in their firm as low, high, or about right? What is the impact of your answers on the stock price depression hypothesis?

5. The current value of an equity investment includes a discounted present value summation of all future income flows. If a firm acts to sacrifice future income for present income when the present value of the future income is higher than the amount of present income generated, what is the effect on the value of the firm's stock? Can a manager sacrifice long-term profit for short-term returns and increase the firm's stock price? Does the stock price depression theory assert, in essence, that participants in liquid stock markets often do not accurately value future income flows? Even assuming that stock prices are not perfectly rational indicators of future income, are managers more accurate predictors? Why?

6. Is the fifth reason just the dark side of the first? Can single firms act to disadvantage nonshareholder constituencies? If so, why do mergers and acquisitions create special problems? How can nonshareholder constituencies protect themselves from the "event risk" of a possible takeover? How, for example, can bondholders protect themselves from a dilution of the security behind their bonds caused by an acquisition? Does society have a special interest in limiting a firm and its creditors from contracting to create excessive leverage in the firm's capital structure?

7. If the supply function for outstanding shares is upward-sloping for any given bidder because of the heterogeneous beliefs of target shareholders on the value of their shares, takeovers at a premium price provide a windfall for approving shareholders who believe that the price substantially exceeds the actual value of their shares and a loss for dissenters forced to sell their shares for less than they think they are worth. Should the law allow takeovers only when an acquisition price generates more gain for the approving majority than loss suffered by a dissenting minority? Does the fact that all the shareholders (including both pessimistic and optimistic types) will revise their estimates of stock value a bit in reaction to news of a bid affect your answer? (The bid itself shifts the top end of the supply curve for the bidder upwards.) What if the losers were willing to sell at prices below the bid before the bid was announced and have now decided that the bid price is low because other bidders might now appear and bid more? In other words, does it matter that losers become losers only after the bid is announced? If not, what legal rules will permit mergers only if a net calculation is positive? A unanimous vote requirement? A two-thirds vote requirement? Should we delegate the responsibility to target managers? Can we expect target managers to be able to make such a calculation when they choose to thwart takeovers of their firm? How much do target managers know about the subjective valuations of target stock by individual shareholders who are not active participants in the trading markets?

8. If a significant number of acquisitions in the eighties were not socially beneficial, should the government legislate to block acquisitions or should it rely on the market to correct itself? Is the falloff in leveraged acquisitions in late 1989 a market correction?

SUBCHAPTER B. THE VARIOUS TOPOLOGIES OF MERGERS, ACQUISITIONS, AND REORGANIZATIONS

When tax, accounting, antitrust, state corporate code, and securities law experts use terms such as *merger, asset* or *stock acquisition,* and *reorganization* to describe an acquisition, they are not necessarily describing the same transaction. The various regulatory systems that attach consequences to transaction forms define those basic forms using different criteria, criteria appropriate to the regulatory purpose at hand. Critical to an understanding of regulatory systems that affect large transactions is a careful delineation and comparison of the various classification systems that experts of each system use.

Accounting principles and tax law distinguish corporate transactions based on characteristics that are, perhaps, commonly understood by laypeople. At the primary level, sales are separated from classic mergers. If one of the two participating firms receives, either at the firm level or at the shareholder level, cash or cash equivalents (debt securities) in exchange for the transfer of substantially all the firm's assets or a controlling block of the firm's stock, it is a sale. On the other hand, if two constituent firms pool their assets and the equity holders of both firms become equity holders in the surviving firm holding the pooled assets, then the transaction is a classic merger or consolidation. In a sale the shareholders of the selling firm lose their equity (ownership) interest in their firm's assets and replace that interest with cash (or cash equivalents such as debt securities in the buyer); in a classic merger the shareholders of both firms pool their equity interests in an ongoing entity. Sales are also divided into stock sales and asset sales based on the identity of the selling entity and the character of the assets acquired; in stock sales the selling entities are individual shareholders selling stock; in asset sales the selling entity is a firm selling its assets.

For policy reasons that are not obvious (we will investigate them in later chapters), accounting principles and tax law use the merger-sale distinction as a cornerstone of their systems of rules. In accounting, a merger sale distinction affects the accounting conventions that the surviving firm may use in its financial statements. In a sale the market price paid to the target firm or its shareholders must be reflected in the financials of the purchasing firm. In a merger the categories in the financials of the two constituent firms are merely added together to create the financials of the surviving firm. Since the financials of any one firm do not accurately reflect the market value of its assets (we will explain these accounting conventions in the accounting chapter), the two methods produce very different financials for the acquiring firm. There is considerable debate among economists over why, in an efficient capital market, this ought to matter, but there can be no doubt that businesspeople believe that it does.

In tax law a merger-sale distinction determines whether or not a transaction is taxed. In a stock sale, for example, a selling shareholder in a sale realizes and recognizes taxable gain or loss; she has changed the form of her investment. A shareholder in a merger is said to continue her investment in the same firm, and we ought not to impose a tax. In an asset sale the selling firm must recognize and pay a tax on the proceeds received for its assets, and if these proceeds are distributed to the selling-firm shareholders, those shareholders recognize taxable gain and loss as well.

State corporate codes are the fallen angels. Originally designed around the basic merger-sale distinction noted above, they evolved in the mid–1960s into something quite different. State corporate codes regulate the procedure firms must follow to effect any given transaction. The principal procedural matters include the shareholders' right to vote on a given transaction and the appraisal rights of dissenting shareholders should a given transaction go forward over their objection. Other important procedural questions include the mechanics of transferring title to assets and debt obligations in the transaction.

In midcentury state corporate codes also depended on the merger-sale distinction to stipulate proper procedure. In a classic merger the shareholders of both corporations vote and have appraisal rights. In a classic sale the shareholders of the selling firm vote and have appraisal rights. Clever lawyers manipulated the statutory language with ease, casting sales under the "statutory merger" section and casting mergers under the "statutory sales" of assets sections to suit the purposes of their client, usually to avoid select procedural requirements. Rather than attempt to protect the distinction, as the accounting principles and the tax code have done with rules on integrated transactions and the like, the state legislatures and their courts, after a brief skirmish, not only abandoned the classic distinction but amended their codes to legitimize the lawyers' efforts.

The movement among state legislatures is now to synchronize the requirements of the various sections so that it matters less which section applies. The goal of the drafters of the legislation is to make the shareholders' voting rights for a given transaction the same, whatever section the lawyers use. As we shall see, the New York Stock Exchange has also stepped in with rules designed to the same effect. Interestingly, as we shall see, in state law the classic merger-sale distinction has reappeared in a fashion in the state courts: the Delaware Supreme Court may use the distinction as part of its new definition of a fiduciary standard for boards of directors involved in takeover acquisitions.

Some of the defined effects in state corporate codes have also been modified by case law. By state statute a surviving firm in a merger assumes all the liabilities of the constituent firms, but an acquiring firm in an asset sale can choose not to assume the selling firm's liabilities. Case law on effect of acquisitions on the tort obligations (and related obligations such as environmental or employment discrimination claims) of the acquired firm, known as successor liability, has substantially modified this basic merger-sale distinction. Tort obligations may attach to buying firms in asset sales, for example, even though the buying firms contracted not to assume them. The statutory systems that provide for the survival of pension obligations under ERISA follow the classic distinction more closely, however.

Other systems of regulation affecting acquisitions do not use the classic merger-sale distinction at all but rely on other basic distinctions. The Securities Act of 1933, for example, is concerned primarily with the public sale of new securities, be they debt or equity securities. Thus rule 145 requires that whenever shareholders exchange their old securities for new securities, whether debt or equity, in an acquisition, the protections of the 1933 act apply. This can occur in either a classic merger (stock in one firm exchanged for stock in the surviving firm) or a classic sale (stock in one firm exchanged for debt securities in the surviving firm). Moreover, the Securities and Exchange Act of 1934 regulates public tender offers, regardless of whether the consideration is stock, as in a classic merger, or cash, as in a sale. The exchange act also regulates certain events that occur routinely as part of major acquisitions—proxy solicitations by publicly held firms for example—and the timing and content of public disclosures about planned transactions.

The federal antitrust act specific to acquisitions, the Clayton Act, regulates all business combinations that pose a threat to competition in relevant product and service markets. The focus is on a combination of the assets of two firms in one entity, regardless of who the shareholders are. Classic mergers and classic sales are both combinations of otherwise distinct entities, so both are similarly regulated by the Clayton Act, and antitrust lawyers often refer to either as a merger. The size of the acquisition and the effect of the acquisition on relevant product markets, not whether it is a merger or a sale, are the focus of the legislation. Amendments to the Clayton Act, known as the Hart–Scott–Rodino Act, affect the timing of public disclosure of acquisition plans. In a similar vein, the law controlling various regulated industries, banking or insurance, requires the approval of all large-scale combinations, both classic mergers and sales in the industry, because officials are interested in passing on the capabilities to the new owners. It is unimportant how they came to be new owners.

In sum, the legal vocabulary one uses to describe an acquisition varies with the regulatory system in issue. The concept of a merger in a "statutory merger" under state corporate law is not the same as the concept of a merger in an "A reorganization" under the tax code. A business person's definition of a transaction, however, does not typically depend on legal terminology. A businessperson is interested primarily in who ends up with control of the assets of the constitutent firms and how much (and in what form) those controlling individuals have to pay others who gave up control over those assets. Such a person is likely to have the following definitions in mind:

Merger: In a merger the owners of separate firms pool their interests in a single firm. The surviving firm owns the assets and owes the debt previously owned or owed by the separate firms. If the firms are corporations, the shareholders of the separate firms become shareholders of the surviving firm. In other words, the owners of the constituent firms are owners in the surviving firm. *The businessperson's definition depends on the final position of the shareholders of the constituent firms.* The relative voting power of a shareholder in either firm is diluted significantly in the surviving firm as a result of the combination. For example, corporation A (acquirer) and corporation T (target), of roughly equal size, pool their assets and liabilities into a new corporation AT (or A as the surviving entity), with the shareholders of corporation A holding 50 percent of AT stock and the shareholders of corporation T holding 50 percent of AT stock.

There are two major definitional problems. First, can we include transactions in which either some or all of the shareholders of one of the constituent firms end up with cash or nonownership interests in the surviving firm (debt instruments such as mortgage bonds) or, similarly, all of the shareholders of one of the constituent firms end up with some equity in the surviving firm and some cash or debt? In our example, what if the shareholders of T, in exchange for their T stock, receive an equal value in voting stock in AT, which gives them only a 25 percent interest in AT, and in AT bonds. If too much of the consideration for the shareholders of one firm is not equity instruments in the surviving firm, the transaction is not a merger but an acquisition.

Second, if one of the firms is much larger than the other, common usage would label the transaction a sale. If, for example, A is IBM, a $55 billion corporation, and the corner gas station is T, a $30,000 corporation, even though the firms pool their assets, with the owners of the gas station receiving shares in IBM, the surviving entity, we would more naturally refer to the transaction as a sale of the gas station to IBM rather than a merger with IBM.

Our layperson is unconcerned, however, with the posttransaction position of debtors in either of the constituent firms. In other words, if the bondholders in A are given cash rather than bonds in AT, it would not affect the classification of the transaction as a merger. Is this true if the bondholders in A are given a significant amount of voting stock in AT along with the shareholders of A and T?

Acquisition: In an acquisition one firm, A, pays for all the assets or all the stock of another, T. It is a sale. Consideration may be anything but equity instruments in the purchasing firm—cash or debt instruments in the purchasing firm, for example. The acquiring firm can buy all the assets from the selling firm (an asset sale) or, if the firm is a corporation, can buy all the stock from the selling-firm shareholders (a stock sale). Either way the owners of the selling firm lose control and interest in the selling firm's assets. *After the transaction the shareholders of the selling firm have no ownership interest in the surviving firm.* Absent special payment provisions, the shareholders of the selling firm no longer have a direct stake in the management of their firm's assets. On the other hand, the shareholders in the acquiring firm retain their relative voting power in the surviving firm. In their view their firm has merely changed the form of its assets: cash on the balance sheet has been replaced by a factory, for example.

In an asset sale the acquiring firm may choose not to assume the selling firm's liabilities, and the selling firm continues to exist, unless dissolved, holding the cash received in the sale. In a stock sale the acquiring firm has bought ownership of the legal entity and holds the entity as a new subsidiary, unless the subsidiary is dissolved into the parent. The liabilities of the selling firm remain with the firm after the control change.

The basic definitional problem involves distinguishing between the sale of a firm as a business and the sale of some of the firm's property or the sale of some of the firm's stock. How much property or stock must be sold before we can say that one firm has purchased a second? Our layperson might answer that the sale of substantially all a firm's operating assets or the sale of a controlling block of stock constitutes a sale.

Recapitalization: In a recapitalization a firm changes its capital structure, changing the nature and mix of the outstanding investment instruments in the firm. *Unlike a merger or an acquisition, a recapitalization does not involve the combination of two separate entities, and a substantial number of shareholders of the firm involved remain with the firm.* There are two possible kinds of recapitalization. The first, and traditional, recapitalization involves an exchange of outstanding investment instruments for newly issued investment instruments with different rights and preferences. A firm, for example, exchanges its common stock for outstanding preferred stock subject to substantial dividend arrearages.

A broader definition of recapitalization could include (but usually does not in our regulatory systems) firm acts that affect the underlying investment nature of firm securities (by affecting their leverage within the firm, for example) without changing the written form of the securities themselves. A firm can change the underlying nature of outstanding investments absent a formal exchange of one instrument for another. For example, corporation A has assets of $200,000, has issued $100,000 of thirty-year debentures, and has outstanding common stock with a market value of $100,000. If firm A borrows $95,000 from a commercial bank and pays its shareholders the entire amount in cash dividends, the market value of the shareholders' stock will drop to a value of $5,000. This ought not to concern us since the shareholders also have the cash (unless the shareholders cannot invest the cash as profitability as the firm could), but the market value of the debentures will fall as well, reflecting the fact that their underlying security—their call on the firm's assets in the event of default—has been reduced. The basic definitional problem for the broader definition involves deciding when a firm's act effects a substantial enough change to warrant its special classification as a recapitalization.

Questions

Using the businessperson's generic definitions of *merger, acquisition,* and *reorganization,* label the following transactions:

1. A stock-for-stock exchange: Corporation A exchanges part of its voting stock for the voting stock of corporation T so that, immediately after the transaction, corporation A controls corporation T. Does it make a difference if the exchange is negotiated with the second firm as an entity (a compulsory share exchange) or if the exchange is offered publicly to all individual shareholders of the second firm (an exchange tender offer)?

2. An assets-for-stock-exchange: Corporation A exchanges part of its voting stock for all the assets of corporation T. Does it make a difference if a corporation exchanges *substantially all* its voting stock for the assets of a second? Who is acquiring whom?

3. A triangular exchange: Corporation A creates a shell subsidiary, which holds only stock in the parent. The subsidiary exchanges the parent stock for all the assets or all the voting stock in a second corporation, T.

4. A leveraged buyout (LBO): A group of managers, holding less than 3 percent of the equity in their firm, borrow money at a high interest rate and with a short repayment term and buy with these funds all the outstanding voting shares of their firm. The managers pay off the loans with money raised through selling "junk bonds"—below investment grade (very risky) subordinated debt instruments in the firm—to the public and through selling some firm assets.

5. A squeeze-out (or freeze-out):

a. Cashing out minority shareholders in a single firm: Corporation A with a control group of shareholders owning collectively 80 percent of A stock cause A to form a wholly owned shell corporation, A'. A and A' pool their assets; A' is the surviving entity. The control group shareholders exchange their A shares for A' shares, and the minority shareholders exchange their A shares for cash. (This is a version of diagram 1.) Ought the control group in A to be able to force such a transaction over the objection of all the minority shareholders?

b. Cashing out minority shareholders in a subsidiary: Corporation A owns 80 percent of the shares of corporation T. A forms a second wholly owned subsidiary, A'. A' and T pool their assets; A' is the surviving entity. The minority shareholders in T receive cash in exchange for their T shares. Ought A to be able to do this over the objection of all the minority shareholders in T?

Chapter Two

SHAREHOLDER VOTING AND APPRAISAL RIGHTS

SUBCHAPTER A. STATE CORPORATE CODES

SECTION 1. INTRODUCTION

Individual states charter corporations at the request and choice of incorporators. Thus the constitution, corporate code, and judicial opinions of the incorporating state control much of the internal governance of a firm. Since the beginning of this century the tiny state of Delaware has been the most popular jurisdiction of incorporation for multistate corporations. Almost half of our largest five hundred corporations and almost a third of the corporations listed on the New York Stock Exchange are Delaware corporations. As a consequence, corporate franchise taxes make up almost 17 percent of Delaware's total tax revenues. Moreover, the Delaware bar profits substantially from legal work generated by Delaware corporations.

Relative to other states Delaware's corporate code gives more leeway to corporate managers in their operation of the firm's business, and Delaware has a more developed and sophisticated body of precedent on corporate law issues, because of the expertise of a specialized court for corporations, the Delaware Chancery Court. At the other end of the spectrum is California's corporate code, which features a heavier regulatory hand. As a consequence, very few of our large multistate corporations are incorporated in California. California does, however, usually have one of the highest number of annual incorporations because of the many new small businesses formed in the state.

Most states fall somewhere between the Delaware and California models. Nevada, Pennsylvania, and Virginia have codes that are similar to Delaware's code, while New York's code is a bit more restrictive. The codes in Pennsylvania and Virginia are new, enacted specifically to compete against Delaware for incorporations. Pennsylvania is also considering the creation of a special corporations court to counter the expertise of the Delaware Chancery Court. The Committee on Corporate Laws of the Section of Corporation, Banking and Business Law of the American Bar Association exerts a very significant influence on state codes. The committee has developed and periodically revises the Model Business Corporation Act. Over thirty-five states have used one of the versions of the Model Act as a basis for their local codes, and states scrutinize each new revision of sections in the Model Act with an eye to adopting the most modern provisions.

SECTION 2. THE BASIC STRUCTURE OF THE CODES

The structure of the Delaware General Corporation Law illustrates the structure of most state corporate codes. The procedure for effecting a statutory merger is outlined in section 251, and the legal effect of a merger is detailed in section 259. A special "short-form" merger procedure for some parent-subsidiary mergers is contained in section 253. There is also an abbreviated procedure for "whale-minnow" mergers in section 252(f). The procedure for an asset sale is contained in section 271. The appraisal rights of dissenting shareholders are outlined in section 262 (we will read this in the next section). As you read the sections, note that the basic merger-sale distinction used in tax and accounting is not followed in state codes. The statutory definitions depend more on the procedure used to effect the transaction. If the parties choose to structure the transaction under section 251, it is a merger. If the parties choose to structure the transaction under section 271, it is an asset sale. In other words, the statutes describe procedures to effect mergers and the operative results of a merger, but the statutes do not define a platonic form of merger. Delaware regulates single-firm reorganizations of capital structure in section 242, which specifies the requirements for amending a corporation's charter.

The main purposes of the corporate codes are, first, to legitimize the various transactions and, second, to specify the role shareholders play when there are major changes in their firm's structure. The statutes supersede the common law, which required unanimous shareholder approval for all extraordinary transactions. As we shall see, the codes preserve a role for shareholders in major corporate transactions, but the codes do not pursue this strategy with consistency or efficacy.

Subsection a. State Statutes on Mergers and Acquisitions

Please read sections 251, 253(a) and (d), and 271 of the Delaware General Corporation Law in your supplement and answer the questions that follow the two notes below.

Note
"Substantially All"

The question of what constitutes "substantially all" of the corporate assets under section 271 is colored by whether "the sale of assets [is] quantitatively vital to the operation of the corporation and is out of the ordinary and substantially affects the existence and purpose of the corporation." Gimbel v. Signal Companies, Inc., 316 A.2d 599, 606 (Del.Ch.1974), affirmed 316 A.2d 619 (1974). As a consequence, the Delaware courts have produced some surprising results in cases in which a firm has two or more forms of assets with widely differing income potentials. Assume a firm with 50 percent of a firm's assets in stock of NYSE companies and 50 percent in an operating factory and inventory. Does section 271 apply if the firm sells only the operating business? If the firm sells only its stock? What if the operating business is twice as profitable as the money market funds? In Katz v. Bregman, 431 A.2d 1274 (Del.Ch.1981), appeal denied 435 A.2d 1044 (Del.1981), the court held that section 271 covered a manufacturing parent's sale of a subsidiary that constituted 51 percent of the parent's total assets, generated about 45 percent of the parent's net sales, and in recent years had been the corporation's only income-producing facility.

Can firms avoid section 271 by mortgaging or pledging all their assets as security for a loan to an acquiring firm and thereafter defaulting on loan repayments, giving the creditor the right to the assets? What if the debtor firm intends to default when it agrees to the mortgage or pledge? In this regard please read section 272 of the Delaware General Corporation Law in your supplement.

Note

State Legislation Restraining Stock Acquisition ("Antitakeover Statutes")

Shareholders in a firm that is the target of a tender offer do not vote to approve or disapprove an acquisition. Since a purchasing firm is buying stock directly from target shareholders rather than proposing a statutory merger, sale of assets, or share exchange, the shareholders' individual choice of whether to sell replaces their right to vote. Recently, however, most states (at last count the number was thirty-nine) have passed takeover legislation that effectively restrains stock acquisitions. Delaware has such a provision in section 203 of its corporation code. Most of the state legislation gives shareholders voting rights not on the acquisition itself but on the effect of the acquisition. If the target board disapproves of the acquisition, the shareholders may, for example, vote on whether the stock acquired by the bidder can vote or on whether the bidder can, subsequent to a stock acquisition in which some shareholders do not sell into the offer, execute a second-stage, cash-out statutory merger to gain 100 percent of the target stock. Delaware's section, known as a business combination, or freeze-out, statute, is of the latter ilk. Of course, by severely restricting the effect of an acquisition, the legislation in essence regulates the acquisition itself. Indeed it would perhaps be more honest and understandable simply to condition stock acquisitions on a shareholder vote, as the state of Ohio once did. See Ohio Rev.Code Ann. § 1701.831(e)(i) (Baldwin 1983). We will discuss state takeover legislation in depth in chapter 4.

Questions

Assume all constituent firms are Delaware corporations:

1. Statutory Mergers (Section 251):

a. Consideration (section 251(b)(5)): Can the stockholders of one of the constituent firms receive cash rather than stock in the surviving firm? In other words, is a statutory merger necessarily a "pooling transaction" or a tax-free "A reorganization"?

Can some of the stockholders in one of the constituent firms receive cash while others in the same firm receive stock in the surviving firm? In other words, do all stockholders in each firm have to receive identical consideration for their stock? Does it depend on whether the stockholders are in the same class (or the same series in a class)?

b. Voting (section 251(b) (first sentence)): Under the merger statute can the stockholders initiate and pass a plan of merger without action or approval from their board of directors? Can the stockholders force a vote on their board of directors' refusal to accept an outstanding offer to merge (and their refusal to submit the offer to the shareholders)?

If there are several classes and series within classes of stock in a constituent firm, which stockholders vote on mergers and what is the standard for approval? See section 251(c). Why do other corporate constituencies (bondholders, employees, and others) have a statutory right to vote?

When is a stockholder vote on one or both of the constituent firms in a merger excused? See sections 251(f) and 253(a). What explains the exceptions?

c. Abandoning or amending merger agreements (section 251(d)): Must the directors go back to the shareholders to abandon a merger already approved by the shareholders? If there is a major change in the stock market between the time of the shareholder vote and the closing that makes the price of the target exorbitant, what can the buyer's managers do?

2. Asset Sales (Section 271):

a. Consideration (section 271(a)): Can the selling firm receive stock in the buying firm as consideration in an asset sale? In other words, is a statutory sale of substantially all the assets a "sale" (taxable transaction)?

After an asset sale, what is the position of the selling firm's shareholders? If the selling firm's shareholders want to receive individually part of the consideration used in the sale, can the buying firm pay them directly (that is, without passing the funds through the selling firm to its shareholders)? If not, how can selling-firm shareholders get part of the consideration? What is the difference between that and a system of direct payment from the buying firm? To whom is this difference important?

b. Voting (section 271(a)): When do the stockholders of the buying firm have a statutory right to vote? Does it matter if the consideration is stock in the buying firm?

Can shareholders of the selling firm vote to sell their firm's assets without approval by their board? Can they vote to reverse their board's refusal to act on an offer to purchase the firm's assets?

3. Tender Offers (See Note on Antitakeover Statutes): When one firm makes a public offer to buy stock from the stockholders of a second firm, do the stockholders of either firm have statutory voting rights? Does the board of directors of the target firm have a statutory right to stop its shareholders from tendering their shares into an outstanding offer? Do target shareholders responding to a tender offer need protections provided by a required shareholder majority vote or by a veto power vested in their board?

Under Delaware state law, do buying-firm shareholders vote if the consideration in the tender offer is stock in the buying firm?

Problem

Corporation A has 100,000 outstanding common shares and 20,000 outstanding preferred shares. A merges with corporation B; A is the survivor. Both A and B are incorporated in Delaware. Corporation B has 1,000 outstanding common shares, 501 of which are held by one large shareholder, Ms. B. Ms. B receives 10,000 shares of A common and $1 million in A debentures convertible into 10,000 shares of A common. The other B shareholders each receive 10 shares of A preferred stock (5,000 shares total) for each share of B common that they hold. Do A shareholders vote on the merger? Can the merger go forward if all the shareholders of corporation B but Ms. B vote against the merger? Can B shareholders other than Ms. B claim that they ought to get A common and A debentures?

Note
Corporate Codes in Other States

The Delaware pattern of shareholder voting rights in major corporate transactions, separate provisions on mergers, asset sales, and reorganizations, and no provision on stock acquisitions is followed in all but a few states, the most important exception being the state of California. We will discuss the California provisions in some detail below. Even the states that follow the basic Delaware pattern have significant deviations from the specific details in the Delaware provisions, however. For example, in 1967, Delaware reduced the required percentage approval to a majority of outstanding shares from a two thirds vote of outstanding shares. Most states have followed suit. New York remains an important holdout, however. N.Y.BUS.CORP.LAW § 903 (McKinney 1986).

The Revised Model Business Corporation Act follows the basic organization in the Delaware General Corporation Law with two significant exceptions. First, section 11.02 provides a procedure for a "share exchange," and other sections contain procedures for statutory mergers and asset sales. In a share exchange, known by some as a compulsory share exchange, one firm acquires all the outstanding stock in a second. A majority of the shareholders of the acquired firm must approve; a majority of the shareholders of the acquiring firm need approve the exchange only if acquired-firm shareholders receive a substantial number of shares in the acquiring firm (usually an amount equal to over 20 percent of the shares outstanding before the acquisition). Over twenty states have adopted such a provision. In California, if immediately after the exchange the acquiring corporation has control of the acquired firm, the transaction is called an exchange reorganization. Such a transaction need be approved only by a majority of each class of the *acquiring* corporation. Why would parties to a merger choose to use a share exchange rather than a straight statutory merger or a statutory asset sale? Why do more states not have the procedure? Is it because a compulsory share exchange operates with the same effect as a triangular merger?

Second, section 11.03(f) provides for class voting on statutory mergers "if the plan contains a provision that, if contained in a proposed amendment to articles of incorporation, would require action by one or more separate voting groups." Thus if preferred stockholders receive stock in the surviving firm with different explicit rights and preferences from the shares they held in the target firm, the preferred shareholders vote as a class on the merger; absence of a favorable majority vote of the preferred stockholders blocks the merger regardless of how the common stockholders vote. In New York preferred stockholders both vote as a separate class and have their votes counted along with the common. In share exchanges under the Model Act class voting is required "by each class or series of shares included in the exchange." If a state has class voting for capital structure reorganizations and not for mergers, what is the effect? See Rauch v. RCA Corp., 861 F.2d 29 (2d Cir.1988) (page 98 infra).

Class voting provisions similar to section 11.03(f) in the Revised Model Act have provided courts with troublesome questions of statutory construction. In Shidler v. All American Life & Financial Corp., 298 N.W.2d 318 (Iowa 1980), the court struggled with the term *cancellation.*

SHIDLER v. ALL AMERICAN LIFE & FINANCIAL CORP.

Supreme Court of Iowa, 1980.
298 N.W.2d 318.

Considered by LeGrand, P.J., and Uhlenhopp, Harris, McCormick, and McGiverin, JJ.

Uhlenhopp, Justice.

* * *

In May 1973 an attempt was made to merge General United Group, Incorporated (GUG), a domestic corporation (and its subsidiary, United Security Life Company (USL), which need not be separately considered), into All American Delaware Corporation, a foreign corporation, which would be the surviving entity. At that time GUG had outstanding 105,000 shares of preferred stock, 2,959,650 shares of common stock, and 10,623,150 shares of class B common stock. The preferred and class B common stock had specified conversion rights into common stock. All of the preferred and class B common stock and 67,043 shares of the common stock were owned by another corporation, All American Life & Casualty Company (Casualty), and 2,892,607 shares of the common stock were owned by the public. Casualty also owned all of the stock of All American Delaware, into which GUG was to merge.

* * *

GUG, the domestic corporation, had three classes of stock, preferred, common and class B common. All of Casualty's shares in GUG would be cancelled, and paragraph 4.3(a) of the merger plan stated that each share of the public GUG common stock would, "by virtue of the Merger and without any action on the part of the holder thereof, be converted into and exchanged for $3.25 cash...." Paragraph 4.5 stated that the public common certificates "shall be surrendered by the holder thereof" to the disbursing agent for cash.

* * *

Section 496A.70 provides in part that if a class of stock is entitled to vote on a merger, "the plan of merger ... shall be approved upon receiving the affirmative vote of the holders of at least two-thirds of the outstanding shares of each class of shares entitled to vote as a class thereon and of the total outstanding shares." It then provides:

> Any class of shares of any such corporation shall be entitled to vote as a class if the plan of merger or consolidation, as the case may be, contains any provision which, if contained in a proposed amendment to articles of incorporation, would entitle such class of shares to vote as a class.

This merger proposal carried by two-thirds of all GUG shares but not by two-thirds of the common stock. Was the common stock entitled to be voted as a class?

Plaintiffs argue that several clauses in section 496A.57 entitled the common to be voted separately. We go no farther than paragraph 3 of that section and specifically to the word "cancellation."[1] [Ed.] Suppose that no merger had been proposed, but an amendment to the articles had been submitted which required that all certificates of GUG common shares be surrendered to a depository for cash, that thereafter the shares of common stock would cease to be stock of the corporation, and that the stock transfer books would be closed. Would not this stock be cancelled in a realistic sense? One day the owner of common stock owns a part of an ongoing enterprise; the next day he does not, he instead has money. His shares are recalled and no further trading is

---

1. [Ed. Section 496A.57 of the Iowa Code reads:

The holders of the outstanding shares of a class shall be entitled to vote as a class upon a proposed amendment, whether or not entitled to vote thereon by the provisions of the articles of incorporation, if the amendment would:

1. Increase or decrease the aggregate number of authorized shares of such class.

* * *

3. Effect an exchange, reclassification, or cancellation of all or part of the shares of such class.]

permitted in them; the books are closed. To "cancel" means to "revoke, annul, invalidate." *Webster's Third New International Dictionary* 325 (1969).

* * *

Defendants voice several arguments contrary to this construction of the statutes. One is that this was a "cash out" merger. They say the common stock was not changed or reduced; it was eliminated and money was substituted. But we find nothing in sections 496A.70 and 496A.57 which differentiates cash out mergers from other varieties. Indeed, the cash out merger is drastic: the stockholder is compelled to give up his stock altogether and separate himself from the ongoing organization; he is ejected. Did not the General Assembly intend that such a class of stock should be entitled to vote separately on its fate?

Defendants further contend that if the General Assembly had intended each class of stock to have separate voting rights on mergers, it could have easily so provided as some states have done. But the Assembly did not desire to give each class separate voting rights automatically. It desired to give a class separate voting rights if that stock was affected in ways designated in section 496A.57, one of which is cancellation.

Then defendants urge that the merger plan does not use the word "cancel" or "cancellation" regarding this stock, and they say section 496A.57 does not apply unless the merger plan contains a provision "identical" to one of those in the section. We think this argument flies in the face of the *Rath* rationale of realism. The substance, not the precise words, controls. A merger draftsman cannot avoid section 496A.57 by calling an actual cancellation something else.

Defendants also insist that under section 496A.76 the assets of GUG could have been sold, the proceeds could have been distributed, and GUG could have been dissolved without a separate class vote; the holders of common stock would then have no stock, but money instead. Why then, defendants ask, may not substantially the same thing be done by merger?

We may assume arguendo that a separate class vote would not be required in such a proceeding, and we lay aside the point that a sale, distribution, and dissolution normally have substantially different consequences than a merger. But the controlling point is that for reasons it found sufficient, the General Assembly made the requirements of section 496A.70 on merger and of section 496A.76 on sale of assets materially different. We may not make the sections identical by judicial legislation.

* * *

The quoted portion of the articles does however purport to prohibit class voting as between common and class B common. This clause was undoubtedly inserted to give control to Casualty. But the articles cannot override the statutes. 18 Am.Jur.2d *Corporations* § 83, at 624

(1965); 18 C.J.S. *Corporations* § 43, at 423 (1939). *See also Ontjes v. Bagley,* 217 Iowa 1200, 1203, 250 N.W. 17, 19 (1933). Section 496A.138 deals with proportions, not class voting. Its words, "or of any class or series thereof," do not authorize a prohibition of class voting. Rather, they constitute an adjective phrase modifying "shares," and "shares" is in an adjective clause modifying "proportion." On the other hand, section 496A.70 provides that any class of shares "shall" be entitled to vote as a class if the merger contains a provision which, as an amendment to articles, would entitle the class to vote separately; and section 496A.57(3) entitles a class to vote separately upon an amendment to cancel shares, "whether or not entitled to vote thereon by the provisions of the articles of incorporation...."

We are not persuaded by defendants' argument.

Finally, defendants urge plaintiffs' claim that the common was entitled to vote as a class is really academic for two reasons. One is that Casualty could have converted its other GUG stock to common and thus obtained a two-thirds affirmative vote by the common on the merger. The other is that under section 496A.138, Casualty could have changed the articles to reduce the two-thirds requirement in section 496A.70 to a lesser proportion and thus carried the merger election.

We lay aside the fact that a conversion of Casualty's other shares to common shares would have involved several other considerations, and that a change in the articles to reduce the two-thirds requirement would today run into the 1978 repeal of the words "or lesser" in section 496A.138. The significant point is that when the vote on the merger actually occurred in May 1973, Casualty had not in fact converted its other stock or reduced the two-thirds requirement. We deal with the election as it occurred, not as it might have occurred. Many corporations have various classes or series of shares which have rights of conversion into other shares. Corporate elections under chapter 496A cannot stand or fall on what would have happened if certain hypothetical conversions had previously taken place or if changes in the articles had previously been made; they must stand or fall on what in fact took place. We do not find merit in defendants' final argument.

We thus answer the question propounded as follows:

> The Iowa law required that the General United Group, Incorporated (GUG) merger into All American Delaware Corporation in May of 1973 be approved by an affirmative vote of at least two-thirds (2/3) of the outstanding GUG Common Stock shares voting separately as a class and by at least two-thirds (2/3) of the total outstanding GUG shares.

Note

The Extraterritorial Effect of Some State Corporate Codes

The protection of local interests has spurred states to enact legislation that affects corporations incorporated in other states ("foreign corporations") that do substantial business within state lines. The purpose of such statutes is to subject "tramp" corporations to minimum statutory safeguards that thereby diminish managerial authority. A tramp corporation is a corporation whose primary contacts are with a foreign jurisdiction and not its state of incorporation. The extraterritorial statutes reduce the benefits for management to incorporate in one state while transacting its principal business in another.

Under these provisions foreign corporations are regulated by local state corporate laws in addition to the laws of the incorporating jurisdiction. Although the constitutionality of these provisions has not been resolved, the statutes are consistent with choice of law rules, are nondiscriminatory between domestic and foreign corporations, and do not cover corporations governed by federal securities laws. See CTS Corp. v. Dynamics Corp. of America, 481 U.S. 69, 107 S.Ct. 1637, 95 L.Ed.2d 67 (1987), infra 425). Currently only two states, California and New York, have promulgated regulatory schemes specifically aimed at foreign corporations doing substantial business in state. Both states apply some part of their corporate code relating to mergers and acquisitions to qualifying foreign corporations doing business within their states. California subjects foreign corporations with a specified presence in the state to its unusual provisions on shareholder voting and appraisal rights. Please read section 2115 of the California Corporations Code in your supplement. New York's legislation is much more limited. A New York statute imposes a section stipulating a procedure for appraisal rights on all foreign corporations registered to do business in New York. Please read section 1319 of the New York Business Corporation Law in your supplement.

Apart from specific state legislation, state courts are nibbling on the advantages of foreign incorporation by interpreting domestic state statutes to be applicable to foreign corporations that transact substantial business in the state. In Jefferson Industrial Bank v. First Golden BanCorporation, 762 P.2d 768 (Colo.App.1988), for example, the Colorado Court of Appeals held that the Colorado shareholder inspection statute preempted an otherwise applicable Delaware statute when a Delaware corporation operated three banks in the state of Colorado. Answering the contention that the Colorado statute had no application to foreign corporations or their agents, the court reasoned that there was nothing in the language of the Colorado inspection statute that indicated legislative intent to limit its effect to domestic corporations. The court reasoned that because the Delaware corporation was a duly authorized foreign corporation, it was "subject to the same duties, restrictions, penalties and liabilities imposed upon a domestic corporation of like character," as provided for in the Colorado corporate code. See Colo.Code Regs. § 7–9–104 (1986).

Subsection b. Single–Firm Capital Reorganizations

Please read sections 102 and 242 in the Delaware General Corporation Law in your supplement and answer the following questions.

Questions

1. Which of the following events require a shareholder vote under section 242?

a. The firm has a general-purpose clause in its charter ("for any lawful purpose"), but the firm has already run a corner grocery store in Ithaca, New York. The managers decide to phase out of the grocery business and move into the racetrack business in New Jersey.

b. The debt-equity ratio of the firm is two to one, and managers decide to issue new subordinated bonds and pass the proceeds from the bond sale to all the shareholders. The bond issue is five times as large as any previous debt placement the firm has undertaken. After the one-time extraordinary dividend, shareholders hold shares worth one-tenth what they were before the transaction, and the debt-equity ratio of the firm is eleven to one. (Is your answer the same for a closely held company?)

c. The firm enters into a long-term labor contract paying abnormally high salaries to all members of the union. (Is your answer the same for a long-term labor contract that pays abnormally low salaries?)

d. The firm enters into long-term executive-employment contracts with very high salaries, few prerequisites, and very liberal severance pay provision (golden parachute) in the event of a "control change."

e. The firm lists debts on the New York Stock Exchange.

f. The firm issues a very large block of preferred stock pursuant to a general grant of authority in its articles of incorporation. The rights and privileges of the stock are not defined in the articles; rather the rights and privileges are set by board resolution (so-called blank check preferred). Please read sections 102(a)(4) and 151(a) (authorizing blank check preferred). The stock is a new type of convertible preferred stock (known as poison pill preferred) designed solely to block hostile takeovers. The stock has no dividend or voting rights. If a large buyer of firm common stock is not approved by the board, all the new preferred stock, except any held by the bidder, is immediately convertible into 1,000 common shares. The poison pill preferred stock is passed out to existing common shareholders as a stock dividend.

g. The firm issues common stock (assume a large quantity of such stock is already outstanding) for assets with questionable or insufficient value (diluting the voting and value of existing shareholders) or issues common stock for an employee stock ownership plan (giving significant equity rights to employees).

h. The firm changes its name from Humble Oil Company to Exxon Oil Company. Why is the right of a shareholder to vote on major corporate changes so limited? Does the distinction between a change in the written rights and preferences of outstanding shares and management decisions that otherwise effect major changes in the type of investment represented by a share of stock have some merit? Why do shareholders not demand more limits on management decision making?

Is there a theory that explains or describes your answers? When businesspeople use the term *reorganization,* are they using a definition that comports with the outlines of a statutory reorganization in section 242?

2. Is there voting by class of stock or by series of stock within a class under section 242? Why is class voting not extended to shareholders voting on statutory mergers under section 251?

SECTION 3. THE DISSENTING SHAREHOLDERS' APPRAISAL REMEDY

All states give some shareholders who dissent to certain types of acquisitions and reorganizations a right to petition a state court for the fair cash value of their shares. If a sizable number of shareholders demand cash in these proceedings, known as appraisal proceedings, it can be a severe cash drain on a deal that otherwise depends on noncash consideration. Many acquisition agreements in noncash deals expressly condition the closing on the absence of even a small percentage of target shareholders claiming their dissenters' rights. Moreover, in all types of deals it can be very embarrassing to a board of directors if a state judge gives a dissenting shareholder more money than the board negotiated for shareholders that supported the acquisition. Supporting shareholders may turn and sue the board for a breach of its fiduciary duty. There are four central issues in the basic definition of the appraisal remedy: First, what kinds of transactions support the right; second, what the procedural requirements are for perfecting the right; third, how courts determine "fair value"; and fourth, whether the right is the exclusive remedy for dissenting shareholders.

Subsection a. State Corporate Codes

Please read section 262 of the Delaware General Corporation Law in your supplement and answer the following questions:

Questions

1. In which kinds of transactions do appraisal rights attach? See section 262(b) (first sentence). Do all voting shareholders in acquisitions and reorganizations have the right? Do the shareholders of the selling firm in an asset sale have appraisal rights? Do dissenting shareholders who vote negatively in a statutory reorganization under section 242 have appraisal rights? Do nonvoting shareholders ever have the right? See sections 251(f) and 253(d).

2. Who pays the lawyer fees and the expert witness fees incurred by the dissenting shareholders? See section 262(j). If there is a good-faith dispute over value, who pays the shareholders' legal fees? Does your answer suggest that shareholders receive less than full value for their shares?

3. If A and T, both cash-poor, decide to merge with all stockholders accepting stock in the surviving entity, and 5 percent of the shareholders seek an appraisal remedy, what is the effect of their election on the transaction? Is this why dissenting shareholders must notify their firms before the shareholder vote of their intention to seek an appraisal if the transaction is approved? Does your answer suggest that a small minority of dissenting shareholders can hold up a transaction favored overwhelmingly by a majority?

Absent fraud, why isn't a majority shareholder vote (or a two-thirds vote in a few states) sufficient protection against the shareholders' receiving inadequate consideration in a merger? Should a firm be able to opt out of the appraisal remedy by a shareholder vote amending the articles of incorporation?

4. Assume a statutory merger between A and T in which the T shares are listed on a national exchange and in which A survives. If T shareholders receive shares in the surviving corporation in a statutory merger, do they have appraisal rights? See section 242(b)(2)(a). Does it matter if the shares of A do not trade on a national exchange or there are otherwise fewer than two thousand A shareholders? If the target shareholders receive shares in the parent corporation of A (assume A is a wholly owned subsidiary), do they have appraisal rights? See section 242(b)(2)(b). If T shareholders receive cash instead of stock in the merger, do the target shareholders have appraisal rights? See section 242(b)(2). Why are the shareholders in each case treated differently?

When the market-out exception applies, the dissenting shareholders must choose between selling their shares in the market and accepting the acquisition price. If a dissenting shareholder owns a large block of stock, will an attempt to liquidate the holding in the market depress market prices?

Note
Other Jurisdictions

Most other jurisdictions give appraisal rights to the shareholders of the selling firm in an asset sale, and almost half the states give appraisal rights to dissenting shareholders when certain amendments to the articles of incorporation are approved. Section 13.02 of the Revised Model Business Corporation Act, for example, gives appraisal rights to dissenting shareholders in the selling firm in an asset sale and to dissenting shareholders in some recapitalization. Michigan and South Carolina grant dissenters' rights to shareholders of a corporation after an acquisition of a controlling block of the shares. In Pennsylvania dissenting shareholders in an asset sale have appraisal rights only if the sale is not followed in one year by a liquidation of the selling corporation. In an unusual twist, the California Corporations Code and the New York Business Corporation Law give appraisal rights to shareholders of corporations selling substantially all their assets for stock in the purchasing corporation but not to shareholders of corporations selling substantially all their assets for cash. The drafters argue that appraisal rights ought to apply only when shareholders receiving stock are forced to become shareholders in a different corporation.

About half the states follow Delaware in providing a market exception for shares listed on national stock exchanges or otherwise traded in liquid markets. The 1978 revision of the Model Act eliminated the exception. The drafters' argument is contained in the following excerpt:

CONARD, AMENDMENTS OF MODEL BUSINESS CORPORATION ACT AFFECTING DISSENTER'S RIGHTS (SECTIONS 73, 74, AND 80)
33 Bus.Law. 2587, 2595–96 (1978).

* * *

The former exception for shares listed on stock exchanges has been eliminated in the light of facts which have become more visible since the stock market exception was added to the Model Act in 1969. The 1970s have demonstrated again the possibility of a demoralized market in which fair prices are not available, and in which many companies publicly offer to buy their own shares because the market grossly under values them. Under these circumstances, access to market value is not a reasonable alternative for a dissenting shareholder. Moreover, a shareholder may be disqualified by state or federal securities laws from using the market because his shares are "restricted," because he is an "insider" who has acquired shares within six months, or because he possesses "inside information." Even if the dissenter is free to use the market, he may find it impractical to do so because his holdings are large and the market is thin. In any event, the market cannot reflect the value of the shares "excluding any appreciation or depreciation in anticipation" of the corporate change which gives rise to the dissenters' rights.

* * *

The removal of the stock market exception will not greatly impede fundamental changes in listed companies; it may even facilitate them. The provision of a cashout right will reduce the occasions for courts to enjoin such changes, or to award damages, because the cashout right will provide the dissenting shareholder with an adequate and relatively noncontentious remedy.

The argument is an assertion that the liquid capital markets often did not accurately reflect all publicly available information about the value of a firm's securities. Financial experts believe the assertion to be contradicted by the evidence. See J. Lorie, M. Hamilton & M. Kispton, *The Stock Market: Theories and Evidence* 70–97 (2d ed. 1985). If a "demoralized" market indicates an "unfair" sale price, do high prices in a boom market indicate a "windfall" gain by shareholders?

KANDA & LEVMORE, THE APPRAISAL REMEDY AND THE GOALS OF CORPORATE LAW
32 UCLA L.Rev. 431, 434–37, 463, 465 (1985).

Most observers have viewed the appraisal statutes as addressing a kind of *ex post* fairness; the minority should be able to jump ship when the master sends it in a new direction. Over time the *ex post* fairness view came under strong attack, especially by (then Professor) Manning. The attack was three-pronged: Appraisal is expensive for the very shareholders it is alleged to protect, it puts undue restraints on those corporations that may need to liquidate assets in order to buy back the appraised shares, and no one was able to distinguish rationally those events that trigger a right to appraisal from those that do not. In short, the attack maintained that appraisal delivered little fairness at odd moments and at high cost. This attack may have been insufficiently sympathetic with dissenters to see that uncertainty and costs for corporations might translate into management's increased sharing of profitable opportunities with passive investors.[11]

A. THE PURPOSE OF THE APPRAISAL REMEDY—BACKGROUND VIEWS

1. Conventional View

The conventional view is built on the idea that appraisal statutes have sought to protect minority shareholders. Under this view minority shareholders gain the right to appraisal at the time of fundamental changes in their enterprise as a substitute for their former right to veto such changes. Thus, appraisal retains the flavor of minority veto power, since the minority shareholder can at least veto his own continuing involvement in a "fundamentally different" corporation.

This view hardly needs another dismembering. It has been correctly attacked as greatly overestimating the protection offered minority shareholders who elect appraisal and, more significantly, as lacking explanatory power. For example, the conventional view does not explain why many appraisal statutes contain a broad market exception, allowing dissenting shareholders simply to sell their shares in an active stock market and reinvest in what might be close substitutes, while other statutes create an exception to the market exception and make appraisal available when shareholders receive cash in return for their widely traded stock. It is hard to see why—and the conventional view does not tell us why—shareholders who receive cash are worse off and more in need of appraisal than shareholders who receive stock of an acquiring or other corporation. More generally, the conventional view does not explain why the various appraisal statutes so differ in detail and why such different corporate changes trigger the availability of appraisal.

2. (Ex Ante) Group Coordination

In a recent article, Professor Fischel advanced a view of the appraisal remedy that we find attractive but of limited descriptive utility. Fischel describes appraisal as an arrangement that shareholders find appealing *ex ante* because they realize that an acquiring bidder can one day try to profit from their lack of coordination.

> Consider the familiar prisoner's dilemma problem where shares of the target are selling at $50. A bidder then announces a tender offer pursuant to which it will pay $60 for 51% of the shares and simultaneously announces that the remaining shares will be obtained in a freeze-out merger for $30. If one shareholder could negotiate for all the shareholders, this offer would be rejected because the pretransaction market value of the target ($50) exceeds the weighted average of the bid (approximately $45). Each shareholder acting individually, however, may rationally conclude to tender at $60 to avoid receiving only $30 for all their shares. Thus the offer might succeed (assuming

---

11. It is possible that appraisal was contemplated as a threat rather than as a recurring reality. Such a threat might be appropriate if managers are viewed as possessing both a good deal of inside information about the firm's opportunities and a means of stripping passive shareholders of their share of these opportunities.

no competition from other bidders) even though shareholders as a class are made worse off.

The appraisal remedy represents a solution to this prisoner's dilemma problem. If the shareholders in the second step of the transaction are likely to receive in excess of $40 in an appraisal proceeding, a bidder who is only willing to pay $45 for all the shares will not go forward. Thus the remedy protects all shareholders from this value-reducing transaction and by decreasing the probability of this negative outcome causes all shares to trade at a higher price.

Unfortunately, this sensible "group coordination" view of appraisal also lacks explanatory power. It does not begin to explain, among other things, why Delaware's statute, which Fischel uses illustratively, denies appraisal when the target's shareholders give up widely traded stock and receive not cash or debt, but the acquirer's stock or *any* widely traded stock. Nor does the group coordination view, or the conventional view for that matter, explain the availability of appraisal in many states, including Delaware, for shareholders of an acquiring corporation that uses a significant amount of its stock to acquire another corporation, unless the acquiring corporation's stock is widely traded. Indeed, the group coordination view does not, on its own, explain any appraisal statute, although it provides a sensible and sophisticated theoretical insight that may be especially useful when coordinated with other appraisal goals.

3. Coattails

Shareholders might reason *ex ante* that in the event of an acquisition, or other organic change affecting their corporation, their investment's security lies in continuing with the new successor enterprise. In particular, shareholders may reason that managers and acquirers know of a corporate secret or other indication of future success and, therefore, that their firm is currently underpriced in the market.[30] The shareholders' aim then becomes to continue in the enterprise and not be frozen out. Shareholders thus wish to ride their representatives' or acquirers' "coattails" to success. One might therefore sympathetically hope that corporate law would give to a shareholder, who owned one percent of a corporation valued at $100x, one-half percent of the stock of an acquirer that was worth $100x and now will be of size $200x, rather than giving the shareholder cash only. Of course if the acquiring corporation's stock is widely traded, then shareholders who receive cash can simply purchase some of the acquirer's stock, thereby finding alternate access to the coattails.

* * *

---

30. The market is unlikely to take all nonpublic information into account. In the extreme case, if a controlling manager knows of the rich discovery of a future profitable contract and does not immediately trade on the basis of this knowledge, the market surely will underprice the firm's stock. *See generally* Gilson & Kraakman, *The Mechanisms of Market Efficiency,* 70 Va.L.Rev. 549 (1984).

The coattails view does have some explanatory power with regard to appraisal statutes. It might, for example, explain the general lack of availability of appraisal for shareholders of a corporation that is acquiring another corporation's assets. It might also explain why some statutes deny appraisal to shareholders when charter amendments fundamentally change their corporations. Nevertheless, we do not take the coattails goal very seriously in this Article because in our view it does not necessarily advance shareholder interests or any convincing fairness or efficiency goal. The shareholder who is not shaken off but continues in the enterprise may simply be given too little in the way of ownership of the surviving corporation. Indeed, there is no reason to think that one who gets cash for stock is on balance any worse off than one who receives an acquirer's stock in exchange for target stock. Imagine, for example, that the original target corporation is valued in the marketplace at $100x. The target may have a terrific business opportunity that its managers have kept secret for no good business reason. They now hope to share the value of this opportunity with an acquirer, also worth $100x—at the expense of the old target shareholders. The new corporation may be worth not $200x but $300x, for example, and a true arm's-length bargain might have yielded $200x for the assets and secrets of the target; allowing the old shareholders to stay on gives them $1.50 for every $2 in value that is really theirs (since they owned pieces of a $200x corporation and are now given half the stock of a $300x corporation). The ride on the coattails may thus sometimes be better than a cash-out that would, for example, give less than $1.50 for what was said to be $1 in value but what was really $2 in value. This is hardly the sort of arrangement, however, that shareholders and legislators should agree upon *ex ante* since it generates unnecessary and inefficient secret keeping, unnecessary and costly mergers, and ultimately, high costs in pooling equity.

The point is thus really a simple one. Allowing shareholders to continue on in the corporate enterprise gives them a share of the upside return but this share may still be less than the share or cash that they would have received in an arm's-length bargain. Nevertheless, since this ride on the coattails seems attractive, conceivably it motivates appraisal statutes' granting appraisal whenever shareholders are threatened with abandonment.

Note

Appraisal Procedure

The appraisal procedures in the Model Act are significantly different from the procedures in Delaware's corporate code. The Model Act seeks to readjust the balance between the corporation and the dissenting stockholders in favor of shareholders. The principal changes are aimed, first, at eliminating much of the delay in getting funds into the hands of dissenting shareholders and, second, at forcing corporations to take more initiative in setting the claims.

Under Delaware law a corporation contemplating a transaction that gives rise to shareholder appraisal rights must notify shareholders of these rights twenty days before the corporation submits the transaction to shareholders for approval. Then each dissenting shareholder electing to demand appraisal rights notifies the corporation before the participating shareholders vote on the transaction. If the transaction passes shareholder approval, the corporation must notify qualifying dissenting shareholders (those who gave notice of their nonconsent) that appraisal rights are available. This second corporate notification must occur within ten days of the transaction's effective date. The shareholder may then, within twenty days of the second notice, demand from the corporation appraisal of his shares. If the shareholder is unsatisfied, he may then within 120 days of the transaction's effective date, file a petition in the court of chancery demanding a determination of the value of his stock. A trial on the petition can take several years. As a result of this lengthy process, the dissatisfied stockholder may not receive any money for his shares for quite some time.

The Model Act, on the other hand, stresses the importance of getting some cash value in the dissenting stockholders' hands quickly. Under the Model Act dissenting shareholders give the corporation a payment demand (as opposed to notice of appraisal right election) before the pivotal shareholder meeting. Once the transaction is approved, the corporation must, within ten days, notify the dissenting shareholders of the maturation of their right. Thereafter if the dissenting shareholder demands payment, the corporation must pay that shareholder the *corporation's* estimated fair value for the shares. If the dissenting shareholder is dissatisfied with the amount, he may, within thirty days of payment, inform the corporation of his *own* estimate. If the corporation fails to settle the discrepancy or commence a proceeding to determine the fair value, it must pay the shareholder his demand. The effect of the Model Act's procedure is to place some money in the hands of dissenters as soon as possible and to place the obligation to petition a court on the corporation rather than the dissenting shareholder.

Lastly, the Model Act gives the court wide discretion in apportioning attorney and expert witness fees "against either the corporation or a dissenter, in favor of any other party, if the court finds that the party against whom the fees and expenses are assessed acted arbitrarily, vexatiously, or not in good faith." Rev. Model Bus.Corp.Act. § 13.31(b)(2). If a corporation does not "substantially comply" with its obligations under the Model Act, it is presumed to have acted in bad faith. Rev. Model Bus. Corp.Act § 13.31(b)(1). If a shareholder's attorney fees are not assessed against a corporation, the court can award "to counsel" (note the omission of financial experts) reasonable fees to be paid out of the amounts awarded all dissenters who benefited from the counsel's efforts. Rev.Model Bus. Corp. Act § 13.31(c).

Questions

1. How many times must a dissenter file papers on a contested valuation under the Revised Model Act? Under Delaware section 262?

2. In exchange for suffering the costs of the additional filing requirements under the Revised Model Act, how is a dissenting stockholder better off than under the Delaware section?

3. Is the attorney and expert fee provision in the Revised Model Act better for dissenters than the attorney fee provision in the Delaware section?

Subsection b. Case Law on Fair Value in Appraisal Proceedings

The fair value issue in appraisal proceedings has three separate components. First, judges, often befuddled by competing financial experts, must value the shares in issue. Second, judges, if the legislation is not specific, must address the bottomless policy question of whether dissenting shareholders should participate in the gains from the acquisition. Third, judges must consider whether claims of fiduciary breach that affect market price ought to be valued in an appraisal proceeding and, if so, how to value such claims. The cases in this section deal, explicitly or implicitly, with the first two of these issues. The *Cavalier* case in the next subsection deals with the third.

The issue of whether and how to account for the potential gains of the merger or acquisition divides states. Should shareholders receive the value of their shares before the announcement of the merger affects share price, or should shareholders claim a portion of the gains generated by the merger itself? Sometimes the question is put in terms of whether the shareholders should receive a part of the "control premium" in acquisitions that involve a change of control. Occasionally the question is explicitly resolved by statute. More often the matter is left to the judiciary. As you will see in the *Weinberger* case below, in Delaware the legislature thought it had resolved the matter, but its supreme court creatively interpreted the statute.

New York is an example of a state legislature that bit the bullet. It amended its statute in 1982 to read: "The court shall ... fix the value of the shares, which for the purposes of this section, shall be the fair value as of the close of business on the day prior to the shareholders' [approval of the action dissented from]. In fixing the fair value of the shares, the court shall consider the nature of the transaction giving rise to the shareholder's right to receive payment of shares and its effects on the corporation and its shareholders, the concepts and methods then customary in the relevant securities and financial markets for determining fair value of shares of a corporation engaging in a similar transaction under comparable circumstances and all other relevant factors." McKinney's—N.Y.Bus.Corp.Law § 623(h)(4).

The New York legislature based the statute on the following finding:

> The case law interpretation of fair value has not always reflected the reality of corporate business combinations. These transactions involve

the sale of the corporation as a whole, and the corporation's value as an entity may be substantially in excess of the actual or hypothetical market price for shares trading among investors. Thus, experience has demonstrated that large premiums over market price are commonplace in mergers and in asset acquisitions. In cases where the transaction involves a restructuring of the shareholders' relative interest in the corporation by amendment of the certificate of incorporation, courts may find it appropriate to determine only the fair value of the dissenters' shares, rather than the value of the corporation as a whole, employing traditional valuation concepts. 1982 N.Y. Laws, Ch. 202, § 1.

Compare N.J.Stat.Ann. 14A:11–3, which states that the "fair value" to be awarded dissenting shareholders "shall exclude any appreciation or depreciation resulting from the proposed action."

BEERLY v. DEPARTMENT OF THE TREASURY
United States Court of Appeals, Seventh Circuit, 1985.
768 F.2d 942 cert. denied 475 U.S. 1010, 106 S.Ct. 1184, 89 L.Ed.2d 301 (1986).

Before CUMMINGS, CHIEF JUDGE, POSNER, CIRCUIT JUDGE, and PECK, SENIOR CIRCUIT JUDGE.[*]

POSNER, CIRCUIT JUDGE.

This appeal requires us to examine the meaning and constitutionality of the little-known statutory provisions for appraisal by the Comptroller of the Currency of shares owned by shareholders dissenting from (1) mergers, consolidations, or conversions of national banks into state banks, 12 U.S.C. § 214a; (2) consolidations of national or state banks under the charter of a national bank, 12 U.S.C. § 215; or (3) mergers of national or state banks into a national bank, 12 U.S.C. § 215a—all transactions that require the Comptroller's approval. The provisions for appraisal go back to 1918, yet, surprisingly in this litigious age, in only one reported case has an appraisal under any of them been challenged. See *Simonds v. Guaranty Bank & Trust Co.*, 492 F.Supp. 1079 (D.Mass.1979).

In the case of a type (3) transaction, the type involved in this case, a dissenting shareholder who gives the proper notice (as was done here) is entitled to receive the "value" of his shares. 12 U.S.C. § 215a(b). Value is determined by a committee of three appraisers of which the dissenters select one, the bank resulting from the merger another, and the two party-designated appraisers the third. 12 U.S.C. § 215a(c). If any dissenter is dissatisfied with the appraisers' valuation of his shares, or if for some reason one of the appraisers is not appointed, or if the appraisers fail to make an appraisal, then the Comptroller shall on request "cause an appraisal [or reappraisal, if the dissenter was dissatisfied with the appraisers' appraisal] to be made which shall be final and binding" on all parties. 12 U.S.C. §§ 215a(c), (d). Similar provi-

[*] Hon. John W. Peck of the Sixth Circuit, sitting by designation.

sions are applicable to transactions of types (1) and (2). See 12 U.S.C. §§ 214a(b), 215(c), (d).

* * *

There are many ways to value a share of stock. The Comptroller considered four: book value, adjusted book value, market value, and investment value.

1. Book value is the difference between the firm's assets and liabilities as valued on its books of account, divided by the number of shares. For Mid–City this comes out to $600.10. But the Comptroller gave book value zero weight in his appraisal.

2. Adjusted book value is book value multiplied by the ratio of the market prices of comparable institutions to their book values. The "peer group" used by the Comptroller to determine the adjusted book value of Mid–City stock consisted of other middle-sized Chicago banks. Their stock was selling at an average of 46 percent of book value. Multiplying this by Mid–City's book value per share produced the figure $294.05; this was the stock's adjusted book value.

3. The meaning of market value is self-evident; but because Mid–City's stock had been very thinly traded (only one-quarter of one percent of its stock had been traded in any recent year), the Comptroller decided to give zero weight to this valuation too. The stock's market value was about $160.

4. Finally, the Comptroller computed an "investment value" for Mid–City by multiplying its most recent annual earnings per share by the price-earnings multiple—which was 6—of Mid–City's peer group; and this produced a figure of $270.72. The Comptroller averaged the two figures he had calculated—the adjusted book value and the investment value—and this yielded his appraisal of $282.39 for each of Beerly's shares.

The methodology of appraisal used by the Comptroller resembles that used in appraising dissenting shareholders' rights under state corporation laws.

* * *

Although this methodology has frequently been criticized (as in the articles just cited), the fact that the Comptroller was following a conventional approach goes far to shield his results from judicial invalidation. It is not for a reviewing court to tell an administrative agency to defy the conventional wisdom, to innovate, to be daring. And one of the principal criticisms of the conventional methodology of appraisal—that market value is a better index of value than any valuation formula—is, as we shall see, inapplicable to this case.

* * *

The purpose of an appraisal is to give the owner of the property being appraised the cash equivalent of what he has given up by relinquishing his ownership. In the case of stock what he gives up is the opportunity to sell the stock or to keep it and obtain an income from it. Ordinarily the best estimate of what an opportunity to sell is worth is found in recent sales of the same thing, which would mean, recent sales of stock in Mid–City National Bank. See, e.g., *Metlyn Realty Corp. v. Esmark, Inc.,* 763 F.2d 826, 835–36 (7th Cir.1985). If the Comptroller had used this method of estimation, it would have turned out very badly for Beerly, because the market value of the stock in the relevant period was only about $160 a share.

It is true that when stock is traded infrequently, past sales may not be a reliable guide to current value, because they impound valuations by only a few buyers and sellers, and because circumstances may have changed since those sales took place. (The other side of the coin is that if a stock has a "thick" market, not only is market value the only rational measure of value, but appraisal rights are unnecessary since the dissenting shareholder can fully protect his interests by selling his shares. On this ground, Delaware does not recognize appraisal rights in such settings. See Del.Gen.Corp.Law § 262(b)(1) (1984).) But the fact remains that if Beerly had wanted to cash in his stock he would have had to take his chances in a market in which the demand was weak. Indeed, since he owned 4 percent of the stock of the company—16 times as much stock as had been sold in any recent year—he might not have been able to unload all of his stock at $160 a share.

And it is necessary to distinguish between a "squeeze-out" and a change merely in the form of the shareholder's rights. When a stock is thinly traded, so that its market value is not a reliable index of its true value, controlling shareholders may be tempted at a time when the market valuation is unreasonably low to force minority shareholders to give up their shares in exchange for the market value of the shares, which by hypothesis is less than their true value. But Beerly was not squeezed out; he was offered what appears to have been equivalent shares in the reorganized firm; he left voluntarily. The Comptroller was generous in giving no weight at all to the (low) market value of Beerly's stock.

Book value is a virtually meaningless index of what a share of stock is worth to the shareholder, and the Comptroller properly disregarded it. The main component of book value is the original cost of the firm's assets, as depreciated. Wholly apart from the well-known vagaries of depreciation, if a firm's assets are specialized to the firm's business they may have very little sale value. Their only value may be to generate the firm's earnings. But then it is clear that the value of the firm is some multiple of its earnings, and not some function of the original cost of its assets. Evidently the book value of middle-sized Chicago banks in the relevant period was greater than their market value, for the stock of Mid–City's "peer group" was trading in the market at an average of only 46 percent of book value per share. Such discounts are common, as any owner of railroad stock knows.

It is true that Beerly presented evidence that some middle-sized Chicago banks had been bought for more than their book value. But there is a big difference between the value of a minority shareholder's interest and the value of a controlling interest, which is what is at stake when the whole firm is acquired and not just some shares of its stock. Someone who thinks he can run a firm better than its present owners—that is, thinks he can get more value out of the firm's assets than they can—naturally will be willing to pay more (if he must!) for a controlling interest than the current market value of the firm's stock; that stock is worth more to him. But the qualification is vital; the stock is worth more to him only if he has control of the firm, so that he can run it; and for control he needs more than 4 percent. Of course the analysis would be more complicated if a buyer were not allowed to pay a premium for a controlling block of stock—if he had to pay all shareholders the same price for their shares. But federal law contains no such requirement, which would make transfers of corporate control more costly and therefore reduce the effectiveness of the market for corporate control in disciplining managers and in moving corporate resources into the hands of those who can get the most value out of them. See Easterbrook & Fischel, *Corporate Control Transactions,* 91 Yale L.J. 698 (1982). All shareholders may be better off, ex ante, with a rule that facilitates takeovers, even though, ex post, some may get lower prices for their shares if a takeover occurs.

The two measures of value that the Comptroller used are more consonant with economic reality than book value is and more favorable to Beerly than market value. The Comptroller's "adjusted book value" was essentially a measure of the market value of a portfolio of comparable banks, and thus corrected for the thinness of the market in Mid–City's own stock. The Comptroller's "investment value" assumed quite sensibly that the value of bank stock is as an income-producing asset and is therefore a function of the bank's income. The precise form of that function depends on investors' estimates of the riskiness of the bank's stock and the prospects for the bank's future earnings; and while it is possible that Mid–City is less risky than its peers or has brighter prospects, the Comptroller was entitled to assume, in the absence of more direct evidence of Mid–City's prospects, that investors were unlikely to consider it a more valuable asset, per dollar of earnings, than a portfolio of stocks of similar banks.

The two measures the Comptroller used are closely related. In effect he made two adjustments to the average market value of the stock of the peer firms to derive the market value of Beerly's shares in Mid–City: He multiplied it first by the ratio of Mid–City's book value to the peer group's average book value and then by the ratio of Mid–City's earnings to the peer group's average earnings, and then he took the average of these two products. He assumed, in other words, that Mid–City's stock would be worth more, relative to the market value of comparable banks' stock, the more its book value exceeded the average book value of the comparable banks and the more its earnings exceeded their earnings. This is a defensible procedure (ratios of book values may be a little more meaningful than absolute book values), and on the whole one generous to Beerly.

* * *

The most questionable feature of the Comptroller's valuation (apart from his giving no weight to the bank's market value—an omission that favored Beerly, however) was the refusal to count any part of the bank's reserve for bad loans as an asset, rather than a liability. The reserve, $2 million, had remained unchanged for many years during which the bank wrote off an average of only $10,000 a year in bad loans. The recent and well-publicized difficulties of large Chicago banks, together with the uncertainties that have been created by the deregulation (though as yet partial) of banking, seem to confirm the prudence of the Comptroller's conservative approach to bank reserves—and in any event we can think of few areas less suitable for judicial second-guessing than the Comptroller's determination of how large a reserve is suitable for a bank of Mid–City's size and condition. But the point is not whether the Comptroller acted reasonably in requiring a large reserve for bad loans; it is whether investors would have considered the reserve excessive, for if so they would have treated the excess as an asset rather than a liability in valuing the firm. However, an adjustment to take account of this possibility would not have altered the appraisal significantly. The reserve was equal to only 7 percent of the bank's book value. Suppose it was twice as large as investors would have thought proper. The effect on adjusted book value (equal to 46 percent of book value) would be to increase that value by only 1.6 percent (46 percent of 3.5 percent is 1.6 percent); and since adjusted book value was given a weight of one-half in valuing Beerly's stock, the result would be a less than 1 percent (0.8 percent, to be precise) increase in the value of his stock. If there was an error in the treatment of the reserve for bad loans—and that is uncertain—it was trifling.

We do not understand Beerly's complaint that the bank paid lower dividends than comparable banks. That would just go to increase the bank's capital, and hence book value, and hence the valuation of Beerly's shares.

* * *

WEINBERGER v. UOP, INC.

Supreme Court of Delaware, 1983.
457 A.2d 701.

Before HERRMANN, C.J., McNEILLY, QUILLEN, HORSEY and MOORE, JJ., constituting the Court en Banc.

MOORE, JUSTICE:

* * *

Turning to the matter of price, plaintiff also challenges its fairness. His evidence was that on the date the merger was approved the stock was worth at least $26 per share. In support, he offered the testimony of a chartered investment analyst who used two basic approaches to valuation: a comparative analysis of the premium paid over market in ten other tender offer-merger combinations, and a discounted cash flow analysis.

In this breach of fiduciary duty case, the Chancellor perceived that the approach to valuation was the same as that in an appraisal proceeding. Consistent with precedent, he rejected plaintiff's method of proof and accepted defendants' evidence of value as being in accord with practice under prior case law. This means that the so-called "Delaware block" or weighted average method was employed wherein the elements of value, i.e., assets, market price, earnings, etc., were assigned a particular weight and the resulting amounts added to determine the value per share. This procedure has been in use for decades. *See In re General Realty & Utilities Corp.*, Del.Ch., 52 A.2d 6, 14-15 (1947). However, to the extent it excludes other generally accepted techniques used in the financial community and the courts, it is now clearly outmoded. It is time we recognize this in appraisal and other stock valuation proceedings and bring our law current on the subject.

While the Chancellor rejected plaintiff's discounted cash flow method of valuing UOP's stock, as not corresponding with "either logic or the existing law" (426 A.2d at 1360), it is significant that this was essentially the focus, i.e., earnings potential of UOP, of Messrs. Arledge and Chitiea in their evaluation of the merger. Accordingly, the standard "Delaware block" or weighted average method of valuation, formerly employed in appraisal and other stock valuation cases, shall no longer exclusively control such proceedings. We believe that a more liberal approach must include proof of value by any techniques or methods which are generally considered acceptable in the financial community and otherwise admissible in court, subject only to our interpretation of 8 *Del.C.* § 262(h), *infra. See also* D.R.E. 702-05. This will obviate the very structured and mechanistic procedure that has heretofore governed such matters.

* * *

Fair price obviously requires consideration of all relevant factors involving the value of a company. This has long been the law of Delaware as stated in *Tri-Continental Corp.*, 74 A.2d at 72:

> The basic concept of value under the appraisal statute is that the stockholder is entitled to be paid for that which has been taken from him, viz., his proportionate interest in a going concern. By value of the stockholder's proportionate interest in the corporate enterprise is meant the true or intrinsic value of his stock which has been taken by the merger. In determining what figure represents this true or intrinsic value, the appraiser and the courts must take into consideration all

factors and elements which reasonably might enter into the fixing of value. Thus, market value, asset value, dividends, earning prospects, the nature of the enterprise and any other facts which were known or which could be ascertained as of the date of merger and which throw any light on *future prospects* of the merged corporation are not only pertinent to an inquiry as to the value of the dissenting stockholders' interest, but *must be considered* by the agency fixing the value. (Emphasis added.)

This is not only in accord with the realities of present day affairs, but it is thoroughly consonant with the purpose and intent of our statutory law. Under 8 *Del.C.* § 262(h), the Court of Chancery:

shall appraise the shares, determining their *fair* value exclusive of any element of value arising from the accomplishment or expectation of the merger, together with a fair rate of interest, if any, to be paid upon the amount determined to be the *fair* value. In determining such *fair* value, the Court shall take into account *all relevant factors* ... (Emphasis added)

See also Bell v. Kirby Lumber Corp., Del.Supr., 413 A.2d 137, 150–51 (1980) (Quillen, J., concurring).

It is significant that section 262 now mandates the determination of "fair" value based upon "all relevant factors". Only the speculative elements of value that may arise from the "accomplishment or expectation" of the merger are excluded. We take this to be a very narrow exception to the appraisal process, designed to eliminate use of *pro forma* data and projections of a speculative variety relating to the completion of a merger. But elements of future value, including the nature of the enterprise, which are known or susceptible of proof as of the date of the merger and not the product of speculation, may be considered. When the trial court deems it appropriate, fair value also includes any damages, resulting from the taking, which the stockholders sustain as a class. If that was not the case, then the obligation to consider "all relevant factors" in the valuation process would be eroded. We are supported in this view not only by *Tri–Continental Corp.,* 74 A.2d at 72, but also by the evolutionary amendments to section 262.

Prior to an amendment in 1976, the earlier relevant provision of section 262 stated:

(f) The appraiser shall determine the value of the stock of the stockholders ... The Court shall by its decree determine the value of the stock of the stockholders entitled to payment therefor ...

The first references to "fair" value occurred in a 1976 amendment to section 262(f), which provided:

(f) ... the Court shall appraise the shares, determining their fair value exclusively of any element of value arising from the accomplishment or expectation of the merger....

It was not until the 1981 amendment to section 262 that the reference to "fair value" was repeatedly emphasized and the statutory mandate that the Court "take into account all relevant factors" appeared [section 262(h)]. Clearly, there is a legislative intent to fully compensate shareholders for whatever their loss may be, subject only to the narrow limitation that one can not take speculative effects of the merger into account.

* * *

IN RE VALUATION OF COMMON STOCK OF LIBBY, McNEILL & LIBBY

Supreme Judicial Court of Maine, 1979.
406 A.2d 54.

Before McKusick, C.J., and Pomeroy, Wernick, Archibald, Godfrey and Nichols, JJ.

McKusick, Chief Justice.

For the first time since the enactment of the Maine Business Corporation Act, effective on January 1, 1972, the courts are in this case called upon to construe and apply the dissenting shareholder appraisal provisions of the Act, 13–A M.R.S.A. § 909 (1974).

In this proceeding, the Superior Court (Cumberland County) had the task of determining the "fair value" as of February 17, 1976, of the common stock of Libby, McNeill & Libby (hereafter "Libby"), a former Maine corporation, engaging primarily in production of canned foods. Libby, McNeill & Libby, Inc. (hereafter "petitioner"), the Delaware successor by merger to the Maine corporation, sought this determination in order to establish the magnitude of its liability to former Libby shareholders who dissented from the merger authorized by all necessary votes on February 18, 1976.[1] The Superior Court valued the Libby stock at $8.55 per share. On appeal, petitioner maintains that the Superior Court justice should have accepted the recommendation of the court-appointed appraiser, who valued the stock at $6.00 per share. Petitioner also contends that the Superior Court erred in ordering petitioner to pay the shareholders' expert fees and expenses. The dissenting shareholders cross-appeal, claiming that the Superior Court's valuation of $8.55 per share is too low, and that the trial justice should have awarded them their attorneys' fees, as well as their experts' fees and expenses.

The major issue generated by this appeal is the proper definition of the term "fair value" as it is used in the dissenting shareholder provisions of the Maine Business Corporation Act. We hold that the

---

1. 13–A M.R.S.A. § 909(1) provides:

"A shareholder having a right under any provision of this Act to dissent to proposed corporate action shall, by complying with the procedure in this section, be paid the fair value of his shares, if the corporate action to which he dissented is effected. The fair value of shares shall be determined as of the day prior to the date on which the vote of the shareholders, or of the directors in case a vote of the shareholders was not necessary, was taken approving the proposed corporate action, excluding any appreciation or depreciation of shares in anticipation of such corporate action."

Superior Court justice's interpretation of the term "fair value" was not entirely correct. On reviewing the record made before the appraiser, we conclude that the Superior Court should have accepted the appraiser's recommendation that a fair value of $6.00 per share be set for the Libby stock. Accordingly, we sustain petitioner's appeal and deny the shareholders' cross-appeal.

* * *

By 1974 Nestle had increased its holdings to over 60%. Then, in 1975, Nestle decided to eliminate all minority shareholders and to turn Libby into a wholly owned subsidiary. Nestle transferred ownership of all its Libby shares to the wholly owned Nestle subsidiary UFS, and on May 29, 1975, UFS made public its tender offer to acquire all remaining shares of Libby common stock. By its tender offer UFS clearly appraised the public that if it received enough Libby stock to raise its holdings to more than 90%, UFS intended to effect a "short form merger" of Libby with UFS. UFS offered to pay $8.125 per share, a price 65% above the stock market price of $4.88 per share on the New York Stock Exchange at which Libby stock traded on May 23, 1975, the last day prior to announcement of the UFS tender offer.[3] More than three quarters of all available shares of Libby common stock were sold to UFS in response to its tender offer, thus giving UFS an aggregate holding of more than 90% of Libby common stock.

On February 18, 1976, petitioner's board of directors approved the plan for a short form merger of Libby and UFS pursuant to 13–A M.R.S.A. § 904. No shareholder vote or further corporate action by Libby was required for authorization of the merger under Maine law. See n. 2 above. Following refusal by both state and federal courts to enjoin the merger, *Tanzer Economic Associates, Inc. Profit Sharing Plan v. Universal Food Specialties, Inc.*, 87 Misc.2d 167, 383 N.Y.S.2d 472 (Sup.Ct., March 10, 1976); *Merrit v. Libby, McNeill & Libby*, 533 F.2d 1310 (2d Cir., April 5, 1976), the merger was completed on April 6,

---

3. The fact that tender offers frequently, if not usually, involve a premium in excess of current market price is established both by the evidence introduced before the appraiser in the case at bar and by reported court decisions, see, e.g., *Gibbons v. Schenley Industries, Inc.*, 339 A.2d 460, 468 (Del.Ch.1975). The investment banker advising the Nestle affiliate in its tender offer for Libby stock recommended the premium in order to overcome shareholder inertia. He testified: "Typically, when a common stock is so widely dispersed not only is it difficult to reach all the shareholders, but many small shareholders are indifferent to tender offers because the process of tendering shares is complicated and it is not worth their while to fill out the necessary papers."

Dissenting shareholders who refused the tender offer and instead insisted on a judicial determination of fair value are not entitled to receive the tender offer premium. In other words, the $8.125 premerger tender offer price does not establish any floor under the amount the court may fix as the value of the Libby stock in the appraisal proceeding. *Id.* That is not to say, however, that the tender offer price might not have some evidentiary significance, at least if no explanation were presented for the tender offer's including a premium. The parties also have not made an issue as to the evidentiary significance, if any, of the surviving corporation's making, as required by 13–A M.R.S.A. § 909(7), "a written offer to each such dissenting shareholder to pay for such shares at a specified price *deemed by such corporation to be the fair value thereof.*" (Emphasis added)

1976. From among those who had rejected the UFS offer of $8.125 per share, 110 shareholders owning 66,140 shares of Libby stock filed written demands for payment of the fair value of their shares and otherwise perfected their right to participate in this valuation proceeding. See 13–A M.R.S.A. § 909(3).

* * * The Superior Court departed from the weighting recommendations of the appraiser,[8] because of the court's belief that the fact the minority shareholders were unwilling sellers, forced to part with their shares in the course of the statutory merger, should be given special consideration. In weighting the three components the Superior Court justice "view[ed] the transaction in terms of the respective losses and benefits to the parties to the actual transaction." Fixing "fair value" at a price which would satisfy a willing buyer and a willing seller would not, according to the Superior Court justice, "adequately compensate the shareholder for his loss of freedom to deal with his property as he sees fit." Thus the justice below rejected the appraiser's recommendation of a 40% weighting for stock market price and instead assigned only a weight of 10% to that element.

In addition, the Superior Court justice asserted that the unsophisticated shareholder carried a mental image of his shareholder rights that focused on his right to part ownership of the assets of the corporation. To compensate the dissenting shareholders for the deprivation of this cherished right of part ownership of corporate assets, the Superior Court ruled that the appraiser erred in assigning net asset value a weight of only 20%. The justice substituted a weighting of 45% for net asset value.

In thus attributing significance to impairment of the dissenting shareholder's economic freedom to dispose of his property when and as he wished and to the shareholder's mental image of his undivided ownership rights in corporate assets, the Superior Court justice committed an error of law that requires the judgment below to be set aside as far as the weighting of the elements of fair value is concerned. The statutory right of a dissenting shareholder to be paid the fair value of his shares is not designed to compensate the shareholder for "psychological" injuries, or to take into account the particular mental image of ownership rights possessed by the shareholder. In the same way,

---

8. The appraiser defined fair value as "what a willing seller would take and a willing buyer would give in a free arm's length transaction in which the parties are informed as to the facts requisite for a rational judgment." We find the appraiser's statement of the law, so far as it goes, to be correct. In approving the "willing buyer/willing seller" approach, however, we do not mean to be understood to say that the market price of the stock in issue is to be taken as the sole criterion of the "fair value" of the stock. The appraiser of course did not so limit his search. We reiterate that all three of the component elements of value should be considered: stock market price, net asset value, and investment value. Each element provides evidence of the price at which a willing buyer and a willing seller would strike a bargain. In any given case, however, after careful consideration of all relevant facts and circumstances, a court may conclude that one of the elements is a highly unreliable indicator of fair value, as compared with the other elements, and may properly decide to assign little or no weight to that element. Thus, the weight to be accorded stock market price will vary, according to the particular circumstances of each case.

compensation for real estate taken under the power of eminent domain disregards whatever emotional or psychological attachments the owner may have to his property, as well as any "nontransferable values arising from [the owner's] unique need for [the] property...." *United States v. 564.54 Acres of Land,* 441 U.S. 506, 516, 99 S.Ct. 1854, 1860, 60 L.Ed.2d 435 (1979), quoting *Kimball Laundry Co. v. United States,* 338 U.S. 1, 5, 69 S.Ct. 1434, 93 L.Ed. 1765 (1949). Furthermore, "fair value" is not measured by any unique benefits that will accrue to the acquiring corporation, any more than the compensable value of property taken by eminent domain is measured by its special value to the condemnor. *Cf., e.g., Gilmore v. Central Maine Power Co.,* 127 Me. 522, 145 A. 137 (1929). The fair value of shares is to be determined on the basis of what a reasonable and objective observer would consider to be a price that reflects the intrinsic value of the right of stock ownership, without regard to any subjective mental processes of the dissenting shareholders or any special benefits to be derived by the acquiring corporation.

The Superior Court's "view[ing] the [merger] in terms of the respective losses and benefits to the parties to the actual transaction" does violence to the statutory mandate, 13–A M.R.S.A. § 909(1), that the value of the dissenters' shares shall be valued without relation to the proposed merger. We cannot read any other way the statutory provision that the fair value of the shares shall be determined as of the day before the merger vote was taken and furthermore shall "exclud[e] any appreciation or depreciation of shares in anticipation of such corporate action." *Id.* The dissenting shareholders are entitled to receive the full fair value of their shares, but that value must be determined independently of the merger transaction that gave the dissenting shareholders the statutory right to be bought out and their corporation the statutory duty to pay them off. The appraisal proceeding is not at all concerned with the losses to the *particular* dissenting shareholders or with the benefits derived by the *particular* acquiring corporation in the merger, except as those losses and benefits would be reflected in the price that would be bargained out in a completely free market between *any* willing buyer and *any* willing seller in absence of the merger.

* * *

Since the fair value of Libby stock is significantly less than the $8.125 per share offered and paid to all Libby shareholders other than the dissenters, we have no statutory basis for awarding the dissenting shareholders attorneys' fees.[16] Nor is there any "good cause" for

---

16. 13–A M.R.S.A. § 909(9)(H) provides in part:

"Such expenses [assessed against the corporation] shall include reasonable compensation for and reasonable expenses of the appraisers, but shall exclude the fees and expenses of counsel for any party and shall exclude the fees and expenses of experts employed by any party, unless the court otherwise orders for good cause. If the fair value of the shares as determined materially exceeds the amount which the corporation offered to pay therefor, or if no offer was made, the court in its discretion may award to any shareholder who is a party to the pro-

awarding the dissenters their experts' fees and expenses.[17] Plainly, circumstances might arise in which a court in its sound discretion would be justified in assessing against the corporation all or part of the dissenters' costs of presenting expert witnesses. For example, such might well be the case where the dissenters provided essential valuation evidence not available otherwise in the proceeding. The experts presented by the shareholders did not perform any such function in the case at bar. The controlling statute does not authorize us to assess against the corporation any of the dissenting shareholders' expenses for attorneys and experts.

* * *

STOUT, ARE TAKEOVER PREMIUMS REALLY PREMIUMS? MARKET PRICE, FAIR VALUE AND CORPORATE LAW
99 Yale L.J. 1235, 1287, 1289–92 (1990).

Appraisal would be both unnecessary and irrelevant if all investors shared identical estimates of stock value: Any merger offer that met with the approval of a majority of shareholders would meet with the approval of all. But if shareholders hold differing opinions of the value of their stock, they can be expected to disagree on the merits of even a premium offer. Appraisal makes sense as a means of recognizing and protecting the interests of those dissenting shareholders who believe that the merger price approved by the majority is less than the actual value of their shares.[286]

ceeding such sum as the court may determine to be reasonable compensation to any expert or experts employed by the shareholder in the proceeding, and may, in its discretion, award to any shareholder all or part of his attorney's fees and expenses."

17. On its appeal petitioner claims that section 909(9)(H), see n. 16 above, should be read to require that, at least where the alleged "good cause" for the assessment of experts' fees against the corporation is an excess of the fair value found by the court over the amount previously offered by the corporation to the dissenting shareholders, that excess must be material. Since the Superior Court found that the excess of $8.55 over $8.125 was not material, petitioner argues the court erred in awarding experts' fees. Since we find fair value to be $6.00, and since we deny the allowance of experts' fees on other grounds, we have no occasion to address the issue of law raised by this point of petitioner's appeal.

286. The modern justification for appraisal is that it protects shareholders from mergers and sales at "unfairly" low prices. * * * This answer is troubling to efficient market theorists. If market prices are accurate, how can a merger at a premium above market be unfair? Scholars argue that merger prices may be inadequate if they do not reflect information withheld from passive shareholders, or if target management has urged shareholders to approve a sale at a low price in return for perquisites such as higher salaries or generous severance provisions.

* * * The downward-sloping demand hypothesis adds the possibility that the price paid dissenters to a merger is "too low" because it fails to reflect their more-optimistic, subjective estimate of stock value.

* * *

Whether appraisal statutes are designed for compensating dissenting shareholders for subjective losses or for mergers tainted by undisclosed information or management misconduct, the stock market exception makes little sense unless one believes that investors in exchange-listed firms suffer smaller losses and are less likely to experience information "blockages" or management knavery.

* * *

* * *

In many ways, however, a downward-sloping demand function for stocks raises as many questions about the appraisal remedy as it answers. The most significant of these may be the question of what the "fair value" of a corporation's shares is. Once market price is rejected as a common standard, the concept of value becomes elusive. In a world where investors disagree sharply in their estimates of the likely return and risk of particular stocks, they cannot all be correct. But which investors are right, and which wrong?

One possibility is that appraisal should measure value as the subjective value each dissenting shareholder attaches to her shares. The dissenter may be a better informed or more experienced judge of intrinsic value than the shareholders who approved the transaction. For example, in a bear market dissenters may be those investors with cooler heads who can objectively estimate earnings without being swayed by market pessimism. A second reason to compensate dissenters for their subjective loss is that the shareholders who voted in favor of the merger or sale received payment that met or exceeded their subjective reservation prices. Perhaps the more-optimistic shareholders who comprise the upper portion of the demand function should be fully compensated as well.

Upon thoughtful consideration, however, the notion of an appraisal remedy designed to compensate dissenting shareholders fully for their perceived losses seems both undesirable and unworkable. Shareholders who believe that the value of their stock substantially exceeds both the market and a premium merger price obviously cannot expect to realize that perceived value by selling the stock in the near future. Presumably, optimists hope to profit from their opinions by holding their stock until the day their bright expectations for the firm's future are realized, either because the market price comes to agree with their assessment of the firm's value or because their optimistic expectations for dividends and other payments are met. That day may come soon, late, or not at all. An appraisal remedy that grants dissenters their subjective expectations without the slightest regard for the reasonableness of those expectations seems somehow unrealistic. Allowing dissenting shareholders to demand their subjective estimates of stock value also provides an incentive for virtually all shareholders dissenting from a merger to seek appraisal, creating a risk that some acquisitions might not take place even though the bidder is willing to pay a price that exceeds the aggregate the target's shareholders would demand in individually negotiated transactions.[299] Finally, and perhaps most signifi-

---

299. A virtual guarantee that dissenting shareholders could receive more for their shares in appraisal than in the merger would raise the risk that extensive (and expensive) appraisal payments would drain cash from merging firms. * * * Moreover, where legal and practical considerations force bidders to make large acquisitions at a uniform price, an appraisal remedy designed to meet the subjective expectations of the most-optimistic of the target's shareholders also would increase the cost of acquisitions to the point where many effi-

cantly, there is no reliable way to determine investors' subjective reservation prices. Direct inquiries for obvious reasons are likely to lead to inflated claims of value: Appraisal makes the heart grow fonder.

Perhaps appraisals of stock value should be based not on the opinions of individual dissenting shareholders, but upon some "average" investor opinion. Courts could attempt to calculate the average estimates of value held by those relatively optimistic investors who are the firm's current shareholders. Alternatively, courts could attempt to compute the average valuation not just of those investors who have actually purchased the stock, but of *all* potential investors. That group would include those individuals who have expressed their pessimistic views of the company's prospects by declining to own it.

The court determined to calculate such average valuations faces obvious practical obstacles. More important, there is no inherent reason why "average" opinion (whether the average of all potential investors or only current shareholders) should be more accurate than any individual dissenting shareholder's opinion. An average valuation culled from the opinions of many uninformed, unexperienced lay investors and relatively few informed experts may differ substantially from the best estimate of share value. Especially in the wake of the 1987 market crash, one cannot avoid the suspicion that, on occasion, average lay opinion departs significantly from rational estimates of value.

A remaining possibility is that appraisal valuation should focus not on the opinions of lay investors or some subset of lay investors, but on the objective estimates of experts who study all available financial information. That appears to be the approach of many state courts in appraisal proceedings.

* * *

As the question of appraisal amply illustrates, under the downward-sloping demand hypothesis the concept of stock "value" becomes problematic. Candidates for "value" include the market price at which marginal shareholders are willing to buy or sell; the varying subjective estimates attached by different shareholders; the average estimates of either existing shareholders or all potential investors; and the informed estimate of the financial expert.[309] Each and every one of these

---

ciency-enhancing transactions might not take place. * * *

Because such efficient transactions increase overall shareholder wealth, from an *ex ante* perspective potential investors may prefer a "minimalist" appraisal remedy that functions as a safety net against unfair merger terms and unreliable market prices rather than one which guarantees each shareholder's hopes are met, no matter how wildly optimistic these may be. * * *

309. Each of these estimates of value may be based on different considerations. For example, some investors may value stock according to their predictions of likely short-term changes in market price, possibly due to investor irrationality. * * * Alternatively, some investors may use orthodox portfolio theory and differ in their estimates of stock value because they differ in their estimates of future risk-discounted earnings. * * * Some investors may also value stock by looking to the underlying

may be the "correct" value under differing circumstances. None can claim to be the only "true" value.

Questions

1. How confident can we be that state court judges can discern "fair" value in a battle of hired financial experts? Are there better procedural rules that would generate less error? For example, what if each party had to submit one price and the judge could choose only between the two figures? Would each party have an incentive to inflate their figures or submit reasonable figures?

2. Should a dissenting shareholder receive a price that reflects a proportion of potential future gains that are generated by the merger itself? If so, how does a judge allocate the gains created by a merger between the target's and the bidder's shareholders?

Assume the following pattern of stock prices: On day one, month one, the market price is $10 per share for corporation B, a Delaware corporation with less than two thousand shareholders; on day one, month two, the board of directors of A announces it is pursuing merger discussions with B, and the market price of B stock rises to $12 per share; on day one, month three, the boards of A and B reach an agreement in principle in which B shareholders will receive one share of A stock and the market price of A stock is $20 a share, and the market price of B stock rises to $15 per share; on day one, month four, the shareholders of B approve the merger, and the market price of B stock is $17 per share; a group of dissenting shareholders vote against the merger, believing that their board left money on the table in the negotiations with A—they believe that B shareholders should receive 1.25 shares of A stock; at the closing a month later B shareholders receive shares of A stock valued on the market immediately after the closing at $19 a share; on day one, month nine, the court decides the case and A has done well—so the value of A stock received by B shareholders who voted in favor of the merger is $30 per share. What amount should a dissenting shareholder receive in an appraisal proceeding in Delaware? See section 262(h). How would Judge Posner decide the case? How would Professor Stout decide the case?

3. Professor Stout's argument against a pure market price standard hinges on her belief that the shareholders' differing subjective evaluations of stock price are not generated primarily by their different perceptions of the value added by the acquisition offer itself, but rather are generated by their different perceptions of the value of the stock neutral of any offer. See Stout, note 309, supra. If this empirical assumption proves to be largely false, what is left of her argument? How should we treat a dissenting shareholder who values his stock before the announcement of a merger at, say, $100 per share when the market is at $95 per share and who values his stock after the merger announcement, in which it is announced he will receive $110 per share in cash under the merger agreement, at $120 per share (based on his belief that his managers could

---

value of the firm's assets rather than current earnings. * * *

bargain for a higher price from the existing bidder or from additional bidders)?

Even if we accept her view that there is an upward-sloping supply curve for any bidder in a stock acquisition, does this necessarily mean that shareholders have a wide range of subjective views on the value of a stock independent of announced acquisitions? How much of the upward slope is explained by transaction costs as opposed to stock valuation? Consider the following individual: He is a passive investor. He is very busy as a professional earning a six-figure income and owns ten shares of stock in A, market price at $100 a share, as part of a diversified portfolio. For him, monitoring the stock price of A and then taking the time to sell into tender offer has high costs relative to his stake in the shares. Assume he values the stock at $100 a share, the market price, and a tender offer is announced at $110 a share. If he does not tender, he is likely to receive securities in a back-end merger equal to close to $110 a share within six months. Why should he bother to sell? The time it takes to inform himself and to sell is more valuable than the few dollars a share he will make if he tenders. It is not that he values the shares at more than $110—he does not—his costs of selling relative to his stake are large. How much sympathy should we have for him in structuring our appraisal remedy?

4. In a two-step transaction, as in the *Libby* case, involving a stock acquisition followed by a cash-out merger, how much evidentiary value should a judge sitting in an appraisal proceeding place on the price offered in the first step? Assume A wants to acquire all the shares of B for $100 per share when the B shares are trading at $75. In case one the firms merge and B shareholders receive $100 in cash. In case two A offers to buy 50.1 percent in a tender offer at $120 and the rest in a cash-out merger at $80. In case three, otherwise the same as case two, A offers $150 in the tender offer and $50 in the merger. In each case what should dissenting shareholders receive through the assertion of their appraisal remedy?

5. If minority shares in a closely held firm generally do, in fact, sell for less per share then control block shares in negotiated transactions, why should a court refuse to apply a "minority discount" in an appraisal proceeding?

Subsection c. The Exclusivity of the Appraisal Remedy

Delaware's Wandering Journey

In the *Weinberger* case in the previous subsection, the Delaware Supreme Court created, prospectively, a rule that limited shareholders with certain kinds of claims to appraisal proceedings. Please review the case as excerpted in the previous section. As you read the cases in this section, ask yourself whether the court has announced a successful and sensible standard. The flip side of the question is presented in this section in the *Cavalier* case. Are there shareholder claims about an acquisition that cannot be made in an otherwise available appraisal proceeding, claims that must be advanced in a class action for damages or injunctive relief?

RABKIN v. PHILIP A. HUNT CHEMICAL CORP.
498 A.2d 1099 (Del.1985).

[The court in *Rabkin v. Philip A. Hunt Chemical Corp.*, 498 A.2d 1099 (Del.1985) rejected a lower court's interpretation of the holding in *Weinberger* as limiting a shareholder's remedy to appraisal even when minority shareholders allege procedural unfairness by majority shareholders when conducting a cash-out merger. In *Rabkin*, Olin Corporation purchased 63.4 percent of Philip A. Hunt Chemical Corporation's stock with the provision that if it purchased all or substantially all of the remaining shares within one year from the closing date, it would pay the same price to the minority shareholders as was paid in the initial transaction. Approximately four weeks after the one-year waiting period Olin's board approved a proposal to cash out the remaining Hunt shareholders at a price of $20 per share, $5 less than the price paid in the original purchase. The fairness of the price was confirmed by both Morgan Lewis and Merrill Lynch. The Hunt board of directors recommended the merger in its proxy statement.

The minority shareholders of Hunt challenged the merger on the grounds that the price offered was grossly inadequate because Olin had unfairly manipulated the timing of the merger to avoid the one-year commitment. The chancery court granted defendant's motion to dismiss, stating that absent claims of fraud or deception, a minority stockholder's rights in a cash-out merger were limited to an appraisal.]

* * *

Thus, the trial court's narrow interpretation of *Weinberger* would render meaningless our extensive discussion of fair dealing found in that opinion. In *Weinberger* we defined fair dealing as embracing "questions of when the transaction was timed, how it was initiated, structured, negotiated, disclosed to the directors, and how the approvals of the directors and the stockholders were obtained." 457 A.2d at 711. While this duty of fairness certainly incorporates the principle that a cash-out merger must be free of fraud or misrepresentation, *Weinberger's* mandate of fair dealing does not turn solely on issues of deception. We particularly noted broader concerns respecting the matter of procedural fairness. *Weinberger*, 457 A.2d at 711, 714. Thus, while "in a non-fraudulent transaction ... price *may* be the preponderant consideration," *id.* at 711 (emphasis added), it is not necessarily so.

* * *

In our opinion the facts alleged by the plaintiffs regarding Olin's avoidance of the one year commitment support a claim of unfair dealing sufficient to defeat dismissal at this stage of the proceedings. The defendants answer that they had no legal obligation to effect the cash-out merger during the one year period. While that may be so, the principle announced in *Schnell v. Chris–Craft Industries* establishes that inequitable conduct will not be protected merely because it is legal.

* * * At the very least the facts alleged import a form of overreaching, and in the context of entire fairness they deserve more considered analysis than can be accorded them on a motion to dismiss.

* * *

Necessarily, this will require the Court of Chancery to closely focus upon *Weinberger's* mandate of entire fairness based on a careful analysis of both the fair price and fair dealing aspects of a transaction. See 457 A.2d at 711, 714. We recognize that this can present certain practical problems, since stockholders may invariably claim that the price being offered is the result of unfair dealings. However, we think that plaintiffs will be tempered in this approach by the prospect that an ultimate judgment in defendants' favor may have cost plaintiffs their unperfected appraisal rights. Moreover, our courts are not without a degree of sophistication in such matters. A balance must be struck between sustaining complaints averring faithless acts, which taken as true would constitute breaches of fiduciary duties that are reasonably related to and have a substantial impact upon the price offered, and properly dismissing those allegations questioning judgmental factors of valuation.

* * *

[On remand, the defendants prevailed, convincing the chancery court judge after a full trial that Olin's decision to purchase Hunt stock was not made until March 1984, after the one-year price commitment had expired. Rabkin v. Olin Corp., Fed.Sec.L.Rep. (CCH) ¶ 95,255 (April 17, 1990).]

CEDE & CO. v. TECHNICOLOR, INC., 542 A.2d 1182 (Del.1988): [The Delaware Supreme Court held that a minority shareholder who had dissented from a cash-out merger and commenced an appraisal proceeding could pursue a later-discovered individual claim of fraud in the merger through an action for rescissory damages against the parties to the merger.]

Policy considerations militate against foreclosing a shareholder electing appraisal rights from later bringing a fraud action based on after-discovered wrongdoing in the merger. Experience has shown that the great majority of minority shareholders in a freeze-out merger accept the cash-out consideration, notwithstanding the possible existence of a claim of unfair dealing, due to the risks of litigation. With the majority of the minority shareholders tendering their shares, only shareholders pursuing discovery during an appraisal proceeding are likely to acquire the relevant information needed to pursue a fraud action if such information exists. Such shareholders, however, would not have any financial incentive to communicate their discovered claim of wrongdoing in the merger to the shareholders who tendered their shares for the consideration offered by the majority and, by tendering, have standing to file suit. Thus, to bar those seeking appraisal from asserting a later-discovered fraud claim may effectively immunize a controlling shareholder from answering to a fraud claim.

> Defendants assert that it is inconsistent (or unfair) to permit both the fraud action and the appraisal action to proceed simultaneously. This argument is misguided. Cinerama is not seeking (nor would our courts permit) inconsistent remedial relief, but rather is simply pleading alternative causes of action. In the instant case, the merger occurred. If the merger was properly consummated, [section 262 of the Delaware Code] affords Cinerama a claim for the fair value of its Technicolor shares. If the merger was not lawfully effected, Cinerama should be entitled to recover rescissory damages, rendering the appraisal action moot.

Id. at 488–89 (citation omitted). [The court then consolidated the fraud and appraisal actions.]

> During the consolidated proceeding, if it is determined that the merger should not have occurred due to fraud, breach of fiduciary duty, or other wrongdoing on the part of the defendants, then Cinerama's appraisal action will be rendered moot and Cinerama will be entitled to receive rescissory damages. If such wrongdoing on the part of the defendants is not found, and the merger was properly authorized, then Cinerama will be entitled to collect the fair value of its Technicolor shares pursuant to statutory appraisal and its fraud action will be dismissed. Under either scenario, Cinerama will be limited to a single recovery judgment.

Id. at 1191.

. . . .

> The Court is aware that consolidation of these two actions may lead to certain procedural difficulties because the remedy available under entire fairness is broader than the scope of valuation permitted under [section 262 of the Delaware Code]. In addition to perfecting statutory appraisal, shareholders may systematically file fraud actions as a method of seeking a larger recovery and thereby cause unnecessary litigation. However, a party who brings an unmeritorious suit asserting violations of entire fairness may be held liable for the costs of the litigation arising therefrom. Given the degree of sophistication our courts have in such matters, the financial risks associated with filing an unmeritorious claim are high. We recognize that we place a sizeable burden upon the Court of Chancery, but to hold otherwise would produce a result that would encourage withholding of material information by a majority shareholder to the minority shareholders' detriment.

Id. at 1192 (citation omitted).

CAVALIER OIL CORP. v. HARNETT

Supreme Court of Delaware, 1989.
564 A.2d 1137.

Before HORSEY, WALSH and HOLLAND, JJ.

WALSH, JUSTICE:

This is an appeal by Cavalier Oil Corporation ("Cavalier") and a cross-appeal by William J. Harnett ("Harnett") from a final judgment of the Court of Chancery determining the fair value of 1,250 shares of stock owned by Harnett in EPIC Mortgage Servicing, Inc. ("EMSI"), a closely-held Delaware corporation. The appraisal action followed a short form merger, pursuant to 8 *Del.C.* § 253, of EMSI into Cavalier on November 20, 1984.

Harnett rejected Cavalier's offer of $93,950 for his EMSI shares, electing instead to assert his appraisal rights under 8 *Del.C.* § 262.

* * *

The Court of Chancery appraisal action was the culmination of a complex and litigious business relationship between Harnett and the two majority shareholders of Cavalier, Tom J. Billman ("Billman") and Clayton C. McCuistion ("McCuistion"). All three individuals were original investors in Equity Programs Investment Corporation ("EPIC"), a Virginia corporation established in 1975. * * *

By 1983, Billman and McCuistion together owned over ninety percent of EPIC's shares while Harnett held the balance of shares.

From its original form, the corporate structure of EPIC changed as various specialized entities were spun off. In 1982, ERSI, which was the companion corporation in the appraisal proceeding, was established as an affiliate of EPIC, with stock ownership reflecting that of the parent. In 1977, EPIC created Epic Mortgage, Inc. ("EMI"), a Delaware corporation, as a subsidiary for servicing mortgages on properties owned by EPIC. In February, 1983, another new subsidiary, also a Delaware corporation, EPIC Mortgage Servicing, Inc. (EMSI), was spun off from EMI and its shares were distributed proportionately. As part of this transaction, EMSI was given the right to service all mortgages in EMI's portfolio. The following month, Community Savings and Loan, Inc. ("CSL"), a Maryland chartered savings and loan association controlled by Billman and McCuistion, effected a merger of EPIC, along with its subsidiary EMI, into CSL.

* * *

Billman and McCuistion, apparently without Harnett's knowledge, arranged for EMSI to enter into an agreement with EMI under which EMI undertook to perform EMSI's mortgage servicing business, thereby gaining significant revenues which were originally intended to accrue to the spun-off EMSI. Harnett received his certificate for 1,250 shares of EMSI, dated March 2, 1983. Harnett claims that he did not learn of the diversion of EMSI's corporate opportunity until he was notified in November, 1984, of the merger of EMSI into Cavalier and was tendered a check for $93,950 for his stock.

* * *

Having concluded that Harnett's corporate opportunity claim was not subject to the bar of *res judicata*, we next consider the related question of whether such a claim may be asserted by a shareholder incident to a section 262 appraisal proceeding. * * *

* * *

Cavalier argues that the Court of Chancery's decision to extend the scope of valuation to embrace Harnett's corporate opportunity claim impermissibly expands the appraisal remedy to include questions of breaches of fiduciary duty, contrary to this Court's holding in *Rabkin. See Rabkin v. Philip A. Hunt Chemical Corp.,* 498 A.2d at 1106. Fiduciary duty/common law fraud claims have been disallowed in appraisal actions under both *Rabkin v. Philip A. Hunt Chemical Corp., id.* (unfair dealing claims, based on breaches of the duties of loyalty and care, raise "issues which an appraisal cannot address") and *Weinberger v. UOP, Inc.,* 457 A.2d at 714 (the appraisal remedy may not be adequate in cases involving fraud, misrepresentation, self-dealing, waste of corporate assets, or gross and palpable overreaching). We believe, however, that our previous rulings do not control this case.

While ordinarily a section 262 appraisal proceeding does not lend itself to any claims other than those incident to the appraisal proceeding itself, the unusual facts of this case, particularly the consent of the parties as reflected in the *Harnett I* settlement order providing that the derivative-like claims are viable for appraisal purposes, require that Harnett's corporate opportunity claim be considered in valuing his shares.

Nor is our decision, upholding the viability of a fraud-based claim on the present facts on the appraisal action, to be viewed as undercutting the holding in *Cede,* that derivative claims are lost in subsequent appraisal proceedings because the derivative plaintiff loses his standing to assert these claims on behalf of the corporation. It is true that this Court in *Cede* held that where allegations of fraud and breaches of fiduciary duty exist in connection with a merger, an action separate and distinct from an appraisal proceeding may and indeed must be maintained. *Cede and Co. v. Technicolor Inc.,* 542 A.2d at 1189. See also *Kramer v. Western Pacific Industries, Inc.,* Del.Supr., 546 A.2d 348, 354 (1988). In *Cede* this Court permitted a separate action for fraud in the merger itself because "... an appraisal action may not provide a complete remedy for unfair dealing or fraud ..." in the merger. *Cede and Co. v. Technicolor, Inc.,* 542 A.2d at 1187. The Court in *Cede* also noted that "[a] determination of fair value does not involve an inquiry into claims of wrongdoing in the merger." *Id.* at 1189. Further, this Court held in *Kramer* that "... direct attacks against a given corporate transaction (attacks involving fair dealing or fair price) give complaining shareholders standing to pursue individual actions even after they are cashed out through the effectuation of a merger." *Kramer v. Western Pacific Industries, Inc.,* 546 A.2d at 354.

The wrongdoing alleged by Harnett relates directly to the fair value of his stock, not to the validity of the merger itself. Harnett does not dispute that there was a legitimate business purpose to be served by the merger. His claim relates strictly to the value of his shares, and is the one issue that all of the parties had agreed to preserve. His claim is thus viewed as more personal than derivative and appropriately so, in view of his status as the sole minority shareholder whose claims of fraud are directed against the two controlling shareholders. The EMSI corporate opportunity claim, if considered on its derivative merits, would inure almost entirely to the benefit of the alleged wrongdoers, an inequitable result at variance with the fair value quest of the appraisal proceeding. In the present case a fair value determination in an appraisal action will satisfactorily redress the claimed wrongdoing. Additionally, the Vice Chancellor found that Harnett did not have knowledge of the basis for the corporate opportunity claim prior to the institution of the appraisal proceeding and that, as a matter of credibility, those claims were based on misrepresentations by the principal shareholders. We conclude that, under the unusual configuration of facts present here, the corporate opportunity claim was assertable in the section 262 proceeding.

On the merits of the corporate opportunity claim, the Court of Chancery, in valuing EMSI, viewed the combined EMSI/EMI mortgage servicing portfolio in light of a finding that the business was a corporate opportunity belonging to EMSI and unlawfully diverted to EMI. The Court ruled that, had this business not been transferred to EMI, EMSI's earnings would have increased, resulting in a higher per share valuation at the time of the merger. This finding was based upon the minutes of EPIC's Directors' meetings, which reflected the purpose for which EMSI was created and representations made to Harnett by Billman and McCuistion. Since Harnett testified before the Vice Chancellor concerning those representations while the other principals declined to do so, the findings supporting the diversion of business from EMSI turns, in large part, on matters of credibility. Under our standard of review, we perceive no basis to disturb those findings. *Levitt v. Bouvier,* 287 A.2d at 673.

Cavalier's final claim of error is directed to the Vice Chancellor's refusal to apply a minority discount in valuing Harnett's EMSI stock. Cavalier contends that Harnett's "de minimus" (1.5%) interest in EMSI is one of the "relevant factors" which must be considered under *Weinberger's* expanded valuation standard. In rejecting a minority or marketability discount, the Vice Chancellor concluded that the objective of a section 262 appraisal is "to value the *corporation* itself, as distinguished from a specific fraction of its *shares* as they may exist in the hands of a particular shareholder" [emphasis in original]. We believe this to be a valid distinction.

* * *

The application of a discount to a minority shareholder is contrary to the requirement that the company be viewed as a "going concern." Cavalier's argument, that the only way Harnett would have received value for his 1.5% stock interest was to sell his stock, subject to market treatment of its minority status, misperceives the nature of the appraisal remedy. Where there is no objective market data available, the appraisal process is not intended to reconstruct a *pro forma* sale but to assume that the shareholder was willing to maintain his investment position, however slight, had the merger not occurred. Discounting individual share holdings injects into the appraisal process speculation on the various factors which may dictate the marketability of minority shareholdings. More important, to fail to accord to a minority shareholder the full proportionate value of his shares imposes a penalty for lack of control, and unfairly enriches the majority shareholders who may reap a windfall from the appraisal process by cashing out a dissenting shareholder, a clearly undesirable result.

* * *

Among the allegations in *Harnett I* was the claim that in June, 1982, Billman and McCuistion had secured from other minority shareholders an assignment of an option to purchase 29,000 shares of EPIC common stock, thereby diluting Harnett's proportionate interest in the entities thereafter spun off from EPIC. In the Court of Chancery, Harnett argued that his share dilution claim, like the corporate opportunity claim, was saved for later assertion in the appraisal proceeding by the terms of the stipulation of dismissal of *Harnett I*. The Vice Chancellor ruled, however, that the share dilution did not survive the demand of *Harnett I* because, it did not "affect the value" of Harnett's stock for appraisal purposes and, in any event, a dispute over the amount of shares held by a dissident shareholder was outside the scope of a statutory appraisal proceeding.

The Court of Chancery correctly ruled that the question of entitlement to a specific number of shares is alien to an appraisal action under Delaware law. Even under *Weinberger's* expanded valuation remedy, the focus continues to be on the determination of the intrinsic worth of the merged corporation, not on the distribution of shares among shareholders. Harnett tacitly concedes that his appraisal remedy here is limited to the fair price component since he alleges no wrongdoing in the merger process itself. As *Weinberger* teaches, fair price means value "per share", *Weinberger v. UOP Inc.*, 457 A.2d at 713, and as was made clear in *Tri–Continental*, the proportionate interest subject to valuation is the dissenting shareholder's "stock which has been taken by the merger" *Tri–Continental Corp. v. Battye*, 74 A.2d at 72. To require the Court of Chancery to conduct a preliminary reallocating of shares based on intra-shareholder disputes, such as dilution claims, would inject into the proceeding a nonvaluation task incompatible with the appraisal purpose. Moreover, we view Harnett's attempt to inject the share dilution claim into the appraisal proceeding as clearly inconsistent with his position on the denial of a minority or marketability discount. If the rationale for rejection of the minority discount is that the valuation focus is limited to the company level and does not involve the size of a particular shareholder's interest, any attempt to reallocate holdings among shareholders is equally irrelevant to the appraisal process.

Question

In the *Cavalier* case, what is the distinction between the corporate opportunity claim and the stock dilution claim that justifies the court's hearing the former and not the latter? Why does the court require an aggrieved shareholder to bring an action separate from the appraisal proceeding on alleged breaches of fiduciary duty that immediately proceed or coincide with a merger?

Other Jurisdictions

STEINBERG v. AMPLICA, INC.

42 Cal.3d 1198, 233 Cal.Rptr. 249, 729 P.2d 683 (1986).

[In a case that determined the exclusivity of the shareholder's appraisal rights under California law, the court in *Steinberg v. Amplica, Inc.*, 42 Cal.3d 1198, 233 Cal.Rptr. 249, 729 P.2d 683 (1986), determined that, at least under the facts of the present case, where plaintiff was aware of all the facts leading to his cause of action for alleged misconduct in connection with the merger *before* the merger was consummated but deliberately opted to sue for compensatory and punitive damages instead of seeking appraisal, section 1312(a)[1] acted as a bar. The court weighed the policy arguments for the opposing positions, stating:]

> On the one hand, some of the evils which an action for appraisal was designed to avoid would occur if a minority shareholder, fully informed as to the facts underlying his claim of breach of fiduciary duty, was permitted to bring an action for damages in excess of the fair market value of his shares against the corporation and individual wrongdoers connected with the merger. The threat of such litigation could, like an action to set aside a merger, prevent the consummation of reorganizations which would benefit the majority and the corporation as a whole.... The prospect of personal liability of those who arranged the merger, including liability for punitive damages, would be almost as powerful a disincentive to legitimate mergers as a threat to unwind the merger.

* * *

[On the other hand, if] a minority shareholder were confined to appraisal when he claimed that the undervaluation of his shares resulted from the breach of fiduciary duty by corporate insiders, the wrongdoers would go unpunished, for only the corporation would be

---

1. Section 1312, subdivision (a) (hereafter section 1312(a)) provides, in pertinent part: "No shareholder of a corporation who has a right under this chapter to demand payment of cash for the shares held by the shareholder shall have any right at law or in equity to attack the validity of the reorganization or short-form merger, or to have (either) set aside or rescinded, except in an action to test whether the number of shares required to authorize or approve the reorganization have been legally voted in favor thereof. ..."

All future references are to the corporations code unless otherwise noted.

liable for the fair market value of the shares. Exemplary damages would not be available, and there would be no deterrent to individual misconduct, since the corporation would be liable for the fair value of the shares no matter what the cause of their undervaluation.

729 P.2d at 691–92.

Fourteen years of litigation over a cash-out merger in Iowa is detailed in two opinions of the Eighth Circuit. At issue is whether, even assuming that an appraisal remedy is the exclusive remedy for valuation disputes, an appraisal remedy is also the exclusive remedy for allegations that a firm violated statutory voting requirements.

SHIDLER v. ALL AMERICAN LIFE & FINANCIAL CORP., 775 F.2d 917 (8th Cir.1985): [Minority shareholders of General United Group, Inc., bought a class action objecting to the 1973 merger of GUG into its parent, All American Delaware Corporation. The minority shareholders had received cash for their shares in the transaction. At the GUG shareholders meeting called to consider the merger, the merger proposal received the votes of more than two-thirds of the outstanding stock but only 42 percent of the outstanding common stock. The transaction closed based on GUG's claim that Iowa's merger statute did not mandate class voting. Less than one month later the surviving firm announced a merger with a third company, USLIFE. The trial court certified the question of voting requirements on the GUG merger to the Iowa Supreme Court, which held that class voting was required. The Eighth Circuit then decided that the dissenting shareholders had stated a valid cause of action in conversion against GUG and its officers, for GUG had wrongfully extinguished their shares.

GUG lawyers were chagrined. There were at least three other methods for structuring the acquisition properly: The acquisition could have been structured as an asset sale, which, under Iowa statutes, did not require class voting; All America could have converted its preferred stock to common stock before the vote to assure a two-thirds margin for each class of stock; or GUG could have amended its articles of incorporation, with a majority vote, to lower the percentage of votes required in a statutory merger.

The court held that the Iowa appraisal statute, which contained language of exclusivity, did not apply to restrict the minority shareholders to an appraisal remedy.]

> The defendants argue first that statutory appraisal, Iowa Code Ann. §§ 496A.78–.79 (West 1962 & Supp.1985), is the sole relief intended by the legislature for disappointed minority shareholders. However, the statute provides for appraisal as the exclusive remedy only where "the proposed corporate transaction [is] approved by the required vote." * * * If the transaction is unlawful, appraisal cannot be

the exclusive remedy. * * * Defendant's position would encourage the corporation to disregard procedural statutes, since dissenting shareholders would be entitled only to the remedy of appraisal regardless of the corporation's conduct:

Clearly the purpose of the dissenters' rights clause of the statute is to enable the majority to act unthwarted by a stubborn, recalcitrant minority or a calculating "striker." * * * On the other hand, if the statute limits the shareholder to a recovery of the value of his shares where fraud or illegality is involved, it would appear to condone wrongdoing and to make the wrong unassailable by an injured party.]

See Note, *Merger and Consolidation in Iowa,* 34 Iowa L.Rev. 67, 79 (1948).

Id. at 922. See also Stepak v. Schey, 553 N.E.2d 1072 (51 Ohio St.3d 8, 1990) (although fiduciary duty claims based on a cash-out merger need not be brought under the Ohio appraisal statute, a claim that managers did not obtain the highest price because of an unlawful lockup option granted a favored bidder must be brought under the statute).

NELSON v. ALL AMERICAN LIFE & FINANCIAL CORP., 889 F.2d 141 (8th Cir.1989). [The district court directed a verdict for the plaintiffs at trial holding GUG strictly liable for conversion. The court refused to consider defendant's claim of good faith, stating that "good faith cannot render an invalid merger suddenly lawful in derogation of Iowa law. Nor does good faith obviate the need to compensate the stockholders for the action which has been taken." Id. at 146. The jury then awarded the plaintiffs compensatory damages and $650,000 in punitive damages. The trial judge entered judgment notwithstanding the verdict against the plaintiffs on punitive damages and allowed the compensatory award to stand, albeit with a reduced interest rate. On appeal, the Eighth Circuit affirmed the award of compensatory damages and the lower court's refusal to award punitive damages. The compensatory damage award consisted of the highest value of the stock within one year of the date of the closing of the GUG merger (the common-law standard of damages when the item converted is fluctuating in value) minus the value given in the GUG acquisition. During the year after the closing of the GUG merger, the surviving company was itself merged into yet another company, and the plaintiffs received the benefit of the merger price in the second acquisition. The merger price was $3.25 a share for the GUG shares; the jury found the value of the GUG shares at the time of merger to be $4.54 a share and the value of the shares ten months after the closing (at the time of the second merger) to be $5.40 a share. The jury awarded $5.40 minus $3.25 with interest from 1973.]

Questions

1. Does the *Shidler* court rest its holding on a breach of fiduciary duty by the General United Group managers or something different? Why did the plaintiff not pursue a claim for breach of fiduciary duty? Should courts

treat the decision to merge and the setting of the merger price or other details of the merger agreement (executive compensation, for example) differently from choices made about shareholder voting procedures?

2. After fourteen years of litigation were the plaintiffs any better off for having not pursued their appraisal rights?

SECTION 4. TRANSACTIONS STRUCTURED TO CIRCUMVENT STATUTORY REQUIREMENTS

The disparate voting and appraisal conditions that attach to the various sections empowering corporations to effect major transactions were not lost on clever lawyers, who soon structured acquisitions to fit the most lenient of the sections. This threw the matter into the state courts, as aggrieved shareholders asked judges to reclassify transactions based on their inherent form. Since a statutory merger has the most substantial voting and appraisal rights requirements, the firms most often structured major acquisitions as asset sales, and aggrieved shareholders asked judges to declare the transactions to be "de facto" mergers. In each of the cases in this section look for the shareholder rights that the parties to transaction sought to avoid. Moreover, ask yourself whether the court in each case should act to recharacterize the transaction in issue to restore those rights. If so, on what standards? Should a court's view on the substance of the exchange (i.e., whether the exchange was for a fair price) affect whether the court's decision about recharacterizing the transaction?

Subsection a. Asset Sales and Reverse Asset Sales

HARITON v. ARCO ELECTRONICS, INC.

Supreme Court of Delaware, 1963.
188 A.2d 123.

SOUTHERLAND, CHIEF JUSTICE, and WOLCOTT and TERRY, JJ., sitting.

SOUTHERLAND, CHIEF JUSTICE.

* * *

A sale of assets is effected under § 271 in consideration of shares of stock of the purchasing corporation. The agreement of sale embodies also a plan to dissolve the selling corporation and distribute the shares so received to the stockholders of the seller, so as to accomplish the same result as would be accomplished by a merger of the seller into the purchaser. Is the sale legal?

The facts are these:

The defendant Arco and Loral Electronics Corporation, a New York corporation, are both engaged, in somewhat different forms, in the electronic equipment business. In the summer of 1961 they negotiated for an amalgamation of the companies. As of October 27, 1961, they entered into a "Reorganization Agreement and Plan." The provisions of this Plan pertinent here are in substance as follows:

1. Arco agrees to sell all its assets to Loral in consideration (inter alia) of the issuance to it of 283,000 shares of Loral.

2. Arco agrees to call a stockholders meeting for the purpose of approving the Plan and the voluntary dissolution.

3. Arco agrees to distribute to its stockholders all the Loral shares received by it as a part of the complete liquidation of Arco.

At the Arco meeting all the stockholders voting (about 80%) approved the Plan. It was thereafter consummated.

Plaintiff, a stockholder who did not vote at the meeting, sued to enjoin the comsummation of the Plan on the grounds (1) that it was illegal, and (2) that it was unfair. The second ground was abandoned.

* * *

The question before us we have stated above. Plaintiff's argument that the sale is illegal runs as follows:

The several steps taken here accomplish the same result as a merger of Arco into Loral. In a "true" sale of assets, the stockholder of the seller retains the right to elect whether the selling company shall continue as a holding company. Moreover, the stockholder of the selling company is forced to accept an investment in a new enterprise without the right of appraisal granted under the merger statute. § 271 cannot therefore be legally combined with a dissolution proceeding under § 275 and a consequent distribution of the purchaser's stock. Such a proceeding is a misuse of the power granted under § 271, and a *de facto* merger results.

* * *

We now hold that the reorganization here accomplished through § 271 and a mandatory plan of dissolution and distribution is legal. This is so because the sale-of-assets statute and the merger statute are independent of each other. They are, so to speak, of equal dignity, and the framers of a reorganization plan may resort to either type of corporate mechanics to achieve the desired end. This is not an anomalous result in our corporation law. As the Vice Chancellor pointed out, the elimination of accrued dividends, though forbidden under a charter amendment (Keller v. Wilson & Co., 21 Del.Ch. 391, 190 A. 115) may be accomplished by a merger. Federal United Corporation v. Havender, 24 Del.Ch. 318, 11 A.2d 331.

* * *

Plaintiff concedes, as we read his brief, that if the several steps taken in this case had been taken separately they would have been legal. That is, he concedes that a sale of assets, followed by a separate proceeding to dissolve and distribute, would be legal, even though the same result would follow. This concession exposes the weakness of his contention. To attempt to make any such distinction between sales under § 271 would be to create uncertainty in the law and invite litigation.

We are in accord with the Vice Chancellor's ruling, and the judgment below is affirmed.

RATH v. RATH PACKING CO.
Supreme Court of Iowa, 1965.
257 Iowa 1277, 136 N.W.2d 410.

GARFIELD, CHIEF JUSTICE.

* * *

Plaintiffs own more than 6000 shares of Rath Packing Co., an Iowa corporation with its principal plant in Waterloo, Iowa, existing under Code 1962, chapter 496A, I.C.A. (Iowa Business Corporation Act). Rath has 993,185 shares outstanding held by about 4000 owners. It is engaged in meat packing and processing, mostly pork and allied products. Its yearly sales for the last five years were from about $267,000,-000 to $296,000,000. Its balance sheet as of January 2, 1965, showed assets of about $56,500,000, current liabilities of about $20,600,000, and long-term debt of about $7,000,000.

Needham Packing Co. is a corporation organized in 1960 under Delaware law with its principal plant in Sioux City, Iowa. Its total shares outstanding, including debentures and warrants convertible into stock, are 787,907, held by about 1000 owners. Both Rath and Needham stock is traded on the American Stock Exchange. Needham is also engaged in meat packing, mostly beef. Its annual sales were from about $80,000,000 to $103,000,000. Its balance sheet as of December 26, 1964, showed assets of $10,300,000, current liabilities of $2,262,000, and long-term debt of $3,100,000.

Pursuant to authority of Rath's board prior to April 2, 1965, it entered into the questioned agreement with Needham, designated "Plan and Agreement of Reorganization," under which Rath agreed to: (1) amend its articles to double the number of shares of its common stock, create a new class of preferred shares and change its name to Rath–Needham Corporation; (2) issue to Needham 5.5 shares of Rath common and two shares of its 80–cent preferred stock for each five shares of Needham stock in exchange for all Needham's assets, properties, business, name and good will, except a fund not exceeding $175,000 to pay expenses in carrying out the agreement and effecting Needham's dissolution and distribution of the new Rath–Needham stock to its shareholders, any balance remaining after 120 days to be paid over to Rath; (3) assume all Needham's debts and liabilities; and (4) elect two Needham officers and directors to its board.

Under the plan Needham agreed to: (1) transfer all its assets to Rath; (2) cease using its name; (3) distribute the new Rath–Needham shares to its stockholders, liquidate and dissolve; and (4) turn over to Rath its corporate and business records.

If the plan were carried out, assuming the new preferred shares were converted into common, the thousand Needham shareholders would have about 54 per cent of the outstanding common shares of Rath–Needham and the four thousand Rath shareholders would have about 46 per cent.

Under the plan the book value of each share of Rath common stock, as of January 2, 1965, would be reduced from $27.99 to $15.93, a reduction of about 44 per cent. Each share of Needham common would be increased in book value, as of December 26, 1964, from $6.61 to $23.90, assuming conversion of the new Rath–Needham preferred.

In the event of liquidation of Rath–Needham, Needham shareholders would be preferred to Rath's under the plan, by having a prior claim to the assets of Rath–Needham to an amount slightly in excess of the book value of all Needham shares. Needham shareholders are also preferred over Rath's under the plan in distribution of income by the right of the former to receive preferred dividends of 80 cents a share—about five per cent of Needham's book value. Shortly prior to the time terms of the plan were made public Rath and Needham shares sold on the American Exchange for about the same price. Almost immediately thereafter the price of Needham shares increased and Rath's decreased so the former sold for 50 per cent more than the latter.

At a meeting of Rath shareholders on April 26, 1965, 60.1 per cent of its outstanding shares, 77 per cent of those voted, were voted in favor of these two proposals: (1) to amend the articles to authorize a class of 80 c preferred stock and increase the authorized common from 1,500,000 shares ($10 par) to 3,000,000 shares (no par); and (2) upon acquisition by Rath of the assets, properties, business and good will of Needham to change Rath's name to Rath–Needham Corporation and elect as its directors Lloyd and James Needham. Holders of 177,000 shares voted against these proposals and 218,000 shares were not voted. The plan was not approved by the shareholders except as above stated.

Rath officers vigorously solicited proxies for the meeting by personal travel, telephone and through a professional proxy soliciting agency. This action was commenced five days prior to the meeting and four days thereafter a supplement and amendment to the petition were filed.

[The next few paragraphs contain a summary of provisions in the Iowa Corporate Code. Section 496A.70 requires a merger to be approved by an affirmative vote of at least two-thirds of the outstanding shares entitled to vote. Section 496A.77 gives dissenting shareholders in merger votes an appraisal remedy. Section 496A.56 allows amendments to a firm's articles on the affirmative vote of the holders of a majority of stock entitled to vote.]

* * *

The above sections are those on which plaintiffs rely. They contend these statutes specifically provide for effecting a merger and the same result cannot legally be attained at least without approval of the holders of two thirds of the shares and according to dissenters "appraisal rights"—i.e., the right to receive the fair value of their stock by compliance with the specified procedure.

Defendants contend and the trial court held compliance with the above sections was not required and defendants could legally proceed under other sections of chapter 496A which merely authorize amendments to articles of incorporation and issuance of stock. The sections just referred to provide (section 496A.55) that a corporation may amend its articles in any respects desired and in particular: change its name, change the number of shares of any class, change shares having a par value to those without par and create new classes of shares with preferences over shares then authorized.

* * *

The principal point of law defendants asked to have adjudicated under rule 105, R.C.P., is that the provisions of chapter 496A last referred to are legally independent of, and of equal dignity with, those relating to mergers and the validity of the action taken by defendants is not dependent upon compliance with the merger sections under which the same result might be attained. The trial court accepted this view.

* * *

We can agree all provisions of our chapter 496A are of equal dignity. But we cannot agree any provisions of the act are legally independent of others if this means that in arriving at the correct interpretation thereof and the legislative intent expressed therein we are not to consider the entire act and, so far as possible, construe its various provisions in the light of their relation to the whole act.

* * *

In seeking the scope and effect of the two sets of sections relied upon at least one fundamental rule of statutory construction is applicable. As stated, the merger sections specifically provide for a particular thing—mergers. The sections authorizing amendment of articles and issuance of stock apply to all amendments and stock issues, whether or not amending the articles or issuing stock is part of a merger, as they may or may not be. As applied to mergers, the sections on which plaintiffs rely are specific provisions, those on which defendants rely are not. * * *

* * *

A closely related rule, many times applied by us, is that where a general statute, if standing alone, would include the same matter as a special statute and thus conflict with it, the latter will prevail and the former must give way. The special provision will be considered an exception to or qualification of the general one.

* * *

It is apparent that if the sections pertaining to amending articles and issuing stock are construed to authorize a merger by a majority vote of shareholders they conflict with the sections specifically dealing with the one matter of mergers which require a two-thirds vote of shareholders. The two sets of sections may be harmonized by holding, as we do, that the merger sections govern the matter of merger and must be regarded as an exception to the sections dealing with amending articles and issuing stock, which may or may not be involved in a merger.

* * *

The merger sections make it clear the legislature intended to require a two-thirds vote of shareholders and accord so-called appraisal rights to dissenters in case of a merger. It is unreasonable to ascribe to the same legislature an intent to provide in the same act a method of evading the required two-thirds vote and the grant of such appraisal rights. The practical effect of the decision appealed from is to render the requirements of a two-thirds vote and appraisal rights meaningless in virtually all mergers. It is scarcely an exaggeration to say the decision amounts to judicial repeal of the merger sections in most instances of merger.

It is obvious, as defendants' counsel frankly stated in oral argument, that corporate management would naturally choose a method which requires only majority approval of shareholders and does not grant dissenters the right to be paid the fair value of their stock. The legislature could hardly have intended to vest in corporate management the option to comply with the requirements just referred to or to proceed without such compliance, a choice that would invariably be exercised in favor of the easier method.

* * * For decree in harmony with this opinion the cause is—Reversed and remanded.

All Justices concur except MASON and RAWLINGS, JJ., who take no part.

Note

Legislative Responses to the De Facto Merger Doctrine

In 1970 the state legislature amended section 496A.68 of the Iowa Business Corporation Act to include the following language:

> The purchase by a corporation of all, or substantially all, of the assets of another corporation, domestic or foreign, followed by dissolution of the selling corporation, shall not, by itself, constitute a merger of such corporations.

What is the effect of the language on the *Rath* case? This pattern is repeated in other states after a successful "de facto merger" argument before a state court. The high-water mark of the de facto merger doctrine is the case of Farris v. Glen Alden Corp., 393 Pa. 427, 143 A.2d 25 (1958), in which the plaintiffs prevailed. Pennsylvania has expressly abolished the doctrine by statute, 15 Pa.Cons.Stat.Ann. § 1904 (Purdon 1956 & Supp. 1989) and added that "structuring a plan or transaction for the purpose or with the effect of eliminating or avoiding the application of dissenters rights is not fraud or fundamental unfairness [justifying an award of equitable relief]." 15 PA.CONS.STAT.ANN. § 1105 (Purdon 1956 & Supp. 1989). Applestein v. United Board & Carton Corp., 60 N.J.Super. 333, 159 A.2d 146 (Ch.1960), affirmed 33 N.J. 72, 161 A.2d 474 (1960) remains a lonely example of a successful and unrepudiated application of the de facto merger argument.

Subsection b. Exchange Tender Offers

IRVING BANK CORP. v. BANK OF NEW YORK CO.

Supreme Court, New York County, 1988.
530 N.Y.S.2d 757.

HERMAN CAHN, JUSTICE.

Irving Bank Corporation ("IBC") moves for summary judgment, or in the alternative for a preliminary injunction, to prevent Bank of New York ("BNY") from implementing its proposed plan of acquisition of IBC. IBC claims that the plan constitutes a de facto merger, and can only be implemented after approval by two-thirds of BNY's shareholders. BNY seeks dismissal of the complaint on the ground that it fails to state a cause of action. (C.P.L.R. 3211(a)(7)). The facts are not in dispute.

THE FACTS

The Parties and Their History

IBC and BNY are both bank holding companies incorporated in the State of New York. In September, 1987, BNY announced its intention to acquire IBC. At that time, BNY made an offer to the Board of Directors of IBC to acquire all of the outstanding shares of IBC, which offer was rejected. Over the following months, the proposed acquisition developed into a contested takeover offer, the Board of IBC having not approved the initial offer, nor any subsequent BNY offer. To the contrary, IBC has contested virtually every action taken by BNY in connection with this matter. As a result, several lawsuits are pending before this court involving the two companies and/or their shareholders.

The IBC Board of Directors has stated that it is now in the process of holding an "auction", in relation to this matter. The "auction" is not relevant to the decision of these motions.

BNY's Plan of Acquisition

BNY's plan of acquisition is basically a two-step process: (1) First, BNY seeks to acquire all or a majority of the outstanding shares of IBC; and (2) thereafter, BNY hopes to consummate a merger between IBC and either BNY or an affiliate of BNY.

The acquisition of IBC's shares would be in exchange for cash and shares of BNY. That is, BNY would pay a certain amount of cash plus between one and two BNY shares for each IBC share acquired....

The De Facto Merger Issue

IBC brings this action as a shareholder of BNY. It seeks a declaration that BNY's plan of acquisition constitutes a merger, within the meaning of BCL Sec. 903,[1] and thus requires a vote of two-thirds of BNY's shareholders to approve the transaction. It argues, that although the form of the plan of acquisition is not one of merger, the substance is that of a merger, and that the court should apply the "de facto merger doctrine", and treat the acquisition plan as a merger.

BNY disputes the existence of the de facto merger doctrine in New York, and furthermore claims that even where the doctrine is recognized, it would not be applicable in these circumstances.

BNY moves for dismissal on the ground that it has properly complied with the BCL provision which permits its Board to issue common shares for "such consideration, not less than par value thereof, as is fixed from time to time by the board." BCL Sec. 504(c). Therefore, BNY claims any exchange of its shares for IBC shares would be valid. Furthermore, it claims that it already has shareholder authority to issue the shares, since the certificate of incorporation authorizes the issuance of 125,000,000 shares, of which less than 40,000,000 have been issued. Issuance of the proposed 31,000,000 shares in the exchange offer, alleges BNY, has already been, in accordance with statutory requirements, approved by the shareholders of BNY. (BCL Sec. 801).[2]

The shareholders of BNY have not approved any merger of IBC into BNY, or other proposed merger, by two-thirds vote. They did approve a corporate resolution authorizing the planned acquisition (which proposal was submitted to them pursuant to the Rules of the New York Stock Exchange), but by less than a two-thirds vote.

* * *

The de facto merger doctrine has been used by some courts of equity to preserve shareholders' rights where the transaction involved, although not a classic merger, is, in essence a merger. The courts will look through the form of the transaction to its substance.

* * * The de facto merger doctrine has been applied in this state, but only where it is apparent that the acquired corporation was quickly to be dissolved.

We need not discuss, at this time, extensively the requirements for a de facto merger. It is clear, however, that two factors are necessary:

---

1. BCL Sec. 903(a)(2): "the plan of merger or consolidation shall be adopted at a meeting of shareholders by vote of the holders of two-thirds of all outstanding shares entitled to vote thereon ..."

2. BCL Sec. 801: "(a) A corporation may amend its certificate of incorporation, from time to time, in any and as many respects as may be desired, if such amendment contains only such provisions as might be lawfully contained in an original certificate of incorporation filed at the time of making such amendment. (b) In particular, and without limitation upon such general power of amendment, a corporation may amend its certificate of incorporation from time to time, so as: ... (7) To increase or decrease the aggregate number of shares, or shares of any class or series, with or without par value, which the corporation shall have authority to issue."

(1) The actual merger must take place soon after the initial transaction, and (2) the seller corporation must quickly cease to exist.

In *Lirosi v. Elkins,* 89 A.D.2d 903, 453 N.Y.S.2d 718 (2d Dep't 1982), the court held that a transfer of assets from one corporation to another, and the subsequent dissolution of the former corporation, constituted a de facto merger. In *Gilbert v. Burnside,* 197 N.Y.S.2d 623 (1959), rev'd 13 A.D.2d 982 (2d Dep't 1961) aff'd 11 N.Y.2d 960, 229 N.Y.S.2d 10, 183 N.E.2d 325, the court held a "reorganization agreement" to be a de facto merger where the agreement provided for the sale of all of the assets of a corporation and its subsequent dissolution. In both cases, the Court found that the dissolution of the acquired corporation was an imminently expected occurrence.

* * *

We note further, that BNY is planning a purchase of the stock, not the assets of IBC. Where the acquiror corporation purchases all the target's assets, leaving the target as a mere shell, the transaction bears a distinct resemblance to a merger. Here, IBC will survive as a corporate entity, with all its assets intact. Although a merger may occur in the future, the instant transaction is not a merger, but the acquisition of a subsidiary.

* * *

Subsection c. Triangular Mergers

EQUITY GROUP HOLDINGS v. DMG, INC.

United States District Court, Southern District of Florida, 1983.
576 F.Supp. 1197.

ARONOVITZ, DISTRICT JUDGE.

* * *

The undisputed facts as stipulated by the parties can be summarized as follows: Defendant, DMG, Inc. ("DMG"), a Florida corporation, is a holding company which has no assets or operations. It is the listed (New York Stock Exchange) parent corporation of a wholly-owned subsidiary, Defendant Diversified Mortgage Investors, Inc. ("DMI"), a Florida corporation. DMG was incorporated in 1980 by DMI for the purpose of carrying out a corporate reorganization. At that time, the shareholders of DMI automatically became shareholders of DMG.

* * *

On October 28, 1983, DMG, Carlsberg and Carlsberg Resources Corporation entered into a Stock Purchase Agreement, pursuant to which DMG agreed to issue two million (2,000,000) shares of DMG voting preferred stock, which had been authorized but unissued, in exchange for forty-four thousand, four hundred, forty-four (44,444) of the one hundred twenty-five thousand (125,000) shares of Carlsberg convertible preferred stock then held by Carlsberg Resources.

Also on October 28, 1983, DMG, DMI and Carlsberg entered into an Agreement and Plan of Merger (the "Merger Agreement"). Pursuant to the Merger Agreement, Carlsberg will merge into DMI; outstanding shares of Carlsberg will then be converted into DMG common. To accomplish this plan, approximately 12.5 million new shares of Common will be issued to shareholders of Carlsberg. Thereafter, some 64% of DMG Common Stock will be owned by Carlsberg shareholders.

* * *

The New York Stock Exchange, wherein DMG is listed, requires that to validate the issuance of the authorized twelve and one-half million shares of DMG common stock that are to be issued to Carlsberg, a majority of DMG shareholders who are represented in person or by proxy at a meeting of shareholders must so vote. See NYSE Company Manual, A–283–284 (January 25, 1978). This election is necessary in order to maintain DMG's listing on the Exchange. Consequently, a shareholders' meeting of DMG has been currently scheduled for December 22, 1983, to vote on a corporate resolution approving the issuance by DMG of the 12.5 million shares of DMG common stock to shareholders of Carlsberg. DMG has also announced that officers and directors of Carlsberg will stand for election to the DMG Board of Directors at the shareholders' meeting scheduled for December 22, 1983, and that Carlsberg will seek to fill by election four of the seven directorial seats on the DMG Board.

* * *

Plaintiff [a DMG shareholder] contends that the two transactions at issue here, i.e., (a) the issuance of two million (2,000,000) voting preferred shares of DMG to Carlsberg, and (b) the merger of DMI and Carlsberg which results in issuance of 12.5 million shares of DMG common to Carlsberg, together constitute a *de facto* merger of *three* corporations: the present DMG, its subsidiary, DMI and Carlsberg; that the real merger is not only that between DMI and Carlsberg, but between DMG, the parent company, and Carlsberg; that, because Carlsberg is approximately three times the size of DMG, it is really Carlsberg which is surviving and DMG which is ceasing to exist after the merger; and that, if in fact these transactions together do constitute a *de facto* merger of DMG into Carlsberg, then Florida Corporation Law Section 607.221 requires a full majority of *all outstanding* shares to approve the transaction, rather than a *quorum of shares voted either at the December 22, 1983 meeting or by proxy,* which is all that is required under the rules of the New York Stock Exchange. See NYSE Company Manual A–283, 284 (January 25, 1978).

Plaintiff concedes that the transactions do not fall within the strict statutory wording of Florida Statute Section 607.221, and that therefore this Court would have to declare the transactions a *de facto* merger in order to find that the statute applies. Plaintiff further argues that if a *de facto* merger were declared in this case, the appropriate relief would be for the Court to issue a preliminary injunction against holding the shareholder vote at which only a quorum, rather than a full majority, would be required to effectuate the merger. * * *

On the foregoing basis, the Court finds that the Plaintiff has not met its burden of proof sufficiently to support the issuance of a preliminary injunction. This is not to say that, given more facts and further discovery, the Court could not find that the transaction at issue is a *de facto* merger requiring a full majority vote of all the outstanding shares of DMG to be approved. * * *

The parties seem to agree that the DMI–Carlsberg Merger, the second of the two transactions at issue here, is a forward triangular merger: a wholly-owned subsidiary is acquiring the assets, liabilities, and stock of the target, a third-party corporation, after which the parent company and its original subsidiary will survive and the target will become part of the subsidiary. The key question before the Court is whether, as Plaintiff alleges, this requires that the Court treat the two transactions—the issuance of two million (2,000,000) shares of DMG voting preferred shares to Carlsberg, and the issuance of 12.5 million shares of common to effectuate a DMI–Carlsberg Merger—as a single transaction.

The reason to do so, Plaintiff alleges, is that in reality, Carlsberg will be taking control of DMG, rather than DMG acquiring Carlsberg as part of its subsidiary, DMI. Plaintiff argues that this is so because: (1) Carlsberg is three times the size of DMG; (2) the Carlsberg family will end up controlling a majority of DMG voting shares; (3) the President of Carlsberg will become the President of DMG; and (4) the DMG Board of Directors will be composed of a majority of persons nominated by, and, essentially, voted in by, Carlsberg. These elements, Plaintiff has repeated in its papers as well as orally, constitute a situation in which, in reality, "the minnow is swallowing the whale".

The Court finds that under these facts and circumstances, on the basis of the record before it, Florida law does not necessarily stop or prevent the minnow from swallowing the whale where the business judgment of both the minnow and the whale is that the event will be mutually beneficial to both parties. Without evidence of a breach of fiduciary duty by the Officers/Directors of DMG or DMI or fundamental unfairness, or without allegations or proof of fraud, misrepresentation, *mala fides* or economic harm resulting from such merger, there is not presented to this Court a basis to invoke its equity jurisdiction.

* * *

The consideration for both of these transactions is adequate under Florida law, or more than adequate. * * *

Carlsberg is becoming a party to the use of a One Hundred Million ($100,000,000) Dollar tax loss carry-forward with DMG, a substantial consideration regardless of its enhanced position of control of DMG. Similarly, DMG will be less likely to suffer a possible default and non-renewal of a Twenty-three Million ($23,000,000) Dollar loan from

Continental Bank due in full December 31, 1983; if default were to occur, it would seriously jeopardize DMG's continued existence. Equity, as well as other shareholders of DMG, will not be harmed *economically* by the Carlsberg–DMG transaction, since the book value of the shares would be roughly equivalent both before and after the DMI–Carlsberg merger. The pre-merger book value would be Two and 77/100 ($2.77) Dollars per share, while the post-merger *pro forma* value would be Two and 70/100 ($2.70) Dollars. * * * In the case at bar, it would be a mistake for the Court to substitute its own judgment for the business judgment of the directors of the corporations involved as to the benefits ultimately to inure to shareholders, absent any evidence of breach of fiduciary duty, or fundamental unfairness, or overreaching.

* * *

The Court does not deny that there is a public interest in corporate democracy at stake here, and that there is merit to Plaintiff's argument that shareholders in a public corporation should be given an opportunity to voice their opinion in a vote on matters of fundamental importance to them. However, it is of importance that the Court is here dealing with shares that were duly authorized by the shareholders of DMG through the 1980 Amendment to DMG's Articles of Incorporation, voted upon by a majority of holders of outstanding stock, which amendments specifically gave the directors the right to issue up to five million (5,000,000) shares of preferred stock *without further shareholder approval.*

The New York Stock Exchange requirement, that a majority of votes cast is required to approve the transaction, also cannot be overlooked. Shareholders are given the right to vote and are free to do so with respect to the DMG issuance of shares to Carlsberg; only the required percentage standard for approval differs between the New York Stock Exchange Rule and the statutory merger standard. The right to vote—or not to do so—is the essence of democracy and is not disregarded in the corporate transactions now before the Court.

Moreover, it cannot be said that corporate suffrage with respect to the shareholders of a parent corporation in a forward triangular merger of its subsidiary with another corporation is a value which the Florida legislature has seen fit to recognize. Florida Statute Section 607.221 guarantees voting rights to the shareholders of the merging subsidiary and the third company, the target or non-surviving corporation; but the section does not contemplate the triangular situation with which the Court is herein faced. The Florida statutes permit the use of the parent's shares as merger consideration. Coupled with the tax advantages and tax-free status of the triangular merger under the Internal Revenue Code, and the convenience of a merger by exchange of stock rather than assets, this is just the type of transaction which the legislature cannot be presumed to have overlooked. In fact, it might be inferred that the legislature intentionally did *not* want to discourage such forms of merger by awarding voting or appraisal rights to the shareholders of the parent.

* * *

Ordered and adjudged that Plaintiff's Motion for Preliminary Injunction be and is hereby denied.

RAUCH v. RCA CORP.
United States Court of Appeals, Second Circuit, 1988.
861 F.2d 29.

Before OAKES, CARDAMONE and MAHONEY, CIRCUIT JUDGES.

MAHONEY, CIRCUIT JUDGE.

* * *

This case arises from the acquisition of RCA Corporation ("RCA") by General Electric Company ("GE"). On or about December 11, 1985, RCA, GE and Gesub, Inc. ("Gesub"), a wholly owned Delaware subsidiary of GE, entered into an agreement of merger. Pursuant to the terms of the agreement, all common and preferred shares of RCA stock (with one exception) were converted to cash, Gesub was then merged into RCA, and the common stock of Gesub was converted into common stock of RCA. Specifically, the merger agreement provided (subject in each case to the exercise of appraisal rights) that each share of RCA common stock would be converted into $66.50, each share of $3.65 cumulative preference stock would be converted into $42.50, and each share of $3.50 cumulative first preferred stock (the stock held by plaintiff and in issue here, hereinafter the "Preferred Stock") would be converted into $40.00.[1] A series of $4.00 cumulative convertible first preferred stock was called for redemption according to its terms prior to the merger.

On February 27, 1986, plaintiff, a holder of 250 shares of Preferred Stock, commenced this diversity class action on behalf of a class consisting of the holders of Preferred Stock. It is undisputed that this action is governed by the law of Delaware, the state of incorporation of both RCA and Gesub. Plaintiff claimed that the merger constituted a "liquidation or dissolution or winding up of RCA and a redemption of the [Preferred Stock]," as a result of which holders of the Preferred Stock were entitled to $100 per share in accordance with the redemp-

---

1. Section 1.6 of the Agreement of Merger provides in part:
As of the Effective Date, by virtue of the Merger and without any action on the part of the holders thereof ...
(e) Each other outstanding share of $3.50 Cumulative First Preferred Stock, without par value, of the Company (a "$3.50 Preferred Share"), except those held by stockholders who have validly perfected appraisal rights under the Delaware General Corporation Law, shall be converted into the right to receive $40.00 in cash, without interest. Notwithstanding the foregoing, if a class vote of the holders of the $3.50 Preferred Shares is required to effect the foregoing and such vote is not obtained, then each outstanding $3.50 Preferred Share shall remain outstanding and represent one validly issued, fully paid and nonassessable $3.50 Preferred Share of the Surviving Corporation [RCA].

tion provisions of RCA's certificate of incorporation,[2] that defendants were in violation of the rights of the holders of Preferred Stock as thus stated; and that defendants thereby wrongfully converted substantial sums of money to their own use. Plaintiff sought damages and injunctive relief.

* * *

According to RCA's Restated Certificate of Incorporation, the owners of the Preferred Stock were entitled to $100 per share, plus accrued dividends, upon the redemption of such stock at the election of the corporation. Plaintiff contends that the merger agreement, which compelled the holders of Preferred Stock to sell their shares to RCA for $40.00, effected a redemption whose nature is not changed by referring to it as a conversion of stock to cash pursuant to a merger. Plaintiff's argument, however, is not in accord with Delaware law.

It is clear that under the Delaware General Corporation Law, a conversion of shares to cash that is carried out in order to accomplish a merger is legally distinct from a redemption of shares by a corporation. Section 251 of the Delaware General Corporation Law allows two corporations to merge into a single corporation by adoption of an agreement that complies with that section. Del.Code Ann. tit. viii, § 251(c)(1983). The merger agreement in issue called for the conversion of the shares of the constituent corporations into cash. The statute specifically authorizes such a transaction:

> The agreement shall state ... the manner of converting the shares of each of the constituent corporations into shares or other securities of the corporation surviving or resulting from the merger or consolidation and, if any shares of any of the constituent corporations are not to be converted solely into shares or other securities of the surviving or resulting corporations, *the cash ... which the holders of such shares are to receive* in exchange for, or upon conversion of such shares ..., *which cash ... may be* in addition to or *in lieu of shares* or other securities of the surviving or resulting corporation....

Id. § 251(b) (emphasis added). Thus, the RCA–GE merger agreement complied fully with the merger provision in question, and plaintiff does not argue to the contrary.

Redemption, on the other hand, is governed by sections 151(b) and 160(a) of the Delaware General Corporation Law. Section 151(b) provides that a corporation may subject its preferred stock to redemption "by the corporation at its option or at the option of the holders of such stock or upon the happening of a specified event." Del.Code Ann. tit.

---

2. RCA's Restated Certificate of Incorporation, paragraph Four, Part I, provides in relevant part:
(c) The First Preferred Stock at any time outstanding *may be redeemed by the Corporation,* in whole or in part, *at its election,* expressed by resolution of the Board of Directors, at any time or times upon not less than sixty (60) days' previous notice to the holders of record of the First Preferred Stock to be redeemed, given as hereinafter provided, at the price of one hundred dollars ($100) per share and all dividends accrued or in arrears.... (emphasis added).

viii, § 151(b) (1983). In this instance, the Preferred Stock was subject to redemption by RCA *at its election. See supra* note 2. Nothing in RCA's certificate of incorporation indicated that the holders of Preferred Stock could initiate a redemption, nor was there provision for any specified event, such as the Gesub–RCA merger, to trigger a redemption.[3]

Plaintiff's contention that the transaction was essentially a redemption rather than a merger must therefore fail. RCA chose to convert its stock to cash to accomplish the desired merger, and in the process chose not to redeem the Preferred Stock. It had every right to do so in accordance with Delaware law. As the district court aptly noted, to accept plaintiff's argument "would render nugatory the conversion provisions within Section 251 of the Delaware Code."

Delaware courts have long held that such a result is unacceptable. Indeed, it is well settled under Delaware law that "action taken under one section [of the Delaware General Corporation Law] is legally independent, and its validity is not dependent upon, nor to be tested by the requirements of other unrelated sections under which the same final result might be attained by different means." *Rothschild Int'l Corp. v. Liggett Group,* 474 A.2d 133, 136 (Del.1984) (quoting *Orzeck v. Englehart,* 41 Del.Ch. 361, 365, 195 A.2d 375, 378 (Del.1963)). The rationale of the doctrine is that the various provisions of the Delaware General Corporation Law are of equal dignity, and a corporation may resort to one section thereof without having to answer for the consequences that would have arisen from invocation of a different section. *See Hariton v. Arco Electronics, Inc.,* 41 Del.Ch. 74, 77, 188 A.2d 123, 125 (Del.1963) (" 'the general theory of the Delaware Corporation Law [is] that action taken pursuant to the authority of the various sections of that law constitute acts of independent legal significance and their validity is not dependent on other sections of the Act' ") (quoting *Langfelder v. Universal Laboratories, Inc.,* 68 F.Supp. 209, 211 n. 5 (D.Del.1946), *aff'd,* 163 F.2d 804 (3d Cir.1947)).

Rothschild Int'l Corp. v. Liggett Group is particularly instructive. In that case, certain preferred shareholders of Liggett were entitled to a $100 per share liquidation preference under Liggett's certificate of incorporation. Liggett, however, undertook a combined tender offer and reverse cash-out merger (similar to the instant transaction) whereby Liggett became a wholly owned subsidiary of Grand Metropolitan Ltd., and the preferred shareholders in question received $70 per share.

---

3. Plaintiff points, however, to Del.Code Ann. tit. viii, § 251(e) (1983), which provides that "[i]n the case of a merger, the certificate of incorporation of the surviving corporation shall automatically be amended to the extent, if any, that changes in the amendment are set forth in the agreement of merger." Plaintiff contends that the agreement of merger "purports to alter or impair existing preferential rights," Brief for Plaintiff–Appellant at 14, thus requiring a class vote under other provisions of Delaware law. There are a number of problems with this contention, but the decisive threshold difficulty is that no "existing preferential rights" are altered or impaired in any way, since the holders of Preferred Stock never had any right to initiate a redemption.

Id., 474 A.2d at 135–36. A preferred shareholder then brought a class action in which it claimed breach of contract and breach of fiduciary duty, asserting that the transaction was the equivalent of a liquidation of Liggett which entitled preferred shareholders to the $100 per share liquidation preference. The Delaware Supreme Court concluded, however, that "there was no 'liquidation' of Liggett within the well-defined meaning of that term" because "the reverse cash-out merger of Liggett did not accomplish a 'liquidation' of Liggett's assets." *Id.* at 136. Accordingly, the Court held that the doctrine of independent legal significance barred plaintiff's claim. *Id.*

In so holding, the Court stated that "[i]t is equally settled under Delaware law that minority stock interests may be eliminated by merger. And, where a merger of corporations is permitted by law, a shareholder's preferential rights are subject to defeasance. Stockholders are charged with knowledge of this possibility at the time they acquire their shares." *Id.* at 136–37 (citing *Federal United Corp. v. Havender,* 24 Del.Ch. 318, 332–34, 11 A.2d 331, 338 (Del.1940)). Thus, the defendants were entitled to choose the most effective means to achieve the desired reorganization, "subject only to their duty to deal fairly with the minority interest." *Id.* at 136.

The instant action presents a most analogous situation. Plaintiff claims that the Gesub–RCA merger was, in effect, a redemption. However, there was no redemption within the well-defined meaning of that term under Delaware law, just as there had been no liquidation in *Liggett.* Thus, because the merger here was permitted by law, defendants legitimately chose to structure their transaction in the most effective way to achieve the desired corporate reorganization, and were subject only to a similar duty to deal fairly.

We note in this regard that plaintiff's complaint nowhere alleges that the $40.00 per share conversion rate for the Preferred Stock was unfair. Rather, "[p]laintiff is complaining of a breach of *contractual* rights, entirely divorced from the purported 'fairness' of the transaction." Brief for Plaintiff–Appellant at 23.[4] Moreover, as the district court stated: "Delaware provides specific protection to shareholders who believe that they have received insufficient value for their stock as the result of a merger: they may obtain an appraisal under § 262 of the General Corporation Law." Plaintiff, however, explicitly disavows any appraisal theory or remedy, consistent with her position that fairness is not the issue.

The doctrine of independent legal significance has been upheld by the Delaware courts in related corporate contexts, as well. *See, e.g., Field v. Allyn,* 457 A.2d 1089 (Del.Ch.), *aff'd mem.,* 467 A.2d 1274

---

4. In view of this statement, we deem it irrelevant that the merger agreement provides for redemption of a series of $4.00 cumulative convertible first preferred stock, but not for redemption of plaintiff's Preferred Stock. Since the holders of Preferred Stock had no right to initiate a redemption, the only conceivable relevance of the redemption of another class of preferred stock would be to a fairness claim, which plaintiff has forsworn.

(Del.1983) (tender offer followed by cash-out merger does not constitute "sale of assets" to which shareholder meeting provisions of Del.Gen. Corp. Law § 271 are applicable); *Orzeck v. Englehart,* 41 Del.Ch. 361, 195 A.2d 375 (Del.1963) (purchase by corporation with its stock of stock of seven other corporations, as a result of which selling stockholders acquire control of purchasing corporation, does not constitute de facto merger to which statutory appraisal rights apply); *Hariton v. Arco Electronics, Inc.,* 41 Del.Ch. 74, 188 A.2d 123 (Del.1963) (sale of corporate assets for shares of stock of purchasing corporation, followed by distribution of those shares to shareholders of, and dissolution of, selling corporation, does not constitute de facto merger to which statutory appraisal rights apply). Plaintiff's attempt to distinguish these cases on their facts is unavailing. While the details of the transactions may vary from case to case, the principle of the rule is clear and its application here cannot be seriously questioned.

* * *

CONCLUSION

The judgment of the district court dismissing the complaint is affirmed.

Subsection d. Mergers as Single-Firm Reorganizations of Capital Structure

WARNER COMMUNICATIONS v. CHRIS–CRAFT IND.

583 A.2d 962 (Del.Ch.1989).

ALLEN, CHANCELLOR.

* * *

Plaintiffs seek a determination that the related holders of Warner Communications Inc.'s Series B Variable Rate Cumulative Convertible Preferred Stock ("Series B Preferred") are not entitled to a class vote upon a proposed merger among Warner, its controlling shareholder Time Incorporated (now renamed Time Warner Inc.) and TW Sub Inc., a wholly owned subsidiary of Time Warner. Plaintiffs in this declaratory judgment action are the parties proposing the merger—Warner, Time and TW Sub, all of which are Delaware corporations. Defendants are two corporations, Chris–Craft Industries, Inc. and its controlled subsidiary, BHC, Inc., which together with its wholly owned subsidiary, is the holder of the Series B Preferred stock. For purposes of this opinion, plaintiffs generally will be referred to as Warner; Time Warner, for purposes of clarity, will be referred to as Time and the holders of the Series B Preferred will be referred to as BHC.

The merger in question is the proposed "back end" of a transaction, the first stage of which was a public tender offer for 51% of Warner's common stock for cash that closed on July 24, 1989. In that merger, the Series B Preferred stock would be cancelled and BHC as the holder of it would receive a new senior security, Time Series BB Convertible

Preferred. For purposes of this motion (but for those purposes only), plaintiffs have stipulated that that substitution would adversely affect defendants.

For the reasons that follow, I conclude that BHC has no right under the Warner certificate of incorporation to a class vote on the proposed merger. In brief, I reach this conclusion upon consideration of the pertinent provisions of the Series B Preferred stock's certificate of designation read in the context of the entire document and in the context of the established corporation law. This consideration compels the conclusion that the drafters of this document did not intend the holder of the Series B Preferred to possess a veto over every merger in which its interest would be adversely affected. Such a right was conferred expressly but only in narrowly defined circumstances concededly not present here. Absent such circumstances, I conclude that there is no right in the holders of the Series B Preferred to a class vote on a merger. The statement of the reasoning that leads to this conclusion entails a separate treatment of each of the two certificate of designation provisions—Section 3.3(i) and Section 3.4(i)—upon which BHC predicates its contrary assertion.

As provided in the certificate of designation creating the Series B Preferred, each share of that stock is entitled to a quarterly dividend equal to the greater of (a) $0.125 or (b) 200% of the regular quarterly dividend, if any, payable on a share of Warner common stock.[1] Each share is convertible into common stock in accordance with a complex formula, and each carries the same voting rights as the common stock, except in the event that a dividend is in default. In that event, the Series B Preferred stock "voting as a class" elects three directors. Generally, however:

Except as otherwise by the Certificate of Incorporation or by law provided, the shares of Series B Stock and the shares of Common Stock ... shall be voted together as one class.

Certificate of Designation, Section 3.1.

Two provisions do otherwise provide, and it is they that provide the ground upon which the parties' ongoing battle[2] is now fought. Section 3.3 of the certificate of designation creates a right in the holders of the Series B Preferred to participate with other holders of Warner preferred in a class vote under certain circumstances. Section 3.4(i) of the certificate creates a right in the holders of Series B Preferred stock alone to a series vote in certain circumstances. Section 3.3 provides in pertinent part as follows:

---

[1]. A two-for-one stock split in 1986 resulted in a proportionate adjustment of the original formula, which was the greater of (a) $0.125 or (b) 100% of the regular quarterly dividend, if any, on common stock.

[2]. These parties have not had harmonious relations. See, e.g., Warner Communications Inc., et al. v. Chris–Craft Industries, Inc., et al., Del.Ch., C.A. No. 10817 (May 15, 1989).

So long as any shares of Series B Stock shall be outstanding and unless the consent or approval of a greater number of shares shall then be required by law, first obtaining the consent or approval of the holders of at least two-thirds of the number of shares of the Series B Stock at the time outstanding, given in person or by proxy either in writing or at a meeting at which the holders of such shares shall be entitled to vote separately as a class, the Corporation shall not (i) amend, alter or repeal any of the provisions of the Certificate of Incorporation or By-laws of the Corporation so as to affect adversely any of the preferences, rights, powers or privileges of the Series B Stock or the holders thereof....

* * *

BHC contends that it is entitled to a class vote on the proposed merger under two distinct provisions of Warner's certificate of incorporation. First, defendants argue that Section 3.3(i) of the certificate of designation gives BHC the right to a class vote. It contends that Section 3.3(i) protects against any corporate action that alters or changes "any rights or preferences" of the preferred stock so as to adversely affect the preferred shareholders. The proposed merger, it says, will alter the rights of the Series B Preferred (and on this motion presumptively in an adverse way) by substituting a new security—Time BB Preferred—for the Series B Preferred. Thus, it concludes, Section 3.3(i) requires that BHC be afforded the opportunity to vote on that merger separately.

Second, defendants argue that Section 3.4(i) of the certificate of designation entitles BHC to a vote on the back-end merger because the Warner certificate of incorporation will admittedly be amended by the merger and necessarily so under Section 243 of the Delaware corporation law. That amendment they say—eliminating the provisions authorizing the Series B Preferred—will adversely affect BHC and will trigger the right to a class vote under Section 3.4(i).

Finally, defendants contend that the fact that Section 3.4(iii) specifically addresses mergers does not preclude other sections, such as Sections 3.3(i) and 3.4(i), from applying to mergers.

So long as any shares of Series B Stock shall be outstanding and unless the consent or approval of a greater number of shares shall then be required by law, (i) the affirmative vote or written consent of the holders of at least two-thirds of the total number of the then outstanding shares of Series B Stock and of any other series of Preferred Stock having the right to vote as a class on such matter, voting as a class, shall be necessary to alter or change any rights, preferences or limitations of the Preferred Stock so as to affect the holders of all of such shares adversely....

Warner answers that it is Section 3.4(iii) of the certificate of designation that is the dispositive provision relating to mergers. That section requires supermajority approval of a merger by the holders of Series B Preferred if in the merger they receive equity securities that are not the highest ranked equity securities of the surviving, resulting or acquiring corporation. Warner points out that under the merger the holders of Series B Preferred stock will receive Time Series BB Preferred stock which will be the senior equity security of Time. Thus, plaintiffs contend that Section 3.4(iii) is the pertinent provision and it grants no right to vote on the back-end merger to the Series B Preferred shareholders.

* * *

Section 3.4(i) provides a right to a series vote (i.e., the Series B Preferred voting alone) in the event of a charter amendment that amends, alters or repeals any provision of the certificate of incorporation so as to adversely affect the Series B Preferred or its holders. Warner will be the surviving corporation in the proposed merger. Its charter will be amended in the merger. It is assumed that the substitution of the merger consideration for the Series B Preferred stock is damaging to defendants. Nevertheless, Section 3.4(i) does not, in my opinion, grant a right to a series vote in these circumstances because the adverse effect upon defendants is not caused by an amendment, alteration or repeal of any provision of Warner's certificate of incorporation. Rather, it is the conversion of the Warner Series B Preferred into Time Series BB Preferred that creates the adverse effect. But the conversion of the Warner Series B Preferred into Time Series BB Preferred does not depend to any extent upon the amendment of the Warner certificate of incorporation under Section 242 of the General Corporation Law. That conversion will occur pursuant to Section 251 of the statute which authorizes mergers and defines the steps necessary to effectuate a merger.

Given that the merger itself is duly authorized,[5] the conversion of the Series B Preferred stock could occur without any prior or contemporaneous amendment to the certificate. Since the merger does contemplate the conversion of the Series B Preferred into the securities of another company, it is to be expected that the certificate would be amended to reflect the removal of these securities from the firm's capital structure. Section 243 requires such a step as a housekeeping matter, but that section does not require that amendment to be contemporaneous with the retirement of the stock and it surely does not make conversion of the stock dependent upon the amendment it contemplates. Rather, the amendment contemplated is necessitated by the merger; such an amendment, like the conversion, flows from the merger and is not a necessary condition of it. Stated in terms of the language of Section 3.4(i), given the existence of the merger, the amendments of the certificate of incorporation can in no event themselves be said to "affect" BHC "adversely," even if one assumes, as I do on this motion, that the substitution of the Time Series BB Preferred stock for Warner Series B Preferred stock does have an adverse affect.

5. There is no claim that Section 242(b)(2), which does create a right to a class vote when a charter amendment alters or changes the rights of the shares of a particular class of stock, itself creates a right to a class vote on the merger.

I turn then to Section 3.3(i). It requires a class vote (the Series B stock voting with any other series of preferred stock that has a vote on the question presented) in order to: "alter or change any rights ... of the Preferred stock so as to affect the holders of all such shares adversely." The central concern of Section 3.3(i) is action that would "alter or change" rights of the "Preferred Stock."[6]

In addressing Section 3.3(i), it is analytically helpful to break down the universe of acts that might arguably "alter or change ... rights of Preferred Stock" into two classes: amendments to a certificate of incorporation and other forms of acts, such as mergers, that might affect the holders of preferred stock.

At first blush, Section 3.3(i) appears to be principally directed to charter amendments, because under Delaware law, special stock rights and preferences are set forth in a corporate charter. Such rights must be stated in, or derivable in a manner clearly set forth in, the certificate of incorporation (8 Del.C. s 151(a)) or set forth in a certificate of designation which, when effective (8 Del.C. s 103), amends and becomes a part of the certificate of incorporation (8 Del.C. s 151(g)).

Insofar as Section 3.3(i) does address charter amendments, the amendments that will follow the Warner–Time merger fail to trigger its provisions for the same reason that those amendments fail to trigger a series vote under Section 3.4(i): the amendments contemplated in the merger will not themselves adversely affect the preferred stock.

The pending motion may thus be seen to come down to the question whether the class vote contemplated by Section 3.3(i) can, in addition to being triggered by an amendment to the certificate of incorporation that "alters ... rights ... adversely," be triggered by other forms of transactions in which the interests of holders of the preferred—and arguably "the rights ... of the Preferred Stock"—are adversely affected. Specifically, does Section 3.3(i) reach mergers?

Will the Series B Preferred be altered or changed in the merger within the meaning of Section 3.3(i)? Concededly, the shares of that stock will be converted into a new security by operation of law in the merger. Did the parties that drafted Section 3.3(i) intend conversion of stock in the merger to be contemplated within the phrase "alter or change?" I cannot conclude, viewing the certificate of designation in its entirety, that there is even a reasonable likelihood that they did.

---

6. For purposes of this motion, I assume but do not decide that defendants are correct that "any rights ... of Preferred Stock" is not limited to those rights necessarily shared by every series of preferred stock because conferred in a provision of the certificate of incorporation of general applicability (i.e., in this instance, the ratability provision quoted in note 4), but would extend to any rights of holders of preferred stock (and perhaps varying rights with respect to a single "matter"). It is remarkable, in any event, how much overlap exists between Sections 3.3(i) and 3.4(i). The latter section is broader in several respects—it covers all charter amendments, not simply those altering the terms of preferred stock; it covers bylaw amendments; it includes adverse effects upon "holders" as well as upon the stock.

The draftsmen of this language—the negotiators to the extent it has actually been negotiated [7]—must be deemed to have understood, and no doubt did understand, that under Delaware law (and generally) the securities whose characteristics were being defined in the certificate of designation could be converted by merger into "shares or other securities of the corporation surviving or resulting from [a] merger or consolidation" or into "cash, property, rights or securities of any other corporation." 8 Del.C. s 251(a); Federal United Corporation v. Havender, Del.Supr., 11 A.2d 331 (1940). Those shares, for example, could be converted into a right to receive cash or other property in a merger and such a conversion would not entitle a holder of stock with a stated value upon liquidation to that value (Rothschild, supra); nor would such a cash out merger constitute a redemption of callable securities. Dart v. Kohlberg, Kravis, Roberts & Co., Del.Ch., C.A. No. 7366, Hartnett, V.C. (May 6, 1985), slip op. at 13.

It is thus elementary that the possibility of a merger represents a possibility of the most profound importance to a holder of stock with special rights or preferences. * * * When one turns to the certificate of designation to ascertain whether the language of Section 3.3(i) was intended to incorporate changes effected through mergers, one is struck by two factors that together compel the conclusion that it was not. The first is the close similarity between the operative language of Section 3.3(i) and Section 242(b)(2) of the General Corporation Law. The second involves a comparison of the language of Section 3.3(i) with other sections of the certificate of designation in which the drafters of that document specifically and expressly treated the possibility of a future merger.

The language of Section 3.3(i) is closely similar to the language of Section 242(b)(2) of the corporation law statute governing amendments to a certificate of incorporation. That section creates a right to a class vote under certain circumstances. It provides in pertinent part:

> The holders of the outstanding shares of a class shall be entitled to vote as a class upon a proposed amendment ... if the amendment would ... alter or change the powers, preferences or special rights of the shares of such class so as to affect them adversely.

8 Del.C. s 242(b)(2) (emphasis added).

The parallel language of Section 3.3(i), as quoted above, provides in pertinent part:

> ... the affirmative vote of at least two-thirds of the ... outstanding shares of Series B Stock ... shall be necessary to *alter or change any rights, preferences or limitations of the Preferred Stock so as to affect* the holders of all such stock adversely.

Certificate of Designation, Section 3.3 (emphasis added).

---

7. In all events, it is agreed that Section 3.3 was not negotiated by Chris–Craft or BHC, but comes precisely from the terms of prior issues of Warner preferred stock.

The parallel is plain. It is therefore significant, when called upon to determine whether Section 3.3(i) creates a right to a class vote on a merger, to note that the language of Section 242(b)(2) does not itself create a right to a class vote on a merger. The voting requirements for a merger are generally set forth in Section 251(c) of our corporation law statute.[8] Under Section 251, unless a charter provision creates a right to a class vote, a merger is authorized by the company's shareholders when "a majority of the outstanding stock of the corporation entitled to vote thereon shall be voted for the adoption of the agreement [of merger]." 8 Del.C. s 251(c). Unlike Section 242(b), Section 251 contains no class vote requirement.

Our bedrock doctrine of independent legal significance (e.g., Orzeck v. Englehart, Del.Supr., 195 A.2d 375 (1963); Rothschild, supra) compels the conclusion that satisfaction of the requirements of Section 251 is all that is required legally to effectuate a merger. It follows, therefore, from rudimentary principles of corporation law, that the language of 242(b)(2), which so closely parallels the language of 3.3(i), does not entitle the holders of a class of preferred stock to a class vote in a merger, even if (as we assume here) the interests of the class will be adversely affected by the merger.[9] See, e.g., Dart v. Kohlberg, Kravis, Roberts & Co., supra. Indeed, this is so apparent that Chris–Craft does not argue that it has such rights under Section 242.

> So long as any shares of Series B Stock shall be outstanding ... without first obtaining the consent or approval of the holders of at least two-thirds of the number of shares of the Series B Stock at the time outstanding ... the Corporation shall not ... (iii) be a party to any transaction involving a merger, consolidation or sale of all or substantially all of the Corporation's assets in which the shares of Series B Stock either remain outstanding or are converted into the right to receive equity securities of the surviving, resulting or acquiring corporation (meaning the corporation whose securities are delivered in exchange for assets or securities of the Corporation) unless such corporation shall have, after such merger, consolidation or sale, no equity securities either authorized or outstanding (except such stock of the Corporation as may have been authorized or outstanding immediately preceding such merger or consolidation or such stock of the surviving, resulting or acquiring corporation as may be issued in exchange therefor) ranking prior, as to dividends or in liquidation, to the Series B Stock or to the stock of the surviving, resulting or acquiring corporation issued in exchange therefor.

Certificate of Designation, Section 3.4 (emphasis added).

---

8. But see 8 Del.C. s 251(f) (stating narrow exceptions to voting requirement).

9. In Dalton v. American Investment Company, Del.Ch., 490 A.2d 574 (1985), aff'd, Del.Supr., 501 A.2d 1238 (1985), this court rejected a claim that because their shares would be adversely affected by a merger, the holders of a class of preferred stock were entitled to a class vote. There the court addressed the matter factually and found no adverse effect. Dalton only accepted per arguendo the theory that Section 242(b)(2) created a right to a class vote on a merger that would adversely affect preferred shares; it would be an error, in my opinion, to read that case as an implicit acceptance of that theory.

Thus, in Section 3.4(iii), the certificate of designation does specifically address the voting requirements of a corporate transaction that would "convert" the Series B Preferred to the securities of another corporation and creates a right to a class vote in a subset of all such cases: when the "surviving, resulting or acquiring corporation" has no equity securities ranking prior to the Series B Preferred except any securities that ranked prior to it before the transaction. The parties agree that Section 3.4(iii) does not require a class vote here.

This section does not explicitly preclude the possibility of a certificate-created requirement for a class vote upon a merger which does not insert prior equity into the capital structure of the firm. Nevertheless, the only fair inference from Section 3.4(iii) is that it was intended to provide the only certificate-created requirement for a series or class vote upon a merger.

* * *

For these reasons, I conclude that the Warner certificate of incorporation does not afford to BHC, as the holder of the Series B Preferred Stock, a right to vote upon the proposed Warner–Time merger as a separate class. Plaintiffs may submit a form of implementing order on notice.

Subsection e. Partnerships and Long–Term Supply Contracts

PRATT v. BALLMAN–CUMMINGS FURNITURE CO., 254 Ark. 570, 495 S.W.2d 509 (1973). In a case dealing with appraisal rights in the wake of the formation of a partnership, the court in *Pratt v. Ballman–Cummings Furniture Co.*, 254 Ark. 570, 495 S.W.2d 509 (1973), reversed a lower court's directed verdict, stating that the lower court incorrectly found that plaintiff's evidence did not support its claim that defendants had accomplished a de facto merger. Plaintiffs, minority shareholders of the Ballman–Cummings Furniture Company, sought recovery of the value of their shares pursuant to the Arkansas appraisal statute. Defendants asserted that the transaction was merely the formation of a partnership by two corporations. While the court stopped short of finding that plaintiffs had established grounds for relief, it did state that a prima facie case of de facto merger had been established and that the trial court thus incorrectly directed verdict for defendants.

The vehicle for establishing the new entity was a sale of the assets of each of the corporation to the partnership. The two corporations would act as partners. Each corporation-partner also sold its merchandise to the partnership. The partnership was responsible for billing, merchandising, collection of accounts receivable, and delivery of furniture to customers, thus eliminating the duplication of expenses of the two former corporations. Furthermore, the two corporation-partners designated one individual to act as general manager of the partnership.

Important to the court's analysis was the subsequent liquidation of one of the constituent corporations.] The court noted that

> There are well recognized in the law, defacto mergers—an association under the guise of a partnership whereby one corporation loses its identity as such and is actually controlled by the management of the partnership. When a particular corporate combination 'is in legal effect a merger or a consolidation, even though the transaction may be otherwise labelled by the parties, the courts treat the transaction as a defacto merger or consolidation so as to confer upon dissenting stockholders the right to receive cash payment for their shares.' [citations omitted]

Id. at 510.

GOOD v. LACKAWANNA LEATHER CO., 96 N.J.Super. 439, 233 A.2d 201 (Ch.Div.1967). [In a case applying the New Jersey defacto merger rules, the court in Good v. Lackawanna Leather Co., 233 A.2d 201 (N.J.1967) failed to find that a defacto merger had taken place between two corporations in the leather industry. Plaintiffs sought appraisal and payment for the value of their shares under N.J.S.A. 14:12–6 and 12–7 and N.J.S.A. 14:3–5, claiming that, while admittedly a statutory merger had not been consummated, the two corporations had engaged in a de facto merger.

The two corporations involved, Good Bros. and Lackawanna Leather, each were involved in the leather goods industry: Good Bros. as a leather processing company and Lackawanna as a finisher and seller of leather products. In April 1958 the two corporations proposed a merger of the two entities, citing as reasons therefor the recent trend among leather finishing companies to develop in-house leather tanning departments, rather than rely on outside suppliers. Likewise, the trend toward in-house tanneries also resulted in Good's dependence upon Lacuna to purchase the bulk of its products. Thus, by combining their operations in a consolidated entity, both Good Bros. and Lackawanna seemingly would benefit.

A merger memorandum circulated among the directors of the two corporations indicated that if any shareholder dissents were filed, the proposed merger would be abandoned. The chief concern of the directors was that any appraisal remedy granted to minority shareholders would cause a burdensome drain of cash from the companies. The boards of both Good Bros. and Lackawanna approved the merger agreement. The agreement was approved by a two-thirds vote of the shareholders of Lackawanna. However, the shares held by plaintiffs, comprising 20% of Lacuna's shares were voted against the transaction, thereby entitling them to receive the appraised value of their stock. Consequently, stockholders of each corporation were informed that the merger would not be consummated because a minority of Lackawanna's stockholders had given written notice of their dissent. A majority of the shareholders of Good Bros. subsequently rejected the merger proposal.

Following the rejection of the merger proposal, Good Bros. and Lackawanna developed a close working relationship. While Good Bros. was not liquidated following the failed merger attempt, it did convert approximately 94% of its plant and equipment to cash and investment securities. Good Bros. thereafter made various loans to Lackawanna and, although purporting to continue to process hides for Lackawanna, Good Bros. actually sold hides processed by another tanner to Lackawanna at cost. Thus, plaintiffs alleged that the purposes of the merger had been accomplished without satisfying the formal requirements of state law.

The court found that in fact there had been no defacto merger, stating that, for a statutory merger to be effected under New Jersey law, one of the corporations must cease to exist following the transaction. Furthermore, the court declared that "a consolidation or a merger always involves a transfer of the assets and business of one corporation to another in exchange for its securities." 233 A.2d at 208. Such a transfer was absent in this case. Also important to the court's analysis was that the two corporations continued to maintain separate, albeit interlocking, boards of directors and that at no time did Good Bros. assume the liabilities of Lackawanna. The development of a close working relationship and the interlocking directorate did not per se constitute a merger. Finally, the court was troubled by the prospect of granting an appraisal remedy when the statute declared that "the *consolidated* corporation shall pay to such stockholder the value of his stock." N.J.S.A. 14:12–6. Since there had been no consolidation of enterprises, there was no corporation to be called upon to pay the dissenters the value of their shares. The mere fact that the corporations accomplished the objectives sought by their merger in another way, without more, did not require a finding of a de facto merger.]

SECTION 5. MAVERICK ATTEMPTS TO TREAT EQUIVALENT TRANSACTIONS ALIKE

Subsection a. The California Corporations Code

The California legislature has taken a different tack from Delaware in the 1977 revisions of its corporate code. California's corporate code, for example, gives voting rights to shareholders of the *buying* firm in asset sales and in stock acquisitions if the consideration is stock in the buying firm. See California Corporations Code sections 181(b) and (c), 1200(b) and (c), and 1201(a) below. A few other states have similar provisions. Ohio Rev.Code Ann. § 1701.83 (Baldwin 1983); Pa.Stat. Tit. 17, § 311(F) (appraisal rights only). The drafters of the California code attempted to synchronize the code provision that regulate mergers and acquisitions by their effect on shareholders, not by their technical form; like transactions should be treated alike.

The California provisions are, in this respect, more like the tax and accounting rules that base their distinctions on the eventual position of target-firm shareholders. In making them so, however, the drafters of the California legislation had to make basic calls on when shareholders in ostensibly different positions deserve similar treatment. Should, for example, cashed-out target shareholders in asset sales be treated the same as target shareholders in asset sales who receive stock in an acquirer? An illustration of both the synchronization argument and some decisions on the merits specific to asset sales is contained in remarks made by one of the principal drafters of the California code:

M. EISENBERG, THE STRUCTURE OF THE CORPORATION
231–32, 250–51 (1976).

Stock-For-Assets Combinations (Including Classical Mergers)

If we put aside the problems raised by the traditional statutes, and consider instead the optimal legislative treatment of stock-for-assets combinations and classical mergers, three things seem clear: (1) A classical merger (that is, a merger so denominated) is simply a special case of a stock-for-assets transaction; (2) Shareholder rights in such transactions should depend on the real impact of the transaction (which may of course include significant changes in legal rights), not on how the transaction is labeled; and (3) The impact of such a transaction on shareholders of a transferor may differ from the impact on shareholders of a survivor, so that the rights of each body of shareholders must be considered separately.

On the transferor's side, the issues are relatively straightforward. If one corporation transfers substantially all of its assets to a second in exchange for stock in the latter (or indeed for any consideration other than cash), from the perspective of the transferor's shareholders the result is a radical reconstitution of the enterprise—so radical that it should not only require approval by the transferor's shareholders, but give rise to appraisal rights for those of the transferor's shareholders who do not choose to participate; and this is true whether the transaction is denominated a merger, or not.

On the survivor's side, the picture is somewhat more complex. If a stock-for-assets combination has a significant economic or legal impact on the survivor's shareholders it should certainly require approval by those shareholders, and give rise to appraisal rights on their part, for much the same reasons that apply to shareholders of the transferor. But if the amount of stock issued by the survivor is not significant in terms of its previously outstanding stock, and no significant change is made in the control structure of the legal entity in which the survivor's corporate enterprise is enveloped, the combination is unlikely to have a significant economic impact on the survivor's shareholders. Such a transaction, therefore, should neither require approval of the survivor's shareholders nor give such shareholders appraisal rights; and this is true even if the combination is denominated a merger.

Cash-For-Assets Combinations

Under the traditional statutes, a sale of substantially all assets for cash requires the approval of the transferor's shareholders. This is as it should be: such a transaction constitutes a radical reconstruction of the enterprise from the transferor's perspective. There is, however, an important difference between a stock-for-assets and a cash-for-assets transaction. Where the transfer is for stock, the result is not only a radically restructured but a continuing enterprise; but where the transfer is for cash and the transferor is immediately liquidated (as is typically the case), the transferor's shareholders are not being brought along in a continuing enterprise, and appraisal rights may therefore be unnecessary, except perhaps as a check on the fairness of price in a self-dealing situation.

A cash-for-assets transaction looks much different from the perspective of the survivor's shareholders. An initial question from this perspective is whether such transactions are mergers within the meaning of the traditional statutes. At one time it would have been fairly clear they were not, since a classical merger involved the issuance of stock by the survivor. Today, however, it is common for merger provisions to contemplate the issuance of cash, and it seems likely that, properly or improperly, these provisions will be interpreted to permit the issuance solely of cash. Under such an interpretation, a cash-for-assets transaction could be viewed as a merger within the meaning of the traditional statutes. On the other hand, such transactions could also be viewed as purchases, and which view should be taken may properly depend on underlying policy considerations. Unlike stock-for-assets combinations, an acquisition of substantially all of a transferor's assets by a survivor for cash may involve neither an increase in the size of the survivor's assets (but instead only a reshuffling of liquid into fixed assets), nor a reallocation of ownership interests. From the survivor's perspective cash-for-assets combinations will therefore frequently be difficult to distinguish from internal expansion; that is, they will frequently not rise to the level of a structural change. Therefore, such transactions should not normally require approval by the survivor's shareholders nor give rise to appraisal rights for such shareholders.

Please read sections 181, 1001(a), 1200, 1201(a) and (b), and 152 of the California Corporations Code in your supplement and answer the following questions:

Questions

1. Compare the voting rights of stockholders in California corporations in statutory mergers, triangular mergers, asset sales, and stock acquisitions with the voting rights of stockholders in Delaware corporations

in the same transactions. In California stock-for-assets transactions are covered in sections 181(c) and 1200(c); cash-for-assets transactions are covered in section 1001; stock-for-stock transactions are covered in sections 181(b) and 1200(b); cash-for-stock is not covered in any of the sections; statutory mergers are covered in sections 181(a) and 1200(a); triangular mergers are covered in section 1200(d). Which code do you prefer? What are the underlying policy choices inherent in each code?

2. How successful is the California code at giving stockholders similar rights under alternative statutory provisions? Why, for example, does a stockholder in a firm selling substantially all its assets for cash not have appraisal rights (appraisal rights attach only to "reorganizations" under West's Cal.Corp.Code § 1300) while a stockholder in a firm receiving cash in a merger has appraisal rights?

3. How easily can parties avoid the requirements of the California code? For example, if planners want to avoid the requirement of a shareholder vote by an acquiring company in a non-cash-asset acquisition, how could they do it? Can the acquirer sell its stock to the target for cash and, in a second step, use the cash proceeds to buy the assets from the target?

Problem

X and Y are incorporated in California. X acquires Y in a triangular merger, paying for Y with 18,000 shares of class A common stock of X. Before the transaction X has 90,000 shares of class A common stock and 10,000 of class B common (which is identical to A common except that B common has diminished voting rights) outstanding and 20,000 of nonvoting preferred stock outstanding. What vote is required of X shareholders to approve the merger? How would your answer change if X were incorporated in Delaware?

Subsection b. Listing Requirements on the New York Stock Exchange Relevant to Shareholder Voting

NEW YORK STOCK EXCHANGE LISTED COMPANY MANUAL

101.00 Introduction

A listing on the New York Stock Exchange is internationally recognized as signifying that a publicly owned corporation has achieved maturity and front-rank status in its industry—in terms of assets, earnings, and shareholder interest and acceptance. Indeed, the Exchange's listing standards are designed to assure that every domestic or non-U.S. company whose shares are admitted to trading in the Exchange market merit that recognition.

* * *

312.00 Shareholder Approval Policy

312.01 Shareholders' interest and participation in corporate affairs has greatly increased. Management has responded by providing more extensive and frequent reports on matters of interest to investors. In addition, an increasing number of important corporate decisions are being referred to shareholders for their approval. This is especially true of transactions involving the issuance of additional securities.

Good business practice is frequently the controlling factor in the determination of management to submit a matter to shareholders for approval even though neither the law nor the company's charter makes such approvals necessary. The Exchange encourages this growth in corporate democracy.

312.02 Companies are urged to discuss questions relating to this subject with their Exchange representative sufficiently in advance of the time for the calling of a shareholders' meeting and the solicitation of proxies where shareholder approval may be involved. All relevant factors will be taken into consideration in applying the policy expressed in this Para. 312.00 and the Exchange will advise whether or not shareholder approval will be required in a particular case.

312.03 Shareholder approval prior to the issuance of securities (under (b), (c) or (d) below) will be prerequisite to listing when: * * *

(c) Common stock or securities convertible into or exercisable for common stock are to be issued in any transaction or series of related transactions, other than a public offering for cash, (i) if the common stock has or will have upon issuance voting power equal to or in excess of 20% of the voting power outstanding before the issuance of such stock or securities convertible into or exercisable for common stock, or (ii) the number of shares of common stock to be issued is or will be equal to or in excess of 20% of the number of shares of common stock outstanding before the issuance of the stock. Exceptions may be made upon application to the Exchange when 1) the delay in securing stockholder approval would seriously jeopardize the financial viability of the enterprise and 2) reliance by the company on this exception is expressly approved by the Audit Committee of the Board.

A company relying on this exception must mail to all shareholders not later than ten days before issuance of the securities a letter alerting them to its omission to seek the shareholder approval that would otherwise be required under the policy of the Exchange and indicating that the Audit Committee of the Board has expressly approved the exception.

(d) The issuance will result in a change of control of the issuer.

(e) Only shares actually issued and outstanding (excluding treasury shares or shares held by a subsidiary) are to be used in making any calculation provided for in this paragraph. Unissued shares reserved for issuance upon conversion of securities or upon exercise of options or warrants will not be regarded as outstanding. * * *

312.05 Where shareholder approval is a prerequisite to the listing of any additional or new securities of a listed company, the minimum vote which will constitute shareholder approval for listing purposes is defined as approval by a majority of votes cast on a proposal in a proxy bearing on the particular matter, provided that the total vote cast on the proposal represents over 50% in interest of all securities entitled to vote on the proposal.

* * *

Questions

1. When are shareholders given the right to vote under a New York Stock Exchange rule and denied that right under the Delaware General Corporation Law code (consider stock-for-assets acquisitions and triangular mergers)? Is a vote under the NYSE rule an adequate substitute for state voting requirements? What is the vote required for passage under the rules? Does the NYSE rule give appraisal rights? See *Equity Group Holdings v. DMG,* supra (a triangular merger).

2. When are shareholders given the right to vote under a NYSE rule and denied the right under the California Corporations Code?

3. Is the right to vote and have an appraisal remedy more important to shareholders in NYSE firms or to shareholders in closely held firms?

EASTERBROOK & FISCHEL, MANDATORY DISCLOSURE AND THE PROTECTION OF INVESTORS
70 Va.L.Rev. 669, 689–90 (1984).

Organized exchanges reduce the costs of transacting. By making it easier for parties with different beliefs about the future to transact, organized exchanges increase liquidity and reduce the unnecessary risk of investing. The greater the liquidity of the secondary market, the more successful the exchange. Because the success of an exchange depends on the amount of trading, exchanges have incentives to adopt rules governing trade that operate to the benefit of investors. Such rules attract more trades, reducing the cost and increasing the profits of those who run the exchanges.

Exchanges gain, for example, by adopting rules that minimize the amount of deceit committed by listed firms, because investors who are misled are less likely to be repeat players. For the same reason, exchanges have an incentive to adopt rules that require listed firms to disclose the amount and type of information that investors demand. Competition among organized exchanges for both the listing of firms and the business of investors, as well as competition between exchanges and other methods of investing, increases the incentives of the exchanges to adopt beneficial rules.

Firms, in turn, have incentives to list their securities on exchanges the rules of which maximize the benefits of investors. To see this, assume for the moment that firms acting by themselves would disclose less (or different) information than that demanded by investors as a class, and that the social loss from this inappropriate level of disclosure is less than the costs to these individual firms of contracting to produce the right amount of information. This might occur, for example, because of the third-party effects discussed in Part II.B. Organized exchanges offer the firms a way to cope with the collective action problem. The firms can agree to be bound by the rules set by the exchange, and these rules can come closer to requiring optimal disclosure because they will "internalize" many of the third-party effects. Firms that bind themselves to follow the exchange's rules will have a competitive advantage in attracting capital. This sort of process is at work in the rivalry among exchanges, with the New York Stock Exchange, which sets rules governing disclosure of information and the issuance of new stock by listed firms, attracting business at the expense of other methods of trading.

* * *

Note
The "Race to Laxity" Debate

An argument that law and economics devotees have used for over fifteen years, see, e.g., Winter, *State Law, Shareholder Protection, and the Theory of the Corporation*, 6 J.Legal Stud. 251 (1977), to justify state incorporation (and resist pleas for federal incorporation) is that competition among states seeking to attract incorporations will lead to optional rules of corporate governance in state corporate codes. Thus Delaware's rules on shareholder voting in acquisitions are superior to the rules of other jurisdictions, notably California, because Delaware's code attracts the largest number of our top five hundred domestic corporations. As noted in the Easterbrook & Fischel article above, stock exchanges compete for listings and trades—the higher the volume of stock trades, the higher the revenue to exchange members. The New York Stock Exchange then competes with other national exchanges such as the American Stock Exchange (AMEX), the Philadelphia Stock Exchange, and the over-the-counter market as well as international exchanges. Since the NYSE is the dominant national exchange, its rules also have a claim of being optional. Yet the NYSE gives additional voting rights to shareholders, even though shareholders of NYSE firms, having a liquid market for their shares, would seemingly have less concern over shareholder voting rights. Why? Which kind of competition, state against state or exchange against exchange, ought to produce sounder rules?

SECTION 0. SHOULD SHAREHOLDERS HAVE THE POWER TO VOTE NOT TO VOTE? FORM AND SUBSTANCE IN STATE CORPORATE CODES

The cases in the previous section demonstrate that the parties to an acquisition can often place the transaction, without altering its fundamental nature and effect, under two or more provisions of a state corporate code and that these alternatives have different requirements for stockholder voting and appraisal rights. Parties are thus free to choose and do choose the provisions with the fewest requirements.

Courts, with very limited and short-lived exceptions, will not nullify the parties' choice by requiring that they meet the requirements of the provision that is most protective of shareholders' rights. Indeed, in *Warner Communication,* the Delaware Chancery Court went to great lengths to construe provisions in a set of articles to preserve a firm's ability to escape class-voting requirements.

State legislatures are moving at differing speeds to coordinate the requirements of the various sections. California has taken the lead with the wholesale revision of its acquisition provisions in 1977. Delaware has also made some effort in this regard. California and, to a lesser extent, the Revised Model Act have attempted to make most acquisitions meet the more stringent standards originating with traditional mergers. Delaware and its imitators, Pennsylvania, for example, have edged in the opposite direction; they relaxed standards for acquisitions to the more lenient standards originating with traditional asset sales. Delaware's exception from voting requirements for mergers in 251(f), for example, gives most mergers between large firms and small firms treatment equivalent to asset sales from the standpoint of the buying firm (but not the selling firm). Delaware has also reduced its two-thirds vote requirement for mergers to a simple majority to match its vote requirement for asset acquisitions.

Whatever a state's view on the need for shareholders' rights in acquisitions, the question remains: Why have state legislatures been slow to redraft their codes to make decisions on the form of an acquisition turn on factors other than the ease of avoiding stockholders' voting and appraisal rights? Or why have courts not stepped into the gap created by state legislation and developed a more active case law on de facto mergers and the like?

We ought not to treat too harshly the hesitancy of our courts and legislatures on the matter. Drafting a corporate code that effectively treats all functionally equivalent transactions alike is a difficult task. We will ask in later chapters whether accounting or tax rules that attempt to do so are successful, and we will find that they often are not. There are three problems that a drafter of a corporate code, intent on treating like exchanges alike, must solve. First, she must decide why a classification of transactions is necessary at all. Why should shareholders vote and have appraisal rights in any kind of major transaction? Second, consistent with her views on the necessity of shareholder voting and appraisal rights, she must subdivide transactions based on whether these rights ought or ought not to adhere. Third, she must devise standards that catch transactions designed primarily to evade her basic distinctions. Each step contains difficult drafting decisions.

To begin our analysis of the difficulty of the task and answer our first question, assume for the sake of argument the classic view: Shareholders ought to vote and have dissenters' rights in all acquisitions in which a group of shareholders undergo a "fundamental and instantaneous" change in the nature of their investment. We can then address the second step. A straightforward application of this principle would produce a rule that gives shareholders a right to vote in all acquisitions except those in which they end up holding stock after the transaction with rights functionally equivalent to those they had before the acquisition.[1] Substantial dilution of the voting power of the stock would count as a fundamental change, as would any change in the form of a stock, whether in type (stock to debt or cash) or in the formal rights and privileges of the stock (participating preferred to nonparticipating preferred). This would justify awarding voting and appraisal rights to stockholders of both parties in most mergers of similarly valued firms and not give voting and appraisal rights to the shareholders of a larger firm in a whale-minnow merger and to the shareholders of a parent in a parent-subsidiary merger as long as the merger did not also constitute, in essence, a single-firm recapitalization of the whale or parent firm (the deal does not include a substantial alteration of the rights and privileges of stock in the larger firm or parent firm). If the drafter believes in class voting for recapitalization, the same system ought to apply to voting in mergers whenever voting rights are given.

So far so good, but now assume that in a merger that is not a whale-minnow or parent-subsidiary merger, the shareholders of one of the firms, the surviving firm, hold stock identical in formal rights to what they held before the merger. That is, the shareholders of the selling firm receive exclusively debt securities in the surviving firm or cash in exchange for their stock. Admittedly stockholders in the selling firm ought to vote, but what of stockholders in the surviving firm? Although the formal rights and privileges attached to their shares are unchanged, they may and probably do have a very different investment as a result of the transaction. Depending on the exchange, they may hold stock in a more risky, highly leveraged business. Should this enable them to vote? If so, how do we define and evaluate the level of increased risk that justifies a stockholder vote? Moreover, should we force shareholder votes on single-firm decisions that add significant leverage (when the directors decide to sell debt, for example) or business risk (when the directors decide to go into a new line of business, for example) to the firm? If we do not, can an acquiring firm leverage itself before a merger to avoid our merger standards?

An application of the basic principle to asset sales (when substantially all the assets of a firm are sold and the sale is outside the normal pattern of the firm's business) is more difficult yet. On the selling side, if one believes that we ought to use changes in the form of, or the rights and privileges attached to, stock as the touchstone for stockholder voting, then stockholders of the selling firm cannot vote unless the firm is dissolved immediately after the sale. If one believes that stockhold-

1. Some would modify the classic view and deny shareholders' voting rights, although not dissenters' rights, when they are cashed out (as opposed to exchanging their stock for different stock), based on the belief that voting protection is necessary only for shareholders forced to remain in a "new" corporation. But if the touchstone is a substantial change in the underlying investment, should not a change to cash qualify?

ers ought to vote whenever the underlying nature of the firm changes dramatically, regardless of whether there is any change in the form of their stock, then an asset sale ought to trigger a vote, because it may affect the underlying value and the risk characteristics of the stock. (Is this situation similar to the situation of buying-firm shareholders in a statutory merger when the selling-firm shareholders receive only cash?) On the buying side, if one believes that we ought to use changes in form as the touchstone, the stockholders of the buying firm ought not to vote. If one believes that stockholders ought to vote whenever the underlying nature of the firm changes dramatically, then an asset purchase of significant size may qualify. A large-scale asset purchase may dramatically affect the risk characteristics of the business and therefore the underlying stock. In other words, once we abandon a convenient but crude reliance on the form of the stock to determine when changes in an investment are fundamental, we are left with some very difficult line-drawing problems.

At this point one needs to ask whether we could avoid all need for this classification system by reassessing the need for a shareholder vote on anything but an election of the board of directors or an amendment to the charter. In other words, can we short-circuit the entire inquiry by answering question one negatively? Why should shareholders have an unequivocal right to vote on mergers, asset sales, and even dissolution decisions? Why do shareholders, at minimum, not have the power to waive the right to vote on such transactions? Under present law is a vote to amend the articles that authorize the board to issue a block of stock in excess of all stock outstanding, as occurred in the *Irwing Bank* case or the *Equity Group Holdings* case, in essence a vote not to vote on mergers? The amendment gives the board the power to make exchange tender offers, as in *Irwing Bank*, or execute triangular mergers, as in *Equity Group Holdings*. Why not make this a more general principle and allow shareholders to vote on whether to vote specifically on mergers and asset sales?

The question easily translates into a more fundamental question of why states ought to have any mandatory provisions on acquisitions in their corporate codes. State law could simply accept and legitimize all charter or bylaw provisions stipulating acquisition procedures or provide standardized terms and procedures that firms could adopt specifically (opt in), or provide terms that firms could replace specifically (opt out) with other arrangements. Under each of the three systems equity investors would choose rules that minimize agency costs associated with faithless or lazy managers and the opportunistic behavior of other groups of investors as well (bondholders' interests can be in conflict with the interest of stockholders once the instruments have been sold) and that, at the same time, give appropriate flexibility to their managers to maximize profits.

What procedures provide the best balance in acquisitions and reorganizations? Investors may decide that they do not care to vote on major corporate changes as long as managers' interests can be effectively aligned with theirs through compensation packages dependent on stock prices (and perhaps appraisal rights for specified changes in their investments). We could let competition for investment dollars determine the content of the corporate charters that produce the most attractive investment alternatives to participants in the capital markets. The results may vary by type of business or size of firm.

At minimum we would get creative answers to the current line-drawing problems that are so crudely resolved by state legislatures. Perhaps this is what we do now; we allow firms to structure their way around a lenient code with little or no judicial interference, finding the alternative that may minimize the voting rights of their stockholders, because we know that those stockholders could, if they so desired, augment the statute with provisions in their charters on voting rights. The Easterbrook and Fischel excerpt that follows makes these points:

EASTERBROOK & FISCHEL, THE CORPORATE CONTRACT
89 Colum.L.Rev. 1416, 1419, 1430 (1989).

How is it that managers came to control such resources?[2] It is not exactly secret that scattered shareholders can't control managers directly. If the investors know that the managers have lots of discretion, why did they give their money to these managers in the first place? If managers promise to return but a pittance, the investors will not put up very much money. The investors simply pay less for the paper the firms issue. There is therefore a limit on managers' efforts to enrich themselves at investors' expense. Managers may do their best to take advantage of their investors, but they find that the dynamics of the market drive them to act as if they had investors' interests at heart. It is almost as if there were an invisible hand.

... In general, all the terms in corporate governance are contractual in the sense that they are fully priced in transactions among the interested parties. They are thereafter tested for desirable properties; the firms that pick the wrong terms will fail in competition with other firms competing for capital. It is unimportant that terms may not be "negotiated"; the pricing and testing mechanisms are all that matters.

---

2. The discussion that follows owes much to Jensen & Meckling, Theory of the Firm: Managerial Behavior, Agency Costs and Ownership Structure, 3 J.Fin.Econ. 305 (1976). They and we write in a tradition that began with Coase, The Nature of the Firm, 4 Economica (n.s.) 386 (1937). Other important contributions include Alchian & Demsetz, Production, Information Costs, and Economic Organization, 62 Am. Econ.Rev. 777 (1972); Fama & Jensen, Agency Problems and Residual Claims, 26 J.L. & Econ. 327 (1983); Fama & Jensen, Separation of Ownership and Control, 26 J.L. & Econ. 301 (1983); Manne, Mergers and the Market for Corporate Control, 73 J.Pol.Econ. 110 (1965); Manne, Some Theoretical Aspects of Share Voting, 64 Colum. L.Rev. 1427 (1964); Winter, State Law, Shareholder Protection, and the Theory of the Corporation, 6 J.Legal Stud. 251 (1977); see also Principals and Agents: The Structure of Business (J. Pratt & R. Zeckhauser eds. 1985); N. Wolfson, The Modern Corporation: Free Markets vs. Regulation (1984); Hansmann, Ownership of the Firm, 4 J.L. Econ. & Organization 267 (1988).

as long as there are no effects on third parties. This should come as no shock to anyone familiar with the Coase Theorem.[14]

* * *

Corporate governance devices that have survived in many firms for extended periods are particularly unlikely candidates for challenge as mistakes. We have emphasized that the durability of a practice both enables people to gauge its effects and allows competition among firms to weed out the practices that do not assist investors. There is no similar process of winnowing out of academic ideas or regulations. Quite the contrary; mandatory terms prescribed by law halt the process of natural selection and evaluation. Unless there is a strong reason to believe that regulation has a comparative advantage over competition in markets in evaluating the effects of corporate contracts, there is no basis for displacing actual arrangements as "mistakes" or "exploitation."

One natural question after all this business of corporation-as-contract is: why law? Why not just abolish corporate law and let people negotiate whatever contracts they please? The short but not entirely satisfactory answer is that corporate law is a set of terms available off-the-rack so that participants in corporate ventures can save the cost of contracting. There are lots of terms, such as rules for voting, establishing quorums, and so on, that almost everyone will want to adopt. Corporate codes and existing judicial decisions supply these terms "for free" to every corporation, enabling the venturers to concentrate on matters that are specific to their undertaking. Even when they work through all the issues they expect will arise, they are apt to miss something. All sorts of complexities will arise later. Corporate law—and in particular the fiduciary principle enforced by courts—fills in the blanks and oversights with the terms that people would have bargained for had they anticipated the problems and been able to transact costlessly in advance. On this view corporate law supplements but never displaces actual bargains—save in situations of third-party effects or latecomer terms.

* * *

The story is not complete, however, because it still does not answer the question "why law?". Why don't law firms or corporate service bureaus or investment banks compile sets of terms on which corporations may be constructed? They can peddle these terms and recover the cost of working through all of the problems. Yet it is costly for the parties (or any private supplier of rules) to ponder unusual situations and dicker for the adoption of terms. Parties or their surrogates must identify problems and then transact in sufficient detail to solve them. This may all be wasted effort if the problem does not occur. Because change is the one constant of corporate life, waste is a certainty. Often the type of problem that the firm encounters does not occur to anyone

---

14. Coase, The Problem of Social Cost, 3 J.L. & Econ. 1, 7 (1960).

until after the venture is under way. Court systems have a comparative advantage in supplying answers to questions that do not occur in time to be resolved ex ante. Common law systems need not answer questions unless they occur. This is an economizing device; it avoids working through problems that do not arise. The accumulation of cases dealing with unusual problems then supplies a level of detail that is costly to duplicate through private bargaining. To put it differently, "contractual" terms for many kinds of problems turn out to be public goods!

* * *

KORNHAUSER, THE NEXUS OF CONTRACTS APPROACH TO CORPORATIONS: A COMMENT ON EASTERBROOK AND FISCHEL
89 Colum.L.Rev. 1449, 1456–57 (1989).

The most problematic information assumption underlying the economic model of contract is the assumption that the parties know every possible state of the world. The law in other contexts often distinguishes between foreseeable and unforeseeable risks. The distinction is not one between high probability and low probability events, or high expected value and low expected value events, but one between imaginable and unimaginable events. At the time of contract, neither party may have contemplated the now-realized state of the world in controversy.[14]

The incongruity of defining the ideal in terms of full information emerges most strongly when we realize that the parties may have contemplated the possibility that they lacked imagination. When an unimaginable event occurs, the parties might consider the imposition of the term they would have negotiated had they imagined the event a highly inappropriate resolution of their dispute. Suppose, for example, that the unimagined event is sufficiently disastrous that, had they anticipated it, the parties would not have contracted at all. The full information ideal gives no guidance in such a situation. Rather, some ex post "fair" division of the loss might best mirror the term they would have chosen to resolve disputes arising from the realization of unimagined events. Even if awareness of a contingency would not have prevented contract formation, the parties might favor a "fair"

---

14. Examples of "unimagined" events are difficult to construct. The closing of the Suez Canal to shipping in 1956 might offer one instance. The development of junk bonds as an effective device for raising large amounts of capital may constitute a second example. Bond indentures drafted prior to 1980 probably did not contemplate or even imagine this financing device and the consequences it would have for the value of bonds. As this example suggests, the concept of unimaginability is vague; it is difficult to designate a precise moment when creditors should have begun to imagine and understand this institutional innovation.

However, unimaginable events may be more frequent than the junk bond example suggests. Individuals often have difficulty imagining how specific contract terms will apply in diverse factual circumstances. At some point, complexity gives rise to something akin to unimaginability.

rule of construction rather than the term they would have acceded to had they imagined the contingency. The price terms of a contract, the terms of management compensation, or the interest rate on corporate bonds will reflect all the risks the parties face. Conceivably, parties can more easily "price" a "fair" default rule than one which specifies "optimal" terms they cannot imagine.

Realization of the complexity of the decision problems faced by corporate actors and the impact of this complexity on defining the ideal contract undermines the appeal of a pure contractual approach. In the face of this complexity, some mandatory rules may appear desirable.

Whether we grant all firms the freedom to cast their own rules based on shareholder choice or we, through state legislatures, attempt to create rules that best approximate what shareholders would otherwise choose, the essential question remains: When will shareholders sensibly request a right to vote or an appraisal right in major acquisitions or reorganizations? At this point we ought to revisit our acceptance of the classic assumption that shareholders will want a vote on all "fundamental" changes in the firm to protect their investment. If shareholders are convinced managers will act in the best interests of the firm in all transactions classified as fundamental, then voting and appraisal rights are unnecessary in these transactions and, perhaps, even dangerous (a class of security holders could block a beneficial transaction to appropriate a larger share of the gains). Coming up with a justification for shareholder voting in this context is not an easy task, as we see in the following extract:

EASTERBROOK & FISCHEL, THE CORPORATE CONTRACT
89 Colum.L.Rev. 1416, 1442–45 (1989).

Much of the discussion has proceeded as if all parts of the corporate contract were established at the beginning. "The beginning" for any participant is when he enters the venture—when he becomes an employee, invests, and so on. This is the critical time for most purposes because the time of entry is when the costs and benefits of governance arrangements are priced. If a term is good or bad at the beginning, adjustments in the prices even everything up. But of course many things change after the beginning. The firm may reincorporate in Nevada. It may adopt staggered terms for members of the board of directors or a "fair price amendment." It may abolish the executive committee of the board, get rid of all the independent directors or create a board with a majority of independent directors. What are we to make of these changes.

Changes of this sort have some things in common: they are proposed by the existing managers (unless approved by the board of directors, no change in an ongoing firm's rules will be adopted), the proposals are accepted by voting among the equity investors, and the winning side in the vote does not compensate the losing side. If the changes are adverse to existing participants in the venture, there will be price adjustments, but these adjustments do not compensate the participants. If an amendment reduces the expected profitability of the firm by an amount worth one dollar per share, the price will fall and existing investors will experience a capital loss of one dollar per share. They can sell, but they can't avoid the loss. The buyers will get shares worth what they pay; the investors at the time of the change are out of luck. The mechanism by which entrepreneurs and managers bear the cost of unfavorable terms does not work—not in any direct way, anyway—for latecomer terms. It will work eventually. Latecomer terms that injure investors will reduce the firm's ability to raise money and compete in product markets. But these eventual reactions are not remedies; they explain why firms that choose inferior governance devices do not survive, and they show why widespread, enduring practices are likely to be beneficial, but they do nothing for participants in the ventures that are about to be ground under by the heel of history.

The process of voting controls adverse terms to a degree but not perfectly. Investors are rationally uninterested in votes, not only because no investor's vote will change the outcome of the election but also because the information necessary to cast an informed vote is not readily available. Shareholders' approval of changes is likely to be unreliable as an indicator of their interests, because scattered shareholders in public firms do not have the time, information, or incentive to review all proposed changes. Votes are not sold, at least not without the shares. The difference between governance provisions established at the beginning and provisions added later suggests some caution in treating the two categories alike. Some of the hardest questions in corporate law concern arrangements that are adopted or changed after the firm is under way and the capital has been raised. Thus doctrines of corporate law refusing to allow shareholders to ratify waste (except unanimously) are well founded. Yet the rules for amending the rules are themselves part of the original articles, and it is (or should be) possible to draft limitations on amendment. These most commonly take the form of provisions designating some amendments as transactions from which investors may dissent and demand appraisal. Moreover, amendments to governance structures may spark proxy contests in which investors' attention is focused, and they also may call forth take-over bids. So voting, or at least the opportunity for review set in place by the voting mechanism, is a partial substitute for the pricing mechanism that applies at the beginning.

One candidate for a rule of law that could overcome a problem in the contracting process is a rule that differentiates among terms according to the time of their adoption. It could provide that terms in place at the beginning (at the time the firm is founded, goes public, or issues significant amounts of stock) are always to be honored unless there are demonstrable third-party effects, while terms adopted later that appear to increase the agency costs of management are valid only if adopted by supermajority vote at successive annual meetings or if dissenting investors are bought out. (The dual-meeting rule would allow an intervening proxy or takeover contest to prevent the change from going into effect.) Yet if such a constraint on amendments is beneficial to investors, why are supermajority and dual-meeting requirements so rare in corporate documents? Investors can and do appreciate the risk that latecomer terms will be damaging, yet perhaps rules that slow down the adoption of changes would be more damaging still on balance. It is not our purpose here to draft rules of law. It is important, however, to keep the latecomer term in mind as a potential problem in a contractual approach to corporate law.

Questions

Under a corporate contract theory, how helpful is the concept of *latecomer terms?* Do investors factor the risk of latecomer terms into the pricing of the *"beginning" terms*? If the risk of latecomer terms is high and beginning investors discount the firm's stock to account for the possibility of increased opportunities for opportunistic behavior by managers, then do incorporators have an incentive to create a charter with provisions that reduce the latecomer term problem? Moreover, when a latecomer term appears, are the investors aggrieved or have they simply taken a chance and lost (that is, assumed the risk that an event may happen, hoping that it will not, and suffered the occurrence of the event)? Indeed, if we protect investors ex post are we not altering the basic contract and affecting its accurate pricing at the beginning? Doesn't a concept of *latecomer terms* that is helpful necessarily include a theory of limited information held by investors? In other words, does the concept depend on a robust theory of investor "surprise"? If we adopt a theory of limited information on the part of investors, is Professor Kornhauser correct in his assessment of the "firm as contract" theory?

What is the difference between a latecomer term that increases board power and one that decreases board power? If an investor believes that maximum board flexibility is the last way to maximize profit, is not the latter latecomer term value decreasing for her?

Can we develop a theory of voting that does not depend on investor surprise? Start with the basic proposition that shareholders should want to vote only in transactions when other control mechanisms (most importantly controls triggered by low stock prices) are less effective than a shareholder vote. Three types of transactions may qualify.

First, transactions in which the management team is "selling out" generate special problems in controlling manager self-interest. If after the transaction the managers are no longer affected by the welfare of their own shareholders, the managers have an incentive to act opportunistically by agreeing to a lower sales price in exchange for personal one-time benefits (side payments, bribes, and the like). Traditional market effects of manager disloyalty—a low stock price—no longer have an impact on a manager's personal future. Termed the final period problem by economists, stockholders could choose to protect themselves in such transactions by voting on appraisal rights. Managers would precommit to shareholder voting procedures to attract investors' cash with binding promises not to engage in final period conduct.

Second, single-firm transactions (or multiple-firm transactions with the same effect) that insulate managers from the traditional control mechanisms and yet are initiated by those managers pose conflict-of-interest problems. Shareholders may want to retain the right to vote to avoid the problems created by the obvious conflict of interest of their managers in such transactions. In other words, managers may seek to void control mechanisms on which shareholders rely. In this context there may be a very important and substantial difference between firm rules on acquisition procedure in general and firm decisions on specific transactions. Shareholders as a consequence may be reluctant to give managers control over changes in acquisition procedures that reduce checks on management behavior in specific transactions. Recall that the Kanda & Levmore article, supra, on appraisal rights makes such a proposal for appraisal rights. Why not extend their proposal to voting as well?

Third, in transactions that involve major one-time changes in the firm, a shareholder vote may be a relatively cost-effective monitory device. A major reason for delegating authority to managers in general is the prohibitively high cost of educating shareholders sufficiently to enable them to make informed business decisions and the prohibitively high cost of soliciting all shareholders' views even if they are educated. On matters of normal business routine these assertions hold true, but in major acquisitions, which instantaneously take one investment and substitute another, shareholders have less of an informational disadvantage; they need only price the new investment against the old, a decision all investors must make routinely in any event, and base their vote on the comparison. Moreover, the "rational apathy" problem facing shareholders (see the Gordon excerpt that follows) may be less apparent in these megadeals. In a one-time, large-size transaction investors are asked to choose among investments in a manner that is otherwise common for them in routine decisions to buy, sell, or hold securities. Thus in large-scale acquisitions, shareholders may believe that they can, at relatively little cost, participate directly in the decision-making process to best protect their investments.

Even if we can identify transactions in which the basic control mechanisms break down, we must ask whether shareholder voting or shareholder appraisal rights provide an effective check on management behavior.

GORDON, THE MANDATORY STRUCTURE OF CORPORATE LAW
89 Colum.L.Rev. 1549, 1575–77, 1580 (1989)

* * *

In voting on a proposed amendment, public shareholders can choose to become informed or remain uninformed on the probable effect on shareholder welfare. Since acquiring information is costly, a shareholder with a small stake will almost always find that the expected returns from becoming informed will be negative, even if her vote (remarkably) turns out to be decisive. Rational apathy is the indicated course. A large public shareholder, by contrast, may find positive expected returns from becoming informed if his vote is decisive, but he faces a different problem: Because other shareholders will be uninformed, his vote cannot be decisive unless he bears the costs necessary to inform them. Since his expected returns from the combined costs of acquiring and disseminating information will probably be negative, he too will follow a course of rational apathy.[82] Thus public shareholders as a group will not be informed on the probable effect of the proposed amendment.[83] The situation is a classic free-rider problem: Because there is no compulsory cost-sharing mechanism, the individually rational course is to be uninformed, even though the collectively rational choice is for shareholders to acquire and disseminate information.[84]

What remains, of course, is to determine what voting rule a rationally apathetic, thus uninformed, shareholder should follow: yea or nay on every proposed amendment. Presumably the shareholder

---

[82]. The large shareholder may nevertheless become informed to keep open another option: to sell into the market where he believes he has a superior analysis of the negative impact of the proposed amendment than the market generally.

[83]. This produces the apparently paradoxical result that markets are efficient but shareholder voting is not, which means that market prices impound all publicly available information but that voting outcomes do not. The difference turns on the nature of decisionmaking in the two cases. In the market, an informed shareholder can earn a return on an individual information acquisition decision, indeed, in direct proportion to the number of uninformed actors. Thus markets will tend toward efficiency. In the shareholder voting case, a joint decision is required for an information acquisition decision to bear fruit. The likelihood of a return is therefore in inverse proportion to the number of uninformed shareholders; thus shareholder voting will have limited utility in producing efficient outcomes. The difference between market aggregation of information and individual decisions to become informed also explains why the innovation hypothesis (based on informed markets) is not inconsistent with shareholder apathy. Compare Romano, supra note 16, at 1604 n. 14.

[84]. These results are sensitive to a number of factors. If a particular public shareholder holds a large enough stake, there may be some information acquisition and dissemination (because of the potentially higher payoff) but the level will still be below the optimum amount for the public shareholders collectively. The presence of other large shareholders will reduce dissemination costs and make it more likely that the costs will be shared. The size of the insider block, on the other hand, is a factor pointing in the opposite direction. As the block increases, the percentage of the public shareholder votes needed to reject the amendment also increases, which reduces the payoff to organized resistance. These factors influence whether the insiders will propose a wealth-reducing amendment. * * *

purchased stock in the belief that management, at least on average, acted in the interests of shareholders. This will generate a strong impetus for a "yes" rule, which the dynamics of rational apathy will tend to reinforce.[85] Thus the stage is set for the insiders to push through wealth-reducing amendments.[86]

2. *Strategic Behavior that Amounts to Economic Coercion.*—The insiders' control over the structure and timing of proposals is another mechanism of opportunistic amendment. This control enables them to obtain approval of wealth-reducing or wealth-neutral amendments even where shareholders are informed. In the insiders' repertoire are "sweeteners," "add-ons" and "chicken" tactics.

a. *Sweeteners.*—The insiders can bundle a wealth-reducing amendment with a "sweetener"—an unrelated proposal that increases shareholder wealth. This is vividly illustrated by the recent wave of dual class common stock recapitalizations, which typically required a charter amendment to establish a class of super-voting common. In many instances firms announced plans to increase cash payouts to shareholders through stock buybacks or higher dividends, but only if the amendment was approved. If the amendment itself increased shareholder wealth, presumably there would have been no reason to tie it to new cash payouts.[88] As this example shows, because the insiders control the packaging, shareholders are obliged to take the bitter with the sweet, and wealth-reducing amendments may be adopted.[89]

85. Because of quorum requirements, abstention by uninformed shareholders would amount to a "no" vote in many circumstances.

86. One question that remains is how all this fits with the efficient market hypothesis. How can it be that the market knows everything and investors know nothing? If the market price quickly and accurately responds to the proposed amendment, then investors can become informed very cheaply and ought to act on that information. However, determining the price effect of a proposal for a specific firm may be very costly, and if the wealth decrease is small, impossible as a practical matter. * * * and accompanying text. Alternatively, investors may not believe the efficient market hypothesis; i.e., despite a negative price change they may believe management's justification for the amendment. Still, it is likely that we would see more shareholder rejections of amendments where the proposal triggered a large negative price effect. This threshold may bound the extent of the information asymmetry explanation for opportunistic amendment.

A second question to ask is whether there are any constraints on the insiders' *proposal* of wealth-reducing amendments. Amendments that are wealth-reducing because of a transfer of cash flows from public shareholders to insiders are likely to be somewhat constrained by the market in corporate control, depending of course on the amount of the transfer relative to the costs of a control shift. Amendments that are wealth-reducing because of entrenchment effects present a different problem because of disabling effects on the corporate control market. Thus, the risk of opportunistic amendment is higher where the subject matter is the insiders' control rather than transfer of cash flows.

* * *

88. Another good example is Inco's combining a vote on a poison pill with a $10 special dividend. Inco "Poison Pill" Tested in Canada, N.Y. Times, Dec. 7, 1988, at D8, col. 3.

89. Another objection is that in bundling the proposal the insiders have added to the public shareholders' information costs. Calculation has become much more difficult, in part because some of the relevant parameters, such as the maintenance of increased payouts, are within management's control. The bundling also means that shareholders will not be able to rely on collective judgments that may emerge if similar amendments are proposed in other

* * *

Interested Shareholder Voting.—Collective action and strategic behavior problems will be exacerbated by interested voting by insiders. Under the laws of most states, amendment requires only a simple majority vote of the outstanding shares.[95] Thus a proposed amendment will succeed so long as it attracts the necessary minority of public shareholder votes that in combination with insider votes form a majority. These votes will be easily won if public shareholders have different views about the wealth effects of the proposal—a likelihood if the amendment is complex or is coupled with a sweetener. So given a significant insider block, a wealth-reducing amendment may pass even if the public shareholders as a group accurately assess the adverse effects. Foreseeing this, public shareholders in firms with significant insider blocks are more likely to be rationally apathetic. By similar argument, such firms can more effectively employ the threats and bluffs of strategic behavior. To attain a simple majority, the insiders need to fool only some of the public shareholders some of the time.

* * *

Professor Gordon considers the question of whether shareholders ought to be able to vote to opt out of requirements in state corporate codes that are now mandatory. Professor Gordon seeks to justify a system with some mandatory rules by attacking the efficiency of shareholder voting. Yet a package of mandatory rules under today's state corporate codes includes rules that *require* shareholder voting in mergers and asset sales. How can one support mandatory rules on shareholder voting by arguing that shareholder voting is inherently problematic? Can we distinguish shareholder votes on acquisition procedures from shareholder votes on specific transactions? Can we argue that votes on the former are more likely to be welfare-decreasing than votes on the latter? In other words, are shareholders better off if they cannot vote not to vote on mergers?[1]

Are there alternative justifications that are not circular? An affirmative answer to the question may come from an analysis of the many rights and procedures that accompany different kinds of shareholder votes. First, consider a pure shareholder vote on whether shareholders will continue to vote in mergers with no identifiable merger partner on the horizon. The correlation in today's law would

---

firms. These added information costs increase the likelihood of rational apathy, and once incurred, are a deadweight cost. In other words, since the decision to become informed is endogenous to the particular case, a complicated proposal may bootstrap its way to approval.

95. Thirty four jurisdictions, including Delaware, follow this position; fifteen require a two-thirds vote. See Revised Model Business Corp. Act Ann. § 10.03 (1989) (summarizing state laws).

1. We will revisit this topic again in chapter 4 when we consider shareholder voting on tender offer defenses.

be a shareholder vote authorizing the board to issue new shares in an amount over 100 percent of the outstanding shares, purely to enable the board to "sell" the firm at its discretion should a willing buyer appear. What are the disclosures required at the time of the vote? They are minimal, entailing only a careful description of the potential power ceded the board to sell the firm. If the board does subsequently decide to sell the firm, shareholders' only legal recourse, if they believe the board has violated its duties of care and loyalty, is to sue in state court. Any detailed information on the board's role in the deed will come through discovery in the litigation. Second, consider a pure shareholder vote ratifying a specific merger. The disclosures required at the time of the vote are specific and detailed. Not only can shareholders use these disclosures to choose how to vote, they can use these disclosures to choose whether to sue their board for a breach of its fiduciary duty. Moreover, shareholders can sue not only for breaches of fiduciary duty but also for breaches of the specific disclosure obligations under federal securities law and state fraud law. Thus in the latter vote shareholders have a considerably easier access to courts if a board does not appear to have fulfilled its obligations to the firm. In summary, a vote not to vote is also a vote on whether shareholders ought to retain an easy route to court to contest specific transactions.

A second rationale for shareholders' favoring a charter that deprives them of the power to vote not to vote on specific acquisitions is based on their belief that they will vote against their interest more often in passing procedural amendment than they will in passing on specific transactions. Shareholders may be better able to assess the likelihood of opportunistic behavior by their managers in the context of a specific deal than in an open-ended delegation of power to their managers that affects future deals. This relates to the point made earlier about why votes on acquisitions may generate less "rational apathy" than other shareholder votes. The stakes are large, and the decision of whether to exchange one investment for another is similar to the basic investment decision that all shareholders necessarily make in the ordinary course. Shareholder votes on procedural questions may be much harder for shareholders to value (what is the increased risk of opportunistic behavior by managers in the future?) and, even if accurately valued, may represent a much smaller change in share price. Thus the costs of gathering information for a procedural vote are higher, and the payoff is lower, increasing the incentive for rational apathy. In light of an increased risk of rational apathy generating affirmative votes on procedural questions that hurt shareholder interests, shareholders choose to disable themselves from voting on acquisition procedure, specifically on voting not to vote on individual transactions. In other words, Professor Gordon's argument on rational apathy may be stronger for some votes than for others.

SUBCHAPTER B. FEDERAL PROXY REGULATIONS

When stockholders vote on acquisitions, state law requires generally that they receive adequate information from their managers on the details of the transaction. State corporate codes often do not detail the specific kinds of information that stockholders should have when they vote. Reread section 251(b)(1)–(6) and (c) (third sentence) of the Delaware General Corporation Law for mergers. Some state court case law has developed, under the rubric of a common law on fiduciary duty, on the obligation of a firm to notify its shareholders of all material facts in a transaction, particularly if the transaction creates a conflict of interest for senior managers (management buyouts (LBOs) and parent-subsidiary mergers that cash out minority shareholders are the classic examples). We will read these cases in chapter 4. Otherwise state law on the matter is basically open-ended.

Federal securities law stands in stark contrast to state law. If a firm is publicly held, that is, it has over five hundred shareholders and $5 million in assets or is traded on a national securities exchange, then section 14(a) of the Securities and Exchange Act of 1934 applies to empower the Securities and Exchange Commission to regulate proxy "solicitations" by the firm. See Exchange Act § 12(a) & (g), Rule 12g–1. A proxy is a delegation of voting power by a shareholder to an agent; as such it is a creation of state law. The SEC rules regulate the "solicitation" of proxies, requiring that a "proxy statement" accompany all solicitations, and contain requirements on the content and form of executed proxies. Since most large firms must solicit proxies from their shareholders in order to have a quorum present at shareholder meetings, the rules have substantial bite. Moreover, even if a registered firm does not solicit proxies for a shareholder meeting, the Exchange Act requires a firm to mail an "information statement" that is substantially the same as a proxy statement. Exchange Act § 14(c), Reg. 14C.

The regulations promulgated by the SEC specifically cover proxy solicitations for votes required by state corporate codes for mergers, asset acquisitions, and reorganizations. The regulations are very detailed on the information that acquisition parties must disclose and yet contain open-ended admonitions to add all other material facts as well. The detail in the schedules can be important even for closely held firms not specifically covered by the Exchange Act. They provide a safe harbor for protection from second-guessing by state judges under the open-ended requirements of state corporate law. The rules give guidance to firm officials on what will satisfy the state codes.

SECTION 1. THE BASICS OF PROXY SOLICITATION DISCLOSURE REQUIREMENTS IN ACQUISITIONS

Regulation 14A, passed by the SEC under the authority of section 14(a) of the Exchange Act, consists of thirteen rules. Under rule 14a–3(a) no solicitation subject to the rules may be made "unless each person solicited is concurrently furnished or has previously been furnished with a written proxy statement containing information specified in Schedule 14A." Preliminary copies of the proxy statement and the form of the proxy, as well as any other soliciting material to be distributed at the same time, must be filed with the commission at least ten days before the final material is used. Rule 14a–6(a). In addition copies of all literature in definitive form must be mailed, concurrently with its distribution, to the commission and to each exchange on which any security of the issuer is listed. Rule 14a–6(c).

The proxy form must itself indicate in boldface type whether or not the proxy is solicited on behalf of the firm's board. Rule 14a–6(h). The proxies can confer authority to vote at only one meeting. Rule 14a–4(d)(2). The proxy must "identify clearly and impartially" any acquisition or reorganization question submitted to a vote and permit the security holder to choose "between approval or disapproval ..., or abstention." Rule 14a–4(a)(3) & (b)(1). A proxy may confer discretionary authority only within specified limitations: matters incident to the conduct of the meeting or unanticipated matters that may come before the meeting; approval of minutes of a prior meeting; shareholder proposals properly omitted from the proxy; or any matter about which the shareholder does not specify a choice, if the form of proxy states in bold type how the proxy holder intends to vote the shares in each such case. Rule 14a–4(c).

The first five items of schedule 14A apply to all proxy statements, regardless of the type of action proposed to be taken. They call for information with respect to the revocability of any executed proxy, dissenters' appraisal rights, the identity of those soliciting the proxy, the special interest of the solicitors and others connected with the solicitors, and a description of the issuer's outstanding securities and their principal holders. Item 12 applies to single-firm reorganizations "if action is to be taken with respect to the modification of any class of securities of the registrant, or the issuance or authorization for issuance of securities of the registrant in exchange for outstanding securities...." Item 14 applies

> if any action is to be taken with respect to any transaction involving (i) the merger or consolidation of the registrant into or with any other person or of any other person into or with the registrant, (ii) the acquisition by the registrant or any of its security holders of securities of another person, (iii) the acquisition by the registrant of any other going business or of the assets thereof, (iv) the sale or other transfer of

all or any substantial part of the assets of the registrant, or (v) the liquidation or dissolution of the registrant....

Please skim item 14 in your supplement. Subsection (a) calls for information about the transactions, and subsection (b) calls for information about both parties to the transaction.

As you can see, section b(3) of schedule 14A incorporates by reference two other SEC regulations, regulation S–X and regulation S–K. Regulation S–X specifies the accounting conventions that filing parties must use in their required financial documents—balance sheets, income statements, and cash flow statements. Regulation S–K is more general and contains a variety of requirements. A few of the provisions of regulation S–K, each heavily edited, are included in your statutory supplement to give you a general flavor of the detail required by the schedule. Note in the excerpts the heavy emphasis on past history and performance and the occasional studied request for forward-looking statements. See, for example, item 102(4) and (5) (estimations on reserves); item 201(b) (future dividends); and item 303(a) (estimates of liquidity capital resources, and unusual events). Must a firm predict the outcome of pending litigation? See item 103.

What is the result of mistakes in the proxy statement? It is the SEC's view that information specifically required by schedule 14A must be disclosed regardless of materiality. Any negligent omissions by the soliciting people subject them to liability under rule 14a–9, the antifraud rule. See, e.g., Gerstle v. Gamble–Skogmo, Inc., 478 F.2d 1281 (2d Cir.1973). When omitted information *is* material, the fact that it is not specifically called for by schedule 14A does not foreclose the possibility of a violation of rule 14a–9. The definition of materiality in this context is left to chapter 6.

SECTION 2. CAN MANAGERS "SELL THE DEAL" TO THEIR SHAREHOLDERS IN THE PROXY MATERIALS?

Consider the position of target shareholders asked to vote on an acquisition and their managers: The shareholders want to know whether the value of the consideration they will receive in the acquisition at the closing, particularly if it is stock in the surviving entity, will be higher than the value of the stock they now hold in their hands, and their managers want badly to so convince them. The buying-firm managers want to assert publicly that there will be synergy gains from the combination or that they have plans for the selling-firm assets that will maximize their value. Yet the firm's lawyers and accountants, fearing lawsuits, discourage the firm's managers from making any predictions of value that the firm does not absolutely have to make under the SEC schedules. The professional experts warn that if the projections are not accurate, the SEC and investors may sue the firm and its experts as, in effect, guarantors on the projections. We are left with three questions in the SEC rules: What types of predictions *must* a firm make in a proxy solicitation on an acquisition or reorganization? What types of predictions *can* a firm make? And finally, what types of predictions are prohibited absolutely, whether or not made in good faith and on reasonable investigation? As noted below, the conservatism of lawyers and accountants has carried the day.

One should begin an inquiry on required disclosures of prospective information in acquisitions or reorganizations by examining items 12 and 14 of regulation 14A. There are three separate bits of language in the items that appear to call for the disclosure of prospective information. First, both items call for financial statements meeting the requirements of article 11 of regulation S–X. Article 11 requires "pro forma" financial information if significant business combinations are "probable." In essence, the pro forma financials present the combined financials of the two constituent corporations as if they had combined on the date of the last financial statements prepared by the surviving company. Thus, in a sense, the information is not protective at all, it is historical in that the companies are combined as of a past date.

> Pro forma financial information should provide investors with information about the continuing impact of a particular transaction by showing how it might have affected historical financial statements if the transaction had been consummated at an earlier time. Such statement should assist investors in analyzing the future prospects of the registrant because they illustrate the possible scope of the change in the registrant's historical financial position and results of operations caused by the transaction.

SEC Reg. § 210.11–02(a).

At issue, however, are the obligations of the firms in an acquisition to adjust or footnote the pro forma financials if the pro formas do not accurately reflect what will in fact occur in the transaction. The SEC regulations on article 11 contain some general language on the matter, requiring that pro formas be adjusted in light of the structure of any planned acquisition "to give effect to the range of possible results." SEC Reg. § 210.1102(b)(8). These adjustments and, in lieu thereof, the footnotes to the pro forma *could* constitute a very valuable kind of prospective information for investors. Yet accountants read this language in article 11 very narrowly. The dominant footnote to pro formas is a disclaimer! The disclaimer states that the pro formas are a "mechanical exercise": They are not an accurate indication of any real results in the acquisition, and they do not include any quantification of synergy gains and other savings that may occur in the acquisition. It is clear, then, that any investor reading the pro forma for information must have a very sophisticated knowledge of accounting principles to make sense of the numbers and qualifications.

Article 11 also has a little-used provision that allows a firm, if it so chooses, to file a "financial forecast" *in lieu of* a pro forma condensed statement under SEC Reg. 210.11–03. The financial forecast must cover a period at least twelve months after the estimated consummation date of the transaction and set out clearly "assumptions particularly relevant to the transaction and effects thereof." Id. Although forecasts are very carefully regulated by generally accepted accounting principles, professional standards generated by accountants themselves, there is room in such forecasts to make predictions about the future results of an acquisition. In fact, accountants advise firms not to use forecast rule.

A second call for prospective information in item 14 could attach to language in (a)(3)(ii) asking for "the reasons for engaging in the transaction." Can the parties brag of synergy gains? In practice, parties disclose only a very general laundry list of reasons; there is no quantification in the disclosures. Item 14(a)(10) comes the closest to asking for some concrete estimates.

> If a report, opinion or appraisal materially relating to the transaction has been received from an outside party, and such report, opinion or appraisal is referred to in the proxy statement, furnish the same....

The requirement is readily avoidable, however.

A third call for prospective information arguably appears in the tame language of instruction 3 to item 303(a) in regulation S–K. Item 303 of regulation S–K is incorporated by reference in items 12 and 14 of regulation 14A. The instruction deals with the "management's discussion and analysis" (MD & A) section of a firm's financial statements. The MD & A is text that helps readers understand the bare numbers in the financials themselves. Instruction 3 requires that "the discussion and analysis shall focus specifically on material events and uncertainties known to management that would cause reported financial information not to be necessarily indicative of future operating results." Major acquisition transactions would appear to qualify, but presumably such information would already be contained in the pro forma financials.

What prospective information can a firm choose to disclose that is not required? Instruction 7 to item 303(a) in regulation S–K provides the basic standard for the MD & A sections of a firm's financials:

> Registrants are encouraged, but not required, to supply forward-looking information. This is to be distinguished from presently known data which will impact upon future operating results, such as known future increases in costs of labor or materials. This latter data may be required to be disclosed. Any forward-looking information supplied is expressly covered by the safe harbor rule for projections. See rule 175.

The SEC has defined "required prospective information" as "currently known trends, events, and uncertainties that are reasonably expected to have material effects" and has defined "optional forward-looking information" as involving "anticipating a future trend or event or anticipating a less predictable impact of a known event, trend or uncertainty." SEC Rel. No. 6711 (April 24, 1987), 52 F.R. 13717. At issue is whether managers can or ought to use instruction 7 to give their official predictions of the firm's future health after an acquisition or reorganization. Such information is of great interest to the investors, but in practice, firms do not make such projections in the MD & A materials.

Rule 175(c)(1) and (2), in conjunction with rule 14a-9, permits a firm to disclose a short list of projections other than those contained in the MD & A sections of the financials. The SEC terms the disclosures "forward-looking information." Read Securities Act rule 175 and Exchange Act rule 14a-9 in your statutory supplement. Rule 175 allows project "revenues, income (loss), earnings (loss) per share, capital expenditures, dividends, capital structure or other financial items" and "a statement of management's plans and objectives for future operations." Presumably each type of projection could be made about the business future of a surviving entity in acquisition or reorganization. Rule 14a-9, in its list of examples of projections that may be misleading, includes "predictions as to specific future market values."

The SEC is generally very suspicious of broad predictions by firm managers, believing that given half a chance, managers will imitate snake oil salesmen. The SEC fears that managers will mislead their shareholders with general exaggerated claims that are not susceptible to correction by after-the-fact litigation based on fraud. As a consequence, the SEC takes the position that predictions are presumed to be fraudulent unless the predictions are, first, specifically required or allowed in disclosure schedules and regulations and, second, made with a "reasonable basis" and "in good faith."

The SEC provisions that allow but do not require disclosure of certain types of prospective information are largely unused, however, as lawyers counsel their client to disclose only that which is required and even then only at minimal levels. As a consequence, most litigation is brought by shareholders who argue that firms should be required to disclose what the SEC allows them to disclose under general antifraud language. As noted in the *South Coast Services* case below, the federal courts have not been very accommodating.

The case presents one of the more difficult issues in the SEC mandatory disclosure debate. It centers around asset appraisals made by the selling firm in an asset sale. Asset appraisals are necessary because balance sheets carry assets at historical cost (with adjustments for depreciation and the like) and do not necessarily reflect current market values. Yet an asset appraisal is very subjective; it predicts market values of fairly illiquid assets—factories, for example. As such, an asset appraisal is a material fact in that it exists and is relied on by the selling-firm managers, and yet it is at the same time an opinion and a projection of future values. All selling-firm shareholders would love to know of all relevant asset appraisals before they vote. It is nonsense to assert to a shareholder with no understanding of legal "terms of art" that such appraisals are not "material."

SOUTH COAST SERVICES, INC. v. SANTA ANA VALLEY IRRIGATION CO.

United States Court of Appeals, Ninth Circuit, 1982.
669 F.2d 1265.

* * *

POOLE, CIRCUIT JUDGE:

This lawsuit concerns the adequacy of proxy statements soliciting shareholder approval of the sale of the assets of Santa Ana Valley Irrigation Company (SAVI) to Intercoast Investments, Inc. (Intercoast).

* * *

Appellants are former shareholders and directors of appellee corporation, Santa Ana Valley Irrigation Company (SAVI). SAVI was organized in 1877 to distribute water to irrigate the farms of its member shareholders in what is now the eastern portion of Orange County, California. As urban sprawl displaced farming in southern California, SAVI's emphasis shifted from irrigation to real estate holding and development. By the end of 1974 all irrigation operations had been phased out. * * * Awareness of this inadequacy and anxiety regarding a possible tender offer from Walker spurred the board to seek the services of a professional appraiser. White, the logical choice, refused on the basis of a conflict of interest, since he had already been retained by Walker. White subsequently asked the board for some information to assist him in making his appraisal. The board conditioned the release of the information on receipt of a copy of the appraisal when finished. White told the board that he could not give them a copy since the appraisal was the property of Walker. White continued his efforts without the information from the board.

Inquiries to other appraisers caused the board to conclude that appraisal of all assets by outside appraisers would be too costly and time consuming. The board settled on a plan whereby professional appraiser Robert Harrison was engaged to appraise only Weir Canyon and a portion of Green River, the two parcels considered the most difficult to evaluate, while management and the board estimated the value of the balance of the properties. In June 1977, the SAVI board instructed its accounting firm to prepare a balance sheet of corporate assets including the historical cost and estimated market value of each property (from information to be furnished by the board and Harrison) with the thought that such figures could be given to the shareholders in response to a possible tender offer from Walker.

To arrive at market values for the properties that were not appraised by Harrison, the board members and general manager, Terry, met and discussed their individual estimates of the value of each separate property. No guidelines were established and no method of evaluation was followed. Instead, each director, on the basis of his own experience and knowledge of the properties, suggested a high, medium and low value for each parcel. Some directors did not give their estimates in writing, and underlying assumptions were not discussed. None of the figures discussed was approved by a vote of the board. Instead, the general manager selected in some fashion from the individual estimates a high, medium and low estimated market value for each property and transmitted this to the accountants. The totals for all the properties if sold individually ranged from a low of $8,150,000 to a high of $12,950,000, compared to a cost basis of $3,349,379.

John Graham, SAVI's accountant, advised the board that, because the estimates were based on speculation and unconfirmed assumptions, the documents he prepared should be restricted to internal use by the board. A cover letter attached to his report contained a disclaimer as to the accuracy or reasonableness of the estimated market values contained therein.

As word circulated that the company was contemplating a sale of all its assets, several potential purchasers surfaced.

* * *

On August 18, 1977, by the same three to two majority, the board voted to approve a final agreement providing for the sale of substantially all of SAVI's assets to Intercoast. On that same date, the board unanimously approved a proxy statement soliciting shareholder approval of the sale and authorized the filing of this statement with the Securities and Exchange Commission (S.E.C.). * * *

The textual portion of the proxy statement noted the three to two division in the board and stated that the majority had considered the alternatives of a possible sale to a third party, a series of separate sales over time, and continued operation, and that it had concluded that a sale to a third party would maximize return and minimize risk to the shareholders. The statement also informed the shareholders that the majority considered the Intercoast offer fair and more favorable than other proposals considered by the board while the dissenters believed that the SAVI properties were worth more than Intercoast was offering. The statement explained that both the majority and the dissenters had reached their conclusions on the basis of their general knowledge of SAVI and the value of its assets.

The materials additionally stated that SAVI had no current appraisals on any of its properties except Green River and Weir Canyon. It was explained that the board had not obtained current appraisals of the other properties because of the expense and because current market information concerning them was more readily available. No mention was made of the balance sheet prepared by the accountants showing the board's valuations of the properties. In another section, the proxy statement set forth a full description of each property, noting factors bearing on development potential. The descriptions of Green River and Weir Canyon were augmented by the Harrison appraisal, and in each instance the appraisal was qualified by a disclaimer stating that an appraisal is only an opinion and that there was no assurance that the appraised value represented the realizable value of the property.

On November 4, 1977, the board sent a supplemental letter to the shareholders partly in response to shareholder inquiries whether the board was aware of any existing appraisal report relating to all of SAVI's properties. The letter referred to the appraisal report made by White on Walker's behalf and stated that SAVI was not involved in its preparation and had no rights to it. The letter further disclosed that the board had been advised that the appraisal placed a value on the properties considerably in excess of the purchase price offered by Intercoast and counselled against overly relying upon appraisals. The letter repeated the majority's recommendation of acceptance and noted the dissenters' belief that the value of the properties was higher than the offer by Intercoast. The board voted three to two against including its own valuations in the supplemental letter.

At a special meeting of the shareholders on November 15, 1977, the proposed sale was approved by a vote of more than 71% (5,987.6 shares to 1,699.5 shares).

* * *

A. FAILURE TO DISCLOSE ESTIMATES OF VALUE.

Appellants argue that disclosure of the board's estimates of the fair market value of the SAVI properties was required by Rule 14a–9 because the listing in the proxy materials of the historic book value of the properties without current market information was misleading. The district court rejected this argument and held that the failure to disclose the estimates was not a proxy violation, stating,

> As a rule the S.E.C. disfavors inclusion of appraisal information in proxy materials because of the inability of the commission to effectively review the accuracy of such estimates of value and the tendency of shareholders to place undue reliance upon them. [Citations]. An exception to this rule is recognized when the proposed estimates of value are objective, reasonably certain data, such as commodity prices prevailing in an active market. [Citations]. This Court finds that the board's appraisals fall in the former category and were properly excluded from the proxy materials.

Appellants claim that the district court erred in its interpretation of the S.E.C.'s position regarding appraisal information and that the S.E.C. in fact favors the disclosure of "current market value appraisal information" in proxy materials. We disagree.

Both the courts and the S.E.C. have consistently discouraged the inclusion of appraised asset valuations in proxy materials. *See, e.g., Gerstle v. Gamble–Skogmo, Inc.,* 478 F.2d 1281, 1292–94 (2d Cir.1973); *Kohn v. American Metal Climax, Inc.,* 458 F.2d 255, 265 (3d Cir.1972); *Denison Mines Limited v. Fibreboard Corporation,* 388 F.Supp. 812, 819 (D.Del.1974). In a note accompanying Rule 14a–9, the S.E.C. has listed examples of "what, depending upon particular facts and circumstances, may be misleading within the meaning of this section." The first example is "[p]redictions as to specific future market values." 17 C.F.R. § 240–14a–9 (1981). Admittedly, this note does not refer specifically to appraisals of current market value. We agree, however, with the Second Circuit that "it is clear that the policy embodied in the note to Rule 14a–9 has consistently been enforced to bar disclosure of asset appraisals as well as future market values...." *Gerstle v. Gamble–Skogmo, Inc., supra,* 478 F.2d at 1292.

Appellants dispute this reading of S.E.C. policy and argue that the position of the S.E.C. on the issue of appraisal disclosure is reflected in an *amicus* brief filed by the S.E.C. staff in *Gerstle v. Gamble–Skogmo, Inc., supra*. Appellants read the position taken in this brief to approve disclosure of appraisal of current fair market value of assets when a liquidation of those assets is contemplated and their current liquidating value is substantially higher than their historic book value. Under such circumstances, according to appellants, the appraisal must be disclosed if reliable.

We are unpersuaded by appellants' argument for two reasons. First, Commission policy is properly expressed through publicly available rules and policy statements. *See, id.* at 1294, n. 13. We have no more reason than did the court in *Gerstle* to recognize a "substantial modification, if not reversal of the SEC's position on disclosure of appraisals in proxy statements" on the basis of an *amicus* brief reflecting staff views which have been neither formally approved by the Commission nor publicly disseminated. *Id.* at 1294. Indeed, we have even less reason. It was noted in *Gerstle* that the Commission was in the process of reevaluating its policy and that new rules regarding appraisals appeared to be forthcoming. *Id.* However, since *Gerstle,* the Commission has issued certain releases, but no new rules changing its position on disclosure of appraisals.[3]

---

3. Appellants point out that a 1976 amendment of the note following Rule 14a–9 deleted future earnings from the list of examples of potentially misleading disclosures. *See,* Securities Act Release No. 5699, *Notice of Adoption of an Amendment to Rule 14a–9, etc.,* [1975–1976 Transfer Binder] CCH Fed.Sec.L.Rep., ¶ 80,461 (1976). We consider this limited amendment to be insufficient to alter the longstanding policy against disclosing appraisal information.

Appellants also point to two recent releases on the subject of disclosure of projections. See, Securities Act Release No. 5992, *Guides for Disclosure of Projections of Future Economic Performance,* [1978 Transfer Binder] CCH Fed.Sec.L.Rep., ¶ 81,756 (1978); and Securities Act Release No. 5993, *Proposed Safe–Harbor Rule for Projections,* [1978 Transfer Binder] CCH Fed.Sec.L.Rep., ¶ 81,757 (1978). These releases are not binding on our decision, as the proxy materials in this case predate their formulation.

Even if these releases had been in effect, they would have affected neither the SEC's position on disclosure of appraisals nor the propriety of withholding the valuations in this case. The 1978 releases deal with net income, and earnings per share. These matters are protected only if disclosed in good faith and if prepared with a reasonable basis. The SEC strongly advocates the disclosure of the assumptions upon which such projections are based. As our later discussion indicates, even if these rules were used as analogous guides, the SAVI board's appraisal valuations could not have been disclosed, as they were not independently reviewed, were not based on uniform or articulated assumptions, and were not prepared with a reasonable basis.

For the same reasons, the board's valuations could not have been disclosed even under the SEC's most recent release, issued after the proxy contest here and after submission of this case, SEC Release No. 34–16833, Fed.Sec.L.Rep. (CCH) ¶ 24,117 (May 23, 1980). The release authorizes disclosure only of appraisals made in good faith and on a reasonable basis in proxy contests in which a principal issue in con-

Second, even if we were to apply the policy stated in the *Gerstle amicus* brief, we would still affirm the district court's ruling that the SAVI board's valuations were properly excluded from the proxy materials. As noted by the court in *Gerstle,* the text of the *amicus* brief stated that "although appraisals generally cannot be disclosed because they may be misleading, existing appraisals of current liquidating value must be disclosed *if they have been made by a qualified expert and have a sufficient basis in fact."* Id. at 1292 (emphasis added). Here, the district court found that the SAVI board's valuations were neither based on objective, reasonably certain data nor prepared by a qualified expert.

> This conclusion rests on several factors. The first is that the board members, though having considerable experience in real estate in some cases, are not uniformly qualified to value real property. None of the directors are professional appraisers. Second, it is not clear what assumptions were made by each member in assigning a high and low value to each parcel. Without precise information as to the method by which these figures were reached, the board's estimates are potentially misleading. It is precisely such subjective information that the S.E.C. policy is designed to exclude. Failure to include the board's valuation figures was, therefore, not a proxy violation.

We cannot say that these findings are clearly erroneous. It is undisputed that the SAVI directors were not professional or expert appraisers. The board members employed no uniform method of valuation in making their estimates. No guidelines or standards were followed for the selection of relevant data nor for the manner in which data were to be weighed and evaluated. There was no agreement as to the basic assumptions underlying the valuation process. Rather, each director, drawing upon his personal knowledge and experience and relying on subjective assumptions, individually arrived at a high, middle and low figure for each property. It appears that these assumptions were not communicated among the board members. One director apparently based his high estimates on a number of contingencies so that his figures did not necessarily reflect his opinion as to the current value of the property. In addition, the board never formally approved the estimates, and some board members did not know what figures had been selected until they saw the accountants' report. Nor did the board know how the individual figures were compiled, that is, whether the highest and lowest figures were chosen, whether the figures were averaged, or whether some other method was used.[4]

---

tention is the liquidation of all or a part of a company's assets or equity.

4. Appellants argue that, because the SAVI board treated the estimates as reliable when it disclosed them to potential purchasers during the course of negotiations, the board is now estopped from contending that the estimates were too unreliable to be disclosed to the shareholders. This contention is not supported by case law. *See Kohn v. American Metal Climax, Inc.,* 458 F.2d 255, 265 (3d Cir.1972). In addition, the determination as to whether the estimates were based on sufficiently objective and reasonably certain data as to allow disclosure does not turn on the subjective views of the board members nor on

Confronted with similarly subjective "appraisals" in *Gerstle,* the court stated that "[w]e seriously doubt that this is what the SEC had in mind when it stated [in its *amicus* brief] that it would allow the work of expert appraisers to be disclosed in proxy statements in some circumstances." 478 F.2d at 1292, n. 10. Thus, even if we were to accept appellants' argument that current S.E.C. policy is reflected in the *Gerstle amicus* brief, that policy would still bar the disclosure of the SAVI board's valuations in the proxy materials.[5]

B. FAILURE TO DISCLOSE INQUIRIES FROM POTENTIAL PURCHASERS.

Appellants further contend that the proxy materials were rendered false and misleading by the failure of the SAVI board to disclose that, in addition to the Intercoast offer, it had received inquiries from four other potential purchasers. Appellants argue that this information was necessary to "clarify the import" of the statement in the proxy materials that "[t]he terms of the proposed sale are more favorable than those of other recent proposals considered by SAVI."

Firm offers from other potential purchasers, if they are more favorable than the offer being endorsed by management, must be disclosed in proxy materials soliciting shareholder approval of a proposed sale of corporate assets. *Gerstle v. Gamble–Skogmo, Inc., supra,* 478 F.2d at 1294–95. There is no duty to disclose inquiries or indications of interest that do not fall within the category of firm or definite offers. *See, e.g., Scott v. Multi–Amp Corporation,* 386 F.Supp. 44, 65 (D.N.J.1974). Here, each of the inquiries from potential purchasers, except that from Shappel Industries, consisted of a single telephone call to the SAVI board during its meeting to consider Intercoast's one-day offer. The purpose of the calls was evidently to request a meeting with the SAVI board to discuss the possibility of a purchase. These last minute expressions of interest clearly do not constitute the type of firm or definite offer that must be disclosed.

While the Shappel proposal poses a slightly more difficult question, we nevertheless find that it was too uncertain and illusory to be considered a firm offer. Shappel informed the SAVI board through Pankey that it was interested in purchasing SAVI for $1,300 per share only if the Weir Canyon property could be developed within three

---

the other uses to which the estimates were put.

5. As additional support for their argument that the board's estimates should have been disclosed, appellants point to the statement in the proxy materials that SAVI had no current appraisals of its properties except for the Green River and Weir Canyon properties that had been appraised by White. Appellants contend that this statement was made misleading by the omission of the board's estimates. This particular argument was not made in the district court and hence the district court made no explicit findings on the point. However, in light of the district court's holding that the board members were neither professional appraisers nor uniformly qualified to appraise real property and that the valuation process was highly subjective, we find that the above statement was not false or misleading. An appraisal is defined as "[a] valuation or an estimation of value of property by disinterested persons of suitable qualifications. The process of ascertaining a value of an asset or liability that involves expert opinion...." Black's Law Dictionary 92 (5th ed. 1979); *see also, United States v. Crowley,* 522 F.2d 427, 429 (7th Cir.1975).

years; if this condition could not be met, the price Shappel would be willing to pay would have apparently dropped to where SAVI would no longer be interested. It appears from the record that there was serious question whether the Weir Canyon property could be developed within three years. In addition, Shappel was not bound by the terms of its proposal, and had SAVI refused the Intercoast offer, Shappel could have withdrawn or changed its proposal. Thus, Shappel's proposal appears to be nothing more than a last minute effort to halt the sale; at best it was but a step in negotiating a purchase, with no assurance whatsoever that such negotiations would bear fruit or, if they did, whether the final terms would have been better than those offered by Intercoast.

* * *

FLETCHER, CIRCUIT JUDGE, dissenting:

* * *

In viewing the sale of SAVI's assets within the framework of this standard of materiality, numerous factors persuade me that a reasonable shareholder would have considered the valuations placed on the assets by the board important in deciding how to vote. SAVI was a company whose value was principally in the liquidation value of its real property assets, which had appreciated dramatically from acquisition costs.[1] SAVI's attractiveness to potential purchasers lay in the liquidation value of its real property assets. Noting that the SAVI board disclosed the valuations in question to both Investors and Shapell, the value of the realty assets must have figured prominently in negotiations and was of material importance. The SAVI shareholders as sellers had just as much need for the information to aid in making informed decisions.

Most of the SAVI stock was in the hands of financially unsophisticated shareholders who, under the terms of the sale, were surrendering forever their interest in the SAVI assets. There was no public market for SAVI stock to serve as an indicator of the current value of these greatly appreciated assets. In these circumstances the board's estimates of the assets' current value would be precisely the kind of information that a reasonable shareholder would need and want to inform his decision and, therefore, the board's failure to disclose the valuations constituted a material omission within the meaning of rule 14a–9.

* * *

The majority's analysis of the problem starts from, the premise that the SEC disfavors inclusion of appraisal information in proxy materials.

---

1. The balance sheet prepared by SAVI's accounting firm listed total assets of $5,416,001. The SAVI realty was carried at acquisition costs totalling $3,396,605. The statement incorporated the board's estimates of the fair market value of the realty, ranging from $8,150,000 low to $12,950,000 high.

To support its characterization of SEC policy the majority relies on *Gerstle v. Gamble–Skogmo, Inc.,* 478 F.2d 1281 (2d Cir.1973), a case involving a merger between General Outdoor Advertising Company (GOA) and Gamble–Skogmo. In *Gerstle* the plaintiffs alleged that the proxy materials seeking approval of the merger were inadequate because, *inter alia,* they failed to include GOA management's valuations of its advertising plants. For additional enlightenment on the asset appraisal issue the district court had asked the SEC to submit an *amicus curiae* brief. This brief stated in pertinent part:

> When a balance sheet in a proxy statement for a merger reflects assets at an amount that is substantially lower than their current liquidating value, and liquidation of those assets is intended or can reasonably be anticipated, the textual or narrative portion of the proxy statement must contain whatever available material information about their current liquidating value is necessary to make the proxy statement not misleading.

478 F.2d at 1291. Further, the brief recognized that appraisals generally may be misleading but stated that appraisals of current liquidating value must be disclosed if they have been made by a qualified expert and have a sufficient basis in fact.

* * * On appeal, Judge Friendly, speaking for the Second Circuit, concluded that the SEC brief did not reflect SEC policy as understood by securities lawyers and accountants in 1963, the year in which the challenged proxy materials were distributed. To the contrary, Judge Friendly observed, it had long been an "article of faith" that appraisals of assets could not be included in proxy statements. *Id.* at 1293. He noted that the considerations underlying this policy against disclosure were distrust of reliability, concern of unwarranted reliance by investors, and the impracticability of the SEC's determining reliability in each instance. While acknowledging that "[t]he SEC may well determine that its policy ... may have deprived those who must decide whether or not to sell their securities ... of valuable information," *id.* at 1294, the court refused to impose liability on Gamble–Skogmo on the basis of a shift in SEC policy since 1963.[2]

* * *

I agree with the drafters of the SEC's *amicus curiae* brief submitted in the *Gerstle* case that in those instances in which the historical cost at which assets are carried in a balance sheet is substantially lower than their current market value, a proxy statement should disclose current appraisals if made by a qualified expert and sufficiently based in fact. In my judgment, this policy is consonant with the purpose underlying the 1934 Act.

* * *

---

2. The court ultimately found liability on the basis of the proxy statement's failure to disclose the fact that Gamble–Skogmo intended vigorously to pursue a plan to dispose of the advertising plants once the merger was effected.

* * * Moreover, it reflects a proper regard for the considerations of materiality critical to analysis under the rule 14a–9.[3]

Laboring under the constraining assumption that appraisal information must in most instances be excluded in deference to a blanket SEC prohibition against its disclosure, the district court found that the SAVI board members were not professional appraisers, not uniformly qualified to value real property, and made their valuations based on unascertained assumptions. These considerations alone, however, are insufficient to support the conclusion that the appraisals were potentially so misleading as to justify their exclusion from the proxy materials.

Although the board members were not professional appraisers and arrived at their estimates of value by an undocumented procedure, their appraisals bear certain indicia of reliability overlooked by the court below. Although some members of the board possessed greater expertise in the field than others, all were experienced in real estate matters. They had intimate knowledge of the SAVI properties and were well acquainted with the factors influencing value in the southern California real estate market. Further, the SAVI board treated the appraisals as reliable when they gave them to two potential purchasers without any disclaimer as to reliability. Most significant, they held themselves out to the shareholders as possessing sufficient expertise to value most of the properties themselves and dispense with a professional appraisal. Thus appellees' contentions that the board lacked the expertise to make a reliable appraisal have a hollow ring to them. The board either had no business marketing the property without securing expert appraisals or they had the requisite expertise to evaluate the properties and should share their opinions with their shareholders.

The final step in an analysis of SAVI's alleged liability for failure to disclose the board appraisals is to weigh the factors bearing on materiality against the likelihood that the estimates would mislead the shareholders. The information is unquestionably material within the meaning of rule 14a–9. However, appraisals by their very nature are susceptible to varying interpretation and even manipulation and the SAVI board estimates, while arguably expert, are not the work of a professional appraiser. Yet when these competing concerns are balanced, it is clear to me that the SAVI shareholders' need for the information outweighs the risk of their being misled. The SAVI board could have alleviated any concern that the shareholders might be misled or that the intent of the disclosure provisions of the securities laws might be subverted simply by qualifying disclosure of the board estimates with the same sort of language of disclaimer used to dissuade the shareholders from placing undue reliance on the Harrison appraisals. It must be noted also that furnishing some appraisals and not

---

3. Recalling that the SAVI proxy materials included the appraisals of two parcels of property, this court is not confronted with the problem troubling the second circuit in *Gerstle*, for appellees' own behavior attests to the fact that by 1977 it was no longer an article of faith that SEC policy barred disclosure of appraisals.

others as was done in this case could be misleading in itself by raising the implication in the minds of some that the value of other properties was unchanged. Reliance on the supposed SEC policy in this case to justify withholding appraisals from shareholders indeed has an ironic twist. The selling shareholders need protection against selling too cheaply. The appraisal information would have helped guard against that. The SAVI shareholders were denied that safeguard. The purchasers, on the other hand, were furnished the information. Thus, I conclude, contrary to the majority, that appellees' omission of the board's valuations rendered the proxy statement materially misleading in violation of rule 14a-9.

In addition to the offer from Investors, the SAVI board received inquiries from four other companies interested in a merger or a purchase of assets. One company, Shapell Industries, signaled the intensity of its interest by suggesting a purchase price of $1,300 per share, $350 more than the Investors offer, if certain contingencies could be met. The board elected not to pursue these so-called "promises in the sky" but rather to accept the firm offer from Investors. Appellants challenge the board's failure to divulge the information regarding other proposals to shareholders who were faced with the same decision whether or not to accept the terms of a proposed sale. Additionally, appellants contend that the information was necessary in order to clarify the reference in the proxy statement to "other recent proposals."

* * *

Again significance attaches to the fact that the proposed transaction involved the sale of assets undervalued in the proxy materials. What in another setting might have been a trivial omission becomes important in light of the fact that the SAVI shareholders had a dearth of information to aid their evaluation of the attractiveness of the recommended offer. Disclosure of information about the interest of three other companies and the conditional offer of a fourth might have provided some insight into the intensity of demand for SAVI's assets, their potential value, and the adequacy of the offer under consideration.

* * *

Because third-party offers generally reflect an objective assessment of a company's worth and do not have the potential for overstatement of value that taints appraisals, * * * there is less danger that shareholders will be misled by the disclosure of material but possibly unreliable information. The fact that the Shapell offer was conditional, however, counsels caution. Reliance on the figure advanced by Shapell might give the shareholders a false sense of SAVI's worth.

However, while there was a risk that the dollar amount attached to the Shapell offer might have sparked a gleam in a shareholder's eye and blinded him to the realities of the SAVI properties' development potential, I am convinced that the undisclosed offer's materiality outweighed the danger of misplaced reliance. A sentence or two of admonishment in the proxy statement would have served to alert shareholders to the dangers of jumping to unwarranted conclusions.

Problem

Buyer, Inc., is acquiring Seller, Inc. Both firms have outstanding equity securities registered under the 1934 act, and both are Delaware corporations. The transaction is structured as a reverse triangular merger with a subsidiary of Buyer, Inc., Subbuyer, Inc., merging into Seller, Inc. Seller, Inc., shareholders receive cash and debt securities in Buyer, Inc., in exchange for all their Seller, Inc., stock. The managers of Seller, Inc., recommend the deal to their shareholders because they believe their firm is not worth as much as the value offered. In other words, they have a sucker on the line. In the proxy materials of Seller, Inc., which of the following statements *must* be included? Of those that need not be included, which *can* be included at the option of Seller, Inc.?

1. The parties structured the transaction as a triangular merger rather than a straight merger of Seller into Buyer *solely* to deprive buyer shareholders of voting and appraisal rights.

2. Buyer, Inc., is likely not to pay dividends for some time because of its poor cash flow position.

3. The earnings per share of Buyer, Inc., are likely to go down after the acquisition because Buyer, Inc., paid a premium price for Seller, Inc.

4. Buyer, Inc., will be hard-pressed to meet its cash obligations on the new subordinated debt it issued to finance the acquisition; it will default if some of Seller's assets cannot be sold in accordance with some rather rosy projections.

5. The financial experts in Seller, Inc., have written a report that Buyer's experts have overvalued Seller in light of anticipated downturns in the industry. (Would it matter if the report is written by outside, independent experts hired by the company?)

6. Seller, Inc., is highly likely to lose a lawsuit pending against it, and damages will exceed 10 percent of the firm's assets.

7. Buyer, Inc., managers plan on selling some Seller, Inc., assets and keeping others, milking them for cash. Buyer will eliminate most research and development expenditures and plans on closing several Seller, Inc., plants in Indiana.

8. Buyer, Inc., managers have written a report claiming and quantifying, with rough figures, synergy gains from the "fit" of the two firms.

SECTION 3. THE MANDATORY DISCLOSURE DEBATE

The disclosure requirements in regulation 14A on proxy statements are one part of a much larger system of mandatory disclosure requirements that include registration statements for public offerings of securities, yearly reporting requirements for registered companies, and schedules for public tender offers. The Easterbrook & Fischel article below raises serious questions about the soundness of the traditional justifications that support these requirements.

EASTERBROOK & FISCHEL, MANDATORY DISCLOSURE AND THE PROTECTION OF INVESTORS
70 Va.L.Rev. 669, 670, 680–87 (1984).

Those who enacted these statutes asserted that they were necessary to eliminate fraud from the market and ensure that investors would receive the returns they expected; otherwise, the argument ran, people would withdraw their capital and the economy would stagnate. This explanation seemed especially pressing in 1933, for there had been frauds preceding the Depression and much disinvestment during. On this public interest story, the interests served by the laws are the same now as they were then, and so the laws have retained their beneficial structure.

No scholar should be comfortable with this simple tale. Fraud was unlawful in every state in 1933; we did not need a federal law to penalize lying and deceit. Fraud in the sale of education is more important to most people of moderate means (the supposed beneficiaries of the securities acts) than fraud in the sale of securities; these people have a much greater portion of their wealth invested in human capital than in the stock market. Yet there are no federal laws addressing these other assets. There were many securities frauds before 1933, and there have been many since. The Investors Overseas Services, National Student Marketing, Equity Funding, and OPM Leasing frauds of the last decade are every bit as spectacular as the frauds of the 1920s.

* * *

A mandatory disclosure system substantially limits firms' ability to remain silent. Just as importantly, it controls the time, place, and manner of disclosure.

* * *

What does a mandatory disclosure system add to the prohibition of fraud? The implicit public-interest justification for disclosure rules is that markets produce "too little" information about securities when the only rule is one against fraud. One often hears the assertion that information is a "public good," meaning that it can be used without being used up and that the producer of information cannot exclude others from receiving the benefits. If the producer of information cannot obtain all of its value, too little will be produced. It seems to follow that there are virtues in a rule requiring production of all information that would be forthcoming were gains fully appropriable.

This rationale gets us only so far. For one thing, it proves too much. No one can fully appropriate the value of information about toothpaste, but there is no federal rule about disclosing the efficacy of toothpaste in preventing cavities. Why are securities different? We leave the other products to competitive markets because of a conclusion that people who make or use a product (or test it as Consumers' Union does) will obtain enough of the gains from information to make the markets reasonably efficient.

Similarly, those who learn about a security may profit from their information. They cannot obtain all of the benefits, because others in the market will infer the news, and the price of the securities will adjust. The new price will "contain" the news, preventing the person who first learned it from taking further gains. This also means, however, that the value of news decays very quickly in securities markets; the information is "used up" as subsequent people see things, and these people then have their own incentives to go out and find information.[19]

The more sophisticated version of the public goods explanation is that although investors produce information, they produce both too much and too little. They produce too little because the benefits are imperfectly appropriable. If information is worth one hundred dollars to investors as a group, but no one can capture more than ten dollars of gains, then no one will obtain more than ten dollars worth of information. Investors produce too much information, though, if several create the *same* ten dollars bit of information (redundant production). Mandatory disclosure will prevent redundant production of information, the argument concludes.

The other source of excessive production is the gain available from forecasting the future. Some information, such as the quarterly earnings of a firm, offers opportunities for trading gains; the person who learns the news first can make great profits. In one important sense, though, the information is worthless. Trading on news that is bound to come out anyway does not change the future or lead to better investment in new securities. The price will ultimately change to reflect the true earnings. That it changes a day or so quicker is not of much moment for allocative efficiency. The lure of trading profits may induce people to spend a lot of effort and other resources "beating the market." Much of this is waste because the profit opportunity is larger than the efficiency gains from expediting the transition of prices. The argument concludes by observing that the prompt disclosure of information by the affected firm will extinguish the trading opportunity. When everyone knows the truth, no one can speculate on it. Investors as a group would pay to have these trading gains (and the costly search for information) eliminated. What better way to do this then mandatory disclosure by the firm that knows the truth?

---

19. See Manne, supra note 4, at 42–43. The dynamic process by which stock markets impound information in prices, extinguishing the value of "old news" while creating incentives to find "new news," is described in Grossman & Stiglitz, On the Impossibility of Informationally Efficient Markets, 70 Am.Econ.Rev. 383 (1980).

These arguments have a common problem: they do not link the benefit of disclosure and the benefit of *mandatory* disclosure. If disclosure is worthwhile to investors, the firm can profit by providing it. The firm is in privity with its investors, and the Coase Theorem suggests that firm and investors can strike a mutually beneficial bargain. A decision by the firm effectively "coordinates" the acts of many investors who could not bargain directly.

To see how this works, take a simple example of a firm that wants to issue new securities. The firm has a project (say, the manufacture of a new computer) that it expects to be profitable. If the firm simply asked for money without disclosing the project and managers involved, however, it would get nothing. Investors would assume the worst, because, they would reason that if the firm had anything good to say for itself it would do so. Silence means bad news. A firm with a good project, seeking to distinguish itself from a firm with a mediocre project (or no project at all), would disclose the optimal amount of information. That is, it would disclose more and more so long as the cost of disclosure (both direct costs of dissemination and indirect costs of giving information to rivals) was worthwhile to investors as a whole.

The firm deals with all actual and prospective investors. Unlike an investor who deals only in a portion of a firm's stock, and thus cannot capture the full value of information, the firm controls all of its investments and can appropriate the full value of information. The firm that discloses more can sell its stock for more, indeed for as much more as the full value of all information.

The process works for bad news as well as for good. Once the firm starts disclosing it cannot stop short of making any critical revelation, because investors always assume the worst. It must disclose the bad with the good, lest investors assume that the bad is even worse than it is. And the firm cannot stand on its say-so alone. Mere disclosure would be enough if the rule against fraud were perfectly enforced, but it is not. Thus the firm uses the verification and certification devices described in Part I. Given these devices, a rule compelling disclosure seems redundant, and if the fraud penalty and verification devices do not work, a rule compelling disclosure is not apt to be enforceable either.

The principle of self-induced disclosure as a solution to the lack of property rights in information applies to trading in the secondary market as well as to the initial issuance of stock. The firm's investors always want to be able to sell their stock in the aftermarket for the highest price. Their ability to do so depends on a flow of believable information (otherwise potential buyers reduce the bid prices, assuming the worst). For most information about a firm, the firm itself can create and distribute the knowledge at less cost than the shareholders, and the firm's decision, because it reflects the value to all shareholders, will be correct at the margin. A firm that wants the highest possible price when it issues stock must take all cost-justified steps to make the stock valuable in the aftermarket, so it must make a believable pledge to continue disclosing.

The evidence bears this out. Firms have been disclosing the most important facts about themselves—and certifying these facts through third parties—as long as there have been firms. It is possible to trace the use of auditors back to the beginning of the corporation, and at the time the '34 Act, which created the requirement of annual disclosure by listed companies, became law, every firm traded on the national markets made voluminous public disclosures certified by independent auditors. Between 1934 and 1964, annual disclosure was required only of those firms traded on national exchanges. (In 1964 the statute was amended to cover all firms with more than a specified number of investors.) Firms could avoid disclosure by delisting or not listing initially. Nonetheless, firms eagerly listed themselves on an exchange and disclosed; firms that were not listed also disclosed substantial amounts of data, following the pattern set by those covered by the statute. Even today, the securities of state and local governments are exempt from the mandatory disclosure rules, yet these issuers routinely supply voluminous information to purchasers.

* * *

That information is a "public good" means that investors acting independently do the wrong amount of information-gathering, but for reasons we have explained, the self-interest of firms' managers lead them to supply roughly the amount of information investors as a group desire. This amount is "rough," however, because of the certification and verification costs in the supply of information. * * * There is one other reason why firms' disclosures may not be optimal: third party effects.

The information produced by one firm for its investors may be valuable to investors in other firms. Firm A's statements may reveal something about the industry in which Firm A operates—if only the size of Firm A's anticipated production—that other participants in the industry can use in planning their own operations. There may be other collateral benefits to investors in rival firms. Yet Firm A cannot charge the investors in these other firms for the benefits, although they would be willing to pay for them. Because they cannot be charged, the information will be underproduced.

* * *

There is a similar free riding problem in the disclosure of information that facilitates comparisons among firms. Firm C may know something that makes it attractive relative to D. It cannot convey this information effectively, however, without conveying information about D's plans and prospects. The information about D will redound partly to the benefit of present or prospective investors in D, and Firm C cannot obtain compensation. Firm C could appropriate part of the gain by buying or selling D's stock, but this is a costly transaction, and Firm C could not appropriate the full gain without owning D, E, F, G, and so on, outright. An increase in the size of firms to allow greater internalization of information has other costs, including monopoly and a reduction in investors' ability to diversify their holdings.

* * *

Or suppose there is an optimal format for communicating information to investors. Some disclosures are easier to understand, verify, etc., than others, while some disclosures tend more to hide than to reveal information. If contracts among all investors in society could be written costlessly, the investors would require all firms to identify and use the optimal format of disclosure. The costs may be too high, though, for one firm acting on its own. The optimal form of disclosure may entail use of some specialized language (one can think of accounting principles, with their detailed definitions, as a specialized disclosure language), yet no one firm can obtain a large share of the benefits of inventing and employing this language; others will be able to use the format without charge. Sometimes, too, the ease of using a given method of disclosure will depend on other firms adopting the same format, so as to facilitate comparisons across investments. Other firms may not be anxious to cooperate.

Mandatory disclosure rules promulgated by the government are one means to achieve standardization, but it does not follow that mandatory disclosure is necessary. Markets frequently devise ingenious solutions to problems of information. Indeed, the problems faced by sellers of securities are not much different from those involved in bringing new products to market. Mass sale of records and stereo systems was facilitated by the development of standard record speeds. Color television was not feasible until manufacturers and broadcasters agreed on a standard method of transmission. The new laser compact disk players are greatly aided in competing against tapes and records by the standard promulgated by Phillips, the holder of an important patent. Sometimes trade associations may devise such standards, as the electronics industry and, in part, the accounting industry have done. Whether standardization may be achieved more cheaply by private or governmental responses is an empirical question.

The point in Easterbrook and Fischel's argument that tends to raise eyebrows is their assertion that firms have an incentive, absent third-party effects, to promptly disclose bad news as well as good. See, e.g., Coffee, *Market Failure and the Economic Case for a Mandatory Disclosure System*, 70 Va.L.Rev. 717, 741 (1984). If the disclosure of bad news will have a negative impact on the personal situation of managers, will they, in the best interests of the *firm*, promptly disclose the news or will they delay the disclosure until they can make personal arrangements to minimize its effect on their lives (engage in insider trading or leave for greener pastures, for example)? Moreover, are managers anxious to disclose good news when such disclosures are in their firm's interest? Could a manager withhold or underplay good news to buy the firm (in a leveraged buyout)? In sum, is a mandatory disclosure system necessary to the proper functioning of a general antifraud rule when managers engage in "final period" behavior?

In the article the authors focus explicitly on the level of voluntary firm disclosures that would attend the initial issuance of stock and on disclosures that would inform the secondary trading market if mandatory disclosure regulations were removed. Would the firm make similar voluntary disclosures that sufficiently inform shareholders exercising their voting privilege if there were no mandatory requirements in this context? What argument would the authors make on the issue of voting disclosures? If selling-firm managers in proxy solicitations are seeking only an affirmative vote rather than a maximum share price in the market, do they have strong incentives to disclose negative information? What is the typical position of the target-firm managers after a successful acquisition? Do such managers have final-period problems?

Chapter Three

SUCCESSOR LIABILITY: THE EFFECT OF AN ACQUISITION ON BONDHOLDERS, PATENT LICENSORS, LESSORS, LABOR UNION MEMBERS, PENSIONERS, AND CONTINGENT PRODUCT, ENVIRONMENTAL, AND CIVIL RIGHTS CLAIMANTS

SUBCHAPTER A. INTRODUCTION TO THE PROBLEMS OF EXTERNALITIES AND OPPORTUNISTIC BEHAVIOR IN ACQUISITIONS

In a sophisticated acquisition negotiation the buyer and the seller do not negotiate solely over a single price for the firm. They often negotiate by item to maximize the joint gains achieved by the parties in the acquisition. The seller and the buyer may disagree on the value of some of the seller's significant rights and obligations. The seller, for example, may value select income-producing assets more highly than the buyer, or the seller may calculate the cost of select obligations to be less than the cost estimated by the buyer. If so, the seller ought not to transfer these assets and obligations in the acquisition. Rather, the seller should dispose of them before or after the acquisition or retain them, as it sees fit. In other words, the parties can maximize the value of the deal by allocating the rights and obligations to the party that puts the highest value on those producing income and the lowest value on those requiring expenditures.

A simple example illustrates the point. A seller with an ongoing business that produces gears for all types of machinery has the prospect of paying on significant product liability claims. The firm has already paid to settle three product liability lawsuits and anticipates several more. The value of the business to the seller without the claims is $575,000. The value of the business to the buyer without the claims is

$600,000. Assume however that the seller, more confident of the quality of the gears it has produced, values the product liability claims (in discounted present value terms) at a negative $50,000, putting the total present value of the firm to the seller at $525,000. The buyer, on the other hand, believes that gears produced during the seller's ownership of the firm will generate liability that will cost, in present dollars, $100,000, putting the total present value of the firm to the buyer at $500,000. As a consequence, there is no room for a deal if the buyer must buy the firm whole and absorb the contingent liabilities.

On the other hand, if the seller agrees to retain responsibility for all product liability claims based on gears produced when the seller owned the firm, the deal can close at a price between $600,000 and $575,000. In essence, the buyer agrees to pay the seller for assuming the contingent claims because the seller places a lower cost on them than does the buyer. From a position of no overlap, the parties have created a joint gain of $25,000 [1] that they are now free to split in negotiations over the purchase price. If we do not allow the parties to allocate the contingent claims in an acquisition, then we destroy the deal at the cost of denying the buyer—the party that values most highly the seller's gear-producing assets, perhaps because it can produce gears at a lower marginal cost—the ability to produce gears.

Our example applies not only to obligations that represent expenditures on the income statement but also to rights and obligations that represent income flows. In our basic example substitute a valuable patent license for the contingent liabilities and assume the same basic valuation of the gear business—$600,000 for the buyer and $575,000 for the seller. The buyer believes the firm is worth only $650,000 because it values an important patent held by the seller, in present dollars, at $50,000. The seller believes the firm is worth $700,000 because it values the patent at $175,000. If the seller retains the patent, the deal works; otherwise it does not. What is the negotiation range if the seller retains the patent? If the buyer must have permission from the patent owner to produce gears, how can the parties structure the deal so that the seller retains the full economic fruits of the patent? How ought the parties to determine the royalty payments?

The darker side of acquisitions (and recapitalizations as well) consists of the parties' creation of joint gains by evading preexisting obligations to third parties who are not represented in the bargaining. If the parties are successful in using an acquisition to avoid or overburden obligations owed to third parties, they can split the gains created by the evasion or additional burden. Consider our example of the gear firm with significant potential product liability claims. The reason for the disparate evaluation of the claims between buyer and seller may be

---

1. The joint gain is calculated by comparing the combined position of the buyer and the seller before the acquisition and their combined position after the acquisition. If, for example, the seller is a poor negotiator and sells the firm, without liabilities, for $575,000, the seller is no better or worse off and the buyer has bought a firm it values at $600,000 for $575,000, for a net gain to the buyer of $25,000.

that the two parties have different predictions about the number and success of future claims, given the quality of the seller's production runs. On the other hand, the buyer and the seller may agree on their predictions on the number and likely success of future claims—that is, both value them at $100,000 if someone has to pay them—but the seller may believe that it can avoid at least half the claims if it sells its business, retains the liabilities, and dissolves, distributing the sale proceeds to its shareholders before putative plaintiffs can sue the firm to collect for their injuries.

Since the product liability claimants are not represented in the acquisition, indeed many future claimants may not know at the time of the acquisition that they are interested parties, the claimants cannot protect themselves from the consequences of the deal. If the seller is correct that it can avoid half the product liability claims in the aftermath of an acquisition, then the seller and the buyer have created a joint gain of $25,000 through the acquisition, which they can divide, at the expense of the contingent claimants. Economists label these costs to product liability claimants, among others, "externalities," or "third-party effects," social costs not borne by the contracting parties.[2] An important function of our legal system is to protect potential victims of externalities.

All contingent claimants, including those with environmental or employment discrimination claims, are potential acquisition victims. Another common victim of acquisitions is the United States government. If the parties to an acquisition are motivated solely by tax savings, that is, the parties pay significantly less total tax after the acquisition than before, then they have created joint gains that the parties can divide at the expense of the United States Treasury. It matters little which of the two parties to an acquisition actually realizes the tax gains, because the parties can allocate the value of the gains among themselves in the purchase price. We will discuss the efforts of Congress and the Internal Revenue Service to combat tax-motivated acquisitions in a later chapter. In the last third of this chapter we focus on the legal protections for contingent claimants.

In designing legal protections for contingent claimants, we could begin with a rule that refuses to allow the seller to retain the liabilities in any acquisition. In other words, the courts could simply attach the liabilities to the buyer, regardless of the parties' efforts to contract otherwise. This stops acquisitions designed largely to avoid future

---

2. The identification of externalities is not an exact science. For example, one could argue that theoretically the purchasers of the gears, when they decided how much they were willing to pay for the gears, ought to have "priced" or "internalized" the possibility that their product liability claims, if any, could be cut off by an acquisition of the producer. In other words, absent a contract warranty that the seller will not attempt to defeat the product liability claims through an acquisition, the purchaser of gears ought to pay fractionally less for the gears. This assumes more knowledge and sophistication on the part of gear customers than is normally the case, however, and in any event the argument does not cover those injured by defective gears that were not gear customers (innocent bystanders, for example).

liabilities, but it also stops legitimate acquisitions in which the seller and the buyer, both intending to pay all valid claims, simply disagree on their assessment of the present value of the future claims. Unless judges can argue successfully that such a rule blocks far fewer legitimate acquisitions than harmful acquisitions, or that an alternative rule that distinguishes the harmful from the beneficial acquisitions is not workable, our courts must design rules that catch the harmful acquisitions and permit legitimate deals. As you read the cases on contingent liabilities in the last third of the chapter, you can assess the success of our courts in this endeavor.

Distinguished from the contingent claimants are parties that have contractual relationships with the seller, the value of which may be adversely affected by an acquisition. This class includes creditors—long-term bondholders to suppliers, licensors of intellectual property rights, real estate or personalty lessors, and employees (white collar or blue collar, unionized or nonunionized). Members of this class can claim damage in any specific acquisition: the creditors can see the value of their debt decrease as the default risk of the debt increases; licensors or lessors may find their grants of permission overburdened or their potential income from royalties or rent diminished; and employees may find themselves out of work or working for less. With the occurrence of any of these events in an acquisition, the injured parties usually call foul and ask for legal redress.

Their argument has bite. In each case the aggrieved party has incurred substantial costs (or foregone significant nonrecurring opportunities) in reliance on a continuing relationship with the firm, and these costs may have put the party at a strategic disadvantage. If the firm refuses (or threatens to refuse, to gain a bargaining advantage) to honor its promises, the aggrieved party loses the value of its sunk costs. Consider, for example, the position of a middle manager who has spent several years learning how to manage a small part of the seller's business. If she is fired, she will lose the value of her skills that are tailored to the specific people and assets that she manages. Other employers will not pay her for the true value of these skills. An employer, realizing her predicament, is tempted to offer her a reduced salary, well below the increases it implicitly promised to pay her when she was hired, and to expropriate some of the value of her asset-specific skills. Yet she resists, relying on her claim for contract damages in court. Can the employer sell the business to a third party, which can threaten to terminate her free of any contract claims and thus extract a reduced salary agreement? This kind of behavior is often labeled opportunistic by economists.

Bondholders have made a similar claim. A firm asks for and receives cash from investors in exchange for the firm's promise to repay the principal in the future and to pay a fixed interest for the privilege of using the money. Is there an implicit promise that the firm will maintain its capital structure in more or less the same basic pattern? Once the firm collects the cash from the bondholders, does it breach the implicit promise by adding so much additional debt that the risk of default on the original bonds is substantially increased? Even if so, can the firm sell to a third party, which materially increases the firm's leverage, without consideration for the selling firm's implicit promise?

In theory, parties who contract with a firm need not be helpless victims of acquisitions. They can protect themselves in a variety of ways in their initial contracts against any potential acquisition. At the time of contracting, they can negotiate for specific promises or warranties against opportunistic behavior or they can simply demand additional compensation for the risk of opportunistic behavior (that is, they can discount the value of the firm's return promise to pay). Our middle manager could, for example, at the time of her hiring have demanded in writing a schedule of raises and a generous severance payment for any loss of her position without cause, or a higher initial salary (with a signing bonus, perhaps) if the firm was unwilling to satisfy her demand for a detailed written contract. In other words, contractual claimants such as the middle manager are not victims of externalities; they can, theoretically, price or internalize the costs of a firm's prospective avoidance of their claims.

If theory matches reality, the role of legal rules is very limited. The judges ought to be empowered only to interpret contract language or to provide gap fillers or default terms if the contract language is silent or ambiguous. Does the middle manager's contract with the seller contain any implicit protections against loss of employment due to control changes? If both parties have perfect information, the courts' choice of default terms as favoring one party or the other does not matter, as long as the courts are predictable over time. We presume the parties have accepted whatever default rule is in force by their choice not to explicitly contract to avoid it. In our example it ought not to matter if courts favor the firm by assuming that the middle managers have no protection against control changes if the contract is silent.

In theory, then, applicable legal rules are relevant in contract cases only to facilitate and order the judge's function of finding and carrying out the intent of the parties to the original bargain. The best example of a system of legal rules that seems, with minor exceptions, to take its basic character from these views is the rules covering the status of creditors (particularly long-term creditors) and real estate lessors in acquisitions. We cover these rules in the first part of the chapter. When reading the materials, ask yourself whether the rules for patent licensors also fit in this category.

On the other hand, theory does not always match fact. Some classes of parties may have bargaining disadvantages stemming from the asymmetric distribution of information, bargaining capacity, perspicacity about the future, or market power. Economists refer to these cases as market failures; we cannot rely on unregulated private autonomy to order the parties' affairs in socially useful ways. When such cases exist, lawmakers must first identify the systemic disadvantages and then design appropriate legal protections. These choices are politically charged, with interest groups claiming special needs. Strong views, couched in morality and political theory but tinged with self-interest, are the order of the day. The examples in the following materials of bargaining situations that our society currently includes in this category of market failures are contained in the second part of the chapter, dealing with collective bargaining agreements and with employee pension and welfare benefit plans.

Indeed, the legislative and judicial process may itself be the vehicle for opportunistic behavior, as some groups who do not deserve or need protection extract value from their contract counterparts that was not part of the original bargain. Our middle manager gets a windfall at the expense of the seller if she explicitly gave up a control change clause in favor of a larger initial salary and is later able to convince a court that she should be awarded damages for the loss of her job due to an acquisition or is able to convince a state legislature to pass a statute protecting her position in acquisitions. Finally, there is the very pragmatic argument advanced by some that acquisitions are one of the time-honored methods of avoiding otherwise overly burdensome governmental regulation. If a firm has negotiated collective bargaining agreements that prove to be too generous in light of economic conditions, it is easier to sell the assets of the firm to another party, which takes the firm free of the contracts, than to negotiate wage concessions.

Note
Bargaining Theory

In our example of a negotiation over the sale of a gear-manufacturing business in which the parties disagreed over the value of future product liability claims and of a patent, we have a classic example of the fundamental tension in multi-issue bargaining between claiming and creating value. The tension is best explained in general terms in D. Lax & J. Sebenius, *The Manager as Negotiator* 29–30, 33–35 (1986):

> We assume that each negotiator strives to advance his interests, whether they are narrowly conceived or include such concerns as improving the relationship, acting in accord with conceptions of equity, or furthering the welfare of others. Negotiators must learn, in part from each other, what is jointly possible and desirable. To do so requires some degree of cooperation. But, at the same time, they seek to advance their individual interests. This involves some degree of competition.
>
> That negotiation includes cooperation and competition, common and conflicting interests, is nothing new. In fact, it is typically understood that these elements are both present and can be disentangled. Deep down, however, some people believe that the elements of conflict are illusory, that meaningful communication will erase any such unfortunate misperceptions. Others see mainly competition and take the cooperative pieces to be minimal. Some overtly acknowledge

the reality of each aspect but direct all their attention to one of them and wish, pretend, or act as if the other does not exist. Still others hold to a more balanced view that accepts both elements as significant but seeks to treat them separately.... [W]e argue that all these approaches are flawed.

A deeper analysis shows that the competitive and cooperative elements are inextricably entwined. In practice, they cannot be separated. This bonding is fundamentally important to the analysis, structuring, and conduct of negotiation. There is a central, inescapable tension between cooperative moves to create value jointly and competitive moves to gain individual advantage. This tension affects virtually all tactical and strategic choice. Analysts must come to grips with it; negotiators must manage it. Neither denial nor discomfort will make it disappear.

* * *

Value creating and value claiming are linked parts of negotiation. Both processes are present. No matter how much creative problem solving enlarges the pie, it must still be divided; value that has been created must be claimed. And, if the pie is not enlarged, there will be less to divide; there is more value to be claimed if one has helped create it first. An essential tension in negotiation exists between cooperative moves to create value and competitive moves to claim it.

* * *

The tension between cooperative moves to create value and competitive moves to claim it is greatly exacerbated by the interaction of the tactics used either to create or claim value.

First, tactics for claiming value (which we will call "claiming tactics") can impede its creation. Exaggerating the value of concessions and minimizing the benefit of others' concessions presents a distorted picture of one's relative preferences; thus, mutually beneficial trades may not be discovered. Making threats or commitments to highly favorable outcomes surely impede hearing and understanding others' interests. Concealing information may also cause one to leave joint gains on the table. In fact, excessive use of tactics for claiming value may well sour the parties' relationship and reduce the trust between them. Such tactics may also evoke a variety of unhelpful interests. Conflict may escalate and make joint prospects less appealing and settlement less likely.

Second, approaches to creating value are vulnerable to tactics for claiming value. Revealing information about one's relative preferences is risky. If the mayor states that she gives relatively greater weight to wage reductions than to civilian review board composition, the union representative may respond by saying (untruthfully) that the union members also feel more strongly about wage reductions, but would be willing to give in a little on wage reductions if the mayor will compensate them handsomely by completely changing the board. (An honest disclosure can be met with a strategic disclosure taking advantage of the revealed preferences.) The information that a negotiator would accept position A in return for a favorable resolution on a second issue can be exploited: "So, you'll accept A. Good. Now, let's move on to discuss the merits of the second issue." The willingness to make a new, creative offer can often be taken as a sign that its proposer is able and willing to make further concessions. Thus, such offers sometimes remain undisclosed. Even purely shared interests can be held hostage in exchange for concessions on other issues. Though a divorcing husband and wife may both prefer giving the wife custody of the child, the husband may "suddenly" develop strong parental instincts to extract concessions on alimony in return for giving the wife custody.

In tactical choices, each negotiator thus has reasons not [to] be open and cooperative. Each also has apparent incentives to try to claim value. Moves to claim value thus tend to drive out moves to create it. Yet, if both choose to claim value, by being dishonest or less than forthcoming about preferences, beliefs, or minimum requirements, they may miss mutually beneficial terms for agreement.

Indeed, the structure of many bargaining situations suggests that negotiators will tend to leave joint gains on the table or even reach impasses when mutually acceptable agreements are available.

Questions

1. If the seller wanted to be a pure "value claimer," it would exaggerate the value of the patent and undervalue the size of potential product liability claims. What is the danger of this approach?

2. On the other hand, if the seller wanted to be a pure "value creator," it would disclose, accurately and fully, its belief about the value of the patent and the size of the potential product liability claims. What is the danger of this approach?

3. How ought a seller to decide whether to disclose or hold back material information?

SUBCHAPTER B. THE EFFECT OF TRANSACTIONS ON DEBT OBLIGATIONS, REAL AND INTELLECTUAL PROPERTY RIGHTS, AND OTHER CONTRACT RIGHTS

SECTION 1. THE BASIC DISTINCTIONS

Statutory Mergers

All state codes have specific statutes on the effect of a statutory merger on the preexisting rights and obligations of the constituent parties. Delaware's provisions are sections 259 and 261 in the Delaware General Corporation Law. Please read these sections in your supplement. As a general matter, the statutes contain language directing that all rights and obligations of the constituent parties pass to the surviving entity in a statutory merger "as a matter of law." Do the merger statutes override contracts that are implicitly or expressly nonassignable? In other words, if one firm holds nonassignable contracts, can a second firm merge with the first and claim rights under the contracts? Does your answer depend on which firm survives in the merger?

PPG INDUSTRIES INC. v. GUARDIAN INDUSTRIES CORP.

United States Court of Appeals, Sixth Circuit, 1979.
597 F.2d 1090, cert. denied 444 U.S. 930, 100 S.Ct. 272, 62 L.Ed.2d 187 (1979).

LIVELY, CIRCUIT JUDGE.

The question in this case is whether the surviving or resultant corporation in a statutory merger acquires patent license rights of the constituent corporations.

* * *

Prior to 1964 both PPG and Permaglass, Inc., were engaged in fabrication of glass products which required that sheets of glass be shaped for particular uses. Independently of each other the two fabricators developed similar processes which involved "floating glass on a bed of gas, while it was being heated and bent." This process is known in the industry as "gas hearth technology" and "air float technology"; the two terms are interchangeable. After a period of negotiations PPG and Permaglass entered into an agreement on January 1, 1964 whereby each granted rights to the other under "gas hearth system" patents already issued and in the process of prosecution.

* * *

Eleven patents are involved in this suit. Nine of them originated with Permaglass and were licensed to PPG as exclusive licensee under Section 3.2, subject to the non-exclusive, non-transferable reservation to Permaglass set forth in Section 3.3. Two of the patents originated with PPG. Section 4.1 granted a non-exclusive, non-transferable license to Permaglass with respect to the two PPG patents. * * *

As of December 1969 Permaglass was merged into Guardian pursuant to applicable statutes of Ohio and Delaware. Guardian was engaged primarily in the business of fabricating and distributing windshields for automobiles and trucks. It had decided to construct a facility to manufacture raw glass and the capacity of that facility would be greater than its own requirements. Permaglass had no glass manufacturing capability and it was contemplated that its operations would utilize a large part of the excess output of the proposed Guardian facility.

The "Agreement of Merger" between Permaglass and Guardian did not refer specifically to the 1964 agreement between PPG and Permaglass. However, among Permaglass' representations in the agreement was the following:

(g) Permaglass is the owner, assignee or licensee of such patents, trademarks, trade names and copyrights as are listed and described in Exhibit "C" attached hereto. None of such patents, trademarks, trade names or copyrights is in litigation and Permaglass has not received any notice of conflict with the asserted rights of third parties relative to the use thereof.

Listed on Exhibit "C" to the merger agreement are the nine patents originally developed by Permaglass and licensed to PPG under the 1964 agreement which are involved in this infringement action.

Shortly after the merger was consummated PPG filed the present action, claiming infringement by Guardian in the use of apparatus and processes described and claimed in eleven patents which were identified by number and origin. The eleven patents were covered by the terms of the 1964 agreement. PPG asserted that it became the exclusive licensee of the nine patents which originated with Permaglass under the 1964 agreement and that the rights reserved by Permaglass were personal to it and non-transferable and non-assignable. PPG also claimed that Guardian had no rights with respect to the two patents which had originated with PPG because the license under these patents was personal to Permaglass and non-transferable and non-assignable except with the permission of PPG. * * *

One of the defenses pled by Guardian in its answer was that it was a licensee of the patents in suit. It described the merger with Permaglass and claimed it "had succeeded to all rights, powers, ownerships, etc., of Permaglass, and as Permaglass' successor, defendant is legally entitled to operate in place of Permaglass under the January 1, 1964 agreement between Permaglass and plaintiff, free of any claim of infringement of the patents...."

* * *

Questions with respect to the assignability of a patent license are controlled by federal law. It has long been held by federal courts that agreements granting patent licenses are personal and not assignable unless expressly made so. * * * This has been the rule at least since 1852 when the Supreme Court decided Troy Iron & Nail v. Corning, 55 U.S. (14 How.) 193, 14 L.Ed. 383 (1852). * * * The district court recognized this rule in the present case, but concluded that where patent licenses are claimed to pass by operation of law to the resultant or surviving corporation in a statutory merger there has been no assignment or transfer.

* * *

Guardian relies on two classes of cases where rights of a constituent corporation have been held to pass by merger to the resultant corporation even though such rights are not otherwise assignable or transferable. It points out that the courts have consistently held that "shop rights" do pass in a statutory merger. * * * A shop right is an implied license which accrues to an employer in cases where an employee has perfected a patentable device while working for the employer. Though the employee is the owner of the patent he is estopped from claiming infringement by the employer. This estoppel arises from the fact that the patent work has been done on the employer's time and that the employer has furnished materials for the experiments and financial backing to the employee.

The rule that prevents an employee-inventor from claiming infringement against a successor to the entire business and good will of his employer is but one feature of the broad doctrine of estoppel which underlies the shop right cases. No element of estoppel exists in the present case. The license rights of Permaglass did not arise by implication. They were bargained for at arms length and the agreement which defines the rights of the parties provides that Permaglass received non-transferable, non-assignable personal licenses. We do not believe that the express prohibition against assignment and transfer in a written instrument may be held ineffective by analogy to a rule based on estoppel in situations where there is no written contract and the rights of the parties have arisen by implication because of their past relationship.

The other group of cases which the district court and Guardian found to be analogous hold that the resultant corporation in a merger succeeds to the rights of the constituent corporations under real estate leases. * * * The most obvious difficulty in drawing an analogy between the lease cases and those concerning patent licenses is that a lease is an interest in real property. As such, it is subject to the deep-rooted policy against restraints on alienation. Applying this policy, courts have construed provisions against assignability in leases strictly and have concluded that they do not prevent the passage of interests by operation of law. * * * There is no similar policy which is offended by the decision of a patent owner to make a license under his patent personal to the licensee, and non-assignable and non-transferable. In fact the law treats a license as if it contained these restrictions in the absence of express provisions to the contrary.

We conclude that the district court misconceived the intent of the parties to the 1964 agreement. We believe the district court put the burden on the wrong party in stating:

> Because the parties failed to provide that Permaglass' rights under the 1964 license agreement would not pass to the corporation surviving a merger, the Court finds that Guardian succeeded to Permaglass' license pursuant to 8 Del.C. § 259, and Ohio Revised Code §§ 1701.81 and 1701.83.

428 F.Supp. at 796.

The agreement provides with respect to the license which Permaglass granted to PPG that Permaglass reserved "a non-exclusive, non-transferable, royalty-free, world-wide right and license *for the benefit and use of Permaglass.*" (emphasis added). Similarly, with respect to its own two patents, PPG granted to Permaglass "a non-exclusive, non-transferable, royalty-free right and license...." Further, the agreement provides that both it and the license granted to Permaglass "shall be personal to PERMAGLASS and non-assignable except with the consent of PPG first obtained in writing."

The quoted language from Sections 3, 4 and 9 of the 1964 agreement evinces an intent that only Permaglass was to enjoy the privileges of licensee. If the parties had intended an exception in the event of a merger, it would have been a simple matter to have so provided in the agreement. Guardian contends such an exception is not necessary since it is universally recognized that patent licenses pass from a licensee to the resultant corporation in case of a merger. This does not appear to be the case. In *Packard Instrument Co. v. ANS, Inc.*, 416 F.2d 943 (2d Cir.1969), a license agreement provided that rights thereunder could not be transferred or assigned "except ... (b) if the entire ownership and business of ANS is transferred by sale, merger, or consolidation,...." 416 F.2d at 944 n. 1. Similarly, the agreement construed in *Freeman v. Seiberling Rubber Co.*, 72 F.2d 124 (6th Cir. 1934), provided that the license was not assignable except with the entire business and good will of the licensee.[1] We conclude that if the parties had intended an exception in case of a merger to the provisions against assignment and transfer they would have included it in the agreement. It should be noted also that the district court in *Packard, supra,* held that an assignment had taken place when the licensee was merged into another corporation.

The district court also held that the patent licenses in the present case were not transferred because they passed by operation of law from Permaglass to Guardian. This conclusion is based on the theory of continuity which underlies a true merger. However, the theory of continuity relates to the fact that there is no dissolution of the constituent corporations and, even though they cease to exist, their essential corporate attributes are vested by operation of law in the surviving or resultant corporation.

* * *

... It does not mean that there is no transfer of particular assets from a constituent corporation to the surviving or resultant one.

The Ohio merger statute provides that following a merger all property of a constituent corporation shall be "deemed to be *transferred* to and vested in the surviving or new corporation without further act or deed,...." (emphasis added). Ohio Revised Code, [former] § 1701.81(A)(4). This indicates that the transfer is by operation of law, not that there is no transfer of assets in a merger situation. The Delaware statute, which was also involved in the Permaglass–Guardian merger, provides that the property of the constituent corporations "shall be vested in the corporation surviving or resulting from such merger or consolidation,...." 8 Del.C. § 259(a). The Third Circuit has

---

1. The parties to the 1964 agreement included language almost identical to that in *Packard* and *Freeman* in a later license agreement which they executed in 1969. See note 2, *infra.*

construed the "shall be vested" language of the Delaware statute as follows: "In short, the underlying property of the constituent corporations is *transferred* to the resultant corporation upon the carrying out of the consolidation or merger...." *Koppers Coal & Transportation Co. v. United States,* 107 F.2d 706, 708 (3d Cir.1939). (emphasis added).

In his opinion in *Koppers,* Judge Biggs disposed of arguments very similar to those of Guardian in the present case, based on the theory of continuity. Terming such arguments "metaphysical" he found them completely at odds with the language of the Delaware statute. *Id.* Finally, on this point, the parties themselves provided in the merger agreement that all property of Permaglass "shall be deemed transferred to and shall vest in Guardian without further act or deed...." A transfer is no less a transfer because it takes place by operation of law rather than by a particular act of the parties. The merger was effected by the parties and the transfer was a result of their act of merging.

Thus, Sections 3, 4 and 9 of the 1964 agreement between PPG and Permaglass show an intent that the licenses held by Permaglass in the eleven patents in suit not be transferable. While this conclusion disposes of the license defense as to all eleven patents, it should be noted that Guardian's claim to licenses under the two patents which originated with PPG is also defeated by Section 11.2 of the 1964 agreement. This section addresses a different concern from that addressed in Sections 3, 4 and 9. The restrictions on transferability and assignability in those sections prevent the patent licenses from becoming the property of third parties. The termination clause, however, provides that Permaglass' license with respect to the two PPG patents will terminate if the ownership of a majority of the voting stock of Permaglass passes from the 1964 stockholders to designated classes of persons, even though the licenses themselves might never have changed hands.

Apparently PPG was willing for Permaglass to continue as licensee under the nine patents even though ownership of its stock might change. These patents originated with Permaglass and so long as Permaglass continued to use the licenses for its own benefit a mere change in ownership of Permaglass stock would not nullify the licenses. Only a transfer or assignment would cause a termination. However, the agreement provides for termination with respect to the two original PPG patents in the event of an indirect takeover of Permaglass by a change in the ownership of a majority of its stock. The fact that PPG sought and obtained a stricter provision with respect to the two patents which it originally owned in no way indicates an intention to permit transfer of licenses under the other nine in case of a merger. None of the eleven licenses was transferable; but two of them, those involving PPG's own development in the field of gas hearth technology, were not to continue even for the benefit of the licensee if it came under the control of a manufacturer of automobiles or a competitor of PPG in the glass industry "other than the present owners" of Permaglass. A consistency among the provisions of the agreement is discernible when the different origins of the various patents are considered.

* * *

Questions

1. Would the result in *PPG Industries* be different if Guardian had merged into Permaglass? If Guardian and Permaglass had combined using a consolidation (both merging into a new shell corporation created for the transaction)? If Guardian had bought all the Permaglass stock? (Note the effects of section 11.2 in the 1964 agreement.) Why is the form of the transaction so critical?

2. Assume PPG Industries is lessee on a real estate lease that is *expressly* "nonassignable." After the merger can Guardian Industries claim to be the lessee under the old lease? How is it that a patent license with no express language on nonassignability does not transfer and a real estate lease with express language does? What is inherently different about the two contracts that justifies this disparate treatment? Can the holding be explained by the nature of the return payments—royalties in licenses and rent in leases?

If a contract is not specific on the effect of statutory mergers, how should the court erect presumptions favoring or disfavoring assignability? Do you agree with the distinction drawn between patent licenses on one hand and shoprights, real estate leases, and insurance coverage on the other?

Should your presumptions on assignability be the same for a statutory merger in which the selling corporation's shareholders receive cash and for a statutory merger in which the selling corporation's shareholders receive stock in the surviving firm?

Draft a clause that would protect the patent licensor in *PPG Industries* from all undesirable control changes (a so-called "control change" clause). If such a clause is in place, what is the strategic position of the patent licensor or the lessor if the licensee or lessee is negotiating to merge with a third party? Are there ways of avoiding a control change clause? What if the clause is not supplemented by a clause on sublicensing or subleasing?

3. Does a surviving firm in a merger become liable for the criminal activity of a disappearing constituent firm? Do statutes like Delaware's section 259 cover criminal liability? See *United States v. Alamo Bank*, 880 F.2d 828 (5th Cir.1989) (a surviving state bank in a merger with a national bank convicted for violations of the National Bank Secrecy Act based on activities of the national bank before the merger). How can a surviving firm act "knowingly" or "willfully" under a criminal statute with respect to acts of a predecessor?

4. In *PPG Industries* why was the contract left incomplete on the effect of mergers when it was drafted? Incompetent lawyers? Or is it more complicated than that? Keep this question in mind when reading the next case, *Mesa Partners*.

MESA PARTNERS v. PHILLIPS PETROLEUM CO.
Court of Chancery of Delaware, 1984.
488 A.2d 107.

WALSH, VICE CHANCELLOR.

This action began as an effort by the plaintiff, Mesa Partners, a Texas partnership, to secure a declaratory judgment that it was not obligated to refrain from attempting to acquire shares of stock, and ultimately control, of Phillips Petroleum Company ("Phillips") by reason of the execution by Mesa Petroleum Company ("Mesa") of an agreement dated January 6, 1983. This agreement ("the Standstill Agreement") between Mesa and General American Oil Company of Texas ("GAO") resolved the competition between Mesa and Phillips for the acquisition of GAO. By virtue of that agreement, Mesa retired from the battle, was compensated for its abortive efforts and Phillips acquired GAO. Phillips claims the agreement had the further effect of restricting Mesa from launching any effort to acquire an interest in Phillips within five years of its execution. In effect, Mesa now seeks a preemptive ruling that the agreement does not limit its proposed plan of acquisition.

* * *

The extensive discovery record which has been developed on an accelerated basis provides an insight into the events which transpired on January 5 and 6, 1983, when Mesa and Phillips negotiated the fate of GAO. The scenario began on December 20, 1982, when Mesa launched a hostile tender offer for a 51% controlling interest in GAO. Mesa's tender offer was two-tiered but its only price commitment was to purchase shares in the first step at $40 per share. GAO responded three days later with a self-tender offer for 31% of its shares at $50 per share. The usual flurry of litigation followed in several jurisdictions as Mesa sought to enjoin GAO's self-tender. By December 30, 1982, Mesa claimed to have achieved a tender of more than 77% of GAO stock but was unable to take down those shares because the depositing shareholders were free to withdraw their shares in favor of GAO's self-tender by January 7, 1983. * * *

In the meanwhile, GAO's investment banker, First Boston Corporation, was seeking a "white knight" to rescue GAO from the unwanted attention of Mesa. Phillips expressed interest in such a role and began negotiations with GAO looking toward a possible acquisition. Eventually, Phillips and GAO were able to agree on the basic terms of merger which included, *inter alia*, the payment by Phillips of $45 per share through direct acquisitions from certain large shareholders and by securing the shares to be realized from the GAO self-tender which would continue. Key to the consummation of the deal, however, was a settlement with Mesa. Acting through their investment bankers, GAO and Mesa began negotiating for Mesa's exit from the scene. At first, GAO would not identify its white knight but eventually Phillips was disclosed and direct negotiations ensued with Joseph G. Fogg, of Morgan Stanley acting on behalf of Mesa and Geoffrey Boisi of Goldman, Sachs acting for Phillips. Phillips' basic approach was to persuade Mesa to abandon its tender offer in favor of the GAO self-tender. In the process Mesa would be able to sell its previously acquired block of GAO shares and be compensated for its expenses.

By January 5, the negotiations had reached the point where it was desirable for the Chief Executive Officers of both companies to talk directly. On the evening of January 5, T. Boone Pickens, Mesa's CEO, who was in New York, spoke by telephone to William C. Douce, Phillips' CEO, who was at a hunting lodge in Georgia. Douce described the conversation as a candid and friendly one in which the terms of Mesa's withdrawal were discussed. Pickens appeared interested in broadening the negotiations to include the sale of oil rigs and "other deals" but Douce indicated he was interested only in securing GAO and its assets for Phillips. Eventually, it was agreed that Mesa would be paid $15 million for its "expenses" in the GAO affair. Douce claims that he also told Pickens that it would be necessary for Mesa to execute a standstill agreement as to "GAO and its assets" but he did not talk "specifically" about Phillips Petroleum. Pickens does not recall any discussion concerning a standstill agreement.

After the respective CEOs had reached agreement on the terms of Mesa's withdrawal, Douce contacted Phillips' headquarters in Bartlesville, Oklahoma, advised them of the terms and requested that an implementing agreement be prepared and sent to Pickens in New York. At this point events become disputed with each side offering a different version of the circumstances under which the agreement was prepared and executed. It is clear, however, that basic responsibility for the drafting of the Standstill Agreement fell to GAO's counsel, Wachtell, Lipton, Rosen & Katz ("Wachtell Lipton") while Phillips' counsel, Fried, Frank, Shriver, Harris and Jacobsen ("Fried Frank") were assigned responsibility for preparing the voluminous documents needed to effectuate the GAO–Phillips agreement. The two firms did confer concerning the language of the Standstill Agreement and reached an understanding to use a "subtle" approach to secure Phillips inclusion in the Standstill Agreement without specific use of its name. It was agreed to use language in the agreement which by implication could be construed to apply to Phillips. This approach was consistent with the views later expressed by Phillips' executives that it did not want to appear apprehensive over the need to protect itself from a "raid" by Pickens through insisting on a specific identification in the Standstill Agreement. In other words, if Phillips were perceived to be "running scared" it might whet Pickens' appetite.

* * *

Once the Standstill Agreement had been drawn, it was delivered on January 6, 1983, to Mesa's representatives who were gathered in the conference room at Morgan Stanley. When the agreement arrived it was reviewed and discussed. Present at that time in addition to

Pickens were: Messers. Madden, Batchelder and Tassin, all executives of Mesa; Joseph Fogg, Simon Orme and Charles Short of Morgan Stanley, accompanied by Jesse Lovejoy counsel for Morgan Stanley; and Joseph Flom and Blaine Fogg of Skadden Arps. Each of these individuals has been deposed and have given varying recitals of what occurred prior to Pickens' execution of the agreement. The Mesa executives, including Pickens' claim they were advised the Standstill Agreement did not cover Phillips. The Morgan Stanley representatives, with varying degrees of certitude, contend that Fogg advised Pickens that Phillips was covered by the agreement. Flom, whose recollection was less than categorical, testified that he did not advise Pickens that Phillips was not covered by the agreement but he is unsure whether anyone advised Pickens that Phillips was covered by the agreement. He indicated that "various possibilities of interpretation" were discussed but the issue of a Phillips standstill was not of prime concern to him because Pickens had indicated on that occasion, and earlier, that he had no interest in Phillips "because they were friends of his."

Two other lawyers present have clearer recall of the discussion. Blaine Fogg recalled that there was a general agreement that because the Standstill Agreement didn't specifically mention Phillips, it did not include it. Lovejoy, who no longer represents Morgan Stanley but is employed by another investment banker, specifically recalls the discussion concerning whether the agreement covered Phillips. He expressed the judgment that since the agreement did not mention Phillips or any other possible acquiror and did appear to restrict purchases of the securities of any company but GAO, it did not apply to Phillips.

The agreement was signed by Pickens and accepted by GAO. Phillips thereafter completed its negotiations with GAO, with the latter proceeding to complete its self-tender. By virtue of a short form merger under Section 253 of the Delaware Corporation Code on March 8, 1983, GAO ceased to exist and Phillips became the survivor. In subsequent press releases, public announcements and filings with the Securities and Exchange Commission Phillips did not indicate that it was the recipient of a Standstill Agreement which protected it from future acquisition of its stock by Mesa.

* * *

Phillips first points to the language in subpart (a) which restricts Mesa from "directly or indirectly" acquiring any voting securities or voting rights in GAO. * * * In any event, the language "directly and indirectly" as it applies to a restriction on acquisition, is commonly understood as embracing the use of a third party or an intermediary device to accomplish the prohibited objective. * * *

Phillips does not suggest that Mesa intends the use of a third-party or intermediary in its effort to control Phillips. Moreover, GAO ceased to exist as a separate entity capable of issuing any securities as of

March 8, 1983, and it presently cannot be the subject of any acquisition by Mesa. There is no merit to this claim of ambiguity.

Phillips next contends that subsection (d) of paragraph 2 which prohibits Mesa from seeking "to control or influence the management, board of directors or policies of GAO" extends the standstill to Phillips by virtue of its subsequent acquisition of GAO. This contention is subject to the infirmity previously noted. With the demise of GAO as a functioning corporate entity there was no management, board or policies subject to interference.

Finally, Phillips points to the final sentence of paragraph 2 which provides:

> Notwithstanding the foregoing, the preceding restrictions on us pursuant to this paragraph 2 shall terminate in the event that GAO or any of its Affiliates should take any action with respect to us or our voting securities which action, if taken by us or any Affiliate of ours with respect to GAO or its voting securities, would violate this paragraph 2.

This provision of the Standstill Agreement is, in effect, a reciprocity agreement, *i.e.,* Mesa is not required to refrain from acquisition if GAO commences similar acquisition activity against Mesa. The linchpin of Phillips' argument of ambiguity is the use of the term "affiliates." It argues that the reciprocity provision indicates that other parties, *i.e.,* affiliates of GAO or affiliates of Mesa, were deemed to be covered by the agreement. Phillips does not suggest who Mesa's affiliates might be, but it maintains that in view of its conceded "white knight" status the agreement obviously included it as GAO's affiliate. At least an ambiguity is created.

Although this is a slim reed upon which to set aside the parol evidence rule, it will suffice. The intent and object of the writing is thus subject to review in the light of the circumstances which surround the execution of the document so long as the document is not altered or changed. * * * There is little doubt that the Standstill Agreement represented the culmination of the negotiations between Mesa and Phillips over who would acquire GAO. There is also no question that Phillips was to acquire GAO and, in the process, assure that Mesa received $15 million if, in the words of one of the investment bankers "it retired from the fray." When Douce and Pickens finalized the terms of Mesa's withdrawal they took a simplistic approach. Pickens wanted to be compensated and Douce wanted to make sure that Phillips acquired all GAO's property without further interference from Mesa. While Douce may have wanted a standstill agreement he wanted it to protect the valuable assets his company was about to acquire. Douce candidly admitted that the future of Phillips, as such, was never discussed, and the evidence fairly supports the assumption that Pickens, at that time, had no designs on Phillips.

The oral agreement reached between the respective CEOs required formalizing. Douce set the wheels in motion by advising Phillips' personnel of the terms of the deal and they, in turn, looked to Phillips'

New York counsel, working with GAO's counsel, to structure the agreement. There was a great deal to be done in a short period of time in order to avoid the preliminary injunction hearing facing Mesa and GAO on January 7. In adopting a Standstill Agreement based on the Cities agreement, which contained the same "affiliates" provision and "interference with management" language, counsel for GAO and Phillips, in what is conceded to be "subtle fashion", inserted language which avoided "overtly mentioning" Phillips. There is no direct evidence that Mesa's counsel participated in this drafting but in any event the agreement when delivered for Pickens' signature contained language which Phillips' counsel hoped would provide Phillips with a Standstill Agreement without saying so, and more importantly, without alerting the other side that such was intended. So much for a meeting of the minds.

As previously noted, there is disagreement among the Mesa, Morgan Stanley and Skadden Arps entourage as to whether Pickens signed the agreement with the understanding that it provided Phillips with a five year standstill undertaking. The Morgan Stanley representatives who claim to have advised Pickens are now handsomely paid to act as financial advisors to Phillips in planning takeover defenses. The Skadden Arps firm labored under a similar disability of past representation. Although Joseph Fogg, who is not a lawyer, claims to have advised Pickens that the Standstill Agreement definitely included Phillips, no other lawyer in the room tendered a similar opinion. Indeed, Morgan Stanley's own counsel, Lovejoy, was of a different view. The most reasonable explanation, however, is that inclusion of Phillips in the agreement was simply a non-issue. It had not been mentioned by Douce and in view of its "coded" insertion in the agreement was not of direct concern to Pickens.

Apart from his claim that he was not then interested in going after Phillips, there is clear circumstantial evidence that such a move was not within Pickens' contemplation when he signed the GAO Standstill Agreement. As noted, both Skadden Arps and Morgan Stanley had longstanding and continuing takeover advisory relationships with Phillips. Indeed, Joseph Fogg claims to have advised Pickens during the GAO battle that if certain of Morgan Stanley's oil company clientele, including Phillips, became acquisition targets, Morgan Stanley's first loyalty would be to them. Flom described Morgan Stanley's and his firm's relationship and its significance to whether Pickens was being asked to negotiate a Standstill Agreement with Phillips through GAO:

> "Now, as a point of fact, not only did I, but Morgan Stanley, would not have represented Boone if we thought it was an active possibility of him going after Phillips."

* * *

The evidence which most strongly supports Phillips' argument is the testimony of Joseph Fogg and his Morgan Stanley associates. However, Fogg claims his reason for believing, as a non-lawyer, that the agreement might extend to Phillips was his reading of the "directly and indirectly" language in subpart 2(a). But, as noted, the ambiguity dispute centers on the "affiliates" provision not the "directly and indirectly" language. Thus even if Fogg's layman's view of the meaning of an agreement prepared by lawyers who wished to convey a hidden meaning in a subtle fashion was expressed, it did not extend to the principal, if not sole, substantial ambiguity in the agreement.

* * *

Phillips' effort to transform the Standstill Agreement into a document reflecting Phillips' present position based on its disguised past intention, in effect, results in a reformation of the agreement. In the absence of a mutually-shared understanding that Phillips was to be a beneficiary of paragraph 2, reformation would not be available.

* * *

In addition to its argument that the Standstill Agreement might be interpreted to include it, Phillips contends that it succeeded to its benefits by operation of law upon the merger of GAO into Phillips. It relies upon the language of 8 *Del.C.* § 259 which confers upon the surviving corporation in a merger all "rights, privileges, powers, and franchises" of the constituent corporations. Mesa points out that had the parties intended that the agreement would extend to the "successors and assigns" of the designated parties such language could have been easily inserted. Indeed, such language was used in paragraph 3 as part of the mutual release of claims and litigation.

Phillips' argument has a surface appeal since under Delaware corporate law the survival of contractual obligations is recognized even in the absence of a "successors and assigns" clause. *Fitzsimmons v. Western Airlines, Inc.,* Del.Ch., 290 A.2d 682 (1972); *Western Airlines, Inc. v. Allegheny Airlines, Inc.,* Del.Ch., 313 A.2d 145, 153 (1973). Both *Fitzsimmons* and *Western Airlines* involved the survival of contractual obligations, not powers. As the Court in *Western Airlines* noted, there is a strong public policy, designed primarily for the protection of creditors and third parties who dealt in good faith with the predecessor corporation, which supports this view. The Court further noted that, notwithstanding the Delaware merger statute, contractual obligations do not pass if the parties "by their objective contractual language contemplated that such obligations would not pass." *Id.* at 153.

Apart from the fact that the party now sought to be obligated under the survival theory is Mesa not Phillips, viewing Phillips as a successor beneficiary of the agreement does violence to the mutual intention of the parties. If the agreement was intended, as seems most plausible, to address only the right of GAO to require Mesa to desist in its acquisition efforts while Phillips proceeded with its plan of acquisition, that "power," possessed by GAO and presumably acquired by Phillips, had at the time of the merger accomplished its purpose. To the extent the "power" was exercised against Mesa, it had achieved full satisfaction. Phillips too achieved the benefit of that power upon the completion of the merger.

Asset Acquisitions

The state codes have no specific sections on the effect of asset acquisitions or of stock acquisitions on the preexisting rights and obligations of the target firm. States treat asset acquisitions as a large collection of individual sales contracts on specific items. Thus in an asset sale a patent license or a real estate lease is treated as if the license or lease were individually assigned. This means that for a patent license to transfer in an asset sale, it must be expressly assignable, and that for a real estate lease to transfer in an asset sale, it must not contain an express prohibition on assignment. It also means that a buyer can choose *not* to assume selected obligations of the seller. Some preexisting creditors of the seller would rather have the buyer assume their obligations. They sue to force the buyer to pay on their debts. In rare cases, courts, under the rubric of the de facto merger doctrine, will step in and protect debtors in asset sales when their obligations are not assumed by the buyer.

BUD ANTLE, INC. v. EASTERN FOODS, INC.

United States Court of Appeals, Eleventh Circuit, 1985.
758 F.2d 1451.

PITTMAN, DISTRICT JUDGE.

* * *

The appellant, Eastern Foods, Inc. (Eastern), appeals from a jury verdict in which it was held liable under the theory of de facto merger for a debt on open account owed by B & B Produce Processors, Inc. (B & B) to the plaintiff-appellee Bud Antle, Inc. (Bud Antle). Eastern contends that the district court erred in its refusal to direct a verdict in its favor on the de facto merger count and in its charge to the jury on the de facto merger doctrine. This court agrees and must reverse the district court's judgment.

The plaintiff-appellee Bud Antle, which is in the wholesale produce business, sold lettuce on open account to B & B. B & B processed and packaged the lettuce and sold it to its customers, principally fast food franchises. B & B experienced cash flow problems, and by September 30, 1978, it owed Bud Antle $158,659.57 on open account.

During September, 1978, the defendant-appellant Eastern, a corporation that produces, sells, and distributes food products, met with B & B and showed interest in a possible merger with B & B. Eastern, B & B, and B & B's shareholders on September 29, 1978 entered an "Option Agreement" under which Eastern paid B & B $50,000.00 for "the option to purchase all of the business and affairs of B & B." The agreement provided:

If such option is exercised then at Eastern's election, either the Shareholders [of B & B] will transfer to Eastern all of the issued and outstanding stock of B & B or B & B will transfer all of its assets, real, personal, tangible and intangible to Eastern which at closing shall assume all of the disclosed liabilities of B & B. The exercise price under such option shall be a total of $50,000 payable at closing.

Contemporaneously with the execution of this option agreement, Eastern and B & B entered into a "Management Agreement" which gave Eastern certain authority to manage the operations of B & B. The purported purpose of this arrangement was to give Eastern an opportunity to evaluate in detail the financial condition of B & B and thus enable Eastern to reach an informed decision about whether to exercise its option. On October 1, 1978, Eastern and B & B entered a more comprehensive "Restated Management Agreement" which gave Eastern greater control over the management of B & B. This agreement provided that Eastern "shall be the exclusive manager of [B & B's] business, and hereby agrees to provide such services and perform such duties as are customarily provided for in such instances." It provided that Eastern agreed "to advise, consult with, and issue directions" on a variety of matters including all sales activities; the hiring, paying, and discharging of B & B's employees; the ordering of inventory and supplies; the conducting of promotional activities; and the maintenance of all machinery, fixtures, vehicles, and other operating equipment. The agreement authorized Eastern to place any or all B & B employees on Eastern's payroll. It authorized Eastern to terminate or renegotiate B & B's equipment rental contracts and leases. It authorized Eastern, where feasible, to consolidate the two companies' existing branch facilities. It authorized Eastern to negotiate with B & B's creditors to obtain voluntary reductions of B & B's outstanding debt. The agreement stated that Eastern would provide these services as an independent contractor, and it provided for Eastern to be compensated for the services based on the volume of B & B's production and sales during the operation of the agreement.

Pursuant to this agreement, Eastern undertook the management and operation of B & B from October 1, 1978 to February 29, 1979. It instituted a number of management actions authorized by the agreement. It loaned money to B & B without interest, receiving in return promissory notes executed by B & B and personally guaranteed by two of B & B's officers. Eastern renegotiated several of B & B's leases which were in default. It consolidated five of the two companies' branch warehouse facilities. There was no separate accounting by either B & B or Eastern for the cost or rent associated with the joint use of the other's offices and warehouses. Eastern also assumed the responsibility of making B & B's payroll, and the employees of B & B were paid by checks drawn on Eastern's account.

Since the management agreement provided that all funds derived from the operation of B & B would be received by Eastern, Eastern established a separate bank account for B & B. This account was entitled "Bell and Brook Account." Eastern used the name "Bell & Brook" in place of "B & B" on invoices and stationery. The Bell & Brook invoices listed the products sold by B & B as well as certain products sold by Eastern. Each product was identified by a unique product code number which enabled Eastern to keep separate records for the sale of B & B products and the receivables they generated. The name "Bell & Brook" allegedly was used in place of "B & B" to distinguish the sales, receipts, and expenses that B & B generated prior to the management agreement from those it generated after the agreement. Most of B & B's receivables generated prior to the signing of the management agreement had been sold to a factoring company.

During this period Eastern advised B & B's creditors, including Bud Antle, that Eastern and B & B had entered into a management agreement and option agreement and that the two corporations were considering a merger. Eastern also sought to ascertain from B & B's creditors the outstanding balances on B & B's accounts. Eastern, B & B, and Bud Antle engaged in a series of discussions and communications concerning B & B's outstanding debt and the possible merger. Eastern attempted to persuade Bud Antle to accept a reduction in B & B's debt, but Bud Antle insisted on full payment.

During the operation of the Restated Management Agreement, Eastern purchased produce from Bud Antle. All of these purchases were invoiced to Eastern even though some of the shipments were made to B & B at various warehouse locations. Eastern paid Bud Antle for all of the produce it purchased. During the term of the Restated Management Agreement, Bud Antle made no sales of lettuce directly to B & B.

Eastern terminated the Restated Management Agreement in February of 1979 as the agreement provided it could do. Eastern ceased doing business with B & B's customers and notified them that its management relationship with B & B had been terminated. There was conflicting testimony about whether Eastern retained any of B & B's assets after terminating the agreement. It is clear that most of B & B's assets were seized by creditors and state taxing authorities.

It is undisputed that there was no statutory merger between Eastern and B & B. There was never a transfer of the capital stock of one corporation to the other corporation or its shareholders, officers, or directors. No shareholder, officer, or director of either corporation ever became a shareholder, officer, or director of the other.

* * *

As a general rule, a corporation that purchases or otherwise acquires the assets of a second corporation does not assume the debts and liabilities of the second corporation. * * * Most jurisdictions recognize four exceptions to this rule, however, and will hold the buying corporation liable for the seller's debts if (1) the buyer expressly or impliedly agreed to assume such debts; or (2) the transaction amounts to a de facto merger of the buyer and seller; or (3) the buying corporation is a "mere continuation" of the selling corporation; or (4) the transaction is entered into fraudulently in order to escape liability for such debts. * * *

Another exception, which courts often incorporate into one of the previous four, to-wit: the fraudulent transaction exception, is the absence of adequate consideration for the sale or transfer.

* * * Although Georgia courts have not expressly adopted all of these exceptions, early Georgia cases indicate agreement with the majority rule.

* * *

All four of these exceptions require a transfer of assets in order to hold the acquiring corporation liable. The existence of such a transfer is a disputed issue of fact in this case; and under the trial court's instructions to the jury, it cannot be determined whether the jury found such a transfer to have occurred. There was evidence from which the jury might have found such a transfer to have taken place *during* the operation of the management agreement. The jury might have found that Eastern controlled B & B's assets and used them for its own operations. There was also some testimony that Eastern retained some of B & B's assets after the management agreement was terminated. Assuming that Eastern's control and retention of such assets was sufficient to raise a jury question on the issue of transfer of assets, Eastern's contention that the district court should have directed a verdict in its favor on this issue would be without merit.

Even with that assumption, Eastern can be held liable for B & B's pre-existing debts only if Bud Antle has proven the applicability of one of the exceptions listed above. Bud Antle did not raise in its complaint all of the exceptions. Only the fraud and de facto merger exceptions were raised expressly in independent counts, and only the de facto merger exception reached the jury. The exceptions for fraud and the express or implied assumption of debts, therefore, are not before this court.

* * *

Although the Georgia courts have not recently addressed the concept of de facto merger, Georgia likely would follow the majority view concerning the requirements and applicability of the de facto merger doctrine. The Eighth Circuit recently set out the elements that must be present to find a de facto merger:

> (1) There is continuation of the enterprise of the seller corporation, so that there is a continuity of management, personnel, physical location, assets, and general business operations.
>
> (2) There is a continuity of shareholders which results from the purchasing corporation paying for the acquired assets with shares of its own stock, this stock ultimately coming to be held by the shareholders of the seller corporation so that they become a constituent part of the purchasing corporation.

(3) The seller corporation ceases its ordinary business operations, liquidates, and dissolves as soon as legally and practicably possible.

(4) The purchasing corporation assumes those liabilities and obligations of the seller ordinarily necessary for the uninterrupted continuation of normal business operations of the seller corporation.

Keller v. Clark Equipment Co., 715 F.2d 1280, 1291 (8th Cir.1983), cert. denied, ___ U.S. ___, 104 S.Ct. 713, 79 L.Ed.2d 176 (1984).

It is undisputed that one of these four elements was not present in this case: a continuity of shareholders resulting from the acquiring corporation paying for the acquired assets with shares of its own stock. Several courts have held that "[a] consolidation or merger always involves a transfer of the assets and business of one corporation to another in exchange for its securities." *Good v. Lackawanna Leather Co.,* 96 N.J.Super. 439, 233 A.2d 201, 208 (Ch.Div.1967).[1] * * *

At the very least, there must be some sort of continuation of the stockholders' ownership interests.

* * * The reason for this requirement is that corporate liability adheres not to the nature of the business enterprise but to the corporate entity itself. * * * The corporate entity and its shareholders ultimately are responsible for the disposition of the corporation's assets and the payment of its debts.

* * * Even if the corporation sells to another corporation its entire business operation and all its assets, in exchange for some consideration other than stock, the two corporate entities remain distinct and intact. The corporate entities have not merged, and each is liable for its own debts, absent fraud or one of the other exceptions listed above.

* * *

In the case at bar, the evidence was undisputed that no transfer of stock took place. Therefore, there could not have been a de facto merger to make Eastern liable for B & B's debts. The district court should have directed a verdict in Eastern's favor on the issue of de facto merger.

* * *

The mere continuation exception applies when the purchasing corporation is merely a continuation or reincarnation of the selling corporation. * * * In other words, the purchasing corporation is mere-

---

1. Some courts, applying the de facto merger doctrine to products liability cases, have modified the requirements for finding a de facto merger. The Supreme Court of Michigan has distinguished the doctrine's application in products liability cases. See *Turner v. Bituminous Casualty Co.,* 397 Mich. 406, 244 N.W.2d 873 (1976). In a very recent opinion, the Fifth Circuit similarly modified the mere continuation exception.

* * *

Since the modification was carved out for products liability cases, it has no application here.

ly a "new hat" for the seller, with the same or similar management and ownership. * * * In determining whether one corporation is a continuation of another, the test is whether there is a continuation of the corporate entity of the seller—not whether there is a continuation of the seller's business operation.

* * * Therefore, "[t]he key element of a 'continuation' is a common identity of the officers, directors and stockholders in the selling and purchasing corporations." *Leannais v. Cincinnati, Inc.*, 565 F.2d 437, 440 (7th Cir.1977). *But see Rivers v. Stihl, Inc.*, 434 So.2d 766, 771–72 (Ala.1983) (applies a "basic continuity of enterprise" test in the context of products liability).

The evidence was undisputed that there was no such continuation of management or ownership in the case at bar. None of B & B's officers, directors, or stockholders ever became an officer, director, or stockholder of Eastern. Although some of B & B's officers may have been employed by Eastern, mere employment is insufficient to warrant application of the continuation exception. * * * Therefore, Eastern was not, as a matter of law, a continuation of B & B, and the district court should have directed a verdict in Eastern's favor on this issue.

* * *

Questions

1. In an asset acquisition, if the buyer explicitly does not agree to assume *contractual* obligations of the seller and the transaction is not fraudulent (that is, the assets are sold for fair value), why should the creditors of the seller be able to attach their obligations to the buyer? In other words, do the de facto merger and the mere continuation doctrines make sense in this context? Assume in *Bud Antle* that Eastern Foods chose to exercise its option to buy the assets of B & B for $50,000 and left B & B with its debt to Bud Antle (i.e., assume the option did not require, as it does in the case, that Eastern Foods assume all B & B's liability in an asset sale). Should the court declare Eastern Foods liable on the Bud Antle debt?

2. In normal applications of the de facto merger doctrine, preexisting creditors of the selling firm, often tort claimants, argue that the buying firm in an asset sale ought to be liable on their obligations. Can the argument work in reverse? Can the buying firm in an asset sale that qualifies under the de facto merger doctrine (same shareholders, same business) argue that it is a successor to the seller's otherwise nonassignable contracts? Can the buying firm in an asset sale claim use the de facto merger doctrine to claim rights under a patent license held by the selling firm? See Syenergy Methods, Inc. v. Kelly Energy Systems, Inc., 695 F.Supp. 1362 (D.R.I.1988) (a buying firm in an asset sale can, under the de facto merger doctrine, claim benefits of a "personal" covenant not to compete). Is this sound?

Stock Acquisitions

On the other hand, states treat stock acquisitions as if they have no effect on a target's preexisting rights and obligations. Since the identity of a target's shareholders does not affect the entity itself, courts consider all contracts with the firm to survive the acquisition. Thus a patent license with the target is unaffected and a real estate lease is unaffected, regardless of express general language of nonassignability in either.

BRANMAR THEATRE CO. v. BRANMAR, INC.
Court of Chancery of Delaware, 1970.
264 A.2d 526.

SHORT, VICE CHANCELLOR.

This is an action for a declaratory judgment in which plaintiff seeks to enjoin defendant from cancelling a lease agreement previously executed by the parties. Defendant, by its answer, prays the court to find that it was entitled to treat the lease agreement as terminated because of a violation of a covenant therein prohibiting assignment by the lessee. * * *

Plaintiff was incorporated under the laws of Delaware on June 7, 1967. The owners of its outstanding capital stock were the Robert Rappaport family of Cleveland, Ohio. On June 9, 1967 plaintiff and defendant entered into a lease agreement for a motion picture theatre in the Branmar Shopping Center, New Castle County, Delaware. The lease, sixteen pages in length, recites that the lessor is to erect a theatre building in the shopping center. It provides for the payment of rent by the lessee to the lessor of $27,500 per year plus a percentage of gross admissions receipts, plus five per cent of any amounts paid to the lessee by refreshment concessionaires. The percentage of admissions figure is regulated by the type of attractions in the theatre, the minimum being five per cent and the maximum ten. The lease provides for a twenty year term with an option in the lessee to renew for an additional ten years. The lessee is to provide the lessor with a loan of $60,000, payable in installments, to be used for construction. The lessee is to provide, at its cost, whatever fixtures and equipment are necessary to operate the theatre. Paragraph 12 of the lease, the focal point of this lawsuit, provides:

> "Lessee shall not sublet, assign, transfer or in any manner dispose of the said premises or any part thereof, for all or any part of the term hereby granted, without the prior written consent of the Lessor, such consent shall not be unreasonably withheld."

Joseph Luria, the principal for Branmar Shopping Center testified at trial that he negotiated the lease agreement with Isador Rappaport; that he made inquiries about Rappaport's ability to manage a theatre and satisfied himself that Rappaport had the competence and the important industry connections to successfully operate the theatre. It appears that Rappaport and his son operate a successful theatre in Cleveland, Ohio and have owned and operated theatres elsewhere.

Following execution of the lease the Rappaports were approached by Muriel Schwartz and Reba Schwartz, operators of ten theatres in the Delaware and neighboring Maryland area, with an offer to manage the theatre for the Rappaports who had no other business interests in the Wilmington area. This offer was not accepted but the Schwartzes subsequently agreed with the Rappaports to purchase the lease from plaintiff and have it assigned to them. An assignment was executed by plaintiff to the Schwartzes. Defendant rejected the assignment under the power reserved in Paragraph 12 of the lease. On May 29, 1969 the Schwartzes purchased the outstanding shares of plaintiff from the Rappaports. Upon receipt of notice of the sale defendant advised plaintiff that it considered the sale of the shares to the Schwartzes to be a breach of Paragraph 12 of the lease and the lease to be null and void.

* * *

Defendant argues that the sale of stock was in legal effect an assignment of the lease by the Rappaports to the Schwartzes, was in breach of Paragraph 12 of the lease, and that it was, therefore, justified in terminating plaintiff's leasehold interest. That in the absence of fraud, and none is charged here, transfer of stock of a corporate lessee is ordinarily not a violation of a clause prohibiting assignment is clear from the authorities. * * * Defendant contends, however, that this is not the ordinary case. Here, it says, due to the nature of the motion picture business, the performance required was by the Rappaports personally. But while defendant's negotiations were with a member of the Rappaport family when the lease was executed it chose to let the theatre to a corporation whose stock might foreseeably be transferred by the then stockholders. In the preparation of the lease, a document of sixteen pages, defendant was careful to spell out in detail the rights and duties of the parties. It did not, however, see fit to provide for forfeiture in the event the stockholders sold their shares. Had this been the intent it would have been a simple matter to have so provided.
* * *

Defendant contends that the evidence clearly shows that the Schwartzes do not have the connections in the industry to obtain first quality motion pictures which is of prime importance to a landlord under "a percentage rental agreement." If these were the facts defendant's theory that the lease called for personal performance by the Rappaports might have some merit.

* * *

If the question of ability to perform to defendant's best advantage is material at all it is as between the Schwartzes and the Rappaports and there is simply no competent evidence in the record to answer this question. Moreover, defendant's characterization of the lease as "a percentage rental agreement" is not justified. The rental terms are not based solely on percentages but on a substantial stipulated annual rent plus percentages. What difference in dollars the percentages would amount to depending upon the identity of the theatre's management does not appear.

Conditions and restrictions in a deed or lease which upon a breach work a forfeiture of estate are not favored by the law. Old Time Petroleum Co. v. Turcol, 18 Del.Ch. 121, 156 A. 501. * * * This rule rests on the principle that the party having the power to stipulate in his own favor should not neglect to make his exactions clear and further 'that every man's grant is to be taken most strongly against himself.' * * * The disfavor in which forfeitures are viewed gives a special reason for invoking this general rule of construction against the person whose granting language is appealed to as the source of a claimed forfeiture. * * *

Defendant suggests that since "the Rappaports" could not assign the lease without its consent they should not be permitted to accomplish the same result by transfer of their stock. But the rule that precludes a person from doing indirectly what he cannot do directly has no application to the present case. The attempted assignment was not by the Rappaports but by plaintiff corporation, the sale of stock by its stockholders. Since defendant has failed to show circumstances to justify ignoring the corporation's separate existence reliance upon the cited rule is misplaced.

* * *

Questions

What reasons did the court give for refusing to interpret the nonassignability clause to apply to stock acquisitions when the refusal operated to frustrate the clear intent of one (and arguably both) of the parties to the lease? Are there better justifications for the court's holding?

SECTION 2. THE SPECIAL PROBLEMS OF PROTECTING PREEXISTING BONDHOLDERS IN LEVERAGED BUYOUTS AND LEVERAGED RECAPITALIZATIONS

Subsection a. Fiduciary Duty for Bondholders?

The contested leveraged buyout of RJR Nabisco described in the following case is the largest leveraged buyout to date and featured some of Wall Street's best-known lawyers and investment bankers. A bestseller was written about the contest. B. Burrough & J. Helyar, *Barbarians at the Gate: The Fall of RJR Nabisco* (1990). All serious students of mergers, acquisitions, and reorganizations should read the book.

METROPOLITAN LIFE INS. CO. v. RJR NABISCO, INC.

United States District Court, Southern District of New York, 1989.
716 F.Supp. 1504.

WALKER, DISTRICT JUDGE:

The corporate parties to this action are among the country's most sophisticated financial institutions, as familiar with the Wall Street investment community and the securities market as American consumers are with the Oreo cookies and Winston cigarettes made by defendant RJR Nabisco, Inc. (sometimes "the company" or "RJR Nabisco"). The present action traces its origins to October 20, 1988, when F. Ross Johnson, then the Chief Executive Officer of RJR Nabisco, proposed a $17 billion leveraged buy-out ("LBO") of the company's shareholders, at $75 per share.[1] Within a few days, a bidding war developed among the investment group led by Johnson and the investment firm of Kohlberg Kravis Roberts & Co. ("KKR"), and others. On December 1, 1988, a special committee of RJR Nabisco directors, established by the company specifically to consider the competing proposals, recommended that the company accept the KKR proposal, a $24 billion LBO that called for the purchase of the company's outstanding stock at roughly $109 per share.

* * *

Plaintiffs now allege, in short, that RJR Nabisco's actions have drastically impaired the value of bonds previously issued to plaintiffs by, in effect, misappropriating the value of those bonds to help finance the LBO and to distribute an enormous windfall to the company's shareholders. As a result, plaintiffs argue, they have unfairly suffered a multimillion dollar loss in the value of their bonds.[4]

* * *

The bonds implicated by this suit are governed by long, detailed indentures, which in turn are governed by New York contract law.[10] No one disputes that the holders of public bond issues, like plaintiffs here, often enter the market after the indentures have been negotiated and memorialized. Thus, those indentures are often not the product of face-to-face negotiations between the ultimate holders and the issuing company. What remains equally true, however, is that underwriters ordinarily negotiate the terms of the indentures with the issuers. Since the underwriters must then sell or place the bonds, they necessarily negotiate in part with the interests of the buyers in mind. Moreover, these indentures were not secret agreements foisted upon unwit-

---

1. A leveraged buy-out occurs when a group of investors, usually including members of a company's management team, buy the company under financial arrangements that include little equity and significant new debt. The necessary debt financing typically includes mortgages or high risk/high yield bonds, popularly known as "junk bonds." Additionally, a portion of this debt is generally secured by the company's assets. Some of the acquired company's assets are usually sold after the transaction is completed in order to reduce the debt incurred in the acquisition.

4. Agencies like Standard & Poor's and Moody's generally rate bonds in two broad categories: investment grade and speculative grade. Standard & Poor's rates investment grade bonds from "AAA" to "BBB." Moody's rates those bonds from "AAA" to "Baa3." Speculative grade bonds are rated either "BB" and lower, or "Ba1" and lower, by Standard & Poor's and Moody's, respectively. See, e.g., Standard and Poor's Debt Rating Criteria at 10–11. No one disputes that, subsequent to the announcement of the LBO, the RJR Nabisco bonds lost their "A" ratings.

10. Both sides agree that New York law controls this Court's interpretation of the indentures, which contain explicit designations to that effect.

ting participants in the bond market. No successive holder is required to accept or to continue to hold the bonds, governed by their accompanying indentures; indeed, plaintiffs readily admit that they could have sold their bonds right up until the announcement of the LBO. * * *

Instead, sophisticated investors like plaintiffs are well aware of the indenture terms and, presumably, review them carefully before lending hundreds of millions of dollars to any company.

* * *

The indentures at issue clearly address the eventuality of a merger. They impose certain related restrictions not at issue in this suit, but no restriction that would prevent the recent RJR Nabisco merger transaction. * * * The indentures also explicitly set forth provisions for the adoption of new covenants, if such a course is deemed appropriate. * * *

In their first count, plaintiffs assert that

[d]efendant RJR Nabisco owes a continuing duty of good faith and fair dealing in connection with the contract [i.e., the indentures] through which it borrowed money from MetLife, Jefferson–Pilot and other holders of its debt, including a duty not to frustrate the purpose of the contracts to the debtholders or to deprive the debtholders of the intended object of the contracts—purchase of investment-grade securities.

* * *

In effect, plaintiffs contend that express covenants were not necessary because an *implied* covenant would prevent what defendants have now done.

* * *

Thus, in cases like *Van Gemert v. Boeing Co.*, 520 F.2d 1373 (2d Cir.), *cert. denied*, 423 U.S. 947, 96 S.Ct. 364, 46 L.Ed.2d 282 (1975) ("*Van Gemert I*"), and *Pittsburgh Terminal Corp. v. Baltimore & Ohio Ry. Co.*, 680 F.2d 933 (3d Cir.), *cert. denied*, 459 U.S. 1056, 103 S.Ct. 475, 74 L.Ed.2d 621 (1982)—both relied upon by plaintiffs—the courts used the implied covenant of good faith and fair dealing to ensure that the bondholders received the benefit of their bargain as determined from the face of the contracts at issue. In *Van Gemert I*, the plaintiff bondholders alleged inadequate notice to them of defendant's intention to redeem the debentures in question and hence an inability to exercise their conversion rights before the applicable deadline. The contract itself provided that notice would be given in the first place. *See, e.g., id.* at 1375 ("A number of provisions in the debenture, the Indenture Agreement, the prospectus, the registration statement ... and the Listing Agreement ... dealt with the possible redemption of the debentures ... and the notice debenture-holders were to receive ..."). Faced with those provisions, defendants in that case unsurprisingly admitted that the indentures specifically required the company to provide the bondholders with notice. *See id.* at 1379. While defendant there issued a press release that mentioned the possible redemption of outstanding convertible debentures, that limited release did not "mention even the tentative dates for redemption and expiration of the conversion rights of debenture holders." *Id.* at 1375. Moreover, defendant did not issue any general publicity or news release. Through an implied covenant, then, the court fleshed out the full extent of the more skeletal right that appeared in the contract itself, and thus protected plaintiff's bargained-for right of conversion.[21] As the court observed,

> What one buys when purchasing a convertible debenture in addition to the debt obligation of the company ... is principally the expectation that the stock will increase sufficiently in value that the conversion right will make the debenture worth more than the debt ... *Any loss occurring to him from failure to convert, as here, is not from a risk inherent in his investment but rather from unsatisfactory notification procedures.*

Id. at 1385 (emphasis added, citations omitted).[22] I also note, in passing, that *Van Gemert I* presented the Second Circuit with "less sophisticated investors." *Id.* at 1383. Similarly, the court in *Pittsburgh Terminal* applied an implied covenant to the indentures at issue because defendants there "took steps to prevent the Bondholders from receiving information which they needed *in order to receive the fruits of their conversion option should they choose to exercise it.*" *Pittsburgh Terminal*, 680 F.2d at 941 (emphasis added).

The appropriate analysis, then, is first to examine the indentures to determine "the fruits of the agreement" between the parties, and then to decide whether those "fruits" have been spoiled—which is to say, whether plaintiffs' contractual rights have been violated by defendants.

* * *

A review of the parties' submissions and the indentures themselves satisfies the Court that the substantive "fruits" guaranteed by those contracts and relevant to the present motions include the periodic and regular payment of interest and the eventual repayment of principal. *See, e.g.,* Bradley Aff.Exh. L, § 3.1 ("The Issuer covenants ... that it will duly and punctually pay ... the principal of, and interest on, each of the Securities ... at the respective times and in the manner provided in such Securities ..."). According to a typical indenture, a default shall occur if the company either (1) fails to pay principal when due; (2) fails to make a timely sinking fund payment; (3) fails to pay within 30 days of the due date thereof any interest on the date; or (4) fails duly to

---

21. Since newspaper notice, for instance, was promised in the indenture, the court used an implied covenant to ensure that meaningful, reasonable newspaper notice was provided. *See id.* at 1383.

22. *See also id.* at 1383 ("An issuer of [convertible] debentures has a duty to give adequate notice either on the face of the debentures, ... or in some other way, of the notice to be provided in the event the company decides to redeem the debentures. Absent such advice as to the specific notice agreed upon by the issuer and the trustee for the debenture holders, the debenture holders' reasonable expectations as to notice should be protected.").

observe or perform any of the express covenants or agreements set forth in the agreement. * * * Plaintiffs' Amended Complaint nowhere alleges that RJR Nabisco has breached these contractual obligations; interest payments continue and there is no reason to believe that the principal will not be paid when due.

It is not necessary to decide that indentures like those at issue could never support a finding of additional benefits, under different circumstances with different parties. Rather, for present purposes, it is sufficient to conclude what obligation is *not* covered, either explicitly or implicitly, by these contracts held by these plaintiffs. Accordingly, this Court holds that the "fruits" of these indentures do not include an implied restrictive covenant that would prevent the incurrence of new debt to facilitate the recent LBO. To hold otherwise would permit these plaintiffs to straightjacket the company in order to guarantee their investment. These plaintiffs do not invoke an implied covenant of good faith to protect a legitimate, mutually contemplated benefit of the indentures; rather, they seek to have this Court create an additional benefit for which they did not bargain.

Although the indentures generally permit mergers and the incurrence of new debt, there admittedly is not an explicit indenture provision to the contrary of what plaintiffs now claim the implied covenant requires. That absence, however, does *not* mean that the Court should imply into those very same indentures a covenant of good faith so broad that it imposes a new, substantive term of enormous scope. This is so particularly where, as here, that very term—a limitation on the incurrence of additional debt—has in other past contexts been expressly bargained for; particularly where the indentures grant the company broad discretion in the management of its affairs, as plaintiffs admit, * * * particularly where the indentures explicitly set forth specific provisions for the adoption of new covenants and restrictions, * * * and *especially* where there has been no breach of the parties' bargained-for contractual rights on which the implied covenant necessarily is based. While the Court stands ready to employ an implied covenant of good faith to ensure that such bargained-for rights are performed and upheld, it will not, however, permit an implied covenant to shoehorn into an indenture additional terms plaintiffs now wish had been included. * * *

Plaintiffs argue in the most general terms that the fundamental basis of all these indentures was that an LBO along the lines of the recent RJR Nabisco transaction would never be undertaken, that indeed *no* action would be taken, intentionally or not, that would significantly deplete the company's assets. Accepting plaintiffs' theory, their fundamental bargain with defendants dictated that nothing would be done to jeopardize the extremely high probability that the company would remain able to make interest payments and repay principal over the 20 to 30 year indenture term—and perhaps by logical extension even included the right to ask a court "to make sure that plaintiffs had made a good investment." * * * But as Judge Knapp aptly concluded in *Gardner,* "Defendants ... were under a duty to carry out the terms of the contract, but not to make sure that plaintiffs had made a good investment. The former they have done; the latter we have no jurisdiction over." *Id.* Plaintiffs' submissions and MetLife's previous undisputed internal memoranda remind the Court that a "fundamental basis" or a "fruit of an agreement" is often in the eye of the beholder, whose vision may well change along with the market, and who may, with hindsight, imagine a different bargain than the one he actually and initially accepted with open eyes.

The sort of unbounded and one-sided elasticity urged by plaintiffs would interfere with and destabilize the market. And this Court, like the parties to these contracts, cannot ignore or disavow the marketplace in which the contract is performed. Nor can it ignore the expectations of that market—expectations, for instance, that the terms of an indenture will be upheld, and that a court will not, *sua sponte,* add new substantive terms to that indenture as it sees fit. The Court has no reason to believe that the market, in evaluating bonds such as those at issue here, did not discount for the possibility that any company, even one the size of RJR Nabisco, might engage in an LBO heavily financed by debt. That the bonds did not lose any of their value until the October 20, 1988 announcement of a possible RJR Nabisco LBO only suggests that the market had theretofore evaluated the risks of such a transaction as slight.

The Court recognizes that the market is not a static entity, but instead involves what plaintiffs call "evolving understanding[s]." * * * Just as the growing prevalence of LBO's has helped change certain ground rules and expectations in the field of mergers and acquisitions, so too it has obviously affected the bond market, a fact no one disputes. * * * To support their argument that defendants have violated an implied covenant, plaintiffs contend that, since the October 20, 1988 announcement, the bond market has "stopped functioning." * * *

They argue that if they had "sold and abandoned the market [before October 20, 1988], the market, if everyone had the same attitude, would have disappeared." * * * What plaintiffs term "stopped functioning" or "disappeared," however, are properly seen as natural responses and adjustments to market realities. Plaintiffs of course do not contend that no new issues are being sold, or that existing issues are no longer being traded or have become worthless.

To respond to changed market forces, new indenture provisions can be negotiated, such as provisions that were in fact once included in the 8.9 percent and 10.25 percent debentures implicated by this action. New provisions could include special debt restrictions or change-of-control covenants. There is no guarantee, of course, that companies like RJR Nabisco would accept such new covenants; parties retain the freedom to enter into contracts as they choose. But presumably, multi-billion dollar investors like plaintiffs have some say in the terms of the investments they make and continue to hold. And, presumably, companies like RJR Nabisco need the infusions of capital such investors are capable of providing.

Whatever else may be true about this case, it certainly does not present an example of the classic sort of form contract or contract of adhesion often frowned upon by courts. In those cases, what motivates a court is the strikingly inequitable nature of the parties' respective bargaining positions. * * * Plaintiffs here entered this "liquid trading market," with their eyes open and were free to leave at any time. Instead they remained there notwithstanding its well understood risks.

Ultimately, plaintiffs cannot escape the inherent illogic of their argument. On the one hand, it is undisputed that investors like plaintiffs recognized that companies like RJR Nabisco strenuously opposed additional restrictive covenants that might limit the incurrence of new debt or the company's ability to engage in a merger. Furthermore, plaintiffs argue that they had no choice other than to accept the indentures as written, without additional restrictive covenants, or to "abandon" the market. * * *

Yet on the other hand, plaintiffs ask this Court to imply a covenant that would have just that restrictive effect because, they contend, it reflects precisely the fundamental assumption of the market and the fundamental basis of their bargain with defendants. If that truly were the case here, it is difficult to imagine why an insistence on that term would have forced the plaintiffs to abandon the market. * * *

In the final analysis, plaintiffs offer no objective or reasonable standard for a court to use in its effort to define the sort of actions their "implied covenant" would permit a corporation to take, and those it would not.[28] Plaintiffs say only that investors like themselves rely upon the "skill" and "good faith" of a company's board and management, * * * and that their covenant would prevent the company from "destroy[ing] . . . the legitimate expectations of its long-term bondholders." *Id.* at 54. As is clear from the preceding discussion, however, plaintiffs have failed to convince the Court that by upholding the explicit, bargained-for terms of the indenture, RJR Nabisco has either exhibited bad faith or destroyed plaintiffs' *legitimate,* protected expectations.

Plaintiffs argue that defendants have sought to blame plaintiffs themselves for whatever losses they may have incurred. Yet this Court need not address whether plaintiffs are at fault, or whether they assumed a risk in any tort sense, or whether they should never have agreed to exchange the specific debt provisions in at least two of the covenants at issue for alternative benefits and public covenants. Instead, it concludes that courts are properly reluctant to imply into an

---

28. Under plaintiffs' theory, bondholders might ask a court to prohibit a company like RJR Nabisco not only from engaging in an LBO, but also from entering a new line of business—with the attendant costs of building new physical plants and hiring new workers—or from acquiring new businesses such as RJR Nabisco did when it acquired Del Monte.

integrated agreement terms that have been and remain subject to specific, explicit provisions, where the parties are sophisticated investors, well versed in the market's assumptions, and do not stand in a fiduciary relationship with one another.

It is also not to say that defendants were free willfully or knowingly to misrepresent or omit material facts to sell their bonds. Relief on claims based on such allegations would of course be available to plaintiffs, if appropriate [29]—but those claims properly sound in fraud, and come with requisite elements. Plaintiffs also remain free to assert their claims based on the fraudulent conveyance laws, which similarly require specific proof.[30] Those burdens cannot be avoided by resorting to an overbroad, superficially appealing, but legally insufficient, implied covenant of good faith and fair dealing.

* * *

Plaintiffs advance a claim that remains based, their assertions to the contrary notwithstanding, on an alleged breach of a fiduciary duty. Defendants go to great lengths to prove that the law of Delaware, and not New York, governs this question. Defendants' attempt to rely on Delaware law is readily explained by even a cursory reading of *Simons v. Cogan,* 549 A.2d 300, 303 (Del.1988), the recent Delaware Supreme Court ruling which held, *inter alia,* that a corporate bond "represents a contractual entitlement to the repayment of a debt and does not represent an equitable interest in the issuing corporation necessary for the imposition of a trust relationship with concomitant fiduciary duties." Before such a fiduciary duty arises, "an existing property right or equitable interest supporting such a duty must exist." *Id.* at 304. A bondholder, that court concluded, "acquires no equitable interest, and remains a creditor of the corporation whose interests are protected by the contractual terms of the indenture." *Id.* * * *

* * * This Court finds *Simons* persuasive, and believes that a New York court would agree with that conclusion. * * * Before a court recognizes the duty of a "punctilio of an honor the most sensitive," it must be certain that the complainant is entitled to more than the "morals of the market place," and the protections offered by actions based on fraud, state statutes or the panoply of available federal securities laws. This Court has concluded that the plaintiffs presently before it—sophisticated investors who are unsecured creditors—are not entitled to such additional protections.

* * *

Questions

1. There are two separate arguments advanced by the bondholders in the case. The first is a contract argument based on the indenture agree-

---

29. The Court, of course, today takes no position on this issue.

30. As noted elsewhere, plaintiffs can also allege violations of express terms of the indentures.

ment. The second is a fiduciary duty argument based on common-law principles. What law applies to control each argument?

In responding to the contract argument, the court noted that there had been no defaults on the payment obligations under the bonds. Why were the bondholders so angry? Are there practical problems with a request to a judge for an implied contract term or for general obligation of fiduciary duty that obligates the board to protect the trading value of the bonds?

2. In the last eight years over twenty-five states have passed statutes, known as constituency statutes, that permit but do not require directors to consider the interests of constituencies other than shareholders when making decisions in the best interests of the corporation. Such statutes often specifically include creditors as well as employees and suppliers in their lists of other relevant constituencies. New York has such a provision. Please read N.Y.—McKinney's Business Corporation Law § 717(b) in your supplement. Assume the New York statute controls in the *RJR Nabisco* case; does it affect the result?

Most states have statutes that require attention to shareholders' interests and *allow* attention to the interests of other constituencies. See, e.g., Ill.—S.H.A. ch. 32, ¶ 8.85; and Wis.Stat.Ann. 180.305. Two states have statutes that ask directors not to regard any one constituent's interest as the dominant interest. West's Ann.Ind.Code 23–1–35–1(d); Pa.Bus.Corp.L. § 511. Please read the Pennsylvania statute in your supplement. One state, Connecticut, makes consideration of nonshareholder constituencies, including creditors, mandatory rather than permitted. Conn.Gen.Stat. Ann. § 33–133(e). If the Connecticut or Pennsylvania statute applied in the *RJR Nabisco* case, would it change the result?

3. Can a firm's board enter into debt covenants with bondholders that give bondholders a veto over any control changes, whether by merger, asset sale, or stock acquisition? Does a board have the power to enter into such agreements? If so, is a board's use of such a power limited by its fiduciary obligation to its shareholders? See Gearhart Industries, Inc. v. Smith International, Inc., 592 F.Supp. 203 (N.D.Tex.1984), affirmed in part, modified in part 741 F.2d 707 (5th Cir.1984) (a target responded to a creeping open-market acquisition by issuing a package of debentures and warrants to a group of institutional investors; the exercise price on the warrants dropped substantially on the occurrence of an unapproved tender offer; the injunction was refused).

If enforcing a fiduciary duty to bondholders would decrease a firm's capital costs by lowering its cost of borrowing, why do firms not voluntarily agree to offer such a duty? A firm voluntarily agreeing to such a duty ought to be able to sell its bonds at better prices and have a distinct advantage in the capital markets. If a firm offered voluntarily to be bound by a fiduciary duty to bondholders, what would happen to its stock prices? Would they decrease in value by less than the bonds would increase? If the courts force all firms to have a fiduciary relationship with their bondholders as well as their stockholders, will the total value of each firm's stock and bonds increase? Why do bondholders not have a right to vote for directors?

Please read Wyoming Statutes 1977, §§ 17–18–201 to 17–18–206 in your supplement. What is the effect of the unique Wyoming bondholder provisions? If you held stock in a Wyoming corporation, would you vote your shares in favor of an amendment to the articles of incorporation that would permit "notices of bondholder protections"?

Note
Leveraged Recaps

Leveraged buyouts are not the only method of releveraging a firm to the detriment of bondholders. Firms fearing takeovers by unwanted suitors have discovered that an effective takeover defense is a leveraged reorganization, also called a leveraged recap. By boosting debt and shrinking equity, companies exhaust their cash and borrowing capacity. Cash poor bidders, also known as raiders, cannot use the firm's cash or borrowing capacity to finance an acquisition. In a typical leveraged recap, a firm borrows a huge sum of cash (there are several ways to effect the debt placement) and pays the cash out in a one-time special dividend to its shareholders, leaving the firm encumbered by the new debt and the shareholders holding "stub" stock, valued at less than 10 percent of its pretransaction price. Shareholders are happy, the value of the cash dividend plus the value of the stub stock often exceeds the value of the stock before the announcement of the recapitalization. But bondholders can lose large amounts, as the market value of outstanding bonds tumbles to reflect the debtor firm's higher default risk. See Anders, *"Recapitalizations" Are a Bonanza for Some, but Bondholders Can Take a Terrific Beating,* Wall St.J., June 1, 1987 at 53, col. 3.

Note
The Empirical Evidence

Studies of leveraged transactions in the early to mid eighties showed that bondholders experienced only insignificant losses from takeovers and leveraged buyouts, but the data were thin. Coffee, *Unstable Coalitions: Corporate Grievance as a Multi–Player Game,* 78 Geo.L.J. 1495, 1516–18 (1990) (summarizing studies). In these early studies, however, significant wealth losses did occur when there was substantial increase in a firm's leverage. In four recent studies of the mid to late eighties the results changed. Researchers found significant negative average returns on outstanding publicly traded, nonconvertible bonds after the announcement of an LBO. Id. at 1518–19. Yet the amount of bondholder losses was not significantly related to the amount of shareholder gains. Thus the researchers concluded that the motive for LBOs did not appear to be the naked pursuit of wealth transfers from bondholders. In one study bondholder losses were on average only 3.3 percent of shareholder gains, and another found that bondholder losses could not be accurately predicted from equity gains for any one LBO.

Note
The Market Response

After leveraged buyouts and leveraged recaps became popular, issuers of debt securities were forced to increase yields to place new issues. Some, however, found that they could lower yields by offering "poison put" covenants in the trust indenture agreements that spell out the rights of the debt holders. The covenants enable investors to sell the bonds back to the issuer on the occurrence of a "triggering event," defined to include changes of control, leveraged recapitalizations, and, in most cases, a severe credit downgrade (to triple B minus or lower). A second strategy is to increase the coupon rate on bonds with the occurrence of a specified triggering event that results in a credit downgrade (some also decrease the coupon rate on a credit upgrade).

COFFEE, UNSTABLE COALITIONS: CORPORATE GOVERNANCE AS A MULTI-PLAYER GAME
78 Geo.L.J. 1495, 1519-20 (1990).

In brief, the poison put is a right given in the debt instrument to bondholders to demand repayment at their option of the full principal amount of the indebtedness (possibly plus a premium) in the event of certain occurrences such as a takeover, restructuring, recapitalization, or merger.[83] Between only January and June 1989, over fifty debt issues, totaling approximately $14 billion in principal amount, have contained such event risk protections.[87]

* * *

83. To date, poison puts have been used more to compensate bondholders against event risk than to deter hostile takeovers. Generally, poison puts (or "super poison puts" in the more extravagant language of the financial press) are triggered if a "designated event" (as defined) occurs and a specified decline also takes place in the debt's rating by either Standard & Poor's Corp. or Moody's Investors Services, Inc. Sometimes, a decline in the rating of both rating agencies is required. "Designated events" are typically defined as (1) a change in control, usually demonstrated by the acquisition of either 20% or 30% of the issuer's stock by a person or group; (2) a merger or acquisition of the issuer, including a sale of substantially all its assets; (3) a buy-back by the issuer of some percentage (usually 30%) of its stock within a defined period (usually a 365-day period); (4) a recapitalization that, either through repurchases or dividends, meets the 30% mark in a 365-day period; or sometimes (5) a change in continuing directors—that is, a failure of a majority of the directors to remain in office. *See* Heiberling, *Event Risk Provisions Protect Bondholders Against Takeovers*, Nat'l L.J., June 5, 1989, at 22, col. 1. Generally, these puts have had a five or ten year life, and thus do not last for the life of the bond. Sometimes, the issuer also has the option to override the put provision by increasing the interest rate to a level that in the judgment of a designated investment banking firm compensates the bondholders for the increase in event risk. For a more recent variant that gives event risk protection without being a takeover deterrent, see *infra* text accompanying note 89.

87. Indeed, the early evidence suggests that bond purchasers have placed a high premium on these new "put" provisions. For example, the Harris debenture issue, which was one of the first debenture issues to contain this provision, traded at 120 basis points over U.S. Treasury securities, instead of at the 160-190 basis points at which other debentures of similar risk levels were traded. *See* Heiberling, *supra* note 83, at 25, col. 4. In short, the market valued this poison put at from 40 to 70 basis points. In addition, the market estimated the value of the 10-year term of the Harris put (as compared to the more typical 5-year term) at 10-20 basis points. *Id.* However, there is also evidence that on close inspection, many of these puts are not as protective as they initially seem. So far, Standard & Poor's has given only one out of 14 issuers rated its highest "event protection" rating.

The defensive utility of the poison put as an antitakeover device is only marginal; it will not block those takeovers in which the bidder is willing to pay off the debt. Yet, its defensive impact is hardly accidental. This is clearer once one recognizes that the most obvious protection for bondholders from event risk is not a put, but an upward interest rate shift in the event of a rating downgrading. Given an active secondary market, such a provision adequately compensates diversified bondholders and permits nondiversified bondholders to sell into the market. Moreover, such contingent rate shifting bonds, which also first appeared in 1989, permit the issuer to reduce the interest rate slightly if the bond rating is upgraded.[89] Given this option and the fact that the issuer benefits under the shifting rate formula if there is a credit upgrading, the suspicion grows that those managements choosing to adopt the poison put format are utilizing the bondholders' anxiety for their own self-protective ends.

The rights of bondholders in leveraged buyouts and leveraged recaps are the subject of much debate.

TAULCE, SHOULD BONDS HAVE MORE FUN? A REEXAMINATION OF THE DEBATE OVER CORPORATE BONDHOLDERS RIGHTS
1 Col.Bus.L.Rev. 1, 53–67, 131–132 (1989).

* * *

In refusing to adopt any such broad notion of fiduciary rights of bondholders courts have shown sound judgment for two fundamental reasons.

First * * * the reasons for questioning the traditional contract approach to determining bondholder rights do not go so far as to say that the contracting process and market forces are highly ineffective in protecting the interests of bondholders. Rather, the criticisms of the traditional rule establish only that there are some circumstances in which the traditional rule's presumption of the adequacy of the contracting process and market forces does not hold up. There is no basis for maintaining that the contract process and market forces are so ineffectual in protecting the interests of bondholders that sweeping judicial policing in the form of enforcement of fiduciary rights to bondholders is necessary. A broad grant of fiduciary rights to bondholders would undermine completely the allocations of risks under

---

89. In June 1989, Enrop Corp. of Houston issued the first of these bonds pegging the yield to the credit rating. Its bonds are rated BBB–, just above the floor in investment grade. Thus, investors had special reason to fear a rating decline, and Enrop responded to this need. Under its indenture, if the credit rating is moved up to A–, the interest rate moves from 9.5% to 9.4%, but if the rating falls one notch (to below investment grade), the rate goes from 9.5% to 12%. *See* Light, *supra* note 84, at 78. Such two-sided adjustments protect both sides.

bond contracts even though there is little reason to believe bondholders have been extensively victimized by debtor corporation opportunistic behavior.[122]

Second, creating a corporate fiduciary duty to bondholders would raise fundamental problems of impairing the efficiency of the capital structure of the corporation. Because bondholders have only a fixed claim on the income of the corporation and do not share in the corporate profits, maximization of profits is not in the best interests of the bondholders. Their best interest is to have the corporation engage in the least risky activities that are consistent with earning sufficient income to cover the payments due the bondholders under the bond contract. The recognition of fiduciary duties to bondholders would be inefficient because it would prohibit the corporation from engaging in other activities if there would be any greater level of risk associated with such other activities, even though such other activities would produce a higher expected return for the corporation. Subject to the problem of debtor corporation opportunistic behavior, stockholders, as the takers of residual profits and the bearers of residual risks, have the incentive to make the proper trade-off between risks and expected return from any given choice of corporate activities. Bondholders do not have the same incentive.

* * *

Several problems arise in attempting to fashion a standard of fiduciary duty from the vague mandates to the corporate board to exercise independent judgment or act in the best interests of the corporation as a whole.

First, such a standard of fiduciary duty in fact provides no alternative to analysis of the bondholder-corporation contractual relationship. Any attempt to mandate that corporate management act only in the best interests of all corporate investors must take account of what rights the various investors have bargained for. If bondholders have contracted to allow the corporation to retain certain powers and have received appropriate compensation for allowing the corporation to retain those powers, determining what is in the best interests of the corporation "as a whole" must take account of how the relationship of the various corporate investors has been structured. * * * In this light the "fiduciary" standard of requiring management to act only in the best interests of all investors is nothing more than requiring management to honor the terms of the bond contract. The only task is to interpret the bond contract in the proper fashion.

The second problem with this approach—mandating that corporate managers act for the benefit of all investors—is that it rests on a false premise. The false premise is that requiring directors to make deci-

---

122. * * *

* * *

* * * History shows that the market has responded, albeit somewhat belatedly, * * * by demanding the inclusion of increasingly stringent "event risk" protections in the indentures of most new bond issues.

sions in the best interests of the "corporation as a whole" will somehow overcome the inherent tension between investor groups. In fact, that tension cannot be so easily overcome. For example, one of the most basic of corporate decisions, whether or not to pay a dividend, raises a fundamental conflict of interests between bondholders and stockholders. If the corporation has no immediate use for funds, stockholders ordinarily will benefit from the payment of a dividend or at least be left no worse off by its payment. On the other hand, bondholders will frequently prefer to have the corporation's funds not paid out in dividends and will instead prefer to have the funds retained for eventual payment of bondholder claims. It is far from clear just what the best interests of the corporation "as a whole" are in such circumstances.

* * *

A third problem with the fiduciary duty notion of acting in the best interests of the corporation as a whole is that under existing institutional arrangements it is not realistic to expect corporate management to exercise independent judgment when faced with conflicts between bondholder and stockholder interests. Corporate management is elected by stockholders, not bondholders. Corporate management may have significant stock ownership in the corporation, management compensation levels in many instances may be tied to stock prices and management is constrained by the market for corporate control to maximize the price of corporate stock or else face the danger of a hostile takeover. One could argue that the existing institutional arrangements that tie the fortunes of corporate management to the fortunes of stockholders could be altered to take account of the fact that bondholders provide a substantial portion of the capital of many enterprises. For example, it is possible for bondholders to be given proportional representation on corporate boards of directors so as to have some leverage to protect their interests. It has also been suggested that management compensation packages should be structured in terms of proportionate interests in both the stock and bonds of the corporation. But it is far from clear that changes in existing institutional arrangements are desirable. Looking to the market provides the most damaging criticism of these proposals. If there were value to either of them (or to other alterations of existing institutional arrangements) they would have been adopted long ago. A corporation that adopted some such proposal would thereby signal to the capital markets that the interests of bondholders would be protected in such a corporation. Investors would then demand lower compensation for providing bond capital to the corporation and the corporation would thereby have a competitive advantage over firms that fail to adopt such proposals. Yet, such arrangements are exceedingly rare in practice.

* * *

Finally, there are problems of how such a standard of fiduciary obligation could ever be enforced. Given that boards of directors will rarely state an intention to favor one group over another and that claims of non-discriminatory justification could be made for most corporate actions, it seems likely that very few decisions by a board could be challenged as favoring one group of investors over another. * * * The question of what is best for the corporation in the long run is a highly subjective one that courts are not likely to be adept at deciding or willing to decide. * * *

Note

Insolvency Standards for Corporate Distributions

Although courts have been reluctant to impose general duties on boards of directors in favor of bondholders and other creditors, the law does provide creditors with minimum protections against firm distributions of capital that impair the firm's repayment obligations on the debt. McDaniel's position assumes not only that contractual protections are inadequate but also that the protections of these legal rules are inadequate. The rules are designed to provide redress once a creditor has suffered an actual default on the debtor's payment obligations. State legal capital statutes, affecting corporate distributions to shareholders, limit leveraged recaps. State fraudulent conveyance laws (and a similar provision in the federal bankruptcy code), limiting transfers for inadequate return consideration, limit leveraged buyouts. Dissolution provisions in state corporate codes condition payments to shareholders in liquidation and dissolution of a firm on the payment of all outstanding credit obligations. Finally, state bulk sales acts require that buyers in asset acquisitions give notice to creditors before the transaction if the buyer is not assuming the seller's debts. Legal capital, fraudulent conveyance, and bulk sales statutes are covered in the succeeding subsections. Dissolution statutes are covered in the chapter's final section on contingent liabilities.

Subsection b. State Corporate Code Provisions Restricting Dividends and Redemptions

B. MANNING & J. HANKS, A CONCISE TEXTBOOK ON LEGAL CAPITAL

13–16, 63–64 (3rd ed. 1990)

The shareholder is willing to admit the "priority" of the creditor's interest claim and claim for principal payment on maturity. That does *not* imply, however, that the shareholder is willing to stand by chronologically until such time as the creditors have been paid in full. The shareholder will usually insist, that if, as he hopes, the enterprise makes money (and perhaps even if it does not), the shareholders will receive some return on (or of) their investment from time to time, regardless of the fact that there are creditor claims outstanding. Such periodic payments to shareholders are characterized as "dividends"; and, in the usual and normal case of the healthy incorporated enterprise, it is assumed that some assets will be regularly distributed out from the corporate treasury to the shareholder investors in dividend form.

Simple as this observation may be, its implications are far-reaching. If it were the case that all creditors had to be paid off before *any* payment could be made to shareholder investors, and if shareholders received nothing until ultimate liquidation of the enterprise when they would divide the residuum left after payment of all creditors—if, in other words, the terms "prior" and "before" were chronological as well as hierarchical—the creditor would not have to worry about assets being drained away into the hands of junior claimants and he would sleep better at night. But that arrangement would be wholly unacceptable to shareholders. Shareholders insist—and ultimately creditors must concede—that, *during the life* of the creditor's claim, assets may be passed out to an investing group that hierarchically ranks below the creditors. The question becomes unavoidable: How much of the assets in the treasury of the incorporated enterprise may be distributed to shareholders, when, and under what circumstances?

While "dividends" are the most common form in which distributions are made to shareholders out of corporate assets, the distributive process is potentially Protean. If it is decided that an incorporated enterprise should be broken up, or that some of its assets or separable operations should be sold for cash, extraordinary cash distributions may be made to shareholders; these will be referred to as liquidating distributions, or distributions in partial liquidation. Similarly, the decision-makers in a going economic enterprise may conclude that the company has more cash or other liquid assets on hand than it needs, that no interesting investment opportunities are visible, and that the best thing to do is to distribute the excess assets to the shareholders; such a transaction may be referred to as a partial return of capital. Substantially the same transaction may occur where, for one reason or another, it seems desirable to those who are making the decisions to transfer a major nonliquid asset (such as a parcel of land or a separable business operation) to the shareholders, either by transferring to each shareholder a proportionate undivided interest in the asset, or by putting the asset into a subsidiary and distributing the subsidiary's shares to the parent's shareholders. Or those in control of an incorporated enterprise may decide to "buy in" or "repurchase" some of the outstanding stock of the corporation—a transaction that pays assets out of the corporate treasury to shareholders but brings in to the corporation nothing but pieces of paper in the hands of the corporation.

* * *

These instances do not exhaust the numbers of ways in which assets can be transferred by corporate managers out of the corporate till into the hands of shareholders. Distributions of corporate assets to a shareholder may be denominated as "salary payments" though in excess of a compensation level that would be reasonable for the services performed for the corporation by the shareholder. Corporate assets can be sold to shareholders for less than their market value. Corporate assets can be loaned to shareholders, or leased to shareholders, on terms that in effect reduce the aggregate resources of the corporate treasury. If the corporation guarantees the debt of a shareholder to a third party, the corporation's credit is put in jeopardy to the benefit of the shareholder. Corporate assets can be pledged or mortgaged to shareholders through arrangements under which, upon nonpayment of the loan by the corporation (at the decision of the board), the assets will be forfeited to the shareholders.[3] These same transactions, with the same consequences, can be carried out through dealings between the shareholders of the corporation and subsidiaries of the corporation. In all these instances, and others, the problem of the creditor of the corporation is the same. Assets have left the corporate pot, have gone beyond his reach, and, worst of all, have been paid out to that group of investors whose claim to the assets of the corporation is junior to his.

Finally, it must be observed, there are two other factors that contribute to the creditor's unease. It is not just that there are many ways by which corporate assets *can* be channeled out of the corporate pot and into the shareholders' pockets. More worrisome is the shareholders' keen desire and incentive to do just that. The shareholder knows that so long as his money is at stake in the enterprise he will be the last one paid—or will not be paid at all—if the weather gets stormy. His instinct is to limit that risk by arranging for some kind of payout of at least his initial investment as soon as possible.

A closely related consideration is the dynamic known as "leverage". The creditor wants a thick equity cushion under him; the equity investors tend to prefer a thick debt slice in the company's capitalization, up to the capacity of the enterprise to meet the carrying charges of the debt. The shareholder sees an obvious advantage in a funding plan under which he puts in $1 and the lender puts in $2, the lender agreeing to a fixed return of 5¢ for each dollar loaned; if the enterprise earns 10¢ on each of the three dollars invested, the end result is that the creditor's $2 investment yields him 10¢ while the shareholder's $1 investment yields him 20¢. Shareholders greatly relish such leveraged arrangements under which the entrepreneurial harvest, if any, will come to them while the risk of capital loss is largely that of lenders.

The second thought that disturbs the sweet slumber of the creditor is the knowledge that virtually all responsibility and power for the conduct of the enterprise is in the hands of the members of the board of directors, who are elected by and mainly interested in the shareholders, and of corporate officers selected by the board. As the creditor sees it, hungry goats have been set to watch the cabbages.

---

3. In addition, of course, one who is a shareholder can legitimately lend money to the corporation and thus become both a creditor and an equity owner. In that case, however, a payment made by the corporation on the loan is not, as an analytic matter, a distribution to shareholders, but a payment to a creditor.

Out of the conflict between the creditor's desire to keep corporate assets from being distributed to shareholders, and the shareholder's insistence upon receiving asset distributions despite the existence of outstanding creditors' claims, arises the major problem to which the par and stated capital provisions—the legal capital provisions—of state corporation codes are directed.

* * *

The basic thesis of *Wood v. Dummer* is incontestable. If the hierarchical relationship of creditor to shareholder is to have any meaning at all, then the management must not be left free to shovel all the assets in the corporate treasury out to the shareholders when the corporation has insufficient assets to pay its creditors or when the shareholder distribution itself renders the corporation unable to pay its creditors. The central point is to avoid insolvency.

"Insolvency" has, of course, long had a recognized duality of meaning. The first was developed over the centuries by the English chancery courts—the equity courts. In the equity courts, the test of a debtor's insolvency was whether he was unable to meet his obligations as they became due. This is often referred to as the "equity insolvency test", a term that will appear frequently hereafter in this book.

As was often the case, the English law courts across the street from the chancery court went their own way in developing a concept of insolvency for use in bankruptcy proceedings. In the law courts, the test for bankruptcy was whether the aggregate amount of the debtor's assets was less than the total amount of his liabilities. This is often referred to as the "bankruptcy test".

The difference between these two conceptions can be very great. The equity insolvency test is concerned with current liquidity of the going enterprise; the emphasis of the bankruptcy sense of insolvency is upon liquidation of the enterprise. It is easily possible for an enterprise to be short of cash and other liquid means of payment while at the same time holding illiquid assets of great value; such an enterprise may well fail the equity insolvency test. It is also a quite possible occurrence for an enterprise to have a large current cash flow while steadily operating at a loss and suffering a continuing erosion of its asset base; in time, such an enterprise will fail to meet the bankruptcy test of insolvency.

* * *

Please read Revised Model Business Corporation Act sections 6.40 and 8.33 and their official comments in your supplement.

Questions

1. Why does the Model Act contain two tests? Massachusetts corporate law has always contained only the equity insolvency test, and Massa-

chusetts creditors do not appear to have suffered any severe disadvantage as a result. See the official comment to section 6.40.

2. Why does the balance sheet test in section 6.40 not require the use of Generally Accepted Accounting Principles? Why do state codes say nothing about how corporations or their accountants keep their books or prepare their financial statements?

At the present time a few states have adopted the current version of the Model Act, which was amended in 1980 and in 1987. Some states have the pre–1987 version and some states have the pre–1980 version. Several states, including Delaware, also have their own version of the legal capital statutes, which use very different standards. Del.Gen.Corp.Law § 170 (capital surplus and nimble dividend standard); N.Y.—McKinney's Bus. Corp.Law § 510(b) (capital surplus test).

Subsection c. Fraudulent Conveyance Acts and Leveraged Buyouts

Fraudulent conveyance laws are aimed at protecting the creditors' right to execute judgments on assets of debtors in the event of defaults. If a debtor has transferred property to frustrate collection efforts by creditors, creditors may sue under state law to set aside any improper transfers and obtain a lien on the transferred property to the full extent of their claims. Trustees in bankruptcy (or debtors in possession) are empowered under federal law to recover for the benefit of creditors the value of any property improperly removed from the bankrupt debtor's estate. Fraudulent conveyance provisions are found in section 548 of the Federal Bankruptcy Code, 11 U.S.C.A. § 548, and in state acts, which are typically modeled on either the Uniform Fraudulent Conveyance Act or the newer Uniform Fraudulent Transfer Act. A trustee in bankruptcy is also empowered to invoke state fraudulent conveyance law to invalidate prebankruptcy transfers. 11 U.S.C.A. § 144(b). The statutes have a long heritage, deriving from Statute of 13 Elizabeth, passed by the English Parliament in 1571.

In 1983 and 1984 a federal district court sent shock waves through the merger and acquisition community by applying fraudulent conveyance law to a primitive leveraged buyout. United States v. Gleneagles Investment Co., 565 F.Supp. 556 (M.D.Pa.1983); 571 F.Supp. 935 (1983); and 584 F.Supp. 671 (1984). The Third Circuit affirmed the district court's basic analysis in the opinion below. Before you read the case, please read Uniform Fraudulent Conveyance Act sections 2, 4, 5, 7, and 9 in your supplement.

UNITED STATES OF AMERICA v. TABOR COURT REALTY CORP.

United States Court of Appeals, Third Circuit, 1986.
803 F.2d 1288, cert. denied 483 U.S. 1005, 107 S.Ct. 3229, 97 L.Ed.2d 735 (1987).

ALDISERT, CHIEF JUDGE.

* * *

These appeals arise from an action by the United States to reduce to judgment delinquent federal income taxes, interest, and penalties assessed and accrued against Raymond Colliery Co., Inc. and its subsidiaries (the Raymond Group) for the fiscal years of June 30, 1966 through June 30, 1973 and to reduce to judgment similarly assessed taxes owed by Great American Coal Co., Inc. and its subsidiaries for the fiscal year ending June 30, 1975.

The government sought to collect these tax claims from surface and coal lands owned by the Raymond Group as well as from lands formerly owned by it but which, as a result of allegedly illegal and fraudulent county tax sales, were later owned by Gleneagles Investment Co., Inc. In addition, the government sought to assert the priority of its liens over liens held by others. The district court held in favor of the government on most of its claims and concluded the litigation by promulgating an order of priority of liens on Raymond Group lands.

* * *

Very serious problems surfaced in 1971 when Raymond's chief stockholders—the Gillens and Clevelands—started to have disagreements over the poor performance of the coal producing companies. The stockholders decided to solve the problem by seeking a buyer for the group. * * * Although the litigation in the district court was far-reaching, most of the central issues have their genesis in 1973 when the Raymond Group was sold to Durkin in a leveraged buy-out through the vehicle of Great American.

A leveraged buy-out is not a legal term of art. It is a shorthand expression describing a business practice wherein a company is sold to a small number of investors, typically including members of the company's management, under financial arrangements in which there is a minimum amount of equity and a maximum amount of debt. The financing typically provides for a substantial return of investment capital by means of mortgages or high risk bonds, popularly known as "junk bonds." The predicate transaction here fits the popular notion of a leveraged buy-out. Shareholders of the Raymond Group sold the corporation to a small group of investors headed by Raymond's president; these investors borrowed substantially all of the purchase price at an extremely high rate of interest secured by mortgages on the assets of the selling company and its subsidiaries and those of additional entities that guaranteed repayment.

To effectuate the buy-out, Great American obtained a loan commitment from Institutional Investors Trust on July 24, 1973, in the amount of $8,530,000. The 1973 interrelationship among the many creditors of the Raymond Group, and the sale to Great American—a seemingly empty corporation which was able to perform the buy-out only on the strength of the massive loan from IIT—forms the backdrop for the relevancy of the Pennsylvania Uniform Fraudulent Conveyance Act, one of the critical legal questions presented for our decision.

The loan from IIT was structured so as to divide the Raymond Group into borrowing companies and guarantor companies. The loan was secured by mortgages on the assets of the borrowing companies, but was also guaranteed by mortgages on the assets of the guarantor companies. We must decide whether the borrowers' mortgages were invalid under the UFCA and whether there was consideration for the guarantors' mortgages.

The IIT loan was closed on November 26, 1973. The borrowing companies in the Raymond Group received $7 million in direct proceeds from IIT. The remaining $1.53 million was placed in escrow as a reserve account for the payment of accruing interest. The loans were to be repaid by December 31, 1976, at an interest rate of five points over the prime rate but in no event less than 12.5 percent. In exchange, each of the borrowing companies—Raymond Colliery, Blue Coal, Glen Nan, and Olyphant Associates—created a first lien in favor of IIT on all of their tangible and intangible assets; each of the guarantor companies—all other companies in the Raymond Group—created a second lien in favor of IIT on all of their tangible and intangible assets. The loan agreement also contained a clause which provided IIT with a priority lien on the proceeds from Raymond's sales of its surplus lands. Finally, the agreement provided that violations of any of the loan covenants would permit IIT to accelerate the loan and to collect immediately the full balance due from any or all of the borrowers or guarantors.

The exchange of money and notes did not stop with IIT's advances to the borrowing companies. Upon receipt of the IIT loan proceeds, the borrowing companies immediately transferred a total of $4,085,000 to Great American. In return, Great American issued to each borrowing company an unsecured promissory note with the same interest terms as those of the IIT loan agreement. In addition to the proceeds of the IIT loan, Great American borrowed other funds to acquire the purchase price for Raymond's stock.

When the financial dust settled after the closing on November 26, 1973, this was the situation at Raymond: Great American paid $6.7 million to purchase Raymond's stock, the shareholders receiving $6.2 million in cash and a $500,000 note; at least $4.8 million of this amount was obtained by mortgaging Raymond's assets.

Notwithstanding the cozy accommodations for the selling stockholders, the financial environment of the Raymond Group at the time of the sale was somewhat precarious. At the time of the closing, Raymond had multi-million dollar liabilities for federal income taxes, trade accounts, pension fund contributions, strip mining and backfilling obligations, and municipal real estate taxes. * * *

Under Durkin's control after the buy-out, Raymond's condition further deteriorated. Following the closing the Raymond Group lacked the funds to pay its routine operating expenses, including those for materials, supplies, telephone, and other utilities. It was also unable to pay its delinquent and current real estate taxes. Within two months of the closing, the deep mining operations of Blue Coal were shut down; within six months of the closing, the Raymond Group ceased all strip mining operations. * * * Finally, on September 15, 1976, IIT notified the borrowing and guarantor Raymond companies that their mortgage notes were in default. On September 29, 1976, IIT confessed judgments against the borrowing companies for the balance due on the loan and began to solicit a buyer for the Raymond Group mortgages.

* * *

Pagnotti Enterprises, another large anthracite producer, was the prime candidate to purchase the mortgages from IIT. In December 1976, James J. Tedesco, on behalf of Pagnotti, commenced negotiations for the purchase. Tedesco signed an agreement on December 15, 1976. Pursuant to the mortgage sale contract—and prior to the closing of the sale and assignment of the mortgages—IIT and Pagnotti each placed $600,000 in an escrow account to be applied to the payment of delinquent real estate taxes on properties listed for the county tax sales or to be used as funds for bidding on the properties at the tax sales.

* * *

On January 26, 1977, the sale and assignment of the IIT mortgages took place. Pagnotti paid approximately $4.5 million for the IIT mortgages; at that time, the mortgage balance was $5,817,475.69. Pagnotti thereafter assigned the mortgage to McClellan, * * * McClellan did just that—it foreclosed.

* * *

McClellan initially challenges the district court's application of the Pennsylvania Uniform Fraudulent Conveyances Act (UFCA), 39 Pa. Stat. §§ 351–363, to the leveraged buy-out loan made by IIT to the mortgagors, and to the acquisition of the mortgages from IIT by McClellan. The district court determined that IIT lacked good faith in the transaction because it knew, or should have known, that the money it lent the mortgagors was used, in part, to finance the purchase of stock from the mortgagors' shareholders, and that as a consequence of the loan, IIT and its assignees obtained a secured position in the mortgagors' property to the detriment of creditors. * * *

Section 354 of the UFCA is a "constructive fraud" provision. It establishes that a conveyance made by a person "who is or will be thereby rendered insolvent, is fraudulent as to creditors, without regard to his actual intent, if the conveyance is made ... without a fair consideration." 39 Pa.Stat. § 354. Section 353 defines fair consideration as an exchange of a "fair equivalent ... in good faith." 39 Pa.Stat. § 353. Because section 354 excludes an examination of intent, it follows that "good faith" must be something other than intent; because section 354 also focuses on insolvency, knowledge of insolvency is a rational interpretation of the statutory language of lack of "good faith."

* * *

We have decided that the district court reached the right conclusion here for the right reasons. It determined that IIT did not act in good faith because it was aware, first, that the exchange would render Raymond insolvent, and second, that no member of the Raymond Group would receive fair consideration. We believe that this determination is consistent with the statute and case law.

McClellan and amicus curiae also argue that as a general rule the UFCA should not be applied to leveraged buy-outs. They contend that the UFCA, which was passed in 1924, was never meant to apply to a complicated transaction such as a leveraged buy-out. The Act's broad language, however, extends to any "conveyance" which is defined as "every payment of money ... and also the creation of any lien or incumbrance." 39 Pa.Stat. § 351. This broad sweep does not justify exclusion of a particular transaction such as a leveraged buy-out simply because it is innovative or complicated. If the UFCA is not to be applied to leveraged buy-outs, it should be for the state legislatures, not the courts, to decide.

In addition, although appellants' and amicus curiae's arguments against general application of the Act to leveraged buy-outs are not without some force, the application of fraudulent conveyance law to certain leveraged buy-outs is not clearly bad public policy.[2] In any event, the circumstances of this case justify application. Even the policy arguments offered against the application of fraudulent conveyance law to leveraged buy-outs assume facts that are not present in this case. For example, in their analysis of fraudulent conveyance law, Professors Baird and Jackson assert that their analysis should be applied to leveraged buy-outs only where aspects of the transaction are not hidden from creditors and the transaction does not possess other suspicious attributes. *See* Baird and Jackson, *Fraudulent Conveyance Law and Its Proper Domain,* 38 Vand.L.Rev. 829, 843 (1985). In fact, Baird and Jackson conclude their article by noting that their analysis is limited to transactions in which "the transferee parted with value when he entered into the transaction and that transaction was entered in the ordinary course." *Id.* at 855 (footnote omitted). In the instant case, however, the severe economic circumstances in which the Raymond Group found itself, the obligation, without benefit, incurred by the Raymond Group, and the small number of shareholders benefited

---

2. A major premise of the policy arguments opposing application of fraudulent conveyance law to leveraged buy-outs is that such transactions often benefit creditors and that the application of fraudulent conveyance law to buy-outs will deter them in the future. * * * An equally important premise is that creditors can protect themselves from undesirable leveraged buy-outs by altering the terms of their credit contracts. * * * This second premise ignores, however, cases such as this one in which the major creditors (in this instance the United States and certain Pennsylvania municipalities) are involuntary and do not become creditors by virtue of a contract. The second premise also ignores the possibility that the creditors attacking the leveraged buy-out (such as many of the creditors in this case) became creditors before leveraged buy-outs became a common financing technique and thus may not have anticipated such leveraged transactions so as to have been able to adequately protect themselves by contract.

* * *

by the transaction suggest that the transaction was not entered in the ordinary course, that fair consideration was not exchanged, and that the transaction was anything but unsuspicious. The policy arguments set forth in opposition to the application of fraudulent conveyance law to leveraged buy-outs do not justify the exemption of transactions such as this.[3]

* * *

McClellan next argues that the district court erred in holding that the mortgages were invalid under section 357 of the UFCA, 39 Pa.Stat. § 357. * * *

As distinguished from the "constructive fraud" sections of the UFCA discussed *supra,* section 357 invalidates conveyances made with an intent to defraud creditors: "Every conveyance made and every obligation incurred with actual intent, as distinguished from intent presumed in law, to hinder, delay, or defraud either present or future creditors, is fraudulent as to both present and future creditors." 39 Pa. Cons.Stat. § 357. Under Pennsylvania law, an intent to hinder, delay, or defraud creditors may be inferred from transfers in which consideration is lacking and where the transferor and transferee have knowledge of the claims of creditors and know that the creditors cannot be paid.
* * *

Direct evidence is not necessary to prove "actual intent." * * * In Pennsylvania, the existence of actual intent is a question of fact, * * * therefore, the court's determination is reviewed on the clearly erroneous standard.

The evidence recited by the district court supports its finding of an intent to hinder creditors.

* * *

A. LEON HIGGINBOTHAM, JR., CIRCUIT JUDGE, concurring in part and dissenting in part.

I concur in the majority's judgment that Pennsylvania's fraudulent conveyance laws may be applied to a leveraged buyout where, as here, a few shareholders seek to use it as a device to benefit themselves and take advantage of the creditors of a clearly faltering corporation. Since I find that the purposes underlying Pennsylvania's fraudulent conveyance law dictate that only a portion of the disputed transfer of funds be set aside, however, I must dissent from that part of the majority's opinion which declares the IIT mortgage loans wholly void. * * * IIT made four separate loans totaling $8,530,000. Of this, $4,085,000 was passed through Raymond Group companies to shareholders and $1,530,-

---

3. It should also be noted that another basic premise of the Baird and Jackson analysis is that as a general matter fraudulent conveyance law should be applied only to those transactions to which a rational creditor would surely object. * * * Although a rational creditor might under certain circumstances consent to a risky but potentially beneficial leveraged buy-out of a nearly insolvent debtor, no reasonable creditor would consent to the intentionally fraudulent conveyance the district court correctly found this transaction to be.

* * *

000 was retained by IIT as an interest reserve as part of the invalid transaction. However, $2,915,000 was used to pay existing debts (including an existing mortgage loan owned by Chemical Bank). To the extent that the IIT funds were used to pay existing creditors, the assets available to creditors generally were not diminished and the Raymond Group's estate was not improperly depleted.[1] I would therefore hold that only the transfer of the $4,085,000 between IIT and the Raymond Group's shareholders and the creation of the $1,530,000 interest reserve for IIT should be set aside.

Questions:

1. There are three separate primary transactions in the case, the loan from IIT to Raymond Colliery, the loan from Raymond Colliery to Great American, and the purchase by Great American of the Raymond Colliery stock held by the Gillens and Clevelands. Which of the transactions are voidable under the Uniform Fraudulent Conveyance Act? Does the court consider them one at a time or as one transaction? IIT loaned money to the firm in exchange for a repayment promise and security interests in firm land (mortgages). How can the court hold that IIT did not give fair value for what it received?

2. In a classic leveraged buyout, the buyout group forms a shell acquisition vehicle that gathers a war chest of cash by placing loans. The vehicle buys a controlling block of stock in the target firm and merges the vehicle into the target. With the merger, the target becomes obligated on all the acquisition financing. If soon after the LBO the target is in bankruptcy, can creditors of the target sue under the *Tabor Court Realty* case? Can the buyout group avoid fraudulent conveyance claims restricting an acquisition? Assume, for example, the buyout group uses the proceeds of a loan (secured by all assets including those after-acquired in the acquisition) to purchase the assets and assume the liabilities of the target. If the firm fails, can the creditors bring suit under the UFCA?

If an LBO does violate the UFCA, who is liable? Selling shareholders (controlling and noncontrolling)? New shareholders? LBO lenders (who have and have not yet been paid)? Purchasers of junk bonds sold by the firm after the transaction to pay off LBO debts? For how much?

3. Is it constructive fraud on preexisting firm creditors whenever an LBO fails? How should courts determine what is fair value under fraudulent conveyance statutes? Is fair value present in LBOs because the target receives nonmonetary value from the new purchasers, such as new management expertise? See Credit Managers Ass'n v. Federal Co., 629 F.Supp. 175, 182 (C.D.Cal.1986). Does a firm need to include in its calculation of debt obligations for its cash flow projections threatened lawsuits on product liability or employment discrimination claims and the like?

---

1. It is clear that Pennsylvania's fraudulent conveyance laws would have permitted the Raymond Group to take out a loan to pay existing debts. *Trumbower Co. v. Noe Construction Corp.,* 64 D. & C.2d 480 (1973). To an extent, this is what the Raymond Group did with IIT loan proceeds.

4. Does the holding in the case apply to leveraged recaps? Assume, for example, a firm borrows money from a small group of lenders and passes the funds on to its shareholders in dividends. If the firm is in bankruptcy soon thereafter, do the creditors have a valid fraudulent conveyance claim? Does the case apply to large-scale stock redemptions? Assume that a firm with four shareholders redeems the stock of three of them with cash and then cannot meet its obligations. See In re Anderson Industries, Inc., 55 B.R. 922 (Bkrtcy.Mich.1985).

5. Can employees file suit under a fraudulent conveyance act to protect wages, vacation and sick leave pay, and life insurance, health insurance, and pension benefits? See International Ass'n of Machinists v. United States Can Co., 150 Wis.2d 479, 441 N.W.2d 710 (1989).

6. Two parties that benefited enormously from the LBO wave in the late eighties were investment bankers and Wall Street lawyers. The investment bankers collected huge fees for structuring the buyout, writing fairness opinions on the buyout price and underwriting the junk bonds that often were part of the financing package. Wall Street lawyers charged large fees for legal advice and for shepherding the transaction through the many applicable legal requirements. In the $1.2 billion leveraged buyout of Revco D.S., Inc., for example, the company paid $80 million in fees and other expenses to various professionals who had rendered services in the buyout. The buyout entity engaged the professionals, and when the entity merged into Revco after a successful stock acquisition, Revco was obligated to pay the fees. If the surviving firm in an LBO soon becomes insolvent, can aggrieved creditors sue the bankers and lawyers for a return of the fees on the grounds that payments were a fraudulent conveyance? See In re Revco D.S. Inc., Cas. Nos. 588–1308 through 588–1321 (Bankr.N.Ohio 7/16/90) (Preliminary Examiner's Report).

7. In light of the possibility of an attack under fraudulent conveyance laws (especially if the LBO fails), what should the buyout group and its lenders do at the time of the buyout to establish a paper record to protect themselves in litigation? Most buyout groups try to hire outside experts to give "solvency opinions," letters opining that the firm will be solvent after the buyout. How much protection do favorable opinions provide an LBO group? Ought creditors to be able to sue these experts for favorable letters when the predictions of solvency do not bear out? On what standards? Cf. Wells v. Shearson Lehman/American Express, Inc., 127 A.D.2d 200, 514 N.Y.S.2d 1 (1st Dept. 1987), reversed on other grounds 72 N.Y.2d 11, 530 N.Y.S.2d 517, 526 N.E.2d 8 (1988) (investment bankers can be liable to shareholders on fairness opinions).

If the board of directors of a firm agreeing to an LBO relies on a solvency opinion to assure itself and other participants in an LBO of the future viability of the firm, can the board soliciting the opinion agree to indemnify the provider of the solvency opinion for all liabilities that may be associated with the opinion? Can the board agree to waive any claims it may have against the provider of a solvency opinion? If so, who is bound by the waiver? Can a provider of a solvency opinion limit its liability exposure by circumscribing its conclusions with a long list of "assumptions and limitations" (for example, "The opinion giver has relied without independent verification on the data supplied by the firm")? If a board agrees to indemnification or waiver provisions on the "assumption and limitation" provisions, do the provisions affect the ability of the board to rely on the solvency opinion? The ability of the board to argue justifiable reliance on the solvency opinion? See Del.Gen.Corp. Law § 141(e) (a director may rely on an outside expert in "good faith" if the expert "has been selected with reasonable care by or on behalf of the corporation".

KUPETZ v. WOLF

United States Court of Appeals, Ninth Circuit, 1988.
845 F.2d 842.

SNEED, CIRCUIT JUDGE:

The district court, by way of a summary judgment and directed verdict, determined that the bankrupt made neither fraudulent conveyances under various California fraudulent conveyance statutes and section 548 of the Bankruptcy Code nor improper corporate distributions under California law. * * * We affirm.

Wolf & Vine, a mannequin manufacturing company, is the debtor in proceedings before the United States Bankruptcy Court for the Central District of California. Prior to July 31, 1979, Wolf & Vine had been owned 50% by Morris Wolf and 50% by the Marmon Group, Inc. (Marmon). Wolf announced his intention to retire and dispose of his share in the business. Marmon, being obligated under an earlier agreement to purchase the business, began looking for a suitable purchaser of the entire business. After reviewing several potential buyers they decided that David Adashek, an individual backed by Continental Illinois National Bank (the Bank), was suitable.

On July 31, 1979, a series of transactions took place that essentially left Adashek in full control of the company. These transactions amounted to what is known as a leveraged buyout (LBO). There was no evidence in the proceedings below that either Marmon or Wolf knew how the purchase of their stock was to be financed.

The separate transactions were as follows:

(1) Adashek formed Little Red Riding Hood (Riding Hood), a Wisconsin corporation having $100.00 in capital;

(2) Riding Hood purchased all the shares of Wolf & Vine from Wolf and Marmon for $3 million, $1.1 million paid immediately and $1.9 million to be paid in installments over the next two years;

(3) Riding Hood financed the transaction with a $1.1 million loan from the Bank and the Bank issued letters of credit in favor of the sellers for the remaining amount;

(4) Riding Hood merged into Wolf & Vine, which, as the survivor corporation, assumed the obligation of Riding Hood to the sellers, Wolf and Marmon; and

(5) Wolf & Vine pledged its assets to the Bank to secure the $1.1 million loan and the letters of credit. Thus, Adashek effectively pledged the assets of Wolf & Vine to finance his acquisition of that corporation.

All would be well if only Wolf & Vine could service its debt. Adashek, presumably aware of this fact, proceeded to make significant changes in the way the company was run. Apparently Wolf, who had been retained as president, disagreed with some of the changes and several months later resigned. For a time Wolf & Vine made payments to Mr. Wolf and Marmon pursuant to the purchase agreement. For example, in July 1980, Wolf was paid $401,235.75 and Marmon was paid $142,427.32. A year later, however, in July 1981, although Wolf and Marmon were each paid $798,750, the payment to Wolf was made by the Bank under the letter of credit.[1] During this time Wolf & Vine failed to perform as well as Adashek had anticipated and in December 1981 it filed for bankruptcy under Chapter 11. It later changed its petition to a Chapter 7 liquidation proceeding.

In May 1983, the Trustee filed a complaint in the district court alleging that the manner in which the sale was financed constituted fraudulent conveyances to Wolf and Marmon under state law and bankruptcy law, improper distributions to shareholders, breaches of fiduciary duty, and civil conspiracy. The Trustee argues that Wolf and Marmon were the beneficiaries of fraudulent conveyances in the form of payments of the purchase price that left the company's creditors without a chance of collecting the amounts owed to them. The Trustee's claims against Adashek and the Bank were settled leaving only Wolf and Marmon as defendants.

* * *

The Trustee makes three primary claims on appeal, two based on state law and one on federal law. First, he argues that the payments to the selling shareholders are subject to attack under the state fraudulent conveyance law. Section 544(b) of the Bankruptcy Code permits the Trustee to stand in the shoes of a creditor to assert any state law claims that a creditor may have. Second, the Trustee argues that the 1981 payments were fraudulent transfers under Bankruptcy Code section 548. That section in part prohibits transfers by the debtor made without fair consideration when the debtor is left insolvent or with unreasonably small capital. Inasmuch as the purpose of California fraudulent conveyance law in no way differs from that of Bankruptcy Code § 548, the discussion applicable to the first disposes of claims under the latter as well. Third, it is contended by the Trustee that the payments to the selling shareholders were improper distributions under Cal.Corp.Code §§ 500 and 501, which prohibit payments made when the corporation does not have enough retained earnings, or is unable to

---

1. Apparently, there is some confusion about whether the 1981 payment to Marmon was also under a letter of credit.

meet its liabilities, at the time of, or as a result of, the transaction. For reasons discussed below, we find that none of these claims has merit.

LBOs pose difficult issues when the purchased corporation becomes bankrupt. An LBO is a purchase transaction based on pledging the assets of the purchased entity to secure the purchase price. Typically, a small group of investors and managers combine to purchase the outstanding shares of a company by creating a large debt by either issuing high-yield "junk bonds" or obtaining a loan from a financial institution. Almost no equity capital is invested. The debt, to repeat, is secured by pledging the assets of the acquired company as security.

Existing unsecured creditors are vulnerable in an LBO. From their perspective, a pledge of the company's assets as collateral to finance the purchase of the company reduces the assets to which they can look for repayment. As some of the acquired companies have failed, creditors have begun to assert that LBOs are fraudulent as to creditors. In this case, the Trustee's attack is, at bottom, such an assertion.

The present law of fraudulent conveyances has its roots in the Statute of 13 Elizabeth passed by Parliament in 1571. The statute was directed at a practice by which debtors sold their property to friends or relatives for a nominal sum, thus defeating creditors' attempts to satisfy their claims against the debtor. Once the creditor had given up its claim against the debtor, the debtor would reclaim the property that purportedly had been transferred.

The basic thrust of that early statute was to prohibit transfers that hinder, delay, or defraud creditors. Such transfers were prevented by making the collusive transferee liable to the creditor in the amount of the transfer. For four centuries, the primary difficulty has been how to decide which transfers in fact hinder, delay, or defraud creditors. Because intent to defraud is difficult to prove, courts rely on "badges of fraud." Thus, certain indicia of fraud may lead to the conclusion that the debtor had fraudulent intent. The most common of these, now found in the UFCA and in Bankruptcy Code section 548, is to assume fraudulent intent when an *insolvent debtor makes a transfer and gets nothing or very little in return.*

In an LBO, the lender, by taking a security interest in the company's assets, reduces the assets available to creditors in the event of failure of the business. The form of the LBO, while not unimportant, does not alter this reality. Thus, where the parties in an LBO fully intend to hinder the general creditors and benefit the selling shareholders the conveyance is fraudulent under UFCA § 7. The per se rules of the UFCA also may apply. A transfer made by an insolvent debtor who does not receive *fair* consideration is a fraudulent conveyance. And if a transaction leaves the firm with unreasonably small capital the transaction may be attacked.

The few courts [10] that have looked at the reach of fraudulent conveyance law in the context of LBOs have based their decisions, implicitly at least, on whether there was evidence of intentional fraud. Thus, those transactions in which all was "above board" to begin with have been "ratified" by the courts even though the creditors may have suffered in the end. In *Credit Managers Ass'n v. Federal Co.*, 629 F.Supp. 175 (C.D.Cal.1985), the court dealt with an attack on an LBO transaction on the basis of theories the same as those of the Trustee in this case: fraudulent conveyance, improper distribution, and equitable subordination. The court, after noting the possibility that fraudulent conveyance law could vitiate all LBOs, refused to employ this approach and declined to overturn the LBO.

In contrast, when the LBO was intentionally designed to defraud the creditors, the courts have had little difficulty in finding the transaction fraudulent. In *United States v. Gleneagles Inv. Co.*, 565 F.Supp. 556 (M.D.Pa.1983), for example, the court found violations of both the intentional and constructive fraud sections of the UFCA. This decision was upheld by the Third Circuit in *United States v. Tabor Court Realty Corp.*, 803 F.2d 1288 (3d Cir.1986), cert. denied, ___ U.S. ___, 107 S.Ct. 3229, 97 L.Ed.2d 735 (1987), which relied substantially on the suspicious circumstances surrounding the transaction that evidenced actual intent to defraud. *Tabor*, 803 F.2d at 1297.

---

10. Academics have recently joined the fray. Professors Baird and Jackson believe that fraudulent conveyance law should not be applied to LBOs. Baird & Jackson, *supra* note 3. They argue that LBOs are often economically efficient and may therefore benefit creditors. Thus, LBOs must not be penalized by a law designed to prevent "genuinely" fraudulent conveyances. From their perspective, the problem with applying fraudulent conveyance law to these transactions is that it gives creditors the ability to "whipsaw" the debtor, taking advantage of the successful LBO and suing under fraudulent conveyance theories if it is unsuccessful. Baird and Jackson also assume that creditors can protect themselves from dangers posed by LBOs by adjusting the terms on which they grant credit. In conclusion, Baird & Jackson find that "the inability of creditors to contract around the fraudulent conveyance remedy when it is in their interest may suggest that fraudulent conveyance law should be applied in bankruptcy to a narrow range of cases in which there is little chance that creditors would find the transfer in their interest." * * * Presumably these cases would be those in which actual intent to defraud is present.

In *United States v. Tabor Court Realty Co.*, 803 F.2d 1288 (3d Cir.1986), cert. denied, ___ U.S. ___, 107 S.Ct. 3229, 97 L.Ed.2d 735 (1987), the court noted that Baird and Jackson's "analysis is limited to transactions in which 'the transferee parted with value when he entered into the transaction and [the] transaction was entered in the ordinary course.'" *Id.* at 1297 (quoting Baird & Jackson, *supra*, at 855). In several footnotes the court more directly criticized Baird & Jackson's premise that creditors could protect themselves from LBOs through contract provisions, noting that they fail to consider that some creditors, such as tax and judgment creditors, are involuntary creditors. *Id.* at 1297 n. 2. That, in fact, was the particular situation that court confronted. These involuntary creditors, such as tax claimants and tort judgment holders, have had no chance to agree to restrict LBO transactions. Another commentator has pointed out that realities of the marketplace make it likely that the creditors with the economic power to force a debtor to forego an LBO, or restrict the conditions under which one may take place, are more likely to take a security interest than they are to contract for restrictive conditions. This leaves only small trade creditors, with little relative economic power, at the mercy of a decision to undergo a buyout. Note, *Fraudulent Conveyance Law and Leveraged Buyouts*, 87 Colum.L.Rev. 1491, 1512 (1987).

We decline to use the law of fraudulent conveyances to force the selling shareholders in this case to give up the payments they have received. We are so moved by a combination of factors. First, there is no evidence of any intention on the part of the selling shareholders to defraud the corporation's creditors. Second, the selling shareholders did not know that Adashek intended to finance the purchases through an LBO. Third, the Trustee represents no creditors whose claims against the estate arose before July 31, 1979, and who did not have full opportunity to evaluate the effect of the LBO on Wolf & Vine's creditworthiness. Fourth, the form of the transactions employed by the LBO reflects a sale by Wolf and Marmon to an entity other than Wolf & Vine. Each of these factors requires amplification.

Turning to intent to defraud, there is no evidence that the selling shareholders intended to defraud the Wolf & Vine creditors. Indeed, the Trustee has dropped any such claim on appeal and our review of the trial transcript indicates this was proper. Although lack of fraudulent intent does not bar a fraudulent conveyance claim under a constructive intent provision of the law, we hesitate to utilize constructive intent to frustrate the purposes intended to be served by what appears to us to be a legitimate LBO. Nor do we think it appropriate to utilize constructive intent to brand most, if not all, LBOs as illegitimate. We cannot believe that virtually all LBOs are designed to "hinder, delay, or defraud creditors."

The legitimacy of the LBO in this case is reinforced not only by the absence of an intent to defraud Wolf & Vine creditors, but also by the fact that Wolf did not know that his buyout would be leveraged. There was, in fact, uncontradicted evidence that Wolf did not know that Adashek had pledged Wolf & Vine assets to make the acquisition until the bankruptcy petition was filed more than two years after the sale of the Wolf stock. * * * Whether Marmon knew about the method of acquisition is not clear from the record.

The Trustee makes much of the fact that the selling shareholders did not thoroughly investigate Adashek and his proposed business plan for acquiring and running the company. The suggestion is that the ignorance of Wolf and possibly Marmon was the result of indifference. We are sensitive to the issue and in some circumstances would find it of controlling importance.[12] Here Marmon and Wolf appear to have been fairly careful in selecting a purchaser for the company. Clearly there was a screening of prospective purchasers. Several purchasers were rejected outright as not being financially sound enough to make the acquisition. * * * Of greater importance is the fact that Wolf and Marmon knew that Adashek was backed by the Continental Illinois Bank which had agreed to issue a letter of credit to back the transac-

---

12. In some circumstances, of course, controlling shareholders of a corporation are obligated to make certain that the business's creditors are not harmed by transactions in which the business enters. *See,* *e.g., Pepper v. Litton,* 308 U.S. 295, 306–07, 60 S.Ct. 238, 245–46, 84 L.Ed. 281 (1939); *Brown v. Presbyterian Ministers Fund,* 484 F.2d 998, 1005 (3d Cir.1973).

tion. * * * Admittedly, the LBO's legitimacy is not strengthened by the fact that neither Wolf nor Marmon asked Adashek for a financial statement, acquisition plan, or business plan. * * * But they were aware that Adashek's net worth was in excess of $5 million, that he was a successful investor, and that Continental was willing to back his purchase by the issuance of irrevocable letters of credit. We conclude the selling shareholders neither knew nor had reason to know that Adashek planned a leveraged acquisition of Wolf & Vine.

Our comfort with that conclusion is enhanced by the absence of presently existing creditors with claims that arose prior to the LBO. * * * All existing creditors had the opportunity to gain the knowledge of Wolf & Vine's financial status and its heavy debt structure prior to extending credit to it.[16] Creditors easily could have asked for financial information before extending credit. Moreover, the transaction was well-publicized within the industry. To ask Wolf to underwrite the creditors' losses, due partially at least to their failure to inquire adequately, would not be just.

As already mentioned, we are influenced by the formal structure of this LBO. The sale was complete as of July 31, 1979. Payments were spread over a three-year period. A large portion of the purchase price

---

16. The relevant statutes dictate, in most cases, that a transfer cannot be set aside as a fraudulent conveyance unless the creditor had a claim in existence at the time of the purported fraudulent conveyance. Under section five of the UFCA, Cal.Civ.Code § 3439.05, however, a conveyance made without fair consideration that leaves the transferor with unreasonably small capital is fraudulent, despite lack of fraudulent intent, "as to creditors *and as to other persons who become creditors during the continuance of such business or transaction.*" (emphasis added). Thus, it would appear that even a post-purchase transaction creditor, such as those present in this case, may attack a transaction if the other grounds of § 3439.05 are met. The California courts do not seem to have doubted the plain language of the statute that later-arising creditors may attack conveyances that meet the other requirements of the statute. (At least one California court, however, has stated that only a person that was a creditor at the time of the transaction has standing to sue under section five. *Pope v. National Aero Finance Co.,* 236 Cal.App.2d 722, 728, 46 Cal.Rptr. 233, 237 (1965) (referring to § 3439.04, .05, .06) (citing *TWM Homes, Inc. v. Atherwood Realty & Inv. Co.,* 214 Cal.App.2d 826, 843, 29 Cal.Rptr. 887, 896 (1963) (referring only to § 3439.04)).) But like Judge Rafeedie in *Credit Managers,* we believe this grant of standing to sue must be modified in light of an LBO in which there was no actual intent to defraud. Judge Rafeedie put it well:

[W]hen the California legislature passed [the predecessor statute to § 3439.05] in 1939, it clearly did not intend to cover leveraged buyouts which are very public events. The legislature was addressing instead transactions that have the earmarks of fraud.... If there is no limit on when a creditor can sue to set aside a transfer, fraudulent conveyance law becomes an insurance policy for creditors.... Credit could liberally be extended to such companies regardless of their assets or cash flow with the knowledge that the buyout could always be attacked later if the company folded.

Credit Managers, 629 F.Supp. at 181. Because fraudulent conveyance statutes were designed to protect creditors from *secret* transactions by debtors, the same rules should not apply when the transaction is made public. Future creditors may not complain when they knew or could easily have found out about the transaction. This certainly appears to be the case in this particular LBO. The transaction was well-publicized and the Trustee has not claimed or presented evidence that any of the future creditors were not aware of Wolf & Vine's financial dealings. In the context of this well-publicized LBO, this court will not permit later-arising creditors to attack an LBO purchase transaction as a fraudulent conveyance under section five of the UFCA.

was paid on July 31, 1979, and the remainder was secured by an *irrevocable* letter of credit. Thus, the transaction bore the indicia of a "straight" sale rather than the marks of a serial redemption by Wolf & Vine of its own stock. The Trustee's case would be stronger had the "selling" shareholders known, or should have known, that their stock was being paid for by an asset depleting transfer by Wolf & Vine. This case, however, does not present such facts. In this case the creditors of Wolf & Vine were placed at risk by Adashek's failure to manage the business properly. Wolf and Marmon should not be considered Adashek's guarantor.

There is no evidence that Wolf and Marmon did not act in good faith throughout the transaction. They sold their shares for a fair price to another company that, though very thinly capitalized, was backed by the substantial personal assets of a wealthy purchaser and his relationship with a major bank. While we should not be understood as insulating all LBOs from fraudulent conveyance laws, we do affirm the district court's decision on the state fraudulent conveyance law claim and the § 548 bankruptcy claim in this case.

We now address the Trustee's argument that the payments to Wolf and Marmon were improper distributions under Cal.Corp.Code §§ 500 and 501. * * * The Trustee's contention that he has standing to attack the July 1980 payments and perhaps the July 1981 payment to Marmon is more substantial. To establish that the 1980–81 payments constituted improper distributions, the Trustee must show that at the time the payments were made, the corporation did not have enough retained earnings or was unable to meet its liabilities at the time of, or as a result of, the payments.

* * *

We are convinced, however, that the district court reached the correct result. As already indicated, we do not view the 1980–81 payments as a distribution by Wolf & Vine to its former shareholders, Wolf and Marmon. They received the installment payments to which they were entitled under the sales agreement with Riding Hood. These payments, if distributions at all within the meaning of Cal.Corp.Code §§ 500 and 501, were distributions by Wolf & Vine to its then existing shareholder, Adashek, for whose benefit the distributions were made. In substance, no distributions to Wolf and Marmon were made. Adashek was the beneficiary of these distributions. What was said in Part B of this opinion concerning the appropriateness of creditors of Wolf & Vine, whose claims accrued subsequent to the sale by Wolf and Marmon, looking to former shareholders for relief from the consequences of the subsequent failure of Wolf & Vine is equally applicable at this point. Were the proceeding arising from the bankruptcy of Adashek it would be pertinent to inquire whether Wolf and Marmon received a preference as a result of the 1980–81 payments. That, however, is not the issue before us.

* * *

Questions

1. Did the *Kupetz* court correctly interpret the *Tabor Court Realty* opinion as limited to cases of actual fraud? See In re Morse Tool, Inc., 108 B.R. 389 (Bkrtcy.D.Mass.1989) (rejecting *Kupetz* v *Wolf* analysis).

2. The *Kupetz* court, in answer to the charge of constructive fraud under section 4 of the Uniform Fraudulent Conveyance Act, noted that the selling shareholders did not know the transaction was financed by pledges of their firm's assets. Is such a defense in the statute? Does a lender making a loan to a leveraged buyout target have a complete defense based on good faith? See In re Morse Tool, Inc., 108 B.R. 389 (Bkrtcy.Mass.1989) (rejecting the *Kupetz* analysis).

3. At the core of the Ninth Circuit's strained construction of precedent and statute is, perhaps, a conviction that fraudulent conveyance acts simply should not apply to LBOs absent actual fraud. The argument is based on the incentives of the LBO lenders. In the typical fraudulent conveyance act case, a person on the edge of bankruptcy sells a prized asset to his mother for five cents on the dollar. His mother is happy to close the transaction for obvious reasons; she has no stake in the ongoing health of the firm. An LBO is very different because the buyout group itself has equity in the firm, and it has convinced lenders to fund the acquisition based on the firm's cash flow. The equity participants are not anxious to lose their stake, and their lenders expect to be repaid. Why would a buyout group, Adashek in the *Kupetz* case, and its LBO lenders, Continental Illinois National Bank in the *Kupetz* case, agree to fund an LBO if the firm is likely to end up in bankruptcy? If the major lender will not give funds absent assurances of credit-worthiness of the surviving entity in an LBO, why should we second-guess the business calculations of the buyout ground and its lenders absent some evidence of actual fraud? Does your answer depend on whether you are seeking protection for pre-LBO creditors of the firm? For contingent claimants of the firm? See note 2 in the *Tabor Court Realty* case.

4. The court also refused to hold that the payments made to Wolf and Marmon were distributions that violated California's legal capital statutes. Assume for the purpose of argument that section 6.40 of the Revised Model Business Corporation Act applies. Would you, as judge, find that the payments violated the section? Why does the court refuse to treat the payments as a redemption of the Wolf and Marmon stock?

Note

Post–LBO Creditors

In *Kupetz* the court concludes that since no creditors were shown to have claims that arose before the LBO and there were no creditors who did not have a full chance to evaluate the LBO's effect, none could challenge it. Does the Uniform Fraudulent Conveyance Act distinguish between subsequent and prior creditors? A bankruptcy judge followed this part of the *Kupetz* opinion in In re Ohio Corrugating Co., 91 B.R. 430, 435 (Bkrtcy.N.D. Ohio 1988):

It appears to the Court that subsequent creditors are in a substantially different position from existing creditors. In this case, creditors appear to have willingly extended credit to the Debtor after the buyout in reliance on the performance of the "new" company.... We see no basis here for holding that the constructive fraud provisions of 11 U.S.C. Sec. 548 may be utilized as a form of insurance for creditors whose claims matured after the buyout.

In In re Morse Tool, Inc., 108 B.R. 389 (Bkrtcy.Mass.1989), however, Judge Kenner rejected the *Kupetz* analysis as "contrary to the plain language of sections 5 and 7," which "expressly extend their benefits to future creditors."

The Uniform Fraudulent Transfer Act, a more recent uniform act followed by more states (twenty-four) than the Uniform Fraudulent Conveyance Act, explicitly recognizes, in part, the holdings in *Kupetz* and *Ohio Corrugating.* Post–LBO creditors can attack an LBO only under section 4—if they can prove there was actual fraud, unreasonably small assets remain, or there was an intent to incur debts beyond the ability to pay. Pre–LBO creditors can also void the transaction under section 5—by showing that it involved a transfer without reasonably equivalent value when a debtor was, or thereby became, insolvent.

Subsection d. Bulk Sales Acts

U.C.C. §§ 6–102—6–107 (1987 Official Text)

§ 6–102. "Bulk Transfers"; Transfers of Equipment; Enterprises Subject to This Article; Bulk Transfers Subject to This Article

(1) A "bulk transfer" is any transfer in bulk and not in the ordinary course of the transferor's business of a major part of the materials, supplies, merchandise or other inventory (Section 9–109) of an enterprise subject to this Article.

* * *

(3) The enterprises subject to this Article are all those whose principal business is the sale of merchandise from stock, including those who manufacture what they sell.

§ 6–103. Transfers Excepted From This Article

The following transfers are not subject to this Article.

* * *

(6) Transfers to a person maintaining a known place of business in this State who becomes bound to pay the debts of the transferor in full and gives public notice of that fact, and who is solvent after becoming so bound;

(7) A transfer to a new business enterprise organized to take over and continue the business, if public notice of the transaction is given and the new enterprise assumes the debts of the transferor and he

receives nothing from the transaction except an interest in the new enterprise junior to the claims of creditors;

* * *

Public notice under subsection (6) or subsection (7) may be given by publishing once a week for two consecutive weeks in a newspaper of general circulation where the transferor had its principal place of business in this state an advertisement including the names and addresses of the transferor and transferee and the effective date of the transfer.

* * *

§ 6–104. Schedule of Property, List of Creditors

(1) Except as provided with respect to auction sales (Section 6–108), a bulk transfer subject to this Article is ineffective against any creditor of the transferor unless:

(a) The transferee requires the transferor to furnish a list of his existing creditors prepared as stated in this section; and

(b) The parties prepare a schedule of the property transferred sufficient to identify it; and

(c) The transferee preserves the list and schedule for six months next following the transfer and permits inspection of either or both and copying therefrom at all reasonable hours by any creditor of the transferor, or files the list and schedule in (a public office to be here identified).

* * *

§ 6–105. Notice to Creditors

In addition to the requirements of the preceding section, any bulk transfer subject to this Article except one made by auction sale (Section 6–108) is ineffective against any creditor of the transferor unless at least ten days before he takes possession of the goods or pays for them, whichever happens first, the transferee gives notice of the transfer in the manner and to the persons hereafter provided (Section 6–107).

[§ 6–106. Application of the Proceeds

In addition to the requirements of the two preceding sections:

(1) Upon every bulk transfer subject to this Article for which new consideration becomes payable except those made by sale at auction it is the duty of the transferee to assure that such consideration is applied so far as necessary to pay those debts of the transferor which are either shown on the list furnished by the transferor (Section 6–104) or filed in writing in the place stated in the notice (Section 6–107) within thirty days after the mailing of such notice. This duty of the transferee runs to all the holders of such debts, and may be enforced by any of them for the benefit of all.

(2) If any of said debts are in dispute the necessary sum may be withheld from distribution until the dispute is settled or adjudicated.

(3) If the consideration payable is not enough to pay all of the said debts in full distribution shall be made pro rata.]

* * *

§ 6-107. The Notice

(1) The notice to creditors (Section 6-105) shall state:

(a) that a bulk transfer is about to be made; and

(b) the names and business addresses of the transferor and transferee, and all other business names and addresses used by the transferor within three years last past so far as known to the transferee; and

(c) whether or not all the debts of the transferor are to be paid in full as they fall due as a result of the transaction, and if so, the address to which creditors should send their bills.

(2) If the debts of the transferor are not to be paid in full as they fall due or if the transferee is in doubt on that point then the notice shall state further:

(a) the location and general description of the property to be transferred and the estimated total of the transferor's debts;

(b) the address where the schedule of property and list of creditors (Section 6-104) may be inspected;

(c) whether the transfer is to pay existing debts and if so the amount of such debts and to whom owing;

(d) whether the transfer is for new consideration and if so the amount of such consideration and the time and place of payment * * *

(3) The notice in any case shall be delivered personally or sent by registered or certified mail to all the persons shown on the list of creditors furnished by the transferor (Section 6-104) and to all other persons who are known to the transferee to hold or assert claims against the transferor.

NATIONAL CONFERENCE OF COMMISSIONERS ON UNIFORM STATE LAWS, PREFATORY NOTE AND OFFICIAL COMMENT TO SECTION 6-101 ON REVISING DISCUSSION DRAFT

Uniform Commercial Code, Article 6, Bulk Sales, (1988).

PREFATORY NOTE

Background. Bulk sale legislation originally was enacted in response to a fraud perceived to be common around the turn of the century: a merchant would acquire his stock in trade on credit, then sell his entire inventory ("in bulk") and abscond with the proceeds, leaving creditors unpaid. The creditors had a right to sue the merchant on the unpaid debts, but that right often was of little practical value. Even if the merchant-debtor was found, in personam jurisdiction over him might not have been readily available. Those creditors who succeeded in obtaining a judgment often were unable to satisfy it because the defrauding seller had spent or hidden the sale proceeds. Nor did the creditors ordinarily have recourse to the merchandise sold. The transfer of the inventory to an innocent buyer effectively immunized the goods from the reach of the seller's creditors. The creditors of a bulk seller thus might be left without a means to satisfy their claims.

To a limited extent, the law of fraudulent conveyances ameliorated the creditors' plight. When the buyer in bulk was in league with the seller or paid less than full value for the inventory, fraudulent conveyance law enabled the defrauded creditors to avoid the sale and apply the transferred inventory toward the satisfaction of their claims against the seller. But fraudulent conveyance law provided no remedy against persons who bought in good faith, without reason to know of the seller's intention to pocket the proceeds and disappear, and for adequate value. In those cases, the only remedy for the seller's creditors was to attempt to recover from the absconding seller.

State legislatures responded to this perceived "bulk sale risk" with a variety of legislative enactments. Common to these statutes was the imposition of a duty on the buyer in bulk to notify the seller's creditors of the impending sale. The buyer's failure to comply with these and any other statutory duties generally afforded the seller's creditors a remedy analogous to the remedy for fraudulent conveyances: the creditors acquired the right to set aside the sale and reach the transferred inventory in the hands of the buyer.

Like its predecessors, Article 6 (1987 Official Text) is remarkable in that it obligates buyers in bulk to incur costs to protect the interests of the seller's creditors, with whom they usually have no relationship. Even more striking is that Article 6 affords creditors a remedy against a good faith purchaser for full value without notice of any wrongdoing on the part of the seller. The Article thereby impedes normal business transactions, many of which can be expected to benefit the seller's creditors. For this reason, Article 6 has been subjected to serious criticism. * * *

Recommendation. The National Conference of Commissioners on Uniform State Laws and the American Law Institute believe that changes in the business and legal contexts in which sales are conducted have made regulation of bulk sales unnecessary. The Conference and the Institute therefore withdraw their support for Article 6 of the Uniform Commercial Code and encourage those states that have enacted the Article to repeal it. * * * For those states that are disinclined to repeal Article 6, they have promulgated a revised version of Article

6. The revised Article is designed to afford better protection to creditors while minimizing the impediments to good-faith transactions.

* * *

§ 6–101.

OFFICIAL COMMENT

* * *

Article 6 (1987 Official Text) imposes upon transferees in bulk several duties toward creditors of the transferor. These duties include the duty to notify the creditors of the impending bulk transfer and, in those jurisdictions that have adopted optional Section 6–106, the duty to assure that the new consideration for the transfer is applied to pay debts of the transferor.

Compliance with the provisions of Article 6 can be burdensome, particularly when the transferor has a large number of creditors. When the transferor is actively engaged in business at a number of locations, assembling a current list of creditors may not be possible. Mailing a notice to each creditor may prove costly. When the goods that are the subject of the transfer are located in several jurisdictions, the transferor may be obligated to comply with Article 6 as enacted in each jurisdiction. The widespread enactment of nonuniform amendments makes compliance with Article 6 in multiple-state transactions problematic. Moreover, the Article requires compliance even when there is no reason to believe that the transferor is conducting a fraudulent transfer, *e.g.*, when the transferor is scaling down the business but remaining available to creditors.

Article 6 imposes strict liability for noncompliance. Failure to comply with the provisions of the Article renders the transfer ineffective, even when the transferor has attempted compliance in good faith, and even when no creditor has been injured by the noncompliance. The potential liability for minor noncompliance may be high. If the transferor should enter bankruptcy before the expiration of the limitation period, Bankruptcy Code §§ 544(b), 550(a), 11 U.S.C. §§ 544(b), 550(a), may enable the transferor's bankruptcy trustee to set aside the entire transaction and recover from the noncomplying transferee all the goods transferred or their value. The trustee has this power even though the noncompliance was with respect to only a single creditor holding a small claim.

The benefits that compliance affords to creditors do not justify the substantial burdens and risks that the Article imposes upon good faith purchasers of business assets. The Article requires that notice be sent only ten days before the transferee takes possession of the goods or pays for them, whichever happens first. Given the delay between sending the notice and its receipt, creditors have scant opportunity to avail themselves of a judicial or nonjudicial remedy before the transfer has been consummated.

In some cases Article 6 may have the unintended effect of injuring, rather than aiding, creditors of the transferor. Those transferees who recognize the burdens and risks that Article 6 imposes upon them sometimes agree to purchase only at a reduced price. Others refuse to purchase at all, leaving the creditors to realize only the liquidation value, rather than the going concern value, of the business goods.

As a response to these inadequacies and others, the National Conference of Commissioners on Uniform State Laws has completely revised Article 6. This revision is designed to reduce the burdens and risks imposed upon good-faith buyers of business assets while increasing the protection afforded to creditors. Among the major changes it makes are the following:

—this Article applies only when the buyer has notice, or after reasonable inquiry would have had notice, that the seller will not continue to operate the same or a similar kind of business after the sale (Section 6–102(1)(c)).

—this Article does not apply to sales in which the value of the property otherwise available to creditors is less than $10,000 or those in which the value of the property is greater than $25,000,000 (Section 6–103(3)(l)).

—the choice-of-law provision (Sections 6–103(1)(b) and 6–103(2)) limits the applicable law to that of one jurisdiction.

—when the seller is indebted to a large number of persons, the buyer need neither obtain a list of those persons nor send individual notices to each person but instead may give notice by filing (Sections 6–105(2) and 6–104(2)).

—the notice period is increased from 10 days to 45 days (Section 6–105(5)), and the statute of limitations is extended from six months to one year (Section 6–110).

—the notice must include a copy of a "schedule of distribution," which sets forth how the net contract price is to be distributed (Sections 6–105(3) and 6–106(1)).

—a buyer who makes a good faith effort to comply with the requirements of this Article or to exclude the sale from the application of this Article, or who acts on the good faith belief that this Article does not apply to the sale, is not liable for noncompliance (Section 6–107(3)).

—a buyer's noncompliance does not render the sale ineffective or otherwise affect the buyer's title to the goods; rather, the liability of a noncomplying buyer is for damages caused by the noncompliance (Sections 6–107(1) and 6–107(8)).

* * *

Questions

1. Do bulk sales acts apply to statutory mergers or stock acquisitions? Does it matter that selling-firm shareholders may receive exclusively cash in the merger? Do bulk sales acts apply to leveraged buyouts? Does it matter whether the LBO is accomplished through a statutory merger or an asset sale?

2. Assume that one firm buys all the assets of a second firm but takes on none of the liabilities. Assume also that the firm's assets include those covered by a bulk sales act (U.C.C. § 6–102(1)). The second firm's managers find later that the proceeds are insufficient to pay all the firm's creditors. Can the creditors sue the buyer under a fraudulent conveyance act or a bulk sales act? Now assume that the buyer in an asset sale does agree to take on all the seller's liabilities and after the transaction defaults on some of the liabilities. Can the aggrieved creditors sue the buyer under bulk sales act? To what advantage?

If the buyer is intent on keeping an acquisition confidential as long as possible so as not to tip off other potential bidders, what is the effect of choosing to structure the acquisition as an asset sale?

3. There is a split of opinion on the wisdom of section 6–106 in the Uniform Commercial Code; more states omit the section than adopt it. In the context of large-scale asset acquisitions, is the section sound?

4. If a selling firm receives escalating bids from two or more buyers, has it "auctioned" the firm for the purposes of the bulk sales provisions? If so, do the firm and its directors escape liability?

Problem

Ms. Kluge, the CEO of Able, Inc., a solvent manufacturing company that is publicly traded, decides to buy the company. She sets up a wholly owned shell corporation, Baker, Inc., and borrows money from several banks at very high interest and for very short terms ("bridge loans"), secured only by her promise that she will use the funds to buy her firm and will repay the loan once she has done so by pulling cash out of the business. Baker, Inc., uses the loaned money to buy all the assets of Able, Inc., assuming all its liabilities. Baker pays its sole shareholder, Ms. Kluge, a large cash dividend with cash generated by selling some of the assets and by pledging others for new loans. Ms. Kluge uses the money to pay off the bridge loans. Soon thereafter Baker, Inc., can no longer pay its creditors, many of whom began as creditors of Able, Inc. Can the creditors sue under legal capital, fraudulent conveyance, or bulk sales statutes? What relief can they pursue under each statute?

SUBCHAPTER C. EMPLOYEE CONTRACTS: COLLECTIVE BARGAINING AGREEMENTS AND PENSION PLANS

SECTION 1. COLLECTIVE BARGAINING AGREEMENTS

In 1935 Congress enacted the Wagner Act (the National Labor Relations Act), which gave employees the right to organize, to bargain collectively with employers, and to engage in strikes, picketing, and other concerted activities. See generally *The Developing Labor Law* (C. Morris ed. 1983 as suppl.). The process of collective bargaining generally results in a collective bargaining agreement setting the terms and conditions of employment. Most of the contracts contain an agreement to arbitrate disputes under the agreement. Assuming a collective bargaining agreement to be in force when a firm is negotiating to sell its business, there are two overriding questions. First, do the employees have rights under the agreement to block a sale, particularly if the purchasing firm intends to lay off employees or substantially change the terms of employment for retained employees? This is the subject of subsection a below. Second, after the acquisition can the employees assert rights against the purchasing firm based on their dealings with the selling firm? This is the subject of subsection b.

Subsection a. Control Change Clauses in Collective Bargaining Agreements

The cases below are based on the Railway Labor Act, a statute originally passed in 1926 that establishes the collective bargaining policy for public carriers. At issue in the *P & LE* case is, first, whether a sale of a railroad violates the terms and conditions of an employment agreement when the agreement does not contain an explicit clause on acquisitions, and if not, whether the employees can force a selling firm to bargain about adding such terms. The importance of the case stretches beyond the Railway Labor Act in its decision; the majority relies on and interprets cases limiting the duty to bargain under the National Labor Relations Act in the event of an asset sale. The *UAL* opinions that follow deal with the question of whether express terms in a collective bargaining agreement on control changes are void if they conflict with a firm's fiduciary obligation to its shareholders.

PITTSBURGH AND LAKE ERIE R.R. CO. v. RAILWAY LABOR EXECUTIVES' ASS'N

Supreme Court of the United States, 1989.
491 U.S. 490, 109 S.Ct. 2584, 105 L.Ed.2d 415.

JUSTICE WHITE delivered the opinion of the Court.

These cases involve the interaction of three federal statutes with respect to the proposed sale of the rail line of the Pittsburgh and Lake Erie Railroad (P & LE). The statutes are the Railway Labor Act (RLA), 44 Stat. 577, amended, 45 U.S.C. § 151 *et seq.;* the Interstate Commerce Act (ICA), 49 U.S.C. § 10101 *et seq.* (1982 ed. and Supp. V); and the Norris–LaGuardia Act (NLGA), 47 Stat. 70, 29 U.S.C. § 101 *et seq.*

Petitioner, P & LE, is a small rail carrier owning and operating 182 miles of rail line serving points in Ohio and western Pennsylvania and possessing trackage rights over other lines extending into New York. P & LE has experienced financial problems of increasing severity, having lost $60 million during the five years preceding the onset of this case. After other efforts to improve its condition failed, notably work force reductions, concessions from its employees, and market expansion, P & LE decided that in order to recoup for its owners any part of their investments it must sell its assets.[1] On July 8, 1987, P & LE agreed to sell its assets for approximately $70 million to a newly formed subsidiary, P & LE Rail Co., Inc. (Railco), of Chicago West Pullman Transportation Corporation (CWP).[2] Railco intended to operate the railroad as P & LE had except that Railco would not assume P & LE's collective-bargaining contracts with its various unions and would need only about 250 employees rather than the 750 then working for P & LE.[3] When the unions representing P & LE's employees were notified of the proposed sale, they asserted that the sale would have an effect on the working conditions of the carrier's employees and therefore was subject to the requirements of RLA, 45 U.S.C. § 152, Seventh and § 156, which provide:

"§ 152 ... Seventh: Change in pay, rules, or working conditions contrary to agreement or to section 156 forbidden

"No carrier, its officers, or agents shall change the rates of pay, rules, or working conditions of its employees, as a class, as embodied in agreements except in the manner prescribed in such agreements or in section 156 of this title."

"§ 156. Procedure in changing rates of pay, rules, and working conditions

"Carriers and representatives of the employees shall give at least thirty days' written notice of an intended change in agreements affecting rates of pay, rules, or working conditions, and the time and place for the beginning of conference between the representatives of the parties interested in such intended changes shall be agreed upon within ten days after the receipt of said notice, and said time shall be within the thirty days provided in the notice. In every case where such notice of intended change has been given, or conferences are being held with reference thereto, or the services of the Mediation Board have been requested by either party, or said Board has proffered its services, rates of pay, rules, or working conditions shall not be altered by the carrier until the controversy has been finally acted upon, as required by section 155 of this title, by the Mediation Board, unless a period of ten days has elapsed after termination of conferences without request for or proffer of the services of the Mediation Board." [4]

---

1. Attempts to interest major rail lines in the property were unavailing because of the high cost of labor protection that would have been mandatory under the section of the ICA applicable to purchases by an existing carrier. 49 U.S.C. § 11347, *infra*, n. 7.

2. P & LE would keep certain real estate and some 6,000 rail cars.

3. CWP anticipated inviting all P & LE employees to submit applications and intended to give preference to them in hiring. CWP also expected to bargain for new contracts with the existing unions.

4. Disputes about proposals to change rates of pay, rules, or working conditions are known as major disputes. Minor disputes are those involving the interpretation or application of existing contracts. The latter are subject to compulsory arbitration. The former are subject to the procedures set out in § 156 and in § 155, which specify the functions of the Mediation Board. In *Railroad Trainmen v. Terminal Co.*, 394 U.S. 369, 378, 89 S.Ct. 1109, 1115, 22 L.Ed.2d 344 (1969), we described the procedures applicable to major disputes:

"The Act provides a detailed framework to facilitate the voluntary settlement of major disputes. A party desiring to effect a change of rates, pay, rules, or working

The unions advised that they stood ready to negotiate all aspects of the matter, including the decision to sell the railroad assets. P & LE responded that it was willing to discuss the matter but that § 156 notice and bargaining were not required since the transaction was subject to the jurisdiction of the Interstate Commerce Commission (ICC or Commission) under the ICA and since the requirements of §§ 155 and 156 would intrude on that regime as well as upon management's prerogatives to conduct the affairs of the company with respect to the sales transaction.

Most of the unions then responded by themselves filing § 156 notices proposing changes in existing agreements to ameliorate the adverse impacts of the proposed sale upon P & LE's employees. The unions sought guarantees that the sale would not cause any employee to be deprived of employment or to be placed in any worse position with respect to pay or working conditions and that P & LE would require that the purchaser of its rail line assume P & LE's collective-bargaining agreements.[5] P & LE again declined to bargain, asserting that the transaction was within the exclusive jurisdiction of the ICC. * * * On September 15, 1987, the unions went on strike. * * *

The proposed sale of assets could not be carried out without compliance with the terms of the ICA, 49 U.S.C. § 10901, which requires that noncarriers seeking to acquire a rail line first obtain a certificate of public convenience and necessity from the ICC. Section 10901(e) specifies the procedures for this purpose and provides that the

conditions must give advance written notice. § 6. The parties must confer, § 2 Second, and if conference fails to resolve the dispute, either or both may invoke the services of the National Mediation Board, which may also proffer its services *sua sponte* if it finds a labor emergency to exist. § 5 First. If mediation fails, the Board must endeavor to induce the parties to submit the controversy to binding arbitration, which can take place, however, only if both consent. §§ 5 First, 7. If arbitration is rejected and the dispute threatens 'substantially to interrupt interstate commerce to a degree such as to deprive any section of the country of essential transportation service, the Mediation Board shall notify the President,' who may create an emergency board to investigate and report on the dispute. § 10. While the dispute is working its way through these stages, neither party may unilaterally alter the *status quo*. §§ 2 Seventh, 5 First, 6, 10."

5. The unions' proposals were essentially these:

"1. No employee of the P & LE Railroad Company who [was actively employed or on authorized leave of absence] between August 1, 1986 and August 1, 1987 ... shall be deprived of employment or placed in a worse position with respect to compensation or working conditions for any reason except resignation, retirement, death or dismissal for justifiable cause.... The formulae for the protective allowances, with a separation option, shall be comparable to those established in the *New York Dock* conditions.

"2. If an employee is placed in a worse position with respect to compensation or working conditions, that employee shall receive, in addition to a make-whole-remedy, penalty pay equal to three times the lost pay, fringe benefits and consequential damages suffered by such employee.

"3. P & LE agrees to obtain binding commitments from any purchaser of its rail line operating properties and assets to assume all [P & LE's] collective bargaining agreements ... to hire P & LE employees in seniority order without physicals, and to negotiate with the P & LE and this Organization an agreement to apply this Agreement to the sale transaction and to select the forces to perform the work over the lines being acquired." App. 38, 42, 46, 50, 54, 58, 62, 66, 122, 126.

ICC "may" require the acquiring company "to provide a fair and equitable arrangement for the protection of railroad employees who may be affected thereby no less protective of and beneficial to the interests of such employees than those established pursuant to section 11347 of this title." Section 10505, however, authorizes the Commission to grant exemptions from the requirements of the Act when not necessary to carry out the national transportation policy. Based on its experience with acquisitions under § 10901, the ICC had issued what is known as the Ex Parte No. 392 Class Exemption, * * * which provides abbreviated procedures for seeking approval for acquisitions by non-carriers such as Railco of an operating railroad or its assets. The regulatory procedure, see 49 CFR § 1150.32(b) (1987), involved the filing of an application for exemption which would become effective seven days after filing absent contrary notice from the Commission. An interested party could oppose the exemption by filing a petition to revoke at any time, after consideration of which the ICC could revoke the exemption in whole or in part or impose labor protective provisions. The ICC had indicated, however, that only in exceptional situations would such protective provisions be imposed.

Accordingly, Railco on September 19, 1987, filed a notice of exemption pursuant to *Ex Parte 392*. After denying various requests by the unions to reject the notice of exemption and stay the sale, the Commission allowed the exemption to become effective on September 26. A petition to revoke filed by the union on October 2 is still pending before the Commission. At no time did the union request imposition of labor protective provisions pursuant to the Commission's authority under § 10901.

* * *

P & LE submits that neither its decision to sell nor the impact that sale of the company might have had on its employees was a "change in *agreements* affecting rates of pay, rules, or working conditions" (emphasis added) within the meaning of the RLA, 45 U.S.C. § 156 and that P & LE therefore had no duty to give notice or to bargain with respect to these matters. The Court of Appeals rejected this submission, focusing on the effects the sale would have on employees and concluding that the "loss of jobs by possibly two-thirds of the employees clearly would require a 'change in agreements affecting rates of pay, rules, or working conditions.'" * * * The court did not point out how the proposed sale would require changing any specific provision of any of its collective-bargaining agreements. It did not suggest that any of those agreements dealt with the possibility of the sale of the company, sought to confer any rights on its employees in the event of the sale, or guaranteed that jobs would continue to be available indefinitely.[14]

---

14. Indeed, the Court of Appeals stated that "P & LE's agreements with its unions, however, do not appear to contemplate this type of transaction [*i.e.*, sale of the rail lines], and thus neither expressly permit nor prohibit the sale." * * * RLEA asserts that P & LE had granted job security guarantees to some of its employees, see

What P & LE proposed to do would remove it from the railroad business and terminate its position as a railroad employer; and like the Court of Appeals, RLEA does not explain how such action would violate or require changing any of the provisions of the unions' written contracts with P & LE.

Of course, not all working conditions to which parties may have agreed are to be found in written contracts. *Detroit & Toledo Shore Line Railroad Co. v. Transportation Union,* 396 U.S. 142, 154–155, 90 S.Ct. 294, 301–302, 24 L.Ed.2d 325 (1969) (*Shore Line*). It may be that "in the context of the relationship between the principals, taken as a whole, there is a basis for implying an understanding on the particular practice involved." *Id.,* at 160, 90 S.Ct., at 304 (Harlan, J., dissenting). But the Court of Appeals did not purport to find an implied agreement that P & LE would not go out of business, would not sell its assets, or if it did, would protect its employees from the adverse consequences of such action. Neither does RLEA. We therefore see no basis for holding that P & LE should have given a § 156 notice of a proposed "change" in its express or implied agreements with the unions when it contracted to sell its assets to Railco. Nor was it, based on its own decision to sell, obligated to bargain about the impending sale or to delay its implementation. We find RLEA's arguments to the contrary quite unconvincing.

There is more substance to the Court of Appeals' holding, and to RLEA's submission, that the unions' § 156 notices proposed far-reaching changes in the existing agreements over which P & LE was required to bargain and that the status quo provision of § 156 prohibited P & LE from going forward with the sale pending completion of the "purposely long and drawn out" procedures which the Act requires to be followed in order to settle a "major" dispute. *Railway Clerks v. Florida E.C.R. Co.,* 384 U.S. 238, 246, 86 S.Ct. 1420, 1424, 16 L.Ed.2d 501 (1966). Section 156 provides that when a notice of change in agreements has been given, "rates of pay, rules, or working conditions shall not be altered by the carrier until the controversy has been finally acted upon, as required in section § 155." Relying on *Shore Line,* RLEA argues, and the Court of Appeals held, that when a rail labor union files a § 156 notice to change the terms of an agreement, the "working conditions" that the carrier may not change pending conclusion of the bargaining process are not limited to those contained in express or implied agreements but include, as *Shore Line* held, "those actual, objective working conditions and practices, broadly conceived, which were in effect prior to the time the pending dispute arose and which are involved in or related to that dispute." 396 U.S., at 153, 90 S.Ct., at 301. RLEA submits that the relationship of employer-employee and the state of being employed are among those working conditions

Brief for Respondent 3, but the record does not contain the collective bargaining contracts, and if there were such guarantees, there is no claim that they would survive the sale of the rail line.

that may not be changed until the RLA procedures are satisfied. We are unconvinced, for several reasons, that this is the case.

* * *

In *Textile Workers v. Darlington Mfg. Co.*, 380 U.S. 263, 85 S.Ct. 994, 13 L.Ed.2d 827 (1965), an employer closed its textile mill when a union won a representation election. The National Labor Relations Board concluded that this action was an unfair labor practice under §§ 8(a)(1) and (3) of the National Labor Relations Act (NLRA). The Court of Appeals disagreed holding that the complete or partial liquidation of an employer's business even though motivated by antiunion animus was not an unfair practice. We affirmed in part,[16] ruling that insofar as the NLRA is concerned, an employer "has an absolute right to terminate his entire business for any reason he pleases...." 380 U.S., at 268, 85 S.Ct., at 998. Whatever may be the limits of § 8(a)(1), we said, an employer's decision to terminate its business is one of those decisions "so peculiarly matters of management prerogative that they would never constitute violations" of that section. *Id.*, at 269, 85 S.Ct., at 999. Neither would ceasing business and refusing to bargain about it violate § 8(a)(3) or § 8(a)(5) even if done with antiunion animus. 380 U.S., at 267, n. 5, 269–274, 85 S.Ct., at 998, n. 5, 999–1002. "A proposition that a single businessman cannot choose to go out of business if he wants to would represent such a startling innovation that it should not be entertained without the clearest manifestation of legislative intent or unequivocal judicial precedent so construing the Labor Relations Act." *Id.*, at 270, 85 S.Ct., at 999. We found neither.[17]

---

16. We thought that a partial liquidation might present a different case and remanded for further findings. See 380 U.S., at 268, 276–277, 85 S.Ct. at 1002–1003.

17. In *First National Maintenance Corp. v. NLRB*, 452 U.S. 666, 101 S.Ct. 2573, 69 L.Ed.2d 318 (1981), which, like *Textile Workers v. Darlington Mfg. Co.*, 380 U.S. 263, 85 S.Ct. 994, 13 L.Ed.2d 827 (1965), arose under the NLRA, we concluded that "the harm likely to be done to an employer's need to operate freely in deciding whether to shut down part of its business purely for economic reasons outweighs the incremental benefit that might be gained through the union's participation in making the decision." 452 U.S., at 686, 101 S.Ct., at 2584. Further, we held that the employer's decision to close down a segment of its business "is *not* part of § 8(d)'s 'terms and conditions,' ... over which Congress has mandated bargaining." *Ibid.* In so holding, we did not feel constrained by the Court's decision in *Railroad Telegraphers v. Chicago & N.W.R. Co.*, 362 U.S. 330, 80 S.Ct. 761, 4 L.Ed.2d 774 (1960). * * * In *Telegraphers* a railroad was seeking simply to eliminate or consolidate some of its little-used local stations. The railroad here, by contrast, sought to sell all its lines and go out of business. There is nothing in *Telegraphers* that forces us to reach the result, in this extreme case, that P & LE was prohibited from terminating its operations without first bargaining with the unions. Notwithstanding the policy considerations prompting the enlarged scope of mandatory bargaining under the RLA, in light of *Darlington*, which *First National Maintenance* reaffirmed, we are not inclined to extend *Telegraphers* to a case in which the railroad decides to retire from the railroad business.

The dissent, *post*, at ___, seems to assert that *Shore Line* and *Telegraphers* dealt with a railroad's freedom to leave the market. But as we point out, that is precisely what those cases did not involve. We are plainly at odds with the dissent with respect to the significance of P & LE's decision to leave the railroad business.

Although *Darlington* arose under the NLRA, we are convinced that we should be guided by the admonition in that case that the decision to close down a business entirely is so much a management prerogative that only an unmistakable expression of congressional intent will suffice to require the employer to postpone a sale of its assets pending the fulfillment of any duty it may have to bargain over the subject matter of union notices such as were served in this case. Absent statutory direction to the contrary, the decision of a railroad employer to go out of business and consequently to reduce to zero the number of available jobs is not a change in the conditions of employment forbidden by the status quo provision of § 156. In this case, P & LE concluded that it must sell its assets, and its agreement to sell to Railco, if implemented, would have removed it from the railroad business; no longer would it be a railroad employer. No longer would it need the services of members of the rail unions. The RLEA concedes that had the collective-bargaining agreements expressly waived bargaining concerning sale of P & LE's assets, the unions' § 156 notices to change the agreements could not trump the terms of the agreements and could not delay the sale. * * *

We think the same result follows where the agreement is silent on the matter and the railroad employer has proceeded in accordance with the ICA. In these circumstances, there is little or no basis for the unions to expect that a § 156 notice would be effective to delay the company's departure from the railroad business. Congress clearly requires that sales transactions like P & LE's proposal must satisfy the requirements of the ICA, but we find nothing in the RLA to prevent the immediate consummation of P & LE's contract to sell. When the ICC approved the sale by permitting the *Ex Parte 392* exemption to become effective, P & LE was free to close the transaction and should not have been enjoined from doing so.

* * *

Our holding in this case, which rests on our construction of the RLA and not on the pre-emptive force of the ICA, is that petitioner was not obligated to serve its own § 156 notice on the unions in connection with the proposed sale. We also conclude that the unions' notices did not obligate P & LE to maintain the status quo and postpone the sale beyond the time the sale was approved by the Commission and was scheduled to be consummated. We do not hold, however, that P & LE had no duty at all to bargain in response to the unions' § 156 motions. The courts below held and RLEA agrees that P & LE's decision to sell, as such, was not a bargainable subject. The disputed issue is whether P & LE was required to bargain about the effects that the sale would or might have upon its employees. P & LE, in our view, was not entirely free to disregard the unions' demand that it bargain about such effects. When the unions' notices were served, however, the terms of P & LE's agreement with Railco were more or less settled, and P & LE's decision to sell on those terms had been made. To the extent that the unions' demands could be satisfied only by the assent of the buyers, they sought to change or dictate the terms of the sale, and in effect challenged the decision to sell itself. At that time, P & LE was under no obligation to bargain about the terms it had already negotiated. To the extent that the unions' proposals could be satisfied by P & LE itself, those matters were bargainable but only until the date for closing the sale arrived, which, of course, could not occur until the *Ex Parte 392* exemption became effective.[19] * * *

* * *

JUSTICE STEVENS, with whom JUSTICE BRENNAN, JUSTICE MARSHALL, and JUSTICE BLACKMUN join, concurring in part and dissenting in part.

Regulated utilities do not have the same freedom to respond to market pressures that unregulated firms have. They may not raise rates or cut services, for example, without permission from a regulatory agency. Most significantly for this case, they may neither enter nor leave the market without agency approval.

* * *

The railroad industry long has been the subject of governmental regulation. A year after this Court held that individual States were powerless to regulate rail lines extending beyond their boundaries, * * * Congress established the Interstate Commerce Commission (ICC) to regulate economic aspects of the rail industry. * * * Regulation of employment relationships within the rail industry followed, and in 1926, Congress enacted the Railway Labor Act (RLA). * * * The intervening six decades were marked by relatively peaceful coexistence between the two statutes. During the course of the employment relationship, the RLA provided the means for resolving disputes. * * * If a railroad sought to end that relationship by sale, consolidation, or abandonment, the ICC routinely conditioned approval on the railroad's acceptance of either job protection or some form of severance pay for employees who would be affected by the change.

This symbiosis ended in 1985, when the ICC announced that it no longer would impose labor-protective conditions on sales of short-line railroads unless exceptional circumstances were shown.

* * *

Suddenly it became important for railroad unions to obtain such labor protections through collective bargaining. Unlike other employment contracts, however, rail labor agreements are altered not by periodic renegotiation but by notification, pursuant to § 6 of the RLA, 45 U.S.C. § 156, of a desire to change terms in the agreements. * * * Thus it is not surprising that the unions in this case did not seek labor

---

19. We address the duty to bargain about the effects of the sale only in the context of the facts existing when the unions' notices were served. We do not deal with a railroad employer's duty to bargain in response to a union's § 156 notice proposing labor protection provisions in the event that a sale, not yet contemplated, should take place.

protective provisions until—just 18 months after the ICC abdicated its traditional protective role—plans to sell the railroad surfaced.[6]

There is no disagreement that labor-protective provisions related to the effects of an abandonment or sale may be the subject of collective bargaining. It follows, I believe, that when railway labor unions request the inclusion of such provisions in their collective-bargaining agreements by proper statutory notice, * * * the employer must maintain the status quo during the statutorily mandated negotiating process or risk a strike as a consequence of its breach of that duty. * * * The Court admits the force of this proposition and acknowledges that an employer has some duty to bargain when a sale is announced. * * * Nevertheless, it indicates that this particular dispute did not obligate the railroad to preserve the status quo, for the Court would prohibit any bargaining that "in effect challenged the decision to sell," and would allow negotiations to cease as soon as the sale is closed. Ante, at 19.[7] This diminution of the employer's duty contravenes two of our decisions interpreting the Railway Labor Act.

* * *

To evade the natural result of adherence to Shore Line and Telegraphers, the Court relies on two later opinions declaring that "an employer has the absolute right to terminate his entire business for any reason he pleases," *Textile Workers v. Darlington Manufacturing Co.,* 380 U.S. 263, 268 (1965), and that the consequences of a partial closure are not a mandatory subject of bargaining, *First National Maintenance Corp. v. NLRB,* 452 U.S. 666 (1981). See ante, at 14–16, and n. 17. But those opinions interpreted the strictures that the National Labor Relations Act places on an unregulated industry. As we noted in *First National Maintenance Corp.,* that is a situation far different from the Railway Labor Act's governance of a regulated industry.[9]

* * *

---

6. The railroad might have had a greater duty to bargain, the Court suggests, had the unions served notice before sale negotiations had commenced. See ante, at 19, n. 19. Yet in the two opinions that I believe should control this case, we did not fault the unions for filing § 6 notices in reaction to—rather than in anticipation of—the railroads' initiatives * * *

In light of the ICC's abrupt halt to its practice of requiring labor protections, moreover, the Court's distinction unfairly penalizes the unions in this case.

7. The Court neglects to mention that a sale may be closed within a matter of months, whereas resort to RLA procedures may entail "virtually endless 'negotiation, mediation, voluntary arbitration, and conciliation.'" * * * If the railroad knows its obligations will end when the sale is consummated, it will have no incentive to expedite bargaining. Thus the Court's imposition of a minimal bargaining duty affords employees scarcely more protection than they would have absent any duty.

9. We stressed that the decision in *Telegraphers* "rested on the particular aims of the Railway Labor Act and national transportation policy. See 362 U.S., at 336–338. The mandatory scope of bargaining under the Railway Labor Act ... [is] not coextensive with the National Labor Relations Act and the [National Labor Relations] Board's jurisdiction over unfair labor practices. See *Chicago & N.W.R. Co. v. Transportation Union,* 402 U.S. 570, 579, n. 11 (1971) ('parallels between the duty to bargain in good faith and the duty to exert every reasonable effort, like all parallels between the NLRA and the Railway Labor Act, should be drawn with the utmost care and with full awareness of the differences between the statutory schemes')." *First National Maintenance Corp. v. NLRB,* 452 U.S. 666, 686–687, n. 23 (1981).

Questions

1. P & LE was a failing business that needed to release employees and extract wage concessions from retained employees to survive. Why did P & LE choose to sell to a "noncarrier" rather than itself lay off unneeded employees and bargain for wage concessions? Once P & LE decided to sell, why did it not sell to a second "carrier" that could lay off unneeded employees and bargain for wage concessions? See footnote 1 in the case. Does the opinion affirm the reasons for P & LE's choice? Should the RLA contain such a "loophole"?

2. The are two arguments in the case. The first deals with whether managers of a firm, by selling the firm, change the terms and conditions of employment so that collective bargaining is required. (Must P & LE file a section 156 notice to sell the company?) Absent an express provision in a collective bargaining agreement dealing with control changes, is it a violation of the agreement for a company to sell a business to another firm that intends to release selling-firm employees or otherwise to change the terms and conditions of employment for employees?

The second argument deals with the union's request to change the terms and conditions of their collective bargaining agreement in light of an anticipated sale of the company. (Can the union file a section 156 notice to negotiate about the effect of the sale of the company?) Can a collective bargaining agreement expressly give employees a veto over mergers and acquisitions? Should a manager ever agree to such a provision? Why does the dissent argue that railroads should be treated differently from "unregulated industry"? Now that railroad unions have read the case, should they all file section 156 notices to seek new contractual protections against acquisitions? Do you believe that railroads will readily accede to a union demand to put provisions in labor contracts that protect employees from acquisitions?

AIR LINE PILOTS ASS'N INTERN. v. UAL CORP., INTERN. ASS'N OF MACHINISTS & AEROSPACE WORKERS

United States Court of Appeals, Seventh Circuit, 1989.
874 F.2d 439.

POSNER, CIRCUIT JUDGE.

This suit arises out of efforts by United Air Lines' pilots to take over the airline, and by the airline's directors and the union representing the airline's machinists to prevent the takeover. When these efforts were first mounted, the airline was a subsidiary of a larger enterprise, and the contemplated takeover was of the entire enterprise. But the pilots wanted to divest the enterprise of its nonairline assets, so that when all the dust settled the pilots would own the airline and nothing else. To simplify exposition we shall pretend that the planned takeover was of a free-standing airline company—which United has since become as a result of a decision by the board of directors of the parent corporation to sell the nonairline assets.

Concretely the plan was for the airline pilots' union, representing United's pilots, to make a tender offer for all of United's common stock. For tax purposes the stock would be owned not by the pilots directly but in trust for them by an employee stock ownership plan (an "ESOP," as it is called). To finance this ambitious offer, which when first proposed in April 1987 carried a price tag of $4.5 billion, the pilots' union lined up a consortium of banks and other lenders to whom the pilots agreed to pledge the unencumbered assets of United if the tender offer succeeded. In short, a leveraged buyout was contemplated. (The union also planned to invest some of its pension assets in the venture.) To enable United to repay the lenders, the pilots offered to accept sharp reductions in their wages and benefits for several years (such concessions are called "give ups") and to effect other economies as well. Shares in the ESOP would be assigned to the pilots in proportion to their give-ups; other employees would obtain interests in the ESOP (or in additional ESOPs that would own the stock of United in concert with the pilots' ESOP) in proportion to their own give-ups.

* * *

No tender offer has yet been made. The pilots cannot get final commitments on financing their takeover bid unless the anti-takeover defenses challenged in this litigation are rescinded.

United's directors did not want a tender offer by the pilots to succeed or even to be made. They were seconded in this wish by the machinists (most of whom in fact are baggage handlers rather than mechanics), who feared that among the economies the pilots would attempt to effect if they succeeded in taking over the airline would be a reduction in machinists' wages, benefits, and employment. The directors explored with the machinists the possibility of inserting in the collective bargaining agreement between United and the machinists' union what the plaintiffs dub with some imprecision "labor contract poison pills."

* * *

In fact United's directors and the machinists' union agreed to insert in the machinists' collective bargaining agreement with the airline two provisions designed to thwart the pilot's impending takeover bid. Neither is a poison pill although the second resembles one. In at least one respect they are more lethal than poison pills: the board of directors cannot unilaterally rescind them, no matter how attractive the tender offer.

The first provision, which is section B(1)(b) of the collective bargaining agreement, provides that if United is taken over, the union shall have "the unilateral option . . . [t]o serve a Section 6 notice immediately." The reference is to section 6 of the Railway Labor Act, 45 U.S.C. § 156, which provides that before either the union or the employer may propose a change in their collective bargaining agreement, thereby inaugurating negotiations that if unsuccessful could result (following statutorily required mediation) in a strike, it must issue a notice of its intentions to the other party. So the issuance of a section 6 notice begins the countdown to a strike, although most of the time the parties are able to settle their differences eventually and a strike is averted. Airlines as well as railroads are subject to the Railway Labor Act.

Since either party to a railroad or airline collective bargaining agreement has a unilateral right to issue a section 6 notice at any time, section B(1)(b) is merely declaratory of the machinists' statutory rights. However, there was unrebutted testimony that the existence of this provision would deter the pilots' consortium of lenders from committing themselves to finance United's takeover bid. For they would be "lending into a strike," and banks won't do this. This testimony is a bit hard to credit, since the same lenders testified that they would take the risk of a machinists' strike provided section B(1)(b) was stricken. Why this superfluous section—and superfluous it is, for if the machinists want to begin the countdown that leads to a strike they will do so whether or not section B(1)(b) remains in their collective bargaining agreement with United—should have so fell an impact eludes us. On the other hand, the district judge found that section B(1)(b) was inserted solely to thwart the pilots' takeover bid, and this finding is not clearly erroneous.

The other section that United and the machinists inserted in the collective bargaining agreement is more like a poison pill because it would dilute the pilots' share position, though what the device is called is supremely unimportant. Again the district judge found on adequate evidence that its only purpose was to thwart a takeover bid by the pilots. The device, section C of the machinists' agreement, must be set out in full:

> In the event the Company or any other party provides or agrees to provide any union-represented labor group with a common stock, preferred stock, stock option, warrant, Employee Stock Ownership Program, or employee equity/participatory ownership of any type ("employee stock plan"), or profit-sharing, such plan shall be offered and allocated to each union-represented labor group on the same basis by reference to "market" wages, benefits and work rules relative to those in effect upon implementation of such plan.
>
> In the first instance, the determination of "market" levels of wages, benefit levels and work rules for the purposes of this agreement shall be by the carrier for all employee groups. A joint arbitration procedure including all parties will be established for the settlement of any dispute over market wages, benefit levels and work rules for all employee groups. Such arbitration procedures and standards shall be detailed in a stipulation agreement entered as soon as practicable.

The pilots are a "union-represented labor group"—they are represented by the Air Line Pilots Association. So if they succeed in taking over United, United will have to offer its other unionized employees—the machinists and the flight attendants—a similar deal. The machinists call section C a "most favored nation" or "me too" clause, but it is more than that. It requires the stock of United to be allocated among the various unionized groups of employees (pilots, machinists, and flight attendants) on the basis of the wage and other concessions that each group makes relative to the arbitrators' determination of each group's "market wage." Suppose the arbitrators determined that the market wage for pilots (not the wage they are receiving from United, but the wage they would receive in a competitive, i.e., nonunionized, labor market) was $40 an hour, and the market wage for machinists was $10 an hour. Suppose that the wages United was actually paying them were $50 and $10. Suppose the pilots were willing to offer "give-ups" worth $11 an hour and the machinists $2. (Ignore the question *why* the machinists would be willing to work for wages below what they could get elsewhere.) And for simplicity suppose that pilots and machinists work the same number of hours on average. Then as we understand section C it would entitle each machinist to twice as much stock as each pilot, because the machinist would be giving up twice as much *relative to the market benchmark* as the pilot ($2 versus $1). The pilots, in contrast, envisage allocating stock in the ESOP among the unionized groups in proportion to the absolute, rather than relative, value of their give-ups, which in our hypothetical example would give each pilot more than five times as many shares in the ESOP as each machinist. The effect of the machinists' agreement with United, if it went into effect upon a takeover by the pilots, would thus be to dilute the pilots' ownership and control.

* * * Corporation law places limits on efforts to fend off hostile takeovers, but the district judge held that the Railway Labor Act preempts state regulation of such efforts when they are embodied in a collective bargaining agreement subject to the Act. United and the machinists acknowledge as they must that the logic of the judge's reasoning applies equally to collective bargaining agreements regulated not by the Railway Labor Act but by the National Labor Relations Act.

If a federal and a state statute create inconsistent duties, the state statute must of course give way; the supremacy clause requires no less. If they do not create inconsistent duties yet enforcement of the state statute would (having due regard for the strength of the state interest) stand as a substantial and unwarranted obstacle to attaining the objectives of the federal statute, again the state statute is preempted. This is done by interpreting the federal statute to outlaw any such obstacles, and then bringing the supremacy clause into play again.

* * *

This is an example of creative interpretation, since ordinarily Congress will not have foreseen, and by hypothesis will not have made express provision for, the creation by the state of an (ordinarily unintended) obstacle to the fulfillment of Congress's purposes.

Insofar as Delaware law requires that the board of directors proceed with all due deliberation in deciding whether to adopt defensive measures against a takeover, see, e.g., *Smith v. Van Gorkom*, 488 A.2d 858 (Del.1985); *Ivanhoe Partners v. Newmont Mining Corp.*, 535 A.2d

1334, 1341–42 (Del.1987)—measures that may include a management-sponsored ESOP, * * * which in a realistic sense section C of the machinists' agreement with United is—there is a theoretical possibility of conflict with the employer's duty under federal labor law to bargain collectively. Bargaining often continues down to the wire and if negotiators are not vested with broad authority the bargaining may collapse and a strike ensue. So if a union sprung a demand for a poison pill at the eleventh hour, the employer might find itself caught between its duty under state law to refer the matter to the board of directors, which in turn would be required to consult with its financial advisors, and a duty under federal law to respond immediately to the union's démarche. But this is theory, not practice, at least as far as the present case is concerned. And even as theory it is suspect because any illegal proposal could be made at the last minute, and it cannot be right that this bare possibility preempts all state laws that set limits on what parties to collective bargaining agreements can agree to.

The next question is whether Delaware corporation law, while not inconsistent with the Railway Labor Act in the strict sense of imposing inconsistent duties, nevertheless might thwart the Act's objectives. Having to negotiate with one eye on state corporation law could complicate collective bargaining negotiations between United and its unions. United might find itself in a position where to buy labor peace it had to grant the machinists the protection they sought against a takeover that might result in a diminution in their wages, benefits, or employment, yet where it could not do so without violating Delaware's corporation law. But of course this would be equally true if the machinists wanted a provision in their collective bargaining agreement that machinists shall receive half their pay in cocaine or that replacement workers shall be poisoned within 24 hours of being hired. The federal statutes that encourage collective bargaining do not seek to do so by granting employers and unions an exemption from state laws of general applicability, whether they are laws against poisoning people, or beating up people, * * * or laws limiting the use of poison pills or other anti-takeover devices designed to poison not people but transactions, or even laws seeking to reduce the costs of employers, * * * or guaranteeing workers minimum health benefits, * * * or severance pay. * * *

United and the machinists do not contend that Delaware's legislature and courts are seeking to create and impose a rival labor code to the RLA or the NLRA * * *

They contend that the even-handed application of Delaware corporation law might forbid an anti-takeover measure contained in a labor contract. And so it might. But this is not a persuasive argument for federal preemption, unless it can be shown that allowing poison pills or other anti-takeover devices to be written into such contracts regardless of whether the devices violate state law is necessary in order to reduce the number or severity of transportation strikes or otherwise to attain the essential objectives of the Railway Labor Act. United and the machinists make no such showing. This is the first case that has come to our attention where anti-takeover devices have been planted in a collective bargaining agreement, and this makes it hard for us to believe, in the absence of evidence, that freedom to negotiate for their inclusion unhampered by state law is necessary to the system of collective bargaining established by the Act.

Although preemption does not seem required to further the objectives of federal law, it could have a catastrophic effect on the efforts of states to regulate takeovers, and this consideration is germane since, realistically, a judgment about preemption requires a weighing of federal and state interests. * * *

Any firm that had a collective bargaining agreement with a significant fraction of its work force could adopt anti-takeover measures with complete impunity, simply by writing them into the collective bargaining agreement. Unionized firms would be immune to hostile takeovers if, as is common, the union feared that a buyer of the company would seek to economize on its labor costs by renegotiating the company's collective bargaining agreements or even by selling off the company's assets to purchasers who would take free of any obligation under such agreements. For us to create in the name of preemption so enormous a loophole in state regulation, without any evidence that the loophole is necessary to protect the objectives of federal labor law, would be reckless. Like the criminal law, the regulation of corporations is, as the Supreme Court reminded us in the *CTS* case, a matter of primary state responsibility. * * * In such areas the presumption is against federal preemption. * * * And presumption or not, we do not think that the framers of the Railway Labor Act meant to deal the body blow to state regulation of corporations that a finding of preemption in this case would administer.

All this is not to suggest that there could never be preemption by the Railway Labor Act of state corporation law. If the pilots were seeking to enjoin the issuance by the machinists of a section 6 notice, on the ground that the machinists, acting in cahoots with United's board of directors, were trying to thwart a takeover bid, in violation of Delaware law, a real issue of preemption would be presented. We need not decide how it should be resolved. We hold only that wholesale preemption, which would make all anti-takeover measures inviolate, provided only that they were written into collective bargaining agreements, is not required by the purposes of the Railway Labor Act.

* * *

AIR LINE PILOTS ASS'N INTERN. v. UAL CORP., INTERN. ASS'N OF MACHINISTS & AEROSPACE WORKERS

United States Court of Appeals, Seventh Circuit, 1990.
897 F.2d 1394.

POSNER, CIRCUIT JUDGE. This case returns to us following our remand to the district judge to consider questions of state law left undecided on the first round. ...

* * *

Under Delaware law an anti-takeover provision is lawful only if the corporation adopting it has given due consideration to shareholder welfare; the business-judgment rule in Delaware allows less scope for an anti-takeover provision than for provisions less likely to generate a conflict of interest between management, eager to retain control of the corporation, and the shareholders, eager to maximize the value of their shares. *Revlon, Inc. v. MacAndrews & Forbes Holdings, Inc.,* 506 A.2d 173, 180 (Del.1985). The proper characterization of Sections B(1)(b) and C, which the pilots contend are anti-takeover provisions and United and the machinists contend are provisions regulating the company's labor relations, is a fact-bound issue on which Judge Zagel's determination, unless clearly erroneous, binds us. His determination that these are anti-takeover provisions is not clearly erroneous; it is not erroneous at all. There is abundant evidence that these provisions were adopted not to resolve a conflict between United and the machinists and thus head off a possible strike, as United and the machinists contend in this litigation, but to prevent the pilots from taking over the company.

Section C is particularly transparent; its only possible purpose is to discourage the pilots from making a takeover attempt by diluting the value of the stock that the pilots' employee stock plan would acquire by taking over the company. Although one can imagine the company's acceding to the machinists' request for such a provision not because the company wanted to defeat a takeover by the pilots but because it wanted to buy labor peace with the machinists, Judge Zagel found with ample support in the record that the object of both parties was to defeat a takeover by the pilots. As for Section B(1)(b), the evidence was again ample that its purpose was to scare off the lenders to whom the pilots might turn for the financing of their takeover attempt.

So these are anti-takeover devices, and of a unique lethality because unlike the usual "poison pills" the company could not rescind them. They were written into a collective bargaining agreement that the company could not alter unilaterally other than through the cumbersome process of a section 6 notice, followed by protracted mediation and cooling-off periods. They are the Doomsday Bomb in the arsenal of corporate defensive measures. Delaware law requires that defensive measures, and a fortiori defensive measures as irrevocable as these, be adopted with due concern for the interests of shareholders. The challenged covenants were adopted in haste and with due regard for nothing except their probable efficacy in defeating the pilots' takeover attempt. They violate Delaware law.

The History of the UAL Buyout

COFFEE, UNSTABLE COALITIONS: CORPORATE GOVERNANCE AS A MULTI–PLAYER GAME
78 Geo. L.J. 1495, 1523–25 (1990)

By far the most publicized transaction involving unions in 1989 was the abortive effort by UAL's pilots' union to structure a $6.75 billion leveraged buyout of UAL.[101] The UAL buyout attempt had a long history, as the pilots' union had played a central role in a loose coalition with several large investors that succeeded in ousting UAL's chief executive officer, Richard J. Ferris, in 1987. At one point, the union, assisted by an investment banking firm acting as an adviser, had considered and almost made a hostile tender offer. Its efforts were thwarted, however, in large part because of the constant and bitter opposition of UAL's other principal union—the machinists' union—which negotiated a labor contract with management that effectively blocked the pilots' proposed buyout through an ESOP. Nonetheless, following a hostile bid by Marvin Davis for UAL in 1989, UAL's management quickly switched sides and formed an alliance with the pilots' union to propose a leveraged buyout under which employees would acquire seventy-five percent of UAL (with the remaining equity being divided between management and a third party investor, British Airways). The corporate governance provisions negotiated to hold together this shotgun marriage of labor and management were specially tailored and appear to be unprecedented. Although the unions were to have only three seats on a fifteen-member board (with eight seats held by independent directors), two out of the three labor directors' votes would be necessary to approve any major decision. This insistence by the pilots' union on a special veto power over important decisions seemingly reflected a distrust of UAL's management and a fear that management would otherwise be in a position to breach its implicit deal once the transaction was complete. For their interests to be protected, the union's representatives felt it necessary to insist on a veto power over any major divestiture or acquisition of assets or any move toward diversification. In short, contractual provisions were not enough; governance had to be shared—possibly so that free cash flow would be kept locked in the core business.

The UAL story does not end, however, with a happy marriage of labor and management. The machinists' union remained bitterly opposed to the buyout throughout 1989, and their hostility, according to press reports, caused the "unraveling [of] the deal by frightening potential lenders." Following the inability of the original buyout proposal to obtain adequate financing, the UAL board withdrew its support for the buyout. Nonetheless, arbitrageurs, who had been left holding substantial blocks of UAL stock whose value had declined precipitously after the buyout's failure, began a consent solicitation to remove the board and approached the pilots' union for support. Both the unions and shareholder groups showed that they could form a coalition against the board as well as with it.

Finally, in early 1990 the rival unions did form an alliance and formulated a buyout proposal based on the use of an ESOP that would

---

101. * * *

In April 1990, a revised and reduced buyout for $4.38 billion was made by all three of UAL's principal unions and was accepted in principle by UAL's board of directors.

* * *

give employees seventy-five percent ownership of UAL. This proposal, however, excluded UAL's chief executive officer, Stephen Wolf, from any significant equity participation, and he apparently resisted it as a result. In effect, by early 1990 the unions had come full circle back to their original position in opposition to management. What is most striking about the UAL story is that over the course of an almost three-year period, every coalition that could be formed was formed: management allied with one union against another; the unions allied with each other and with management; and ultimately the unions allied with a powerful shareholder to outflank management. Machiavelli would have understood this world of alternating coalition formation and defection.

* * *

[The April 1990 bid of $4.38 billion ($201 a share) also failed for want of financing, and the three unions made a fifth attempt in October. The union's bankers valued the fifth offer at $3.38 billion ($155 a share); traders valued it at 15 percent less. The offer consisted of $20 a share in cash; $31 a share in senior notes paying 12 percent interest; $41.50 a share in notes secured by aircraft paying 11.5 percent interest; $32.50 a share in preferred stock paying a 12 percent dividend; and a contingency payment obligation valued at as much as $30 a share (Wall St.J., p. D3, col. 2 (Oct 10, 1990)). The UAL board rejected the offer. UAL stock dropped to $88 a share. Unhappy shareholders, many of whom had bought UAL stock at $160 a share, and disgruntled unions are pondering their next move.]

Questions

1. Must all provisions in union contracts that protect employees in acquisitions, potentially deterring some bidders who would otherwise buy the firm, meet the heightened *Unocal* standard? Does your answer depend on whether a firm is responding to a pending bid or is responding to a general concern that the firm could be a takeover target? Is your answer different for a control change clause in a union contract that applies only to hostile control changes (that is, stock acquisitions that do not have the approval of the preacquisition target board) than for a control change clause that applies to all major firm restructurings (including, among others, friendly mergers)?

2. Once a control change provision has been adopted in a collective bargaining agreement, as one was in the *UAL* case, and the court holds that such a provision is a violation of state law, should the court enjoin the provision or enforce the provision and allow the firm's shareholders to collect damages from their directors for making the agreement? If a court enjoins the provision, can the union claim damages from the firm for breach of contract? Assume the union gave up wage demands (or made express wage concessions) in exchange for the now invalidated provision. Was this scenario likely in *UAL*? If a court enjoins a control change provision in a collective bargaining agreement, as Judge Posner did in the

UAL case, should the other parts of the collective bargaining agreement remain valid?

3. Is the *UAL* case consistent or inconsistent with the argument that boards of directors, among other things, should not by law be required to owe general fiduciary duties to employees as well as shareholders? Please read N.Y.—McKinney's Business Corporation Law § 717(6) and Connecticut General Statutes Ann. § 33–133(e) in your supplement. What is the effect of these statutes, if any, on the *UAL* holdings?

4. Are "tin parachutes" legal?

NEW PLOY: "TIN PARACHUTES"
N.Y. Times Mar. 19, 1987 at D1.

* * *

Under the tin parachute plan, Herman Miller employees, depending on their tenure and other considerations, are entitled to cash payments up to two and a half times their annual compensation, including bonus and incentive pay, if the company changes hands against the board of directors' wishes.

Nearly half the Fortune 500 companies already have golden parachutes protecting key employees. But Herman Miller is among the first to have a plan that reaches down to the lowest ranks. The Mobil Corporation, the Accuray Corporation, America West Airlines and the Diamond Shamrock Corporation have similar plans.

"Because of the sheer number of employees they apply to, it can be a significant expense" for the raider, said Douglas Shaw, a compensation consultant. * * * America West, for example, not only awards longstanding employees lump sum payments, it also insists that an unwelcome raider pick up the tab for employees' legal expenses of up to $1 million. "That can obviously add up," Mr. Shaw said.

In the case of golden parachutes of a multibillion-dollar company, said Graef Crystal, a business school professor at the University of California at Berkeley, "the bidding is in hundred-million-dollar increments, and three times pay for 20 people may get lost in the bidding. But when you're going to cover 5,000 employees, that doesn't get lost in the rounding."

Unlike golden parachutes for executives, which must be disclosed publicly, tin parachutes are often kept secret—at least until a hostile bidder appears on the scene.

"They don't put it in their proxy; they don't put out press releases, and by and large, unless it comes to light in a takeover fight, you never find out about it," said Richard D. Greenfield, a Philadelphia lawyer specializing in shareholder litigation.

* * *

There are those, however, who do not buy the argument that companies are concerned about their rank and file in setting up the tin parachutes. One is Professor Crystal, who said, "If they were so participative, why don't they offer that same protection if the dirty deed was done by them and not a raider?" Most of the parachute plans are written so that they do not apply if there is a friendly takeover of the company, which would include a management-led leveraged buyout.

In addition, some feel these plans become excessive and are installed at shareholders' expense.

Professor Crystal calls these devices a "highly reprehensible" takeover defense. * * *

Others advise against the tin parachutes simply because, like any poison pill, they can be all too toxic. "At least you can usually negotiate poison pills away," said Mr. Schaeffer of the Hay Group. "But here you're creating rights with your employees. It's going to be hard to take them away."

* * *

Does your answer depend on whether the severance payments in a tin parachute vest only in hostile control changes or whether they vest in all job dislocations resulting from any large-scale firm restructurings? See Ryan, Corporate Directors and the "Social Costs" of Takeovers—Reflections on the Tin Parachute, 64 Tul.L.Rev. 3 (1989) (the former are much more common than the latter).

Subsection b. Must the Buyer Adopt the Seller's Labor Contracts or Bargain With the Seller's Union?

Assume a firm has signed a collective bargaining agreement with a union that enjoys the majority support of the firm's employees. If the managers of the firm sell the firm's business, must the buyer adopt the collective bargaining agreement? If so, the new employer has the same obligations to employees as the original employer, including the obligation to arbitrate all contract differences, liability for the predecessor's unremedied unfair labor practices, and the duty to bargain with the predecessor's union. If not, must the buyer bargain with the seller's union about the initial terms and conditions of employment for any rehired employees? Or is the buyer completely free from any labor obligations of the seller? If so, the seller's employees rehired by the buyer, in conjunction, perhaps, with other employees of the buyer, must reorganize and seek renewed recognition as a bargaining unit. These questions are the subject of the following four Supreme Court cases.

JOHN WILEY & SONS, INC. v. LIVINGSTON
Supreme Court of the United States, 1964.
376 U.S. 543, 84 S.Ct. 909, 11 L.Ed.2d 898.

MR. JUSTICE HARLAN delivered the opinion of the Court.

* * *

District 65, Retail, Wholesale and Department Store Union, AFL–CIO, entered into a collective bargaining agreement with Interscience Publishers, Inc., a publishing firm, for a term expiring on January 31, 1962. The agreement did not contain an express provision making it binding on successors of Interscience. On October 2, 1961, Interscience merged with the petitioner, John Wiley & Sons, Inc., another publishing firm, and ceased to do business as a separate entity. There is no suggestion that the merger was not for genuine business reasons.

At the time of the merger Interscience had about 80 employees, of whom 40 were represented by this Union. It had a single plant in New York City, and did an annual business of somewhat over $1,000,000. Wiley was a much larger concern, having separate office and warehouse facilities and about 300 employees, and doing an annual business of more than $9,000,000. None of Wiley's employees was represented by a union.

In discussions before and after the merger, the Union and Interscience (later Wiley) were unable to agree on the effect of the merger on the collective bargaining agreement and on the rights under it of those covered employees hired by Wiley. The Union's position was that despite the merger it continued to represent the covered Interscience employees taken over by Wiley, and that Wiley was obligated to recognize certain rights of such employees which had "vested" under the Interscience bargaining agreement. Such rights, more fully described below, concerned matters typically covered by collective bargaining agreements, such as seniority status, severance pay, etc. The Union contended also that Wiley was required to make certain pension fund payments called for under the Interscience bargaining agreement.

Wiley, though recognizing for purposes of its own pension plan the Interscience service of the former Interscience employees, asserted that the merger terminated the bargaining agreement for all purposes. It refused to recognize the Union as bargaining agent or to accede to the Union's claims on behalf of Interscience employees. All such employees, except a few who ended their Wiley employment with severance pay and for whom no rights are asserted here, continued in Wiley's employ.

No satisfactory solution having been reached, the Union, one week before the expiration date of the Interscience bargaining agreement, commenced this action to compel arbitration. * * * Wiley, objecting to arbitration, argues that it never was a party to the collective bargaining agreement, and that, in any event, the Union lost its status as representative of the former Interscience employees when they were mingled in a larger Wiley unit of employees. The Union argues that Wiley, as successor to Interscience, is bound by the latter's agreement, at least sufficiently to require it to arbitrate. The Union relies on § 90 of the N.Y. Stock Corporation Law, which provides, among other things, that no "claim or demand for any cause" against a constituent corporation shall be extinguished by a consolidation. Alternatively, the Union argues that, apart from § 90, federal law requires that arbitration go forward, lest the policy favoring arbitration frequently be undermined by changes in corporate organization.

Federal law, fashioned "from the policy of our national labor laws," controls. * * * State law may be utilized so far as it is of aid in the development of correct principles or their application in a particular case, * * * but the law which ultimately results is federal. We hold that the disappearance by merger of a corporate employer which has entered into a collective bargaining agreement with a union does not automatically terminate all rights of the employees covered by the agreement, and that, in appropriate circumstances, present here, the successor employer may be required to arbitrate with the union under the agreement.

* * *

Employees, and the union which represents them, ordinarily do not take part in negotiations leading to a change in corporate ownership. The negotiations will ordinarily not concern the well-being of the employees, whose advantage or disadvantage, potentially great, will inevitably be incidental to the main considerations. The objectives of national labor policy, reflected in established principles of federal law, require that the rightful prerogative of owners independently to rearrange their businesses and even eliminate themselves as employers be balanced by some protection to the employees from a sudden change in the employment relationship. The transition from one corporate organization to another will in most cases be eased and industrial strife avoided if employees' claims continue to be resolved by arbitration rather than by "the relative strength ... of the contending forces," * * *

The preference of national labor policy for arbitration as a substitute for tests of strength between contending forces could be overcome only if other considerations compellingly so demanded. We find none. While the principles of law governing ordinary contracts would not bind to a contract an unconsenting successor to a contracting party,[3] a collective bargaining agreement is not an ordinary contract. "... [I]t is a generalized code to govern a myriad of cases which the draftsmen cannot wholly anticipate.... The collective agreement covers the whole employment relationship. It calls into being a new common law—the common law of a particular industry or of a particular plant." * * * Central to the peculiar status and function of a collective bargaining agreement is the fact, dictated both by circumstance, * * * and by the requirements of the National Labor Relations Act, that it is not in any real sense the simple product of a consensual relationship. Therefore, although the duty to arbitrate, as we have said, * * * must be founded on a contract, the impressive policy considerations favoring

3. But cf. the general rule that in the case of a merger the corporation which survives is liable for the debts and contracts of the one which disappears. 15 Fletcher, Private Corporations (1961 rev. ed.), § 7121.

arbitration are not wholly overborne by the fact that Wiley did not sign the contract being construed. This case cannot readily be assimilated to the category of those in which there is no contract whatever, or none which is reasonably related to the party sought to be obligated. There was a contract, and Interscience, Wiley's predecessor, was party to it. We thus find Wiley's obligation to arbitrate this dispute in the Interscience contract construed in the context of a national labor policy.

We do not hold that in every case in which the ownership or corporate structure of an enterprise is changed the duty to arbitrate survives. As indicated above, there may be cases in which the lack of any substantial continuity of identity in the business enterprise before and after a change would make a duty to arbitrate something imposed from without, not reasonably to be found in the particular bargaining agreement and the acts of the parties involved. So too, we do not rule out the possibility that a union might abandon its right to arbitration by failing to make its claims known. Neither of these situations is before the Court. Although Wiley was substantially larger than Interscience, relevant similarity and continuity of operation across the change in ownership is adequately evidenced by the wholesale transfer of Interscience employees to the Wiley plant, apparently without difficulty. The Union made its position known well before the merger and never departed from it. In addition, we do not suggest any view on the questions surrounding a certified union's claim to continued representative status following a change in ownership. * * * This Union does not assert that it has any bargaining rights independent of the Interscience agreement; it seeks to arbitrate claims based on that agreement, now expired, not to negotiate a new agreement.[5]

* * *

NLRB v. BURNS INTERN. SEC. SERVICES, INC.

Supreme Court of the United States, 1972.
406 U.S. 272, 92 S.Ct. 1571, 32 L.Ed.2d 61.

Mr. Justice White delivered the opinion of the Court.

Burns International Security Services, Inc. (Burns), replaced another employer, the Wackenhut Corp. (Wackenhut), which had previously

---

5. The fact that the Union does not represent a majority of an appropriate bargaining unit in Wiley does not prevent it from representing those employees who are covered by the agreement which is in dispute and out of which Wiley's duty to arbitrate arises. * * * There is no problem of conflict with another union, * * * since Wiley had no contract with any union covering the unit of employees which received the former Interscience employees.

Problems might be created by an arbitral award which required Wiley to give special treatment to the former Interscience employees because of rights found to have accrued to them under the Interscience contract. But the mere possibility of such problems cannot cut off the Union's right to press the employees' claims in arbitration. While it would be premature at this stage to speculate on how to avoid such hypothetical problems, we have little doubt that within the flexible procedures of arbitration a solution can be reached which would avoid disturbing labor relations in the Wiley plant.

provided plant protection services for the Lockheed Aircraft Service Co. (Lockheed) located at the Ontario International Airport in California. When Burns began providing security service, it employed 42 guards; 27 of them had been employed by Wackenhut. Burns refused, however, to bargain with the United Plant Guard Workers of America (UPG) which had been certified after a National Labor Relations Board (Board) election as the exclusive bargaining representative of Wackenhut's employees less than four months earlier.

* * *

[W]here the bargaining unit remains unchanged and a majority of the employees hired by the new employer are represented by a recently certified bargaining agent there is little basis for faulting the Board's implementation of the express mandates of § 8(a)(5) and § 9(a) by ordering the employer to bargain with the incumbent union.

* * *

It does not follow, however, from Burns' duty to bargain that it was bound to observe the substantive terms of the collective-bargaining contract the union had negotiated with Wackenhut and to which Burns had in no way agreed. Section 8(d) of the Act expressly provides that the existence of such bargaining obligation "does not compel either party to agree to a proposal or require the making of a concession."

* * *

* * * The claim is that Burns must be held bound by the contract executed by Wackenhut, whether Burns has agreed to it or not and even though Burns made it perfectly clear that it had no intention of assuming that contract. *Wiley* suggests no such open-ended obligation. Its narrower holding dealt with a merger occurring against a background of state law that embodied the general rule that in merger situations the surviving corporation is liable for the obligations of the disappearing corporation. See N.Y. Stock Corp. Law § 90 (1951); 15 W. Fletcher, Private Corporations § 7121 (1961 rev. ed.). Here there was no merger or sale of assets, and there were no dealings whatsoever between Wackenhut and Burns. On the contrary, they were competitors for the same work, each bidding for the service contract at Lockheed. Burns purchased nothing from Wackenhut and became liable for none of its financial obligations. Burns merely hired enough of Wackenhut's employees to require it to bargain with the union as commanded by § 8(a)(5) and § 9(a). But this consideration is a wholly insufficient basis for implying either in fact or in law that Burns had agreed or must be held to have agreed to honor Wackenhut's collective-bargaining contract.

* * *

We also agree with the Court of Appeals that holding either the union or the new employer bound to the substantive terms of an old collective-bargaining contract may result in serious inequities. A potential employer may be willing to take over a moribund business only if he can make changes in corporate structure, composition of the labor force, work location, task assignment, and nature of supervision. Saddling such an employer with the terms and conditions of employment contained in the old collective-bargaining contract may make these changes impossible and may discourage and inhibit the transfer of capital. On the other hand, a union may have made concessions to a small or failing employer that it would be unwilling to make to a large or economically successful firm.

* * *

It therefore follows that the Board's order requiring Burns to "give retroactive effect to all the clauses of said [Wackenhut] contract and, with interest of 6 percent, make whole its employees for any losses suffered by reason of Respondent's [Burns'] refusal to honor, adopt and enforce said contract" must be set aside.

* * *

Although Burns had an obligation to bargain with the union concerning wages and other conditions of employment when the union requested it to do so, this case is not like a § 8(a)(5) violation where an employer unilaterally changes a condition of employment without consulting a bargaining representative. It is difficult to understand how Burns could be said to have *changed* unilaterally any pre-existing term or condition of employment without bargaining when it had no previous relationship whatsover to the bargaining unit and, prior to July 1, no outstanding terms and conditions of employment from which a change could be inferred. The terms on which Burns hired employees for service after July 1 may have differed from the terms extended by Wackenhut and required by the collective-bargaining contract, but it does not follow that Burns changed *its* terms and conditions of employment when it specified the initial basis on which employees were hired on July 1.

* * *

Affirmed.

MR. JUSTICE REHNQUIST, with whom THE CHIEF JUSTICE, MR. JUSTICE BRENNAN, and MR. JUSTICE POWELL join, concurring in No. 71–123 and dissenting in No. 71–198.

* * * I would enforce neither the Board's bargaining order nor its order imposing upon Burns the terms of the contract between the union and Wackenhut.

* * *

Phrased another way, the doctrine of successorship in the federal common law of labor relations accords to employees the same general protection against transfer of assets by an entity against which they have a claim as is accorded by other legal doctrines to nonlabor-related claimants against the same entity. Nonlabor-related claimants in such transfer situations may be protected not only by assumption agreements resulting from the self-interest of the contracting parties participating in a merger or sale of assets but also by state laws imposing upon the successor corporation of any merger the obligations of the merged corporation (see, *e.g.*, § 90 of the N.Y. Stock Corp. Law (1951), cited in *Wiley, supra*), and by bulk sales acts found in numerous States. These latter are designed to give the nonlabor-related creditor of the predecessor entity some claim, either as a matter of contract right against the successor, or as a matter of property right to charge the assets that pass from the predecessor to the successor. The implication of *Wiley* is that the federal common law of labor relations accords the same general type and degree of protection to employees claiming under a collective-bargaining contract.

* * *

HOWARD JOHNSON CO. v. DETROIT LOCAL JOINT EXECUTIVE BD., AFL–CIO

Supreme Court of the United States, 1974.
417 U.S. 249, 94 S.Ct. 2236, 41 L.Ed.2d 46.

MR. JUSTICE MARSHALL delivered the opinion of the Court.

Once again we are faced with the problem of defining the labor law obligations of a "successor" employer to the employees of its predecessors. In this case, petitioner Howard Johnson Co. is the bona fide purchaser of the assets of a restaurant and motor lodge. Respondent Union was the bargaining representative of the employees of the previous operators, and had successfully concluded collective-bargaining agreements with them. In commencing its operation of the restaurant, Howard Johnson hired only a small fraction of the predecessors' employees. The question presented in this case is whether the Union may compel Howard Johnson to arbitrate, under the arbitration provisions of the collective-bargaining agreements signed by its predecessors, the extent of its obligations under those agreements to the predecessors' employees.

Prior to the sale at issue here, the Grissoms—Charles T. Grissom, P.L. Grissom, Ben Bibb, P.L. Grissom & Son, Inc., and the Belleville Restaurant Co., a corporation wholly owned by P.L. Grissom & Son—had operated a Howard Johnson's Motor Lodge and an adjacent Howard Johnson's Restaurant in Belleville, Michigan, under franchise agreements with the petitioner. Employees at both the restaurant and motor lodge were represented by the respondent Hotel & Restaurant Employees & Bartenders International Union. The Grissoms had entered into separate collective-bargaining agreements with the Union covering employees at the two establishments. Both agreements contained dispute settlement procedures leading ultimately to arbitration. Both agreements also provided that they would be binding upon the employer's "successors, assigns, purchasers, lessees or transferees."

On June 16, 1972, the Grissoms entered into an agreement with Howard Johnson to sell it all of the personal property used in connection with operation of the restaurant and motor lodge. The Grissoms retained ownership of the real property, leasing both premises to Howard Johnson. Howard Johnson did not agree to assume any of the Grissoms' obligations, except for four specific contracts relating to operation of the restaurant and motor lodge. On June 28, Howard Johnson mailed the Grissoms a letter, which they later acknowledged and confirmed, clarifying that "[i]t was understood and agreed that the Purchaser ... would not recognize and assume any labor agreements between the Sellers ... and any labor organizations," and that it was further agreed that "the Purchaser does not assume any obligations or liabilities of the Sellers resulting from any labor agreements...."

Transfer of operation of the restaurant and motor lodge was set for midnight, July 23, 1972. On July 9, the Grissoms notified all of their employees that their employment would terminate as of that time. The Union was also notified of the termination of the Grissoms' business. On July 11, Howard Johnson advised the Union that it would not recognize the Union or assume any obligations under the existing collective-bargaining agreements.

After reaching agreement with the Grissoms, Howard Johnson began hiring its own work force. It placed advertisements in local newspapers, and posted notices in various places, including the restaurant and motor lodge. It began interviewing prospective employees on July 10, hired its first employees on July 18, and began training them at a Howard Johnson facility in Ann Arbor on July 20. Prior to the sale, the Grissoms had 53 employees. Howard Johnson commenced operations with 45 employees, 33 engaged in the restaurant and 12 in the motor lodge. Of these, only nine of the restaurant employees and none of the motor lodge employees had previously been employed by the Grissoms. None of the supervisory personnel employed by the Grissoms were hired by Howard Johnson.

* * *

When the focus is placed on the facts of these cases, it becomes apparent that the decision below is an unwarranted extension of *Wiley* beyond any factual context it may have contemplated. Although it is true that both *Wiley* and this case involve § 301 suits to compel arbitration, the similarity ends there. *Wiley* involved a merger, as a result of which the initial employing entity completely disappeared. In contrast, this case involves only a sale of some assets, and the initial employers remain in existence as viable corporate entities, with substantial revenues from the lease of the motor lodge and restaurant to Howard Johnson. Although we have recognized that ordinarily there is no basis for distinguishing among mergers, consolidations, or purchases of assets in the analysis of successorship problems, * * * we think these distinctions are relevant here for two reasons. First, the merger in *Wiley* was conducted "against a background of state law that embodied the general rule that in merger situations the surviving corporation is liable for the obligations of the disappearing corporation," * * * which suggests that holding Wiley bound to arbitrate under its predecessor's collective-bargaining agreement may have been fairly within the reasonable expectations of the parties. Second, the disappearance of the original employing entity in the *Wiley* merger meant that unless the union were afforded some remedy against Wiley, it would have no means to enforce the obligations voluntarily undertaken by the merged corporation, to the extent that those obligations vested prior to the merger or to the extent that its promises were intended to survive a change of ownership. Here, in contrast, because the Grissom corporations continue as viable entities with substantial retained assets, the Union does have a realistic remedy to enforce their contractual obligations. Indeed, the Grissoms have agreed to arbitrate the extent of their liability to the Union and their former employees; presumably this arbitration will explore the question whether the Grissoms breached the successorship provisions of their collective-bargaining agreements, and what the remedy for this breach might be.[3]

Even more important, in *Wiley* the surviving corporation hired *all* of the employees of the disappearing corporation. Although, under *Burns,* the surviving corporation may have been entitled to make substantial changes in its operation of the enterprise, the plain fact is that it did not. * * * The claims which the union sought to compel Wiley to arbitrate were thus the claims of Wiley's employees as to the benefits they were entitled to receive in connection with their employment. It was on this basis that the Court in *Wiley* found that there was the "substantial continuity of identity in the business enterprise," * * * which it held necessary before the successor employer could be compelled to arbitrate.[4]

Here, however, Howard Johnson decided to select and hire its own independent work force to commence its operation of the restaurant and motor lodge.[5] It therefore hired only nine of the 53 former

3. * * * The mere existence of the successorship clauses in the bargaining agreements between the Union and the Grissoms, however, cannot bind Howard Johnson either to the substantive terms of the agreements or to the arbitration clauses thereof, absent the continuity required by *Wiley,* when it is perfectly clear the Company refused to assume any obligations under the agreements.

4. Subsequently, the Interscience plant was closed and the former Interscience employees were integrated into Wiley's work force. The arbitrator, relying in part on the NLRB's decision in *Burns,* held that the provisions of the Interscience collective-bargaining agreement remained in effect for as long as Wiley continued to operate the former Interscience enterprise as a unit in substantially the same manner as prior to the merger, but that the integration of the former Interscience employees into Wiley's operations destroyed this continuity of identity and terminated the effectiveness of the bargaining agreement. 55 Lab.Arb., at 218–220.

5. It is important to emphasize that this is not a case where the successor corporation is the "alter ego" of the predecessor, where it is "merely a disguised continuance of the old employer." * * * Such cases involve a mere technical change in the structure or identity of the employing entity, frequently to avoid the effect of the labor laws, without any substantial change in its ownership or management. In these circumstances, the courts have had little difficulty holding that the successor is in

Grissom employees and none of the Grissom supervisors. The primary purpose of the Union in seeking arbitration here with Howard Johnson is not to protect the rights of Howard Johnson's employees; rather, the Union primarily seeks arbitration on behalf of the former Grissom employees who were *not* hired by Howard Johnson. It is the Union's position that Howard Johnson was bound by the pre-existing collective-bargaining agreement to employ all of these former Grissom employees, except those who could be dismissed in accordance with the "just cause" provision or laid off in accordance with the seniority provision. It is manifest from the Union's efforts to obtain injunctive relief requiring the Company to hire all of these employees that this is the heart of the controversy here. Indeed, at oral argument, the Union conceded that it would be making the same argument here if Howard Johnson had not hired any of the former Grissom employees, and that what was most important to the Union was the prospect that the arbitrator might order the Company to hire all of these employees.

What the Union seeks here is completely at odds with the basic principles this Court elaborated in *Burns*. We found there that nothing in the federal labor laws "requires that an employer ... who purchases the assets of a business be obligated to hire all of the employees of the predecessor though it is possible that such an obligation might be assumed by the employer." 406 U.S., at 280 n. 5. * * * *Burns* emphasized that "[a] potential employer may be willing to take over a moribund business only if he can make changes in corporate structure, composition of the labor force, ... and nature of supervision." 406 U.S., at 287–288. We rejected the Board's position in part because "[i]t would seemingly follow that employees of the predecessor would be deemed employees of the successor, dischargeable only in accordance with provisions of the contract and subject to the grievance and arbitration provisions thereof. Burns would not have been free to replace Wackenhut's guards with its own except as the contract permitted." *Id.*, at 288. Clearly, *Burns* establishes that Howard Johnson had the right not to hire any of the former Grissom employees, if it so desired.[8] * * *

reality the same employer and is subject to all the legal and contractual obligations of the predecessor. * * *

There is not the slightest suggestion in this case that the sale of the restaurant and motor lodge by the Grissoms to Howard Johnson was in any sense a paper transaction without meaningful impact on the ownership or operation of the enterprise. Howard Johnson had no ownership interest in the restaurant or motor lodge prior to this transaction. Although the Grissoms' operation of the enterprise as Howard Johnson's franchisee was subject to substantial restraints imposed by the franchise agreements on some aspects of the business, the franchise agreements imposed no restrictions on the Grissoms' hiring or labor relations policies. There is nothing in the record to indicate that Howard Johnson had had any previous dealings with the Union, or had participated in any way in negotiating or approving the collective-bargaining agreements.

8. See *Crotona Service Corp.*, 200 N.L. R.B. 738 (1972). Of course, it is an unfair labor practice for an employer to discriminate in hiring or retention of employees on the basis of union membership or activity under § 8(a)(3) of the National Labor Relations Act. * * * Thus, a new owner could not refuse to hire the employees of his predecessor solely because they were union members or to avoid having to recognize

We do not believe that *Wiley* requires a successor employer to arbitrate in the circumstances of this case. The Court there held that arbitration could not be compelled unless there was "substantial continuity of identity in the business enterprise" before and after a change of ownership, for otherwise the duty to arbitrate would be "something imposed from without, not reasonably to be found in the particular bargaining agreement and the acts of the parties involved." 376 U.S., at 551. This continuity of identity in the business enterprise necessarily includes, we think, a substantial continuity in the identity of the work force across the change in ownership. The *Wiley* Court seemingly recognized this, as it found the requisite continuity present there in reliance on the "wholesale transfer" of Interscience employees to Wiley. *Ibid.* This view is reflected in the emphasis most of the lower courts have placed on whether the successor employer hires a majority of the predecessor's employees in determining the legal obligations of the successor in § 301 suits under *Wiley.* * * *

Since there was plainly no substantial continuity of identity in the work force hired by Howard Johnson with that of the Grissoms, and no express or implied assumption of the agreement to arbitrate, the courts below erred in compelling the Company to arbitrate the extent of its obligations to the former Grissom employees. * * *

Mr. Justice Douglas, dissenting.

* * *

The contract between the Grissoms and the Union explicitly provided that successors of the Grissoms would be bound,[1] and certainly there can be no question that there was a substantial continuity—indeed identity—of the business operation under Howard Johnson, the successor employer. * * *

FALL RIVER DYEING & FINISHING CORP. v. NLRB

Supreme Court of the United States, 1987.
482 U.S. 27, 107 S.Ct. 2225, 96 L.Ed.2d 22.

Justice Blackmun delivered the opinion of the Court.

* * *

For over 30 years before 1982, Sterlingwale operated a textile dyeing and finishing plant in Fall River, Mass. * * *

In the late 1970's the textile-dyeing business, including Sterlingwale's, began to suffer from adverse economic conditions and foreign

---

the union. * * * There is no suggestion in this case that Howard Johnson in any way discriminated in its hiring against the former Grissom employees because of their union membership, activity, or representation.

1. "This Agreement shall be binding upon the successors, assigns, purchasers, lessees or transferees of the Employer whether such succession, assignment or transfer be effected voluntarily or by operation of law or by merger or consolidation with another company provided the establishment remains in the same line of business." 482 F.2d 489, 491.

competition. After 1979, business at Sterlingwale took a serious turn for the worse because of the loss of its export market, * * * and the company reduced the number of its employees. * * * Finally, in February 1982, Sterlingwale laid off all its production employees, primarily because it no longer had the capital to continue the converting business. * * * It retained a skeleton crew of workers and supervisors to ship out the goods remaining on order and to maintain the corporation's building and machinery. * * * In the months following the layoff, Leonard Ansin, Sterlingwale's president, liquidated the inventory of the corporation and, at the same time, looked for a business partner with whom he could "resurrect the business." * * * Ansin felt that he owed it to the community and to the employees to keep Sterlingwale in operation. * * *

For almost as long as Sterlingwale had been in existence, its production and maintenance employees had been represented by the United Textile Workers of America, AFL–CIO, Local 292 (Union). * * *

In late summer 1982, however, Sterlingwale finally went out of business. It made an assignment for the benefit of its creditors, * * * primarily Ansin's mother, who was an officer of the corporation and holder of a first mortgage on most of Sterlingwale's real property, * * * and the Massachusetts Capital Resource Corporation (MCRC), which held a security interest on Sterlingwale's machinery and equipment. * * * Ansin also hired a professional liquidator to dispose of the company's remaining assets, mostly its inventory, at auction. * * *

During this same period, a former Sterlingwale employee and officer, Herbert Chace, and Arthur Friedman, president of one of Sterlingwale's major customers, Marcamy Sales Corporation (Marcamy), formed petitioner Fall River Dyeing & Finishing Corp. * * * Chace and Friedman formed petitioner with the intention of engaging strictly in the commission-dyeing business and of taking advantage of the availability of Sterlingwale's assets and work force. * * * Accordingly, Friedman had Marcamy acquire from MCRC and Ansin's mother Sterlingwale's plant, real property, and equipment, * * * and convey them to petitioner.[1] * * * Petitioner also obtained some of Sterlingwale's remaining inventory at the liquidator's auction. * * * Chace became petitioner's vice president in charge of operations and Friedman became its president. * * *

In September 1982, petitioner began operating out of Sterlingwale's former facilities and began hiring employees. * * * It advertised for workers and supervisors in a local newspaper, * * * and Chace personally got in touch with several prospective supervisors. * * * Petitioner hired 12 supervisors, of whom 8 had been supervisors with Sterlingwale and 3 had been production employees there. * * * In its hiring decisions for production employees, petitioner took into consideration

---

1. Petitioner did not acquire one of the three buildings formerly used by Sterlingwale, App. 200–201, and closed one that it did acquire, *id.*, at 195.

recommendations from these supervisors and a prospective employee's former employment with Sterlingwale. * * *

Petitioner's initial hiring goal was to attain one full shift of workers, which meant from 55 to 60 employees. * * *

Petitioner planned to "see how business would be" after this initial goal had been met and, if business permitted, to expand to two shifts. *Ibid.* The employees who were hired first spent approximately four to six weeks in start-up operations and an additional month in experimental production. * * *

By letter dated October 19, 1982, the Union requested petitioner to recognize it as the bargaining agent for petitioner's employees and to begin collective bargaining. * * *

Petitioner refused the request, stating that, in its view, the request had "no legal basis." * * * At that time, 18 of petitioner's 21 employees were former employees of Sterlingwale. * * * By November of that year, petitioner had employees in a complete range of jobs, had its production process in operation, and was handling customer orders, * * * by mid-January 1983, it had attained its initial goal of one shift of workers. * * * Of the 55 workers in this initial shift, a number that represented over half the workers petitioner would eventually hire, 36 were former Sterlingwale employees. * * * Petitioner continued to expand its work force, and by mid-April 1983, it had reached two full shifts. For the first time, ex-Sterlingwale employees were in the minority but just barely so (52 or 53 out of 107 employees). * * *

Although petitioner engaged exclusively in commission dyeing, the employees experienced the same conditions they had when they were working for Sterlingwale. The production process was unchanged and the employees worked on the same machines, in the same building, with the same job classifications, under virtually the same supervisors. * * * Over half the volume of petitioner's business came from former Sterlingwale customers, and, in particular, Marcamy. * * *

* * *

Although petitioner does not challenge the Board's "substantial continuity" approach, it does contest the application of the rule to the facts of this case. Essentially for the reasons given by the Court of Appeals, * * * however, we find that the Board's determination that there was "substantial continuity" between Sterlingwale and petitioner and that petitioner was Sterlingwale's successor is supported by substantial evidence in the record. Petitioner acquired most of Sterlingwale's real property, its machinery and equipment, and much of its inventory and materials.[10] It introduced no new product line. Of

---

10. Petitioner makes much of the fact that it purchased the assets of Sterlingwale on the "open market." * * * Petitioner, however, overlooks the fact that it was formed with the express purpose of acquiring Sterlingwale's assets, a purpose it accomplished by having its parent company acquire some of Sterlingwale's major assets and then transferring them to petitioner. So long as there are other indicia

particular significance is the fact that, from the perspective of the employees, their jobs did not change. Although petitioner abandoned converting dyeing in exclusive favor of commission dyeing, this change did not alter the essential nature of the employees' jobs, because both types of dyeing involved the same production process. The job classifications of petitioner were the same as those of Sterlingwale; petitioner's employees worked on the same machines under the direction of supervisors most of whom were former supervisors of Sterlingwale. The record, in fact, is clear that petitioner acquired Sterlingwale's assets with the express purpose of taking advantage of its predecessor's work force.

We do not find determinative of the successorship question the fact that there was a 7–month hiatus between Sterlingwale's demise and petitioner's start-up. Petitioner argues that this hiatus, coupled with the fact that its employees were hired through newspaper advertisements—not through Sterlingwale employment records, which were not transferred to it—resolves in its favor the "substantial continuity" question.[11] * * * We thus must consider if and when petitioner's duty to bargain arose.

In *Burns,* the Court determined that the successor had an obligation to bargain with the union because a majority of its employees had been employed by Wackenhut. * * * The "triggering" fact for the bargaining obligation was this composition of the successor's work force.[12] The Court, however, did not have to consider the question *when* the successor's obligation to bargain arose: Wackenhut's contract expired on June 30 and Burns began its services with a majority of former Wackenhut guards on July 1. * * *

In other situations, as in the present case, there is a start-up period by the new employer while it gradually builds its operations and hires

---

of "substantial continuity," the way in which a successor obtains the predecessor's assets is generally not determinative of the "substantial continuity" question. * * *

11. Similarly, in light of the general continuity between Sterlingwale and petitioner from the perspective of the employees, we do not find determinative the differences between the two enterprises cited by petitioner. Petitioner's change in marketing and sales, * * * appears to have had no effect on the employer-employee relationship. That petitioner did not assume Sterlingwale's liabilities or trade name, *id.,* at 16, also is not sufficient to outweigh the other factors. * * * Moreover, the mere reduction in petitioner's size, in comparison to that of Sterlingwale, * * * does not change the nature of the company so as to defeat the employees' expectations in continued representation by their Union. * * *

12. After *Burns,* there was some initial confusion concerning this Court's holding. It was unclear if work force continuity would turn on whether a majority of the successor's employees were those of the predecessor or on whether the successor had hired a majority of the predecessor's employees. Compare 406 U.S., at 281 ("[A] majority of the employees hired by the new employer are represented by a recently certified bargaining agent"), with *id.,* at 278 ("[T]he union had been designated bargaining agent for the employees in the unit and a majority of these employees had been hired by Burns"). See also *Howard Johnson Co. v. Hotel Employees,* 417 U.S., at 263 ("[S]uccessor employer hires a majority of the predecessor's employees"); *Golden State Bottling Co. v. NLRB,* 414 U.S., at 184, n. 6 (same). The Board, with the approval of the Courts of Appeals, has adopted the former interpretation. * * * This issue is not presented by the instant case.

employees. In these situations, the Board, with the approval of the Courts of Appeals, has adopted the "substantial and representative complement" rule for fixing the moment when the determination as to the composition of the successor's work force is to be made. If, at this particular moment, a majority of the successor's employees had been employed by its predecessor, then the successor has an obligation to bargain with the union that represented these employees. * * *

* * * The Court of Appeals observed that by mid-January petitioner "had hired employees in virtually all job classifications, had hired at least fifty percent of those it would ultimately employ in the majority of those classifications, and it employed a majority of the employees it would eventually employ when it reached full complement." 775 F.2d, at 431–432. At that time petitioner had begun normal production. Although petitioner intended to expand to two shifts, and, in fact, reached this goal by mid-April, that expansion was contingent expressly upon the growth of the business. Accordingly, as found by the Board and approved by the Court of Appeals, mid-January was the period when petitioner reached its "substantial and representative complement." Because at that time the majority of petitioner's employees were former Sterlingwale employees, petitioner had an obligation to bargain with the Union then. * * *

JUSTICE POWELL, with whom THE CHIEF JUSTICE and JUSTICE O'CONNOR join, dissenting.

In this case the undisputed evidence shows that petitioner is a completely separate entity from Sterlingwale. There was a clear break between the time Sterlingwale ceased normal business operations in February 1982 and when petitioner came into existence at the end of August. In addition, it is apparent that there was no direct contractual or other business relationship between petitioner and Sterlingwale. * * * Although petitioner bought some of Sterlingwale's inventory, it did so by outbidding several other buyers on the open market. Also, the purchases at the public sale involved only tangible assets. Petitioner did not buy Sterlingwale's trade name or goodwill, nor did it assume any of its liabilities. And while over half of petitioner's business (measured in dollars) came from former Sterlingwale customers, apparently this was due to the new company's skill in marketing its services. There was no sale or transfer of customer lists, and given the 9-month interval between the time that Sterlingwale ended production and petitioner commenced its operations in November, the natural conclusion is that the new business attracted customers through its own efforts. No other explanation was offered. * * * Any one of these facts standing alone may be insufficient to defeat a finding of successorship, but together they persuasively demonstrate that the Board's finding of "substantial continuity" was incorrect. * * *

Even if the evidence of genuine continuity were substantial, I could not agree with the Court's decision. As we have noted in the past, if the presumption of majority support for a union is to survive a change in ownership, it must be shown that there is both a continuity of conditions *and* a continuity of work force. * * * This means that unless a majority of the new company's workers had been employed by the former company, there is no justification for assuming that the new employees wish to be represented by the former union, or by any union at all. * * * Indeed, the rule hardly could be otherwise. It would be contrary to the basic principles of the NLRA simply to presume in these cases that a majority of workers supports a union when more than half of them have never been members, and when there has been no election. * * *

In my view, the Board's decision to measure the composition of petitioner's work force in mid-January is unsupportable. * * * In fact, less than three months after the duty to bargain allegedly arose, petitioner had nearly doubled the size of its mid-January work force by hiring the remaining 50–odd workers it needed to reach full production. This expansion was not unexpected; instead, it closely tracked petitioner's original forecast for growth during its first few months in business. Thus there was no reasonable basis for selecting mid-January as the time that petitioner should have known that it should commence bargaining.

* * *

Questions

1. The alter ego employer: Why was the buyer in *Wiley* bound by the seller's collective bargaining agreement, and why were the buyers in *Howard Johnson* and *Fall River* not so bound? Does the form of the transaction (asset sale, merger, or stock purchase) determine whether the buyer is bound by collective bargaining agreements negotiated with the seller? If not, does transaction form have any impact on the issue? Is your answer for unions seeking arbitration on behalf of the workers absorbed by the buyer (or a division of the buyer) different from your answer for a union seeking arbitration on behalf of workers *not* hired by the buyer?

What is the relevance of a collective bargaining agreement lacking a clause that makes the provisions of the agreement binding on "successors and assigns, purchasers, lessees, or transferees" of the seller's business? If a collective bargaining agreement between the union and a selling firm does bind "successors and assigns," must the buyer adhere to the bargaining agreement despite contrary terms in an asset sale? A statutory merger? See Graphic Arts, etc. v. Martin Podany Associates, Inc., 531 F.Supp. 169 (D.Minn.1982). How can good lawyers draft an agreement to resolve these questions? Why do we not see more control change clauses in collective bargaining agreements? In Icahn's takeover of TWA the unions gave Icahn wage concessions (to allow him to outbid Lorenzo, whom the unions feared) in exchange for covenants limiting Icahn's ability to sell the firm's assets or merge with another firm.

2. The successor employer: Why did the new businesses in *Burns* and *Fall River* have a duty to bargain with the seller's union? Is the test that a

majority of the new employer's work force is hired from the ranks of the seller's employees, or that the new employer has hired a majority of the seller's employees? Why is Burns not an alter ego employer and yet a successor employer? What is the difference?

If a union of the seller can bargain with the buyer on behalf of the seller's employees absorbed by the buyer along with the seller's business, what rights does the union have to bargain on behalf of employees who are hired anew by the buyer, never having been employed by the seller?

3. How are the standards for successor liability on labor contracts different from the standards for successor liability on a seller's other contractual debts? Do all the justices of the Supreme Court agree on the difference? What explains the difference?

4. For nonunion employees how does new doctrine in many jurisdictions prohibiting "terminations at will" affect bust-up takeovers (acquisitions in which the buyer liquidates the acquired firm)? See, e.g., Cleary v. American Airlines, 111 Cal.App.3d 443, 168 Cal.Rptr. 722 (1980).

Subsection c. *New State Legislation Protecting Employees in Acquisitions*

Several states have, at the request of state labor leaders, passed legislation that protects employees in acquisitions. Delaware has such a statute. Please read Delaware General Corporation Law sections 706 and 3302(9)(H) and (I) in your statutory supplement. In chapter 11 of title 19, mentioned in section 706, the state department of labor may sue on behalf of aggrieved employees, or employees may sue on their own behalf, to recover unpaid wages. A defendant must pay reasonable attorney's fees if judgment is entered for any plaintiff. An employer is also liable for fines of $200 "for each violation."

Massachusetts and Pennsylvania have passed a section similar to Delaware's for labor contracts—Massachusetts General Law Ann. c. 149, § 20E, and Pennsylvania Business Corporation Law chapter 25I—and have added a more general section protecting all employees, union and nonunion, with a mandatory severance pay provision in transfers of control. Mass.Gen.L.Ann. c. 149, § 183 (1989), Pa.Bus.Corp.Law tit. 15, ch. 25I, § 2581–2583. The severance sections, in essence, provide a mandatory "tin parachute" for target employees. The operative language of the Massachusetts section is as follows:

> (b) Any employee of a control transferor whose employment is terminated within twenty-four calendar months after the transfer of control of his employer is entitled to a one time lump sum payment from the control transferee equal to the product of twice his weekly compensation multiplied by each completed year of service. Such severance pay to eligible employees shall be in addition to any final wage payment to the employee and shall be made within one regular pay period after the employee's last day of work.

Id. § 183(b). The section also provides for severance payments of twice the weekly compensation times the years in service if an employee is terminated twelve months before a control transfer or in the period of time when a control transferee owns between 5 percent and 50 percent of the firm. Id. § 183(c). The act does not cover employees who have been employed less than three years and does not apply if the employee is "covered by an express contract providing for such payment ... in excess of that provided by this section." Id. § 183(d)(1) & (2). The Massachusetts statute applies to all control changes, and a firm may not opt out of the section; the Pennsylvania statute applies only to hostile control changes (unapproved by the preacquisition board but approved by a vote of target shareholders), and a firm can opt out only by bylaw amendment adopted within two months of the passage of the act (July 26, 1990). Can an employee waive these severance rights by contract?

Questions:

1. Does section 706 change federal law on alter ego and successor employers? If so, is the Delaware provision constitutional?

2. Section 706 does not apply in the *UAL* cases in subsection a. Why? If the Delaware statute omitted section 3302(9) requirements and instead applied the statute to all Delaware corporations, would the statute be constitutional? Should the policies implicit in the section as passed have had an impact on the reasoning in the *UAL* opinions?

3. Does section 706 prohibit clauses in labor contracts that expressly provide for termination of seller employees at the will of buyer on the occurrence of mergers or acquisitions? If not, the statute merely alters the "default" rule, that is, the rule that applies when the union agreement is otherwise silent on the question or when section 259 (on the effect of statutory mergers) does not apply. If so, does the statute generate the economic stagnancy that worried the Supreme Court in the *P & LE* case?

Federal Plant Closing Statute

WORKER ADJUSTMENT AND RETRAINING ACT

29 U.S.C.A. §§ 2101, 2102, 2104.

§ 2101 DEFINITIONS: EXCLUSIONS FROM DEFINITION OF LOSS OF EMPLOYMENT.

(a) DEFINITIONS.—As used in this Act—

(1) the term "employer" means any business enterprise that employs—

(A) 100 or more employees, excluding part-time employees; or

(B) 100 or more employees who in the aggregate work at least 4,000 hours per week (exclusive of hours of overtime);

(2) the term "plant closing" means the permanent or temporary shutdown of a single site of employment, or one or more facilities or operating units within a single site of employment, if the shutdown results in an employment loss at the single site of employment during any 30–day period for 50 or more employees excluding any part-time employees;

(3) the term "mass layoff" means a reduction in force which—

(A) is not the result of a plant closing; and

(B) results in an employment loss at the single site of employment during any 30–day period for—

(i)(I) at least 33 percent of the employees (excluding any part-time employees); and

(II) at least 50 employees (excluding any part-time employees); or

(ii) at least 500 employees (excluding any part-time employees);

* * *

(6) subject to subsection (b), the term "employment loss" means

(A) an employment termination, other than a discharge for cause, voluntary departure, or retirement,

(B) a layoff exceeding 6 months, or

(C) a reduction in hours of work of more than 50 percent during each month of any 6–month period;

* * *

(b) Exclusions From Definition of Employment Loss.—

(1) In the case of a sale of part or all of an employer's business, the seller shall be responsible for providing notice for any plant closing or mass layoff in accordance with section 3 of this Act, up to and including the effective date of the sale. After the effective date of the sale of part or all of an employer's business, the purchaser shall be responsible for providing notice for any plant closing or mass layoff in accordance with section 3 of this Act. Notwithstanding any other provision of this Act, any person who is an employee of the seller (other than a part-time employee) as of the effective date of the sale shall be considered an employee of the purchaser immediately after the effective date of the sale.

§ 2102 **NOTICE REQUIRED BEFORE PLANT CLOSINGS AND MASS LAYOFFS.**

(a) NOTICE TO EMPLOYEES, STATE DISLOCATED WORKER UNITS, AND LOCAL GOVERNMENTS.—An employer shall not order a plant closing or mass layoff until the end of a 60–day period after the employer serves written notice of such an order—

(b) REDUCTION OF NOTIFICATION PERIOD.—(1) An employer may order the shutdown of a single site of employment before the conclusion of the 60-day period if as of the time that notice would have been required the employer was actively seeking capital or business which, if obtained, would have enabled the employer to avoid or postpone the shutdown and the employer reasonably and in good faith believed that giving the notice required would have precluded the employer from obtaining the needed capital or business.

(2)(A) An employer may order a plant closing or mass layoff before the conclusion of the 60-day period if the closing or mass layoff is caused by business circumstances that were not reasonably foreseeable as of the time that notice would have been required.

§ 2104 ADMINISTRATION AND ENFORCEMENT OF REQUIREMENTS.

(a) CIVIL ACTIONS AGAINST EMPLOYERS.—(1) Any employer who orders a plant closing or mass layoff in violation of section 3 of this Act shall be liable to each aggrieved employee who suffers an employment loss as a result of such closing or layoff for—

(A) back pay for each day of violation at a rate of compensation not less than the higher of—

(i) the average regular rate received by such employee during the last 3 years of the employee's employment; or

(ii) the final regular rate received by such employee; and

(B) benefits under an employee benefit plan. Such liability shall be calculated for the period of the violation, up to a maximum of 60 days, but in no event for more than one-half the number of days the employee was employed by the employer.

* * *

(3) Any employer who violates the provisions of section 3 with respect to a unit of local government shall be subject to a civil penalty of not more than $500 for each day of such violation, except that such penalty shall not apply if the employer pays to each aggrieved employee the amount for which the employer is liable to that employee within 3 weeks from the date the employer orders the shutdown or layoff.

* * *

Questions

1. Does the Worker Adjustment and Retraining Act apply to layoffs arising from mergers and acquisitions? If so, what is the effect of the act? WARN has emerged as a major hurdle in the merger of failing securities houses, necessitated by a slump in the securities business. A healthy brokerage house buys a failing brokerage house to absorb the failing house's customer accounts and recapitalize its business (brokerage houses are required by Treasury Regulation to maintain a minimum net capital

cushion to protect their customers from their insolvency). The surviving entity in such mergers must often lay off institutional securities salespeople, traders, back-office people, and investment bankers.

In general, what is the effect of the law on takeovers in which the buyer plans after the transaction to sell a significant portion of the seller's business? What is the effect of WARN on transactions in which (1) the closing date is subject to change, (2) the parties desire confidentiality, or (3) the entire transaction is to be completed in less than sixty days? In such deals must the parties simply pay the penalty under the act and divide the cost in the transaction price? Is the payment of compensatory funds deductible as an ordinary business expense? Are the payments a penalty, which is not deductible, or back pay, which is?

Which firm in an acquisition is obligated to give a WARN notice if the buyer does not plan to hire a significant number of the seller's employees? If the seller gives notice of mass layoffs thirty days (rather than the required sixty days) before the closing and the buyer fires all the seller's employees at the closing, who is liable? For how much? Are your answers different if the buyer fires the seller's employees two days after the closing?

2. After an acquisition in which no WARN notice was given, can the buyer encourage employees to leave with generous severance packages rather than give a WARN notice and keep them on for sixty days? In other words, can employees waive their rights under the act and release the firm from the act's civil penalty provisions? If the surviving firm must carry unproductive salespeople, how much must the surviving firm pay institutional salespeople on commission who can, due to an economic downturn, no longer make their normal commissions during the sixty-day shutdown period?

3. If notices of plant closings are valuable to employees, why do we not see such provisions more often in negotiated collective bargaining agreements?

Note

Union Strategy in Seeking Protections through Legislation Rather Than Collective Bargaining

Most collective bargaining agreements do not have complex control change clauses with provisions similar to those provided in the Delaware or Massachusetts statutes and do not have plant closing notification provisions similar to those contained in WARN. In the *UAL* case the takeover protections in the machinists' collective bargaining agreement were mild, containing a type of equal price provision, and affected only Employee Stock Ownership Plan buyouts, even though other bidders (Marvin Davis, for example) were also making hostile bids for the company. "Tin parachutes" are not widely used, and when used, cover *only* hostile takeovers, leaving managers free to avoid labor obligations to the fullest extent they can under existing law through leveraged buyouts and friendly acquisitions. Presumably this is because unions have decided they would rather trade these rights for higher wages or other benefits in open bargaining with firms.

Why then do labor unions and their employees vigorously support the protective legislation that mandates terms in their collective bargaining agreements that they otherwise would not usually agree to in bargaining? The Delaware act, for example, was the product of intense lobbying by union interests. See Wall St.J., Dec. 20, 1989, at A16, col. 1 (describing labor's support for a Pennsylvania bill that guarantees as much as twenty-six weeks' severance pay to any employee remaining out of work within two years after a company has been put into play and guarantees preservation of union contracts regardless of who gains control of a company). Is it because the unions believe such legislation provides them a costless boost to a previously agreed-on labor contract ("we negotiate for our best wage package and then run to the state houses to improve on our deal")? This is very short-sighted. What happens when the labor contracts come up for renegotiation and the parties cannot change the new standard terms imposed by legislation? Unless one believes in "rachet negotiating" of union contracts (once gained, never lost), won't management factor the cost of the new terms into the bargaining over wages and benefits? Moreover, how ought a firm price a wage and benefit package when it believes that a union may run to a legislature and seek additional new terms?

From the point of view of the union, at renegotiation time, after the legislation has been passed, how are the trade-offs between higher wages and legislation any different from the trade-offs between higher wages and protective terms in collective bargaining agreements? In other words, if unions routinely choose not to bargain for such protections in individual collective bargaining agreements, choosing instead higher wages or other benefits, why do unions not oppose protective legislation as wealth-reducing? Can we explain the apparent incongruity by looking at the motivations of labor leaders and the difficulties encountered by union membership in getting their representatives to act in the membership's best interest?

SECTION 2. FEDERAL REGULATION OF PENSION PLANS

Significant successor liabilities can arise out of the assumption or termination of employee benefit plans in the context of corporate acquisitions. The complexity of the topic merits a separate book. See B. Miller, *Employee Benefits: Mergers and Acquisitions* (1985). The matter is controlled by statute, the Employee Retirement Income Security Act of 1974 (ERISA) and its amendments. The statute deals with the issue of successor liability quite differently from the way the courts deal with the question in collective bargaining and product liability cases. ERISA treats pension plan obligations like real estate leases and other basic contractual obligations.

A defined benefit pension plan is a promise to pay retiring workers a stated accrued sum, usually in the form of an annuity with monthly payments, determined on the basis of a fixed formula. The required amount of plan contributions by a sponsoring employer are based on actuarial calculations, which are estimates based on anticipated investment return on plan assets, mortality, turnover of employees, and salary levels. Risk of investment loss on plan funds remains with the employer. A defined contribution plan, on the other hand, is a promise to pay workers at retirement (or at any other termination of employment) the amounts that have accumulated in the workers' pension plan account over the years. The risk of investment loss on contributions in these plans falls on the plan participant. Either type of plan may be maintained pursuant to a collective bargaining agreement negotiated by a union. A few of the major acquisition issues connected with pension plans are discussed below.

A plan is "tax-qualified" if it satisfies all the requirements prescribed in section 401(a) or 403(a) of the Internal Revenue Code. In tax-qualified plans, employees do not recognize taxable income until benefits are distributed, and all investment income earned by the plan itself is not taxed currently. IRC section 501. At the same time an employer may deduct, at the time of payment, contributions within certain prescribed limits to the plan as a business expense. IRC section 404. Employers and employees are not required to maintain pension plans, but the tax incentives to have a tax-qualified pension plan are very powerful. The tax deferral aspect of qualified plans means that employers and employee can split the benefits of the tax savings. Without the tax provisions an employee must save for retirement with after-tax wages and pay tax on any investment income earned by his retirement investments. With a qualified plan an employee does not pay tax on the retirement contributions or on the income earned thereby until he actually receives the money on retirement.

Buying-Firm Liability for Selling-Firm Terminations

Defined benefit pension plans, reflecting a long-term promise to pay by employers, are liabilities of a selling firm that are significant in all major acquisitions.[3] In an acquisition the buyer may choose to assume the seller's plan or refuse to assume the seller's plan, if a collective bargaining agreement between the seller and its employees does not constrict the choice. The form of the acquisition affects the buyer's ability to avoid primary liability for the seller's preacquisition plan operations when the buyer does not want to assume and continue the plan. In a statutory merger or stock acquisition, if the buyer does not want to assume the plan, the seller terminates the plan before the acquisition. In an asset acquisition the seller usually terminates its plan after the acquisition if the buyer does not assume it.

---

3. Restrictive regulations promulgated by the IRS have made defined benefit plans less attractive than defined contribution plans. Many firms are now choosing contribution plans over benefit plans to reduce administrative costs and liability exposure. With contribution plans the risk of investment loss shifts from the employer to the employee. In benefit plans the company makes promises to pay retirement benefits that can be outstanding for twenty or more years (depending on the age of the employee). In contribution plans the employer promises only to make periodic payments into employees' accounts, so an employer's exposure on unpaid promises is limited to the length of the payment period (less than a year). In acquisitions the liability on contribution plans is therefore not usually a significant factor in the transaction.

When an employer terminates its plan, the Pension Benefit Guaranty Corporation steps in and guarantees payment of all benefits vested as of the date of the termination. If the assets of the plan are insufficient to pay the benefits, the PBGC will pay the difference and will sue the terminating employer to recover its outlays. Moreover, if the seller has consistently underfunded its plan or made other errors in administration, it may be liable to the Internal Revenue Service for both excise taxes and income taxes, as the plan will be judged to have lost its qualified status. See section 4791(b), 404 of the Internal Revenue Code.

If the seller terminates its plan on the eve of an acquisition, the buyer is liable to the PBGC or the IRS for the seller's underfunding of its plan or for the seller's tax penalties for improperly operating its plan only if the buyer uses a statutory merger or stock purchase form of acquisition. See 29 U.S.C.A. § 1369(b)(3). In an asset sale a seller's liability to the PBGC and the IRS, even if the seller liquidated immediately after the sale, do not attach to the buyer, with three exceptions: First, the transaction has, as its principal purpose, evading ERISA or IRS liability (see 29 U.S.C.A. § 1369(a) and I.R.C. § 482). Second, the PBGC and the IRS are considered ordinary creditors under state law, and as we have seen, under state law on fraudulent conveyances, bulk sales, or on de facto mergers, the buyer in an asset sale may be accountable to the seller's creditors. See I.R.C. § 6901(a)(2). Third, it is possible that a PBGC or IRS lien may have attached to the assets purchased by the buyer, if the PBGC or the IRS had filed their claims on the seller's assets before the acquisition closing. See ERISA 4068(a), I.R.C. § 6323. The buyer may avoid even the possibility of a PBGC lien, however, by asking the seller in an asset sale to terminate its plan only after the acquisition closing date.

EMPLOYEE'S RETIREMENT INCOME SECURITY ACT, SEC. 1369

29 U.S.C.A. § 1369.

§ 1369. Treatment of transactions to evade liability; effect of corporate reorganization

(a) Treatment of transactions to evade liability. If a principal purpose of any person in entering into any transaction is to evade liability to which such person would be subject under this subtitle and the transaction becomes effective within five years before the termination date of the termination on which such liability would be based, then such person and the members of such person's controlled group (determined as of the termination date) shall be subject to liability under this subtitle in connection with such termination as if such person were a contributing sponsor of the terminated plan as of the termination date.

(b) Effect of corporate reorganization. For purposes of this subtitle, the following rules apply in the case of certain corporate reorganizations:

(1) Change of identity, form, etc. If a person ceases to exist by reason of a reorganization which involves a mere change in identity, form, or place of organization, however effected, a successor corporation resulting from such reorganization shall be treated as the person to whom this subtitle applies.

(2) Liquidation into parent corporation. If a person ceases to exist by reason of liquidation into a parent corporation, the parent corporation shall be treated as the person to whom this subtitle applies.

(3) Merger, consolidation, or division. If a person ceases to exist by reason of a merger, consolidation, or division, the successor corporation or corporations shall be treated as the person to whom this subtitle applies.

Selling–Firm Liability When Buying Firm Assumes and Terminates a Plan

If the buyer assumes all the seller's pension plan liabilities in a merger or stock sale and the *buyer* terminates the plan, with resulting liability to the PBGC, the seller or its former shareholders are not secondarily liable for any shortfall. On the other hand, if the buyer assumes all the seller's pension plan liabilities in an asset sale and the buyer terminates the plan, the PBGC takes the position that the seller may be secondarily liable to the PBGC for any deficiency (state law on fraudulent conveyances also ought to apply). Although there is no statute on point for single-employer plans, the PBGC will issue a letter indicating that the seller has no continuing liability only if the plan has sufficient assets to satisfy all guaranteed benefits and if the net worth of the buyer is greater than any potential funding insufficiency. E.g., PBGC Opinion Letters 78–29 (Dec. 12, 1978), 78–7 (May 25, 1978), 77–167 (Oct. 13, 1977) & 77–147 (May 24, 1977).

A special provision affecting seller liability applies to multi-employer plans, plans maintained by two or more corporations not under common control pursuant to one or more collective bargaining agreements. 29 U.S.C.A. § 1384. A sale of assets is construed to be a termination by the seller unless the buyer agrees to continue the same plan for at least five years and posts a bond as a guarantee. Even so, the seller must agree in the acquisition contract to be secondarily liable for five years and must post a bond if it wishes to liquidate before the five year period expires. The PBGC can grant waivers of the bond es crow requirements if there is not a substantial risk of underfunding in the transaction. See 29 U.S.C.A. § 1384(a).

EMPLOYEE'S RETIREMENT INCOME SECURITY ACT, § 1384(a)

29 U.S.C.A. § 1384.

§ 1384. Sale of assets

(a) **Complete or partial withdrawal not occurring as a result of sale and subsequent cessation of covered operations or cessa-

tion of obligation to contribute to covered operations; continuation of liability of seller. (1) A complete or partial withdrawal of an employer (hereinafter in this section referred to as the "seller") under this section does not occur solely because, as a result of a bona fide, arm's-length sale of assets to an unrelated party (hereinafter in this section referred to as the "purchaser"), the seller ceases covered operations or ceases to have an obligation to contribute for such operations, if—

(A) the purchaser has an obligation to contribute to the plan with respect to the operations for substantially the same number of contribution base units for which the seller had an obligation to contribute to the plan;

(B) the purchaser provides to the plan for a period of 5 plan years commencing with the first plan year beginning after the sale of assets, a bond issued by a corporate surety company that is an acceptable surety for purposes of section 412 of this Act, * * * or an amount held in escrow by a bank or similar financial institution satisfactory to the plan, in an amount equal to the greater of—

(i) the average annual contribution required to be made by the seller with respect to the operations under the plan for the 3 plan years preceding the plan year in which the sale of the employer's assets occurs, or

(ii) the annual contribution that the seller was required to make with respect to the operations under the plan for the last plan year before the plan year in which the sale of the assets occurs,

which bond or escrow shall be paid to the plan if the purchaser withdraws from the plan, or fails to make a contribution to the plan when due, at any time during the first 5 plan years beginning after the sale; and

(C) the contract for sale provides that, if the purchaser withdraws in a complete withdrawal, or a partial withdrawal with respect to operations, during such first 5 plan years, the seller is secondarily liable for any withdrawal liability it would have had to the plan with respect to the operations (but for this section) if the liability of the purchaser with respect to the plan is not paid.

(2) If the purchaser—

(A) withdraws before the last day of the fifth plan year beginning after the sale, and

(B) fails to make any withdrawal liability payment when due,

then the seller shall pay to the plan an amount equal to the payment that would have been due from the seller but for this section.

(3)(A) If all, or substantially all, of the seller's assets are distributed, or if the seller is liquidated before the end of the 5 plan year period described in paragraph (1)(C), then the seller shall provide a bond or amount in escrow equal to the present value of the withdrawal liability the seller would have had but for this subsection.

(B) If only a portion of the seller's assets are distributed during such period, then a bond or escrow shall be required, in accordance with regulations prescribed by the corporation, in a manner consistent with subparagraph (A).

(4) The liability of the party furnishing a bond or escrow under this subsection shall be reduced, upon payment of the bond or escrow to the plan, by the amount thereof. * * *

Note

Buyer Termination of Overfunded Target Plans for Acquisition Financing

A buyer's termination of a seller's overfunded defined benefit pension plan after an acquisition followed by the use of the excess cash to pay off acquisition financing has irked organized labor. An employer may recover excess assets on a plan termination if the plan expressly permits such a recovery (ERISA § 4044(d)). Most do. In the bullish stock market of the eighties overfunding was a recurring phenomenon. A 1986 study found that in the single-employer defined benefit plans there was a net of $218 billion surplus available on a termination basis. As yet, however, labor's efforts to get Congress or the Treasury to stop the practice of terminating overfunded plans to get at the excess assets have failed. Labor representatives want excess plan assets to go to employees on plan termination, not employers. The Treasury has responded as follows:

Leading Testimony of Secretary of Labor William E. Brock before a Joint Hearing of House and Senate Labor Committee (March 24, 1987), Pension Plan Guide (CCH) ¶ 25,825

* * *

> Sen. Howard M. Metzenbaum, co-chairman of the joint hearing panel, asked Brock to whom the money belongs in an overfunded pension. Brock answered by saying that in enacting ERISA, Congress said a defined benefit plan was owned by the corporation. Metzenbaum disagreed, arguing that if the worker must accept the loss of an underfunded plan, then he should receive the rewards of an overfunded plan.

* * *

A study released in 1990 by the PBGC found that the great majority of overfunded pension plan terminations are not caused by hostile takeovers. Sec.Reg.Law Rptr. 794 (June 25, 1990). In the study the great majority of pension fund terminations were not related to leveraged buyouts. Two-thirds of the LBOs in the study did not take excess pension fund assets. Of the third that did, the excess funds averaged less than 5 percent of the equity value of the target. The study found no statistically significant relationship between the existence of excess pension fund assets and the decision to effect an LBO. Moreover, there was no evidence that LBOs had a negative effect on employment. The number of vested participants in ongoing plans did not fall after an LBO. The study also concluded that reversions cannot "finance" an LBO; as long as the market properly values excess pension fund assets, the value of these assets is simply priced in the deal. Fund reversions only pare debt used to finance the retention of the excess assets in the first place. The study did find a slight positive correlation between LBO announcements and subsequent terminations of overfunded plans, however.

Congress put up roadblocks to the practice in the Pension Protection Act of 1987 and in the Omnibus Reconciliation Act of 1990. Before the 1987 act, buyers absorbing plans that did not expressly provide for reversion to a sponsoring employer of any excess funds merely amended the plan to include such a provision and then terminated the plan. After the 1987 act, any plan amendment providing for reversion of excess assets to employers takes effect no sooner than five years after the date of adoption (ERISA § 4044(d)(2)(A)), and the period applies to plans transferred in acquisitions (ERISA § 4044(d)(2)(C)). Thus buyers can no longer amend plans of targets to allow reversion to employers and then terminate the fund. The plan must already contain an explicit reversion provision. The impact of this development, of course, is that firms have an incentive now to either raid their *own* pension funds to take out excess funds as one method of protecting themselves from potential hostile bidders or amend their plans to provide a reversion right to employees. Which are they likely to choose?

In the 1990 act, Congress raised the tax on plan assets that revert to employers upon plan termination and mandated benefit increases or replacement plans for the benefit of the employees. As of October 1, 1990, an employer that receives assets after the termination of a defined benefit plan is subject to a 50% excise tax unless specific requirements are met which qualify the reversion for a 20% excise tax (the previous tax was 15%). The 20% tax applies when the employer establishes a qualified replacement plan or amends the terminating plan to provide for pro rata benefit increases for employees. A replacement plan must cover 95% of the plan employee and contain at least 25% of the assets of the terminating plan.

Can a firm pull out excess funds without terminating its plan? Congress recently refused to pass a bill proposed by the Treasury that would allow the practice explicitly, so firms resort to several well-known ploys—terminating and reestablishing plans or splitting one plan into two and terminating the one with excess assets (typically the one containing only retirees)—to withdraw assets from ongoing overfunded defined benefit plans and yet retain some part of the plan. Can a buyer of a firm with an overfunded plan that does not have a provision for reversion for excess assets to a sponsoring employer use one of these techniques to avoid the five-year rule? (See, e.g., ERISA § 4044(d)(2)(B) (if a plan has been in effect for less than five years and the plan has provided for the distribution of residual assets to the employer since its effective date, the distribution of excess assets on termination is allowed)).

Questions

1. Why do we not require that a buyer assume a seller's pension plan? How would you draft such a rule in light of the possibility of single-firm plan terminations? Why do the successorship rules for liabilities caused by funding deficiencies in terminated single-employer plans mirror rules for ordinary contractual debts (rather than rules for, say, union bargaining recognition)? Why, for example, can a buyer refuse to assume a seller's liability to the Pension Benefit Guaranty Corporation in an asset sale but not a statutory merger? How does the guarantee of the United States (through the PBGC) affect the acquisition rules for pension plans? There is, of course, no federal guarantee of employment backing the National Labor Relations Act, but we do have a national system of unemployment compensation payments.

2. Why are there special rules for selling-firm liability when a buyer assumes and continues the seller's obligations under a multi-employer plan? Again, why are the rules *not* applicable to the liability of the selling firm in a statutory merger? How could the selling firm in a merger be secondarily liable when it ceases to exist? Could we condition the seller's dissolution on the posting of a bond or the escrow of funds? See ERISA § 1384(a)(3).

3. Should the PBGC be concerned about the rash of LBOs? Financial stress is the most important cause of plan terminations, and if highly leveraged firms are more likely to fail, the PBGC may be asked to step in as guarantor more frequently. Moreover, an LBO drastically reduces the assets available to the PBGC as an unsecured creditor in the event of bankruptcy. Are the PBGC, and other unsecured creditors, such as retired employees with unfunded health benefits, compensated for accepting the increased risk of default in an LBO?

4. What kind of transaction would run afoul of ERISA section 1369(a)?

The interplay between pension and benefit plans and collective bargaining agreements has produced some odd results. Consider the position of those Chromalloy workers who retired before the asset sale in the following case.

RYAN v. CHROMALLOY AMERICAN CORP.
United States Court of Appeals, Seventh Circuit, 1989.
877 F.2d 598.

MANION, CIRCUIT JUDGE.

Plaintiffs, retired hourly employees of Chromalloy American Corporation ("Chromalloy"), appeal from the district court's order granting summary judgment for the defendants in this class action involving claims under the Employee Retirement Income Security Act of 1974, 29 U.S.C. § 1001 *et seq.*, and Section 301(a) of the Labor Management

Relations Act of 1947, 29 U.S.C. § 185(a). The plaintiffs seek reinstatement of their retiree welfare benefits, which were terminated by Chromalloy after it sold its Kewanee Division where plaintiffs were employed. * * *

In 1972, Chromalloy purchased Kewanee Machinery & Conveyor Co. * * * Chromalloy maintained the predecessor company's existing Group Benefit Program according to the governing trust, program, and plan documents. * * *

The Group Benefit Program ("Program") provided for "death, accident and sickness, hospital, surgical, medical expense and extended compensation benefits for [the Divisions'] employees and retired employees and their eligible dependents." More specifically, eligible retired hourly employees and their dependents were covered for basic hospital, surgical, and medical expenses up to the age of 65. After the age of 65, the retiree's hospital, surgical, and medical coverage was not only limited in its scope, but also to an overall lifetime total of $5000 in coverage per person.

Each of the documents governing the Program contained either an express termination clause or a reference to the Division's right to terminate the entire program or plan. Article IX–3 of the Trust document, for example, stated that if, among other things, the company were to sell "all or substantially all of the assets of an employer, then this trust shall be deemed terminated as respects the employees of such employer, unless provision is made whereby this trust will be continued by ... [the] purchaser of all or substantially all of such assets." Section 7.10 of the Program document entitled *"No Vested Interest"* stated that:

> Except as otherwise expressly provided in subsection 8.3 and except with respect to his rights to receive any benefits that shall have accrued under the contract, no person shall have any right, title, or interest in or to the assets of the fund, or in or to any company contributions thereto, such contributions being made to and held under the trust fund for the sole purpose of providing benefits under the program in accordance with its terms.

In turn, Section 8 of the Program document authorized the Division to amend or terminate the Program. Specifically, Section 8.1 entitled *"Termination"* expressly provided that the "program, the trust agreement and any portion of the contract providing non-insured benefits may be terminated by the division at any time ..." The only limitation on this right was contained in Section 8.3, which prescribed the manner in which any excess assets of the Program were to be disposed of upon termination. Similarly, the Plan document provided that:

> The Plan Administrator reserves the right to amend, modify or terminate this Plan at any time, provided, however, no amendment, modification, or termination shall adversely affect the right of a Covered Person to receive reimbursement for medical expenses incurred by

reason of an illness or injury for which he was receiving medical treatment at the time of such amendment, modification or termination.

Finally, the Summary Plan Descriptions distributed to the hourly employees of each of the three Kewanee Division plants set forth the respective schedule of benefits for eligible employees and their dependents, and made clear that:

> This booklet is a Summary Plan Description. It is intended to explain the benefits provided by the Kewanee Machinery Division of Chromalloy American Corporation Group Benefit Program. It does not constitute the Plan. Your rights and benefits are determined in accordance with the provisions of the Plan.
>
> * * *
>
> *Individual Termination of Coverage.* The coverage of any covered person under the plan shall terminate on the earliest of the following dates:
>
> 1) the date of termination of the Plan;
>
> 2) the date employment terminates for reasons other than leave of absence, disability, retirement or death of employee;
>
> * * *
>
> 4) the date all coverage or certain benefits are terminated in a particular class by modification of the Plan;
>
> * * *
>
> * * * This plan is referred to in the Collective Bargaining Agreement between Kewanee Machinery Division and Local 21, International Brotherhood of Teamsters and in the Collective Bargaining Agreement between Kewanee Machinery Division and Local 208, International Brotherhood of Boilermakers. Copies are available upon written request to the Plan Administrator.

The collective bargaining agreements between both the Kewanee and Evansville plants and their respective unions made the following reference to the plan:

> SECTION 3—Retiring employees who are eligible for pension benefits as established in the Hourly Employees' Pension Trust and their dependents, if insured at the time of retirement, will be provided life insurance [employee only], sickness and accident and hospitalization insurance at no cost to the employee. Benefits will be similar to those provided active employees except they will be less and more limited in certain coverages as recommended by the insurance company and will not duplicate the Medicare Program.
>
> * * *
>
> SECTION 5—The Company will provide and distribute to employees a booklet describing the insurance plan and benefits.

The collective bargaining agreement at the Kirksville, Missouri plant did not contain any references to coverage for retired employees.

On October 7, 1983, Chromalloy sold the assets of the Kewanee Machinery Division to the Allied Products Corporation ("Allied"). Although Allied chose not to maintain the Division's Group Benefits Program, Chromalloy continued to pay welfare benefits under the plan up to June 30, 1984, because approximately $100,000 remained in the Trust, and in accordance with paragraph 8.3 of the Program, had to be distributed to covered employees until the funds were exhausted. On May 10, 1984, Chromalloy notified all of the plan participants that it was terminating their benefit coverage as of June 30, 1984.

John Ryan, a retired hourly employee of the Division, brought suit and subsequently became the named plaintiff representing a class certified by the district court on May 14, 1986, and defined in a supplemental order as follows:

> All former hourly employees of the Kewanee Machinery Division of Chromalloy American Corporation including its Kewanee, Illinois, Evansville, Indiana and Kirksville, Missouri plants, eligible for pension benefits under the Kewanee Division hourly pension plan on or before October 7, 1983, and their dependents, all of whom would be eligible for benefits under the Chromalloy American Corporation Group Benefit Trust, Program, and Plan (together constituting an "employee welfare benefit plan" as defined in 29 U.S.C. Sec. 1002(1), (3)), but for its termination on October 7, 1983.

* * * Plaintiffs allege that their retirement benefits, which constituted a welfare benefit plan under ERISA, vested upon their retirement. Defendant moved for summary judgment, arguing that no genuine issues of material fact existed since plaintiffs' benefits did not vest under the applicable provisions of ERISA, the governing plan documents, or the collective bargaining agreements between Chromalloy and the respective unions representing the hourly employees at each of the three plants within the Division.

* * *

On appeal, appellants concede that it was appropriate to grant summary judgment on their claim that their retiree welfare benefits automatically vested under the provisions of ERISA. Appellants now recognize that their claims concern the termination of "employee welfare benefits" [4] and that Congress explicitly exempted such welfare

---

4. ERISA's extensive regulations extend to "employee benefit plans" which, in turn, are divided into two categories. Congress distinguished "employee pension benefit plans" from "employee welfare benefit plans," *compare* 29 U.S.C. § 1002(2)(A) *with* § 1002(1), and explicitly exempted the latter from the full breadth of the statute's requirements. Welfare benefit plans are defined as:

> [A]ny plan, fund, or program which was heretofore or is hereafter established or maintained by an employer or by an employee organization, or by both, to the extent that such plans, fund, or program was established or is maintained for the purpose of providing for its participants or their beneficiaries, through the purchase of insurance or otherwise, (A) medical, surgical, or hospital care or benefits, or benefits in the event of sickness, accident, disability, death or unemployment, or vacation benefits, apprenticeship or other training programs, or day care centers or scholarship funds, or prepaid legal services, or (B) any benefit described in section 185(c) of this title

benefits from the statute's accrual, vesting, and funding requirements. * * * Therefore, the efficacy of appellants' claim under ERISA turns solely upon the terms of the written instruments governing the plan.

ERISA requires that "[e]very employee benefit plan ... be established and maintained pursuant to a written instrument." 29 U.S.C. § 1102(a)(1). Through those instruments, the parties are free to subject such welfare benefits to vesting requirements not provided by ERISA, or they may reserve the power to terminate such plans. * * * We agree with the district court's decision, which reflects a careful examination of the documents, that they unambiguously provided for the right to terminate the plan.

The Trust document provided that the Trust would be terminated if "all or substantially all" of the assets of an employer were sold, the very contingency at issue here. * * *

With reference to the remaining Plan documents, both the Program and Plan documents specifically provided that the Plan could be terminated at any time. Finally, the Summary Plan Descriptions distributed to the employees of each of the plants within the Division all emphasized that the beneficiaries' "rights and benefits are determined in accordance with the provisions of the Plan," and that individual coverage would terminate with "the date of termination of the Plan." The appellants argue that this reading of the Summary Plan Description is erroneous because the termination language falls under the heading INDIVIDUAL TERMINATION OF COVERAGE rather than the specific heading for RETIREE BENEFITS. We find this argument unavailing based on our own reading of the Summary Plan Description as an integrated whole so that all of the provisions, if possible, will be given effect.

* * *

To begin with, the section on retiree benefits merely explained the extent of the benefits provided under the plan. It makes no reference to the retiree's vested right to the benefits. Furthermore, we are persuaded that the coverage of retirees was fully embraced in the provisions referring to "any Covered Person under the Plan." For example, the preceding section dealing with the nature of coverage for various types of employees noted that coverage for retirees is available to those who are eligible for pension benefits—that is, "any Covered Person under the Plan." We can not accept appellants' attempt to read the parts of the Summary Plan Description in isolation. In sum, the district court's order of summary judgment on the appellants' count under ERISA was appropriate.

We also agree with the district court's determination that appellant's benefits did not vest under the provisions of the collective

(other than pension or retirement or death, and insurance to provide such pensions).

29 U.S.C. § 1002(1).

bargaining agreements at the Kewanee and Evansville plants. The language in Section 3 of these collective bargaining agreements (under the heading "Group Insurance"), the provision upon which appellants most heavily rely, merely refers to a retiree's eligibility for welfare benefits. Section 3 contains no references to the duration of the benefits or whether they vest upon retirement. On the contrary, Section 5 of the agreements (both under the same heading) makes reference to the fact that a booklet describing the plan would be distributed by the company, presumably the Summary Plan Descriptions, which, as we have previously emphasized, expressly referred to the fact that individual coverage was governed by the Program documents and would terminate upon the termination of the plan. Accordingly, the district court's entry of summary judgment on behalf of the defendant was also appropriate with regard to appellants' claim under Section 301(a) of the LMRA.

* * *

Questions

1. Employees of the Kewanee Machinery Division received only a "summary plan description." How would most employees, upon receiving only these booklets, have interpreted their rights under the plan as retirees? What is the effect on retirees of a pension benefit plan termination? If an employee has vested rights to pension payments, who now pays? What is the effect on retirees of a welfare benefit plan termination? Can an employee have vested rights in a pension plan and, at the same time, no vested rights in a welfare benefit plan? If termination of a pension plan has a very different effect from termination of a welfare benefit plan, should an employer be able to use general termination language to apply to both types of plans? Assume the employee also read section 3 of his or her collective bargaining agreement. How would most employees contemplating retirement have interpreted their rights to sickness, accident, and hospitalization coverage? After the case, what's the position of Kewanee retirees? Can they readily buy health and life insurance?

2. Should the plaintiffs sue the employer for misleading them about the extent of their rights? Should the plaintiffs sue their own union under a similar theory? Should courts impose a disclosure obligation on unions or employers to inform members clearly of the length of the members' coverage?

SUBCHAPTER D. SUCCESSOR FIRM AND ACQUISITION LENDER LIABILITY FOR PRODUCT LIABILITY, EMPLOYMENT DISCRIMINATION, AND ENVIRONMENTAL CLAIMS

In asset acquisitions if the acquiring firm buys all the assets from a selling firm and expressly assumes none of its outstanding liabilities, and the seller dissolves, passing on the sale proceeds to its shareholders before paying off all its creditors, can the creditors sue the buying firm regardless of the language in the sale agreement? We have already considered the position of voluntary creditors, those who entered into contracts with the seller, and in section 1 below we consider the position of involuntary creditors, those who are victims of a seller's unlawful acts undertaken before the acquisition.

In a statutory merger or consolidation the surviving firm is liable on all the outstanding claims of both the constituent firms, including those of the firms that cease to exist as a result of the transaction. In a stock acquisition a firm sold by its shareholders to a second group of shareholders continues to be liable on all outstanding claims. The critical question in stock acquisitions and triangular statutory mergers is whether the assets of the new stockholder, a parent corporation, can be attached by claimants of the subsidiary. Traditional doctrine says no, but a new wind may be blowing, as we note in section 2.

Finally, one of the more dramatic developments in recent case law is a move to hold major lenders liable for environmental claims against loan recipients. This will have an impact on acquisition financing, as we will see in section 3.

SECTION 1. LIABILITY OF THE BUYER IN ASSET ACQUISITIONS

Subsection a. Basic Standards

KELLER v. CLARK EQUIPMENT CO.
United States Court of Appeals, Eighth Circuit, 1983.
715 F.2d 1280, cert. denied 464 U.S. 1044, 104 S.Ct. 713, 79 L.Ed.2d 176.

* * *

HEANEY, CIRCUIT JUDGE.

This case began as a challenge to the validity of three patents covering various aspects of a successful four-wheel loader marketed initially by Melroe Manufacturing Company (Melroe), and subsequently by Clark Equipment Company (Clark), under the trade name "Bobcat." The present appeal involves one of the three patents—a manufacturing patent entitled "tractor vehicle and drive therefore"—which this Court declared invalid under 35 U.S.C. § 102(b) because the application for it was not filed within one year after the invention had been offered for sale. * * * Clark now appeals from the district court's holding that Melroe was liable to Cyril and Louis Keller—two of the owners of the manufacturing patent in question—for its negligent failure to file the patent application in a timely manner and that Clark assumed that liability when it purchased Melroe in 1969. We affirm.

* * *

CONTRACTUAL ASSUMPTION

As a general rule, when one company sells or otherwise transfers all of its assets to another company, the transferee is not liable for the debts and liabilities of the transferor. * * *

That general rule is inapplicable, however, when the transferee expressly or impliedly agrees to assume the transferor's debts and liabilities. * * *

The district court found that in this case the plain terms of the 1969 purchase agreement between Clark and Melroe demonstrated Clark's intent to assume the Keller liability. We agree with this determination.

In the whereas portion of the purchase agreement, Clark agreed to "assume all the liabilities, obligations and covenants of Melroe, except as specifically excluded herein, all as hereinafter provided." The written assumption attached to the purchase agreement pursuant to sections 3.1 and 3.2 of the agreement stated:

> [Clark] * * * assumes and agrees to pay * * * to the extent that they are existing and outstanding on the date hereof, * * * such liabilities of Melroe * * * as are to be assumed by Clark * * * under the terms of [the 1969 agreement].

The district court found that Clark assumed Melroe's liability to the Kellers under the above-stated provisions of the purchase agreement. The court first found that the liability was a contingent one because although the negligent act occurred prior to the closing of the purchase agreement in 1969, the injury to the Kellers—Clark's cessation of royalty payments—did not occur until after the closing. The court then found that because Clark did not exclude this contingent liability from those obligations, it agreed to assume responsibility for Melroe's liability to the Kellers.

Clark contends that because the district court held that the Kellers' negligence claim did not accrue until 1972 for statute of limitations purposes, it must follow that the claim did not exist at all in 1969. Therefore, Clark argues that it could not have agreed to assume responsibility for the Keller liability since it assumed only those obligations "existing and outstanding" on the date of the purchase agreement. We cannot agree.

The district court properly recognized that in 1969 Melroe's contingent liability to the Kellers was already in existence because the negligent conduct had occurred in 1962. The 1969 purchase agreement demonstrates that Clark considered such contingent liabilities to be "existing and outstanding" obligations since it lists several contingent debts which Clark agreed to pay if Melroe's liability for them was established after the agreement was closed. Moreover, because the Kellers were continuing to receive royalties at the time of the closing, and Melroe thus had no reason to believe that the Kellers would assert their contingent negligence claim, the failure of the 1969 purchase agreement to list the Kellers' claim as a contingent liability evinces no intention to exclude that liability from those assumed by Clark.

Clark alternatively urges that even if the Kellers' claim existed in 1969, it was expressly excluded from the assumption agreement because

Clark agreed to assume only those liabilities disclosed by Melroe, and Melroe did not disclose the Kellers' claim. Specifically, Clark relies on section 3.1 of the agreement which stated that Clark did not assume "any liabilities arising out of the breach of any representation or warranty of Melroe contained herein" nor "any liabilities not disclosed due to any misrepresentation by Melroe herein." Clark contends that the Keller liability arises from Melroe's misrepresentation in not disclosing the contingent negligence claim.

* * *

In section 1.6 of the agreement, Melroe represented that the listed contingent liabilities—which did not include the Kellers' claim—reflected all "known" claims, and that to the "best of its knowledge," no legal action was threatened which would materially affect the company's liabilities. Similarly, in section 1.8 of the agreement, Melroe warranted that "to the best of its knowledge" there were no infringement claims relating to the company's patent except those disclosed— which again did not include the Kellers' claim with respect to the 117 patent. Again, in section 1.14, Melroe warranted that to the "best of its knowledge" it was not engaged in or threatened with any legal action.

The foregoing sections demonstrate that the "misrepresentations" which Clark excluded in section 3.1 from its general assumption of liability were only those knowingly made. Even though Melroe was aware of the late-filing problem raised in the Universal and Owatonna litigation in 1966 and 1968, Melroe had no reason to believe in 1969 that the Kellers would assert any claim with respect to the 117 patent. Melroe never failed to fulfill its contractual obligation to pay royalties to the Kellers for use of the 117 patent. Indeed, if Clark had not ceased making royalty payments in 1972, the Kellers' contingent claim never would have become a present one and they would not have filed suit. Thus, Melroe's failure to disclose the Kellers' contingent claim did not constitute a "misrepresentation" within the meaning of section 3.1 of the purchase agreement, and Clark cannot rely on that section to urge that it excluded the Kellers' claim from the liabilities it assumed in 1969.

Notwithstanding the above analysis, Clark argues that Melroe's failure to disclose its contingent liability constituted a misrepresentation within the meaning of section 1.21 of the agreement because it contains no "best knowledge" provisions.[10]

The district court, however, held that in order to construe section 1.21 in harmony with the other warranty provisions in the agreement, an omission would be misleading only if it violated the specific disclo-

---

10. Section 1.21 stated:

Section 1.21. *No Misleading Statements.* Neither the financial statements of Melroe and Melroe, Ltd. * * * nor this Agreement contain any untrue statement of a material fact or omit to state a material fact necessary in order to make the statements contained therein or herein not misleading.

sure requirements contained in sections 1.4, 1.8 and 1.14. * * * Accordingly, because in 1969, Melroe did not know, nor have reason to know, of the contingent liability to the Kellers, it committed no misrepresentations under the specific disclosure sections or section 1.21 of the purchase agreement.[11] The district court, therefore, did not err in finding that Clark assumed the Keller liability in the 1969 agreement.

DE FACTO MERGER

The district court alternatively held that Clark was liable for Melroe's negligence under the de facto merger doctrine. We affirm.

Although the North Dakota courts have not addressed *de facto* merger questions, the court below found that North Dakota would likely follow the majority view concerning the requirements and applicability of the doctrine. The district court concluded that to find a *de facto* merger, the following elements must be present:

> (1) There is a continuation of the enterprise of the seller corporation, so that there is a continuity of management, personnel, physical location, assets, and general business operations.
>
> (2) There is a continuity of shareholders which results from the purchasing corporation paying for the acquired assets with shares of its own stock, this stock ultimately coming to be held by the shareholders of the seller corporation so that they become a constituent part of the purchasing corporation.
>
> (3) The seller corporation ceases its ordinary business operations, liquidates, and dissolves as soon as legally and practically possible.
>
> (4) The purchasing corporation assumes those liabilities and obligations of the seller ordinarily necessary for the uninterrupted continuation of normal business operations of the seller corporation.

We find no error in this construction of the *de facto* merger test.

* * *

The district court found that each of these four factors was present in this case.[12] Clark does not seriously dispute these findings. Instead, Clark contends a *de facto* merger did not occur here because two indispensable requirements of the doctrine are lacking: (1) the corpora-

---

11. This construction also controls section 1.11 of the agreement in which Melroe warranted that it did not have "any indebtedness, contingent or otherwise, except as set forth in [its] balance sheets." Melroe did not breach this warranty by not listing the Kellers' negligence claim because to the best of its knowledge the Kellers were going to continue receiving royalties and they were not intending to assert their claim.

12. In the 1969 purchase agreement, Melroe transferred all its assets to Clark in exchange for 475,000 shares of Clark common stock worth approximately $15 million. The Melroe operations—including most management officials, employees and assets—became the Melroe Division of Clark. The former Melroe company, in turn, changed its name to Gwinner Holding Company. It agreed to cease business operations, liquidate and dissolve as soon as legally and practically possible.

tion selling its assets must not have been amenable to suit after the sale; and (2) the sale must have been performed to actually or constructively defraud the selling corporation's creditors.

Clark urges that the Kellers could have pursued their negligence action under various provisions of North Dakota and Delaware law which purportedly permit creditors to sue a dissolving corporation which is winding up its affairs or to proceed against the former stockholders of a dissolved corporation to whom the assets were distributed. The district court rejected this claim, finding that the Kellers had no effective remedy under either Delaware or North Dakota law. We agree.

Gwinner, the holding company which succeeded Melroe, never was anything but a corporate shell with essentially no assets or business activities. While Gwinner technically remained in business until 1974,[13] it effectively liquidated its assets promptly after the closing of the 1969 purchase agreement by distributing the Clark common stock to the former Melroe shareholders. Gwinner's remaining assets consisted of only $50,000, which the 1969 purchase agreement provided for winding up expenses. It had no employees or business activities capable of producing income. Indeed, the former shareholders of Melroe had covenanted not to compete with Clark's business activities. In addition, Clark has not demonstrated that the Kellers could have held the former Melroe shareholders personally liable for the corporation's negligence nor even that the Kellers in 1973, when they filed suit, could have traced the Clark stock to the former Melroe shareholders to whom the shares were distributed after the 1969 closing.

Clark's other primary contention is that the *de facto* merger doctrine is inapplicable here because there is no showing that the 1969 sale was consummated to defraud creditors. We cannot agree.

While evidence of fraudulent intent may strengthen the case for finding a *de facto* merger, such evidence simply is not an indispensable requirement in every case. * * * Indeed, the existence of a fraudulent transfer in and of itself generally is considered to be an exception, in addition to the *de facto* merger doctrine, to the general rule that a purchasing corporation is not liable for the debts and liabilities of the selling corporation.

* * *

Questions

1. If Melroe had manufactured a defective Bobcat in 1962 that caused injury to a plaintiff in 1972, would Clark have assumed the liability under sections 3.1 and 3.2 of the acquisition agreement?

2. If the Kellers had brought suit promptly in 1972, when the royalties stopped and when Melroe's successor, Gwinner, was still in existence,

---

13. Delaware revoked Gwinner's corporate charter in 1974 for failure to file an annual report.

could they have sued Gwinner in tort? Could they have sued Gwinner or Melroe shareholders for any distributions of the acquisition payment? Could they have sued Gwinner or Melroe directors for effecting corporate distributions that put the firm into insolvency? Do legal capital or fraudulent conveyance statutes apply?

3. If the Kellers had brought suit in 1974, after Melroe had dissolved, could they have sued Melroe shareholders for any dissolution distributions? Why did the court put the burden on Clark to demonstrate that this remedy was available? What would the result in the case have been if Clark had carried the burden? Does the de facto merger doctrine require proof that the plaintiffs cannot collect from a predecessor's shareholders?

4. Do the courts apply the same de facto merger doctrine in cases bought by aggrieved shareholders (see chapter 2, subchapter A, section 4) as they do in cases bought by aggrieved creditors? Does your answer for creditors depend on whether the plaintiffs are contract or tort claimants?

Rights of Contingent Claimants against a Dissolved Corporation

An alternative to allowing suit against a buying firm in an asset sale over express language in an acquisition agreement to the contrary is a suit against the recipients of the acquisition proceeds. If the selling firm has dissolved, or has otherwise distributed the sale proceeds to its shareholders, the question becomes whether the victim should sue the directors or shareholders of the selling firm personally. Assume in *Keller* for example, the court held in favor of Clark Equipment and against Keller on both the contract and the de facto merger argument. Can Keller sue Melroe or its shareholders? For how much? Remember that Melroe had no funds when it dissolved in 1974. Can Keller claim the Clark stock distributed to Melroe shareholders in 1969? The effectiveness or ineffectiveness of remedies against the selling firm and its participants are a material part of any argument in support of the de facto merger and alter ego doctrines that permit suit against an otherwise nonassenting buyer.

We have already covered rights against directors and shareholders when a firm makes a distribution that puts it in insolvency. If the legal capital statutes or the fraudulent conveyance acts apply, a creditor has relief against shareholders and, in some cases, directors of the firm. What rights do the creditors have against the shareholders and directors of a *dissolved* corporation? Please read sections 14.05(a), 14.06, and 14.07 of the Revised Model Business Corporation Act and sections 278 and 280 to 282 of the Delaware General Corporation Law in your supplement.

CORPORATE LIFE AFTER DEATH: CERCLA PREEMPTION OF STATE CORPORATE DISSOLUTION LAW
88 Mich.L.Rev. 131, 149–55 (1989).

State statutes giving corporations the capacity to sue and be sued after dissolution were enacted as a reaction to the harshness of the common law rule that all actions by and against a corporation were abated at dissolution.

* * *

Under the English common law, all actions both by and against a corporation abated upon dissolution and the assets of the corporation escheated to the King. In the United States, with the institution of the business corporation in the 1800s, the English common law rule was changed so that the assets of the corporation constituted a trust fund upon dissolution for creditors and shareholders with outstanding claims. This development, known as the trust fund theory, allowed a creditor to bring suit against the directors and shareholders of a dissolved corporation under the theory that the assets were distributed to these shareholders under a lien held by the creditor. Claims brought under the trust fund theory were only subject to general statutes of limitations applicable to the particular claim asserted.

It is unclear to what extent the common law trust fund theory continues to exist after the advent of state statutes governing corporate dissolution. Although claims clearly covered by statute are controlled by the statutory provisions and barred if not brought within the statute's time limitations, some claims against dissolved corporations do not fall clearly within the statute; for these claims, the argument for continuing the trust fund theory is still made, especially in the field of products liability.

The corporate dissolution statutes in many states today are patterned substantially after section 105 of the Model Business Corporation Act ("1979 Model Act"). The relevant portion of the 1979 Model Act provides:

> The dissolution of a corporation ... shall not take away or impair any remedy available to or against such corporation, its directors, officers, or shareholders, for any right or claim existing, or any liability incurred, prior to such dissolution if action or other proceeding thereon is commenced within two years after the date of such dissolution.

The Revised Model Business Corporation Act of 1985 ("1985 Model Act") made substantial changes to this provision, but most state statutes are patterned after the 1979 Model Act, varying only the amount of time in which to bring suit.

The 1979 Model Act's provision authorizing suits for two years after dissolution is typically described as a survival statute, determining capacity to be sued, and not a statute of limitations. Suit must be commenced within two years of dissolution for any claim against the dissolved corporation, even if the appropriate statute of limitations for the claim is longer. The Model Act thus ameliorates the harsh effects of the common law rule of complete abatement of claims at dissolution by allowing claimants a restricted period of time after dissolution in which to bring claims against the corporation. However, the statutory period is limited to allow the corporation a point of repose after which it may be secure in winding up its affairs and distributing its assets.

* * *

Courts also have had difficulty in applying section 105 (and statutes modeled after it) because its language provides no guidance regarding claims that arise after dissolution. Consequently, courts that have struggled with post-dissolution claims brought under statutes based on the 1979 Model Act have reached inconsistent and unpredictable results. These results have ranged from allowing post-dissolution claims to be brought at any time after dissolution to allowing no post-dissolution claims to be brought whatsoever.

Because the statutes based on the 1979 Model Act generally do not address post-dissolution claims, it appears that courts have often decided these claims based on whether the survival period seems unreasonably short for the particular claim at issue. For example, courts have allowed claims against dissolved corporations if there is some element of self-dealing by the corporation's directors before dissolution, or if some other contingency has occurred which, in the court's judgment, makes barring the claim after two years seem unfair.

The failure of the 1979 Model Act to clearly address claims arising after dissolution was resolved by the Revised Model Business Corporation Act of 1985. However, in the large number of states that still have corporate dissolution statutes based on section 105 of the 1979 Model Act, the result of a claim brought after the corporation has dissolved is unpredictable.

* * *

The 1985 Model Act alleviates the problems caused by the 1979 Model Act by creating a longer survival period and by directly addressing claims that arise after dissolution. The 1985 Model Act addresses pre-dissolution and post-dissolution claims separately: section 14.06 provides for claims that are known at the time of dissolution and section 14.07 provides for claims that are unknown at the time of dissolution.

* * *

Questions:

1. How should Melroe have provided for Keller's claim on dissolution? Under the Model Act was Keller's claim against Melroe in 1973 a "known claim" when Melroe dissolved in 1974? What is a "contingent" claim under the Model Act? Under Delaware sections 280 and 281 is Keller's claim "contingent, conditional or unmatured"? Under the Delaware sections is Keller's claim against Melroe treated differently from product liability claims? Assume Keller had been injured by a defective Bobcat manufactured by Melroe, how should Melroe have provided for his claim on dissolution?

2. If Keller had sued Melroe in 1975, would section 14.07 apply? If not, how do we decide whether Keller's claim is time-barred? Could Keller sue Melroe in 1975 under Delaware section 278?

Problem

Toy, Inc., makes playhouses for children. Mr. Consumer buys one for his children. Immediately thereafter, and before Mr. Consumer gives the playhouse to his children for Christmas, Toy, Inc., sells its assets to Playthings, Inc., and, in the transaction, does not transfer any of its liabilities, actual or contingent. Toy, Inc., then passes the sale proceeds back to its shareholders in a proper liquidation, paying all known debts and giving appropriate newspaper notice. Years after the sale Playthings, Inc., discovers that Toy, Inc., used potentially toxic materials in its playhouse design, and Playthings, Inc., changes it production process to use different construction materials. Six years after the dissolution, Mr. Consumer discovers that toxic materials used in the playhouse have injured his now-teenage children. Who can the children sue for recompense?

Should we favor a stricter approach that prohibits asset distributions in dissolution until the firm makes adequate provisions for all postdissolution claims, including contingent product liability and environmental claims?

GREEN, SUCCESSOR LIABILITY: THE SUPERIORITY OF STATUTORY REFORM TO PROTECT PRODUCTS LIABILITY CLAIMANTS
72 Cor.L.Rev. 17, 49–55, 57 (1986).

* * *

The 1984 revision of the Model Act for the first time recognized the problems faced by the long-tail claimant. However, the drafters' solution—a five-year limitation on claims against dissolved corporations and their shareholders—does little to alleviate the situation. In the vast majority of successor liability cases suits are not filed within five years of the predecessor's sale of assets. The limitation on a shareholder's liability to the lesser of her pro rata share of the claim or the amount of assets distributed to her in connection with the dissolution further reduces the utility of the expanded abatement period. Although the expanded period in which to bring suit may provide a practical remedy for a few successor liability claims, it does not resolve the problems of most long-tail claimants—problems that lead to the development of liberal successor liability law.

The proposed statute confronts the long-tail products claimant problem more directly and effectively than do the Model Act and existing state dissolution statutes. The proposed statute is also flexible enough to accommodate the varying circumstances surrounding sales of corporate assets by dissolving corporations.

§ 1 LIMITATIONS ON DISSOLUTION AND DISTRIBUTIONS IN CONNECTION WITH DISSOLUTION

* * *

(b) Notwithstanding the provisions of this Act, no corporation that has engaged in manufacturing products that it sells or leases may dissolve or distribute its assets to its shareholders in connection with its dissolution until the corporation has made adequate provision for postdissolution products liability claims.

* * *

(1) Provision for postdissolution products liability claims may be made by:

(A) obtaining liability insurance for postdissolution products liability claims;

(B) transferring, as part of the sale of the corporation's assets, liability for future products liability claims to the purchaser of the corporation's assets; or

(C) any other method that provides protection for those asserting postdissolution products liability claims against the corporation equivalent to the protection that would have existed if the corporation had continued to carry on its business and not undergone dissolution.

(2) Provision for postdissolution products liability claims shall be adequate if the amount of insurance coverage or other assets available to satisfy postdissolution products liability claims is not less than:

(A) the corporation's net current value at the time of dissolution; plus

(B) the value of any prior distributions made to shareholders in contemplation of dissolution.

* * *

(d) A corporation may bring a proceeding in the [name of appropriate court] to seek modification of its obligation to make adequate provision for postdissolution products liability claims.

(1) Upon the filing of a petition for modification, the court shall appoint a guardian to represent the interests of all potential postdissolution products liability claimants.

(2) After conducting a hearing, the court may enter an order modifying the corporation's obligation to make adequate provision for postdissolution products liability claims if it finds that:

(A) despite diligent efforts by the corporation to make adequate provision for postdissolution products liability claimants, it cannot reasonably do so;

(B) the shareholders of the corporation will suffer manifest injustice unless modification of the obligation of adequate provision is permitted; and

(C) an alternative plan to protect postdissolution products liability claimants strikes a reasonable balance between the interests of the postdissolution products liability claimants and the stockholders' interest in avoiding the manifest unfairness identified in section 1(d)(2)(B).

* * *

The statute's enforcement mechanism imposes personal liability on any director who approves, and any officer who furthers, a distribution to stockholders in violation of the statute. Officers and directors may obtain contribution from stockholders who receive distributions but directors and officers—not long-tail claimants—bear the onerous burden of asserting a claim against a potentially large and geographically diverse group of stockholders.

* * *

Questions

1. If an insurance company will insure against all future product liability claims against a seller in an asset acquisition, why does it matter whether we put the burden of paying those claims unequivocally on the seller or the buyer in the acquisition? If the burden is allocated to the buyer, can the parties simply reallocate the burden by discounting the premium payments to present value and deducting them from the purchase price?

2. The troublesome case in asset acquisitions occurs when a seller *cannot* buy insurance against all future product liability claims because the claims are too uncertain. In other words, no insurance company will offer a policy to the seller. How does Professor Green's statute handle these tough cases?

3. Under Professor Green's statute would a seller who could not insure have an incentive, after the asset sale, to pass the proceeds back to its shareholders in an extraordinary dividend and continue the firm as a shell? How does his statute apply in the *Keller* case (the Gwinner Holding Company was dissolved by the state of North Dakota for not filing its annual report and paying its annual incorporation fees)? Do legal capital statutes or fraudulent conveyance law give the same protection that the proposed dissolution statute provides?

Subsection b. Product Liability Claims

NICCUM v. HYDRA TOOL CORP.

Supreme Court of Minnesota.
438 N.W.2d 96.

On March 21, 1985, Michael Niccum severely and permanently injured his right hand while operating a Forcemaster Press Brake on the premises of the A & D Fabricating Company. * * * In May 1973, [Wisconsin Equipment Corporation ("WEC")] manufactured and sold a Wisconsin Forcemaster Press Brake, Model 10 FM 100, serial number 73384, to Alloy Hard Facing & Engineering Co. located in Minneapolis,

Minnesota. The chain of ownership of this particular machine is unknown; however, in 1985 it was owned by A & D Fabricating in Blaine where Niccum was injured.

After the sale of the press brake by WEC to Alloy, another company known as HTC, Inc. purchased all of the assets of WEC on July 22, 1977. HTC, Inc. is a wholly owned subsidiary of Hydra Tool Corporation and was incorporated in the summer of 1977 to enter the agreement with WEC. The purchase agreement required HTC to provide a certain amount of cash and in return HTC would receive essentially all of the assets of WEC, including land, buildings, inventory, contracts, customer lists, accounts receivable, patents, trademarks and "good will." It expressly provided HTC would assume no liability for injuries caused by WEC products already on the market. Such liability was to be retained by WEC. Following the sale to HTC, WEC dissolved on October 3, 1977. Hydra Tool had no prior knowledge that WEC would dissolve following the transaction.

For approximately three months, HTC, Inc., continued to use the WEC facility in Wisconsin, manufacturing press brakes of the WEC design and using WEC inventory. HTC, Inc., then dissolved and its assets were assumed by Hydra Tool Corporation. The officers and directors of HTC, Inc., and Hydra Tool Corporation were essentially the same. Hydra Tool moved its manufacturing operations to Greenwood, Mississippi, and continued to manufacture mechanical press brakes there for approximately one year.

* * *

Minnesota follows the traditional approach to corporate successor liability. In *J.F. Anderson Lumber Co. v. Myers,* 296 Minn. 33, 206 N.W.2d 365 (1973), we set forth four circumstances under which successor corporations may be held liable for actions of a transferor corporation:

> [W]here one corporation sells or otherwise transfers all of its assets to another corporation, the latter is not liable for the debts and liabilities of the transferor, except: (1) where the purchaser expressly or impliedly agrees to assume such debts; (2) where the transaction amounts to a consolidation or merger of the corporation; (3) where the purchasing corporation is merely a continuation of the selling corporation; and (4) where the transaction is entered into fraudulently in order to escape liability for such debts.

Id. at 37–38, 206 N.W.2d at 368–69. Appellant concedes none of these traditional exceptions to the non-liability rule are applicable in this case. Instead appellant asks this court to expand the *Anderson* rule to include other exceptions.

In 1981, the Minnesota legislature addressed the question of transferee liability in Act of May 27, 1981, ch. 270, § 97, 1981 Minn.Laws 1208; Minn.Stat. § 302A.661 (1988). The statute states in part:

Transferee liability. The transferee is liable for the debts, obligations, and liabilities of the transferor only to the extent provided in the contract or agreement between the transferee and the transferor or to the extent provided by this chapter or other statutes of this state.

Minn.Stat. § 302A.661, subd. 4. The reporter's notes to this section commented:

> Subdivision 4 of this section is aimed at limiting the civil liabilities of transferors assumed by transferees to those agreed to between the parties or imposed by law, even if the transferee is operating the corporation in exactly the same manner as it was operated by the transferor. This limits, for example, exposure to product liability claims for items manufactured by the transferor.

General Comment–1981, Minn.Stat.Ann. 302A.661 (West 1985). This statute indicates an intent of the legislature to limit any further extension of successor liability beyond the traditional exceptions already provided in *Anderson*.

Appellant seeks to have the third exception to the non-liability rule, mere continuation, expanded to include cash-for-assets sales. Under the traditional rule mere continuation "refers principally to a 'reorganization' of the original corporation" under federal bankruptcy law or through state statutory devices. *J.F. Anderson*, 296 Minn. at 38, 206 N.W.2d at 369. This court held that "continuity of business, name, and management alone, is not, we think, sufficient basis for holding a transferee liable for the debts of the transferor." *Id.* If there is no continuation of the corporate entity—shareholders, stock, and directors—the successor corporation is not liable. Expansion of the "mere continuation" exception focuses on the continuity of the business operation, not the corporate entity.

The Michigan Supreme Court expanded the mere continuation exception in *Turner v. Bituminous Casualty Co.*, 397 Mich. 406, 244 N.W.2d 873 (1976). The court held there should be no distinction between a merger and a sale of assets for cash in imposing liability on a successor corporation. *Id.* at 429, 244 N.W.2d at 883. The *Turner* decision has not received strong support in other states. Eight states—Kentucky, Missouri, Nebraska, New York, North Dakota, South Dakota, Vermont and Wisconsin—have declined to expand the mere continuation exception. Opponents of the expansion argue liability should not be imposed on a successor corporation because (1) the successor corporation did not create the risk by placing the defective product into the market; (2) any profit realized on the product is only received in a remote way; and (3) the successor has not represented to the public the safety of the predecessor's product. We find these arguments persuasive and decline to expand the continuation exception.

Appellant also argues for an imposition of successor liability under the product line exception adopted by the California Supreme Court in *Ray v. Alad Corp.*, 19 Cal.3d 22, 560 P.2d 3, 136 Cal.Rptr. 574 (1977). Under the product line theory, a successor corporation which continues to manufacture a product of the business it acquires, regardless of the method of acquisition or any possible attribution of fault, assumes strict liability for products manufactured and sold before the change of corporate ownerships. *Id.* at 34, 560 P.2d at 11, 136 Cal.Rptr. at 582.

The majority of courts which examined the product line exception have declined the invitation to adopt it. These courts have generally based their decisions on one or more of the following arguments: (1) the exception is inconsistent with elementary products liability principles, and strict liability principles in particular, in that it results in an imposition of liability without a corresponding duty; (2) the exception threatens small successor businesses with economic annihilation because of the difficulty involved in obtaining insurance for defects in a predecessor's product; and (3) the exception is essentially a radical change in the principles of corporation law, and, as such, should be left to legislative action. We agree with this reasoning and decline to adopt the product line exception. Accordingly, we hold the traditional limitations on successor liability remain the law in this state.

[The court affirmed a grant of summary judgment for the defendant.]

* * *

Questions

1. Doesn't section 302A.661 nullify *all* de facto merger or continuation theories? The section is an unusual statutory effort to specify the position of liabilities in asset sales. Why have more state legislatures not spoken on the matter?

2. What situations justify liability under traditional de facto merger, "continuation of business," and the fraud exceptions? How do the new continuity and product line rules compare with the traditional exceptions? Which of the new rules is the broader?

3. Should product liability claimants be treated the same as preexisting contractual creditors (bondholders or trade creditors) in acquisitions? If not, what should the additional protection look like?

4. If a court were to apply one of the newer successor liability theories in *Niccum,* what is the relevance of the fact that Hydra Tool (through its subsidiary) manufactured press brakes only one year and three months after the asset sale in 1977, and thus stopped manufacturing them well before the accident in 1985?

5. How can the buyer structure an acquisition to minimize the risk of product liability claims in Minnesota? In Michigan? In California? If you are an advocate of the California or Michigan rule for successorship to product liability claims, should you not also advocate collapsing subsidiaries into their parents for the purpose of satisfying product liability claims against an insolvent subsidiary? Otherwise, won't corporate parents have an incentive to keep their manufacturing subsidiaries significantly undercapitalized?

6. Do bulk sales laws, fraudulent conveyance laws, and shareholder distribution laws provide protection for contingent tort claimants? See Koons v. Walker, 76 Mich.App. 726, 257 N.W.2d 229 (1977) (bulk sales).

7. State courts appear to be refusing to follow the Michigan or California courts' more liberal successor liability rules. Why? What is the effect of imposing successor liability with respect to product defects that were not, and could not have been, foreseen at the time of manufacture? How effectively can parties negotiating an asset sale predict potential liability exposure so that they can structure their predictions into the price asked and offered?

SMITH, GREEN, AND BERNSTEIN, RISK MANAGEMENT: THE DANGERS FOR BUYERS WHO INHERIT FLAWED PRODUCTS

Mergers & Acquisitions, July/August 1989 at 48–53.

* * *

Courts created new methods of imposing liability on the successor corporation by expanding upon the four historical exceptions. The expansion occurred amid increasing numbers of acquisitions and developing theories of product liabilities, and created new opportunities for injured plaintiffs to recover for product defects. These new methods of imposing successor liability are commonly referred to as the continuity exception, the product line exception, and the buyer's duty to warn. However, they are not applied the same way by all courts, and some courts have not accepted them at all.

Courts may impose liability on successor corporations based on the continuity exception when the successor continues to produce the same product as the seller, through some of the seller's employees, in the same physical plant, and under similar supervision as the seller. This outcome is especially likely when the successor uses the same name as the seller and holds itself out to the world as the same enterprise.

The "continuity" method of imposing liability on successors differs from the traditional exception to the rule of nonliability concerning the continuation of the seller (continuation of business) in that the traditional exception was applied only in limited circumstances where the successor was, for all practical purposes, identical to the predecessor. The new approach is more liberal since it does not require that the buyer and seller be exactly the same.

One of the theories underlying the continuity exception is that the successor, having reaped the benefits of continuing to manufacture its predecessor's products, exploiting its accumulated goodwill, and enjoying the patronage of its established customers, should be made to bear some of the burdens of continuity, such as liability for defective products.

* * *

Under the product line exception, if a successor continues to manufacture and sell the same line of products under the same name as the predecessor, the successor may be responsible for the product liability of the predecessor. The seminal case in the development of the product line exception was Ray v. Alad Corp. decided in California in 1977.

The difference between the product line exception and the continuity exception is that the product line exception imposes liability on the successor for continuing to manufacture the same products as the seller. The continuity exception is more difficult to satisfy in that it imposes liability on the successor when the successor retains the seller's personnel, assets, and trade name in addition to continuing to manufacture the products of the seller. It is easier for a plaintiff to recover from a successor based on the product line exception, as long as the jurisdiction in which he or she is suing recognizes this exception.

One court justified application of the product line exception based on three policies, although they are not particular to the product line exception. First, plaintiff's remedies against the original manufacturer are nonexistent because of the acquisition, since the seller's assets are transferred to the buyer. Second, the successor is better able than the injured plaintiff to assume a risk-spreading role, by estimating the risk of injuries and obtaining insurance (if possible) or passing along the costs of compensating injured parties to consumers through higher prices. Third, it is fairer to require the successor to assume the burden of responsibility for defective products. In continuing the operation of the seller's business, the successor benefits from the seller's goodwill. It is, therefore, appropriate for the successor to accept the responsibility for the seller's product defects.

Successors also have been held responsible for their failure to warn customers of defects in the seller's products that were or should have been discovered by the successor before the injury occurred, if there is a continuing relationship between the successor and the seller's customers. Although the precise relationship required for finding a duty to warn is unclear, courts have considered a succession by the buyer to its seller's service contract and the buyer's subsequent service of the product to be relevant.

A successor must pay careful attention to where the seller's products are sold. The more states in which the products are distributed, the greater the number of potential jurisdictions for deciding questions of successor liability. And the law on successor liability may vary significantly from state to state. For instance, under one state's law, the successor may be liable and under another state's it may not be. Indeed, the newly created exceptions to the general rule may be applied differently in different states, and in some states, they may not be applied at all.

Some states have not confronted the issue of expanding the traditional rules governing successor liability or have declined to widen the traditional rules. Other states may apply the new rules in circumstances such as where there is some similarity between the predecessor and successor (e.g., in the continuity or product line exceptions). In a classic assets acquisition, of course, that similarity may not be difficult to find. The proliferation of rules may prevent a successor from being able to predict precisely when it is likely to acquire liabilities.

The checkered experience of Amsted Industries Inc. as a defendant in five separate cases between 1975 and 1982 illustrates the difficulties in trying to deal with varying state laws. Amsted's problems were further compounded by a series of acquisitions and successorships that began in 1956 when Bontrager acquired the assets and liabilities of Johnson, a manufacturer of presses. Amsted entered the picture in 1962 when it acquired Bontrager for cash and continued Bontrager's practice of manufacturing presses under the Johnson name. But Amsted sold its press business in 1975 to LWE Inc., which also continued to manufacture Johnson presses.

In a 1975 case decided in California two years before another California court enunciated the "product line" rule in Ray v. Alad Corp., Amsted was held not liable under the state's laws for the defective products of its predecessor.

Amsted's litigation scorecard thereafter read:

Michigan, 1979—The U.S. District Court for the Eastern District of Michigan, applying Michigan law, used the continuity exception to hold Amsted liable as a successor.

Illinois, 1979—An Illinois court rejected the product line exception and held Amsted not liable as a successor under that state's law.

New Jersey, 1981—The state Supreme Court, in an application of New Jersey law, applied the product line exception and found Amsted liable as a successor.

Nebraska, 1982—The state Supreme Court rejected the product line exception and held Amsted not liable under Nebraska law as a successor.

The confusion surrounding the Amsted cases underscores the importance in acquisitions of determining where the selling company has distributed products that may be potentially defective and trigger product liability for the buyer.

* * *

The expanded imposition of successor liability on corporations that purchase manufacturing assets can have a chilling effect on the ability of the small manufacturer to sell its business assets for a fair purchase price rather than liquidate. In order to divest itself of its business assets, the small manufacturing corporation may have to sacrifice by lowering its price to such an extent that it may not net a sum commensurate with the true worth of the business assets.

* * *

YAMIN, THE ACHILLES HEEL OF THE TAKEOVER: NATURE AND SCOPE OF SUCCESSOR CORPORATION PRODUCTS LIABILITY IN ASSET ACQUISITIONS
7 Harv. J. of Law & Pub. Pol, 187, 248–256 (1984).

* * *

* * * Products liability in the asset acquisition context is indeed becoming increasingly difficult to avoid. Nevertheless, the resourceful corporate lawyer is far from helpless to respond.

A composite of the factors which comprise the relatively insulated asset acquisition can be synthesized out of the cases. From this list of factors the acquiring corporation should choose those that fit best—or conflict least—with its acquisition plans. It should be cognizant that some will be inapposite because they directly interfere with its primary purpose(s) for seeking to acquire the assets. This process of choosing from among factors which may help prevent a transfer of liability concomitant with the transfer of assets may indicate that it can comfortably accommodate so few of the factors in its acquisition plan as to call into question the wisdom of the purchase itself. On the other hand, after balancing costs, including the possibility of successor liability, against the benefits expected to be derived from the acquisition, it may wish to proceed without the protection these factors might provide. If it chooses the latter course—to proceed in the time-honored "damn the torpedoes" fashion—it can do so secure at least in the knowledge that a number of ameliorative strategies are available by which to contain some of the liability that may be incurred.

* * *

When examining the particular list of preventive factors set out below, the reader should be aware that they are not intended to be exhaustive. Surely an ingenious business lawyer could formulate many other plausible strategies.

1. PREVENTIVE FACTORS

* * *

(a) Avoidance of Indicia of Continuity

Continuity of the enterprise as between buyer and seller is a theme which runs through all the expanded successor liability cases. Thus, to the maximum extent possible the corporate planner should avoid the appearance of or, preferably, the fact of continuity. One obvious way to accomplish this is to structure the sale such that the seller actually survives as a viable *operating* entity. For example, the successor could avoid purchasing all of the assets, choosing instead only those which it can put to the most effective use and leaving the seller with sufficient assets with which to sustain an ongoing enterprise. Failing that, the buyer should avoid retention of key personnel or even ordinary employees of the seller. Of course, this suggestion may be academic if management and other personnel are among the chief assets the buyer seeks. Continuity of ownership by a majority of the shareholders should, of course, be eschewed. Finally, while we may not think of it in terms of "indicia of continuity," failure to tender adequate consideration can readily trigger the "mere continuity" label.

(b) Avoidance of Continuity in Seller's "Product Line"

This is a fall-back position from compliance with the first factor, but it may still be useful in avoiding liability under the *Ray* product line doctrine. The most thorough way to root out product line indicia is to actually change the seller's product lines after the asset purchase.

* * *

(c) Avoidance of Appearance of Benefit From Seller's "Goodwill"

This is a subset of the indicia of continuity factor, but is independent enough from continuity to suggest that it may be avoided in the absence of the ability to eschew other continuity factors. All reference to goodwill and related assets should be omitted from the contract of sale. Moreover, purchase of trademarks, customer lists, trade names and the like should be avoided as being so analogous to "goodwill" itself as to be nearly indistinguishable from it. It may also be worthwhile to give notice to the seller's customers and suppliers specifically and to the public in general that a new entity has replaced the seller. This will tend to preclude the possibility that a court could reasonably claim that the buyer is benefitting by trading on the seller's reputation.

* * *

(d) Payment of Consideration in Cash, Not Acquirer's Stock

There are several risks that can be reduced by purchasing assets for cash rather than stock. The chief advantage to doing so is the avoidance of liability under the de facto merger doctrine. Aside from the connection between payment in stock and the de facto merger doctrine, payment in stock may also constitute an important indicium of continuity under any of the alternative tests of successor liability.

Note that valuation problems can occur when consideration takes the form of stock. Overvaluation of the stock paid (in effect, payment of inadequate consideration) could trigger a finding of the "mere continuation" exception, or, if the resulting shortfall is egregious enough, a labeling of the transaction as fraudulent.

(e) Payment of Consideration to Selling Corporation, Not to Its Shareholders

The purchasing corporation should not only avoid payment of consideration directly to the seller's shareholders, but also a contract for the sale of assets which includes as one of its terms a requirement that consideration be paid over to the seller's shareholders. Payment to the seller's shareholders would constitute a determinative indicium of continuity, since by definition such a transfer assures a continuing interest on the part of those equity owners in the successor enterprise. Moreover, payment in that fashion would probably be sufficient to trigger liability under any of the theories canvassed in this article, but its most serious effect could be to trigger liability flowing from the fraudulent transaction exception.

(f) Avoidance of Express or Implied Agreement for Post–Sale Liquidation or Dissolution

The reason for inclusion of this factor as one to be avoided will be made clear by referring to the concurring opinion of Justice Schreiber in *Ramirez*, a quotation from which appears earlier in this article. The Justice stated that successor liability "is premised on the *elimination* by the successor of an effective remedy[,]" meaning elimination by the successor of the *selling corporation*. This factor is omnipresent in the justifications appearing in the cases imposing liability upon successors in products liability suits by consumers and constitutes the essence of the "plaintiff's plight." The most effective way to avoid this ground for liability is to structure the transaction so that the seller survives.

If the purchaser neither requires, as part of the agreement of sale, that the seller dissolve, nor participates in such dissolution if it actually occurs, he reserves to himself the option to later frame an argument to the effect that *he* did not "eliminate an effective remedy," i.e., a viable defendant, for the injured plaintiff.

* * *

B. Ameliorative Strategies

* * *

* * *

(a) Adjustment in Price of Assets

The most effective response to successor liability may well be the most obvious: adjustment of the price of the assets to reflect the estimated risk and magnitude of successor liability. * * * Of course, the *extreme* difficulty of arriving at an estimated cost of future product liability judgments should in no wise be gainsaid.[389]

(b) Insurance Protection Against Liability

* * * The buyer may arrange with the seller simply to maintain the latter's products liability insurance in force covering the purchased assets, especially if the seller will survive the asset sale. Such an arrangement would, of course, entail an upward adjustment in the price paid to the seller for the assets to reflect his continued payment of premiums. Alternatively, the buyer could take an assignment of the seller's policy or purchase its own. In the latter situations the cost of insurance presumably would be deducted from the price of the assets.

* * *

---

389. Ironically, this problem for counsel is analogous to one of the elements that plight of the plaintiff which motivates courts to activism in this field, i.e., here, the difficulty of estimating the size of the fund necessary to be reserved by the selling corporation under statutory safeguards for creditors blends into the problem of adjusting the price of the assets.

Insurance may well be the "best resolution" of the successor liability problem—but only if it can be obtained. According to a multitude of commentators on the subject, this country is in the midst of a products liability insurance crisis, and this predicament is most acute for smaller businesses. Thus, the successor today often finds himself on the horns of a dilemma: either he cannot secure products liability insurance at all, or it is available only at a price that is prohibitive. Faced with this problem, he may attempt to self-insure, deducting the estimated costs of doing so from the price offered for the assets. * * *

(c) Indemnification by Seller

The first order of business with respect to indemnification against successor liability claims is for the buyer to negotiate a strong indemnification clause in the contract of sale itself. If the seller will survive the asset transfer, indemnification can run directly from it to the buyer. On the other hand, if the seller is scheduled to dissolve after the transaction, the buyer might obtain indemnification from the seller's principals, its corporate parent, or another party related to the seller. Of course, full (as opposed to partial) indemnity should be the purchaser's objective. Again, appropriate adjustments in the amount of consideration paid likely will be made.

(d) Reservation of Portion of Sales Price in Escrow

This tactic is closely related to indemnification, but may, in some cases, provide the successor with greater peace of mind. This added assurance flows from the fact that the escrowed fund is normally delivered to a third party stakeholder, thus reducing or eliminating the successor's fear that the seller will renege on its undertaking. As with all ameliorative strategies, valuation (i.e., price adjustment) problems abound.

(e) Formation of Insulating Subsidiary

A parent corporation generally cannot be held directly responsible for any liabilities incurred by a bona fide subsidiary. It follows, then, that a subsidiary formed for the purpose will constitute an ideal vehicle through which to purchase assets. * * * After formation of the subsidiary, the parent would be liable for successor liability against the subsidiary only to the extent of its investment in that wholly owned but separate corporate entity, "so long as corporate formalities are preserved and there is genuine substance to the subsidiary's separate existence as a profit oriented business."

(f) Discharge of Actual or Potential Duty to Warn

This strategy is self-explanatory and is followed simply by discovering any potential duty to warn and seeking to satisfy it. The cost of fulfilling this duty could be reflected in the price of the assets, or compensated for through other media we have just surveyed, such as insurance, escrow, or indemnity. Ideally, investigation of the potential for duty to warn liability will have been made before the closing of the asset sale.

* * *

Subsection c. Employee Discrimination Claims

EEOC v. VUCITECH

United States Court of Appeals, Seventh Circuit, 1988.
842 F.2d 936.

POSNER, CIRCUIT JUDGE.

These appeals present a variety of interesting questions arising out of a protracted effort by the Equal Employment Opportunity Commission to fix personal liability on an employer's officers for a practice not authoritatively determined to be discriminatory until years after they committed it, and on a successor of the employer.

The three individual defendants, whom we shall refer to as the "Vucitech group," were (together with a fourth person, now dead) the officers and shareholders of MTC Gear Corporation, a closely held corporation engaged in the manufacture of gears and other mechanical devices used in motor vehicles. MTC employed between 75 and 100 workers, who were represented by a union. In 1979 the Vucitech group negotiated on behalf of MTC a new collective bargaining agreement with the union. After counsel advised that the recently enacted Pregnancy Discrimination Act of 1978, 42 U.S.C. § 2000e(k) (amending Title VII of the Civil Rights Act of 1964), did not require the payment of maternity benefits as part of the fringe benefits for employees' dependents (as opposed to the employees themselves), the Vucitech group offered the union, in lieu of dependents' maternity benefits, a "baby bonus" plan. Under the plan every male employee would receive a lump sum of $750 for every baby that his wife gave birth to while he was employed by the corporation. The union agreed, and agreed again in the 1982 collective bargaining negotiations with the Vucitech group, when the baby bonus was raised to $1,000.

* * * At all events, all of the parties assume, and so shall we, that once the Pregnancy Discrimination Act had been interpreted to apply to dependents' benefits, the baby bonus plan was unquestionably in violation of the Act. The plan may have violated Title VII even without the Pregnancy Discrimination Act. * * *

The Commission notified MTC of the charges. Conciliation efforts, with the Vucitech group representing the company, followed, but they failed in March 1982. The Commission decided, however, to postpone formal action until the Supreme Court resolved the question of benefits for pregnant dependents, which it did a few months after our *Joslyn* decision, holding in *Newport News Shipbuilding & Dry Dock Co. v. EEOC,* 462 U.S. 669, 103 S.Ct. 2622, 77 L.Ed.2d 89 (1983), that the Act forbids discrimination not only with respect to the wages and benefits of pregnant (necessarily female) employees but also with respect to benefits for pregnant dependents of male employees. We quickly vacated *Joslyn,* and in May 1984 the EEOC filed suit under Title VII against MTC, charging sex discrimination in the failure to pay maternity benefits for the wives of ten (later reduced to eight) employees of MTC but not naming any individuals as defendants.

MTC was a much different entity in 1984 from what it had been at the beginning of 1982. For shortly after the conciliation efforts had broken down, the Vucitech group, whose members were in their sixties and wanted to retire, had sold all their stock in MTC to Muzzamil Niazi, who as part of the deal assumed all of MTC's liabilities, expressly including any liability growing out of the charges of sex discrimination that had been filed with the EEOC. The Vucitech group retired, but their quiet life was soon interrupted. Niazi was a crook. He embezzled money from MTC on a grand scale, driving the company into the ground. In November 1983 the secured creditors seized all of MTC's assets and shut it down. Niazi exited, still owing the Vucitech group $2.8 million for the sale of their stock to him. As the members of the group had been counting on this money to finance their retirement, the Niazi fiasco forced them out of retirement. In December 1983, using the proceeds of a $2.8 million loan that they obtained from a bank in Chicago, they bought for $3 million all of MTC's machinery and equipment at public auction and placed these assets in a new corporation, Profile Gear Corporation, which they owned together with two former employees of MTC and which opened for business in January 1984. Except for the change in name and partial change in ownership, Profile was essentially the same entity (in nature of business, and in customers and employees, though naturally there was some turnover in both of these groups) as MTC, now defunct. So when the EEOC sued MTC in 1984 it named Profile as an additional defendant.

* * * But it is not, because, as noted earlier, two of the employees whom the EEOC is representing in this litigation were denied maternity benefits after Niazi took over MTC and the Vucitech group retired. The members of the group were not personally involved in the discrimination against these two workers; the only possible defendant, with MTC down the tubes, is Profile.

The entire issue of successor liability, which is so important in regard both to common law torts (especially of the delayed-action variety, where the culpable act and the injury may be separated by many years) and to statutory torts such as discrimination in violation of Title VII, is dreadfully tangled, reflecting the difficulty of striking the right balance between the competing interests at stake. * * * In favor of successor liability is the interest in preventing tortfeasors from externalizing the costs of their misconduct by selling their assets free of any liabilities and distributing the proceeds to their shareholders. * * * Against is the interest in a fluid market in corporate assets, which is impeded if purchasers acquire along with the assets legal liabilities of unknown, sometimes unknowable, dimensions. The latter consideration dominated common law thinking until recent years, producing a rule, now eroding, * * * that in a sale of assets (as here), as distinct from a merger or consolidation, the purchaser took free of any liabilities not expressly assumed, including tort liabilities. * * *

A similar but looser approach, in which the focus is on the continuity between the predecessor's and successor's businesses and the latter's notice of the former's acts, has long been followed in labor cases in which the issue is the successor's duty to honor the obligations assumed by its predecessor in a collective bargaining agreement. See, e.g., *Fall River Dyeing & Finishing Corp. v. NLRB*, ___ U.S. ___, 107 S.Ct. 2225, 2235–37, 96 L.Ed.2d 22 (1987); *NLRB v. Burns International Security Services, Inc.*, 406 U.S. 272, 278–81 and n. 4, 286, 92 S.Ct. 1571, 1577–79 and n. 4, 1581, 32 L.Ed.2d 61 (1972). These cases have in turn been thought to provide an appropriate model for dealing with successorship questions in Title VII cases. See, e.g., *Bates v. Pacific Maritime Ass'n*, 744 F.2d 705 (9th Cir.1984); *EEOC v. MacMillan Bloedel Containers, Inc.*, 503 F.2d 1086, 1089–92 (6th Cir.1974). A liability is a liability, whatever its legal source; and while circumstances alter cases, the basic issue in every successorship case is how to strike a proper balance between on the one hand preventing wrongdoers from escaping liability and on the other hand facilitating the transfer of corporate assets to their most valuable uses.

There is, however, the following difference between the tort and labor contexts: in the latter, there is no question that the successor knows of any collective bargaining agreements that his predecessor has signed; in the former, the successor may be ignorant of the predecessor's liability. Employment discrimination, a tort in a labor context, is thus a mixed case. Another mixed case is the successor's liability for a predecessor's unfair labor practice; and here as we would expect there must be a showing of notice to the successor. See *Golden State Bottling Co. v. NLRB*, 414 U.S. 168, 185, 94 S.Ct. 414, 425, 38 L.Ed.2d 388 (1973).

Whatever the precise formulation of the rule should be in employment-discrimination cases, there can be little doubt that Profile is liable as MTC's successor. Although the particular discrimination in question occurred after the Vucitech group had temporarily departed from the scene, it was merely a continuation of the baby bonus policy which the group had adopted and, as it were, bequeathed to its successor, Niazi. The collective bargaining agreement that the group negotiated in 1982 and that contained the $1,000 baby bonus did not expire until February 1985. By that time the group was back in control, and knew or should have known that the original charges of sex discrimination had not been resolved—and upon inquiry of the EEOC about their status would quickly have learned that two additional charges had been filed. So there was no surprise; or at least there should not have been, and of course the Vucitech group's knowledge, actual or constructive, must be imputed to Profile, which they controlled. In addition, the Vucitech group was at least somewhat implicated in Niazi's violations of the Pregnancy Discrimination Act, which were pursuant to the collective bargaining agreement that the group had negotiated in 1982. The amount in controversy is again very small—a mere $2,000—making us wonder at the motives behind the defendants' steadfast resistance to paying the maternity benefits that they unlawfully denied their employees' wives. And these amounts were known from the outset; there was no open-ended liability as in a tort suit.

Finally, there is the "substantial continuity" between predecessor and successor of which the cases speak; indeed, the facts in *Fall River Dyeing* are rather similar to those of the present case. This bears not only on the issue of notice, but also on the issue of maintaining the fluidity of corporate assets, which is impeded if assets sold piecemeal are each encumbered by the liabilities of their previous owner. When the successor company knows about its predecessor's liability, knows the precise extent of that liability, and knows that the predecessor itself would not be able to pay a judgment obtained against it, the presumption should be in favor of successor liability, even if the successor (as here) purchased the assets of its predecessor rather than merged the predecessor into it or consolidated with it. This solution prevents the externalizing of the liability without disappointing the reasonable expectations of investors (and hence impeding the market for corporate assets). The successor, if he knows of his potential liability, will demand compensation in the form of a lower price for the assets, and in this way the burden of liability will be shifted back to the owners of those assets, where it belongs.

In rejecting successor liability, the district court attached great and in our view undue weight to the fact that because MTC had gone broke, there was an element of windfall in making Profile liable as its successor; had it not been for the succession, the two employees involved in this aspect of the case would have been out of luck. Two recent decisions of this court, *Musikiwamba v. ESSI, Inc., supra,* and *Wheeler v. Snyder Buick, Inc.,* 794 F.2d 1228, 1236 (7th Cir.1986), say that successor liability is inappropriate where prior to the succession the predecessor lost its ability to pay a judgment, so that as in this case, but for the succession, the plaintiffs would depart empty-handed. However, we do not understand these decisions to have imposed an ironclad requirement in all cases of successor liability. Certainly in an equity case, as *Wheeler* was and this case is (as the Vucitech group tirelessly emphasizes), the proper approach to the issue of successor liability is not to erect a set of hoops to force plaintiffs to jump through but to ask whether such liability would strike a reasonable balance between the interest in fully sanctioning unlawful conduct and the interest in facilitating the market in corporate and other productive assets.

* * *

The disappearance of the tortfeasor (the predecessor in liability) before the succession is relevant, because it reduces the likelihood both that the succession was a device for escaping the consequences of liability and that the successor had notice of its predecessor's legal liability. MTC did not go broke as part of some elaborate scheme to escape the trivial liability arising from the failure to pay maternity benefits, and to this extent the point emphasized by the district court and our previous decisions does indeed weigh against successor liability. But the point is outweighed by the fact that MTC's discrimination was a legacy of the Vucitech group, which operating in the corporate form of Profile took over the company once again after Niazi's defalcation. The Niazi interlude is an irrelevance; the discriminations, built as they were into the collective bargaining agreement that the Vucitech group had negotiated, would have occurred even if the group had never sold their stock to Niazi, in which event MTC rather than Profile would be liable to the two employees in question. We conclude that Profile is liable as a successor employer, and hence that the EEOC must succeed on its cross-appeal.

GOLDEN STATE BOTTLING CO. v. NLRB

Supreme Court of the United States, 1973.
414 U.S. 168, 94 S.Ct. 414, 38 L.Ed.2d 388.

MR. JUSTICE BRENNAN delivered the opinion of the Court.

The principal question for decision in this case is whether the bona fide purchaser of a business, who acquires and continues the business with knowledge that his predecessor has committed an unfair labor practice in the discharge of an employee, may be ordered by the National Labor Relations Board to reinstate the employee with backpay.

Petitioners are Golden State Bottling Co., Inc. (Golden State), and All American Beverages, Inc. (All American). All American bought Golden State's soft drink bottling and distribution business after the National Labor Relations Board had ordered Golden State, "its officers, agents, successors, and assigns" to reinstate with back pay a driver-salesman, Kenneth L. Baker, whose discharge by Golden State was found by the Board to have been an unfair labor practice. In a subsequent backpay specification proceeding to which both Golden State and All American were parties, see 29 CFR §§ 102.52–102.59, the Board found that All American continued after the acquisition to carry on the business without interruption or substantial changes in method of operation, employee complement, or supervisory personnel. In that circumstance, although All American was a bona fide purchaser of the business, unconnected with Golden State, the Board found that All American, having acquired the business with knowledge of the outstanding Board order, was a "successor" for purposes of the National Labor Relations Act and liable for the reinstatement of Baker with backpay. * * *

We affirm.

* * *

We in no way qualify the *Burns* holdings in concluding that the Board's order against All American strikes an equitable balance.[6] When a new employer, such as All American, has acquired substantial assets of its predecessor and continued, without interruption or substantial change, the predecessor's business operations, those employees who have been retained will understandably view their job situations as essentially unaltered. Under these circumstances, the employees may well perceive the successor's failure to remedy the predecessor employer's unfair labor practices arising out of an unlawful discharge as a continuation of the predecessor's labor policies. To the extent that the employees' legitimate expectation is that the unfair labor practices will be remedied, a successor's failure to do so may result in labor unrest as the employees engage in collective activity to force remedial action. Similarly, if the employees identify the new employer's labor policies with those of the predecessor but do not take collective action, the successor may benefit from the unfair labor practices due to a continuing deterrent effect on union activities. Moreover, the Board's experience may reasonably lead it to believe that employers intent on suppressing union activity may select for discharge those employees most actively engaged in union affairs, so that a failure to reinstate may result in a leadership vacuum in the bargaining unit.

* * * Since the successor must have notice before liability can be imposed, "his potential liability for remedying the unfair labor practices is a matter which can be reflected in the price he pays for the business, or he may secure an indemnity clause in the sales contract which will indemnify him for liability arising from the seller's unfair labor practices."

* * *

Questions

1. Does the *Vucitech* case rest on its unusual facts or has Judge Posner established an expanded standard for all employee discrimination claims? Why does the traditional continuation doctrine not apply?

2. How does the notice standard in *Vucitech* compare to either the successorship rules in collective bargaining case law or case law on contract obligations? Does, for example, the notice requirement supplement the successorship rule in collective bargaining case law when title XII claims are in issue?

3. How does the notice standard work in practice? Does a buying firm have to have specific notice of the claims asserted against it? If general notice of the *possibility* of title XII claims or unfair labor practice

---

[6]. A purchasing company cannot be obligated to carry out under § 10(c) every outstanding and unsatisfied order of the Board. For example, because the purchaser is not obligated by the Act to hire any of the predecessor's employees, see *NLRB v. Burns International Security Services, Inc.*, supra, at 280 n. 5, the purchaser, if it does not hire any or a majority of those employees, will not be bound by an outstanding order to bargain issued by the Board against the predecessor or by any order tied to the continuance of the bargaining agent in the unit involved. *Id.*, at 280–281.

claims will suffice, does not the rule catch all acquisitions? If specific notice is required, what is the effect of the rule on the common practice in acquisitions of asking selling firms to disclose all known claims in the closing documents?

4. Does implying a notice requirement affect the "right balance" between victim compensation and ease of transferability of assets? What is the effect of notice if buyers cannot calculate the value of claims against Vucitech, even if they are known?

Subsection d. Environmental Law Claims

DEPARTMENT OF TRANSP. v. PSC RESOURCES, INC.

Superior Court of New Jersey, Law Division, 1980.
175 N.J.Super. 447, 419 A.2d 1151.

YOUNG, J.S.C.

The single issue submitted for determination is whether a corporation which purchases the assets of another corporation for cash is liable for damages arising from the environmental tort of its predecessor. Plaintiff Department of Transportation of the State of New Jersey (DOT) moves for summary judgment against defendant PSC Resources, Inc. (PSC) for damages to plaintiff's property caused by PSC's predecessor, codefendant Diamond Head Oil Refining Co., Inc. (Diamond Head). The facts are not in dispute, making the motion appropriate for disposition on the law. * * *

Plaintiff alleges that between February 1, 1946 and November 1, 1973 Diamond Head operated waste oil reprocessing and canning facilities at 1401 and 1427 Harrison Turnpike in Kearny, N.J. The facility at 1427 Harrison Turnpike was shut down in 1955 while operations continued at 1401 Harrison Turnpike. The complaint further alleges that in the operation of its facilities Diamond Head discharged oily wastes, sludge and contaminated waste water onto the adjacent property and into a body of water known as Oil Lake. DOT acquired the property upon which Oil Lake was situated March 6, 1968.

Defendant PSC was incorporated as a subsidiary of Phillips Screw Company, Inc. under the laws of the State of Delaware as Phillips Resources Inc. on October 23, 1973 and received a certificate of authority to transact business in this State on October 31, 1973. PSC was incorporated for the purpose of acquiring the stock and/or assets of Diamond Head. This purpose was effectuated on October 26, 1973 when PSC entered into a stock purchase agreement which resulted in the acquisition of 100% of the issued and outstanding stock of Diamond Head on November 1, 1973. The terms of the agreement required the officers and directors of Diamond Head to resign on November 1, 1973, while PSC's nominees, Arthur M. Vash, president and director of PSC, John J. Casey, treasurer and director of PSC, and Jerome E. Rosen, secretary and director of PSC, became the new directors and officers of Diamond Head. On the same date, within hours after their appointments, these new directors submitted a "Plan of Complete Liquidation and Dissolution" which PSC as sole stockholder adopted. After a certificate of dissolution was filed pursuant to *N.J.S.A.* 14A:12–2 the assets of Diamond Head, consisting of the plant and property located at 1401 Harrison Turnpike, Kearny, New Jersey, were transferred to PSC for less than $100.

From November 1, 1973 until November 3, 1976 PSC continued to operate the plant at 1401 Harrison Turnpike under the name "Diamond Head Oil Refining Company, Division of PSC Resources, Inc." DOT alleges that PSC continued Diamond Head's practice of pumping the accumulated waste water, which contained oil, solids, soluble organic compounds, heavy metals, sodium hydroxide and sodium silicate, from the low area of the facility into Oil Lake located on DOT's property. * * *

On November 3, 1976 the Diamond Head facility was purchased by Ag–Met Oil Service, Inc., predecessor to Newtown Refining Corporation. Newtown is a codefendant in this action, but is not a party to the pending motion.

In 1977 plaintiff commenced the construction of a highway, Interstate 280. In the course of that construction, and as represented by plaintiff's counsel, under the direction and supervision of state and federal environmental authorities DOT had to remove and dispose of more than 10 million gallons of oil-contaminated water and more than 200,000 cubic yards of oily sludge from Oil Lake. Plaintiff alleges that the cost of such removal amounted to $4,918,436.

Suit was instituted by DOT against Diamond Head and PSC on September 14, 1977. Default was entered against Diamond Head on November 21, 1977. * * *

Notwithstanding the general rule of nonliability in asset acquisitions, a successor corporation will be liable if any one of the following four exceptions is met: (1) where the purchaser expressly or impliedly agrees to assume debts and liabilities; (2) where the transaction amounts to a consolidation or merger of the seller and purchaser; (3) where the purchasing corporation is merely a continuance of the selling corporation; or (4) where the transaction is entered into fraudulently in order to evade liability for debts. *Ibid.* "A fifth exception sometimes incorporated as an element of one of the above exceptions is the absence of adequate consideration for the sale or transfer."

* * *

The DOT argues that PSC is liable for the tortious conduct of Diamond Head on application of the principles here summarized. A reading of the affidavits, depositions and various agreements and documents before this court makes clear that the issue of successor liability is narrowed as to whether PSC is a continuation of Diamond Head. Although PSC acquired Diamond Head by obtaining all the outstanding shares, the officers and directors of Diamond Head and

PSC, as sole shareholder, dissolved the corporate entity. A paucity of evidence exists to substantiate a finding that with the transfer of assets PSC was effecting a merger, either statutory or *de facto;* that PSC had agreed to assume Diamond Head's debts or liabilities, or that PSC was intent upon defrauding Diamond Head's creditors.

Maintaining that PSC is a continuation of Diamond Head, the DOT relies on Judge Pindar's opinion in *Jackson v. Diamond T. Trucking Co.* * * * Judge Pindar abstracted the common elements delineated in the following passage:

> ... [I]n each case there was (1) transfer of corporate assets (2) for less than adequate consideration (3) to another corporation which continued the business operation of the transferor (4) when both corporations had at least one common officer or director who was, in fact, instrumental in the transfer ... and (5) the transfer rendered the transferor incapable of paying its creditors claims because it was dissolved in either fact or law. [*Jackson v. Diamond T. Trucking Co.,* 100 *N.J.Super.* at 196, 241 *A.*2d at 477]

The DOT urges the court to apply strictly the five criteria to the transfer of Diamond Head's assets to PSC. It is clear that all five criteria are satisfied. Diamond Head transferred its assets for less than $100 to PSC, which continued the refining operations. At the time of the transfer both companies had the same officers and directors, who submitted a plan for the dissolution of Diamond Head and the transfer of assets to PSC. This plan, which was adopted by PSC as sole shareholder, rendered Diamond Head unable to pay the claims of its creditors. It should be noted, however, that in all the cases relied on by Judge Pindar in the *Diamond T.* opinion, as well as that opinion, the principals of each corporation were aware of an outstanding debt, * * * or an underlying obligation. * * * Although a tort claimant becomes a creditor of the defendant on the date of the tort, * * * nothing before this court substantiates the assertion that PSC had knowledge, or should have known, of an underlying claim by DOT when the assets of Diamond Head were transferred. While knowledge of a contingent tort claim may be irrelevant to establish successor liability, such a factor was important in the *Diamond T.* decision, and the opinions cited therein.

Another distinction should also be noted. The Diamond T. Trucking Co. and its transferor, Phillips Specials, shared the same principals for almost one year. In the case at bar PSC and Diamond Head shared the same principals for, at most, a few hours. PSC acquired the assets of Diamond Head by a method known as a "two-step asset acquisition." Generally, a corporation acquires all or most of the stock of another corporation, transfers the latter's assets, and then dissolves or liquidates that company.[5] In essence, the principals of Diamond Head, as

---

5. These transactions are planned in such a fashion for the purposes of corporate taxation and are considered a direct purchase of the assets by virtue of I.R.C. § 332, 26 *U.S.C.A.* § 332, if certain provi-

appointed by PSC on November 1, 1973, were officers as a matter of form.

* * *

The holding in *Ramirez* represents the abandonment of the traditional approach to successor liability in product liability cases. Judge King synthesized the strict liability rationale of *Ray* and the continuity of the business operation approach of *Turner*.

* * *

Before deciding if the traditional corporate test should likewise be abandoned in the case at bar, the issue whether the *Ramirez* standard is an appropriate substitute in the area of environmental torts must be addressed. The DOT maintains that an application of this test would be appropriate because the underlying policy rationale in product cases is similar to that in environmental cases. PSC argues, however, that plaintiff's cause of action does not lie in the realm of environmental tort, but rather in the area of trespass and nuisance. Defendant further asserts that, even if the gravamen of the complaint lies in environmental tort, such a tort cannot be analogized to one of product liability.

Addressing the defendant's first contention, this court determines that PSC's attempt to distinguish an environmental tort from those of nuisance and trespass does not succeed. Torts against the environment find their origin in the law of nuisance and trespass. * * *

As noted above, defendant further argues that the alleged tort committed by the defendant is not sufficiently analogous to products liability to warrant the use of the successor liability criteria as set forth in *Ramirez*. The salient characteristic in the product liability cases in which successor liability was found is that in each the tort was declared to be one of strict liability. The threshold question becomes whether the alleged pollution of Oil Lake by PSC is a strict liability tort.

Absolute liability for nuisance has been recognized at common law where the defendant carries on an abnormally dangerous activity in an inappropriate place, or where an enterprise involves so great a risk to its surroundings that its location may be considered unreasonable.
* * *

Having reviewed decisional law and the statutes designed to safeguard the State's waters vis-à-vis pertinent product liability opinions, it is evident that claims to enforce such law sound in strict tort liability. The policy rationale for the imposition of strict liability in a defective product action is equally applicable to the present wrong for which relief is sought. The refinery is in a better position to protect itself and bear the costs of a discharge of pollutants from its facility into bodies of water than would be the public. In addition, the refiner is the instrumentality to look to for improvement of the waste disposal process, cf.

sions of I.R.C. § 334, 26 *U.S.C.A.* § 334, are met.

Cyr v. B. Offen & Co., Inc., 501 F.2d at 1154 (in which the court stated that the manufacturer of a product is the instrumentality to look to for improvement). * * *

The nature and policy considerations of a product liability action are sufficiently analogous to those of the present action to warrant an abandonment of the traditional approach, and an application of the current test for successor liability as set forth in *Ramirez*. * * * The *Ramirez* court recognized that liability, as well as the philosophy of spreading the risk to society at large for cost of injuries resulting from the wrong, have been fully embraced in New Jersey. The adoption of such an approach prohibits the result in any particular case to "turn on the intricacies of the law of corporate mergers and disclaimers." 171 N.J.Super. at 275, 408 A.2d at 826. A like rationale was advanced in *Wilson v. Fare Well Corp.*, wherein the court—intent on protecting the innocent, injured party who is unable to proceed against the original tortfeasor—observed, "When an ongoing business assumes all the benefits of its predecessor and continues to function in the same manner as its predecessor, *tort* liability should attach." 140 N.J.Super. at 491, 356 A.2d at 467 (emphasis supplied).

PSC as sole stockholder dissolved Diamond Head, thus rendering DOT incapable of pursuing its cause of action against that entity. As a result plaintiff, with no recourse, seeks to recover from PSC.

* * * Defendant here engaged in the same enterprise as its predecessor. Since PSC derived the benefit of an established refining company's expertise and system of operation, it should also bear the burden of the operation. The successor is also in a better position to spread the cost of clean-up and removal costs. One commentator noted that oil "should be priced to bear all of its costs, including the hidden costs of clearing up pollution...." Comment, 36 Brooklyn L.Rev. 350, 367 (1970). * * *

An application of this test to the facts in the present action indicates that PSC is the successor of Diamond Head. On November 1, 1973 PSC purchased *all* of Diamond Head's assets for less than $100 cash. PSC conducted business at the facility under the name "Diamond Head Oil Refining Company, Division of PSC Resources, Inc." until 1976. The refinery was manned by virtually the same operating personnel. Several members of lower-level management remained in the employ of PSC after its takeover of the facility. More importantly, however PSC continued the same waste disposal process of Diamond Head, which is alleged to be the source for the pollution of Oil Lake. Based on these facts, it is apparent that PSC indeed continued essentially the same operation as Diamond Head.

PSC raises several arguments against the imposition of successor liability. First, PSC asserts that to burden it with such liability is unfair. Second, PSC states that it did not insure against such a risk, a determinative factor in products liability cases. Finally, after postulating a policy which would assure a profitable disposal of industrial waste, PSC argues that the expense of clean-up that ensues from the imposition of successor liability would derogate from such a policy.

The assertion that the doctrine of successor liability is unfair and creates surprise on the successor has been met by the courts in the product liability cases. * * *

Describing the argument of surprise as "without merit," the court in *Turner v. Bituminous* phrased its rebuttal in this language:

> It is clear that once corporations considering such transactions become aware of the possibility of successor products liability, they can make suitable preparations. Whether this takes the form of ... insurance, indemnification agreements or of escrow accounts, or even a deduction from the purchase price is a matter to be considered between the parties. [397 *Mich.* at 429, 244 *N.W.*2d at 883]

Likewise, the courts have not been persuaded by the argument that the imposition of successor liability might create unpredictability in the market place or stifle commercial transfers of assets. * * * Liability for contingent obligations exists with mergers, "[y]et corporate mergers continue to occur ..." Turner v. Bituminous, 397 Mich. at 428, 244 N.W.2d at 882. This court adopts the reasoning of the *Turner* court and is likewise not persuaded by the argument of surprise.

Equally lacking merit is defendant's assertion that PSC was not insured against damages caused by such discharges. * * * The burden of bearing the risk being clearly delegated to a facility that discharges, defendant's argument regarding lack of insurance is unpersuasive. * * * This court finds that PSC is the successor to Diamond Head, and is subject to liability for any claims against it arising from the discharge of pollutants onto the plaintiff's property.

Questions

1. What is the nature of Diamond Head's liability? Was Diamond Head or PSC liable as an "owner" of the land on which Oil Lake is located?

Why did the court need a "new" approach to successor liability? Why doesn't the old exception for continuation of a business give the same result? Does your answer depend on whether we view the two steps of the acquisition separately (a stock acquisition for full value plus a formal asset sale for nominal value) or collapse them into a sale of assets for a substantial price?

2. Why did Diamond Head sell assets in liquidation rather than simply pass assets back to shareholders in a liquidating distribution? What happened to the $100 purchase price? Why was the transaction structured this way rather than as a straight asset sale?

3. The court looked to *Ramirez*, a product liability case following the minority position of California on the product line rule, for guidance in an environmental law case. Will states that do not follow the California rule for product liability reject the rule for environmental torts as well? Or are courts more likely to impose more liberal successor liability rules in

environmental law cases than product liability cases? The New Jersey Spill Act, like the Comprehensive Environmental Response, Compensation, and Liability Act, imposes a tax on select industries to create a state fund for cleaning up wastes if no "responsible" parties can be charged. Does the existence of this fund affect the court's efforts to attach liability to successors?

4. Do the avoidance strategies mentioned in the Yarmin article above on product liability claims work for environmental claims as well?

CERCLA

In 1980 Congress enacted the Comprehensive Environmental Response, Compensation, and Liability Act, 42 U.S.C.A. §§ 9601–9675, to provide for the cleanup of hazardous substances that have been released into the environment. CERCLA imposes liability for cleanup costs on those responsible for generating, transporting, or disposing of such hazardous substances. Suit may be brought by the Environmental Protection Agency or a private party responsible under CERCLA for cleaning up waste left by previous owners. CERCLA also established a "superfund" for cleanup of hazardous substances when responsible parties cannot be found or are unable to finance cleanup operations. The fund is financed by general tax revenues, excise taxes on the petrochemical industry, and the proceeds of successful litigation against responsible parties.

Since CERCLA liability can be unpredictably large, parties to major acquisitions are often troubled by successor liability questions on potential CERCLA claims. The successor liability issue has two parts. First, the act provides a defense to successor *owners* of polluted land if the pollution was caused by an unrelated third party. Is the seller of assets in an asset acquisition an unrelated third party? See 42 U.S.C.A. §§ 9601(35)(A), 9607(b)(3) below. Second, if the purchaser of another firm's business does not buy the contaminated land but continues the predecessor's business, as in the *PSC Resources* case above, do common-law theories of successor liability apply? Moreover, assume the purchase of another firm's business does buy the contaminated land but is protected by the innocent landowner defense; do common-law theories of successor liability apply if the purchaser continues the seller's business (without adding any more pollutants to the already contaminated area)?

§ 9607. Liability

(a) Covered persons; scope; recoverable costs and damages; interest rate; "comparable maturity" date. Notwithstanding any other provision or rule of law, and subject only to the defenses set forth in subsection (b) of this section—

(1) the owner and operator of a vessel or a facility,

(2) any person who at the time of disposal of any hazardous substance owned or operated any facility at which such hazardous substances were disposed of, * * * shall be liable for—

(A) all costs of removal or remedial action incurred by the United States Government or a State or an Indian tribe not inconsistent with the national contingency plan;

(B) any other necessary costs of response incurred by any other person consistent with the national contingency plan;

(C) damages for injury to, destruction of, or loss of natural resources, including the reasonable costs of assessing such injury, destruction, or loss resulting from such a release; and

(D) the costs of any health assessment or health effects study carried out under section 104(i) [42 USCS § 9604(i)].

The amounts recoverable in an action under this section shall include interest on the amounts recoverable under subparagraphs (A) through (D).

* * *

(b) Defenses. There shall be no liability under subsection (a) of this section for a person otherwise liable who can establish by a preponderance of the evidence that the release or threat of release of a hazardous substance and the damages resulting therefrom were caused solely by—

* * *

(3) an act or omission of a third party other than an employee or agent of the defendant, or than one whose act or omission occurs in connection with a contractual relationship, existing directly or indirectly, with the defendant (except where the sole contractual arrangement arises from a published tariff and acceptance for carriage by a common carrier by rail), if the defendant establishes by a preponderance of the evidence that (a) he exercised due care with respect to the hazardous substance concerned, taking into consideration the characteristics of such hazardous substance, in light of all relevant facts and circumstances, and (b) he took precautions against foreseeable acts or omissions of any such third party and the consequences that could foreseeably result from such acts or omissions.

* * *

(35)(A) The term "contractual relationship", for the purpose of section 107(b)(3) [42 USCS § 9607(b)(3)], includes, but is not limited to, land contracts, deeds or other instruments transferring title or possession, unless the real property on which the facility concerned is located was acquired by the defendant after the disposal or placement of the hazardous substance on, in, or at the facility, and one or more of the circumstances described in clause (i), (ii), or (iii) is also established by the defendant by a preponderance of the evidence:

> (i) At the time the defendant acquired the facility the defendant did not know and had no reason to know that any hazardous substance which is the subject of the release or threatened release was disposed of on, in, or at the facility.

* * *

In addition to establishing the foregoing, the defendant must establish that he has satisfied the requirements of section 107(b)(3)(a) and (b) [42 USCS § 9607(b)(3)(a) and (b)].

* * *

The EPA takes a very aggressive position on the issue, arguing that the more liberal rules of successor liability found in California—the product line theory—ought to apply. The only major case to date on the matter, *Smith Land & Improvement Corp. v. Celotex Corp.*, is excerpted below. The comment by two former EPA officials, Burak and Brown, that follows the case demonstrates that the EPA approach is not without critics. The effect on acquisition negotiations of the aggressive enforcement of environmental claims against successors is devastating. When unknown or uncertain environmental liabilities appear in an acquisition negotiation, they kill some deals outright, sharply raise the price tags of others, and cause others to crash later on. Negotiation over environmental issues in the later 1980s became the most time-consuming issue in many negotiations. See "Poison Pills in the Takeover Game, Hidden Waste Dumps Haunt Buyer and Seller," Wall St.J., p. 1, col. 5 (April 2, 1990).

SMITH LAND & IMPROVEMENT CORP. v. CELOTEX CORP.

United States Court of Appeals, Third Circuit, 1988.
851 F.2d 86, cert. denied 488 U.S. 1029, 109 S.Ct. 837, 102 L.Ed.2d 969 (1989).

* * *

WEIS, CIRCUIT JUDGE.

This is a suit by a purchaser of land seeking contribution toward expenses incurred in the clean-up of a hazardous waste site. * * *

Plaintiff owns a tract of land in Plymouth Township, Pennsylvania, on which is deposited a large pile of manufacturing waste containing asbestos. In July 1984, the Environmental Protection Agency informed plaintiff that unless it took steps to alleviate the asbestos hazard the federal government would perform the work and then pursue reimbursement. Plaintiff proceeded to correct the condition to EPA's satisfaction, allegedly incurring costs of $218,945.44. * * * Plaintiff asserts that defendants are corporate successors to the Philip Carey Company (Carey), which had created the large waste pile in the course of manufacturing asbestos products. Carey sold the land to the plaintiff's predecessor in 1963. As defendants point out, they never owned or operated the facility. We assume at this juncture—but absent findings do not determine—that Carey previously owned the land and produced the asbestos scrap pile which precipitated the EPA action. Through a series of transactions beginning in 1967, the interest of Carey apparently settled in the hands of defendants Celotex and Rapid-American. The parties do not dispute these facts in the current procedural posture of the case; however, plaintiff argues that defendants are responsible for Carey's derelictions on a theory of corporate successor liability.

* * *

The record here indicates that nothing other than statutory mergers or consolidations occurred; therefore, the sale of assets or the de facto merger doctrines [2] do not appear pertinent.

It is not surprising that, as a hastily conceived and briefly debated piece of legislation, CERCLA failed to address many important issues, including corporate successor liability. The meager legislative history available indicates that Congress expected the courts to develop a federal common law to supplement the statute.

* * *

The concerns that have led to a corporation's common law liability of a corporation for the torts of its predecessor are equally applicable to the assessment of responsibility for clean-up costs under CERCLA. The Act views response liability as a remedial, rather than a punitive, measure whose primary aim is to correct the hazardous condition. Just as there is liability for ordinary torts or contractual claims, the obligation to take necessary steps to protect the public should be imposed on a successor corporation.

The costs associated with clean-up must be absorbed somewhere. Congress has emphasized funding by responsible parties, but if they cannot be ascertained or cannot pay the sums necessary, federal monies may be used.

Expenses can be borne by two sources: the entities which had a specific role in the production or continuation of the hazardous condition, or the taxpayers through federal funds. CERCLA leaves no doubt that Congress intended the burden to fall on the latter only when the responsible parties lacked the wherewithal to meet their obligations.

Congressional intent supports the conclusion that, when choosing between the taxpayers or a successor corporation, the successor should

---

2. * * * The EPA in a 1984 memorandum of its counsel has taken the position that a successor corporation is liable for the acts of its predecessor under a "continuity of business operation approach." EPA Memorandum, "Liability of Corporate Shareholders and Successor Corporations for Abandoned Sites under CERCLA," Courtney M. Price, Assistant Admin. for Enforcement and Compliance Monitoring (June 13, 1984).

bear the cost. Benefits from use of the pollutant as well as savings resulting from the failure to use non-hazardous disposal methods inured to the original corporation, its successors, and their respective stockholders and accrued only indirectly, if at all, to the general public. We believe it in line with the thrust of the legislation to permit—if not require—successor liability under traditional concepts.

* * *

As recounted above, because the district court in this case held that the caveat emptor doctrine precluded the plaintiff's recovery, it had no occasion to consider the question of successor liability. Consequently, the record contains no factual findings or rulings on the legal effect of the various statutes which might affect the liability passed on through merger or consolidation.

In resolving the successor liability issues here, the district court must consider national uniformity; otherwise, CERCLA aims may be evaded easily by a responsible party's choice to arrange a merger or consolidation under the laws of particular states which unduly restrict successor liability. * * * The general doctrine of successor liability in operation in most states should guide the court's decision rather than the excessively narrow statutes which might apply in only a few states.

To summarize, our study of CERCLA persuades us that Congress intended to impose successor liability on corporations which either have merged with or have consolidated with a corporation that is a responsible party as defined in the Act. We will remand to the district court for further proceedings to fully explore that issue in light of the circumstances.

* * *

BURAK & BROWN, EPA'S POLICY ON CORPORATE SUCCESSOR LIABILITY UNDER SUPERFUND

Chem. & Rad.Waste Litigation Rptr. 649, 651–52 (1981).

Part II[5] of EPA's July, 1984, Enforcement Policy, dealing with corporate successor liability, is of great concern to any company that has acquired industrial property or intends to do so in the future. On its face, the Policy purports to add another layer of liability to Superfund, *i.e.*, derivative liability for the "successors" of hazardous waste generators and transporters, as well as the successors of site owners and operators. EPA's extremely thin legal justification in the Policy cites a minority state common law rule known as the "product line exception," as well as several federal statutory cases in the labor and civil rights areas. EPA does not explain whether it intends to abide by the limitations or qualifications articulated in both the state "product

---

5. Part I of the Policy focuses on the liability of corporate shareholders and is not discussed in this article.

line" and federal statutory cases, and does not articulate a justification for applying either set of cases to Superfund. * * *

Hypothetical (1): A purchases the assets of B, including a real estate parcel (site Z) formerly used for manufacturing. Two years later, EPA lists site Z on the NPL and sends a notice letter to A.

In this hypothetical, the issue of successor liability is moot because A is automatically liable as a current owner under Superfund Section 107(a).

Hypothetical (2): A purchases the assets of B, excluding the above site Z, which is kept as the only remaining corporate asset for a year, at which time it is sold to X. B subsequently dissolves. When EPA lists site Z on the NPL, X declares bankruptcy. EPA then sends a notice letter to A, alleging that A is the corporate successor of B.

In hypothetical (2), successor liability is clearly inappropriate. The fact that A has taken over much of the general business formerly operated by B does not establish the requisite "continuity" because A never owned or derived any benefit from site Z. Moreover, since A does not presently own site Z, the policy factors relating to "spreading the risk" are of questionable relevance. Another factor militating against liability is that A did not really deprive the government of a remedy by acquiring B's assets, since B retained a substantial asset and dissolved a year later after another transaction.

Hypotheticals (1) and (2) represent a large percentage of conceivable owner liability situations. As illustrated above, successor liability will be either inappropriate or moot altogether in these situations. * * *

* * *

Hypothetical (4): A purchases the assets of B, including facility X, which sent waste to site Z in 1970. A operates facility X in a similar fashion as B. B dissolves. EPA lists site Z on the NPL and sends a notice letter to the address of facility X. A responds to EPA that they had nothing to do with site Z. EPA responds that A is liable as B's successor.

The facts in hypothetical (4) potentially satisfy the "continuity of business" criterion of both the product line approach and the federal cases. * * *

In terms of policy and "equitable" factors, hypothetical (4) would arguably fit within the product line theory because A presently enjoys the profits from the operation of facility X and is a logical candidate, under products liability "deep pocket" thinking, to assist in "spreading the risk." Under the federal statutory cases, however, the desirability of forcing the successor to remedy or compensate for injuries caused by the action of a predecessor is not assumed—an equitable balance must be achieved between the goals of the statute and the burden on the successor. EPA conveniently overlooks this central theme in *Golden*

State by assuming that federal courts will use a product line-type theory.

A critical factor in *Golden State, Marlene Industries, supra,* and *Service Envelope, supra,* is notice of the pending claim at the time of acquisition. Without such notice, the equitable balance cannot be achieved. In Superfund terms, this means that the generator successor in hypothetical (4) should not be deemed liable unless it knew at the time of acquisition that there was a liability risk from waste previously shipped off site.

The most equitable approach would be to consider receipt of a notice letter as the operative event for determining notice. As a practical matter, a successor is unlikely to have had notice unless the predecessor had already received a notice letter at the time of acquisition and the predecessor disclosed this to the successor. Therefore, there would be no successor liability for the majority of generator cases.
* * *

Aside from notice, *Golden State* requires inquiry as to whether successor liability is consistent with the goals of the statute in question. Superfund provides for broad liability on its face, and courts have recently interpreted generator liability in a liberal fashion. Nevertheless, there is nothing in the legislative history of Superfund to support the conclusion that Congress intended for EPA to track down the successors of off-site, non-negligent hazardous waste generators and to force them to pay for Superfund cleanup.

Indeed, Congress created a multibillion dollar revolving fund fed by tax revenues, specifically so that EPA would never be in the position of being "deprived of a remedy," like the plaintiff in *Ray v. Alad.* Thus, the product liability concept of "someone must pay" cannot be blindly applied to Superfund. * * *

This is not to say that the government will be barred from recovery or remediation in most cases, it only means that in some cases the absence of a financially viable party will have to be accepted and the Trust Fund created under CERCLA for such situations will have to be used. Just as the initial reluctance of the Reagan administration to spend funds and the desire to "conserve the Fund" received criticism in Congress, this latest attempt to avoid funding limitations is destined to receive criticism in the courts. Creative interpretations of the law are understood, but when the stretch proposed by the successor corporate liability policy is examined, it will be revealed to go beyond creativity into fantasy.

In most instances, successor liability for a site owner would be inappropriate because the requisite continuity and the policy justification for spreading the risk are absent if the site is not presently owned. Where the site is presently owned, the issue of successor liability is moot. Therefore, successor liability should only be applied to successors of owners where the traditional de facto merger/mere continuation criteria dictate.

Where generators are concerned, application of the product line theory requires both a holding out as being the predecessor and the dissolution of the predecessor, in addition to continuity of operations. Federal statutory case law clearly establishes that in addition to continuity, prior notice is essential to holding a corporate successor liable under an "equitable balance" approach. Thus, no generator should have derivative liability unless they had notice at the time of acquisition that the entity they were acquiring was a potentially responsible party. Absent meaningful notice, the equitable balance required by federal cases should tip in favor of the corporate successor.

Another gap in the Policy that must be filled is the lack of any meaningful justification for broad successor liability based on the language of Superfund or its legislative history. Federal statutory cases require this justification as a factor in the "equitable balance" approach, and in any event, the regulated community is entitled to be informed of the perceived basis for such a far-reaching enforcement policy. Convenience of the government, ease of prosecution, or availability of more funds for remediation are all practical reasons for such an approach, but they do not supply the legal rationale necessary to impose such a far-reaching interpretation.

Problem

Officials of Buyer, Inc., are assessing whether to acquire Seller, Inc., a family-held business from which the founding three brothers, now all in their sixties, want to retire. Apparently, none of the sons or daughters of the brothers are interested in continuing the business. Seller, Inc., has manufactured high-quality, handcrafted shotguns for over forty years. The manufacturing process uses petrochemicals and other toxic materials. Seller disposes of its wastes in accordance with modern pollution statutes, but in earlier years the firm deposited some of these materials in deep wells, long since covered over and forgotten. Moreover, the firm has had a stormy relationship with its 150 employees, who are unionized and have struck the factory on at least three occasions en route to obtaining the current collective bargaining agreement. Furthermore, by threatening title XII litigation the union has succeeded in forcing the firm to agree to retain a number of workers who now are over seventy years old. The employees want to resist the sale, because Buyer, Inc., if it purchases Seller, Inc., will continue to make shotguns but with an automated process requiring fewer employees. Finally, a court in California has recently ruled, in a case against another shotgun manufacturer, that the manufacturer is strictly liable for injuries generated by dropped loaded shotguns because the gun manufacturer failed to design a gun that would not fire accidently if dropped. Trial lawyers all over the country have formed an "educational" association to discuss the filing of new suits based on the California case. Buyer will agree to buy the firm if it does not have to absorb Seller's environmental liabilities, product liability claims, and labor contract. Can you structure the sale so that the transaction can close?

SECTION 2. PARENT LIABILITY FOR CLAIMS AGAINST A SUBSIDIARY

Do cases such as *Kayser–Roth* affect either of the following two basic strategies? First, using a stock acquisition or a triangular merger, the buying firm attempts to isolate its assets from the potential liabilities of the target. Does your answer depend on whether the liabilities are from preacquisition or postacquisition acts of the target? Second, a buying firm in a stock acquisition attempts to protect a target's healthy businesses from its sick businesses by separating the assets of the target into two separate corporations, one containing a target business subject to large potential claims and the other containing all other healthy target businesses. The buying firm then sells the risky subsidiary to a third party and merges into the nonrisky subsidiaries. Does your answer depend on whether the target had, long before the acquisition, separated its sick from its healthy businesses using corporate subsidiaries?

UNITED STATES v. KAYSER–ROTH CORP.

United States Court of Appeals, First Circuit, 1990.
910 F.2d 24.

BOWNES, SENIOR CIRCUIT JUDGE.

Kayser–Roth Corporation (Kayser) appeals from a decision by the district court of Rhode Island holding it liable as both an "owner" and "operator" for the cleanup costs incurred by the Environmental Protection Agency in response to a spill of trichloroethylene (TCE) at the Stamina Mills textile plant (the site). Stamina Mills, Inc. (Stamina), the nominal owner of the site, was a wholly owned subsidiary of Kayser prior to Stamina's dissolution in 1977. The government has sought to recover its cleanup costs from Kayser under the Comprehensive Environmental Response, Compensation, and Liability Act, 42 U.S.C. § 9601 et seq. (CERCLA), based on direct liability (Kayser as operator of the site) and indirect liability (Kayser as owner by "piercing the corporate veil"). Kayser argues that the parent company of a dissolved subsidiary cannot, as a matter of law, be held liable on either ground. We disagree, and affirm on the basis that Kayser is liable as an operator.

CERCLA was enacted in response to the increasing concern about the vast problems of the disposal of and contamination from hazardous waste throughout the country. It is a remedial statute designed to protect and preserve public health and the environment. Because CERCLA is a remedial statute, we ... construe its provisions liberally to avoid frustration of the beneficial legislative purpose. With this in mind, we join the Second Circuit in proclaiming that "we will not interpret section 9607(a) in any way that apparently frustrates the statute's goals." Dedham Water Co. v. Cumberland Farms Dairy, Inc.,

805 F.2d 1074, 1081 (1st Cir.1986) (quoting New York v. Shore Realty, 759 F.2d 1032, 1045 (2d Cir.1985)) (Dedham I).

The Act empowers the government to use money from the "superfund" to clean up hazardous waste sites. 42 U.S.C. § 9604(a). Any "person" who is the "owner" or "operator" of a facility at the time of the disposal of a hazardous substance shall be liable for, among other things, all of the costs of removal or other remedial action incurred by the United States. 42 U.S.C. § 9607(a)(2). Liability for the cost incurred is strict and joint and several.

I.

We begin our discussion with the issue of whether a parent corporation may be held directly liable as an operator. "Operator" is defined circularly in the statute as any person [5] operating a facility. 42 U.S.C. § 9601(20)(A)(ii). Congress, by including a liability category in addition to owner ("operators") connected by the conjunction "or," implied that a person who is an operator of a facility is not protected from liability by the legal structure of ownership. Given this grammatical construction and the broad definition of "person," corporate status, while relevant to determine ownership, cannot shield a person from operator liability. In addition, the legislative history provides no indication that Congress intended "all persons" who are "operators" to exclude parent corporations. Thus, our analysis of the statute and its legislative purpose and history reveals no reason why a parent corporation cannot be held liable as an operator under CERCLA.

Our decision is supported by the interpretation given "operator" by other courts. See, e.g., United States v. Northeastern Pharmaceutical, 810 F.2d 726, 743–44 (8th Cir.1986), cert. denied, 484 U.S. 848, 108 S.Ct. 146, 98 L.Ed.2d 102 (1987) (individual liability under § 9607(a)(3)); Idaho v. Bunker Hill Co., 635 F.Supp. 665 (D.Idaho 1986) (parent corporation liable as operator). For example, the majority shareholder of a corporation has been held individually liable as an operator under CERCLA. Shore, 759 F.2d at 1052. In addition, a corporation that was an owner through holding a security interest and became active in the management of the corporation has been held liable. United States v. Fleet Factors Corp., 901 F.2d 1550, 1557 (11th Cir.1990).

We are unpersuaded by the case upon which Kayser relies most heavily to support its position. Joslyn Mfg. Co. v. T.L. James & Co., 893 F.2d 80 (5th Cir.1990). Although there is some broad language in Joslyn that might support Kayser's position, the opinion is concerned primarily with owner rather than operator liability. The Joslyn court framed its issue as whether to "impose direct liability on parent corporations for the violations of their wholly owned subsidiaries." Joslyn, 893 F.2d at 81. On the theory of the case presently under consideration, Kayser is being held liable for its activities as an opera-

---

5. The statute defines "person" extremely broadly and certainly includes a parent corporation. 42 U.S.C. § 9601(21). Kayser does not seriously contest that it is a person within the meaning of the statute.

tor, not the activities of a subsidiary. Our reading of the Joslyn case is bolstered by a fifth circuit district court's narrow interpretation of the Joslyn case. Riverside Market Devel. Corp. v. International Building Products, 1990 WL 72249, 1990 U.S.Dist. LEXIS 6375 (E.D.La.1990) (distinguishing Joslyn and following Shore Realty and Northeastern Pharmaceutical in holding individual liable as operator and noting that in Joslyn there was no participation by parent in activities of subsidiary).

In sum, we believe that a fair reading of CERCLA allows a parent corporation to be held liable as an operator of a subsidiary corporation.

II.

We now examine whether the district court correctly held that Kayser was an operator. Without deciding the exact standard necessary for a parent to be an operator, we note that it is obviously not the usual case that the parent of a wholly owned subsidiary is an operator of the subsidiary. To be an operator requires more than merely complete ownership and the concomitant general authority or ability to control that comes with ownership. At a minimum it requires active involvement in the activities of the subsidiary.

The district court's excellent opinion found that "Kayser–Roth ... exerted practical total influence and control over Stamina Mills' operations." United States v. Kayser–Roth Corp., 724 F.Supp. 15, 18 (D.R.I. 1989). The court summarized the evidence as follows:

Kayser–Roth exercised pervasive control over Stamina Mills through, among other things: 1) its total monetary control including collection of accounts payable; 2) its restriction on Stamina Mills' financial budget; 3) its directive that subsidiary-governmental contact, including environmental matters, be funneled directly through Kayser–Roth; 4) its requirement that Stamina Mills' leasing, buying or selling of real estate first be approved by Kayser–Roth; 5) its policy that Kayser–Roth approve any capital transfer or expenditures greater than $5000; and finally, its placement of Kayser–Roth personnel in almost all Stamina Mills' director and officer positions, as a means of totally ensuring that Kayser–Roth corporate policy was exactly implemented and precisely carried out.

Id. at 22. Kayser's control included environmental matters including the approval of the installation of the cleaning system that used the TCE.[8] The district court found Kayser had the power to control the release or threat of release of TCE, had the power to direct the mechanisms causing the release, and had the ultimate ability to prevent and abate damage. Kayser–Roth knew that Stamina Mills employed a scouring system that used TCE; indeed [it] approved the

---

8. Although indicia of ability to control decisions about hazardous waste are indicative of the type of control necessary to hold a parent corporation liable as an operator, we do not think the presence of such indicia is essential, assuming there are other indicia of the pervasive control necessary to prove operator status.

installation of that system . . . [and] was able to direct Stamina Mills on how the TCE should have been handled.

Id. Such control is more than sufficient to be liable as an operator under CERCLA.

Kayser argues vehemently that it was blameless for the spill, which was caused by a third party and was not brought to Kayser's attention until years later. Kayser misunderstands CERCLA. Under this strict liability statute, all that it is necessary to prove is that Kayser was an operator at the time of the spill. Although CERCLA includes a limited affirmative defense that the spill was caused by a third party, that defense does not help Kayser because it only applies if the third party was not in a contractual relationship with the operator, which was not the case here. 42 U.S.C. § 9607(b)(3).

Based on the record, we find that the district court did not err in finding that Kayser was an operator and in holding it liable for the cost of the cleanup.[11]

The First Circuit did not reach the district court's alternative holding that Kayser–Roth Corporation was liable as an owner.

U.S. v. KAYSER–ROTH CORP.
United States District Court, District of Rhode Island, 1989.
724 F.Supp. 15.

FRANCIS J. BOYLE, CHIEF JUDGE.

* * *

CERCLA liability based upon piercing the corporate veil is a species of owner, rather than operator, liability. While an owner may be, in most cases, an operator, the converse is not necessarily true. Imputing CERCLA liability upon a parent corporation by piercing the corporate veil is, in essence, concluding that the parent is an owner for CERCLA's purposes. * * * Upon analysis of the factors relevant to piercing Stamina Mills' veil, and mindful of the liberal construction CERCLA must be afforded so as not to frustrate probable legislative intent, the Court concludes that Kayser–Roth is an owner for CERCLA's purposes.

An analysis of piercing Stamina Mills' veil to hold Kayser–Roth liable begins with the general proposition that a corporate entity may be disregarded in the interest of public convenience, fairness and equity. As the First Circuit has stated:

> . . . [F]ederal courts will look closely at the purpose of the federal statute to determine whether the statute places importance on the

---

11. Because we decide that the district court was not clearly erroneous in finding that Kayser was an operator, we do not need to consider the various arguments advanced regarding Kayser's liability as an owner.

corporate form ... an inquiry that usually gives less respect to the corporate form that does the strict common law alter ego doctrine....

Alman v. Danin, 801 F.2d 1, 3 (1st Cir.1986) (quoting *Town of Brookline v. Gorsuch,* 667 F.2d 215, 221 (1st Cir.1981)).

CERCLA's language attempts to address nationwide public health and environmental problems. In fashioning a remedial framework by which some of these problems could be resolved, Congress had two basic purposes in mind:

First, Congress intended that the federal government be immediately given the tools necessary for a prompt and effective response to the problems of national magnitude resulting from hazardous waste disposal. Second, Congress intended that those responsible for problems caused by the disposal of chemical poisons bear the costs and responsibility for remedying the harmful conditions they created.

Dedham Water Co. v. Cumberland Farms Dairy, Inc., 805 F.2d 1074, 1081 (1st Cir.1986) (quoting *United States v. Reilly Tar & Chemical Corp.,* 546 F.Supp. 1100 (D.Minn.1982)). CERCLA's provisions should thus be viewed expansively, so as not to frustrate these "beneficial legislative purposes."[6] *Id.; Shore Realty,* 759 F.2d at 1045. It is against this backdrop that it is concluded that CERCLA places no special importance upon the corporate structure. * * *

Kayser–Roth has exhibited overwhelming pervasive control over Stamina Mills. Many of the same factors used in holding Kayser–Roth liable as an operator are relevant. * * * Accordingly, Stamina Mills' veil should be pierced to hold Kayser–Roth liable, not only because public convenience, fairness, and equity dictate such a result, but also due to the all encompassing control which Kayser–Roth had over Stamina Mills as, in fact and deed, an owner. Any other result would provide too much solace to deliberate polluters, who would use this device as an escape.

* * *

Note

Restructurings After an LBO

In late 1987 Kohlberg, Kravis, Roberts and Company, through Hillsborough Holdings Corporation, arranged a $2.4 billion leveraged buyout of Jim Walter Corporation on the assumption that the asbestos product claims against a Jim Walter subsidiary, Celotex Corporation, that had once made asbestos products could be confined to the subsidiary. In the LBO, KK & R split Jim Walter into two separate entities. One consisted solely of Celotex and its subsidiaries, which face massive potential tort liabilities arising out of asbestos claims in an aggregate amount far exceeding their net worth. The other entity consisted of all Jim Walter's other subsidiaries, which

---

6. The *Dedham Water* court further stated that "'[W]e will not interpret section 9607(a) in any way that apparently frustrates the statute's goals, in the absence of a specific congressional intent otherwise.'" *Dedham Water,* 805 F.2d at 1081 (quoting *New York v. Shore Realty,* 759 F.2d 1032, 1045 (2d Cir.1985)).

were profitable and financially sound. The Celotex entity was sold three months after the buyout. Hillsborough then merged with the second entity and proceeded to sell the remaining Jim Walter assets, which it believed were free of the Celotex liabilities.

A suit against Hillsborough brought by eighty thousand asbestos victims so unsettled bond investors and potential asset buyers that Hillsborough was forced to seek bankruptcy court protection. See Wall St. J., p. 1, col. 5 (April 2, 1990). The plaintiffs seek to have the corporate veil between Jim Walter and its subsidiary, Celotex, removed, leaving the former company and its successors liable for any judgment against Celotex. One of the several theories in the case is that the LBO was, in effect, a fraudulent conveyance carried out to shield Jim Walter's assets from the asbestos-related claims. Other theories include allegations that Celotex operated as a mere tool of Jim Walter and was therefore its alter ego. The plaintiffs rely on language in an earlier federal district court decision, Nixon v. Celotex, 693 F.Supp. 547 (W.D.Mich.1988), in which the judge held that because of Jim Walter's active participation in the affairs of Celotex, the court had personal jurisdiction over Jim Walter under Michigan law, even though the corporation would otherwise not be subject to the court's jurisdiction.

LBOs are particularly vulnerable to such claims. In any LBO of a company such as Jim Walter, with subsidiaries having significant tort exposure from asbestos, tobacco, chemicals, or other potentially hazardous substances, tort creditors will sue to block or recharacterize the transaction based on the belief that the additional debt in the deal will, if unopposed, hurt the value of their claims. Moreover, the surviving companies in the buyouts have such a small equity cushion that, as happened in the Jim Walter case, even the threat of a significant judgment assessed against the parent can throw the buyout group's financing plans into a tailspin.

SCHMOLL v. ACANDS, INC.
United States District Court, District of Oregon, 1988.
703 F.Supp. 868.

* * *

PANNER, CHIEF JUDGE.

Plaintiff Raymond Schmoll brings this products liability action against Raymark Industries Inc. and Raytech Corporation (Raytech). The issue is whether Raytech is liable as a successor for Raymark Industries' production, sale and distribution of products containing asbestos. I find that Raytech is a successor in liability to Raymark Industries.

* * *

Raymark Industries manufactured and distributed energy absorption and transmission products, including asbestos and asbestos-containing products. Since the early 1970's, Raymark Industries [1] has

---

1. Until 1982 Raymark Industries was called Raybestos–Manhattan, Inc. The name was changed as part of the corporate reorganization in which Raymark Corpora-

been named in an ever-increasing number of asbestos related personal injury lawsuits. By June 26, 1988, Raymark Industries had been named as a defendant in more than 68,000 cases. Approximately 1,000 new cases are filed each month.

Raymark Industries has suffered severe financial declines as a result of the asbestos litigation. In 1981, Raymark Corporation [2] had a net worth of $112.4 million. By 1985, the reported net worth of the company had dropped to $3.6 million. Between 1982 and 1988, Raymark Corporation reorganized its corporate structure in response to this financial decline. Raymark told its shareholders that the corporate restructuring would:

> permit the Company to gain access to sources of capital and borrowed funds and thereby finance the acquisition and operation of new businesses unrelated to Raymark Corporation in a corporate structure that should not subject the holding company or such acquired businesses to asbestos-related liabilities of Raymark Corporation.

The corporate restructuring involved a complex series of transactions that transformed Raybestos–Manhattan into Raymark Industries and Raytech. The steps of this restructuring are diagrammed and described below.

```
            RAYBESTOS–MANHATTAN (RAYBESTOS)

                  RAYMARK CORPORATION

              RAYMARK INDUSTRIES (RAYBESTOS)
    ┌─────────────┬──────────┬──────────┬──────────────┐
WET CLUTCH &  DRY CLUTCH &  RIPG   R/M FORMED    DAIKIN–R/M
  BRAKE         BRAKE                PRODUCTS
```

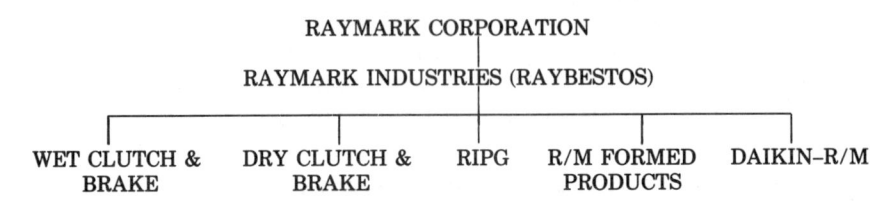

STEP 1: Raybestos–Manhattan (Raybestos), originally organized as a New Jersey corporation in 1929, was reorganized as a Connecticut corporation in 1976. In 1982, Raybestos–Manhattan changed its name to Raymark Industries and created Raymark Corporation as a holding company for Raymark Industries. Raymark Corporation's only asset was the stock of Raymark Industries. In 1985, Raymark Industries' assets included two operating divisions, Wet Clutch & Brake (WC & B) and Dry Clutch & Brake (DC & B); the stock of a German subsidiary, Raybestos Industrie—Produkte G.m.b.H. (RIPG); the stock of a shell corporation, R/M Formed Products; and a 50% interest in a foreign joint venture, Daiken—R/M.

tion became the parent and sole shareholder of Raymark Industries.

2. The corporate structure and reorganization will be discussed in detail at a later point. However, for clarification, Raymark Corporation was a holding company and operated through its subsidiary, Raymark Industries.

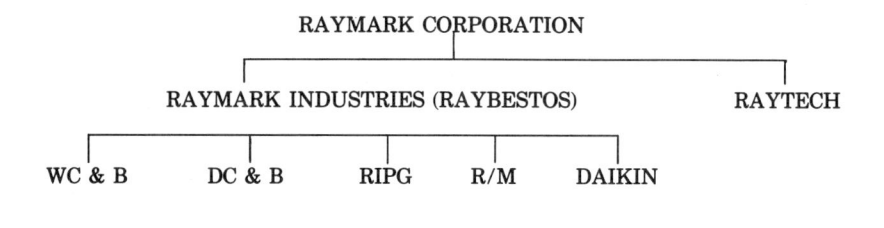

```
                    RAYMARK CORPORATION
         ┌─────────────────┴─────────────────┐
    RAYMARK INDUSTRIES (RAYBESTOS)         RAYTECH
  ┌──────┬──────┼──────┬──────┐
WC & B  DC & B  RIPG   R/M   DAIKIN
```

STEP 2: In June 1986, Raymark Corporation created Raytech as a wholly owned subsidiary.

```
                    RAYMARK CORPORATION
         ┌─────────────────┴─────────────────┐
    RAYMARK INDUSTRIES (RAYBESTOS)         RAYTECH
                                              │
                                           RAYSUB
  ┌──────┬──────┼──────┬──────┐
WC & B  DC & B  RIPG   R/M   DAIKIN
```

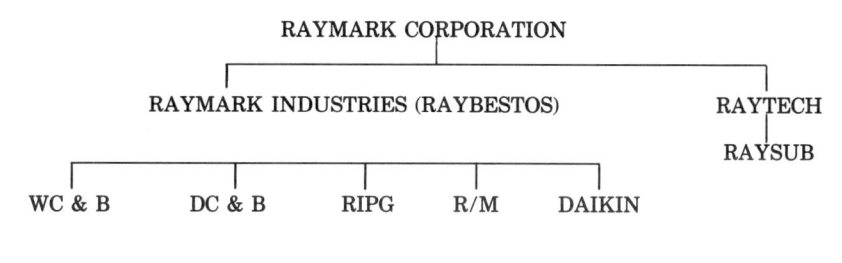

STEP 3: Raytech then created Raysub as a wholly-owned subsidiary. Raytech and Raysub were created solely to carry out the merger described in the next step.

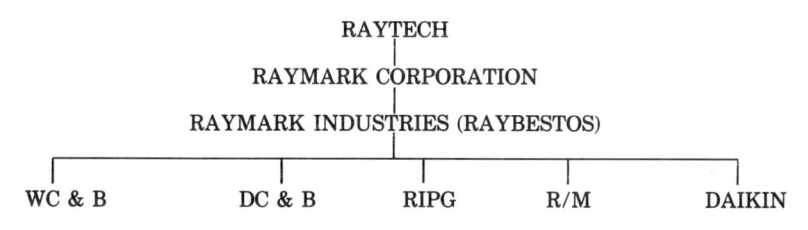

```
                    RAYTECH
                       │
              RAYMARK CORPORATION
                       │
         RAYMARK INDUSTRIES (RAYBESTOS)
  ┌──────────┬──────────┼──────────┬──────────┐
WC & B    DC & B      RIPG        R/M       DAIKIN
```

STEP 4: In October 1986, Raymark Corporation merged into Raysub, with Raymark Corporation surviving as a wholly-owned subsidiary of Raytech. In this merger, each outstanding share of Raymark common stock was converted into one share of Raytech stock. Raytech, designated the "holding company," was entirely owned by the former shareholders of Raymark Corporation. As a result of this merger, Raytech, the parent of Raysub, became the parent of Raymark Corporation. Raytech then owned 100 percent of the stock of Raymark Corporation, which owned 100 percent of the stock of Raymark Industries.

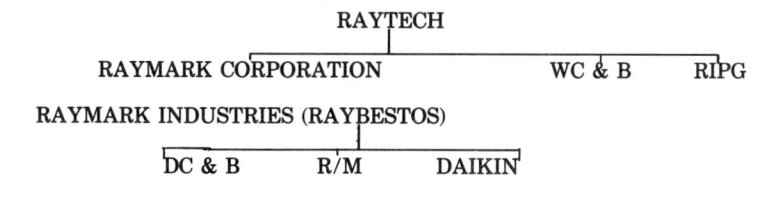

```
                         RAYTECH
         ┌──────────────────┼──────────┬──────┐
   RAYMARK CORPORATION              WC & B   RIPG
            │
 RAYMARK INDUSTRIES (RAYBESTOS)
     ┌──────┼──────┐
   DC & B  R/M   DAIKIN
```

STEP 5: In 1987, Raytech purchased Raymark Industries' two most profitable assets, the Wet Clutch and Brake Division and RIPG stock. Raytech purchased the Wet Clutch and Brake Division for $76.9 million. Payment consisted of approximately $15 million in cash, $10 million worth of Raytech stock at closing with another $6 million in stock to be transferred later,[3] and $46 million in unsecured notes. The Wet Clutch and Brake Division, the largest of Raymark Industries' business operations, had significant profit potential.[4] Furthermore, the asbestos claims against Raymark Industries did not arise from the Wet Clutch and Brake Division.[5]

Raytech also purchased the RIPG stock owned by Raymark Industries for $8.2 million. RIPG does not manufacture or sell its asbestos products in the United States and has never been named in asbestos-related litigation. Terms of the sale included a cash payment of $3.9 million, with the balance financed by an unsecured note.

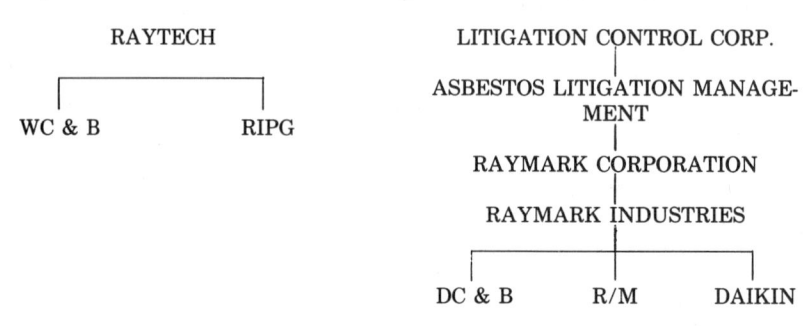

```
         RAYTECH                    LITIGATION CONTROL CORP.
      ┌─────┴─────┐                            │
                                   ASBESTOS LITIGATION MANAGE-
    WC & B       RIPG                        MENT
                                              │
                                    RAYMARK CORPORATION
                                              │
                                    RAYMARK INDUSTRIES
                                     ┌────────┼────────┐
                                   DC & B    R/M     DAIKIN
```

STEP 6: In 1988, Raytech sold Raymark Corporation, and thus Raymark Industries, to Asbestos Litigation Management (ALM) for $1 million. ALM paid $50,000 in cash and a $950,000 unsecured promissory note for all Raymark Corporation's assets and liabilities.

ALM is a wholly owned subsidiary of Litigation Control Corporation (LCC), whose business includes claims processing, document control and retention, and other services to companies involved in complex litigation. ALM serves only companies defending asbestos litigation. ALM now owns the stock of Raymark Corporation, whose only asset is Raymark Industries' stock.

---

3. Though stock transferred to Raymark had an apparent market value of $10 million, it is unlikely that Raymark could have sold those shares for anything approaching that value. Any attempt by Raymark to market large blocks of these shares would have had a devastating effect on the price of Raytech shares. Dr. Albert Fitzpatrick, plaintiff's business expert, stated that Raymark probably would have had to accept a 90% discount in order to sell these shares as a block.

4. Of the portfolio of businesses owned by Raymark Industries, the Wet Clutch and Brake division was the best current performer in 1986.

5. The Wet Clutch division purchased asbestos paper as a component of products but the asbestos paper operated in an oil-immersed environment.

As a result of this involved corporate restructuring, Raytech now owns WC & B and RIPG, the two historically lucrative businesses of Raymark Industries, without the drain of asbestos-related litigation. By selling the stock of Raymark Corporation, Raytech was able to dispose of a subsidiary whose asbestos-related expenses had decreased its earnings by $8.6 million during the first quarter of 1988.

* * * Raymark Industries had valuable assets, RIPG and Wet Clutch & Brake. It conveyed these assets to Raytech, which was owned by Raymark Industries' former shareholders. This transaction left Raymark Industries with staggering asbestos liabilities, unprofitable operations, unsecured notes, and stock which could not be sold in large blocks without a deep discount.

Present and future asbestos tort claimants, as Raymark Industries' potential creditors, were likewise left with little in the transaction. The money Raytech paid for Raymark Industries' profit-generating assets will not adequately compensate present and future claimants. If Raytech escapes liability for Raymark Industries' torts, these creditors will no longer have access to Raymark Industries' valuable assets or to the potential stream of profits generated by these assets.

In the present case, the context of the corporate restructuring and the participants' statements show that the elaborate transfer of assets was designed to escape liability. Raymark Industries has experienced severe financial problems because of asbestos litigation. By April 1, 1988, nearly 34,000 asbestos related personal injury cases were pending against Raymark Industries. These claims exceed $33 billion. Trying cases to verdict has cost an average of $59,000. Raymark Industries has been assessed more than $75,000,000 in punitive damages from asbestos litigation.[7] Raymark Industries has already exhausted approximately 71% of its almost $400 million in insurance coverage.

In response to Raymark Corporation's financial difficulties, Craig Smith[8] and other officers and directors, with the advice of counsel, developed the sophisticated corporate restructuring scheme. The New York law firm of Debevoise & Plimpton advised Raytech's board of directors that:

7. A consolidated case against Raymark Industries involving more than 2,200 plaintiffs is currently pending in the United States District Court for the Eastern District of Texas. The verdict in that case could far exceed Raymark Industries' insurance policy limits.

8. From 1980 to 1985, Craig Smith was employed by Raymark Corporation as a division president. In 1985, Smith became the President and Chief Executive Officer of Raymark Corporation. Presently Smith is the President and Chief Executive Officer of Raytech.

Smith established Litigation Control Corporation on August 27, 1987. Its purpose is to provide services to corporations which have high volumes of litigation particularly in the field of product liability and toxic tort. Litigation Control Corporation currently holds 100 percent of the shares of Raymark Corporation. Craig Smith owns 45 percent of the shares of LCC and his son, Bradley Smith, owns another 15 percent of the shares of LCC.

It should be possible under existing case law for Raytech to acquire assets or businesses of Raymark without thereby subjecting Raytech or such acquired assets or businesses to liability for the asbestos-related claims against Raymark under the doctrines of successor liability, piercing the corporate veil or fraudulent conveyance....

Raymark Corporation's 1985 annual report stated that the company's long term strategy was:

to protect and enhance shareholder investment, to maximize the amounts available for deserving asbestos-injured claimants [9] and to limit exposure for asbestos claims only to businesses currently threatened, thus enabling our other businesses and any new business opportunities to grow, unshadowed by the cloud of asbestos liability.

Another purpose of the corporate restructuring was:

to gain access to new sources of capital and borrowed funds which could be used to finance the acquisition and operation of new businesses in a corporate restructure that should not subject Raytech or such acquired businesses to the asbestos related liabilities of Raymark.

* * *

I find that, although the corporate restructuring meets the technical formalities of corporate form, it was designed with the improper purpose of escaping asbestos-related liabilities.[11] Raymark Corporation changed from the parent of Raymark Industries to the subsidiary of Raytech to the subsidiary of ALM. Raytech purchased Raymark Corporation's two valuable assets and then sold the remainder to ALM for $1 million. It is inconceivable that in an armslength corporate transaction, a buyer would have purchased an entity so lacking in assets and laden with liabilities.

There is no just reason to respect the integrity of these transactions. Raymark Industries made substantial profits from the production of asbestos-containing products. Raymark Industries should not be allowed to avoid liability by transferring its profitable assets leaving no more than a corporate shell unable to satisfy its asbestos-related obligations.

This case presents serious equitable considerations. At least 21 million American workers have been directly exposed to significant amounts of asbestos at the work place since 1940 and millions more have been indirectly exposed. * * * Tens of thousands of people

---

9. Raymark Industries' 1988 Settlement Guidelines provides a maximum payment of $452. In a recent case involving clear asbestos liability and death from mesothelioma, Raymark Industries offered nothing. The jury returned a verdict of $1.7 million in compensatory damages against Raymark Industries. *Sawyer v. Raymark Industries, Inc.*, No. 87–542 (D.Haw. Dec. 6, 1988).

11. Plaintiff notes that if he were attempting to set aside the transactions, rather than hold Raytech responsible for Raymark Industries' torts, the court could hold as a matter of law that the transactions constituted fraudulent conveyances under the Uniform Fraudulent Transfer Act, Or.Rev.Stat. § 95.200–310.

become ill or die from asbestos-related diseases every year. * * * Asbestos-related lawsuits are filed in corresponding numbers.[12]

It is ironic that, while Raymark Industries prides itself for not following Johns–Manville Corporation's (Manville) lead by filing bankruptcy, Raymark is in effect attempting a bankruptcy-like reorganization without affording creditors the protections of formal bankruptcy. In December 1986, the United States Bankruptcy Court for the Southern District of New York confirmed a Plan of Reorganization of Manville. The Plan created a personal injury trust of $3 billion to cover all of Manville's present and future, known and unknown asbestos injury liabilities.

* * *

The success or failure of Raymark Corporation's attempts to escape asbestos liability will provide direction to other companies seeking to avoid such responsibility. Upholding the integrity of such transactions would unjustly elevate form over substance.

* * *

SECTION 3. LENDER LIABILITY

In traditional acquisition financing, major lenders are concerned about the potential claims against the surviving firm and about effect of the claims on the repayment obligation. United States v. Fleet Factors Corp., 901 F.2d 1550 (11th Cir.1990) has dramatically changed the rules of the game. In the following case a Ninth Circuit court discusses the *Fleet Factors* opinion.

IN RE BERGSOE METAL CORP.
United States Court of Appeals, Ninth Circuit, 1990.
910 F.2d 668.

* * *

KOZINSKI, CIRCUIT JUDGE:

The Comprehensive Environmental Response, Compensation and Liability Act, 42 USC §§ 9601 et seq. (CERCLA), provides that the "owner" of a contaminated facility is liable for the costs of cleanup. It is left for the courts, however, to clean up the mess left behind by complicated financial transactions. We search for the CERCLA owner. * * * Bergsoe Metals is a Delaware corporation formed in 1978 for the purpose of conducting a lead recycling operation. The East Asiatic Company, Ltd., The East Asiatic Company, Inc. and Heidelberg Eastern, Inc. (collectively, EAC) are owners of Bergsoe's stock. The Port of

---

12. Through April 1, 1988, Raymark Industries has been named in 68,057 separate actions involving 84,724 individual plaintiffs. In 1988, 1,209 cases have been filed per month. Raymark Industries projects additional filings through 1997 of approximately 61,200 cases.

More than 165 companies are involved in the asbestos litigation across the nation. Asbestos Litig.Rep. 4667–70 (Feb. 26, 1982).

St. Helens is a municipal corporation organized under the laws of Oregon and empowered to issue revenue bonds to promote industrial development in the St. Helens, Oregon area.

Sometime in 1978, representatives of Bergsoe contacted the Port to discuss the building of a lead recycling facility in St. Helens. These discussions resulted in a Memorandum of Agreement signed December 13, 1978. The Port therein agreed to issue industrial development revenue bonds and pollution control revenue bonds to provide funds for the acquisition of land and the construction of a secondary lead recycling plant and related pollution control equipment in St. Helens.

On December 28, 1979, the Port sold Bergsoe 50 acres of land on which to construct the plant. In exchange, Bergsoe gave the Port a promissory note for $400,000 and a mortgage on the property.

Through a series of interlocking transactions that closed on June 5, 1981, Bergsoe, the Port and the United States National Bank of Oregon completed the financing for the recycling operation. At the heart of this financing were the revenue bonds, issued by the Port. The Bank held the bonds in trust for the bondholders. The revenue from the bond sales went to Bergsoe, which was obligated to pay the money owed on the bonds to the Bank.

The first transaction was a sale-and-lease-back arrangement between Bergsoe and the Port. Bergsoe conveyed to the Port by warranty deed the 50 acres and the recycling plant to be built there. The Port and Bergsoe then entered into two leases to cover the property and the plant. Bergsoe agreed to construct the plant and to pay rent on the leases directly to the Bank. That rent was equal to the principal and interest to come due on the bonds. The leases gave Bergsoe the option of purchasing the entire facility for $100 once the bonds had been paid in full.

The second transaction involved two mortgage and indentures of trust between the Port and the Bank, corresponding to the two leases. The Port agreed to issue its revenue bonds, and mortgaged to the Bank, as trustee for the bondholders, the property and recycling plant. The Port also assigned to the Bank all its rights under, and revenues to be generated from, the leases. The Bank agreed to hold the amounts generated from sale of the bonds in a construction fund to be paid to Bergsoe. The indentures obligated the Bank to collect rent under the leases and to apply them in retirement of the bonds.

In addition to acting as trustee, the Bank purchased the bonds. In partial consideration for this purchase, the Port signed a subordination agreement whereby the Port subordinated all its rights under the prior $400,000 obligation to the Bank's rights under the leases.

The Port also placed in escrow with the Bank the warranty deeds, bills of sale and UCC release statements, with instructions to deliver the documents to Bergsoe when the company exercised its option to purchase the facility.

The Bergsoe recycling plant began operation in the spring of 1982 and soon experienced financial difficulties. In September 1983, the Bank declared Bergsoe in default on the leases. Subsequently, the Bank and Bergsoe agreed upon a workout arrangement, whereby Front Street Management Corporation would manage the recycling facility. In exchange, the Bank and the Port would agree not to foreclose under the leases or bond indentures. On June 30, 1984, the Bank, Bergsoe, Front Street and the Port executed various workout documents.

The plant did no better under Front Street's management than it had under Bergsoe's, and the plant shut down in 1986. On October 21 of that year, the Bank put Bergsoe into involuntary bankruptcy under Chapter 11 of the Bankruptcy Code. By that time, the Oregon Department of Environmental Quality had determined that various hazardous substances had contaminated the plant site. In September 1987, the Bank and the trustee in bankruptcy filed suit against EAC, the companies who own Bergsoe, to collect on Bergsoe's debts. The plaintiffs subsequently amended their complaint to request a declaration that EAC is liable for the costs of cleaning up the environmental contamination.

The defendants filed a counterclaim, including a third party complaint against the Port, alleging that the Bank and the Port are liable for the costs of cleanup under CERCLA. The Port moved for summary judgment, alleging that it does not own the recycling plant for CERCLA purposes, and therefore has no CERCLA liability.

* * *

CERCLA holds the "owner" of a facility liable for the costs of cleaning up hazardous substances released at the facility. 42 USC §§ 9607(a)(1) & (2). The CERCLA definition of "owner" is not, however, coextensive with all possible uses of that term; it specifically excludes "a person, who, without participating in the management of a vessel or facility, holds indicia of ownership primarily to protect his security interest in the vessel or facility." 42 USC § 9601(20)(A).

* * *

There is no question that, in at least one sense, the Port owns the Bergsoe recycling plant: the deed to the property is in the name of the Port. The Port nonetheless maintains that it is not a CERCLA owner because it falls within the security interest exception.

In order for the Port to win on summary judgement, the undisputed facts must demonstrate both that the Port holds indicia of ownership primarily to protect its security interest in the Bergsoe plant and that it did not participate in the management of the plant. * * *

That the Port holds paper title to the Bergsoe plant does not, alone, make it an owner of the facility for purposes of CERCLA; under the security interest exception the court must determine *why* the Port holds such indicia of ownership. Here, there is no doubt that the Port has the deed in the plant primarily to ensure that Bergsoe would meet its obligations under the leases and therefore under the bonds. In other words, the Port has a security interest in the property.

* * * Here, the Port held title to the property not to ensure that *it* would receive payment, but to guarantee that Bergsoe would cover the Port's own indebtedness under the bonds. * * *

The relevant evidence that the Port's ownership was merely part of the financing arrangement is to be found in the Port/Bergsoe leases. These documents do grant to the Port the deeds to the property, and each document is described as a "lease" rather than as a "security agreement." Nonetheless, the leases give to Bergsoe all other traditional indicia of ownership, such as responsibility for the payment of taxes and for the purchase of insurance; significantly, the leases assign to Bergsoe the risk of loss from destruction or damage to the property.

Even more telling, however, are the terms of repayment under the leases. Bergsoe's "rent" was equal to the principal and interest due under the bonds. The money was to be paid directly to the Bank as trustee for the bondholders. The leases expired not on a specific date, but when the money owed under the bonds was paid off. And, when the bonds were paid off, Bergsoe could purchase full title to the property for the nominal sum of $100. To facilitate this transaction, the Port had placed the deeds and other relevant documents in escrow with the Bank.

* * *

The Port may nonetheless be liable under CERCLA if it participated in the management of the Bergsoe plant. Unfortunately, CERCLA does not define the phrase "participating in the management ... of a facility." The statute thus provides little guidance as to how much control over a facility a secured creditor can exert before it will be liable for cleanup.

To date, only one federal circuit has addressed this question. In *Fleet Factors*, the Eleventh Circuit considered several alternative rules. The government proposed that a secured creditor that participates in any manner in the management of a facility is excluded from the security interest exemption. * * * Fleet Factors proposed a rule adopted by certain district courts, that participation in financial management is allowable, but participation in the day-to-day or operational management of a facility will subject the creditor to liability. The Eleventh Circuit adopted an intermediate rule:

> [A] secured creditor may incur section 9607(a)(2) liability ... by participating in the financial management of a facility to a degree indicating a capacity to influence the coproration's treatment of hazardous wastes. It is not necessary for the secured creditor actually to involve itself in the day-to-day operations of the facility in order to be liable—although such conduct will certainly lead to the loss of the protection of the statutory exemption. Nor is it necessary for the secured creditor to participate in management decisions related to hazardous waste. Rather, a secured creditor will be liable if its involvement with the

management of the facility is sufficiently broad to support the inference that it could affect hazardous waste disposal decisions if it so chose.

Id. at 2915.

We leave for another day the establishment of a Ninth Circuit rule on this difficult issue, it is clear from the statute that, whatever the precise parameters of "participation," there must be *some* actual management of the facility before a secured creditor will fall outside the exception. Here there was none, and we therefore need not engage in line drawing.

EAC points to several facts that it claims demonstrate that the Port participated in the management of the Bergsoe plant. First, that the Port "negotiated and encouraged" the building of the Bergsoe plant. * * * Were this sufficient to remove a creditor from the security interest exception, the exception would cease to have any meaning. Creditors do not give their money blindly, particularly the large sums of money needed to build industrial facilities. Lenders normally extend credit only after gathering a great deal of information about the proposed project, and only when they have some degree of confidence that the project will be successful. A secured creditor will always have some input at the planning stages of any large-scale project and, by the extension of financing, will perforce encourage those projects it feels will be successful. If this were "management," no secured creditor would ever be protected.[2]

EAC next points to certain of the Port's rights under the leases, such as the right to inspect the premises and to reenter and take possession upon foreclosure. This argument suffers from the same flaw as the last: nearly all secured creditors have these rights. That a secured creditor reserves certain rights to protect its investment does not put it in a position of management. What is critical is not what rights the Port had, but what it did. The CERCLA security interest exception uses the active "participating in management." Regardless of what rights the Port may have had, it cannot have participated in management if it never exercised them.[3] And there is no evidence that the Port exercised any control over Bergsoe once the two parties signed the leases.

Finally, EAC argues that the Port participated in management through its actions in giving Front Street control at the plant as part of

---

2. No doubt the Port, as a municipal corporation empowered to promote industrial development, encouraged Bergsoe to build the plant for reasons other than the Port's own financial gain. A creditor's motivation is irrelevant, however, to the issue of whether its actions constitute management.

3. * * *
EAC generally errs in equating the power to manage with actual management.

As did the Eleventh Circuit in *Fleet Factors,* we hold that a creditor must, as a threshold matter, exercise actual management authority before it can be held liable for action or inaction which results in the discharge of hazardous wastes. Merely having the power to get involved in management, but failing to exercise it, is not enough.

the 1984 workout. There is, however, no evidence that the Port participated in the decision to hire Front Street; those negotiations were entirely between the Bank, Bergsoe and Front Street. The Port's participation was limited to an agreement between itself, the Bank and Bergsoe. The Port's sole obligation under the agreement was to forego exercising any of its default remedies under the leases so that the workout might proceed. There were separate agreements between Bergsoe and Front Street and between the Bank and Bergsoe. The Port never entered into a contract with Front Street, and there is no evidence of any negotiations between the two.

EAC contends, nonetheless, that the Port is responsible for the Bank's actions in placing Front Street in control because the Bank was acting as the Port's agent, enforcing the Port's rights under the leases. This assertion is belied by the terms of the mortgage and indentures of trust between the Port and the Bank, wherein the Port assigns to the Bank "all right, title and interest of the [Port] in the Lease[s]." * * * Thus, to the extent the Bank was attempting to enforce the lease terms, it did so pursuant to its own rights under the leases. More to the point, it was not the leases that the Bank was worried about, but the bonds. As trustee for the bondholders, the Bank had a duty to try to keep the plant running so that Bergsoe could pay the principal and interest under the bonds. In negotiating the workout, the Bank was acting not as the Port's agent, but as the bondholders'.

There being no material issue of fact, we conclude that the Port holds indicia of ownership primarily to protect its security interest and that it did not participate in the management of the Bergsoe recycling plant. * * *

Question

Is the bank in *Bergsoe Metal Corp.* liable under CERCLA? Is EAC liable under CERCLA?

Chapter Four

INTRODUCTION TO STOCK ACQUISITIONS: THE WILLIAMS ACT AND STATE ANTITAKEOVER STATUTES

Two types of statutes regulate the form and effect of major stock acquisitions, the Williams Act, a federal securities statute, and state antitakeover legislation. Congress passed the Williams Act in 1968, amending the Securities and Exchange Act of 1934 by adding, among others, sections 13(d) to (g) and 14(d) and (e). The provisions established substantive rules on stock acquisitions and delegated authority to the Securities and Exchange Commission to supplement the sections with regulations, rules, and schedules. State antitakeover legislation is a relatively recent phenomenon, having been given renewed life by the Supreme Court in 1987. In this chapter we explore the mechanics of the Williams Act and state antitakeover legislation.

SUBCHAPTER A. FEDERAL REGULATION: THE WILLIAMS ACT

SECTION 1. SECTION 13(d): DISCLOSURE OF A 5 PERCENT ACQUISITION

Please read sections 13(d) and (g) of the Securities and Exchange Act of 1934, Securities and Exchange Commission rules 13d–1 to 13d–6, and skim schedule 13D (focusing on general instruction C and item 4) in your statutory supplement.

Note

Proposed Rules Under Section 13(d)

The Securities and Exchange Commission proposed on March 14, 1989, to amend rules 13d–1 (filing of schedule 13D and 13G), 13d–2 (filing of amendments to schedules 13D and 13G), 13d–7 (fees for filing), 13d–101 (schedule 13D), and 13d–102 (schedule 13G). The rules are part of an integrated scheme to expand the number of people that would be eligible to file short-form schedule 13G. If adopted, the rules would allow passive noninstitutional investors to file short-form schedule 13G in lieu of schedule 13D. The scheme would also add a ten-day maximum cooling-off period for investors who lose 13G filing privileges. During the cooling-off period the investor would be prohibited from voting the shares or acquiring additional shares in the issuer.

On March 13, 1989, the commission proposed to change general instruction C on schedules 13D (acquirer disclosure) and 14D–1 (tender offer statement) and 13E–3 (self-tender offer transaction statement). The revised instructions would require "significant participants" in major transactions of securities (i.e., large block purchases, tender offers, proxy contests, going-private transactions) to respond to specified items on the required filed schedule. Most significantly, the commission would expand the disclosure requirements to cover any person who contributes more than 10 percent of the equity capital, has the right to receive more than 10 percent of the profits, or has the right to receive more than 10 percent of the assets upon liquidation of the filing person.

The effect of the change would place equity participants in limited partnerships, closely held corporations, and similar entities within the purview of the SEC disclosure regulations. Specifically, these qualified equity participants, like those controlling these entities under the current rule, would have to disclose information about their identity, their background, their funding, and the purposes of their investments. The proposed change was spurred by the SEC's concern that the current instructions did not adequately provide shareholders and the market with material information about significant participants in large security transactions.

Questions

1. Who must file a schedule 13D and who must file a schedule 13G? See rule 13d–1(a) and (b)(1). What are the significant differences in timing and content between the two schedules? To whom must the filing person send copies of either schedule?

2. How does the Securities and Exchange Commission treat options to buy common stock or bonds convertible into common stock in calculating whether a person has a 5 percent stake in the stock? See rule 13d–3.

3. Three individuals, each holding 2 percent of an outstanding registered equity security, contract to vote in concert on all firm matters (a majority vote among the three determines how all three will vote their stock). Must they file a schedule 13D? See rule 13d–3(a) & (b) and rule 13d–5(b)(1). What if the contract is solely to sell all stock together, based on a majority vote of the pooling shareholders, in the event of a tender offer? See generally GAF Corp. v. Milstein, 453 F.2d 709 (2d Cir.1971); Champion Parts Rebuilders, Inc. v. Cormier Corp., 661 F.Supp. 825 (N.D.Ill. 1987).

4. Three investors form a limited partnership in which each of the three is a limited partner. The general partner is an investment firm. The limited partnership is formed exclusively for acquiring an identified

target. When the limited partnership acquires 5 percent of the target's voting stock and must file a schedule 13D, must the partnership reveal the identity of each of the limited partners and the terms and conditions of their participation? If the three investors incorporate a shell corporation, formed exclusively for the acquisition, must the corporation's schedule 13D disclose the identity of the shareholders? See schedule 13D, instruction C. What kinds of investors are particularly sensitive about public disclosure of their investment in acquisitions? (Consider, for example, the position of state pension plans and corporate pension plans.)

5. Assume that a bidder decides that the least expensive way, neutral of legal requirements, of purchasing a target is the accumulation of 15 percent of the target's stock in the open market followed by a public tender offer for 36 percent at a slight premium over market price. The bidder estimates that its open market purchases will gradually drive stock prices up but that it can buy 15 percent before the market fully understands its intentions. Once its intentions are public knowledge, a public tender offer is the least costly method of obtaining the remaining 36 percent stake that it seeks. Can a bidder structure such an acquisition program within the requirements of section 13(d)? See section 13(d)(1)(a) and rule 13d–1(a) and review the *Icahn* case. Does this practice frustrate the intent of the section?

6. "Waffling": Can a bidder obscure a disclosure of its future intentions by listing numerous "possibilities"? For example, Raider has considered but not decided whether to pursue various courses of action relating to Target, including (1) seeking control through a tender offer or additional private or open market purchases, (2) proposing a merger between Raider and Target, (3) seeking representation on Target's board, (4) holding for investment, or (5) reselling. Raider intends to review its options from time to time in light of circumstances then prevailing.

7. Stock "parking": A potential bidder, itself owning no stock in a target, orally contracts with several dealers. Each dealer buys 4.99 percent of the target stock and agrees to sell the stock to the bidder on the bidder's request. The bidder will reimburse each dealer for any decline in the value of the stock suffered while in the dealer's hands and pay the broker-dealer a healthy commission (spread). The bidder does not disclose these arrangements under section 13(d). Is this illegal? See rule 13d–3. See also SEC v. First City Financial Corp., 688 F.Supp. 705 (D.D.C.1988).

8. Proxy solicitations: A potential bidder, owning 4.9 percent of the stock of a target, solicits proxies to oust the target board (complying with the proxy rules and regulations under section 14(a) of the Securities and Exchange Act; see chapter 2). Must the bidder also file a schedule 13D? See rule 13d–5.

9. Stock "warehousing": A potential bidder, itself owning no stock in a target, selectively informs institutional investors of its interest in a particular target. There is no actual or implicit agreement to repurchase. The selective disclosure helps the bidder accumulate stock in the hands of holders disposed to resell once a tender offer is announced. Is this illegal? See rules 13d–3(a) & (b) and 13d–5(b)(1).

10. Amendments: An investor who has filed a schedule 13D or 13G indicating only an investment intent in the target changes its mind and buys additional stock for the purpose of seeking control. When must the investor amend its schedule? See rule 13d–2. If an investor seeking control of a target files a schedule 13D, indicating a general intent to gain control but no firm plans or financing for its effort, must the investor file amendments as its financing becomes certain, as the details of its acquisition plan become clear, or as it changes its plans in light of the appearance of a competitive bid? If so, how many amendments would you expect have to be filed in a large stock acquisition?

Note
The Effect of Section 13(d)

Critics of the Williams Act argue that the effect of section 13(d) is to reduce the incentives for investors to make investments that trigger the disclosure requirements of the rule, especially when there are significant search costs necessary in locating firms that are good buys. After the disclosure other parties can take a "free ride" on the disclosing purchaser's search costs and also jump in and buy target stock without compensating the disclosing purchaser. See Macey & Netter, *Regulation 13D and the Regulatory Process,* 65 Wash.U.L.Q. 131 (1987).

The argument is strongest in light of item 4 in schedule 13D, requiring disclosure of the purpose behind a 5 percent acquisition. A bidder intent on making a public tender offer in the near future will not want to trigger the disclosure requirement in section 13(d) in advance of the announcement of its tender offer. The earlier the bidder must disclose its plans, the more time other bidders will have to make competing offers and the more time target managers will have to erect defenses to the bid. Moreover, competitors and target managers will have the benefit, free of cost, of the initial bidder's views, generated at considerable cost, on how best to change the operation of the target to maximize its worth. Thus unless bidders can avoid preliminary disclosure under the section, the number of bidders willing to make initial bids for targets will decrease significantly at the margin.

The net effect of the section, it is argued, is that shareholders of target firms are the big losers, and the big winners are the target managers, who protect their jobs and their ability to shirk their responsibility to their shareholders, law and accounting firms, which protect a source of revenue, and the Securities and Exchange Commission, which protects its role as regulator, are the big winners.

A second argument against the section focuses on the ability of the target to file lawsuits under the section that are designed, not to vindicate rights under the section, but to stall swiftly moving and unwanted takeover attempts. Lawyers can file lawsuits, within the limits of their professional code of ethics, whenever they have a good-faith belief that the litigation is "nonfrivolous," not a good-faith belief that they will win. When a target board discovers a takeover threat, it hires buyers, who file with a federal judge, within hours of the disclosure, a request for, first, a temporary restraining order (TRO) and, second, a preliminary injunction based on alleged violations of section 13(d). In response to a request for a TRO the judge, if impressed with the urgency of the situation and persuaded by the target's lawyers of the legitimacy of the allegations (even if the bidder's lawyers have, because of the short notice, not been able to attend the hearing) can grant a temporary injunction against the takeover. In a request for a preliminary injunction a judge can stop the takeover pending a full hearing on the merits of the claim. The target board hopes that even if a court ultimately rejects the target's allegations that the bidder has violated section 13(d), the court will have delayed the takeover during the proceedings. Why is delay such a powerful defense in takeovers? Whose money is financing the stock purchases? It is argued, section 13(d) just provides target boards with another bargaining chit in its negotiations with the bidder. If the bidder ups the price, the target will withdraw its court filings. See Jarrell, The Wealth Effects of Litigation by Targets: Do Interests Diverge in a Merger?, 28 J.L. & Econ. 151 (1985) (in over 75 percent of the cases litigious targets significantly increased the takeover premium either by encouraging competitive bidding or by sweetening the offers from the only suitor).

The critical question, and a possible answer to the critics, is the following: If shareholders of all potential stock acquisition targets (uninfluenced by their managers) had a costless choice on whether to adopt section 13(d) with respect to purchases of target stock, how would they vote? What factors would enter into their decision? Does your answer depend on whether the shareholders are deciding in anticipation of presently unannounced acquisitions (ex ante) or are deciding once an acquisition has been announced and is in progress (ex post)? Which perspective is more important to lawmakers?

Could target shareholders rationally believe ex ante that their stock is *more* valuable as a result of section 13(d)? Without disclosure under section 13(d) they may be hurt as sellers but benefited as buyers when they engage in securities transactions without knowledge of a pending acquisition plan. Does this balance out for diversified investors? If so, must we look to other benefits or costs to evaluate the social value of the rule? Do fewer acquisitions translate into lower stock prices? Or does the increased power to bargain with a potential bidder translate into higher stock prices?

Relief for Section 13(d) Violations

Most lower federal courts have recognized an implied private right of action in the target (issuer) to cure violations of section 13(d). E.g., Florida Common-Banks v. Culverhouse, 772 F.2d 1513 (11th Cir.1985). Gerhart Industries, Inc. v. Smith Intern., Inc., 741 F.2d 707 (5th Cir.1984). But see Liberty Nat. Ins. Holding Co. v. Charter Co., 734 F.2d 545 (11th Cir.1984) (no implied right in target to seek divestment). Relief is usually limited to an order requiring the filing of a corrected schedule and enjoining, pending the amended filing (or a short period after the amending filing), further acquisitions or the exercise of voting rights on already acquired stock. Moreover, shareholders who sold stock during the period in which the bidder failed to file a proper schedule 13D have a private cause of action for damages under, among other sections and rules, rule 10b–5. There is substantial disagreement, however, over whether permanent divestment or sterilization (loss of voting rights) of stock acquired after the filing of an incomplete schedule is appropriate once the offender makes a correct amended filing. The dispute centers on how one interprets the following case.

RONDEAU v. MOSINEE PAPER CORP.

Supreme Court of the United States, 1975.
422 U.S. 49, 95 S.Ct. 2069, 45 L.Ed.2d 12.

Mr. Chief Justice Burger delivered the opinion of the Court.

* * *

Respondent Mosinee Paper Corp. is a Wisconsin company engaged in the manufacture and sale of paper, paper products, and plastics. Its principal place of business is located in Mosinee, Wis., and its only class of equity security is common stock which is registered under § 12 of the Securities Exchange Act of 1934, 15 U.S.C. § 78*l*. At all times relevant to this litigation there were slightly more than 800,000 shares of such stock outstanding.

In April 1971 petitioner Francis A. Rondeau, a Mosinee businessman, began making large purchases of respondent's common stock in the over-the-counter market. Some of the purchases were in his own name; others were in the name of businesses and a foundation known to be controlled by him. By May 17, 1971, petitioner had acquired 40,413 shares of respondent's stock, which constituted more than 5% of those outstanding. He was therefore required to comply with the disclosure provisions of the Williams Act, by filing a Schedule 13D with respondent and the Securities and Exchange Commission within 10 days. That form would have disclosed, among other things, the number of shares beneficially owned by petitioner, the source of the funds used to purchase them, and petitioner's purpose in making the purchases.

Petitioner did not file a Schedule 13D but continued to purchase substantial blocks of respondent's stock. By July 30, 1971, he had acquired more than 60,000 shares. On that date the chairman of respondent's board of directors informed him by letter that his activity had "given rise to numerous rumors" and "seems to have created some problems under the Federal Securities Laws...." Upon receiving the letter petitioner immediately stopped placing orders for respondent's stock and consulted his attorney.[2] On August 25, 1971, he filed a Schedule 13D which, in addition to the other required disclosures, described the "Purpose of Transaction" as follows:

"Francis A. Rondeau determined during early part of 1971 that the common stock of the Issuer [respondent] was undervalued in the over-the-counter market and represented a good investment vehicle for future income and appreciation. Francis A. Rondeau and his associ-

---

2. Although some outstanding orders were filled after July 30, 1971, petitioner placed no new orders for respondent's stock after that date.

ates presently propose to seek to acquire additional common stock of the Issuer in order to obtain effective control of the Issuer, but such investments as originally determined were and are not necessarily made with this objective in mind. Consideration is currently being given to making a public cash tender offer to the shareholders of the Issuer at a price which will reflect current quoted prices for such stock with some premium added."

Petitioner also stated that, in the event that he did obtain control of respondent, he would consider making changes in management "in an effort to provide a Board of Directors which is more representative of all of the shareholders, particularly those outside of present management...." One month later petitioner amended the form to reflect more accurately the allocation of shares between himself and his companies.

On August 27 respondent sent a letter to its shareholders informing them of the disclosures in petitioner's Schedule 13D.[3] The letter stated that by his "tardy filing" petitioner had "withheld the information to which you [the shareholders] were entitled for more than two months, in violation of federal law." In addition, while agreeing that "recent market prices have not reflected the real value of your Mosinee stock," respondent's management could "see little in Mr. Rondeau's background that would qualify him to offer any meaningful guidance to a Company in the highly technical and competitive paper industry."

* * *

The Court of Appeals' conclusion that respondent suffered "harm" sufficient to require sterilization of petitioner's stock need not long detain us. The purpose of the Williams Act is to insure that public shareholders who are confronted by a cash tender offer for their stock will not be required to respond without adequate information regarding the qualifications and intentions of the offering party. By requiring disclosure of information to the target corporation as well as the Securities and Exchange Commission, Congress intended to do no more than give incumbent management an opportunity to express and explain its position. The Congress expressly disclaimed an intention to provide a weapon for management to discourage takeover bids or prevent large accumulations of stock which would create the potential for such attempts. Indeed, the Act's draftsmen commented upon the "extreme care" which was taken "to avoid tipping the balance of regulation either in favor of management or in favor of the person making the takeover bid."

* * *

The short of the matter is that none of the evils to which the Williams Act was directed has occurred or is threatened in this case. Petitioner has not attempted to obtain control of respondent, either by

---

3. Respondent simultaneously issued a press release containing the same information. Almost immediately the price of its stock jumped to $19–$21 per share. A few days later it dropped back to the prevailing price of $12.50–$14 per share, where it remained.

a cash tender offer or any other device. Moreover, he has now filed a proper Schedule 13D, and there has been no suggestion that he will fail to comply with the Act's requirement of reporting any material changes in the information contained therein.[9] * * * On this record there is no likelihood that respondent's shareholders will be disadvantaged should petitioner make a tender offer, or that respondent will be unable to adequately place its case before them should a contest for control develop. Thus, the usual basis for injunctive relief, "that there exists some cognizable danger of recurrent violation," is not present here. *United States v. W.T. Grant Co.*, 345 U.S. 629, 633 (1953). See also *Vicksburg Waterworks Co. v. Vicksburg*, 185 U.S. 65, 82 (1902).

Nor are we impressed by respondent's argument that an injunction is necessary to protect the interests of its shareholders who either sold their stock to petitioner at predisclosure prices or would not have invested had they known that a takeover bid was imminent. * * * As observed, the principal object of the Williams Act is to solve the dilemma of shareholders desiring to respond to a cash tender offer, and it is not at all clear that the type of "harm" identified by respondent is redressable under its provisions. In any event, those persons who allegedly sold at an unfairly depressed price have an adequate remedy by way of an action for damages, thus negating the basis for equitable relief.[10] * * * Similarly, the fact that the second group of shareholders for whom respondent expresses concern have retained the benefits of their stock and the lack of an imminent contest for control make the possibility of damage to them remote at best. * * *

* * *

MR. JUSTICE MARSHALL dissents.

MR. JUSTICE BRENNAN, with whom MR. JUSTICE DOUGLAS joins, dissenting.

* * *

The violation itself establishes the actionable harm and no showing of other harm is necessary to secure injunctive relief. Today's holding completely undermines the congressional purpose to preclude inquiry into the results of the violation.

Questions

1. Using the language in the *Rondeau* case, how can one argue both for and against the position that permanent divesture or sterilization is appropriate for section 13(d) violations?

---

9. Because this case involves only the availability of injunctive relief to remedy a § 13(d) violation following compliance with the reporting requirements, it does not require us to decide whether or under what circumstances a corporation could obtain a decree enjoining a shareholder who is currently in violation of § 13(d) from acquiring further shares, exercising voting rights, or launching a takeover bid, pending compliance with the reporting requirements.

10. The Court was advised by respondent that such a suit is now pending in the District Court and class action certification has been sought. Although we intimate no views regarding the merits of that case, it provides a potential sanction for petitioner's violation of the Williams Act.

2. The *Rondeau* court details the policies behind the Williams Act in general, of which section 13(d) is a small part. Do the policy arguments articulated by the court justify section 13(d)? Or is section 14(d) a rough protection for the harms generated by totally unregulated tender offers? Indeed, what does section 13(d) have to do in particular with tender offers?

CHROMALLOY AMERICAN CORP. v. SUN CHEMICAL CORP.

United States Court of Appeals, Eighth District, 1979.
611 F.2d 240.

HENLEY, CIRCUIT JUDGE.

* * *

In January, 1978 Sun Chemical Corporation began purchasing significant amounts of Chromalloy stock on the New York Stock Exchange. Chromalloy is a diversified corporation with revenues in fiscal year 1978 of nearly $1.4 billion and net earnings of $47 million, while Sun is a considerably smaller corporation with 1978 revenues of $394 million and net earnings of $20 million. Norman E. Alexander is Chief Executive Officer and Chairman of Sun's Board of Directors, and has been instrumental in instigating and furthering the purchase of Chromalloy stock by Sun Chemical Corporation.

By February 5, 1979 Sun had acquired 605,620 shares, or 5.2 per cent, of Chromalloy's total outstanding shares. Sun was therefore required to comply with the disclosure provisions of § 13(d) of the Securities Exchange Act, 15 U.S.C. § 78m(d)(1) (1976). Pursuant to the disclosure requirements, Sun on February 5, 1979 filed its first Schedule 13D. Sun stated that its acquisitions were for investment; that it had no present intention of seeking control of Chromalloy; that it presently intended to continue to increase its holdings; that the amount of such increase had not been determined; that Sun had been discussing with certain directors and members of Chromalloy management the possible increase in Sun's holdings; and that Sun might "at any time determine to seek control of Chromalloy." In four subsequent amendments to the Schedule 13D between April, 1979 and late July, 1979 Sun reported its plans to purchase additional stock, its unsuccessful attempt to gain representation on the Chromalloy Board, and its negotiations regarding a "stand-still" agreement whereby Sun would limit its purchases for a period of time as a condition of representation on the Chromalloy Board. In each of the amendments to its Schedule 13D Sun disclaimed any intent to control Chromalloy.

By late July, 1979 Sun's ownership had increased to nearly ten per cent of Chromalloy's outstanding stock. * * *

Under the provisions of the revised SEC regulations, we are confronted with two distinct questions: first, whether the district court erred in finding that Sun has a disclosable purpose to acquire control, and second, whether the district court abused its discretion in refusing to order disclosure of Sun's proposals for corporate changes aside from Sun's control intent.

In assessing Sun's obligation to disclose a control purpose, we look to the definition of "control" appearing in Rule 12b–2(f), 17 C.F.R. § 240.12b–2(f) (1979), made applicable to Schedule 13D filings by 17 C.F.R. § 240.12b–1 (1979).[12] Rule 12b–2(f) provides:

> *Control.* The term "control" (including the terms "controlling", "controlled by" and "under common control with") means the possession, directly or indirectly, of the power to direct or cause the direction of the management and policies of a person, whether through the ownership of voting securities, by contract, or otherwise.

17 C.F.R. § 240.12b–2(f) (1979).

* * *

Contrary to Sun's first contention, Sun's desire to influence substantially the policies, management and actions of Chromalloy amounts to a purpose to control Chromalloy. There is ample support in the record for the finding of a control purpose. Sun has disclosed its plans to acquire twenty per cent of Chromalloy's stock, its attempts to gain representation on Chromalloy's Board, and its intention to review continually its position with respect to Chromalloy. The district court further found that Sun has prepared an "acquisition model" with Chromalloy as a "target"; that Norman Alexander first learned of the investment opportunities in Chromalloy when a brokerage firm informed him that the thirty-five per cent of common stock held by insiders was not in a solid management block; that Norman Alexander's private memoranda have been concerned from the start with the split on Chromalloy's Board of Directors as a possible avenue to power; and that according to an investment banker, Sun's projected twenty per cent interest in Chromalloy would be a wise business decision only if Sun is attempting to gain control. Taken together, these facts support the finding that Sun proposes to control Chromalloy through a combination of numbers and influence.

As a matter of law, Rule 12b–2(f) contemplates that influence can be an element of control. Control is defined to include "the [*indirect*] power to ... cause the direction of ... policies." Disclosure of a control purpose may be required where the securities purchaser has a perceptible desire to influence substantially the issuer's operations. * * *

---

12. Although revised Item 4 does not use the term "control", we assume that any control purpose is still measurable against the definition of control appearing in Rule 12b–2(f).

Cases decided before the revision of Item 4 have considered the definition of "control" in Rule 12b–2(f) to be controlling. *TSC Industries, Inc. v. Northway, Inc.,* 426 U.S. 438, 451 n. 13, 96 S.Ct. 2126, 48 L.Ed.2d 757 (1976); *Graphic Sciences, Inc. v. International Mogul Mines Ltd.,* 397 F.Supp. 112, 125 & n. 37 (D.D.C.1974). The Southern District of New York, in a case decided after the effective date of the revised form, considered a number of circumstances in determining control intent without reference to the definition of control in Rule 12b–2(f). *Transcon Lines v. A.G. Becker, Inc.,* 470 F.Supp. 356, 376–78 (S.D. N.Y.1979).

Moreover, the Securities Exchange Act is remedial legislation and is to be broadly construed in order to give effect to its intent. * * * To protect the investing public through full and fair disclosure of Sun's intentions, the district court was justified in defining control to include working control and substantial influence.

Sun next contends that the district court failed to find a "fixed plan" to acquire control of Chromalloy. This fact is not determinative. Item 4 of Schedule 13D requires disclosure of a purpose to acquire control, even though this intention has not taken shape as a fixed plan. We do not agree with Sun's contention that disclosure of Sun's control purpose will mislead investors by overstating the definiteness of Sun's plans. *Cf. Missouri Portland Cement Co. v. Cargill, Inc.*, 498 F.2d 851, 872 (2d Cir.), *cert. denied,* 419 U.S. 883, 95 S.Ct. 150, 42 L.Ed.2d 123 (1974) (disclosure of intention to substantially expand target company would be misleading where purchaser's twenty year study included this possibility but where no plan was adopted); *Susquehanna Corp. v. Pan American Sulphur Corp.,* 423 F.2d 1075, 1084–85 (5th Cir.1970) (disclosure of plan for merger would be misleading where plan subsisted for only two days before repudiation); *Electronic Speciality Co. v. International Controls Corp.,* 409 F.2d 937, 948 (2d Cir.1969) (disclosure that purchaser "would give consideration" to merger was sufficient disclosure, where merger was proposed as alternative to tender offer). The cited cases stress that disclosure of plans for specific corporate changes can be misleading until these assume definite, non-contingent form. Disclosure of a purchaser's *purpose* in acquiring stock is a different matter. Item 4 specifically requires disclosure of a purpose to acquire control, regardless of the definiteness or even the existence of any plans to implement this purpose.

Finally, we find no merit in Sun's argument that SEC Rule 12b–22 limits the obligation to disclose a control purpose. Rule 12b–22 allows registrants under Sections 13 and 15(d) of the Securities Exchange Act to disclaim the *existence* of control:

> *Disclaimer of control.* If the existence of control is open to reasonable doubt in any instance, the registrant may disclaim the existence of control and any admission thereof; in such case, however, the registrant shall state the material facts pertinent to the possible existence of control.

17 C.F.R. § 240.12b–22 (1970). This rule on its face is inapposite to Item 4 of Schedule 13D, since Item 4 requires disclosure of "the *purpose* of the acquisition," while Rule 12b–22 is concerned with *existing* control. We have found no relevant authority, nor has Sun offered any, to support the contention that Rule 12b–22 modifies the obligation of a purchaser to disclose a control purpose.

* * *

We also perceive no abuse of discretion in the district court's refusal to order disclosures beyond Sun's court-approved Schedule 13D.

* * *

In the present case, Sun's long-range hopes for certain corporate changes could prove misleading to investors if disclosed as firm proposals. The district court's findings of fact indicate that Sun has made the following tentative overtures towards corporate changes: Norman Alexander once told Moody's Investor Services that any deal with Chromalloy "would be done with Chromalloy's money or they would get out"; Alexander "hoped" Chromalloy would eventually seek to acquire the assets of Sun; Sun commissioned a study to recommend which divisions of Chromalloy are most feasible to sell off; Alexander expressed the opinion that a profit could be realized if a trim-down of Chromalloy were properly executed; and Alexander offered to "take care of" certain Chromalloy Board members in return for their support. Each of these items involves little more than an unconsummated hope, feasibility study, or opinion, not a firm plan or proposal. We note also that Sun and Alexander have to date been denied a seat on Chromalloy's Board of Directors, and are seemingly not in a position to precipitate any of the hoped-for changes.

The degree of specificity with which future plans must be detailed in Schedule 13D filings presents a difficult question. * * * Thus, within the scope of its discretion, the district court might have required further disclosures of Sun. However, given the arguable danger of overstatement and the rule that parties are not required to disclose plans which are contingent or indefinite, * * * we hold that the district court's order refusing further disclosures involved no abuse of discretion.

The final issue on appeal is whether the district court abused its discretion in refusing Chromalloy's request for a cooling-off period, the mailing of a restated Schedule 13D to Chromalloy shareholders at Sun's expense, and the publication of a restated Schedule 13D in the press.

We consider the argument for additional injunctive relief in light of the principles set forth by the Supreme Court in *Rondeau v. Mosinee Paper Corp.,* 422 U.S. 49, 95 S.Ct. 2069, 45 L.Ed.2d 12 (1975). The Court in *Rondeau* considered the availability of injunctive relief to remedy a § 13(d) violation following compliance with the reporting requirements. Recognizing that the injunctive process is designed to deter, not to punish, *id.,* at 61, the Court held that injunctive relief under the Williams Act was subject to traditional equitable limitations. Relief beyond compliance with the reporting requirements is justified only if the petitioner can show irreparable harm in the absence of such relief. *Id.*[18]

We have concluded that the Schedule 13D approved by the district court adequately discloses Sun's control intention. Given Sun's compli-

---

18. Because this case involves only the availability of injunctive relief *following compliance* with § 13(d), we are not required to decide what circumstances might justify a decree enjoining a shareholder who is *currently* in violation of § 13(d) from acquiring further shares or exercising voting rights, pending compliance with the reporting requirements. The posture of the case is identical to *Rondeau* in this respect. *Rondeau v. Mosinee Paper Corp., supra,* 422 U.S. at 59 n. 9, 97 S.Ct. 926.

ance with § 13(d), we do not perceive such ongoing harm to Chromalloy or its present shareholders [19] as would justify a cooling-off period or a stockholder mailing. Shareholders who were misinformed by Sun's original Schedule 13D and amendments have been reapprised by the same form of communication.

* * *

There is also no precedent for a cooling-off period. In the closely analogous context of misleading tender offers, courts have held that a misleading tender offer is adequately cured by an amended offer.

* * *

The disclosure requirements established by Congress are not intended to provide a weapon for current management to discourage takeover bids or prevent large accumulations of stock. * * * Further injunctive relief, particularly a cooling-off period, would in the present case serve largely as a dilatory tool in the hands of current management, and for this reason was properly denied.

* * *

Questions

1. Why isn't the danger of misleading investors through "overstating the definiteness of plans" the winning argument on the issue of disclosing plans for changes, applicable to Sun's relatively unspecified (and, in the end, feeble) plans to acquire "control"?

2. Why were Sun managers hesitant to state a purpose "to acquire control" even though they freely disclosed their intention to buy more stock and gain representation on the board? Were they just splitting hairs? What is the effect of using the word *control* on existing managers? On other shareholders?

DAN RIVER, INC. v. ICAHN

United States Court of Appeals, Fourth Circuit, 1983.
701 F.2d 278.

MURNAGHAN, CIRCUIT JUDGE

* * *

More significantly, however, the recognition that the case involves, in the end, the omission of one identifiable and allegedly material fact raises the question whether the "sterilization" order which we review here is an appropriate remedy for the supposed wrong. On the facts of the particular case before us, we are constrained to hold that the order

---

19. We do not reach the issue of harm to former Chromalloy shareholders who may have sold to Sun without attempting to garner a control premium. Chromalloy on appeal has pressed the interests of present shareholders and the public in requesting additional relief, perhaps recognizing that a cooling-off period and additional dissemination of information cannot redress the harm, if any, suffered by past shareholders who have already sold to Sun. These shareholders have an adequate remedy at law through an action for damages. * * *

"sterilizing" Icahn's stock cannot be justified on the basis of the insufficient disclosure alleged.

A conclusion that an offeror has failed to make full disclosure must, at bottom, rest upon a finding that the shareholders are being deprived of information necessary to evaluate and act upon the offer. The best remedy for such a problem is to get more information to the shareholders before they have to decide whether or not to tender their shares. Had management been serious in its desire to get all relevant information to its shareholders, it easily could have directed the district court's attention to the omitted contingent liability and sought an order holding up the tender offer unless and until Icahn amended its 14D statements, and appealed the refusal of the district court to do so.

Management has not followed such a course, however. Dan River has not appealed the district court's refusal to enjoin the tender offer. Rather, it merely argues on appeal that the more limited "sterilization" order is nevertheless an appropriate remedy for perceived disclosure violations.

* * *

The so-called lesser remedy of "sterilization" is most certainly acceptable to management, for management is the chief beneficiary of the order. "Sterilization" of Icahn's shares immunizes management from any challenges to its control of the company. Yet the thrust of disclosure laws is to protect shareholders, not management. Management's right of action under the Williams Act is primarily in the interest of the Dan River stockholders to ensure "truthful and complete" information.

* * *

Manifestly, the "sterilization" order affords shareholders no more "truthful and complete" information than that already provided by Icahn in its filings.

* * *

At most, the "sterilization" order is an attempt to foreclose any harm that shareholders might suffer as a consequence of Icahn's purchase of shares under the tender offer. In that regard, "sterilization" of Icahn's shares exacts a heavy toll from Icahn while, at best, yielding stockholders a small measure of premature relief. Icahn is enjoined from actions which can hardly be said to pose harm to shareholders. There is little to be feared, for instance, in permitting Icahn to solicit proxies. Nor does there appear to be much cognizable harm in allowing Icahn to press a vote for new management—a vote the result of which could, if the need arises, be voided or enjoined from taking effect upon the motion of the current management or upon the filing of a suit by interested shareholders.

* * *

The SEC as Plaintiff

Please read sections 21(d)(3) and 21C(a)–(c) of the Securities and Exchange Act contained in your statutory supplement. The case, decided before the provisions were passed in 1990 (the Court implied the remedy under the earlier provisions), nevertheless may impact on the question of how to calculate disgorgement relief under the new provisions.

SEC v. FIRST CITY FINANCIAL CORP.
United States Court of Appeals, District of Columbia Circuit, 1989.
890 F.2d 1215.

SILBERMAN, CIRCUIT JUDGE:

* * *

The SEC charged appellants, First City Financial Corporation, Ltd. ("First City") and Marc Belzberg, with deliberately evading section 13(d) and its accompanying regulations in their attempted hostile takeover of Ashland Oil Company ("Ashland") by filing the required disclosure statement after the 10 day period. * * *

After carefully examining appellants' lengthy briefs and the record in this case, then, we conclude the district court's finding, that appellants deliberately violated section 13(d), should be affirmed, and we turn to the remedies the trial court fashioned.

* * *

There remains, of course, the question of how the court measures those illegal profits. Appellants vigorously dispute the $2.7 million figure that the district court arrived at by simply calculating all of the profits First City realized (in its eventual sale back to Ashland) on the 890,000 shares First City purchased between March 14 and 25. * * * The SEC's claim to disgorgement, which the district court accepted, is predicated on the assumption that had First City made its section 13(d) disclosure on March 14, at the end of the statutory 10 day period, the stock it purchased during the March 14–25 period would have been purchased in a quite different and presumably more expensive market. That hypothetical market would have been affected by the disclosure that the Belzbergs had taken a greater than 5 percent stake in Ashland and would soon propose a tender offer.

Since disgorgement primarily serves to prevent unjust enrichment, the court may exercise its equitable power only over property causally related to the wrongdoing. The remedy may well be a key to the SEC's efforts to deter others from violating the securities laws, but disgorgement may not be used punitively. * * * Therefore, the SEC generally must distinguish between legally and illegally obtained profits. * * * Appellants assert that the hypothetical market between March 14–25 that the SEC urged and the district court accepted was simplistic, quite unrealistic, and so *de facto* punitive. It did not take into account other variables—besides the section 13(d) disclosure—which caused the post-March 25 price of the stock to rise above that which prevailed during the March 14–25 period. At trial appellants' expert witness testified that four independent factors combined to increase the stock price to the level it reached on March 25 and that these factors were not present on March 14, when the defendants should have disclosed. He identified these factors as: (1) the Belzbergs by the 25th held between 8 and 9 percent of Ashland, (2) the Belzbergs had prior to the 25th communicated to Ashland the size of their holdings, (3) Ashland publicly disclosed the Belzbergs' position on the 25th before the 13(d) disclosure, and (4) by the 25th, rumors swirled of an imminent takeover bid at $55 per share. In an attempt to hypothesize how the Belzbergs would have acted—had they disclosed on March 14—and how the market would have responded to those actions, the witness presented three alternative scenarios that in his view more accurately measured the impact of the nondisclosure and which yielded disgorgement figures of zero, $496,050, and $864,588. Perhaps not surprisingly, appellants' witness testified that the most realistic scenario required no disgorgement at all.[23]

If exact information were obtainable at negligible cost, we would not hesitate to impose upon the government a strict burden to produce that data to measure the precise amount of the ill-gotten gains. Unfortunately, we encounter imprecision and imperfect information. Despite sophisticated econometric modelling, predicting stock market responses to alternative variables is, as the district court found, at best speculative. Rules for calculating disgorgement must recognize that separating legal from illegal profits exactly may at times be a near-impossible task. * * *

Accordingly, disgorgement need only be a reasonable approximation of profits causally connected to the violation.

* * *

Although the SEC bears the ultimate burden of persuasion that its disgorgement figure reasonably approximates the amount of unjust enrichment, we believe the government's showing of appellants' actual profits on the tainted transactions at least presumptively satisfied that burden. Appellants, to whom the burden of going forward shifted, were then obliged clearly to demonstrate that the disgorgement figure was not a reasonable approximation. Defendants in such cases may make such a showing, for instance, by pointing to intervening events from the time of the violation. In *SEC v. MacDonald*, 699 F.2d 47 (1st Cir.1983)

---

23. The expert witness concluded that disgorgement was unnecessary because if First City had disclosed on March 14, as the SEC claims it should have, we should assume that the 890,000 shares actually bought in the March 17–25 period (the 10–day window in Belzberg's view) would have been purchased in the lawful March 4–14 10–day window. Since Ashland prices were lower in the March 4–14 period than during March 17–25, the witness believed that no disgorgement was appropriate. This analysis, however, does not consider the impact of buying these 890,000 shares within this 10–day period—in addition to the 330,000 shares the Belzbergs actually purchased then—which presumably would have itself pushed up the price.

(*en banc*), the First Circuit reversed a district court order requiring the defendant to disgorge all profits from an illegal insider trade when the defendant had held on to the stock for more than a year. The court restricted the amount to a figure based on the price of the stock "a reasonable time after public dissemination of the inside information." * * * Similarly, the Second Circuit in *SEC v. Manor Nursing Centers, Inc.*, 458 F.2d 1082 (2d Cir.1972), refused to extend the disgorgement remedy to income subsequently earned on the initial illegal profits. In those cases, the defendant demonstrated a clear break in or considerable attenuation of the causal connection between the illegality and the ultimate profits.

Here, appellants took a different approach using a sophisticated expert witness. As we noted, they maintained that the post-March 25 price was influenced by four other independent factors besides the belated section 13(d) disclosure, so even if First City had disclosed on March 14, the price would not have run up then to the extent it did after March 25. The difficulty we see with appellants' argument is that none of the four factors are independent of the section 13(d) disclosure determination. Thus, although by March 25 First City had accumulated 8–9 percent of Ashland, whereas on March 14 it had slightly over 5 percent (and although the market might react more strongly to the higher figure), we do not see why we should not assume that First City would have acquired 8–9 percent before March 14—if they knew they had to disclose on the earlier date. Second, it seems likely that First City would have notified Ashland's management on March 13 if they had planned to disclose on the next day, just as they did on March 25. Third, Ashland's premature disclosure of First City's holdings (prior to the section 13(d) notice) would likely have also occurred. And finally, the March 25 market takeover rumors were probably associated with all of the above activity, which is inextricably linked with the impending section 13(d) notice. We therefore agree with the district court that appellants' efforts to hypothesize both the takeover efforts of a First City that complied with section 13(d) and the market reaction to that are impossibly speculative.

* * *

Question

Why did the court refuse "alternative B" in footnote 22? Doesn't this figure represent the most Belzberg can be said to have made as a result of his refusal to disclose until March 25? Is the remedy aimed at calculating the damages suffered by all selling shareholders or at disgorging all gains made by Belzberg as a result of the violation?

SECTION 2. THIRD–PARTY TENDER OFFERS

The classic tender offer is a publicly announced offer by an acquirer that it will purchase stock tendered to its depository agent, usually an investment bank, for a set price, typically significantly higher than the current market price, within a limited period of time, if certain market conditions hold true (the market does not crash during the pendency of the offer, for example) and if a specified number of shareholders tender (enough to give the offeror 51 percent of the stock, for example). Rather than buying a controlling block of stock of a diffusely held public company in small bits and pieces, through numerous private negotiations or open market purchases, the offeror hopes to save time and expense by asking publicly that all interested shareholders come to him with their shares. Why is such an approach less expensive?

In a partial tender offer the offeror wants less than all the stock and will accept no more even if more is tendered. In an any-and-all tender offer, the offeror seeks all the stock and will usually buy all that is tendered even if not all the outstanding stock is tendered, if the amount tendered is substantial (over 66 percent). A tender offer made by a firm independent of the target is sometimes called a third-party tender offer (the firm and its shareholders are the other two parties); if it is made by a firm to its own shareholders, it is sometimes called a self-tender offer. Third-party tender offers are regulated by the Securities and Exchange Commission under the authority of section 14(d) of the Exchange Act, and self-tender offers are regulated by the SEC under the authority of section 13(e) of the Exchange Act.

The Form and Disclosure Requirements for a Bidder

Please read section 14(d) of the Exchange Act and Securities and Exchange Commission rules 14d–1, 14d–3, 14d–4, 14d–6, 14d–8, 14d–10, 14e–1, 10b–4, and 10b–13 and skim SEC schedule 14D–1 (focus on general instructions C and D and items 4, 8, 9, and 10) in your statutory supplement.

Questions

1. What kinds of public offers to buy securities are regulated by section 14(d)? See section 14(d)(1) and (8). Is "tender offer" defined in the statute or rules?

2. What are the basic disclosure requirements for a regulated tender offer? See section 14(d)(1) (referring to section 13(d)), rules 14d–4 and 14d–6 (tender offer itself), rule 14d–3, and schedule 14D (tender offer "statement"). When must offerors file a schedule 14D and to whom? See rule 14d–3.

Must a tender offeror disclose its bottom line or reservation price for the target stock when it has offered less? If not, must a tender offeror disclose the financial projections or asset appraisals that it used to calculate its bottom-line price? What if the projections or appraisals are based on information voluntarily given by the target managers and the target managers support the offer? What if managers use the asset appraisals in setting the value in an issuer tender offer? See Radol v. Thomas, 772 F.2d

244 (6th Cir.1985); Flynn v. Bass Bros. Enterprises, Inc., 744 F.2d 978 (3d Cir.1984).

Must a tender offeror disclose that it intends to keep several top-level target managers if the offer is successful or that it intends to honor the severance plan for top-level target managers that are not retained?

Must a tender offeror disclose that if successful, it intends to close a factory and fire workers, sell a factory, or make other major changes in the target firm's asset configuration that impact on labor?

3. What form must a regulated tender offer take? How long must the offer be open? Is there a maximum time allowed? While it is open, can shareholders who have tendered withdraw their shares if they change their mind? Whose shares must the buyer accept if more shares are tendered than the buyer wants? If a buyer changes the tender offer price while the tender offer is open, do shareholders who have tendered before the price change get the benefit of the higher price? See sections 14(d)(5) to (7), rules 14d–7, 14d–10, 14e–1.

If a bidder announces a change from an any-or-all cash tender offer to a partial cash offer followed by a squeeze-out merger, is this an amendment with a ten-day minimum offering period or a new offer with a twenty-day minimum offering period? See CRTF Corp. v. Federated Dept. Stores, Inc., 683 F.Supp. 422 (S.D.N.Y.1988).

4. Can a tender offeror buy stock privately during its tender offer? Before or after a tender offer? See rule 10b–13.

5. Can an arbitrageur tender stock in a tender offer that he does not possess? That he has borrowed from a third party? See rule 10b–4.

6. What is the source of the Securities and Exchange Commission's authority to promulgate rules 14d–7, 14d–10, and 14e–1? Don't the rules change rather than supplement the statutory language?

7. What conditions precedent can a buyer place on its obligations to accept stock tendered in an outstanding tender offer? See rule 12d–1(b)(5). Are there limits in the statutes or rules?

Can a bidder commence a tender offer without firm financing for the cash it needs to buy the asked-for shares, claiming instead that it is highly confident that it will be able to arrange financing in the near future (presumably before it accepts tendered shares)? See item 4 in schedule 14D–1; Newmont Mining Corp. v. Pickens, 831 F.2d 1448 (9th Cir.1987). Can the same firm condition its acceptance of the shares on having the financing in place at the end of the tender offer period?

Can a bidder condition a tender offer on general market conditions? Can a bidder condition a tender offer on the absence of acts by the target managers during the pendency of the tender offer (suppose the target announces a huge one-time cash dividend, for example, on the common stock) that affect the value of the stock? Should all tender offers include such conditions? What other conditions ought a tender offer to include? Rather than specify all conditions, can a tender offer just stipulate that the buyer makes an offer terminable "at will"?

Tender Offer Conditions: The Role of Contract Law

GILBERT v. EL PASO CO.
Supreme Court of Delaware, 1990.
575 A.2d 1131.

MOORE, CHIEF JUSTICE.

* * *

On the afternoon of December 20, 1982, Travis Petty, El Paso's chairman and chief executive officer, received a telephone call from Richard Bressler, the chairman and chief executive officer of Burlington. Bressler confirmed long-circulating rumors of Burlington's interest in acquiring El Paso, and notified Petty that Burlington's board of directors had recently authorized him to initiate a tender offer to gain control of El Paso. The following day, December 21, 1982, Petty received a letter from Bressler confirming that Burlington had launched a tender offer for up to 25,100,000 common shares of El Paso, representing approximately 49.1% of the company's outstanding common stock. The ownership of these shares, when added to the 537,800 already beneficially owned by Burlington, would give Burlington control of over 51.8% of all outstanding El Paso common shares.

The offer stipulated that tendered shares could be withdrawn until January 12, 1983, and that the offer would expire at 12:00 midnight on January 19, 1983. Burlington stated that if the December offer was oversubscribed, any shares tendered before December 30, 1982 would be entitled to proration rights.[7] Significantly, Burlington revealed no future plans to purchase the remaining 49% of El Paso's common shares upon completion of a fully-subscribed December offer. In fact, Burlington specifically cautioned that any future second-step transaction with El Paso's minority shareholders "might be on terms (including the consideration offered per share) the same as, or more or less favorable than, those of the [December] offer." Additionally, Burlington expressly reserved the right to terminate its highly-conditional offer upon the occurrence of any one of a number of specified events.[8]

* * *

---

[7]. We have previously observed that granting such proration rights, in the absence of adequate protections for the company's remaining or back-end shares, has been universally recognized as a "classic coercive measure designed to stampede shareholders into tendering" their shares. *Unocal*, 493 A.2d at 956. This stratagem has primarily been criticized by us and has met a timely demise. *See id. See also* 17 C.F.R. § 240.14d–8 (1988).

[8]. Burlington reserved the right to terminate the offer if: (a) any legal action challenging the offer were instituted or threatened; (b) any governmental body took action which might affect or delay the offer; (c) there were substantial and material changes or threatened changes in the business or assets of El Paso; (d) El Paso authorized or proposed to authorize an extraordinary dividend or the creation of new capital stock; (e) El Paso adopted or proposed to adopt any amendments to its articles of incorporation or By-laws; or (f) El Paso and Burlington entered into a definitive agreement or understanding involving a business combination. Not surprisingly, each of these events occurred at some point during the course of this takeover contest.

Based in part upon these presentations, the El Paso board unanimously rejected Burlington's December offer, concluding that it was not in the best interests of the company or its shareholders. The directors were principally concerned with the perceived inadequacy of the $24 offering price, the partial nature of the bid, and the potentially adverse impact upon remaining shareholders if the December offer were successful. The directors also adopted several resolutions, upon the recommendation of legal counsel, designed to impede Burlington's bid. These measures include "golden parachute" employment agreements with El Paso's senior managers; amendments to El Paso's by-laws and Employee Savings and Stock Ownership plans; creation of a new series of preferred stock, with detachable share rights intended to forestall any business combination between El Paso and a 25% or greater shareholder without the approval of 90% of the outstanding preferred shares.[9]

* * *

Throughout the weekend of January 8th and 9th, the parties' financial and legal advisors negotiated the essential components of a possible accord between the companies. Central to these negotiations was the amount which Burlington would ultimately invest in El Paso. Despite the apparent urging of El Paso's representatives, Burlington steadfastly refused to increase its front-end offer beyond the minimal amount required under its December offer to gain control of El Paso—approximately $600,000,000. Therefore, in order to reconcile these conflicting points with both companies' desire to augment El Paso's capital structure, the parties agreed in principle to Burlington's acquisition of a majority of El Paso's common stock through a consensual, two-part transaction. Under this proposal, Burlington was granted an option of purchase 4,166,667 treasury shares directly from El Paso for $100,000,000. These funds would then be used to increase El Paso's equity base. Burlington would then terminate the December offer, and would substitute in its place a new offer (the January offer), for a reduced total of 21,000,000 shares at $24 per share,[16] which would then be open to all El Paso shareholders. Notably, in addition to enhancing the equity base of the company, this arrangement satisfied El Paso's objective that all shareholders should benefit from an improved Burlington offer.

As part of this record, Burlington agreed in principle to El Paso's demand for enhanced procedural safeguards and protections for El Paso's remaining back-end shareholders. Burlington also agreed that Petty and four other El Paso representatives would continue as di-

9. This novel security, issued as an integral part of a Share Purchase Rights Plan, is generally recognized as the first use and forerunner of the contemporary "poison pill" anti-takeover device. * * *

16. It appears that the number of shares to be purchased by Burlington under the January offer was established after Burlington had agreed to directly invest $100,000,000 in El Paso. The record suggests that the parties worked backwards from Burlington's total investment ceiling of $600,000,000, and determined that the remaining $500,000,000 available for Burlington's acquisition effort could be used to purchase approximately 21,000,000 El Paso shares at $24 per share.

rectors of El Paso ("the Continuing Directors"). Finally, Burlington acknowledged that any contemplated second-step for El Paso's remaining minority shares would be subject to the majority approvals of both the Continuing Directors and El Paso's minority (i.e., non-Burlington) shareholders.

* * *

Burlington thereafter terminated its December offer, and on the next day, January 11, 1983, instituted the new January offer for 21,000,000 shares at $24 per share. In response to the January offer, 40,246,853 shares were tendered, including most of the shares owned by El Paso's directors.

* * *

Plaintiffs primarily challenge two aspects of the settlement agreement between Burlington and El Paso: the substitution of the January offer for the December offer, and the direct purchase by Burlington of 4,166,667 treasury shares from El Paso. Plaintiffs claim, without dispute from the defendants, that those transactions (i) reduced the number of shares that Burlington directly purchased from El Paso's shareholders and (ii) diluted the proration pool initially established under the December offer by allowing *all* shareholders, including those who were not members of the class, to tender into the January offer.

* * *

We first address the Court of Chancery's decision in *Gilbert I* dismissing the breach of contract allegations against Burlington. The court noted that "[p]laintiffs' principal complaint is that Burlington breached its contractual obligation to complete its December tender offer." As characterized, the plaintiffs' breach of contract claim is fundamentally dependent upon their assertion that the class had a recognizable, vested and defendable right to have their shares purchased under the December offer. The plaintiffs' action for contractual breach is contingent upon their presumption that, by tendering their shares into Burlington's highly conditional December offer, the class was vested with certain rights with which neither Burlington nor El Paso could interfere.

It is undisputed that Burlington had conditioned its acceptance of shares tendered into the December offer upon the non-occurrence of a number of specified events, and that *each* of these conditions occurred in the three weeks following the announcement of Burlington's December offer. * * * It is also well settled that under general contract law an offeror may condition the performance contemplated in his offer upon the occurrence or non-occurrence of specific events. Such conditions may effectively limit the obligation of the promisor to perform. * * * Under New Jersey law, an offeror has wide latitude over the terms of its offer and is free to engraft any number of conditions or terms upon it. * * * Similarly, in connection with a tender offer, an offeror may specify any number of conditions qualifying its obligation to perform, subject to Securities and Exchange Commission limitations and the requirements established under the Williams Act. * * * These fundamental principles are clear and are apparently uncontested by the plaintiffs.

Among their ancillary contractual claims, however, plaintiffs argue that Burlington deliberately invoked these conditions solely to acquire El Paso on more advantageous terms, and in so doing, breached its implied covenant of good faith and fair dealing with the class. Although an implied covenant of good faith and honest conduct exists in every contract, * * * such subjective standards cannot override the literal terms of an agreement.

As part of the December offer, Burlington expressly reserved the right to terminate the offer upon the occurrence of a number of objective, factual events over which Burlington exercised no discretion or control. Although an implied covenant of good faith may preclude an offeror from escaping its obligations by deliberately causing the occurrence of a condition precedent, there is no evidence of such activity here. We agree with the Vice Chancellor's finding that an offeror "is free to pursue its economic interests through the application of conditions intended to limit the cost of proceeding." * * * In tendering their shares to Burlington, the class accepted these express limitations and qualifications, and acknowledged that Burlington could be relieved of its promise to perform upon the occurrence of any of the reserved conditions. Thus, Burlington's mere exercise of its contractual right to terminate its tender offer, without more, does not constitute a breach of its implied covenant of good faith and fair dealing.

* * *

[The court concluded that the plaintiff's allegations of fiduciary breach against the target directors failed as well.]

Note
The Effect of the Williams Act

The classic defense of the Williams Act is contained in Chief Justice Burger's opinion in *Rondeau v. Mosinee Paper Corp.,* supra: The act gives the target shareholders adequate information about the bid and the time to digest the information. Absent the act, bidders can make a raw offer, without information on itself or its plans, at premium prices and stampede shareholders into tendering by announcing that the offer will be open for a short time and that the buyer will accept less than all the shares on a first-come-first-served basis.

Critics of the Williams Act view the act as a hinderance to tender offers that replace inefficient managers. Without the threat of such tender offers, managers have more room to shirk their responsibilities. First, the act's requirement that the offeror disclose all material facts about the target, including its plans for the target if it obtains control, reduces the incentive to make initial bids, because other bidders and the target can use the information revealed without compensation, free-riding on the initial bidder's search costs, to defeat the offeror's bid. Second, the act's waiting period enhances the possibility of competitive bids or defensive maneuvers by target managers. And third, the Securities and Exchange Commission rules promulgated under the authority of the act prohibit price discrimination among target shareholders, raising the costs of a control acquisition to the price demanded by the last shareholder (the holdout shareholder) whose shares are needed to complete the control block.

As a consequence, the act raises the cost of successful takeovers and shelters managerial inefficiency. If the Williams Act were repealed, the argument runs, "lightning fast" bids ("Saturday night specials") could be launched, competitive bidders and target managers would not have time to react, and it would become possible to consummate a tender offer at a lower price. Managers would be more concerned about their job performance, lest they encourage a tender offer from depressed stock prices caused by their subpar efforts, and shareholders would receive the benefit of higher stock prices across the board from consistently better performing managers.

In the years immediately following the passage of the Williams Act in 1968, takeover premiums increased from 32 percent to 53 percent, and the frequency of takeovers declined. See Jarrell & Bradley, The Economic Effects of Federal and State Regulation of Cash Tender Offers, 23 J.L. & Econ. 371, 373, 388, 405 (1980). After the act the number of takeovers did not exceed pre-act levels for eleven years.

Note

Equal Treatment of Shareholders in Tender Offers

OESTERLE, THE RISE AND FALL OF STREET SWEEP TAKEOVERS
Duke L.J. 202, 249–56 (1989).

* * *

Williams Act supporters focus on one or both of the Act's two goals. * * * The Act's first goal is to enable target shareholders to evaluate an offer's merits more effectively. The Act thus requires disclosures by bidders and relaxes deadline pressure. The provisions mandating a minimum offering period, withdrawal periods, and pro rata acceptance for oversubscribed offers all act to delay any tender offer's closing date in order to ensure that target shareholders have time to consider and act on the offer's merits.

* * *

The Act's second goal, which is independent of and not necessary to the first, is to protect shareholder equality in control changes. Bidders must include all shareholders in an offer, must accept oversubscribed offers pro rata, may not purchase in the markets during an offer's pendency, must give any price increases to all those who tendered before the increases, and must legally commence their tender offer on the date of the first offer-specific public announcement. Moreover, the

Act prevents those who tender from avoiding the pro rata limitations through short tenders or hedged tenders. These provisions prohibit price discrimination among shareholders once a tender offer has begun, arguably to protect small shareholders who otherwise could not command the premiums that large shareholders could command. The Act's shareholder equality goal, however, is much less defensible than the shareholder evaluation goal.

* * *

The statutory language of the Williams Act does not require that all tender offers for more than 5% of any equity security registered under section 12 of the Securities Exchange Act of 1934 go to all shareholders, nor does the Act prohibit a tender offeror from privately buying shares during a tender offer. The SEC added those obligations by rule. The statute requires only that all shareholders be allowed to participate proportionately in oversubscribed offers and that all receive the highest price offered to any shareholder. The provision on proportionate participation is necessary not as an equal-opportunity rule, but to relieve deadline pressure on target shareholders. A minimum offering period does not relieve a rush to tender if at the end of the period the bidder accepts stock on a first-tendered basis. The provision on price increases also encourages shareholders to tender during the offer period rather than wait until the last minute before the offer expires.

Absent SEC regulatory interference, a bidder could comply with the Act even if it purchased stock outside the tender offer before, during, and after the tender offer and at prices differing from the tender offer price. The Act's language also allows a bidder to discriminate among shareholders in the tender offer itself.[224]

* * * Professors Easterbrook and Fischel have directly challenged rules that require the gains in control transactions to be shared. They argue that target shareholders would prefer a rule that allowed unequal division of control acquisition gains if the total gains produced in such acquisitions were maximized in the aggregate, regardless of how the gains were distributed in any one transaction.[228] Through diversification, according to their view, shareholders can eliminate the risk of adverse discrimination in any one control transaction and enjoy a proportionate share of the larger aggregate gains that such a rule would produce, a share that would exceed their share of the gains under an equal-division rule.

---

224. Section 14(d)(7)'s best-price rule does not literally require inclusion of all shareholders in any one tender offer. One could comply with the statute by excluding some shareholders from a tender offer completely or by making two tender offers at different prices for mutually exclusive groups of shareholders.

228. *Id.* at 711–14. Recent empirical evidence suggests that transfer of control at a premium benefits minority shareholders, a finding that supports the Easterbrook and Fischel thesis. *See* Holderness & Sheehan, *The Rate of Majority Shareholders in Publicly Held Corporations: An Exploratory Analysis,* 21 J.FIN.ECON. 317, 327–33 (1988).

Arguments favoring an unequal division of control transaction gains must answer two charges. First, some might claim that unequal-division rules would consistently advantage insiders and that small shareholders would be unable to diversify against such a systematic risk. Second, others might claim that if an unequal-division rule produced aggregate gains exceeding those produced by an equal-division rule, then that merely shows a broader problem in need of correction. According to this second charge, unequal-division rules would produce gains only if the law were lax and allowed insiders to exploit their control positions to the detriment of other shareholders.

An equal-treatment rule designed to protect small shareholders is not an unqualified good.[235] Such a rule allows small shareholders to benefit from gains created by others *outside* the firm itself (although not from insider trading). Bidders create information (i.e., that they will bid), and speculators with superior market-monitoring capabilities first disclose that information. Both bidders and speculators invest resources in order to create or discover such information in the trading markets. If we allow small shareholders to free-ride on these investments, under the rubric of equal protection, then bidders and speculators will underinvest, and the entire stock market will be poorer as a result. Not only will the market's price discovery function be compromised, but investors will also have less incentive to invest in large blocks of stock. Large block holders are better able to monitor managers' actions and reduce the transaction costs of control changes. The reason that the market works fairly well now is because the equal-protection rule has seen so much slippage from theory to practice. Vigilant egalitarians, though, are always pushing to reduce this slack.

The second charge made by equal-opportunity advocates is that an unequal-division rule allows shareholder control groups to exploit other shareholders. According to this argument, if control-group stock has more value than other stock solely because control-group shareholders can divert a disproportionate share of the firm's income to themselves, then an unequal-division rule would allow control groups to sell this right of exploitation, presumably to a new control group that will be best able to maximize its disproportionate share of corporate income—the highest-valued user. The need for an unequal division rule is thus a symptom of an inadequate system of insider controls. If the law, or firms, better regulate insider behavior, the unequal-division rule becomes superfluous.

In the context of street sweeps, however, this argument makes no sense. Most street sweeps respond to insiders' refusal to sell a company. Acquirers accumulate stock from noncontrolling shareholders in

---

235. It is surprising that the antidiscrimination rule is so uncritically accepted in this area, when it has met with so thorough a rebuke in others. *See, e.g.,* Department of Justice, Report on the Robinson–Patman Act 251–59 (1977) (Robinson–Patman Act's price discrimination provisions, which embody "equality of opportunity" principles, cannot be justified in light of great economic inefficiencies that Act imposes on society).

order to form a control group that can oust a preexisting control group. Hence, in a street sweep, the acquirer is not buying out the existing control group, but ousting it.[238] Such street sweeps do not reward control groups holding disproportionate shares of firm income, but rather act as a check on such groups.

The unequal prices that acquirers pay to shareholders in accumulating a control block reflect (1) transaction-cost savings when acquirers can buy a block of stock rather than having to pursue individual solicitations, (2) informational disparities among shareholders, and (3) different price evaluations by those with similar information. The first and third reasons for unequal price should trouble no one, but the second reason might trouble some. It ought not, however, since acquirers who create this valuable information—i.e., their intent to buy—ought to be able to exploit that information.

* * *

Question

Can we design the Williams Act to eliminate the "stampede effect" generated by public short-lived first-come-first-served tender offers and yet preserve a bidder's ability to offer different prices to different kinds of shareholders?

The Definition of a "Tender Offer": When Is a "Street Sweep" Included?

Please read rule 14d–2 in your statutory supplement.

HANSON TRUST PLC v. SCM CORP.
United States Court of Appeals, Second Circuit, 1985.
774 F.2d 47.

MANSFIELD, CIRCUIT JUDGE:

* * *

---

238. Even if an acquirer purchases a preexisting control block in a street sweep, the claim against an unequal division of the gains has two answers. First, assuming that control groups can extract some disproportionate share of the gain to the rest of the shareholders' disadvantage, one could not characterize all acquirers as paying a premium solely because they can better exploit small shareholders. Many acquirers only exploit small shareholders to the same extent that the preexisting control group can. Thus, the premium paid for control is not based on an expectation of enhanced minority shareholder exploitation, but on an expectation that the acquirer can create socially useful gains, such as economies of scale. Second, the assumption that all disproportionate shares of gains enjoyed by shareholder control groups are inappropriate is not necessarily true. As Professor Gilson notes, minority shareholders might be better off giving a disproportionate share of the gains to a shareholder control group if the group effectively monitors managers to the advantage of all shareholders. This argument assumes, however, that the agency cost that firm managers visit on a diverse group of shareholders is larger than the agency cost generated by managers monitored by a control group of shareholders plus the agency cost generated by the control group itself. If managers and a shareholder control group simply gang up on all other shareholders to divert corporate income, minority shareholders might be worse off.

SCM is a New York corporation with its principal place of business in New York City. Its shares, of which at all relevant times at least 9.9 million were outstanding and 2.3 million were subject to issuance upon conversion of other outstanding securities, are traded on the New York Stock Exchange (NYSE) and Pacific Stock Exchange. Hanson Trust PLC is an English company with its principal place of business in London. * * *

On August 21, 1985, Hanson publicly announced its intention to make a cash tender offer of $60 per share for any and all outstanding SCM shares. Five days later it filed the tender offer documents required by § 14(d)(1) of the Williams Act and regulations issued thereunder. The offer provided that it would remain open until September 23, unless extended, that no shares would be accepted until September 10, and that

> "Whether or not the Purchasers [Hanson] purchase Shares pursuant to the Offer, the Purchasers may thereafter determine, subject to the availability of Shares at favorable prices and the availability of financing, to purchase additional Shares in the open market, in privately negotiated transactions, through another tender offer or otherwise. Any such purchases of additional Shares might be on terms which are the same as, or more or less favorable than, those of this Offer. The Purchasers also reserve the right to dispose of any or all Shares acquired by them." *Offer to Purchase For Cash Any and All Outstanding Shares of Common Stock of SCM Corporation* (Aug. 26, 1985) at 21.

On August 30, 1985, SCM, having recommended to SCM's stockholders that they not accept Hanson's tender offer, announced a preliminary agreement with Merrill under which a new entity, formed by SCM and Merrill, would acquire all SCM shares at $70 per share in a leveraged buyout sponsored by Merrill. Under the agreement, which was executed on September 3, the new entity would make a $70 per share cash tender offer for approximately 85% of SCM's shares. If more than two-thirds of SCM's shares were acquired under the offer the remaining SCM shares would be acquired in exchange for debentures in a new corporation to be formed as a result of the merger. On the same date, September 3, Hanson increased its tender offer from $60 to $72 cash per share. However, it expressly reserved the right to terminate its offer if SCM granted to anyone any option to purchase SCM assets on terms that Hanson believed to constitute a "lock-up" device. * * *

The next development in the escalating bidding contest for control of SCM occurred on September 10, 1985, when SCM entered into a new leveraged buyout agreement with its "White Knight," Merrill. The agreement provided for a two-step acquisition of SCM stock by Merrill at $74 per share. The first proposed step was to be the acquisition of approximately 82% of SCM's outstanding stock for cash. Following a merger (which required acquisition of at least 66⅔%), debentures would be issued for the remaining SCM shares. If any investor or group other than Merrill acquired more than one-third of SCM's outstanding shares, Merrill would have the option to buy SCM's two most profitable businesses, pigments and consumer foods, for $350 and $80 million respectively, prices which Hanson believed to be below their market value.

Hanson, faced with what it considered to be a "poison pill," concluded that even if it increased its cash tender offer to $74 per share it would end up with control of a substantially depleted and damaged company. Accordingly, it announced on the Dow Jones Broad Tape at 12:38 P.M. on September 11 that it was terminating its cash tender offer. A few minutes later, Hanson issued a press release, carried on the Broad Tape, to the effect that "all SCM shares tendered will be promptly returned to the tendering shareholders."

At some time in the late forenoon or early afternoon of September 11 Hanson decided to make cash purchases of a substantial percentage of SCM stock in the open market or through privately negotiated transactions. Under British law Hanson could not acquire more than 49% of SCM's shares in this fashion without obtaining certain clearances, but acquisition of such a large percentage was not necessary to stymie the SCM–Merrill merger proposal. If Hanson could acquire slightly less than one-third of SCM's outstanding shares it would be able to block the $74 per share SCM–Merrill offer of a leveraged buyout. This might induce the latter to work out an agreement with Hanson, something Hanson had unsuccessfully sought on several occasions since its first cash tender offer.

Within a period of two hours on the afternoon of September 11 Hanson made five privately-negotiated cash purchases of SCM stock and one open-market purchase, acquiring 3.1 million shares or 25% of SCM's outstanding stock. The price of SCM stock on the NYSE on September 11 ranged from a high of $73.50 per share to a low of $72.50 per share. Hanson's initial private purchase, 387,700 shares from Mutual Shares, was not solicited by Hanson but by a Mutual Shares official, Michael Price, who, in a conversation with Robert Pirie of Rothschild, Inc., Hanson's financial advisor, on the morning of September 11 (before Hanson had decided to make any private cash purchases), had stated that he was interested in selling Mutual's Shares' SCM stock to Hanson. Once Hanson's decision to buy privately had been made, Pirie took Price up on his offer. The parties negotiated a sale at $73.50 per share after Pirie refused Price's asking prices, first of $75 per share and, later, of $74.50 per share. This transaction, but not the identity of the parties, was automatically reported pursuant to NYSE rules on the NYSE ticker at 3:11 P.M. and reported on the Dow Jones Broad Tape at 3:29 P.M.

Pirie then telephoned Ivan Boesky, an arbitrageur who had a few weeks earlier disclosed in a Schedule 13D statement filed with the SEC that he owned approximately 12.7% of SCM's outstanding shares. Pirie negotiated a Hanson purchase of these shares at $73.50 per share after rejecting Boesky's initial demand of $74 per share. At the same time Rothschild purchased for Hanson's account 600,000 SCM shares in the open market at $73.50 per share. An attempt by Pirie next to negotiate the cash purchase of another large block of SCM stock (some 780,000 shares) from Slifka & Company fell through because of the latter's inability to make delivery of the shares on September 12.

Following the NYSE ticker and Broad Tape reports of the first two large anonymous transactions in SCM stock, some professional investors surmised that the buyer might be Hanson. Rothschild then received telephone calls from (1) Mr. Mulhearn of Jamie & Co. offering to sell between 200,000 and 350,000 shares at $73.50 per share, (2) David Gottesman, an arbitrageur at Oppenheimer & Co. offering 89,000 shares at $73.50, and (3) Boyd Jeffries of Jeffries & Co., offering approximately 700,000 to 800,000 shares at $74.00. Pirie purchased the three blocks for Hanson at $73.50 per share. The last of Hanson's cash purchases was completed by 4:35 P.M. on September 11, 1985.

* * *

Sir Gordon White [Hanson's United States Chairman] testified that on September 11, 1985, after learning of the $74 per share SCM–Merrill leveraged buyout tender offer with its "crown jewel" irrevocable "lock up" option to Merrill, he instructed Pirie to terminate Hanson's $72 per share tender offer, and that only thereafter did he discuss the possibility of Hanson making market purchases of SCM stock. Pirie testified that the question of buying stock may have been discussed in the late forenoon of September 11 and that he had told White that he was having Hanson's New York counsel look into whether such cash purchases were legally permissible.

* * *

Since, as the district court correctly noted, the material relevant facts in the present case are not in dispute, this appeal turns on whether the district court erred as a matter of law in holding that when Hanson terminated its offer and immediately thereafter made private purchases of a substantial share of the target company's outstanding stock, the purchases became a "tender offer" within the meaning of § 14(d) of the Williams Act. Absent any express definition of "tender offer" in the Act, the answer requires a brief review of the background and purposes of § 14(d).

Congress adopted § 14(d) in 1968 "in response to the growing use of cash tender offers as a means of achieving corporate takeovers ... which ... removed a substantial number of corporate control contests from the reach of existing disclosure requirements of the federal securities laws." *Piper v. Chris–Craft Industries,* 430 U.S. 1, 22, 97 S.Ct. 926, 939, 51 L.Ed.2d 124 (1977).

* * *

The typical tender offer, as described in the Congressional debates, hearings and reports on the Williams Act, consisted of a general, publicized bid by an individual or group to buy shares of a publicly-owned company, the shares of which were traded on a national securities exchange, at a price substantially above the current market price. * * * The offer was usually accompanied by newspaper and other publicity, a time limit for tender of shares in response to it, and a provision fixing a quantity limit on the total number of shares of the target company that would be purchased.

Prior to the Williams Act a tender offeror had no obligation to disclose any information to shareholders when making a bid. * * * The average shareholder, pressured by the fact that the tender offer would be available for only a short time and restricted to a limited number of shares, was forced "with severely limited information, [to] decide what course of action he should take." * * * "Without knowledge of who the bidder is and what he plans to do, the shareholder cannot reach an informed decision. He is forced to take a chance. For no matter what he does, he does it without adequate information to enable him to decide rationally what is the best possible course of action."

* * *

The purpose of the Williams Act was, accordingly, to protect the shareholders from that dilemma by insuring "that public shareholders who are confronted by a cash tender offer for their stock will not be required to respond without adequate information."

* * *

Congress took "extreme care," * * * however, when protecting shareholders, to avoid "tipping the balance of regulation either in favor of management or in favor of the person making the takeover bid." * * * Indeed, the initial draft of the bill, proposed in 1965, had been designed to prevent "proud old companies [from being] reduced to corporate shells after white-collar pirates have seized control." * * * Williams withdrew that draft following claims that it was too biased in favor of incumbent management.

* * *

Congress finally settled upon a statute requiring a tender offer solicitor seeking beneficial ownership of more than 5% of the outstanding shares of any class of any equity security registered on a national securities exchange first to file with the SEC a statement containing certain information specified in § 13(d)(1) of the Act, as amplified by SEC rules and regulations. Congress' failure to define "tender offer" was deliberate. Aware of "the almost infinite variety in the terms of most tender offers" and concerned that a rigid definition would be evaded, Congress left to the court and the SEC the flexibility to define the term.

* * *

Although § 14(d)(1) clearly applies to "classic" tender offers of the type described above (pp. 54–55), courts soon recognized that in the case of privately negotiated transactions or solicitations for private purchases of stock many of the conditions leading to the enactment of § 14(d) for the most part do not exist. The number and percentage of stockholders are usually far less than those involved in public offers. The solicitation involves less publicity than a public tender offer or none. The solicitees, who are frequently directors, officers or substantial stockholders of the target, are more apt to be sophisticated, inquiring or knowledgeable concerning the target's business, the solicitor's objectives, and the impact of the solicitation on the target's business prospects. In short, the solicitee in the private transaction is less likely to be pressured, confused, or ill-informed regarding the businesses and decisions at stake than solicitees who are the subjects of a public tender offer.

These differences between public and private securities transactions have led most courts to rule that private transactions or open market purchases do not qualify as a "tender offer" requiring the purchaser to meet the pre-filing strictures of § 14(d). The borderline between public solicitations and privately negotiated stock purchases is not bright and it is frequently difficult to determine whether transactions falling close to the line or in a type of "no man's land" are "tender offers" or private deals. This has led some to advocate a broader interpretation of the term "tender offer" than that followed by us in *Kennecott Copper Corp. v. Curtiss–Wright Corp., supra,* 584 F.2d at 1207, and to adopt the eight-factor "test" of what is a tender offer, which was recommended by the SEC and applied by the district court in *Wellman v. Dickinson,* 475 F.Supp. 783, 823–24 (S.D.N.Y.1979), *aff'd on other grounds,* 682 F.2d 355 (2d Cir.1982), *cert. denied,* 460 U.S. 1069, 103 S.Ct. 1522, 75 L.Ed.2d 946 (1983), and by the Ninth Circuit in *SEC v. Carter Hawley Hale Stores, Inc., supra.* The eight factors are:

"(1) active and widespread solicitation of public shareholders for the shares of an issuer;

(2) solicitation made for a substantial percentage of the issuer's stock;

(3) offer to purchase made at a premium over the prevailing market price;

(4) terms of the offer are firm rather than negotiable;

(5) offer contingent on the tender of a fixed number of shares, often subject to a fixed maximum number to be purchased;

(6) offer open only for a limited period of time;

(7) offeree subjected to pressure to sell his stock;

(8) public announcements of a purchasing program concerning the target company precede or accompany rapid accumulation of large amounts of the target company's securities." (475 F.Supp. at 823–24).

Although many of the above-listed factors are relevant for purposes of determining whether a given solicitation amounts to a tender offer, the elevation of such a list to a mandatory "litmus test" appears to be both unwise and unnecessary. As even the advocates of the proposed test recognize, in any given case a solicitation may constitute a tender offer even though some of the eight factors are absent or, when many factors are present, the solicitation may nevertheless not amount to a tender offer because the missing factors outweigh those present. *Id.*, at 824; *Carter, supra*, at 950.

We prefer to be guided by the principle followed by the Supreme Court in deciding what transactions fall within the private offering exemption provided by § 4(1) of the Securities Act of 1933, and by ourselves in *Kennecott Copper* in determining whether the Williams Act applies to private transactions. That principle is simply to look to the statutory purpose. In *S.E.C. v. Ralston Purina Co.*, 346 U.S. 119, 73 S.Ct. 981, 97 L.Ed. 1494 (1953), the Court stated, "the applicability of § 4(1) should turn on whether the particular class of persons affected need the protection of the Act. An offering to those who are shown to be able to fend for themselves is a transaction 'not involving any public offering.'" *Id.*, at 125, 73 S.Ct. at 984. Similarly, since the purpose of § 14(d) is to protect the ill-informed solicitee, the question of whether a solicitation constitutes a "tender offer" within the meaning of § 14(d) turns on whether, viewing the transaction in the light of the totality of circumstances, there appears to be a likelihood that unless the pre-acquisition filing strictures of that statute are followed there will be a substantial risk that solicitees will lack information needed to make a carefully considered appraisal of the proposal put before them.

Applying this standard, we are persuaded on the undisputed facts that Hanson's September 11 negotiation of five private purchases and one open market purchase of SCM shares, totalling 25% of SCM's outstanding stock, did not under the circumstances constitute a "tender offer" within the meaning of the Williams Act. Putting aside for the moment the events preceding the purchases, there can be little doubt that the privately negotiated purchases would not, standing alone, qualify as a tender offer, for the following reasons:

> (1) In a market of 22,800 SCM shareholders the number of SCM sellers here involved, six in all, was miniscule compared with the numbers involved in public solicitations of the type against which the Act was directed.

> (2) At least five of the sellers were highly sophisticated professionals, knowledgeable in the market place and well aware of the essential facts needed to exercise their professional skills and to appraise Hanson's offer, including its financial condition as well as that of SCM, the likelihood that the purchases might block the SCM–Merrill bid, and the risk that if Hanson acquired more than 33⅓% of SCM's stock the SCM–Merrill lock up of the "crown jewel" might be triggered. Indeed, by September 11 they had all had access to (1) Hanson's 27–page detailed disclosure of facts, filed on August 26, 1985, in accordance with § 14(d)(1) with respect to its

$60 tender offer, (2) Hanson's 4–page amendment of that offer, dated September 5, 1985, increasing the price to $72 per share, and (3) press releases regarding the basic terms of the SCM–Merrill proposed leveraged buyout at $74 per share and of the SCM–Merrill asset option agreement under which SCM granted to Merrill the irrevocable right under certain conditions to buy SCM's consumer food business for $80 million and its pigment business for $350 million.

(3) The sellers were not "pressured" to sell their shares by any conduct that the Williams Act was designed to alleviate, but by the forces of the market place. Indeed, in the case of Mutual Shares there was no initial solicitation by Hanson; the offer to sell was initiated by Mr. Price of Mutual Shares. Although each of the Hanson purchases was made for $73.50 per share, in most instances this price was the result of private negotiations after the sellers sought higher prices and in one case price protection, demands which were refused. The $73.50 price was not fixed in advance by Hanson. Moreover, the sellers remained free to accept the $74 per share tender offer made by the SCM–Merrill group.

(4) There was no active or widespread advance publicity or public solicitation, which is one of the earmarks of a conventional tender offer. Arbitrageurs might conclude from ticker tape reports of two large anonymous transactions that Hanson must be the buyer. However, liability for solicitation may not be predicated upon disclosures mandated by Stock Exchange Rules. See *S.E.C. v. Carter–Hawley Hale Stores, Inc., supra,* 760 F.2d at 950.

(5) The price received by the six sellers, $73.50 per share, unlike that appearing in most tender offers, can scarcely be dignified with the label "premium." The stock market price on September 11 ranged from $72.50 to $73.50 per share. Although risk arbitrageurs sitting on large holdings might reap sizeable profits from sales to Hanson at $73.50, depending on their own purchase costs, they stood to gain even more if the SCM–Merrill offer of $74 should succeed, as it apparently would if they tendered their shares to it. Indeed, the $73.50 price, being at most $1 over market or 1.4% higher than the market price, did not meet the SEC's proposed definition of a premium, which is $2.00 per share or 5% above market price, whichever is greater. SEC Exchange Act Release No. 16,385 (11/29/79) [1979–80] Fed.Sec.L.Rep. ¶ 82,374.

(6) Unlike most tender offers, the purchases were not made contingent upon Hanson's acquiring a fixed minimum number or percentage of SCM's outstanding shares. Once an agreement with each individual seller was reached, Hanson was obligated to buy, regardless what total percentage of stock it might acquire. Indeed, it does not appear that Hanson had fixed in its mind a firm limit on the amount of SCM shares it was willing to buy.

(7) Unlike most tender offers, there was no general time limit within which Hanson would make purchases of SCM stock. Concededly, cash transactions are normally immediate but, assuming an inability on the part of a seller and Hanson to agree at once on a price, nothing prevented a resumption of negotiations by each of the parties except the arbitrageurs' speculation that once Hanson acquired 33⅓% or an amount just short of that figure it would stop buying.

In short, the totality of circumstances that existed on September 11 did not evidence any likelihood that unless Hanson was required to comply with § 14(d)(1)'s pre-acquisition filing and waiting-period requirements there would be a substantial risk of ill-considered sales of SCM stock by ill-informed shareholders.

There remains the question whether Hanson's private purchases take on a different hue, requiring them to be treated as a *"de facto"* continuation of its earlier tender offer, when considered in the context of Hanson's earlier acknowledged tender offer, the competing offer of SCM–Merrill and Hanson's termination of its tender offer. After reviewing all of the undisputed facts we conclude that the district court erred in so holding.

In the first place, we find no record support for the contention by SCM that Hanson's September 11 termination of its outstanding tender offer was false, fraudulent or ineffective. Hanson's termination notice was clear, unequivocal and straightforward. Directions were given, and presumably are being followed, to return all of the tendered shares to the SCM shareholders who tendered them. Hanson also filed with the SEC a statement pursuant to § 14(d)(1) of the Williams Act terminating its tender offer. As a result, at the time when Hanson made its September 11 private purchases of SCM stock it owned no SCM stock other than those shares revealed in its § 14(d) pre-acquisition report filed with the SEC on August 26, 1985.

The reason for Hanson's termination of its tender offer is not disputed: in view of SCM's grant of what Hanson conceived to be a "poison pill" lock up option to Merrill, Hanson, if it acquired control of SCM, would have a company denuded as the result of its sale of its consumer food and pigment businesses to Merrill at what Hanson believed to be bargain prices. Thus, Hanson's termination of its tender offer was final; there was no tender offer to be "continued." Hanson was unlikely to "shoot itself in the foot" by triggering what it believed to be a "poison pill," and it could not acquire more than 49% of SCM's shares without violating the rules of the London Stock Exchange.

Nor does the record support SCM's contention that Hanson had decided, before terminating its tender offer, to engage in cash purchases. Judge Kram referred only to evidence that "Hanson had *considered* open market purchases before it announced that the tender offer was dropped" (emphasis added) but made no finding to that effect. Absent evidence or a finding that Hanson had decided to seek control of SCM through purchases of its stock, no duty of disclosure existed under the federal securities laws.

Second, Hanson had expressly reserved the right in its August 26, 1985, pre-acquisition tender offer filing papers, whether or not tendered shares were purchased, "*thereafter* ... to purchase additional Shares in the open market, in privately negotiated transactions, through another tender offer or otherwise." (Emphasis added). See p. 46, *supra*. Thus, Hanson's privately negotiated purchases could hardly have taken the market by surprise. Indeed, professional arbitrageurs and market experts rapidly concluded that it was Hanson which was making the post-termination purchases.

Last, Hanson's prior disclosures of essential facts about itself and SCM in the pre-acquisition papers it filed on August 26, 1985, with the SEC pursuant to § 14(d)(1), are wholly inconsistent with the district court's characterization of Hanson's later private purchases as "a deliberate attempt to do an 'end run' around the requirements of the Williams Act." On the contrary, the record shows that Hanson had already filed with the SEC and made public substantially the same information as SCM contends that Hanson should have filed before making the cash purchases. The term "tender offer," although left somewhat flexible by Congress' decision not to define it, nevertheless remains a word of art. Section 14(d)(1) was never intended to apply to *every* acquisition of more than 5% of a public company's stock. If that were the case there would be no need for § 13(d)(1), which requires a person, *after* acquiring more than 5%, to furnish the issuer, stock exchange and the SEC with certain pertinent information. Yet the expansive definition of "tender offer" advocated by SCM, and to some extent by the SEC as amicus, would go far toward rendering § 13(d)(1) a dead letter. In the present case, we were advised by Hanson's counsel upon argument on September 23 that on that date it was filing with the SEC the information required by § 13(d)(1) of the Williams Act with respect to its private purchases of SCM stock. In our view this is all that is required by the Act in the present circumstances.

It may well be that Hanson's private acquisition of 25% of SCM's shares after termination of Hanson's tender offer was designed to block the SCM–Merrill leveraged buyout group from acquiring the 66⅔% of SCM's stock needed to effectuate a merger. It may be speculated that such a blocking move might induce SCM to buy Hanson's 25% at a premium or lead to negotiations between the parties designed to resolve their differences. But we know of no provision in the federal securities laws or elsewhere that prohibits such tactics in "hardball" market battles of the type encountered here. *See Treadway Companies, Inc. v. Care Corp.*, 638 F.2d 357, 378–79 (2d Cir.1980) ("We also see nothing wrong in Care's efforts to acquire one third of Treadway's outstanding stock, and thus to obtain a 'blocking position'.").

Thus the full disclosure purposes of the Williams Act as it now stands appear to have been fully satisfied by Hanson's furnishing to the public, both before and after termination of its tender offer, all of the essential relevant facts it was required by law to supply.

* * *

FIELD v. TRUMP

United States Court of Appeals, Second Circuit, 1988.
850 F.2d 938, cert. denied 489 U.S. 1012, 109 S.Ct. 1122, 103 L.Ed.2d 185 (1989).

WINTER, CIRCUIT JUDGE.

* * *

This dispute originates in Pay'n Save's acquisition of Schuck's Auto Supply, Inc. in January 1984. That transaction left the former owners of Schuck's, defendants Samuel N. Stroum and Stuart M. Sloan and members of their families ("Stroums" or "Stroum Group"), holding 18.4% of Pay'n Save's outstanding common stock. The Stroums were not happy shareholders, however, and had their own ideas about how to run Pay'n Save. Looking for ways to pacify the Stroums, Pay'n Save management sought and obtained a standstill agreement dated March 30, 1984. The Stroums agreed not to sell or otherwise dispose of their shares, or to offer to purchase Pay'n Save. In return, Stroum and Sloan received seats on the company's board.

Friction between the Stroums and management nevertheless continued. As a result, management retained Kidder Peabody and later Merrill Lynch Capital Markets to find a purchaser for the company. To the same end, defendant Calvin Hendricks, Pay'n Save's Chief Financial Officer and Vice–Chairman of its board, undertook discussions with Eddie Trump, President of the Trump Group, Ltd., about acquiring Pay'n Save. According to its subsequent Offer to Purchase, the Trump Group took the position that it "would only consider an acquisition of the company if management would participate in the equity of the resulting entity." * * * Management agreed, and on August 31 the Trumps proposed to the Pay'n Save board a cash tender offer at $22.00 per share for two-thirds of the company's outstanding shares, to be followed by a cash-out merger at the same price. One week later, in the early morning hours of a late-night Pay'n Save board meeting, the Trumps raised their offer to $22.50 but warned that it would be withdrawn if it were not approved. Merrill Lynch opined that $22.50 was a fair price, and a majority of Pay'n Save's board approved it. Stroum and Sloan dissented. That morning, September 7, 1984, Pay'n Save issued a press release announcing that it had reached a merger agreement with the Trumps and that the Trumps were initiating a tender offer at $22.50. In a statement of their own, the Stroums called the Trump offer "skimpy" and accused management of acting in "unseemly haste."

During the next few days, according to the Offer to Purchase, "Eddie Trump contacted Messrs. Stroum and Sloan and the parties had several conversations concerning the possibility of settling the objections of Messrs. Stroum and Sloan to the Transactions." * * * At 5:10 p.m. on September 12, after a meeting between the Trumps, Stroum and Sloan, the Trumps told Pay'n Save's board that they were withdrawing their previously announced tender offer in order "to facilitate the negotiations with Messrs. Stroum and Sloan." * * * The Trumps also issued a press release announcing both the withdrawal of their tender offer and their negotiations with the Stroums. These negotiations quickly bore fruit. Later that night, the Trumps and the Stroums entered into a Settlement Agreement under which the Trumps paid the Stroums $3,300,000 for an option to purchase the Stroums' shares at $23.50 per share. In addition, the Trumps paid the Stroums $900,000 for the Stroums' "fees and expenses." The Settlement Agreement was subject to the Pay'n Save board's approval of an amendment to the September 7 merger agreement that would provide for an increased price of $23.50 per share for the tender offer and merger. The $4,200,000 payment (option price plus "fees and expenses"), when added to the $23.50 per share purchase price, amounted to a price of $25.00 per share for the Stroums.

The next day, September 13, the Pay'n Save board approved the amendment to the merger agreement, and Pay'n Save issued a press release announcing that the Trumps would soon proceed with a tender offer at the new $23.50 price. According to the complaint, the press release announcing the new price and the September 12 press release announcing the "withdrawal" reached the public simultaneously.

Claiming to have been a Pay'n Save shareholder who tendered shares for $23.50, $1.50 less than the price paid to the Stroums, plaintiff brought this putative class action against Pay'n Save, its officers, * * * its pro-management directors, * * * and the Trumps and their affiliated entities, * * *.

Plaintiff's principal claim arises under Section 14(d)(7) of the Williams Act, the so-called "best-price" provision. * * * To the same end, the SEC has promulgated a rule prohibiting side transactions involving purchases of securities subject to a tender offer. Rule 10b–13. * * * The essence of plaintiff's claim is that the $4,200,000 paid to the Stroums during the brief "withdrawal" of the offer was in law and fact a payment of a $1.50 per share premium intended to induce the Stroums to accept the tender offer. The failure to pay this premium to the other tendering shareholders, plaintiff argues, violated the "best-price rule."

No party disputes the proposition that payment of a premium to one shareholder and not others during a tender offer is illegal. The issue rather is whether the purported withdrawal effectively ended the offer so that the $4,200,000 payment was not during or part of a tender offer. In dismissing the Section 14(d)(7) claim, the district court relied upon SEC rules governing the commencement of a tender offer, specifically Rule 14d–2(b). * * * While the public announcement of the essential terms of a tender offer results in the technical "commencement" of a tender offer, the offer will nevertheless be legally deemed not to have commenced if its withdrawal is announced within five business days. In the instant case, the initial announcement of the Trumps' tender offer came on the morning of Friday, September 7, 1984, and the purported withdrawal was announced on the afternoon of Wednesday, September 12, four business days later. Based on these facts, the district court concluded that, for purposes of Section 14(d)(7), "there was no tender offer in place at the time of the Settlement Agreement, and thus, as a matter of law, no violation of [that] Section." * * * We disagree, however, and believe that the allegations of the complaint state a claim under the Williams Act.

* * *

Similarly, giving effect to every purported withdrawal that allows a discriminatory premium to be paid to large shareholders would completely undermine the "best-price rule." For example, plaintiff has alleged that the purported withdrawal of the original tender offer was intended solely to allow the Trumps to pay a premium of $1.50 per share to the Stroums that was not offered to shareholders who tendered pursuant to the "new" tender offer announced immediately thereafter.[1] The "best-price rule" of Section 14(d)(7) and Rule 14d–10 is completely unenforceable if offerors may announce periodic "withdrawals" during which purchases at a premium are made and thereafter followed by "new" tender offers. Unless successive tender offers interrupted by withdrawals can in appropriate circumstances be viewed as a single tender offer for purposes of the Williams Act, the "best-price rule" is meaningless.

Whether the purchase of the Stroum shares was a private purchase or part of a continuing tender offer is not determined simply by the Trumps' use of the labels "withdrawal" and "new" offer. * * * Indeed, we have explicitly recognized that purchases after a purported withdrawal of a tender offer may constitute a continuation of the offer in light of the surrounding circumstances. * * *

Finally, Section 14(d)(7) itself explicitly treats a material change in the terms of a tender offer in the form of an increased price as a continuation of the original offer rather than as a new tender offer. Clearly, therefore, purchases of shares by an offeror after a purported withdrawal of a tender offer may constitute a continuation of the original tender offer.

Rule 14d–2(b) is not to the contrary. That Rule merely creates a window of time during which a genuine withdrawal leaves matters for all legal purposes as though a tender offer had never been commenced.

---

1. Whether the "fees and expenses" for which the Trumps paid $900,000 to the Stroums were actually incurred is irrelevant under the "best-price rule." Some or all of those sums were expended in order to obtain a premium for the Stroums, and it would thwart the purposes of Section 14(d)(7) to allow reimbursement. Moreover, we believe the "best-price rule" would be unworkable if offerors were permitted to discriminate among shareholders according to expenses that were not uniformly incurred, such as broker's or attorney's fees.

The Rule does nothing to alter the principle that the mere announcement of a withdrawal may not be effective if followed by purchases of shares and other conduct inconsistent with a genuine intent to withdraw. The Rule is also irrelevant because a bidder is always free to withdraw a tender offer. The argument advanced by defendants, if correct, would thus apply even in cases in which the provisions of Rule 14d–2(b) governing withdrawal announcements did not.[2]

For purposes of the "best-price rule," therefore, an announcement of a withdrawal is effective when the offeror genuinely intends to abandon the goal of the original offer. * * * The complaint here alleges that the Trumps' Offer to Purchase explicitly stated that the purported withdrawal was intended to allow negotiations with the Stroums. Such negotiations indicate a continuing intent to obtain control of Pay'n Save.

* * *

The parties and the district court have correctly assumed that Section 14(d)(7) impliedly affords a private right of action to shareholders.

* * *

Street Sweeps

OESTERLE, THE RISE AND FALL OF STREET SWEEP TAKEOVERS

Duke L.J., 219–33 (1989).

* * *

Since it is impossible for a street sweep to comply with the tender offer rules, a bidder's primary concern in planning a street sweep is whether the proposed method of acquisition constitutes a "tender offer." The Williams Act, however, does not define the term, and the drafters appear to have purposely avoided placing any useful definitional guidance in the Act's legislative history. Yet the Act contains implicit limitations on the concept's scope. The Act does not explicitly require that all large-scale stock acquisitions be made in the form of a regulated tender offer, and no one asserts that such a requirement can be read into the Act. Thus, the Act must leave some room for large-scale stock acquisitions through open-market trades or privately negotiated deals. * * * Apparently, Congress expected the SEC to define the boundaries of the Act's coverage.

---

2. Defendants have emphasized that "the public shareholders of Pay'n Save ultimately received $23.50 per share, or approximately $5.00 per share in excess of the market value of their shares on the last full trading date prior to the announcement of the proposed tender offer and merger." Appellees' Joint Brief at 2–3. They apparently wish to stress that application of the "best-price rule" where a payment of a premium above the offer to a large shareholder is necessary to consummate the transaction will ultimately work to the detriment of shareholders generally by decreasing such transactions. This point, however, can be made about the Williams Act generally, * * * and thus must be addressed to Congress.

The SEC, however, has been reluctant to provide guidance on the definition of a tender offer. For twenty years, the SEC has successfully resisted the bench and bar's requests for meaningful assistance on the issue. The SEC argues that a precise definition would enable purchasers, whose transactions should be regulated, to structure transactions in ways that would avoid any definition the agency could provide. The SEC seems to fear that acquirers might follow the law if they could understand it.

The only SEC rule relevant to the definition of a tender offer is Rule 14d–2, a product of the SEC's concern with premature tender offer announcements.

* * *

Rule 14d–2, however, assumes a definition of tender offer and thus is not informative of the SEC's views on what constitutes a tender offer. Considering the SEC's general position on street sweeps, Rule 14d–2(d)'s safe harbor provision, which describes what does *not* constitute public announcement of a tender offer, makes little sense. Under that provision an offeror can issue a press release, make a public statement, or purchase a newspaper advertisement announcing its intention to commence a tender offer for a specific company, as long as the offeror does not include the amount of securities sought and the price to be offered. Research indicates that disclosure of an offeror's and target's identity is all that is necessary to stimulate substantial arbitrage activity in the target stock. Therefore, the type of press release that Rule 14d–2(d) permits will put a target into play and begin takeover speculation in the target stock. If, however, a bidder made a similar public announcement about a street sweep—giving only its and the target's identity and indicating its intention to engage in a street sweep—the SEC would argue that the resulting sweep was in fact a tender offer.

In addition to Rule 14d–2, the SEC periodically stresses its position that, under the Williams Act, the scope of the term tender offer goes "beyond the conventional tender offer to include acquisition programs that present the type of abuses that Congress intended to eliminate." This position leaves us to speculate on what constitutes an "unconventional" tender offer and, as we shall see, on what "abuses" Congress intended to correct. In defining an unconventional tender offer, the SEC help is limited to an eight-part "flexible factors" test,[92] set forth in amicus briefs condemning particular acquisitions.

The SEC's eight-part test is hopelessly inadequate. The SEC describes each factor in the test only vaguely, and some of the factors appear to overlap. The SEC also routinely attaches a catchall equivo-

---

92. The factors that indicate a tender offer are: (1) an active and widespread solicitation of public shareholders, (2) for a substantial percentage of the issuer's stock, (3) at a premium over prevailing market price, (4) on firm rather than negotiable terms, (5) contingent on the tender of a fixed minimum number of shares and with a ceiling of a fixed maximum number of shares, (6) open for a limited period of time, (7) putting pressure on offerees to sell their stock, (8) and using public announcements of the purchasing program. *See id.* at 1548 n. 16.

cation to the test: "The Commission repeatedly has cautioned that not all eight factors are entitled to equal weight and that neither all, nor even a majority, of the eight factors need be present." The SEC has not, however, indicated which of these factors are determinative or which can be missing in a determination.

* * *

Judicial interpretations of the SEC's eight-factor test fall all over the map. One district court interpreted the test to include in its definition of tender offer "all methods of takeover by a large-scale stock purchase program." While this interpretation is reasonable, and the SEC commonly cites the case favorably, the judge erred in even accepting the test as a legitimate interpretation of the Williams Act. Indeed, one court has explicitly rejected the test as too vague. Finally, other courts have viewed the test as a shapeless authority, finding in it whatever they want to find.

The common thread throughout these opinions, if one can be found, is the notion that street sweeps do not violate the Williams Act unless, prior to a sweep, a purchaser publicizes its intention to use a sweep to gain control of a target. Publicity can take the form of general press releases, public announcements aimed at all shareholders, or communications to a large number of individual shareholders. Courts view (or ought to view) such publicity, when followed by large-scale private and open-market purchases at premium prices, as too close to traditional tender offers. This judicial approach has legitimate underpinnings: street sweep publicity creates the same shareholder uncertainty as tender offer publicity—i.e., the uncertainty of whether shareholders will lose the premium values offered in the acquisition if they hold their shares.

The SEC also distinguishes between privately negotiated purchases and open-market purchases. In privately negotiated purchases, the SEC focuses on the number of direct solicitees and, to a lesser extent, the sophistication of those solicitees, as critical variables. Apparently, if the acquirer solicits enough shareholders, the SEC considers the street sweep to be a tender offer, even when general publicity of the sweep is absent. The general market notification (which creates the pressure to sell) results from the large number of individual contacts, rather than a simple press release. The SEC's approach finds support in some judicial opinions. On its face, though, this approach seems inconsistent in that it allows an acquirer to purchase from sellers, regardless of sophistication and number, in the open markets with no public comment and the enticement of a steadily rising price, but prohibits the same acquirer from directly contacting shareholders with an unadorned offer to purchase at a price slightly in excess of market.[109]

109. The irony is perhaps best evident in Hanson Trust PLC v. SCM Corp., 774 F.2d 47 (2d Cir.1985). In *Hanson Trust,* the court stated that it would define a tender offer using as guidance the principles that define a private offering under

The inconsistency, though, is more theoretical than real. The fundamental problem with direct solicitations is the communication that normally accompanies face-to-face offers. An acquirer usually, if not always, tells each solicitee that it intends to stop purchasing once it acquires a set amount of target stock, and urges the solicitee to tender in order to participate in the acquisition and collect any part of the acquisition premium. If this kind of sales dialogue occurs, the number and sophistication of the solicitees becomes important. As the number increases, notification of the sweep becomes more public and the solicitees' collective ability to resist decreases. As the solicitees' sophistication increases, the less susceptible they become to this type of sales talk. Informed traders who know about a firm, a buyer, and some of the practices in the acquisition market are better able to decide when to call the buyer's bluff and, indeed, when to run their own bluffs. If acquirers could avoid such sales talk and make only pure, unadorned offers to shareholders, the face-to-face acquisition programs should be indistinguishable from straight open-market acquisition programs. In sum, the communication to potential sellers that a one-time acquisition program of limited duration is in progress creates the pressure to sell.

* * *

The first problem with the current tender offer definition is that a rule based on publicity is somewhat extraordinary in light of the federal securities laws' general purpose—to require and police public disclosure by market insiders. Rather than encouraging public disclosure in street sweeps, the courts and the SEC, in effect, discourage acquirers from disclosing their true intentions. If acquirers may undertake street sweeps on the condition that they are careful not to reveal their intentions to the market, then those who sell their stock during a street sweep might not even know that a street sweep is under way. In other words, in the name of helping target shareholders, the SEC is encouraging acquirers to disclose less.

The existence of a street sweep is surely material to those trading in a target's stock. Yet the SEC encourages acquirers to withhold this information, not because the information is false or misleading, but because the information is too important—it creates pressure to sell. In its paternalistic approach to street sweeps, the SEC considers that shareholders are better off not knowing of an ongoing street sweep despite the shareholders' desire to know that information and the acquirer's desire to disclose it. Whether the SEC is correct in its assessment of street sweep dangers will be discussed later in the context of the SEC's newly proposed rules.

the Securities Act of 1933. The acquisition program in *Hanson Trust* involved both privately negotiated transactions and open-market purchases. Focusing solely on the privately negotiated transactions, the court found that the number of solicitees was "minuscule." *Id.* at 57. One might ask how this finding squares with the 600,000 shares that Hanson purchased in the open market. Were those shareholders who sold in the open market not solicitees? The court assumed, without explanation, that they were not. Presumably, this assumption hinged on the absence of any contemporaneous public communication of Hanson's intent to sweep the street.

The second problem with the current definition is that a policy of discouraging acquirers from publicizing street sweeps is doomed in practice. The SEC recognizes this problem in its proposal to ban street sweeps during or following tender offers. Any notification to the market of an impending tender offer creates opportunities for street sweeps. Even if the SEC rule were adopted, acquirers could still mount street sweeps with methods that would satisfy a no-publicity rule. Word that a company is in play can come from a variety of sources and travels very fast through the markets. For example, word that an acquirer is making an ostensibly friendly offer to another company's board (a "bear hug") for a merger or purchase of all its assets can have the same effect on the market as notification of a tender offer.

Even street sweeps that commence in total secrecy do not remain secret for long. At a minimum, market reporting tapes inform market professionals of the first large trades in a street sweep, and discovering a purchaser's identity is not difficult. Even more likely is immediate dispersal, among a network of market professionals, of information that an acquirer had given to a few initial solicitees. Perhaps the SEC could consider initial solicitees as agents of the acquirer in spreading the news, but an information trail would be very difficult to reconstruct in an enforcement proceeding. In sum, any rule that acts to suppress valuable information in the capital markets is likely to be honored more in the breach than in the observance.

Third, the current tender offer definition might contradict some disclosure requirements established in the Securities Exchange Act of 1934. Section 13(d) and its accompanying rules require that anyone acquiring more than 5% of a registered firm's equity securities must disclose that acquisition to the issuer, the markets, and the SEC. The purchaser must also disclose the "purpose ... of the acquisition," and the existence of any plan to acquire additional securities, in a Schedule 13D filing. If acquirers had to disclose immediately upon acquisition of a 5% stake, then Schedule 13D would require every acquirer in a street sweep to inform the market that a street sweep was in progress. Section 13(d)'s ten-day window, however, allows acquirers to comply with both the Williams Act and Schedule 13D, since most street sweeps conclude in a shorter period. Despite the ten-day window, though, it remains unclear whether an acquirer that chooses to file a Schedule 13D promptly, rather than waiting the full ten days, mounts an illegal tender offer in violation of the Williams Act, since it will have given specific public notice of the street sweep in the Schedule. If so, it seems odd that an acquirer violates one rule by following another. If not, a Schedule 13D filing becomes a safe method of avoiding the basic prohibition against street sweep publicity.

* * *

Other Exchange Act provisions that mandate early disclosure of street sweep plans include section 14(d) and its accompanying rules. The SEC rules require a tender offeror to disclose all material information in a Schedule 14D-1. If the offeror intends to mount a street sweep upon the tender offer's failure, the offeror should arguably include this intention in the Schedule. Similarly, when an issuer intends to mount a street sweep to defend against a hostile bidder, the issuer should disclose this intention in filings under Schedule 14D-9 and Rule 13e-1. These intentions might also be material information that an issuer must disclose under Rule 10b-5's general antifraud provisions. In the context of tender offers and issuers' large-scale stock repurchases, a rule discouraging public announcement of information that the market considers important will invariably conflict with many rules mandating disclosure of material information.

One added incongruity in the current definition of tender offer is the effect that such an expansive definition has on other provisions incorporating the term. For example, whether an individual receives notice of an acquisition from an acquirer or its insiders, Rule 14e-3 prohibits any trading on advance notice of a tender offer. Assuming Rule 14e-3 does not apply to street sweeps, individuals who trade on advance notice of a street sweep might still find themselves in violation of that Rule if the acquirer is too public about its acquisition plans. Arbitrageurs who have bought stock in anticipation of a street sweep will be at risk if their information about the potential sweep came from the acquirer or its insiders. If the acquirer has contacted too many solicitees, such an arbitrageur becomes an inside trader. Thus, the SEC's expansive definition of tender offer has possibly unforeseen rippling effects on other provisions of the securities laws.

* * *

The Definition of "Bidder" in Rule 14d-1(b)(1)

MAI BASIC FOUR, INC. v. PRIME COMPUTER, INC.

United States Court of Appeals, First Circuit, 1989.
871 F.2d 212.

COFFIN, SENIOR CIRCUIT JUDGE.

This expedited appeal arises out of the efforts of a group of companies in the computer industry, MAI Basic Four, Choice Corporation, and Brooke Partners, L.P. (collectively Basic), to take over control of Prime Computer, Inc. (Prime). * * * In this counterclaim Prime alleged, principally, that Basic had violated the Williams Act Amendments to the Securities Exchange Act (the Act), * * * by failing to disclose in its Offer to Purchase sufficient information concerning the involvement, interests, and condition of its investment advisor, investor, and underwriter, Drexel Burnham Lambert, Inc. (Drexel). It contended that Drexel fell under the Act's disclosure requirements because it was in reality a "bidder." SEC Rule 14d-1(b)(1), 17 C.F.R. § 240.14d-1(b)(1); Rule 14d-6, 17 C.F.R. § 14d-6; SEC Schedule 14D-1, 17 C.F.R. § 240.14d-100. * * *

Basic is offering $20 a share in cash for all shares of Prime, a price that exceeds the pre-offer market price. As of the date of oral argument, March 2, 1989, approximately 61 percent of Prime stock had been tendered, 46 percent on a fully diluted basis.[1] The offer is conditioned upon there being tendered, prior to its expiration, 67 percent of the shares on a fully diluted basis. * * * The financing consists of $20 million in cash, supplied by Brooke Partners, L.P.; $650 million in bank financing; and $875 million in high yield, interest bearing, increasing rate notes (*i.e.,* "junk bonds"), placement to be arranged by Drexel. Upon consummation of the offer, Basic intends to merge itself and Prime and cash out any remaining Prime stockholders at $20 a share.

Drexel's past, present, and contemplated roles in connection with the offer lie at the heart of this appeal. Since 1986 Drexel has been associated in arranging financing for Basic's principal stockholders, Bennett S. LeBow and William Weksel, in several other acquisitions (of Liggett Group, Inc. and of Western Union Corp.) in which Drexel has obtained both substantial fees and equity positions. In the spring of 1988, Drexel tried unsuccessfully to interest Prime in buying MAI Basic Four. Subsequently, Basic decided to be the acquirer. Drexel's undertaking, as financial advisor for this transaction, is to "include, but not be limited to ... advising and assisting [Basic] in determining the possible alternative ways in which the Transaction might be structured, and advising and assisting [Basic] with respect to the completion of the Transaction." * * *

Drexel has an equity interest in MAI Basic Four, Inc., which will be 5 percent on a diluted basis, with a right to purchase at half price another 9 percent. In addition to this 14 percent of direct interest, it possesses, through two intermediary partnership entities, a one-third equity interest in LeBow, Inc., and, through another entity, a 17 percent equity interest in Brooke Partners. LeBow, Inc., is the sole owner of L. Holdings, which is Brooke's sole general partner. As of the date of the offer, Drexel also, through a stockholders agreement, had the right to name one of the three directors of LeBow, Inc., with veto power over some corporate actions. During this litigation, the agreement was changed to remove Drexel's right to a board member, but Drexel continues to have the right to attend board meetings and is guaranteed first refusal in future underwriting and placement.

Drexel's role in placing $875 million in junk bonds will entitle it to $65 million in fees, if the placement is successful. At the moment, the record indicates that none of these notes have been sold. Even if the offer fails, Drexel will be entitled to 15 percent of any profit Basic realizes from selling Prime stock now held. There is some ambiguity with regard to a further role Drexel may have in relation to the notes. The offer to Purchase merely reflects Drexel's view that it is "highly

---

1. That is, after taking into account additional shares projected to be issued in connection with (or in response to) the tender offer.

confident" that it can place the $875 million of notes and its agreement "to use its best efforts to arrange the financing." * * *

But Weksel testified in a deposition that he expected Drexel to furnish any funds needed to complete the transaction even if all the notes were not sold.

* * *

The positions taken by the parties could not be farther apart. Basic first contends that it has furnished all the information required by the court and that the court has acknowledged as much. Then it challenges the court's finding that Drexel is a bidder. Finally it argues that even if Drexel could be considered a bidder, no additional disclosure is required by the Act. When asked why Basic could not readily furnish the kind of information concerning Drexel that was provided in *Interco,* counsel's response was that other questions would be asked and that "no amount of disclosure is ever going to be enough."[3]

Prime, on the other hand, maintains that Drexel should, as a bidder, furnish all items of information required for compliance with Schedule 14D–1. In oral argument counsel stated, without citing any authority, that even if Drexel is not a bidder, it is still such a key participant that its financial condition was material information which must be more thoroughly disclosed under the Williams Act.

* * *

The facts in this case bear some similarity to those in *Koppers Co. v. American Express Co.,* 689 F.Supp. 1371 (W.D.Pa.1988), where an investment bank was held to be a bidder for purposes of Rule 14d. In *Koppers,* two Shearson entities, Shearson Holdings and its subsidiary Shearson Lehman, and their indirect subsidiary, SL–Merger, Inc., were found collectively to have become aggressively involved in a takeover plan at an early stage; to have contributed $23.05 million for purchasing shares of the target; to own 46 percent of the Class B common stock in the target; to have committed themselves to a contribution of $570 million for notes or preferred stock; and to have earned large brokerage fees. The court accepted, as criteria for a bidder, "those who are central to the offer," 689 F.Supp. at 1388 (citation omitted), "playing a central participatory role," being "a motivating force," "one of the principal planners and players." *Id.* at 1390. It acknowledged the multiple roles of the Shearson entities—advisor, underwriter, equity partner, financier, broker-dealer—deeming these roles as far surpassing that of an investment banker. The court labelled Shearson "a major equity participant," "one of the entities on whose behalf the tender offer is made." *Id.*

In the case at bar, Drexel has equity interests in various affiliates associated with LeBow. It has a background of association with Basic and other LeBow interests. Like Shearson in *Koppers,* Drexel partici-

---

3. In its brief, Basic stated that it pursued this expedited appeal "to get off the judicial carousal [sic] it has been riding for the last two months."

pated in the planning of the Prime tender offer very early, well before the offer. It had a director with veto power in LeBow, Inc., the sole owner of the general partner of Brooke Partners. Brooke in turn supplied the entire $20 million of equity for this highly leveraged deal, which funds Drexel was instrumental in raising through earlier tender offers. Drexel has relinquished this directorship, but only after commencement of the tender offer and without explication. Of course the projected equity position of Drexel is far less than Shearson's 46 percent interest in *Koppers*. Finally, Drexel will enjoy substantial fees, perhaps in excess of $65 million, for its heavy participation in the offer.

In a similar vein, the present case is at least somewhat distinguishable from *City Capital Assocs. Ltd. Partnership v. Interco, Inc.*, 860 F.2d 60 (3d Cir.1988). In *Interco*, the court of appeals pointed out that Drexel was not engaged by the acquirer until after the tender offer was made. The court distinguished *Koppers* on the basis that Drexel was to have no representation on the board of the surviving entity, *id.* at 63 n. 5., and emphasized that there was no indication that Drexel had any control over the offer or that it would have any other role than that of investor. *Id.* at 63. The court chose not to determine the significance of a recent development, that (apparently due to its inability to secure outside financing) Drexel had committed itself to purchase $609 million of preferred securities, implying that on this basis the district court might properly reach a different result on the bidder issue.

Given Drexel's early and pervasive role in the planning and execution of the present offer, its erstwhile board representation in the corporation controlling the sole equity participant in the bidder group, and record evidence sufficient to reasonably suggest an expectation, though not a contractual obligation, that Drexel would itself provide additional financing if it could not place the $875 million in junk bonds elsewhere, we might accept the approach of the Third Circuit while distinguishing *Interco* on its facts. Such a decision on our part would be consistent with one of the formulations of the test in *Interco*, that if a stockholder in an acquirer "is in a position to have a significant impact on the future of that corporation, information about the stockholder may well be material to a decision of stockholders of the target whether to take the offer or hang on with the hope of a greater return." *Id.* at 65.

But we recognize that in the end the court in *Interco* concluded that financial statements are not required from an entity that will wind up as a minority stockholder. It reached this result based on the perceived need for a bright-line test in the takeover context, requiring a narrow construction of Rule 14d–1(b)(1), and a strict application of Schedule 14D–1, General Instruction G, Item 9, 17 C.F.R. § 240.14d–100, reading the latter to indicate that "bidder" under the SEC regulations means an entity formally making a tender offer and those who *control* it. Because the traditional indicia of control were lacking, ipso facto Drexel was deemed not to be a bidder. We think the more realistic prescription is that of *Interco's* dissenter, who wrote:

> [I]n the event of doubt on a particular disclosure question, courts should exercise liberality in order to carry out the remedial purposes of the [Williams Act]. Excess information may well be harmless, but inadequate disclosure could be disastrous to the shareholder.

860 F.2d at 68 (Weis, J., dissenting). The more flexible, fact-based approach advocated by Judge Weis is consistent with our reading of the Williams Act.[5]

The SEC Rule, 14d–1(b)(1), 17 C.F.R. § 240.24d–1(b)(1), uses the word "bidder" in place of "person" in the statute. It defines a bidder as "any person who makes a tender offer or on whose behalf a tender offer is made." The SEC, in a 1979 Release, stated that bidder was a "shorthand reference[ ] to [a] principal participant[ ] in a tender offer." * * * We read the "on whose behalf" language of Rule 14d–1(b)(1) to incorporate the "group" concept of sections 13(d) and 14(d) of the Williams Act.

* * *

We distill from these guides, which use the words "directly or indirectly," "on whose behalf," "principal participant[ ]," and "any contract, understanding, relationship, agreement or other arrangement" that there is no bright, hard-line test for bidder under the regulation. We empathize with the Third Circuit when it said in *Interco*, "[t]his is an area of law in which predictability is of crucial importance." * * * But we are skeptical. We suspect that any bright-line test, separating those who are subject to the Williams Act from those who are not, would merely invite the ingenuity of resourceful counsel to place their client formally on the desired side of the line, whatever the underlying reality may be.

In this case we cannot say that, as a matter of law, an active advisor-broker-financier-participant who owns less than a majority interest in the surviving entity is not a bidder where, as here, there has been a history of close association, equity sharing, board representation and involvement from the beginning of the present offer, and where there is the possibility of the advisor-broker being the indispensable key to the offer's success. Nor can we say that while a 46 percent stockholder qualifies as a bidder, a 14 percent direct stockholder with other indirect equity interests cannot qualify.[9] At a minimum it is evident that Drexel has "act[ed] as a partnership, limited partnership, . . . or other group for the purpose of acquiring, holding, or disposing of securities of an issuer." 15 U.S.C. § 78n(d)(2). We are not convinced

---

5. The appellant in *Interco* disavowed that Drexel was part of a "group," and the majority therefore declined to reach this issue. 860 F.2d at 65 n. 6. In view of our interpretation and application of the group concept, *infra,* our analysis may not ultimately contradict that of the Third Circuit.

9. We recognize, too, the possibility that the prospect of Drexel becoming a major creditor by itself purchasing the junk bonds might, in light of all the circumstances, make its financial condition material for purposes of § 14(e) irrespective of the bidder issue. Prime has not pressed this argument, and we decline to reach it.

that the district court erred in determining that Prime demonstrated a likelihood of success on the merits, and therefore affirm the court's ruling that Drexel is a bidder.

This does not end our inquiry. We must determine whether the information still required by the court is "material."

* * *

It is not clear to us that the financial strength or vulnerability of Drexel, including the adverse impact of Drexel's plea bargain and other legal difficulties, is immaterial to Prime shareholders' deliberations. As opposed to the "highly confident" opinion of Drexel and the conclusory report that Drexel has over $2 billion of capital, and despite the argument that Drexel has recently financed far larger deals, the *Interco* submission indicated an equity of $1.4 billion as of June 24, 1988, *before* the $650 million plea bargain. As Judge Friendly put it:

> In applying [the materiality] test to a cash tender offer, it is necessary to appreciate the problem faced by a stockholder of the target company in deciding whether to tender, to sell or to hold part or all of his securities. It is true that, in the case of an "any and all" offer such as that here at issue, a stockholder who has firmly decided to tender has no interest in the financial position of the offeror *other than its ability to pay* ... since he will have severed all financial connections with the target.

Prudent Real Estate Trust v. Johncamp Realty, Inc., 599 F.2d 1140, 1147 (2d Cir.1979) (emphasis added). Even assuming the professed ability to pay the offered price,

> [T]he shareholder of the target company faces a hard problem in determining the most advantageous course of action, a problem whose difficulty is enhanced by his usual ignorance of the course other shareholders are adopting. If the bidder is in a flourishing financial condition, the stockholder might decide to hold his shares in the hope that, if the offer was only partially successful, the bidder might raise his bid after termination of the offer.... *Per contra,* a poor financial condition of the bidder might cause the shareholder to accept for fear that control of the company would pass into irresponsible hands.

Id. That shareholders might reasonably hold out for a higher offer is supported by the determination of the Delaware Chancery Court, rejecting Basic's challenge to the institution of takeover defenses by Prime directors, that the directors reasonably relied on independent investment bankers' valuation of Prime stock between $23 and $28 per share.
* * *

In turn, whether Drexel be seen as weak or strong is a legitimate datum for Prime stockholders.

Nor can we discount the possible impact of Drexel's plea bargain and other legal difficulties as immaterial. This area of corporate cannibalism is not a neat and tidy one. We must rely to a large extent on the judgment of the trial judge who lives with the case. * * *

Consequently, we defer to the district court's judgment that the kind of information voluntarily submitted in *Interco* is material in the present case.

* * *

We affirm the order of the district court. We further direct that if Basic files with the SEC [11] 1) current financial statements of Drexel, 2) identification of all Drexel-affiliated officers and directors, and 3) disclosure of recent trading in shares by Drexel, then the district court, upon determining that these disclosures appear accurate and reasonably equivalent to the information voluntarily disclosed in *Interco* (but brought up to date), shall vacate the injunction insofar as it is based on nondisclosure.

Questions

1. What is the difference between being a member of a bidding "group" and having an ownership interest in a business entity that is a bidder? Does it depend on who will be the legal owner of the target stock? How does the legislative history of the concept of a "group" help here? How should this difference be reflected in the disclosure requirements of the Williams Act? Should we apply a "control" standard both to members of bidder groups and to partners or shareholders of bidders?

2. Are your answers for question one different for exchange tender offers in which the consideration pay is securities in the bidding firm?

3. The *Prime Computer* court, like many other courts in all types of disclosure controversies under the Williams Act, construed the act and its rules with a bias toward disclosure. What are the costs of detailed disclosures by all those aiding the bidder or associated with the bidder in a tender offer? Is there a point at which there is too much disclosure required?

4. As all students of America's financial markets well know, Drexel filed for bankruptcy within a year of its plea bargain, which was based on the securities violations of one of its major owners, Michael Millken. Does this vindicate the court's holding on materiality?

The Obligations of a Target Subject to a Third–Party Tender Offer

Please read rules 13e–1, 14e–2, and 14d–9 and skim schedule 14D–9 in your statutory supplement.

Questions

1. If a target is the subject of a pending tender offer, what is its minimum disclosure obligation? Can it avoid filing a schedule 14D–9? See rules 14e–2 and 14d–9(f). If your answer is yes, would you recommend that

---

11. We leave it to the district court to determine whether and to what extent such additional disclosures must be broadcast to target shareholders, in light of the additional costs involved.

it do so? If the tender offer is conditioned on the target board's waiver of in-place protections under state antitakeover statutes or a firm poison pill plan, can a board refuse to waive those protections and still satisfy rule 14e–2(2) or (3)?

2. If a target is attempting to find an alternative purchaser and is therefore in preliminary discussions with several potential purchasers ("white knights"), when does the target have to reveal the names of these parties? The terms of its offer to sell? See schedule 14D–9, item 7.

An Introduction to Bidder–Target Tactical Litigation over Disclosure Requirements

As noted above, the bidder must disclose information in a schedule 14D–1, and the target typically must disclose information in a schedule 14D–9. Violations of the requirements in the specific items of both schedules and omissions of all other material facts are actionable under section 14(e) of the Securities and Exchange Act of 1934. The next chapter focuses on lines of cases detailing this disclosure obligation. The following case, however, illustrates the general quagmire often confronted by courts in contested tender offers, as a bidder and a target make crossing allegations of disclosure violations a routine part of their overall battle plans. Has the Williams Act turned into an excuse to sue on long-shot claims for the purpose of exacting costs and effecting delay?

KOPPERS CO., INC. v. AMERICAN EXPRESS CO.
United States District Court, Western District of Pennsylvania, 1988.
689 F.Supp. 1371.

Opinion of COHILL, CHIEF JUDGE.

Presently before the Court are cross-motions for preliminary injunctions. The plaintiff, Koppers Company, Inc. ("Koppers") brought this action to enjoin a hostile tender offer attempt commenced by defendant BNS, Inc. on March 3, 1988. In its request for a preliminary injunction, Koppers argues that there is a great likelihood that the tender offer violates federal securities and other laws and that irreparable harm will be caused its shareholders if the offer is not enjoined. Defendant BNS, Inc. requests a preliminary injunction ordering Koppers to correct allegedly misleading statements in its Schedule 14D–9 statement, a statement which is required to be filed with the Securities and Exchange Commission ("SEC") by a target company which is the subject of a tender offer. 15 U.S.C. § 78n(d)(4).

This is a difficult case. The facts are intricate and complicated; the law is fuzzy. Because of the unusual posture of the American Express/Shearson interests, apparently as broker-dealer-investment banker-advisor-owner in this takeover transaction, we have had to find the way by looking at cases, statutes and regulations which merely give us clues as to the direction the court should take. We have found little to serve as an actual roadmap.

The facts are similarly muddled because of the intricate arrangements of the tender offerors. This is demonstrated by the fact that more than the first one-third of this document is devoted to a description of those arrangements. * * * We have analyzed the acts of this case and concluded that it is more prudent to err on the side of disclosure than obfuscation.

* * *

On October 16, 1987, Beazer, NatWest, and Shearson Holdings formed BNS Partners under the Delaware Uniform Partnership Act. The partnership consisted of Bright Aggregates, Speedward, and SL–Merger each of which jointly contributed $50 million in capital.

Beazer, through Bright Aggregates, has contributed $24.5 million in capital and received a 49% interest in the partnership; Shearson through SL–Merger, contributed $23.05 million and received a 46.1% interest in the partnership; and NatWest, through Speedward, contributed $2.45 million and obtained a 4.9% interest. The sole purpose of the partnership was to acquire shares of Koppers prior to the tender offer, which was not made until March 3, 1988. Bright Aggregates, with Mr. Beazer as its President, is the managing partner of BNS Partners and has sole authority to manage the partnership's affairs.

Defendant BNS, Inc. ("BNS Inc.") is a corporation organized under the laws of the State of Delaware and has its principal place of business in Dallas, Texas. The shareholders of BNS Inc. are Bright Aggregates, Speedward, and SL–Merger. These three shareholders own stock in BNS Inc. in apparent direct proportion to the capital contributions of their progenitors; the relationship is somewhat obscured, however, by the fact that each of the three owns a fraction of one share of a different class of stock, with the three holdings coming to a total of one share.

Thus, Bright Aggregates owns .490 shares of Class A common stock, which is all the Class A common stock outstanding; SL–Merger holds .461 shares of Class B common stock; Speedward holds .024 shares of Class B common stock and .025 shares of Class C common stock. We will discuss this unusual arrangement later.

BNS Inc. was formed for the sole purpose of acquiring the shares of Koppers from the tender offer.

Bright Aggregates began purchasing Koppers' stock through Shearson prior to the tender offer. As of October 21, 1987, Bright Aggregates had accumulated 343,400 common shares of Koppers stock. Bright Aggregates now owns 458,100 shares of common stock which it purchased in the open market.

Between October, 1987, and March 3, 1988, BNS Partners used its $50 million in capital and an additional $21 million in margin loans to purchase 1,636,000 shares of Koppers stock in the open market through its broker, Shearson Lehman. In order to comply with the stock purchasing notification requirements of the Hart–Scott–Rodino Antitrust Improvements Act of 1976, 15 U.S.C. § 18a(a), BNS Inc. filed their Hart–Scott–Rodino Notification and Report forms with the SEC on March 3, 1988, the same day it commenced its tender offer. The timing of the purchases relative to the infusion of capital was called into question at the hearing.

On March 3, 1988, BNS Inc., Bright Aggregates, and Beazer each filed a Schedule 14D–1 with the Securities and Exchange Commission ("SEC"), as required by 15 U.S.C. § 78n(d)(1), and commenced an unsolicited tender offer for Koppers' common stock at a price of $45.00 per share and its cumulative preferred stock 4% series at a price of $107.75 per share. The stated purpose of the tender offer is to acquire all the stock of Koppers and to seek to have Koppers consummate a merger or similar business combination transaction with BNS Inc., or an affiliate of BNS Inc. The tender offeror was identified as BNS Inc. There have since been at least 20 amendments to the original Schedule 14D–1.

No entity identified with the Shearson interests—SL–Merger, Shearson Lehman, American Express, or Shearson Holdings—filed a Schedule 14D–1 relating to the tender offer. In addition to its part ownership of BNS Inc. through SL–Merger, Shearson is the financial advisor for BNS Inc. and one of the dealer-managers for the tender offer.

To complete the tender offer, the BNS Inc. tender offer statement reveals that financing of approximately $1.7 billion is needed. Shearson is to provide approximately $570 million; a syndicate of banks led by Citibank is to lend approximately $864 million, and Beazer is to contribute $298 million for preferred stock issued by BNS Inc. and the 458,100 common shares of Koppers that it holds. Beazer's contribution is largely financed by NatWest.

Upon completion of the tender offer, BNS Partners will transfer its shares of Koppers to BNS Inc.; the partnership will be dissolved, and BNS Inc. will assume the liabilities and obligations of BNS Partners. BNS Inc., will, in turn, issue common shares to be distributed among the partners of BNS Partners, so that immediately after the distribution Bright Aggregates will hold 490 shares of Class A Common Stock, SL–Merger will hold 461 shares of Class B Common Stock, and Speedward will hold 24 shares of Class B Common Stock and 25 shares of Class C Common Stock. * * *

On March 16, 1988, the Koppers Board of Directors ("The Board") declared the $45 per share offer of March 3 to be inadequate. The Board did conclude, however, that the offer price of $107.75 for the preferred stock was adequate. As required by 15 U.S.C. § 78n(d)(4), Koppers filed a Schedule 14D–9 with the SEC.

On March 21, 1988, defendants increased their tender offer proposal to $56 per share of common stock. On March 22, 1988, the Board declared the $56 per share offer to be inadequate.

On March 25, 1988, the defendants increased their offer to $60 per share of common stock. On April 5, 1988, The Board met to consider the $60 offer, and announced that it was unable to take a position as to the adequacy of the offer, although Mr. Charles Pullin, Chairman and Chief Executive Officer of Koppers, indicated in his testimony at the hearing before this court that he feels the offer is inadequate.

The original offer of $107.75 per share of preferred stock has not been modified.

The tender offer is scheduled to expire April 15, 1988.

* * *

Koppers alleges that the defendants are soliciting tenders of Koppers' stock through a materially false and misleading Offer to Purchase that fails to disclose information required by the Securities Exchange Act of 1934.

Count 1 of Koppers' Amended Complaint alleges that the defendants violated * * * the Williams Act, * * * by (1) failing to provide adequate information regarding the role of the Shearson entities; (2) failing to disclose that a subsidiary of Shearson, E.F. Hutton & Company, Inc. has pled guilty to certain criminal charges and that certain of its former employees face legal actions and SEC investigations; (3) failure to file financial information with respect to "bidders" Shearson Lehman and NatWest; (4) failure to file other material information concerning the bidders; and (5) failure to state which jurisdictions are encompassed in a disclaimer that tenders will not be accepted from jurisdictions in which the making of the offer would not be in compliance with state securities laws.

Count 2 alleges that the Schedule 14D-1 fails to disclose (1) the conditional and speculative nature of the financing; (2) that the terms of the financing would violate Section 7 of the Exchange Act; (3) that Shearson purchased and sold Koppers' securities between the date on which BNS Partners was formed and the date the tender offer commenced; (4) that Shearson Lehman contacted Koppers in February, 1988, and offered to assist Koppers in any defense of a tender offer; and (5) that significant criminal, civil, and administrative investigations have been undertaken.

Count 3 alleges that the Schedule 14D-1 fails to disclose that the transaction contemplated by the tender offer violates Section 7 of the Exchange Act, * * * and Federal Reserve Board Regulations G, T, U, and X, * * * in that the banks and broker-dealers involved in this transaction are prohibited from lending more than 50% of the funds used to purchase stock if such stock is to be used to secure a loan. It is further alleged that BNS Inc. is a shell corporation that will incur debt as a result of the tender offer which will exceed the 50% limitation.

Count 4 alleges that the Schedule 14D-1 fails to disclose that the transaction contemplated by the tender offer violates Section 4(a)(1) of the Bank Company Holding Act, § 1843(a)(1), which prohibits a bank holding company from acquiring "direct or indirect ownership or control of any voting shares of a company which is not a bank," in that NatWest is a bank holding company which will acquire 4.9% indirect ownership of Koppers' stock if the tender offer is successful.

* * *

Count 5 alleges that Shearson Holdings and/or Shearson Lehman violated Section 10(b) of the Exchange Act, 15 U.S.C. § 78j, and the rules and regulations promulgated thereunder by executing transactions in Koppers' stock from October 17, 1987, through March 2, 1988, during which period Koppers repurchased 476,000 shares of its stock. Koppers alleges that the stock price was artificially inflated and manipulated during that period and seeks a judgment for all damages it sustained as a result of Shearson Holdings' and/or Shearson Lehman's actions.

In its Second Amended Complaint, Koppers added Count 6, alleging that defendants violated the Williams Act by failing to disclose that BNS Inc. had violated the Hart–Scott–Rodino Antitrust Improvements Act, 15 U.S.C. §§ 18a(a) & (d) by its transaction in Koppers stock prior to commencement of the tender offer.

* * *

BNS Inc., BNS Partners, Bright Aggregates, and Beazer PLC have filed a counterclaim alleging that the Schedule 14D–9 filed by Koppers in response to the tender offer is materially false and misleading and is therefore in violation of the Williams Act, in that Koppers has failed to disclose material information about: (1) its rejection of the original tender offer price of $45 a share; (2) the terms of Koppers' suggested plan of recapitalization and proposed substantial cash dividend or distribution; (3) the terms for financing Koppers' suggested plan of recapitalization; (4) the sale of Koppers' stock to its employee stock ownership plan; (5) the potential sale of all or part of Koppers' construction materials and service business; (6) the effect of Koppers' proposed plans on the price of Koppers' stock; (7) how Koppers will service the debt it will incur if its plan is executed; and (8) how Koppers' plan is more advantageous than BNS Inc.'s offer.

* * *

IX. DISCLOSURE OF INFORMATION REGARDING KOPPERS' ENVIRONMENTAL LIABILITIES

A. The Arguments of the Commonwealth of Pennsylvania and the Governor of Pennsylvania as Amici Curiae

The Commonwealth of Pennsylvania and the Governor of the Commonwealth were granted leave to file briefs as *amici curiae*. The thrust of the Commonwealth's arguments (as do some of Koppers') expresses environmental concerns; in addition the *amici* argued that the transaction would adversely affect the economy—"jobs, communities and families" in Pennsylvania.

While these arguments for the public interest have great emotional appeal, and were well-argued by counsel for the Commonwealth and the Governor, we do not believe that those issues are relevant to the Williams Act questions before us at this time.

The Commonwealth makes an analogy to the Uniform Fraudulent Conveyances Act, 39 P.S. §§ 351–63, but we do not agree that this argument applies here. No provision of the Williams Act, so far as we can determine, speaks to environmental concerns.

B. The Arguments of Koppers

Koppers argues that the Schedule 14D–1 filed by BNS Inc. fails to disclose Koppers' potential environmental liabilities. At the hearing, Koppers provided substantial and highly detailed evidence that (1) Koppers is and will remain indebted for enormous quantifiable and unquantifiable expenses of cleaning up and monitoring numerous hazardous substance infected work sites; (2) Koppers' Construction and Materials operations have steady earnings that are necessary to solve (and pay for) the environmental problems of the Chemical and Allied Products Systems business that Beazer has indicated its intention to sell off; and (3) Koppers cannot sell any of its businesses from the Chemical and Allied Products operations without retaining liability for past environmental problems.

Koppers argues that the agreement that BNS Inc. has with Citibank grants Citibank the right to reject tender offer financing if it finds problems with Koppers' environmental liabilities and that therefore BNS Inc. should disclose the extent of Koppers liabilities so that the shareholders may make their own reasoned analysis as to whether Citibank will continue with the financing arrangements.

There are several serious problems with Koppers' position on environmental concerns. First, Koppers cites no provision in Schedule 14D–1, no other statutory or regulatory provisions, and no case law to support its argument.

Second, we find no environmental review condition to Citibank's commitment to fund the tender offer for Koppers' stock. While Citibank's financing of the proposed merger after the tender offer is contingent upon, inter alia, Citibank's receipt of a satisfactory environmental review report concerning Koppers, it is highly speculative that further disclosures about this environmental audit are relevant to the decisions to be made by Koppers' shareholders. We do not believe that a reasonable investor would find facts regarding this very contingent loan arrangement to be material in determining whether to tender his shares in Koppers.

Third, to require the tender offeror to supply such detailed information about the target company would be giving the target company the key to perpetual freedom. If the target company refused to disclose such highly private information then the tender offeror would never be able to meet its Schedule 14D–1 requirements.

Last, we are hesitant to open a Pandora's Box where one has not been provided by the SEC. (Enough exist already!) Extending Koppers' argument to its logical conclusion, the tender offeror would have to disclose to the shareholders of the target company all of the problems with their own corporation that may give a future lender of the tender offeror cause to reconsider a decision to lend.

* * *

On the basis of the foregoing analysis, [after twenty-five pages of technical analysis of the transaction and applicable law] we conclude that Koppers has a reasonable probability of proving at the trial on the merits that the tender offer, as proffered, would violate Sections 14(d) and (e) of the Williams Act in the following respects:

    1. There is no Schedule 14D–1 filed on behalf of the Shearson Interest bidders.

    2. The tender offer fails adequately to disclose how the bidders intend to discharge debts incurred as a result of the tender offer, and in particular to redeem the Shearson Interests.

    3. The tender offer fails to disclose adequately possible violations of the margin requirements of the Securities and Exchange Act and regulations promulgated by the Federal Reserve Board.

* * *

Accordingly, the interests of justice will be best served by preserving the status quo and granting Koppers' motion for a preliminary injunction. Until a trial on the merits shall be held, the defendants will be restrained from (1) soliciting the tender of any Koppers stock, (2) acquiring or attempting to acquire any shares of Koppers stock and (3) voting any shares of Koppers stock previously acquired, or using such shares to control or affect the management of Koppers.

* * *

SECTION 3. ISSUER REPURCHASES OF ITS OWN STOCK OR DEBT: BUYBACKS AND BUYOUTS

A large-scale share and debt repurchase by an issuer, or a "buyback," is a distribution of cash by a firm in exchange for a return of a substantial portion of its outstanding stock or debt securities. In recent years buybacks by public firms have become increasingly important in distributions of earnings to shareholders, restructurings to avoid unwanted third-party tender offers (defensive buybacks), and restructurings to avoid default on debt obligations. Public firms typically repurchase shares in one of four ways: self-tender offers, open market purchases, private purchases, and the exercise of redemption rights on outstanding stock. The newest strategy is a sophisticated variant of redemption; if an issuer's stock is not already callable, the firm issues transferable put rights (TPRs) on its outstanding shares.

Open market repurchases are made on secondary markets at the then-prevailing price, while private or targeted repurchases are made from a few sellers at a price that usually exceeds market value. If the private seller is itself a potential unwanted acquirer and the firm eliminates the acquisition threat by buying the acquirer's stock, the payment is known as greenmail. Under a TPR plan, the firm issues put options to each shareholder in proportion to the number of shares owned. For example, if the firm wants to repurchase 10 percent of its outstanding shares, each shareholder would receive one TPR per ten shares of stock, with each TPR giving the shareholder the right to sell back one share of stock at a fixed price within a specified period. The price is "in the money," that is, the exercise price is set higher than the prevailing market price so that all puts are likely to be exercised by the end of the option period.

Self-tender offers must be made in accordance with regulations similar to those governing ordinary tender offers. TPRs are subject to regulation under the Securities Act of 1933. Open market purchases and private purchases, unless they constitute a nonconventional tender offer, are largely unregulated. If, as the result of a large share buyback, the number of outstanding shareholders declines to below three hundred, the firm no longer has to register its equity securities under the Securities and Exchange Act of 1934, and the firm is said to have been taken private through a buyout. Of course, all buybacks are subject to Securities and Exchange Commission rule 10b–5, which prohibits a firm from buying back its shares without full disclosure of all material information to its shareholders. See chapter 6.

Self–Tender Offers

Please read rule 13e–4 and skim schedule 13E–4 in your statutory supplement.

Questions

1. Are there any major differences between the regulatory requirements for an issuer tender offer and a third-party tender offer? See rule 13e–4(f)(6). In other words, in a bidding contest between an issuer and an independent firm does either party have an advantage due solely to requirements in federal securities law?

2. If a chief executive officer and other members of a top management team decide to buy their own firm in a leveraged buyout, must they file a schedule 13E–4? See rule 13e–4(a)(2).

Transferable Put Rights (TPRs)

KALE, NOE, & GAY, SHARE REPURCHASE THROUGH TRANSFERABLE PUT RIGHTS

25 J.Fin.Econ. 141 (1989).

Gillette, a maker of razor blades, toothbrushes, toiletries, and pens, is the second company to initiate a share buy-back plan with the use of TPRs.

* * *

Recently, Gillette has been under constant threat of a hostile takeover. Because of its constant takeover battles, Gillette has been dubbed "the single most shopped company in the world".

* * *

In February 1988, Coniston Partners, a New York-based partnership, disclosed that it owned 6.8% of Gillette's stock and was considering a corporate control challenge by seeking four seats on Gillette's board. Gillette, as it always had, urged its shareholders to reject Coniston's bid to unseat four Gillette directors in a proxy fight. * * * In a too-close-to-call proxy fight, Gillette defeated Coniston by a vote of 52% to 48%. Seeking to have these results nullified, Coniston filed a suit charging that Gillette made false and misleading claims during the proxy contest. * * *

When Coniston was on the verge of winning the court battle, the two companies agreed to a settlement. Gillette agreed to initiate a stock repurchase through TPRs. Under this plan, Gillette, with approximately 112 million shares outstanding, was to repurchase 16 million shares by issuing one put per seven shares to each shareholder. Each put gave shareholders the right to sell back one share at $45 (the market price then was around $39) by September 19. A secondary market for trading these TPRs was provided by the New York Stock Exchange (NYSE). In return, Coniston agreed to "stand still" and not wage a proxy fight for the next three years. When the settlement between Coniston and Gillette was announced on August 1, Gillette's stock price fell from $40.125 on the previous day to $37.50. The next day, it fell further, to $36.50. This price change reflects the combined effect of the announcement that Coniston would not takeover Gillette and that a repurchase through TPRs was to be initiated.[7] Tender puts were issued to all shareholders of record as of August 12 with the expiration date set for September 19. The puts started trading on the NYSE on August 16. In the third week of August, Coniston announced that it had purchased additional puts from other shareholders in addition to the approximately one million it had received under the buyback program. By mid-September, Coniston had accumulated between 2.6 and 2.7 million puts. In early October, Gillette announced that it had bought back the 15.6 million shares tendered through put exercise, or approximately 98.4% of the puts issued. Coniston Partners, which originally had a 6.8% stake (approximately 7.62 million

---

7. This negative announcement effect is consistent with Dann and DeAngelo (1983) who report a two-day announcement effect of −4.52% for a sample of 30 firms entering into standstill agreements. Vista Chemical, another firm that announced a share repurchase through TPRs, experienced a two-day decline in share price from $62 to $56.25 on announcement. However, this repurchase was only a part of a major restructuring announcement that also included new debt financing, the creation of an employee stock-option plan and the giving of additional nonqualified stock options to management and certain employees. Also, it appears from publicly available information that Vista Chemical, unlike Gillette, was not in the midst of a takeover battle.

shares), owned 4.5% (or approximately 4.34 million shares) after the repurchase.

* * *

In addition to being a prime takeover target because of its market position. Gillette had a significant fraction of low-reservation-price ("LR") shareholders such as arbitragers and speculators in its ownership. Arbitragers and speculators owned approximately 15% of the stock at the time of the takeover threat from Revlon and, subsequently, because of persistent rumors of a takeover, speculative activity continued to be high. Management and employees, who would have a high reservation price ("HR") for the stock in case of a takeover threat, owned a relatively small fraction: 1.5% and 0.5%. The reservation prices of the remaining shareholders, mostly institutions with a total stake of 50%, were generally unknown. It may have been reasonable for a potential raider to conjecture, however, that a sufficient number of them, particularly non-taxpaying institutions, had low reservation prices. These factors made Gillette difficult to defend against hostile takeovers.

To deter a takeover, one of the things Gillette needed to do was to significantly reduce the fraction of low-reservation-price shareholders.

* * *

The Gillette–Coniston control battle was an interesting situation for the deployment of TPRs. First, it was important for Gillette not to initiate a targeted share repurchase. * * * Using TPRs in the Coniston repurchase ensured that all shareholders were given the chance to participate in the gains.

* * *

Those shareholders with low private values, arbitragers and others, could exercise their put rights and could even sell back a disproportionate number of shares by purchasing puts from HR shareholders. Thus, LR shareholders were satisfied. HR shareholders also gained because they received some of the premium paid in the repurchase in the price received for the put rights sold to the LR shareholders. These gains may have been partly offset if the TPR share repurchase further entrenched management and that entrenchment lowered the value of the firm. That Coniston was able to buy over two million puts, in addition to its allotment of approximately one million, and that trading in Gillette's TPRs was heavy (the average daily trading volume was 359,600) lend strong support to the differential private value hypothesis.

Second, no greenmail was perceived to have been paid. * * *

Gillette's management also apparently benefited from using TPRs. First, it averted a takeover. Second, it was not perceived as having paid greenmail in the process, and thus may have avoided subsequent legal action by shareholders. Finally, the repurchase through TPRs enabled it to ensure that only the lowest-reservation-price shareholders sold back, so, the postrepurchase ownership structure had a substantially higher proportion of HR shareholders, which would help in deterring future takeover bids.

* * *

Going-Private Stock Repurchases

KAUFMANN v. LAWRENCE

United States District Court, Southern District of New York, 1974.
386 F.Supp. 12, affirmed 514 F.2d 283 (2d Cir.1975).

CARTER, DISTRICT JUDGE.

* * *

WRG, a full-service advertising agency, is a New York corporation with principal offices in New York City. It proposes advertising programs for its clients, writes and produces television and radio commercials, contracts for advertising terms and space, and arranges for distribution of advertising materials. The individual defendants are directors and officers of the company. Defendant Mary Wells Lawrence was the founder of the company and is its chief executive officer.

The company was organized in 1966. Between approximately April, 1966, and June, 1968, the officers and directors acquired 1,450,600 shares of common stock of the company at an aggregate cost to them of $548,600. Thereafter, in 1968, a public offering of WRG common stock was made for the first time, consisting of a total of 409,900 shares at $17.50 per share. Of these 409,900 shares offered, 359,900 shares belonged to officers and directors of the company. In 1968, through this offering, the public invested $7,173,250 in the company. The officers and directors netted some $5,866,370 from this investment of funds from the public. Defendant Lawrence, who had bought founders' shares in 1966 for $30,100, realized some $1,266,575 as a result of this 1968 sale of stock to the public.[1] As of August 31, 1974, the issuance of 5,000,000 shares of WRG common stock was authorized; 1,631,588 shares had been issued, of which 265,052 shares were held by WRG officers, directors and employees.

WRG stock was listed and traded on the American Stock Exchange beginning in 1970, and in connection with the second public offering in 1971, the stock was transferred for listing and trading to the New York Stock Exchange. In 1971, some 333,739 shares, all owned by WRG directors, officers and employees, were sold to the public at $21.75 per share. The public invested some $7,258,823.25 in the company in the purchase of WRG shares in the 1971 offering. The aggregate net amount realized from this second public sale was $6,841,649, of which defendant Lawrence received $2,272,425.

---

1. This net figure is not all profit. It is the amount received by the individuals after deductions for commissions and other costs involved in the offering.

The corporation has prospered. Its gross billings grew from $77 million in the fiscal year ended October 31, 1969, to $115 million in fiscal year ended October 31, 1973. Earnings per share rose from $1.02 in fiscal 1969 to $2.04 in the fiscal year ended October 31, 1973. The company was described by plaintiff's expert at the November 25th hearing, as having developed a fine reputation, being noted for creativity in advertising, the possession of excellent business management and first-rate clients. Its common stock rose to a high of 27⅞ in 1972, but was selling at 5½ immediately prior to the exchange offer which is the subject of this controversy.

The idea of buying back the public stock was planted in the winter of 1973. Apparently what helped further the idea of removing the company from the public realm was an abortive attempt to buy out another company. These were sensitive negotiations, and we are advised that because the nature of the negotiations had to be fully disclosed to the SEC, they had to be terminated.

The decision to pursue going "private" further was made in August, 1974. Just prior to the September 4, 1974, WRG Board meeting, the advice of Paul Hallingby, Jr., President and chief Executive Officer of White, Weld & Co., Inc. was sought about the wisdom, fairness and advisability of the proposed exchange offer. White, Weld & Co., Inc., had acted as managing underwriter for the 1968 and 1971 public offerings, and since 1968 had been WRG's investment banking advisor and consultant. Hallingby in a letter dated September 4, 1974, advised Mrs. Lawrence that the exchange offer would be attractive and that the offering price of $3 in cash and $8 principal amount of 10% subordinated sinking fund debentures constituted fair value for the company's stock in the light of current market conditions. The transaction as finally approved by the Board at the September 4, 1974, meeting and offered to the public, was an offer to purchase from holders of its common stock, up to 1,405,008 shares of common stock, representing all of the issued outstanding shares except approximately 226,850 shares owned by members of the Board of Directors. The Board had agreed not to participate in this exchange offer. A holder would receive for each share tendered $3 in cash and $8 principal amount of a newly created 10% subordinated sinking fund debenture maturing on November 1, 1984, and bearing interest at 10% per annum. The debentures are unsecured obligations of the company limited to an aggregate principal amount of $11,240,064. Payment of the principal and interest is subordinated to all prior debt, and payment in any case is contingent upon the company being solvent and having a surplus at the time of payment. The debentures are redeemable at WRG's option. WRG is to pay into the sinking fund, on or before November 1, of each year from 1975 to 1983 in cash 10% of the aggregate principal amount of the originally outstanding debentures. WRG has the right to reduce its cash payments to the sinking fund by filing debentures with the Trustee which the company had acquired. The package is estimated to have a current value of $9 per share, but is actually selling at roughly a

30% discount. White, Weld & Co., Inc. has agreed to guarantee an over-the-counter market for any shares not tendered, and at the November 25th hearing, one of its officers, Brian Little, testified that a market could be made with as few as 50,000 shares.

The offer expired at 5 p.m. on November 25, and all tenders became irrevocable after November 12th. White, Weld & Co. is dealer-manager of the offer and Chase Manhattan Bank is the exchange agent. The Prospectus bears the statement, *"Participation in the Exchange Offer is completely voluntary and the Company makes no recommendations with respect thereto"* (italics in the original). The Prospectus further states that neither the company nor the Board is making any recommendation as to whether the offer should be accepted or rejected.

* * * The issue raised is undeniably serious and troublesome. The public has invested some $14 million in the company. The decision to buy out the public during the current depressed market will enable the public shares to be repossessed at a fraction of the original cost to the public shareholders. Moreover, if the exchange offer is successful, i.e., if the number of shareholders is reduced to fewer than 300, the company will be able to operate as a private corporation free from public regulation and oversight.

A member of the Securities and Exchange Commission, A.A. Sommer, Jr., has manifested concern about the trend of public companies to go "private," and is quoted as suggesting that "under well established legal principles such conduct may also be unlawful." (*Wall Street Journal,* November 15, 1974). The statement places stress on the benefits to, and large profits realized by, insiders when a company goes "private" because the stock market's depressed state enables the shares, previously purchased at high prices, to be repurchased at bargain rates.

This is really the basic issue and principle which plaintiff seeks to litigate. Plaintiff stresses the small capital investment of the directors prior to the 1968 offering, and the subsequent huge gains realized in the sale of their stock to the public in 1968 and 1971. Plaintiff contends that the exchange offer is an attempt to squeeze out the public and the package does not give the public fair value. At the hearing, plaintiff's expert testified that the appropriate way to measure true value was by what he called "intrinsic value"; that figure is arrived at by looking at the history of the price-earnings ratios of a company. Using that formula, he placed the current value of WRG shares at a high of $22 and a low of $19—$20. Defendants are, of course, using current market value to measure the fairness of the exchange offer, and that certainly is regarded as a fair indication of value. * * * Whether the offer is fair or unfair or a good or a bad transaction, however, does not raise a federal question. * * *

Plaintiff alleges that the statement in the Prospectus to the effect that the shareholders' response to the exchange offer is voluntary is a misrepresentation. He contends that the proposal is really intended as an immediate or ultimate squeeze-out of the public. He may well be right, but I do not think that helps his cause. Obviously, defendants are seeking to capitalize on the current economic downtrend and are offering their shareholders a package which is attractive only because of unfavorable economic conditions. In fact, the package is saleable only because of those conditions. The shareholder may tender his stock and sell the debentures at a discount in order to get out while he can. He may, however, gamble and refuse to tender, or tender and indicate his faith in WRG's future prosperity by holding the debentures until maturity. The Prospectus gives him all the relevant facts and he can act on the basis of full information.

This is not the case of any hidden or secret action by an outside group to take over control of the company. Nor does there appear to be any sizeable group of shareholders opposed to the exchange proposal. Indeed, if such opposition does exist, defendants' plans to go "private" will be frustrated by a sizeable number of shareholders refusing to tender their shares.

While Sections 10(b) and 14(e) must be read flexibly, and not technically or restrictively, * * * there is nothing invalid *per se* in a corporate effort to free itself from federal regulations, provided the means and the methods used to effectuate that objective are allowable under the law. Nor has the federal securities law placed profit-making or shrewd business tactics designed to benefit insiders, without more, beyond the pale. Those laws in respect of their design and interpretive reach, as I understand them, including the provisions relied on here, are satisfied if a full and fair disclosure is made, so that the decision of the holders of WRG stock to accept or refuse the exchange offer can be said to have been freely based upon adequate information. See Popkin v. Bishop, 464 F.2d 714, 721 (2d Cir.1972).

A public company going "private" may indeed raise serious questions concerning protection of the public interest. There is, however, no foundation on the record before me from which the ramifications of that interest within the reach of the federal securities laws might conceivably be explored. Thus plaintiff has failed to meet the alternative test pursuant to which a preliminary injunction might appropriately be granted.

* * *

Questions

1. Eleven days before the court heard the *Kaufman* case, a Securities and Exchange Commission commissioner publicly condemned the WRG transaction as unethical and illegal. Sommer, "Going Private: A Lesson in Corporate Responsibility," Fed.Sec.L.Rep. (CCH) ¶ 80,010 (1974). He complained that if all the public shares were tendered in response to the exchange offer, the dominant shareholder would go from a 7 percent interest to a 43 percent interest with "over $3.7 million (less taxes)

provided by the public safely locked up for her benefit ... and without a single dime of additional investment by her." Would he have been as concerned had the company done well and offered a package of cash and debentures worth $35 to take the company private when the stock was trading at $30 rather than a package worth $6.50 when the stock was trading at $5.50? Or is he concerned about the coercive nature of the exchange offer, regardless of price?

What is the position of shareholders who do not tender, hoping enough others will join them to defeat the offer, and find that the offer succeeds? What will be the value of their shares in a closely held company? The prospectus announcing the exchange offer noted that nontendering shareholders risked holding stock that would be delisted from the New York Stock Exchange and deregistered under the Securities and Exchange Act of 1934 (which requires quarterly and annual reports and regulates the solicitation of proxies of registered companies). It noted that the "reduced float may adversely affect the market price of Common Stock not exchanged and may also make such price more volatile." Would this disclosure be different if WRG stock was trading at $30 and the exchange offered a package of cash and debentures valued at $35? Would this disclosure be different if WRG stock were being purchased on the same terms by a third party? Is it the inherently coercive nature of any tender offer to take a company private that troubles Sommer?

2. There is no detailed discussion in the case of the reasons for WRG's going private. Are some reasons illegitimate? Consider each of the following reasons. Assume that the WRG managers believe that the costs of complying with the regulations applicable to publicly traded companies are too steep. On the other hand, assume the WRG managers believe the market undervalues the firm because (a) it has developed a new product, (b) orders for its products are up, (c) it has better managers than its competitors, or (d) general economic conditions have unduly depressed all stock prices. Or assume that WRG has a glut of cash, its existing facilities generate a healthy rate of return, but no new internal projects appear with rates of return that meet the rates of return on existing projects or exceed those available to its investors if they took the cash in the form of dividends and invested in other firms. Finally, assume that WRG management wants to effect a major business restructuring, does not believe the market will accurately value their plans ex ante, and thus seeks to implement their program when the firm is private and then to take the firm public again (with a new issue of stock; a "reverse LBO") once the program is in place (a "round trip").

3. Consider the position of the WRG shareholders as new holders of debentures. If fewer than three hundred shareholders are left after the exchange offer, and the company is no longer a registered company under the Securities and Exchange Act of 1934, see Exchange Act section 15(d), it is permitted to stop filing annual and quarterly financial reports one year after going private. How do debenture holders get information about the firm? Is this important to a trading market in the debentures? Can the firm withhold information to drive down the bond prices in anticipation of a repurchase offer for the bonds?

Please read rule 13e–3 and skim schedule 13E–3 in your statutory supplement.

Comparing the Regulation of Issuer Buybacks and Leveraged Buyouts

Most modern going-private transactions are not self-tender offers or street sweeps. Rather the management group sponsoring the acquisition itself forms an acquisition vehicle, a shell corporation or a limited partnership; the acquisition vehicle makes an any-and-all tender offer for the target; and if the tender offer is successful, the vehicle merges into the target, cashing out all the nontendering minority shareholders in the second-stage transaction (a "back-end" statutory merger). A leveraged buyout gives an acquisition group more flexibility in arranging the complicated new financing necessary to buy all the outstanding stock. For example, in an LBO it is easier for the management group to give some of their new financial partners equity participation in the deal, which may be necessary to "sweeten" their debt placements or to reduce the debt load to attract additional creditors.

OESTERLE & NORBERG, MANAGEMENT BUYOUTS: CREATING OR APPROPRIATING SHAREHOLDER WEALTH
41 Vand.L.Rev., 207, 246–49 (1988).

The conceptual difficulties of defining disclosure obligations in many management buyouts stems from their hybrid nature; a management buyout has some of the characteristics of an issuer repurchase and an outside bid. In issuer repurchases, the consensus seems to be that there are heavy disclosure obligations because the issuer should not be able to strike opportunistic deals with its own shareholders, that is, deals that take advantage of asymmetric information about the firm itself. In bids by outside parties, however, the disclosure obligations are less demanding, although there is no consensus on how much less demanding. The bidder has spent funds to acquire valuable information, information that the sellers themselves often could also acquire (as shareholders or through their agents, the firm managers). To deprive the bidder of the fruits of its efforts would deter bidders from investing in the collection of information on potential targets and reduce the number of beneficial buyouts. A management buyout, however, has elements of both an issuer repurchase, because members of the buyout group are fiduciaries and have superior access to firm information as a result of their privileged position, and an outside bid, because the buyout group is a new entity purchasing control of the firm, often in competition with other bidders and, perhaps, even an existing control group. The legal history of the SEC's treatment of issuer repurchases and tender offers by outside bidders illustrates a hazy, and intermittent recognition of management buyouts' relationship to the basic conceptual dichotomy.

The SEC, sensitive to the problems of defining proper disclosures in issuer repurchases, attempted both in 1975 and 1977 to assume the authority to prohibit going private transactions through issuer or issuer affiliate repurchases that the SEC deemed "unfair." Faced with criticism that the Commission had no authority to promulgate such a rule, the SEC adopted in 1979 a substitute rule, Rule 13e–3, that specifically requires the disclosure of itemized information and generally requires the disclosure of all material inside information. * * *

Rule 13e–3 may have a limited application to management buyouts, however. The Rule applies only to issuer repurchases or repurchases by an "affiliate" of the issuer. An affiliate is a person who "controls, is controlled by, or under common control" with the issuer. The SEC has noted that determinations of control are a question of fact and are "not limited to control obtained through ownership of equity securities." Presumably, a CEO leading a management buyout group would qualify the group as an affiliate. If less powerful members of the management team participate in the buyout without the CEO, or the CEO is not a major participant in the buyout group, the group may not have the status of an affiliate. * * *

If the buyout is structured as a tender offer, however, the buyout group must comply with Rule 14d–1 and file a Schedule 14D–1, if it is not an affiliate, or must comply with Rule 13e–4 and file a Schedule 13E–4 (in addition to a Schedule 13E–3) if it is an affiliate. In sum, there are no specific disclosure schedules for management buyouts by nonaffiliates that do not involve a tender offer. Moreover, management buyouts by nonaffiliates that do involve tender offers are subject to the same specific disclosure schedules as tender offers by third-party bidders. Since the possibility of abuse of insider information and position by management buyout groups that are not technically "affiliates," although slightly less severe on average, approaches the potential problems in issuer repurchases, one would expect the SEC to give management buyouts by nonaffiliates more individualized attention.

In any event, the major differences between Schedules 13E–3 for issuer repurchases and Schedule 14D–1 for third-party tender offers is in items 8 and 9 of Schedule 13E–3; these items have no specific corresponding disclosure requirements in the Schedule 14D–1. Item 8 of Schedule 13E–3 requires a statement on the fairness of the transaction with supporting rationale and includes a reference to item 9 that requires the disclosure of all reports or appraisals from outside parties "materially relating" to the fairness of the offer. In Schedule 13E–3, the issuer, as a fiduciary to the selling shareholders, must, in essence, disclose all its valuation information while outside bidders, using Schedule 14D–1, can presumably be more secretive. The courts, however, may not be sensitive to the difference, and may apply the same definition of "material" to both situations. The United States Court of

Appeals for the Third Circuit, for example, has held that asset appraisals commissioned by an outside bidder should be disclosed, if the appraisals are made by unbiased experts after a thorough investigation. If there is a real difference in the schedules, however, management buyouts may enjoy the luxury of the more lenient standard in Schedule 14D-1, depending on the composition of the buyout group and the structure of the transaction.

Neither a judicial approach, based on a unitary definition of "material" in all control contests, nor the SEC's approach, placing emphasis on control of the firm by the dominant members of the buyout group, is very satisfying. To the extent that a management buyout group acts on inside information and without serious intervention by nonparticipating managers or directors on behalf of the firm's shareholders, the buyout poses the same dangers as a large issuer repurchase of shares. If the buyout group acts largely on public information and is contested vigorously by a group of outside directors acting on behalf of shareholders, the buyout resembles a third-party offer. The SEC, and the courts, should focus on the specific character of the buyout process before deciding which disclosure obligations to apply to the particular transaction. There are many indications that the present disclosure tools are too crude.

* * *

Questions

1. When must an issuer file a schedule 13E-3? See rule 13e-3(3). If an issuer uses a self-tender offer to go private, must it also file a schedule 13E-4? If an issuer, subject to an outstanding third-party tender offer, uses a self-tender offer to take itself private, must it also file a rule 13e-1 notice and a schedule 14D-9?

The Securities and Exchange Commission promulgated rule 13e-3 after the *Kaufman* case. If the rule had been in force for the case, would WRG have had to file a schedule 13E-3? In the schedule would WRG have had to disclose any of the reasons for going private listed in question 2, infra, after the case? Would WRG have had to disclose the exact amount of the market's "undervalue" of the firm ("The price ought to be closer to $7 a share.")?

Though rule 13e-3 did not exist, WRG was under significant filing obligations from rule 13e-4 (schedule 13E-4) and from the Securities Act of 1933 (form S-1) (the exchange offer was a public offer and sale of the WRG's debenture securities; see chapter 6). What does schedule 13e-3 add to the requirements of these two disclosure regulations? Note the contents of the prospectus (required by the 1933 act) filed in the case. Does it meet the requirements of rule 13e-3?

2. Are the obligations of an issuer taking the company private greater or less than the obligations of a third party who, through an any-and-all tender offer, takes the company private? Does schedule 14d-1 contain anything similar to items 8 and 9 in schedule 13E-3? What purpose is

served by the items in a self-tender offer? What is the difference between a regulation that requires all going-private transactions to be at a "fair price" and one that requires the firm to state whether the going-private transaction is at a "fair price"?

3. Are the obligations of an issuer taking the company private greater or less than the obligations of an issuer that recommends its shareholders accept a tender offer from an independent firm? Should they be?

4. A limited partnership is formed that includes some members of senior management, currently owning less than 3 percent of the outstanding voting equity of the firm but with a 30 percent equity interest in the partnership, and various other outside investors. The partnership makes a tender offer for the firm, intending to take the firm private. What schedule or schedules must the partnership file? In other words, what is the critical distinction between a 13e–3 and a 14d–1 transaction?

5. In a management buyout (MBO), in which a partnership of several senior managers and other new equity investors (investment banks, perhaps) buy all outstanding stock in the firm, must the MBO group file a schedule 14D–1, a schedule 13E–3, or a schedule 13E–4?

Note

The Puzzle of the Large Premiums in Stock Buybacks

Open market repurchases and self-tenders are both greeted on announcement with significant stock price increases. Buckley, When the Medium Is the Message: Corporate Buybacks as Signals, 65 Ind.L.J. 493, 499–500 (1990) (the two-day announcement return is 16.2 percent for a self-tender and 3.6 percent for an open market repurchase). More dramatically, management buyouts, a tender offer by a purchasing group that includes firm managers as substantial equity participants, can offer shareholders a premium of 30 to 40 percent over predeal market prices. See Oesterle & Norberg, Management Buyouts: Creating or Appropriating Shareholder Wealth?, 41 Vand.L.Rev. 207 (1988). In buybacks and MBOs, unlike third-party tender offers, there are no new gains from synergy (the combination of the operations of two independent firms) or from replacing inferior managers. Since stock repurchases do not necessarily change the management structure of the firm nor the essential nature of the firm's business, where does the new value come from?

There are explanations that suggest buybacks and leveraged buyouts are socially undesirable. First, for example, the managers could use buybacks to benefit shareholders at the expense of other constituencies—bondholders, employees, and middle managers—by severely leveraging the capital structure of the firm. We covered some of these issues in chapter 3. Second, the managers could use buybacks to engage in the purest form of insider trading. This is a suspicion whenever, as a result of the buyback or LBO, the insiders gain a larger stake in the firm. The managers may know, based on their inside access to private firm information, that the firm's stock is undervalued. They take this value away from some or all the public shareholders through buybacks or LBOs. The information does not have to be solely in the form of advance knowledge of favorable business events. It can be in the knowledge that the firm ought to restructure itself to be more profitable. If the managers of the firm after a successful buyback or LBO implement dramatic and profitable changes in the management or business structure, why did they not implement such changes before the buyback, when they were fiduciaries for now cashed-out public shareholders?

Are there explanations that justify buybacks or LBOs? If so, can our legal system distinguish between value-creating and value-appropriating buybacks?

In buybacks that do not take a firm private, Professor Buckley has argued that the repurchase is a "signaling" phenomenon. Through a repurchase a firm signals the market, in ways that cannot be imitated by other firms and that cannot be duplicated by other methods such as stock dividends, that the market is undervaluing the firm. Buckley, When the Medium Is the Message: Corporate Buybacks as Signals, 65 Ind.L.J. 493 (1990). Thus buybacks in which the firm's managers repurchase only a portion of the outstanding shares increase the allocative efficiency of stock markets by dissipating informational asymmetries between the firm and outside investors. Insider trading may not be a problem, because all nontendering shareholders, many of whom are not insiders, can share in buyback gains reflected in the price of their stock. Moreover, if the repurchase itself effectively and accurately signals the market about the value of the inside information at the time of the repurchase, then insiders cannot effect wealth transfers from selling shareholders either, as the sales price will reflect the value of the information.

Signaling, by itself, cannot justify going-private transactions, however. Self-tender offers and LBOs that take a firm private are not concerned about the future public pricing of the firm's securities. Nontendering shareholders have no liquid market for their stock and thus do not enjoy positive buyback gains reflected in the value of their stock. Moreover, in LBOs, more prevalent than self-tender offers in modern going-private transactions, nontendering minority shareholders are typically cashed out in a second-stage merger between the acquisition vehicle and the target, disabling them from participating in the future prospects of the firm. The sales price offered to nonparticipating shareholders may reflect the strategic difficulties of their choice in responding to a going-private offer rather than the value of any inside information. How can we justify the premium price in going-private transactions?

OESTERLE & NORBERG, MANAGEMENT BUYOUTS: CREATING OR APPROPRIATING SHAREHOLDER WEALTH?
41 Vand.L.Rev. 207, 222–33 (1988).

What can the managers do privately that they could not or should not have done as salaried executives of a publicly held company? * * *

First, private companies are not subject to the many burdens imposed by the Securities Exchange Act of 1934 and other governmentally imposed regulations on public companies. * * * One wonders, however, how substantial these savings are; it seems highly unlikely that these savings can explain the millions of dollars in profits earned by members of the purchasing groups. Moreover, these savings would seem to be more than offset by the fees paid to the investment bankers who structure the buyout. * * *

Second, assuming that no material, nonpublic information is involved, the management group simply may have a forecast of the firm's future different than that held by the public market. * * * Adherents of the semi-strong or strong version of the efficient market theory would scoff at this claim, for, according to those theories, the public market price best incorporates the value of all public information. In other words, the management purchaser group paying a premium over market for undervalued stock is more likely to be wrong than right. This is not to say, however, that the firm's shareholders should be prohibited from enjoying the benefits of their managers' foolishness. * * *

Third, until the Tax Reform Act of 1986, management buyouts provided unique and substantial tax advantages. * * * Moreover, the interest deduction, which is often advanced as a significant motivation for buyouts, is not unique to buyouts. A firm's existing management can recapitalize the company without selling it in order to take advantage of the interest deduction. Without demonstrating that buyouts are a substantially cheaper method of acquiring large interest deductions than floating more debt securities or adopting stock repurchase programs, which also increase the debt-equity ratio, the interest deduction cannot, by itself, be a justification for management buyouts.

* * *

Fourth, management buyouts may be justified because top managers recognize that a particular firm is suffering substantial agency costs or, in other words, that the management team is performing marginally because of an ineffective corporate monitoring process. A management buyout, which will give managers a more substantial equity stake in the corporation, will induce the management team to perform more faithfully the goal of maximizing the worth of the business. The unadorned agency cost position, however, is not very satisfying. If a firm has shirking managers, an alternative way of encouraging better management performance is to increase the amount of compensation contingent on corporate performance through, for example, option plans or stock appreciation rights. Since managers themselves have a good deal of control over their own compensation plans, management buyouts carried out to improve the monitoring process seemingly involve a taking of corporate opportunity—the opportunity to motivate managers—for personal gain. This situation is not materially different from undertaking a management buyout with more conventional kinds of inside information such as the discovery of a valuable ore field under the obsolete factory, for example. * * *

In an extreme case, it seems that management buyouts could create a moral hazard. The opportunity for management buyouts may encourage managers of publicly held firms to shirk their responsibilities, allowing managers strategically to increase their personal profits from successful buyouts. Of course, the countervailing pressure from outside bidders ought to eliminate such temptations because excessive shirking ought to attract outside bidders as well. Perhaps the most favorable gloss that can be put on this form of the agency cost argument is that management buyouts (if they are the first to bid for control of the firm, that is, the bid is not in response to an outside bid) will encourage outsiders to bid for the firm. The resulting auction between the outsiders and the management group will maximize the public shareholders' slice of any gains attributable to the owner-managers' success at reducing overall agency costs after the buyout. In other words, management buyout proposals may signal to the market that a firm is a prime takeover target. * * *

The final justification is a more refined version of the agency cost problem. While the fourth justification focuses primarily on laziness—managers work harder when they are owners—this justification focuses on the risk preferences of typical managers. Managers are confronted with a high risk business decision that they are unwilling to take as agents of a public corporation but are willing to take as owners. * * *

Modern finance theory postulates that managers are more risk averse than most shareholders because managers cannot diversify their investment of human capital in an employing firm.

* * * As a consequence, managers suffer firm-specific risk (unsystematic risk) that other shareholders can avoid more easily by maintaining a diverse investment portfolio, although shareholders must pay managers to accept such risks. Moreover, managers, within broad boundaries imposed by the monitoring capability of the shareholders, faced with specific business choices will favor alternatives that sacrifice expected value for less variance in outcome, to the detriment of the interests of their shareholders. The conflict is the most pronounced when the choice on the table is dramatic; that is, when it involves a radical deviation from past business practices. The choice is a high risk, one-time gamble with high stakes.

How do shareholders encourage their managers to take the high risk gambles that hold positive expected values? The best choice is a redivision of the gains from the gamble so that managers get a larger return per dollar invested. Shareholders get less than they would get if the managers would take the gamble as salaried employees without a redivision of the gains, but managers may refuse to do this for the high risk business decisions. However, if shareholders are willing to accept some redistribution of gains, they still may get more than they would if the managers do nothing and the gains are never realized, which is the more likely scenario for the high risk gambles. * * *

In management buyouts top executives get a higher rate of return and assume a higher risk (they put a higher percentage of their personal assets at risk in the firm), but presumably the degree of the increase in return exceeds the degree of the increase in risk for an enhanced expected value per dollar of investment. Shareholders get some positive returns for selling the firm to the managers, because the managers will act and the shareholders assume no risk for the success of the act, which is better than holding shares in a corporation which does nothing at all that is risky.

* * *

Note
Reverse LBOs: Buying Back Debt

Many firms that took on additional debt in the eighties now find themselves unable to make the huge interest and principal payments. In early 1990 over twenty-five major companies have floated exchange offers to replace nearly $13 billion of high-yield junk bonds with equity or deferred payment debt. "Many Firms Find Debt They Piled on in 1980s Is a Cruel Taskmaster," Wall St.J. p. 1 col. 6 (Oct. 9, 1990). Forstmann and Company, for example, is asking bondholders to accept new securities that pay no cash but will accrue interest at a higher rate for three years. Western Union is asking note holders to accept a package that includes some cash, stock, and new bonds with interest rates far lower than the old notes and deferred for several years. Bondholders are not happy and are in some cases uniting to get better terms or defeat the offer. JPS Textile had so few tenders into its exchange offer that even after upping the ante by throwing in some common stock, it had to cancel its offer.

The Securities and Exchange Commission is looking into debt tender offers because the SEC rules covering tender offers for stock do not apply to exchange and cash tender offers for debt. See section 14(d). Currently the SEC has promulgated several rules applicable to debt offers under the authority of section 14(e), however. Please read section 14(e) and SEC rules 14e–1. The SEC has in the past granted exemptions from these rules for debt tender offers in "no action" letters but seems less inclined to do so at present. Do the proration rule, rule 14d–8, and the all-holders rule, rule 14d–10, apply to debt tender offers?

The most controversial of the new debt tender offers is the product of acrimonious negotiations with a new player on the acquisition scene—the "vulture fund." A vulture fund buys bonds that are the subject of an issuer exchange offer when the issuer is desperate to reduce its debt load. The fund holds out, playing the firm's precarious situation, demanding a higher payment for its securities than that received by other bondholders. In response, issuers have reduced the incentive for vulture funds to buy the firm's bonds by including a minimum acceptance condition in its tender offer that is equal to that required to amend the bond's indenture. Most indentures provide that a supermajority of the debt holders can amend most of its terms.[1] The firm thus threatens to amend the indenture by voting the tendered bonds to strip the indenture of all its financial covenants. If a vulture fund appears and holds out and the firm responds by

---

1. If the debt is publicly held, the Trust Indenture Act does not allow the modification of the principal amount, interest rate, and maturity date. The firm can, however, amend the financial covenants that trigger cross-defaults, acceleration, and bankruptcy.

amending the indenture, the fund ends up with virtually worthless paper. See Coffee, "Coercive Debt Tender Offers," 204 New York L.J. p. 5 (July 19, 1990).

KATZ v. OAK INDUSTRIES, INC.
Court of Chancery of Delaware, 1986.
508 A.2d 873.

ALLEN, CHANCELLOR.

* * *

Plaintiff is the owner of long-term debt securities issued by Oak Industries, Inc. ("Oak"), a Delaware corporation; in this class action he seeks to enjoin the consummation of an exchange offer and consent solicitation made by Oak to holders of various classes of its long-term debt.

* * *

Even a casual review of Oak's financial results over the last several years shows it unmistakably to be a company in deep trouble.

* * *

The Company and Allied–Signal, Inc. entered into two agreements. The first, the Acquisition Agreement, contemplates the sale to Allied–Signal of the Materials Segment for $160 million in cash. The second agreement, the Stock Purchase Agreement, provides for the purchase by Allied–Signal for $15 million cash of 10 million shares of the Company's common stock together with warrants to purchase additional common stock.

The Stock Purchase Agreement provides as a condition to Allied–Signal's obligation that at least 85% of the aggregate principal amount of all of the Company's debt securities shall have tendered and accepted the exchange offers that are the subject of this lawsuit. Oak has six classes of such long term debt.[3] If less than 85% of the aggregate principal amount of such debt accepts the offer, Allied–Signal has an option, but no obligation, to purchase the common stock and warrants contemplated by the Stock Purchase Agreement. An additional condition for the closing of the Stock Purchase Agreement is that the sale of the Company's Materials Segment contemplated by the Acquisition Agreement shall have been concluded.

Thus, as part of the restructuring and recapitalization contemplated by the Acquisition Agreement and the Stock Purchase Agreement, the Company has extended an exchange offer to each of the

---

3. The three classes of debentures are: 13.65% debentures due April 1, 2001, 10½% convertible subordinated debentures due February 1, 2002, and 11⅞% subordinated debentures due May 15, 1998. In addition, as a result of the 1985 exchange offer the company has three classes of notes which were issued in exchange for debentures that were tendered in that offer. Those are: 13.5% senior notes due May 15, 1990, 9⅝% convertible notes due September 15, 1991 and 11⅝% notes due September 15, 1990.

holders of the six classes of its long-term debt securities. These pending exchange offers include a Common Stock Exchange Offer (available only to holders of the 9⅝% convertible notes) and the Payment Certificate Exchange Offers (available to holders of all six classes of Oak's long-term debt securities). The Common Stock Exchange Offer currently provides for the payment to each tendering noteholder of 407 shares of the Company's common stock in exchange for each $1,000 9⅝% note accepted. The offer is limited to $38.6 million principal amount of notes (out of approximately $83.9 million outstanding).

The Payment Certificate Exchange Offer is an any and all offer. Under its terms, a payment certificate, payable in cash five days after the closing of the sale of the Materials Segment to Allied–Signal, is offered in exchange for debt securities. The cash value of the Payment Certificate will vary depending upon the particular security tendered. In each instance, however, that payment will be less than the face amount of the obligation. The cash payments range in amount, per $1,000 of principal, from $918 to $655. These cash values however appear to represent a premium over the market prices for the Company's debentures as of the time the terms of the transaction were set.

The Payment Certificate Exchange Offer is subject to certain important conditions before Oak has an obligation to accept tenders under it. First, it is necessary that a minimum amount ($38.6 million principal amount out of $83.9 million total outstanding principal amount) of the 9⅝% notes be tendered pursuant to the Common Stock Exchange Offer. Secondly, it is necessary that certain minimum amounts of each class of debt securities be tendered, together with consents to amendments to the underlying indentures.[4] Indeed, under the offer one may not tender securities unless at the same time one consents to the proposed amendments to the relevant indentures.

The condition of the offer that tendering security holders must consent to amendments in the indentures governing the securities gives rise to plaintiff's claim of breach of contract in this case. Those amendments would, if implemented, have the effect of removing significant negotiated protections to holders of the Company's long-term debt including the deletion of all financial covenants. Such modification may have adverse consequences to debt holders who elect not to tender pursuant to either exchange offer.

Allied–Signal apparently was unwilling to commit to the $15 million cash infusion contemplated by the Stock Purchase Agreement, unless Oak's long-term debt is reduced by 85% (at least that is a condition of their obligation to close on that contract). Mathematically, such a reduction may not occur without the Company reducing the

---

4. The holders of more than 50% of the principal amount of each of the 13.5% notes, the 9⅝% notes and the 11⅝% notes and at least 66⅔% of the principal amount of the 13.65% debentures, 10½% debentures, and 11⅞% debentures, must validly tender such securities and consent to certain proposed amendments to the indentures governing those securities.

principal amount of outstanding debentures (that is the three classes of outstanding notes constitute less than 85% of all long-term debt). But existing indenture covenants (See Offering Circular, pp. 38–39) prohibit the Company, so long as any of its long-term notes are outstanding, from issuing any obligation (including the Payment Certificates) in exchange for any of the debentures. Thus, in this respect, amendment to the indentures is required in order to close the Stock Purchase Agreement as presently structured.

Restrictive covenants in the indentures would appear to interfere with effectuation of the recapitalization in another way. Section 4.07 of the 13.50% Indenture provides that the Company may not "acquire" for value any of the 9⅝% Notes or 11⅝% Notes unless it concurrently "redeems" a proportionate amount of the 13.50% Notes. This covenant, if unamended, would prohibit the disproportionate acquisition of the 9⅝% Notes that may well occur as a result of the Exchange Offers; in addition, it would appear to require the payment of the "redemption" price for the 13.50% Notes rather than the lower, market price offered in the exchange offer.

In sum, the failure to obtain the requisite consents to the proposed amendments would permit Allied–Signal to decline to consummate both the Acquisition Agreement and the Stock Purchase Agreement.

* * *

Plaintiff's claim is that no free choice is provided to bondholders by the exchange offer and consent solicitation. Under its terms, a rational bondholder is "forced" to tender and consent. Failure to do so would face a bondholder with the risk of owning a security stripped of all financial covenant protections and for which it is likely that there would be no ready market. A reasonable bondholder, it is suggested, cannot possibly accept those risks and thus such a bondholder is coerced to tender and thus to consent to the proposed indenture amendments.

It is urged this linking of the offer and the consent solicitation constitutes a breach of a contractual obligation that Oak owes to its bondholders to act in good faith. Specifically, plaintiff points to three contractual provisions from which it can be seen that the structuring of the current offer constitutes a breach of good faith. Those provisions (1) establish a requirement that no modification in the term of the various indentures may be effectuated without the consent of a stated percentage of bondholders; (2) restrict Oak from exercising the power to grant such consent with respect to any securities it may hold in its treasury; and (3) establish the price at which and manner in which Oak may force bondholders to submit their securities for redemption.

* * *

This case does not involve the measurement of corporate or directorial conduct against that high standard of fidelity required of fiduciaries when they act with respect to the interests of the beneficiaries of their trust. Under our law—and the law generally—the relationship between a corporation and the holders of its debt securities, even convertible debt securities, is contractual in nature. * * * Arrangements among a corporation, the underwriters of its debt, trustees under its indentures and sometimes ultimate investors are typically thoroughly negotiated and massively documented. The rights and obligations of the various parties are or should be spelled out in that documentation. The terms of the contractual relationship agreed to and not broad concepts such as fairness define the corporation's obligation to its bondholders.[7]

Thus, the first aspect of the pending Exchange Offers about which plaintiff complains—that "the purpose and effect of the Exchange Offers is to benefit Oak's common stockholders at the expense of the Holders of its debt"—does not itself appear to allege a cognizable legal wrong. It is the obligation of directors to attempt, within the law, to maximize the long-run interests of the corporation's stockholders; that they may sometimes do so "at the expense" of others (even assuming that a transaction which one may refuse to enter into can meaningfully be said to be at his expense) does not for that reason constitute a breach of duty. It seems likely that corporate restructurings designed to maximize shareholder values may in some instances have the effect of requiring bondholders to bear greater risk of loss and thus in effect transfer economic value from bondholders to stockholders. * * * But if courts are to provide protection against such enhanced risk, they will require either legislative direction to do so or the negotiation of indenture provisions designed to afford such protection.

* * *

Modern contract law has generally recognized an implied covenant to the effect that each party to a contract will act with good faith towards the other with respect to the subject matter of the contract. * * *

It is this obligation to act in good faith and to deal fairly that plaintiff claims is breached by the structure of Oak's coercive exchange offer. Because it is an implied *contractual* obligation that is asserted as the basis for the relief sought, the appropriate legal test is not difficult to deduce. It is this: is it clear from what was expressly agreed upon that the parties who negotiated the express terms of the contract would have agreed to proscribe the act later complained of as a breach of the implied covenant of good faith—had they thought to negotiate with respect to that matter. If the answer to this question is yes, then, in my opinion, a court is justified in concluding that such act constitutes a breach of the implied covenant of good faith. * * *

---

7. To say that the broad duty of loyalty that a director owes to his corporation and ultimately its shareholders is not implicated in this case is not to say, as the discussion below reflects, that as a matter of contract law a corporation owes no duty to bondholders of good faith and fair dealing. *See, Restatement of Law, Contracts 2d,* § 205 (1979). Such a duty, however, is quite different from the congeries of duties that are assumed by a fiduciary.

Applying the foregoing standard to the exchange offer and consent solicitation, I find first that there is nothing in the indenture provisions granting bondholders power to veto proposed modifications in the relevant indenture that implies that Oak may not offer an inducement to bondholders to consent to such amendments. Such an implication, at least where, as here, the inducement is offered on the same terms to each holder of an affected security, would be wholly inconsistent with the strictly commercial nature of the relationship.

Nor does the second pertinent contractual provision supply a ground to conclude that defendant's conduct violates the reasonable expectations of those who negotiated the indentures on behalf of the bondholders. Under that provision Oak may not vote debt securities held in its treasury. Plaintiff urges that Oak's conditioning of its offer to purchase debt on the giving of consents has the effect of subverting the purpose of that provision; it permits Oak to "dictate" the vote on securities which it could not itself vote.

The evident purpose of the restriction on the voting of treasury securities is to afford protection against the issuer voting as a bondholder in favor of modifications that would benefit it as issuer, even though such changes would be detrimental to bondholders. But the linking of the exchange offer and the consent solicitation does not involve the risk that bondholder interests will be affected by a vote involving anyone with a financial interest in the subject of the vote other than a bondholder's interest. That the consent is to be given concurrently with the transfer of the bond to the issuer does not in any sense create the kind of conflict of interest that the indenture's prohibition on voting treasury securities contemplates. Not only will the proposed consents be granted or withheld only by those with a financial interest to maximize the return on their investment in Oak's bonds, but the incentive to consent is equally available to all members of each class of bondholders. Thus the "vote" implied by the consent solicitation is not affected in any sense by those with a financial conflict of interest.

In these circumstances, while it is clear that Oak has fashioned the exchange offer and consent solicitation in a way designed to encourage consents, I cannot conclude that the offer violates the intendment of any of the express contractual provisions considered or, applying the test set out above, that its structure and timing breaches an implied obligation of good faith and fair dealing.

One further set of contractual provisions should be touched upon: Those granting to Oak a power to redeem the securities here treated at a price set by the relevant indentures. Plaintiff asserts that the attempt to force all bondholders to tender their securities at less than the redemption price constitutes, if not a breach of the redemption provision itself, at least a breach of an implied covenant of good faith and fair dealing associated with it. The flaw, or at least one fatal flaw, in this argument is that the present offer is not the functional equivalent of a redemption which is, of course, an act that the issuer may take unilaterally. In this instance it may happen that Oak will get tenders of a large percentage of its outstanding long-term debt securities. If it does, that fact will, in my judgment, be in major part a function of the merits of the offer (i.e., the price offered in light of the Company's financial position and the market value of its debt). To answer plaintiff's contention that the *structure* of the offer "forces" debt holders to tender, one only has to imagine what response this offer would receive if the price offered did not reflect a premium over market but rather was, for example, ten percent of market value. The exchange offer's success ultimately depends upon the ability and willingness of the issuer to extend an offer that will be a financially attractive alternative to holders. This process is hardly the functional equivalent of the unilateral election of redemption and thus cannot be said in any sense to constitute a subversion by Oak of the negotiated provisions dealing with redemption of its debt.

Accordingly, I conclude that plaintiff has failed to demonstrate a probability of ultimate success on the theory of liability asserted.

* * *

Questions

1. Could rational bondholders have decided that they did not want an equal opportunity to receive a premium because it would expose them to coercive offers? Is there a collective action problem because the bondholders cannot collectively agree to hold out, the prospect of being left with debt securities having a value below the pre-tender market price for a player that holds out when enough other players tender causes a debt holder to tender even though he is worse off than he was before the offer was made?

2. If an issuer directs a tendering bondholder how to vote the bonds as a condition of tendering, is the issuer the beneficial owner of the bonds and therefore subject to the sterilization provision in the bond indenture?

3. Should we worry about the bondholders in the case when 80 percent of the notes in one of the classes were owned by four institutions? Is there a collective action problem?

SUBCHAPTER B. STATE REGULATION OF STOCK ACQUISITIONS: ANTITAKEOVER STATUTES

States have enacted three generations of takeover statutes since the seventies. The generations are defined by two Supreme Court cases, one in 1982 and one in 1987. Before the 1982 case, *Edgar v. Mite Corp.*, states had begun to pass statutes similar to the Illinois statute declared unconstitutional in that case. The states took their cue from the statute on regulated industries that allowed, for example, state banking officials to pass on the merits of bank mergers that involved a state chartered bank. The statutes were severe, forbidding acquisitions of firms with substantial assets in the state unless the bidder secured approval of the acquisition from a designated public official. After

Edgar v. Mite Corp. states passed second-generation statutes designed to satisfy the hazy criteria of the case. The most popular were control share acts and fair price acts. Most observers, including the state legislatures that passed them, assumed that the second-generation statutes were unconstitutional, and federal courts routinely threw out the statutes that came before them. States continued to pass the statutes, primarily to give local targets something to sue on in court to effect delay in unwanted takeover bids.

In 1987 the Supreme Court surprised almost everyone and decided that one of these odd-looking second-generation statutes, the Indiana Control Share Act, was constitutional. After the 1987 case, states rushed to pass a third generation of statutes, designed to push the limits of what the Supreme Court indicated it might accept in subsequent litigation. States passed business combination acts and then pushed forward, passing appraisal acts. The lower federal courts, perhaps burned by their approach to the second-generation statutes, completely reversed field and have, with a few exceptions, upheld many of the third-generation statutes. When the Supreme Court recently refused to hear an appeal from a 1989 Sixth Circuit case upholding a popular third-generation statute—a business combination statute—the states took the bit in their teeth. Pennsylvania, in a move that will undoubtedly be followed by others, passed the newest and most restrictive statute—a disgorgement act. It appears that states will push as far as allowed by the Supreme Court to limit takeovers of domestic corporations. A study of state antitakeover legislation is therefore a study of the interaction of state legislatures and the Supreme Court.

The Frequency of the Statutes

A rough current count of states with one or more of the statutes is as follows: about twenty states have control share acts, fifteen have business combination acts, fifteen have fair price statutes, and two have redemption statutes. Several states layer their takeover statutes to include more than one type. Pennsylvania, for example, has a control share act, a business combination statute, and a disgorgement statute. The total count of states with some form of antitakeover legislation is about thirty-five.

State legislatures passed many of the state statutes in extreme haste at the request of an individual or local firm worried about a takeover threat. When rumors circulated about a takeover of Boeing Corporation, for example, the Washington legislature met in emergency session and approved a bill, signed immediately by the governor, that had been drafted by Boeing counsel. Arizona state officials, at the request of Greyhound Corporation, introduced, adopted, and signed into law the Arizona Control Share Act in three days. It took Illinois only two days and Minnesota only one to pass their statutes. The governor of Massachusetts signed the Massachusetts statute in the offices of Gillette, a takeover target at the time. Whose interests were state officials representing in promulgating the legislation?

EDGAR v. MITE CORP.

Supreme Court of the United States, 1982.
457 U.S. 624, 102 S.Ct. 2629, 73 L.Ed.2d 269.

JUSTICE WHITE delivered an opinion, Parts I, II, and V–B of which are the opinion of the Court.*

The issue in this case is whether the Illinois Business Take–Over Act, Ill.Rev.Stat., ch. 121½, ¶ 137.51 *et seq.* (1979), is unconstitutional under the Supremacy and Commerce Clauses of the Federal Constitution.

I

* * * Under the Illinois Act any takeover offer for the shares of a target company must be registered with the Secretary of State. Ill.Rev. Stat., ch. 121½, ¶ 137.54.A (1979). A target company is defined as a corporation or other issuer of securities of which shareholders located in Illinois own 10% of the class of equity securities subject to the offer, or for which any two of the following three conditions are met: the corporation has its principal executive office in Illinois, is organized under the laws of Illinois, or has at least 10% of its stated capital and paid-in surplus represented within the State. * * * An offer becomes registered 20 days after a registration statement is filed with the Secretary unless the Secretary calls a hearing. * * * The Secretary may call a hearing at any time during the 20–day waiting period to adjudicate the substantive fairness of the offer if he believes it is necessary to protect the shareholders of the target company, and a hearing must be held if requested by a majority of a target company's outside directors or by Illinois shareholders who own 10% of the class of securities subject to the offer. * * * If the Secretary does hold a hearing, he is directed by the statute to deny registration to a tender offer if he finds that it "fails to provide full and fair disclosure to the offerees of all material information concerning the take-over offer, or that the take-over offer is inequitable or would work or tend to work a fraud or deceit upon the offerees...." * * *

III

We first address the holding that the Illinois Takeover Act is unconstitutional under the Supremacy Clause. We note at the outset that in passing the Williams Act, which is an amendment to the Securities Exchange Act of 1934, Congress did not also amend § 28(a) of

---

* The Chief Justice joins the opinion in its entirety; Justice Blackmun joins Parts I, II, III, and IV; Justice Powell joins Parts

the 1934 Act, 15 U.S.C. § 78bb(a).[6] In pertinent part, § 28(a) provides as follows:

> "Nothing in this title shall affect the jurisdiction of the securities commission (or any agency or officer performing like functions) of any State over any security or any person insofar as it does not conflict with the provisions of this title or the rules and regulations thereunder." 48 Stat. 903.

Thus Congress did not explicitly prohibit States from regulating takeovers; it left the determination whether the Illinois statute conflicts with the Williams Act to the courts. Of course, a state statute is void to the extent that it actually conflicts with a valid federal statute; and

> "[a] conflict will be found 'where compliance with both federal and state regulations is a physical impossibility ...,' * * * where the state 'law stands as an obstacle to the accomplishment and execution of the full purposes and objectives of Congress.' * * *"

Our inquiry is further narrowed in this case since there is no contention that it would be impossible to comply with both the provisions of the Williams Act and the more burdensome requirements of the Illinois law. The issue thus is, as it was in the Court of Appeals, whether the Illinois Act frustrates the objectives of the Williams Act in some substantial way.

The Williams Act, passed in 1968, was the congressional response to the increased use of cash tender offers in corporate acquisitions, a device that had "removed a substantial number of corporate control contests from the reach of existing disclosure requirements of the federal securities laws." * * * The Williams Act filled this regulatory gap. The Act imposes several requirements.

* * *

There is no question that in imposing these requirements, Congress intended to protect investors. * * * But it is also crystal clear that a major aspect of the effort to protect the investor was to avoid favoring either management or the take-over bidder. * * * This policy of "evenhandedness," * * * represented a conviction that neither side in the contest should be extended additional advantages vis-à-vis the investor, who if furnished with adequate information would be in a position to make his own informed choice.

* * *

IV

The Court of Appeals identified three provisions of the Illinois Act that upset the careful balance struck by Congress and which therefore

---

I, and V–B; and Justice Stevens and Justice O'Connor join Parts I, II, and V.

6. There is no evidence in the legislative history that Congress was aware of state takeover laws when it enacted the Williams Act. When the Williams Act was enacted in 1968, only Virginia had a takeover statute. The Virginia statute, Va. Code § 13.1–528 (1978), became effective March 5, 1968; the Williams Act was enacted several months later on July 19, 1968. Takeover statutes are now in effect in 37 States.

* * *

stand as obstacles to the accomplishment and execution of the full purposes and objectives of Congress. We agree with the Court of Appeals in all essential respects.

The Illinois Act requires a tender offeror to notify the Secretary of State and the target company of its intent to make a tender offer and the material terms of the offer 20 business days before the offer becomes effective. * * * During that time, the offeror may not communicate its offer to the shareholders. * * * Meanwhile, the target company is free to disseminate information to its shareholders concerning the impending offer. The contrast with the Williams Act is apparent. Under that Act, there is no pre-commencement notification requirement; the critical date is the date a tender offer is "first published or sent or given to security holders." 15 U.S.C. § 78n(d)(1). * * *

We agree with the Court of Appeals that by providing the target company with additional time within which to take steps to combat the offer, the precommencement notification provisions furnish incumbent management with a powerful tool to combat tender offers, perhaps to the detriment of the stockholders who will not have an offer before them during this period. These consequences are precisely what Congress determined should be avoided, and for this reason, the precommencement notification provision frustrates the objectives of the Williams Act.

It is important to note in this respect that in the course of events leading to the adoption of the Williams Act, Congress several times refused to impose a precommencement disclosure requirement. * * *

For similar reasons, we agree with the Court of Appeals that the hearing provisions of the Illinois Act frustrate the congressional purpose by introducing extended delay into the tender offer process. The Illinois Act allows the Secretary of State to call a hearing with respect to any tender offer subject to the Act, and the offer may not proceed until the hearing is completed. * * * The Secretary may call a hearing at any time prior to the commencement of the offer, and there is no deadline for the completion of the hearing. * * * Although the Secretary is to render a decision within 15 days after the conclusion of the hearing, that period may be extended without limitation. Not only does the Secretary of State have the power to delay a tender offer indefinitely, but incumbent management may also use the hearing provisions of the Illinois Act to delay a tender offer. The Secretary is required to call a hearing if requested to do so by, among other persons, those who are located in Illinois "as determined by post office address as shown on the records of the target company and who hold of record or beneficially, or both, at least 10% of the outstanding shares of any class of equity securities which is the subject of the takeover offer." * * * Since incumbent management in many cases will control, either directly or indirectly, 10% of the target company's shares, this provision allows management to delay the commencement of an offer by insisting on a hearing. As the Court of Appeals observed, these provisions potentially afford management a "powerful weapon to stymie indefinitely a takeover." * * * In enacting the Williams Act, Congress itself "recognized that delay can seriously impede a tender offer" and sought to avoid it.[13]

* * *

The Court of Appeals also concluded that the Illinois Act is preempted by the Williams Act insofar as it allows the Secretary of State of Illinois to pass on the substantive fairness of a tender offer. Under ¶ 137.57.E of the Illinois law, the Secretary is required to deny registration of a takeover offer if he finds that the offer "fails to provide full and fair disclosure to the offerees ... or that the take-over offer is inequitable ..." (emphasis added).[15] The Court of Appeals understood the Williams Act and its legislative history to indicate that Congress intended for investors to be free to make their own decisions. We agree. * * * Thus, as the Court of Appeals said, "[t]he state thus offers investor protection at the expense of investor autonomy—an approach quite in conflict with that adopted by Congress." * * *

V

The Commerce Clause provides that "Congress shall have Power ... [t]o regulate Commerce ... among the several States." U.S. Const., Art. I, § 8, cl. 3. "[A]t least since *Cooley v. Board of Wardens,* 53 U.S. (12 How.) 299, 13 L.Ed. 996 (1852), it has been clear that 'the Commerce Clause.... even without implementing legislation by Congress is a limitation upon the power of the States.'" * * * Not every exercise of state power with some impact on interstate commerce is invalid. A state statute must be upheld if it "regulates evenhandedly to effectuate a legitimate local public interest, and its effects on interstate commerce are only incidental ... unless the burden imposed on such commerce is clearly excessive in relation to the putative local benefits." *Pike v. Bruce Church, Inc.,* 397 U.S. 137, 142, 90 S.Ct. 844, 847, 25 L.Ed.2d 174 (1970), * * *

The Commerce Clause, however, permits only *incidental* regulation of interstate commerce by the States; direct regulation is prohibited. * * * The Illinois Act violates these principles for two reasons. First, it

---

13. According to the Securities and Exchange Commission, delay enables a target company to:

"(1) repurchase its own securities;

"(2) announce dividend increases or stock splits;

"(3) issue additional shares of stock;

"(4) acquire other companies to produce an antitrust violation should the tender offer succeed;

"(5) arrange a defensive merger;

"(6) enter into restrictive loan agreements; and

"(7) institute litigation challenging the tender offer." Brief for Securities and Exchange Commission as *Amicus Curiae* 10, n. 8.

15. Appellant argues that the Illinois Act does not permit him to adjudicate the substantive fairness of a tender offer. Brief for Appellant 21–22. On this state-law issue, however, we follow the view of the Court of Appeals that ¶ 137.57.E allows the Secretary of State "to pass upon the substantive fairness of a tender offer...." 633 F.2d 486, 493 (1980).

directly regulates and prevents, unless its terms are satisfied, interstate tender offers which in turn would generate interstate transactions. Second, the burden the Act imposes on interstate commerce is excessive in light of the local interests the Act purports to further.

A

States have traditionally regulated intrastate securities transactions,[16] and this Court has upheld the authority of States to enact "blue-sky" laws against Commerce Clause challenges on several occasions. * * * The Court's rationale for upholding blue-sky laws was that they only regulated transactions occurring within the regulating States. "The provisions of the law ... apply to dispositions of securities *within* the State and while information of those issued in other States and foreign countries is required to be filed ..., they are only affected by the requirement of a license of one who deals with them *within* the State.... Such regulations affect interstate commerce in [securities] only incidentally." *Hall v. Geiger–Jones Co., supra,* 242 U.S., at 557–558, 37 S.Ct., at 223 (citations omitted). * * *

The Illinois Act differs substantially from state blue-sky laws in that it directly regulates transactions which take place across state lines, even if wholly outside the State of Illinois. A tender offer for securities of a publicly held corporation is ordinarily communicated by the use of the mails or other means of interstate commerce to shareholders across the country and abroad. Securities are tendered and transactions closed by similar means. Thus, in this case, MITE Corp., the tender offeror, is a Delaware corporation with principal offices in Connecticut. Chicago Rivet is a publicly held Illinois corporation with shareholders scattered around the country, 27% of whom live in Illinois. MITE's offer to Chicago Rivet's shareholders, including those in Illinois, necessarily employed interstate facilities in communicating its offer, which, if accepted, would result in transactions occurring across state lines. These transactions would themselves be interstate commerce. Yet the Illinois law, unless complied with, sought to prevent MITE from making its offer and concluding interstate transactions not only with Chicago Rivet's stockholders living in Illinois, but also with those living in other States and having no connection with Illinois. Indeed, the Illinois law on its face would apply even if not a single one of Chicago Rivet's shareholders were a resident of Illinois, since the Act applies to every tender offer for a corporation meeting two of the following conditions: the corporation has its principal executive office in Illinois, is organized under Illinois laws, or has at least 10% of its stated capital and paid-in surplus represented in Illinois. Ill.Rev.Stat., ch. 121½, ¶ 137.52–10(2) (1979). Thus the Act could be applied to regulate a tender offer which would not affect a single Illinois shareholder.

16. For example, the Illinois blue-sky law, Ill.Rev.Stat. ch. 121½, ¶ 137.1 *et seq.* (1979 and Supp.1980), provides that securities subject to the law must be registered "prior to sale in this State...." ¶ 137.5.

It is therefore apparent that the Illinois statute is a direct restraint on interstate commerce and that it has a sweeping extraterritorial effect. Furthermore, if Illinois may impose such regulations, so may other States; and interstate commerce in securities transactions generated by tender offers would be thoroughly stifled.

* * *

B

The Illinois Act is also unconstitutional under the test of *Pike v. Bruce Church, Inc.,* 397 U.S., at 142, 90 S.Ct., at 847, for even when a state statute regulates interstate commerce indirectly, the burden imposed on that commerce must not be excessive in relation to the local interests served by the statute. The most obvious burden the Illinois Act imposes on interstate commerce arises from the statute's previously described nationwide reach which purports to give Illinois the power to determine whether a tender offer may proceed anywhere.

The effects of allowing the Illinois Secretary of State to block a nationwide tender offer are substantial. Shareholders are deprived of the opportunity to sell their shares at a premium. The reallocation of economic resources to their highest valued use, a process which can improve efficiency and competition, is hindered. The incentive the tender offer mechanism provides incumbent management to perform well so that stock prices remain high is reduced.

* * *

Appellant claims the Illinois Act furthers two legitimate local interests. He argues that Illinois seeks to protect resident security holders and that the Act merely regulates the internal affairs of companies incorporated under Illinois law. We agree with the Court of Appeals that these asserted interests are insufficient to outweigh the burdens Illinois imposes on interstate commerce.

While protecting local investors is plainly a legitimate state objective, the State has no legitimate interest in protecting nonresident shareholders. Insofar as the Illinois law burdens out-of-state transactions, there is nothing to be weighed in the balance to sustain the law. We note, furthermore, that the Act completely exempts from coverage a corporation's acquisition of its own shares. * * * Thus Chicago Rivet was able to make a competing tender offer for its own stock without complying with the Illinois Act, leaving Chicago Rivet's shareholders to depend only on the protections afforded them by federal securities law, protections which Illinois views as inadequate to protect investors in other contexts. This distinction is at variance with Illinois' asserted legislative purpose, and tends to undermine appellant's justification for the burdens the statute imposes on interstate commerce.

We are also unconvinced that the Illinois Act substantially enhances the shareholders' position. The Illinois Act seeks to protect shareholders of a company subject to a tender offer by requiring disclosures regarding the offer, assuring that shareholders have adequate time to decide whether to tender their shares, and according shareholders withdrawal, proration, and equal consideration rights. However, the Williams Act provides these same substantive protections.

* * *

As the Court of Appeals noted, the disclosures required by the Illinois Act which go beyond those mandated by the Williams Act and the regulations pursuant to it may not substantially enhance the shareholders' ability to make informed decisions. * * * It also was of the view that the possible benefits of the potential delays required by the Act may be outweighed by the increased risk that the tender offer will fail due to defensive tactics employed by incumbent management. We are unprepared to disagree with the Court of Appeals in these respects, and conclude that the protections the Illinois Act affords resident security holders are, for the most part, speculative.

Appellant also contends that Illinois has an interest in regulating the internal affairs of a corporation incorporated under its laws. The internal affairs doctrine is a conflict of laws principle which recognizes that only one State should have the authority to regulate a corporation's internal affairs—matters peculiar to the relationships among or between the corporation and its current officers, directors, and shareholders—because otherwise a corporation could be faced with conflicting demands. * * * That doctrine is of little use to the State in this context. Tender offers contemplate transfers of stock by stockholders to a third party and do not themselves implicate the internal affairs of the target company. * * * Furthermore, the proposed justification is somewhat incredible since the Illinois Act applies to tender offers for any corporation for which 10% of the outstanding shares are held by Illinois residents. * * * The Act thus applies to corporations that are not incorporated in Illinois and have their principal place of business in other States. Illinois has no interest in regulating the internal affairs of foreign corporations.

We conclude with the Court of Appeals that the Illinois Act imposes a substantial burden on interstate commerce which outweighs its putative local benefits. It is accordingly invalid under the Commerce Clause.

The judgment of the Court of Appeals is

Affirmed.

JUSTICE POWELL, concurring in part.

* * *

I join Part V–B because its Commerce Clause reasoning leaves some room for state regulation of tender offers. This period in our history is marked by conglomerate corporate formations essentially unrestricted by the antitrust laws. Often the offeror possesses resources, in terms of professional personnel experienced in takeovers as well as of capital, that vastly exceed those of the takeover target. This disparity in resources may seriously disadvantage a relatively small or regional target corporation. Inevitably there are certain adverse consequences in terms of general public interest when corporate headquarters are moved away from a city and State.*

The Williams Act provisions, implementing a policy of neutrality, seem to assume corporate entities of substantially equal resources. I agree with Justice Stevens that the Williams Act's neutrality policy does not necessarily imply a congressional intent to prohibit state legislation designed to assure—at least in some circumstances—greater protection to interests that include but often are broader than those of incumbent management.

* * *

Control Share Acts

Please read the NASAA–ABA Model Control Share Act in your statutory supplement.

Questions

1. Can a bidder avoid the effect of a control share act by making its tender offer contingent on receiving full voting rights with the tendered stock? How do tendering shareholders satisfy the condition? Can shareholders who have tendered into a pending offer vote their shares?

2. If a state legislature has not adopted a control share act, can a firm amend its charter to include a provision modeled after a control share act? If so, why does the state legislature need to adopt a control share act for all firms? If a firm incorporated in a state that has a control share act does not want to be bound by the act, what must the firm do? Why does the act have an "opt-out" rather than an "opt-in" provision?

3. A control share act affects the voting power of shares held by an interested shareholder. Why did the drafters of the control share act not just require an affirmative vote of existing shareholders for any large stock acquisition by an interested shareholder?

Ohio has the oldest and the most straightforward of the state control share statutes. Ohio prevents the acquisition of control shares without a favorable vote of disinterested shareholders, while the Indiana statute prevents those holding control shares from voting them without a favorable vote of disinterested shareholders. Ohio Rev.Code Ann. (Page's) § 170.83.1 (1985 Repl. Vol.). Under the Indiana statute the target does, however, have the right to redeem control shares that have not been allowed to vote. The aberrant form of the Indiana statute was an effort to find a home in the language of a Sixth Circuit opinion that had declared the Ohio statute

---

* The corporate headquarters of the great national and multinational corporations tend to be located in the large cities of a few States. When corporate headquarters are transferred out of a city and State into one of these metropolitan centers, the State and locality from which the transfer is made inevitably suffer significantly. Management personnel—many of whom have provided community leadership—may move to the new corporate headquarters. Contributions to cultural, charitable, and educational life—both in terms of leadership and financial support—also tend to diminish when there is a move of corporate headquarters.

unconstitutional in Fleet Aerospace Corp. v. Holderman, 796 F.2d 135 (6th Cir.1986), vacated 481 U.S. 1026, 107 S.Ct. 1949, 95 L.Ed.2d 521 (1987). Arguably at the heart of the opinion was language denouncing prohibitions on the act of purchase. See also Icahn v. Blunt, Fed.Sec.L.Rep. (CCH) ¶ 92,096, 612 F.Supp. 1400 (W.D.Mo. June 24, 1985) (invalidating a Missouri statute modeled after the Ohio statute). The drafters felt that they could deflect much of the fire of these two courts if they did not stop purchases per se but only controlled the rights of the shares so purchased. This is presumably closer to the traditional function of state corporate codes. The Sixth Circuit opinion in *Fleet Aerospace* predated the *CTS* case that follows the Maryland Fair Price Statute and was vacated by the Supreme Court in light of its opinion in *CTS*.

4. Assume that a shareholder of a corporation resident in a jurisdiction that has enacted the Model Control Share Act owns 5 percent of the outstanding shares and solicits proxies from shareholders holding another 16 percent of the outstanding shares. Can the shareholder vote his shares or the proxies at a shareholders' meeting without section 5 approval? Is your answer different if a shareholder first holds proxies for 16 percent of the outstanding shares and then buys another 5 percent of the outstanding shares?

Fair Price Statutes

Please read Maryland Close Corporations Law sections 3–601 through 3–603 in your statutory supplement.

Questions

1. A fair price statute normally requires that a shareholder triggering the statute cannot effect a back-end merger unless the merger consideration for disinterested shareholders meets certain price criteria or unless two-thirds of the disinterested shareholders vote for the merger. The price criteria are set to eliminate front-end loading in acquisition programs, that is, the triggering shareholder must pay the back-end shareholders as least as much as the price the buyers paid to acquire their initial controlling block of stock. If the price criteria are not set unreasonably high, a fair price statute could, in theory, allow back-end mergers that do not have the approval of two-thirds of the disinterested shareholders.

How do statutes that affect only back-end mergers between bidders who have made successful partial tender offers (for, say, 51 percent of the outstanding common stock) and target firms act as a deterrent to hostile tender offers? What kinds of hostile tender offers are affected by the statute? Does your answer depend on the bidder's financing? Does a fair price statute create more or less trouble for hostile bidders than does a control share act?

2. Is the following claim accurate? A fair price statute only requires that a bidder treat all shareholders equally in an acquisition, offering the same price for all shares purchased. As such, one cannot dispute the statute's social value.

3. Could a firm adopt, through a charter amendment, a fair price requirement for back-end mergers? If so, what purpose is served by a fair price statute?

CTS CORP. v. DYNAMICS CORP. OF AMERICA
Supreme Court of the United States, 1987.
481 U.S. 69, 107 S.Ct. 1637, 95 L.Ed.2d 67.

JUSTICE POWELL delivered the opinion of the Court.

This case presents the questions whether the Control Share Acquisitions Chapter of the Indiana Business Corporation Law * * * is pre-empted by the Williams Act, * * * or violates the Commerce Clause of the Federal Constitution. * * *

On March 4, 1986, the Governor of Indiana signed a revised Indiana Business Corporation Law, Ind.Code § 23-1-17-1 et seq. (Supp. 1986). That law included the Control Share Acquisitions Chapter (Indiana Act or Act). Beginning on August 1, 1987, the Act will apply to any corporation incorporated in Indiana, * * * unless the corporation amends its articles of incorporation or bylaws to opt out of the Act. * * * Before that date, any Indiana corporation can opt into the Act by resolution of its board of directors. * * * The Act applies only to "issuing public corporations." The term "corporation" includes only businesses incorporated in Indiana. * * * An "issuing public corporation" is defined as:

"a corporation that has:

"(1) one hundred (100) or more shareholders;

"(2) its principal place of business, its principal office, or substantial assets within Indiana; and

"(3) either:

"(A) more than ten percent (10%) of its shareholders resident in Indiana;

"(B) more than ten percent (10%) of its shares owned by Indiana residents; or

"(C) ten thousand (10,000) shareholders resident in Indiana." * * *

The Act focuses on the acquisition of "control shares" in an issuing public corporation. Under the Act, an entity acquires "control shares" whenever it acquires shares that, but for the operation of the Act, would bring its voting power in the corporation to or above any of three thresholds: 20%, 33⅓%, or 50%. * * * An entity that acquires control shares does not necessarily acquire voting rights. Rather, it gains those rights only "to the extent granted by resolution approved by the shareholders of the issuing public corporation." * * * Section 9 requires a majority vote of all disinterested [2] shareholders holding each class of stock for passage of such a resolution. * * *

2. "Interested shares" are shares with respect to which the acquiror, an officer or an inside director of the corporation "may exercise or direct the exercise of the voting

Oesterle, Law of Mergers ACB—16

The practical effect of this requirement is to condition acquisition of control of a corporation on approval of a majority of the pre-existing disinterested shareholders.[3]

The shareholders decide whether to confer rights on the control shares at the next regularly scheduled meeting of the shareholders, or at a specially scheduled meeting. The acquiror can require management of the corporation to hold such a special meeting within 50 days if it files an "acquiring person statement,"[4] requests the meeting, and agrees to pay the expenses of the meeting. * * * If the shareholders do not vote to restore voting rights to the shares, the corporation may redeem the control shares from the acquiror at fair market value, but it is not required to do so. * * * Similarly, if the acquiror does not file an acquiring person statement with the corporation, the corporation may, if its bylaws or articles of incorporation so provide, redeem the shares at any time after 60 days after the acquiror's last acquisition. * * *

The Indiana Act differs in major respects from the Illinois statute that the Court considered in *Edgar v. MITE Corp.*, 457 U.S. 624, 102 S.Ct. 2629, 73 L.Ed.2d 269 (1982). After reviewing the legislative

---

power of the corporation in the election of directors." § 23-1-42-3. If the record date passes before the acquiror purchases shares pursuant to the tender offer, the purchased shares will not be "interested shares" within the meaning of the Act; although the acquiror may own the shares on the date of the meeting, it will not "exercise ... the voting power" of the shares.

As a practical matter, the record date usually will pass before shares change hands. Under SEC regulations, the shares cannot be purchased until 20 business days after the offer commences. 17 CFR § 240.14e-1(a) (1986). If the acquiror seeks an early resolution of the issue—as most acquirors will—the meeting required by the Act must be held no more than 50 calendar days after the offer commences, about three weeks after the earliest date on which the shares could be purchased. * * * The Act requires management to give notice of the meeting "as promptly as reasonably practicable ... to all shareholders of record as of the record date set for the meeting." * * *

It seems likely that management of the target corporation would violate this obligation if it delayed setting the record date and sending notice until after 20 business days had passed. Thus, we assume that the record date usually will be set before the date on which federal law first permits purchase of the shares.

3. The United States and appellee Dynamics Corporation suggest that § 23-1-42-9(b)(1) requires a second vote by *all* shareholders of record. Indiana disputes this interpretation of its Act. Section 23-1-42-9(b)(1) provides:

"[T]he resolution must be approved by:

"(1) each voting group entitled to vote separately on the proposal by a majority of all the votes entitled to be cast by that voting group, with the holders of the outstanding shares of a class being entitled to vote as a separate voting group if the proposed control share acquisition would, if fully carried out, result in any of the changes described in [Indiana Code § 23-1-38-4(a) (describing fundamental changes in corporate organization)]."

The United States contends that this section always requires a separate vote by all shareholders and that the last clause merely specifies that the vote shall be taken by separate groups if the acquisition would result in one of the listed transactions. Indiana argues that this section requires a separate vote only if the acquisition would result in one of the listed transactions. Because it is unnecessary to our decision, we express no opinion as to the appropriate interpretation of this section.

4. An "acquiring person statement" is an information statement describing, *inter alia*, the identity of the acquiring person and the terms and extent of the proposed acquisition. * * *

history of the Williams Act, Justice White, joined by Chief Justice Burger and Justice Blackmun (the plurality), concluded that the Williams Act struck a careful balance between the interests of offerors and target companies, and that any state statute that "upset" this balance was pre-empted.

* * *

As the plurality opinion in *MITE* did not represent the views of a majority of the Court, we are not bound by its reasoning. We need not question that reasoning, however, because we believe the Indiana Act passes muster even under the broad interpretation of the Williams Act articulated by Justice White in *MITE*. As is apparent from our summary of its reasoning, the overriding concern of the *MITE* plurality was that the Illinois statute considered in that case operated to favor management against offerors, to the detriment of shareholders. By contrast, the statute now before the Court protects the independent shareholder against both of the contending parties. Thus, the Act furthers a basic purpose of the Williams Act, " 'plac[ing] investors on an equal footing with the takeover bidder,' " *Piper v. Chris–Craft Industries*, 430 U.S., at 30, 97 S.Ct., at 943 (quoting the Senate Report accompanying the Williams Act, S.Rep. No. 550, 90th Cong., 1st Sess., 4 (1967)).[7]

The Indiana Act operates on the assumption, implicit in the Williams Act, that independent shareholders faced with tender offers often are at a disadvantage. By allowing such shareholders to vote as a group, the Act protects them from the coercive aspects of some tender offers. If, for example, shareholders believe that a successful tender offer will be followed by a purchase of nontendering shares at a depressed price, individual shareholders may tender their shares—even if they doubt the tender offer is in the corporation's best interest—to

---

7. Dynamics finds evidence of an intent to favor management in several features of the Act. It argues that the provision of the Act allowing management to opt into the Act, see § 23–1–17–3(b), grants management a strategic advantage because tender offerors will be reluctant to take the expensive preliminary steps of a tender offer if they do not know whether their efforts will be subjected to the Act's requirements. But this provision is only a temporary option available for the first 17 months after enactment of the Act. The Indiana Legislature reasonably could have concluded that corporations should be allowed an interim period during which the Act would not apply automatically. Because of its short duration, the potential strategic advantage offered by the opportunity to opt into the Act during this transition period is of little significance.

The Act also imposes some added expenses on the offeror, requiring it, *inter alia*, to pay the costs of special shareholder meetings to vote on the transfer of voting rights, see § 23–1–42–7(a). In our view, the expenses of such a meeting fairly are charged to the offeror. A corporation pays the costs of annual meetings that it holds to discuss its affairs. If an offeror—who has no official position with the corporation—desires a special meeting, solely to discuss the voting rights of the offeror, it is not unreasonable to have the offeror pay for the meeting.

Of course, by regulating tender offers, the Act makes them more expensive and thus deters them somewhat, but this type of reasonable regulation does not alter the balance between management and offeror in any significant way. The principal result of the Act is to grant shareholders the power to deliberate collectively about the merits of tender offers. This result is fully in accord with the purposes of the Williams Act.

protect themselves from being forced to sell their shares at a depressed price. As the SEC explains: "The alternative of not accepting the tender offer is virtual assurance that, if the offer is successful, the shares will have to be sold in the lower priced, second step."

* * *

* * * In such a situation under the Indiana Act, the shareholders as a group, acting in the corporation's best interest, could reject the offer, although individual shareholders might be inclined to accept it. The desire of the Indiana Legislature to protect shareholders of Indiana corporations from this type of coercive offer does not conflict with the Williams Act. Rather, it furthers the federal policy of investor protection.

In implementing its goal, the Indiana Act avoids the problems the plurality discussed in *MITE*. Unlike the *MITE* statute, the Indiana Act does not give either management or the offeror an advantage in communicating with the shareholders about the impending offer. The Act also does not impose an indefinite delay on tender offers. Nothing in the Act prohibits an offeror from consummating an offer on the 20th business day, the earliest day permitted under applicable federal regulations. * * * Nor does the Act allow the state government to interpose its views of fairness between willing buyers and sellers of shares of the target company. Rather, the Act allows *shareholders* to evaluate the fairness of the offer collectively.

* * *

* * * Dynamics reasons that no rational offeror will purchase shares until it gains assurance that those shares will carry voting rights. Because it is possible that voting rights will not be conferred until a shareholder meeting 50 days after commencement of the offer, Dynamics concludes that the Act imposes a 50–day delay. This, it argues, conflicts with the shorter 20–business–day period established by the SEC as the minimum period for which a tender offer may be held open. * * * We find the alleged conflict illusory.

The Act does not impose an absolute 50–day delay on tender offers, nor does it preclude an offeror from purchasing shares as soon as federal law permits. If the offeror fears an adverse shareholder vote under the Act, it can make a conditional tender offer, offering to accept shares on the condition that the shares receive voting rights within a certain period of time. The Williams Act permits tender offers to be conditioned on the offeror's subsequently obtaining regulatory approval. * * * There is no reason to doubt that this type of conditional tender offer would be legitimate as well.[9]

---

9. Dynamics argues that conditional tender offers are not an adequate alternative because they leave management in place for three extra weeks, with "free rein to take other defensive steps that will diminish the value of tendered shares." * * * We reject this contention. In the unlikely event that management were to take actions designed to diminish the value of the corporation's shares, it may incur liability under state law. But this problem does not control our pre-emption analysis.

Even assuming that the Indiana Act imposes some additional delay, nothing in *MITE* suggested that *any* delay imposed by state regulation, however short, would create a conflict with the Williams Act. The plurality argued only that the offeror should "be free to go forward without *unreasonable* delay." 457 U.S., at 639, 102 S.Ct., at 2639 (emphasis added). In that case, the Court was confronted with the potential for indefinite delay and presented with no persuasive reason why some deadline could not be established. By contrast, the Indiana Act provides that full voting rights will be vested—if this eventually is to occur—within 50 days after commencement of the offer. This period is within the 60–day maximum period Congress established for tender offers in 15 U.S.C. § 78n(d)(5). We cannot say that a delay within that congressionally determined period is unreasonable.

Finally, we note that the Williams Act would pre-empt a variety of state corporate laws of hitherto unquestioned validity if it were construed to pre-empt any state statute that may limit or delay the free exercise of power after a successful tender offer. State corporate laws commonly permit corporations to stagger the terms of their directors. * * *

By staggering the terms of directors, and thus having annual elections for only one class of directors each year, corporations may delay the time when a successful offeror gains control of the board of directors. Similarly, state corporation laws commonly provide for cumulative voting. * * * By enabling minority shareholders to assure themselves of representation in each class of directors, cumulative voting provisions can delay further the ability of offerors to gain untrammeled authority over the affairs of the target corporation. * * *

In our view, the possibility that the Indiana Act will delay some tender offers is insufficient to require a conclusion that the Williams Act pre-empts the Act. The longstanding prevalence of state regulation in this area suggests that, if Congress had intended to pre-empt all state laws that delay the acquisition of voting control following a tender offer, it would have said so explicitly. The regulatory conditions that the Act places on tender offers are consistent with the text and the purposes of the Williams Act. Accordingly, we hold that the Williams Act does not pre-empt the Indiana Act.

As an alternative basis for its decision, the Court of Appeals held that the Act violates the Commerce Clause of the Federal Constitution. * * *

The principal objects of dormant Commerce Clause scrutiny are statutes that discriminate against interstate commerce. * * * The Indiana Act is not such a statute. It has the same effects on tender offers whether or not the offeror is a domiciliary or resident of Indiana. Neither the Act nor any other federal statute can assure that shareholders do not suffer from the mismanagement of corporate officers and directors. * * *

Thus, it "visits its effects equally upon both interstate and local business." * * *

Dynamics nevertheless contends that the statute is discriminatory because it will apply most often to out-of-state entities. This argument rests on the contention that, as a practical matter, most hostile tender offers are launched by offerors outside Indiana. But this argument avails Dynamics little. "The fact that the burden of a state regulation falls on some interstate companies does not, by itself, establish a claim of discrimination against interstate commerce." * * * Because nothing in the Indiana Act imposes a greater burden on out-of-state offerors than it does on similarly situated Indiana offerors, we reject the contention that the Act discriminates against interstate commerce.

This Court's recent Commerce Clause cases also have invalidated statutes that adversely may affect interstate commerce by subjecting activities to inconsistent regulations.

* * * The Indiana Act poses no such problem. So long as each State regulates voting rights only in the corporations it has created, each corporation will be subject to the law of only one State. No principle of corporation law and practice is more firmly established than a State's authority to regulate domestic corporations, including the authority to define the voting rights of shareholders. * * * Accordingly, we conclude that the Indiana Act does not create an impermissible risk of inconsistent regulation by different States.

The Court of Appeals did not find the Act unconstitutional for either of these threshold reasons. Rather, its decision rested on its view of the Act's potential to hinder tender offers. We think the Court of Appeals failed to appreciate the significance for Commerce Clause analysis of the fact that state regulation of corporate governance is regulation of entities whose very existence and attributes are a product of state law. * * * Every State in this country has enacted laws regulating corporate governance. By prohibiting certain transactions, and regulating others, such laws necessarily affect certain aspects of interstate commerce. This necessarily is true with respect to corporations with shareholders in States other than the State of incorporation. Large corporations that are listed on national exchanges, or even regional exchanges, will have shareholders in many States and shares that are traded frequently. The markets that facilitate this national and international participation in ownership of corporations are essential for providing capital not only for new enterprises but also for established companies that need to expand their businesses. This beneficial free market system depends at its core upon the fact that a corporation—except in the rarest situations—is organized under, and governed by, the law of a single jurisdiction, traditionally the corporate law of the State of its incorporation.

These regulatory laws may affect directly a variety of corporate transactions. Mergers are a typical example. In view of the substantial effect that a merger may have on the shareholders' interests in a corporation, many States require supermajority votes to approve mergers. * * * By requiring a greater vote for mergers than is required for other transactions, these laws make it more difficult for corporations to merge. State laws also may provide for "dissenters' rights" under which minority shareholders who disagree with corporate decisions to take particular actions are entitled to sell their shares to the corporation at fair market value. * * * By requiring the corporation to purchase the shares of dissenting shareholders, these laws may inhibit a corporation from engaging in the specified transactions.[12]

It thus is an accepted part of the business landscape in this country for States to create corporations, to prescribe their powers, and to define the rights that are acquired by purchasing their shares. A State has an interest in promoting stable relationships among parties involved in the corporations it charters, as well as in ensuring that investors in such corporations have an effective voice in corporate affairs.

There can be no doubt that the Act reflects these concerns. The primary purpose of the Act is to protect the shareholders of Indiana corporations. It does this by affording shareholders, when a takeover offer is made, an opportunity to decide collectively whether the resulting change in voting control of the corporation, as they perceive it, would be desirable. A change of management may have important effects on the shareholders' interests; it is well within the State's role as overseer of corporate governance to offer this opportunity. The autonomy provided by allowing shareholders collectively to determine whether the takeover is advantageous to their interests may be especially beneficial where a hostile tender offer may coerce shareholders into tendering their shares.

Appellee Dynamics responds to this concern by arguing that the prospect of coercive tender offers is illusory, and that tender offers generally should be favored because they reallocate corporate assets into the hands of management who can use them most effectively.[13]
* * *

12. Numerous other common regulations may affect both nonresident and resident shareholders of a corporation. Specified votes may be required for the sale of all of the corporation's assets. * * * The election of directors may be staggered over a period of years to prevent abrupt changes in management. * * * Various classes of stock may be created with differences in voting rights as to dividends and on liquidation. * * * Provisions may be made for cumulative voting. * * * Corporations may adopt restrictions on payment of dividends to ensure that specified ratios of assets to liabilities are maintained for the benefit of the holders of corporate bonds or notes. * * * Where the shares of a corporation are held in States other than that of incorporation, actions taken pursuant to these and similar provisions of state law will affect all shareholders alike wherever they reside or are domiciled.

* * *

13. It is appropriate to note when discussing the merits and demerits of tender offers that generalizations usually require qualification. No one doubts that some successful tender offers will provide more effective management or other benefits such as needed diversification. But there is no reason to *assume* that the type of conglomerate corporation that may result from repetitive takeovers necessarily will result in more effective management or otherwise be beneficial to shareholders.

As indicated *supra,* at 1646, Indiana's concern with tender offers is not groundless. Indeed, the potentially coercive aspects of tender offers have been recognized by the Securities and Exchange Commission, * * * and by a number of scholarly commentators. * * * The Constitution does not require the States to subscribe to any particular economic theory. We are not inclined "to second-guess the empirical judgments of lawmakers concerning the utility of legislation." * * *

In our view, the possibility of coercion in some takeover bids offers additional justification for Indiana's decision to promote the autonomy of independent shareholders.

Dynamics argues in any event that the State has " 'no legitimate interest in protecting the nonresident shareholders.' " * * * We agree that Indiana has no interest in protecting nonresident shareholders *of nonresident corporations.* But this Act applies only to corporations incorporated in Indiana. We reject the contention that Indiana has no interest in providing for the shareholders of its corporations the voting autonomy granted by the Act. Indiana has a substantial interest in preventing the corporate form from becoming a shield for unfair business dealing. Moreover, unlike the Illinois statute invalidated in *MITE,* the Indiana Act applies only to corporations that have a substantial number of shareholders in Indiana. * * * Thus, every application of the Indiana Act will affect a substantial number of Indiana residents, whom Indiana indisputably has an interest in protecting.

Dynamics' argument that the Act is unconstitutional ultimately rests on its contention that the Act will limit the number of successful tender offers. There is little evidence that this will occur. But even if true, this result would not substantially affect our Commerce Clause analysis. We reiterate that this Act does not prohibit any entity—resident or nonresident—from offering to purchase, or from purchasing, shares in Indiana corporations, or from attempting thereby to gain control. It only provides regulatory procedures designed for the better protection of the corporations' shareholders. We have rejected the "notion that the Commerce Clause protects the particular structure or methods of operation in a ... market." *Exxon Corp. v. Governor of Maryland,* 437 U.S., at 127, 98 S.Ct., at 2215. The very commodity that is traded in the securities market is one whose characteristics are defined by state law. Similarly, the very commodity that is traded in the "market for corporate control"—the corporation—is one that owes its existence and attributes to state law. Indiana need not define these commodities as other States do; it need only provide that residents and nonresidents have equal access to them. This Indiana has done. Accordingly, even if the Act should decrease the number of successful tender offers for Indiana corporations, this would not offend the Commerce Clause.

The divergent views in the literature—and even now being debated in the Congress—reflect the reality that the type and utility of tender offers vary widely. Of course, in many situations the offer to shareholders is simply a cash price substantially higher than the market price prior to the offer.

On its face, the Indiana Control Share Acquisitions Chapter evenhandedly determines the voting rights of shares of Indiana corporations. The Act does not conflict with the provisions or purposes of the Williams Act. To the limited extent that the Act affects interstate commerce, this is justified by the State's interests in defining the attributes of shares in its corporations and in protecting shareholders. Congress has never questioned the need for state regulation of these matters. Nor do we think such regulation offends the Constitution. Accordingly, we reverse the judgment of the Court of Appeals.

It is so ordered.

JUSTICE SCALIA, concurring in part and concurring in the judgment.

* * * This case is a good illustration of the point. Whether the control shares statute "protects shareholders of Indiana corporations," * * * or protects incumbent management seems to me a highly debatable question, but it is extraordinary to think that the constitutionality of the Act should depend on the answer. Nothing in the Constitution says that the protection of entrenched management is any less important a "putative local benefit" than the protection of entrenched shareholders, and I do not know what qualifies us to make that judgment—or the related judgment as to how effective the present statute is in achieving one or the other objective—or the ultimate (and most ineffable) judgment as to whether, given importance-level x, and effectiveness-level y, the worth of the statute is "outweighed" by impact-on-commerce z.

* * *

As long as a State's corporation law governs only its own corporations and does not discriminate against out-of-state interests, it should survive this Court's scrutiny under the Commerce Clause, whether it promotes shareholder welfare or industrial stagnation. Beyond that, it is for Congress to prescribe its invalidity.

* * *

I do not share the Court's apparent high estimation of the beneficence of the state statute at issue here. But a law can be both economic folly and constitutional. The Indiana Control Shares Acquisition Chapter is at least the latter. I therefore concur in the judgment of the Court.

JUSTICE WHITE, with whom JUSTICE BLACKMUN and JUSTICE STEVENS join as to Part II, dissenting.

* * *

The Williams Act expressed Congress' concern that individual investors be given sufficient information so that they could make an informed choice on whether to tender their stock in response to a tender offer. The problem with the approach the majority adopts today is that it equates protection of individual investors, the focus of the Williams Act, with the protection of shareholders as a group. Indiana's

Control Share Acquisitions Chapter undoubtedly helps protect the interests of a majority of the shareholders in any corporation subject to its terms, but in many instances, it will effectively prevent an individual investor from selling his stock at a premium. Indiana's statute, therefore, does not "furthe[r] the federal policy of *investor* protection," *ante,* at 1646 (emphasis added), as the majority claims.

* * *

The majority claims that if the Williams Act pre-empts Indiana's Control Share Acquisitions Chapter, it also pre-empts a number of other corporate-control provisions such as cumulative voting or staggering the terms of directors. But this view ignores the fundamental distinction between these other corporate-control provisions and the Chapter: unlike those other provisions, the Chapter is designed to prevent certain tender offers from ever taking place. * * *

The Control Share Acquisitions Chapter will effectively prevent minority shareholders in some circumstances from selling their stock to a willing tender offeror. It is the practical impact of the Chapter that leads to the conclusion that it is pre-empted by the Williams Act.

Given the impact of the Control Share Acquisitions Chapter, it is clear that Indiana is directly regulating the purchase and sale of shares of stock in interstate commerce. Appellant CTS's stock is traded on the New York Stock Exchange, and people from all over the country buy and sell CTS's shares daily. Yet, under Indiana's scheme, any prospective purchaser will be effectively precluded from purchasing CTS's shares if the purchaser crosses one of the Chapter's threshold ownership levels and a majority of CTS's shareholders refuse to give the purchaser voting rights. This Court should not countenance such a restraint on interstate trade.

The United States, as *amicus curiae,* argues that Indiana's Control Share Acquisitions Chapter "is written as a restraint on the *transferability* of voting rights in specified transactions, and it could not be written in any other way without changing its meaning. Since the restraint on the transfer of voting rights is a restraint on the transfer of shares, the Indiana Chapter, like the Illinois Act [in *MITE*], restrains 'transfers of stock by stockholders to a third party.'" * * * I agree.

* * *

The State of Indiana, in its brief, admits that at least one of the Chapter's goals is to protect Indiana Corporations. The State notes that the Chapter permits shareholders "to determine ... whether [a tender offeror] will liquidate the company or remove it from the State." * * * A state law which permits a majority of an Indiana corporation's stockholders to prevent individual investors, including out-of-state stockholders, from selling their stock to an out-of-state tender offeror and thereby frustrate any transfer of corporate control, is the archetype of the kind of state law that the Commerce Clause forbids.

* * *

Can a State Constitutionally Protect Nonshareholder Constituencies Through Antitakeover Legislation?

OESTERLE, DELAWARE'S TAKEOVER STATUTE: OF CHILLS, PILLS, STANDSTILLS AND WHO GETS ICED

13 Del.J.Corp.L., 879, 937–42.

The Court's focus in *CTS* is too narrow in two respects. First, and foremost, it overlooks the competition between existing managers and bidders for control of the firm. Second, it fails to consider, as Justice White does in the dissent, both the competition between local and out-of-state employees for job opportunities and the competition between local and out-of-state taxing districts for subjects to tax.

The first argument turns on a distinction between the local market and the players. The protected market in this case is control of firms; existing managers, despite the fact that they are in place, are competitors in that market. To the extent that their position is solidified by the statute, the statute discriminates in their favor. This suggests that the Indiana statute in the *CTS* case could be viewed, and perhaps ought to be viewed, as an effort by the Indiana legislature to intentionally discriminate between in-state (existing managers) and out-of-state (potential managers) parties in a competitive market for corporate control. Thus viewed, the Indiana statute should have been struck down as unconstitutional under the commerce clause. For states other than Delaware, bidders are almost always out-of-state concerns (whether defined by physical location or by state of incorporation) and existing managers are almost always in-state parties. In this context, an alternative construction of state legislative intent that saves the statute—the legislature intended to protect shareholders of Indiana corporations, most of whom are out of state—is difficult to sell.

The second argument supporting a finding of discrimination is that the Indiana legislature intended to protect in-state resources from leaving the state, to the detriment of out-of-state employees and out-of-state taxing districts. In short the state is attempting to lock in assets that are located in the state. This discrimination should also be unconstitutional, although some commentators argue that a slight shift in emphasis may save the statute. Professor Donald Regan suggests that if a state statute were motivated substantially by concern over the disruption of established economic relations, it would not constitute unlawful discrimination under the commerce clause. In other words, the state is not attempting to lock in assets absolutely in the state, but rather is providing a mechanism for minimizing the disruption and dislocation caused by major business restructurings. Presumably, if such regulation does not discriminate between economic disruptions caused by intrastate and interstate relocations of capital, and if it does not operate to lock in assets to disadvantage out-of-state workers and taxing districts, the legislation is constitutional. The statute would, in effect, operate as a substitute for the milder forms of plant-closing legislation that require advance notice of closings and expenditures by the firm to mitigate the effects of worker relocation.

In the context of tender offer legislation, however, the argument is most likely to be an artifice. First, since most bidders are out-of-state, protecting existing relations usually is at the expense of potential out-of-state relocations. Whenever local facilities are established and there is a threat that they will be relocated or liquidated out-of-state, any legislation that retards the closing or liquidation of facilities will harm those out-of-state parties who would be benefited by a relocation of the capital languishing in existing local facilities. Second, and more significantly, if dislocation costs are the core concern of the legislature, there are more direct ways of dealing with the problem. Plant-closing legislation (requiring advance notice of closings) or other forms of labor legislation (retraining programs or severance provisions) more directly address the problems created by plant closings or major personnel changes. Takeover statutes are a very crude device for limiting dislocation costs. Such statutes allow friendly control changes that can and often do effect major relocations, while disallowing hostile control changes, not all of which effect major relocations. Given the availability of more direct methods of addressing relocation disruption, one must conclude that some states, in passing takeover statutes, are really attempting to lock in assets already in the state rather than to mitigate the effects of major business restructurings.

The Delaware legislature, however, does not seem to have the problems of justification that should have been (but, in fact, were not) a cause of trouble for Indiana's legislature. The Delaware statute is unique in that it applies principally to firms with their principal headquarters in other states. As a result, Delaware is perhaps the only state able to make the claim that its legislature could not have intended its statute to discriminate against out-of-state parties in favor of in-state parties. Neither bidders nor potential targets that are incorporated in Delaware have a significant physical or ownership presence in Delaware. So, while Indiana ought to have trouble justifying its statute as neither discriminatory against out-of-state players in the control market nor against out-of-state employees or taxing districts, Delaware can smugly assert that it has no similar problems of proof. If the commerce clause test is hinged solely on a finding of local protectionism, the Delaware statute has a uniquely favorable position because it cannot be said to be protective of a Delaware-based constituency.[231] This is true unless, of course, one includes Delaware corporate

---

231. Under a construction of the commerce clause that depends entirely on a finding of protectionist discrimination, is there a constitutional limitation on Delaware's ability to regulate the affairs of firms that have no physical assets or owner location in the state? Professor Donald Regan seems to say no. See Regan, *Siamese Essays, supra* note 206. If so, can Delaware pass, as part of its corporate

lawyers and the Delaware treasury, but even so considered, the legislation cannot be said to discriminate against out-of-state lawyers.

Delaware, however, should not escape so easily. By virtue of its statute, Delaware is, in effect, a stand-in or an agent for other state legislatures when it enacts blatantly protectionist legislation. The Delaware legislature, instead of the Indiana legislature, is doing explicitly what Indiana should itself not be able to do—that is, protecting Indiana managers from out-of-state competitors in the control market for firms with their headquarters in Indiana. By virtue of the expediency of incorporating in Delaware, should firms enjoy the protection of potentially identical legislation? Suppose Delaware were willing to code, a provision prohibiting all factories of firms incorporated in Delaware, wherever located in the United States, from purchasing from out-of-state suppliers or hiring out of state workers? Professor Regan seems to say that the commerce clause would allow it, but argues that limits on Delaware legislation must come from limits on extraterritorial legislation found elsewhere in the constitution.

Regan has suggested that the extraterritorial problem for takeover legislation may be resolved by a declaration of "location": We can declare that control changes are located in the state of incorporation and, presumably, factory purchasing or hiring is located at the site of the factory. Control change regulations are therefore local regulations, while factory purchasing and hiring regulations are not. On the surface this approach, as Professor Regan recognizes, appears to be only formalistic. We ought to be uncomfortable defining away the extraterritorial effects of takeover statutes by declaring that firm control changes are somehow located in the state of incorporation when the bidder, the firm operating facilities and the headquarters, and most all of the firm shareholders are located out of state. Professor Regan, tentatively suggests a justification of this fiction on the grounds of avoiding inconsistent and overlapping regulations. This suggestion is plausible but not very satisfying. See id. at 1869. At minimum the justification seems to require that we increase the formalism because a location of control changes in the state of incorporation not only allows Delaware to pass a takeover statute affecting shareholders and firm assets located exclusively in other states, but also precludes other states, where all the shareholders and assets are physically located, from passing any regulations.

The flaw in the position is that an argument based on inconsistent state regulation does not itself conclusively determine which states should regulate which firms. Presumably we would be uncomfortable with a constitutional rule that sanctions parceling out exclusive regulatory authority over individual firms by random drawing or by the first letter in the corporate name, but either rule would eliminate inconsistent state regulations. If the elimination of inconsistent regulation is the dominant concern, one could argue that a more sensible system of regulation (than one that allocates regulatory authority to the place of incorporation) would be a system that allocates such authority based on exclusivity in shareholder or asset location. Why not locate control changes in the one state with the most resident firm shareholders or in the one state with the most firm assets? In sum, there must be more to the extraterritorial principle than the avoidance of inconsistent state regulation.

The classic answer to the extraterritorial question posed above refers, in the context of corporate codes, to the choice of the governed; firms and their shareholders could have chosen to be governed by the laws of another state, the state with the most shareholders, for example, but they did not do so. They chose to be governed by the law of Delaware instead and we respect their choice. This suggests a second criterion that has bearing on extraterritoriality: Among possible systems of nonconflicting state regulation over firms, we tend to respect the choice of the participants as long as all substantial players have an adequate voice. If all the substantial players are local and can participate in the political process, then adequate voice may perhaps be presumed, but the inquiry is more problematic when the substantial players are all located outside a state's boundaries, as they are with Delaware corporations. Once the analysis turns to the question of whether the legislation is legitimate in light of all the parties, the inquiry reverts to an analysis very similar to the one in the text: is the legislature furthering shareholder interests?

provide Indiana this "service" for a lucrative commission—incorporation fees from firms physically located in Indiana that, together with fees from firms located in other states, support the Delaware state treasury and the local bar. In theory, can Delaware maximize its revenues by passing a statute that effects discrimination on behalf of local firms in other states? Or can one argue that Delaware, as a de facto agent of Indiana, should not be able to do what Indiana itself cannot do, that is, favor local managers in the competition for control of firms located in Indiana?

Also troubling is the thought that Delaware can provide firms located in Indiana with a service that the Indiana legislature may have refused to provide. As an example, assume that firms incorporated in Indiana with local facilities and local ownership ask the Indiana legislature to enact takeover legislation to protect local managers, employees, and taxing districts at the expense of the Indiana shareholders. Assume further that the Indiana legislature declines, favoring instead the interests of shareholders or deciding to enact a milder law than the firms requested. As a result, assume that the Indiana firms reincorporate in Delaware and the Delaware legislature provides takeover legislation protecting the local Indiana interests, the very interests that the Indiana legislature had itself refused to protect. This scenario is far from fictitious. California, for example, having recognized the futility of adopting its own takeover statute when most firms located in California are incorporated in Delaware, may take the extraordinary step of asking Congress to preempt all state legislation in the area and set minimum standards at the federal level.[233]

Questions

1. Can a state statute apply to resident corporations regardless of an operating or ownership presence in the state? Can a state statute apply to nonresident corporations with a substantial operating or ownership presence in the state? See TLX Acquisition v. Telex Corp., 679 F.Supp. 1022 (W.D.Okl.1987).

2. Does the Indiana statute discriminate against out-of-state bidders? If the relevant market is for control of Indiana firms, are not existing managers, despite the fact that they are in place, competitors in that market? In other words, did the Supreme Court omit players in the

---

233. A bipartisan California Senate commission is urging state legislators to pass a resolution urging Congress to enact legislation that sets minimum corporate governance standards. * * * The commission shelved proposed takeover legislation designed to increase California's surveillance and control over takeovers because it would have been "rendered ineffective by less stringent Delaware law [regulating target board of directors behavior]". * * * Some of the recommendations favor the commission's position on takeovers. It recommends, among other things, that Congress pass a requirement that shareholders must approve all poison pills and that poison pills expire in three years, unless the shareholders reapprove the pill or pass a limitation on supermajority rules.

control market when it assessed whether the statute is protectionist of in-state interests?

3. Does the Indiana statute discriminate against out-of-state employees and out-of-state taxing districts by locking in assets that are located in Indiana?

4. Assuming for the sake of argument that the answer to either question 2 or 3 is affirmative, can Delaware, which has no in-state managers or assets, pass an identical statute for corporations incorporated in Delaware but located in Indiana? In other words, can Delaware provide firms in Indiana with a service that the Indiana legislature can not?

5. Is the Indiana statute justifiable because it is one of several plausible attempts to protect target shareholders of domestic corporations or because it specifically gives target shareholders the right to vote on offers? If the latter statement is accurate, will the following Delaware statute pass constitutional muster?

Business Combination (Freeze-Out) Acts

Please read Delaware General Corporation Law section 203 in your statutory supplement.

Note

New York's Act

In New York although the triggering acquisition amount is 20 percent, the cooling-off period is potentially indefinite.[1] Assuming that the board does not approve an acquisition, a majority of disinterested shareholders (excluding the 20 percent owner but including the inside managers) must vote to allow a business combination with an interested shareholder but can do so only after the expiration of an initial five-year moratorium.[2] Absent such a vote, interested shareholders can effect business combinations with a target only if they pay a statutorily defined "fair price" in the transaction. The fair price is the greater of the following: (1) the highest price per share paid by the interested shareholder for firm shares after he becomes a 5 percent owner and within either five years of the start of the business combination or five years before the interested shareholder becomes a 20 percent owner, (2) the market value of the stock on the announcement date of the business combination, or (3) the market value of the stock on the date the acquirer becomes a 20 percent owner. Moreover, the holders of all outstanding shares of stock are entitled to receive compensation. The essence of the New York statute, then, is the fair price release rather than a vote of disinterested shareholders. New York's opt-out provision is also more onerous, with an eighteen-month waiting period for charter amendments.

1. N.Y.—McKinney's Bus.Corp.Law § 912(a)10(A), (b) & (c).

2. See § 912(c)(2). Moreover, the New York statute's definition of "business combinations" is much broader, including liquidations, see § 912(a)(5)(D), and large dividend distributions. See § 912(a)(5)(B).

Questions

1. The Delaware statute, at its core, prohibits an entity (an "interested shareholder") that has acquired a specified stock position in a publicly traded Delaware corporation—15 percent or more of the voting stock—from engaging in any business combination with the corporation for a cooling-off period of three years. There are several ways to avoid triggering the cooling-off period as well as several ways to terminate prematurely ("thaw") a running cooling-off period. What are they? See section 203(a) and (b).

2. The statute does not stop acquisitions, but it limits the ability of those who have made successful partial acquisitions to restructure the parent-subsidiary relationship created by the acquisition. What kind of acquisitions, if any, will the statute deter?

Consider a skeleton example of a typical leveraged deal, popular in the early eighties: A small partnership of investors, with a reputation for success in takeovers, forms a shell corporation. The shell gathers cash (a war chest) by selling high interest, short-term, unsecured debt with a promise to repay the debt through a sale of the assets acquired in a future takeover. With this cash the shell makes a cash tender offer for 51 percent control of a publicly traded company. After control of the board passes, the new board effects a back-end merger between the shell and the publicly traded company, exchanging the shares of the minority shareholders for preferred stock or debt in the residual firm. A properly structured merger of a publicly held corporation avoids giving the minority shareholders any appraisal rights. The acquirer (a "bootstrapper" or "bust-up artist" to opponents) uses control of the assets of the target to pay off the short-term debt: it applies all cash and cash equivalents directly to the debt, it sells sluggish operating divisions to generate cash, and it streamlines the remaining business operations to maximize immediate and substantial cash flow.

If the shell were prevented from consummating a merger or its economic equivalent (for example, a special asset sale or a recapitalization), then the shell could claim only 51 percent of the cash potential of the target through dividends or their equivalents. If the acquirer can apply 100 percent of the cash generated by the target to service the debt, lenders are encouraged to lend more cash to the acquirer at better rates than they would if the acquirer could apply only 51 percent of the cash potential in the target to any acquisition financing.

3. One can argue that the statute does not adversely affect bidders that have sufficient capital or long-term borrowing capacity to purchase targets as longer term investments. Firms with strong balance sheets and plenty of cash need not force the target to generate cash to meet immediate and severe short-term interest obligations. These firms can be comfortable with a three-year cooling-off period because they do not need 100 percent control of the target's assets to service otherwise unserviceable debt; they have sufficient external resources to service a substantial amount of the acquisition financing and are content with pro rata distributions of the acquired firm's cash. Why are firms with strong balance sheets the preferred purchasers? Is it because there are fewer of them? Or because

it is hoped they will effect less-radical changes in the target's operating structure?

Returning to the basic assumption of the argument, if the most profitable method of acquiring a firm is through a two-step leveraged acquisition of 100 percent of the shares, if we deny even healed firms this form of acquisition, don't we, at the margin, discourage these firms from making as many takeover bids?

4. What strategies are available to a bidder to avoid the effect of the statute? The most obvious, of course, is to accumulate enough cash to tender for over 85 percent of the target stock. But what if the bidder cannot finance such an offer or the target has placed over 15 percent of the outstanding shares in friendly hands? Consider the possible success of the following strategies:

a) Make a partial bid at a substantial premium over preoffer prices contingent on the target board's waiving the effect of the statute, or contingent on the shareholders' voting to thaw the three-year moratorium. The latter contingency depends on a substantial oversubscription of the tender offer. An offeror could make a tender offer for 51 percent of the stock with a promise to cash out the remaining stockholders at above pre-tender offer prices. Typically the tender offer will be oversubscribed, and many of those whose shares are prorated can be expected to vote in favor of the subsequent cash-out merger in order to cash out their speculative positions. Ironically, under this scenario a bidder who cannot purchase 85 percent at the tender offer price is better off tendering for just 51 percent rather than a higher percentage, such as 60 percent. This is so because it may be easier to get a two-thirds vote of the remaining shareholders to effect the back-end merger since more arbitrageurs will be in the voting pool.

b) Make a tender offer in combination with a consent solicitation to get control of the target board and have the board waive the provisions of the statute. A bidder tenders for 51 percent of the stock conditioned on the receipt of written consents from shareholders sufficient to replace the board of directors with a slate favorable to the bidder. Once sufficient written consents are obtained, the bidder replaces the board, has the new board waive the section's protections, and closes the tender offer. A firm can destroy the strategy by staggering the election of directors or eliminating the written consent procedure through an amendment to its certificate of incorporation. If a firm has eliminated the use of a written consent procedure, can a bidder seek proxies instead? When can the bidder vote the proxies?

c) A bidder buys 51 percent of the stock, triggering the three-year cooling-off period, gets control of the board, and creates a wholly owned subsidiary with a provision in its charter opting out of the statute. The bidder then transfers the parent's assets to the subsidiary, distributes the subsidiary's stock to all shareholders pro rata (in a stock dividend), and, finally, executes a squeeze-out merger with the subsidiary, eliminating all the minority shareholders. Again, a firm could slow this process by staggering the election of its board of directors.

5. What can targets do to buttress the power of the statute? The two defenses that, with the statute, can most obviously lock up a target are standstill agreements with white squires and poison pill plans. In the former, target management places a large block of stock in friendly hands (a white squire) under an informal or formal agreement (a standstill agreement) that the third party will not tender the stock absent the assent of the target board. Available figures indicate that a standstill agreement on as small a portion as 4 percent of the outstanding target stock may often suffice to eliminate the risk of a bidder's satisfying the statute's 85 percent cap. Insider shareholdings combined with the number of shares that are never tendered in even the most lucrative offers often total 10 or 11 percent of the outstanding shares.

Standstill agreements are, however, somewhat risky. First, placing stock with a white squire under an informal agreement is risky, because money can break down trust; the prospect of substantial profits may override the white squire's promise. Second, placing stock with a white squire under a formal agreement may backfire because courts may construe the stock to be under the control of the target board and exclude it from the denominator in a calculation of the 85 percent cap. The task of planners, then, is to draft an agreement that rides the ridge of these two positions. The agreement should effectively constrain a white squire from tendering and be specifically enforceable. Also, the agreement should not qualify the stock under the statute as being controlled by the board for the purposes of the statute.

Poison pill plans with a discriminatory call feature, see chapter 5, may provide the optimal protection against the cap. In a call plan the board distributes, as a stock dividend, rights to acquire firm stock at a large discount. The rights are created to be contingent on a substantial acquisition of stock by an unapproved purchaser and to discriminate against the purchaser; that is, if a purchaser triggers the rights by purchasing a specified amount of stock, it cannot exercise rights attached to any stock that it has purchased. The discrimination feature of the plan, together with the Delaware statute, works to effect a lockup of a target firm. Once a bidder acquires over 85 percent of the stock of the target, any residual shareholders (other than officers and directors) can exercise their rights to purchase additional firm stock and reduce the bidder's ownership percentage to below the 85 percent cap. Moreover, the value of the acquirer's stock in the firm will suffer a substantial dilution.

The existence of the pill will also, of course, have the planned effect of making it difficult for the bidder to acquire the initial 85 percent position (neutral of the exercise of any rights), because a substantial number of target shareholders will refuse to tender. In refusing to tender, the shareholders are anticipating an opportunity to exercise their rights as residual shareholders, thus acquiring firm stock at a large discount at the expense of the bidder. Like all poison pill plans, the existing target board has the power to waive the rights, usually by redeeming them for an insignificant amount of money any time before the triggering acquisition and, often, for a short time thereafter. In essence, the goal of a poison pill plan is to create an event so onerous that no one can afford to trigger the plan with an unapproved acquisition, thus forcing all potential acquirers to seek the blessing of the existing board.

Note

Arguments Against, for, and Neutral on the Value of Business Combination Statutes to Shareholders

Against: What is troubling about the statute's concern over bootstrappers is that bootstrappers may provide the best curative for lazy, inept, or self-interested managers. Raiders search for, seize on, and profit from opportunities to enhance the operation of publicly held companies; they are less concerned with so-called synergy gains from combinations of two independent operating entities and seek gains from major changes in the target firm itself. The best opportunities for bootstrappers, then, are firms that are languishing because of lazy, inept, or corrupt management. If the cost to the firm of such conduct is substantial, then bootstrappers and their backers can turn a handsome profit by buying the firm and restructuring its operations.

Studies of hostile takeovers indicate that such bootstrap takeovers often occur in industries on the decline or in industries suffering other sharp business changes, where managers fail to shrink operations rapidly enough or fail to make other necessary adjustments rapidly enough. The problem of sluggish management is most severe, perhaps, when a firm in a declining industry continues to generate substantial cash flows; the managers hold and reinvest the cash in inefficient programs rather than paying it out to shareholders who can make better use of it. In the oil industry, for example, managers were continuing costly explorations for additional oil reserves despite a declining market for oil. In the airline industry managers were slow to adjust to the demands of deregulation; they failed to readjust union wage scales that had reached excessive levels under regulation. The forest products, food, and broadcasting industries are additional examples of industries with excess capacity and substantial cash flows. In all these industries existing managers, perhaps because of inertia or a desire to protect personal turf or nonshareholder constituencies, maintained full-scale traditional operations for too long in the face of substantial changes in the business climate.

The disciplining effect of hostile takeovers in these industries, once they appeared, was dramatic. Not only were the firms actually acquired in these industries radically restructured, but other firms in the industry that were not the subjects of takeovers also swiftly undertook major restructurings. It appears that incumbent managers who worry about bootstrappers are more likely to effect appropriate changes in their firm's operations to keep firm share prices high, offering less temptation to potential purchasers. It should be no surprise, then, that the industries most affected by the threats of bootstrappers contain firms that, on their own, have engaged in some of the more radical restructurings of late. In sum, it may be the bootstrappers that provide the strongest incentive for incumbent managers to keep agency costs down. If so, the drafters of business combination statutes have done shareholders a serious disservice by styling their statutes to discriminate against bootstrappers.

For: In response to the argument above, however, the drafters of the Delaware statute argue that the statute does not discriminate against all bootstrappers but only against bootstrappers that take advantage of the collective action problem suffered by shareholders in responding to tender offers. Some bidders, they argue, will stampede shareholders into tendering control of the firm for bargain prices and then follow up with a squeeze-out of the back-end minority shareholders at even worse prices. The collective action problem is created when a bidder threatens all target shareholders with the prospect that those who tender will be better off than those who do not. Absent a collective response providing that no shareholders will tender unless the price is raised, each shareholder's best response is to tender immediately, even if she believes that "give" exists in the bidder's price or that other bidders could pay higher prices. The primary example of this problem is the two-tier tender offer, which begins with an initial front-end offer for a percentage of the target's shares and then concludes with a back-end cash-out of the remaining shareholders, often at a lower price than that offered at the front end of the transaction.

Those who argue against the significance of the shareholder coercion argument make two points. First, they doubt the coercive power of two-tier tender offers and in support cite a Securities and Exchange Commission study that found that, on average, fewer shareholders tender for two-tier than for any-and-all tender offers.[1] The study further found that the average total premiums received by shareholders in the two types of offers differ only insignificantly. From these data, the coercive argument opponents assert that two-tier tender offers cannot be overly coercive. If such tender offers are coercive, they argue, the tender offers induce a significantly larger percentage of shareholders to tender and should induce tenders at lower average premiums when compared to any-and-all tender offers. Second, they argue that since two-tier tender offers are now rare, concern over them should be minimized. If the argument that most hostile tender offers are not, in fact, coercive is valid, then the Delaware statute loses much of its legitimate underpinnings.

There are, however, two plausible rebuttals to data supporting the position that tender offers are not coercive, each suggesting that shareholder coercion in tender offers is real. The first rebuttal rests on the possibility that the collective action problem is not unique to two-tier tender offers but may also be found in any-and-all tender offers. Those who assume that any-and-all tender offers are not coercive (and who use them as a basis for comparison with two-tier tender offers or suggest that the absence of two-tier tender offers nullifies the problem) underestimate the basic power of the shareholder collective action problem. Because shareholders must decide to tender individually, any time the tender offer

---

[1]. Comment & Jarrel, *Two-Tier and Negotiated Tender Offers, the Imprisonment of the Free-riding Shareholder,* 19 J.Fin.Econ. 283 (1987) (an article based on a 1985 memorandum of the Office of the Chief Economist, Securities and Exchange Commission, The Economics of Any-or-All, Partial and Two-Tier Tender Offers (Apr. 19, 1985)). Blended premiums in two-tier tender offers resulted in a median premium paid of 54.5 percent; in any-or-all offers the median premium equaled 51.8 percent. Id. at 298. Furthermore, in over two-thirds of the successful two-tier offers less than a 20 percent difference existed between the premiums offered in the front and back ends. Id. at 300–301.

price is higher than the present value of the potential back-end price (discounted for risk due to uncertainty), shareholders may be forced to individually tender when, as a group, they would most likely refuse to tender, holding out for a higher price. This scenario can occur with any-and-all tender offers as well as with two-tier tender offers. Thus the prevalence of any-and-all tender offers is not necessarily synonymous with the elimination of the collective action problem.[2]

A second rebuttal focuses on the reasons both for the equivalence of two-tier offers to any-and-all offers in premiums paid and for the diminishing role of two-tier tender offers. The studies may only reflect that target firms have learned to take care of themselves and blunt the problem. Arguably, two-tier tender offers occur less frequently, because firms have blocked them with a variety of firm-specific defenses, principally shark repellent amendments to corporate charters and poison pill plans. Board-out supermajority amendments (in which the board can, by resolution, waive the provisions), for example, may operate very similarly to the Delaware statute; and back-end mergers must be approved by a supermajority of the voters, with the size of the required vote dependent on whether the bidder can vote (if the bidder can vote its shares, the percentage of votes required for approval can be very high—as high as 80 percent). The popular fair price amendment that requires a bidder to pay the front-end tender offer price to minority shareholders who lose their stock in a back-end merger also significantly reduces a bidder's incentive to use a two-tier offer instead of an any-and-all offer. The data then may simply reflect the ability of firms to deal with the problems of two-tier offers with firm-specific defenses.

The follow-up from the critics of the state statutes is, however, that proponents have just admitted that state legislation is unnecessary; firms can defend themselves. The drafters of the Delaware statute can argue in sur-rebuttal that the statute is a legislative legitimization of these amendments and serves a valuable function by eliminating the firm-by-firm expenses of charter amendments and, more importantly, by reducing the potential uncertainties associated with an unstable judicial climate. State courts (and federal courts interpreting state law) have failed to rule with any uniformity concerning target company defenses; invalidations of defenses seemingly occur almost randomly, and with disastrous consequences to the defending firm. See, e.g., Bank of New York Co. v. Irving Bank

---

2. The any-and-all tender offer does have one significant difference from the two-tier tender offer, but the difference does not eliminate, nor necessarily even reduce, its coercive effect. All tendering shareholders in any-and-all tender offers completely escape from the firm and thus avoid holding minority shares once the tender offer has been consummated. In two-tier tender offers that are oversubscribed, as most are, tendering shareholders cannot escape holding minority shares once the tender offer has been executed. Theoretically an any-and-all tender offer can attract and pay off all of a firm's existing shareholders. This has significant appeal to many who perceive any-and-all tender offers as inherently fair—anyone who wants out can get out at the tender offer price. Yet an any-and-all tender offer that attracts 100 percent of the shares may have done so by convincing each tendering shareholder that the consequences of not tendering are so severe that it would be foolish to refuse to tender, holding out in the hopes that at least 51 percent of the other shareholders would also hold out for a higher but reasonable price. Ultimately, however, the question of the intensity and frequency of shareholder coercion in any-and-all offers is an empirical question.

Corp., 139 Misc.2d 665, 528 N.Y.S.2d 482 (1988), affirmed 143 A.D.2d 1073, 533 N.Y.S.2d 411 (1988) [followed by N.Y.Bus.Corp.Law § 4603]; Amalgamated Sugar Co. v. NL Industries, Inc., 644 F.Supp. 1229 (D.N.Y.1986) [followed by N.J.Bus.Corp.Act § 14D:7-7(3)]. In light of the uncertain legality of these devices, it should come as no surprise that firms have lobbied state legislatures and asked that their privately created devices be, in essence, legitimized by statute. Indeed, some state statutes do no more than empower firms specifically to adopt popular private defenses.

Neutral: The Delaware statute, by itself, does not present a substantial deterrent to hostile takeovers; it increases the effectiveness of already potent poison pill plans. The choice by target managers first to implement a poison pill plan and then not to waive the plan, coupled with the three-year moratorium in the statute, should, if left unchecked, block most unwanted acquisitions. In recent years, however, the courts have questioned whether target managers, in creating or refusing to waive takeover defenses, are acting in the best interests of their shareholders. Delaware courts will inevitably be faced with legal challenges to both a board's decision to adopt a poison pill plan to buttress the moratorium in the Delaware statute and its decision not to waive the plan or the statutory three-year cooling-off period. In other words, before the adoption of the statute the Delaware courts had been faced with supervising the decisions of target boards; the statute will not materially change their responsibility.

The only real change brought about by the statute relates to the timing of the decisions of the target boards. The statute does not affect the nature of the essential inquiry into the managers' motives. Target boards can choose (1) to opt out of the statute within ninety days of its passage, (2) to sponsor a charter amendment to opt out of the statute, (3) to erect defenses that supplement the statute, with or without a shareholder vote, and (4) to waive the firm-specific defenses and the statutory moratorium altogether. These choices can be motivated by self-interest or by an interest in serving their shareholders.

The effectiveness of the Delaware statute will, therefore, ultimately turn on the performance of the Delaware courts. The courts must decide whether they will actively supervise the acts of target managers under the new statute, when the appropriate time for doing so is, and what standards and presumptions will aid such decisions. The statute does nothing more than revest in the Delaware courts the matter of supervision. If one believes that the Delaware courts are too lenient in assessing the conduct of target managers—that too many hostile takeovers are deterred or repelled—then one ought to believe that the statute will add only marginally to the problem. If, on the other hand, one believes that the Delaware courts are too harsh in assessing the conduct of target managers—that too many hostile takeovers succeed because target managers fear court discipline—then one ought to believe that the statute will increase, though only marginally, manager protections. In the end, the Delaware courts will define the parameters.

Redemption or Appraisal Statutes

Please read Pennsylvania Corporations and Unincorporated Associations Code sections 2541–48 in your statutory supplement.

AMANDA ACQUISITION CORP. v. UNIVERSAL FOODS CORP.

United States Court of Appeals, Seventh Circuit, 1989.
877 F.2d 496, cert. denied ___ U.S. ___, 110 S.Ct. 366, 107 L.Ed.2d 353 (1989).

EASTERBROOK, CIRCUIT JUDGE.

* * *

Wisconsin has a third-generation takeover statute. Enacted after *CTS*, it postpones the kinds of transactions that often follow tender offers (and often are the reason for making the offers in the first place). Unless the target's board agrees to the transaction in advance, the bidder must wait three years after buying the shares to merge with the target or acquire more than 5% of its assets. We must decide whether this is consistent with the Williams Act and Commerce Clause.

* * *

No firm incorporated in Wisconsin and having its headquarters, substantial operations, or 10% of its shares or shareholders there may "engage in a business combination with an interested stockholder ... for 3 years after the interested stockholder's stock acquisition date unless the board of directors of the [Wisconsin] corporation has approved, before the interested stockholder's stock acquisition date, that business combination or the purchase of stock". * * * An "interested stockholder" is one owning 10% of the voting stock, directly or through associates (anyone acting in concert with it). * * * A "business combination" is a merger with the bidder or any of its affiliates, sale of more than 5% of the assets to bidder or affiliate, liquidation of the target, or a transaction by which the target guarantees the bidder's or affiliate's debts or passes tax benefits to the bidder or affiliate. * * * The law, in other words, provides for almost hermetic separation of bidder and target for three years after the bidder obtains 10% of the stock—unless the target's board consented before then. No matter how popular the offer, the ban applies: obtaining 85% (even 100%) of the stock held by non-management shareholders won't allow the bidder to engage in a business combination, as it would under Delaware law.

* * * Wisconsin firms cannot opt out of the law, as may corporations subject to almost all other state takeover statutes. In Wisconsin it is management's approval in advance, or wait three years. Even when the time is up, the bidder needs the approval of a majority of the remaining investors, without any provision disqualifying shares still held by the managers who resisted the transaction.[3] * * * As a practical matter, Wisconsin prohibits any offer contingent on a merger between bidder and target, a condition attached to about 90% of contemporary tender offers.

* * *

---

3. Acquirors can avoid this requirement by buying out the remaining shareholders at a price defined by § 180.726(3)(c), but this is not a practical option.

If our views of the wisdom of state law mattered, Wisconsin's takeover statute would not survive. Like our colleagues who decided *MITE* and *CTS,* we believe that antitakeover legislation injures shareholders.[5] * * * Managers frequently realize gains for investors via voluntary combinations (mergers). If gains are to be had, but managers balk, tender offers are investors' way to go over managers' heads. If managers are not maximizing the firm's value—perhaps because they have missed the possibility of a synergistic combination, perhaps because they are clinging to divisions that could be better run in other hands, perhaps because they are just not the best persons for the job—a bidder that believes it can realize more of the firm's value will make investors a higher offer. Investors tender; the bidder gets control and changes things. * * * The prospect of monitoring by would-be bidders, and an occasional bid at a premium, induces managers to run corporations more efficiently and replaces them if they will not.

Premium bids reflect the benefits for investors. The price of a firm's stock represents investors' consensus estimate of the value of the shares under current and anticipated conditions. Stock is worth the present value of anticipated future returns—dividends and other distributions. Tender offers succeed when bidders offer more. Only when the bid exceeds the value of the stock (however investors compute value) will it succeed. A statute that precludes investors from receiving or accepting a premium offer makes them worse off. It makes the economy worse off too, because the higher bid reflects the better use to which the bidder can put the target's assets. (If the bidder can't improve the use of the assets, it injures itself by paying a premium.)

Universal, making an argument common among supporters of anti-takeover laws, contends that its investors do not appreciate the worth of its business plans, that its stock is trading for too little, and that if investors tender reflexively they injure themselves. If only they would wait, Universal submits, they would do better under current management. A variant of the argument has it that although smart investors know that the stock is underpriced, many investors are passive and will tender; even the smart investors then must tender to avoid doing worse on the "back end" of the deal. State laws giving

---

5. Because both the district court and the parties—like the Williams Act—examine tender offers from the perspective of equity investors, we employ the same approach. States could choose to protect "constituencies" other than stockholders. Creditors, managers, and workers invest human rather than financial capital. But the limitation of our inquiry to equity investors does not affect the analysis, because no evidence of which we are aware suggests that bidders confiscate workers' and other participants' investments to any greater degree than do incumbents—who may (and frequently do) close or move plants to follow the prospect of profit. Joseph A. Grundfest, a Commissioner of the SEC, showed in *Job Loss and Takeovers,* address to University of Toledo College of Law, Mar. 11, 1988, that acquisitions have no logical (or demonstrable) effect on employment. See also Brown & Medoff, *The Impact of Firm Acquisitions on Labor,* in *Corporate Takeovers: Causes and Consequences* 9 (A. Auerbach ed. 1988); Roberta Romano, *The Future of Hostile Takeovers: Legislation and Public Opinion,* 57 U.Cin. L.Rev. 457 (1988); C. Steven Bradford, *Protecting Shareholders from Themselves? A Policy and Constitutional Review of a State Takeover Statute,* 67 Neb.L.Rev. 459, 529–34 (1988).

management the power to block an offer enable the managers to protect the investors from themselves.

Both versions of this price-is-wrong argument imply: (a) that the stock of firms defeating offers later appreciates in price, topping the bid, thus revealing the wisdom of waiting till the market wises up; and (b) that investors in firms for which no offer is outstanding gain when they adopt devices so that managers may fend off unwanted offers (or states adopt laws with the same consequence). Efforts to verify these implications have failed. The best available data show that if a firm fends off a bid, its profits decline, and its stock price (adjusted for inflation and market-wide changes) never tops the initial bid, even if it is later acquired by another firm.

* * *

* * * Stock of firms adopting poison pills falls in price, as does the stock of firms that adopt most kinds of anti-takeover amendments to their articles of incorporation.

* * * Studies of laws similar to Wisconsin's produce the same conclusion: share prices of firms incorporated in the state drop when the legislation is enacted.

* * *

Although a takeover-*proof* firm leaves investors at the mercy of incumbent managers (who may be mistaken about the wisdom of their business plan even when they act in the best of faith), a takeover-*resistant* firm may be able to assist its investors. An auction may run up the price, and delay may be essential to an auction. Auctions transfer money from bidders to targets, and diversified investors would not gain from them (their left pocket loses what the right pocket gains); diversified investors would lose from auctions if the lower returns to bidders discourage future bids. But from targets' perspectives, once a bid is on the table an auction may be the best strategy. The full effects of auctions are hard to unravel, sparking scholarly debate. Devices giving managers some ability to orchestrate investors' responses, in order to avoid panic tenders in response to front-end-loaded offers, also could be beneficial, as the Supreme Court emphasized in *CTS*, 481 U.S. at 92–93, 107 S.Ct. at 1651–52. ("Could be" is an important qualifier; even from a perspective limited to targets' shareholders given a bid on the table, it is important to know whether managers use this power to augment bids or to stifle them, and whether courts can tell the two apart.)

State anti-takeover laws do not serve these ends well, however. Investors who prefer to give managers the discretion to orchestrate responses to bids may do so through "fair-price" clauses in the articles of incorporation and other consensual devices. Other firms may choose different strategies. A law such as Wisconsin's does not add options to firms that would like to give more discretion to their managers; instead it destroys the possibility of divergent choices. Wisconsin's law applies even when the investors prefer to leave their managers under the gun, to allow the market full sway. Karpoff and Malatesta found that state anti-takeover laws have little or no effect on the price of shares if the firm already has poison pills (or related devices) in place, but strongly negative effects on price when firms have no such contractual devices. To put this differently, state laws have bite only when investors, given the choice, would deny managers the power to interfere with tender offers (maybe already *have* denied managers that power). * * *

Skepticism about the wisdom of a state's law does not lead to the conclusion that the law is beyond the state's power, however. We have not been elected custodians of investors' wealth. States need not treat investors' welfare as their summum bonum. Perhaps they choose to protect managers' welfare instead, or believe that the current economic literature reaches an incorrect conclusion and that despite appearances takeovers injure investors in the long run. Unless a federal statute or the Constitution bars the way, Wisconsin's choice must be respected.

Amanda relies on the Williams Act of 1968, incorporated into §§ 13(d), (e) and 14(d)–(f) of the Securities Exchange Act of 1934, 15 U.S.C. §§ 78m(d), (e), 78n(d)–(f). The Williams Act regulates the conduct of tender offers. Amanda believes that Congress created an entitlement for investors to receive the benefit of tender offers, and that because Wisconsin's law makes tender offers unattractive to many potential bidders, it is preempted. See *MITE*, 633 F.2d at 490–99, and Justice White's views, 457 U.S. at 630–40.

* * *

The Williams Act regulates the *process* of tender offers: timing, disclosure, proration if tenders exceed what the bidder is willing to buy, best-price rules. It slows things down, allowing investors to evaluate the offer and management's response. Best-price, proration, and short-tender rules ensure that investors who decide at the end of the offer get the same treatment as those who decide immediately, reducing pressure to leap before looking.[7] After complying with the disclosure and delay requirements, the bidder is free to take the shares. *MITE* held invalid a state law that increased the delay and, by authorizing a regulator to nix the offer, created a distinct possibility that the bidder would be unable to buy the stock (and the holders to sell it) despite compliance with federal law. Illinois tried to regulate the process of tender offers, contradicting in some respects the federal rules. Indiana, by contrast, allowed the tender offer to take its course as the Williams Act specified but "sterilized" the acquired shares until the remaining investors restored their voting rights. Congress said nothing about the voting power of shares acquired in tender offers. Indiana's law reduced the benefits the bidder anticipated from the acquisition but left the process alone. So the Court, although accepting Justice White's views

---

[7]. To reduce is not to eliminate. Investors' options include selling to arbitrageurs in the market. This price fluctuates daily and may drop suddenly if the prospects of the bid's success dim.

for the purpose of argument, held that Indiana's rules do not conflict with the federal norms.

CTS observed that laws affecting the voting power of acquired shares do not differ in principle from many other rules governing the internal affairs of corporations. Laws requiring staggered or classified boards of directors delay the transfer of control to the bidder; laws requiring supermajority vote for a merger may make a transaction less attractive or impossible. 481 U.S. at 85–86, 107 S.Ct. at 1647–48. Yet these are not preempted by the Williams Act, any more than state laws concerning the *effect* of investors' votes are preempted by the portions of the Exchange Act, 15 U.S.C. § 78n(a)–(c), regulating the process of soliciting proxies. Federal securities laws frequently regulate process while state corporate law regulates substance. Federal proxy rules demand that firms disclose many things, in order to promote informed voting. Yet states may permit or compel a supermajority rule (even a unanimity rule) rendering it all but impossible for a particular side to prevail in the voting. * * * Are the state laws therefore preempted? How about state laws that allow many firms to organize without traded shares? Universities, hospitals, and other charities have self-perpetuating boards and cannot be acquired by tender offer. Insurance companies may be organized as mutuals, without traded shares; retailers often organize as co-operatives, without traded stock; some decently large companies (large enough to be "reporting companies" under the '34 Act) issue stock subject to buy-sell agreements under which the investors cannot sell to strangers without offering stock to the firm at a formula price; Ford Motor Co. issued non-voting stock to outside investors while reserving voting stock for the family, thus preventing outsiders from gaining control (dual-class stock is becoming more common); firms issue and state law enforces poison pills. All of these devices make tender offers unattractive (even impossible) and greatly diminish the power of proxy fights, success in which often depends on buying votes by acquiring the equity to which the vote is attached. * * * None of these devices could be thought preempted by the Williams Act or the proxy rules. If they are not preempted, neither is Wis.Stat. § 180.726.

Any bidder complying with federal law is free to acquire shares of Wisconsin firms on schedule. Delay in completing a second-stage merger may make the target less attractive, and thus depress the price offered or even lead to an absence of bids; it does not, however, alter any of the procedures governed by federal regulation. Indeed Wisconsin's law does not depend in any way on how the acquiring firm came by its stock: open-market purchases, private acquisitions of blocs, and acquisitions via tender offers are treated identically. Wisconsin's law is no different in effect from one saying that for the three years after a person acquires 10% of a firm's stock, a unanimous vote is required to merge. Corporate law once had a generally-applicable unanimity rule in major transactions, a rule discarded because giving every investor the power to block every reorganization stopped many desirable changes. (Many investors could use their "hold-up" power to try to engross a larger portion of the gains, creating a complex bargaining problem that often could not be solved.) Wisconsin's more restrained version of unanimity also may block beneficial transactions, but not by tinkering with any of the procedures established in federal law.

Only if the Williams Act gives investors a right to be the beneficiary of offers could Wisconsin's law run afoul of the federal rule. No such entitlement can be mined out of the Williams Act, however. *Schreiber v. Burlington Northern, Inc.*, 472 U.S. 1, 105 S.Ct. 2458, 86 L.Ed.2d 1 (1985), holds that the cancellation of a pending offer because of machinations between bidder and target does not deprive investors of their due under the Williams Act. The Court treated § 14(e) as a disclosure law, so that investors could make informed decisions; it follows that events leading bidders to cease their quest do not conflict with the Williams Act any more than a state law leading a firm not to issue new securities could conflict with the Securities Act of 1933. * * * Investors have no right to receive tender offers. More to the point—since Amanda sues as bidder rather than as investor seeking to sell—the Williams Act does not create a right to profit from the business of making tender offers. It is not attractive to put bids on the table for Wisconsin corporations, but because Wisconsin leaves the process alone once a bidder appears, its law may co-exist with the Williams Act.

* * *

When state law discriminates against interstate commerce expressly—for example, when Wisconsin closes its border to butter from Minnesota—the negative Commerce Clause steps in. The law before us is not of this type: it is neutral between inter-state and intra-state commerce. Amanda therefore presses on us the broader, all-weather, be-reasonable vision of the Constitution. Wisconsin has passed a law that unreasonably injures investors, most of whom live outside of Wisconsin, and therefore it *has* to be unconstitutional, as Amanda sees things. Although *Pike v. Bruce Church, Inc.*, 397 U.S. 137, 90 S.Ct. 844, 25 L.Ed.2d 174 (1970), sometimes is understood to authorize such general-purpose balancing, a closer examination of the cases may support the conclusion that the Court has looked for discrimination rather than for baleful effects. * * * Although the scholars whose writings we cited in Part II.A conclude that laws such as Wisconsin's injure investors, Wisconsin is entitled to give a different answer to this empirical question—or to decide that investors' interests should be sacrificed to protect managers' interests or promote the stability of corporate arrangements.

Illinois's law, held invalid in *MITE*, regulated sales of stock elsewhere. Illinois tried to tell a Texas owner of stock in a Delaware corporation that he could not sell to a buyer in California. By contrast, Wisconsin's law, like the Indiana statute sustained by *CTS*, regulates the internal affairs of firms incorporated there. Investors may buy or sell stock as they please. Wisconsin's law differs in this respect not only from that of Illinois but also from that of Massachusetts, which forbade any transfer of shares for one year after the failure to disclose any material fact, a flaw that led the First Circuit to condemn it.

* * *

Buyers of stock in Wisconsin firms may exercise full rights as investors, taking immediate control. No interstate transaction is regulated or forbidden. True, Wisconsin's law makes a potential buyer less willing to buy (or depresses the bid), but this is equally true of Indiana's rule. Many other rules of corporate law—supermajority voting requirements, staggered and classified boards, and so on—have similar or greater effects on some persons' willingness to purchase stock. * * * States could ban mergers outright, with even more powerful consequences. * * * Wisconsin did not allow mergers among firms chartered there until 1947. We doubt that it was violating the Commerce Clause all those years. * * * Every rule of corporate law affects investors who live outside the state of incorporation, yet this has never been thought sufficient to authorize a form of cost-benefit inquiry through the medium of the Commerce Clause.

Wisconsin, like Indiana, is indifferent to the domicile of the bidder. A putative bidder located in Wisconsin enjoys no privilege over a firm located in New York. So too with investors: all are treated identically, regardless of residence. Doubtless most bidders (and investors) are located outside Wisconsin, but unless the law discriminates according to residence this alone does not matter. * * *

Wisconsin could exceed its powers by subjecting firms to inconsistent regulation. Because § 180.726 applies only to a subset of firms incorporated in Wisconsin, however, there is no possibility of inconsistent regulation. Here, too, the Wisconsin law is materially identical to Indiana's. * * * This leaves only the argument that Wisconsin's law hinders the flow of interstate trade "too much". CTS dispatched this concern by declaring it inapplicable to laws that apply only to the internal affairs of firms incorporated in the regulating state. * * * States may regulate corporate transactions as they choose without having to demonstrate under an unfocused balancing test that the benefits are "enough" to justify the consequences.

To say that states have the power to enact laws whose costs exceed their benefits is not to say that investors should kiss their wallets goodbye. States compete to offer corporate codes attractive to firms. Managers who want to raise money incorporate their firms in the states that offer the combination of rules investors prefer. * * * Laws that in the short run injure investors and protect managers will in the longer run make the state less attractive to firms that need to raise new capital. If the law is "protectionist", the protected class is the existing body of managers (and other workers), suppliers, and so on, which bears no necessary relation to state boundaries. States regulating the affairs of domestic corporations cannot in the long run injure anyone but themselves.

* * * The long run takes time to arrive, and it is tempting to suppose that courts could contribute to investors' welfare by eliminating laws that impose costs in the short run.

* * * The price of such warfare, however, is a reduction in the power of competition among states. Courts seeking to impose "good" rules on the states diminish the differences among corporate codes and dampen competitive forces. Too, courts may fail in their quest. How do judges know which rules are best? Often only the slow forces of competition reveal that information. Early economic studies may mislead, or judges (not trained as social scientists) may misinterpret the available data or act precipitously. Our Constitution allows the states to act as laboratories; slow migration (or national law on the authority of the Commerce Clause) grinds the failures under. No such process weeds out judicial errors, or decisions that, although astute when rendered, have become anachronistic in light of changes in the economy. Judges must hesitate for these practical reasons—and not only because of limits on their constitutional competence—before trying to "perfect" corporate codes.

The three district judges who have considered and sustained Delaware's law delaying mergers did so in large measure because they believed that the law left hostile offers "a meaningful opportunity for success". * * *

Delaware allows a merger to occur forthwith if the bidder obtains 85% of the shares other than those held by management and employee stock plans. If the bid is attractive to the bulk of the unaffiliated investors, it succeeds. Wisconsin offers no such opportunity, which Amanda believes is fatal.

Even in Wisconsin, though, options remain. Defenses impenetrable to the naked eye may have cracks. Poison pills are less fatal in practice than in name (some have been swallowed willingly), and corporate law contains self-defense mechanisms. Investors concerned about stock-watering often arranged for firms to issue pre-emptive rights, entitlements for existing investors to buy stock at the same price offered to newcomers (often before the newcomers had a chance to buy in). Poison pills are dilution devices, and so pre-emptive rights ought to be handy countermeasures.[11] So too there are countermeasures to statutes deferring mergers. The cheapest is to lower the bid to reflect the costs of delay. Because every potential bidder labors under the

---

11. Imagine a series of Antidote rights, issued by would-be bidding firms, that detach if anyone exercises flip-over rights to purchase the bidder's stock at a discount. Antidote rights would entitle the bidder's investors, *other than those who exercise flip-over rights*, to purchase the bidder's stock at the same discount available to investors exercising flip-over rights. Antidotes for flip-in rights also could be issued. In general, whenever one firm can issue rights allowing the purchase of cheap stock, another firm can issue the equivalent series of contingent preemptive rights that offsets the dilution.

same drawback, the firm placing the highest value on the target still should win. Or a bidder might take down the stock and pledge it (or its dividends) as security for any loans. That is, the bidder could operate the target as a subsidiary for three years. The corporate world is full of partially owned subsidiaries. If there is gain to be had from changing the debt-equity ratio of the target, that can be done consistent with Wisconsin law. The prospect of being locked into place as holders of illiquid minority positions would cause many persons to sell out, and the threat of being locked in would cause many managers to give assent in advance, as Wisconsin allows. (Or bidders might demand that directors waive the protections of state law, just as Amanda believes that the directors' fiduciary duties compel them to redeem the poison pill rights.) Many bidders would find lock-in unattractive because of the potential for litigation by minority investors, and the need to operate the firm as a subsidiary might foreclose savings or synergies from merger. So none of these options is a perfect substitute for immediate merger, but each is a crack in the defensive wall allowing some value-increasing bids to proceed.

At the end of the day, however, it does not matter whether these countermeasures are "enough". The Commerce Clause does not demand that states leave bidders a "meaningful opportunity for success". * * * A state with the power to forbid mergers has the power to defer them for three years. Investors can turn to firms incorporated in states committed to the dominance of market forces, or they can turn on legislators who enact unwise laws. The Constitution has room for many economic policies. "[A] law can be both economic folly and constitutional." *CTS*, 481 U.S. at 96–97, 107 S.Ct. at 1653–54 (Scalia, J., concurring). Wisconsin's law may well be folly; we are confident that it is constitutional.

Questions

1. If Judge Easterbrook believes the Wisconsin statute to be unwise, why does he refuse to hold it unconstitutional under the contract clause?

2. How convincing is Judge Easterbrook's position that states will eventually see the light and repeal antitakeover statutes, when the current trend is an avalanche in the opposite direction? What distinguishes antitakeover statutes from other provisions of corporate codes? From state blue-sky laws?

3. Why did Judge Easterbrook not apply commerce clause analysis to employee effects or taxpayer effects?

Note

Will States Eventually Repeal Antitakeover Statutes?

In *Amanda Acquisition* Judge Easterbrook places his faith in the self-corrective power of the competition among states to promulgate optimal corporate charters. Eventually states will see the light and begin to reverse the current avalanche of ever more restrictive statutes. Is he correct? Consider section 203 of Delaware's business combination statute. Traditionally Delaware's primary interest in creating and amending its corporate code has been to establish a set of basic structural rules for its firms with which the participants are most comfortable—that is, a set of rules that the participants themselves would have negotiated had not the cost of such a large-scale negotiation been prohibitive. Is section 203 such a provision? If not, will Delaware move to repeal the section?

Do not expect to see Delaware retreat from section 203 anytime soon. The Delaware legislature, for many of the same reasons that make a private negotiation prohibitive, is more accessible to firm managers than to firm shareholders and other nonshareholder constituencies. Fortunately most aspects of the Delaware corporate code present no substantial problems in this regard. For the most part it is in the joint interests of the firm's managers and shareholders to adopt basic structural provisions that maximize firm value. But when conflicts between managers and shareholders arise, as in the case of provisions establishing methods of executive compensation or of provisions establishing methods of executing contracts between managers in their personal capacity and the firm, we are less comfortable if it appears that firm managers have the upper hand in dealing with the Delaware legislature. Yet even in many of these matters, managers' interests in their professional reputations, and their interests in the firm's earnings and share prices (through compensatory bonus and option programs), provide some restraint on the degree to which managers will push for lopsided legislation.

On the other hand, the efficacy of mechanisms for ousting managers when they have significantly diminished firm value by their poor or corrupt performance will inherently split managers and shareholders into separate interest groups. Effective policing mechanisms will have substantial value to shareholders and are unlikely to be received enthusiastically by managers.[1] To the extent that managers have more influence with the Delaware legislature, one would expect managers to limit the efficacy of the more powerful policing mechanisms. The costs of such laws are spread over a large number of stockholders in many firms who are dispersed geographically. Managers, who are more concentrated, can lobby the Delaware legislature with firm funds, while shareholders have to fund lobbying efforts out of their own pockets. The cost of lobbying to defeat the legislation is likely to be greater than the cost of the legislation to any one stockholder, and the cost of organizing a concerted effort to defeat the legislation is high.

One of the most powerful policing devices is the threat of a hostile acquisition. Any effort by managers to derail this threat through legisla-

---

1. Prof. Michael Jensen sums the problem up as follows: "[C]onsider the simple situation in which a principal (stockholder) hires an agent (managers and board of directors) to take some actions on his or her behalf.... The principal may want to delegate a wide range of decision rights to the agent. In no event, however, will it be sensible for the principal to delegate the ultimate control rights to the agent: the rights to hire, fire, and set the compensation of the agent.... If the principal were to delegate the control rights, ... the agent would become the effective owner of the decision rights (although he probably could not alienate them) and could be expected to use them in his own interests. Jensen, *Takeovers: Their Causes and Consequences*, 2 J.Econ.Persp. 42 (1988).

tion ought to be viewed with healthy suspicion. Unless the Delaware legislature can show that it is not sacrificing shareholder interests in passing section 203, the statute ought to be struck down as unconstitutional. If the statute is not struck down, managers will have profited from the poor representation of shareholder interests in the Delaware legislature. The statute's burden on interstate commerce ought to be premised on the grounds that it lines the pockets of a discrete group that has substantial advantages in accessing the Delaware legislature.[2] For such statutes to survive, it must be clear that the Delaware legislature intended to pass section 203 in the shareholders' best interests and that there is a supportable basis in fact for the legislation's actually doing what the legislature intended it to do. The key to the statute's constitutionality, then, ought to be whether the statute is intended to serve, and does, arguably, in fact serve, the interests of the shareholders of Delaware corporations. Otherwise the net effect of the section will be to transfer wealth away from largely nonconstituent shareholders to constituent managers and, possibly, other constituents. Moreover, some wealth may simply be dissipated through less efficient management of the enterprise.

The Supreme Court's *CTS* opinion can be read without strain as consistent with this approach. At issue is how specifically the language that approves the Indiana statute in the case can be read. The Court's language can be read on two levels: first, that the Indiana statute is one of several plausible attempts to protect shareholders or, second, that the Indiana statute provides the only legitimate form of protection short of giving special voting rights to noninterested shareholders. The first reading seems to be the more plausible; the Court appears more concerned with the right of states to allocate power within chartered corporations than with specifically how the power ought to be distributed. If so, the Delaware statute again appears to be on more solid ground.

If, however, the Supreme Court is more sensitive to the problem of unequal access of the managers and the shareholders to the Delaware lawmakers, then the Court may want to police the allocation of power between the two groups in state takeover regulation. If so, the Delaware statute would seem to be on thinner ice than the Indiana statute, mainly because shareholder voting is less important under the Delaware statute than under the Indiana statute.

Under the Indiana statute shareholders can opt out of the statute by charter amendment before a control share acquisition occurs. After a control share acquisition has occurred or when it is pending, the acquisition can be approved by a majority vote of preexisting shareholders (excluding shares held by officers, inside directors, and the acquirer). While one can argue that the vote to opt out, which can only be initiated by the target board, is heavily influenced by the target board through its control of the firm proxy machinery, it is also true that after a control share acquisition occurs, the Indiana statute makes shareholder participation mandatory.

---

2. See Tribe, *American Constitutional Law* 408–09 (2d ed. 1988) (discussing the theme of political representation that often underlies commerce clause analysis). Cf. J. Ely, *Democracy and Distrust* 73 (1980) (discussing the effect of the interpretivist approach to constitutional analysis).

On the other hand, shareholder voting is secondary in the Delaware statute. The statute vests primary control of the process in the target board, which has the power to waive the moratorium. Bidders who cannot wait three years to effect a back-end merger are not likely to bypass board disapproval; they depend instead on the act's supermajority provision, which provides that two-thirds of the disinterested shareholders can also approve a back-end merger.

Most tender offers will be conditioned on a board waiver, not a shareholder vote: if the board grants a waiver, the vote is unnecessary; if the board refuses, it is a foregone conclusion that it will also refuse to send the matter to the shareholders for their approval. In sum, the method of forcing a shareholder vote under the Delaware statute is substantially different from the Indiana procedure in that it requires a bidder to make a large initial acquisition and take a substantial risk before the shareholder vote. An acquirer must buy enough stock to control the board of directors and cause the board to submit to all disinterested shareholders a proposal to allow a merger.

Indeed, it may be disingenuous for Delaware to argue otherwise. Delaware's first circulated proposal for takeover legislation, in June 1987, was a control share acquisition statute. The proposal received heavy criticism from those convinced that the Indiana statute was an ineffective check on leveraged acquisitions, and those responsible for drafting the statute conceded to this claim.

Their charge against the Indiana statute has two parts. First, the statute takes control of a target's defense away from target managers and vests it in target shareholders, because acquirers can force a shareholder vote. By conditioning any tender offer on a favorable vote, which may be fifty days away, the bidder need not have financing in place or even be seriously committed to the acquisition—he may just want to publicize the company's availability for sale. Second, the shareholder vote, when taken, will always favor the bidder. After the announcement of a potential acquisition, arbitrageurs will, it is argued, acquire shares (either before the record date or, if after the record date, with proxies attached) and along with institutional investors, vote for a short-term profit.[3] In sum, the statute may help put a firm in play.

The Pennsylvania Disgorgement Statute

Please read sections 2571–2574 of title 15 of the Pennsylvania Consolidated Statutes in your statutory supplement.

Questions

1. How does the disgorgement provision deter takeover attempts? What is the effect of the provision on an unsuccessful bidder? What is the effect of the provision on "greenmailers"? If a bidder appears despite the

---

3. Invoking the play of arbitrageurs is a smoke screen and overlooks the point that shareholders who sell to arbitrageurs would themselves have decided to favor the offer—that is, they would have voted for the bid had they held their shares.

provision, what is the effect of the provision on the ability of the target board to find competing bidders, including a "white knight"?

2. Does the provision apply to proxy contests or consent solicitations for control of a Pennsylvania firm? What is the effect of either an unsuccessful or a successful proxy solicitation for control of the board by a shareholder who holds less than 20 percent of the outstanding shares in the firm? What is the consequence under the statute of a shareholder seeking proxies not to unseat the board but to counteract board proposals on takeover provisions in the firm's charter?

3. What is the effect of the provision on the acquirer in the following situation? A bidder, holding 15 percent of a target's stock, negotiates a preliminary agreement with a target board for a statutory merger. After the agreement is announced, a third-party bidder appears with a higher offer. The board accepts the higher offer. Is the initial friendly purchaser subject to the statute?

4. The statute contains a three-month opt-out period that ended July 26, 1990. Sixty-seven of the approximately three hundred public companies subject to the act—including eleven of the sixteen Fortune 500 companies—opted out. See 22 Sec.Reg. & Law Rptr. 1177 (Aug. 10, 1990). Is this a victory or a loss for the act's drafters?

Note
The Effect of the State Statutes on Share Prices

Lawrence Schumann analyzed the 205-day period before the passage of the New York takeover statute. In that period the New York legislature passed one statute that was vetoed by the governor and passed a second statute, recommended by the governor, which he subsequently signed. For the entire period stock prices of New York firms exhibited abnormal returns, returns not explained by a market basket of stocks in firms not subject to the law, of negative 9.7 percent. In the final eighty-six days of the period, from the time the eventually successful bill was introduced to the time it passed, stock prices of New York firms exhibited abnormal returns of negative 4.4 percent. See Schumann, *State Regulation of Takeovers and Shareholder Wealth: The Case of New York's 1985 Takeover Statute,* 19 Rand J. of Econ. 557 (1988). Messrs. Sidak and Woodward found that Indiana's Control Share Act reduced the value of Indiana corporations by more than 6 percent. Woodward, *How Much Indiana's Anti-takeover Law Cost Shareholders,* Wall St.J., May 5, 1988, at 32, col. 3. Not all authors agree. See Quirin, *Letter to the Editor, Indiana's Anti-takeover Law,* Wall St.J., May 24, 1988, at 39, col. 1 (disputing the conclusions of the Sidak and Woodward study). Professor Romano studied Connecticut's Fair Price Statute, Pennsylvania's Redemption Statute, and Missouri's Control Share Acquisition Statute and found no effect on stock prices. Romano, *The Political Economy of Takeover Statutes,* 73 Va.L.Rev. 111, 180–87 (1987).

The methodology of these studies is not free from controversy, however. Compare Ryngaert & Netter, "Shareholder Wealth Effects of the Ohio Antitakeover Law," 4 J. of Law, Econ. & Org. 373 (1988) (finding a 2 percent drop in share prices of Ohio firms accompanying the passage of the

Ohio law), with Margotta, McWilliams & McWilliams, "An Analysis of the Stock Price Effect of the 1986 Ohio Takeover Legislation," 6 J. of Law, Econ. & Org. 235 (1990) (finding no effect after disputing Ryngaert & Netter's assumptions on event windows and portfolio composition.)

The most comprehensive study to date, investigating forty antitakeover bills introduced in state legislatures from 1982 to 1987, found that, on average, the press announcement of the legislation corresponded with a small but statistically significant decrease in the stock value of the firms incorporated in the state considering the law. Karpoff & Malatesta, The Wealth Effects of Second Generation State Takeover Legislation, J.Fin. Econ. (1990). The study also found that the stock prices of large firms headquartered in the state, regardless of their states of incorporation, decreased by small but statistically significant amounts. Focusing on the Pennsylvania disgorgement statute (which was combined with a control share statute and a constituency statute), these authors noted in a later study that the first press announcement of the bill, on December 1, 1989, corresponded with an average decrease in the price of Pennsylvania firms relative to the S & P 500 of a statistically significant 1.27 percent. On the day of the first news wire coverage of the bill, October 13, 1989, which was not picked up by any newspaper, Pennsylvania firms' average market-adjusted stock return was a negative 1.58 percent. The average market-adjusted return slipped an additional .8 percent on the day the bill was introduced in the state Senate, October 20, 1989, and an additional 2.9 percent during the first two weeks in December, when the bill was discussed and passed by the state senate. Summing up, the authors concluded that from the date of the first wire-service story through the time the bill was introduced into the House of Representatives after it had passed the Senate, the average Pennsylvania company's cumulated abnormal stock return was a whopping negative 6.9 percent. Karpoff & Malatesta, PA Law: State Antitakeover Laws and Stock Prices, Fin.Anal.J. 8 (July–Aug. 1990).

Chapter Five

THE POWER AND FIDUCIARY RESPONSIBILITY OF BOARDS OF DIRECTORS ATTEMPTING, DEFENDING AGAINST, OR AGREEING TO TAKEOVERS

As we have seen in chapter 2, boards of directors have the power under state corporate codes (unless a firm's articles are to the contrary) to contract for statutory mergers and asset sales, usually subject to shareholder ratification. Boards also have the power to contract for stock acquisitions, subject to either a shareholder vote (for compulsory share exchanges) or their shareholders' willingness to sell. In some cases the shareholders' ability to vote or sell in their own best interest is prejudiced by inappropriate board conduct. Conflicts of interest on the board or simple board laziness may lead the board to make incomplete or ill-formed recommendations to their shareholders. In such cases state courts step in and enforce general fiduciary duties of care and loyalty.

More problematic, perhaps, are cases in which the board of a potential target firm decides to block acquisition overtures. Without board approval the shareholder cannot vote on a proposal for a statutory merger or an asset sale. Acquirers are left to either mount a proxy fight to oust the board or make their acquisition offer directly to the shareholders in the form of a stock acquisition. Boards are not powerless in such situations, however. They promulgate structural impediments to both proxy solicitations and stock acquisitions. Aggrieved shareholders and frustrated bidders run to state courts for relief. As you will see, the response of the courts has been disjointed and conflicted. Some courts have found, for example, that state corporate codes place limits on a board's power to erect some kinds of takeover defenses to stock acquisitions. Other courts have held that although a board has the power to erect structural defenses, this power is also subject to the board's general duties of care and loyalty. Yet there is considerable debate over how to evaluate whether, in any given case, these duties have been violated.

Subchapter A focuses on the power of the board to erect takeover defenses, and subchapters B and C deal with a board's general duties of care and loyalty in attempting, defending against, or agreeing to takeovers.

SUBCHAPTER A. THE POWER OF BOARDS OF DIRECTORS TO ERECT TAKEOVER DEFENSES

SECTION 1: INTRODUCTION TO FIRM-SPECIFIC TAKEOVER DEFENSES

Firms concerned about reducing their vulnerability to unwanted takeovers have fashioned a growing number of defenses. Indeed the state antitakeover statutes we studied in the previous chapter are often just versions of otherwise widely adopted firm-specific takeover defenses. There are two severable legal questions that appear anytime one of these takeover devices is contested in court. First, are the defenses void ad initio as outside the power of the board of directors to adopt, and second, if the defenses are prima facie valid on the facts of a particular case, have the directors abused their discretion in deploying or refusing to defuse a defense? The first question is the subject of this subchapter, and the second question is the subject of subchapter B.

There are three different kinds of takeover defenses relevant to our study of board power. The categories are defined by the role of shareholders in the erection of each defense: First, takeover defenses that require specific shareholder ratification (e.g., "shark repellent" charter amendments); second, takeover defenses put in place by the board using very general grants of authority contained in a firm's charter (e.g., a firm uses a charter provision authorizing the issuance of "blank check" preferred stock to promulgate a poison pill plan); and third, takeover defenses based on the board's general powers as granted in a state corporate code (e.g., a board uses a code provision authorizing a board to contract for the sale of firm assets to erect a "crown jewel" defense). In the first category, shareholders must vote to approve the specific defense in question. In the second category, shareholders, unless the general grant is in a firm's original charter, must vote to amend a firm's charter to give the board the general power. And in the third category, shareholders do not necessarily vote at all, unless they vote to amend a charter to remove the board's power to effectuate the defense.

The shareholders are not powerless, however, with respect to defenses promulgated without specific ratification (categories two and three). They can, using the shareholder resolution procedure provided under Securities and Exchange Commission rule 14a–8, vote to recommend that a board withdraw specific defenses that it has chosen to put in place. Moreover, a board deciding to use a takeover defense in categories two or three could choose to ask for a positive shareholder ratification, although unnecessary, to protect them from shareholder-derivative litigation. The courts that have addressed the issue have held that some kinds of defenses that fall in each of the three categories are beyond the power of the board. Moreover, our national exchanges prohibit takeover defenses that would otherwise fall in the first category.

The following is a general introduction to some of the popular defenses that fall in each of the three categories. This list is intended to be neither exhaustive nor thoroughly explanatory; I leave this to the rich facts of the cases we will study in this chapter and the next. As you read each case in the next two chapters, note the details of each defense employed and consider the usefulness of each defense.

Charter amendments that require a specific shareholder vote are called "shark repellent" amendments. Drafters of early shark repellent amendments designed them to retard the ability of someone with newly acquired voting power from taking control of the firm's board of directors. The amendments provided for a "staggered" board of directors (only a minority, usually one-third, of the board seats are the subject of an election in any one year), for eliminating shareholder voting through the written consent procedure (a method of voting that does not require a formal shareholders' meeting), for limiting the right of shareholders to call a special meeting of shareholders, for prohibiting the removal of a sitting director unless "for cause," for limiting the creation of new seats on the board of directors, and for giving the remaining members of the board the sole authority to appoint new directors if a director resigned in midterm. By mid–1989, 54 percent of the 1,440 largest public companies had adopted staggered terms for directors, 23 percent had adopted charter amendments limiting shareholders' rights to act by written consent, and 21 percent had adopted charter amendments limiting a shareholder's right to call a special shareholders' meeting. See IRRC, Corporate Takeover Defenses 1989 (1989).

Shark repellent charter amendments proved to be only marginally effective. Once an acquiror gained voting control of the stock, existing board members owed the new owner fiduciary duties, and most board members who could not respond to the new owner's requests simply resigned rather than continue in an uncomfortable lame duck capacity, at constant risk of being the object of a suit brought by the new controlling shareholder. Moreover, courts prohibit the existing board from finding ways of diluting the ownership of a new controlling owner once the new owner has the controlling block of stock. Condec Corp. v. Lukenheimer Co., 43 Del.Ch. 353, 230 A.2d 769 (1967) (the court enjoined the issuance of a large block of new shares to a friendly party after an unwanted buyer had otherwise obtained control).

Lawyers, therefore, designed a second round of charter amendments with much more punch—indeed, state antitakeover legislation often mimics these second-generation charter amendments. The more powerful amendments contain provisions for a supermajority vote for all business combinations between a controlling shareholder and the firm if the controlling shareholder acquired control without the specific approval of a preexisting board of directors (recall the business combination acts of Delaware and New York) or if the controlling shareholder did not meet fair price criteria in the merger (recall the Maryland fair price statute). By mid–1989, 32 percent of the largest 1,440 public companies had adopted fair price charter amendments, and 17 percent had adopted supermajority amendments. Some charter amendments give nontendering shareholders the right to put their stock to the firm for a specified period of time at a generous price after a successful stock acquisition (recall the Pennsylvania redemption statute). Others reduce the voting rights of one who has made a successful stock acquisition unless the acquisition meets specified fair price requirements or is approved by nonselling shareholders (recall the control share acts). The most extreme form of this sophisticated class of charter amendments is amendments that create two classes of voting stock ("two-tier voting stock"). One class, held by insiders, has concentrated voting power and diluted rights to the firm's equity.

The major disadvantages of charter amendments adopted by shareholder vote are, first, they take time to put in place, second, they are not flexible, and third, the firm must justify them in comprehensive disclosure documents required by the federal proxy solicitation regulations. In response, clever corporate lawyers designed new defenses that could be implemented without a shareholder vote—the firms could employ them in less time and did not have to justify them in proxy statements. The most popular of these defenses is a poison pill plan, a dividend distribution of stock, stock rights, or other securities notes that have special redemption or conversion provisions. The conversion options in these instruments are activated by an unapproved stock acquisition of a specified percentage of a firm's stock (a "trigger") and make the issuer prohibitively expensive to buy. By mid–1989, 43 percent of the 1,440 largest public companies had adopted poison pill plans. A second member of this category, less popular and more controversial, is stock exchange offers that create, without charter amendment, a two-tier voting stock system. The firm offers stock with diluted voting power and concentrated claims on equity for its outstanding common stock. The insiders do not tender, the outsiders do, and the insiders end up with concentrated voting power.

The poison pill plans, which began as distributions of convertible preferred stock, have evolved into distributions of stock rights and convertible debt. A board, to be able to create one of the popular poison pill plans, must have blanket authority in a firm's charter to issue rights, debt, or preferred stock with rights and privileges set by board resolution at the time of issuance. A charter provision on preferred stock that empowers the board to issue novel kinds of preferred stock is called a blank check preferred provision. Moreover, if a plan allows shareholders to exchange one kind of stock for another in the issuer, the firm must have sufficient authorization in its charter to issue the new stock. Thus poison pill plans often are preceded by charter amendments, voted on by shareholders, that enable a board to craft the novel securities that are the backbone of these plans. In the proxy materials that accompany a proxy solicitation for such charter amendments, detailed disclosures of the specifics of any one plan or any one takeover defense may not be necessary. Only a general comment that the amendments will empower the board to adopt a defense in the future will usually suffice.

Most poison pill plans are designed so that no bidder can afford to trigger them with an unapproved stock acquisition. Boards retain the right to waive the effects of a plan, usually through a reservation of a right to redeem the outstanding securities for a nominal fee. Thus buyers must negotiate with the board before acquiring a triggering block of stock, seeking the board's approval of the acquisition and the board's agreement that it will redeem the outstanding conversion rights. In other words, poison pill plans force bidders to negotiate with the target board in stock acquisitions, acquisitions that the bidder could otherwise consummate without the board's approval.

The third category of defenses—those that do not require any shareholder vote—is the most wide-ranging. Boards of directors use their inherent power over firm assets to make the firm unattractive to unwanted bidders. These defenses are often less attractive than a poison pill plan, because the defenses in category three usually require that the board expend assets or make major changes in the capital structure of the firm.[1] The board sells the key firm asset (the "crown jewel" defense), buys the stock of an unwanted bidder ("greenmail"), gives top managers handsome severance payments contingent on control changes ("golden parachutes"), or issues stock to a friendly party (a "white squire") subject to reselling restrictions (a "standstill agreement"). The firm makes acquisitions of its own to create antitrust problems for the bidder, to create national defense concerns if the bidder is foreign (the "Pentagon play"), or to acquire control of the bidder in a reverse acquisition (the "Pac-Man" defense). The most common modern defense in this category is a radical restructuring—the target releverages itself by selling debt and passing the cash proceeds of the placement back to its own shareholders in a huge one-time stock dividend. By releveraging, a firm exhausts its debt capacity and its cash reserves so that a bidder cannot use the firm's own assets to finance an acquisition.

Note
Empirical Data on the Use and Effect of the Takeover Defenses

Researchers are engaged in an ongoing study of the effect of tender offers and tender offer defenses on corporate constituencies. A recent

---

1. The important exception is the lock-up option, in which a board sells an option to buy its prime asset for a bargain price and the option is triggered by an unwanted acquisition.

paper by Bradley, Desai & Kim, "Synergistic Gains from Corporate Acquisitions and Their Division between the Stockholders of the Target and Acquiring Firms," 21 J.Fin.Econ. 3 (1988), reported that successful tender offers increase the combined value of the target and the acquiring firms by an average of 7.4 percent. The study also found that target stockholders captured most, if not all, the gains; acquiring firms showed, on average, neither positive nor negative short-term effects. See also Jarrell & Poulsen, *The Returns to Acquiring Firms in Tender Offers: Evidence from Three Decades,* (1989) (gains to acquirers average close to zero). Another study found that average premiums to target shareholders from 1961 to 1986 were almost 48 percent, or an estimated $134.4 billion. Black & Grundfest, Shareholder Gains from Takeovers and Restructuring between 1981 and 1986, 1 J. Applied Corp.Fin. 5 (1988).

Where does the new value come from? Please reread the Shleifer & Vishny excerpt in chapter 1, supra. The studies are in conflict. Stock price evidence does not support the theory that target firms are victims of market undervaluation. Stock prices of targets successful at fending off hostile bidders decline to approximately prebid levels within two years of the failed bid. Bhagat, Brickley & Lowenstein, *The Pricing Effects of Interfirm Cash Tender Offers,* 42 J.Fin. 965 (1987). Moreover, one researcher, using analysts' consensus forecasts of the target's stand-alone earnings, found that the forecasts did not change with bids (supporting a synergy theory of takeovers) but did drop 10 percent with management resistance. Pound, *The Information Effects of Takeover Bids and Resistance,* 22 J.Fin. Econ. 207 (1988). Some stock price studies find no support for the claims that, on average, tender offers harm bondholders, labor, or the government (through decreased tax payments). See Dennis & McConnell, *Corporate Mergers and Security Returns,* 16 J.Fin.Econ. 143 (1986); Breen, The Potential for Tax Gains as a Merger Motive, Federal Trade Commission, Bureau of Economics (July 1987); Shleifer & Summers, Hostile Takeovers and Breaches of Trust in Corporate Takeover: Causes and Consequences (A. Auerback ed. 1988). But see Coffee, Unstable Coalitions: Corporate Governance as a Multi-player Game, 78 Geo.L.J. 1495, 1516–18 (1990) (a summary of studies that show bondholders suffer losses in leveraged buyouts). On the other hand, business line financial data seem to indicate that acquiring firms do not experience increases in profitability and productivity in using target assets that would justify the acquisitions. D. Ravenscraft & F. Scherer, Mergers, Sell-offs and Economic Efficiency 220–21 (1987).

Researchers have conducted studies on the effects of antitakeover charter amendments on stock prices. Fair price amendments have been found to have no significant effects, while classified board and supermajority clauses have been found in some studies to have significant negative impacts on target shareholder wealth. See Jarrell & Poulsen, *Shark Repellents and Stock Prices: The Effects of Antitakeover Amendments since 1980,* 19 J.Fin.Econ. 127 (1987); Jarrell, Brickley & Netter, *The Market for Corporate Control: The Empirical Evidence since 1980,* 2 J.Econ.Persp. 49 (1988). The more harmful supermajority amendments correlated with lower levels of institutional stockholding and with higher levels of insider stockholding. Jarrell & Poulsen, infra. Similarly, dual-class voting stock recapitalizations are associated with significant negative stock price effects. Jarrell & Poulsen, *Dual–Class Recapitalizations as Antitakeover Mechanisms,* 20 J.Fin.Econ. 130 (1988). Yet 95 percent of all proposed shark repellent amendments pass. Why do shareholders vote for such charter amendments?

Pound found, first, that the inefficiencies in proxy solicitation give managers an advantage in proxy contests (it is difficult to contact shareholders, and time can be short), second, that institutional investors operating under personal conflicts of interest may vote with management against their fiduciary interests, and third, that credible dissidents have to incur significant costs to signal to other shareholders that the dissidents are not cranks. Pound, *Proxy Contexts and the Efficiency of Shareholders Oversight,* 20 J.Fin.Econ. 237 (1988).

Studies of target defenses undertaken without a ratifying shareholder vote also show negative effects on stock prices. The adoption of the more restrictive of the poison pill plans causes stock price declines. Ryngaert, *Effects of Poison Pills on Shareholder Wealth,* 20 J.Fin.Econ. 377 (1988). Some of the least restrictive plans, however, may even increase stock prices (perhaps because the adoption signals to the market positive information about the takeover value of the firm or because the plans give target managers negotiating leverage to secure a higher tender offer premium). Court decisions validating a poison pill also cause price declines, while price increases follow a court decision to invalidate a pill. Id. Another study compared the wealth effects of poison pill adoptions by Delaware-incorporated firms with those of firms incorporated in other states. Choi, Kamma & Weintrop, *The Delaware Courts, Poison Pills, and Shareholder Wealth,* 2 J.Law, Econ. & Org. 375 (1989). The overall wealth effect for 267 publicly traded firms was a decline in market value of their shares by $2.14 billion, $1.97 billion for 133 Delaware firms and $.17 billion for 134 firms incorporated outside Delaware. The authors theorized that the absence of significant wealth effects of poison pill adoptions by non-Delaware firms may be due to the uncertainty about the legality of the antitakeover tactic in states other than Delaware.

Who adopts poison pill plans and why? A study found that firms that adopt poison pill plans, first, are less profitable than average in their industries and, second, are run by managers with smaller fractions of their own firm's stock than average in their industries. Malatesta & Walking, 20 J.Fin.Econ. 347 (1988). We may be on the edge of a new wave of shareholder activism, however. Institutional investors have led a widespread proxy solicitation campaign against poison pills in recent years, placing shareholder resolutions calling for the revocation of the plans. In the spring 1990 annual meeting season one-third of the anti-poison pill resolutions garnered a majority of the votes cast. See chapter 5 at 527–28.

Severe corporate restructuring of assets through acquisition programs or divestiture or of stock structure through stock issuances or repurchases, undertaken without a shareholder vote, also results in significant negative stock price effects. Dann & DeAngelo, *Corporate Financial Policy and Corporate Control: A Study of Defensive Adjustments in Asset and Ownership Structure,* 20 J.Fin.Econ. 87 (1988). There is evidence, however, that some kinds of restructuring, specifically leveraged recapitalizations, do have a positive impact on stock prices. Fortier, *Hostile Takeovers and the Market for Corporate Control,* 2 J.Econ.Persp. 2 (1988). Finally, studies demonstrate that greenmail payments create negative abnormal returns if not followed by a successful bid. Mikkelson & Ruback, Target Repurchases and Common Stock Returns, MIT Working Paper (June 1986).

At this point available data seem to suggest two interrelated phenomena for takeover defenses. First, when a firm employs takeover defenses before a tangible bid is on the table, the announcement of the defenses reduces the value of the firm's stock. The more effective the defense, the larger the reduction in value. Second, once a bidder appears, however, takeover defenses enable target firm shareholders to claim more value if the acquisition is successful. The defenses give target firm managers the ability to negotiate for a higher acquisition price. Moreover, some claim that if two bidders are vying for a target firm, defenses that reduce the value of the firm for one bidder and not the other may make target shareholders better off. See Berkovitch & Khanna, *How Target Shareholders Benefit from Value–Reducing Defensive Strategies in Takeovers,* 45 J.Fin. 137 (1990).

How do we reconcile the first phenomenon—defenses decrease the value of a firm—with the second—defenses increase the acquisition price to the benefit of target shareholders? There are, among others, three possible explanations. First, stock declines on the adoption of takeover defenses reflect the market's judgment that the advantages of a higher acquisition price are outweighed by the risk that target managers will misuse defenses to discourage bidders completely. Second, stock declines on the adoption of takeover defenses reflect the new disincentive that the defenses create for search efforts by all potential bidders. Although firms can use takeover defenses to increase acquisition prices, the defenses reduce returns on search and bidding costs for bidders. But see Berkovitch, Bradley & Khanna, *Tender Offer Auctions, Resistance Strategies, and Social Welfare,* 5 J.L., Econ. & Org. 395 (1989) (contracts between first bidders and a target can compensate first bidders for search and bidding costs.) Takeover defenses increase the probability that target managers will be able to defeat a pending offer or entice a second bidder to create an auction. Both possibilities increase the potential cost of any potential takeover, discourage first bidders at the margin, and thereby deny some target-firm shareholders a significant potential increase in the value of their shares by discouraging bidders from putting their firms "in play." Compare Berkovitch, Bradley & Khanna, Tender Offer Auctions, Resistance Strategies, and Social Welfare, 5 J.L., Econ. & Org. 395 (1989), with Schwartz, Defensive Tactics and Optimal Search, 5 J.L., Econ. & Org. 413 (1989). Third, stock price declines on the adoption of takeover defenses may not be effective estimates of the value of the defenses. If the important variable is the ability of target managers to use takeover defenses, then most of the effect of the availability of the defenses may be reflected in a firm's price before the defenses are actually adopted. If this third theory is correct, the more suitable test for the value of such defenses would be based on exogenous changes in the ability of firms to use the defenses—we should monitor stock price effects on changes in the law. See Kamma, Sreenivas,

Weintrop & Weir, *Investors' Perceptions of the Delaware Supreme Court Decision in Unocal v. Mesa,* 20 J.Fin.Econ. 419 (1988) (the Delaware Supreme Court decision in *Unocal v. Mesa Petroleum* generated negative wealth effects for Delaware firms).

SECTION 2. SHARK REPELLENT AMENDMENTS: WHEN IS AN AFFIRMATIVE VOTE NOT ENOUGH?

Subsection a. State Corporate Codes

Shark repellent amendments to a firm's charter must be approved by a shareholder vote. Common first-generation shark repellents are designed to retard the ability of someone with newly acquired voting power to take immediate control of a firm's board of directors. Thus the basic package of amendments retards an acquirer's ability to place a new majority on the board by (i) removing and replacing a majority of the sitting directors whose terms have not expired, (ii) electing a new majority when the terms of enough sitting directors have expired, or (iii) more than doubling the size of the board and packing it with a new majority.

The aim of these amendments is not to preserve existing control arrangements once an unwanted party has successfully obtained voting control but to deter unwanted parties from ever seeking to acquire control. In a stock acquisition the amendments generate significant additional financing costs for unwanted acquirers by delaying their ability to use or control target assets to repay acquisition financing. In a proxy contest the amendments dilute the effect of a winning proxy campaign at any one shareholders' meeting.

The following case illustrates the removal and vacancy portions of a traditional shark repellent package of charter amendments. It also illustrates that shark repellents must be carefully drafted to meet the specific requirements of the applicable state corporate code.

GEORGIA–PACIFIC CORP. v. GREAT NORTHERN NEKOOSA CORP.

United States District Court, District of Maine, 1990.
731 F.Supp. 38.

GENE CARTER, JUDGE:

This action arises out of Georgia–Pacific's attempt to take over Great Northern Nekoosa Corporation by a cash tender offer commenced on October 31, 1989. In its complaint Georgia–Pacific seeks declaratory and injunctive relief against certain impediments to Georgia–Pacific's offer, which has been twice rejected by Great Northern's Board of Directors. These allegedly unlawful impediments include the director removal and vacancy amendments to Great Northern's articles of incorporation and bylaws. At a shareholders' meeting, specially called for March 2, 1990, Georgia–Pacific hopes to oust Great Northern's

Board, which opposes the takeover, and to fill the vacancies thus created with its own candidates.

* * *

In May, 1984, Great Northern amended its articles of incorporation to include the following, so-called supermajority provision for removal of directors:

> Subject to the rights of the holders of any series of preferred stock then outstanding, any director, or the entire Board of Directors, may be removed from office at any time, but only by the affirmative vote of the holders of at least 75% of the voting power of all the shares of the Corporation entitled to vote generally in the election of directors, voting together as a single class.

* * *

Article IV, Section 2 of Great Northern's bylaws requires the same seventy-five percent vote in order to remove a director or directors.

The Maine Business Corporation Act ("MBCA") also specifically provides for removal of directors in section 707:

> 1. At a special meeting of shareholders called expressly for that purpose, the entire board of directors or any individual directors may be removed, with or without cause, by a vote of the shareholders as provided in this section.
>
> 2. ... [S]uch removal may be accomplished by the affirmative vote of ⅔ of the outstanding shares entitled to vote for directors. The articles of incorporation may provide that such removal may be accomplished by a lesser vote, but in no case by a vote of less than a majority of shares voting on the proposed removal.

13–A M.R.S.A. § 707. Georgia–Pacific contends that the removal provisions in Great Northern's articles of incorporation and bylaws are void because, in requiring a seventy-five percent majority to remove directors rather than the two-thirds majority set forth in § 707, they conflict with the MBCA. The MBCA makes clear that the bylaws and amendments to articles of incorporation may not be inconsistent with the MBCA or other law. See, e.g., 13–A M.R.S.A. §§ 402(1)(E)(3), 202(1)(E), 802(2)(0), and 601(1). It has also long been established in Maine that the powers of a corporation are derived from law and may not be enlarged by any act of the corporate body.

* * *

Great Northern's argument that section 611 of the MBCA expressly permits corporation to ignore the two-thirds majority requirement in section 707 is unpersuasive.... Section 611 establishes that a majority vote will authorize any corporate action, "[e]xcept to the extent that the vote of a greater number of shares ... is required by this Act or by the articles or bylaws...." It is clear to the Court that in framing section 611, the drafters meant to defer to section 707 and other sections like it which specify increased voting requirements for certain corporate acts. The general rule stated in section 611, referring as it does, in the alternative, to voting requirements set forth in the Act or the articles, cannot be read as providing license for corporation to bypass the Act's specific provisions when drafting their articles of incorporation and bylaws. The fact that the articles or bylaws may sometimes require a vote greater than a majority does not, when both the articles and the Act set voting requirements, establish the relationship between such provisions.[2] As discussed previously, however, the Act makes it very clear in other sections that the bylaws and articles of incorporation may not be inconsistent with the Act.

Even if section 611 could read as conflicting with section 707, Maine rules of statutory construction require that specific statutory provisions take precedence over general ones.... Section 611 provides the general voting requirements for corporate acts, but section 707 specifically addresses the voting requirements for removal of directors. Therefore, section 611 must yield to section 707 in circumstances dealing with the removal of directors.

The Great Northern articles of incorporation and bylaws also include sections providing that any vacancies in the Board of Directors "shall only be filled by a majority vote of the directors then in office though less than a quorum." The MBCA has one section dealing generally with vacancies in the board of directors and another dealing specifically with the filling of vacancies in the board when the directors have been removed at a shareholders' meeting. 13-A M.R.S.A. §§ 706(1)(B), 707(5). Section 706(1)(B) states: "Unless the articles of incorporation or the bylaws reserve to the shareholders the right to fill vacancies, any other vacancy, however occurring, in the board of directors may be filled by a majority of the remaining directors or by a sole remaining director." 13-A M.R.S.A. § 706(1)(B). The section purports to cover vacancies, "however occurring," but the next section of the statute expressly covers the filling of vacancies created by removal of directors at a shareholders' meeting: "If any or all directors are removed at such meeting of the shareholders, new directors may be elected at the same meeting without express notice being given of such election." 13-A M.R.S.A. § 707(5). As previously discussed, under Maine rules of statutory construction, general statutory provisions usually yield to specific ones.... Thus, election of new directors in cases of removal by the shareholders is governed by section 707(5).

---

2. Great Northern asserts that section 611 "makes it clear that (i) the requisite shareholder vote required for a particular matter is the highest vote required by the MBCA or the corporation and that (ii) a corporation may establish a higher voting standard than is otherwise established by the MBCA." Defendant's Memorandum of Law in Opposition to Georgia-Pacific's Motion at 9. There is no basis for this construction of the statute. Nowhere does it say that if there is a conflict between the articles and the Act, the one requiring the highest vote applies, and nowhere is there any abrogation of the oft-repeated rule that the articles and bylaws may not be inconsistent with the Act.

Section 707(5) permits the shareholders to elect new directors at the meeting. The provision in Great Northern's articles and bylaws mandating that vacancies in the board of directors resulting from removal from office be filled by a majority vote of the directors then in office is plainly inconsistent with the section 707(5).... Therefore, the vacancy-filling provisions of Great Northern's articles of incorporation and bylaws are void to the extent that they attempt to mandate an election procedure in cases of removal.

Section 707(5) of the MBCA expressly permits the election of new directors at a shareholders' meeting without prior notice, when the election is occasioned by the removal of directors at the same shareholders' meeting. To the extent that Article II, Section 9 of Great Northern's By-Laws attempts to impose a 90-day notice requirement for nomination of director candidates after removal of the directors at a meeting of the shareholders, it, too, is inconsistent with the Act and, therefore, void.

* * *

Questions

1. Since Great Northern Nekoosa's shareholders approved the shark repellent amendments, who is the court protecting? Can a firm require a supermajority vote for election of a director? For approval of a statutory merger? Why is removal of a director unique?

The larger question hidden in the case is why state corporate codes are not completely permissive. Why should a corporate code contain mandatory provisions that shareholders are unable to alter by charter amendment? See the materials in chapter 2.

2. Why do shareholders routinely pass shark repellent packages created by firm managers? Are they voting against their best interest or in their best interest in passing these amendments? If the former, what explains their behavior?

3. The traditional package of shark repellent amendments aimed at retarding a new controlling shareholder from placing nominees on the board has not proven to be an effective deterrent to unwanted stock acquisitions. Consider, for example, the effect of a staggered board charter amendment: one-third of the board is elected in any given year, and all directors have three-year terms. A successful acquirer must wait two years to elect a majority of the directors (unless the drafters of the shark repellent amendments have carelessly forgotten to tie up removal proceedings as well). Yet what is the position of the lame duck directors immediately after the acquisition? Do they owe a fiduciary duty to the new controlling shareholder? If the lame duck directors refuse to act at the request of the new controlling shareholder, do they risk personal litigation? How long do you expect the lame duck directors to voluntarily hold their positions?

A stronger type of shark repellent amendment, which was the foundation for second-generation state antitakeover amendments discussed in the previous chapter, consisted of fair price and supermajority provisions. Both provisions require that an acquirer of a set percentage of the target's stock cannot engage in second-stage merger or asset sale transactions with the target unless a supermajority, often over 85 percent, of the outstanding target shareholders approve. The fair price version exempts transactions from the supermajority vote if the price offered shareholders in the transaction meets certain criteria, usually indexed to the highest price paid by the acquirer for its initial block of target stock. Moreover, most of the provisions also contained a clause that prohibited firms from repealing them unless by supermajority vote. Most of the more sophisticated provisions came to contain a "board-out" clause, empowering a target board to waive the provision for a specific acquirer before it had made the triggering acquisition. If the provisions did not contain a board-out clause, what was the effect of the provisions on the firm?

4. The Great Northern Nekoosa Corporation takeover represents the latest method of mounting a hostile takeover when the target is protected by state antitakeover legislation and poison pill plans. The bidder makes its offer (careful not to trigger any poison pill state legislation) and then moves to oust the board with a follow-up proxy contest. A target board responds by passing shark repellent amendments, some of which are legal and, as we see in the case, some of which may be outside the boundaries of a state corporate code. The shark repellent amendments have not proven to be effective, however. Can a target firm erect more-potent defenses? In this regard, consider the following case:

STAHL v. APPLE BANCORP. INC.
Court of Chancery of Delaware, 1990.
579 A.2d 1115.

Opinion of ALLEN, CHANCELLOR.

* * * Upon effectuation of the reorganization in September 1989, Stahl became the owner of approximately 20% of the then outstanding shares of Bancorp. By November 7, 1989, he owned approximately 30.3% of the outstanding Bancorp shares. As Stahl's proportionate share of Bancorp stock rose above 20%, Bancorp's financial advisor, and a large stockholder, each expressed concern to Mr. McDougal that Stahl might obtain control of the company without paying a control premium.

On November 15, 1989, the company's board of directors met to consider what action, if any, should be taken with respect to Stahl's stock accumulation. Two proposals were suggested: negotiating a standstill agreement with Stahl and adopting a stock purchase rights plan (a "rights plan"). The board authorized the preparation of the rights plan.

* * *

On November 17, the board adopted the rights plan. Stahl responded on November 22, 1989, by delivering to the company a proposal to be submitted to a vote at the next annual meeting of stockholders, calling for an amendment to the company's bylaws increasing the number of directors of the company from 12 to 21. In the proposal Stahl nominated 13 individuals (including himself) to be named to the board if his bylaw proposal were approved.[3] He nominated four individuals to be elected if his bylaw proposal were defeated. Later, Stahl stated in a Schedule 13D filing that he would solicit proxies in favor of his proposal and for the election of his nominees to the board. That filing also stated that, if elected, Stahl intended to recommend to the full board that the rights under the rights plan be redeemed and that the board evaluate the performance of management and make any changes it deemed necessary to improve overall management performance.

On March 19, 1990 the board fixed April 17, 1990 as the record date for determining the shareholders entitled to vote at the company's 1990 annual meeting. While no date for the annual meeting was fixed, it was anticipated that the meeting would be held in May 1990. Section 213 of the Delaware General Corporation Law provides that the record date for an annual meeting shall not be less than 10 or more than 60 days before the date the meeting is held. Thus, the latest date at which an annual meeting could be held with an April 17 record date would be June 16.

On March 28, 1990, Stahl commenced a tender offer to purchase any and all outstanding shares of common stock of the company at $38 cash per share.[4] The offer is conditioned upon the expansion of the company's board of directors to 21 members and the election of Stahl's 13 nominees to serve on the board. The offer is also conditioned upon the stock purchase rights being redeemed or Stahl otherwise being satisfied that the rights are invalid.

* * *

On April 9 and 10, the company's board of directors held a special meeting. The company's proxy solicitor informed the board that it was likely if the board did not present the stockholders with an economic alternative to Stahl's offer that Stahl would prevail in a proxy fight by a significant margin. The company received from its financial advisors a written opinion that Stahl's offer, which represented a 17% premium over the prior market price, was inadequate and unfair to the stockholders from a financial point of view. The financial advisors advised the board that greater value for the stockholders could be obtained through certain alternative strategies. They further advised the board that adequate exploration of those alternatives would require more time than was available before the meeting, if the record date stood at April 17.

---

3. Apple has a staggered board. Under the company's certificate of incorporation and bylaws, only 4 seats are open for election this year. Thus, in order for Stahl to gain majority control of the board, the bylaw proposal must be approved.

4. The closing market price of Bancorp stock on March 27, 1990 was $32¼ (per share). On May 8, 1990, the shares closed at $43⅛.

The board resolved to recommend to Bancorp's stockholders that they reject Stahl's offer. It further resolved to withdraw the April 17 record date in order to allow itself more time to pursue alternatives to the Stahl offer. The directors decided that "it is not in the best interest of the company and its stockholders to hold the annual meeting until the company has had a fair opportunity to explore and pursue alternatives to the Stahl offer which would enable the company to maximize stockholder value." These alternatives included the sale of the company or the merger of the company with another financial institution.

* * *

Plaintiff contends that the deferral of the annual meeting and the rescission of the record date together constitutes a direct and intended interference with the exercise of the shareholders' right of franchise. It is said that to be sustained this action requires the directors to establish a compelling justification, which, plaintiff asserts, defendants cannot do. Plaintiff invokes the authority of a series of cases in support of his position: *e.g., Aprahamian v. HBO & Co.,* Del.Ch., 531 A.2d 1204 (1987); *Blasius Industries, Inc. v. Atlas Corp.,* Del.Ch., 564 A.2d 651 (1988); *Gintel v. Xtra Corp.,* Del.Ch., C.A. No. 11422, Allen, C. (February 27, 1990) (oral ruling).

* * *

[I]n *Blasius* and in *Aprahamian* this court held that action designed primarily to impede the effective exercise of the franchise is not evaluated under the business form of review:

> Action designed principally to interfere with the effectiveness of a vote inevitably involves a conflict between the board and a shareholder majority. Judicial review of such action involves a determination of the legal and equitable obligations of an agent towards his principal. This is not, in my opinion, a question that a court may leave to the agent finally to decide so long as he does so honestly and competently; that is, it may not be left to the agent's business judgment.

Blasius, 564 A.2d at 660. *See also Aprahamian,* 531 A.2d at 1207 ("The business judgment rule ... does not confer any presumption of propriety on the acts of the directors in postponing the annual meeting.") * * * *Blasius* did, however, go on to reject the notion of *per se* invalidity of action taken to interfere with the effective exercise of the corporate franchise; it admitted the possibility that in some circumstances such action might be consistent with the directors equitable obligations. It was suggested, however, that such circumstances would have to constitute "compelling justification," given the central role of the stockholder franchise.

Thus, *Blasius'* reference to "compelling justification" reflects only the high value that the prior cases had placed upon the exercise of voting rights and the inherently particularized and contextual nature of any inquiry concerning fiduciary duties. Neither it nor *Aprahamian* represent new law.

Thus the fundamental question when the motion is evaluated under these cases may be expressed as whether the defendants have exercised corporate power inequitably. In answering that question, it is necessary to ask, in the context of this case, whether they have taken action for the purpose of impairing or impeding the effective exercise of the corporate franchise and, if they have, whether the special circumstances are present (compelling justification) warranting such an unusual step.

In my opinion one employing this method of analysis need not inquire into the question of justification in this instance, for I cannot conclude that defendants have taken action for the primary purpose of impairing or impeding the effective exercise of the corporate franchise. I reach this conclusion understanding that the Bancorp board had planned to call the annual meeting of stockholders for May and that it changed that plan in response to the risk that the combination of the proposed Stahl proxy contest and tender offer would result in a change in board control and the sale of the company.

For these purposes I do not accept that the Stahl tender offer, conditioned on the outcome of a stockholder vote, would have a coercive effect on that vote, nor do I rest my opinion on the ground that a board may always postpone a meeting for a substantial period on the eve of an annual meeting if it concludes that it will lose a proxy contest and thus decides to authorize a significant new development, such as the sale of the company.[8]

Rather, I place my opinion on the narrow ground that the action of deferring this company's annual meeting where no meeting date has yet been set and no proxies even solicited does not impair or impede the effective exercise of the franchise to any extent. To speak of the effective exercise of the franchise is to imply certain assumptions concerning the structure and mechanism that define the vote and govern its exercise. Shares are voted at meetings; meetings are generally called as fixed in bylaws. While the refusal to call a shareholder meeting when the board is not obligated to do so might under some imaginable circumstances breach a fiduciary duty, such a decision does not itself constitute an impairment of the exercise of the franchise that sparked the close judicial scrutiny of *Schnell, Blasius,* etc.

In no sense can the decision not to call a meeting be likened to kinds of board action found to have constituted inequitable conduct relating to the vote. In each of these franchise cases the effect of the board action—to advance (*Schnell*) or defer (*Aprahamian*) a meeting; to adopt a bylaw (*Lerman*); or to fill board vacancies (*Blasius*)—was practically to preclude effective stockholder action (*Schnell, Blasius, Lerman*) or to snatch victory from an insurgent slate on the eve of the

---

8. *See Gintel v. Xtra Corp.,* Del.Ch., C.A. No. 11422, Allen, C. (February 27, 1990) (oral ruling) (board required to hold annual meeting close to the time set where, on the eve of the meeting, the board—upon receiving advice that it would lose the election—declared that the meeting would be postponed in order that it might find a buyer for and negotiate a sale of the company).

noticed meeting (*Aprahamian*). Here the election process will go forward at a time consistent with the company's bylaws and with Section 211 of our corporation law. Defendant's decision does not preclude plaintiff or any other Bancorp shareholder from effectively exercising his vote, nor have proxies been collected that only await imminent counting. Plaintiff has no legal right to compel the holding of the company's annual meeting under Section 211(c) of the Delaware General Corporation Law, nor does he, in my opinion, have a right in equity to require the board to call a meeting now.

* * *

Thus, since I do not see the board's decision to defer the annual meeting to a later time in conformity with the company's bylaws and Section 211 as a decision that does threaten the legitimacy of the electoral process, I conclude that the propriety of that decision is to be measured by the permissive business judgment form of review. * * * This determination would ordinarily end the matter, practically speaking.

It is the case, however, that the decision to rescind the April 17 record date and defer the planned annual meeting was taken in response to the threat of losing a prospective proxy contest and the sale of the company that would, in these circumstances, result. It thus was a decision that arguably was taken within that zone in which the threat recognized by *Unocal* (493 A.2d at 954) is present. Thus, I will assume for purposes of this motion that the intermediate form of business judgment review identified in *Unocal* is called for here.

* * * Here I will look only to *Unocal's* core inquiry: did the directors reasonably perceive a threat to a valid corporate or shareholder interest when they made the decision under review, and is the board's response a reasonable one in relation to that threat. I conclude both core elements of the *Unocal* test are satisfied here.

In so concluding I do not accept the notion that the prospect that the shareholders might vote differently than the board recommends can alone constitute any threat to a corporate interest. * * *

But the Bancorp board did not simply face a prospective proxy contest. Rather it faced a special situation in which the proxy contest was tied to a tender offer. * * * Where the shareholders are in effect to be asked to decide whether the company should be sold in a given transaction, the board may properly recognize the shareholders need for information, other than the market prices of their stock, relevant to that decision. The disaggregated shareholders are incapable of obtaining appropriate information on alternatives other than the Stahl proposal and the market for their stock; only the board can accomplish that task. Thus, the absence of relevant information, in my opinion, may reasonably be seen as posing a threat to the vote of the Bancorp shareholders in the particular context presented.

The essence of the *Unocal* form of review is a judicial assessment of the proportionality of a response to a threat. Here the response to the threat was extremely mild. Thus, in this instance one need not focus finely on how great was the threat posed by the prospect of an early vote, in order to conclude that the board's response in delaying the annual meeting to a later time (consistent with the company's bylaws and Section 211) was reasonable under *Unocal*. To delay a meeting once called would constitute a more substantial question of disproportionality. As one moves closer to a meeting date and attempts to postpone a meeting would likely require a greater and greater showing of threat in order to justify interfering with the conclusion of an election contest. Thus, in this way, the "enhanced" business judgment form of review of *Unocal* and the non-business judgment review of *Schnell, Condec, Aprahamian,* and *Blasius* come in the context of action arguably affecting the voting process, to resemble each other. * * * This, of course, is not surprising. What is new in *Unocal* —judicial review of board decisions under an "objective" standard—is old in cases dealing with explicitly self-interested transactions or actions designed to affect the vote.

* * *

Subsection b. NYSE Restrictions on Charter Amendments That Restrict the Voting Rights of Outstanding Stock

It did not take long for target managers and their advisers to decide that a traditional shark repellent package of amendments would not stem the tide of unwanted acquirers, so they looked for stronger medicine. The most obvious new strategy was to change the voting power of the outstanding common stock. There were several ways to limit the voting power of outstanding stock and several ways to effect the limitation.

The firm could, for example, cap the voting power of any one shareholder, regardless of the number of shares held, or could restrict the voting power of shares for three years after any transfer. The firm could either amend its articles of incorporate to limit the voting rights of outstanding shares or issue new supervoting shares with tenure restrictions (see the *Unilever* case, supra) as stock dividends on the existing common. Capping voting power based on the number of shares held or the length of time the shares were held, however, severely disadvantaged existing control groups. What are the disadvantages?

The technique most favored by target managers was the creation of two classes of stock. One class would have the predominant equity interest in the firm—holders would receive full dividends and have full rights on liquidation—but would also have limited voting rights. The second class would have very limited equitable rights—holders would receive little or no portion of any dividend or liquidation distributions—but would also have supervoting rights. The control group would hold some of the first class and all of the second class. By mid-1989, 7.4

percent of our largest 1,440 public companies had adopted dual-class capitalization plans.

There are two methods of implementing a two-tier voting stock plan. First, the firm can amend its articles of incorporation to limit the rights of outstanding shares and authorize the issuance of the new supervoting shares, which are sold or distributed exclusively to insiders. Second, the firm can amend its articles of incorporation to authorize the issuance of nonvoting or limited-voting shares, if the articles did not do so already, and then distribute the new nonvoting shares through a self-tender offer, exchanging the new shares for the outstanding voting shares. Insiders would not participate in the exchange and would retain the voting shares.

The New York Stock Exchange had a long-standing rule that required listed companies to provide one vote per share of common stock. The rule stopped our largest companies from implementing voting plans as takeover defenses. In 1986, however, under pressure from listed firms that wanted to adopt such plans and threatened to jump to a smaller rival stock exchange that allowed such plans, the American Stock Exchange, the NYSE petitioned the Securities and Exchange Commission to relax the one-vote-one-share rule. The SEC, after a failed round of negotiations in which it attempted to get all the national exchanges to adopt a one-vote-one-share rule, promulgated rule 19c–4, barring national securities exchanges and national securities associations from listing stock of a corporation that had taken any corporate action "with the effect of nullifying, restricting or disparately reducing the per share voting rights of [existing common shareholders]." Please read the rule in your statutory supplement.

The NYSE, Amex, and NASDAQ promptly adopted a version of the SEC rule. The United States Court of Appeals for the District of Columbia held, however, that the SEC did not have the power to promulgate the rule. Business Roundtable v. SEC, 905 F.2d 406 (D.C. Cir.1990). The case does not affect the ability of the national exchanges to adopt such a rule voluntarily. At present the NYSE still has the rule in its listing requirements. NYSE Listed Company Manual Sec. 313.00 (1990). It is unclear whether the exchange will revoke its adoption of the rule. The SEC release discussing the merits of its rule is excerpted below.

EXCHANGE ACT RELEASE NOS. 25,891 & 25,891A, JULY 7 AND 13, 1988

Fed.Sec.L.Rep. (CCH) ¶ 84,247.

* * *

The Commission recognizes that under state law, disparate voting rights plans generally are permitted subject to shareholder approval. The Commission also recognizes, however, that collective action problems may make defeating an issuer recapitalization proposal extremely difficult.[73] Many commentators in both the December and July hearings, including institutional investors, individual investors, and law professors, testified extensively about the difficulties involved in shareholders acting together in their collective best interest. Frequently, a disparate voting rights plan is presented to shareholders in a form, such as an offer to exchange higher vote stock for lower vote stock with a dividend sweetener, that provides shareholders with an incentive to accept less than voting rights stock rather than oppose the recapitalization, although, acting collectively, shareholders as a group might prefer to retain their voting rights and reject the sweetener offered by management. The coercive nature of some disparate voting rights plans may also be exacerbated by management's ability to set the proxy agenda and use corporate funds to lobby shareholders in favor of its proposal. The Commission also has heard testimony from institutional investors describing the pressure placed on managers of corporate pension plans during the shareholder voting process.

Although the Commission does not believe that shareholders invariably are powerless to defeat an issuer-sponsored proposal to recapitalize, the Commission does believe that, because of the forces cited above, the shareholder voting process is not fully effective in preventing the adoption of disparate voting rights plans that disenfranchise shareholders. The Commission believes that it is preferable for a company's insiders wishing to gain voting control to do so through a repurchase of shares, in which such repurchase is subject to market discipline and judicial review regarding state corporate fiduciary requirements.

Moreover, the Commission is concerned about the rights of minority shareholders, who are permanently disenfranchised by a proposal against which they voted. While the shareholder voting mechanism may be of limited effectiveness in protecting against disenfranchisement by management, it nonetheless has value in ensuring management accountability. For example, shareholders have occasionally elected dissidents in proxy contests for control of a company's Board of Directors. Moreover, the potential that shareholders will vote against management or at least amass a sufficient opposition vote to embarrass the company contributes to ongoing accountability.

* * *

The Commission's Office of Chief Economist ("OCE"), now the Office of Economic Analysis, in an update to its initial study of the wealth effects of disparate voting rights plans, did find significant

73. * * *
Professor Weiss referred to the "substantial body of literature" explaining why the shareholder vote is not always an accurate representation of shareholder preference. For example, Professor Weiss cited the "rational apathy" problem, which leads shareholders to support management proposals because the expected cost to any one shareholder of carefully evaluating these proposals will greatly exceed any potential benefit to the shareholder. Second, Professor Weiss outlined the "free rider" problem, which acknowledged that the typical shareholder will not make the effort to evaluate a management-sponsored proposal, but will rely on other shareholders to do that and "free ride" on their efforts.

negative wealth effects in connection with such recapitalizations. In particular, the OCE Update found that negative price effects were concentrated in companies that had recapitalized after the NYSE announced its moratorium on enforcing its one share, one vote rule. Importantly, the OCE Update also noted that the post-moratorium firms were characterized by substantially lower insider holdings and substantially higher institutional holdings, as compared to companies that had recapitalized prior to the NYSE moratorium.

* * *

"Time Phased" Voting

The Rule presumes to prohibit corporate action to impose any restriction on voting power of shares based on the length of time the shareholder has held the stock. * * * Those plans usually involve a recapitalization in which all shareholders at the time of the recapitalization receive multiple votes per share for their holdings. Any investor that purchases stock subsequent to the commencement of the plan receives one vote per share unless and until that investor holds the stock for a stated period of time (usually three or four years). * * * As outside shareholders sell their high vote shares which converts them to low vote shares, insiders, by holding their shares, gain voting control from the outside shareholders. * * *

"Capped" Voting Plans

The Rule also presumes to prohibit, with one exception, corporate action to impose any limitation on the voting power of shares based on the number of shares owned. So-called capped voting plans generally are designed to insulate management from the threat of a hostile takeover by restricting the ability of the potential acquiror to obtain voting control. * * * By instituting a capped voting plan shareholders who purchase shares in excess of the triggering amount are disenfranchised of the voting rights for the excess shares.

Super Voting Stock Distributions

* * * The Rule then essentially presumes to prohibit all issuances of super voting stock. * * * Super voting stock usually is employed in recapitalizations in the following manner: super voting stock is issued as a stock dividend with transfer restrictions that require the stock to be converted into lower voting stock if sold. As a result, insiders will be able to gain voting control of the company by holding the super voting stock received as a dividend, while outside shareholders are forced by the transfer restriction to convert their super voting stock to limited voting stock when they want to sell.

* * *

Exchange Offers

* * * These recapitalizations can be structured as a one-time opportunity to receive less than full voting rights stock in exchange for shares of the existing class of common stock. For example, a company will issue a new class of lower voting stock with a higher dividend, and make the existing voting stock convertible into the lower voting, higher dividend stock. * * *

In these transactions, shareholders will face the choice of surrendering their voting control and receiving a small economic benefit (the dividend sweetener), or bypassing the exchange offer and maintaining the greater voting stock. The exchange offer is coercive because those shareholders wishing to hold the greater voting stock to defeat the plan would be taking a substantial risk that an insufficient number of outside shareholders will do likewise and majority voting control will shift to insiders. Accordingly, such shareholders may be "coerced" individually to opt for lower voting stock with a dividend sweetener to avoid holding ineffective full voting stock, without any dividend benefit.

* * *

Commentators also have questioned the effect of Rule 19c–4 on tender offer defensive shareholder rights plans.[126] * * *

The Commission has determined that such plans generally should not be covered by the Rule. As with any recapitalization or disparate voting rights plan, the focus should be placed upon the effect of the plan on the voting rights of existing shareholders. It is important, therefore, to note that unlike transactions prohibited by the Rule, shareholder rights plans are not adopted to restructure a corporation by disenfranchising an existing class or classes of shareholders in order to solidify the voting power of management or a control group. Rather, these plans are adopted by corporations to discourage tender offers, or to encourage the development of an auction for the company resulting in shareholders receiving a higher price for their stock. In fact such plans are adopted with the intent that they will never be implemented.[128]

---

126. * * *

Predominantly, these inquiries questioned the applicability of the Rule to so-called flip-in shareholder rights plans. Under certain flip-in plans, rights or warrants are attached to the common stock of a company, entitling the holder, upon the right being triggered, to buy additional shares of common stock at a price substantially below market value. These rights generally are redeemable at any time by the Board of Directors of the company prior to being triggered and exercised. The rights, however, are not exercisable until the occurrence of a so-called triggering event, usually the acquisition of a specified percentage of the company's stock by a hostile bidder or the commencement of a tender offer. Upon the occurrence of the triggering event, all shareholders except the potential acquiror may then purchase shares at below market value, crippling the takeover effort by the acquiror.

128. The Commission emphasizes, however, that its position on anti-takeover shareholder rights plans should not be misconstrued as a blanket exception for all restructurings adopted under the guise of a "poison pill." If a corporation develops an anti-takeover device designed specifically to transfer voting control from existing shareholders to insiders, or a group favored by insiders, it may violate Rule 19c–4 irrespective of the fact that it is termed a "poison pill." The Commission notes that several firms have adopted "poison pills" which would affect voting rights of a large purchaser of the company's stock. *See, e.g., Asarco, Inc. v. MRH Holmes A Court,* 611 F.Supp. 468 (D.N.J.1985). * * *

Commentators also questioned the effect Rule 19c–4 would have on the use of lock-ups, in which newly issued shares or options to buy additional shares, often at a discount, are issued to another party. * * * The Commission believes that the fairness of the compensation paid for voting stock generally should be determined by state law, with the addition of possible shareholder voting requirements imposed by SRO rules.[130]

* * *

COMMISSIONER GRUNDFEST, Concurring:

* * *

Rule 19c–4 also does not prohibit any corporation from adopting any capital structure. Corporations can continue to issue any number of classes of stock, some with little or no voting power and others with substantial or even dominant control.[4] The rule is, instead, carefully crafted to address concerns about the process by which disenfranchisement occurs. The transactions that most consistently cause concern involve exchange offers, dividends, or other distributions that dramatically increase the voting power of a relatively small, well defined group of stockholders at the expense of a larger group of public stockholders.

* * *

While every electoral process is potentially subject to a collective action problem, there are sound reasons for the Commission to focus its concern on decisions that can lead to disenfranchisement. All voting choices fall into one of two categories: they are either "constitutional" or "parliamentary." A constitutional choice involves a decision about how other decisions will be made. A parliamentary choice involves the application to a particular problem of a decision rule previously determined by a constitutional choice. An election that proposes to disenfranchise certain shareholders is a constitutional choice because it permanently alters the process by which later corporate decisions are made.

---

130. For example, Section 312 of the NYSE's Listed Company Manual requires shareholder approval where additional issuances of stock in an acquisition would increase the outstanding common stock by 18½% or more. See also Section 712 of the Amex Company Guide. * * *

4. For example, suppose a corporation with a twenty percent shareholder seeks to concentrate voting powers in that shareholder. It can achieve that result by offering to repurchase the eighty percent of its outstanding voting shares held by the public and raising the necessary capital through the issuance of nonvoting shares. If control in the hands of the twenty percent shareholder truly enhances the corporation's value, this transaction will be financially feasible. If, however, the primary effect of the transaction is to transfer wealth from public shareholders to the dominant shareholder, then the transaction may be more difficult to finance. Further, if a corporation wants to raise additional equity capital without diluting the voting control of existing shareholders, Rule 19c–4 allows the issuance and sale of nonvoting shares. The market mechanism, which is a substitute for the electoral mechanism generally relied upon in transactions that raise disenfranchisement concerns, thus acts as a filter allowing beneficial recapitalizations and financings to continue while deterring transactions that tend primarily to disenfranchise and transfer wealth from public to inside shareholders without competitive compensation. * * *

Constitutional choices are legitimately subject to greater scrutiny than parliamentary choices and are rationally subject to more stringent safeguards. These safeguards can include supermajority requirements or absolute prohibitions on disenfranchisements. They can also include requirements such as Rule 19c–4 that channel constitutional decisions through mechanisms less susceptible to collective choice problems. Indeed, the greater scrutiny rationally accorded to constitutional choices provides a sound and consistent rationale for the Commission's decision at least initially to focus its attention on the disenfranchisement process.

* * *

More fundamentally, however, it should be recognized that Rule 19c–4 deals with one of the more intricate and difficult areas in all the social sciences: the problem of social choice. The entire field is rife with paradoxes, contradictions, and impossibility theorems.[15] Indeed, when subject to close scrutiny, even the simple majority voting procedure that we often take for granted as a fair and generally accepted method of social decisionmaking is revealed to be full of potential contradictions that can make it appear arbitrary and capricious. Accordingly, it is neither reasonable nor possible to hold Rule 19c–4 to a standard that requires perfect logical consistency in all circumstances and all applications. No voting rule or rule regulating voting behavior can achieve that result, and Rule 19c–4 should not be held to such an unattainable standard. The rule should, instead, be understood for what it is: an effort to craft a carefully targeted standard that operates prospectively to substitute market mechanisms for voting processes in situations that involve a substantial danger of collective action problems and that raise disenfranchisement concerns of constitutional magnitude.

* * *

Questions

1. Does the Securities and Exchange Commission rule apply to recapitalizations in which the shareholders vote to amend the firm's articles of incorporation to change the rights and privileges of outstanding stock? If shareholders are unable to vote their interests effectively against a two-tier voting stock recapitalization plan, why are they able to vote their interests on other acquisition questions, such as approving a statutory merger between two independent firms or approving a shark repellent amendment requiring a supermajority vote for a "back-end" merger with an unap-

---

15. The most famous of these is Arrow's impossibility theorem which demonstrates, among other things, that no voting rule satisfies a set of four seemingly innocuous and desirable conditions. See K.J. Arrow, *Social Classic and Individual Values* (1963); A.K. Sen, *Social Choice and Justice: A Review Article*, 23 J.Econ.Lit. 1764 (1985). For other discussions of the difficulties encountered in this area see, e.g., Ordeshook, *supra* note 7, at 65–71 (the paradoxes of voting) and A.K. Sen, *Collective Choice and Social Welfare* (1970).

proved acquirer? Should a shareholder vote to approve a poison pill plan be respected?

2. Does the SEC rule prohibit all supervoting poison pill plans? See *Unilever Acquisition Corp.*, infra. In *Unilever* the firm issued supervoting stock as a stock dividend. Does the rule prohibit self-tender offers in which a firm exchanges supervoting stock for its common stock? In which a firm exchanges debt securities for its common stock?

Does the rule affect state control share act statutes? In a state that does not have a control share act, can a firm amend its charter to implement protections that mimic a control share act?

Does the "collective action" problem that worries Commissioner Grundfest apply equally to two-tier voting stock plans that are put in by shareholder vote and those that are the result of stock dividends or exchange offers?

3. Can a firm issue to its officers as compensation stock that, although otherwise identical to the common in all respects, enables them to vote as a class on all reorganizations, statutory mergers, and asset sales?

4. Can a clever lawyer avoid the SEC rule with a complex spin-off? Consider whether the rule would, by itself, prohibit the following recapitalization: A firm drops down its assets into two wholly owned corporate subsidiaries. One of the subsidiaries, A, contains the firm's most valuable and irreplaceable assets; the other, B, contains the remainder of the firm's working operations. A's assets and B's assets are interrelated in that both are needed to produce the firm's ultimate product. The firm then distributes the stock of A predominantly to insiders and the stock of B to all other shareholders. See, e.g., Robert M. Bass Group v. Evans, 552 A.2d 1227 (Del.Ch.1988) (reorganization rejected as a breach of the manager's fiduciary duty).

SECTION 3. POISON PILL PLANS: THE POWER OF THE BOARD TO ADOPT TAKEOVER DEFENSES WITHOUT RESORT TO SHAREHOLDER RATIFICATION

MORAN v. HOUSEHOLD INTERNATIONAL, INC.

Supreme Court of Delaware, 1985.
500 A.2d 1346.

MCNEILLY, JUSTICE:

* * *

This case presents to this Court for review the most recent defensive mechanism in the arsenal of corporate takeover weaponry—the Preferred Share Purchase Rights Plan ("Rights Plan" or "Plan"). The validity of this mechanism has attracted national attention. *Amici curiae* briefs have been filed in support of appellants by the Security and Exchange Commission ("SEC")[1] and the Investment Company

---

1. The SEC split 3–2 on whether to intervene in this case. The two dissenting Commissioners have publicly disagreed

Institute. An *amicus curiae* brief has been filed in support of appellees ("Household") by the United Food and Commercial Workers International Union.

* * *

On August 14, 1984, the Board of Directors of Household International, Inc. adopted the Rights Plan by a fourteen to two vote.[2] The intricacies of the Rights Plan are contained in a 48–page document entitled "Rights Agreement". Basically, the Plan provides that Household common stockholders are entitled to the issuance of one Right per common share under certain triggering conditions. There are two triggering events that can activate the Rights. The first is the announcement of a tender offer for 30 percent of Household's shares ("30% trigger") and the second is the acquisition of 20 percent of Household's shares by any single entity or group ("20% trigger").

If an announcement of a tender offer for 30 percent of Household's shares is made, the Rights are issued and are immediately exercisable to purchase $1/100$ share of new preferred stock for $100 and are redeemable by the Board for $.50 per Right. If 20 percent of Household's shares are acquired by anyone, the Rights are issued and become non-redeemable and are exercisable to purchase $1/100$ of a share of preferred. If a Right is not exercised for preferred, and thereafter, a merger or consolidation occurs, the Rights holder can exercise each Right to purchase $200 of the common stock of the tender offeror for $100. This "flip-over" provision of the Rights Plan is at the heart of this controversy.

* * *

Household did not adopt its Rights Plan during a battle with a corporate raider, but as a preventive mechanism to ward off future advances. The Vice–Chancellor found that as early as February 1984, Household's management became concerned about the company's vulnerability as a takeover target and began considering amending its charter to render a takeover more difficult. After considering the matter, Household decided not to pursue a fair price amendment.[3]

In the meantime, appellant Moran, one of Household's own Directors and also Chairman of the Dyson–Kissner–Moran Corporation, ("D–K–M") which is the largest single stockholder of Household, began discussions concerning a possible leveraged buy-out of Household by D–K–M. D–K–M's financial studies showed that Household's stock was significantly undervalued in relation to the company's break-up value.

with the other three as to the merits of the Rights Plan. * * *

2. Household's Board has ten outside directors and six who are members of management. Messrs. Moran (appellant) and Whitehead voted against the Plan. The record reflects that Whitehead voted against the Plan not on its substance but because he thought it was novel and would bring unwanted publicity to Household.

3. A fair price amendment to a corporate charter generally requires supermajority approval for certain business combinations and sets minimum price criteria for mergers. *Moran,* 490 A.2d at 1064, n. 1.

It is uncontradicted that Moran's suggestion of a leveraged buy-out never progressed beyond the discussion stage.

Concerned about Household's vulnerability to a raider in light of the current takeover climate, Household secured the services of Wachtell, Lipton, Rosen and Katz ("Wachtell, Lipton") and Goldman, Sachs & Co. ("Goldman, Sachs") to formulate a takeover policy for recommendation to the Household Board at its August 14 meeting.

* * *

Representatives of Wachtell, Lipton and Goldman, Sachs attended the August 14 meeting. The minutes reflect that Mr. Lipton explained to the Board that his recommendation of the Plan was based on his understanding that the Board was concerned about the increasing frequency of "bust-up"[4] takeovers, the increasing takeover activity in the financial service industry, such as Leucadia's attempt to take over Arco, and the possible adverse effect this type of activity could have on employees and others concerned with and vital to the continuing successful operation of Household even in the absence of any actual bust-up takeover attempt. Against this factual background, the Plan was approved.

Thereafter, Moran and the company of which he is Chairman, D–K–M, filed this suit.

* * *

The primary issue here is the applicability of the business judgment rule as the standard by which the adoption of the Rights Plan should be reviewed. Much of this issue has been decided by our recent decision in *Unocal Corp. v. Mesa Petroleum Co.*, Del.Supr., 493 A.2d 946 (1985). In *Unocal*, we applied the business judgment rule to analyze Unocal's discriminatory self-tender. We explained:

> When a board addresses a pending takeover bid it has an obligation to determine whether the offer is in the best interests of the corporation and its shareholders. In that respect a board's duty is no different from any other responsibility it shoulders, and its decisions should be no less entitled to the respect they otherwise would be accorded in the realm of business judgment.

Id. at 954 (citation and footnote omitted).

* * *

Pre-planning for the contingency of a hostile takeover might reduce the risk that, under the pressure of a takeover bid, management will fail to exercise reasonable judgment. Therefore, in reviewing a pre-planned defensive mechanism it seems even more appropriate to apply the business judgment rule.

* * *

---

4. "Bust-up" takeover generally refers to a situation in which one seeks to finance an acquisition by selling off pieces of the acquired company.

While appellants contend that no provision of the Delaware General Corporation Law authorizes the Rights Plan, Household contends that the Rights Plan was issued pursuant to 8 *Del.C.* §§ 151(g) and 157. It explains that the Rights are authorized by § 157 [7] and the issue of preferred stock underlying the Rights is authorized by § 151.[8] Appellants respond by making several attacks upon the authority to issue the Rights pursuant to § 157.

Appellants begin by contending that § 157 cannot authorize the Rights Plan since § 157 has never served the purpose of authorizing a takeover defense. Appellants contend that § 157 is a corporate financing statute, and that nothing in its legislative history suggests a purpose that has anything to do with corporate control or a takeover defense. Appellants are unable to demonstrate that the legislature, in its adoption of § 157, meant to limit the applicability of § 157 to only the issuance of Rights for the purposes of corporate financing. Without such affirmative evidence, we decline to impose such a limitation upon the section that the legislature has not.

* * *

Secondly, appellants contend that § 157 does not authorize the issuance of sham rights such as the Rights Plan. They contend that the Rights were designed never to be exercised, and that the Plan has no economic value. In addition, they contend the preferred stock made subject to the Rights is also illusory, citing *Telvest, Inc. v. Olson*, Del.Ch., C.A. No. 5798, Brown, V.C. (March 8, 1979).

Appellants' sham contention fails in both regards. As to the Rights, they can and will be exercised upon the happening of a triggering mechanism, as we have observed during the current struggle of Sir James Goldsmith to take control of Crown Zellerbach. *See* Wall Street Journal, July 26, 1985, at 3, 12. As to the preferred shares, we agree with the Court of Chancery that they are distinguishable from sham securities invalidated in *Telvest, supra*. The Household pre-

---

7. The power to issue rights to purchase shares is conferred by 8 *Del.C.* § 157 which provides in relevant part:

Subject to any provisions in the certificate of incorporation, every corporation may create and issue, whether or not in connection with the issue and sale of any shares of stock or other securities of the corporation, rights or options entitling the holders thereof to purchase from the corporation any shares of its capital stock of any class or classes, such rights or options to be evidenced by or in such instrument or instruments as shall be approved by the board of directors.

8. 8 *Del.C.* § 151(g) provides in relevant part:

When any corporation desires to issue any shares of stock of any class or of any series of any class of which the voting powers, designations, preferences and relative, participating, optional or other rights, if any, or the qualifications, limitations or restrictions thereof, if any, shall not have been set forth in the certificate of incorporation or in any amendment thereto but shall be provided for in a resolution or resolutions adopted by the board of directors pursuant to authority expressly vested in it by the provisions of the certificate of incorporation or any amendment thereto, a certificate setting forth a copy of such resolution or resolutions and the number of shares of stock of such class or series shall be executed, acknowledged, filed, recorded, and shall become effective, in accordance with § 103 of this title.

ferred, issuable upon the happening of a triggering event, have superior dividend and liquidation rights.

Third, appellants contend that § 157 authorizes the issuance of Rights "entitling holders thereof to purchase from the corporation any shares of *its* capital stock of any class ..." (emphasis added). Therefore, their contention continues, the plain language of the statute does not authorize Household to issue rights to purchase another's capital stock upon a merger or consolidation.

Household contends, *inter alia,* that the Rights Plan is analogous to "anti-destruction" or "anti-dilution" provisions which are customary features of a wide variety of corporate securities. While appellants seem to concede that "anti-destruction" provisions are valid under Delaware corporate law, they seek to distinguish the Rights Plan as not being incidental, as are most "anti-destruction" provisions, to a corporation's statutory power to finance itself. We find no merit to such a distinction. We have already rejected appellants' similar contention that § 157 could only be used for financing purposes. We also reject that distinction here.

"Anti-destruction" clauses generally ensure holders of certain securities of the protection of their right of conversion in the event of a merger by giving them the right to convert their securities into whatever securities are to replace the stock of their company. * * * The fact that the rights here have as their purpose the prevention of coercive two-tier tender offers does not invalidate them.

* * *

Having concluded that sufficient authority for the Rights Plan exists in 8 *Del.C.* § 157, we note the inherent powers of the Board conferred by 8 *Del.C.* § 141(a),[11] concerning the management of the corporation's "business and *affairs* " (emphasis added), also provides the Board additional authority upon which to enact the Rights Plan. *Unocal,* 493 A.2d at 953.

Appellants contend that the Board is unauthorized to usurp stockholders' rights to receive tender offers by changing Household's fundamental structure. We conclude that the Rights Plan does not prevent stockholders from receiving tender offers, and that the change of Household's structure was less than that which results from the implementation of other defensive mechanisms upheld by various courts.

Appellants' contention that stockholders will lose their right to receive and accept tender offers seems to be premised upon an under-

---

11. 8 *Del.C.* § 141(a) provides:

(a) The business and affairs of every corporation organized under this chapter shall be managed by or under the direction of a board of directors, except as may be otherwise provided in this chapter or in its certificate of incorporation. If any such provision is made in the certificate of incorporation, the powers and duties conferred or imposed upon the board of directors by this chapter shall be exercised or performed to such extent and by such person or persons as shall be provided in the certificate of incorporation.

standing of the Rights Plan which is illustrated by the SEC *amicus* brief which states: "The Chancery Court's decision seriously understates the impact of this plan. In fact, as we discuss below, the Rights Plan will deter not only two-tier offers, but virtually all hostile tender offers."

The fallacy of that contention is apparent when we look at the recent takeover of Crown Zellerbach, which has a similar Rights Plan, by Sir James Goldsmith. Wall Street Journal, July 26, 1985, at 3, 12. The evidence at trial also evidenced many methods around the Plan ranging from tendering with a condition that the Board redeem the Rights, tendering with a high minimum condition of shares and Rights, tendering and soliciting consents to remove the Board and redeem the Rights, to acquiring 50% of the shares and causing Household to self-tender for the Rights. One could also form a group of up to 19.9% and solicit proxies for consents to remove the Board and redeem the Rights. These are but a few of the methods by which Household can still be acquired by a hostile tender offer.

In addition, the Rights Plan is not absolute. When the Household Board of Directors is faced with a tender offer and a request to redeem the Rights, they will not be able to arbitrarily reject the offer. They will be held to the same fiduciary standards any other board of directors would be held to in deciding to adopt a defensive mechanism, the same standard as they were held to in originally approving the Rights Plan. *See Unocol,* 493 A.2d at 954–55, 958.

In addition, appellants contend that the deterence of tender offers will be accomplished by what they label "a fundamental transfer of power from the stockholders to the directors." They contend that this transfer of power, in itself, is unauthorized.

The Rights Plan will result in no more of a structural change than any other defensive mechanism adopted by a board of directors. The Rights Plan does not destroy the assets of the corporation. The implementation of the Plan neither results in any outflow of money from the corporation nor impairs its financial flexibility. It does not dilute earnings per share and does not have any adverse tax consequences for the corporation or its stockholders. The Plan has not adversely affected the market price of Household's stock.

Comparing the Rights Plan with other defensive mechanisms, it does less harm to the value structure of the corporation than do the other mechanisms. Other mechanisms result in increased debt of the corporation. *See Whittaker Corp. v. Edgar, supra* (sale of "prize asset"), *Cheff v. Mathes, supra,* (paying greenmail to eliminate a threat), *Unocal Corp. v. Mesa Petroleum Co., supra,* (discriminatory self-tender).

There is little change in the governance structure as a result of the adoption of the Rights Plan. The Board does not now have unfettered discretion in refusing to redeem the Rights. The Board has no more discretion in refusing to redeem the Rights than it does in enacting any defensive mechanism.

The contention that the Rights Plan alters the structure more than do other defensive mechanisms because it is so effective as to make the corporation completely safe from hostile tender offers is likewise without merit. As explained above, there are numerous methods to successfully launch a hostile tender offer.

Appellants' third contention is that the Board was unauthorized to fundamentally restrict stockholders' rights to conduct a proxy contest. Appellants contend that the "20% trigger" effectively prevents any stockholder from first acquiring 20% or more shares before conducting a proxy contest and further, it prevents stockholders from banding together into a group to solicit proxies if, collectively, they own 20% or more of the stock.[12] In addition, at trial, appellants contended that read literally, the Rights Agreement triggers the Rights upon the mere acquisition of the right to vote 20% or more of the shares through a proxy solicitation, and thereby precludes any proxy contest from being waged.

Appellants seem to have conceded this last contention in light of Household's response that the receipt of a proxy does not make the recipient the "beneficial owner" of the shares involved which would trigger the Rights. In essence, the Rights Agreement provides that the Rights are triggered when someone becomes the "beneficial owner" of 20% or more of Household stock. Although a literal reading of the Rights Agreement definition of "beneficial owner" would seem to include those shares which one has the right to vote, it has long been recognized that the relationship between grantor and recipient of a proxy is one of agency, and the agency is revocable by the grantor at any time. * * * Therefore, the holder of a proxy is not the "beneficial owner" of the stock. As a result, the mere acquisition of the right to vote 20% of the shares does not trigger the Rights.

The issue, then, is whether the restriction upon individuals or groups from first acquiring 20% of shares before waging a proxy contest fundamentally restricts stockholders' right to conduct a proxy contest. * * *

We conclude that there was sufficient evidence at trial to support the Vice-Chancellor's finding that the effect upon proxy contests will be minimal. Evidence at trial established that many proxy contests are won with an insurgent ownership of less than 20%, and that very large holdings are no guarantee of success. There was also testimony that the key variable in proxy contest success is the merit of an insurgent's issues, not the size of his holdings.

Having concluded that the adoption of the Rights Plan was within the authority of the Directors, we now look to whether the Directors have met their burden under the business judgment rule.

---

12. Appellants explain that the acquisition of 20% of the shares trigger the Rights, making them non-redeemable, and thereby would prevent even a future friendly offer for the ten-year life of the Rights.

The business judgment rule is a "presumption that in making a business decision the directors of a corporation acted on an informed basis, in good faith and in the honest belief that the action taken was in the best interests of the company." *Aronson v. Lewis,* Del.Supr., 473 A.2d 805, 812 (1984) (citations omitted). Notwithstanding, in *Unocal* we held that when the business judgment rule applies to adoption of a defensive mechanism, the initial burden will lie with the directors. The "directors must show that they had reasonable grounds for believing that a danger to corporate policy and effectiveness existed.... [T]hey satisfy that burden 'by showing good faith and reasonable investigation....'" *Unocal,* 493 A.2d at 955 (citing *Cheff v. Mathes,* 199 A.2d at 554–55). In addition, the directors must show that the defensive mechanism was "reasonable in relation to the threat posed." *Unocal,* 493 A.2d at 955. Moreover, that proof is materially enhanced, as we noted in *Unocal,* where, as here, a majority of the board favoring the proposal consisted of outside independent directors who have acted in accordance with the foregoing standards. *Unocal,* 493 A.2d at 955; *Aronson,* 473 A.2d at 815. Then, the burden shifts back to the plaintiffs who have the ultimate burden of persuasion to show a breach of the directors' fiduciary duties. *Unocal,* 493 A.2d at 958.

There are no allegations here of any bad faith on the part of the Directors' action in the adoption of the Rights Plan. There is no allegation that the Directors' action was taken for entrenchment purposes. Household has adequately demonstrated, as explained above, that the adoption of the Rights Plan was in reaction to what it perceived to be the threat in the market place of coercive two-tier tender offers. Appellants do contend, however, that the Board did not exercise informed business judgment in its adoption of the Plan.

Appellants contend that the Household Board was uninformed since they were, *inter alia,* told the Plan would not inhibit a proxy contest, were not told the plan would preclude all hostile acquisitions of Household, and were told that Delaware counsel opined that the plan was within the business judgment of the Board.

As to the first two contentions, as we explained above, the Rights Plan will not have a severe impact upon proxy contests and it will not preclude all hostile acquisitions of Household. Therefore, the Directors were not misinformed or uninformed on these facts.

Appellants contend the Delaware counsel did not express an opinion on the flip-over provision of the Rights, rather only that the Rights would constitute validly issued and outstanding rights to subscribe to the preferred stock of the company.

To determine whether a business judgment reached by a board of directors was an informed one, we determine whether the directors were grossly negligent. *Smith v. Van Gorkom,* Del.Supr., 488 A.2d 858, 873 (1985). Upon a review of this record, we conclude the Directors were not grossly negligent. The information supplied to the Board on August 14 provided the essentials of the Plan. The Directors were given beforehand a notebook which included a three-page summary of the Plan along with articles on the current takeover environment. The extended discussion between the Board and representatives of Wachtell, Lipton and Goldman, Sachs before approval of the Plan reflected a full and candid evaluation of the Plan. Moran's expression of his views at the meeting served to place before the Board a knowledgeable critique of the Plan. The factual happenings here are clearly distinguishable from the actions of the directors of Trans Union Corporation who displayed gross negligence in approving a cash-out merger. *Id.*

In addition, to meet their burden, the Directors must show that the defensive mechanism was "reasonable in relation to the threat posed". The record reflects a concern on the part of the Directors over the increasing frequency in the financial services industry of "boot-strap" and "bust-up" takeovers. The Directors were also concerned that such takeovers may take the form of two-tier offers.[14] In addition, on August 14, the Household Board was aware of Moran's overture on behalf of D–K–M. In sum, the Directors reasonably believed Household was vulnerable to coercive acquisition techniques and adopted a reasonable defensive mechanism to protect itself.

* * *

While we conclude for present purposes that the Household Directors are protected by the business judgment rule, that does not end the matter. The ultimate response to an actual takeover bid must be judged by the Directors' actions at that time, and nothing we say here relieves them of their basic fundamental duties to the corporation and its stockholders. * * * Their use of the Plan will be evaluated when and if the issue arises.

* * *

Note

Poison Pill Plan Typology

R. FERRARA, M. BROWN & J. HALL, TAKEOVERS
337–43, 355–56 (1987).

* * *

The first shareholder rights agreement, more commonly known as a "poison pill," appeared in the defensive arsenal of a target company in June 1983, when Lenox, Inc. adopted a pill during its battle with Brown–Forman Distillers Corp. A poison pill can substantially increase the cost of a hostile merger, often making such a transaction economically unsound. But pills do not necessarily deter friendly mergers, because the target's board typically may redeem a pill at a

---

14. We have discussed the coercive nature of two-tier tender offers in *Unocal*, 493 A.2d at 956, n. 12. We explained in *Unocal* that a discriminatory self-tender was reasonably related to the threat of two-tier tender offers and possible greenmail.

nominal price. Thus, a poison pill ultimately may serve to bring a would-be hostile bidder to the bargaining table.

The two principal types of rights plans are (a) a "call" plan, under which a holder of a right can buy securities at a discount under certain circumstances, and (b) a "put" or "back-end" plan, under which the holder of a right can require the rights issuer or the acquiring company to purchase securities under certain circumstances.

* * *

1. THE CALL PLAN

a. *How a Call Plan Works*

Call plans are much more common than are put plans. A call plan is intended to encourage a potential acquiror to negotiate with the target, rather than launch a hostile bid, by making it extremely costly for a hostile bidder to accomplish a post-tender offer merger or to engage in certain self-dealing transactions with the target.

The typical call right, such as that issued by Household, essentially entitles the holder (once the right becomes exercisable) to buy stock at half price in certain situations. In the case of a merger between the rights issuer and an acquiror, the rights holders can buy, at half price, the stock of the company surviving the merger (whether the survivor be the issuer or the acquiror). Alternatively, if an acquiror of the issuer's shares engages in certain kinds of self-dealing transactions, the rights holders can purchase shares of the issuer at half price. The call right thus allows the issuer's stockholders to share in any benefit reaped by the acquiror through a squeeze-out merger or through self-dealing.

To implement a call plan, a company issues to its stockholders one right for each share of common stock. The issuance is in the nature of a dividend authorized by the directors and need not be approved by the shareholders.

b. *Terms of a Typical Call Right*

A typical call right has the following terms:

- *Trading and exercisability.* The right is initially "stapled" to the common stock—that is, it trades together with the common stock—and is not exercisable until ten days after a third party acquires 20 percent or more of the company's stock or has started a tender offer for 20 percent or more of those shares. As soon as practicable thereafter, the company issues separate rights certificates, and the rights become exercisable and transferable separately in the market from the common stock.

- *Exercise price.* The right permits a holder to buy a share of the common stock of the issuer or acquiror (depending on the circumstances) at a price based on an estimate of the long-term value of the company's stock over the life of the right. The exercise price is typically a multiple of the market price (for example, three times) of the common stock on the date of issuance of the right.

- *Term and redeemability.* The right has a stated term of ten years, but it is redeemable by the target's directors at a nominal price (for example, ten cents) at any time before, or for a limited time after, the occurrence of a triggering event, such as the announcement that a third party has acquired 20 percent of the company's stock. The redemption feature allows the board to negotiate an acquisition of the company on terms favorable to all shareholders. Once the rights become nonredeemable, they affect white knight transactions as well as hostile bids.
- *Right to buy stock at half price under certain circumstances.* The call right permits its holder, under certain circumstances, to buy stock having a market value of twice the exercise price of the right. For example, if a merger occurs after the rights have become exercisable, the holder of each right is entitled to purchase that number of the surviving company's shares whose market value is twice the exercise price of the right. This feature is sometimes referred to as a "flip-over" provision because the target shareholder's right "flips over" into a right to buy stock in the surviving company, even if that company is not the same as the original issuer of the right.

Similarly, if a third party acquires 20 percent or more of the target's stock and then engages in certain self-dealing transactions, the holder of each right (other than the 20–percent holder, whose rights become null and void) may receive that number of the issuer's shares whose market value is twice the exercise price of the right. Self-dealing transactions typically are defined to include any transaction in which the 20–percent holder or one of its affiliates merges into the target, transfers assets to the target in exchange for target stock, buys any target assets whose aggregate fair market value exceeds a specified amount, receives any compensation from the target other than for full-time employment, or receives disproportionate benefits as a result of any loan, advance, financial assistance, or tax advantage provided by the target. This feature is sometimes referred to as a "flip-in," because the right can be "flipped" into a position in the stock of the target company.

- *Voting.* The rights have no voting power.
- *Amendment.* The target may amend the rights agreement from time to time in any manner that does not adversely affect the interests of the rights holders. Amendments may extend either the term of the rights or, in the absence of a 20–percent shareholder, the period of time during which the rights may be redeemed.

c. Variants From Typical Call Plans

- *Automatic flip-in.* Some recent call plans have contained "flip-in" provisions under which the rights become exercisable to buy stock of the issuer or an acquiror at a fraction of market value whenever the acquiror buys more than a threshold amount of the issuer's stock, even if the acquiror does not engage in any coercive or self-dealing transactions. * * *

- *Window period for redemption.* A number of companies have adopted call plans that allow redemption of rights for a limited period of time following a bidder's acquisition of a threshold amount of shares. Such a "window period" may give the target's directors more time to react to the supposed acquisition attempt and may prevent premature triggering of the rights, especially if the acquiror reached the threshold amount by mistake (for example, through the inadvertent formation of a "group" under the securities laws). This redemption provision, however, may significantly reduce the call plan's deterrent effect because it lessens the risks to the bidder of exceeding the threshold and may pressure the target into finding a white knight once the company has been put in play during the "window period."
- *Redemption with shareholder approval.* Some call plans grant the stockholders the power to redeem the rights, by either a supermajority vote or a vote of a majority of the stockholders other than the 20–percent stockholder, even after an acquiror crosses the 20–percent line.
- *No flip-over for approved transactions.* In another variant of the plan, the "flip-over" provision applies only to transactions involving persons who acquire more than 20 percent of the target's stock without prior approval of the target's board of directors, whether or not the right already has become exercisable by reason of an unapproved 20–percent stock acquisition. The right thus is "poisonous" only to unsolicited acquirors, and the board may enter into a white-knight transaction, without regard to the pill, even after the flip-over provision has taken effect against a hostile bidder. This variation, however, might tend to undercut the deterrent effect of the rights because, it might encourage a bidder who is not interested in acquiring 100 percent of the company to cross the 20–percent threshold in the hope of forcing the target to make a deal with a white knight.

d. Tax and Accounting Aspects

Neither the distribution of the rights, nor the subsequent "unstapling" of the rights from the common stock and the distribution of rights certificates, constitutes a taxable event for the company or its shareholders; rather, the rights are treated for tax purposes as capital assets in the hands of most shareholders. Each right probably would have a basis of zero, and its holding period would relate back to the holding period of the common stock from which the right was separated. If the rights become exercisable to purchase the target's stock at half price, the rights holder may recognize taxable income. If the rights become exercisable to purchase the acquiror's stock at half price, the holders would probably have to recognize taxable income even if they do not exercise the rights. The rights may also have some impact on the issuer's ability to engage in a tax-free reorganization.

Because the rights would be "out of the money" (*i.e.*, too expensive for anyone to want to exercise) when issued, they would not dilute earnings per share. Moreover, because the redemption date is neither fixed nor determinable, accounting guidelines would not require recognition of the redemption amount as a long-term obligation of the issuer. Under certain circumstances, however, the rights could impair the issuer's ability to consummate a business combination that qualifies for pooling of interests treatment.

The rights issuer need not register with the SEC the common stock issuable upon exercise of the rights because the rights will not be exercised—and the stock will not be issued—until some future triggering event has occurred. The SEC staff, however, has taken the position that such stock must be registered once the rights have been exercised and the stock actually has been issued.

* * *

2. The Put Plan

a. *How a Put Plan Works*

While historically less common than "call" rights plans, "put" rights plans have been adopted by a number of companies, including Phillips, Revlon, Great Lakes International, and CTS. Put plans are used most often when target companies need a defense against specific bidders under specific circumstances.

Under a put plan, as under a call plan, a company's board issues rights to shareholders as a dividend, without shareholder approval. A put right typically enables its holder (other than a holder of more than a specified percentage of the company's stock) to "put" to the issuer a share of common stock for a specified amount of cash, debt securities, preferred stock, or a combination of the above, in the event that a third party acquires more than a specified percentage of the company's stock and does not offer to buy the rest of the stock at a specified price (which is usually equal to the value of the cash or securities receivable if the rights are exercised). The price can be a fixed amount, as under the Revlon plan, which gave shareholders (other than a 20–percent holder) the right to exchange a Revlon share for $65 in notes if a third party acquired 20 percent of Revlon's stock and did not offer to buy the remaining shares for $65 each. Alternatively, the price can be set by a formula to equal the highest price per share paid by a bidder in acquiring the issuer's stock. * * *

The issuer should be aware that a put plan may raise certain legal questions not raised by a call plan, including the need to comply with restrictions under loan agreements and state corporation statutes concerning the redemption of stock. A put plan also might raise fraudulent conveyance issues, on the theory that the company has given rights holders the right to put shares to the company for excessive consideration. In addition, if the put right is not available to the bidder (or to other shareholders owning in excess of a specified threshold percentage of the target's stock), there is at least a question whether the put plan constitutes an exclusionary tender offer and thus is inconsistent with the "all holders" rule that the SEC adopted in 1986.

* * *

Questions

1. The plan used in the *Moran* case is commonly called a "flip-over call" plan. How does a flip-over plan put in place by a target firm bind a nonconsenting bidder to honor rights to buy bidder stock at bargain prices? Recall that the plan affects second-stage, or back-end, statutory mergers between a bidder that has acquiring voting control of a target and the target. Why did the Household International plan include an illusory right to buy preferred stock (the exercise price is far greater than the value of the preferred stock acquired; the right is "out of the money")? Did the drafters believe it helped their section 157 argument? After the case do flip-over plans need an out-of-the-money option on preferred to be valid?

2. What is the effect of a flip-over plan on a back-end merger in which the unapproved bidder merges into the target (a reverse merger)? In which the unapproved bidder causes the target to sell all its assets to the bidder? How can the drafters of poison pill plans protect against such actions? Does a "flip-in" feature help?

3. What is the effect of a flip-over call plan on a bidder who acquires 51 percent of the outstanding common stock of the target and then does not execute a back-end merger or asset sale? How can the drafters of poison pill plans protect against this? Does an automatic flip-in plan help?

4. Judge Easterbrook suggests, in *Amanda Acquisition,* pp. 447–458, supra, that bidders can avoid flip-over plans with their own plans that counter the dilutive effects of a triggered flip-over plan. What would a bidder countermeasure look like and how would it work in practice? Why do we not see such measures in practice? Can a bidder counter the dilutive effects of a "flip-in" feature in a call plan?

5. Why does a flip-over call plan not need a discriminatory vesting condition while a flip-in call plan does? In a discriminatory plan a shareholder who triggers the vesting of the poison pill rights may not exercise the rights that it holds.

6. Why are put plans less attractive to targets than call plans?

7. Are there risks in using an automatic flip-in provision in a call plan? Can an existing management group rather than a raider trigger the plan? In September 1990 shareholders of a Massachusetts corporation, Instron Corporation, sued to claim the lucrative call rights under a poison pill plan when the firm's founders declared in a news release that they and family members owned 39 percent of the firm's stock. The plan had a 20 percent trigger, and although no one person owned more than 20 percent of the stock, the suing shareholders claimed the news release created a "group" of shareholders whose shares were consolidated under the language of the plan.

DYNAMICS CORP. OF AMERICA v. CTS CORP.

United States Court of Appeals, Seventh Circuit, 1986.
805 F.2d 705.

POSNER, CIRCUIT JUDGE.

This case involves a challenge under the corporate law of Indiana to a "poison pill," which is a device used by corporate managers to fend off hostile tender offers.

* * *

On March 10 of this year Dynamics Corporation of America, which already owned 9.6 percent of the common stock of CTS Corporation, made a tender offer that if accepted would bring its stock holdings up to 27.5 percent. CTS's stock was trading at $36 a share (all dollar figures are rounded to the nearest dollar). The price in the tender offer was $43. On March 22, after very hurried consideration, CTS adopted a shareholders' rights plan of the kind known as a "poison pill." Under the plan, if and when one shareholder (namely Dynamics) obtained 15 percent or more of the company's common stock, every other shareholder would be entitled to buy a package of stock and debentures for 25 percent of the market price of the package. In April the district court issued a preliminary injunction against the poison pill. * * * We affirmed. The tender offer then went through, and Dynamics used its newly obtained 27.5 percent position in CTS to begin a proxy fight to oust CTS's existing board of directors.

Meanwhile CTS had responded to the district court's injunction by referring the question of further defensive measures to a committee of outside directors. After several days of intensive deliberation the committee returned to the full board with a recommendation that the company be sold and that pending sale a new poison pill be adopted under which, if any shareholder obtained 28 percent of the company's common stock, all the other shareholders would be entitled to turn in their shares and receive in exchange for each share a $50 debenture (bond), payable after one year, with interest at 10 percent per annum. The plan would remain in effect for one year but could be cancelled by the board of directors at any time. It would be cancelled automatically if anyone made a cash tender offer for all outstanding shares at a price of $50 or more.

The board adopted the plan on the same day we upheld the district court's preliminary injunction (April 23). At the time, CTS's stock was selling at $38 a share, but it rose to $45 the next day, when CTS announced that it had adopted the plan as part of a strategy for selling the company—though this was also the first day after we affirmed the district court's preliminary injunction. Dynamics moved immediately to enjoin this second "poison pill," but on May 3 the district judge denied the motion. * * * The election for the board of directors was held on May 16. CTS's board, which had campaigned on a platform of selling the company and had represented that the second poison pill was designed to maximize the price at which the company would be sold, won reelection by a narrow margin.

* * *

Our previous opinion noted that the irreparable harms from granting or denying the preliminary injunction appeared to be in equipoise in this case, so that analysis would have to focus on the likelihood that Dynamics would prevail on the merits if its suit to invalidate the poison pill was tried. After pointing out that the controlling law was that of Indiana and that in matters of corporation law the Indiana courts normally take their cue from the Delaware courts, which are more experienced in such matters, we observed that while the board of directors of a corporation that is a target or potential target of hostile tender offers has the power to adopt a poison pill, the particular poison pill it adopts must be reasonably related to the goal of shareholder wealth maximization. Since, moreover, there is a potential conflict of interest between the managers and shareholders of the target, courts are not simply to rubber stamp the board's judgment but must review it carefully to make sure that in adopting the poison pill the board really was acting in the best interests of the corporation. * * * In making this determination the court must consider the procedures leading up to the adoption of the poison pill and the terms of the poison pill. CTS's counsel acknowledged at the argument of the present appeal that the action of a board of directors in adopting a poison pill is subject to "enhanced scrutiny" by the courts, because of the potential conflict of interest between the board and the shareholders. In nevertheless and inconsistently insisting that the standard of judicial review is whether the board acted with gross negligence, counsel was misstating the test set forth in the Delaware decisions and in our previous opinion to govern review of poison pills.

The first poison pill that CTS adopted clearly flunked the test. The circumstances of its adoption indicated that the board's objective was to block Dynamics' tender offer regardless of the consequences for the welfare of CTS's shareholders. So did the terms of that poison pill. If Dynamics completed its tender offer the pill would be administered and Dynamics would find that its 27.5 percent ownership position had shrunk to 20.7 percent, the dilution being caused by the stock component of the pill. It would also find that it had incurred a capital loss in excess of $20 million, for the value of the company would be no greater as a result of the exercise of the rights conferred by the poison pill but Dynamics' share of the company would be smaller. And CTS would be saddled with a heavy ($80 million) new long-term debt, for no value received.

* * *

The second poison pill was adopted in different circumstances and has different provisions from the first. The second was devised by the outside directors (constituted as a special committee) in consultation with the company's investment advisor, Smith Barney. The district court found that unlike the board the first time around, the special committee did not start with the preconceived idea of preventing a takeover of CTS whether by Dynamics or any other person or firm that might make a tender offer; that after thoroughly and impartially considering a variety of alternative methods of maximizing the shareholders' wealth the committee decided that the company should be sold;

and that it adopted the poison pill (the second pill, the one challenged in this appeal) in order to maximize the price at which the company would be sold. The trigger was set at 28 percent to allow Dynamics to complete its tender offer but prevent it from acquiring any more shares. The committee's main concern was that if Dynamics acquired enough shares to have a "blocking position" other potential acquirers would be deterred from trying to buy the company. A secondary concern was that Dynamics would be able to acquire the additional shares without having to pay a premium for thereby obtaining control of the company, thus depriving all shareholders of any participation in a "control premium."

The district court also found that the committee had made an honest-to-goodness effort to value the company and had come up with a price of $50 per share. Anyone who thinks the company is worth at least that much can take it over simply by making a cash tender offer for all outstanding shares of the company, at a price of $50 or better per share; for if such an offer is made, the poison pill will self-destruct. The shareholders are unlikely to refuse such an offer, since $50 is the company's own valuation (and not a modest one, either, as we shall see). Should a lower price become attractive to shareholders because the market price of CTS's stock falls—for example, at a market price of $29 (the current market price) even a sale price as low as $42 would yield a higher premium than a sale price of $50 if the market price were still $38—the board of directors has the power to cancel the pill, and would be under considerable pressure to exercise that power. During the proxy fight Dynamics said that if it got control of the board it would sell the company for $46 a share; and though this may just have been puffing, it is some evidence that the board's valuation of the company was not too far off target. The stock market may have considered the second poison pill, unlike the first, a positive development, for the price of CTS stock rose (though only temporarily) after the announcement of the second pill; it had fallen after the announcement of the first. (But the cause may have been our affirmance of the preliminary injunction against the first poison pill, rather than the announcement of the second poison pill.) Finally, this poison pill is to remain in the medicine chest for only a year; and if at the end of that time the board has not sold the company as the board said the poison pill would help it do, the board will have a lot of explaining to do and may lose the next election, having barely squeaked by in this one after promising to sell the company.

If the facts we have recited were the only facts established by the record, we would affirm the district judge's decision. But there are more. To begin with, regarding the procedural adequacy of CTS's decision to adopt a second poison pill, the role of the investment advisor is troubling. As noted in our first opinion, Smith Barney's compensation package for advising the board on how to respond to Dynamics' original tender offer included a bonus if the offer was defeated ("the independence fee"). For the second round Smith Barney was again the advisor but this time it was retained by the committee of outside directors rather than by the entire board, and, according to an uncontradicted affidavit, its compensation package does not include an "independence fee." What it does include is unknown, however, since Smith Barney's agreement with the committee is not in the appellate record. But Judge Getzendanner said that Smith Barney will obtain an "incentive fee for the white knight strategy," which we understand to mean that it will be paid more if CTS is sold to a buyer agreeable to the board than if it is acquired in a hostile takeover. In the record is a letter to Smith Barney from CTS's treasurer describing the fee that Smith Barney is to receive under different scenarios and fixing a generous fee for sale to a "white knight" (a buyer acceptable to the board) and a negligible fee if Dynamics obtains control of the board in a proxy fight. The letter contains no mention of a fee if there is a hostile takeover. The letter was written before the special committee of outside directors retained Smith Barney, but we are unable to determine from the record whether it is still in effect. Besides providing for the independence fee, the original compensation agreement had included a large bonus for a sale to a white knight, and again we are unable to determine from the record whether that agreement (presumably minus the independence fee) is still in effect. The situation regarding Smith Barney's compensation in the second round thus is thoroughly confused, suspicious, and not clarified by the district court's opinions. The scheme of compensation may involve a bonus of some sort for sale to a white knight, even if a "black knight" offers the shareholders more money for their shares. More generally, there is no indication to what extent the amount of compensation is linked to the price at which the company was sold—though some such link might be necessary to align Smith Barney's self-interest with the interests of the shareholders.

Standing alone, this impurity in the procedures leading up to the adoption of the second pill would not warrant reversal, or even a remand. Nor would the fact that the outside directors aren't really disinterested, since they will probably lose their directorships (and directors' fees) if CTS is acquired, unless the acquiror is a foreign company. A lack of disinterest cannot be equated to bad faith or procedural unfairness; otherwise defensive measures would be unlawful per se, which they are not. It is true that the special committee acted with some haste, but given its concern (the reasonableness of which we shall examine later) that Dynamics might, after completing its initial tender offer, seek to buy enough additional shares to acquire a blocking position, it had to move rapidly.

* * * True, the consultation may have been contaminated by the method of compensating the advisor. But we are not minded to hold directors to a standard of procedural scrupulousness that would transform their role from that of businessmen to that of Article III judges. Furthermore, if directors can be sued both for selling their company too hastily (*Van Gorkom*), that is, at too low a price, and for selling it too slowly (this case), that is, for setting too high a price, they are placed on a legal razor's edge.

More serious than any procedural irregularities in the decision by CTS's board to adopt the second poison pill are the substantial, and as yet unanswered, questions regarding the relationship between the terms of the second poison pill and the welfare of CTS's shareholders— but of course these questions make the issue of Smith Barney's compensation more serious than it would otherwise be. The first question is, why is the poison pill activated when one shareholder obtains 28 percent of the shares, rather than 50 percent? Despite much talk of "blocking positions," the record contains no evidence as to how Dynamics could use 28 percent or any other fractional ownership short of 50 percent to block anything. Although Indiana law authorizes corporations to require a supermajority vote for certain structural changes, such as a merger, CTS has not imposed such a requirement; it can do anything by a simple majority of the shares. See Ind.Code § 23–1–5–2(b). Dynamics can no more block majority decisions with 49.99 percent of the company than with 27.5 percent. If someone tenders for more than 50 percent of the shares (however slightly more), and succeeds in the tender, he can if he wants squeeze out Dynamics and become sole owner of CTS. Of course, squeezing out a minority shareholder is not completely painless, for the shareholder has appraisal rights that, depending on how a court values them, may make the transaction a costly one for the majority shareholder; recent developments in Delaware law have strengthened (some think too much) the position of the dissenting shareholder. * * * And the larger the minority shareholder, the greater the pressure the majority shareholder may feel to squeeze him out rather than tolerate his continued presence. For even though the minority shareholder, whether large or small, can't wrest control of the board of directors from the majority shareholder, he may by virtue of the size of his stake in the company have an incentive to play a more vigorous role as corporate monitor and gadfly than would a smaller shareholder (CTS in its brief calls Dynamics a "contentious" and "unruly" minority shareholder). So all things considered, CTS might indeed be a somewhat less attractive acquisition target with a very large minority shareholder. But whether the difference between a 27.5 percent shareholder and a 49 percent shareholder is material with respect to these concerns is an issue unexplored on this record.

We do not want to be understood as holding that ownership of 28 percent of CTS's stock could *not* create a "blocking position" in some sense that might justify the use of this percentage to trigger a poison pill. Poison pills with lower triggering percentages have been upheld. But every poison pill is *sui generis,* and there must be evidence justifying setting the triggering percentage below the level that would give a minority shareholder an actual legal right to block decisions taken by the majority. We cannot find that evidence. It is true that the board obtained the opinion of a qualified financial expert (other than Smith Barney) that the 28 percent trigger was proper, but the opinion was offered as a conclusion; its basis was not explained. The district court's opinions do not illuminate the issue.

The secondary ground for the 28 percent trigger, that it is necessary in order to assure that all shareholders will participate in any premium for conveying control of the company, is also unexplained. It is true that the more shares Dynamics has of CTS's stock, the fewer additional shares it need buy to take control of CTS; but it is hard to see how this can hurt the shareholders. If someone tenders for 51 percent of the company, Dynamics is in a good position to make a counteroffer, since it has a big base to start from. But of course the counteroffer will succeed only if it is at a higher price. Dynamics' position as a large minority shareholder, far from discouraging the auction of the company—CTS's avowed goal in adopting the second poison pill—should encourage it. Nor can we see how this conclusion would be altered if Dynamics had 28 percent instead of 27.5 percent of CTS's stock—or for that matter 49 percent. A recent study finds that the existence of a large minority shareholder encourages takeovers, see Schleifer & Vishny, *Large Shareholders and Corporate Control*, 94 J.Pol.Econ. 461, 463 (1986), and while the study neither is conclusive nor shows that shareholders of CTS would be better off if Dynamics had more than 27.5 percent of CTS's shares, it does underscore the absence from the record of persuasive or even plausible reasons for the "blocking position" or "stalking horse" or "control premium" grounds for the 28 percent trigger.

* * *

A further consideration is that the larger Dynamics' position is, the easier it will be for another firm to take over the company by making a deal with Dynamics, for acquiring Dynamics' shares will bring it closer to owning a majority. The stated premise of CTS's hostility to Dynamics' increasing its position in CTS stock is that Dynamics doesn't care for the long-run health of CTS, that it is just a short-run profit maximizer. But if so, this means that Dynamics should be willing and eager to sell its shares to anyone that will offer it a good profit. It is true that if Dynamics had 49 percent of the company and then sold out to the owner of another one percent plus, the remaining shareholders would not obtain a control premium. But that is an argument for a fair-price amendment, which would guarantee all shareholders the same price as paid for control, rather than for a poison pill. Again these are matters not illuminated by the record or the district judge's opinions.

Dynamics' principal argument against the second poison pill is simply that $50 a share is too high a valuation of CTS; no one will pay $50 a share for CTS, so the practical effect of the poison pill is to make the company invulnerable to being taken over. In principle Dynamics or anyone else can make a tender offer at a lower price but if it does so the poison pill will be activated and the tender offeror (assuming it succeeds in taking over the company) will end up owing every shareholder who refuses to tender his stock but instead asserts his right under the poison pill more money than the stock is worth. Indeed, by tendering for an additional half percent of the stock Dynamics could end up as the only shareholder in a company whose liabilities (which would now include the $50 debentures received by the other shareholders along with CTS's other debts) might greatly exceed its assets: a bankrupt company. If owners of all 72 percent of the shares not owned by Dynamics after our hypothetical .5 percent tender (100 percent—28 percent) asserted their rights under the poison pill, CTS would have acquired an additional debt of $200 million, compared to only $80 million of additional debt under the original poison pill. Additional debt of $200 million would be equal to three-quarters of the net worth of the company even if the company is valued (very generously, as it appears) at $50 a share. Any shareholder who tenders his stock to the tender offeror gives up his rights under the poison pill; but so long as the tender offer price is below $50, many and perhaps most shareholders will refuse.

The $50 figure is only a face value and of course securities frequently trade for less or more than their face value. In this case, if the company is worth less than $50, so that if all or most of the shareholders claimed their rights under the poison pill the company might be forced into bankruptcy, it might seem to follow that the shareholders would accept less than $50 to surrender their rights through sale of their stock to a tender offeror. But this is not correct. As soon as enough shareholders tender to give the tender offeror 28 percent, the poison pill will be triggered and some fraction of the remaining shareholders will try to make more than the tender offer price by swapping their stock for the debentures. If enough do so, the tenderer will find himself in control of a company with tremendous debt, and little value; he will have bought not a company but a mass of debt. The prospect will deter tender offers at prices below $50, whatever the debentures may really be worth.

But this only shows that the poison pill is indeed likely to be effective in its stated purpose of discouraging tender offers at less than $50. That purpose is not unlawful provided the board was trying reasonably and in good faith to sell the company at the highest possible price. The trigger price, however, is highly relevant to the issues of reasonableness and good faith, since if set too high it will prevent all tender offers, not just those that are below the corporation's sale value. Since the entire premise of the second poison pill was that it was designed to facilitate the sale of the company, the pill cannot be upheld if the trigger price is an unreasonably high sale price.

The district judge's determination that, at least on the basis of the evidence presented at the preliminary injunction hearing, the valuation was reasonable and in good faith is a finding of fact, * * * so we must uphold it unless it is clearly erroneous. And her finding that $50 was a reasonable and good-faith price for a security for which Dynamics had been willing to pay $43 (the price in its tender offer) is not on its face unreasonable, especially when we consider that once one departs from market values the process of valuing an asset becomes fraught with uncertainty.

* * *

Of course this might be a reason for forbidding corporate management (or even a committee of outside directors) to set a reservation price for the sale of the corporation rather than giving the market a free hand, but the law does not go so far.

Nevertheless the method by which the $50 figure was chosen is sufficiently troublesome to make this another issue on which further consideration by the district judge is necessary before we can determine whether her conclusion regarding reasonableness and good faith was clearly erroneous. Smith Barney determined CTS's sale value primarily by multiplying CTS's expected earnings for the coming year by a price-earnings multiple of 15.5. The multiple was based on the multiples commanded by other manufacturers of electronic components, but no effort was made to establish comparability. A price-earnings multiple reflects investor expectation concerning the company's entire stream of future earnings (suitably discounted), not just a one-year projection. CTS is a troubled company and even if it were forecasting its next year's earnings correctly, investors might not value the company at the same multiple of those earnings that other companies in its field are valued at. CTS has, moreover, a history of extravagant earnings projections. This history would tend to depress its price-earnings multiple in the stock market, at least when the earnings component is a projection, as distinct from actually realized earnings.

Even if the multiple of 15.5 was reasonable, the earnings figure that Smith Barney multiplied by 15.5—$3.23 per share for 1987—was a wildly extravagant forecast. As recently as April 1986 the company had reduced its estimate of expected earnings for 1987 from $1.50 to only 89¢. The $3.23 figure was based on an expectation—for which no ground other than optimism has been suggested—that both CTS and its industry would show dramatic growth in the coming year. Smith Barney had estimated just a month before making its $50 valuation that while at a price of $40 a share the probability of selling the company would be 85 percent, at $43 it would be only 35 percent. By this method of estimation, at $50 a share the probability of selling the company would be close to zero. In a separate opinion issued on May 3, upholding Dynamics' claim that CTS's board had made misleading representations in the course of the proxy fight, the district judge had described $50 a share as "an outside high value based substantially on untested, optimistic management projections," had noted CTS's history of overly optimistic earnings projections, had said that "CTS really does not expect a triggering event and hence $50 notes very probably never will be issued," and had pointed out that Smith Barney in estimating the company to be worth $50 a share had taken the board's $3.23

projection at face value without attempting to verify it. It is true that Merrill Lynch advised the board of directors that Smith Barney's methodology in valuing the company was sound, but Merrill Lynch, like Smith Barney, took for granted the earnings projection which the board had supplied Smith Barney. That projection, never independently validated, is the weakest link in the valuation chain. The affidavit of CTS's other independent financial expert was prepared after the fact to bolster CTS's litigating position.

When these facts are put together with the history recounted in our previous opinion, we are left with considerable uncertainty regarding the basis on which the district judge was able to reject the inference that the second poison pill was designed to keep CTS from being sold without the board's consent and to keep Dynamics from expanding its base of stock holdings from which to wage another proxy fight for control of the board—so that, in the end, the current management and directors would keep their jobs. As the district judge herself said, "That the defendants are determined to stop [Dynamics] is evident, as they consider it better to sell CTS at a potentially depressed price than watch [Dynamics] take control." 635 F.Supp. at 1181. About CTS's determination to stop Dynamics, even at the price of selling the company for less than it was worth, the district judge said only that "this hostility towards [Dynamics], even if unreasonable, cannot be simply equated with a goal of entrenchment." *Id.* We are not clear why not.

But it is possible that other facts outweigh those we have just reviewed and may justify the district judge's conclusion that the $50 valuation was not either deliberately inflated or unreasonably high, though this we cannot determine from her opinions. In her separate opinion dealing with CTS's alleged misrepresentations in the proxy fight, she faulted CTS for having failed to convey to the shareholders another valuation of CTS's stock that Smith Barney had made—this one at $75 per share. If $75 was somehow in the ballpark (though how it could have been is unclear), her evident skepticism concerning $50 becomes difficult to understand; this is an inconsistency that can be cleared up on remand. Another point is that if the 15.5 multiple were applied to CTS's earlier estimate of its 1987 earnings—89¢—it would mean that the stock was worth less than $14 a share, which no one thinks reasonable; remember that Dynamics' tender was at $43. So though Smith Barney's valuation procedure seems deeply flawed, the $50 valuation may not be invalidated by the flaws. Further considerations bearing on the reasonableness of the second poison pill are that it was to remain in effect for only a short period (one year), that it was before the shareholders (though not formally submitted to them for ratification) during the proxy fight, and that it is cancellable by the board. Concerning the last point, if the board turned down an objectively favorable tender offer for less than $50 by refusing to cancel the pill, it might have a hard time explaining this to the shareholders at the next proxy fight—a fight that Dynamics no doubt will wage with as much vigor and determination as the one just past, which it narrowly lost and perhaps only lost because of the promise by CTS's board to sell the company. Unless that promise is redeemed or the company's performance dramatically improved, the present board will probably lose the next proxy fight, just as it expected to lose the last one if Dynamics' tender offer went through.

Yet these facts are not decisive either. The cancellable feature of the poison pill just permits the board to sell the company to a "white knight," which it could do without a poison pill. And the authenticity of the stockholders' indirect approval of the poison pill in the proxy campaign is undermined by the misrepresentations that CTS made concerning the value of the company, misrepresentations calculated to make the shareholders think (despite the absence of any grounds) that if they kept the old board it would sell the company within a year for at least $50 a share. It is true that Judge Getzendanner ordered corrective action—another mailing to the shareholders, to correct the misrepresentations—but the efficacy of this action, carried out as it was only a few days before the election, may be doubted.

Judge Getzendanner may not have clearly erred in finding that CTS had acted reasonably and in good faith in adopting the second poison pill, but there are enough doubts on this score—doubts concerning Smith Barney's incentives, the choice of a 28 percent trigger in the particular circumstances, and the method by which a $50 valuation was arrived at—doubts not dispelled by the district court's findings of facts—to require that the case be remanded for further consideration of Dynamics' request for a preliminary injunction. And since nothing is to be gained by decision on an obsolete record, the parties should be allowed to present evidence of relevant developments since the last hearing, including evidence bearing on CTS's efforts to find a buyer for the company and on the realism of its earnings projections back in May in light of the company's experience since then. A forecast of earnings is not invalidated by failure to achieve it; even a realistic forecast is just an estimate, implying some probability that actual performance will deviate from it. But consistent failure to achieve or even approach forecasted performance is relevant evidence on the realism of a company's methods of forecasting, an important issue in the present case.

We expressed in our last opinion and we repeat our skepticism concerning the propriety of poison pills. The present pill essentially prevents the shareholders from deciding to sell the company at less than $50 per share unless the directors approve. We grant that there is at least an arguable concern with two-tiered tender offers. The offeror offers a high price for enough shares to wrest control of the company from its present management in the expectation of being able to buy the remaining shares later at a lower price; knowing this, shareholders may fall over each other to tender their shares in response to the first offer; as a result, the time for holding an auction of the company with more than one bidder is drastically foreshortened. But this problem can be solved by a fair-price amendment to the corporation's charter, which merely forbids different prices between the tiers. And any defensive provision that commands the support of a majority (and, *a fortiori,* if it commands a super-majority) of the corporation's shareholders, as a charter amendment must do, is more likely to be in the shareholders' best interests than a measure adopted by the board of directors alone.

* * *

The poison pill, typically and here adopted by vote of the board rather than of the shareholders, eliminates the market for corporate control at any price below the value of the pill to the shareholder electing to take it (or rather, to administer it to the corporation). Eliminates it, period, when, as may be the case here, the value of the pill exceeds the maximum reasonable sale value of the company. The poison pill turns every tender offer into a two-tier offer with a higher rather than lower back-end: the offeror offers at one price and then is forced to buy out nontendering shareholders at a higher price. If it is enough higher, the incentive to make a tender offer is destroyed.

* * *

We need not speculate on whether in some circumstances a poison pill might be a reasonable element of a plan for a corporate auction. The poison pill in this case operated, as we have said, as a reservation price: no one could bid lower than the value of the poison pill to the shareholders and hope to induce a significant number of them to sell their shares. Auctioneers frequently establish reservation prices, that is, refuse (or reserve the right to refuse) to sell the item to be auctioned unless a bid higher than the specified price is received. The analogy, however, is imprecise. The owner of the auctioned property is selling his own property; the management of a corporation is selling property that belongs to others, the shareholders, whose ability to ensure management's faithful performance of its fiduciary duties to them is limited. Also, items usually are auctioned because there is no ready market for them, hence no market price. CTS's stock is traded on the New York Stock Exchange, though it can be argued that the value fixed by the market is the value of the marginal share rather than the sale value of the entire company as a unit.

We need not pursue these issues further. It would be premature to decide in this case that, as a matter of Indiana law, a board of directors intent on selling the corporation for the highest possible price cannot set a reservation price and cannot use a poison pill as the means of doing so. But even if it can, the reservation price must be reasonably related to the value of the corporation, and the decision to establish such a price and do so by means of a poison pill must be made in good faith after proper consideration. The record before us creates a serious doubt whether CTS has satisfied this standard.

* * *

Questions

1. Judge Posner applies Indiana law, looking to Delaware precedents for guidance. Has he correctly applied Delaware law? Is the case consistent with the *Moran* opinion? Is Judge Posner convincing in his arguments in favor of severely limiting a firm's ability to use a poison pill plan?

2. Must put plans, according to Judge Posner, have a reasonable price floor, a trigger of 50 percent, a cancelable feature, and a short life? If so, most modern plans fail his test. Is Judge Posner correct in his assertion that under the second poison pill plan no one will make a tender offer below $50? Can a bidder condition a tender offer priced at $40 on the target board's redemption of its pill? If a target board refuses and stock price falls to $35 a share, can angry shareholders sue the board? What will happen if the frustrated bidder mounts a proxy contest to remove the board? See *Georgia–Pacific Corp.*, infra.

3. Does the Securities and Exchange Commission "all-holders" rule in rule 14(d)–10, supra, affect put poison pill plans? Is a firm's obligation to exchange notes or cash for its outstanding stock, once a poison pill plan is triggered, a tender offer? Why does the rule contain an express exclusion of calls and redemptions but not puts? Similarly, does the rule apply to flip-in call poison pill plans? If the all-holders rule does apply to flip-in call or put plans, what is the effect of the rule on such plans? See Div. Corp. Fin., SEC No–Action Letter (Feb. 7, 1987), "Registration of Rights Issuable Pursuant to Stockholder Rights Plans," Fed.Sec.L.Rep. (CCH) ¶ 74,811 [1987 Transfer Binder].

Early Court Defeats for Discriminatory Plans and Curative State Legislation

Some of the first courts to deal with poison pill plans found them to violate state corporate codes by discriminating among shares of stock in the same class, establishing unreasonable restraints on the alienability of stock, and effecting without a shareholder vote a major delegation of power to a firm's board. *Minstar* is an example of such a case.

MINSTAR ACQUIRING CORP. v. AMF, INC.

United States District Court, Southern District of New York, 1985.
621 F.Supp. 1252.

LOWE, DISTRICT JUDGE:

* * *

At the board of directors meeting on May 9, 1985 the AMF board declared a dividend of one "Right" per share of its outstanding common stock, as of the close of business on May 20, 1985. Each Right entitled the holder to exchange one share of AMF common stock for a "unit" comprised of one-tenth of a share of a new series of AMF stock designated "Series B Preference Stock" and $5.75 principal share of 14.5% Subordinated debentures, due in 1995. The Indenture covering these Debentures contained certain restrictions including: (1) a moratorium on incurring further debt, except for working capital used in the ordinary course of business and to fund the Rights Plan; (2) a restriction on the sale or transfer of assets of AMF exceeding 1% of Consolidated Adjusted Net Assets, except as conducted in the ordinary course of business; and (3) a prohibition on the making of investments with affiliates of AMF.

In the event of default, the holders of at least 25% of all debentures then outstanding may declare the principal of all the debentures and the interest accrued thereon due and payable. AMF claims that the combined liquidation preference of Series B Preference Stock and the principal amount of the Debenture (per unit) amounts to $23.00.

The Rights assigned are not transferable and may be exercised only during a forty day period beginning on the date that a person acquires 30% or more of the shares of AMF common stock without having proposed a plan to acquire all the remaining shares on terms which are deemed fair by the board of directors. The Rights expire on November 15, 1985 if not triggered prior to that date.

In the event the Rights are exercised, the holders of Series B Preference Stock are entitled to receive dividends at an annual rate of 15.5% calculated on the liquidation price of $172.50 per share. The Series B Stock is not redeemable until 1990, and then is redeemable only at a specified premium. The Series B stockholders are not entitled to vote for directors, except if accrued dividends are not paid. In this event the B stock, as a class, may elect two members of the Board. The Rights are redeemable for $.10 per Right by action of the AMF board at any time prior to a change in control, however, upon a change in control they become irredeemable.

* * *

Minstar argues that the Rights Plan discriminates against post May 20th stockholders. The Rights are not transferable. Thus, only the shareholders as of May 20, have any right to convert their stock. AMF contends that it did not discriminate against Minstar because, to the extent that Minstar owned any stock on May 20th, it too may convert. We find AMF's argument unpersuasive.

The May 20th date was not simply the record closing date as in the case of the usual dividends declaration. Normally, the record date closes the class of shareholders eligible to receive the dividend. Thereafter, the shareholder may transfer his dividend if he so chooses. The non-transferability of the Rights in the instant case is the fatal flaw.

We believe that as a matter of New Jersey law this type of discrimination between holders of a class of securities is illegal.[4] * * *

---

4. We recognize that the Board was empowered to issue as a dividend these rights to all common shareholders pursuant to the corporate charter. However, the non-transferability of the rights constituted a division of the common stock into two classes (pre-May 20/post-May 20). The bundle of rights possessed by pre-May 20 shareholders is significantly greater than those that would be possessed by purchas-

A second ground for invalidating this Plan is that the non-transferability of the Rights constitutes an unreasonable restraint on the alienability of the underlying common stock. Under normal circumstances Rights have real value when exercised in conjunction with common stock. However, the transfer of the common stock herein cannot be accomplished with the Rights, thus the value of stock in the hands of a post-May 20th purchaser is significantly reduced. Moreover, the seller would destroy much of the value of the Right by transferring the stock. Under these circumstances we find that the non-transferability of the Right is an unreasonable restraint on alienation.[5]

We must infer that the effect of the Rights, as now constituted, is to restrict the transferability of the underlying stock. Therefore AMF's arguments that the restraint only limits the Rights is unpersuasive. Moreover, despite the rationalizations of the AMF board, this effect seems to have been clearly intended.

We note that AMF claims the Rights are intended to protect the non-tenderors, however, anyone who purchased AMF common on the market would not be protected. In fact such a shareholder is distinctly more disadvantaged due to the Rights Plan. He would be unable to seek the "protection" of Class B stock, nor would he be part of the Minstar majority. Because many of the non-tendering shareholders would convert to Class B, the open market purchaser would be left out in the cold, without any large block of similarly situated non-tendering shareholders.

Finally we note the Rights Plan has the impermissible effect of vesting a veto power over any merger in the hands of the non-tendering May 20th stockholders. As discussed above only May 20th stockholders can become Class B shareholders. The Rights Plan requires approval of a merger by the Class B stock as a class, thus the May 20th shareholders may have effective control over any merger. The only way Minstar could ever merge would be to conduct a second tender offer after the Rights have been exercised to gain control of now non-existent Class B stock. We believe that such major changes in structure and voting rights may only be approved by the shareholders.

---

ers of the common stock on the open market, post-May 20. We consider this discriminatory reclassification of the common stock as improper. We believe that the Board may not do this without shareholder approval under New Jersey Law. N.J. Stat.Ann. § 14A:9–1(2)(f); 14A:9–2(4). See Asarco.

5. At the hearing on the motion, AMF's counsel argued that the restrictions on transfer were specifically authorized by New Jersey Statute. They first cited N.J. Stat.Ann. § 14A:7–7(1). We hold that § 7–7(1) is inapplicable. It appears that § 7–7(1) merely requires that any restraint on transferability appear on a certificate legend. That section does not substantively authorize restrictions. Counsel next asserted that § 14A:7–12(2) authorizes the restriction. While we agree that § 7–12(2) does authorize some restraints on alienation, it does not authorize the type of restriction at issue here. To the contrary, that section specifically indicates that a restraint must be "reasonable." We can find no authority in New Jersey law or the common law which authorizes a complete, absolute restraint on alienation. We therefore hold that the restriction is unreasonable. * * *

The Board's unilateral action, in this Court's opinion, was improper under New Jersey law.

* * *

The argument in *Minstar* that has had the most bite is its holding that a discriminatory rights plan improperly distinguishes among shares of stock in the same class. Several other courts have at one time agreed. Compare *Amalgamated Sugar Co. v. NL Industries, Inc.*, 644 F.Supp. 1229 (S.D.N.Y.1986); *Minstar Acquiring Corp. v. AMF, Inc.*, 621 F.Supp. 1252 (S.D.N.Y.1985); *Asarco, Inc.*, infra, with *Harvard Industries, Inc. v. Tyson*, Fed.Sec.L.Rep. (CCH) ¶ 93,064 (E.D.Mich.1986); *Dynamics Corp. of America v. CTS Corp.*, 637 F.Supp. 406 (N.D.Ill.1986), affirmed 794 F.2d 250 (7th Cir.1986), reversed on other grounds 481 U.S. 69, 107 S.Ct. 1637, 95 L.Ed.2d 67 (1987); Gelco Corp. v. Coneston Partners, 652 F.Supp. 829 (D.Minn.1986). The Delaware Supreme Court reached the question in Revlon, Inc. v. MacAndrews & Forbes Holdings, Inc., 506 A.2d 173, 180 (Del.1985). The court said a board "clearly had the power to adopt" a put poison pill plan that had a discriminatory feature similar to the one that so troubled Judge Low in *Minstar*.

Under the rights plan in *Revlon*, Revlon's shareholders received one note purchase right as a dividend on each share of common stock. The right entitled the holder to exchange one share of common stock for a $65 Revlon note bearing interest at the rate of 12 percent per annum with a one-year maturity. The rights would be triggered when anyone acquired beneficial ownership of 20 percent or more of Revlon's shares unless the acquirer promptly announced and consummated a transaction to buy Revlon's shares for cash at $65 or more per share. Those rights could not be exercised by the acquirer and could be redeemed for ten cents each anytime before the triggering event.

Questions

1. The New Jersey legislature passed the following amendment to its corporate code after the *Minstar* case recognizing the right of directors to discriminate among shareholders in *rights* or *option* offerings. How does this amendment affect the holding of the case? Does it alter Judge Lowe's position on discriminatory stock rights? On restraints on stock alienation? On transfers of shareholder power to managers without shareholder ratification?

> (3) * * * Unless otherwise provided in the certificate of incorporation * * * a corporation may before, * * * act, authorize and issue rights or options which include conditions that prevent the holder of a specified percentage of the outstanding shares of the corporation, including subsequent transferees of the holder, from exercising those rights or options or which invalidate any rights or options beneficially

owned by the holder of a specified percentage of the outstanding shares of the corporation, including subsequent transferees of the holder. N.J.Bus.Corp.Act § 14D:7–7(3). Several states have similar statutes. E.g., Colo.Corp.Code § 7–4–106(2); Official Code Ga.Ann. § 14–2–601; Fla.Gen. Corp.Act § 607.058; N.Y.—McKinney's Bus.Corp.Law §§ 4603(a)(1) & (2), 912(a)(10); Ohio Rev.Code § 1701.01.

2. In *Amalgamated Sugar,* cited above, the acquirer took an extraordinary gamble, triggering a call poison pill plan (containing both flip-over and flip-in features with a second trigger based on business transactions between the unwanted bidder and the target), and then litigated the effect of a triggered plan on the firm in court. What was the position of the firm after the plan had been triggered? Can the target negotiate with other potential buyers, even white knights, to sell the firm? What happens to the value of target stock held by the bidder if the court refuses to enjoin the plan? The bound-up position of the firm under the triggered plan was a substantial factor in the judge's decision to invalidate the plan. Should a judge always invalidate a triggered plan to free an otherwise trussed-up firm? Is it relevant that the plans are designed not to be triggered, that is, not to create discrimination among shareholders?

3. Would Judge Lowe have approved the plan in *Minstar* if shareholders had voted to approve the plan? Can shareholders vote to approve disparities in voting rights among shareholders holding a single class of stock or to approve restraints on transferability of outstanding shares?

4. Does the judge's argument that the plan discriminates among shareholders of the same class or series make sense? Consider the following counterargument:

The statutes at issue in the case are intended to protect existing shareholders from dilution of their equity position by unilateral board action after the shareholder has invested. The board cannot unilaterally assign a dividend to all shareholders with last names beginning with A, for example. The discrimination in poison pills is not of this type, however, because all shareholders who purchased stock triggering the rights knew, at the time of purchase, that they would be excluded from exercising such rights. Thus these purchasers were not disadvantaged by a change in their positions after they had purchased their stock. Indeed, if one asks whether the plans discriminated among shareholders at the time of the rights dividend, the technical answer would be no; the bidder's act created the discrimination. On the other hand, everyone agrees that if a board adopts a plan that discriminates against a bidder who has already bought his stock, the plan is unlawful. In any event, asking whether the plan created the discrimination or whether the bidders knowingly triggered the discriminatory effects completely misses the point. The real issue is whether the poison pill plans provide a benefit to target shareholders by forcing bidders to negotiate with the board. If plans enable target managers to better protect their own shareholders in acquisition negotiations, they are sound; if they enable target managers to protect their personal positions in the firm at the expense of their shareholders, they are infirm.

5. Is a poison pill plan vulnerable to proxy or written consent contests? Can a bidder seeking to acquire Revlon buy 19.9 percent of Revlon's

shares, make a generous tender offer conditional on the board's approval (expecting the target board will reject it by refusing to redeem its poison pill), solicit proxies or consents to oust the members of the existing board based on their refusal to accept the offer, elect new, sympathetic directors who redeem the poison pill rights, and, finally, complete the tender offer? See *Georgia–Pacific Corp. v. Great Northern Nekoosa Corp.*, supra. If arbitrageurs take significant positions in the stock, who will they vote for in the proxy contest? Proxy solicitation rules, of course, add significant expense to a hostile takeover (the expense of proxy materials and the added financing costs of the delay), but is the added expense a significant obstacle? How can a target protect itself against proxy or written consent contests? Can shark repellent charter amendments solve the problem? See section 3. Can target firms design their poison pill plans to protect against proxy solicitations as well as stock acquisitions? This last question is the subject of the next two cases.

THE BANK OF NEW YORK CO. v. IRVING BANK CORP.

Supreme Court, New York County, 1988.
139 Misc.2d 665, 528 N.Y.S.2d 482, affirmed 143 A.D.2d 1070, 533 N.Y.S.2d 411 (1988).

* * *

HERMAN CAHN, JUDGE:

The Bank of New York Company, Inc. ("BNY"), plaintiff, moves for an order enjoining defendant Irving Bank Corporation ("IBC") from enforcing a certain "rights" agreement as amended on March 15, 1988, and specifically enjoining the enforcement of the March 15, 1988 amendment.

In September 1987 BNY announced its intention to commence a tender offer for all of the outstanding shares of IBC.

* * *

The board of directors of IBC believes that acceptance of the offer is not beneficial for IBC's shareholders, stemming in large part from the fact that federal regulations limit the number of prospective tender offerors. However, these regulations have recently been modified, which modifications will slowly deregulate the banking system over the next few years. The result of the deregulation may be to allow more large banking institutions, not presently able to bid for IBC, to do so. It is asserted that this will produce an auction type bidding during which, it is believed, a higher price can be negotiated by the board of directors. This argument has presumably been communicated to IBC's shareholders in response to BNY's tender offer. On October 9, 1987 the board of IBC adopted a "rights" plan. Pursuant thereto, one right per share of outstanding common stock was made payable to shareholders of record on October 19, 1987. If an acquisition is approved by the board, the rights can be redeemed by the board at .01 per right. The right to redeem is exercisable prior to the time a person or entity obtains ownership or control of twenty per cent or more of stock of IBC.

The rights become exercisable when certain triggering events occur and thereupon entitle the holders thereof to either purchase shares in IBC or in any new company formed as the result of an acquisition:

1) Ten days following an announcement that 20% or more of IBC's outstanding common stock has been acquired by one person or entity, the rights issued entitle the holders thereof to purchase one share of IBC for $200. (This exercise price is much greater than the present or recent market value of a share of IBC [1] and therefore is properly labeled by plaintiffs as "illusory," having "nothing to do with the reason for the poison pill.") * * *

2) If IBC is consolidated or merged with another company, or if 50% or more of IBC's assets or earning power are transferred or sold, the rights entitle the holders thereof to purchase shares of common stock of the surviving company at 50% of market value. (This provision is commonly referred to as a "flip-over.")

The purpose for adopting the rights plan was to make it unattractive and unprofitable for IBC to be taken over by another company unless the board of directors of IBC approves the acquisition.

A) THE MARCH 15TH AMENDMENT

On March 15, 1988, approximately one month after BNY had commenced a proxy contest seeking election of a new board, the IBC board adopted an amendment to the heretofore described rights agreement. Said amendment, Section 23, provided for the redemption of the rights by the board at any time "prior to such time as any person becomes an acquiring person." [3] However, the basic thrust of Section 23 is to severely limit the authority of any board of directors other than the present board to redeem the rights. The relevant portion of Section 23 reads as follows:

"... the Board of Directors of the company shall be entitled so to redeem the Rights only if it consists of a majority of Continuing Directors (as hereinafter defined) or, if the Board of Directors of the Company is not so constituted, only if the members of the Board of Directors of the Company who are not Continuing Directors were elected to immediately succeed Continuing Directors and either (i) were elected by the affirmative vote of the holders of at least two-thirds of the issued and outstanding Shares of the Company or (ii) in connection with the election of the members of the Board of Directors of the Company who are not Continuing Directors, no merger, consolidation, liquidation, business combination or similar transaction or series of transactions with respect to the Company is or was proposed. The term "Continuing Director" shall mean a director who either was a member of the Board of Directors of the Company prior to March 15, 1988 or who subsequently became a director of the Company and whose

---

1. For example, the market value of IBC at the close of business on April 13, 1988 was $65.00/share.

3. An "acquiring person" is defined as "... any person ... who or which ... shall be the Beneficial Owner (as such term is hereinafter defined) of 20% or more of the shares then outstanding ..."

election, or nomination for election by the Company's shareholders, was approved by a vote of a majority of the Continuing Directors then on the Board of Directors of the Company."

An analysis of the above will show that it creates several different classes of directors. The first are directors who were in office prior to March 15, 1988, and who have all rights of directors. The second group are directors who are elected after March 15, 1988 and whose election was approved by a vote of the majority of the first group. This group also has all the rights of directors.

The third group are directors elected after March 15, 1988 and who have not postponed or agreed to certain actions relating to mergers. These are the actions which the first group has decided to block.

The fourth and final group are directors who were elected by the vote of the holders of at least two-thirds of the shares. This group also has all the rights of directors.

It is to be further noted that a single plurality is required for election to the board.

What Section 23 thus does is several things. First, it creates several different classes of directors—having different powers, or having to be elected by different majorities to exercise all of the powers. Second, it effectively limits the powers of a future board which is not a continuation of the present board or which is not approved by it, while still leaving those powers to a board which is approved. For example, the present board, or one approved by it, may redeem the rights. A future board, properly elected by a fifty-one percent majority, but not approved by the present board, may not redeem the shares.

BNY and shareholders of IBC seek to enjoin enforcement of this provision. The court notes that Section 23 as amended March 15, 1988 is the only provision of the rights agreement herein contested.

* * *

Recently, there has been an abundance of case law recognizing the propriety of the adoption by the board of directors of a corporation of a rights plan, both as a preventative mechanism to ward off future tender offers (See, e.g., *Moran v. Household International, Inc.*, 500 A.2d 1346 (Del.Supr.1985)), and as a defense measure during battle with a corporate raider (see, e.g., *Revlon, Inc. v. MacAndrews & Forbes Holdings*, 506 A.2d 173 (Del.Supr.1986)). These cases address the duties of directors to their corporations and their protections under the business judgment rule.

At issue here is not the propriety of the adoption of the plan, but rather the legality of Section 23, the provision restricting the power of duly elected directors to conduct business of the corporation otherwise conductable by directors elected in a specified manner. The Court turns therefore, to the Business Corporation Law.

Business Corporation Law Sec. 614 governs the voting requirements for the election of directors of a corporation:

> "(a) Directors shall, except as otherwise required by this chapter or by the certificate of incorporation as permitted by this chapter, be elected by a plurality of the votes cast at a meeting of shareholders by the holders of shares entitled to vote in the election." (Underlining added.)

A duly elected board is empowered to manage the business of the corporation (B.C.L. Sec. 701) by vote of a majority present, if a quorum is present at the time of the vote (B.C.L. Sec. 708). A restriction of the board's power to manage the business of the corporation is invalid unless (1) all of the incorporators or all of the shareholders of record have authorized such provision on the certificate of incorporation; (2) subsequent shareholders have notice of the provision; and (3) no shares of the corporation are listed on a national securities exchange or in an over-the-counter market. (B.C.L. Sec. 620).

By statute any restriction on the power of the board of directors must be placed in the Certificate of Incorporation * * * which was not done by IBC. Accordingly, the board of directors was without authority to adopt a provision restricting the action of a future board.

That a board could be elected which possesses the full power to redeem the rights herein does not resolve the issue; IBC's board went beyond its power when it adopted a provision which would require a super-majority vote for BNY's slate in order to elect a new board. Again, no such provision was placed in the certificate of incorporation requiring such supermajority vote (B.C.L. Sec. 614).

The evil of Section 23, is not that it deprives a Board of certain powers; it is that it is selective in the deprivation. In other words, the present Board members could have the powers, if they were reelected to the Board, but the insurgents would not if they were elected by the same plurality. Those new members of the Board approved by the current Board would have the powers, but those not so approved would not. This retention of authority is beyond the powers of the Board.

It is no answer to say that the insurgents would possess all the powers, if elected by a supermajority. The illegal discrimination between Boards is not thereby cured.

* * *

Questions

1. The case raised the fear among the managers of New York corporations, who did not read the case carefully, that in New York poison pill plans were illegal. The New York State legislature responded to the outcry by passing a statute that amended its corporate code to legitimize poison pills. Please read sections 4603(a)(1) and (2) and 912(a)(10) in the New York Business Corporation Law. Does the statute overrule the *Irving Bank* case? How is the statute different from the New Jersey statute above?

2. In Davis Acquisition, Inc. v. NWA, Inc., Fed.Sec.L.Rep. (CCH) ¶ 95,434 (Del.Ch.1989), a flip-in-flip-over call rights plan contained a provision that, in effect, provided that any board that comprised predominantly members who were not nominated by the incumbent board and for whom there had not been forty-five days' prior notice that they would be nominated could not redeem the stock rights for a period of 180 days after its election, if to do so would facilitate a transaction with a bidder who was not approved by the incumbent board. The incumbent board, or a successor predominantly composed of people nominated to office by the incumbent board, was not subject to such a limitation. The plan was authorized by the target board after a frustrated bidder (his merger negotiations with the target board had failed) had announced an intention to mount a proxy solicitation seeking to elect a full slate of directors to the board. The chancery court, hoping to clear the way for an unbiased shareholder vote, denied a motion for preliminary injunction on the condition that the target inform its shareholders that the redemption provision had been challenged in court and, *if* found invalid, might not substantially delay effectuation of a sale transaction by the bidder's slate.

3. If a firm cannot protect the redemption rights in a poison pill plan from a successful proxy solicitation, can a firm adopt a put poison pill plan that is triggered by an unapproved stock acquisition *or* an unapproved proxy consent solicitation? In other words, can a firm stop a proxy solicitation *before* the votes are counted? Consider the poison pill plan in the following case:

STAHL v. APPLE BANCORP., INC.

Court of Chancery of Delaware, 1990.
Fed.Sec.L.Rep. ¶ 95,412.

[The facts are on pages 473–478, supra.]

Opinion of ALLEN, CHANCELLOR.

* * *

Currently pending is plaintiff's motion for partial summary judgment, principally, with respect to a claim that the definition of beneficial ownership of stock in the rights plan causes the rights to have certain impermissible or inequitable effects upon the exercise of the corporate franchise. * * * The stock rights plan in issue, as do most such plans, reflects the concept of Rule 13d–5 in defining that relationship broadly. For purposes of the triggering mechanisms of the stock rights plan a shareholder is deemed to own any shares:

> (iii) which are beneficially owned, directly or indirectly, by any other person with which such person or any such person's affiliates has any agreement, arrangement or understanding ... for the purpose of acquiring, holding, voting or disposing of any securities of the [company].

The plan, however, exempts from this definition of "agreement, arrangement or understanding" to vote [the Company's securities] any agreement, etc., that "arises solely from a revocable proxy or consent given in response to a public proxy or consent solicitation."

It is assumed by both parties (and thus not an issue for the court on this motion) that Mr. Stahl is precluded from entering into an agreement with other shareholders (if those shareholders own .7% of Bancorp's stock) to serve on the same slate of directors in opposition to the management slate; from agreeing to indemnify (or be indemnified by) other shareholders in connection with running for office; and from asking for and receiving permission to use the name of another stockholder for purposes of endorsing his slate, even if there were no irrevocable proxy given or other promises made.

In other words Stahl contends, and the company agrees, that the *in terrorem* effect of the beneficial ownership definition upon him is to isolate him; to prevent him from reaching agreements with other shareholders (whether revocable or not) that would not direct the voting of stock, but that would otherwise concern the election contest. Mr. Stahl does not contend that a definition preventing him from entering into contracts, agreements or understandings that *bind* another to vote for his slate or that *bind* another not to vote in favor of the management nominees would be invalid. The formation of blocks of committed (legally bound) shares, he implicitly concedes, involves circumstances and considerations closely analogous to those arising from the existence of a large single shareholder, which considerations have been held to present threats justifying the rights that poison pill plans contemplate. But agreements that broadly *relate* to the vote but that do not bind other shareholders (such as agreements of the kind specified above) cannot, he says, be seen as presenting a sufficient risk to justify the direct imposition on the fairness of the proxy contest that, he asserts, the broad definition of beneficial ownership in the rights plan entails.

* * *

As indicated above, the relief sought in the amended complaint and in the motion before the court appears to be a judicial declaration that the beneficial ownership provision of Bancorp's stock rights plan cannot validly be applied to agreements or understandings that *direct the voting of shares but are unconditionally revocable* or agreements that relate to the proxy contest *but do not legally bind any person to vote* in one way or another.

There is a strong normative argument that might be offered in support of such a position. While corporate elections are not perfectly parallel to civic elections (one can, for example, accumulate votes by buying shares) notions of what a fair election means and entails do inescapably carry over to some extent from one setting to the other. It is troubling in either context if the side in control of the levers of power employs them with respect to an election to coerce its opposition to restrict its legitimate electioneering activities. One need not assume bad faith on the part of incumbents to foresee in such a situation the prospects for unfairness; honest men seeking their (disputable) vision of what is best, if not bound-in by rules, are capable of gross impositions. Thus, it offers cold comfort that the law will assume that directors are acting in good faith. Where the franchise is involved a special obligation falls upon courts to review with care action that impinges upon legitimate election activities.

In *Moran v. Household International, Inc.*, this court, and later of course our Supreme Court, faced the question of the statutory validity of a poison pill stock rights plan. The proxy contest implications of the pill were reviewed, if not exhaustively. Responding to the obvious problems that arise in recognizing a board's ability to, in effect, regulate the legitimate election activities of shareholder-adversaries, this court referred to "a troubling aspect of the Rights Plan ... its potential restriction on proxy contests." 490 A.2d at 1079. The relief sought in *Moran*, was the invalidation in its entirety of the stock rights plan there in issue. 490 A.2d at 1063. In the trial court it was argued that the rights plan would adversely affect the ability to mount an effective proxy contest. The court found "[t]he concern ... somewhat speculative." 490 A.2d at 1079. On appeal the stockholder argued:

that the Board was unauthorized to fundamentally restrict stockholders' rights to conduct a proxy contest.... that the "20% trigger" effectively prevent[ed] any stockholder from first acquiring 20% or more shares before conducting a proxy contest and further, *it prevent[ed] stockholders from banding together into a group to solicit proxies if, collectively, they own[ed] 20% or more of the stock....*

Moran, 500 A.2d at 1355 (emphasis added). The Supreme Court quoted the Vice Chancellor's ruling on this point:

Thus, while the Rights Plan does deter the formation of proxy efforts of a certain magnitude, it does not limit the voting power of individual shares. On the evidence presented *it is highly conjectural* to assume that a particular effort to assert shareholder views in the election of directors or revisions of corporate policy will be frustrated by the proxy feature of the Plan. Household's witnesses, Troubh and Higgins described recent corporate takeover battles in which insurgents holding less than 10% stock ownership were able to secure corporate control through a proxy contest or the threat of one.

Moran, 500 A.2d at 1355 (emphasis added). The Supreme Court then found that:

There was sufficient evidence at trial to support the Vice Chancellor's finding that *the effect upon proxy contests will be minimal.*

Moran, 500 A.2d at 1355 (emphasis added). Having concluded that the impact on proxy contests would be minimal, the court rejected the contention that the rights plan would impermissibly burden a proxy contest.

The Supreme Court's determination that the flip-over pill considered in *Moran* involved acceptable ("minimal") effects on proxy contests, points us first to the recognition that validity of stock rights must be assessed at the time of the corporate action creating them; validity of corporate securities cannot rise or fall on future contingencies once issued. Thus, with respect to the point here being considered, it is an assessment of the reasonably foreseeable consequences that a pill is likely to have on legitimate election activities, made as of the time that the board acted, that is relevant for a determination whether the action was authorized and whether it constituted a breach of duty of loyalty. *Moran* held that there was only "conjecture" and "speculation" to support the conclusion that the effects of the pill were other than "minimal" on proxy contests in that instance. It also held that board action taken in good faith and advisedly may be valid even though it affects in some respects the exercise of the franchise. Thus, I deduce that plaintiff can prevail on the initial invalidity position only if one can say (1) that *Moran* did not address, and thus did not authorize restrictions on the proxy process arising from, agreements relating to the voting process that do not conditionally or otherwise bind votes and (2) the board has no valid interest in forcing shareholders to abstain from such agreements.

The Supreme Court did not focus upon unconditionally revocable voting agreements or upon agreements relating to the proxy contest process that are not proxies and do not legally bind a shareholder to vote. It stated the issue it addressed as: "whether the restriction on individuals and *groups* from first acquiring 20% of the shares before waging a proxy contest fundamentally restricts stockholders rights ..." 500 A.2d at 1355. There was no need to specifically consider whether shareholders who do not legally bind themselves to vote together but who might wish to enter into understandings or agreements relating to the proxy contest (*e.g.*, serve on the same insurgent slate), are a "group" that can legitimately be discouraged (prevented) from doing so.

The thrust of the Supreme Court's reasoning in *Moran* was simply that the restrictions imposed by the stock rights plan on a proxy contest were immaterial to conducting a proxy fight effectively. In adopting the stock rights plan here, it has not been shown that the Bancorp board could not have reasonably concluded similarly. If it did the restrictions here at issue should be valid, as were those in *Moran,* unless the kinds of revocable voting agreements or other agreements not covering the voting of stock that are our focus can be said to require or deserve the same treatment received by revocable proxies, which the Supreme Court in *Moran* in effect exempted from the language of the rights plan. *See* 500 A.2d at 1355. But while the kinds of agreements we consider now are the same as revocable proxies in that they are revocable, they may be different in many particulars of practical significance. The most salient difference, however, arises from the fact that an exemption for revocable proxies from the beneficial ownership definition is mandated by the Supreme Court's "immateriality" test. The acceptance of proxies is the essence of a proxy contest. A prohibition on accepting them beyond the triggering point could never be immaterial; it would be fatal to a proxy contestant's position. But voting agreements or understandings of the type here in question plainly could be (and in this instance probably are) immaterial in the sense that a shareholder may put forth a slate of candidates and communicate her position to others, and others may vote for that slate without restriction.

In light of *Moran*, I am unable to say that stockholders have an absolute right to reach agreements with each other concerning the voting of stock (excepting agreements reflected in the granting of a revocable proxy). In the absence of such an absolute right, and given the fact that the summary judgment record does not permit me to say that the Bancorp board could not have reasonably concluded that the restrictions here addressed would not materially impair the ability of the shareholders to turn out the existing board, I cannot now conclude that the provision of the stock rights plan that defines beneficial ownership constitutes an invalid provision beyond the board's power to adopt.

* * *

Question

Time Warner stock, one year after Time's successful defense of Paramount Communications' bid of $200 a share, was trading at about $85. Will dissident shareholders mount a proxy fight? Time Warner has adopted a "divide and rule" poison pill plan. Here's how it works: If a person or group unseats five out of eight Time Warner directors who stand for election in any given year (Time Warner has staggered elections for its twenty-four directors), the company will immediately issue a new lot of Time Warner common shares—in some cases more than a $1 billion worth—to its giant class of preferred shareholders. These investors also get the option to convert their nonvoting preferred shares into voting common, at, roughly, then-current market prices for common. Currently Time Warner's Class C and D preferred shares can be converted into common only for $200 and $225, respectively. Existing common shareholders get nothing, with the effect that their stake in Time Warner is heavily diluted. Common holders, knowing in advance of a proxy contest that Time Warner would effectively take money out of their pockets and give it to preferred holders if the insurgents prevail, will have little reason to throw their votes to the insurgent. Is the plan valid under Delaware law? The company argues that the purpose of the device is not to stop proxy contests but to protect the preferred stock from major control changes—much like the event risk protection for junk bond holders. The "divide and rule" plan also protects against stock acquisitions. Preferred holders get similar benefits if any person or group buys 40 percent of the common. See Wall St.J. p. C1, col. 3 (Dec. 12, 1990).

Supervoting Poison Pill Plans

The *Irving Bank Corp.* case and the *Unilever* case that follows suggest that courts apply a much stricter standard to stock dividend plans that directly affect shareholder voting rights than to stock dividend plans that give shareholders puts or call rights at handsome premiums. Is this justifiable? All put or call poison pill plans affect a shareholder's right to sell his shares by blocking unapproved bids, a right just as fundamental and probably more valuable than a shareholder's right to vote. If a firm can adopt put or call poison pill plans without a shareholder vote, why should courts not allow a stock dividend of the type attempted in the following case?

UNILEVER ACQUISITION CORP. v. RICHARDSON–VICKS, INC.

United States District Court, Southern District of New York, 1985.
618 F.Supp. 407.

OWEN, DISTRICT JUDGE.

Richardson–Vicks Inc., * * * is resisting a takeover attempt by the Unilever Acquisition Corp.

* * *

Richardson–Vicks is a publicly-held Delaware corporation, with some one-third or more of its stock controlled or held by various Richardsons.

* * * The Richardson–Vicks board of directors voted and announced the issuance of a "Series A $4.00 Participating Cumulative Convertible Preferred Stock" to be distributed as a stock dividend to common stockholders of record as of September 27, 1985. Under the proposal, one share of the new preferred stock is to issue for each 5 shares of common. Among other benefits, each preferred share will entitle the holder to cast 25 votes on all issues on which the common can vote. However, if the preferred share is transferred, the new holder may exercise only 5 of those 25 votes for the first 36 months the stock is held. Thus, if the stock dividend is made as planned, the result will be that while each common stockholder will have the same voting power as theretofore, that stockholder will be unable to transfer those voting rights, since two-thirds will be unexercisable for 36 months following the transfer. This, it appears, would make it impossible for Unilever to acquire Richardson–Vicks at this time, for without the consent of the Richardson group, even were Unilever to succeed in purchasing all non-Richardson shares, the effect would be to increase the Richardson group's command of the total exercisable vote from about one-third to an absolute majority for the following 36 months.

* * *

Under Delaware statute, each share of common stock is entitled to one vote, unless the corporate certificate of incorporation provides otherwise. Del.Gen.Corp.Law § 212. Furthermore, to change the certificate of incorporation in matters affecting shareholder rights, the board must ordinarily submit the proposed amendments to the shareholders at an annual or special meeting. Del.Gen.Corp.Law § 242.

However, the board is also empowered to authorize by resolution, without shareholder approval, the issuance of new stock not authorized in the certificate of incorporation if it is explicitly authorized to do so by the provisions of the certificate of incorporation and it files a certificate meeting certain requirements with the Secretary of State. Del.Gen.Corp.Law § 151(g). One unreported decision of the Delaware Chancery court has relied on this provision in refusing to enjoin issuance without stockholder authorization of a "piggyback preferred stock" which would have the effect of increasing from 75% to 80% the majority necessary to consummate certain mergers. See *National Education Corporation v. Bell & Howell Co., et al.,* # 7278 (Del.Ch.Ct. 1983). While defendant has filed a certificate pursuant to this section, plaintiff maintains that the board acted beyond its authority in so doing, since while the Richardson–Vicks certificate of incorporation authorizes the board to issue preferred stock with the terms to be set by the board, it does so only with the restriction that all shares of any series of preferred stock have identical voting rights.

In addition, the Delaware statute explicitly provides that "no restriction [on transfer of shares] shall be binding with respect to securities issued prior to the adoption of the restriction unless the holders of the securities are parties to an agreement or voted in favor of the restriction." Del.Gen.Corp.Law § 202(b).

The proposed dividend both restricts transferability of Richardson–Vicks common stock and affects its voting rights, since after the issuance of the dividend, a common stockholder will be unable to transfer two-thirds of his voting power. In addition, it undoubtedly will discriminate hereafter among different holders of shares of the same issue of preferred stock, since some will, while others will not be able to vote the full number, depending on the circumstances of acquisition.

Defendant points out that discrimination among stockholders, when authorized by the stockholders or under extreme circumstances, is not in itself a violation of Delaware law and has been upheld by the Delaware courts, although under significantly different circumstances. See *Providence & Worchester Co. v. Baker,* 378 A.2d 121 (Del.Sup.1977) (where authorized for over one hundred years by corporate charter, large stockholders may be restricted to fewer votes per share than small stockholders); *Unocal Corp. v. Mesa Petroleum Co.,* 493 A.2d 946 (Del.Sup.Ct. 1985) (in fending off well known "greenmailer," corporation permitted to make exchange offer to all shareholders other than the greenmailer). However, these cases are not applicable where the discrimination strips the shareholder of the ability to transfer voting rights without prior warning, compensation or shareholder authorization, creating two classes within one series of shares—those that have been recently acquired, with reduced votes, and those that have not, with full votes—and it does this in the face of a provision of the corporation's certificate of incorporation explicitly providing that "[a]ll shares of any one series of preferred stock shall be identical with each other in all respects." Art. 4, § B–III. Under Delaware law, a change in corporate structure of this magnitude, reducing the transferability of a shareholder's ability to vote and the value of his or her asset to this degree, requires stockholder approval which has not been obtained. Del.Gen.Corp.Law § 202(b).

* * *

There are other early stock distribution cases that found supervoting right plans unlawful. E.g., Asarco, Inc. v. Court, 611 F.Supp. 468, 477 (D.N.J.1985); R.D. Smith & Co. v. Preway Inc., 644 F.Supp. 868 (W.D.Wis.1986); Spinner Corp. v. Princeville Development Corp., Civ. No. 86–0701 (D.Iowa, Oct. 31, 1986). In *Asarco* the court rejected as ultra vires an amendment of the certificate of incorporation providing for issuance of Series C preferred stock. The amendment authorized the board to issue a dividend of $^1\!/_{10}$ of a share of Series C for each share of common. Initially Series C shares possessed no voting rights except on matters related to preferential rights. However, if any shareholder became the beneficial owner of more than 20 percent of either Asarco's common stock or its Series C shares, then each $^1\!/_{10}$ of a Series C share owned by anyone other than the 20 percent holder entitled its owner to five votes on all matters submitted to common stockholders. The Series C shares owned by the 20 percent holder who had triggered the voting rights did not acquire voting rights. Judge Debevoise reasoned that

> Asarco's board created a situation where the same class of stock will have different voting rights. This can be viewed as occurring with respect to two classes of stock. The new preferred will have differing voting rights depending on whether it is held by a 20 percent holder. The new preferred is piggy-backed onto the outstanding common stock, and therefore there has also been created a situation in which certain common stockholders,—those who acquire 20 percent of the shares,—will have their voting power diluted five-fold vis-à-vis the other common stockholders. This is to be distinguished from a situation where a new class of stock has superior voting rights to all common stockholders or to all stockholders holding some other class. I conclude that while the Business Corporation Act permits changes of voting rights as between classes or series of stock; it does not permit an amendment under section 7–2 which would redistribute voting power within a class or series.

611 F.Supp. at 477.

Questions

1. If the shareholders of Richardson–Vicks voted to approve by a simple majority the convertible preferred stock dividend in issue, would the plan be legal? Or must such a vote be unanimous? Note that the court in *Asarco* declared that an amendment to a certificate of incorporation was ultra vires and void.

2. Does the New Jersey statute on pages 513–514 legitimize supervoting plans? Does the New York Stock Exchange rule against the creation of two tiers of voting stock on pages 478–484 prohibit list companies from using supervoting poison pill plans?

3. Would the Richardson–Vicks plan in *Unilever* be legal if the plan contained a provision allowing the board to waive the effects of the vote dilution, that is, if the board could approve specific transactions? If Richardson–Vicks issued to common shareholders a stock right to acquire Series C preferred, what would be the result if an approved bidder acquired 20 percent of the firm's shares and the right were redeemable by the board before the triggering acquisition? After the triggering acquisition?

4. Is the *Unilever* case good law in Delaware? The case was decided before the Delaware Supreme Court opinions in *Moran* and *Revlon*. Can one make the argument that the discrimination claim in *Unilever* is similar to the discrimination claim in *Minstar* that the Delaware Supreme Court rejected in *Revlon?* In other words, does a supervoting plan discriminate among shareholders, which is legal, and not among shares in the same class, which is not? Or is shareholder voting treated differently from put or call rights attached to shares?

Note
Shareholder Resolutions Under Rule 14a–8 Attacking Management Conduct in Takeovers

Rule 14a–8, promulgated under section 14 of the 1934 Exchange Act, grants a security holder owning at least 1 percent or $1,000 in market value of voting securities the right to present proposals for inclusion in the corporation's proxy solicitation materials for upcoming shareholder meetings. The security holder must have held the securities for at least one year (ownership through an employee stock ownership plan counts), and the proposals must be timely. The proponent may not only ask for a shareholder vote on a specific proposition but also draft a five-hundred-word supporting statement that the firm must include in the corporation's proxy statement. The rule gives even small shareholders an opportunity to initiate a referendum on various aspects of corporate policy and operation. Without the rule (or if a shareholder proposal does not come under the rule), a shareholder has to bear the expense of preparing and mailing his own proxy and proxy statement, complying with all the proxy solicitation rules continued in Securities and Exchange Commission regulation 14A. For all but the largest shareholders this is prohibitively expensive. Thus rule 14a–8 is an essential and often exclusive mechanism for shareholder activism.

The scope of rule 14a–8 is carefully circumscribed, however. Section (c) of the rule details circumstances under which a corporation may omit a proposal from an upcoming proxy statement. Please read SEC rule 14a–8(c) in your statutory supplement. The scope of these exemptions is frequently a matter of contention as shareholders attempt to put the choices of their managers in acquisitions to a shareholder vote. Can a shareholder use rule 14a–8 to have shareholders vote on the appropriateness of a takeover defense adopted by their managers without a ratifying vote (i.e., a poison pill plan)? See, e.g., In re National Intergroup, Inc., Fed.Sec.L.Rep. (CCH) ¶ 95,355 (Del.Ch.1990) (a proposed resolution attacking a poison pill plan led to a negotiated substitute shareholder resolution, supported by management, that placed a shortened expiration date on the plan and mandated that all future plans be subject to shareholder approval; it received 96 percent of the vote). The SEC has not been a model of consistency in its approach to shareholder resolution requests relating to acquisitions.

On February 23, 1990, for example, the SEC's Division of Corporate Finance ruled that UAL Corporation could not omit a proposal that called for the company's board to censure its chief executive officer for his role in promoting a recent failed leveraged buyout. The SEC held that the attempted LBO was extraordinary in nature and thus fell outside the rule 14a–8(c)(7) ordinary business exception. Less than one month later, however, the division reversed itself, holding that the issue did fall under rule 14a–8(c)(7); the decision to censure did constitute the ordinary business of the company. The division decided similarly when it held on March 22, 1990, that Time–Warner could omit a proposal that called for censure of company directors for rejecting the recent Paramount takeover bid. The division, however, relied on rule 14a–8(c)(8), which allows the exclusion of proposals that relate to an election to office; the proposal attacked the business judgment of directors up for reelection.

On January 10, 1990, the SEC, in a major reversal of a previous policy, held that a corporation could not omit, under rule 14a–8(c)(7), a proposal recommending that the board adopt a policy barring golden parachute payments. The division concluded that significant policy issues surrounded the current public debate over antitakeover devices such as golden parachutes. The SEC ruling led to a spate of shareholder resolutions attacking golden parachutes in the spring 1990 annual meeting season. The proposals received an average of 24.2 percent of the votes cast. On February 6, 1990, the division decided that Wendy's International could omit a proposal asking the board to eliminate all antitakeover measures and not to consider future measures. The division relied on 14a–8(c)(3), concluding that the proposal was too vague and thus potentially misleading. The division implied that a more narrowly drawn proposal might survive scrutiny. On June 30, 1990, the SEC stated that Philips Industries could not omit from its proxy materials a shareholder proposal asking that the company's officers and directors personally reimburse Philips for all fees and expenses associated with a stalled leveraged buyout and related litigation.

The evidence on the success of shareholder resolutions on acquisition defenses shows a trend in favor of dissident shareholders. See 22 Sec.Reg. & Law Rptr. (B.N.A.) 1073 (July 20, 1990) (summarizing data compiled by the Investor Responsibility Research Center). Proposals attacking poison pill plans captured record numbers of favorable votes during the spring 1990 annual meeting season. The average level of support was 42.8 percent. This represents a steady increase in the level of support for the anti-poison pill shareholder proposals. The first year that shareholders launched a campaign against poison pills was 1987, and the proposals garnered an average of only 27.4 percent of the vote. In 1988 the proposals received an average of 38.2 percent, and in 1989 an average of 39.5 percent of the vote. The 1990 season also generated a resurgence of popularity in the number of antipill resolutions filed. In 1987 shareholders filed over fifty resolutions. The number had fallen to twenty in 1988 and 1989. In 1990 the number rose to thirty-nine, twelve of which won a majority of the votes cast (compared to only two in 1987 and 1988, for example).

The question remains, however: When a single shareholder takes the lead and files a rule 14a–8 resolution, complete with explanatory statement, why are other shareholders who take a moment to execute and send in their proxies not voting in larger numbers against the plans? Would rules making shareholder proxy executions confidential help? Shareholder proposals to make proxy voting confidential received an average of 34 percent of the votes cast in 1990, up from 27.4 percent in 1989, 18.8 percent in 1988, and 9.9 percent in 1987. Why are institutional shareholders sensitive about incumbent firm managers knowing how the shareholders voted? Do the managers of large funds of investors' money have a stake in keeping open the information flow from inside publicly traded firms?

SUBCHAPTER B. FIDUCIARY DUTIES OF CONTROLLING OFFICIALS AND SHAREHOLDERS

SECTION 1. THE DECISION TO SELL: MUST THE TARGET BOARD PUBLICLY AUCTION OFF THE FIRM?

As you will note in the cases below, the Delaware Supreme Court uses four basic tests for the propriety of a selling firm's board in an acquisition. The basic business judgment rule test in *Smith v. Van Gorkom,* the enhanced business judgment rule test in *Unocal v. Mesa Petroleum,* the fair auction test in *Revlon v. MacAndrews,* and the intrinsic fairness test in *Mills Acquisition v. MacMillan.* Look for the basic definition of each test and for the facts that are crucial to the court's choice of a test in any given case.

SMITH v. VAN GORKOM
Supreme Court of Delaware, 1985.
488 A.2d 858.

HORSEY, JUSTICE (for the majority):

* * *

This appeal from the Court of Chancery involves a class action brought by shareholders of the defendant Trans Union Corporation ("Trans Union" or "the Company"), originally seeking rescission of a cash-out merger of Trans Union into the defendant New T Company ("New T"), a wholly-owned subsidiary of the defendant, Marmon Group, Inc. ("Marmon"). Alternate relief in the form of damages is sought against the defendant members of the Board of Directors of Trans Union, New T, and Jay A. Pritzker and Robert A. Pritzker, owners of Marmon.

* * *

On September 5, at another Senior Management meeting which Van Gorkom attended, Romans again brought up the idea of a leveraged buy-out as a "possible strategic alternative" to the Company's acquisition program. Romans and Bruce S. Chelberg, President and Chief Operating Officer of Trans Union, had been working on the matter in preparation for the meeting. According to Romans: They did not "come up" with a price for the Company. They merely "ran the numbers" at $50 a share and at $60 a share with the "rough form" of their cash figures at the time. Their "figures indicated that $50 would be very easy to do but $60 would be very difficult to do under those figures." This work did not purport to establish a fair price for either the Company or 100% of the stock. It was intended to determine the cash flow needed to service the debt that would "probably" be incurred in a leveraged buy-out, based on "rough calculations" without "any benefit of experts to identify what the limits were to that, and so forth." These computations were not considered extensive and no conclusion was reached.

At this meeting, Van Gorkom stated that he would be willing to take $55 per share for his own 75,000 shares. He vetoed the suggestion of a leveraged buy-out by Management, however, as involving a potential conflict of interest for Management. Van Gorkom, a certified public accountant and lawyer, had been an officer of Trans Union for 24 years, its Chief Executive Officer for more than 17 years, and Chairman of its Board for 2 years. It is noteworthy in this connection that he was then approaching 65 years of age and mandatory retirement.

* * *

Van Gorkom decided to meet with Jay A. Pritzker, a well-known corporate takeover specialist and a social acquaintance. However, rather than approaching Pritzker simply to determine his interest in acquiring Trans Union, Van Gorkom assembled a proposed per share price for sale of the Company and a financing structure by which to accomplish the sale. Van Gorkom did so without consulting either his Board or any members of Senior Management except one: Carl Peterson, Trans Union's Controller. Telling Peterson that he wanted no other person on his staff to know what he was doing, but without telling him why, Van Gorkom directed Peterson to calculate the feasibility of a leveraged buy-out at an assumed price per share of $55. Apart from the Company's historic stock market price,[5] and Van Gorkom's long association with Trans Union, the record is devoid of any competent evidence that $55 represented the per share intrinsic value of the Company.

---

5. The common stock of Trans Union was traded on the New York Stock Exchange. Over the five year period from 1975 through 1979, Trans Union's stock had traded within a range of a high of $39½ and a low of $24¼. Its high and low range for 1980 through September 19 (the last trading day before announcement of the merger) was $38¼–$29½.

* * *

Van Gorkom then reviewed with Pritzker his calculations based upon his proposed price of $55 per share. Although Pritzker mentioned $50 as a more attractive figure, no other price was mentioned. However, Van Gorkom stated that to be sure that $55 was the best price obtainable, Trans Union should be free to accept any better offer. Pritzker demurred, stating that his organization would serve as a "stalking horse" for an "auction contest" only if Trans Union would permit Pritzker to buy 1,750,000 shares of Trans Union stock at market price which Pritzker could then sell to any higher bidder. * * *

On Thursday, September 18, Van Gorkom met again with Pritzker. At that time, Van Gorkom knew that Pritzker intended to make a cash-out merger offer at Van Gorkom's proposed $55 per share.

* * * There was no further discussion of the $55 price. However, the number of shares of Trans Union treasury stock to be offered to Pritzker was negotiated down to one million shares; the price was set at $38—75 cents above the per share price at the close of the market on September 19. At this point, Pritzker insisted that the Trans Union Board act on his merger proposal within the next three days, stating to Van Gorkom: "We have to have a decision by no later than Sunday [evening, September 21] before the opening of the English stock exchange on Monday morning." * * *

On Friday, September 19, Van Gorkom called a special meeting of the Trans Union Board for noon the following day. He also called a meeting of the Company's Senior Management to convene at 11:00 a.m., prior to the meeting of the Board. No one, except Chelberg and Peterson, was told the purpose of the meetings. Van Gorkom did not invite Trans Union's investment banker, Salomon Brothers or its Chicago-based partner, to attend.

Of those present at the Senior Management meeting on September 20, only Chelberg and Peterson had prior knowledge of Pritzker's offer. Van Gorkom disclosed the offer and described its terms, but he furnished no copies of the proposed Merger Agreement. Romans announced that his department had done a second study which showed that, for a leveraged buy-out, the price range for Trans Union stock was between $55 and $65 per share. Van Gorkom neither saw the study nor asked Romans to make it available for the Board meeting.

Senior Management's reaction to the Pritzker proposal was completely negative. No member of Management, except Chelberg and Peterson, supported the proposal. Romans objected to the price as being too low;[6] he was critical of the timing and suggested that consideration should be given to the adverse tax consequences of an all-cash deal for low-basis shareholders; and he took the position that

---

6. Van Gorkom asked Romans to express his opinion as to the $55 price. Romans stated that he "thought the price was too low in relation to what he could derive for the company in a cash sale, particularly one which enabled us to realize the values of certain subsidiaries and independent entities."

the agreement to sell Pritzker one million newly-issued shares at market price would inhibit other offers, as would the prohibitions against soliciting bids and furnishing inside information to other bidders. Romans argued that the Pritzker proposal was a "lock up" and amounted to "an agreed merger as opposed to an offer." Nevertheless, Van Gorkom proceeded to the Board meeting as scheduled without further delay.

Ten directors served on the Trans Union Board, five inside (defendants Bonser, O'Boyle, Browder, Chelberg, and Van Gorkom) and five outside (defendants Wallis, Johnson, Lanterman, Morgan and Reneker). All directors were present at the meeting, except O'Boyle who was ill. Of the outside directors, four were corporate chief executive officers and one was the former Dean of the University of Chicago Business School. None was an investment banker or trained financial analyst. All members of the Board were well informed about the Company and its operations as a going concern. They were familiar with the current financial condition of the Company, as well as operating and earnings projections reported in the recent Five Year Forecast. The Board generally received regular and detailed reports and was kept abreast of the accumulated investment tax credit and accelerated depreciation problem.

Van Gorkom began the Special Meeting of the Board with a twenty-minute oral presentation. Copies of the proposed Merger Agreement were delivered too late for study before or during the meeting.[7] He reviewed the Company's ITC and depreciation problems and the efforts theretofore made to solve them. He discussed his initial meeting with Pritzker and his motivation in arranging that meeting. Van Gorkom did not disclose to the Board, however, the methodology by which he alone had arrived at the $55 figure, or the fact that he first proposed the $55 price in his negotiations with Pritzker.

Van Gorkom outlined the terms of the Pritzker offer as follows: Pritzker would pay $55 in cash for all outstanding shares of Trans Union stock upon completion of which Trans Union would be merged into New T Company, a subsidiary wholly-owned by Pritzker and formed to implement the merger; for a period of 90 days, Trans Union could receive, but could not actively solicit, competing offers; the offer had to be acted on by the next evening, Sunday, September 21; Trans Union could only furnish to competing bidders published information, and not proprietary information; the offer was subject to Pritzker obtaining the necessary financing by October 10, 1980; if the financing contingency were met or waived by Pritzker, Trans Union was required to sell to Pritzker one million newly-issued shares of Trans Union at $38 per share.

7. The record is not clear as to the terms of the Merger Agreement. The Agreement, as originally presented to the Board on September 20, was never produced by defendants despite demands by the plaintiffs. Nor is it clear that the directors were given an opportunity to study the Merger Agreement before voting on it. All that can be said is that Brennan had the Agreement before him during the meeting.

Van Gorkom took the position that putting Trans Union "up for auction" through a 90-day market test would validate a decision by the Board that $55 was a fair price. He told the Board that the "free market will have an opportunity to judge whether $55 is a fair price." Van Gorkom framed the decision before the Board not as whether $55 per share was the highest price that could be obtained, but as whether the $55 price was a fair price that the stockholders should be given the opportunity to accept or reject.[8]

Attorney Brennan advised the members of the Board that they might be sued if they failed to accept the offer and that a fairness opinion was not required as a matter of law.

Romans attended the meeting as chief financial officer of the Company. He told the Board that he had not been involved in the negotiations with Pritzker and knew nothing about the merger proposal until the morning of the meeting; that his studies did not indicate either a fair price for the stock or a valuation of the Company; that he did not see his role as directly addressing the fairness issue; and that he and his people "were trying to search for ways to justify a price in connection with such a [leveraged buy-out] transaction, rather than to say what the shares are worth." Romans testified:

> I told the Board that the study ran the numbers at 50 and 60, and then the subsequent study at 55 and 65, and that was not the same thing as saying that I have a valuation of the company at X dollars. But it was a way—a first step towards reaching that conclusion.

Romans told the Board that, in his opinion, $55 was "in the range of a fair price," but "at the beginning of the range."

Chelberg, Trans Union's President, supported Van Gorkom's presentation and representations. He testified that he "participated to make sure that the Board members collectively were clear on the details of the agreement or offer from Pritzker;" that he "participated in the discussion with Mr. Brennan, inquiring of him about the necessity for valuation opinions in spite of the way in which this particular offer was couched;" and that he was otherwise actively involved in supporting the positions being taken by Van Gorkom before the Board about "the necessity to act immediately on this offer," and about "the adequacy of the $55 and the question of how that would be tested."

The Board meeting of September 20 lasted about two hours. Based solely upon Van Gorkom's oral presentation, Chelberg's supporting representations, Romans' oral statement, Brennan's legal advice, and their knowledge of the market history of the Company's stock,[9] the

---

8. In Van Gorkom's words: The "real decision" is whether to "let the stockholders decide it" which is "all you are being asked to decide today."

9. The Trial Court stated the premium relationship of the $55 price to the market history of the Company's stock as follows:

* * * the merger price offered to the stockholders of Trans Union represented a premium of 62% over the average of the high and low prices at which Trans Union stock had traded in 1980, a premium of 48% over the last closing price, and a premium of 39% over the highest

directors approved the proposed Merger Agreement. However, the Board later claimed to have attached two conditions to its acceptance: (1) that Trans Union reserved the right to accept any better offer that was made during the market test period; and (2) that Trans Union could share its proprietary information with any other potential bidders. While the Board now claims to have reserved the right to accept any better offer received after the announcement of the Pritzker agreement (even though the minutes of the meeting do not reflect this), it is undisputed that the Board did not reserve the right to actively solicit alternate offers.

The Merger Agreement was executed by Van Gorkom during the evening of September 20 at a formal social event that he hosted for the opening of the Chicago Lyric Opera. Neither he nor any other director read the agreement prior to its signing and delivery to Pritzker.

* * *

[The court then detailed the events at two subsequent board meetings, on October 8 and January 26.]

* * *

On February 10, the stockholders of Trans Union approved the Pritzker merger proposal. Of the outstanding shares, 69.9% were voted in favor of the merger; 7.25% were voted against the merger; and 22.85% were not voted.

* * *

Under Delaware law, the business judgment rule is the offspring of the fundamental principle, codified in 8 *Del.C.* § 141(a), that the business and affairs of a Delaware corporation are managed by or under its board of directors. * * * In carrying out their managerial roles, directors are charged with an unyielding fiduciary duty to the corporation and its shareholders. * * *

The business judgment rule exists to protect and promote the full and free exercise of the managerial power granted to Delaware directors. * * * The rule itself "is a presumption that in making a business decision, the directors of a corporation acted on an informed basis, in good faith and in the honest belief that the action taken was in the best interests of the company." * * * Thus, the party attacking a board decision as uninformed must rebut the presumption that its business judgment was an informed one.

The determination of whether a business judgment is an informed one turns on whether the directors have informed themselves "prior to making a business decision, of all material information reasonably available to them."

price at which the stock of Trans Union had traded any time during the prior six years.

Under the business judgment rule there is no protection for directors who have made "an unintelligent or unadvised judgment." * * * A director's duty to inform himself in preparation for a decision derives from the fiduciary capacity in which he serves the corporation and its stockholders. * * *

Since a director is vested with the responsibility for the management of the affairs of the corporation, he must execute that duty with the recognition that he acts on behalf of others. Such obligation does not tolerate faithlessness or self-dealing. But fulfillment of the fiduciary function requires more than the mere absence of bad faith or fraud. Representation of the financial interests of others imposes on a director an affirmative duty to protect those interests and to proceed with a critical eye in assessing information of the type and under the circumstances present here. * * *

Thus, a director's duty to exercise an informed business judgment is in the nature of a duty of care, as distinguished from a duty of loyalty. Here, there were no allegations of fraud, bad faith, or self-dealing, or proof thereof. Hence, it is presumed that the directors reached their business judgment in good faith, *Allaun v. Consolidated Oil Co.*, Del.Ch., 147 A. 257 (1929), and considerations of motive are irrelevant to the issue before us.

The standard of care applicable to a director's duty of care has also been recently restated by this Court. In *Aronson, supra,* we stated:

> While the Delaware cases use a variety of terms to describe the applicable standard of care, our analysis satisfies us that under the business judgment rule director liability is predicated upon concepts of gross negligence. (footnote omitted)

473 A.2d at 812.

We again confirm that view. We think the concept of gross negligence is also the proper standard for determining whether a business judgment reached by a board of directors was an informed one.

In the specific context of a proposed merger of domestic corporations, a director has a duty under 8 *Del.C.* 251(b), along with his fellow directors, to act in an informed and deliberate manner in determining whether to approve an agreement of merger before submitting the proposal to the stockholders. Certainly in the merger context, a director may not abdicate that duty by leaving to the shareholders alone the decision to approve or disapprove the agreement. * * * Only an agreement of merger satisfying the requirements of 8 *Del.C.* § 251(b) may be submitted to the shareholders under § 251(c). * * *

On the record before us, we must conclude that the Board of Directors did not reach an informed business judgment on September 20, 1980 in voting to "sell" the Company for $55 per share pursuant to the Pritzker cash-out merger proposal. Our reasons, in summary, are as follows:

The directors (1) did not adequately inform themselves as to Van Gorkom's role in forcing the "sale" of the Company and in establishing the per share purchase price; (2) were uninformed as to the intrinsic value of the Company; and (3) given these circumstances, at a minimum, were grossly negligent in approving the "sale" of the Company upon two hours' consideration, without prior notice, and without the exigency of a crisis or emergency.

As has been noted, the Board based its September 20 decision to approve the cash-out merger primarily on Van Gorkom's representations. None of the directors, other than Van Gorkom and Chelberg, had any prior knowledge that the purpose of the meeting was to propose a cash-out merger of Trans Union. No members of Senior Management were present, other than Chelberg, Romans and Peterson; and the latter two had only learned of the proposed sale an hour earlier. Both general counsel Moore and former general counsel Browder attended the meeting, but were equally uninformed as to the purpose of the meeting and the documents to be acted upon.

Without any documents before them concerning the proposed transaction, the members of the Board were required to rely entirely upon Van Gorkom's 20-minute oral presentation of the proposal. No written summary of the terms of the merger was presented; the directors were given no documentation to support the adequacy of $55 price per share for sale of the Company; and the Board had before it nothing more than Van Gorkom's statement of his understanding of the substance of an agreement which he admittedly had never read, nor which any member of the Board had ever seen.

Under 8 *Del.C.* § 141(e), "directors are fully protected in relying in good faith on reports made by officers."

* * * The term "report" has been liberally construed to include reports of informal personal investigations by corporate officers. * * * However, there is no evidence that any "report," as defined under § 141(e), concerning the Pritzker proposal, was presented to the Board on September 20.[16] Van Gorkom's oral presentation of his understanding of the terms of the proposed Merger Agreement, which he had not seen, and Romans' brief oral statement of his preliminary study regarding the feasibility of a leveraged buy-out of Trans Union do not qualify as § 141(e) "reports" for these reasons: The former lacked substance because Van Gorkom was basically uninformed as to the essential provisions of the very document about which he was talking. Romans' statement was irrelevant to the issues before the Board since it did not purport to be a valuation study. At a minimum for a report

---

16. In support of the defendants' argument that their judgment as to the adequacy of $55 per share was an informed one, the directors rely on the BCG study and the Five Year Forecast. However, no one even referred to either of these studies at the September 20 meeting; and it is conceded that these materials do not represent valuation studies. Hence, these documents do not constitute evidence as to whether the directors reached an informed judgment on September 20 that $55 per share was a fair value for sale of the Company.

to enjoy the status conferred by § 141(e), it must be pertinent to the subject matter upon which a board is called to act, and otherwise be entitled to good faith, not blind, reliance. Considering all of the surrounding circumstances—hastily calling the meeting without prior notice of its subject matter, the proposed sale of the Company without any prior consideration of the issue or necessity therefor, the urgent time constraints imposed by Pritzker, and the total absence of any documentation whatsoever—the directors were duty bound to make reasonable inquiry of Van Gorkom and Romans, and if they had done so, the inadequacy of that upon which they now claim to have relied would have been apparent.

The defendants rely on the following factors to sustain the Trial Court's finding that the Board's decision was an informed one: (1) the magnitude of the premium or spread between the $55 Pritzker offering price and Trans Union's current market price of $38 per share; (2) the amendment of the Agreement as submitted on September 20 to permit the Board to accept any better offer during the "market test" period; (3) the collective experience and expertise of the Board's "inside" and "outside" directors; and (4) their reliance on Brennan's legal advice that the directors might be sued if they rejected the Pritzker proposal. We discuss each of these grounds *seriatim:*

A substantial premium may provide one reason to recommend a merger, but in the absence of other sound valuation information, the fact of a premium alone does not provide an adequate basis upon which to assess the fairness of an offering price. Here, the judgment reached as to the adequacy of the premium was based on a comparison between the historically depressed Trans Union market price and the amount of the Pritzker offer. Using market price as a basis for concluding that the premium adequately reflected the true value of the Company was a clearly faulty, indeed fallacious, premise, as the defendants' own evidence demonstrates.

The record is clear that before September 20, Van Gorkom and other members of Trans Union's Board knew that the market had consistently undervalued the worth of Trans Union's stock, despite steady increases in the Company's operating income in the seven years preceding the merger. The Board related this occurrence in large part to Trans Union's inability to use its ITCs as previously noted. Van Gorkom testified that he did not believe the market price accurately reflected Trans Union's true worth; and several of the directors testified that, as a general rule, most chief executives think that the market undervalues their companies' stock. Yet, on September 20, Trans Union's Board apparently believed that the market stock price accurately reflected the value of the Company for the purpose of determining the adequacy of the premium for its sale.

In the Proxy Statement, however, the directors reversed their position. There, they stated that, although the earnings prospects for Trans Union were "excellent," they found no basis for believing that this would be reflected in future stock prices. With regard to past trading, the Board stated that the prices at which the Company's common stock had traded in recent years did not reflect the "inherent" value of the Company. But having referred to the "inherent" value of Trans Union, the directors ascribed no number to it. Moreover, nowhere did they disclose that they had no basis on which to fix "inherent" worth beyond an impressionistic reaction to the premium over market and an unsubstantiated belief that the value of the assets was "significantly greater" than book value. By their own admission they could not rely on the stock price as an accurate measure of value. Yet, also by their own admission, the Board members assumed that Trans Union's market price was adequate to serve as a basis upon which to assess the adequacy of the premium for purposes of the September 20 meeting.

The parties do not dispute that a publicly-traded stock price is solely a measure of the value of a minority position and, thus, market price represents only the value of a single share. Nevertheless, on September 20, the Board assessed the adequacy of the premium over market, offered by Pritzker, solely by comparing it with Trans Union's current and historical stock price.

* * *

Indeed, as of September 20, the Board had no other information on which to base a determination of the intrinsic value of Trans Union as a going concern. As of September 20, the Board had made no evaluation of the Company designed to value the entire enterprise, nor had the Board ever previously considered selling the Company or consenting to a buy-out merger. Thus, the adequacy of a premium is indeterminate unless it is assessed in terms of other competent and sound valuation information that reflects the value of the particular business.

Despite the foregoing facts and circumstances, there was no call by the Board, either on September 20 or thereafter, for any valuation study or documentation of the $55 price per share as a measure of the fair value of the Company in a cash-out context. It is undisputed that the major asset of Trans Union was its cash flow. Yet, at no time did the Board call for a valuation study taking into account that highly significant element of the Company's assets.

We do not imply that an outside valuation study is essential to support an informed business judgment; nor do we state that fairness opinions by independent investment bankers are required as a matter of law. Often insiders familiar with the business of a going concern are in a better position than are outsiders to gather relevant information; and under appropriate circumstances, such directors may be fully protected in relying in good faith upon the valuation reports of their management. *See* 8 *Del.C.* § 141(e). * * *

Here, the record establishes that the Board did not request its Chief Financial Officer, Romans, to make any valuation study or review of the proposal to determine the adequacy of $55 per share for sale of the Company. On the record before us: The Board rested on Romans' elicited response that the $55 figure was within a "fair price range" within the context of a leveraged buy-out. No director sought any further information from Romans. No director asked him why he put $55 at the bottom of his range. No director asked Romans for any details as to his study, the reason why it had been undertaken or its depth. No director asked to see the study; and no director asked Romans whether Trans Union's finance department could do a fairness study within the remaining 36-hour period available under the Pritzker offer.

Had the Board, or any member, made an inquiry of Romans, he presumably would have responded as he testified: that his calculations were rough and preliminary; and, that the study was not designed to determine the fair value of the Company, but rather to assess the feasibility of a leveraged buy-out financed by the Company's projected cash flow, making certain assumptions as to the purchaser's borrowing needs. Romans would have presumably also informed the Board of his view, and the widespread view of Senior Management, that the timing of the offer was wrong and the offer inadequate.

The record also establishes that the Board accepted without scrutiny Van Gorkom's representation as to the fairness of the $55 price per share for sale of the Company—a subject that the Board had never previously considered. The Board thereby failed to discover that Van Gorkom had suggested the $55 price to Pritzker and, most crucially, that Van Gorkom had arrived at the $55 figure based on calculations designed solely to determine the feasibility of a leveraged buy-out.[19] No questions were raised either as to the tax implications of a cash-out merger or how the price for the one million share option granted Pritzker was calculated.

We do not say that the Board of Directors was not entitled to give some credence to Van Gorkom's representation that $55 was an adequate or fair price. Under § 141(e), the directors were entitled to rely upon their chairman's opinion of value and adequacy, provided that such opinion was reached on a sound basis. Here, the issue is whether the directors informed themselves as to all information that was reasonably available to them. Had they done so, they would have learned of the source and derivation of the $55 price and could not reasonably have relied thereupon in good faith.

19. As of September 20 the directors did not know: that Van Gorkom had arrived at the $55 figure alone, and subjectively, as the figure to be used by Controller Peterson in creating a feasible structure for a leveraged buy-out by a prospective purchaser; that Van Gorkom had not sought advice, information or assistance from either inside or outside Trans Union directors as to the value of the Company as an entity or the fair price per share for 100% of its stock; that Van Gorkom had not consulted with the Company's investment bankers or other financial analysts; that Van Gorkom had not consulted with or confided in any officer or director of the Company except Chelberg; and that Van Gorkom had deliberately chosen to ignore the advice and opinion of the members of his Senior Management group regarding the adequacy of the $55 price.

None of the directors, Management or outside, were investment bankers or financial analysts. Yet the Board did not consider recessing the meeting until a later hour that day (or requesting an extension of Pritzker's Sunday evening deadline) to give it time to elicit more information as to the sufficiency of the offer, either from inside Management (in particular Romans) or from Trans Union's own investment banker, Salomon Brothers, whose Chicago specialist in merger and acquisitions was known to the Board and familiar with Trans Union's affairs.

Thus, the record compels the conclusion that on September 20 the Board lacked valuation information adequate to reach an informed business judgment as to the fairness of $55 per share for sale of the Company.[20]

This brings us to the post-September 20 "market test" upon which the defendants ultimately rely to confirm the reasonableness of their September 20 decision to accept the Pritzker proposal. In this connection, the directors present a two-part argument: (a) that by making a "market test" of Pritzker's $55 per share offer a condition of their September 20 decision to accept his offer, they cannot be found to have acted impulsively or in an uninformed manner on September 20; and (b) that the adequacy of the $17 premium for sale of the Company was conclusively established over the following 90 to 120 days by the most reliable evidence available—the marketplace. Thus, the defendants impliedly contend that the "market test" eliminated the need for the Board to perform any other form of fairness test either on September 20, or thereafter.

Again, the facts of record do not support the defendants' argument. There is no evidence: (a) that the Merger Agreement was effectively amended to give the Board freedom to put Trans Union up for auction sale to the highest bidder; or (b) that a public auction was in fact permitted to occur. The minutes of the Board meeting make no reference to any of this. Indeed, the record compels the conclusion that the directors had no rational basis for expecting that a market test was attainable, given the terms of the Agreement as executed during the evening of September 20.

* * *

The Merger Agreement, specifically identified as that originally presented to the Board on September 20, has never been produced by the defendants, notwithstanding the plaintiffs' several demands for production before as well as during trial. No acceptable explanation of this failure to produce documents has been given to either the Trial Court or this Court.

* * *

---

20. For a far more careful and reasoned approach taken by another board of directors faced with the pressures of a hostile tender offer, see *Pogostin v. Rice, supra* at 623–627.

Van Gorkom states that the Agreement as submitted incorporated the ingredients for a market test by authorizing Trans Union to receive competing offers over the next 90-day period. However, he concedes that the Agreement barred Trans Union from actively soliciting such offers and from furnishing to interested parties any information about the Company other than that already in the public domain. Whether the original Agreement of September 20 went so far as to authorize Trans Union to receive competitive proposals is arguable. * * *

The defendants attempt to downplay the significance of the prohibition against Trans Union's actively soliciting competing offers by arguing that the directors "understood that the entire financial community would know that Trans Union was for sale upon the announcement of the Pritzker offer, and anyone desiring to make a better offer was free to do so." Yet, the press release issued on September 22, with the authorization of the Board, stated that Trans Union had entered into "definitive agreements" with the Pritzkers; and the press release did not even disclose Trans Union's limited right to receive and accept higher offers. Accompanying this press release was a further public announcement that Pritzker had been granted an option to purchase at any time one million shares of Trans Union's capital stock at 75 cents above the then-current price per share.

Thus, notwithstanding what several of the outside directors later claimed to have "thought" occurred at the meeting, the record compels the conclusion that Trans Union's Board had no rational basis to conclude on September 20 or in the days immediately following, that the Board's acceptance of Pritzker's offer was conditioned on (1) a "market test" of the offer; and (2) the Board's right to withdraw from the Pritzker Agreement and accept any higher offer received before the shareholder meeting.

The directors' unfounded reliance on both the premium and the market test as the basis for accepting the Pritzker proposal undermines the defendants' remaining contention that the Board's collective experience and sophistication was a sufficient basis for finding that it reached its September 20 decision with informed, reasonable deliberation.[21]
* * *

Part of the defense is based on a claim that the directors relied on legal advice rendered at the September 20 meeting by James Brennan, Esquire, who was present at Van Gorkom's request. * * *

---

21. Trans Union's five "inside" directors had backgrounds in law and accounting, 116 years of collective employment by the Company and 68 years of combined experience on its Board. Trans Union's five "outside" directors included four chief executives of major corporations and an economist who was a former dean of a major school of business and chancellor of a university. The "outside" directors had 78 years of combined experience as chief executive officers of major corporations and 50 years of cumulative experience as directors of Trans Union. Thus, defendants argue that the Board was eminently qualified to reach an informed judgment on the proposed "sale" of Trans Union notwithstanding their lack of any advance notice of the proposal, the shortness of their deliberation, and their determination not to consult with their investment banker or to obtain a fairness opinion.

Several defendants testified that Brennan advised them that Delaware law did not require a fairness opinion or an outside valuation of the Company before the Board could act on the Pritzker proposal. If given, the advice was correct. However, that did not end the matter. Unless the directors had before them adequate information regarding the intrinsic value of the Company, upon which a proper exercise of business judgment could be made, mere advice of this type is meaningless; and, given this record of the defendants' failures, it constitutes no defense here.[22]

* * *

A second claim is that counsel advised the Board it would be subject to lawsuits if it rejected the $55 per share offer. It is, of course, a fact of corporate life that today when faced with difficult or sensitive issues, directors often are subject to suit, irrespective of the decisions they make. However, counsel's mere acknowledgement of this circumstance cannot be rationally translated into a justification for a board permitting itself to be stampeded into a patently unadvised act. While suit might result from the rejection of a merger or tender offer, Delaware law makes clear that a board acting within the ambit of the business judgment rule faces no ultimate liability. * * * Thus, we cannot conclude that the mere threat of litigation, acknowledged by counsel, constitutes either legal advice or any valid basis upon which to pursue an uninformed course.

* * *

[The court also held that the board did not "cure" its breach of its duty of care at the October 6 and January 26 meetings.]

Whether the directors of Trans Union should be treated as one or individually in terms of invoking the protection of the business judgment rule and the applicability of 8 *Del.C.* § 141(c) are questions which were not originally addressed by the parties in their briefing of this case. This resulted in a supplemental briefing and a second rehearing en banc on two basic questions: (a) whether one or more of the directors were deprived of the protection of the business judgment rule by evidence of an absence of good faith; and (b) whether one or more of the outside directors were entitled to invoke the protection of 8 *Del.C.* § 141(e) by evidence of a reasonable, good faith reliance on "reports," including legal advice, rendered the Board by certain inside directors and the Board's special counsel, Brennan.

The parties' response, including reargument, has led the majority of the Court to conclude: (1) that since all of the defendant directors, outside as well as inside, take a unified position, we are required to treat all of the directors as one as to whether they are entitled to the

---

22. Nonetheless, we are satisfied that in an appropriate factual context a proper exercise of business judgment may include, as one of its aspects, reasonable reliance upon the advice of counsel. This is wholly outside the statutory protections of 8 *Del.C.* § 141(e) involving reliance upon reports of officers, certain experts and books and records of the company.

protection of the business judgment rule; and (2) that considerations of good faith, including the presumption that the directors acted in good faith, are irrelevant in determining the threshold issue of whether the directors as a Board exercised an informed business judgment. * * *

The defendants ultimately rely on the stockholder vote of February 10 for exoneration. The defendants contend that the stockholders' "overwhelming" vote approving the Pritzker Merger Agreement had the legal effect of curing any failure of the Board to reach an informed business judgment in its approval of the merger.

The parties tacitly agree that a discovered failure of the Board to reach an informed business judgment in approving the merger constitutes a voidable, rather than a void, act. Hence, the merger can be sustained, notwithstanding the infirmity of the Board's action, if its approval by majority vote of the shareholders is found to have been based on an informed electorate. * * * In *Lynch v. Vickers Energy Corp., supra,* this Court held that corporate directors owe to their stockholders a fiduciary duty to disclose all facts germane to the transaction at issue in an atmosphere of complete candor. We defined "germane" in the tender offer context as all "information such as a reasonable stockholder would consider important in deciding whether to sell or retain stock." * * * In reality, "germane" means material facts.

Applying this standard to the record before us, we find that Trans Union's stockholders were not fully informed of all facts material to their vote on the Pritzker Merger and that the Trial Court's ruling to the contrary is clearly erroneous. We list the material deficiencies in the proxy materials:

(1) The fact that the Board had no reasonably adequate information indicative of the intrinsic value of the Company, other than a concededly depressed market price, was without question material to the shareholders voting on the merger.

Accordingly, the Board's lack of valuation information should have been disclosed. Instead, the directors cloaked the absence of such information in both the Proxy Statement and the Supplemental Proxy Statement. Through artful drafting, noticeably absent at the September 20 meeting, both documents create the impression that the Board knew the intrinsic worth of the Company. * * *

(2) We find false and misleading the Board's characterization of the Romans report in the Supplemental Proxy Statement. Nowhere does the Board disclose that Romans stated to the Board that his calculations were made in a "search for ways to justify a price in connection with" a leveraged buy-out transaction, "rather than to say what the shares are worth," and that he stated to the Board that his conclusion thus arrived at "was not the same thing as saying that I have a valuation of the Company at X dollars." * * *

(3) We find misleading the Board's references to the "substantial" premium offered. The Board gave as their primary reason in support of the merger the "substantial premium" shareholders would receive. But the Board did not disclose its failure to assess the premium offered in terms of other relevant valuation techniques, thereby rendering questionable its determination as to the substantiality of the premium over an admittedly depressed stock market price.

(4) We find the Board's recital in the Supplemental Proxy of certain events preceding the September 20 meeting to be incomplete and misleading. It is beyond dispute that a reasonable stockholder would have considered material the fact that Van Gorkom not only suggested the $55 price to Pritzker, but also that he chose the figure because it made feasible a leveraged buy-out. * * *

CHRISTIE, JUSTICE, dissenting:

The majority opinion reads like an advocate's closing address to a hostile jury. And I say that not lightly. Throughout the opinion great emphasis is directed only to the negative, with nothing more than lip service granted the positive aspects of this case. * * *

Directors of this caliber are not ordinarily taken in by a "fast shuffle". I submit they were not taken into this multi-million dollar corporate transaction without being fully informed and aware of the state of the art as it pertained to the entire corporate panorama of Trans Union. * * *

These men knew Trans Union like the back of their hands and were more than well qualified to make on the spot informed business judgments concerning the affairs of Trans Union including a 100% sale of the corporation. Lest we forget, the corporate world of then and now operates on what is so aptly referred to as "the fast track". These men were at the time an integral part of that world, all professional business men, not intellectual figureheads.

* * *

Note

The Effect of *Van Gorkom* on D & O Insurance

Researchers have found that in spite of all the attention the case has received in the business community, it had no effect on the market value of Delaware corporations. Bradley & Schipani, The Relevance of the Duty of Care Standard in Corporate Governance, 75 Iowa L.Rev. 1 (1989). The finding is consistent with the view that the decision had no real impact on the way Delaware corporations were managed or the way the stock of these firms was priced by the market. Perhaps investors believed that later courts would construe the decision narrowly, applying it only to takeovers, and that liability under the decision's reasoning could be easily avoided, by obtaining a fairness opinion from an investment banker and otherwise creating a proper paper trail for any acquisition decision. Interestingly, however, directors' and officers' liability insurance (D & O insurance) increased more than twelvefold in the year the decision was rendered. Id. at 73. Moreover, the common stock of firms that write D & O insurance rose significantly. This increase in equity led the authors of the study to suggest that "insurers were able to increase their premiums beyond the actuarially fair level.... Increase in liability premiums was not due to an expected increase in liability claims. Rather, the increase in premiums was due to the inelasticity of demand for corporate liability insurance and the hyperbole surrounding the *Trans Union* decision." Id. at 75.

REVLON, INC. v. MacANDREWS & FORBES HOLDINGS, INC.

Supreme Court of Delaware, 1986.
506 A.2d 173.

MOORE, JUSTICE:

* * *

The prelude to this controversy began in June 1985, when Ronald O. Perelman, chairman of the board and chief executive officer of Pantry Pride, met with his counterpart at Revlon, Michel C. Bergerac, to discuss a friendly acquisition of Revlon by Pantry Pride. Perelman suggested a price in the range of $40–50 per share, but the meeting ended with Bergerac dismissing those figures as considerably below Revlon's intrinsic value. All subsequent Pantry Pride overtures were rebuffed, perhaps in part based on Mr. Bergerac's strong personal antipathy to Mr. Perelman.

Thus, on August 14, Pantry Pride's board authorized Perelman to acquire Revlon, either through negotiation in the $42–$43 per share range, or by making a hostile tender offer at $45. Perelman then met with Bergerac and outlined Pantry Pride's alternate approaches. Bergerac remained adamantly opposed to such schemes and conditioned any further discussions of the matter on Pantry Pride executing a standstill agreement prohibiting it from acquiring Revlon without the latter's prior approval.

On August 19, the Revlon board met specially to consider the impending threat of a hostile bid by Pantry Pride.[3] At the meeting, Lazard Freres, Revlon's investment banker, advised the directors that $45 per share was a grossly inadequate price for the company. Felix Rohatyn and William Loomis of Lazard Freres explained to the board that Pantry Pride's financial strategy for acquiring Revlon would be through "junk bond" financing followed by a break-up of Revlon and the disposition of its assets. With proper timing, according to the experts, such transactions could produce a return to Pantry Pride of

---

3. There were 14 directors on the Revlon board. Six of them held senior management positions with the company, and two others held significant blocks of its stock. Four of the remaining six directors were associated at some point with entities that had various business relationships with Revlon. On the basis of this limited record, however, we cannot conclude that this board is entitled to certain presumptions that generally attach to the decisions of a board whose majority consists of truly outside independent directors. * * *

$60 to $70 per share, while a sale of the company as a whole would be in the "mid 50" dollar range. Martin Lipton, special counsel for Revlon, recommended two defensive measures: first, that the company repurchase up to 5 million of its nearly 30 million outstanding shares; and second, that it adopt a Note Purchase Rights Plan. Under this plan, each Revlon shareholder would receive as a dividend one Note Purchase Right (the Rights) for each share of common stock, with the Rights entitling the holder to exchange one common share for a $65 principal Revlon note at 12% interest with a one-year maturity. The Rights would become effective whenever anyone acquired beneficial ownership of 20% or more of Revlon's shares, unless the purchaser acquired all the company's stock for cash at $65 or more per share. In addition, the Rights would not be available to the acquiror, and prior to the 20% triggering event the Revlon board could redeem the rights for 10 cents each. Both proposals were unanimously adopted.

Pantry Pride made its first hostile move on August 23 with a cash tender offer for any and all shares of Revlon at $47.50 per common share and $26.67 per preferred share, subject to (1) Pantry Pride's obtaining financing for the purchase, and (2) the Rights being redeemed, rescinded or voided.

The Revlon board met again on August 26. The directors advised the stockholders to reject the offer. Further defensive measures also were planned. On August 29, Revlon commenced its own offer for up to 10 million shares, exchanging for each share of common stock tendered one Senior Subordinated Note (the Notes) of $47.50 principal at 11.75% interest, due 1995, and one-tenth of a share of $9.00 Cumulative Convertible Exchangeable Preferred Stock valued at $100 per share. Lazard Freres opined that the notes would trade at their face value on a fully distributed basis.[4] Revlon stockholders tendered 87 percent of the outstanding shares (approximately 33 million), and the company accepted the full 10 million shares on a pro rata basis. The new Notes contained covenants which limited Revlon's ability to incur additional debt, sell assets, or pay dividends unless otherwise approved by the "independent" (non-management) members of the board.

At this point, both the Rights and the Note covenants stymied Pantry Pride's attempted takeover. The next move came on September 16, when Pantry Pride announced a new tender offer at $42 per share, conditioned upon receiving at least 90% of the outstanding stock. Pantry Pride also indicated that it would consider buying less than 90%, and at an increased price, if Revlon removed the impeding Rights. While this offer was lower on its face than the earlier $47.50 proposal, Revlon's investment banker, Lazard Freres, described the two bids as essentially equal in view of the completed exchange offer.

4. Like bonds, the Notes actually were issued in denominations of $1,000 and integral multiples thereof. A separate certificate was issued in a total principal amount equal to the remaining sum to which a stockholder was entitled. Likewise, in the esoteric parlance of bond dealers, a Note trading at par ($1,000) would be quoted on the market at 100.

The Revlon board held a regularly scheduled meeting on September 24. The directors rejected the latest Pantry Pride offer and authorized management to negotiate with other parties interested in acquiring Revlon. Pantry Pride remained determined in its efforts and continued to make cash bids for the company, offering $50 per share on September 27, and raising its bid to $53 on October 1, and then to $56.25 on October 7.

In the meantime, Revlon's negotiations with Forstmann and the investment group Adler & Shaykin had produced results. The Revlon directors met on October 3 to consider Pantry Pride's $53 bid and to examine possible alternatives to the offer. Both Forstmann and Adler & Shaykin made certain proposals to the board. As a result, the directors unanimously agreed to a leveraged buyout by Forstmann. The terms of this accord were as follows: each stockholder would get $56 cash per share; management would purchase stock in the new company by the exercise of their Revlon "golden parachutes";[5] Forstmann would assume Revlon's $475 million debt incurred by the issuance of the Notes; and Revlon would redeem the Rights and waive the Notes covenants for Forstmann or in connection with any other offer superior to Forstmann's. The board did not actually remove the covenants at the October 3 meeting, because Forstmann then lacked a firm commitment on its financing, but accepted the Forstmann capital structure, and indicated that the outside directors would waive the covenants in due course. Part of Forstmann's plan was to sell Revlon's Norcliff Thayer and Reheis divisions to American Home Products for $335 million. Before the merger, Revlon was to sell its cosmetics and fragrance division to Adler & Shaykin for $905 million. These transactions would facilitate the purchase by Forstmann or any other acquiror of Revlon.

When the merger, and thus the waiver of the Notes covenants, was announced, the market value of these securities began to fall. The Notes, which originally traded near par, around 100, dropped to 87.50 by October 8. One director later reported (at the October 12 meeting) a "deluge" of telephone calls from irate noteholders, and on October 10 the Wall Street Journal reported threats of litigation by these creditors.

Pantry Pride countered with a new proposal on October 7, raising its $53 offer to $56.25, subject to nullification of the Rights, a waiver of the Notes covenants, and the election of three Pantry Pride directors to the Revlon board. On October 9, representatives of Pantry Pride, Forstmann and Revlon conferred in an attempt to negotiate the fate of Revlon, but could not reach agreement. At this meeting Pantry Pride announced that it would engage in fractional bidding and top any Forstmann offer by a slightly higher one. It is also significant that Forstmann, to Pantry Pride's exclusion, had been made privy to certain

---

5. In the takeover context "golden parachutes" generally are understood to be termination agreements providing substantial bonuses and other benefits for managers and certain directors upon a change in control of a company.

Revlon financial data. Thus, the parties were not negotiating on equal terms.

Again privately armed with Revlon data, Forstmann met on October 11 with Revlon's special counsel and investment banker. On October 12, Forstmann made a new $57.25 per share offer, based on several conditions.[6] The principal demand was a lock-up option to purchase Revlon's Vision Care and National Health Laboratories divisions for $525 million, some $100–$175 million below the value ascribed to them by Lazard Freres, if another acquiror got 40% of Revlon's shares. Revlon also was required to accept a no-shop provision. The Rights and Notes covenants had to be removed as in the October 3 agreement. There would be a $25 million cancellation fee to be placed in escrow, and released to Forstmann if the new agreement terminated or if another acquiror got more than 19.9% of Revlon's stock. Finally, there would be no participation by Revlon management in the merger. In return, Forstmann agreed to support the par value of the Notes, which had faltered in the market, by an exchange of new notes. Forstmann also demanded immediate acceptance of its offer, or it would be withdrawn. The board unanimously approved Forstmann's proposal because: (1) it was for a higher price than the Pantry Pride bid, (2) it protected the noteholders, and (3) Forstmann's financing was firmly in place.[7] The board further agreed to redeem the rights and waive the covenants on the preferred stock in response to any offer above $57 cash per share. The covenants were waived, contingent upon receipt of an investment banking opinion that the Notes would trade near par value once the offer was consummated.

* * *

We turn first to Pantry Pride's probability of success on the merits. The ultimate responsibility for managing the business and affairs of a corporation falls on its board of directors. 8 *Del.C.* § 141(a). In discharging this function the directors owe fiduciary duties of care and loyalty to the corporation and its shareholders. * * * These principles apply with equal force when a board approves a corporate merger pursuant to 8 *Del.C.* § 251(b); * * * and of course they are the bedrock of our law regarding corporate takeover issues. * * * While the business judgment rule may be applicable to the actions of corporate directors responding to takeover threats, the principles upon which it is

---

6. Forstmann's $57.25 offer ostensibly is worth $1 more than Pantry Pride's $56.25 bid. However, the Pantry Pride offer was immediate, while the Forstmann proposal must be discounted for the time value of money because of the delay in approving the merger and consummating the transaction. The exact difference between the two bids was an unsettled point of contention even at oral argument.

7. Actually, at this time about $400 million of Forstmann's funding was still subject to two investment banks using their "best efforts" to organize a syndicate to provide the balance. Pantry Pride's entire financing was not firmly committed at this point either, although Pantry Pride represented in an October 11 letter to Lazard Freres that its investment banker, Drexel Burnham Lambert, was highly confident of its ability to raise the balance of $350 million. Drexel Burnham had a firm commitment for this sum by October 18.

founded—care, loyalty and independence—must first be satisfied.
* * *

If the business judgment rule applies, there is a "presumption that in making a business decision the directors of a corporation acted on an informed basis, in good faith and in the honest belief that the action taken was in the best interests of the company." *Aronson v. Lewis,* 473 A.2d at 812. However, when a board implements anti-takeover measures there arises "the omnipresent specter that a board may be acting primarily in its own interests, rather than those of the corporation and its shareholders..." *Unocal Corp. v. Mesa Petroleum Co.,* 493 A.2d at 954. This potential for conflict places upon the directors the burden of proving that they had reasonable grounds for believing there was a danger to corporate policy and effectiveness, a burden satisfied by a showing of good faith and reasonable investigation. *Id.* at 955. In addition, the directors must analyze the nature of the takeover and its effect on the corporation in order to ensure balance—that the responsive action taken is reasonable in relation to the threat posed. *Id.*

The first relevant defensive measure adopted by the Revlon board was the Rights Plan, which would be considered a "poison pill" in the current language of corporate takeovers—a plan by which shareholders receive the right to be bought out by the corporation at a substantial premium on the occurrence of a stated triggering event. *See generally Moran v. Household International, Inc.,* Del.Supr., 500 A.2d 1346 (1985). By 8 *Del.C.* §§ 141 and 122(13),[11] the board clearly had the power to adopt the measure. *See Moran v. Household International, Inc.,* 500 A.2d at 1351. Thus, the focus becomes one of reasonableness and purpose.

The Revlon board approved the Rights Plan in the face of an impending hostile takeover bid by Pantry Pride at $45 per share, a price which Revlon reasonably concluded was grossly inadequate. Lazard Freres had so advised the directors, and had also informed them that Pantry Pride was a small, highly leveraged company bent on a "bust-up" takeover by using "junk bond" financing to buy Revlon cheaply, sell the acquired assets to pay the debts incurred, and retain the profit for itself.[12] In adopting the Plan, the board protected the shareholders from a hostile takeover at a price below the company's intrinsic value, while retaining sufficient flexibility to address any proposal deemed to be in the stockholders' best interests.

---

11. The relevant provision of Section 122 is:

"Every corporation created under this chapter shall have power to:

(13) Make contracts, including contracts of guaranty and suretyship, incur liabilities, borrow money at such rates of interest as the corporation may determine, issue its notes, bonds and other obligations, and secure any of its obligations by mortgage, pledge or other encumbrance of all or any of its property, franchises and income, ...". 8 *Del.C.* § 122(13). * * *

12. As we noted in *Moran,* a "bust-up" takeover generally refers to a situation in which one seeks to finance an acquisition by selling off pieces of the acquired company, presumably at a substantial profit. *See Moran,* 500 A.2d at 1349, n. 4.

To that extent the board acted in good faith and upon reasonable investigation. Under the circumstances it cannot be said that the Rights Plan as employed was unreasonable, considering the threat posed. Indeed, the Plan was a factor in causing Pantry Pride to raise its bids from a low of $42 to an eventual high of $58. At the time of its adoption the Rights Plan afforded a measure of protection consistent with the directors' fiduciary duty in facing a takeover threat perceived as detrimental to corporate interests. *Unocal,* 493 A.2d at 954–55. Far from being a "show-stopper," as the plaintiffs had contended in *Moran,* the measure spurred the bidding to new heights, a proper result of its implementation. *See Moran,* 500 A.2d at 1354, 1356–67.

Although we consider adoption of the Plan to have been valid under the circumstances, its continued usefulness was rendered moot by the directors' actions on October 3 and October 12. At the October 3 meeting the board redeemed the Rights conditioned upon consummation of a merger with Forstmann, but further acknowledged that they would also be redeemed to facilitate any more favorable offer. On October 12, the board unanimously passed a resolution redeeming the Rights in connection with any cash proposal of $57.25 or more per share. Because all the pertinent offers eventually equalled or surpassed that amount, the Rights clearly were no longer any impediment in the contest for Revlon. This mooted any question of their propriety under *Moran* or *Unocal.*

The second defensive measure adopted by Revlon to thwart a Pantry Pride takeover was the company's own exchange offer for 10 million of its shares. The directors' general broad powers to manage the business and affairs of the corporation are augmented by the specific authority conferred under 8 *Del.C.* § 160(a), permitting the company to deal in its own stock. * * * However, when exercising that power in an effort to forestall a hostile takeover, the board's actions are strictly held to the fiduciary standards outlined in *Unocal.* These standards require the directors to determine the best interests of the corporation and its stockholders, and impose an enhanced duty to abjure any action that is motivated by considerations other than a good faith concern for such interests.

* * *

The Revlon directors concluded that Pantry Pride's $47.50 offer was grossly inadequate. In that regard the board acted in good faith, and on an informed basis, with reasonable grounds to believe that there existed a harmful threat to the corporate enterprise. The adoption of a defensive measure, reasonable in relation to the threat posed, was proper and fully accorded with the powers, duties, and responsibilities conferred upon directors under our law. * * *

However, when Pantry Pride increased its offer to $50 per share, and then to $53, it became apparent to all that the break-up of the company was inevitable. The Revlon board's authorization permitting management to negotiate a merger or buyout with a third party was a recognition that the company was for sale. The duty of the board had thus changed from the preservation of Revlon as a corporate entity to the maximization of the company's value at a sale for the stockholders' benefit. This significantly altered the board's responsibilities under the *Unocal* standards. It no longer faced threats to corporate policy and effectiveness, or to the stockholders' interests, from a grossly inadequate bid. The whole question of defensive measures became moot. The directors' role changed from defenders of the corporate bastion to auctioneers charged with getting the best price for the stockholders at a sale of the company.

This brings us to the lock-up with Forstmann and its emphasis on shoring up the sagging market value of the Notes in the face of threatened litigation by their holders. Such a focus was inconsistent with the changed concept of the directors' responsibilities at this stage of the developments. The impending waiver of the Notes covenants had caused the value of the Notes to fall, and the board was aware of the noteholders' ire as well as their subsequent threats of suit. The directors thus made support of the Notes an integral part of the company's dealings with Forstmann, even though their primary responsibility at this stage was to the equity owners.

The original threat posed by Pantry Pride—the break-up of the company—had become a reality which even the directors embraced. Selective dealing to fend off a hostile but determined bidder was no longer a proper objective. Instead, obtaining the highest price for the benefit of the stockholders should have been the central theme guiding director action. Thus, the Revlon board could not make the requisite showing of good faith by preferring the noteholders and ignoring its duty of loyalty to the shareholders. The rights of the former already were fixed by contract. * * * The noteholders required no further protection, and when the Revlon board entered into an auction-ending lock-up agreement with Forstmann on the basis of impermissible considerations at the expense of the shareholders, the directors breached their primary duty of loyalty.

The Revlon board argued that it acted in good faith in protecting the noteholders because *Unocal* permits consideration of other corporate constituencies. Although such considerations may be permissible, there are fundamental limitations upon that prerogative. A board may have regard for various constituencies in discharging its responsibilities, provided there are rationally related benefits accruing to the stockholders. *Unocal,* 493 A.2d at 955. However, such concern for non-stockholder interests is inappropriate when an auction among active bidders is in progress, and the object no longer is to protect or maintain the corporate enterprise but to sell it to the highest bidder.

Revlon also contended that * * * it had contractual and good faith obligations to consider the noteholders. However, any such duties are limited to the principle that one may not interfere with contractual relationships by improper actions. Here, the rights of the noteholders were fixed by agreement, and there is nothing of substance to suggest that any of those terms were violated. The Notes covenants specifically contemplated a waiver to permit sale of the company at a fair price. The Notes were accepted by the holders on that basis, including the risk of an adverse market effect stemming from a waiver. Thus, nothing remained for Revlon to legitimately protect, and no rationally related benefit thereby accrued to the stockholders. Under such circumstances we must conclude that the merger agreement with Forstmann was unreasonable in relation to the threat posed.

A lock-up is not *per se* illegal under Delaware law. * * * Such options can entice other bidders to enter a contest for control of the corporation, creating an auction for the company and maximizing shareholder profit. Current economic conditions in the takeover market are such that a "white knight" like Forstmann might only enter the bidding for the target company if it receives some form of compensation to cover the risks and costs involved. * * *

However, while those lock-ups which draw bidders into the battle benefit shareholders, similar measures which end an active auction and foreclose further bidding operate to the shareholders' detriment. * * * Forstmann had already been drawn into the contest on a preferred basis, so the result of the lock-up was not to foster bidding, but to destroy it. The board's stated reasons for approving the transactions were: (1) better financing, (2) noteholder protection, and (3) higher price. As the Court of Chancery found, and we agree, any distinctions between the rival bidders' methods of financing the proposal were nominal at best, and such a consideration has little or no significance in a cash offer for any and all shares. The principal object, contrary to the board's duty of care, appears to have been protection of the noteholders over the shareholders' interests.

While Forstmann's $57.25 offer was objectively higher than Pantry Pride's $56.25 bid, the margin of superiority is less when the Forstmann price is adjusted for the time value of money. In reality, the Revlon board ended the auction in return for very little actual improvement in the final bid. The principal benefit went to the directors, who avoided personal liability to a class of creditors to whom the board owed no further duty under the circumstances. Thus, when a board ends an intense bidding contest on an insubstantial basis, and where a significant by-product of that action is to protect the directors against a perceived threat of personal liability for consequences stemming from the adoption of previous defensive measures, the action cannot withstand the enhanced scrutiny which *Unocal* requires of director conduct. See *Unocal*, 493 A.2d at 954–55.

In addition to the lock-up option, the Court of Chancery enjoined the no-shop provision as part of the attempt to foreclose further bidding by Pantry Pride. * * * The no-shop provision, like the lock-up option, while not *per se* illegal, is impermissible under the *Unocal* standards when a board's primary duty becomes that of an auctioneer responsible for selling the company to the highest bidder. The agreement to negotiate only with Forstmann ended rather than intensified the board's involvement in the bidding contest.

It is ironic that the parties even considered a no-shop agreement when Revlon had dealt preferentially, and almost exclusively, with Forstmann throughout the contest. After the directors authorized management to negotiate with other parties, Forstmann was given every negotiating advantage that Pantry Pride had been denied: cooperation from management, access to financial data, and the exclusive opportunity to present merger proposals directly to the board of directors. Favoritism for a white knight to the total exclusion of a hostile bidder might be justifiable when the latter's offer adversely affects shareholder interests, but when bidders make relatively similar offers, or dissolution of the company becomes inevitable, the directors cannot fulfill their enhanced *Unocal* duties by playing favorites with the contending factions. Market forces must be allowed to operate freely to bring the target's shareholders the best price available for their equity.[16] Thus, as the trial court ruled, the shareholders' interests necessitated that the board remain free to negotiate in the fulfillment of that duty.

The court below similarly enjoined the payment of the cancellation fee, pending a resolution of the merits, because the fee was part of the overall plan to thwart Pantry Pride's efforts. We find no abuse of discretion in that ruling.

* * *

MILLS ACQUISITION CO. v. MACMILLAN, INC.

Supreme Court of Delaware, 1989.
559 A.2d 1261.

MOORE, JUSTICE.

In this interlocutory appeal from the Court of Chancery, we review the denial of injunctive relief to Mills Acquisition Co., a Delaware corporation, and its affiliates Tendclass Limited and Maxwell Communications Corp., PLC, both United Kingdom corporations substantially controlled by Robert Maxwell. Plaintiffs sought control of Macmillan, Inc. ("Macmillan" or the "company"), and moved to enjoin an asset option agreement—commonly known as a "lockup"—between Macmillan and Kohlberg Kravis Roberts & Co. ("KKR"), an investment firm specializing in leveraged buyouts. The lockup was granted by Macmillan's board of directors to KKR, as the purported high bidder, in an "auction" for control of Macmillan.

* * *

---

16. By this we do not embrace the "passivity" thesis rejected in *Unocal*. *See* 493 A.2d at 954–55, nn. 8–10. The directors' role remains an active one, changed only in the respect that they are charged with the duty of selling the company at the highest price attainable for the stockholders' benefit.

Macmillan is a large publishing, educational and informational services company. It had approximately 27,870,000 common shares listed and traded on the New York Stock Exchange. In May, 1987, Macmillan's chairman and chief executive officer, Edward P. Evans, and its president and chief operating officer, William F. Reilly, recognized that the company was a likely target of an unsolicited takeover bid. They began exploring various defensive measures, including a corporate restructuring of the company.[4]

* * *

As the Vice Chancellor noted in *Macmillan I,* for one year following the initial study of management's proposed restructuring plans:

> two central concepts remained constant. First Evans, Reilly and certain other members of management would end up owning absolute majority control of the restructured company. Second, management would acquire that majority control, not by investing new capital at prevailing market prices, but by being granted several hundred thousand restricted Macmillan shares and stock options.

Id. at 1229.

Management's plan was to "exchange" these options and shares granted by the company into "several million shares of the recapitalized company." * * *

In addition, a Macmillan Employee Stock Option Plan ("ESOP") would purchase, with borrowed funds provided by the company, a large block of Macmillan shares. The then-existing independent ESOP trustee would be replaced by Evans, Reilly, Beverly C. Chell, Vice President, General Counsel, and Secretary, and John D. Limpitlaw, Vice President—Personnel and Administration. * * * This arrangement would have given these persons voting control over all of the unallocated ESOP shares.

* * *

After the June 11 board meeting, management initiated various anti-takeover measures, including new lucrative severance contracts, known as "golden parachute" agreements, for several top executives in the event of a hostile takeover. Earlier, at the June 11 meeting, the board had approved generous five year "golden parachute" agreements for Evans and Reilly. The board also approved the adoption of a rights plan, commonly known as a "poison pill", from which the management-controlled ESOP was exempted. * * *

---

4. Evans and Reilly consulted the same lender and investment banker involved in the Harcourt restructuring, Morgan Guaranty & Trust Company and The First Boston Corporation, respectively. * * * In February, 1988, a group of First Boston bankers formed their own firm, Wasserstein, Perella & Co., Inc. Wasserstein, Perella was similarly retained to represent Macmillan along with First Boston. After the retention of Wasserstein, Perella by management, it appears that First Boston's role was a mere formality, as they had little, if any, discernible involvement thereafter.

Until August, 1987, the restructuring plan contemplated a "one company" surviving entity. This concept was changed, however, to provide for the company to be split into two distinct and separately traded parts: the Information business ("Information") and the Publishing business ("Publishing"). * * *

As initially planned, Information would trade two classes of common stock. One class, wholly owned by management, would be entitled to ten votes per share (constituting absolute voting control). * * *

The second class would have one vote per share and would be held by the public stockholders. The management owned shares were all to be deposited in a voting trust designating Evans as the sole voting trustee. Further, Information would hold a "blocking preferred" stock in Publishing (constituting 20% of Publishing's voting power).

At the September 22, 1987 board meeting the directors were informed of the new two company restructuring concept, including its anti-takeover features and management's substantial voting and equity participation in Information. The board approved the plan without objection.[5]

On October 21, 1987, the Robert M. Bass Group, Inc., a Texas corporation controlled by Robert M. Bass, together with certain affiliates (hereafter collectively, "the Bass Group" or "Bass"), emerged as a potential bidder. By then, Bass had acquired approximately 7.5% of Macmillan's common stock. Management immediately called a special board meeting on October 29, where a rather grim and uncomplimentary picture of Bass and its supposed "*modus operandi*" in prior investments was painted by management. Bass was portrayed, among other things, as a "greenmailer."

At the meeting, the previously adopted poison pill was modified to reduce the "flip-in" trigger from 30% to 15%.[6]

In its decisions the Macmillan board completely relied on management's portrayal of Bass. As it turned out, and the Vice Chancellor so found in *Macmillan I*, management's characterization of the Bass Group, including most if not all of the underlying "factual" data in support thereof, was "less than accurate." *Id.* at 1232 & n. 15. Indeed, it was false. * * *

At a regularly scheduled board meeting on March 22, 1988, the Macmillan directors voted to: (1) grant 130,000 more shares of restricted stock to Evans, Reilly, Chell and Charles G. McCurdy, Vice President—Corporate Finance; (2) seek shareholder approval of a "1988 stock option and incentive plan" and the issuance of "blank check" preferred stock "having disparate voting rights;" (3) increase the di-

---

5. In addition, the board granted options to management to purchase 202,500 shares of Macmillan at an exercise price of $74.24 per share. 552 A.2d at 1232.

6. A "flip-in" poison pill is one which grants shareholders additional financial rights in the target corporation when the pill is triggered by a cash offer or a large acquisition of target shares—here a threshold level of 15%.

* * *

rectors' compensation by some 25% per year; and (4) adopt a "non-Employee Director Retirement Plan." [8]

Due to the significant financial interests of Evans, Reilly, Chell, McCurdy and other managers in the proposed restructuring, management decided in February or March to establish a "Special Committee" of the Board to serve as an "independent" evaluator of the plan. The Special Committee was hand picked by Evans, but not actually formed until the May 18, 1988 board meeting. This fact is significant because the events that transpired between the time that the Special Committee was conceived and the time it was formed illuminate the actual working relationship between management and the allegedly "independent" directors. It calls into serious question the actual independence of the board in *Macmillan I and II*.

As the Vice Chancellor observed, starting in April, 1988, Evans and others in management, interviewed, and for four weeks thereafter maintained intensive contact with, the investment banking firm of Lazard Freres & Co. ("Lazard"), which was to eventually become the Special Committee's financial advisor. * * * All of these meetings involved extensive discussions concerning the proposed recapitalization.

Thus, the Vice Chancellor found that "[i]n total, Lazard professionals worked with management on the proposed restructuring for over 500 hours before their 'client', the Special Committee, formally came into existence and retained them."

On May 17, the day before the Macmillan annual stockholders' meeting, Evans received a letter from the Bass Group offering to purchase, consensually, all of Macmillan's common stock for $64 per share. The offer was left open for further negotiation. On May 18, the annual meeting was held at which the board recommended, and the shareholders approved, the previously mentioned 1988 Stock Option Plan and the "blank check" preferred stock. The Bass offer was not disclosed to the shareholders, although Bass had made the offer public in a filing with the Securities and Exchange Commission, which occurred simultaneously with the delivery of Bass' offer to Evans.

The Macmillan board convened immediately after the shareholders' meeting. Evans disclosed the Bass offer to the board. He then described the proposed restructuring, including the management group's planned equity position in Information. Thereafter, the Special Committee was selected.[9] However, the Committee was not given any

---

8. Under this plan, all directors aged sixty years or older who had served on the Macmillan Board for at least five years (constituting seven of the eleven non-management directors) would be paid lifetime benefits equal to the directors' fees being paid at the time of "termination." In addition to the seven directors who would immediately qualify, three of the five members of the Special Committee who were considering the restructuring would also instantly qualify. Under this plan, as later amended, benefits also were to be paid to surviving spouses of board members. * * *

9. The Special Committee consisted of Lewis A. Lapham, an old college classmate of Evans' father, (Chairman), James H. Knowles, Jr., Dorsey A. Gardner, Abraham L. Gitlow and Eric M. Hart. Hart failed to

negotiating authority regarding the terms of the restructuring. Evans apparently designated himself to "negotiate" that matter with the board.

At this May 18 meeting, the directors also amended the earlier "golden parachute" agreements; authorized a $125 million mortgage on Macmillan's building in New York City in order to finance the contemplated restructuring; and further amended the "Retirement Plan" to include severance benefits for *spouses* of directors. *Id.* However, the board deferred discussion of the Bass proposal.

* * *

The Special Committee met on May 28 to hear Lazard's presentation. Evans, Reilly, Chell and McCurdy attended. *Id.* at 1235 n. 23.
* * *

Macmillan's financial advisors valued the recapitalization at $64.15 per share. Lazard valued Macmillan at $72.57 per share, on a pre-tax basis, but advised the "independent" directors that it found the restructuring, valued at $64.15 per share, to be "fair." Lazard also recommended rejection of the $64 Bass offer because it was "inadequate." Wasserstein, Perella valued Macmillan at between $63 and $68 per share and made the same recommendations as Lazard concerning the restructuring and the Bass offer. All of these valuations will gain added significance in *Macmillan II*.

* * *

The restructuring that was approved, and later preliminarily enjoined, treated the public shareholders and the management group differently. In exchange for their Macmillan shares, the public stockholders were to receive a dividend of $52.35 cash, a $4.50 debenture, a "stub share" of Publishing ($5.10) and a one-half share of Information ($2.20). The management group, and the ESOP, would not receive the cash and debenture components. Instead, they would "exchange" their restricted stock and options for restricted shares of Information, representing a 39.2% stake in that company.

The Information stock received by management could not be sold, pledged, or transferred for two years, and would not fully vest for five years. The management holders could, however, vote the shares and receive dividends. Management would also own 3.2% of Publishing. The ESOP would own 26% of Publishing.[13]

The effect of all this would increase management's then-combined holdings of 4.5% in Macmillan to 39% in Information. Additionally, management would receive substantial cash and other benefits from the transaction. * * *

---

attend a single meeting of the Committee.
* * *

13. Although the *Macmillan I* opinion did not further discuss this point, it appears that the combination of the ESOP and management holdings, along with the 20% "blocking preferred" that Information holds in Publishing, would give management effective control over Publishing as well.

Following the board's public announcement on May 31, the Bass Group made a second offer for all Macmillan stock at $73 per share. In the alternative, Bass proposed a restructuring, much like the one the board had approved, differing only in the respect that it would offer $5.65 per share more, and management would be treated the same as the public stockholders.[14]

Two days after the revised offer was announced, Lazard concluded that it could furnish an "adequacy" opinion that would enable the Special Committee to reject the $73 per share cash portion of Bass' offer. They gave an oral opinion the following day, June 7, at a joint meeting of the Special Committee and the board that the Bass $73 cash offer, as distinguished from Bass' alternative restructuring proposal, was inadequate, given Lazard's earlier opinion that the "pre-tax break up" value of Macmillan was between $72 and $80 per share. Wasserstein, Perella expressed a similar opinion, having previously valued the company at between $66 and $80 per share. * * * These valuation ranges, obviously intended to accord with management's restructuring in *Macmillan I*, will assume an interesting significance in *Macmillan II*, when less than three months later, on August 25, these same advisors, at Evans' behest, found Maxwell's $80 all cash offer inadequate.

Upon the Special Committee's recommendation, the board again rejected the revised Bass offer and reaffirmed its approval of the management restructuring. It is noteworthy that Bass' alternative restructuring proposal was never determined to be financially inadequate or unfair by Lazard or Wasserstein, Perella. * * *

* * *

On July 14, 1988, the Vice Chancellor preliminarily enjoined the Evans designed restructuring, and held that both of the revised Bass offers were "clearly superior to the restructuring." The Court further inferred that the only real "threat" posed by the Bass offers was to the incumbency of the board "or to the management group's expectation of garnering a 39% ownership interest in Information on extremely favorable terms."

* * *

Within a few hours after the Court of Chancery issued its preliminary injunction, Evans and Reilly formally authorized Macmillan's investment advisors to explore a possible sale of the entire company.
* * *

On July 20, a most significant development occurred when Maxwell intervened in the Bass–Macmillan bidding contest by proposing to

---

14. The Vice Chancellor determined that "[t]here is no evidence that any member of the Board or the Special Committee questioned how a sale of 39% of Information would constitute a sale of the company if sold to the Bass Group, yet would not be if that same 39% interest is sold to the management group. The defendants have failed to explain that reasoning, and its logic continues to elude the Court." 552 A.2d at 1242.

Evans a consensual merger between Macmillan and Maxwell at an all-cash price of $80 per share. This was $5.00 higher than any other outstanding offer for the company. Maxwell further stated his intention to retain the company's management, and additionally, to negotiate appropriate programs of executive incentives and compensation.

Macmillan did not respond to Maxwell's overture for five weeks. Instead, during this period, Macmillan's management intensified their discussions with KKR concerning a buyout in which senior management, particularly Evans and Reilly, would have a substantial ownership interest in the new company. Upon execution of a confidentiality agreement, KKR was given detailed internal, non-public, financial information of Macmillan, culminating in a series of formal "due diligence" presentations to KKR representatives by Macmillan senior management on August 4 and 5, 1988.

On August 12, 1988, after more than three weeks of silence from the company, Maxwell made an $80 per share, all-cash tender offer for Macmillan, conditioned solely upon receiving the same non-public information which Macmillan had given to KKR three weeks earlier. * * *

Later that day, Evans received a letter from Maxwell confirming that he had initiated a tender offer, but also reiterating his desire to reach a friendly accord with Macmillan's management. Alternatively, Maxwell offered to purchase Information from the company for $1.1 billion. Significantly, no Macmillan representative ever attempted to negotiate with Maxwell on any of these matters. Notwithstanding the fact that on May 30 both Wasserstein, Perella and Lazard had given opinions that the management restructuring, with a value of $64.15, was fair, and on June 7 had advised the board that the company had a maximum breakup value of $80 per share, Wasserstein, Perella and Lazard issued new opinions on August 25 that $80 was unfair and inadequate. Accordingly, the Maxwell offer was rejected by the Macmillan board.

* * *

Nonetheless, on September 6, 1988, representatives of Macmillan and KKR met to negotiate and finalize KKR's buyout of the company. In this transaction Macmillan senior management would receive up to 20% ownership in the newly formed company. During this meeting, Evans and his senior managers suggested that they would endorse the concept and structure of the buyout to the board of directors, *even though KKR had not yet disclosed to Evans and his group the amount of its bid.* With this extraordinary commitment, KKR indicated that it would submit a firm offer by the end of the week—September 9. Following this meeting with KKR, Macmillan's financial advisors were instructed by Evans to notify the six remaining potential bidders, during September 7 and 8, that "the process seems to be coming to a close" and that any bids for Macmillan were due by Friday afternoon, September 9. It is particularly noteworthy that Maxwell was given less than 24 hours to prepare its bid, not having received this notification until the night of September 8.

In a September 8 meeting with Robert Maxwell and his representatives, Evans announced that the company's management planned to recommend a management-KKR leveraged buyout to the directors of Macmillan, and that he would not consider Maxwell's outstanding offer despite Maxwell's stated claim that he would pay "top dollar" for the entire company. Evans then declared that now he would only discuss the possible sale of up to $750 million worth of assets to Maxwell in order to facilitate this buyout. Furthermore, Evans flatly told Maxwell that senior management would leave the company if any other bidder prevailed over the management sponsored buyout offer. Following this meeting, Robert Maxwell expressed his concern to Evans that no lockup or other "break up" arrangements should be made until Macmillan had properly considered his proposal. Additionally, he volunteered to either negotiate his offering price or to purchase Information for $1.4 billion, subject to a minimal due diligence investigation.

* * *

In the late afternoon of September 9, Evans received another letter from Robert Maxwell, offering to increase his all-cash bid for the company to $84 per share. This revised offer was conditioned solely upon Maxwell receiving a clear understanding of which managers would be leaving Macmillan upon his acquisition of the company.

* * *

By 5:30 p.m. on September 9, two bidders remained in the auction: Maxwell, by virtue of his written $84 all-cash offer, and KKR, which had submitted only an oral bid to Macmillan's advisors. However, Macmillan representatives continued to negotiate overnight with KKR until an offer was reduced to writing on the next day, September 10, despite the bid deadline previously mandated by the company. In their written bid, KKR offered to acquire 94% of Macmillan's shares through a management participation, highly-leveraged, two-tier, transaction, with a "face value" of $85 per share and payable in a mix of cash and subordinated debt securities. Additionally, this offer was strictly conditioned upon the payment of KKR's expenses and an additional $29.3 million "break up" fee if a merger agreement between KKR and Macmillan was terminated by virtue of a higher bid for the company.

On September 10 and 11, Macmillan's directors met to consider Maxwell's all-cash $84 bid and KKR's blended bid of $85. Although Macmillan's financial advisors discounted KKR's offer at $84.76 per share, they nevertheless formally opined that the KKR offer was both higher than Maxwell's bid and was fair to Macmillan shareholders from a financial point of view. The Macmillan board, inferring from Maxwell's September 9 letter that he would not top a bid higher than $84 per share, approved the KKR offer and agreed to recommend KKR's offer to the shareholders. The Macmillan–KKR merger agreement was publicly announced the following day, accompanied by Macmillan's affirmation that it would take all action necessary to insure the inapplicability of its shareholder rights plan, i.e., "poison pill," to the KKR offer.

Subsequently, on September 15—and in seeming contradiction to his September 9 statement that he would not top his previous offer—Maxwell announced that he was increasing his all-cash offer to $86.60 per share. * * *

After considering the increased Maxwell bid, on September 22 the Macmillan board withdrew its recommendation of the KKR offer to shareholders, and declared its willingness to consider higher bids for the company. The board therefore instructed its investment advisors to attempt to solicit higher bids from Maxwell, KKR or any other potential bidders, in an effort to maximize the company's value for shareholders. Additionally, the board directed that the shareholder rights plan be applied to all bidders in order to enhance the auction process.

On September 23, 1988, Wasserstein, Perella began establishing the procedures for submission of the Maxwell and KKR final bids. In partial deference to Maxwell's vocal belief that the auction would be "rigged" in KKR's favor, and in order to promote an appearance of fairness in the bidding process, a "script" was developed which would be read over the telephone to both KKR and Maxwell. According to this script, both bidders were called and advised on September 24 that "the process appears to be drawing to a close" and that any final amended bids were due by 5:30 p.m., September 26.

After receiving this information on September 24, Robert Pirie, Maxwell's financial advisor, once again expressed concern to Macmillan that KKR would be favored in the auction process, and would receive "break up" fees or a lockup agreement without Maxwell first being allowed to increase its bid. Perhaps as a result of this concern, Robert Maxwell stated unequivocally in a September 25 letter to Macmillan that he was prepared, if necessary, to exceed a higher competing offer from KKR.[20]

* * *

By the auction deadline on that evening, both Maxwell and KKR had submitted bids. Maxwell made an all-cash offer, consistent with its previous bids, of $89 per share. Like its past bids, KKR submitted another "blended", front-loaded offer of $89.50 per share, consisting of $82 in cash and the balance in subordinated securities. However, this nominally higher KKR bid was subject to three conditions effectively designed to end the auction: (1) imposition of the "no-shop" rule, (2) the grant to KKR of a lockup option to purchase eight Macmillan subsidiar-

20. Later that day, Maxwell was finally given the additional financial information which KKR received in early August.

ies for $950 million, and (3) the execution of a definitive merger agreement by 12:00 noon, the following day, September 27.

While Macmillan's financial analysts considered the value of KKR's bid to be slightly higher, they decided that the bids were too close to permit the recommendation of either offer, and that the auction should therefore continue. However, shortly after the bids were received, Evans and Reilly, who were present in the Macmillan offices at the time, asked unidentified financial advisors about the status of the auction process. Inexplicably, these advisors told Evans and Reilly that both bids had been received, informed them of the respective price and forms of the bids, and stated that the financial advisors were unable to recommend either bid to the board.[22]

Thereafter, in the presence of Reilly and Charles J. Queenan, a Pittsburgh lawyer * * * Evans telephoned a KKR representative and "tipped" Maxwell's bid to him. In this call, Evans informed KKR that Maxwell had offered "$89, all cash" for the company and that the respective bids were considered "a little close." After a few minutes of conversation, the KKR representative realized the impropriety of the call and abruptly terminated it.

Meanwhile, Macmillan's financial advisors, apparently ignorant of Evans' "tip" to KKR, began developing procedures for a supplemental round of bidding. Bruce Wasserstein, the leading financial advisor to Macmillan management, who primarily orchestrated the auction process, developed a second "script" which was to be read over the telephone to both bidders. It stated:

> We are not in a position at this time to recommend any bid. If you would like to increase your bid price, let us know by 10:00 p.m.

At approximately 8:15 p.m., Wasserstein first read this prepared text to a Maxwell representative, and then relayed the same message to KKR. However, the actual document in evidence, which purports to be the "script", significantly varies in what was said to KKR. Allegedly in response to questions from KKR, Wasserstein and other financial advisors impressed upon KKR "the need to go as high as [KKR] could go" in terms of price. Additionally, the Wasserstein "script" discloses the further statement:

> To KKR: Focus on price but be advised that we do not want to give a lockup. If we granted a lockup, we would need: (1) a significant gap in your bid over the competing bid; (2) a smaller group of assets to be bought; and (3) a higher price for the assets to be bought.

At approximately 10:00 p.m., near the auction deadline of midnight, Pirie on behalf of Maxwell telephoned Wasserstein to inquire whether Macmillan had received a bid higher than the Maxwell offer. During the call, Pirie flatly stated that upon being informed that a

---

22. This epitomizes the problem of conducting an auction without board oversight, and under uncontrolled circumstances that gave Evans and Reilly, themselves interested bidders with KKR, complete and improper access to the process.

higher bid had been received by Macmillan, Maxwell would promptly notify the company whether it would increase its standing offer. Pirie also said that if Maxwell had already submitted the highest bid for the company, he would not "bid against himself" by increasing his offer.

While Wasserstein could reasonably infer from this message that Maxwell intended to top any KKR offer, it is clear that Pirie wanted to know whether KKR had in fact submitted a higher bid. Wasserstein claims to have believed that such a revelation might violate KKR's "no-shop" condition, and would have terminated the KKR offer. Therefore, he replied that if Maxwell had "anything further to say, tell us by midnight." Additionally, Wasserstein told Pirie to assume that Macmillan would not call Maxwell to inform it of a higher offer. After this conversation, and upon the advice of legal counsel, Wasserstein called Pirie back and reemphasized that he was not in a position to recommend a bid to the Macmillan board, and that Maxwell should submit its highest bid to the company by 12:00 midnight.

From the bulk of these conversations, Maxwell and Pirie reasonably, but erroneously, concluded that Wasserstein was attempting to force Maxwell to bid against itself, and that its offer was indeed higher than the competing KKR bid. Furthermore, the record is clear that Wasserstein, who later acknowledged this fact to the Macmillan board, knew that Pirie mistakenly believed that Maxwell was already the high bidder for the company. Yet, despite his responsibilities as "auctioneer" for the company, Wasserstein never sought to correct Maxwell's mistaken belief that it had prevailed in the auction. The cumulative effect of all this was that Maxwell did not increase its bid before the Macmillan board met on the next day, September 27.

At 11:50 p.m., September 26, ten minutes before the bid deadline, KKR submitted a final revised offer with a face value of $90 per share. Furthermore, the bid was predicated upon the same three previous conditions—except that the revised lockup option, apparently reflecting the additional information relayed by Wasserstein in his special KKR "script," was reduced to include only four subsidiaries at a purchase price of $775 million.

In the early morning hours of September 27, after the midnight auction deadline, Macmillan negotiated with both parties over wholly different matters. Macmillan's advisors negotiated with Maxwell's representatives for several hours over the specific and unresolved terms of Maxwell's otherwise unconditional merger proposal. However, during these sessions Macmillan never suggested that Maxwell increase its bid. On the other hand, for almost eight hours Macmillan and KKR negotiated to increase KKR's offer. By the next morning, while only increasing its total bid by approximately $1.6 million, to $90.05 ($.05 per share), KKR extracted concessions from Macmillan which increased KKR's exercise price under the lockup by $90 million after adding three more Macmillan divisions to the group of optioned assets.

Significantly, the sale of the assets under the KKR lockup agreement was structured on a "cash" basis, which would immediately result in a $250 million current tax liability for Macmillan. Moreover, both KKR and Macmillan knew that this tax liability could have been avoided through an "installment" basis sale of the assets. Above all, they knew that it would produce a *de facto* financial "poison pill" which would effectively end the auction process.

On the morning of September 27, the Macmillan board met with its investment advisors to consider these competing bids. During the course of the meeting, chaired by Evans and with Reilly present, the company's financial advisors with Wasserstein as the lead spokesman (some directors said he presided), made presentations describing their communications with both Maxwell and KKR during the auction process. Wasserstein falsely claimed that the advisors had conducted "a level-playing field auction where both parties had equal opportunity to participate." Additionally, in answer to questioning, Wasserstein mistakenly assured the board that he had been the "only conduit of information" during the process and, falsely, that both parties had received *identical* information during the auction. Despite the obvious untruth of these assertions, Evans and Reilly remained silent, knowing also that Evans had clandestinely, and wrongfully, tipped Maxwell's bid to KKR.

Wasserstein then announced the results of the second round of the auction along with the specific aspects of KKR's $90.05 "face amount" offer and Maxwell's $89 cash bid. Wasserstein, whose firm was originally retained as *management's* financial advisor, not the board's, then opined that the KKR offer was the higher of the two bids. The Lazard representative, who was retained as the financial advisor to the independent directors of the board, but throughout acquiesced in Wasserstein's predominant role, thereafter concurred in Wasserstein's assessment. Wasserstein additionally explained the ramifications of the conditions of KKR's offer, including the "deterrent" effect of the $250 million tax liability produced by the KKR lockup agreement.

However, through its deliberations on September 27, Macmillan's board, whether justified or not, was under the impression that the two bids were the product of a fair and unbiased auction process, designed to encourage KKR and Maxwell to submit their best bids.[25] The directors were not informed of Evans' and Reilly's "tip" to KKR on the previous day. Nor were they told of Wasserstein's extended "script" giving to KKR, but denying to Maxwell, additional information about the bidding process. Throughout the board meeting Evans and Reilly remained silent, deliberately concealing from their fellow directors their misconduct of tipping Maxwell's bid to KKR.

After these presentations, the Macmillan directors held extensive and closed discussions concerning the choices available to the board,

25. Even though neither the Board as a whole, nor the allegedly "independent" directors, had taken any action to ensure such a process.

including the possibility that Maxwell might increase its bid if the board "shopped" the KKR offer. Yet, as they believed that the risk of terminating the KKR offer outweighed the potential advantage of an increased Maxwell bid, the directors decided to accept the higher face value KKR proposal, and granted the KKR merger and lockup option agreements.

* * *

On September 29, 1988, KKR filed documents required by the Securities and Exchange Commission, amending its outstanding tender offer to reflect the increased $90.05 face amount bid accepted by the Macmillan board. In this filing, and for the first time, KKR disclosed Evans' September 26 "tip" to KKR that Maxwell's cash bid was $.50 lower than KKR's.

On that same day, Robert Maxwell delivered a letter to Evans announcing that he had amended his cash tender offer to $90.25 per share, conditioned upon invalidation of the KKR lockup agreement. In his letter, Maxwell emphasized that he had previously stated his willingness to top any offer higher than his earlier $89 offer, and that he was nevertheless willing to purchase for $900 million the same four divisions which KKR originally proposed to purchase for $775 million.

On October 4, the Macmillan board met to consider both the revised Maxwell bid and Evans' September 26 "tip" to KKR. After some discussion and deliberation, the board rejected Maxwell's increased offer because it was conditioned on invalidating the KKR lockup. Furthermore, the board considered that Evans' "tip" to KKR was immaterial in light of the second round of bidding that occurred. Additionally, after consultation with counsel, the board concluded that their ignorance of this "tip", at the time they approved the merger with KKR, was insufficient grounds for repudiating the lockup agreement.

After a hearing on Maxwell's motion for a preliminary injunction, on October 17, the Court of Chancery denied Maxwell's request to enjoin the lockup agreement, the break-up fees and expenses granted by the Macmillan board to KKR. In ruling for Macmillan, the trial court found that although KKR was consistently and deliberately favored throughout the auction process, Maxwell was not prevented from, or otherwise misled to refrain from, submitting a higher bid for the company. However, the court found that Macmillan's shareholders should have the opportunity to consider an alternative offer for the company, and therefore enjoined the operation of Macmillan's "poison pill" shareholder rights plan as a defensive measure to Maxwell's still open tender offer. In this appeal neither party has challenged that limited injunction. Thus, the sole issue before us is the validity, under all of the foregoing circumstances, of the asset lockup option granted pursuant to the KKR–Macmillan merger agreement with its attendant breakup fees and expenses.

* * *

We have held that when a court reviews a board action, challenged as a breach of duty, it should decline to evaluate the wisdom and merits of a business decision unless sufficient facts are alleged with particularity, or the record otherwise demonstrates, that the decision was not the product of an informed, disinterested, and independent board. * * * Yet, this judicial reluctance to assess the merits of a business decision ends in the face of illicit manipulation of a board's deliberative processes by self-interested corporate fiduciaries. Here, not only was there such deception, but the board's own lack of oversight in structuring and directing the auction afforded management the opportunity to indulge in the misconduct which occurred. In such a context, the challenged transaction must withstand rigorous judicial scrutiny under the exacting standards of entire fairness. * * * What occurred here cannot survive that analysis.

The Vice Chancellor correctly found that Evans and Reilly, as participants in the leveraged buyout, had significant self-interest in ensuring the success of a KKR bid. Given this finding, Evans' and Reilly's deliberate concealment of material information from the Macmillan board must necessarily have been motivated by an interest adverse to Macmillan's shareholders. Evans' and Reilly's conduct throughout was resolutely intended to deliver the company to themselves in *Macmillan I*, and to their favored bidder, KKR, and thus themselves, in *Macmillan II*. The board was torpid, if not supine, in its efforts to establish a truly independent auction, free of Evans' interference and access to confidential data. By placing the entire process in the hands of Evans, through his own chosen financial advisors, with little or no board oversight, the board materially contributed to the unprincipled conduct of those upon whom it looked with a blind eye.

* * *

The voluminous record in this case discloses conduct that fails all basic standards of fairness. While any one of the identifiable breaches of fiduciary duty, standing alone, should easily foretell the outcome, what occurred here, including the lack of oversight by the directors, irremediably taints the design and execution of the transaction.

It is clear that on July 14, 1988, the day that the Court of Chancery enjoined the management-induced reorganization, and with Bass' $73 offer outstanding, Macmillan's management met with KKR to discuss a management sponsored buyout. This was done without prior board approval. By early September, Macmillan's financial and legal advisors, originally chosen by Evans, independently constructed and managed the process by which bids for the company were solicited. Although the Macmillan board was fully aware of its ultimate responsibility for ensuring the integrity of the auction, the directors wholly delegated the creation and administration of the auction to an array of Evans' hand-picked investment advisors. It is undisputed that Wasserstein, who was originally retained as an investment advisor to Macmillan's senior management, was a principal, if not the primary, "auctioneer" of the company. While it is unnecessary to hold that Wasserstein lacked independence, or was necessarily "beholden" to management, it appears that Lazard Freres, allegedly the investment advisor to the independent directors, was a far more appropriate candidate to conduct this process on behalf of the board. Yet, both the board and Lazard acceded to Wasserstein's, and through him Evans', primacy.

While a board of directors may rely in good faith upon "information, opinions, reports or statements presented" by corporate officers, employees and experts "selected with reasonable care," 8 *Del.C.* § 141(e), it may not avoid its active and direct duty of oversight in a matter as significant as the sale of corporate control. That would seem particularly obvious where insiders are among the bidders. This failure of the Macmillan board significantly contributed to the resulting mismanagement of the bidding process. When presumably well-intentioned outside directors remove themselves from the design and execution of an auction, then what occurred here, given the human temptations left unchecked, was virtually inevitable.

Clearly, this auction was clandestinely and impermissibly skewed in favor of KKR. The record amply demonstrates that KKR repeatedly received significant material advantages to the exclusion and detriment of Maxwell to stymie, rather than enhance, the bidding process.

As for any "negotiations" between Macmillan and Maxwell, they are noteworthy only for the peremptory and curt attitude of Macmillan, through its self-interested chief executive officer Evans, to reject every overture from Maxwell. In Robert Maxwell's initial letter to Evans of July 21, he proposed an $80 all-cash offer for the company. This represented a substantial increase over any other outstanding offer. Indeed, it equalled the highest per share price, which both Wasserstein, Perella and Lazard had previously ascribed to the value of the company on June 7, when the Evans' sponsored restructuring was before the board. Now, not only was Maxwell ignored, but Evans convinced Wasserstein, Perella and Lazard, contrary to their June 7 opinions, ascribing a maximum value to the company of $80 per share, to declare Maxwell's August 12 bid of $80 inadequate.[28] Not only did Macmillan's financial advisors dismiss all Maxwell offers for negotiations, but they also deliberately misled Maxwell in the final stage of the auction by perpetuating the mistaken belief that Maxwell had the high bid. Additionally, Maxwell was subjected to a series of short bid deadlines in a seeming effort to prevent the submission of a meaningful bid. The defendants have totally failed to justify this calculated campaign of resistance and misinformation, despite the strict duties of care and loyalty demanded of them.

* * *

28. Yet, on May 30 these same advisors had found management's $64.15 restructuring to be fair.

The tone and substance of the communications between Macmillan and Maxwell dispel any further doubt that Maxwell was seen as an unwelcome, unfriendly and unwanted bidder. Evans, a self-interested fiduciary, repeatedly stated that *he* had no intention of considering a merger with Maxwell, and that *he* would do everything to prevent Maxwell from acquiring Macmillan. Nonetheless, Robert Maxwell's response was a diplomatic, yet persistent, pursuit of Macmillan, emphasizing his desire to work with existing management and his intent to operate the company as a going concern. With the sole exception of his September 9th letter, declining to exceed a "fully financed" offer above $84, Maxwell never retreated from his stated intent to continue bidding for Macmillan, or his willingness to negotiate any other aspect of his offer.

This continuing hostility toward Maxwell cannot be justified after the Macmillan board actually decided on September 10–11 to abandon any further restructuring attempts, and to sell the entire company. Although Evans had begun negotiations with KKR on July 14, the board's action in September formally initiated the auction process. Further discriminatory treatment of a bidder, without any rational benefit to the shareholders, was unwarranted. The proper objective of Macmillan's fiduciaries was to obtain the highest price reasonably available for the company, provided it was offered by a reputable and responsible bidder.[29] *Revlon*, 506 A.2d at 182, 184. At this point, there was no justification for denying Maxwell the same courtesies and access to information as had been extended to KKR. *Id.* at 184. Without board planning and oversight to insulate the self-interested management from improper access to the bidding process, and to ensure the proper conduct of the auction by truly independent advisors selected by, and answerable only to, the independent directors, the legal complications which a challenged transaction faces under *Revlon* are unnecessarily intensified. * * *

In examining the actual conduct of this auction, there can be no justification for the telephonic "tip" to KKR of Maxwell's $89 all-cash offer following the first round of bidding held on September 26th. Although the defendants contend that this tip was made "innocently" and under the impression that the auction process had already ended, this assertion is refuted by the record. The recipient of the "tip", KKR, immediately recognized its impropriety. Evans' and Reilly's knowing concealment of the tip at the critical board meeting of September 27th utterly destroys their credibility. Given their duty of disclosure under

---

29. In assessing the bid and the bidder's responsibility, a board may consider, among various proper factors, the adequacy and terms of the offer; its fairness and feasibility; the proposed or actual financing for the offer, and the consequences of that financing; questions of illegality; the impact of both the bid and the potential acquisition on other constituencies, provided that it bears some reasonable relationship to general shareholder interests; the risk of nonconsummation; the basic stockholder interests at stake; the bidder's identity, prior background and other business venture experiences; and the bidder's business plans for the corporation and their effects on stockholder interests. *Cf. Ivanhoe*, 535 A.2d at 1341–42; *Unocal*, 493 A.2d at 955–56; *Revlon*, 506 A.2d at 182–83.

the circumstances, this silence is an explicit acknowledgment of their culpability. * * *

Defendants maintain that the Evans–Reilly tip was immaterial, because it did not prevent Maxwell from submitting a higher bid in the second and final round of the auction on September 26th. However, this "immaterial" tip revealed both the price and form of Maxwell's first round bid, which constituted the two principal strategic components of their otherwise unconditional offer. With this information, KKR knew every crucial element of Maxwell's initial bid. The unfair tactical advantage this gave KKR, since no aspect of its own bid could be shopped, becomes manifest in light of the situation created by Maxwell's belief that it had submitted the higher offer. Absent an unprompted and unexpected improvement in Maxwell's bid, the tip provided vital information to enable KKR to prevail in the auction.

Similarly, the defendants argue that the subsequent Wasserstein "long script"—in reality another form of tip—was an immaterial and "appropriate response" to questions by KKR, providing no tactical information useful to KKR. As to this claim, the eventual auction results demonstrate that Wasserstein's tip relayed crucial information to KKR: the methods by which KKR should tailor its bid in order to satisfy Macmillan's financial advisors. It is highly significant that both aspects of the advice conveyed by the tip—to "focus on price" and to amend the terms of its lockup agreement—were adopted by KKR. They were the very improvements upon which the board subsequently accepted the KKR bid on Wasserstein's recommendation. Nothing could have been more material under the circumstances. It violated every principle of fair dealing, and of the exacting role demanded of those entrusted with the conduct of an auction for the sale of corporate control. * * *

Given the materiality of these tips, and the silence of Evans, Reilly and Wasserstein in the face of their rigorous affirmative duty of disclosure at the September 27 board meeting, there can be no dispute but that such silence was misleading and deceptive. In short, it was a fraud upon the board. * * *

Under 8 *Del.C.* § 141(e), when corporate directors rely in good faith upon opinions or reports of officers and other experts "selected with reasonable care", they necessarily do so on the presumption that the information provided is both accurate and complete. Normally, decisions of a board based upon such data will not be disturbed when made in the proper exercise of business judgment. However, when a board is deceived by those who will gain from such misconduct, the protections girding the decision itself vanish. Decisions made on such a basis are voidable at the behest of innocent parties to whom a fiduciary duty was owed and breached, and whose interests were thereby materially and adversely affected.[32] This rule is based on the unyielding principle that

---

32. In this context we speak only of the traditional concept of protecting the deci-

corporate fiduciaries shall abjure every temptation for personal profit at the expense of those they serve.[33] *Guth,* 5 A.2d at 510.

In *Revlon,* we addressed for the first time the parameters of a board of directors' fiduciary duties in a sale of corporate control. There, we affirmed the Court of Chancery's decision to enjoin the lockup and no-shop provisions accepted by the Revlon directors, holding that the board had breached its fiduciary duties of care and loyalty.[34]

Although we have held that such agreements are not *per se* illegal, we recognized that like measures often foreclose further bidding to the detriment of shareholders, and end active auctions prematurely. * * * If the grant of an auction-ending provision is appropriate, it must confer a substantial benefit upon the stockholders in order to withstand exacting scrutiny by the courts. * * * Moreover, where the decision of the directors, granting the lockup option, was not informed or was induced by breaches of fiduciary duties, such as those here, they cannot survive.

* * *

This case does not require a judicial determination of *when* Macmillan was "for sale."[35] By any standards this company was for sale

sion itself, sometimes referred to as the business judgment doctrine. *Revlon,* 506 A.2d at 180 n. 10. The question of the independent directors' personal liability for these challenged decisions, reached under circumstances born of the board's lack of oversight, is not the issue here. However, we entertain no doubt that this board's virtual abandonment of its oversight functions in the face of Evans' and Reilly's patent self-interest was a breach of its fundamental duties of loyalty and care in the conduct of this auction. More than anything else it created the atmosphere in which Evans, Reilly and others could act so freely and improperly. Given these facts, a board can take little comfort in what was said under far different circumstances in *Graham v. Allis–Chalmers Mfg. Co.,* Del. Supr., 41 Del.Ch. 78, 188 A.2d 125, 130–31 (1963). * * * Nor can decisions reached under such circumstances be sustained.

33. Although Wasserstein was not a Macmillan officer or director, it is bedrock law that the conduct of one who knowingly joins with a fiduciary, including corporate officials, in breaching a fiduciary obligation, is equally culpable. Thus, decisions based on the advice of such persons share the same defects as those discussed in n. 32, *supra.* * * *

34. Following *Revlon,* there appeared to be a degree of "scholarly" debate about the particular fiduciary duty that had been breached in that case, i.e. the duty of care or the duty of loyalty. In *Ivanhoe,* 535 A.2d at 1345, we made it abundantly clear that *both* duties were involved in *Revlon,* and that both had been breached.

35. This Court has been required to determine on other occasions since our decision in *Revlon,* whether a company is "for sale". * * * Clearly not every offer or transaction affecting the corporate structure invokes the *Revlon* duties. A refusal to entertain offers may comport with a valid exercise of business judgment.

* * *

Circumstances may dictate that an offer be rebuffed, given the nature and timing of the offer; its legality, feasibility and effect on the corporation and the stockholders; the alternatives available and their effect on the various constituencies, particularly the stockholders; the company's long term strategic plans; and any special factors bearing on stockholder and public interests. * * * In *Ivanhoe* we recognized that a change in corporate structure under the special facts and circumstances of that case did not invoke *Revlon.* * * *

Specifically, Newmont's management faced two potentially coercive offers. In responding to such threats management's efforts were viewed as reasonable decisions intended to guide the corporation through the minefield of dangers directly posed by one bidder, and potentially by another. * * * While it was argued that the transaction benefited management by strengthen-

both in *Macmillan I* and *II.* In any event, the board of directors formally concluded on September 11 that it would be in the best interests of the stockholders to sell the company. * * *

What we are required to determine here is the scope of the board's responsibility in an active bidding contest once their role as auctioneer has been invoked under *Revlon.* Particularly, we are concerned with the use of lockup and no-shop clauses.

* * *

In this case, a lockup agreement was not necessary to draw any of the bidders into the contest. Macmillan cannot seriously contend that they received a final bid from KKR that materially enhanced general stockholder interests. By all rational indications it was intended to have a directly opposite effect. As the record clearly shows, on numerous occasions Maxwell requested opportunities to further negotiate the price and structure of his proposal. When he learned of KKR's higher offer, he increased his bid to $90.25 per share.

* * * Further, KKR's "enhanced" bid, being nominal at best, was a *de minimis* justification for the lockup. When one compares what KKR received for the lockup, in contrast to its inconsiderable offer, the invalidity of the agreement becomes patent. * * *

Here, the assets covered by the lockup agreement were some of Macmillan's most valued properties, its "crown jewels." [37] Even if the lockup is permissible, when it involves "crown jewel" assets careful board scrutiny attends the decision. When the intended effect is to end an active auction, at the very least the independent members of the board must attempt to negotiate alternative bids before granting such a significant concession. * * *

Maxwell invited negotiations for a purchase of the same four divisions, which KKR originally sought to buy for $775 million. Maxwell was prepared to pay $900 million. Instead of serious negotiations with Maxwell, there were only concessions to KKR by giving it a lockup of seven divisions for $865 million.

Thus, when directors in a *Revlon* bidding contest grant a crown jewel lockup, serious questions are raised, particularly where, as here, there is little or no improvement in the final bid. *Revlon,* 506 A.2d at 184, 187. The care and attention which independent directors bring to this decision are crucial to its success. * * *

As for the no-shop clause, *Revlon* teaches that the use of such a device is even more limited than a lockup agreement. Absent a

ing its position, at most this was a secondary effect. There was no proof of self-dealing, and the evidence clearly sustained the conclusion that the board of Newmont punctiliously met its fiduciary obligations to the stockholders in the face of two major threats.

37. In the current takeover parlance, these are valuable assets or lines of business owned by a target company. The attempt is to sell them to third parties or place them under option at bargain prices as a device to defeat an unwanted takeover attempt.

material advantage to the stockholders from the terms or structure of a bid that is contingent on a no-shop clause, a successful bidder imposing such a condition must be prepared to survive the careful scrutiny which that concession demands. * * *

Directors are not required by Delaware law to conduct an auction according to some standard formula, only that they observe the significant requirement of fairness for the purpose of enhancing general shareholder interests. That does not preclude differing treatment of bidders when necessary to advance those interests. Variables may occur which necessitate such treatment. However, the board's primary objective, and essential purpose, must remain the enhancement of the bidding process for the benefit of the stockholders.

We recognize that the conduct of a corporate auction is a complex undertaking both in its design and execution. * * * We do not intend to limit the broad negotiating authority of the directors to achieve the best price available to the stockholders. To properly secure that end may require the board to invoke a panoply of devices, and the giving or receiving of concessions that may benefit one bidder over another. * * *

But when that happens, there must be a rational basis for the action such that the interests of the stockholders are manifestly the board's paramount objective.

* * *

When *Revlon* duties devolve upon directors, this Court will continue to exact an enhanced judicial scrutiny at the threshold, as in *Unocal*, before the normal presumptions of the business judgment rule will apply. However, as we recognized in *Revlon*, the two part threshold test, of necessity, is slightly different. * * *

At the outset, the plaintiff must show, and the trial court must find, that the directors of the target company treated one or more of the respective bidders on unequal terms. It is only then that the two-part threshold requirement of *Unocal* is truly invoked, for in *Revlon* we held that "[f]avoritism for a white knight to the total exclusion of a hostile bidder might be justifiable when the latter's offer adversely affects shareholder interests, but ... the directors cannot fulfill their enhanced *Unocal* duties by playing favorites with the contending factions." *Id.* 506 A.2d at 184.

In the face of disparate treatment, the trial court must first examine whether the directors properly perceived that shareholder interests were enhanced. In any event the board's action must be reasonable in relation to the advantage sought to be achieved, or conversely, to the threat which a particular bid allegedly poses to stockholder interests. *Unocal*, 493 A.2d at 955.

If on the basis of this enhanced *Unocal* scrutiny the trial court is satisfied that the test has been met, then the directors' actions necessarily are entitled to the protections of the business judgment rule.

The latitude a board will have in responding to differing bids will vary according to the degree of benefit or detriment to the shareholders' general interests that the amount or terms of the bids pose. We stated in *Revlon*, and again here, that in a sale of corporate control the responsibility of the directors is to get the highest value reasonably attainable for the shareholders. *Revlon*, 506 A.2d at 182. Beyond that, there are no special and distinct "Revlon duties". Once a finding has been made by a court that the directors have fulfilled their fundamental duties of care and loyalty under the foregoing standards, there is no further judicial inquiry into the matter. * * *

The Special Problems of LBOs

Please reread the Jensen excerpt in chapter 1 at pp. 12–21, and the Oesterle excerpt in chapter 4 at pp. 401–03A.3.b. and read section 1203 of the California Corporation Code in your statutory supplement. How does the California provision approach the conflict-of-interest problems inherent in leveraged buyouts that include firm managers as principals?

ALLEN, INDEPENDENT DIRECTORS IN MBO TRANSACTIONS: ARE THEY FACT OR FANTASY?
45 Bus. Lawyer 2055 (1990).
By William T. Allen [*]

* * *

I want to address one of these questions—and not the most far-reaching or glamorous of them. I want to inquire into the role of outside directors—special committees of outside directors—when the corporation is to be sold, and whether such committees can or do function adequately to protect appropriate interests in such a setting. Addressing that subject requires, as well, that one explore, a bit, the role of the investment bankers and lawyers who guide the board in a change of control transaction.

To relieve any suspense, I will report now that I am going to conclude that, as one who has reviewed in one way or another a fair number of special committees in a sale context, I remain open to the possibility that such committees can be employed effectively to protect corporate and shareholder interests. But I must confess a painful awareness of the ways in which the device may be subverted and rendered less than useful. I conclude, as well, that it is the lawyers and the investment bankers who in many cases hold the key to the effectiveness of the special committee. * * *

On this foundational question, there is a disturbing dichotomy of views. A prominent view is the view that outside directors serve a largely ornamental role in the month-to-month direction of the enterprise. Peter Drucker, a leading scholar of business management, asserts that boards of directors are "an important ceremonial and legal

---

[*] William T. Allen is Chancellor of the Delaware Court of Chancery.

fiction" that "do not function." Another scholar quotes a CEO as saying, "the board rubber-stamps the action of management and the board members are there to mollify the outside stockholders." Outside directors are widely seen as so bound up with management in a variety of ways that it is delusion or pretense to expect them to represent shareholder views when a conflict transaction arises. * * *

Yet our statutory corporation law has long assumed that disinterested directors can exercise a business judgment unaffected by the fact that the CEO of the firm may be self-interested. * * *

More recently, and perhaps most significantly, outside directors have been pressed into service on special committees charged with negotiating a sale of the company to management or to the highest bidder. * * *

A search for a reliable answer to the question—"which view is correct?"—could begin with a large-scale empirical inquiry into how committees of outside directors have in fact tended to act in various settings. But I am aware of no effort to address that question empirically, and the methodological problems of such an inquiry would be daunting.

A review of some of the cases from the Delaware Court of Chancery is no substitute for a rigorous empirical study, but there have been a reasonably large number of takeover cases in our court in which committees of outside directors have functioned or purported to function. What do they suggest about the utility of this device?

Well, there are a number of cases that can be cited in support of the cynical view. In *Bass v. Evans*, for example, Vice Chancellor Jacobs found the functioning of a special committee of directors to be "little more than a charade," and the Delaware Supreme Court later characterized the outside members of the board of this same company as "torpid, if not supine." Indeed, a slow reading of the facts reported in *Bass* is a painful exercise for someone not already persuaded to the cynical view. Nor is that case unique. * * * More recently, the court of chancery opinion *In re Trans World Airlines, Inc. Shareholder Litigation* reflects a situation which would meet the expectations of those who expect little of outside directors. Indeed, insofar as the functioning of a special committee is concerned, that case appeared, on an application for preliminary injunction, to reflect the hollow posturing that is the risk that validation of the special committee structure entails.

But despite these and other cases that might support this cynical position, I remain unconvinced. I confess to skepticism but not cynicism. I have seen counter-examples in which a committee of structurally independent directors has appeared to function quite adversarily. One recent case involving a special board committee that received wide attention is the *RJR Nabisco* buyout transaction. At least as that case appeared at the time of a hearing on preliminary injunction, the outside directors were seen as energetically exercising informed and independent judgment in the sale of the enterprise. Their decision was accorded the deference that courts grant to a valid exercise of business judgment.

* * *

Thus, in the sale context, the Delaware cases suggested that it *is* possible for "outside" directors to function independently, in a way that at least at a preliminary injunction stage, satisfies the standards of a dispassionate and experienced reviewing court. But those cases demonstrate as well that not every decision by an apparently disinterested special committee deserves or will be accorded that respect.

The factor that distinguishes those circumstances in which the decision of a committee of outside directors has been accorded respect and those in which its decision has not, is not mysterious. The court's own implicit evaluation of the integrity of the special committee's process marks that process as deserving respect or condemns it to be ignored. When a special committee's process is perceived as reflecting a good faith, informed attempt to approximate aggressive, arm's-length bargaining, it will be accorded substantial importance by the court. When, on the other hand, it appears as artifice, ruse or charade, or when the board unduly limits the committee or when the committee fails to correctly perceive its mission—then one can expect that its decision will be accorded no respect.

But how likely is it that these outside directors—who have had feelings of solidarity with and, to some extent, dependency upon management—will pursue a process that will be later seen as having integrity?

Consider the outside director who is asked to serve on a special committee to preside over a sale of the company. While he may receive some modest special remuneration for this service, he and his fellow committee members are likely to be the only persons intensely involved in the process who do not entertain the fervent hope of either making a killing or earning a princely fee. Couple that with the pressure that the seriousness and urgency of the assignment generate; the unpleasantness that may be required if the job is done right; and, the fact that no matter what the director does he will probably be sued for it, and you have, I think, a fairly unappetizing assignment.

Combine these factors with those mentioned earlier that create feelings of solidarity with management directors, particularly the corporation's CEO, and it becomes, I would think, quite easy to understand how some special committees appear as no more than, in T.S. Eliot's phrase, "an easy tool, deferential, glad to be of use."

Only one factor stands against these pressures towards accommodation of the CEO: that is a sense of duty. When special committees have appeared to push and resist their colleagues, it has been, I submit, because the men and women who comprised the committee have understood that as a result of accepting this special assignment, they have a new duty and stand in a new and different relationship to the firm's management or its controlling shareholder. When, as in *Mills v. Macmillan,* a special committee has appeared to perform this special assignment badly, it is probably because its members have been ill-served by their advisors and, as a result, have failed to understand or to accept the radical change in that relationship that had occurred.

I fully appreciate that corrupt conduct does occur. But I believe—especially in the context of the larger public companies—that when outside directors serving on a special committee fail to meet our expectations, it is likely that they fail because they have not understood what was expected of them. Directors must know what is right before courts can expect them to do what is right.

Thus, I come to the role of the committee's advisors—the lawyers and investment bankers who guide the committee through the process of the sale of a public company. I regard the role of the advisors in establishing the integrity of this process as absolutely crucial. Indeed, the motives and performance of the lawyers and bankers who specialize in the field of mergers and acquisitions is to my mind the great, largely unexamined variable in the process. In all events, it is plain that quite often the special committee relies upon the advisors almost totally. It is understandable why. Frequently, the outside directors who find themselves in control of a corporate sale process have had little or no experience in the sale of a public company. They are in *terra incognito.* Naturally, they turn for guidance to their specialist advisors who will typically have had a great deal of relevant experience.

Thus, in my opinion, if the special committee process is to have integrity, it falls in the first instance to the lawyers to unwrap the bindings that have joined the directors into a single board; to instill in the committee a clear understanding of the radically altered state in which it finds itself and to lead the committee to a full understanding of its new duty.

Much, of course, will turn on the court's evaluation of the integrity of the special committee's process. In reaching that evaluation, the court will be mindful—and the lawyers advising the committee need to be mindful as well—that the committee, if respected, holds the shareholders' welfare in its hands; the court will be mindful that claims of so-called structural bias in the process are plausible; and, that the court's own power of perception is limited. Thus, in a sale context, counsel for a special committee must accept from the outset that as a practical matter she will have to demonstrate that the special committee's process had integrity; that the committee was informed, energetic and committed in this transaction to the single goal of maximizing the shareholders' interest.

Please don't mistake me. This is not a call to pay even greater attention to appearances; it is advice to abandon the theatrical and to accept and to implement the substance of an arm's-length process. To do this, the lawyers and the bankers must be independent of management. They must accept in their hearts that in the MBO or the auction context, their client is the committee and not management. They must clearly and emphatically remind their client that, at this juncture, the CEO and his associates are to be treated at arm's-length. And the lawyers and bankers must act on that view. That means that from the outset, the advisors must be prepared to forego future business. It comes to that.

If all of that is done, the resulting process will be unmistakably imbued with the character of a genuine attempt to maximize advantage on behalf of the shareholders. The outside directors will have in mind the nature of the changed relationship between themselves and the company's management and will have in mind the nature of the legal duties that they bear.

This process has, on occasion, appeared to have worked well. When it works well, it is, I think, superior to later judicial review for substantive fairness because courts are more poorly equipped than are business persons to assess business risks and rewards. But the process of referring conflict matters to a special committee has on other occasions failed, collapsing into a disgraceful charade. What remains to be determined by some future systematic inquiry is whether the benefits associated with successful invocation of the device outweigh the cost to shareholders of the failures.[31] But that large scale project, if it is possible, is for the future. For the present, as in the past, case law, and in this area statutory law as well, will be informed largely by shared perceptions or intuitions that fall short of such systematic understanding.

My intuition is that the jury is still out on the question whether the special committee device works well enough, often enough, for the law to continue to accord it weight. I am sure, however, of this: if the future leads us to view that that process does offer to shareholders protections that are consistent with justice, it will in large measure be because lawyers have been true to their professional responsibilities and have used their talent and power to see that outside directors understand and strive to satisfy their duty.

I conclude now. In doing so, I wish to refer to the special role of the lawyer. I do not mean to be moralistic, but I do wish to remind you that lawyers are not engaged in a strictly commercial enterprise. You have accepted an obligation that transcends the obligations of investment bankers or businessmen or women. That obligation is to justice. While such a grand word may seem quaint at the close of the decade of self-promotion and the mega-deal, it *is* in pursuit of that concept that laws are made, courts established, and lawyers trained and licensed.

* * *

---

31. The cost to shareholders of a failed or corrupt process would be reflected in a sub-optimal price. The cost to the economy as a whole would be the inefficiency of transferring the asset (the firm) to one other than the buyer with the most socially productive use. In our system, we tend to treat the willingness to pay the highest price as a good proxy for determining the highest social good—an assumption the correctness of which could, of course, sustain debate.

BARKAN v. AMSTED INDUSTRIES, INC.

Supreme Court of Delaware, 1989.
567 A.2d 1279.

Opinion of WALSH, JUSTICE.

This is an appeal from a Court of Chancery decision that approved the settlement of several class action lawsuits. The litigation arose out of a management-sponsored leveraged buyout ("MBO") of all of the common stock of Amsted Industries, Inc. ("Amsted") by members of Amsted's management and a newly formed employee stock ownership plan ("ESOP"). * * * In early 1985, Charles Hurwitz ("Hurwitz") began acquiring a significant number of shares of Amsted common stock through an entity known as MAXXAM Associates. Although Hurwitz claimed that the shares were being purchased for investment purposes only, he was widely recognized as a sophisticated investor in the market for corporate control. Accordingly, Amsted's board of directors retained Goldman, Sachs & Co. in May, 1985 to counsel them concerning possible responses to Hurwitz's overture. Goldman Sachs advised the board that Hurwitz had earned a reputation for attempting to acquire control of a corporation at a price below its real value or, alternatively, to extract "greenmail." The investment bankers suggested an array of possible defenses to the challenge posed by Hurwitz. These included a stock purchase rights plan, a stock repurchase by the corporation, a friendly acquisition by a third party, a management-sponsored leveraged buyout, and a management-sponsored leveraged buyout involving an ESOP.

Amsted's board chose to adopt a common stock purchase rights plan, commonly referred to as a "poison pill". Under its terms, in the event that any person or group acquired 20% or more of Amsted's common shares or announced an offer that would enable any person or group to own 30% or more of such shares, holders of rights issued pursuant to the plan would be entitled to purchase newly issued Amsted stock. More important, the plan contained a "flip-over" provision, which enabled rights holders to buy the stock of any acquiring corporation at a significant discount. The goal of the plan was to prevent any business combination of which the board did not approve. The board could give a merger its blessing by redeeming the plan rights.

With the rights plan in place, Amsted began to consider the possibility of undertaking a leveraged buyout involving an ESOP. Because such a transaction offered significant tax advantages, it was felt that it would provide shareholders with the highest possible price for their shares. On September 26, 1985, the Amsted board authorized the establishment of an ESOP, although no definite proposal for undertaking an MBO was discussed at that time. On October 22, 1985, however, the Amsted board established a Special Committee of its members to investigate the merits of any transaction involving a change of corporate control. The Special Committee was composed of directors who were neither officers of Amsted nor beneficiaries of the ESOP. Although the Special Committee was given the power to evaluate the fairness of any acquisition proposal made by a third party, the Committee was instructed not to engage in an active search for alternatives to an MBO.

Several days later, on October 29, 1985, the Amsted board terminated certain pension plans covering substantially all Amsted employees who were not subject to collective bargaining agreements. The board's goal was to make the excess assets in the plans (estimated by Goldman Sachs to be worth approximately $75 million) available to finance an MBO. On November 4, 1985, an MBO proposal was finally presented to the Amsted board by the ESOP trustees and members of Amsted senior management (the "MBO Group"). Under the proposal, the MBO Group would purchase all of Amsted's outstanding stock for $37 per share of cash and $27 per share in principal amount of a new issue of subordinated discount debentures, valued at $11 per share.[1]

* * *

The MBO proposal hit a roadblock. Citibank, which had informally agreed to assemble financing for the deal, concluded that the proposed transaction was too highly leveraged and withdrew its support. On November 13, 1985, First National Bank of Chicago ("First National") agreed to take Citibank's place. However, First National proposed that $3 per share of cash in the original proposal be replaced with preferred stock having a face value of $4 and a market value of $3. The total value of this package of consideration remained $48 per share.

Through the rest of November, December, and much of January, Goldman Sachs and the MBO Group worked to arrange financing for the transaction proposed by First National. By late January, however, the MBO Group decided that the value of the consideration offered would have to be reduced. Decreased earnings in the first quarter of fiscal year 1986 (which ended December 31, 1985) led the MBO Group to doubt Amsted's ability to perform at the level previously anticipated. Accordingly, when the MBO Group finally went to Amsted's board with a proposal on January 29, 1986, they offered a $45 per share package, with $31 per share in cash, $4 per share in preferred stock valued at $3 per share, and $27 in principal amount of subordinated discount debentures valued at $11 per share.

The Special Committee met that day to consider the proposal. Salomon Brothers, the Special Committee's investment advisors, opined that a price of $45 was "high in the range of fairness." The Special Committee, however, directed Salomon Brothers to seek an increase in the cash component of the package. The MBO Group quickly agreed to

---

1. Barkan's suit was not filed until March 12, 1986.

offer an additional $1.25 in cash, making the total consideration worth $46.25 per share. The Special Committee approved the increased offer and recommended it to the full board, which also gave its blessing to the MBO. The board also voted to redeem the common stock purchase rights plan in order to make the transaction possible. An Exchange Offer followed shortly thereafter on February 5, 1986.

At this point, the long-quiescent Hurwitz approached Goldman Sachs and voiced his dissatisfaction with the adequacy of the offer. After some negotiation, Hurwitz agreed to tender his shares if the cash component of the transaction were increased again, by $.75 per share to $33 per share. Goldman Sachs agreed to recommend such an increase if the plaintiffs in the four lawsuits filed in November, 1985 could be persuaded to reach a settlement. The plaintiffs had not yet conducted any discovery nor amended their complaints to reflect the developments that had occurred since November. Nevertheless, on February 10, 1986, the plaintiffs agreed to a full settlement, conditioned upon their being permitted to conduct "confirmatory discovery" at a later date. On February 19, 1986, the Exchange Offer was amended to reflect the increased cash consideration. The Offer closed on March 5, 1986, with 89% of the outstanding stock having been tendered. The MBO itself was closed on June 2, 1986.

* * *

There is some dispute among the parties as to the meaning of *Revlon,* as well as its relevance to the outcome of this case. We believe that the general principles announced in *Revlon,* in *Unocal Corp. v. Mesa Petroleum Co.,* Del.Supr., 493 A.2d 946 (1985), and in *Moran v. Household International, Inc.,* Del.Supr., 500 A.2d 1346 (1985) govern this case and every case in which a fundamental change of corporate control occurs or is contemplated. However, the basic teaching of these precedents is simply that the directors must act in accordance with their fundamental duties of care and loyalty. * * * It is true that a court evaluating the propriety of a change of control or a takeover defense must be mindful of "the omnipresent specter that a board may be acting primarily in its own interests, rather than those of the corporation and its shareholders." *Unocal,* 493 A.2d at 954. Nevertheless, there is no single blueprint that a board must follow to fulfill its duties. A stereotypical approach to the sale and acquisition of corporate control is not to be expected in the face of the evolving techniques and financing devices employed in today's corporate environment. * * * Rather, a board's actions must be evaluated in light of relevant circumstances to determine if they were undertaken with due diligence and in good faith. If no breach of duty is found, the board's actions are entitled to the protections of the business judgment rule. * * *

This Court has found that certain fact patterns demand certain responses from the directors. Notably, in *Revlon* we held that when several suitors are actively bidding for control of a corporation, the directors may not use defensive tactics that destroy the auction process.

* * * When it becomes clear that the auction will result in a change of corporate control, the board must act in a neutral manner to encourage the highest possible price for shareholders. However, *Revlon* does not demand that every change in the control of a Delaware corporation be preceded by a heated bidding contest. *Revlon* is merely one of an unbroken line of cases that seek to prevent the conflicts of interest that arise in the field of mergers and acquisitions by demanding that directors act with scrupulous concern for fairness to shareholders. When multiple bidders are competing for control, this concern for fairness forbids directors from using defensive mechanisms to thwart an auction or to favor one bidder over another. When the board is considering a single offer and has no reliable grounds upon which to judge its adequacy, this concern for fairness demands a canvas of the market to determine if higher bids may be elicited. * * * When, however, the directors possess a body of reliable evidence with which to evaluate the fairness of a transaction, they may approve that transaction without conducting an active survey of the market. As the Chancellor recognized, the circumstances in which this passive approach is acceptable are limited. "A decent respect for reality forces one to admit that ... advice [of an investment banker] is frequently a pale substitute for the dependable information that a canvas of the relevant market can provide." *In re Amsted Indus. Litig.,* letter op. at 19–20. The need for adequate information is central to the enlightened evaluation of a transaction that a board must make. Nevertheless, there is no single method that a board must employ to acquire such information. Here, the Chancellor found that the advice of the Special Committee's investment bankers, when coupled with the special circumstances surrounding the negotiation and consummation of the MBO, supported a finding that Amsted's directors had acted in good faith to arrange the best possible transaction for shareholders. Our own review of the record leads us to rule that the Chancellor's finding was well within the scope of his discretion.

Several factors provide the basis for the Chancellor's finding. First, the investment community had been aware that Amsted was a likely target for a takeover or an MBO from the moment that Hurwitz announced his sizeable interest in the corporation. In the parlance of the market, Hurwitz's actions put Amsted "in play." Yet in the ten months that passed between Hurwitz's appearance on the scene and the closing of the Exchange Offer, not one bidder emerged to make an offer for control of Amsted. Of course, Amsted was shielded by its stock purchase rights plan during much of this period. Nevertheless, the spate of takeover litigation that has confronted Delaware courts in recent years readily demonstrates that such "poison pills" do not prevent rival bidders from expressing their interest in acquiring a corporation. * * *

When properly employed, the function of a "poison pill" is to protect shareholders from coercive takeover tactics and to enhance the bidding for a corporation that is for sale. * * *

Because potential bidders know that a pill may not be used to entrench management or to unfairly favor one bidder over another, they have no reason to refrain from bidding if they believe that they can make a profitable offer for control of the corporation. Moreover, the Amsted board redeemed the rights plan five weeks before the closing of the Exchange Offer, thereby leaving an extended period of time during which Amsted was wholly unshielded from competing tender offers. We do not suggest that the absence of rival bids is sufficient to certify as correct a board's decision that a given transaction is fair to shareholders. However, when it is widely known that some change of control is in the offing and no rival bids are forthcoming over an extended period of time, that fact is supportive of the board's decision to proceed.

More important, the Amsted board had valid reasons for believing that no rival bidder would be able to surpass the price offered by the MBO Group. Including an ESOP in the transaction allowed the MBO Group to receive significant tax advantages that could be reflected in the price offered to shareholders. Even so, the MBO Group had some difficulty arranging financing for its proposal because lenders felt that the performance of the corporation might be dampened by cyclical downturns. In fact, such an event occurred in late 1985, as Amsted's earnings for the first quarter of fiscal year 1986 suffered a significant decline. Thus, when in late January, 1986, Salomon Brothers opined that $45 per share was a very fair price, the Board had good reason not only to accept Salomon Brothers opinion, but also to believe that no alternative deal could give shareholders a better price. As the MBO Group increased its offer to $46.25 and then to $47 per share, the evidence supporting the fairness of the deal increased still further. Thus, we believe that when the Exchange Offer was made, the directors could conclude in good faith that they had approved the best possible deal for shareholders.

We certainly do not condone in all instances the imposition of the sort of "no-shop" restriction that bound Amsted's Special Committee. Where a board has no reasonable basis upon which to judge the adequacy of a contemplated transaction, a no-shop restriction gives rise to the inference that the board seeks to forestall competing bids. Even here, a judicious market survey might have been desirable, since it would have made it clear beyond question that the board was acting to protect the shareholder's interests. Thus, while numerous factors—timing, publicity, tax advantages, and Amsted's declining performance—point to the directors' good faith belief that the shareholders were getting the best price, we decline to fashion an ironclad rule for determining when a market test is not required. The evidence that will support a finding of good faith in the absence of some sort of market test is by nature circumstantial; therefore, its evaluation by a court must be open-textured. However, the crucial element supporting a finding of good faith is knowledge. It must be clear that the board had sufficient knowledge of relevant markets to form the basis for its belief that it acted in the best interests of the shareholders. The situations in which a completely passive approach to acquiring such knowledge is appropriate are limited. The Chancellor found this to be such a situation, however, and we believe his finding to be within the scope of his discretion.

* * *

CITRON v. FAIRCHILD CAMERA AND INSTRUMENT CORP.

Supreme Court of Delaware, 1989.
569 A.2d 53.

Opinion of HORSEY, JUSTICE.

Plaintiff, Edith Citron, brings a class action on behalf of all stockholders of Fairchild Camera and Instrument Corporation ("Fairchild"), a Delaware corporation, who sold their shares to Schlumberger (California) Inc. ("Schlumberger"), a Delaware corporation, pursuant to a May 29, 1979 tender offer, or who had their shares converted into cash in the subsequent merger of Schlumberger into Fairchild on September 28, 1979. * * *

On May 18, Gould's board of directors approved a revised proposal for Fairchild (hereafter referred to as Gould's "third proposal"). It was cast in the form of a *proposed* conditional cash tender offer to Fairchild's stockholders at *$70* per share for up to *2,250,000* shares. Gould's offer was also conditioned on its board's being assured by Gould's counsel and auditors that the term of Gould's outstanding loan agreements would not be violated by such a tender offer.

Higgins received Gould's letter, containing its third proposal, either late on the 18th or early on the 19th. Finding it lacking *any* details on the second tier of the offer, Higgins immediately telephoned Slusser to express surprise at the lack of specifics of the second tier of Gould's offer. According to Higgins' later testimony, Slusser responded that the omission of specifics of the second tier of its proposed tender offer was an "oversight" and that Gould *intended* the "back-end" of its two-stage tender offer to be worth $70 per share. However, Slusser also stated that Gould could not be firm about the specifics of the "back-end" and that Gould assumed that such matters could be negotiated at a later date. * * *

About 8:00 a.m. the following day, May 19, Rohatyn telephoned Gilpatric to communicate Schlumberger's "non-negotiable" offer for all of Fairchild's five million plus shares for $66 cash. The offer was subject to the following conditions:

(1) rejection of the Gould proposal;

(2) acceptance of Schlumberger's offer by noon that day;

(3) unanimous approval by Fairchild's board; and

(4) execution of an agreement and a joint public announcement before the close of business that day.

Rohatyn told Gilpatric to inform Fairchild's board that Schlumberger would not entertain any negotiations or discussions.[12]

Fairchild's board meeting, attended by eight of its nine directors, began at 9:00 a.m. on May 19th and lasted nearly three hours. At Corrigan's request, Gilpatric led the board's discussion of the two proposals by outlining the terms of Gould's third proposal and then the terms of the Schlumberger proposal.

Higgins, speaking for Salomon Brothers, criticized Gould's third proposal for failing to value the Gould preferred to be received by Fairchild's shareholders in the second step of the proposed merger. According to the minutes, Higgins had "no explanation"[14] for Gould's failure to include specifics of its proposed "back-end" that would confirm its intention that it be valued at $70 per share. While he assumed that continued to be Gould's intention, Higgins advised the board that Gould's proposal was "impossible to value" for lack of specifics of the "back-end" of its proposal. Finally, Higgins pointed out that, assuming the Gould preferred were provided a 9% dividend rate, the dividend requirements alone of the Gould preferred would exceed Fairchild's earnings in its last fiscal year.

Higgins contrasted the uncertainty of Gould's third proposal with Schlumberger's $66 all-cash offer for all shares. He noted that Schlumberger's cash offer represented a substantial premium over the market price of Fairchild stock prior to its recent upsurge. In conclusion, Higgins opined that Schlumberger's $66 all-cash, all-shares offer represented an "adequate" price for Fairchild.

Nussbaum of Wachtell Lipton reiterated his firm's continuing antitrust concerns over a Fairchild–Gould combination. Wachtell Lipton's research showed substantially fewer antitrust concerns as a result of a Fairchild–Schlumberger combination. Finally, he reminded the board of its duty in choosing between the two offers to exercise its sound business judgment in the best interests of Fairchild's stockholders.

---

12. Gilpatric had been acquainted with Rohatyn for a number of years and had observed Riboud's "continental no-nonsense, no-bargaining, take-it-or-leave-it" style. Gilpatric "believed ... that Schlumberger meant what it said and that it was a take-it-or-leave-it, $66 that day, or Schlumberger was gone." The court found Gilpatric's belief was shared by other Fairchild directors (Burke, Bowers, and Corrigan) and by Salomon Brothers. The court found the "reasonableness of this belief [was] fully supported by the record."

14. Citron emphasizes the contradiction between Higgins' trial testimony of what he told the board and what the board minutes reflect his statements to have been. Plaintiff points out that the minutes do not reflect that Higgins informed the board of the substance of his follow-up telephone conversation with Slusser (presumably earlier that day) and Slusser's assurance that Gould's omission of the specifics of its second tier was an "oversight" and that Gould intended it to have a value of $70 per share.

Once again, Corrigan expressed management's persistent concerns that the delay inherent in consummating the Gould proposal would have a negative impact on Fairchild's ability to retain many of its key employees, especially technicians. He believed that if these employees left the firm, the value of the second tier of Gould's offer would be substantially less than $70.

Following an executive session, the board voted unanimously to recommend the Schlumberger proposal to the stockholders of Fairchild. The board considered the following, "among other factors," to be important:

> 1) The opinion of Salomon Brothers that the Schlumberger proposal was adequate and Salomon Brothers' inability to express an opinion either as to the value of the latest Gould proposal or as to whether such proposal was more or less adequate than the Schlumberger proposal due to the uncertainties as to the value and the terms of the proposed Gould preferred stock issue included in such proposal.[16]
>
> 2) The opinion of the Wachtell, Lipton firm that the Schlumberger proposal ... did not appear to present antitrust issue of the seriousness involved in the Gould proposal;
>
> 3) Fairchild management's judgment that the delay—possibly as much as four months—that would be encountered in consummating the Gould proposal could have a materially adverse effect on Fairchild's operations in the meantime, particularly in the hiring and retention of key personnel.

Later the same day, Schlumberger and Fairchild executed a merger agreement and issued a joint press release, stating that Fairchild would operate as a subsidiary of Schlumberger under its present management and that Schlumberger would continue present or comparable benefit programs.

* * *

Plaintiff's second argument against the business judgment rule's application to this case is lack of due care; that is, that Fairchild's board, in accepting Schlumberger's offer over Gould's final proposal, failed to act in an informed manner as required under *Smith v. Van Gorkom,* Del.Supr., 488 A.2d 858 (1985). * * *

The standard for determining "whether a business judgment reached by a board of directors was an informed one" is gross negligence. *Van Gorkom* at 873. In our case law since *Van Gorkom,* our due care examination has focused on a board's decision-making process. We look for evidence as to whether a board has acted in a deliberate and knowledgeable way in identifying and exploring alternatives. Within the context of this analysis, we are, of course, ever mindful of

---

16. Salomon Brothers reaffirmed its inability to determine whether the Gould offer was worth more or less than the Schlumberger offer in an opinion letter dated June 7, 1979.

the realities of corporate directorship. We recognize that management is often the catalyst in the decision-making process. We further recognize that a board will receive substantial information from third-party sources. As we have noted on various occasions, however, in change of control situations, sole reliance on hired experts and management can "taint[ ] the design and execution of the transaction." *Mills Acquisition Co. v. Macmillan, Inc.,* Del.Supr., 559 A.2d 1261, 1281 (1988). Thus, we look particularly for evidence of a board's active and direct role in the sale process.

In this case we find ample evidence in the record of the board's involvement. An overriding, and eminently reasonable, concern of the directors was the indefinite nature of Gould's final proposal. Bowers and Stenson believed that Gould's omission of any terms of the second step of the merger was a deliberate tactical maneuver to get rid of Schlumberger. They also believed that Ylvisaker had had more than enough time to propose specific terms and was simply "hedging his bet." Stenson viewed Gould's $70 proposal as not constituting an offer, but simply a "monkey wrench" thrown in by "very savvy" people. He was also concerned about Gould's ability to finance the cash portion of the offer. Burke noted that Gould had been unable two months earlier to complete a private placement of a $125 million preferred stock offering. Burke, Bowers, and Stenson were concerned about Gould's general financial wherewithal, not simply to complete the transaction, but to sustain, after acquisition, Fairchild's capital-intensive semiconductor business. They were especially concerned over Gould's ability to assume Fairchild's substantial debt requirements and that Gould's proposed preferred stock dividend requirement would exceed Fairchild's earnings. Bowers, in particular, expressed serious misgivings over whether Gould's debt undertakings to acquire Fairchild would not breach the terms of Gould's outstanding revolving credit and term loan agreements with its lenders. Under these agreements, Gould was required to maintain certain financial ratios and Gould's ability to issue new securities and dispose of assets required lender approval. In contrast, there was no uncertainty in Schlumberger's offer; Bowers characterized it as "cash on the barrel head" from a company rich in cash resources. All of these are classic factors upon which a board may base a proper business decision to accept or reject a proposal. * * *

Plaintiff's attempt to compare this case to *Van Gorkom* is strained and juxtaposes superficial similarities while ignoring crucial differences. In *Van Gorkom,* the chairman of the board, unbeknownst to the other directors, devised a plan to sell the company and picked a sale price based on how long he felt it would take an acquirer to pay back borrowed funds. Neither the chairman nor the board obtained a valuation of the company. After he found a buyer, he called a board meeting to approve a merger—despite the fact that the board had never before considered a sale of the company. *Van Gorkom,* 488 A.2d at 866–67. The Fairchild board, however, had been considering the possibility that the company would be sold for two years prior to receipt of

Gould's unsolicited first proposal. The board, also in contrast with the Trans Union board, received investment advice from four leading investment banking firms, commissioned financial evaluations by three of them, shopped the company to roughly 75 potential buyers, and discussed the sale of the company at three separate board meetings over the course of three weeks. The present case is significantly different from *Van Gorkom* and the comparison fails.

Concededly, the board ultimately acceded to Schlumberger's three-hour deadline. The Chancellor concluded, however, that the board knew enough as of May 19 concerning the value of the company to make a rational choice with respect to the two offers. * * * The imposition of artificial time limits on the decision-making process of a board of directors may compromise the integrity of that deliberative process. See *Van Gorkom*. However, whether the constraints are self-imposed or attributable to bargaining tactics of an adversary seeking a final resolution to a belabored process must be considered. Boards that have failed to exercise due care are frequently boards that have been rushed. We conclude that the time constraints placed on the Fairchild board were not of the board's making and did not compromise its deliberative process under *Van Gorkom*.

We turn to plaintiff's subordinate argument that the Chancellor erred in his consideration of the plaintiffs' *Revlon* claim. The Chancellor concluded that the board, "once it became clear that a control transaction would be forced upon the company, acted in good faith to try and arrange and support the transaction that seemed to offer the best option for the Fairchild shareholders." * * * To the extent that *Revlon* instructs a board to obtain the best available transaction for its shareholders, the Fairchild directors complied with *Revlon*. * * * Gould's failure to submit a firm and unconditional offer precluded a bidding contest foreclosing plaintiffs' reliance on *Revlon*. * * *

The actions of Fairchild's board under the circumstances are entirely consonant with well-established Delaware law. We have rejected the thesis that a board of directors should be a passive instrumentality when addressing a takeover bid. * * * We emphatically restate that principle here. The Fairchild board, actively led by its outside independent directors, had a right, indeed a firm duty, to consider a host of factors in determining whether to entertain Gould's offer. * * *

The record also sustains the Chancellor's findings that Fairchild's board of directors studiously endeavored to avoid "playing favorites," consistent not only with *Revlon* but with any "enhanced" duty which, also six years later, was enunciated under *Unocal Corp. v. Mesa Petroleum Co.*, Del.Supr., 493 A.2d 946, 954 (1985). Fairchild's board did not erect any defensive barriers to prevent a Gould tender offer.

* * * The record firmly supports the trial court's finding that whatever personal dislike Corrigan had for Gould did not skew the bidding process or influence the board's ultimate decision. Fairchild's bankers were at all relevant times in contact with Gould; and Gould

was not deprived of a fair opportunity to formulate and present both a firm proposal and a later counterbid. The facts are: (a) that Corrigan as well as Higgins of Paine Webber timely advised Ylvisaker and Slusser, Gould's financial advisor, of Fairchild's immediate need of a definitive offer; and (b) that Ylvisaker as well as Slusser replied that Fairchild's deadline posed "no problem." Moreover, Higgins affirmatively offered to assist Slusser to provide Gould with any further information needed for it to make a final, best and firm offer. Gould's third proposal fell far short of the mark. Fairchild's board came under no legal duty to give Gould one more opportunity to submit a firm unconditional bid and risk losing the Schlumberger offer. We will not hold a target board of predominantly disinterested directors liable for allegedly failing to exhibit due care when the bidder does not provide the target board with a definitive bid.

Given our controlling standard of review, we must reject plaintiff's claim that Fairchild's board failed to make a business judgment concerning the value of Gould's proposal because it arguably never placed a monetary value on the indefinite offer.

* * *

We conclude that the directors of Fairchild acted in good faith and with due care in recommending Schlumberger, Inc.'s $66 all-cash, all-shares tender offer over Gould, Inc.'s two-tiered offer of cash and securities. Accordingly, the board's decision is entitled to the presumption of the business judgment rule.

* * *

GILBERT v. THE EL PASO COMPANY
Supreme Court of Delaware, 1990.
575 A.2d 1131.

Opinion of MOORE, JUSTICE.

[See facts on pages 354–357.]

* * *

We turn to *Gilbert II*, where the Court of Chancery dismissed the remaining counts against all defendants. The Vice Chancellor concluded that the settlement agreement was "part of an overall rapprochement [sic] between Burlington and El Paso," and that the actions of the El Paso directors "cannot properly be regarded as antitakeover defense measures that would trigger the enhanced judicial scrutiny mandated by *Unocal*." *Gilbert II*, slip op. at 17. In rejecting plaintiffs' argument that *Unocal* should govern the actions of the El Paso board, the trial court characterized the enhanced *Unocal* standard as prescribing "the standard for evaluating the conduct of directors adopting antitakeover measures to defend against a threat to the corporate enterprise resulting from a potential change of control." *Id.* at 16–17. The court thus settled upon the business judgment rule—ostensibly by default—as the appropriate standard of review in assessing the conduct of El Paso's directors.

In our opinion the failure to apply *Unocal* in *Gilbert II* was erroneous. When evaluating the probability of success of plaintiffs' claim, the enhanced *Unocal* standard clearly was applicable. Given the vice Chancellor's finding that El Paso had adopted and conducted a defensive strategy against an attempted takeover, the negotiations by which El Paso's directors successfully extracted material concessions from Burlington constituted a protective response to a potential perceived harm of the type contemplated by *Unocal*. Under these circumstances, the board clearly remained subject to *Unocal*'s enhanced duties.

* * *

The law is clear that *Unocal* is invoked as the result of any defensive measures taken in response to some threat to corporate policy and effectiveness which touch upon issues of control. *Unocal*, 493 A.2d at 955. Here, everything that El Paso did was in reaction to Burlington's tender offer. Unlike *Time*, there is no independent transaction having any legal significance which stands apart from the directors' initial efforts to thwart Burlington, or their later attempts to settle with it and attenuate the effects of the takeover. Among those latter efforts were agreements which permitted the directors to tender into the January offer and which, significantly, allowed Petty and four other designees to retain their positions on the El Paso board. Bearing in mind that *Unocal*'s enhanced scrutiny arises from the appearance of certain inherent conflicts attendant to the invocation of defensive measures designed to thwart or impede a takeover, no clearer application of *Unocal* could be conceived than under the circumstances here.

* * *

It is apparent that the adversarial negotiations which ensued at El Paso's request on January 8, 1983 can only be viewed as the culmination of final efforts to resist Burlington's coercive December offer. Thus, we cannot agree that the settlement between El Paso and Burlington represented a consensual, voluntary adjustment of their grievances. In the face of Burlington's takeover, El Paso's board was anything but a willing partner to the settlement agreement. The settlement cannot be properly characterized as a rapprochement between the parties, but rather as a capitulation by El Paso on the most favorable terms that it could muster.

* * *

In reviewing plaintiffs' claims, we must first analyze the nature of the December offer to determine whether it endangered the interests of El Paso and its shareholders. We have repeatedly recognized the coercive nature of two-tier, partial tender offers. *Newmont*, 535 A.2d at 1342; *Unocal*, 493 A.2d at 956. The December offer, which provided neither for a second-step transaction nor any back-end protections for

El Paso's remaining minority shareholders, was an archetype of this coercive mechanism. Indeed, the plaintiffs hardly deny the serious threat to the corporation and its shareholders which the December offer posed.

* * *

The record indicates that by the special board meeting of January 7, 1983, the situation faced by the El Paso directors was materially changed. With only days remaining before the December offer would be successfully completed, it had become apparent that the breakup of the company was inevitable. Thus, it was incumbent upon the El Paso board to seek the best transaction and maximum value reasonably attainable under the circumstances. *Macmillan,* 559 A.2d at 1288; *Revlon,* 506 A.2d at 182. * * *

Having reasonably determined that Burlington's price of $24 was the highest price likely obtainable for the company, one cannot say that the board acted improperly by entering into negotiations which materially enhanced the structural protections afforded El Paso's stockholders. Even the plaintiffs concede that the January offer provided substantial improvements in the terms extended to all shareholders. In sum, the record attests to the diligence of the El Paso board, and suggests that the directors fulfilled their fiduciary duties of care and loyalty to the company and its shareholders. *Contrast Macmillan,* 559 A.2d at 1280–82, 1282–84; *Van Gorkom,* 448 A.2d at 873–88.

As to the plaintiffs' contention that self-dealing can be inferred from the El Paso directors' role in arranging the January offer, into which the board could tender their own El Paso shares, it is undisputed that El Paso's directors did not stand on both sides of the transaction. * * * By tendering into the January offer, no board member received any special benefit which was not also extended to all shareholders. * * * Conceivably, the retention of five El Paso directors on the board, after Burlington assumed control of the company, suggests self-interest and a motive for entrenchment. However, there is not a scintilla of evidence to intimate that this arrangement was the result of improper motives.

If anything, the record suggests that the directors had an abiding concern for El Paso's shareholders, who remained subject to a backend, freezeout merger. Their presence on the new board assured that the interests of these minority stockholders would continue to be represented. Without more, the mere fact that one is elected by a controlling shareholder is not an indicia of faithlessness.

* * *

Questions

1. What facts are crucial to whether the test in *Van Gorkom, Unocal, Revlon,* or *Mills Acquisition* applies to any one case?

2. When a target board decides to sell a firm, must it shop the firm or conduct a formal auction before agreeing to an acquisition price? If so,

does the board have a fiduciary duty to erect takeover defenses that give time for shopping or auctioning the firm? If not, how can a board be sure that it has obtained the best price for its shareholders? When is shopping the firm or auctioning the firm not in the best interests of the target shareholders?

If the only pending offer is from a management buyout (MBO) group, is the case for requiring the target to shop or auction the firm stronger or weaker? Do the facts of *Barkan* comport with your answer?

3. What procedural rules emerge from the cases? Can a board accede to a very short decision deadline imposed by a bidder? Compare *Citron* with *Van Gorkom*. Do the decisions affect as a practical matter a requirement that the selling board obtain a fairness opinion from an outside financial adviser? Compare *Barkan* with *Van Gorkom*. If a board does obtain the advice of an outside financial adviser, is the board necessarily in a better position in subsequent litigation over the acquisition? See *Mills Acquisition*.

4. When, if at all, can the selling firm favor one bidder in a contest between two or more bidders with a lockup, leg-up, no-shop, or cancellation fee agreement? The sale of treasury stock to Pritzker in *Van Gorkom* is a classic stock lockup. The option to purchase Revlon's Vision Care and National Health Laboratories divisions in *Revlon* is a classic asset lockup. Lockups also come in the form of contingent stock options; the options have a striking price that is well in the money and are contingent on someone other than the holder buying the firm. Recall Pritzker's refusal to bid for Trans Union because he would only serve as a "stalking horse," initiating an auction contest. Would the sale of the treasury shares allow him to cover his expenses if he should lose a bidding war for the firm?

When does the granting of lockups result in the enticement of higher bids from the recipients than would be made without the use of the devices? A stock lockup given to a second bidder is often called a leg-up. Can a leg-up give the recipient an incentive to aid the target in inducing third parties to bid?

5. In the Delaware cases can a board, in deciding between bids of competing bidders, consider nonshareholder corporate constituencies—employees, debt holders, customers, suppliers, and local citizens? See *Revlon*. In *Revlon* do the aggrieved note holders have a cause of action, based on the board's waiver of the note covenants, on the board's acceptance (after the opinion) of the Pantry Pride bid, or on the board's exchange offer (of notes for outstanding common stock)?

6. Consider the chronological order of the cases. Do the later cases, *Barkan, Citron,* and *Gilbert,* suggest that the court is retreating from *Van Gorkom* and *Revlon* ?

The High–Water Mark of LBOs?

IN RE RJR NABISCO

Court of Chancery of Delaware, 1989.
Fed.Sec.L.Rep. (CCH) ¶ 94,194.

Opinion of ALLEN, CHANCELLOR.

These consolidated actions, which are said to be brought on behalf of the shareholders of RJR Nabisco, Inc., a Delaware corporation, seek to enjoin the closing of a pending tender offer for up to 74% of the outstanding stock of RJR Nabisco ("RJR"). The offer is extended by entities organized for that purpose by the investment firm Kohlberg Kravis Roberts & Co. ("KKR") and presently has been extended so as to close on February 6, 1989. The tender offer, if consummated, is intended to be followed promptly by a merger. The blended consideration to be received by each shareholder should these transactions be effectuated will consist of cash and securities valued, by the Company's investment bankers, at approximately $108 to $108.50 per share. The value of the total transaction is by all measures extraordinary—approximately $25 billion.

* * *

RJR is a Delaware corporation formed following the 1985 merger of RJ Reynolds Tobacco Company and Nabisco Brands, Inc. The Company's principal offices are now in Atlanta, Georgia. Through its subsidiaries, which include RJ Reynolds, Nabisco Brands, Inc., Del Monte Corporation and Planters Life Savers Company, the Company holds leading positions in the tobacco, food and consumer products industries. The Company has 225,519,911 shares of common stock and 1,251,904 shares of preferred stock issued and outstanding. Immediately prior to the events here in question, RJR's common stock was trading on the New York Stock Exchange in the mid 50's.

At an October 19, 1988 RJR board of directors meeting, F. Ross Johnson, speaking on behalf of the Management Group, informed the board that that group was seeking to develop a transaction to take the Company private by means of a leveraged buyout. He suggested a price of $75 per share.

* * *

On October 20, 1988, the board issued a press release announcing the proposed transaction. It announced the appointment of a special committee of the board ... The Special Committee retained two financial advisors, Dillon, Read & Co. (the company's regular investment banker) and Lazard Freres, Inc. The Committee also retained ... Skadden Corps, Slate, Meegher & Flom to render legal advice to the Committee and to the company's outside directors ...

On October 24, KKR, who had purportedly earlier been rebuffed in an effort to entice management to join it in a leveraged buyout, informed the Special Committee that it was planning to extend an offer to acquire the Company for $90 per share in cash and securities. On October 27, KKR commenced a tender offer at $90 per share cash for up to 87% of the Company's stock. The offer stated that the balance of RJR's shares were to be exchanged for new securities in a second step merger.

On November 2, the Special Committee issued a press release announcing that it was interested in receiving proposals to acquire the Company. On November 7, the Committee disseminated Rules and Procedures for Submission of Proposals. This provided, *inter alia,* for a deadline of 5:00 p.m. November 18, 1988 for the final submission of bids. The rules specified that "[t]he rules and procedures outlined above are intended to constitute a single round of bidding. Any Proposal should reflect the potential purchaser's highest offer." The Special Committee also stated that it "encourage[d] proposals that provided to current RJR shareholders a prospect for a substantial common stock related interest in the purchasing entity." *Id.*

Three bids were in the hands of the Special Committee on the appointed deadline of November 18. The Management Group bid was valued by the Management Group at $100 per share, consisting of $90 in cash, $6 preferred stock and an equity interest of $4. KKR's bid came in at a claimed $94 per share, ($75 in cash, $11 in preferred stock and $8 in convertible debt which would convert into 25% of the purchasing entity's equity). The third bidder was the First Boston Corporation. Its proposal, while not fully developed, was in some respects the most interesting. It contemplated an acquisition of the Company's tobacco business in 1989 for approximately $15.75 billion in cash and warrants, and an installment sale of the Company's food businesses immediately (by year end 1988), with the proceeds of such sale to be held for the account of the Company's shareholders. The total value of the First Boston Group proposal, if it could be realized, was estimated to be in the range of $98 to $110 in cash and cash equivalents, securities valued at $5, and warrants valued at $2–$3. The warrants would entitle RJR shareholders to acquire up to 20% of the Company's tobacco business.

The First Boston approach was innovative, appealing and problematic. Its primary appeal lay in the fact that the installment sale mechanism would provide tax advantages estimated to be as high as $3 billion. There were two difficulties, however, with this proposal. First, its terms were not fully worked out. Second, impending changes in the tax code created time constraints which placed the realization of those tax benefits at risk.

In view of the fact that the First Boston Group's proposal was at this point potentially the most attractive, and that more time was necessary to develop it further, the Committee decided to extend the bidding until November 29. In its press release announcing the terms of the extension, it also published the terms of the three bids it had received, including the percentage of potential equity participation each contemplated.

* * *

At 5:00 p.m. November 29, the Committee again received three bids. The Management Group raised its bid only minimally; it valued its new bid at $101 per share ($88 cash; $9 preferred stock; $4 convertible preferred). It was the lowest of the three bids. KKR's bid jumped appreciably to a claimed value of $106 ($80 cash; $17 preferred stock; $8 automatically converting debenture), the First Boston Group's bid was said to be in a range from $103 to $115.

The Special Committee concluded early on that the First Boston Group's bid, while attractive, was subject to too much uncertainty to be practicable. Between the remaining bids, KKR's bid plainly appeared to be the higher if the securities included in the bids were worth what the bidders claimed. The Committee determined that before it would choose between these two bids it would seek to assure that KKR's higher bid was worth what it claimed. Accordingly, it directed its lawyers and investment bankers to negotiate concerning the terms of the securities and the details of a merger agreement. This was done during the course of the evening of the 29th and the morning of the 30th.

Some time late in the evening of November 29, the Management Group learned of these talks, apparently from a newspaper reporter. The Management Group apparently realized that it had made a tactical error in raising its bid only $1 when, as later events show, it was willing to pay substantially more. It attempted to recoup by advising the Committee that it had yet to submit its best bid. It requested an opportunity to do so. This request was not responded to before the Management Group pressed ahead late in the following morning to present another bid.

The Special Committee reconvened at 7:45 a.m. on November 30, together with its financial advisors and six independent outside directors of RJR. Once convened, this group, with a few recesses, remained in session throughout the day.

The independent directors were first informed that the terms of the merger agreement with KKR were essentially complete, but that KKR had expressed displeasure because of its suspicion that its bid had been leaked to the press and from there to the Management Group. In light of its fears, KKR had requested, first informally and then by letter, that its bid be acted upon that day. The letter required action on the bid by 1:00 p.m. November 30. This assertedly created concern in the minds of some of the directors that the KKR bid might be withdrawn if not acted upon in a timely manner.

At some time early on in the meeting on November 30, before the Committee turned to its consideration of the competing bids, the meeting was informed that a letter had been hand-delivered from the Management Group protesting the board's negotiation the night before of the KKR bid as a final offer. The letter stated the Management Group's willingness to discuss all aspects of its proposal. The Committee agreed to waive the terms of the rules and procedures and consider new bids from both parties should such bids be forthcoming. It did not, however, invite or encourage further bidding. Further bidding did, however, eventuate; before describing it, I turn to a brief outline of the alternatives before the Committee on the morning of the 30th.

The KKR proposal of $106, made on the night of November 29, consisted of $80 in cash, $17 in cumulative exchangeable pay-in-kind preferred stock and $8 in face value senior converting debentures, which KKR valued at $9 because of the conversion feature.

The terms of the KKR PIK preferred eventually agreed to were designed to achieve the aim that the security would trade at par at some point following distribution.[5] The concern was that a massive public sale of securities, anticipated in order to refinance the bridge loans used to fund the purchase of RJR shares, would push down the value of the preferred stock. This problem was addressed by a provision to reset the rate after the market had absorbed the securities needed to pay off the bridge loans. The Committee also sought to achieve as brief an interval as possible in which the yield on the preferred would float. KKR eventually agreed to reset the rate at the earlier of one year following the refinancing of the bridge loan or two years after the tender offer closed. In light of these agreements, the Committee's investment advisors informed the Committee of their view that the securities should trade at close to their face value of $17 per share.

The senior converting debentures were to convert automatically into common stock of the Company at the end of three [6] years unless the holder "opts out" during a two week option period which then arises. If none of the debenture holders were to opt out, the debenture holders as a class would own 25% of the equity of the Company at the end of four years. These securities were to pay interest in kind for the first ten years following their issuance, and generate cash distributions thereafter. The interest rate was to float initially, subject to a reset identical to the preferred stock reset. The rate initially would be approximately 14.5%.

On the morning of the 30th, before the Management Group presented further proposals, the Special Committee also considered the apparently lower bid, the Management Group's November 29 bid of $101, consisting of $88 per share in cash, $9 cumulative PIK preferred

---

5. The terms of the pay-in-kind preferred are as follows: Initially, that is, for the first six years, the stock pays dividends "in kind." The dividend rate would initially be a floating rate set at 5½% over a basket of interest rates (defined as the highest of (i) the three month Treasury bill rate, (ii) the 10 year Treasury bond rate, and (iii) the 30 year Treasury bond rate), subject to a ceiling of 16⅝% and a floor of 12⅝%. The dividend rate is subject to a reset mechanism that will reset the rate at a fixed rate within one year of any refinancing of the bridge loans used to finance the transaction or two years after consummation of the tender offer. The fixed rate is to be set in an arbitration proceeding among the advisors to KKR, the advisors to the Company, and, if necessary, a third party investment banker. The hope is to permit the security to trade at par at the time the fixed rate is determined.

6. This was negotiated up from two years in the original November 29 proposal and was later increased to four years in the final proposal.

stock, and $4 face amount 13% junior convertible exchangeable preferred stock.

At the time of submission, the terms of the cumulative PIK preferred stock were not final. The other security proposed—the 13% junior convertible exchangeable preferred stock—would initially accrue, but not pay, dividends calculated at a rate of 13%. By its terms, this stock could be converted at any time into a maximum of 15% of the fully diluted stock of the surviving tobacco entity. The stock, however, had a "call" feature that allowed the Company to redeem it at any time at par plus accrued and unpaid dividends. RJR's investment advisors were of the view that this unrestricted call provided the issuer with the ability to destroy the equity aspects of the security before it would make financial sense to exercise them. This was said to deprive Management's convertible preferred of any premium value in addition to its value as a straight debt instrument. This security remained unchanged in the final bid and was assigned a value of $2–$2.50.

* * *

* * * The Special Committee invited Messrs. Kravis and Roberts to make a presentation to the meeting concerning their plans should they acquire the Company. Following the presentation, which took place around 11:00 a.m., Mr. Hugel asked Mr. Roberts to extend the 1:00 p.m. deadline for consideration of KKR's bid. Mr. Roberts gave no assurances that the deadline would be extended.

Following a brief recess, the meeting was reconvened at about 12:30 p.m. A representative of the Management Group then reported to the Committee orally that the Management Group was raising its bid to $108 per share consisting of $84 cash, $20 in PIK preferred stock, and $4 in convertible preferred (i.e., $4 less cash and $11 more preferred stock than the bid of the prior evening). No terms for the component securities were given, but it was stated that the Management Group was willing to negotiate all terms, including price, with the Committee.

With this in mind, the Special Committee told KKR that another bid had been received and again requested an extension of the 1:00 p.m. deadline. This time an extension until 2:00 p.m. was granted.[7] The minutes of the November 30 board meeting reflect that the Management Group had been asked to make its highest and best bid shortly after 1:00 p.m. Mr. Hugel testified that the directors discussed the need to obtain their highest and best bid and agreed that this was to be relayed to the Management Group. * * * James A. Stern, an Officer of Shearson Lehman involved in the process, testified that the Management Group was told about 1:00 p.m. or 1:30 p.m. to "[s]harpen your pencils and put your best bid on the table." * * * In response to

---

7. In consideration, KKR got the Company to agree to reimburse KKR's expenses up to $.20 per share in the event that no merger agreement was signed between the Company and KKR. KKR agreed, on its part, to reduce the topping fee provision in its proposed merger agreement from $1 to $.75 per share.

which the Management Group "reached back and submitted a final proposal, final bid that again had $84 a share in cash, a $24 a share of PIK preferred and the same 15% equity interest via the convertible preferred."

The Management Group's last proposal was submitted to the Committee shortly before 1:30 p.m. The Management Group asserted it to be worth $112; the additional $4 of value was all additional preferred stock, raising the face amount of the PIK preferred securities from $20 to $24. Like the previous bid, Management's $112 offer left open certain significant terms, including provisions of the PIK preferred stock and the convertible preferred. As it had done the previous evening with KKR's $106 bid, the Special Committee began negotiating with the Management Group to determine if it could achieve terms for the securities offered which would allow them to trade at their stated value.

In view of KKR's actions in extracting assurance of $.20 per share expense reimbursement provision before it agreed to an extension (see note 7 supra), the Special Committee and its advisors assert that they were concerned that KKR might simply withdraw its bid altogether at this point. * * * This would, it is said, have left the Committee in a markedly worse negotiating position than the position it was in with competing bids on the table.

Assertedly in order to protect the shareholders from the risk of losing the bird in hand, after receiving the Management Group's face value $112 proposal, the Committee offered to KKR to enter into the now fully negotiated merger agreement with it at $106 per share, subject to a $1 topping fee should the Company accept another offer within seven days, but with the agreement that no further expenses would be paid. It also offered KKR the opportunity to bid again prior to the acceptance of any other offer. In response to the Committee's offer to enter into a contract, KKR declined but delivered a revised bid which it claimed to be worth $108 per share.[8] The new bid, which was not subject to a deadline, consisted of $80 per share in cash, $18 PIK preferred and converting debentures which KKR valued at $10. The terms of the PIK preferred remained the same as those of the previous bid, but the conversion period for the other security, the automatically converting debentures, was extended another year which was the basis for KKR's assertion that the same face amount of converting debt was now worth $1 per share more. The Committee's advisors gave their preliminary opinion that the revised KKR bid was worth between $107 and $108 per share.

There were no on-going discussions with KKR for the remainder of the afternoon of November 30; during that time, the Special Committee's investment advisors negotiated with the Management Group in an

---

8. As to other matters, it proposed that its topping fee would be $1 per share and the $.20 payment for expenses, should another offer be accepted, would remain in force.

attempt to improve the terms of the Management Group's securities. Specifically, there was an attempt to get the Management Group to agree to tie the length of the reset period on its PIKs to the refinancing of the bridge loans used to finance the stock acquisition. The Management Group declined to do so. Its PIK preferred had the potential, indeed the likelihood, of not being reset to the market for almost three years.

Attempts to increase the lower rate on Management's PIK were unavailing. The Management Group also declined to put a reset mechanism on its convertible preferred.

By about 6:00 p.m., when the Special Committee reconvened to confer concerning the discussions with the Management Group, it was reported to the Special Committee that no significant progress had been made with respect to the terms of the Management Group's securities. It was further reported by the Committee's investment advisors that in its view, the securities were unlikely to trade at the values assigned them by the Management Group. The Committee apparently decided to return to both bidders one last time. * * * KKR responded to this further invitation after receiving reassurances that the members of the Management Group would not be in attendance at any board meeting at which the offers were considered. It submitted a merger agreement with its final bid of $109; $1 more in cash. This final bid consisted of $81 in cash, $18 PIK preferred, and $10 converting debentures. KKR placed a 30-minute fuse on this offer when it was submitted.

The Management Group replied to a last communication from the Committee that "they had our final proposal." Stern Dep. at 131. It is possible, however, that an imperfect communication occurred at this point. The Committee's advisor had been negotiating with the Management Group concerning the reset provision of the preferred stock. The communication at about 5:00 p.m. or 6:00 p.m. on November 30 may have been thought to relate only to that subject or may have been thought to relate to all subjects concerning the bids. * * *

The Special Committee's Investment Advisors' Presentations Concerning the Bids

The Special Committee's investment advisors, Lazard Freres and Dillon Read, met with the Special Committee after both "final" bids were received. It estimated the Management Group's proposal to be worth between $108.50 and $109 per share, based on its conclusions that (1) the Management Group's PIK preferred stock should be discounted approximately $2 per share because of the longer term of its reset provisions, its below market dividend rate, and its weaker yield curve protections;[9] and (2) that the Management Group's convertible

---

[9]. The fluctuating rate on the Management Group security was pegged to LIBOR (London Inter-Bank Offering Rate) which is a short term rate, as opposed to the "basket" of rates against which the KKR security was measured. By opting for the highest of several rates with different maturities to fix the current interest rate, as opposed to a single rate, an investor is offered greater protection against market

preferred should be discounted from $4 to $2.50 because it had no reset mechanism, also carried a low dividend rate and was callable at any time.

The advisors only discounted the KKR PIK preferred stock between $.50 and $1. With respect to the KKR converting debentures, they advised the Special Committee that they should trade at their estimated value of $10 and determined as a result that the KKR bid was worth approximately $108 to $108.50 per share.

Based on these valuations, the unprecedented size of the debt offerings of high yield securities involved, and the inherent limitations of predicting future markets, the investment advisors concluded that the bids were substantially equivalent. Both investment bankers advised the Committee that, in their view, the Committee could exercise sound business judgment in recommending either offer, and that they were prepared to give fairness opinions on either transaction.

According to the minutes of the meeting (which are attacked as *post hoc* creations by lawyers for use in litigation), the Committee then reviewed the following factors:

1. the risk that further negotiating with either the management group or KKR could result in the withdrawal of either party from the bidding process;

2. the 15% equity interest in the management group proposal as contrasted with the 25% equity interest in the KKR proposal;

3. the fact that the KKR structure contemplated that the tobacco and a substantial part of the food businesses would remain going forward versus the tobacco only business contemplated by the management group proposal;

4. the greater amount of permanent equity in the KKR proposal;

5. the fact that the amount of PIK securities in both proposals was unprecedented and that there would be an additional $1.5 billion in PIK securities issued in the management group transaction;

6. the fact that the management group proposal provided for $84 in cash per share of common stock while the KKR proposal provided for $81 in cash per share of common stock;

7. the potential issues arising under the Company's debt indentures in connection with the management group's proposal but not in connection with the KKR proposal; and

8. the KKR (but not the management group) was willing to provide for the presentation of benefits for employees whose jobs were terminated as the result of business divestitures.

changes with respect to different maturities.

Based on these considerations, and without attempting to seek a higher bid from either party, the Committee elected to recommend the KKR bid and the board shortly thereafter authorized the execution of the KKR merger agreement that had been negotiated.

* * *

The argument * * * is that the Special Committee was not motivated in good faith to seek the best available transaction regardless of whose deal it was, but rather, was motivated to see that the Management Group did not succeed even if it would, marginally at least, pay more. This motivation is explained by a posited desire by the members of the Special Committee to disassociate themselves from public criticism directed against Mr. Johnson [14] and the avarice his initial proposal was said to represent. This inappropriate desire resulted, it is claimed, in (1) the premature termination of the auction, and (2) the choice of a demonstratively lower bid.

* * *

As to this, defendants offer their real defense, which is that in fact they acted in utter good faith throughout. They sought to achieve the best available transaction for the shareholders and can explain every decision they made on that basis.

Plaintiffs' argument with respect to motivation is built upon inferences from a series of acts or decisions that are claimed to be explicable only by a desire to favor KKR even if it meant not getting the best available transaction for the Company's shareholders.

> (1) Most importantly, they say that the directors aborted a tied auction in circumstances in which, had they been properly motivated, they would have sought to break the tie;

> (2) They chose an offer that had $3 less cash per share and which, upon honest evaluation, was worth about $3 a share less;

> (3) They accepted a bid that presented antitrust problems when the competing bid which everyone admits offered at least equivalent value had no such problems;

> (4) They sought higher bids from KKR when it appeared KKR had an inferior bid but failed to solicit a higher bid from the Management Group when they could say KKR's bid was higher;

> (5) They failed to respond to Management Group's November 29 letter offering to pay more; and

> (6) They offered to sign a merger agreement with KKR at its $106 price subject to a right to solicit other bids but never made a similar offer to the Management Group.

---

14. It is, for example, noted in the briefs that the December 5 issue of *Time* magazine (which was on the stands before November 30) placed a picture of Mr. Johnson on its cover and trumpeted the Management Group's proposal under the caption "A Game of Greed." Anderson Dep. at 193–96.

Consideration of this argument does not, however, require consideration of each of these elements. For present purposes, consideration of the critical elements would appear sufficient.

Those critical elements include the decision at the end of the day on November 30, after the Committee was told by its investment bankers that the KKR nominal value $109 offer and the Management Group's nominal value $112 bid offered to shareholders substantially equivalent value, to accept one of the offers without returning to the contestants once more. The second critical decision is, of course, the choice to accept the KKR proposal and to reject the Management Group's bid. * * *

In reviewing, with respect to *bona fides,* the Special Committee's decision to accept one of the proposals in the early evening of November 30, two circumstances must be first noted. First, the consideration offered in both proposals contained complex securities not susceptible to intuitive evaluation. Sophisticated and effective business generalists of the type likely to be found on the board of such companies as RJR will seldom have the specialized skills useful to most accurately value such securities. Our law, of course, recognizes the appropriateness of directors relying upon the advice of experts when specialized judgment is necessary as part of a business judgment. *See* 8 *Del.C.* § 141(e). In this instance, the Committee did receive the advice of Lazard Freres and of Dillon Read that when the respective securities were appropriately valued, they regarded the bids as substantially equivalent.

Plaintiffs spend a good deal of effort in attacking this judgment. The effort (as it relates to this theory of liability) is to show that the opinion was not only incorrect but was implausible. From this plaintiffs would infer a motive to favor KKR (the unspoken link being the assumption that the bankers detected a preference by the Committee and fell in with it). I have reviewed the competing affidavits by the investment bankers. I cannot conclude that plaintiffs have shown the Lazard Freres or Dillon Read work to be flawed. Briefly, that is because it is quite apparent, even to one with modest sophistication in techniques of financial analysis, that the value of the reset provision for the interest rate of a subordinated security issued in these circumstances (when very large amounts of senior debt is shortly to be issued) is of great importance to the value of the security. It is plausible (more than that really, but I need go no further) that the KKR reset provision made its convertible debentures relatively more valuable than was the Management Group's analogous convertible preferred. This fact, together with the higher rate that the converting debentures were to bear and the fact that the convertibility feature of the Management Group's preferred stock could be mooted by exercise of a call provision at any time (thus diminishing the value of the prospect of a later equity participation), provides quite sufficient bases to conclude that the opinions of the Special Committee's advisors concerning prospective value of the respective packages (which largely reduced to quite different assessments of the relative values of the converting debentures and the convertible preferred) were competent and reached in good faith.

Thus, the fact that the board was faced with what it could reasonably believe were bids that were essentially equivalent from a financial point of view is a relevant circumstance in assessing its good faith in acting as it did.

The second especially relevant circumstances with respect to the Committee's decision to act when it did relates to the fact that the Committee had been placed under severe time constraints by KKR in submitting its final proposal—the Committee was given thirty minutes to accept the bid on pain of its being withdrawn. Of course, this may have been an empty threat. I suppose that few thought the chances of such a withdrawal very high but no one, of course, was in a position to assure that it would not happen. Were it to have happened, it is plain that the recap option would have provided a poor substitute at the range of values the bidding had been driven to. Thus, the Committee would have been left with the Management Group's proposal of substantially equivalent value but with some important terms that were plainly less appealing.

* * *

In the light of these circumstances, the decision not to attempt to break the tie but to accept one of the bids at that point and thus avoid the risk of the loss of that bid—no matter that my personal view might be that the risk was rather small—can in no event be seen as justifying an inference that those who made such a choice must have had some motivation other than the honest pursuit of the corporation's welfare.
* * *

Nor can the decision to prefer KKR's bid with $3 less cash and with less nominal or face value per share be seen as so beyond the bounds of reasonable judgment as to raise an inference of bad faith in my opinion. The larger equity stub, the different future business plans of the two bidders, and the superior reset provision of KKR's proposed converting debentures, all provide a basis to support the notion that the choice was a rational one. That KKR as an acquiror presented antitrust questions or offered a somewhat lower proportion of cash simply presents an occasion for the exercise of judgment; the judgment reached does not, as indicated, appear so far afield as to raise a question of the motivation of the board.

* * *

The obligation then is in the first instance to be informed of "all material information reasonably available." When the question is what is the best available price for an asset, the market for such an asset provides a valuable source, and where the relevant market is "thick," the most useful source of such information. In the sale of a very special, perhaps unique asset such as control of a corporation, a regular market will be unavailable. In that instance, an auction market can provide important information as to what is the best available transaction for sale of the Company. * * *

If plaintiffs' argument that the Special Committee was negligent is to be rejected for present purposes, it is necessary to show that the Committee had "all material information reasonably available" at the time it decided to act to accept the KKR proposal without going back to invite a tiebreaking round of bids. Presumably, at that point the auction could have continued and more information might have been gotten about what could be achieved.

There is a compelling answer to this position. It is premised upon the insight, upon the fact, that information has costs and it focuses verbally on the word "reasonably" in the *Aronson* formulation. It concludes that the amount of information that it is prudent to have before a decision is made is itself a business judgment of the very type that courts are institutionally poorly equipped to make. * * *

The answer need only be briefly expanded. Clearly, more information was available to the Committee on the central question would either party pay more. Just ask and you may find out (if the answer is yes, time would of course be necessary to evaluate if another proposal *was* worth more). But in this setting, the act of asking another time for a highest and best bid *might* itself have costs. It is not inconceivable that KKR (by that time protected by a $.20 per share expense reimbursement agreement given in exchange for extending its 1:00 p.m. deadline earlier in the day) could have walked away from the transaction. Thus, the risks (costs) associated with getting more information had to be weighed by the Committee against the likely benefits. The Rohatyn testimony (and it is not alone in this) tends to establish that the Committee addressed this question with due care. It concluded that in the circumstances (the stage of the auction, the level of the prices, the events of the day, etc.), the risks outweighed the potential rewards. In my opinion, this important decision is itself entitled to the deference courts give to business decisions made by disinterested directors with care in the honest pursuit of the corporation's interest. * * *

Accordingly, I conclude that the Committee had at the time it made its decision "all material information reasonably available" to it. * * * Moreover, there is, in my opinion, no sufficient evidence that it then failed "to act with requisite care" thereafter in reaching the particular decision to prefer the KKR proposal. It is the case that that decision was made under extreme time pressure. But where an arm's-length negotiating adversary imposes time limits, a board is forced to contend with that circumstance. If it exercises informed judgment in the circumstances, considers the risks posed by the deadline imposed, and concludes that it is prudent to act and acts with care, it has satisfied its duty. * * * Plaintiffs have failed to demonstrate a reasonable likelihood that the defendants did otherwise in this instance.

* * *

But with the central assertion—that when substantially equivalent bids are received, the concept "auction," which has been given such currency by its use in the *Revlon* opinion, itself requires the board to ask for other bids—I simply cannot agree. Surely the board may not use its power to exercise judgment in that context as a sham or pretext to prefer one bidder for inappropriate reasons—as occurred, one supposes, in *Holly Farms* and certainly occurred in *Revlon* itself. But the board of directors continues, in the auction setting as in others, to bear the burden imposed and exercise the power conferred by Section 141(a). Assuming it does exercise a business judgment, in good faith and advisedly, concerning the management of the auction process, it has, in my opinion, satisfied its duty. It appears that such a judgment was reached in the early evening of November 30 and I can find no basis in the principle that explains the *Revlon* case for the court to set it aside.

* * *

Questions

1. What did the special committee do correctly that the directors in *Mills Acquisition* did incorrectly? Consider the difficult position of the special committee attempting to value the "final" bids, consisting of unusual and sophisticated investment instruments (PIK preferred stock and convertible preferred stock). Did they accept the lower of the two bids?

2. How can a firm stop an auction? If a public deadline set by the target board for "final" bids has passed, and a losing bidder makes a new bid for a higher price, must the target board reauction the firm? How can a firm force bidders to make their best offers before the deadline? Does a "topping fee" (the firm grants the highest bidder at the time of the deadline a large fee contingent on the firm's acceptance of another, higher offer) help? Can the firm use a generic lockup option, offering the option to the highest bidder at a given point in time? Why did the special committee in *RJR Nabisco* continue to retreat from "deadlines" when it had a tipping fee in place? What led the committee to finally stop the bidding? If you were a bidder in an auction contest, would you put your "final offer" on the table when a target board announces for the first time (for the second time, the third time), a "deadline for all final offers"?

3. Is the RJR Nabisco buyout the last of the large leverage buyouts?

B. BURROUGH & J. HELYAR, BARBARIANS AT THE GATE
512–14 (1990).

* * *

In the months following the RJR Nabisco buyout many on Wall Street sensed a new civility in the takeover world, a backlash, they reasoned, against the unfettered displays of greed and hubris seen during the momentous fight. "This transaction was a watershed event," Peter Cohen said in August. "Everybody on Wall Street looks and acts very differently when they look at deals now. It's made everyone a little bit more conservative, calmed them down, took some of the fight out of them. No one's got the appetite after RJR."

Certainly that seemed so in Cohen's case. Shearson's merchant-banking effort quieted significantly in the wake of RJR. "If it happened again, I wouldn't make a lot of the same mistakes," Cohen admitted. "Today, we're still doing transactions, but they're five hundred million, a billion, and they're not contested."

* * *

For the most part, though, Wall Street's takeover machine slept in 1989. LBO activity dropped sharply. The prospect of anti-LBO legislation delayed many deals, while new tremors in the junk-bond market stalled others. The first eight months of 1989 saw $4 billion worth of junk-bond defaults and debt moratoriums, the most spectacular being the troubles of Canadian entrepreneur Robert Campeau's retail empire. Then, in October, the unraveling of a $6.79 billion buyout of United Airlines's parent prompted momentary panic on Wall Street, sending the Dow Jones Industrial Average down nearly 200 points and prompting fears of a new market crash.

Ted Forstmann, of course, felt thoroughly vindicated. During 1989 Forstmann continued to spend more time bashing Kravis than pursuing leveraged buyouts. He took his anti-junk bond crusade to Washington, where it found a warm reception among lawmakers eager to smite the "LBO menace." By the fall Congress was pondering a number of anti-LBO measures, including one that would eliminate the deductibility of certain key junk bonds, a move that could sharply increase the costs of completing many LBOs. "The worm has finally turned," Forstmann said in October. "People are finally beginning to understand what this stuff is all about."

Faced with possible new legislative curbs and a faltering junk-bond market, many Wall Street observers began publicly predicting the twilight of the modern takeover era. *USA Today,* displaying pictures of Kravis and the indicted Mike Milken, announced that October's stock slide "marked an end to the 1980s and the time of takeover mania and the quick buck." Among these pessimists, it was de rigueur to suggest that RJR Nabisco, the largest deal of the eighties, would also be its tombstone.

But others weren't so inclined to write off the resources—or the greed—of Wall Street. Nearly $20 billion in money remained available worldwide for LBOs. With the decline in junk bonds, Kravis began to concoct new ways to structure LBOs. Injecting equity into new deals, perhaps as much as 15 percent, was one way he considered to insulate the firm from its longtime dependence on junk bonds. Whether these and other ideas will in fact work and prolong the takeover era should depend both on the appetites of bond buyers and the future activities of congressional critics.

* * *

Note

Statutes Empowering Firms to Waive Director Liability in Acquisitions

In footnote 34 the Delaware court responded with a rather testy footnote to "scholars" who had been trying to determine whether the *Unocal* test was a duty of care or a duty of loyalty test. The debate has significance because of section 102(b)(7) in the Delaware General Corporation Law. Please read the section in your statutory supplement. Almost forty states have adopted a version of the Delaware provision. See also sections 512 and 1721(h) of the Pennsylvania Business Corporation Law. Within six months of the adoption of section 102(b)(7) in Delaware, over three hundred firms, at their first annual meeting held after the effective date of the section, passed charter amendments waiving director liability to the full extent allowed under the provision. In a sense the section represents the ultimate shark repellent amendment: The firm adopts a charter amendment that exonerates its officers and directors from liability (to the maximum extent politically feasible) in acquisitions. What is the effect of such exoneration on the basic definition of their fiduciary duty of care?

Researchers studying the effect of section 102(b)(7) found that the passage of the law correlated with a significant decrease in the equity value of firms incorporated in Delaware relative to those incorporated elsewhere. Bradley & Schipani, The Relevance of the Duty of Care Standard in Corporate Governance, 75 Iowa L.Rev. 1 (1989). The results startled the authors of the study: The cumulative abnormal return to Delaware firms over the months surrounding the effective date of the section was a negative 2.96 percent, the largest drop found in any recent research on various other takeover defenses. See section 1, supra. Moreover, the researchers found that most of the 559 firms that elected to adopt the protections of the Delaware statute experienced a second significant decrease in the market value of their common stock when they first announced their intention to pass amendments to their articles to make use of the section. The authors concluded that "available evidence seems to be mounting that legal rules are important constraints on the behavior of corporate managers." Id. at 70.

Why are shareholders voting against their best interest in supporting charter amendments based on the section? Are the costs to any one shareholder of waging a proxy campaign to defeat a management-sponsored proxy proposal greater than the slight decrease in market value that the shareholder will suffer if the proposal passes? Can managers use proxy machinery to extract wealth from their own shareholders?

Questions

1. Do the statutes affect equitable relief (injunctions, for example) for due care violations?

2. Why do shareholders vote to adopt charter amendments that waive the due care liability of their directors?

3. How does the Delaware statute affect director liability for a violation of the standard of conduct specified in the *Van Gorkom, Revlon,* or *Mills Acquisition* cases? For an application of the section see John Hancock Capital Growth Management, Inc. v. Aris Corp., Fed.Sec.L.Rep. (CCH) ¶ 95,461 (Del.Ch.1990). The defendant firm sold its principal assets to another firm. Under bond indenture covenants the defendant's bondholders had to approve the sale or the proceeds of the sale had to be used to pay off the bonds. The defendant induced the bondholders to vote their approval by increasing the interest rate on the bonds, paying the bondholders some cash, and issuing warrants to the bondholders. Preferred shareholders sued the firm's nine directors, alleging that the board was grossly negligent in not repurchasing the bonds before the asset sale, when the bonds could have been bought at a substantial discount in a sagging market. Could the repurchase offer have been conditioned on the receipt of bondholder consents sufficient to waive the protective covenants? See chapter 4. The court dismissed the action against the directors, because the defendant had a charter provision eliminating director liability for gross negligence.

4. Should corporations be able to amend their charters to limit directors' liability for duty of loyalty violations as well?

Liability of Investment Bankers in LBOs

Since *Smith v. Van Gorkom* directors have been on notice that they can be held liable for not making an informed decision on the fairness of the price in an acquisition. This has led directors to demand "fairness opinions" from investment bankers before the directors will approve any acquisition. The opinions are particularly important when the self-interest of management in a leveraged buyout creates a need for a decision by a subcommittee of the board consisting of independent directors. The independent directors have come to rely heavily on investment banker fairness opinions to inform and support their decisions. As can be seen from the performance of the investment bankers in the *Mills Acquisition* case, the quality of the service provided by investment bankers in some acquisitions is open to serious question. In *Mills Acquisition* the court reached out and almost invited a lawsuit against Mr. Wesserstein. Since the court enjoined the acquisition, however, such a suit became unnecessary. But it is quite another matter when the shareholders fail in their efforts to enjoin an acquisition. Disgruntled shareholders, having lost in their claims against their directors who have successfully hidden behind fairness opinions, have turned to suing the investment bankers who issued the opinions.

WELLS v. SHEARSON LEHMAN/AMERICAN EXP., INC.
Supreme Court, Appellate Division, 1987.
127 A.D.2d 200, 514 N.Y.S.2d 1, reversed on other grounds 72 N.Y.2d 11, 530 N.Y.S.2d 517, 526 N.E.2d 8 (1988).

KUPFERMAN, JUSTICE.

In 1984, the principal officers of Metromedia paid approximately $1.1 billion for the company's publicly held shares. This was the culmination of a process begun in December, 1983.

* * *

Nevertheless, Shearson Lehman and Bear Stearns were tangentially involved in the buyout process in the following manner: after plaintiffs filed the Delaware lawsuits, Metromedia selected four of its directors to form a committee to evaluate the fairness of the buyout. This committee hired Shearson Lehman and Bear Stearns to give their opinion on that issue for the stockholders. Before the settlement, Shearson Lehman and Bear Stearns rendered an opinion that the total assets of the corporation were worth $1.114 billion. Later, their opinion was included in proxy material sent to shareholders. On the basis of that proxy material, the shareholders voted overwhelmingly to approve management's buyout.

Allegedly, Metromedia paid Shearson Lehman $750,000 for its opinion, $685,000 in brokers fees, and agreed to pay an additional $3.2 million if the merger went through. Allegedly, Metromedia paid Bear Stearns $500,000 for its opinion and agreed to pay an additional $2 million if the merger were effected. Additionally, through a special deal on the stock price, it allegedly provided Bear Stearns the opportunity to realize an $8.1 million trading profit.

Within a year of the buyout, Metromedia sold its television assets (one portion of the company) for $2 billion, or $886 million more than Shearson Lehman and Bear Stearns had valued all Metromedia's assets. Subsequently, Metromedia sold most of its remaining assets for $2.5 billion, for a total of $4.5 billion.

Ms. Wells who, as mentioned, had been a plaintiff in the Delaware litigation, brought suit in New York against Shearson Lehman and Bear Stearns. She claims defendants either failed to use due care or intentionally issued erroneous opinions with the motive that only an opinion favorable toward the merger would bring them substantial monetary gain.

* * * On a motion to dismiss for legal insufficiency, we must deem the factual allegations to be true and accord them every favorable inference. * * * Plaintiffs claim that they, as stockholders, lost money due to the negligent or wrongful preparation of defendants' opinion. Shearson Lehman and Bear Stearns make the untenable assertion that they represented the officers and therefore were not in privity to the shareholders. The officers, however, created a committee whose purpose was to serve the shareholders by determining the fairness of the buyout. The committee hired Shearson Lehman and Bear Stearns. Anybody hired by the committee, aiding in its endeavor, was actually retained to advise the shareholders. Assuming Ms. Wells' complaint is true, and assuming Shearson Lehman and Bear Stearns were aware (as they must have been) that their opinion would be used to help shareholders decide on the fairness of Metromedia's stock offer, they can be liable to the shareholders. *Credit Alliance Corporation et al. v. Arthur Andersen & Co.,* 65 N.Y.2d 536, 493 N.Y.S.2d 435, 483 N.E.2d 110.

* * *

SCHNEIDER v. LAZARD FRERES & CO.
159 A.D.2d 291, 552 N.Y.S.2d 571.

Plaintiffs, a group of shareholders in RJR Nabisco, Inc., a Delaware corporation, claim that an unfairly conducted auction of RJR stock resulted in the acceptance of a bid by the RJR Board of Directors more than a billion dollars less than what could have been obtained by a fair auction. They sued the RJR Board and the successful bidder, Kohlberg, Kravis, Roberts & Co., in the Delaware Court of Chancery for an injunction against consummation of the tender offer Kohlberg won the right to have as high bidder. * * * When a motion by the shareholders for a preliminary injunction in the Delaware action was denied, they brought the instant action in New York against the two investment bankers hired by the Special Committee to advise it conducting the auction, Lazard Freres & Co. and Dillon Read & Co., Inc., the gist of which is that the Special Committee conducted the auction in the unfair manner it did because of faulty advice given to it by the bankers. More particularly, the shareholders allege that the bankers advised the Special Committee that the final bids submitted by Kohlberg and the Management Group were "substantially equivalent from a financial point of view" when, in fact, the latter was superior; alternatively, the shareholders allege that if the Management Group's bid was inferior, then, given the dynamics of the auction, the bankers should have advised the Special Committee to invite another bid from the Management Group, or, if the two bids were, as they were represented to be, substantially equivalent in value, then the bankers should have advised the Special Committee to solicit a set of tie-breaking bids. The failure to invite tie-breaking bids is presented only as the final and most egregious example of an auction that was throughout run in a way to give Kohlberg an unfair advantage over the Management Group.

The bankers moved before IAS for an order dismissing the complaint for failure to state a cause of action, their main argument being that their advice was addressed to the Special Committee, not the shareholders, and that they therefore owed no duty to the shareholders to render non-negligent advice; in addition, the bankers argued that if they did owe a duty of care to the shareholders, the complaint does not allege how it was breached.

* * *

Turning to whether the bankers owed the shareholders a duty of care, the argument on this question is somewhat distractingly presented mainly in terms of whether the relationship between the shareholders and the bankers was or was not one "approaching privity" within the meaning of Credit Alliance Corporation v. Arthur Andersen & Co.,

65 N.Y. 536, 493 N.Y.S.2d 435, 483 N.E.2d 110. No claim is made by the shareholders that any of them actually relied on any advice the bankers gave the Special Committee concerning either the conduct of the auction or the relative values of the competing bids. Nor is there any allegation that any such advice was passed on, or intended to be passed on, to any of the shareholders for the purpose of influencing them to take any particular action in connection with the auction. On the contrary, underlying the complaint is the notion that it was the expectation of all concerned that the shareholders were not to do anything other than passively follow the recommendation of the Special Committee, which was up specifically to protect their interests in the auction. Thus, the shareholders, in the complaint, speak of the Special Committee as "their" committee, the directors constituting it as their "representatives", and advice given to and relied on by the Special Committee as advice given to and relied on by the shareholders "acting through the Special Committee". Viewing the relationship between the shareholders and the Special Committee thus, that is, as one of principal and agent, we do not see how it can be said that a duty of care owed by the bankers to the Special Committee was not intended for the benefit of the shareholders. The existence of a fiduciary relationship between the Special Committee and the shareholders itself establishes the requisite privity between the shareholders and any persons in contractual privity with the Special Committee. We do not think it a startling proposition that a principal is in privity with his agent's agent, or with anyone else his agent deals with on his behalf (see, Credit Alliance Corporation v. Arthur Andersen & Co., supra, at 550, fn. 9, 493 N.Y.S.2d 435, 483 N.E.2d 110; 3 N.Y. Jur. 2d, Agency and Independent Contractors, Section 271), so that a negligent statement made by a third person to an agent and relied on by the agent to the principal's detriment is actionable by the principal. In contrast, in the typical Credit Alliance situation, a negligent statement is made not to an agent, but by an agent, and is relied on by a third person outside of the agency relationship for purposes of entering into a transaction with the agent's principal.

In determining whether the bankers owed the shareholders a duty of care, we think the question is not whether the relationship between them was one approaching privity, but whether the relationship between the shareholders and the Special Committee was one governed by the law of agency or the law of corporations, the bankers argue that well settled principles of corporate law make corporate management the responsibility and prerogative of the board, not the shareholders; that directors at all times, no more so in the present context than in others, act as fiduciaries for the shareholders, this being their reason for being; that it was for the RJR Board to decide, in the exercise of its business judgment and as the shareholders' fiduciary, whether the bankers were negligent, and, if so, whether RJR should sue them for it; and that to permit this action to go forward would be to permit shareholders to decide whether any lawyer, accountant or other professional hired by a board to advise it with respect to corporate business should be sued for malpractice. We reject this argument because we agree with the shareholders that sale of the control of a corporation is not corporate business of the type governed by traditional principles of corporate governance, and that the Special Committee stood in a relationship to the shareholders different from that which normally obtains between a corporation's board and shareholders. The Special Committee's purpose was not to judge transactions accruing to the benefit of the corporate treasury; nor was it concerned with any matters affecting RJR's internal affairs. Rather, its purpose was to advise the shareholders with respect to a transaction that contemplated RJR's demise and whose end and aim was to obtain for the shareholders the highest possible price for their stock. In this "buyout" context, if something less than the highest possible price was obtained, the loss was sustained by the shareholders, not the corporation, and, for that reason, we are of the view that the relationship between the shareholders and the Special Committee was essentially that of principal and agent on which principles of corporate law should not be superimposed....

We agree with the shareholders that the complaint gives adequate notice of how the bankers were negligent. With respect to the valuation of the bids, the financial facts allegedly disregarded by the bankers are set forth with particularity, and it will be the shareholders' burden to show that a failure to consider these facts was a failure to exercise that degree of care that a reasonably prudent investment banker would have exercised under the same circumstances. With respect to the conduct of the auction, it will be necessary for the shareholders to show that a reasonably prudent person, intent on obtaining the highest possible price for the shareholders' stock, would not have conducted the auction in the manner advised by the bankers.

Questions

1. In *Wells* the fairness opinion was referenced in proxy materials sent to shareholders. In *Schneider* was the content of the fairness opinion communicated to shareholders?

2. In *Wells* did Shearson Lehman have a conflict of interest when it rendered its fairness opinion? Should it be liable under a duty of loyalty or duty of care theory?

3. How can an investment bank limit its liability to a client's shareholders? Should the law permit investment banks to contract with client firms for complete indemnification against shareholder lawsuits? *See In re RJR Nabisco, Inc.,* 576 A.2d 654, 656 note 2 (Del.Ch.1990):

> For example, RJR has indemnified these investment banks from certain losses or damages. Pursuant to their undertaking to advise the special committee of the RJR board of directors, both investment banks secured indemnification from RJR for damages or loss that they incur as a result of those services. That indemnification appears to be broad,

excluding, by its terms, only loss or damage judicially determined to arise primarily out of gross negligence, willful misconduct or bad faith of the banks.

Should it be a breach of duty for a board to agree to the fee arrangement in *Wells* or the indemnification provision in *RJR Nabisco?*

4. The extraordinary tale of the Metromedia leveraged buyout deserves special attention. On December 6, 1983, four senior officers of Metromedia proposed an LBO, giving $40 in cash and debentures to existing shareholders. The total purchase price of $1.1 billion was to be obtained through loans secured by Metromedia assets. Several shareholders started a class action, alleging the price was too low. Four outside Metromedia directors were appointed to a special committee to represent the interests of shareholders in the acquisition. The special committee hired Shearson Lehman and Bear Stearns and Company, which, on January 31, informed the committee that the offered price was fair. Defendants settled the shareholder lawsuits by increasing the price per share $0.69 ($16.5 million) and by paying the plaintiffs' attorneys fees of about $1 million. The plaintiffs' attorneys pushed for judicial approval, asserting that the settlement was "fair and reasonable." The proposed release provided that "all claims ... that have been and could have been asserted by the plaintiffs against any defendant ... or anyone else in connection with ... the Action ... shall be ... released and dismissed with prejudice." The shareholders approved the merger on June 21, 1984, having received proxy statements that included written opinions from both Shearson Lehman and Bear Stearns on the appropriateness of the price. On the same date the Delaware Chancery Court entered final judgment approving the settlement as "fair, reasonable and adequate." In May 1985 the new owners of Metromedia sold seven television stations for over $2 billion, and in February 1986 they sold the remaining Metromedia shares in liquidation of the firm for an additional $2.5 billion. Had the shareholders received the proceeds from the sales, they would have collected around $84 more per share. 72 N.Y.2d at 26. The shareholders sued the investment bankers and defeated a motion to dismiss at trial court and at the Appellant Division. The court of appeals held, however, that the release in the shareholder litigation against the buyout group also protected the investment bankers. Metromedia's management reaped an enormous personal profit, as did the investment bankers and the lawyers.

Did the managers steal from its shareholders? What arguments might exonerate the principals? Why could shareholders not protect themselves? Do we need additional legal protections? Should the shareholders be able to reopen the settled case? On what grounds?

SECTION 2. DEFENSIVE REORGANIZATIONS: THE TARGET BOARD'S DECISION NOT TO SELL

In light of *Revlon* can a target firm refuse to sell to anyone once a bidder puts the firm in play? If so, what standards govern the board's conduct? The following cases deal with these questions.

IVANHOE PARTNERS v. NEWMONT MINING CORP.
Supreme Court of Delaware, 1987.
535 A.2d 1334.

MOORE, JUSTICE:

We accepted this expedited interlocutory appeal from a decision of the Court of Chancery, denying a preliminary injunction to plaintiffs, in order to address certain defensive maneuvers taken in a battle for the control of Newmont Mining Corporation ("Newmont"), one of the largest gold producers in North America. In an attempt to block a hostile tender offer by Ivanhoe Partners and Ivanhoe Acquisition Corporation (collectively "Ivanhoe"), Newmont declared a $33 per share dividend to all its stockholders, which helped its largest shareholder, Consolidated Gold Fields PLC ("Gold Fields"), to engage in a "street sweep" of Newmont stock, thereby increasing Gold Field's ownership of Newmont from 26% to 49.7%.[3] The "street sweep" and its related transactions, including the dividend, and the extension of and amendments to a previously existing standstill agreement with Newmont, if proper, will effectively defeat Ivanhoe's bid.

* * *

In 1981 Gold Fields began vigorously acquiring Newmont stock. Newmont immediately sued to enjoin Gold Fields' acquisition of a significant or controlling interest. Ultimately, Newmont agreed to allow Gold Fields to purchase up to a one-third interest in the company, but in return Newmont demanded that Gold Fields sign a standstill agreement. That accord, which in 1983 was amended and extended for ten years, limited Gold Fields' interest in Newmont to 33$\frac{1}{3}$%, restricted Gold Fields' representation on the board to one third the total number of directors, required Gold Fields and Newmont to support the other's director nominees, and gave Newmont a right of first refusal in the event Gold Fields decided to sell its interest. * * * Of particular significance is that the standstill agreement also provided that Gold Fields could terminate the arrangement at its option upon acquisition by a third party of 9.9% or more of Newmont's outstanding shares. Gold Fields maintained a 26% interest from 1981 until recently, when Ivanhoe's purchase of 9.95% triggered Gold Fields' option to terminate the contract.

On August 13, 1987 Ivanhoe announced that it had acquired 8.7% of Newmont. Significantly, Ivanhoe soon took the deliberate step to increase its Newmont holdings to 9.95%, which thereby freed Gold Fields to terminate the standstill agreement. This was done intentionally with the hope that Gold Fields then would ally itself with Mr. Pickens and his Ivanhoe affiliates, either to take over Newmont and to divide it among themselves, or to reach some other mutually advantageous arrangement. This Ivanhoe tactic prompted a series of strategic

---

3. "Street sweep" refers to the rapid acquisition of securities on the open market during and shortly after the pendency of a tender offer for the same class of securities. The shares are ordinarily purchased at a premium from arbitrageurs.

maneuvers and responses by each of the three parties. In anticipation of a battle with Ivanhoe, Newmont began implementing traditional defensive measures.[7] However, in doing so Newmont found itself in the peculiar position of having simultaneously to fear and to court Gold Fields. Although Newmont and Gold Fields had enjoyed a compatible business association for some time, Gold Fields now was freed of its prior constraints. It had the option to acquire control of Newmont. In order to maintain a balance in their relationship, Newmont exempted Gold Fields from these defensive measures. Nonetheless, the Vice Chancellor found that Gold Fields' was rationally perceived as a threat to Newmont's continued independence. Specifically, throughout its relationship with Newmont, Gold Fields had demonstrated that it had its own independent objectives which were not necessarily congruent with Newmont's.

On August 31 Ivanhoe sent Newmont a letter requesting a meeting to discuss the acquisition by Ivanhoe of all of the remaining Newmont common stock. By separate letter, Ivanhoe solicited Gold Fields to discuss "a broad range of alternatives" concerning the disposition of their Newmont stock. On September 8, when these letters proved fruitless, Ivanhoe commenced a hostile tender offer for 42% of Newmont at $95 per share. Among other things the tender offer was contingent upon Ivanhoe's obtaining financing, the source of which was not disclosed.

Furthermore, the Offer to Purchase disclosed that Ivanhoe would seek to acquire all remaining shares in a second step transaction at $95 per share cash which, likewise, was subject to obtaining financing. The offer stated that no specific second step transaction had been devised, and that there was no firm commitment to do so.

The Newmont directors had to quickly address numerous problems.[10] Based in part upon a presentation by its independent financial adviser, Goldman, Sachs and Company ("Goldman Sachs"), the board determined that the $95 offer was inadequate. When Ivanhoe attempted to remove the current board by shareholder consent, the directors amended the bylaws to delay the effect of any consent solicitation for twenty days. The board also undertook two major tasks to defend against the perceived Ivanhoe and Gold Fields threats. First, in an effort to protect Newmont's independence, the board began exploring alternatives with Gold Fields to discourage it from terminating the

---

7. On August 18, 1987 the Newmont board approved "golden parachutes" which called for substantial severance payments to twenty-five key management employees.

On September 7, Newmont's board approved a 2.25 billion dollar revolving credit agreement which provided for default of the loans if an entity acquired 50% or more of Newmont.

10. Newmont's board consisted of nine members: three management directors; two outside directors affiliated with Gold Fields; and four independent directors. Throughout the board's consideration and adoption of the various defensive mechanisms described here, the two Gold Fields' directors recused themselves. Thus all relevant actions taken by the remaining directors bore the imprimatur of a board majority consisting of four independent directors.

standstill agreement. Second, the board proposed an aggressive business and capital program (the "Gold Plan") which included the disclosure of liberal estimates of reserves and a corresponding increase in the gold production estimates by 50%.[11] * * *

Ivanhoe then raised its tender offer price to $105 on September 16. Two days later the Newmont Board met to consider the revised offer and found that it, too, was inadequate. The Board's decision was made after a second presentation by Goldman Sachs which included revised figures based on the Gold Plan.[12] At the same meeting Newmont's management offered a "restructuring" proposal designed to deal with the threats posed by Gold Fields and Ivanhoe. This proposal consisted of the declaration of a large dividend to be financed by the sale of Newmont's non-gold assets, and the signing of a new standstill agreement with Gold Fields to insure Newmont's independence. The purpose of the dividend was to reduce liquidity, thus making Newmont a less attractive target, to distribute the value of its non-gold assets to all of the shareholders (including Ivanhoe), and to facilitate Gold Fields' street sweep. Significantly, the proposed standstill agreement would limit Gold Fields' control of Newmont, thereby assuring the latter's continued independence.

Although Gold Fields had considered breaking the standstill agreement and going into the open market to purchase control of Newmont, * * * the prospect of accomplishing a similar yet more restricted objective with only a small capital investment was very attractive.[13] Thus, the dividend became the linchpin for negotiating the new standstill agreement.

By September 20, 1987 Newmont and Gold Fields had reached an accord. This new agreement allowed Gold Fields to purchase up to 49.9% of Newmont stock, but effectively limited its representation on the Newmont board to 40% of the total directors. Additionally, Gold Fields was required to support the board's slate of nominees for the remaining board positions, and was prohibited from transferring its interest to any third party who refused to be bound by the standstill.

Once executed, the new agreement was delivered to Newmont in escrow conditioned upon the declaration of a $33 dividend.[14] On September 21 and 22, Gold Fields, consistent with the terms of the accord, and facilitated by the dividend, "swept the street", purchasing

---

11. The Gold Plan called for the acceleration of exploration and production activities. Although Ivanhoe strenuously disputes the trial court's findings, there is support for a conclusion that even though the Gold Plan was timed to defeat the Ivanhoe offer, the adoption of the Gold Plan and the resulting higher Newmont stock valuation, were not mere "puffery".

12. The valuation by Goldman Sachs is a much disputed issue in this case. We find it significant that in its final analysis, Goldman Sachs opined that at a price of $105 per share Ivanhoe would still acquire the two Newmont gold subsidiaries at an 8.7% discount.

13. Throughout this period Gold Fields' investment banker, The First Boston Corporation, urged Gold Fields to break the standstill agreement and independently sweep the street, gain control of Newmont, and declare a dividend.

14. The $33 figure represents the liquidation value of the non-gold assets. * * *

approximately 15.8 million Newmont shares at an average price of $98 per share and increasing their interest to 49.7%.

* * *

* * * Gold Fields and Newmont amended the agreement on September 27: 1) to allow Gold Fields to tender into an "any or all" tender offer if the offeror had firm commitments for financing, and 2) to provide that Gold Fields and Newmont would use their best efforts to establish cumulative voting.

* * *

Since this case involves the actions of a board of directors in the face of a takeover, the probability of success of Ivanhoe's claim must be analyzed under the well established standard of *Unocal*. Ivanhoe contends that the standstill agreement tainted the Newmont directors with a personal interest which requires that the challenged acts be evaluated under the intrinsic fairness test rather than the business judgment rule. * * *

However, the record does not support a conclusion that the directors appeared on both sides of the transaction, or that they derived any personal financial benefit from it which did not devolve upon the corporation and the shareholders generally. * * * Thus, we do not start with an intrinsic fairness analysis.

The board of directors has the ultimate responsibility for managing the business and affairs of a corporation. 8 *Del.C.* § 141(a) (1983). In meeting this responsibility the board is charged with fiduciary obligations of care and loyalty. * * * Under the business judgment rule, directors' decisions are presumed to have been made on an informed basis, in good faith and in the honest belief that the action taken was in the best interests of the company. * * *

This presumption and its underlying fiduciary duties are equally applicable in a takeover context. * * * When directors oppose a hostile takeover there arises "the omnipresent specter that a board may be acting primarily in its own interests, rather than those of the corporation and its shareholders ..." *Unocal*, 493 A.2d at 954. This Court has addressed that potential for conflict by placing upon the directors the burden of proving that they have not acted solely or primarily out of a desire to perpetuate themselves in office, that the threatened takeover posed a danger to corporate policy and effectiveness, and that the defensive measures adopted are reasonable in relation to the threat posed. The target directors must satisfy these prerequisites by showing good faith and reasonable investigation before enjoying the presumptions afforded by the business judgement rule. This requires directorial analysis of the nature of the takeover bid and its effect on the corporate enterprise. Thus, the board may under appropriate circumstances consider the inadequacy of the bid, the nature and timing of the offer, questions of illegality, the impact on constituencies other than shareholders, the risk of nonconsummation, and the basic stockholder interests at stake, including the past actions of the bidder and its affiliates in other takeover contests.

This Court has recognized the coercive nature of two-tier partial tender offers. *Unocal,* 493 A.2d at 956. Here, not only did the Ivanhoe offer fit perfectly the mold of such a coercive device, but after reasonable investigation the offer was found by the Newmont board to be inadequate. The Vice Chancellor held that this finding of inadequacy was justified, and his conclusion is fully supported by the record. * * * Furthermore, Newmont and Gold Fields specifically recognized that Mr. Pickens, who controls Ivanhoe, had been involved in several attempts to acquire and break-up other corporations, resulting in the payment of "greenmail" or severe restructuring of the target companies. * * * Ch., 488 A.2d 107 (1984). The series of Ivanhoe maneuvers, including the secret acquisition of shares, the "bear hug" letter, the coercive partial tender offer and inadequate bid were all viewed by the defendants as classic elements of Mr. Pickens' typical *modus operandi*. Thus, the Newmont board could properly conclude that the Ivanhoe tender offer was not in the shareholders' best interests or those of their company. *Unocal,* 493 A.2d at 952, 956–57.

Gold Fields did not make a public bid for Newmont, and in more recent years there appears to have been a congenial relationship between the two companies. From the outset Gold Fields publicly expressed its support for the Newmont management. A Gold Fields press release stated:

> Consolidated Gold Fields has had a long, close and valued relationship with Newmont. Although Ivanhoe Partners' actions give Gold Fields the right to terminate the standstill agreement, we do not intend to exercise that right at this time, and we have no wish to seek control of Newmont. We strongly support Newmont management and believe it to be in our interest as the largest shareholder, and in the interest of all Newmont shareholders, that management be allowed to continue to direct Newmont's affairs....

Throughout the weeks of harried activity Gold Fields continued to publicly support Newmont's management. Despite this, Newmont contends that it was threatened by the stark possibility that Gold Fields would cancel the 1983 standstill agreement and acquire control of the company, thus leaving the remaining shareholders without protection on the "back end". The record is replete with examples of the reality of this threat. A clear danger was posed by Ivanhoe's deliberate acquisition of 9.95% of Newmont shares, designed to free Gold Fields from the agreement, thereby permitting Ivanhoe and Gold Fields to ally themselves against Newmont. But even without Ivanhoe, Gold Fields now could wrest control away from the public shareholders. In addition, as the Newmont board was aware, Gold Fields had the necessary financial backing to unilaterally "sweep the street" and obtain control of Newmont.

* * *

Finally, the threat which Gold Fields posed was real. The Gold Fields board had in fact paused to weigh its options. Throughout these maneuvers it had considered in earnest the possibility of either independently purchasing control of Newmont or selling its interest to Ivanhoe.

Ivanhoe argues that, even if it and Gold Fields did pose a threat to Newmont's corporate policy and effectiveness, the Newmont directors failed to satisfy the second part of their *Unocal* burden—that their response be reasonable in relation to the threat posed. *Unocal*, 493 A.2d at 955. In examining that contention, *Unocal* requires us to carefully assess the reasonableness of the defensive measures employed and the results achieved. *Id.* Because Newmont's actions here are so inextricably related, the principles of *Unocal* require that they be scrutinized collectively as a unitary response to the perceived threats.

It is significant that throughout the consideration and adoption of these proposals, the Gold Fields directors recused themselves from participation in the Newmont board meetings, leaving an alliance of four independent and three management directors. Thus, with the independent directors in the majority, proof that the board acted in good faith and upon reasonable investigation is materially enhanced.

* * *

Turning to the $33 dividend, it served two significant purposes in defending against Ivanhoe's inadequate and coercive tender offer. First, the dividend distributed the heretofore undervalued non-gold assets to all of Newmont's shareholders. In doing so Newmont effectively eliminated the means by which Ivanhoe might have acquired Newmont's gold assets at a substantial discount to the detriment of the other stockholders. Second, the dividend provided the financial impetus needed to persuade Gold Fields to engage in the street sweep. Although Gold Fields had the requisite financing to implement such action independently of the dividend, its board was reluctant to invest the $1.6 billion dollars needed to obtain a majority interest in Newmont.

The resulting standstill agreement also was a reasonable response to the Gold Fields threat. To forestall Gold Fields entry into the open market to purchase a controlling interest to the detriment of Newmont's public shareholders, Newmont obtained the new standstill agreement which restricted Gold Fields' ability to purchase and exercise control of the corporation. Thus, Newmont exchanged the $33 dividend for a revised standstill agreement, which not only limited Gold Fields' ownership to 49.9%, but, significantly, restricted its board membership to 40%. This guaranteed Newmont's continued independence under a board consisting of 40% Gold Fields directors, 40% independent directors and 20% management nominated directors. Further, the 49.9% limit on Gold Fields' stock ownership protected Newmont's public shareholders from being squeezed out by an unbridled majority shareholder.

The final element of the tripartite defensive measure employed against Ivanhoe was the so-called "street sweep". Ivanhoe contends that Newmont and Gold Fields breached their fiduciary duties to the shareholders who sold their stock in that maneuver. Specifically, Ivanhoe claims that the shareholders were wrongfully coerced into selling in the street sweep, and that Gold Fields was privy to material inside information which facilitated the maneuver. Under *Unocal* we must determine whether the use of the street sweep, aided by Newmont, was a reasonable response to the Ivanhoe threat. Viewed in isolation the measure was a Gold Fields defense to protect its own interest in Newmont. However, for the purpose of evaluating the fiduciary duties of Newmont, we view the street sweep as part of Newmont's own comprehensive defensive strategy.

Ivanhoe's claim that the Newmont board supplied Gold Fields with inside information is without merit. The Vice Chancellor found that Gold Fields did not have access to any confidential material information about Newmont. *Ivanhoe Partners*, 533 A.2d at 604. While Newmont had given Gold Fields a financial analysis of the company, the information furnished was obsolete and immaterial.

Ivanhoe's allegation that the street sweep was inequitably coercive is likewise unsupported by the record. In advancing this argument Ivanhoe relies on conclusory form affidavits executed by arbitrageurs who sold in the street sweep, and on a proposed SEC regulation. Several arbitrageurs signed affidavits stating that they were aware of the amended standstill agreement and the street sweep, and that they had no reasonable alternative but to sell Newmont stock. The Vice Chancellor correctly concluded that the affidavits failed to show that, but for the existence of the standstill, the affiants would have tendered to Ivanhoe. Thus, there was a complete failure of proof in that regard. In any event we are not persuaded on this record that a street sweep has the coercive effect claimed by Ivanhoe.

We, therefore, are satisfied that under all the circumstances Newmont's actions in facilitating the street sweep were reasonable. The measure was an essential part of Newmont's defensive plan, which enabled Newmont to maintain its independent status for the benefit of its other stockholders.

* * *

Ivanhoe claims that the Newmont directors breached the duties imposed upon them in *Revlon* by refusing to entertain Ivanhoe's bid. Ivanhoe argues that under *Revlon* the board was charged with securing the highest available price for the company. However, the facts presented here do not implicate this *Revlon* principle.

Revlon applies here only if it was apparent that the sale of Newmont was "inevitable". The record, however, does not support such a finding for two reasons.

First, Newmont was never for sale. During the short period in which these events occurred, the Newmont board held fast to its decision to keep the company independent. * * * Ultimately, this goal was achieved by the standstill agreement and related defensive measures.

Second, there was neither a bidding contest, nor a sale. The only bidder for Newmont was Ivanhoe. Gold Fields was not a bidder, but wished only to protect its already substantial interest in the company. It did so through the street sweep. Thus, the Newmont board did not "sell" the company to Gold Fields. The latter's purchases were from private sellers. While Gold Fields now owns 49.7% of the stock, its representation on the board is only 40% because of the restrictions of the standstill agreement. These facts do not strip the Newmont board of the presumptions of independence and good faith under the business judgment rule.

Even though Newmont's declaration of the dividend facilitated the street sweep, it did not constitute a "sale" of the company by Newmont.

On this record we are satisfied that the fiduciary obligations imposed by *Revlon* to sell a company to the highest bidder are not applicable here. We, therefore, find no merit in plaintiffs' contentions.

* * *

Question

The case is curious on its face because the court held that Newmont Mining had not put itself up for sale and did not have a duty to auction under *Revlon* when the firm had structured a transfer of effective control to Gold Fields. The Delaware Supreme Court, in footnote 35 of its *Mills Acquisition* decision, supra, attempted to explain its *Ivanhoe* holding. Reread the footnote. Why does the restructuring in *Ivanhoe* not amount to a "sale of the firm" when the aborted reorganization in *Mills Acquisition* was a sale?

SHAMROCK HOLDINGS, INC. v. POLAROID CORP.
Court of Chancery of Delaware, 1988.
559 A.2d 257.

Opinion of BERGER, VICE CHANCELLOR.

This case involves an attack upon the validity of an employee stock ownership plan adopted by Polaroid Corporation ("Polaroid") on July 12, 1988.

* * *

On September 9, 1988 an affiliate of Shamrock Holdings, Inc. commenced a $42 per share cash tender offer for all of Polaroid's outstanding common stock. The offer has been extended repeatedly, in part because, as amended, the offer is conditioned upon a final judicial determination invalidating or rescinding the ESOP shares. According to its original Offer to Purchase, if the ESOP shares are not invalidated or rescinded, Shamrock intends to amend the offer by reducing the price to $40 per share, among other things. * * *

Polaroid is a Delaware corporation with its principal place of business in Cambridge, Massachusetts. Prior to the formation of the ESOP, it had approximately 62 million shares of common stock outstanding, which shares have traded at prices ranging from $16.75 to $44.125 during the past three years.

* * *

For the past few years, financial analysts and members of management have recognized Polaroid's potential as a takeover target. Several factors contributed to the company's vulnerability: (1) profits have been down; (2) Polaroid carries a relatively small amount of debt; and (3) Polaroid has a potentially enormous, as yet unliquidated asset—damages from Kodak for patent infringement (Polaroid is seeking more than $6 billion). The company has taken steps to protect itself against the threat of a takeover. In 1986 the board adopted a stockholder rights plan containing "flip-in" and "flip-over" provisions. In addition, the board is authorized to issue "blank check" preferred stock, stockholders are not permitted to take action by consent and they are not permitted to call special meetings.

* * *

Although management and employee representatives had been considering an ESOP for sometime, the regularly scheduled March 29 board meeting was the first time that the directors considered whether one should be created. * * * The board approved a 5% ESOP at its March meeting.

* * *

As of June 16, 1988, Shamrock had acquired slightly less than 5% of Polaroid's outstanding stock.

* * *

Disney memorialized his interest in having a meeting in a letter to Booth [President and CEO of Polaroid] dated June 17, 1988. The letter confirmed the rumor that Shamrock had a substantial investment in Polaroid and explained that Shamrock was interested in having a meeting with Polaroid management "to establish the ground work for a good relationship with the Company."

* * *

From Polaroid's side, the Shamrock letter, received by Booth on June 22, came as a "cold shower."

* * *

The June 24 strategy meeting was attended by Polaroid's legal and investment advisers. In the context of considering the Shamrock letter, the group discussed various defensive strategies including an

ESOP. Tuchman recalls having been told that the board had approved a 5% ESOP and there were general discussions about increasing the size of the ESOP. Tuchman told the group that an ESOP would add to Polaroid's defensive posture, but there was recognition that a potential disadvantage of a larger ESOP would be the uncertainty as to how employees would react to the "give-ups" that would be necessary to fund a larger ESOP.

* * *

On June 26, 1988, two days after the strategy session over the Shamrock letter, the MEC [Management Executive Committee of Polaroid] held a special Sunday morning meeting. The Polaroid officers discussed the "implications" of Shamrock's letter and Booth announced that he wanted a larger ESOP funded in part by the five year seniority increase. Booth apparently was surprised that the MEC (which in April had been unable to agree upon even a 2% pay cut to fund the ESOP) was aggressively pushing a large ESOP. Booth even got to the point where he had to play "devil's advocate" and point out to his senior people that pay cuts would not be an easy thing to sell to the employees. * * * During the course of the discussion, the committee members were advised that an ESOP greater than 18½% would require stockholder approval. Although the committee members were pushing for an ESOP of 20% or more at this meeting, when they learned of this additional requirement, they agreed that 18½% would be the cap on the ESOP. As Booth explained, there was "no question" but that everyone wanted to put together the ESOP quickly because of the Shamrock letter. * * * By working back from 18½%, using current market prices and allowing for a margin of error, the committee arrived at the round figure of $300 million as the size of the ESOP.

Immediately following the MEC meeting, Norwood was assigned the task of determining appropriate benefit exchanges and pay cuts that would add up to $300 million. His handwritten notes of the same date confirm the link between the implementation of the ESOP and Shamrock's expression of interest in Polaroid. For example, Norwood's time table called for the implementation of the ESOP on July 11—two days before the scheduled Shamrock meeting. In addition, under the head "Issues to Resolve," Norwood noted the need for "acceptable, creative option for trustee when 0 or small % is allocated to employees...." * * * Norwood acknowledged that this note was a reference to 8 *Del.C.* § 203 and the need to have ESOP shares allocated to employees in order to allow them to express their opinions with respect to a potential raider.[5]

5. Pursuant to 8 *Del.C.* § 203, an interested stockholder (one owning more than 15% of the company's stock) may not engage in a business combination with the company for three years after becoming an "interested stockholder" unless, among other things, the stockholder acquires at least 85% of the company's stock in the same transaction that resulted in the stockholder becoming an interested stockholder. § 203(a)(2) Stock held by employee stock plans is excluded from the 85% calculation unless the employees have the

By June 29, 1988, it appears that Booth had decided upon some of the funding sources for the $300 million ESOP. He called a meeting with Graney and Pasquarosa that day and told them that the ESOP would be funded with a 5% pay cut, the § 401(k) matching funds, a delayed pay scale change and the profit-sharing retirement contribution. The two employee representatives argued against the 5% pay cut and pointed out the severe financial impact that would have on employees. After Booth made it clear that his decision was final, the employee representatives then suggested that some adjustment be made for the lowest paid employees, who would find a 5% pay cut the most burdensome. In response to this concern, a modification was made so that the lowest paid employees did not receive an immediate pay cut and the second lowest paid employees received a pay cut of only 2½% instead of 5%.

The next regular board of directors meeting was scheduled to be held on July 26, 1988. However, by July 1, 1988, arrangements were being made to hold a special board meeting before mid-July.

* * *

The special board meeting began at approximately 8 a.m. and lasted for about six hours. The meeting was called on less than one week's notice and, as a result, three outside directors were unable to attend and a fourth had to leave the meeting before any votes were taken. Contrary to general practice, the directors received no written materials prior to the special meeting.

* * *

The ESOP was discussed for about two hours and the witnesses agreed that the one issue that was given the most attention was shareholder neutrality and the financial projections comparing compensation and benefit exchanges to the cost of the ESOP borrowings. Although the directors had approved the concept of an ESOP on March 29 and the plan document on June 14, they had never considered an ESOP as large as $300 million and they had never considered funding an ESOP (regardless of its size) with employee pay cuts. The directors did not question the ESOP size chosen by management and they did not ask about or discuss alternative funding sources. Rather, the directors discussed the following ESOP-related matters:

    1. The ESOP funding sources—5% pay cut, delayed pay scale increase, § 401(k) matching funds and profit-sharing retirement plan contribution;

    2. How the $300 million would be obtained—the terms of the $285 million ESOP borrowing and the fact that Polaroid would make an immediate $15 million cash contribution;

    3. The possible dilutive effect of the ESOP if the borrowed funds were not used to repurchase shares;

right to tender their ESOP shares confidentially.

    4. The prospect that employees would make stockholder decisions (such as tendering and voting decisions) from a long-term rather than short-term perspective;

    5. The likelihood that there would be something of a morale problem when the employees were told about the pay cut and the importance of management/employee communications on that subject;

    6. The prospect that the significant stockholder interest being provided by the ESOP would give the employees greater incentive to make the company profitable; and

    7. The need to amend the ESOP plan document to allow semi-annual allocations of shares in order to have stock in the employees' hands before their pay cut took effect.

Other matters relating to the ESOP were not discussed at the board meeting:

    1. The fact that the Futures Group considered it unacceptable to fund the ESOP in part with a pay cut;

    2. The fact that the EC [Employment Committee] strongly opposed the use of a pay cut as a funding source;

    3. The fact that both committees suggested alternative funding sources that would have been considered acceptable;

    4. The fact that the Compensation Task Force, after two years of study, opposed the elimination of the five year seniority increase or any other cut in current pay;

    5. The fact that Polaroid is subject to 8 *Del.C.* § 203 and the likely effect a 14% ESOP would have under that statute; and

    6. The fact that management viewed the ESOP as a defensive measure and considered it important that the ESOP be in place "before a raider surfaces."

* * *

After the ESOP discussions (which included slide presentations on the key elements of the ESOP plan and the financial ramifications of it) the board unanimously adopted resolutions authorizing the implementation of the $300 million ESOP, including: (i) amendments to the plan document, (ii) authorization to issue Polaroid shares, and (iii) authorization to borrow the funds necessary for the ESOP. The directors authorized the repurchase of up to $300 million in common stock on the open market if and when such purchases are deemed advisable.

* * *

The parties debate at length the applicability of the business judgment rule. On the question of whether the directors were fully informed, plaintiffs point out several similarities between this case and two others where our Supreme Court recently struck down board decisions for lack of information. See *Smith v. Van Gorkom, supra;*

Mills Acquisition Co. v. Macmillan, Inc., Del.Supr., 550 A.2d 35 (1988) (Trans.). Here, as in *Van Gorkom,* the meeting was called on short notice and the directors were given no written materials with which to prepare for the meeting. Only two hours were devoted to the ESOP decision and the Polaroid directors did not have the benefit of all information reasonably available to them because management did not provide it to them and the directors did not ask.[10] Plaintiffs say that the Polaroid directors were not only uninformed, as were their counterparts in *Van Gorkom,* but also misinformed, as were the directors in *Macmillan.* According to plaintiffs, Booth actively misled the Polaroid directors by failing to inform them that the EC, MEC, and Compensation Task Force all opposed employee pay cuts.

On the question of whether *Unocal* applies, plaintiffs point to a variety of Polaroid's internal documents evidencing management's view that the ESOP is defensive. They also note the strategy sessions that immediately followed Shamrock's overture, the speed with which Booth thereafter decided upon the size of the ESOP (three times larger than previously discussed with the board) and the great haste to call a special meeting.

Defendants dispute some of plaintiffs' facts and virtually all of the inferences drawn from those facts. In addition, the parties appear to have differing views as to the applicable law. For example, on the question of due care, defendants rely heavily upon the application of the gross negligence standard. There is no question but that the directors did not know all of the relevant facts.[12] However, defendants argue that a board's failure to become fully informed does not take its decision outside of the protection of the business judgment rule unless its lack of information was so extreme as to reflect gross negligence on the part of the directors.

The Polaroid directors were not, as in *Van Gorkom,* uninformed as to the value of their company when the issue before them was a merger proposal. Rather, in the context of deciding upon an ESOP they were, arguably, uninformed as to the formal position of several groups that opposed pay cuts. Of course, all of the directors knew that employees would not be happy with the idea of a pay cut. In short, defendants say that both the importance of the information and the extent of the directors' general knowledge on the subject in this case are far different from the facts in *Van Gorkom.* Defendants distinguish *Macmillan* by the relative unimportance of the information withheld from the board and Booth's lack of financial interest in the transaction he was proposing.

---

10. The two subjects plaintiffs stress in this regard are the defensive aspects of the ESOP (management's perception that the ESOP would provide protection against a takeover and the operation of 8 *Del.C.* § 203) and alternatives to the funding sources and size of ESOP recommended to the board by management. Plaintiffs argue that this information is material to the ESOP decision.

12. It is undisputed that there was no discussion of § 203 and that the directors were never told about the various committees' opposition to pay cuts.

* * *

The duty of care claim and the issues with respect to the applicability of *Unocal* present legal and factual questions for which answers would be offered if necessary to the disposition of this case. However, neither a board's failure to become adequately informed nor its failure to apply a *Unocal* analysis, where such an approach is required, will automatically invalidate the corporate transaction. Under either circumstance, the business judgment rule will not be applied and the transaction at issue will be scrutinized to determine whether it is entirely fair. *See Mills Acquisition Co. v. Macmillan, Inc.*, Del.Supr., 550 A.2d 35 (1988). * * *

There are several factors to consider in evaluating the fairness of the ESOP. The first and most obvious question is whether the ESOP is funded in whole or in part by the company. Even if the ESOP is "shareholder neutral," consideration must be given to: (1) its impact on business operations (i.e., whether it enhances or impairs productivity); (2) its anti-takeover effect; and (3) its dilutive effect. The burden of proof rests with defendants.

The evidence establishes that the ESOP is being funded by the employees rather than the corporation and the stockholders. The ESOP borrowed a total of $300 million (Polaroid borrowed $285 million with a ten year bank loan and $15 million came from Polaroid's cash on hand) and used those funds to purchase 9.7 million newly issued Polaroid shares. According to management's calculations, approximately $45 million is needed to amortize the ESOP loan. Of that amount, approximately $9 million per year is generated by dividends and tax deductions.[14] The remaining $36 million of the annual amortization payment comes from employee exchanges: (1) the 5% pay cut ($19 million based upon 1988 pay levels); (2) 3% reduction in pay scale increases on April 1, 1989 ($11 million); (3) elimination of § 401(k) match ($6 million); and (4) elimination of profit sharing retirement bonus ($2 million). These figures total $38 million or $2 million more than needed to maintain the "shareholder neutrality" of the ESOP.

Moreover, although it was projected that the "income" from these exchanges would be less than $36 million during 1988 and 1989,[15] the total exchanges are projected to grow from $40 million in 1990 to $60 million in 1997. Norwood calculated the present value of the exchanges using two different discount rates and determined that it exceeded the present value of the loan and debt service. Finally, to the extent that the ESOP accomplishes its purpose by improving productiv-

---

14. Polaroid pays annual dividends and the ESOP is structured so that dividends on ESOP shares are used to repay the loan. In addition, the company is allowed to take a tax deduction on dividends paid on ESOP shares.

15. In 1988 the numbers are less than the annual projection because the diversion of funds did not begin until the year was half over. The numbers for 1989 also represent less than a full year of savings because they include an adjustment to the pay scale increase that will not take place until April 1, 1989.

ity, certain of the exchanges will increase and, instead of being shareholder neutral, the ESOP will become shareholder "positive."

Even though the ESOP is not funded by the company, there are other potential costs that must be considered. There was a great deal of testimony (including corroboration from Shamrock witnesses) that ESOPs generally promote better employee morale and productivity. In corporations such as Polaroid, where there is a close identification between employees and the company, the evidence establishes that ESOPs are even more effective as employee motivators. However, this particular ESOP is funded, in part, with a mandatory 5% pay cut and Polaroid had never instituted an across the board pay cut in its fifty year history. Is it reasonable to expect that employees will become more productive or even remain at their pre-ESOP levels when they are being forced to defer a portion of their current income? Various members of management and several directors thought about this and concluded that the Polaroid ESOP would still serve its purpose of enhancing productivity. However, they did not profess any expertise on the subject of ESOPs funded by pay cuts.

On the other hand, there was no direct evidence that the Polaroid ESOP is likely to do anything but improve productivity. Plaintiffs did stress the fact that the employees (and several committees with management representatives) were opposed to a pay cut. This fact suggests that the ESOP would not have been implemented in its present form if the decision were put to a vote of the Polaroid work force. Does that also mean that the ESOP, having been implemented, will not be effective? I think not. Although the ESOP may not be terribly popular, there is simply no evidence that the employees will express their displeasure by cutting back on productivity. They still have jobs which, one must presume, they wish to retain. In addition, they now have Polaroid stock, which will be more valuable if the company shows greater profits. In sum, I am satisfied that the ESOP does not impose a hidden cost in the form of decreased productivity that would make it less than fair to Polaroid and its stockholders.[16]

Although stockholders have no contractual right to receive tender offers or other takeover proposals, * * * it seems appropriate to consider the ESOP's anti-takeover effect as part of an entire fairness evaluation. Approximately 14% of Polaroid's outstanding stock (9.7 million shares) was issued to the ESOP in late July, 1988. A small portion of that stock was then retroactively allocated to the Polaroid employees entitled to participate in the ESOP. Similar allocations will be made twice a year over the next 10 years so that, at the end of 10 years, all 9.7 million shares will have been allocated to the employees' retirement

---

16. ESOPs are widely recognized as an effective means of providing "strong employee incentive toward productivity." *Edelman v. Phillips,* Del.Ch., Civil Action No. 7899, Walsh, V.C., 1985 WL 11534 (February 12, 1985) (slip op. at 16). A recent article *Harvard Business Review* reported on a study of ESOPs and found that, "[t]he data couldn't be clearer: companies do better after setting up ESOPs." DX 152 at 127.

accounts. The ESOP stock becomes available to the employees (or their estates) only upon termination, retirement or death. For the next ten years, dividends earned on the stock allocated to each employee's account will be used to help pay for the stock. Thereafter, dividends will be credited to the employees' accounts. However, as with the stock itself, the dividends will not be available to the employees until they stop working for Polaroid.

The ESOP provides for confidential and "mirrored" voting and tendering. In the case of a tender offer, for example, the ESOP stockholders may direct the trustee to tender those shares allocated to their accounts. The trustee must honor those directions and maintain their confidentiality. In addition, the trustee must tender the same proportion of unallocated shares. Thus, although most of the ESOP shares have not yet been allocated to employees, they nonetheless control 14% of the stock.

There was great controversy, but not very much evidence, on the issue of how the ESOP affects unsolicited takeover attempts. Plaintiffs clearly believe that ESOP stockholders will be friendly to management. Several factors support such a belief. The ESOP shares allocated to each employee's account represent only a small fraction of that employee's annual salary. Thus, if an employee were being asked to choose between a better return on his ESOP investment and the possibility that he will lose his job, it is reasonable to anticipate that the employee will forego the investment opportunity in favor of job security.

An unsolicited tender offer almost inevitably will raise concerns about job security—concerns which are easily heightened during management's daily contact with the employees. Added to this understandable concern about job security is the fact that an ESOP stockholder is unable to "cash in" on his investment. If an acquiror offers a substantial premium in a tender offer, other stockholders might decide to tender with the idea that they will use the cash proceeds either for other investments or for personal items. The ESOP stockholder who decides to tender receives no cash for personal use and cannot control the reinvestment of the proceeds. For this reason, as well, an ESOP stockholder is less likely to tender than a public stockholder.

The provisions of 8 *Del.C.* § 203 are significant in light of the size of this ESOP (14%) and the factors indicating that ESOP stockholders will be disinclined to tender their shares. Under the newly enacted takeover statute, a prospective acquiror is prohibited from engaging in any business combination with the target corporation for three years after becoming an "interested stockholder" unless, among other things, the acquiror obtains at least 85% of the voting stock of the target company in the same transaction that causes it to become an interested stockholder (i.e., a party owning at least 15% of the company's stock). 8 *Del.C.* § 203(a)(2).[17]

[17]. The other exceptions to the three year bar on business combinations require approval by the existing target board [§ 203(a)(1)] or board approval after the

For purposes of the 85% exception, shares held by inside directors and those held by employee stock plans that do not have confidential tendering are not considered outstanding shares. The stock held by the Polaroid ESOP, which does provide for confidentiality, would be included in the 85% calculation under § 203(a)(2). If, as plaintiffs suggest, the ESOP stockholders will side with management and refuse to tender, then neither Shamrock nor any other potential acquiror will be able to satisfy the 85% requirement of § 203(a)(2).

When viewed as a permanent obstacle to any tender offer, plaintiffs argue that the ESOP cannot possibly be a reasonable response under *Unocal* and, implicitly, it cannot be entirely fair. The Shamrock tender offer, although tending to refute the general statement that the ESOP is an obstacle to tender offers, provides evidence that the ESOP diminishes the acquisition value of the public shares. If the ESOP is invalidated, Shamrock is offering to pay $42 per share to all stockholders. With the ESOP in place, Shamrock's offer is for $40 per share.

I find that the anti-takeover aspect of the ESOP does not make it less than fair. Given its confidentiality provisions, it cannot be said that management controls the employees' tendering decisions. The evidence does establish that management has a leg up based upon its easy access to the employees and their likely concern about job security. However, there is no evidence that the ESOP is a "lock-up" or that the leg up it gives management in any way harms the company or its public stockholders. The ESOP may mean that a potential acquiror will have to gain the employees' confidence and support in order to be successful in its takeover effort. However, there has been no showing that such support is or would be impossible to obtain.

In reaching this conclusion, I find it significant that § 203 excludes from the 85% exception ESOPs that do not have confidential tendering provisions but includes an ESOP such as the one adopted by Polaroid. I do not read the statute as automatically blessing any ESOP with confidential tendering. The statute provides guidance in a negative sense. It is a policy statement that ESOPs with confidential tendering are not suspect—they will not necessarily interfere with an acquiror's ability to obtain 85% of the voting stock of a target corporation.

Two remaining aspects of the ESOP are of some concern. Because the ESOP shares were issued by the company instead of being purchased on the market, the public stockholders' interests have been diluted. The $300 million used to purchase the ESOP stock is available to the company for open market repurchases. If a decision were made to repurchase stock and if the market price were the same as that paid by the ESOP, the net result would be no dilution. However, Polaroid is not obligated to repurchase shares and, based upon the trading prices since Shamrock announced its acquisition proposal, Polaroid would be

stock is acquired plus a ⅔ vote of the shares not held by the interest stockholders [§ 203(a)(3)].

unable to repurchase the same number of shares as were issued to the ESOP.

Management's chart indicates a reduction in earnings per share ranging from $.25 to $.09 on projected earnings per share without the ESOP of $1.79–$2.18 for the period from 1988 through 1990. However, those calculations did not include any increase in Polaroid's earnings resulting from the anticipated increase in productivity associated with the ESOP. If, as Polaroid's management and directors apparently believe, the ESOP will result in increased productivity, any dilution caused by the issuance of the ESOP shares should be more than offset by increased earnings.

There is and can be no hard evidence as to what the dilutive effect of the ESOP will be. There may be no dilutive effect, if the company is able to make open market purchases at prices of approximately $30 per share or if the ESOP generates sufficient additional revenues to increase productivity. Assuming neither, the ESOP will cause a reduction in earnings per share of approximately 5%. If the ESOP's only purpose were to help thwart hostile takeovers, I doubt that it would be considered entirely fair where it dilutes the public stockholders' earnings per share. However, the evidence is uncontradicted that ESOPs promote productivity. If the ESOP shares were purchased on the open market, there would be a cost involved in terms of the delay in implementing a large ESOP.[18] On balance, I find that a minimal reduction in earnings per share is fair where, as here, it is necessary in order to promptly implement a large ESOP that is intended to increase corporate earnings.

A related matter is the price at which the shares were sold to the ESOP—$30.875. That price was the mean of the high and low trading prices on July 12, 1988. The stockholder plaintiffs argue that the price paid by the ESOP was unreasonably low. Defendants knew, when they set the ESOP price, that Shamrock had accumulated a significant amount of stock and was interested in meeting with management to discuss its investment. By setting the ESOP price before Shamrock's position was made public, the stockholder plaintiffs argue that defendants favored their employees over the public stockholders.

I find this argument to be without merit. The information known to defendants but not reflected in the public market was not material under controlling Delaware law or, to the extent that it may be any different, federal law. * * * Here, there were no merger discussions, board resolutions, negotiations or the like. Shamrock simply expressed its interest in a "friendly" meeting. If, as I find, Shamrock's overture was not material, it follows that defendants did not act unfairly in setting the ESOP purchase price before there was any public disclosure of Shamrock's position.

* * *

---

18. Under the rules of the New York Stock Exchange, Polaroid would be limited in the number of shares it could repurchase to about 100,000 shares per day.

In reviewing a decision to establish an ESOP it seems that the same strong indicia of fairness is established where an ESOP is fully funded by the employees and where they control the disposition and voting of the ESOP stock. Such an ESOP, as a general rule, would seem to have the elements necessary to commend itself to a wholly independent board of directors. Admittedly, an ESOP structured in this fashion is not necessarily fair, just as a merger price negotiated by an independent committee may not always be upheld.

After considering all of the evidence, including the timing of the ESOP's establishment, its structure and operation, its purposes and likely impact (both as a motivational device and as an anti-takeover device), I am satisfied that the Polaroid ESOP is fundamentally fair. It is essentially stockholder neutral although it does have some dilutive effect. It is structurally fair in its voting and tendering provisions and I do not find either the timing of its implementation or its possible anti-takeover effect objectionable under the facts of this case. * * *

Defendants rushed to put this ESOP in place before Shamrock took any other steps to express its interest in Polaroid. The timing of the meeting, change in allocation provisions and decision to issue treasury shares all had to have been motivated, at least in part, by a desire to add one more obstacle to Shamrock's potential acquisition bid. The fact that the ESOP was partly defensive, however, does not make it unfair. This is a defensive device (assuming it is one) that is designed to and appears likely to add value to the company and all of its stockholders. It does not prevent the stockholders from receiving or considering alternatives. In sum, the plan adopted by the directors, whether adequately considered or not, is fair and should not be invalidated.

* * *

Note

Tax Advantages of ESOPs

FEDERAL INCOME TAX ASPECTS OF CORPORATE FINANCIAL STRUCTURES, STAFF REPORT.

Joint Committee on Taxation 28–31, 50–52 (Jan. 18, 1989).

* * *

An ESOP is a qualified stock bonus plan or a combination stock bonus and money purchase pension plan which is designed to be invested primarily in employer securities and which may be utilized as a technique of corporate finance. Under an ESOP, employer stock is acquired for the benefit of employees. ESOPs are accorded preferential tax treatment under the Code as an incentive for corporations to finance their capital requirements or their transfers of ownership in such a way that employees have an opportunity to gain an equity interest in their employer. Thus, ESOPs are exempt from tax under the rules generally applicable to qualified pension plans, and, subject to statutory limitations, employer contributions to an ESOP are tax deductible. Further, special tax rules apply to ESOPs that are not available to other types of qualified pension plans.

Under the Code and ERISA, ESOPs have the unique ability (unavailable to any other type of qualified pension plan) to borrow from the employer to acquire employer securities, or to acquire employer securities with a loan guaranteed by the employer. This feature makes ESOPs particularly attractive as a technique of corporate finance. An ESOP that borrows funds to purchase employer securities is referred to as a "leveraged" ESOP. In a leveraged ESOP, employer securities are held in a suspense account and are allocated over time as the acquisition loan is repaid.

A leveraged ESOP must meet certain requirements (secs. 409 and 4975). For example, the loan repayment and allocation formula must be pursuant to a specified schedule. In addition, leveraged ESOPs are required to pass through voting rights to plan participants with respect to employer securities allocated to their accounts. If the employer has a registration-type class of securities, then voting rights must be passed through on all issues. If the employer does not have a registration-type class of securities (e.g., in the case of privately held companies), voting rights are required to be passed through to plan participants only on certain major corporate issues, such as mergers and acquisitions. ESOPs are also required to meet certain distribution requirements. Voting rights are not required to be passed through in the case of shares of stock that have not been allocated to participant's accounts.

Under a leveraged ESOP, the employer makes contributions to repay the acquisition loan and to pay interest on the loan. An employer may deduct the full amount of any contribution to a leveraged ESOP that is used by the ESOP to pay interest on a loan to purchase employer securities and may deduct amounts used to repay loan principal in amounts up to 25 percent of payroll costs.

The Code contains other tax incentives applicable to the establishment and use of ESOPs, including the following:

(1) A taxpayer owning qualified securities in an employer corporation may defer recognition of gain on the sale of the securities to an ESOP that holds at least 30 percent of the employer's securities, to the extent the taxpayer reinvests the proceeds in securities of certain domestic corporations (sec. 1042).

(2) A corporate employer may deduct dividends paid on stock held by an ESOP that are paid currently to employees or are used to repay a loan used to acquire employer securities (sec. 404(k)).

(3) A bank, insurance company, regulated investment company, or corporation actively engaged in the business of lending money may exclude from its gross income 50 percent of the interest earned with respect to any loan the proceeds of which are used by an ESOP to purchase employer securities (sec. 133).

A leveraged ESOP can be used by an employer to obtain funds for working capital or plant expansion, or as a means of financing an acquisition of the assets or stock of another corporation, including a leveraged buyout. Use of this financing technique can result in a lower cost of borrowing than would be available if conventional debt or equity financing were used. In a typical transaction, the employer enters into a contract with the ESOP to sell the ESOP a specified number of shares of its stock. The ESOP borrows the funds needed to purchase the shares from a bank or other lender and pays them over to the employer in exchange for the stock.[41] In subsequent years, the employer makes tax-deductible cash contributions to the ESOP in the amount necessary to amortize the loan principal and interest payments thereon.[42]

Because leveraged ESOPs provide a source of cash to the sponsoring corporation, they may be advantageous in a variety of situations. For example, a leveraged ESOP may be used not only to provide the company with working capital but also to finance an acquisition of the assets or stock of another corporation, including a leveraged buyout. In a typical case, a leveraged ESOP maintained by the acquiring corporation or its subsidiary borrows funds in an amount equal to the amount needed to acquire the target corporation. The proceeds of the loan are used to purchase employer securities from the employer. The employer (or the subsidiary) then uses the proceeds of the sale to purchase the stock or assets of the target company. Within statutory limits, the employer's contributions to the leveraged ESOP to enable it to amortize the loan will be deductible. In this manner, the corporation may reduce its after-tax cost of financing the acquisition.

One variation of this leveraged-ESOP financing technique is for the employer to purchase target stock, either directly or through a subsidiary, using funds borrowed from a financial institution or other lender. Once the acquisition has been completed, the newly-acquired subsidiary establishes a leveraged ESOP. The ESOP borrows money and purchases either newly issued stock of the subsidiary (or stock of the subsidiary from the acquiring corporation); the acquiring corporation then uses the proceeds of this sale to pay off the original acquisition loan. The subsidiary makes annual, deductible contributions sufficient to amortize the ESOP loan and pay interest.[43]

---

41. The lender usually requires either that the employer guarantee the loan or that the stock purchased with the loan proceeds be pledged as collateral. Because of the 50–percent interest exclusion available to the lender, it may be able to lend to the ESOP at a lower rate than it lends to its regular customers not utilizing ESOP financing techniques (or other tax-favored financing techniques).

42. Alternatively, the employer may take out the loan itself and sell its stock to the ESOP in exchange for the ESOP's installment note. The employer will make (deductible) contributions to the ESOP in future years that will enable the ESOP to pay off the note. These payments will be used by the employer to repay its lender.

43. If the management and shareholders of the target company cooperate in the acquisition, it is possible that a portion of the proceeds of the sale of target stock by original target shareholders would qualify for tax-free rollover under sec. 1042. Thus, the acquiring corporation and the target shareholders could agree in advance that a portion (enough to qualify the ESOP as a 30–percent shareholder) of their

Recently, leveraged ESOPs have been used in some situations to thwart hostile corporate takeover attempts. The Proctor and Gamble Company has announced plans to add $1 billion to its existing ESOP (thereby giving the ESOP a 20-percent interest in the company's common stock) in a transaction designed to provide substantial tax benefits and to offer a shield against a hostile takeover. The recent establishment of the J.C. Penney Co. ESOP, in which the employees received a 24-percent interest in the company, is widely viewed as an effort to deter a hostile takeover.

By selling stock to an ESOP, a company may make it difficult for a hostile bidder to acquire control, since stock held by an ESOP might be expected to vote to keep the company independent (i.e., to vote against the takeover). Management generally may use proceeds of a sale of stock to an ESOP for any corporate purpose. Moreover, a sale of stock to the ESOP will not necessarily dilute management's control of the company to the same degree as a sale to outside parties. The stock purchased by the corporation for its employees is held in a suspense account and released for allocations to employees' accounts as the acquisition loan is repaid. Prior to the time the acquisition loan is repaid and stock is allocated to employees' accounts, the shares may be voted by plan trustees on the employees' behalf in accordance with the fiduciary standards of the Employee Retirement Income Security Act of 1974. Whether or not the shares are allocated to participants' accounts, in some cases, the shares sold to the ESOP may have more limited voting rights than are granted to shareholders of public companies.

Leveraged ESOPs also have been used to accomplish leveraged buyouts by persons desiring to take a company private. An example of such a transaction is the leveraged buyout of Parsons Corporation by its ESOP. Prior to the buyout, Parsons' stock traded on the New York Stock Exchange. The ESOP originally owned a minority interest in Parsons. Parsons' management initiated the buyout plan pursuant to which the ESOP acquired all other stock of the corporation so that, according to its chairman; William E. Leonard "we could be in control of our own destiny." The $518 million transaction was fully financed by debt.

* * *

The Revenue Reconciliation Act of 1989 reduced substantially the tax advantages of an employee stock ownership plan. The 1989 act imposes several new conditions on a qualified lender's right to a 50 percent interest exclusion. The ESOP must hold more than 50 percent

shares would be purchased by a leveraged ESOP established by the target and the balance by the acquiring corporation. The proceeds of the sale to the ESOP might qualify for tax-free reinvestment under sec. 1042.

of the firm's stock, excluding nonvoting, nonconvertible preferred. The term of the loan cannot exceed fifteen years, and the ESOP participants must be entitled to direct how the firm's stock acquired with the loan and allocated to their accounts is voted. Moreover, under the 1989 act the firm is subject to an excise tax as high as 10 percent of the amount realized if the ESOP disposes of the firm's stock before the stock has been allocated to participant accounts (and the proceeds of the sale are not so allocated) or within three years. Finally, the tax deferral for shareholders selling to an ESOP (which must own 30 percent of the firm's stock) depends on the shareholder having held the securities for at least three years before the sale.

Note
Empirical Data on ESOPs

A report prepared by the Analysis Group, "ESOP's and Corporate Control: Their Effects since the Polaroid Decision," concluded that when a company announces the formation of an employee stock ownership plan amidst takeover rumors, share prices drop an average of about 4.5 percent. The report concluded that when ESOPs transfer control from outside shareholders to management and ESOP beneficiaries, the transfer results in an average price reduction of 5.1 percent. When ESOPs did not effect a significant control shift, stock prices were not affected, except for firms incorporated in Delaware. Delaware firms experienced a slight raise in stock prices on the adoption of an ESOP that did not effect significant control shifts. The authors reasoned that ESOPs were "signals of anticipated takeover activity." Pension Plan Guide (CCH) ¶ 26,046 (1989).

HANSMANN, WHEN DOES WORKER OWNERSHIP WORK? ESOPs, LAW FIRMS, CODETERMINATION AND ECONOMIC DEMOCRACY
99 Yale L.J. 1749, 1811–12 (1990).

The numerous studies of ESOPs that have been undertaken to date, while not conclusive, have failed to present clear evidence of improvements in either worker productivity or firm profitability once tax subsidies are taken into account. And because ESOPs typically do not provide for substantial worker participation in governance, and hence do not (except where the ESOP owns all of the firm's equity) eliminate the conflict of interest between labor and management, they arguably lack most of the other benefits, in addition to improved incentives for productivity, that might accompany full worker ownership. At the same time, ESOPs yield the poor allocation of risk that is among the most serious disadvantages of worker ownership. Consequently, ESOPs are arguably less desirable, in general, than an alternative package consisting of a well-diversified pension fund and a profit-sharing compensation plan—a combination that offers most of the advantages of ESOPs while lacking the serious disadvantage of requiring that the workers contribute equity capital.

This suggests strongly that ESOPs have been adopted principally to gain tax subsidies. And the tax subsidies are very difficult to justify as a matter of policy. This would be true even if ESOPs brought important improvements in efficiency, since firms would then have an incentive to adopt ESOPs even without encouragement from the tax code. Given the doubtful efficiency of ESOPs, there is no apparent justification for the tax subsidies at all. Moreover, these subsidies are quite costly, and increasingly so. * * *

One could, of course, argue that we have yet to experiment meaningfully with an important variation on the ESOP that might make it efficiency-enhancing: passing votes through to workers in those ESOPs that hold sufficient stock to give the workers a meaningful share in control. But that seems unlikely to offer an improvement. Where the ESOP holds less than one hundred percent of the firm's stock, the workers would have to share voting control with non-worker investors of capital, and the resulting conflicts of interest between the two groups would give strong incentives for inefficient decision-making. And even where the ESOP holds all of the firm's voting stock, so that the workers alone would control the firm, the prognosis seems poor from all that has been said here about the apparent costs of worker governance.

Questions

1. If it is economically superior for a firm to have an employee ownership plan, because employees work harder, why do we need to give tax breaks to such firms? Won't they develop on their own due to the competitive advantage over non-employee-owned firms? Why has this not historically been the case?

2. Are ESOPs for the behalf of employees or for the benefit of the financial community? Who benefits in *Shamrock Holdings*? Did the employees support the plan?

The Fiduciary Duty of ESOP or ERISA Trustees Responding to a Tender Offer

The trustees of an employee stock ownership plan, or an employee retirement plan that has firm stock (see chapter 3), are in a difficult position once a bidder makes a hostile tender offer for the firm stock. Can the trustees cede authorities to the plan beneficiaries? If not, what factors can trustees consider in deciding whether to tender? The first question is the subject of the Labor Department opinion letter; the second question is the subject of the Second Circuit opinion and a joint Department of Labor–Department of Treasury release.

LABOR DEPARTMENT OPINION LETTER ON TENDER OFFERS

February 23, 1989, 16 Pension Rep. (BNA) 390
(March 6, 1989).

Dear Mr. [the names were deleted]:

The Department of Labor has responsibility for administration and enforcement of Title I of the Employee Retirement Income Security Act of 1974 (ERISA). Title I establishes standards governing the operation of employee benefit plans such as the ... Stock Equity Plan and the conduct of fiduciaries with respect to such plans.

It has come to our attention that ... Corporation is currently the subject of competing tender offers. In this connection, you, as trustee of the ... Stock Equity Plan (Plan), have certain obligations, pursuant to Title I of ERISA, which govern your conduct with respect to the issue of tendering ... Stock owned by the Plan. We have reviewed the Plan document with respect to this matter and believe it appropriate to specifically inform you of our view of your responsibilities in this and similar situations.[1]

The Plan is an eligible individual account plan which holds employer securities. Article 14 of the Plan specifically permits each participant to direct the tendering of any employer securities allocated to his account. In part, the provisions of Article 14 provide:

> 14.2 Instructions to Trustee. The Trustee may not take any action in response to a tender offer except as otherwise provided in this Article 14. Each Participant may direct the Trustee to sell, offer to sell, exchange or otherwise dispose of the Common Stock allocated to such Participant's Common Stock Account in accordance with the provisions, conditions and terms of such tender offer and the provisions of this Article 14....
>
> 14.3 Trustee Action on Participant Instructions. The Trustee shall sell, offer to sell, exchange or otherwise dispose of the Common Stock allocated to the Participant's Common Stock Account with respect to whom it has received directions to do so under this Article 14 for Participants or as provided in Section 14.6.
>
> 14.4 Action with Respect to Participants Not Instructing the Trustee or Not Issuing Valid Instructions. To the extent to which Participants do not instruct the Trustee or do not issue valid directions to the Trustee to sell, offer to sell, exchange or otherwise dispose of the Common Stock allocated to their Common Stock Accounts, such Participants shall be deemed to have directed the Trustee that such shares remain invested in Common Stock....
>
> 14.6 Treatment of Unallocated Shares. In the case of shares of Common Stock of the Company that are held in the Unallocated Common Stock Account, the Trustee shall sell, offer to sell, exchange or otherwise dispose of only that number of such shares that bears the same ratio to the total of all such shares as the number of shares in the Common Stock Accounts for which the Trustee has received valid instructions from participants to sell, offer to sell, exchange or other-

---

[1]. The principles described below would also apply with regard to participant-directed proxy voting or plan provisions prescribing a method by which the trustee shall vote proxies appurtenant to shares of stock held by the Plan. In this regard, we are including a copy of the Department's letter to ..., dated February 23, 1988, which provides further discussion on the subject of proxy voting.

wise dispose of bears to the total number of shares in the Common Stock Accounts....

Section 3(21) of ERISA provides that the exercise of any authority or control respecting the management or disposition of plan assets is a fiduciary action. Thus, the decision whether to tender employer stock held by a plan with regard to a tender offer for the plan sponsor is a fiduciary act of plan asset management. Because such decision involves plan asset management, section 403(a) requires that plan trustees have the exclusive authority and responsibility for such, unless one of the two exceptions stated in section 403(a) applies.

ERISA section 403(a) provides that trustees have exclusive authority and discretion to manage and control such assets, with two exceptions: (1) when the plan expressly provides that the trustee(s) are subject to the direction of a named fiduciary who is not a trustee, in which case the trustees are subject to proper directions made in accordance with the terms of the plan and not contrary to ERISA, and (2) when the authority to manage, acquire or dispose the assets of the plan is delegated to one or more investment managers pursuant to section 402(c)(3).

It is the position of the Department that a plan may grant a participant the authority to direct trustees with regard to tendering of stock allocated to his own account and the participant would be considered a named fiduciary for the limited purpose of giving such directions. Under section 403(a)(1), the trustee may follow such direction, subject to the direction being both proper and made in accordance with the plan terms, as well as not being contrary to the provisions of ERISA.[2] Thus, insofar as the previously stated Plan provisions provide for such participant direction, you, as Plan trustee, may follow such directions subject to the standards of section 403(a) described above.

DONOVAN v. BIERWIRTH

United States Court of Appeals, Second Circuit, 1982.
680 F.2d 263, cert. denied 459 U.S. 1069, 103 S.Ct. 488, 74 L.Ed.2d 631 (1982).

FRIENDLY, CIRCUIT JUDGE.

This action was brought on October 19, 1981, by the Secretary of Labor (the Secretary) under § 502(e)(1) of the Employee Retirement Income Security Act of 1974 (ERISA), ... against John C. Bierwirth, Robert G. Freese and Carl A. Paladino, Trustees of the Grumman Corporation Pension Plan (the Plan). The action stems from the

---

[2]. Even with respect to shares voted or tendered by participants, the trustee or other designated fiduciary would still be responsible for assuring that the participants receive necessary and accurate information in order to allow them to be fully informed as they consider how to vote or whether to tender. In addition, if participants were subjected to undue pressure in making their decisions, a trustee would be required to ignore such participant directions. A trustee also remains responsible for determining whether a violation of ERISA would occur if participants' directions were followed.

unsuccessful tender offer by LTV Corporation (LTV) in the fall of 1981 for some 70% of the outstanding common stock and convertible securities of Grumman Corporation (Grumman) at $45 per share. At the time of the offer the Plan owned some 525,000 shares of Grumman common stock, which it had acquired in the mid–1970's. As hereafter recounted, the Plan not only declined to tender its stock but purchased an additional 1,158,000 shares at an average price of $38.27 per share, at a total cost of $44,312,380. These acts, the Secretary's complaint alleged, constituted a violation of §§ 404(a) and 406(b) of ERISA.

* * *

[Trustees appeal from entry of a preliminary injunction stopping them from dealing in Grumman securities and appointing a receiver to serve as an "Investment Manager" for Grumman securities owned by the plan.]

* * *

The LTV offer was made on September 24. It was conditioned upon the tender of a minimum of 50.01% of Grumman's common stock and securities representing or convertible into common stock. The withdrawal/proration date was 12:01 A.M. on October 16, 1981; the termination date was 12:01 A.M. on October 23. ...

Although SEC Rule 14e–2, 17 C.F.R. § 240.14e–2, gave the Grumman board 10 business days from the commencement of the offer to communicate its position, if any, the board lost no time in going into action. It met on September 25. By then the LTV offer had caused the price of Grumman stock to rise to a range of $32 \frac{5}{8}$ to $34 \frac{1}{4}$. The board had before it a two page letter of Dillon, Read & Co., Inc., which had served Grumman as investment banker, stating in a conclusory fashion that it was "of the opinion that the offer is inadequate from a financial point of view to holders of the Grumman securities." The letter said this conclusion was based on

> certain information of a business and financial nature regarding Grumman which was either publicly available or furnished to us by Grumman and [on] discussions with the management of Grumman regarding its business and prospects.

The letter made no attempt at quantification of these factors, and no representative of Dillon, Read attended the meeting for questioning, although apparently there were some supporting financial materials available. Defendant Robert G. Freese had also prepared some projections which are not in the record. The board unanimously adopted a resolution to oppose the tender offer, and issued a press release to that effect, saying that the board had concluded that "the offer is inadequate, and not in the best interests of Grumman, its shareholders, employees or the United States."

On September 28 Grumman began the previously mentioned action which was to lead to the injunction of the tender offer. On the same day defendant Bierwirth, Chairman of the Board of Grumman, sent a letter to the company's shareholders seeking their help in defeating the offer. The letter stated:

> We're very optimistic about our chances of defeating the takeover bid. About a third of all shares are held by Grumman's employee investment and pension plans. These plans are managed by Grummanites who will look long and hard at how well their fellow members would be served by selling off Grumman stock. Much of the rest is owned by Grumman people who, I believe, understand their future is worth more than a quick return on a block of shares.

The reasons given for opposing LTV's offer were the inadequacy of the price and others, relating to the pension fund, set forth in the margin.[3] The letter concluded by announcing that "Grumman's management is totally committed to defeating this takeover attempt", and by pleading "If you own Grumman shares, don't sell out to LTV".

On September 30, at the invitation of George Petrilak, President of the Grumman Retirees Club, Bierwirth met with 300 retirees to discuss the LTV offer. An affidavit of Petrilak avers that "there was great concern expressed by the members as to the possible impact of LTV succeeding in their tender offer upon their pensions," and said that "[t]he overwhelming attitude of the retirees was 'what is good for Grumman is good for retirees'". The Club purchased an advertisement appearing in Newsday, a Long Island newspaper, on October 13, headed

> Grumman retirees protect your pension.
> Do not tender your stock to LTV.

Expectably, Bierwirth spent about 90% of his time during the next fortnight in activity directed to opposing the LTV offer.

* * *

[A]t the Plan trustees' meeting, which was held on October 7, Mullan made a ten minute presentation dealing with ERISA, pointing out that the trustees' decisions "as far as the Grumman stock was concerned had to be predicated solely upon the best interests of the participants of the Plan". There was then a general discussion of how the trustees felt about LTV, the Dillon, Read opinion letter, and Freese's five year financial projections for Grumman. Elaborating on the discussion of LTV, Freese mentioned concern about the underfunding of "their pension plan", LTV's highly leveraged debt situation which would be aggravated by the need for borrowing to finance the acquisition of Grumman, contingent liability with respect to environmental problems and a large number of pending lawsuits and alleged SEC violations, all of which was revealed in a recent LTV prospectus.[5]

---

3. There's one other factor to keep in mind: your pension fund. It's Grumman's policy to fully fund its employee pension fund. In contrast, LTV's pension fund right now is underfunded by almost a quarter of a billion dollars. Grumman people could lose if the two funds were to be merged.

5. The prospectus, dated May 28, 1981 was in connection with a public offering of 4,000,000 shares of LTV at $24.50 per share. The syndicate managers were Lehman Brothers Kuhn Loeb Incorporated and

The same information was contained in LTV's annual report and in its other publicly available filings. Freese expressed concern that the assumed rate of return used by LTV's pension plan was higher than that used by other companies and that LTV would have trouble making contributions to their pension plan. Bierwirth testified that the trustees "were aware of" a report about Grumman by Lehman Brothers Kuhn Loeb Inc. (Lehman Brothers). This report, dated July 8, 1981, which recommended purchase of Grumman common stock, then selling at $28 per share, projected a 1981–84 earnings progression of $2.75, $5.00, $6.50 and $7.50, and contained financial analysis supporting the estimates. The report's projection of greater sales was stated to be based primarily on "[i]ndications * * * that [President] Reagan's request [for increased expenditures for military aircraft] will be approved by Congress" and Grumman's "promising diversification into aerospace subcontracting. * * *"

After a half hour's discussion the trustees voted not to tender the 525,000 Grumman shares held by the Plan. According to Bierwirth the trustees "then discussed whether we should take a second step. If we did not want to tender the stock at $45 a share, should we then consider buying additional shares, the market then being in the 30's?" A merit of such a purchase would be in making it more difficult for LTV to gain control of the pension fund. However, "it was also important that a further investment in Grumman shares be the right thing for us to do." "[A] number of fortuitous events had occurred during the summer and early in September which greatly enhanced the outlook for Grumman" and had made Bierwirth "feel earlier that a further investment in Grumman was desirable and should be recommended to the Trustees come this fall." While it had been "very difficult to accumulate substantial positions in Grumman stock", which ordinarily traded at volumes of 20,000 shares a day, the daily volume of half a million shares induced by the LTV offer made it "possible to accumulate a major position in Grumman stock without affecting the price all that much." Bierwirth was then of the view that "probably a majority of the stock would not be tendered" but could not feel confident about it. He recognized that if the LTV tender offer were abandoned, selling by arbitrageurs would push the price down. Following their discussion of these ideas, the trustees concluded that purchases of Grumman stock up to the maximum of 10% of the value of the Plan's assets permitted by § 407(a)(2) of ERISA, 29 U.S.C. § 1107(a)(2), would be prudent.

* * *

The request to the SEC was granted on Friday, October 9. The trustees met briefly on Monday, October 12, and authorized the Plan's purchase of 1,275,000 additional Grumman shares—just short of ERISA's 10% limitation. A press release issued on October 13 stated

Merrill Lynch White Weld Capital Markets Group. On September 24, 1981, the closing price of these shares was $14.75.

that use of the authorization would increase the Plan's ownership of Grumman stock from 3.8% to approximately 8% of the outstanding fully diluted shares. The Plan, acting through Dillon, Read, purchased 958,000 shares at an average price of $38.61 per share on October 12 and an additional 200,000 shares on October 13 at an average price of $36.62, for a total cost of $44,312,380.

On the next day, October 14, as previously indicated, the district court temporarily enjoined the LTV offer, thereby drastically reducing its chances for success. The price of Grumman stock fell on October 15 to a range of $28\tfrac{1}{4}$–$29\tfrac{1}{2}$. After this court affirmed the temporary injunction, the price of Grumman shares was 28–$28\tfrac{3}{4}$; the market value of the newly purchased shares was approximately $32,500,000. As this is written, the price is $26\tfrac{1}{4}$–$26\tfrac{3}{8}$.

* * *

Sections 404(a)(1)(A) and (B) impose three different although overlapping standards. A fiduciary must discharge his duties "solely in the interests of the participants and beneficiaries." He must do this "for the exclusive purpose" of providing benefits to them. And he must comply "with the care, skill, prudence, and diligence under the circumstances then prevailing" of the traditional "prudent man".

The trustees urge that the mandates of § 404(a)(1)(A) and (B) must be interpreted in the light of two other sections of ERISA. One is § 408(c)(3), 29 U.S.C. § 1108(c)(3), which permits the appointment of officers of the sponsoring corporation as trustees. The other is § 407(a)(3), 29 U.S.C. § 1107(a)(3), which, as here applicable, permitted the Plan to acquire Grumman stock having an aggregate fair market value not exceeding 10% of the fair market value of the assets of the Plan. This provision, the trustees point out, was the result of a lengthy debate in which the Department of Labor played an important role.
* * *

* * *

We accept the argument but not the conclusion which appellants seem to think follows from it. Although officers of a corporation who are trustees of its pension plan do not violate their duties as trustees by taking action which, after careful and impartial investigation, they reasonably conclude best to promote the interests of participants and beneficiaries simply because it incidentally benefits the corporation or, indeed, themselves, their decisions must be made with an eye single to the interests of the participants and beneficiaries. This, in turn, imposes a duty on the trustees to avoid placing themselves in a position where their acts as officers or directors of the corporation will prevent their functioning with the complete loyalty to participants demanded of them as trustees of a pension plan.

There is much to be said for the Secretary's argument that * * * the only proper course was for the trustees immediately to resign so that a neutral trustee or trustees could be swiftly appointed to serve for the duration of the tender offer.[8]

* * *

We are not, however, required to go so far in this case. The record contains specific instances of the trustees' failure to observe the high standard of duty placed upon them. Bierwirth and Freese should have been immediately aware of the difficult position which they occupied as a result of having decided as directors some of the same questions they would have to decide as trustees, and should have explored where their duty lay.[10]

* * *

An even more telling point against the trustees is their swift movement from a decision not to tender or sell [15] the shares already in the fund to a decision to invest more than $44,000,000 in the purchase of additional Grumman shares up to the 10% maximum permitted by § 407(a)(2) of ERISA. Their argument is that once they had reasonably decided not to tender the shares already in the fund since success of the offer would run counter to the interests of the beneficiaries, it followed that they should do everything else they lawfully could do to thwart the offer. This, however, should have involved a calculation of the risks and benefits involved. Bierwirth properly conceded that a further investment in Grumman shares had to be "the right thing for us to do." The trustees' consideration of this was woefully inadequate. Although Grumman shares may have seemed attractive when selling in the high 20's, with what appeared a good chance of appreciation, they were not necessarily attractive when, under the impetus of the tender offer, they had risen to the high 30's. Moreover, and even more important, in purchasing additional shares when they did, the trustees were buying into what, from their own point of view, was almost certainly a "no-win" situation. If the LTV offer succeeded, the Plan would be left as a minority stockholder in an LTV-controlled Grumman—a point that seems to have received no consideration. If it failed, as the Plan's purchase of additional 8% of the outstanding Grumman stock made

---

8. It could be said against this that Bierwirth and Freese were fiduciaries for the Grumman stockholders and that if their actions before the trustees' meeting on October 7 met their duties as such, no harm was done by their prejudgment. However, as Justice Frankfurter observed in a famous passage, "to say that a man is a fiduciary only begins analysis; it gives direction to further inquiry. To whom is he a fiduciary? What obligations does he owe as a fiduciary?" The fiduciary obligations of the trustees to the participants and beneficiaries of the plan are those of trustees of an express trust—the highest known to the law. The trustees do not even contend that the quick judgment made at the directors' meeting of September 25 satisfied their obligations under § 404(a)(1)(A) and (B). Whether it satisfied their obligations to Grumman shareholders is not before us.

10. Bierwirth was a law school graduate and had practiced for 3 years.

15. The record does not indicate that sale was even considered, although that course had some attractions. It would have eliminated the possibilities that if the Plan did not tender and the offer succeeded, the Plan might be left as a minority stockholder in an LTV controlled Grumman, and that, if the Plan did tender and the offer succeeded, the Plan might be left with some Grumman stock, because of the 70% maximum in the tender offer.

more likely, the stock was almost certain to sink to its pre-offer level, as the trustees fully appreciated. Given the trustees' views as to the dim future of an LTV-controlled Grumman, it is thus exceedingly difficult to accept Bierwirth's testimony that the purchase of additional shares was justified from an investment standpoint—or even to conclude that the trustees really believed this. Investment considerations dictated a policy of waiting. If LTV's offer were accepted, the trustees would not want more Grumman shares; if it failed, the shares would be obtainable at prices far below what was paid. Mid–October 1981 was thus the worst possible time for the Plan to buy Grumman stock as an investment. It is almost impossible to believe that the trustees did not realize this and that their motive for purchasing the additional shares was for any purpose other than blocking the LTV offer. Moreover, even if we were to make the dubious assumption that a purchase for this purpose would have been permissible despite all the investment risks that it entailed, the trustees should at least have taken all reasonable steps to make sure the purchase was necessary.

* * *

We do not join in all of the district judge's pejorative adjectives concerning the trustees. They were caught in a difficult and unusual situation—apparently, so far as shown in the briefs, one that had not arisen before. We accept that they were honestly convinced that acquisition of Grumman by the debt-ridden LTV would mean a less bright future for Grumman and also that an LTV acquisition posed some special dangers to the participants of the Plan. However, they should have realized that, since their judgment on this score could scarcely be unbiased, at the least they were bound to take every feasible precaution to see that they had carefully considered the other side, to free themselves, if indeed this was humanly possible, from any taint of the quick negative reaction characteristic of targets of hostile tender offers displayed at the September 24 board meeting, and particularly to consider the huge risks attendant on purchasing additional Grumman shares at a price substantially elevated by the tender offer. We need not decide whether even this would have sufficed; perhaps, after the events of late September, resignation was the only proper course. It is enough that, for the reasons we have indicated, as well as others, the district judge was warranted in concluding, on the materials before him, that the trustees had not measured up to the high standards imposed by § 404(a)(1)(A) and (B) of ERISA. How the situation will appear after a trial is a different matter which we cannot now decide.

* * *

At the conclusion of the case the district court concluded that the fund had lost $4.5 million on the purchase of Grumman stock, Ford v. Bierwirth, 636 F.Supp. 540 (E.D.N.Y.1986). LTV eventually filed for bankruptcy, attempting to escape a huge debt to the Pension Benefit

Guaranty Corporation that was the result of a termination of an unfunded deferred benefit plan. See Pension Benefit Guaranty Corp. v. LTV Corp., ___ U.S. ___, 110 S.Ct. 2668, 110 L.Ed.2d 579 (1990). Did the trustees ultimately serve the interests of their beneficiaries?

JOINT DEPARTMENT OF LABOR/DEPARTMENT OF TREASURY STATEMENT OF PENSION INVESTMENTS

January 31, 1989, 16 Pension Rep. (BNA) 215.
(February 6, 1989).

Questions have recently been raised with the Departments of Labor and Treasury as to the duties of pension fund fiduciaries with respect to tender offers including cash offers at premiums above the market and merger proposals. Given the size and growth of private pension fund equity portfolios in the past 15 years, the significant role that they play in the capital markets, and the recent increase in public attention accorded to related pension investment issues, the Departments would like to reiterate the duties of fiduciaries of pension plans covered by the Employee Retirement Income Security Act of 1974 (ERISA) with respect to tender offers and merger proposals.[1]

Assertions have been made because a tender offer represents a premium over the prevailing market price for shares of the target company's stock, the fiduciary responsibility provisions of ERISA require that pension fund fiduciaries automatically tender their shares. This is not the case. ERISA does require that fiduciaries manage plan investments prudently and solely in the interest of plan participants and beneficiaries. It does not, however, mandate that the plan fiduciary automatically tender shares held by the plan to capture the premium over market represented by the tender offer.

The Department of Labor defines prudence under ERISA with reference to what is in the economic best interest of a plan's participants and beneficiaries, in their capacity as participants and beneficiaries of the plan. Therefore, such decisions must be based on what is in the economic interest of the pension plan, recognizing that the pension trust is a separate legal entity designed to provide retirement income. ERISA's prudence rule also requires fiduciaries to make investment decisions, including tender offer decisions, based on the facts and circumstances applicable to a particular plan. Thus, in evaluating a tender offer, a fiduciary would have to evaluate it on its merits. In doing so, among other things, it will be appropriate to weigh

---

1. Under ERISA, every plan is required to provide for a "named fiduciary" who has the authority to control and manage the operation and administration of the plan. This named fiduciary may be a person or persons such as corporate directors and officers who can have other relationships to the plan sponsor (e.g., corporate officers, directors). In acting as a named fiduciary, however, they are not representing the sponsor or any other organization, but rather are subject to provisions of ERISA, including the requirement that they act solely in the interest of plan participants and beneficiaries.

a tender offer against the underlying intrinsic value of the target company, and the likelihood of that value being realized by current management or by a possible subsequent tender offer. It would also be proper to weigh the long-term value of the company against the value presented by the tender offer and the ability to invest the proceeds elsewhere. In making these determinations, the long-term business plan of the target company's management would be relevant. A similar process should lead to the fund's decision to support or oppose a proposed merger.

The Department of Labor has been and will continue to be particularly watchful for attempts by corporate management to utilize the assets of their own plans either as an offensive or defensive tool in battles for corporate control. The Department wishes to reiterate that any such actions would violate both the requirement that pension funds be managed solely in the interest of plan participants and beneficiaries and the prohibited transaction provisions of ERISA.

In conclusion, the Department of Labor will continue to monitor plan fiduciaries, corporate management, and other interested parties to assure they do not violate ERISA's requirements governing pension plans and are aware of the potential liability for any related violations. The Departments are sensitive to the need to ensure that government policies and actions do not prevent the huge pools of capital represented by private pension plans from being invested in manners that will facilitate our continued economic growth, provide corporate accountability, and enhance our nation's competitiveness. We will insist that plan fiduciaries adhere to ERISA's fiduciary standards and prohibited transaction rules. This is essential if we are to assure the credibility of the private pension system and safeguard the benefit security for the millions of Americans who will rely on their private pension benefit during their retirement years.

PARAMOUNT COMMUNICATIONS, INC. v. TIME INC.

Supreme Court of Delaware, 1989.
571 A.2d 1140.

HORSEY, JUSTICE:

Paramount Communications, Inc. ("Paramount") and two other groups of plaintiffs ("Shareholder Plaintiffs"), shareholders of Time Incorporated ("Time"), a Delaware corporation, separately filed suits in the Delaware Court of Chancery seeking a preliminary injunction to halt Time's tender offer for 51% of Warner Communication, Inc.'s ("Warner") outstanding shares at $70 cash per share. * * * On July 21, 1988, Time's board met, with all outside directors present. The meeting's purpose was to consider Time's expansion into the entertainment industry on a global scale. Management presented the board with a profile of various entertainment companies in addition to Warner, including Disney, 20th Century Fox, Universal, and Paramount.

* * *

The board's consensus was that a merger of Time and Warner was feasible, but only if Time controlled the board of the resulting corporation and thereby preserved a management committed to Time's journalistic integrity. To accomplish this goal, the board stressed the importance of carefully defining in advance the corporate governance provisions that would control the resulting entity. Some board members expressed concern over whether such a business combination would place Time "*in play.*" The board discussed the wisdom of adopting further defensive measures to lessen such a possibility.[5]

* * * Time's board had recognized the potential need to pay a premium in the stock ratio in exchange for dictating the governing arrangement of the new Time–Warner. Levin and outside director Finkelstein were the primary proponents of paying a premium to protect the "Time Culture." The board discussed premium rates of 10%, 15% and 20%. Wasserstein also suggested paying a premium for Warner due to Warner's rapid growth rate. The market exchange ratio of Time stock for Warner stock was .38 in favor of Warner. Warner's financial advisors informed its board that any exchange rate over .400 was a fair deal and any exchange rate over .450 was "one hell of a deal." The parties ultimately agreed upon an exchange rate favoring Warner of .465. On that basis, Warner stockholders would have owned approximately 62% of the common stock of Time–Warner.

On March 3, 1989, Time's board, with all but one director in attendance, met and unanimously approved the stock-for-stock merger with Warner. Warner's board likewise approved the merger. The agreement called for Warner to be merged into a wholly-owned Time subsidiary with Warner becoming the surviving corporation. The common stock of Warner would then be converted into common stock of Time at the agreed upon ratio. Thereafter, the name of Time would be changed to Time–Warner, Inc.

The rules of the New York Stock Exchange required that Time's issuance of shares to effectuate the merger be approved by a vote of Time's stockholders. The Delaware General Corporation Law required approval of the merger by a majority of the Warner stockholders. Delaware law did not require any vote by Time stockholders. The Chancellor concluded that the agreement was the product of "an arms-length negotiation between two parties seeking individual advantage through mutual action."

* * *

At its March 3, 1989 meeting, Time's board adopted several defensive tactics. Time entered an automatic share exchange agreement with Warner. Time would receive 17,292,747 shares of Warner's out-

---

5. Time had in place a panoply of defensive devices, including a staggered board, a "poison pill" preferred stock rights plan triggered by an acquisition of 15% of the company, a fifty-day notice period for shareholder motions, and restrictions on shareholders' ability to call a meeting or act by consent.

standing common stock (9.4%) and Warner would receive 7,080,016 shares of Time's outstanding common stock (11.1%). Either party could trigger the exchange. Time sought out and paid for "confidence" letters from various banks with which it did business. In these letters, the banks promised not to finance any third-party attempt to acquire Time. Time argues these agreements served only to preserve the confidential relationship between itself and the banks. The Chancellor found these agreements to be inconsequential and futile attempts to "dry up" money for a hostile takeover. Time also agreed to a "no-shop" clause, preventing Time from considering any other consolidation proposal, thus relinquishing its power to consider other proposals, regardless of their merits. Time did so at Warner's insistence. Warner did not want to be left "on the auction block" for an unfriendly suitor, if Time were to withdraw from the deal.

* * *

Time representatives lauded the lack of debt to the United States Senate and to the President of the United States. Public reaction to the announcement of the merger was positive. Time–Warner would be a media colossus with international scope. The board scheduled the stockholder vote for June 23; and a May 1 record date was set. On May 24, 1989, Time sent out extensive proxy statements to the stockholders regarding the approval vote on the merger. In the meantime, with the merger proceeding without impediment, the special committee had concluded, shortly after its creation, that it was not necessary either to retain independent consultants, legal or financial, or even to meet. Time's board was unanimously in favor of the proposed merger with Warner; and, by the end of May, the Time–Warner merger appeared to be an accomplished fact.

On June 7, 1989, these wishful assumptions were shattered by Paramount's surprising announcement of its all-cash offer to purchase all outstanding shares of Time for $175 per share. The following day, June 8, the trading price of Time's stock rose from $126 to $170 per share. Paramount's offer was said to be "fully negotiable." [8]

Time found Paramount's "fully negotiable" offer to be in fact subject to at least three conditions. First, Time had to terminate its merger agreement and stock exchange agreement with Warner, and remove certain other of its defensive devices, including the redemption of Time's shareholder rights. Second, Paramount had to obtain the required cable franchise transfers from Time in a fashion acceptable to Paramount in its sole discretion. Finally, the offer depended upon a judicial determination that section 203 of the General Corporate Law of Delaware (The Delaware Anti–Takeover Statute) was inapplicable to any Time–Paramount merger. While Paramount's board had been

8. Subsequently, it was established that Paramount's board had decided as early as March 1989 to move to acquire Time. However, Paramount management intentionally delayed publicizing its proposal until Time had mailed to its stockholders its Time–Warner merger proposal along with the required proxy statements.

privately advised that it could take months, perhaps over a year, to forge and consummate the deal, Paramount's board publicly proclaimed its ability to close the offer by July 5, 1989. Paramount executives later conceded that none of its directors believed that July 5th was a realistic date to close the transaction.

* * *

Over the following eight days, Time's board met three times to discuss Paramount's $175 offer. The board viewed Paramount's offer as inadequate and concluded that its proposed merger with Warner was the better course of action. Therefore, the board declined to open any negotiations with Paramount and held steady its course toward a merger with Warner.

In June, Time's board of directors met several times. During the course of their June meetings, Time's outside directors met frequently without management, officers or directors being present. At the request of the outside directors, corporate counsel was present during the board meetings and, from time to time, the management directors were asked to leave the board sessions. During the course of these meetings, Time's financial advisors informed the board that, on an auction basis, Time's per share value was materially higher than Warner's $175 per share offer. After this advice, the board concluded that Paramount's $175 offer was inadequate.

At these June meetings, certain Time directors expressed their concern that Time stockholders would not comprehend the long-term benefits of the Warner merger. Large quantities of Time shares were held by institutional investors. The board feared that even though there appeared to be wide support for the Warner transaction, Paramount's cash premium would be a tempting prospect to these investors. In mid-June, Time sought permission from the New York Stock Exchange to alter its rules and allow the Time–Warner merger to proceed without stockholder approval. Time did so at Warner's insistence. The New York Stock Exchange rejected Time's request on June 15; and on that day, the value of Time stock reached $182 per share.

The following day, June 16, Time's board met to take up Paramount's offer. The board's prevailing belief was that Paramount's bid posed a threat to Time's control of its own destiny and retention of the "Time Culture." Even after Time's financial advisors made another presentation of Paramount and its business attributes, Time's board maintained its position that a combination with Warner offered greater potential for Time. Warner provided Time a much desired production capability and an established international marketing chain. Time's advisors suggested various options, including defensive measures. The board considered and rejected the idea of purchasing Paramount in a "Pac Man" defense. The board considered other defenses, including a recapitalization, the acquisition of another company, and a material change in the present capitalization structure or dividend policy. The board determined to retain its same advisors even in light of the changed circumstances. The board rescinded its agreement to pay its advisors a bonus based on the consummation of the Time–Warner merger and agreed to pay a flat fee for any advice rendered. Finally, Time's board formally rejected Paramount's offer.

At the same meeting, Time's board decided to recast its consolidation with Warner into an outright cash and securities acquisition of Warner by Time; and Time so informed Warner. Time accordingly restructured its proposal to acquire Warner as follows: Time would make an immediate all-cash offer for 51% of Warner's outstanding stock at $70 per share. The remaining 49% would be purchased at some later date for a mixture of cash and securities worth $70 per share. To provide the funds required for its outright acquisition of Warner, Time would assume 7–10 billion dollars worth of debt, thus eliminating one of the principal transaction-related benefits of the original merger agreement. Nine billion dollars of the total purchase price would be allocated to the purchase of Warner's goodwill.

Warner agreed but insisted on certain terms. Warner sought a control premium and guarantees that the governance provisions found in the original merger agreement would remain intact. Warner further sought agreements that Time would not employ its poison pill against Warner and that, unless enjoined, Time would be legally bound to complete the transaction. Time's board agreed to these last measures only at the insistence of Warner. For its part, Time was assured of its ability to extend its efforts into production areas and international markets, all the while maintaining the Time identity and culture. The Chancellor found the initial Time–Warner transaction to have been negotiated at arms length and the restructured Time–Warner transaction to have resulted from Paramount's offer and its expected effect on a Time shareholder vote.

On June 23, 1989, Paramount raised its all-cash offer to buy Time's outstanding stock to $200 per share. Paramount still professed that all aspects of the offer were negotiable. Time's board met on June 26, 1989 and formally rejected Paramount's $200 per share second offer. The board reiterated its belief that, despite the $25 increase, the offer was still inadequate. The Time board maintained that the Warner transaction offered a greater long-term value for the stockholders and, unlike Paramount's offer, did not pose a threat to Time's survival and its "culture." Paramount then filed this action in the Court of Chancery.

* * *

The Court of Chancery posed the pivotal question presented by this case to be: Under what circumstances must a board of directors abandon an in-place plan of corporate development in order to provide its shareholders with the option to elect and realize an immediate control premium? As applied to this case, the question becomes: Did Time's board, having developed a strategic plan of global expansion to be launched through a business combination with Warner, come under a fiduciary duty to jettison its plan and put the corporation's future in the hands of its shareholders?

While we affirm the result reached by the Chancellor, we think it unwise to place undue emphasis upon long-term versus short-term corporate strategy. Two key predicates underpin our analysis. First, Delaware law imposes on a board of directors the duty to manage the business and affairs of the corporation. 8 *Del.C.* § 141(a). This broad mandate includes a conferred authority to set a corporate course of action, including time frame, designed to enhance corporate profitability. Thus, the question of "long-term" versus "short-term" values is largely irrelevant because directors, generally, are obliged to chart a course for a corporation which is in its best interests without regard to a fixed investment horizon. Second, absent a limited set of circumstances as defined under *Revlon,* a board of directors, while always required to act in an informed manner, is not under any *per se* duty to maximize shareholder value in the short term, even in the context of a takeover. In our view, the pivotal question presented by this case is: "Did Time, by entering into the proposed merger with Warner, put itself up for sale?" A resolution of that issue through application of *Revlon* has a significant bearing upon the resolution of the derivative *Unocal* issue.

* * *

Under Delaware law there are, generally speaking and without excluding other possibilities, two circumstances which may implicate *Revlon* duties. The first, and clearer one, is when a corporation initiates an active bidding process seeking to sell itself or to effect a business reorganization involving a clear break-up of the company. *See, e.g., Mills Acquisition Co. v. Macmillan, Inc,* Del.Supr., 559 A.2d 1261 (1988). However, *Revlon* duties may also be triggered where, in response to a bidder's offer, a target abandons its long-term strategy and seeks an alternative transaction involving the breakup of the company. Thus, in *Revlon,* when the board responded to Pantry Pride's offer by contemplating a "bust-up" sale of assets in a leveraged acquisition, we imposed upon the board a duty to maximize immediate shareholder value and an obligation to auction the company fairly. If, however, the board's reaction to a hostile tender offer is found to constitute only a defensive response and not an abandonment of the corporation's continued existence, *Revlon* duties are not triggered, though *Unocal* duties attach. *See, e.g., Ivanhoe Partners v. Newmont Mining Corp.,* Del.Supr., 535 A.2d 1334, 1345 (1987).

The plaintiffs insist that even though the original Time–Warner agreement may not have worked "an objective change of control," the transaction made a "sale" of Time inevitable. Plaintiffs rely on the subjective intent of Time's board of directors and principally upon certain board members' expressions of concern that the Warner transaction *might* be viewed as effectively putting Time up for sale. Plaintiffs argue that the use of a lock-up agreement, a no-shop clause, and so-called "dry-up" agreements prevented shareholders from obtaining a control premium in the immediate future and thus violated *Revlon*.

We agree with the Chancellor that such evidence is entirely insufficient to invoke *Revlon* duties; and we decline to extend *Revlon's* application to corporate transactions simply because they might be construed as putting a corporation either "in play" or "up for sale." * * * The adoption of structural safety devices alone does not trigger *Revlon*. Rather, as the Chancellor stated, such devices are properly subject to a *Unocal* analysis.

Finally, we do not find in Time's recasting of its merger agreement with Warner from a share exchange to a share purchase a basis to conclude that Time had either abandoned its strategic plan or made a sale of Time inevitable. The Chancellor found that although the merged Time–Warner company would be large (with a value approaching approximately $30 billion), recent takeover cases have proven that acquisition of the combined company might nonetheless be possible. * * * The legal consequence is that *Unocal* alone applies to determine whether the business judgment rule attaches to the revised agreement. Plaintiffs' analogy to *Macmillan* thus collapses and plaintiffs' reliance on *Macmillan* is misplaced.

We turn now to plaintiffs' *Unocal* claim. We begin by noting, as did the Chancellor, that our decision does not require us to pass on the wisdom of the board's decision to enter into the original Time–Warner agreement. That is not a court's task. Our task is simply to review the record to determine whether there is sufficient evidence to support the Chancellor's conclusion that the initial Time–Warner agreement was the product of a proper exercise of business judgment. * * *

We have purposely detailed the evidence of the Time board's deliberative approach, beginning in 1983–84, to expand itself. Time's decision in 1988 to combine with Warner was made only after what could be fairly characterized as an exhaustive appraisal of Time's future as a corporation. After concluding in 1983–84 that the corporation must expand to survive, and beyond journalism into entertainment, the board combed the field of available entertainment companies. By 1987 Time had focused upon Warner; by late July 1988 Time's board was convinced that Warner would provide the best "fit" for Time to achieve its strategic objectives. The record attests to the zealousness of Time's executives, fully supported by their directors, in seeing to the preservation of Time's "culture," i.e., its perceived editorial integrity in journalism. We find ample evidence in the record to support the Chancellor's conclusion that the Time board's decision to expand the business of the company through its March 3 merger with Warner was entitled to the protection of the business judgment rule.

* * *

The Chancellor reached a different conclusion in addressing the Time–Warner transaction as revised three months later. He found that the revised agreement was defense-motivated and designed to avoid the potentially disruptive effect that Paramount's offer would have had on consummation of the proposed merger were it put to a shareholder vote. Thus, the court declined to apply the traditional business judgment rule to the revised transaction and instead analyzed the Time board's June 16 decision under *Unocal*. The court ruled that *Unocal* applied to all director actions taken, following receipt of Paramount's hostile tender offer, that were reasonably determined to be defensive. Clearly that was a correct ruling and no party disputes that ruling.

In *Unocal*, we held that before the business judgment rule is applied to a board's adoption of a defensive measure, the burden will lie with the board to prove (a) reasonable grounds for believing that a danger to corporate policy and effectiveness existed; and (b) that the defensive measure adopted was reasonable in relation to the threat posed. *Unocal*, 493 A.2d 946. Directors satisfy the first part of the *Unocal* test by demonstrating good faith and reasonable investigation. We have repeatedly stated that the refusal to entertain an offer may comport with a valid exercise of a board's business judgment.

* * *

Implicit in the plaintiffs' argument is the view that a hostile tender offer can pose only two types of threats: the threat of coercion that results from a two-tier offer promising unequal treatment for nontendering shareholders; and the threat of inadequate value from an all-shares, all-cash offer at a price below what a target board in good faith deems to be the present value of its shares. * * * Since Paramount's offer was all-cash, the only conceivable "threat," plaintiffs argue, was inadequate value. We disapprove of such a narrow and rigid construction of *Unocal*, for the reasons which follow.

Plaintiffs' position represents a fundamental misconception of our standard of review under *Unocal* principally because it would involve the court in substituting its judgment as to what is a "better" deal for that of a corporation's board of directors.

* * *

The usefulness of *Unocal* as an analytical tool is precisely its flexibility in the face of a variety of fact scenarios. *Unocal* is not intended as an abstract standard; neither is it a structured and mechanistic procedure of appraisal. Thus, we have said that directors may consider, when evaluating the threat posed by a takeover bid, the "inadequacy of the price offered, nature and timing of the offer, questions of illegality, the impact on 'constituencies' other than shareholders ... the risk of nonconsummation, and the quality of securities being offered in the exchange." 493 A.2d at 955. The open-ended analysis mandated by *Unocal* is not intended to lead to a simple mathematical exercise: that is, of comparing the discounted value of Time–Warner's expected trading price at some future date with Paramount's offer and determining which is the higher. Indeed, in our view, precepts underlying the business judgment rule militate against a court's engaging in the process of attempting to appraise and evaluate the relative merits of a long-term versus a short-term investment goal for shareholders. To engage in such an exercise is a distortion of the *Unocal* process and, in particular, the application of the second part of *Unocal*'s test, discussed below.

In this case, the Time board reasonably determined that inadequate value was not the only legally cognizable threat that Paramount's all-cash, all-shares offer could present. Time's board concluded that Paramount's eleventh hour offer posed other threats. One concern was that Time shareholders might elect to tender into Paramount's cash offer in ignorance or a mistaken belief of the strategic benefit which a business combination with Warner might produce. Moreover, Time viewed the conditions attached to Paramount's offer as introducing a degree of uncertainty that skewed a comparative analysis. Further, the timing of Paramount's offer to follow issuance of Time's proxy notice was viewed as arguably designed to upset, if not confuse, the Time stockholders' vote. Given this record evidence, we cannot conclude that the Time board's decision of June 6 that Paramount's offer posed a threat to corporate policy and effectiveness was lacking in good faith or dominated by motives of either entrenchment or self-interest.

Paramount also contends that the Time board had not duly investigated Paramount's offer. Therefore, Paramount argues, Time was unable to make an informed decision that the offer posed a threat to Time's corporate policy. Although the Chancellor did not address this issue directly, his findings of fact do detail Time's exploration of the available entertainment companies, including Paramount, before determining that Warner provided the best strategic "fit." In addition, the court found that Time's board rejected Paramount's offer because Paramount did not serve Time's objectives or meet Time's needs. Thus, the record does, in our judgment, demonstrate that Time's board was adequately informed of the potential benefits of a transaction with Paramount. We agree with the Chancellor that the Time board's lengthy pre-June investigation of potential merger candidates, including Paramount, mooted any obligation on Time's part to halt its merger process with Warner to reconsider Paramount. Time's board was under no obligation to negotiate with Paramount. * * *

Time's failure to negotiate cannot be fairly found to have been uninformed. The evidence supporting this finding is materially enhanced by the fact that twelve of Time's sixteen board members were outside independent directors. * * *

We turn to the second part of the *Unocal* analysis. The obvious requisite to determining the reasonableness of a defensive action is a clear identification of the nature of the threat. * * * Paramount argues that, assuming its tender offer posed a threat, Time's response was unreasonable in precluding Time's shareholders from accepting the tender offer or receiving a control premium in the immediately foreseeable future. Once again, the contention stems, we believe, from a fundamental misunderstanding of where the power of corporate governance lies. Delaware law confers the management of the corporate enterprise to the stockholders' duly elected board representatives. 8 Del.C. § 141(a). The fiduciary duty to manage a corporate enterprise includes the selection of a time frame for achievement of corporate goals. That duty may not be delegated to the stockholders. * * * Directors are not obliged to abandon a deliberately conceived corporate plan for a short-term shareholder profit unless there is clearly no basis to sustain the corporate strategy.

* * *

Here, on the record facts, the Chancellor found that Time's responsive action to Paramount's tender offer was not aimed at "cramming down" on its shareholders a management-sponsored alternative, but rather had as its goal the carrying forward of a pre-existing transaction in an altered form.[19] Thus, the response was reasonably related to the threat. The Chancellor noted that the revised agreement and its accompanying safety devices did not preclude Paramount from making an offer for the combined Time–Warner company or from changing the conditions of its offer so as not to make the offer dependent upon the nullification of the Time–Warner agreement. Thus, the response was proportionate. We affirm the Chancellor's rulings as clearly supported by the record. Finally, we note that although Time was required, as a result of Paramount's hostile offer, to incur a heavy debt to finance its acquisition of Warner, that fact alone does not render the board's decision unreasonable so long as the directors could reasonably perceive the debt load not to be so injurious to the corporation as to jeopardize its well being.

* * *

Questions

1. Do *Ivanhoe Partners* and *Paramount Communications* represent a significant retreat from *Van Gorkom* and *Revlon*? What's left of these two earlier cases?

2. When is a target board entitled to refuse to sell to a willing buyer even if the price is generous? Can a board, protected by a poison pill plan or a state antitakeover statute, simply refuse to negotiate, or otherwise discuss terms, with a bidder who has publicly announced that it will pay a premium over market price for a controlling position in the firm? What additional steps could a well-advised board take to buttress its ability to

---

19. The Chancellor cited *Shamrock Holdings, Inc. v. Polaroid Corp.*, Del.Ch., 559 A.2d 257 (1989), as a closely analogous case. In that case, the Court of Chancery upheld, in the face of a takeover bid, the establishment of an employee stock ownership plan that had a significant anti-takeover effect. The Court of Chancery upheld the board's action largely because the ESOP had been adopted *prior* to any contest for control and was reasonably determined to increase productivity and enhance profits. The ESOP did not appear to be primarily a device to affect or secure corporate control.

reject an unwanted offer, even if the offer is generous? Would the board's adoption of a "strategic plan of global expansion" suffice? Or must a board have its own acquisition program under way?

What is the shareholder's only remedy? A proxy fight for control of the board? Given the poison pill plan in place, see problem, supra 523, is a proxy fight feasible?

3. How can a firm recapitalize to deter any bidders from ever making a bid and thereby save the target board from the embarrassment of having to reject a generous bid? What benefits are provided by a large cash dividend to existing shareholders, a large dividend of notes to existing shareholders, an employee stock ownership plan holding 15 percent of the firm's outstanding common shares, or a sale of 15 percent or more of the firm's outstanding common shares to a friendly party (a "white squire") under a standstill agreement? Did the *Paramount Communications* court correctly interpret the *Shamrock* case?

Can a firm nullify the 85 percent exception in section 203 of the Delaware General Corporation Law more easily by placing 15 percent of its outstanding shares in an ESOP or with a white squire? See pages 439–446. Does a standstill agreement cause the stock held by a white squire to be excluded from the 85 percent calculation? What form of ESOP will also be excluded from the 85 percent calculation?

Who must approve recapitalizations that nullify the 85 percent exception of section 203? Must the employees or shareholders approve a defensive ESOP?

4. The value of Time stock, which was trading in the high $180s soon after the Paramount tender offer, tumbled to $135 after the Delaware courts refused to enjoin Time's defenses. Recall that Time's investment bankers had predicted a price of $150 for Time on the eve of its merger with Warner. Does this have any relevance to an evaluation of the soundness of the courts' decisions? Interestingly, Paramount's share price rose two points on the announcement of the Delaware Supreme Court's decision.

In the *Time* litigation who were the big winners? Warner shareholders were to get a control premium in the abandoned merger of 12 percent and were offered a control premium of 56 percent in the tender offer. Five hundred executives of Warner were paid a record total of $677 million in the tender offer for their stock, option, and bonus plans. This is $12 *per share* of Time. The chief executive officer of Warner personally collected $193 million. He also was given options for 1.8 million shares of Time–Warner and a guaranteed salary of $800,000 per year for ten years with bonuses tied to earnings. At the end of ten years he is guaranteed at least $750,000 per year as an adviser for another five years.

5. Does the *Paramount Communications* opinion legitimize single-firm recapitalizations that are designed to fend off unwanted bidders? In Tomczak v. Morton Thiokol, Inc., Fed.Sec.L.Rep. (CCH) ¶ 95,327 (Del.Ch. 1990), Morton Thiokol, after Dow Chemical had disclosed that it had purchased over 8 percent of Morton's outstanding common stock, sold one of its four divisions to Dow in exchange for Dow's Morton stock. The sale

ended Dow's takeover threat. The chancery court, citing *Paramount Communications,* held that the sale did not constitute a sale of the company, nor effect a breakup reorganization that would trigger the *Revlon* duty to auction; rather "the sale [was] consistent with the company's long-term plans." Id. at ¶ 96,586–87.

The Frustrated Bidder's Standing to Sue the Target for Breach of Fiduciary Duty

CITY CAPITAL ASSOCIATES LTD. PARTNERSHIP v. INTERCO, INC.

Court of Chancery of Delaware, 1988.
551 A.2d 787.

ALLEN, CHANCELLOR.

This case, before the court on an application for a preliminary injunction, involves the question whether the directors of Interco Corporation are breaching their fiduciary duties to the stockholders of that company in failing to now redeem certain stock rights originally distributed as part of a defense against unsolicited attempts to take control of the company. In electing to leave Interco's "poison pill" in effect, the board of Interco seeks to defeat a tender offer for all of the shares of Interco for $74 per share cash, extended by plaintiff Cardinal Acquisition Corporation (CCA) ....

* * *

While CCA is a shareholder, it here asserts interests as a buyer, not a seller of stock. The question of a bidder/shareholder's right to enforce fiduciary duties owed to shareholders does not often arise as a practical matter, because there are typically several stockholder class actions that proceed on the same schedule as an action by the bidder.[18] Therefore, to my knowledge, this court has not been required to focus upon either the question whether a bidder may enforce such rights, qua stockholder, or whether a bidder may, at least in some circumstances, have some other state law source of right to enforce duties owed to shareholders.

As the courts are principally concerned with interests of shareholders in actions in which corporate fiduciary duties are tested, and as the interests of the shareholders of Interco in this instance are implicated here to precisely the same extent as they would have been had the pending class action been consolidated with this action, it seems to make little sense for the court, having determined that the board now has a duty to shareholders to redeem the rights, to fail to protect shareholders by not enforcing that duty specifically. Therefore, in this case, I will hold that CCA, as a shareholder, has standing to assert the rights of a shareholder of Interco to require the board to redeem the stock rights in issue. I note that as to that relief, I perceive no conflict

---

18. Here, while a class action complaint purportedly on behalf of Interco shareholders has been filed in this court, it has been inactive so far as the record discloses.

of interest between CCA and other shareholders since its offer is noncoercive.

Question

Is the action brought by a frustrated bidder as a shareholder a direct or a derivative action? Compare Crane Co. v. Harsco Corp., 511 F.Supp. 294, 303 (D.Del.1981), with Tate & Lyle PLC v. Staley Continental, Inc., Fed.Sec. L.Rep. (CCH) ¶ 93,764 (Del.Ch. May 9, 1988). If it is a derivative action, must the frustrated bidder make a demand on the board that it pursue the action on behalf of the firm? See Fed.R.Civ.P. 23.1.

Note

State Constituency Statutes

Just as state antitakeover statutes grew out of fair price and supermajority charter amendments, constituency statutes grew out of charter amendments that authorize boards to consider nonfinancial matters in reviewing acquisition proposals. By mid–1989, 6 percent of our largest 1,440 public firms had adopted such amendments. It was unclear, however, whether such charter provisions were consistent with the traditional definitions of fiduciary duty that were then commonly contained in state corporate codes. State legislatures, in the past eight years, have moved not only to legitimize the charter provisions but also to build on them. At the time of this writing twenty-five states have adopted statutes that redefine the fiduciary obligation of directors.

Statutes in six states—Connecticut, Iowa, Louisiana, Missouri, Oregon, and Tennessee—apply only to change of control contests. Sixteen statutes permit directors to consider the interests of constituencies other than shareholders, typically employees, creditors, suppliers, customers, and communities, among others (a few allow for consideration of the national and state economies); six statutes list shareholders as one of several groups whose interests a board may consider; two statutes stipulate that a board ought not to consider the interests of any one group dominant; and one statute mandates that the board shall consider interests of nonshareholder groups. Please read section 717(b) of the New York Business Corporation Law, section 23–1–35–1 of the Indiana Statutes Annotated, sections 511 and 1721 of the Pennsylvania Business Corporation Law, and section 33–133(e) of the Connecticut General Statutes Law in your statutory supplement. The New York statute is typical of most of the state statutes. The Indiana and Pennsylvania statutes represent a distinct but growing minority of statutes, and the Connecticut is, thankfully, unique. Sections (d) and (g) of the Indiana statute are typical of the genre, but section (f) is novel (apparently the Indiana legislature did not want federal court judges, particularly Judge Posner in the Sixth Circuit [1] to misinterpret the legislature's intentions). The Pennsylvania statute is one of the newest and most complete. Delaware has yet to adopt one of the provisions.

---

1. See, e.g., Dynamics Corp. of America v. CTS Corp., 805 F.2d 705, 708 (7th Cir. 1986) (Indiana courts normally "take their cue from the Delaware courts, which are much more experienced in such matters").

Questions

1. How do the constituency statutes protect a target board's decision not to sell the firm? If a constituency statute applies, when, if ever, will a court enjoin a board's refusal to cooperate with a bidder offering a generous price? Can clever target managers, primarily intent on saving their jobs, create a paper record to hide behind the interests of one of the affected corporate constituencies? Why are corporate managers the primary sponsors of these statutes? Have they suddenly turned beneficent?

Do the statutes authorize and sanctify a target board's adoption, during a pending tender offer from an unwanted bidder, of golden or tin parachutes, of control change restrictions in collective bargaining agreements, or of control change restrictions, all of which effectively block the offer?

2. Assume that well-intentioned directors, anxious to comply with the statutes, are confronted with an acquisition offer. How do they balance the interests of various constituencies without according primacy to shareholder interests? What standards do they use? Is the reallocation of wealth among various corporate constituencies (including the "national economy") a comfortable role for directors, who, after all, are elected by shareholders? Are the statutes an effective way of imposing on corporations goals that transcend traditional business considerations?

3. Some commentators have suggested that the enactment of most corporate constituency statutes does not effect a change in existing law. See, e.g., Hanks, Non-shareholder constituency Statutes: An Ideal Whose Time Should Never Come, 3 Insights Issue No. 3, p. 20 (1989). They argue that the statutes are a codification of the concept that nonshareholder constituencies may be considered provided that the interests of shareholders are not materially affected. Are they correct? See, e.g., the last sentence of section 717(b) of the New York Business Corporation Law.

Can the directors use the statutes to reject an acquisition proposal that would provide a nonrecurring material benefit to shareholders (a 40 percent increase in the value of their shares, for example) to protect the interests of employees? Of what significance is the fact that only 3 percent (or 10 percent or 30 percent) of all current employees may be adversely affected by the acquisition? Of what significance is the fact that the effect on employees is uncertain, because the acquirer has not firmed up its business plan?

4. Who can sue for breaches of fiduciary duty under the statutes? In the acquisition in question 2 above, can the shareholders sue? On what standards? If the firm refused to protect the interests of the employees and approved the offer, can the employees sue? On what standards? If no one can sue successfully, who oversees the judgment of the directors?

5. If Delaware were to adopt such a statute, what would be its effect on the *Van Gorkom, Unocal,* and *Revlon* opinions?

SECTION 3. BUYING OUT THE UNWANTED BIDDER: GREENMAIL PAYMENTS

CHEFF v. MATHES

Supreme Court of Delaware, 1964.
41 Del.Ch. 494, 199 A.2d 548.

CAREY, JUSTICE.

* * *

Holland Furnace Company, a corporation of the State of Delaware, manufactures warm air furnaces, air conditioning equipment, and other home heating equipment. * * * Mr. Cheff had been Holland's Chief Executive Officer since 1933, received an annual salary of $77,400, and personally owned 6,000 shares of the company. He was also a director.

* * *

During the first five months of 1957, the monthly trading volume of Holland's stock on the New York Stock Exchange ranged between 10,300 shares to 24,200 shares. In the last week of June 1957, however, the trading increased to 37,800 shares, with a corresponding increase in the market price. In June of 1957, Mr. Cheff met with Mr. Arnold H. Maremont, who was President of Maremont Automotive Products, Inc. and Chairman of the boards of Motor Products Corporation and Allied Paper Corporation. Mr. Cheff testified, on deposition, that Maremont generally inquired about the feasibility of merger between Motor Products and Holland. Mr. Cheff testified that, in view of the difference in sales practices between the two companies, he informed Mr. Maremont that a merger did not seem feasible. In reply, Mr. Maremont stated that, in the light of Mr. Cheff's decision, he had no further interest in Holland nor did he wish to buy any of the stock of Holland.

None of the members of the board apparently connected the interest of Mr. Maremont with the increased activity of Holland stock. However, Mr. Trenkamp and Mr. Staal, the Treasurer of Holland, unsuccessfully made an informal investigation in order to ascertain the identity of the purchaser or purchasers. The mystery was resolved, however, when Maremont called Ames in July of 1957 to inform the latter that Maremont then owned 55,000 shares of Holland stock. At this juncture, no requests for change in corporate policy were made, and Maremont made no demand to be made a member of the board of Holland.

Ames reported the above information to the board at its July 30, 1957 meeting. Because of the position now occupied by Maremont, the board elected to investigate the financial and business history of Maremont and corporations controlled by him. Apart from the documentary evidence produced by this investigation, which will be considered infra, Staal testified, on deposition, that "leading bank officials" had indicated that Maremont "had been a participant, or had attempted to be, in the liquidation of a number of companies." Staal specifically mentioned only one individual giving such advice, the Vice President of the First National Bank of Chicago. Mr. Cheff testified, at trial, of Maremont's alleged participation in liquidation activities. Mr. Cheff testified that: "Throughout the whole of the Kalamazoo–Battle Creek area, and Detroit too, where I spent considerable time, he is well known and not highly regarded by any stretch." This information was communicated to the board.

On August 23, 1957, at the request of Maremont, a meeting was held between Mr. Maremont and Cheff. At this meeting, Cheff was informed that Motor Products then owned approximately 100,000 shares of Holland stock. Maremont then made a demand that he be named to the board of directors, but Cheff refused to consider it. Since considerable controversy has been generated by Maremont's alleged threat to liquidate the company or substantially alter the sales force of Holland, we believe it desirable to set forth the testimony of Cheff on this point: "Now we have 8500 men, direct employees, so the problem is entirely different. He indicated immediately that he had no interest in that type of distribution, that he didn't think it was modern, that he felt furnaces could be sold as he sold mufflers, through half a dozen salesmen in a wholesale way."

Testimony was introduced by the defendants tending to show that substantial unrest was present among the employees of Holland as a result of the threat of Maremont to seek control of Holland. Thus, Mr. Cheff testified that the field organization was considering leaving in large numbers because of a fear of the consequences of a Maremont acquisition; he further testified that approximately "25 of our key men" were lost as the result of the unrest engendered by the Maremont proposal. Staal, corroborating Cheff's version, stated that a number of branch managers approached him for reassurances that Maremont was not going to be allowed to successfully gain control. Moreover, at approximately this time, the company was furnished with a Dun and Bradstreet report, which indicated the practice of Maremont to achieve quick profits by sales or liquidations of companies acquired by him. The defendants were also supplied with an income statement of Motor Products, Inc., showing a loss of $336,121.00 for the period in 1957.

On August 30, 1957, the board was informed by Cheff of Maremont's demand to be placed upon the board and of Maremont's belief that the retail sales organization of Holland was obsolete. The board was also informed of the results of the investigation by Cheff and Staal. Predicated upon this information, the board authorized the purchase of company stock on the market with corporate funds, ostensibly for use in a stock option plan.

Subsequent to this meeting, substantial numbers of shares were purchased and, in addition, Mrs. Cheff made alternate personal purchases of Holland stock. As a result of purchases by Maremont,

Holland and Mrs. Cheff, the market price rose. On September 13, 1957, Maremont wrote to each of the directors of Holland and requested a broad engineering survey to be made for the benefit of all stockholders. During September, Motor Products released its annual report, which indicated that the investment in Holland was a "special situation" as opposed to the normal policy of placing the funds of Motor Products into "an active company". On September 4th, Maremont proposed to sell his current holdings of Holland to the corporation for $14.00 a share. * * *

Thereafter, Mr. Trenkamp arranged for a meeting with Maremont, which occurred on October 14–15, 1957, in Chicago.

* * * As a result of the meeting, there was a tentative agreement on the part of Motor Products to sell its 155,000 shares at $14.40 per share. On October 23, 1957, at a special meeting of the Holland board, the purchase was considered. * * * The board was also informed that in order for the corporation to finance the purchase, substantial sums would have to be borrowed from commercial lending institutions. A resolution authorizing the purchase of 155,000 shares from Motor Products was adopted by the board. The price paid was in excess of the market price prevailing at the time, and the book value of the stock was approximately $20.00 as compared to approximately $14.00 for the net quick asset value. The transaction was subsequently consummated. The stock option plan mentioned in the minutes has never been implemented. In 1959, Holland stock reached a high of $15.25 a share.

* * *

Under the provisions of 8 Del.C. § 160, a corporation is granted statutory power to purchase and sell shares of its own stock. Such a right, as embodied in the statute, has long been recognized in this State. * * * The charge here is not one of violation of statute, but the allegation is that the true motives behind such purchases were improperly centered upon perpetuation of control.

* * *

To say that the burden of proof is upon the defendants is not to indicate, however, that the directors have the same "self-dealing interest" as is present, for example, when a director sells property to the corporation. The only clear pecuniary interest shown on the record was held by Mr. Cheff, as an executive of the corporation, and Trenkamp, as its attorney. The mere fact that some of the other directors were substantial shareholders does not create a personal pecuniary interest in the decisions made by the board of directors, since all shareholders would presumably share the benefit flowing to the substantial shareholder. * * * Accordingly, these directors other than Trenkamp and Cheff, while called upon to justify their actions, will not be held to the same standard of proof required of those directors having personal and pecuniary interest in the transaction.

* * *

Plaintiffs urge that the sale price was unfair in view of the fact that the price was in excess of that prevailing on the open market. However, as conceded by all parties, a substantial block of stock will normally sell at a higher price than that prevailing on the open market, the increment being attributable to a "control premium". Plaintiffs argue that it is inappropriate to require the defendant corporation to pay a control premium, since control is meaningless to an acquisition by a corporation of its own shares. However, it is elementary that a holder of a substantial number of shares would expect to receive the control premium as part of his selling price, and if the corporation desired to obtain the stock, it is unreasonable to expect that the corporation could avoid paying what any other purchaser would be required to pay for the stock. In any event, the financial expert produced by defendant at trial indicated that the price paid was fair and there was no rebuttal. Ames, the financial man on the board, was strongly of the opinion that the purchase was a good deal for the corporation. The Vice Chancellor made no finding as to the fairness of the price other than to indicate the obvious fact that the market price was increasing as a result of open market purchases by Maremont, Mrs. Cheff and Holland.

The question then presented is whether or not defendants satisfied the burden of proof of showing reasonable grounds to believe a danger to corporate policy and effectiveness existed by the presence of the Maremont stock ownership. It is important to remember that the directors satisfy their burden by showing good faith and reasonable investigation; the directors will not be penalized for an honest mistake of judgment, if the judgment appeared reasonable at the time the decision was made.

* * *

The Vice Chancellor found that there was no substantial evidence of a liquidation posed by Maremont. This holding overlooks an important contention. The fear of the defendants, according to their testimony, was not limited to the possibility of liquidation; it included the alternate possibility of a material change in Holland's sales policies, which the board considered vital to its future success. The *unrebutted* testimony before the court indicated: (1) Maremont had deceived Cheff as to his original intentions, since his open market purchases were contemporaneous with his disclaimer of interest in Holland; (2) Maremont had given Cheff some reason to believe that he intended to eliminate the retail sales force of Holland; (3) Maremont demanded a place on the board; (4) Maremont substantially increased his purchases after having been refused a place on the board; (5) the directors had good reason to believe that unrest among key employees had been engendered by the Maremont threat; (6) the board had received advice from Dun and Bradstreet indicating the past liquidation or quick sale activities of Motor Products; (7) the board had received professional advice from the firm of Merril Lynch, Fenner & Beane, who recommended that the purchase from Motor Products be carried out; (8) the board had received competent advice that the corporation was over-capitalized; (9) Staal and Cheff had made informal personal investigations from contacts in the business and financial community and had reported to the board of the alleged poor reputation of Maremont. The board was within its rights in relying upon that investigation, since 8 Del.C. § 141(f) allows the directors to reasonably rely upon a report provided by corporate officers.

Accordingly, we are of the opinion that the evidence presented in the court below leads inevitably to the conclusion that the board of directors, based upon direct investigation, receipt of professional advice, and personal observations of the contradictory action of Maremont and his explanation of corporate purpose, believed, with justification, that there was a reasonable threat to the continued existence of Holland, or at least existence in its present form, by the plan of Maremont to continue building up his stock holdings.

* * *

Questions

1. Why are target shareholders often angered by greenmail payments?

2. Are target shareholders better or worse off when their firm is empowered to make greenmail payments? Does the possibility of getting greenmail payments affect the incentives of potential bidders? Why do target boards, as part of shark repellent packages of charter amendments, *disable* themselves from making greenmail payments? By mid–1989, 5.6 percent of our largest 1,440 public companies had enacted charter amendments, as part of their shark repellent amendment packages, that discouraged greenmail.

TOMCZAK v. MORTON THIOKOL, INC.
Court of Chancery of Delaware, 1990.
Fed.Sec.L.Rep. ¶ 95,327.

* * *

Opinion of HARTNETT, VICE CHANCELLOR.

In this purported stockholder's derivative action, plaintiffs challenge the sale by defendant Morton Thiokol, Inc. ("Morton Thiokol") of its Texize Household Products Division ("Texize") to defendant, The Dow Chemical Company ("Dow").

* * *

On November 7th and 8th, 1984, Dow purchased additional shares of Morton Thiokol stock, bringing its total ownership of Morton Thiokol to approximately 8.23%. * * *

Despite Dow's statements to the contrary, Morton Thiokol's inside directors recognized the possibility that Dow was in the second stage of a creeping tender offer. Consequently, Morton Thiokol's executive management (not its complete Board of Directors) met again with Goldman Sachs on November 9th or 10th to discuss its options, including selling Texize to Dow in exchange for cash and Dow's shares of Morton Thiokol. Goldman Sachs believed that such a sale would have the dual benefits of *profitably divesting Texize* and removing the threat of a possible creeping tender offer by Dow. On November 11, 1984, Morton Thiokol instructed Goldman Sachs to approach Dow, through Morgan Stanley, to see if Dow was interested in such a deal.

During this critical period, Goldman Sachs conducted a comprehensive analysis, similar to that done in May of 1984, in order to update its prior analysis of Texize, including an evaluation of its operations, financial performance and future projections. The updated analysis was consistent with Goldman Sachs' earlier valuation of Texize, setting an approximate range of values of Texize at $225–250 million. Thus, when Goldman Sachs contacted Morgan Stanley on November 11th regarding Morton Thiokol's proposed transaction, Goldman Sachs suggested that the aggregate consideration should be $250 million for Texize.

While Morgan Stanley was surprised by such a proposal, it nonetheless reviewed it with Dow. Dow's Chairman and CEO, Mr. Oreffice, viewed $250 million as reasonable because Morgan Stanley had valued Texize within a range of $240–320 million. Consequently, Mr. Oreffice authorized Robert Keil, Dow's Chief Financial Officer, to negotiate the deal, if reasonable. Mr. Keil then instructed Morgan Stanley to advise Goldman Sachs that Dow was interested.

* * *

Ultimately, Morgan Stanley and Goldman Sachs agreed in principle to an exchange of Texize for Dow's 1.4 million shares of Mortan Thiokol's stock, plus $131 million in cash, without attributing an express value to the stock. In essence, however, Morton Thiokol paid approximately $85 per share for the Morton Thiokol stock held by Dow. Morton Thiokol and Dow also entered a standstill agreement under which Dow agreed to refrain from purchasing Morton Thiokol's common stock for ten years. When the investment bankers reported back to their respective principals, the management of both Morton Thiokol and Dow agreed to submit the proposal to their respective Boards.

* * *

At the regularly scheduled Morton Thiokol Board meeting on November 15th, the proposed Letter Agreement between Morton Thiokol and Dow was submitted to the Morton Thiokol Board. Two of Morton's outside directors were absent from the meeting. The Board meeting lasted approximately two hours, with about half that time devoted to considering the proposed transaction. Each of the directors received a copy of the proposed Letter Agreement, and the discussion of the proposed deal included presentations from Mr. Locke, Goldman Sachs, and Wachtell Lipton. Mr. Locke stated his reasons for recommending the transaction and the Board discussed: (1) the long-term prospects for Texize; (2) the capability of Texize to effectively compete in the household products industry; (3) the financial impact of the transaction on Morton Thiokol's balance sheet; and (4) the threat of a creeping tender offer by Dow, which the transaction would eliminate.

A Goldman Sachs representative summarized Goldman Sachs' role in the transaction and detailed the terms of the transaction. After answering the directors' questions, the Goldman Sachs representative informed the Morton Thiokol Board of Goldman Sachs' opinion that the transaction was fair. An attorney from Wachtell Lipton also advised the Morton Thiokol Board that a decision approving the transaction would fall within the parameters of their business judgment. A number of the outside directors also allegedly did independent calculations as to the value of Texize and all concluded that $250 million was a good price for Morton Thiokol. The Morton Thiokol Board then voted unanimously to approve the sale of Texize to Dow on the terms set forth in the Letter Agreement and such consistent changes as might be approved by the managements of Morton Thiokol and Dow.

* * *

The sale of a single division, like Texize, is clearly different from other defensive measures, like poison pills (*Moran*) and discriminatory self-tenders (*Unocal*), which are clearly defensive measures with little or no other independent business purposes. From all the facts and circumstances, however, it is clear that Morton Thiokol sold Texize to Dow, at least in part, to remove Dow as a possible takeover threat. It is undisputed that Morton Thiokol's Board feared the possibility that Dow was conducting a creeping tender offer, and that Morton Thiokol instructed its investment banker, Goldman Sachs, to try to negotiate the disputed transaction with Dow's investment banker, Morgan Stanley, just a few days after Dow had increased its stock holdings in Morton Thiokol to 8.23%, and consequently, the *Unocal* standard applies.

In order to receive the protection of the business judgment rule, therefore, the Morton Thiokol directors must satisfy the two prongs of the *Unocal* standard. First, the Morton Board must show that it had "reasonable grounds for believing there was a danger to corporate policy and effectiveness" from Dow. *Unocal,* 493 A.2d at 954–55. The Morton Thiokol Board can satisfy this prong by "showing good faith and reasonable investigation." *Id.* Furthermore, the showing by the directors is materially enhanced where "a majority of the board favoring the proposal consisted of outside independent directors who have acted in accordance with the foregoing standards." *Moran,* 500 A.2d at 1356.

Here, the vote by all outside directors present (with 2 absent), coupled with the advice rendered by the investment banker (Goldman Sachs) and legal counsel (Wachtell Lipton), constitute a *prima facie* showing of good faith and reasonable investigation. * * * With 8 of the 10 Morton Thiokol directors who approved the sale of Texize to Dow being independent, the plaintiffs bear "a heavy burden of overcoming the presumptions thus attaching to the board's decisions." * * * Plaintiffs here have failed to adduce any facts sufficient to overcome this *prima facie* showing by the board of their good faith and reasonable investigation.

The second prong of the *Unocal* standard requires the Morton Thiokol directors to establish that their action was "reasonable in relation to the threat posed." *Unocal,* 493 at 955. Here, the threat perceived by the Morton Board was the possibility of a creeping tender offer by Dow which would avoid or minimize the payment of any premium to the stockholders of Morton Thiokol. See generally *Telvest v. Bradshaw,* 697 F.2d 576, 577 n. 1 (4th Cir.1983) (stating that a "creeping tender offer" is an "acquisition device which avoids or minimizes the control premium which a would-be acquiror is usually required to pay in a conventional tender offer"). Removing this threat by profitably divesting Texize was reasonable for several reasons. First, unlike many defensive actions, the sale of Texize to Dow did not have a direct negative impact on the value of Morton Thiokol. The price received by Morton for Texize was within the range of values placed on Texize by Morton's investment banker, Goldman Sachs, and essentially no premium was paid by Morton Thiokol for the stock it repurchased from Dow. Second, Morton Thiokol's management had informally considered the possible divestiture of Texize since Morton Thiokol's restructuring in 1982, although Morton's management determined that it was not in the company's best interests to actively "shop" Texize. When Dow entered the picture, however, it presented Morton with a good opportunity to divest Texize at a fair price, while at the same time removing a takeover threat. The sale of Texize also gave Morton the opportunity to use some of the cash received in the sale of Texize to purchase Bee Chemical Co., whose specialty chemical business was a better "strategic fit" with Morton's other divisions than was Texize's household products business.

The Morton Thiokol directors have, therefore, met their burden of showing compliance with the "enhanced duties" espoused in *Unocal.* Consequently, Morton Thiokol's decision to sell Texize to Dow is protected from further judicial scrutiny by the presumption of propriety afforded by the business judgment rule, unless plaintiffs can show facts that remove the action of the Board from the protection of the rule.

* * *

Plaintiffs set forth five reasons in support of their broadly stated claim that the Morton Thiokol Board did not act in good faith and was not disinterested. None of them are persuasive. They are: (1) that the Morton directors were opposing a potential takeover regardless of price because of an April 1, 1984 resolution of the Morton Board to remain independent; (2) that Mr. Oreffice concluded that Morton Thiokol "did not want to be taken over no matter what" based on his discussions with Mr. Locke; (3) that Morton Thiokol ordered Goldman Sachs to come up with an offer to sell Texize to Dow for a price that would provide Dow with a "quickie profit"—a price that was based on Goldman Sachs' perception of what Dow would pay, rather than the inherent and fair value of Texize; (4) that Goldman Sachs failed to set a proper price for the Morton Thiokol stock owned by Dow, because Goldman Sachs set a price for the stock at $2 per share higher than Dow would have sold the stock, thus causing the cash component of the transaction to be lower than it otherwise would have been; and (5) that Morton Thiokol had rejected earlier expressions of interest in Texize.

* * *

* * * Plaintiffs instead argued that there is an issue of "whether the Morton directors fulfilled their duties of obtaining the best possible price as mandated by *Revlon, Inc. v. MacAndrews & Forbes Holdings, Inc.,* Del.Supr., 506 A.2d 173 (1986)."

* * *

The sale of Texize to Dow represented the sale of only one of four divisions of Morton Thiokol and did not constitute the sale of the entire company, or even most of the company, nor was Morton seeking to effect a business reorganization involving a clear break-up of the company. Furthermore, the sale of Texize was not a situation where Morton Thiokol, in response to a bidder's offer, abandoned its long-term strategy and sought a transaction involving the break-up of the company. Rather, the Texize transaction was merely the profitable sale of one division of Morton, with the sale being consistent with the company's long-term plans. Consequently, the sale of Texize could not trigger any *Revlon* duties.

* * *

In summary, I find, from the undisputed facts, that Morton Thiokol and the members of its Board of Directors are entitled to summary judgment as a matter of law on all of plaintiffs' claims against them.
* * *

SECTION 4. RIGHTS OF A FRUSTRATED BUYER UNDER A BROKEN ACQUISITION AGREEMENT

Once the board of a selling firm signs an acquisition agreement and the shareholders vote the approval, can the board terminate the deal before the closing? On what grounds?

Please read sections 251(d) and 271(b) of the Delaware General Corporation Law in your statutory supplement. Please reread the *Smith v. Van Gorkom* case in pp. 529–544, supra, and note the court's reference to and discussion of section 251(d).

There is some conflict in the case law over whether a selling firm's board has the power to make binding promises independent of any shareholder ratification. Moreover, assuming a board can make binding promises before a shareholder vote, when does a preliminary agreement become a contract? Finally, if a selling firm breaches a contract in favor of a later-appearing purchaser, can the frustrated buyer sue the successful buyer? The materials below deal with these questions.

JEWEL COS. INC. v. PAY LESS DRUG STORES NORTHWEST, INC.
United States Court of Appeals, Ninth Circuit, 1984.
741 F.2d 1555.

REINHARDT, CIRCUIT JUDGE:

This case arises out of a takeover battle for the acquisition of a publicly traded company, the Pay Less Drug Stores ("Pay Less"). Plaintiff, the Jewel Companies, Inc. ("Jewel") appeals an order granting summary judgment for the defendant, Pay Less Drug Stores Northwest, Inc., ("Northwest").[1] Jewel alleges that Northwest's actions constitute tortious interference with a merger agreement between Pay Less and Jewel.

* * *

Most of the facts material to this appeal are not in dispute. In September 1979, Pay Less retained the investment banking firm of Goldman, Sachs & Co. to locate a merger partner. Jewel, a Chicago-based company engaged primarily in the retail grocery business, was among the companies contacted. On November 9, 1979, Jewel and Pay Less agreed to a tax-free merger in which each outstanding share of Pay Less stock would be exchanged, for .652 shares of Jewel stock. The merger agreement was executed in writing, formally approved by both boards of directors, signed on behalf of each corporation by its respective president, and made public in a press release on November 9, 1979.[2]

The merger agreement included several covenants the meaning of which is in dispute and is central to the issues before us on appeal. Articles 9.9 and 10.5 of the Jewel–Pay Less merger agreement obligated the board of directors of each firm to "use its best efforts to fulfill those conditions ... over which it has control or influence and to consummate the Merger." Pay Less was further obligated under article 9 of the agreement to forbear from the sale or transfer of any of its properties or assets, and from entering into or terminating any contract

---

1. Although they bear similar corporate names because of a common corporate ancestor, Pay Less and Northwest were entirely unrelated companies prior to the events at issue here.

2. At this time Jewel also agreed to purchase the 297,010 shares of Pay Less stock that were held by a foundation that the founder of Pay Less had established. Jewel also entered into a written agreement for an option to purchase an additional 421,486 shares. The option agreement provided that Mrs. Mary C. Skaggs, the widow of Pay Less's founder and the owner of the 421,486 shares, would vote her shares in favor of the Jewel merger, but if the merger were terminated or cancelled, Jewel would nevertheless have the option to purchase her shares for the same .652 exchange ratio offered to other Pay Less shareholders.

other than in the ordinary course of business. The merger agreement further provided that Pay Less could not "agree to, or make any commitment to" effect any sale, transfer, or extraordinary action prohibited in Article 9. Article 7 of the Jewel–Pay Less merger agreement incorporated several prerequisites to closing the transaction. The obligations of both firms to consummate the merger were conditioned upon Pay Less obtaining the affirmative vote of a majority of the outstanding shares of Pay Less stock. The obligation of each firm to close the transaction was also contingent upon Jewel obtaining the required governmental consents.

Northwest had discussed the possibility of a merger with Pay Less several times in the 1970s. When the Jewel–Pay Less merger agreement was publicly announced, Northwest's management considered making a competing bid to acquire Pay Less. Between December 14 and December 28 Northwest purchased approximately 269,000 shares (over 12% of the outstanding shares) of Pay Less stock in open market transactions. Northwest then filed a schedule 13D, as required by the Williams Act, 15 U.S.C. §§ 78m(d)–(e), 78n(d)–(e). Northwest made public its intention to make a competing bid in a press release issued December 31, 1979. At that time Northwest offered $22.50 per share for Pay Less stock. The press release further stated that Northwest intended "to condition its obligation to purchase tendered shares on Pay Less's Board of Directors abandoning the previously announced proposal to merge with a subsidiary of Jewel Companies, Inc."

* * *

The Northwest tender offer was formally commenced on January 17 by the filing of a schedule 14D–1 statement with the Securities and Exchange Commission. At this point the battle for control of Pay Less escalated. * * * On January 29, as a 10% shareholder of Pay Less, Jewel called a shareholders' meeting to take place on March 4 for the purpose of voting on the Jewel–Pay Less merger agreement, thereby hoping to conclude the balloting before Northwest became record owner of the shares tendered.

Northwest increased its tender offer price to $24 per share on February 1 and Pay Less' Board of Directors unanimously recommended that its shareholders accept the Northwest offer. On this date Northwest and Pay Less, through its Board of Directors, entered into an Indemnity and Record Date Agreement which provided in relevant part that:

(1) Northwest would indemnify Pay Less and its directors for any alleged breach of the Jewel Agreement;

(2) February 23, 1980 would be the record date for determining the shareholders eligible to vote on the Jewel proposal. March 1, 1980, or not less than ten New York Stock Exchange trading days following the expiration date of the tender offer in the event that the tender offer were extended, would be the record date for determining the sharehold-

ers entitled to notice of and to vote on the Northwest merger agreement;

(3) if for some reason a majority of the record owners of Pay Less stock did approve the Jewel merger (a theoretical possibility if the mechanics of recording the transfer of shares on the corporate records were not completed by the Jewel record date, set for February 23, 1980), then the Pay Less Board of Directors would nevertheless abandon the Jewel merger pursuant to Cal.Corp.Code § 1105 (West 1977); and,

(4) Northwest and Pay Less would issue a joint press release in which Pay Less would make a recommendation to its shareholders in favor of acceptance of the tender offer, including a statement to the effect that the price offered under the tender offer is significantly more favorable to its shareholders generally than the terms offered under the Jewel Merger Agreement.

Finally, on February 1, the Pay Less Board signed a merger agreement with Northwest. The board sent all of its shareholders a 29-page letter comparing the two merger offers and setting forth the history of the two proposals. Although it unanimously recommended the Northwest offer, Pay Less advised its shareholders that the March 4 meeting to consider the Jewel merger agreement would go forward as scheduled.

By February 25, a majority of Pay Less's shares had been tendered to Northwest and Jewel withdrew its request for a shareholders' meeting. The meeting nevertheless took place as scheduled on March 4. Northwest, by then the majority shareholder, passed a shareholder resolution rejecting the Jewel merger agreement. The Pay Less Board, which had been reconstituted to include a majority of Northwest representatives, terminated the Jewel agreement. On March 7, Jewel tendered the 297,010 shares of Pay Less stock that it had purchased on November 9, 1979 for $15 a share to Northwest for $24 per share.

* * *

Jewel has dropped all of its claims in this suit except for its claim of tortious interference with contract and prospective commercial advantage for which it now requests damages as its sole relief. On August 17, 1981 Northwest moved for summary judgment on the grounds that (a) the Pay Less–Jewel Agreement did not constitute a valid "contract" and (b) Northwest was privileged to "compete" for the acquisition of Jewel notwithstanding the preexisting Jewel agreement.

* * *

The district court rejected plaintiff's claim that defendant Northwest tortiously induced Pay Less to breach its merger agreement with Jewel on the ground, *inter alia,* that the Jewel–Pay Less agreement was not a valid contract. The district court ruled that under California law, a merger agreement entered into by the boards of directors of two corporations has no legal effect prior to shareholder approval.

The view of negotiated merger transactions expressed by the district court is at odds with the provisions of the California Corporate Code. According to the district court's ruling, the board of directors of a corporation may never bind itself in a merger agreement to exert its best efforts to obtain the requisite shareholders' approval or to forbear from entering into a competing arrangement with another firm pending approval or rejection by the shareholders. In so ruling, the district court has circumscribed the role of corporate boards of directors in a manner which contravenes their traditional management function and which is contrary to the law of California.

The California Corporate Code provides in the broadest terms that "the business and affairs of the corporation shall be managed and all corporate powers shall be exercised by or under the direction of the board." Cal.Corp.Code § 300(a) (West Supp.1984). Accordingly, directors routinely exercise their business judgment to determine whether or not to enter into contracts or to embark on new business ventures.

* * *

Far from diminishing the role of the board in negotiated merger transactions, the California Corporate Code confers considerable latitude on the directors. The Code explicitly provides that the board has broad authority to determine whether to merge its firm, to select a merger partner, and to negotiate the terms on which such a transaction is to take place. To this end, section 1101 of the Code specifically states that a merger agreement embodying these decisions must be negotiated and signed by the two boards prior to consummation of the transaction.

Other provisions of California's Corporate Code strongly indicate that merger agreements contemplated by section 1101 are considered binding contracts between the two boards. Section 1200 of the California Corporate Code requires that all "corporate reorganizations," a definition which includes negotiated merger transactions pursuant to Chapter 11 of the Code, must be approved by the board of each corporation which will either acquire or divest itself of property or assets in a non-cash merger. But where consummation of such a transaction requires shareholder approval, the shareholders need only approve "the principal terms of a reorganization." Cal.Corp.Code § 1201(a) (West Supp.1984). Moreover, section 1201(f) further provides that "[A]ny [shareholder] approval required by this section may be given before or after the approval by the board."

We therefore conclude that the California Corporate Code contemplates that the boards of two corporations seeking merger or reorganization under Chapters 11 and 12 of the California Corporate Code may enter into a binding merger agreement governing the conduct of the parties pending submission of the agreement to the shareholders for approval. The critical issue in the appeal before us then becomes whether such a merger agreement can be exclusive, i.e., whether the board may lawfully agree in such a merger agreement to forbear from entering into competing and inconsistent agreements until the shareholders' vote occurs.

* * *

* * * The Corporate Code of California does not adopt the auction model in regulating negotiated acquisitions. To the contrary, California's regulatory scheme for negotiated merger transactions is predicated on the idea that the board of directors of each merging entity will deliberate upon a decision and then negotiate and execute a merger agreement of the type that it, in its business judgment, deems best for the shareholders. *See* California Corporate Code Chapters 11 and 12 (West Supp.1984).

In light of California's statutory scheme preserving the board's traditional management function in the case of corporate control transactions, we see no reason to conclude that the drafters of the Corporate Code intended to deprive a corporate board of the authority to agree to refrain from negotiating or accepting competing offers until the shareholders have considered an initial offer. That there is no statutory intent to prohibit a board from entering an exclusive merger contract can be readily inferred from the provisions of the California Corporate Code relating to merger agreements that we have previously discussed. These provisions reinforce, and in some circumstances, serve to augment the board's basic discretion as authorized in section 300 of that Code. They seem to us to provide for a proper devolution of responsibility in a negotiated merger transaction: Full initial discretion regarding the terms of the agreement lies with the board, the ultimate determination with the shareholders.

The Code's provision for abandonment of a merger by the board is an example of the broad discretion conferred on boards of directors. That section provides that "[t]he board may, in its discretion, abandon a merger, subject to the contractual rights, if any, of third parties, including other constituent corporations, without further approval by the outstanding shares (Section 152), at any time before the merger is effective." California Corporate Code § 1105 (West 1977). The legislative committee report accompanying the latest revision of the California Corporate Code makes it clear that the provision is intended to extend the board's authority to act on behalf of its corporation beyond the time at which the shareholders have considered a transaction. Report of the Assembly Select Committee on the Revision of the California Corporate Code.[10]

10. The Code's abandonment provision further supports the legality of an exclusive merger agreement between two boards because it recognizes that the acquiring party possesses significant legal rights prior to the time the agreement becomes final. The Code does not expressly state whether the term "third parties" is intended to refer to the other party to a merger agreement. However, leading authorities on California Corporate law have interpreted the section as referring particularly to the acquiring party. *See* 1A Ballantine & Sterling, *California Corporate Law* § 257.02[3] ("... the board of directors of the selling corporation may abandon the proposed transaction without further action by the shareholders, subject to the

We do, of course, recognize that a board may not lawfully divest itself of its fiduciary obligations in a contract. * * * However, to permit a board of directors to decide that a proposed merger transaction is in the best interests of its shareholders at a given point in time, and to agree to refrain from entering into competing contracts until the shareholders consider the proposal, does not conflict in any way with the board's fiduciary obligation. * * *

An exclusive board-negotiated merger agreement may confer considerable benefits upon the shareholders of a firm. A potential merger partner may be reluctant to agree to a merger unless it is confident that its offer will not be used by the board simply to trigger an auction for the firm's assets. Therefore, an exclusive merger agreement may be necessary to secure the best offer for the shareholders of a firm.

* * *

* * * An exclusive merger agreement may also be the least costly means of merging the firm. It increases the likelihood that the firm can be merged without expensive litigation or proxy battles.

It is true that in certain situations the shareholders may suffer a lost opportunity as a result of the board's entering into an exclusive merger agreement. As the district court took great pains to point out, subsequent to a contractual commitment unanticipated business opportunities and exigencies of the marketplace may render a proposed merger less desirable than when originally bargained for. But all contracts are formed at a single point in time and are based on the information available at that moment. The pursuit of competitive advantage has never been recognized at law as a sufficient reason to render void, or voidable, an otherwise valid contract, and in our view, it was not the intention of the drafters of California's Corporate Code to make this any less true of negotiated merger agreements. *See Restatement (Second) of Torts,* § 768(2) (1979).

Moreover, in many ways shareholders have more safeguards from market losses in board negotiated transactions than in others. Even after the merger agreement is signed a board may not, consistent with its fiduciary obligations to its shareholders, withhold information regarding a potentially more attractive competing offer. * * *

While the board can bind itself to exert its best efforts to consum-

contractual rights, if any, of third parties. Such third parties would, of course, most importantly be the purchaser whose rights would be governed by the agreement of sale ..."); *See also* California Corporate Code § 1201(f).

The form for a merger agreement included in Deering's California Code Annotated also supports the legality of exclusive merger agreements. The merger agreement form includes an optional covenant stating that "the merger agreement may be abandoned at any time prior to the effective date upon the unanimous agreement of the board." Cal.Corp.Code § 1101 (Deering's 1977). That this covenant was included in the form suggests that merger agreements may be binding and exclusive absent explicit language indicating that the parties intend otherwise.

mate the merger under California law,[11] it can only bind the corporation temporarily, and in limited areas,[12] pending shareholder approval. The shareholders retain the ultimate control over the corporation's assets. They remain free to accept or reject the merger proposal presented by the board, to respond to a merger proposal or tender offer made by another firm subsequent to the board's execution of exclusive merger agreement, or to hold out for a better offer. Given the benefits that may accrue to shareholders from an exclusive merger agreement, we fail to see how such an agreement would compromise their legal rights.

There are, no doubt, advantages to both exclusive and nonexclusive merger agreements. Determination of the best contract for a given transaction will depend on the particular corporations involved, the intentions of their respective boards, and the preferences for risk and return of both the board and the shareholders. Our role is not to pronounce on general matters of corporate strategic planning. It is, however, our duty to point out that the fears expressed by the district court that exclusive merger agreements are anticompetitive and contrary to public policy because they subvert the welfare of shareholders are without merit.

We therefore hold that the district court erred in ruling that a merger agreement between boards of directors is of no legal effect prior to shareholder approval. To the contrary, we hold that under California law a corporate board of directors may lawfully bind itself in a merger agreement to forbear from negotiating or accepting competing offers until the shareholders have had an opportunity to consider the initial proposal.[13]

* * *

NBT BANCORP, INC. v. FLEET/NORSTAR FINANCIAL GROUP, INC.

Supreme Court, Appellate Division, 1990.
159 A.D.2d 902, 553 N.Y.S.2d 864.

MIKOLL, J.

* * *

---

11. It is not necessary for us to delineate the full scope of a board's "best efforts" obligation. See note 13 infra. The term does, however, include at a minimum a duty to act in good faith toward the party to whom it owes a "best efforts" obligation.

12. The board can bind the corporation temporarily with provisions like those included in the Jewel–Pay Less agreement, which essentially require the board of the target firm to refrain from entering any contract outside the ordinary course of business or from altering the corporation's capital structure. Such provisions are intended, essentially, to preserve the status quo until the shareholders consider the offer.

13. We do not decide the question whether upon the unsolicited receipt of a more favorable offer after signing a merger agreement the board still must recommend to its shareholders that they approve the initial proposal.

Plaintiffs sued defendants claiming (1) interference with contractual relations, (2) tortious inducement of breach of contract, and (3) tortious interference with prospective business relations. These causes of action have as their genesis a proposed merger between plaintiff National Bank and Trust Company of Norwich, a wholly owned subsidiary of plaintiff NBT Bancorp, Inc. (hereinafter NBT), and Central National Bank (hereinafter Central).

* * *

The complaint alleged that plaintiffs and Central executed a merger agreement which required approval by the owners of two thirds of the shares of common stock of Central and the Comptroller of the Currency, a division of the United States Treasury Department, before it would take effect. The agreement, *inter alia,* provided that Central's directors would use their best efforts to secure stockholder approval and refrain from soliciting other merger proposals or disseminating nonpublic information.

Plaintiffs alleged that defendants intentionally interfered with the performance of the merger agreement and their relationship with Central. The complaint alleged the following acts in support of plaintiffs' claims: (1) despite knowledge of the merger agreement, defendants intentionally interfered with its performance in that they conspired with Herbert Kling, a dissident director of Central, to oppose the merger by counseling him on how to oppose it, (2) defendants met with Kling and received nonpublic information from him, (3) defendants secretly accumulated 5% of the outstanding stock of NBT which they dumped on the securities market at below-market prices to create the illusion that the value of NBT's stock was less than that ascribed to it by NBT, so as to discredit the merger, (4) defendants sent a letter to Central's Board of Directors (hereinafter the Board) misrepresenting the value of NBT stock based on the below-market sale defendants engineered and accusing Central's individual directors of placing personal interest ahead of that of the stockholders and of acting improperly in reaching the merger agreement, (5) Kling disseminated the letter to local newspapers which carried stories about the merger, including the allegations contained in the letter, (6) economic pressure was used to foment confusion including separate litigation brought by Kling against NBT in Federal court accusing Central's Board of breach of fiduciary duty, (7) within 24 hours of NBT raising its offer, defendants presented an offer on better terms; this was done to persuade Central not to perform its contract with plaintiffs and, as a result, Central adjourned the scheduled shareholders meeting to approve the merger and terminated the agreement, (8) all the acts were done by defendants to secure an economic advantage at plaintiffs' expense, in which efforts defendants were abetted by Kling who violated his duty of loyalty as a director of Central in seeking to abort the merger, (9) as a result, plaintiffs were deprived of the banking business of Central and the profits for the merger, and (10) plaintiffs agreed to accept $150,000 for permitting Central to terminate the merger agreement.

Addressing the dismissal of the complaint, we conclude that the cause of action for inducement of breach of contract was appropriately dismissed. To succeed on this action a plaintiff must prove, *inter alia,* that a defendant intentionally induced the breach of contract. * * * Assuming for the purposes of this motion, as we must, that plaintiffs' allegations are true, * * * the facts alleged are insufficient to find that defendants induced Central to breach the merger agreement. The complaint alleges that Central's directors, including Kling, breached provisions requiring them to use their best efforts to secure shareholder approval and refrain from soliciting new offers or disclosing nonpublic information. It is not alleged, however, that the Board initiated contact with any person or entity in an attempt to secure an acquisition proposal. The only allegation apropos of other offers is that Central entertained defendants' offer which defendants initiated. Regarding the agreement not to disseminate nonpublic information, the complaint did not state that the Board did so or authorized any director, officer, employee or other party to initiate contact for the purpose of obtaining competing proposals.

Allegations that Central breached the merger agreement by adjourning the special shareholders meeting to consider defendants' offer are totally inadequate to support the cause of action for tortious inducement of breach of contract. It would have been a breach of the Board's fiduciary duty to hold the scheduled meeting without allowing time for notice and evaluation of defendants' offer.

* * *

As a matter of law, such action did not contravene Central's agreement to use its best efforts to secure shareholder approval.

The allegation that Central breached the merger agreement through the acts of Kling is also not supported by the complaint. The provision requiring "best efforts" specifically applied to the individual directors, not Central. The provision cannot be interpreted to interfere with a director's fiduciary duties to his company. Kling never supported the merger agreement and he acted independently of the Board in his opposition. There is no allegation in the complaint that his acts were authorized by Central. Thus, the cause of action for intentionally inducing the breach of contract was properly dismissed because the complaint failed to allege that the acts breached the terms thereof. As a final observation on the issue, we have here interference with a prospective contractual relationship which depended on the approval of stockholders. As the Court of Appeals noted in *Guard–Life Corp. v. Parker Hardware Mfg. Corp.,* 50 N.Y.2d 183, 191, 428 N.Y.S.2d 628, 406 N.E.2d 445, "greater protection is accorded an interest in an existing contract (as to which respect for individual contract rights outweighs the public benefit to be derived from unfettered competition) than to the less substantive, more speculative interest in a prospective relationship (as to which liability will be imposed only on proof of more culpable conduct on the part of the interferer)".

Plaintiffs' cause of action alleging tortious interference with their prospective business relations was, however, improperly dismissed by Supreme Court. Plaintiffs pleaded facts from which it could be concluded that defendants used unlawful means to injure plaintiffs. * * *

Plaintiffs asserted that defendants misrepresented the value of their stock to Central and "dumped" the stock at a price below market although they were informed by their broker that they could obtain a higher price. This accusation, accepted for purposes of the motion as true, supports the conclusion that defendants engaged in unlawful manipulation of stock prices in violation of section 17(A) of the Securities Act of 1933 and section 10(b) of the Securities Exchange Act of 1934. * * *

The complaint also alleged that the disputed stock sale occurred on the day before the merger document was to be signed. The price at which defendants sold the stock was the price which they represented to Central was its true fair market value. These actions indicate that there was a plan to influence Central to terminate the merger agreement. Further, the complaint also alleged that plaintiffs sustained special damages as a result of these actions. It is important to note that we do not have before us a motion for summary judgment but for dismissal for failure to allege a cause of action. This court should not, therefore, decide what inferences would be drawn from the facts pleaded but leave that for the trier of facts to resolve after the presentation of the evidence. Thus, plaintiffs' pleadings set forth a cause of action for tortious interference with prospective business relations.

Next, we affirm Supreme Court's dismissal of plaintiffs' cause of action for tortious interference with contractual relations. To plead a cause of action for intentional interference with contractual relations and/or for intentional and improper interference with the performance of a contract under New York law, the pleader is required to allege a breach of the contract, * * * which plaintiffs have failed to do in this case. * * *

As to defendants' assertion that plaintiffs' acceptance of Central's offer of $150,000 to terminate the merger agreement constituted a waiver of plaintiffs' claims in this action, we find this argument unpersuasive. There is no showing that any such waiver occurred in the record.

* * *

GLASS, MOLDERS, POTTERY, PLASTICS AND ALLIED WORKERS INTERN. UNION v. WICKES COMPANIES, INC., 243 N.J.Super. 44, 578 A.2d 402 (Law Div.1990): [Wickes attempted to take over Owens Corning Fiberglass and failed, after Owens adopted defensive restructuring measures. The restructuring led to job losses. The workers sued Wickes for tortious interference with prospective economic advantage and negligence. Judge Drozdowski of the Superior Court of New Jersey denied a motion to dismiss. The court stated that plaintiffs had a "protectible right" in the "reasonable quantifiable economic advantage and benefit in their jobs, salary and benefits" that gave rise to "some reasonable expectation of economic advantages." The court noted that the complaint alleged intentional interference without justification or excuse by pleading that Wickes "intentionally violated federal laws and regulations in making certain purchases of [Owens] stock without the required reporting and waiting; that this intentional and illegal process was taken with the knowledge of plaintiff's relationship and interest with [Owens]; and that this intentional illicit process would certainly cause harm to the existing and future economic advantage" of plaintiffs.]

TEXACO, INC. v. PENNZOIL, CO.

Court of Appeals of Texas, 1987.
729 S.W.2d 768, writ of error refused 748 S.W.2d 631 (Tex.1988), cert. dismissed 485 U.S. 994, 108 S.Ct. 1305, 99 L.Ed.2d 686 (1988).

WARREN, JUSTICE.

This is an appeal from a judgment awarding Pennzoil damages for Texaco's tortious interference with a contract between Pennzoil and the "Getty entities" (Getty Oil Company, the Sarah C. Getty Trust, and the J. Paul Getty Museum).

The jury found, among other things, that:

(1) At the end of a board meeting on January 3, 1984, the Getty entities intended to bind themselves to an agreement providing for the purchase of Getty Oil stock, whereby the Sarah C. Getty Trust would own 4/7ths of the stock and Pennzoil the remaining 3/7ths; and providing for a division of Getty Oil's assets, according to their respective ownership if the Trust and Pennzoil were unable to agree on a restructuring of Getty Oil by December 31, 1984;

(2) Texaco knowingly interfered with the agreement between Pennzoil and the Getty entities;

(3) As a result of Texaco's interference, Pennzoil suffered damages of $7.53 billion;

(4) Texaco's actions were intentional, willful, and in wanton disregard of Pennzoil's rights; and,

(5) Pennzoil was entitled to punitive damages of $3 billion.

* * *

Though many facts are disputed, the parties' main conflicts are over the inferences to be drawn from, and the legal significance of, these facts. There is evidence that for several months in late 1983,

Pennzoil had followed with interest the well-publicized dissension between the board of directors of Getty Oil Company and Gordon Getty, who was a director of Getty Oil and also the owner, as trustee, of approximately 40.2% of the outstanding shares of Getty Oil. On December 28, 1983, Pennzoil announced an unsolicited, public tender offer for 16 million shares of Getty Oil at $100 each.

Soon afterwards, Pennzoil contacted both Gordon Getty and a representative of the J. Paul Getty Museum, which held approximately 11.8% of the shares of Getty Oil, to discuss the tender offer and the possible purchase of Getty Oil. In the first two days of January 1984, a "Memorandum of Agreement" was drafted to reflect the terms that had been reached in conversations between representatives of Pennzoil, Gordon Getty, and the Museum.

Under the plan set out in the Memorandum of Agreement, Pennzoil and the Trust (with Gordon Getty as trustee) were to become partners on a $3/7$ths to $4/7$ths basis respectively, in owning and operating Getty Oil. Gordon Getty was to become chairman of the board, and Hugh Liedtke, the chief executive officer of Pennzoil, was to become chief executive officer of the new company.

The Memorandum of Agreement further provided that the Museum was to receive $110 per share for its 11.8% ownership, and that all other outstanding public shares were to be cashed in by the company at $110 per share. Pennzoil was given an option to buy an additional 8 million shares to achieve the desired ownership ratio. The plan also provided that Pennzoil and the Trust were to try in good faith to agree upon a plan to restructure Getty Oil within a year, but if they could not reach an agreement, the assets of Getty Oil were to be divided between them, $3/7$ths to Pennzoil and $4/7$ths to the Trust.

The Memorandum of Agreement stated that it was subject to approval of the board of Getty Oil, and it was to expire by its own terms if not approved at the board meeting that was to begin on January 2. Pennzoil's CEO, Liedtke, and Gordon Getty, for the Trust, signed the Memorandum of Agreement before the Getty Oil board meeting on January 2, and Harold Williams, the president of the Museum, signed it shortly after the board meeting began. Thus, before it was submitted to the Getty Oil board, the Memorandum of Agreement had been executed by parties who together controlled a majority of the outstanding shares of Getty Oil.

The Memorandum of Agreement was then presented to the Getty Oil board, which had previously held discussions on how the company should respond to Pennzoil's public tender offer. A self-tender by the company to shareholders at $110 per share had been proposed to defeat Pennzoil's tender offer at $100 per share, but no consensus was reached.

The board voted to reject recommending Pennzoil's tender offer to Getty's shareholders, then later also rejected the Memorandum of Agreement price of $110 per share as too low. Before recessing at 3 a.m., the board decided to make a counter-proposal to Pennzoil of $110 per share plus a $10 debenture. Pennzoil's investment banker reacted to this price negatively. On the morning of January 3, Getty Oil's investment banker, Geoffrey Boisi, began calling other companies, seeking a higher bid than Pennzoil's for the Getty Oil shares.

When the board reconvened at 3 p.m. on January 3, a revised Pennzoil proposal was presented, offering $110 per share plus a $3 "stub" that was to be paid after the sale of a Getty Oil subsidiary ("ERC"), from the excess proceeds over $1 billion. Each shareholder was to receive a pro rata share of these excess proceeds, but in any case, a minimum of $3 per share at the end of five years. During the meeting, Boisi briefly informed the board of the status of his inquiries of other companies that might be interested in bidding for the company. He reported some preliminary indications of interest, but no definite bid yet.

The Museum's lawyer told the board that, based on his discussions with Pennzoil, he believed that if the board went back "firm" with an offer of $110 plus a $5 stub, Pennzoil would accept it. After a recess, the Museum's president (also a director of Getty Oil) moved that the Getty board should accept Pennzoil's proposal provided that the stub be raised to $5, and the board voted 15 to 1 to approve this counter-proposal to Pennzoil. The board then voted themselves and Getty's officers and advisors indemnity for any liability arising from the events of the past few months. Additionally, the board authorized its executive compensation committee to give "golden parachutes" (generous termination benefits) to the top executives whose positions "were likely to be affected" by the change in management. There was evidence that during another brief recess of the board meeting, the counter-offer of $110 plus a $5 stub was presented to and accepted by Pennzoil. After Pennzoil's acceptance was conveyed to the Getty board, the meeting was adjourned, and most board members left town for their respective homes.

That evening, the lawyers and public relations staff of Getty Oil and the Museum drafted a press release describing the transaction between Pennzoil and the Getty entities. The press release, announcing an agreement in principle on the terms of the Memorandum of Agreement but with a price of $110 plus a $5 stub, was issued on Getty Oil letterhead the next morning, January 4, and later that day, Pennzoil issued an identical press release.

On January 4, Boisi continued to contact other companies, looking for a higher price than Pennzoil had offered. After talking briefly with Boisi, Texaco management called several meetings with its in-house financial planning group, which over the course of the day studied and reported to management on the value of Getty Oil, the Pennzoil offer terms, and a feasible price range at which Getty might be acquired. Later in the day, Texaco hired an investment banker, First Boston, to represent it with respect to a possible acquisition of Getty Oil. Meanwhile, also on January 4, Pennzoil's lawyers were working on a draft of a formal "transaction agreement" that described the transaction in more detail than the outline of terms contained in the Memorandum of Agreement and press release.

On January 5, the Wall Street Journal reported on an agreement reached between Pennzoil and the Getty entities, describing essentially the terms contained in the Memorandum of Agreement. The Pennzoil board met to ratify the actions of its officers in negotiating an agreement with the Getty entities, and Pennzoil's attorneys periodically attempted to contact the other parties' advisors and attorneys to continue work on the transaction agreement.

The board of Texaco also met on January 5, authorizing its officers to make an offer for 100% of Getty Oil and to take any necessary action in connection therewith. Texaco first contacted the Museum's lawyer, Lipton, and arranged a meeting to discuss the sale of the Museum's shares of Getty Oil to Texaco. Lipton instructed his associate, on her way to the meeting in progress of the lawyers drafting merger documents for the Pennzoil/Getty transaction, to not attend that meeting, because he needed her at his meeting with Texaco. At the meeting with Texaco, the Museum outlined various issues it wanted resolved in any transaction with Texaco, and then agreed to sell its 11.8% ownership in Getty Oil.

That evening, Texaco met with Gordon Getty to discuss the sale of the Trust's shares. He was informed that the Museum had agreed to sell its shares to Texaco. Gordon Getty's advisors had previously warned him that the Trust shares might be "locked out" in a minority position if Texaco bought, in addition to the Museum's shares, enough of the public shares to achieve over 50% ownership of the company. Gordon Getty accepted Texaco's offer of $125 per share and signed a letter of his intent to sell his stock to Texaco, as soon as a California temporary restraining order against his actions as trustee was lifted.

At noon on January 6, Getty Oil held a telephone board meeting to discuss the Texaco offer. The board voted to withdraw its previous counter-proposal to Pennzoil and unanimously voted to accept Texaco's offer. Texaco immediately issued a press release announcing that Getty Oil and Texaco would merge.

Soon after the Texaco press release appeared, Pennzoil telexed the Getty entities, demanding that they honor their agreement with Pennzoil. Later that day, prompted by the telex, Getty Oil filed a suit in Delaware for declaratory judgment that it was not bound to any contract with Pennzoil. The merger agreement between Texaco and Getty Oil was signed on January 6; the stock purchase agreement with the Museum was signed on January 6; and the stock exchange agreement with the Trust was signed on January 8, 1984.

* * *

[The court held that the jury instructions were correct and that the evidence was sufficient to support the jury verdict.]

The $10.53 billion verdict, which began almost immediately to collect interest at the staggering rate of $3 million a day, pushed Texaco, one of the world's largest corporations, into bankruptcy. The trustee of the Sarah C. Getty Trust, the president of the Paul Getty Museum, and the chief executive officer of Pennzoil had signed a "memorandum of agreement" subject to approval by the Getty Oil board. The events of the January 3 board meeting were at the core of the dispute. The disruption of the meeting is described in the following excerpt.

S. Coll, THE TAKING OF GETTY OIL, 315, 318–22, 328, 330–31 (1987):

* * *

"Look," Liman said to Liedtke. "There is no way that we are going to get acceptance of a proposal today unless you come up with a sweetener. You may not like it, but that's what they're doing to us."

"Okay. Offer them on top of the $110 a stub, a right for all the shareholders to receive an interest in whatever we get in selling ERC above a billion dollars after taxes." Goldman, Sachs had estimated that ERC was worth between $1 billion and $1.5 billion.

"What about some guarantee, in case ERC doesn't go for more than one billion?" Liman asked.

"Okay, if it doesn't yield more than three dollars extra for the shareholders, then at the end of five years, we will make up the difference. So the shareholders will get $110 immediately plus a guarantee that within five years they will get at least another three dollars."

* * *

Just after six, the Getty Oil board members and their coterie of advisors returned to Sutton Room II. Marty Lipton, who had been thrust—or who had thrust himself—to the center of the negotiations, reviewed in detail the terms of the $112.50 offer by Pennzoil and Gordon Getty. When Lipton was finished, several questions were asked about the mechanics of the deal. And then, finally, more than twenty-four hours after they had begun, the directors decided to vote on the $112.50 proposal by Pennzoil and Gordon Getty.

* * *

* * * Harold Williams moved that the board accept Pennzoil's proposal, provided that Liedtke could be persuaded to go to a five-dollar guarantee—a present value of $112.50. All of the directors voted in favor, except Chauncey Medberry, who again voted no.

The $112.50 proposal had passed. Gordon Getty, apparently, would become the chairman of Getty Oil.

Sid Petersen asked if there were any other items to be brought before the board. At Harold Stuart's suggestion, there was a unanimous acclamation praising "the splendid job done by the chairman in handling the meeting under difficult conditions." Thus flattered, Petersen was then enriched. The directors, including Gordon, unanimously approved a proposal by Henry Wendt to indemnify Getty Oil's top executives against future lawsuits arising from their actions during the previous eighteen months, and to favorably amend the employment contracts, or golden parachutes, of "key executives of the company whose careers were likely to be affected by the change in management."

What remained was to persuade Hugh Liedtke to formally raise his offer to $112.50—at the moment, he had not actually authorized anything above the three-dollar ERC guarantee, with a present value of just over $111. Marty Lipton told Petersen that he would carry the news of the directors' vote to Arthur Liman and attempt to get a final confirmation from Liedtke. As Lipton left the room, the board meeting temporarily recessed.

* * *

Liman was told about the 15–1 vote. It was now necessary for Liedtke to formally raise his offer to $112.50. Liman said that he would immediately telephone the Pennzoil chairman at his Waldorf apartment.

* * *

Liman picked up the phone and called Liedtke.

* * *

"You can tell them yes," Liedtke said.

Liman turned to Marty Lipton. "My client accepts."

"We have to go back into session," Lipton replied.

"Why do you have to go back in session?" Liman demanded. "I thought you told me that the board had voted this and it was done."

"No, they voted the counterproposal. Now I have to communicate to them that you have accepted the counterproposal."

"Fine," Liman replied.

"You can come and wait outside the room," Lipton said. "This is only going to take two seconds."

The directors inside Sutton Room II were now standing, putting on their coats, gathering their briefcases and papers. When the door was closed again, Marty Siegel announced that Pennzoil had accepted the board's counterproposal. The meeting was adjourned. Bart Winokur tried to ask about the details of the final negotiations with Pennzoil and whether a document would come back to the board for approval.

Lipton cut him off, saying that normally a final, written takeover agreement would come back to the directors for ratification.

There would later be serious dispute about precisely what happened next. This much was agreed upon by everyone: The door to Sutton Room II opened. The directors and their advisors began to wander out. Arthur Liman was standing in the hallway outside the room. He was waiting to hear what had happened inside.

Liman later testified under oath that either Marty Lipton or Marty Siegel, or perhaps both of them, stepped into the hallway and said, "Congratulations, Arthur, you've got a deal." Lipton testified that he did not remember saying any such thing, and that he was in no mood to congratulate anyone, principally because Goldman, Sachs had not yet agreed to provide a fairness letter sanctifying the transaction. Siegel's memory about the incident was vague. Unlike Lipton, however, Siegel represented Gordon Getty and thus was on the same side of the deal as Liman, who represented Pennzoil. Conceivably, Siegel would have more reason to be pleased about the board's action than Lipton. In any event, Liman testified that after this initial round of congratulations, he asked permission to enter Sutton Room II to thank the Getty Oil directors for their arduous and diligent efforts. Liman said that he shook hands with a number of the board members, who made remarks to him such as "Congratulations" and "Congratulations to you." However, a number of directors and advisors present at the board meeting testified later that they did not recall seeing Liman in the room after the final vote. None of them remembered shaking hands with the Pennzoil attorney.

The issue of who was in a congratulatory or celebratory mood at seven o'clock that Tuesday evening would eventually become a critically important one. At the time, however, there were no pictures taken of smiling or drooping faces, no notes made about the facial expressions of the participants. When the time came to sort the matter out, there was only memory, with all of its conveniences.

* * *

The final press release said: "Getty Oil Company, the J. Paul Getty Museum and Gordon P. Getty, as trustee of the Sarah C. Getty Trust, announced today that they have agreed in principle with Pennzoil to a merger of Getty Oil and a newly-formed entity owned by Pennzoil and the Trustee."

* * *

Was the deal done? Had Gordon Getty and Hugh Liedtke won out? Or was the game still on, was final control of the company still in doubt? That depended, obviously, on how one interpreted the phrase "agreement in principle." If one assumed the perspective of the merger game-player, if one subordinated the objective meaning of language to the rules of the game, then an agreement in principle was no agreement at all. To Geoff Boisi, the Getty Oil banker who had played this game hundreds of times before, an agreement in principle meant simply that nothing was final, that everything was up for grabs.

* * *

To such an investor, armed with a dictionary and reading Getty Oil's press release on the morning of Wednesday, January 4, the phrase "agreement in principle" would hardly have indicated that everything was up for grabs. It would have suggested, to the contrary, that an agreement had been reached. If he wondered at all about the words "in principle," and if he was possessed of an exceptionally sophisticated and subtle mind, the investor might have assumed that only the essential, fundamental terms of the deal had yet been negotiated, and that the parties would now bargain in good faith to hammer out the details of a final document. But even that conclusion was far from self-evident. The phrase "in principle" might also refer to the theoretical, moral certitude of the transaction, to the parties' unyielding determination to conclude a deal. This latter and perfectly plausible interpretation, of course, was precisely the opposite of the Wall Street game-players' definition. To them, "in principle" was a convention, a signal to the bankers and lawyers on the Street that Getty Oil was still in play.

* * *

Meanwhile, negotiations to produce a final merger agreement with Pennzoil had suddenly stalled.

* * *

Questions

1. Can a target board of directors contract to sell the firm to a specified party? If so, what are the firm's obligations *to the first buyer* if a second bidder with a higher offer appears before the initial deal has been submitted to a shareholder vote? What are the target board's obligations *to its shareholders* if a second bidder appears before the initial deal has been submitted to a shareholder vote? Must (should) the answer to these two questions be identical? What legal principles would target firm shareholders favor ex ante (before the emergence of any bidder) to maximize their share value?

Do your answers to these five questions change depending on whether, as in *Texaco*, the board agrees to recommend that its shareholders tender their shares or whether, as in *Jewel*, the board signs an agreement for a statutory merger? Do your answers change if the initial deal for a statutory merger has been submitted to the target's shareholders and received an affirmative vote and the second bidder appears with a higher offer before the initial deal can be closed? Do your answers change if the board runs a formal blind auction between two bidders, contracts with the winning bidder to sell the firm, and then (before a shareholder vote) receives a higher bid from the losing bidder in the auction?

2. Is the question of whether a target board of directors can enter into a binding acquisition contract with one firm essentially the same as the

question of whether a board can bind itself to a bidder with lockup, no-shop, or cancellation clauses?

3. If a court finds that a target has breached a contract with an initial bidder and sold to a later bidder, should the court use its injunctive power to enjoin the acquisition by the second bidder and reinstate the acquisition by the first, or should the court limit its award to contract damages? How ought the damages to be measured?

If the court awards contract damages against the seller, should it also award tort damages against the second, successful bidder? If so, should punitive damages be added to compensatory damages?

4. What form of the business judgment rule applies to the target directors at each stage of the following scenario? A board agrees to a statutory merger with another firm and protects the agreement with covenants that effectively block acquisitions by later-appearing bidders. A bidder appears and offers to buy the firm at a substantial premium if the target will waive the protections in its merger contract. The firm refuses to negotiate with the new bidder and renegotiates its deal with its initial merger partner in order to avoid a shareholder vote on the articles of merger. In place of the statutory merger agreement the parties agree that the firm will make a mixed cash and exchange tender offer for its merger partner's stock. See Paramount Communications, supra at pp. 646–55.

SUBCHAPTER C. THE OBLIGATION OF SHAREHOLDERS SELLING A CONTROLLING BLOCK OF STOCK

Selling to a "Looter"
DeBAUN v. FIRST WESTERN BANK AND TRUST CO.
Court of Appeal, Second District, 1975.
46 Cal.App.3d 686, 120 Cal.Rptr. 354.

THOMPSON, ASSOCIATE JUSTICE.

This appeal primarily concerns the duty of a majority shareholder to the corporation whose shares he holds in selling the shares when possessed of facts establishing a reasonable likelihood that the purchaser intends to exercise the control to be acquired by him to loot the corporation of its assets. We conclude that in those circumstances the majority shareholder owes a duty of reasonable investigation and due care to the corporation.

Alfred S. Johnson Incorporated (Corporation) was incorporated by Alfred S. Johnson in 1955 to process color photographs to be reproduced in printed form. All of the 100 outstanding shares of Corporation were originally owned by Johnson. Subsequently, Johnson sold 20 of his shares to James DeBaun, Corporation's primary salesman, and 10 shares to Walter Stephens, its production manager. In November of 1964, Johnson was seriously ill so that managerial control of Corporation was assumed by DeBaun, Stephens, and Jack Hawkins, Corporation's estimator.

Johnson died testate on January 15, 1965. His will named appellant First Western Bank and Trust Company (Bank) as executor and trustee of a trust created by the will. The 70 shares of Corporation owned by Johnson at the time of his death passed to the testamentary trust. George Furman, an employee of Bank, was charged with the direct administration of the trust. While Bank took no hand in the management of Corporation leaving it to the existing management team, Furman attended virtually all directors' meetings. Bank, through its nominee, voted the 70 shares at stockholders' meetings.

* * *

On October 27, 1966, Bank's trust department determined that the investment in Corporation was not appropriate for the trust and decided to sell the 70 shares.

* * *

On May 15 and 20, 1968, Bank received successive offers for the 70 shares from Raymond J. Mattison, acting in the name of S.O.F. Fund, an inter vivos revocable trust of which he was both settlor and trustee. A sketchy balance sheet of S.O.F. Fund was submitted with the second offer. The offers were rejected. Anticipating a further offer from Mattison and his trust, Furman, acting for Bank, ordered a Dun & Bradstreet report on Mattison and the fund. The report was received on May 24, 1968. It noted pending litigation, bankruptcies, and tax liens against corporate entities in which Mattison had been a principal, and suggested that S.O.F. Fund no longer existed.

As of May 24, I. Earl Funk, a vice-president of Bank, had personal knowledge that: (1) on October 24, 1957, the Los Angeles Superior Court had entered a judgment against Mattison in favor of Bank's predecessor in interest for compensatory and punitive damages as the result of Mattison's fraudulent misrepresentations and a fraudulent financial statement to obtain a loan; and (2) the judgment remained unsatisfied in 1968 and was an asset of Bank acquired from its predecessor in an acquisition of 65 branch banks.

On May 27, 1968, Mattison submitted a third offer to purchase the 70 shares of Corporation held by Bank. The offer proposed that S.O.F. Fund would pay $250,000 for the shares, $50,000 in marketable securities as a down payment with the balance payable over a five-year period. Bank made a counter offer, generally accepting the terms of the Mattison proposal but providing that: (1) the $200,000 balance of the purchase price was to be secured by a pledge of marketable securities valued at a like amount; and (2) Corporation would pay no dividends out of "pre-sale" retained earnings. On June 4, 1968, representatives of Bank met with Oroville McCarrol, who had been a trust officer of Bank's predecessor in interest and was counsel for Mattison. McCarrol proposed that Corporation use its assets to secure the unpaid balance of the purchase price rather than Mattison supplying the security in the form of marketable securities. He proposed also the elimination of the restriction against dividends from pre-sale retained earnings. Despite reservations by Bank personnel on the legality of the use of corporate assets to secure an obligation of a major shareholder, Bank determined to pursue the McCarrol modification further. Troubled by the Dun & Bradstreet report, personnel of Bank met with Mattison and McCarrol on June 27. Mattison explained that it had been his practice to take over failing companies so that the existence of the litigation and tax liens noted in the Dun & Bradstreet report was not due to his fault. Not entirely satisfied, Furman wrote to McCarrol requesting a written report on the status of all pending litigation in which Mattison was involved. McCarrol telephoned his response, declining to represent the status of the litigation but noting that the information was publicly available. Partly because Ralph Whitsett, Furman's immediate superior at Bank, knew McCarrol as a former trust officer of Bank's predecessor in interest, and part'y because during a luncheon with Mattison at the Jonathan Club Robert Q. Parsons, the officer at Daum in charge of the transaction, had noted that Mattison was warmly received by his fellow members and reported that fact to Furman, Bank did not pursue its investigation into the public records of Los Angeles County where a mass of derogatory information lay.

As of July 1, 1968, the public records of Los Angeles County revealed 38 unsatisfied judgments against Mattison or his entities totalling $330,886.27, and 54 pending actions claiming a total of $373,588.67 from them. The record also contained 22 recorded abstracts of judgments against Mattison or his entities totalling $285,704.11, and 18 tax liens aggregating $20,327.97. Bank did not investigate the public record and hence was unaware of Mattison's financial track record.

While failing to pursue the investigation of the known information adverse to Mattison, Bank's employees knew or should have known that if his proposal through McCarrol were accepted the payment of the $200,000 balance of the purchase price would necessarily come from Corporation. They assumed that the payments would be made by Mattison from distributions of the Corporation which he would cause it to make after assuming control. They were aware that Corporation would not generate a sufficient aftertax cash flow to pay dividends in a sufficient amount to permit the payments of interest and principal on the $200,000 balance as scheduled in the McCarrol proposal, and knew that Mattison could make those payments only by resorting to distribution of "pre-sale" retained earnings and assets of Corporation.

On July 11, 1968, Bank accepted the McCarrol modification by entering into an exchange agreement with S.O.F. Fund. The agreement obligated S.O.F. to retain a working capital of not less than $70,000, to refrain from intercompany transactions except in the ordinary course of business for adequate consideration, and to furnish monthly financial statements and a certified annual audit report to Bank. It provides that Bank is to transfer its 70 shares of Corporation to Mattison as trustee of S.O.F. Fund, and that the stock will be held by Bank in pledge to secure the fund's obligation. There is provision for acceleration of the unpaid balance of the purchase price if Mattison defaults in any provision of the agreement. The contract obligated Mattison to cause Corporation to execute a security agreement to secure Mattison's obligation to Bank covering all "furniture, fixtures and equipment of [Corporation]." Mattison agreed also to cause Corporation's principal banking business to be maintained with Bank.

The exchange agreement having been executed, Bank gave Mattison a proxy to vote the 70 shares of Corporation at a special meeting of shareholders of Corporation to be held on July 11 at 3 p.m. Furman attended that meeting and an ensuing directors' meeting, as did Mattison. At the shareholders' meeting, DeBaun and Stephens were told that the shares of Corporation owned by Bank had been sold by it on an installment basis to Mattison and that Bank intended to take a pledge of those shares. A new board of directors was elected of which Mattison had control although DeBaun and Stephens remained as directors. DeBaun and Stephens were informed by Furman that a security agreement had been signed to protect Corporation in the event of death or default of Mattison and that in such an event Bank would "foreclose on the stock." Furman did not supply DeBaun or Stephens with a copy of the security agreement or inform them that in fact in hypothecated corporate assets as security for Mattison's debt to Bank. Relying upon Furman's statement of the effect of the agreement and misled by his failure to disclose its material terms, and by the further representation that the document was simply a formal requirement of Mattison's purchase of the majority shares, DeBaun and Stephens participated in a unanimous vote approving the execution by Corporation of the security agreement. A directors' meeting was then convened at which Mattison was elected president of Corporation.

At the moment of Bank's sale of the controlling shares to Mattison, Corporation was an eminently successful going business with a bright future. It had cash of $76,126.15 and other liquid assets of over $122,000. Its remaining assets were worth $60,000. Its excess of current assets over current liabilities and reserve for bad debts was $233,391.94, and its net worth about $220,000. Corporation's earnings indicated a pattern of growth. Mattison immediately proceeded to change that situation. Beginning with the date that he acquired control, Mattison implemented a systematic scheme to loot Corporation of its assets. His first step was to divert $73,144 in corporate cash to himself and to MICO, a shell company owned by Mattison. The transfer was made in exchange for unsecured noninterest bearing notes but for no other consideration. On August 2, 1968, Mattison caused Corporation to assign to MICO all of Corporation's assets, including its receivables in exchange for a fictitious agreement for management services. He diverted all corporate mail to a post office box from which he took the mail, opened it, and extracted all incoming checks to the corporation before forwarding the mail on. He ceased paying trade creditors promptly, as had been Corporation's practice, delaying payment of trade creditors to the last possible moment and, to the extent he could, not paying some at all. He delayed shipments on new orders. To cover his activities, Mattison removed the corporate books and records.

In September 1968, DeBaun left Corporation's employ as a salesman because of Mattison's policy of not filling orders and because Mattison had drastically reduced DeBaun's compensation. Acting as independent salesman, DeBaun obtained business for Corporation for which Mattison refused to compensate him causing DeBaun to broker the business for a competitor. Mattison continued to loot the corporation, although at a reduced pace by reason of its depleted assets. He collected payments from employees to pay premiums on a voluntary health insurance plan although the policy covering the plan was terminated in September for failure to pay premiums. He issued payroll checks without sufficient funds and continued not to pay trade creditors. Mattison did not supply Bank with the financial reports required by the exchange agreement.

While Bank was not aware of the initial transfer of cash to MICO, it did learn of the other misconduct of Mattison as it occurred. Although the conduct was a breach of the exchange agreement, Bank took no action beyond seeking an oral explanation from Mattison. In December 1968, Stephens also left Corporation's employ.

Bank took no action in the matter until April 25, 1969. On that date, it filed an action in the superior court seeking the appointment of a receiver. On April 30, Bank called a special shareholders' meeting of Corporation at which it voted its shares with those of DeBaun and Stephens to elect a new board of directors replacing the Mattison group. Faced with resistance from Mattison, Bank pursued neither its receivership nor its ouster of the board until June 20, 1969, when it shut down the operations of Corporation. By that time, Corporation was hopelessly insolvent. Its debts exceeded its assets by over $200,000, excluding its contingent liability to Bank, as a result of the fraudulently obtained hypothecation of corporate assets to secure Mattison's debt. Both the federal Internal Revenue Service and California State Board of Equalization had filed liens upon corporate assets and notices to withhold funds. A trade creditor had placed a keeper on the corporate premises.

On July 10, 1969, Bank, pursuant to the security agreement, sold all of Corporation's then remaining assets for $60,000. $25,000 of the proceeds of sale was paid to release the federal tax lien while the remaining $35,000 was retained by Bank. After the sale, Corporation had no assets and owed $218,426 to creditors.

* * *

Early case law held that a controlling shareholder owed no duty to minority shareholders or to the controlled corporation in the sale of his stock.

* * *

Decisional law, however, has since recognized the fact of financial life that corporate control by ownership of a majority of shares may be misused. Thus the applicable proposition now is that "In any transaction where the control of the corporation is material," the controlling majority shareholder must exercise good faith and fairness "from the viewpoint of the corporation and those interested therein." * * * That duty of good faith and fairness encompasses an obligation of the controlling shareholder in possession of facts "[s]uch as to awaken suspicion and put a prudent man on his guard [that a potential buyer of his shares may loot the corporation of its assets to pay for the shares purchased] ... to conduct a reasonable adequate investigation [of the buyer]." * * *

Here Bank was the controlling majority shareholder of Corporation. As it was negotiating with Mattison, it became directly aware of facts that would have alerted a prudent person that Mattison was likely to loot the Corporation. Bank knew from the Dun & Bradstreet report that Mattison's financial record was notable by the the failure of entities controlled by him. Bank knew that the only source of funds available to Mattison to pay it for the shares he was purchasing lay in the assets of the corporation. The after-tax net income from the date of the sale would not be sufficient to permit the payment of dividends to him which would permit the making of payments. An officer of Bank possessed personal knowledge that Mattison, on at least one occasion, had been guilty of a fraud perpetrated on Bank's predecessor in interest and had not satisfied a judgment Bank held against him for damages flowing from that conduct.

Armed with knowledge of those facts, Bank owed a duty to Corporation and its minority shareholders to act reasonably with respect to its dealings in the controlling shares with Mattison. It breached that duty. Knowing of McCarrol's refusal to express an opinion on litigation against Mattison and his entities, and that the information could be obtained from the public records, Bank closed its eyes to that obvious source. Rather, it relied upon Mattison's friendly reception by fellow members of the Jonathan Club and the fact that he was represented by a lawyer who had been a trust officer of Bank's predecessor in interest to conclude that indicators that Mattison was a financial bandit should be ignored. Membership in a club, whether it be the Jonathan or the informal group of ex-trust officers of Bank, does not excuse investigation. Nor can Bank be justified in accepting Mattison's uncorroborated statement that the past financial disasters of his entities reported by Dun & Bradstreet were due to his practice of acquiring failing companies. Only one who loots a failed company at the expense of its creditors can profit from its acquisition. Mattison's constantly repeated entry into the transactions without ever pulling a company from the morass was a strong indication that he was milking the companies profitably. Had Bank investigated, as any prudent man would have done, it would have discovered from the public records the additional detail of Mattison's long, long trail of financial failure that would have precluded its dealings with him except under circumstances where his obligation was secured beyond question and his ability to loot Corporation precluded.

Bank, however, elected to deal with Mattison in a fashion that invited rather than tended to prevent his looting of Corporation's assets. It agreed to a payment schedule that virtually required Mattison to do so. By fraudulently concealing its nature from DeBaun and Stephens, Bank obtained corporate approval of a security agreement which hypothecated corporate assets to secure Mattison's obligation to it. Thus, to permit it to sell its majority shares to Mattison, Bank placed the assets and business of Corporation in peril. Not content with so doing, Bank used its control for still another purpose of its own by requiring Mattison to agree to cause Corporation to give its major banking business to Bank.

Thus the record establishes the duty of Bank and its breach. Appellant Bank seeks to avoid responsibility for its action by reversing the position taken by it in its demurrer to the complaint filed by DeBaun and Stephens individually for injury to their minority stock position by now claiming that its duty ran only to the minority shareholders and not to the controlled corporation. California precedent is to the contrary, holding that the duty runs to both.

* * *

Questions

1. What acts define a "looter"? How does this doctrine relate to the mistreatment by an acquirer of "frozen-in" minority shareholders or "squeezed-out" minority shareholders in chapter 5, infra?

2. Why is the right of shareholders to sue the new controlling shareholder for looting not a sufficient remedy? If it is not sufficient, should we impose an aiding and abetting standard of liability for the selling controlling shareholder rather than establish independent liability as in the *DeBaun* case?

Selling an Office

ESSEX UNIVERSAL CORP. v. YATES

United States Court of Appeals, Second Circuit, 1962.
305 F.2d 572.

LUMBARD, CHIEF JUDGE.

* * *

The defendant Herbert J. Yates, a resident of California, was president and chairman of the board of directors of Republic Pictures Corporation, a New York corporation which at the time relevant to this suit had 2,004,190 shares of common stock outstanding. Republic's stock was listed and traded on the New York Stock Exchange. In August 1957, Essex Universal Corporation, a Delaware corporation owning stock in various diversified businesses, learned of the possibility of purchasing from Yates an interest in Republic. Negotiations proceeded rapidly, and on August 28 Yates and Joseph Harris, the president of Essex, signed a contract in which Essex agreed to buy, and Yates agreed "to sell or cause to be sold" at least 500,000 and not more than 600,000 shares of Republic stock. The price was set at eight dollars a share, roughly two dollars above the then market price on the Exchange. Three dollars per share was to be paid at the closing on September 18, 1957 and the remainder in twenty-four equal monthly payments beginning January 31, 1958. The shares were to be transferred on the closing date, but Yates was to retain the certificates, endorsed in blank by Essex, as security for full payment. In addition to other provisions not relevant to the present motion, the contract contained the following paragraph:

"6. Resignations.

Upon and as a condition to the closing of this transaction if requested by Buyer at least ten (10) days prior to the date of the closing:

(a) Seller will deliver to Buyer the resignations of the majority of the directors of Republic.

(b) Seller will cause a special meeting of the board of directors of Republic to be held, legally convened pursuant to law and the by-laws of Republic, and simultaneously with the acceptance of the directors' resignations set forth in paragraph 6(a) immediately preceding will cause nominees of Buyer to be elected directors of Republic in place of the resigned directors."

Before the date of the closing, as provided in the contract, Yates notified Essex that he would deliver 566,223 shares, or 28.3 per cent of the Republic stock then outstanding, and Essex formally requested Yates to arrange for the replacement of a majority of Republic's directors with Essex nominees pursuant to paragraph 6 of the contract. This was to be accomplished by having eight of the fourteen directors resign seriatim, each in turn being replaced by an Essex nominee elected by the others; such a procedure was in form permissible under the charter and by-laws of Republic, which empowered the board to choose the successor of any of its members who might resign.

On September 18, the parties met as arranged for the closing at Republic's office in New York City. Essex tendered bank drafts and cashier's checks totalling $1,698,690, which was the 37½ per cent of the total price of $4,529,784 due at this time. The drafts and checks were payable to one Benjamin C. Cohen, who was Essex' banker and had arranged for the borrowing of the necessary funds. Although Cohen was prepared to endorse these to Yates, Yates upon advice of his lawyer rejected the tender as "unsatisfactory" and said, according to his deposition testimony, "Well, there can be no deal. We can't close it."

Essex began this action in the New York Supreme Court, and it was removed to the district court on account of diversity of citizenship.

Essex seeks damages of $2,700,000, claiming that at the time of the aborted closing the stock was in actuality worth more than $12.75 a share.[1] Yates' answer raised a number of defenses, but the motion for summary judgment now before us was made and decided only on the theory that the provision in the contract for immediate transfer of control of the board of directors was illegal *per se* and tainted the entire contract. We have no doubt, and the parties agree, that New York law governs.

* * *

It is established beyond question under New York law that it is illegal to sell corporate office or management control by itself (that is, accompanied by no stock or insufficient stock to carry voting control). * * * The same rule apparently applies in all jurisdictions where the question has arisen. * * * The rationale of the rule is undisputable: persons enjoying management control hold it on behalf of the corporation's stockholders, and therefore may not regard it as their own personal property to dispose of as they wish.[3] Any other rule would violate the most fundamental principle of corporate democracy, that management must represent and be chosen by, or at least with the consent of, those who own the corporation.

Essex was, however, contracting with Yates for the purchase of a very substantial percentage of Republic stock. If, by virtue of the voting power carried by this stock, it could have elected a majority of the board of directors, then the contract was not a simple agreement for the sale of office to one having no ownership interest in the corporation, and the question of its legality would require further analysis. Such stock voting control would incontestably belong to the owner of a majority of the voting stock, and it is commonly known that equivalent power usually accrues to the owner of 28.3% of the stock. For the purpose of this analysis, I shall assume that Essex was contracting to acquire a majority of the Republic stock, deferring consideration of the situation where, as here, only 28.3% is to be acquired.

Republic's board of directors at the time of the aborted closing had fourteen members divided into three classes, each class being "as nearly as may be" of the same size. Directors were elected for terms of three years, one class being elected at each annual shareholder meeting on the first Tuesday in April. Thus, absent the immediate replacement of directors provided for in this contract, Essex as the hypothetical new majority shareholder of the corporation could not have obtained managing control in the form of a majority of the board in the normal course of events until April 1959, some eighteen months after the sale of the stock. The first question before us then is whether an agreement to

---

1. In 1959, while this action was pending, the stock was sold to another party for ten dollars a share.

3. The cases have made no distinction between contracts by directors or officers to resign and contracts by persons who in actuality control the actions of officers or directors to procure their resignations, and of course none should exist.

accelerate the transfer of management control, in a manner legal in form under the corporation's charter and by-laws, violates the public policy of New York.

There is no question of the right of a controlling shareholder under New York law normally to derive a premium from the sale of a controlling block of stock. In other words, there was no impropriety *per se* in the fact that Yates was to receive more per share than the generally prevailing market price for Republic stock.

* * *

The next question is whether it is legal to give and receive payment for the immediate transfer of management control to one who has achieved majority share control but would not otherwise be able to convert that share control into operating control for some time. I think that it is.

* * *

The easy and immediate transfer of corporate control to new interests is ordinarily beneficial to the economy and it seems inevitable that such transactions would be discouraged if the purchaser of a majority stock interest were required to wait some period before his purchase of control could become effective. Conversely it would greatly hamper the efforts of any existing majority group to dispose of its interest if it could not assure the purchaser of immediate control over corporation operations. I can see no reason why a purchaser of majority control should not ordinarily be permitted to make his control effective from the moment of the transfer of stock.

Thus if Essex had been contracting to purchase a majority of the stock of Republic, it would have been entirely proper for the contract to contain the provision for immediate replacement of directors. Although in the case at bar only 28.3 per cent of the stock was involved, it is commonly known that a person or group owning so large a percentage of the voting stock of a corporation which, like Republic, has at least the 1,500 shareholders normally requisite to listing on the New York Stock Exchange, is almost certain to have share control as a practical matter. If Essex was contracting to acquire what in reality would be equivalent to ownership of a majority of stock, i.e., if it would as a practical certainty have been guaranteed of the stock voting power to choose a majority of the directors of Republic in due course, there is no reason why the contract should not similarly be legal. Whether Essex was thus to acquire the equivalent of majority stock control would, if the issue is properly raised by the defendants, be a factual issue to be determined by the district court on remand.

Because 28.3 per cent of the voting stock of a publicly owned corporation is usually tantamount to majority control, I would place the burden of proof on this issue on Yates as the party attacking the legality of the transaction. Thus, unless on remand Yates chooses to raise the question whether the block of stock in question carried the equivalent of majority control, it is my view that the trial court should regard the contract as legal and proceed to consider the other issues raised by the pleadings. If Yates chooses to raise the issue, it will, on my view, be necessary for him to prove the existence of circumstances which would have prevented Essex from electing a majority of the Republic board of directors in due course. It will not be enough for Yates to raise merely hypothetical possibilities of opposition by the other Republic shareholders to Essex' assumption of management control. Rather, it will be necessary for him to show that, assuming neutrality on the part of the retiring management, there was at the time some concretely foreseeable reason why Essex' wishes would not have prevailed in shareholder voting held in due course. In other words, I would require him to show that there was at the time of the contract some other organized block of stock of sufficient size to outvote the block Essex was buying, or else some circumstance making it likely that enough of the holders of the remaining Republic stock would band together to keep Essex from control.

* * *

CLARK, CIRCUIT JUDGE (concurring in the result).

* * *

FRIENDLY, CIRCUIT JUDGE (concurring).

* * *

When an issue does arise, the "practical certainty" test is difficult to apply. The existence of such certainty will depend not merely on the proportion of the stock held by the seller but on many other factors— whether the other stock is widely or closely held, how much of it is in "street names," what success the corporation has experienced, how far its dividend policies have satisfied its stockholders, the identity of the purchasers, the presence or absence of cumulative voting, and many others. Often, unless the seller has nearly 50% of the stock, whether he has "working control" can be determined only by an election; groups who thought they had such control have experienced unpleasant surprises in recent years. Judge Lumbard correctly recognizes that, from a policy standpoint, the pertinent question must be the buyer's prospects of election, not the seller's—yet this inevitably requires the court to canvass the likely reaction of stockholders to a group of whom they know nothing and seems rather hard to reconcile with a position that it is "right" to insert such a condition if a seller has a larger proportion of the stock and "wrong" if he has a smaller.

I have no doubt that many contracts, drawn by competent and responsible counsel, for the purchase of blocks of stock from interests thought to "control" a corporation although owning less than a majority, have contained provisions like paragraph 6 of the contract *sub judice*. However, developments over the past decades seem to me to show that such a clause violates basic principles of corporate democracy. To be sure, stockholders who have allowed a set of directors to be placed in office, whether by their vote or their failure to vote, must recognize that death, incapacity or other hazard may prevent a director from serving a full term, and that they will have no voice as to his immediate successor. But the stockholders are entitled to expect that, in that event, the remaining directors will fill the vacancy in the exercise of their fiduciary responsibility. A mass seriatim resignation directed by a selling stockholder, and the filling of vacancies by his henchmen at the dictation of a purchaser and without any consideration of the character of the latter's nominees, are beyond what the stockholders contemplated or should have been expected to contemplate. This seems to me a wrong to the corporation and the other stockholders which the law ought not countenance, whether the selling stockholder has received a premium or not. Right in this Court we have seen many cases where sudden shifts of corporate control have caused serious injury.

* * *

* * * To hold the seller for delinquencies of the new directors only if he knew the purchaser was an intending looter is not a sufficient sanction. The difficulties of proof are formidable even if receipt of too high a premium creates a presumption of such knowledge, and, all too often, the doors are locked only after the horses have been stolen. Stronger medicines are needed—refusal to enforce a contract with such a clause, even though this confers an unwarranted benefit on a defaulter, and continuing responsibility of the former directors for negligence of the new ones until an election has been held. Such prophylactics are not contraindicated, as Judge Lumbard suggests, by the conceded desirability of preventing the dead hand of a former "controlling" group from continuing to dominate the board after a sale, or of protecting a would-be purchaser from finding himself without a majority of the board after he has spent his money. A special meeting of stockholders to replace a board may always be called, and there could be no objection to making the closing of a purchase contingent on the results of such an election. I perceive some of the difficulties of mechanics such a procedure presents, but I have enough confidence in the ingenuity of the corporate bar to believe these would be surmounted.

Hence, I am inclined to think that if I were sitting on the New York Court of Appeals, I would hold a provision like Paragraph 6 violative of public policy save when it was entirely plain that a new election would be a mere formality—i.e., when the seller owned more than 50% of the stock.

* * *

Questions

1. When can a director or officer holding a block of stock sell for a premium price and agree to resign? Can a large shareholder who is not a director sell her block of stock and agree to deliver resignations of the board? What if the board members refuse to resign?

2. What is the effect of section 14(f) of the Securities Exchange Act of 1934 on the doctrine announced in the *Essex* case? Please read the section in your statutory supplement.

3. How effective as a takeover defense is a "staggered" board provision (providing for the election of only one-third of the board in any one year) in the articles of incorporation? Can a bidder condition its tender offer for 51 percent of the outstanding stock on the resignation of existing directors and the appointment of a designated slate? What is the obligation of the sitting board if over 51 percent of the outstanding shares are tendered?

Sharing the Proceeds From the Sale

ZETLIN v. HANSON HOLDINGS, INC.

Court of Appeals of New York, 1979.
48 N.Y.2d 684, 421 N.Y.S.2d 877, 397 N.E.2d 387.

OPINION OF THE COURT

Plaintiff Zetlin owned approximately 2% of the outstanding shares of Gable Industries, Inc., with defendants Hanson Holdings, Inc., and Sylvestri together with members of the Sylvestri family, owning 44.4% of Gable's shares. The defendants sold their interests to Flintkote Co. for a premium price of $15 per share, at a time when Gable was selling on the open market for $7.38 per share. It is undisputed that the 44.4% acquired by Flintkote represented effective control of Gable.

Recognizing that those who invest the capital necessary to acquire a dominant position in the ownership of a corporation have the right of controlling that corporation, it has long been settled law that, absent looting of corporate assets, conversion of a corporate opportunity, fraud or other acts of bad faith, a controlling stockholder is free to sell, and a purchaser is free to buy, that controlling interest at a premium price.

* * *

Certainly, minority shareholders are entitled to protection against such abuse by controlling shareholders. They are not entitled, however, to inhibit the legitimate interests of the other stockholders. It is for this reason that control shares usually command a premium price. The premium is the added amount an investor is willing to pay for the privilege of directly influencing the corporation's affairs.

In this action plaintiff Zetlin contends that minority stockholders are entitled to an opportunity to share equally in any premium paid for a controlling interest in the corporation. This rule would profoundly affect the manner in which controlling stock interests are now transferred. It would require, essentially, that a controlling interest be transferred only by means of an offer to all stockholders, i.e., a tender offer. This would be contrary to existing law and if so radical a change is to be effected it would best be done by the Legislature.

* * *

Questions

1. If courts required majority shareholders to allow all minority shareholders to participate in a sale of control (an "equal opportunity" rule), how would private parties have to structure their stock acquisitions?

2. Why do courts not adopt an equal opportunity rule for all corporations? Is the rule in the best interest of target shareholders? Should we require, as has been proposed, that all large-scale acquisitions of publicly held firms be in the form of tender offers regulated under the Williams Act?

3. Given the reluctance of state courts to impose an equal opportunity rule, why has the Securities and Exchange Commission adopted an equal opportunity rule for tender offers? Please read SEC rule 14d–10 in your statutory supplement.

Corporate Opportunity

DAVID J. GREENE & CO. v. DUNHILL INTERN., INC. (PART I)

Court of Chancery of Delaware, 1968.
249 A.2d 427.

DUFFY, CHANCELLOR:

Plaintiffs collectively own 30,685 shares of defendant A.G. Spalding & Bros., Inc., a Delaware corporation ("Spalding"); they seek an injunction prohibiting the consummation of a proposed merger between Spalding and Dunhill International, Inc., a Delaware corporation ("Dunhill"), in which the latter will be the surviving corporation. Dunhill owns 80.3% of Spalding's stock. Plaintiffs contend that the terms of the merger are grossly unfair and inequitable to Spalding's minority stockholders. * * *

Spalding is a name known to every boy who ever owned or coveted a baseball or glove. For present purposes it is sufficient to say that it is one of the nation's leading producers of athletic equipment, with 1967 sales of approximately $58,000,000. About $2,000,000 of these resulted from sales made by its toy division under the tradename "Tinkertoy."

Dunhill is a diversified operating company which manufactures and sells both automotive and infant-feeding equipment and other products equally different from both of those. It is a conglomerate and still merger-minded.

* * *

I next consider plaintiffs' contentions that Dunhill took over a corporate opportunity which rightfully belonged to Spalding. The law as to corporate opportunity is settled in Delaware by Supreme Court decisions. The cornerstone case is Guth v. Loft, Inc., 23 Del.Ch. 255, 5 A.2d 503 (1939), which was reaffirmed * * * in Equity Corporation v. Milton, Del.Ch., 221 A.2d 494 (1966). In the latter case Chief Justice Daniel Wolcott wrote:

"The rule of the *Guth* case is that when there is presented to a corporate officer a business opportunity which the corporation is financially able to undertake, and which, by its nature, falls into the line of the corporation's business and is of practical advantage to it, or is an opportunity in which the corporation has an actual or expectant interest, the officer is prohibited from permitting his self-interest to be brought into conflict with the corporation's interest and may not take the opportunity for himself."

While our law on corporate opportunity has developed around the duty owed by directors and officers, I am of the view that comparable duties and standards should be imposed when the party whose conduct is in question is a stockholder. In some circumstances a stockholder has opportunities to express and prefer his self-interest to that of the corporation. But we are concerned with circumstances in which a stockholder, by virtue of his control of corporate functions, makes a choice advantageous to himself and against the corporate interest.
* * *

The rule of *Guth* is applicable in determining whether a majority stockholder, acting as a result of his control of a corporate function, has preempted an opportunity which rightfully belongs to the corporation.
* * *

Child Guidance Toys, Inc., was acquired by Dunhill on May 31, 1968; it manufactures and distributes educational toys and visual aid teaching devices. In 1967 Child Guidance had net sales of about $8,000,000. Prior to the acquisition Spalding had a toy division, which made and sold "Tinkertoys," Dunhill did not make or sell toys of any kind.

Plaintiffs allege that Dunhill diverted to itself the opportunity to acquire Child Guidance and that this was done in violation of its fiduciary duty to the public stockholders. Dunhill argues that this issue is not relevant to the fairness of the merger terms but I cannot say, on this record, that as a matter of law it is not. Duff, Anderson's valuation is based on the inclusion of Child Guidance as part of Dunhill and not of Spalding. And Mr. Benjamin's uncontested affidavit states that if Child Guidance belongs to Spalding "this would confer a significant advantage and an additional element of value for Spalding." It follows that the contention is relevant to valuation.

Next, Dunhill argues that plaintiffs have not sustained their burden of proof to show that there has been an unlawful diversion. The record on this issue is limited, but such as it is, I believe, favors plaintiffs. Thus the affidavit filed by Morris Shilensky, whose firm is counsel to Dunhill, shows that shortly after a prior merger by that company "there was widely circulated a description of a program for acquisition of businesses for Dunhill as well as for Spalding." He states that the Child Guidance opportunity came to Dunhill and not Spalding. That is perfectly understandable. The program Dunhill publicized *included* Spalding but asked that proposals be submitted to *Dunhill.* A reasonable inference from all of this is that Dunhill had taken over any acquisition program Spalding had. And in the same literature the Platt & Munk division of Dunhill, to which Child Guidance was later assigned, is identified as a "book publishing company;" it was said that it had areas of interest in "book publishing concerns * * * games, greeting cards and book clubs." Not a word about toys. And the Tinkertoy operation of Spalding is identified as the division interested in educational toys and equipment. Finally, the acquisition was apparently made for cash and there is no dispute about Spalding's ability to secure the amount actually paid.

In sum, the record makes out a sufficient showing of a business opportunity in the line of Spalding's business, which would have been of practical advantage to it and which it was financially able to undertake; that opportunity was acquired by Spalding's controlling stockholder.

* * *

Questions

1. An acquisition of a toy company is in the normal line of business for both the parent, a "merger-minded" conglomerate, and the subsidiary, a producer of athletic equipment with a small toy division. Why should the subsidiary get the benefit of the new acquisition?

2. If a buyer originally approaches target-firm managers with an offer to buy sufficient treasury shares from the firm to gain control, can the managers sell their controlling block of personal stock instead? Is this a violation of the corporate opportunity doctrine? See Brown v. Halbert, 271 Cal.App.2d 252, 76 Cal.Rptr. 781 (1969).

SUBCHAPTER D. FIDUCIARY DUTIES OF THE MANAGERS OF AN ACQUIRING FIRM

SECTION 1. DUTIES TO ACQUIRING-FIRM SHAREHOLDERS

Studies of stock prices in takeovers during the 1980s show large premiums paid to target shareholders, averaging 50 percent over pre-deal market price, and no gains or slightly negative gains to the bidders. Black, Bidder Overpayment in Takeover, 41 Stan.L.Rev. 597, 601–03 (1989). Moreover, postacquisition data on the performance of many of the surviving firms are not rosy. See Herman & Lowenstein, The Efficiency Effects of Hostile Takeovers, in *Knights, Raiders, and Targets: The Impact of the Hostile Takeover* 211 (J. Coffee, L. Lowenstein & S. Rose–Ackerman eds. 1988). The data suggest that managers of bidders may not be serving the interests of their own shareholders in acquisitions. Moreover, as we have seen in earlier chapters, shareholders of the bidder often do not vote on major acquisitions. In such cases the courts are often asked to stop unwanted acquisitions. As we see in the next case, however, the courts view their role in these controversies as very limited.

MUSCHEL v. WESTERN UNION CORP.
Court of Chancery of Delaware, 1973.
310 A.2d 904.

BROWN, VICE CHANCELLOR:

Plaintiffs are the record owners of 83,920 shares of the Defendant Western Union Corporation (hereafter referred to as Western Union) and claim to bring this action individually, derivatively on behalf of and for the benefit of Western Union, and representatively on behalf of all other shareholders of Western Union similarly situated. The Defendant Western Union and the Defendant Regrem, Inc. a wholly-owned subsidiary of Western Union are corporations of the State of Delaware as is the Defendant National Sharedata Corporation (hereafter referred to as NSC). NSC is primarily engaged in providing data processing management services to commercial banking institutions. On or about April 16, 1973, it was announced by Western Union that it had agreed in principle to acquire NSC through an exchange of securities.

By agreements dated May 25, 1973, Western Union, Regrem and NSC agreed to a plan of merger under which Regrem would merge into NSC, with NSC thereafter being the surviving corporation and thus a wholly-owned subsidiary of Western Union. As part of this merger Western Union is to issue approximately 880,000 shares of its common stock to the shareholders of NSC with the agreed upon exchange ratio being 0.387 of a share of Western Union common stock for each of 2,278,727 shares of NSC common stock then outstanding. Based on the closing sale price for Western Union common stock on April 13, 1973, the shares to be received by the shareholders of NSC had a total value of approximately $23.5 million. The Western Union shares to be issued under the proposed merger would constitute about 7 percent of the presently outstanding shares of Western Union. In this reverse three-party merger Western Union, through its board of directors, provides stockholder approval for Regrem and therefore no approval of the transaction has been sought from the shareholders of Western Union.

* * *

Throughout all their arguments, is the underlying premise that Western Union is paying a greatly excessive price for NSC. By example, they point out that according to the prospectus figures (a) by respective market value of the securities involved Western Union is paying $23.5 million for NSC stock worth $16 million; (b) that based on a price-earnings comparison for the past fiscal year of NSC, Western Union is paying at 60–1 ratio; and (c) that based on a comparison of the book value of assets to be acquired Western Union is issuing shares worth $23.5 million to acquire assets of approximately $1.7 million.

* * *

Western Union acknowledges that it is paying a premium to NSC stockholders of some 45 percent and that there will be an initial dilution of Western Union stock of 11.6 cents per share. It offers evidence, however, to show that such a premium is not unrealistic in a merger of this type wherein a going concern is being acquired for immediate entry into a new field for the purpose of future growth, and also offers projections which indicate $7 per share earnings for the combined Western Union—NSC operation by 1978.

* * *

* * * I am of the opinion that the business judgment rule is the standard that must be applied, and that consequently the burden is on Plaintiffs to establish some fraud, or what amounts to fraud, on the part of Western Union in order to prevail at this stage of the proceedings. It is well established that in order to enjoin a proposed merger on the theory of constructive fraud based on a claimed discriminatory undervaluation or overvaluation of corporate assets, it must be plainly demonstrated that the overvaluation or undervaluation, as the case may be, is such as to show a conscious abuse of discretion before fraud at law can be made out.

* * *

Mere inadequacy of price will not reveal fraud, but rather the disparity must be so gross as to lead the Court to conclude that it was not due to an honest error of judgment, but rather to bad faith, or to reckless indifference to the rights of others interested. Wide discretion in the matter of valuation is confided to directors, and as long as they appear to act in good faith, with honest motives, and for honest ends, the exercise of their discretion will not be interfered with.

* * *

Plaintiffs do not dispute these principles, but argue that the business judgment rule does not come into effect where it appears that not all material facts concerning the transaction were presented to the board. They claim that during discovery, and subsequent to the filing of suit, it has been learned that two critical factors related to a proper evaluation of NSC were not brought to the attention of the Western Union board. * * * Second, the board was not advised that a certain 5 year projection of revenues and earnings of NSC which was presented to the board was substantially inflated from similar projections prepared by the management of NSC.

* * *

In addition, there is evidence that although the 5 year projection presented to the board was brighter than a separate 5 year projection prepared by NSC, the one presented to the board contemplated the 5 year potential of NSC after and as the result of the proposed merger with Western Union. In other words, the projection offered was premised on a combined effort of the resources of the merged companies, and was not intended to be a projection for NSC alone.

Therefore, there is evidence in the record to indicate that what Plaintiffs feel to be critical was considered by others to be non-material for the reasons stated. There is also evidence that the allegedly inflated projection of NSC potential was not that at all. In view of this, I do not feel at this time that I can conclude that the Western Union board failed to make an informed judgment. I therefore feel, based on the present status of the record, that they are entitled to the presumption of having made an informed judgment in good faith which can be attributed to a rational business purpose.

* * *

Questions

1. Why do bidders seem to make so many questionable acquisitions?

2. Can we devise legal standards that better protect bidder shareholders from improvident acquisitions? Should the law require approval by the shareholders of the bidder for all major acquisitions (including tender offers, triangular mergers, and all-asset purchases)? (Recall the California Corporations Code and New York Stock Exchange provisions on pages 111 and 114, respectively.) Should courts enjoin acquisitions if the bidder's stock price declines abnormally relative to other industry stocks on the announcement of an acquisition? (Compare the importance of stock price declines in *Paramount*, at 646, supra, and in *CTS Corporation*, at 498, supra.)

3. If a bidder makes an improvident acquisition, are there self-enforcing market penalties? For example, will a foolish bidder find itself the target of a bid? See chapter 1. See also Mitchell & Lehn, Do Bad Bidders Become Good Targets?, 98 J.Pol.Econ. 372 (1990) (acquisitions that reduce the equity value of the bidder led to later divestitures in subsequent bust-up takeovers of the bidder or in defensive restructuring programs by the bidder). Should we rely on the market to deter foolish acquisitions?

SECTION 2. DUTIES TO TARGET–FIRM SHAREHOLDERS

In a leveraged acquisition the bidder raises cash to buy control of a target, usually through a cash tender offer. In raising the cash, the bidder often solicits very short-term, high-interest loans with a promise to repay with cash from the sale of target assets or from the sale of debt secured by the target assets. These promises require the bidder to extract cash from the target after the acquisition. If the bidder has the target pay a large dividend once the target has sold assets or issued new debt, the minority shareholders of the target receive a pro rata portion of the cash distinction. Most bidders cannot afford such a cash drain, so they must take steps to stop minority shareholders from receiving a large portion of any cash distribution. There are two methods: the freeze-in and the freeze-out.

In the freeze-in the bidder, as majority shareholder, organizes the affairs of the target so that cash distributions come out as lease payments, salary, and other kinds of payments that do not involve minority shareholders. Since these payments are limited in amount and must be distributed over a period of time (unless the distributions are illegal), most leveraged buyouts, with immediate and crushing cash needs, must rely on the second method, the cash-out or freeze-out. In a freeze-out the bidder gains 100 percent control by forcing the minority shareholders out of the target, paying those shareholders in noncash consideration (notes or preferred stock in the bidder) for their shares. The success of either method is, of course, crucial to the first step of the acquisition—the cash tender offer. The more a bidder can exclude minority shareholders from cash distributions generated after the tender offer, the higher the price the bidder can, and is willing to, pay in the tender offer.

"Frozen-in" Minority Shareholders

SUMMA CORP. v. TRANS WORLD AIRLINES, INC.

Supreme Court of Delaware, 1988.
540 A.2d 403, cert. denied 488 U.S. 853, 109 Ct. 140, 102 L.Ed.2d 112 (1988).

MOORE, JUSTICE.

This accounting action has consumed more than twenty-five years of litigation between Trans World Airlines, Inc. ("TWA"), and the late Howard R. Hughes and his wholly owned enterprise, Hughes Tool Company ("Toolco"). * * *

In 1962 TWA sued Hughes and Toolco in the Court of Chancery alleging that the defendants had breached their fiduciary duty of loyalty by deliberately interfering with TWA's commercial success to benefit themselves. After trial the Court of Chancery assessed damages plus interest of $48,349,022.48 against Toolco.

* * *

We find no error in the trial court's calculation of damages and interest. Accordingly, we affirm.

* * *

In 1939 Howard R. Hughes, through Toolco, began acquiring stock in TWA. In 1942 Toolco had working control of TWA, owning 40% of its common stock. By 1958, Toolco had increased its holdings to 78%, and exercised control over TWA's day-to-day operations. * * *

Between 1950 and 1960 Toolco used its control position to TWA's detriment. Because of Hughes' evasive nature and difficult temperament, Toolco was slow to order the then novel jet airplanes which TWA needed to remain competitive. Toolco refused to allow TWA to purchase its own aircraft, preferring instead to buy the planes and sell or lease them to TWA at a profit. Several of the planes ordered for TWA, once delivered, were diverted to other airlines. Some planes never arrived due to Toolco's deliberate efforts to delay or stop their production. Many of those actions were designed to minimize both Hughes' and Toolco's tax exposure, but they also resulted in losses of profits to TWA.

* * *

It is well established in Delaware that one who stands on both sides of a transaction has the burden of proving its entire fairness. * * * In the absence of arms length bargaining, clearly the situation here, this obligation inheres in, and invariably arises from the parent-subsidiary relationship. * * * This rule applies when "the parent, by virtue of its domination of the subsidiary, causes the subsidiary to act in such a way that the parent receives something from the subsidiary to the exclusion of, and detriment to the minority stockholders of the subsidiary." *Sinclair Oil,* 280 A.2d at 720.

Toolco was a 78% shareholder in TWA, and, exerting its control position, Toolco refused to allow TWA to purchase its own jets, delayed the production of jets which were ordered, unjustifiably rejected acceptable aircraft, forced TWA to enter into leases for aircraft, and sold airplanes to TWA at a profit—all to Toolco's benefit, but materially detrimental to the productivity and effectiveness of TWA. By fixing the terms of the leases and sales to TWA, Toolco thereby accrued substantial profits, reportable as capital gains, as well as other tax benefits. Furthermore, Toolco structured the transactions to minimize its exposure to risk at the expense of TWA's profits. Such conduct hardly comports with basic concepts of fair dealing under the fiduciary standards of Delaware corporation law.

Toolco's defense is essentially one of minimizing its actions. For example, it argues that TWA had no need for a full fleet of certain jet aircraft in 1955 because those planes did not have non-stop transatlantic capability. Thus, Toolco contends, it should not be held accountable for TWA's lost profits due to Toolco's failure to order such aircraft.

However, this argument, like Toolco's others, ignores the fact that the intrinsic fairness test placed the burden upon Toolco to prove that it was not the cause of TWA's lost profits. It could have done so by showing that the outcome of the transaction, had it been approved by an independent board of directors, would have been the same. The trial court found, and we agree, that Toolco failed to meet that burden.

Mr. Robert W. Rummel, a longtime employee of Toolco and TWA, testified that Hughes would not allow him to negotiate with one aircraft manufacturer because it refused to give Toolco the highest priority for delivery. The record also demonstrates that this manufacturer found Hughes to be a very difficult person. This adversely affected TWA because it caused Toolco to lose the little priority it did establish for delivery of the aircraft. Substantial evidence indicates that had Toolco been willing to negotiate, TWA would have had a delivery priority competitive with other airline companies. Toolco's argument that it was waiting for jets with true transatlantic capability is without merit. Other airlines, who were willing to negotiate with this particular manufacturer put the same planes to use on their transatlantic routes until the later models were available. When updated transatlantic jets were produced, the manufacturer negotiated with the airlines to "roll over" the earlier models for the later ones.

Thus, for reasons clearly attributable to the eccentric or idiosyncratic business methods of Howard Hughes, TWA was unable to establish a jet fleet as quickly as its competitors. Given this record, it is manifest that no independent board of directors could have taken such action in good faith and in the honest belief that it was in the best interests of TWA. * * * That point becomes even more apparent when one considers the application of the intrinsic fairness test here, and Toolco's failure to meet its burden of proof in that regard.

* * *

"Frozen–Out" Minority Shareholders

WEINBERGER v. UOP, INC.

Supreme Court of Delaware, 1983.
457 A.2d 701.

MOORE, JUSTICE:

This post-trial appeal was reheard en banc from a decision of the Court of Chancery. It was brought by the class action plaintiff below, a former shareholder of UOP, Inc., who challenged the elimination of UOP's minority shareholders by a cash-out merger between UOP and its majority owner, The Signal Companies, Inc.

* * *

In ruling for the defendants, the Chancellor re-stated his earlier conclusion that the plaintiff in a suit challenging a cash-out merger must allege specific acts of fraud, misrepresentation, or other items of misconduct to demonstrate the unfairness of the merger terms to the minority. We approve this rule and affirm it.

The Chancellor also held that even though the ultimate burden of proof is on the majority shareholder to show by a preponderance of the evidence that the transaction is fair, it is first the burden of the plaintiff attacking the merger to demonstrate some basis for invoking the fairness obligation. We agree with that principle. However, where corporate action has been approved by an informed vote of a majority of the minority shareholders, we conclude that the burden entirely shifts to the plaintiff to show that the transaction was unfair to the minority. * * * But in all this, the burden clearly remains on those relying on the vote to show that they completely disclosed all material facts relevant to the transaction.

Here, the record does not support a conclusion that the minority stockholder vote was an informed one. Material information, necessary to acquaint those shareholders with the bargaining positions of Signal and UOP, was withheld under circumstances amounting to a breach of fiduciary duty. We therefore conclude that this merger does not meet the test of fairness, at least as we address that concept, and no burden thus shifted to the plaintiff by reason of the minority shareholder vote. Accordingly, we reverse and remand for further proceedings consistent herewith.

* * *

While looking to invest this cash surplus, Signal became interested in UOP as a possible acquisition. * * * In the arm's length bargaining that followed, an understanding was reached whereby Signal agreed to purchase from UOP 1,500,000 shares of UOP's authorized but unissued stock at $21 per share.

This purchase was contingent upon Signal making a successful cash tender offer for 4,300,000 publicly held shares of UOP, also at a price of $21 per share. This combined method of acquisition permitted Signal to acquire 5,800,000 shares of stock, representing 50.5% of UOP's outstanding shares. * * *

Although UOP's board consisted of thirteen directors, Signal nominated and elected only six. Of these, five were either directors or employees of Signal. The sixth, a partner in the banking firm of Lazard Freres & Co., had been one of Signal's representatives in the negotiations and bargaining with UOP concerning the tender offer and purchase price of the UOP shares.

However, the president and chief executive officer of UOP retired during 1975, and Signal caused him to be replaced by James V. Crawford, a long-time employee and senior executive vice president of one of Signal's wholly-owned subsidiaries. Crawford succeeded his predecessor on UOP's board of directors and also was made a director of Signal.

By the end of 1977 Signal basically was unsuccessful in finding other suitable investment candidates for its excess cash, and by February 1978 considered that it had no other realistic acquisitions available to it on a friendly basis. Once again its attention turned to UOP.

The trial court found that at the instigation of certain Signal management personnel, including William W. Walkup, its board chairman, and Forrest N. Shumway, its president, a feasibility study was made concerning the possible acquisition of the balance of UOP's outstanding shares. This study was performed by two Signal officers, Charles S. Arledge, vice president (director of planning), and Andrew J. Chitiea, senior vice president (chief financial officer). Messrs. Walkup, Shumway, Arledge and Chitiea were all directors of UOP in addition to their membership on the Signal board.

Arledge and Chitiea concluded that it would be a good investment for Signal to acquire the remaining 49.5% of UOP shares at any price up to $24 each. Their report was discussed between Walkup and Shumway who, along with Arledge, Chitiea and Brewster L. Arms, internal counsel for Signal, constituted Signal's senior management.
* * *

It was ultimately agreed that a meeting of Signal's executive committee would be called to propose that Signal acquire the remaining outstanding stock of UOP through a cash-out merger in the range of $20 to $21 per share.

The executive committee meeting was set for February 28, 1978. As a courtesy, UOP's president, Crawford, was invited to attend, although he was not a member of Signal's executive committee.

* * *

Thus, Crawford voiced no objection to the $20 to $21 price range, nor did he suggest that Signal should consider paying more than $21 per share for the minority interests. * * * For many reasons, Signal's management concluded that the acquisition of UOP's minority shares provided the solution to a number of its business problems.

Thus, it was the consensus that a price of $20 to $21 per share would be fair to both Signal and the minority shareholders of UOP. Signal's executive committee authorized its management "to negotiate" with UOP "for a cash acquisition of the minority ownership in UOP, Inc., with the intention of presenting a proposal to [Signal's] board of directors ... on March 6, 1978".

* * *

The closing price of UOP's common stock on that day was $14.50 per share.

Between Tuesday, February 28, 1978 and Monday, March 6, 1978, a total of four business days, Crawford spoke by telephone with all of UOP's non-Signal, i.e., outside, directors. Also during that period, Crawford retained Lehman Brothers to render a fairness opinion as to the price offered the minority for its stock. He gave two reasons for this choice. First, the time schedule between the announcement and the board meetings was short (by then only three business days) and since Lehman Brothers had been acting as UOP's investment banker for many years, Crawford felt that it would be in the best position to respond on such brief notice. Second, James W. Glanville, a long-time director of UOP and a partner in Lehman Brothers, had acted as a financial advisor to UOP for many years. Crawford believed that Glanville's familiarity with UOP, as a member of its board, would also be of assistance in enabling Lehman Brothers to render a fairness opinion within the existing time constraints.

Crawford telephoned Glanville, who gave his assurance that Lehman Brothers had no conflicts that would prevent it from accepting the task. Glanville's immediate personal reaction was that a price of $20 to $21 would certainly be fair, since it represented almost a 50% premium over UOP's market price. Glanville sought a $250,000 fee for Lehman Brothers' services, but Crawford thought this too much. After further discussions Glanville finally agreed that Lehman Brothers would render its fairness opinion for $150,000.

During this period Crawford also had several telephone contacts with Signal officials. In only one of them, however, was the price of the shares discussed. In a conversation with Walkup, Crawford advised that as a result of his communications with UOP's non-Signal directors, it was his feeling that the price would have to be the top of the proposed range, or $21 per share, if the approval of UOP's outside directors was to be obtained. But again, he did not seek any price higher than $21.

Glanville assembled a three-man Lehman Brothers team to do the work on the fairness opinion. These persons examined relevant documents and information concerning UOP, including its annual reports and its Securities and Exchange Commission filings from 1973 through 1976, as well as its audited financial statements for 1977, its interim reports to shareholders, and its recent and historical market prices and trading volumes. In addition, on Friday, March 3, 1978, two members of the Lehman Brothers team flew to UOP's headquarters in Des Plaines, Illinois, to perform a "due diligence" visit, during the course of which they interviewed Crawford as well as UOP's general counsel, its chief financial officer, and other key executives and personnel.

As a result, the Lehman Brothers team concluded that "the price of either $20 or $21 would be a fair price for the remaining shares of UOP". They telephoned this impression to Glanville, who was spending the weekend in Vermont.

On Monday morning, March 6, 1978, Glanville and the senior member of the Lehman Brothers team flew to Des Plaines to attend the scheduled UOP directors meeting. Glanville looked over the assembled information during the flight. The two had with them the draft of a "fairness opinion letter" in which the price had been left blank. Either during or immediately prior to the directors' meeting, the two-page "fairness opinion letter" was typed in final form and the price of $21 per share was inserted.

On March 6, 1978, both the Signal and UOP boards were convened to consider the proposed merger. Telephone communications were maintained between the two meetings. Walkup, Signal's board chairman, and also a UOP director, attended UOP's meeting with Crawford in order to present Signal's position and answer any questions that UOP's non-Signal directors might have. Arledge and Chitiea, along with Signal's other designees on UOP's board, participated by conference telephone. All of UOP's outside directors attended the meeting either in person or by conference telephone.

First, Signal's board unanimously adopted a resolution authorizing Signal to propose to UOP a cash merger of $21 per share as outlined in a certain merger agreement and other supporting documents. This proposal required that the merger be approved by a majority of UOP's outstanding minority shares voting at the stockholders meeting at which the merger would be considered, and that the minority shares voting in favor of the merger, when coupled with Signal's 50.5% interest would have to comprise at least two-thirds of all UOP shares. Otherwise the proposed merger would be deemed disapproved.

UOP's board then considered the proposal. Copies of the agreement were delivered to the directors in attendance, and other copies had been forwarded earlier to the directors participating by telephone. They also had before them UOP financial data for 1974–1977, UOP's most recent financial statements, market price information, and budget projections for 1978. In addition they had Lehman Brothers' hurriedly prepared fairness opinion letter finding the price of $21 to be fair. Glanville, the Lehman Brothers partner, and UOP director, commented on the information that had gone into preparation of the letter.

* * *

After consideration of Signal's proposal, Walkup and Crawford left the meeting to permit a free and uninhibited exchange between UOP's non-Signal directors. Upon their return a resolution to accept Signal's offer was then proposed and adopted. While Signal's men on UOP's board participated in various aspects of the meeting, they abstained from voting. However, the minutes show that each of them "if voting would have voted yes".

On March 7, 1978, UOP sent a letter to its shareholders advising them of the action taken by UOP's board with respect to Signal's offer. This document pointed out, among other things, that on February 28, 1978 "both companies had announced negotiations were being conducted".

Despite the swift board action of the two companies, the merger was not submitted to UOP's shareholders until their annual meeting on May 26, 1978. In the notice of that meeting and proxy statement sent to shareholders in May, UOP's management and board urged that the merger be approved. * * * The proxy statement indicated that the vote of UOP's board in approving the merger had been unanimous. It also advised the shareholders that Lehman Brothers had given its opinion that the merger price of $21 per share was fair to UOP's minority. However, it did not disclose the hurried method by which this conclusion was reached.

As of the record date of UOP's annual meeting, there were 11,488,302 shares of UOP common stock outstanding, 5,688,302 of which were owned by the minority. At the meeting only 56%, or 3,208,652, of the minority shares were voted. Of these, 2,953,812, or 51.9% of the total minority, voted for the merger, and 254,840 voted against it. When Signal's stock was added to the minority shares voting in favor, a total of 76.2% of UOP's outstanding shares approved the merger while only 2.2% opposed it.

By its terms the merger became effective on May 26, 1978, and each share of UOP's stock held by the minority was automatically converted into a right to receive $21 cash.

A primary issue mandating reversal is the preparation by two UOP directors, Arledge and Chitiea, of their feasibility study for the exclusive use and benefit of Signal. This document was of obvious significance to both Signal and UOP. Using UOP data, it described the advantages to Signal of ousting the minority at a price range of $21–$24 per share.

* * *

It is clear from the record that neither Arledge nor Chitiea shared this report with their fellow directors of UOP. We are satisfied that no one else did either. This conduct hardly meets the fiduciary standards applicable to such a transaction.

* * *

None of UOP's outside directors who testified stated that they had seen this document. * * *

The Arledge–Chitiea report speaks for itself in supporting the Chancellor's finding that a price of up to $24 was a "good investment" for Signal. It shows that a return on the investment at $21 would be 15.7% versus 15.5% at $24 per share. This was a difference of only two-tenths of one percent, while it meant over $17,000,000 to the minority. Under such circumstances, paying UOP's minority shareholders $24 would have had relatively little long-term effect on Signal, and the Chancellor's findings concerning the benefit to Signal, even at a price of $24, were obviously correct.

Certainly, this was a matter of material significance to UOP and its shareholders. Since the study was prepared by two UOP directors, using UOP information for the exclusive benefit of Signal, and nothing whatever was done to disclose it to the outside UOP directors or the minority shareholders, a question of breach of fiduciary duty arises. This problem occurs because there were common Signal–UOP directors participating, at least to some extent, in the UOP board's decision-making processes without full disclosure of the conflicts they faced.[7]

* * *

Given the absence of any attempt to structure this transaction on an arm's length basis, Signal cannot escape the effects of the conflicts it faced, particularly when its designees on UOP's board did not totally abstain from participation in the matter. There is no "safe harbor" for such divided loyalties in Delaware. When directors of a Delaware corporation are on both sides of a transaction, they are required to demonstrate their utmost good faith and the most scrupulous inherent fairness of the bargain. * * *

---

7. Although perfection is not possible, or expected, the result here could have been entirely different if UOP had appointed an independent negotiating committee of its outside directors to deal with Signal at arm's length. * * * Since fairness in this context can be equated to conduct by a theoretical, wholly independent, board of directors acting upon the matter before them, it is unfortunate that this course apparently was neither considered nor pursued. * * * Particularly in a parent-subsidiary context, a showing that the action taken was as though each of the contending parties had in fact exerted its bargaining power against the other at arm's length is strong evidence that the transaction meets the test of fairness. * * *

The requirement of fairness is unflinching in its demand that where one stands on both sides of a transaction, he has the burden of establishing its entire fairness, sufficient to pass the test of careful scrutiny by the courts. * * * There is no dilution of this obligation where one holds dual or multiple directorships, as in a parent-subsidiary context. * * * Thus, individuals who act in a dual capacity as directors of two corporations, one of whom is parent and the other subsidiary, owe the same duty of good management to both corporations, and in the absence of an independent negotiating structure (see note 7, *supra*), or the directors' total abstention from any participation in the matter, this duty is to be exercised in light of what is best for both companies. * * * The record demonstrates that Signal has not met this obligation.

The concept of fairness has two basic aspects: fair dealing and fair price. The former embraces questions of when the transaction was timed, how it was initiated, structured, negotiated, disclosed to the directors, and how the approvals of the directors and the stockholders were obtained. The latter aspect of fairness relates to the economic and financial considerations of the proposed merger, including all relevant factors: assets, market value, earnings, future prospects, and any other elements that affect the intrinsic or inherent value of a company's stock.

* * * However, the test for fairness is not a bifurcated one as between fair dealing and price. All aspects of the issue must be examined as a whole since the question is one of entire fairness. However, in a non-fraudulent transaction we recognize that price may be the preponderant consideration outweighing other features of the merger. Here, we address the two basic aspects of fairness separately because we find reversible error as to both.

Part of fair dealing is the obvious duty of candor required by *Lynch I, supra*. Moreover, one possessing superior knowledge may not mislead any stockholder by use of corporate information to which the latter is not privy. * * * With the well-established Delaware law on the subject, and the Court of Chancery's findings of fact here, it is inevitable that the obvious conflicts posed by Arledge and Chitiea's preparation of their "feasibility study", derived from UOP information, for the sole use and benefit of Signal, cannot pass muster.

The Arledge–Chitiea report is but one aspect of the element of fair dealing. How did this merger evolve? It is clear that it was entirely initiated by Signal. The serious time constraints under which the principals acted were all set by Signal. It had not found a suitable outlet for its excess cash and considered UOP a desirable investment, particularly since it was now in a position to acquire the whole company for itself. For whatever reasons, and they were only Signal's, the entire transaction was presented to and approved by UOP's board within four business days. Standing alone, this is not necessarily indicative of any lack of fairness by a majority shareholder. It was what occurred, or more properly, what did not occur, during this brief period that makes the time constraints imposed by Signal relevant to the issue of fairness.

The structure of the transaction, again, was Signal's doing. So far as negotiations were concerned, it is clear that they were modest at best. Crawford, Signal's man at UOP, never really talked price with Signal, except to accede to its management's statements on the subject, and to convey to Signal the UOP outside directors' view that as between the $20–$21 range under consideration, it would have to be $21. The latter is not a surprising outcome, but hardly arm's length negotiations. Only the protection of benefits for UOP's key employees and the issue of Lehman Brothers' fee approached any concept of bargaining.

As we have noted, the matter of disclosure to the UOP directors was wholly flawed by the conflicts of interest raised by the Arledge–Chitiea report. All of those conflicts were resolved by Signal in its own favor without divulging any aspect of them to UOP.

This cannot but undermine a conclusion that this merger meets any reasonable test of fairness. The outside UOP directors lacked one material piece of information generated by two of their colleagues, but shared only with Signal. True, the UOP board had the Lehman Brothers' fairness opinion, but that firm has been blamed by the plaintiff for the hurried task it performed, when more properly the responsibility for this lies with Signal. There was no disclosure of the circumstances surrounding the rather cursory preparation of the Lehman Brothers' fairness opinion. Instead, the impression was given UOP's minority that a careful study had been made, when in fact speed was the hallmark, and Mr. Glanville, Lehman's partner in charge of the matter, and also a UOP director, having spent the weekend in Vermont, brought a draft of the "fairness opinion letter" to the UOP directors' meeting on March 6, 1978 with the price left blank. We can only conclude from the record that the rush imposed on Lehman Brothers by Signal's timetable contributed to the difficulties under which this investment banking firm attempted to perform its responsibilities. Yet, none of this was disclosed to UOP's minority.

Finally, the minority stockholders were denied the critical information that Signal considered a price of $24 to be a good investment. Since this would have meant over $17,000,000 more to the minority, we cannot conclude that the shareholder vote was an informed one. Under the circumstances, an approval by a majority of the minority was meaningless. * * *

[The court's discussion of fair price includes a discussion of the valuation standards that apply in appraisal proceedings. This discussion is contained in pages 64–67.]

ROSENBLATT v. GETTY OIL CO.

Supreme Court of Delaware, 1985.
493 A.2d 929.

MOORE, JUSTICE:

In this class action brought on behalf of the minority stockholders of Skelly Oil Company (Skelly) we review a Court of Chancery decision holding that the 1977 stock-for-stock merger of Skelly and Mission Corporation (Mission) into Getty Oil Company (Getty) was entirely fair to the plaintiffs.

* * *

Immediately before this merger Getty directly owned 7.42% of Skelly's outstanding shares and 89.73% of Mission, which in turn held 72.6% of Skelly's stock.

* * *

On July 12, 1976, Berg [Getty executive vice president and chief operating officer] called James E. Hara, president of Skelly, to inform him that a combination of Getty, Skelly, and Mission was being considered. Berg suggested a conference of high-level Getty and Skelly personnel. This meeting was held in Dallas, Texas, on July 15, 1976, attended by the principal officers of both companies. All acknowledged the desirability of a merger. The consensus was that the fairest way to achieve this result would be an exchange of common stock, continuing shareholder participation in a larger post-merger company. * * *

Generally, it was agreed at the July 15 meeting that DeGolyer and MacNaughton (D & M), a Dallas, Texas, petroleum engineering firm with an outstanding reputation, would assist the parties in evaluating their respective oil, gas and mineral reserves. D & M had worked periodically with both Skelly and Getty since 1939, and had prepared annual estimates of oil and gas reserves for both companies for many years. In addition, D & M had begun preparing annual reports on Getty's mineral properties for the last several years prior to the merger. Accordingly, D & M was contacted on July 15, 1976 by Getty and Skelly and asked to estimate the reserves of both companies, to make an economic valuation based on those estimates, and then to deliver this analysis to the companies for their use in negotiating the merger exchange ratio.

After the July 15 Dallas meeting, Getty and Skelly promptly began evaluating their respective surface and subsurface assets. It is clear that both parties devoted substantial internal resources in preparing to negotiate the exchange ratio of Getty and Skelly stock. In addition, both companies hired reputable investment banking firms to assist in the valuation task, and to render opinions on the fairness of the merger's ultimate terms. Getty retained Blyth, Eastman, Dillon & Co. ("Blyth Eastman"), and Skelly chose Smith Barney, Harris Upham & Co. ("Smith Barney").

* * *

As to their surface properties, each company began compiling an asset book cataloging an item by item value of all their respective above-ground holdings, such as refineries, manufacturing plants, pipelines, transport facilities, etc. Along with the dollar amount accorded each item, there also was a description of the valuation method or methods used to calculate that figure. The asset books, once completed, were to be exchanged. The two companies would then negotiate surface property values for inclusion in their asset factors under the Delaware Block formula. As to their respective subsurface holdings, D & M was to update the reserve estimates of Getty and Skelly with the assistance of each company's personnel. D & M was then to make an economic projection, based on these estimates, for use by the parties in negotiating an exchange ratio.

On September 29, 1976, Getty and Skelly exchanged asset books. Getty immediately discovered that for every item of property listed, Skelly had selected the particular valuation method, irrespective of consistency, which produced the highest asset value. There is testimony that this adversarial approach angered Getty personnel. In contrast, Getty had applied a more consistent, conservative technique of valuing its surface assets. It claims to have done so because of the threat of post-merger litigation. Despite this disparity in approach, Getty and Skelly maintained contact and sought to resolve their differences through hard bargaining. Eventually, they reached accord.

However, while the surface asset books were compiled, exchanged, and their contents negotiated, the companies had numerous meetings with D & M regarding the valuation of their reserves. D & M had begun a field-by-field, lease-by-lease analysis of the oil, gas, and mineral reserves of the parties, working with the Getty or Skelly personnel most familiar with the specific field under study. D & M also examined proprietary information each company maintained regarding its own reserve estimates. * * * Invariably, disputes arose between the two sides as to the values used by D & M, particularly regarding future prices of petroleum products. * * *

On October 25th and 26th, Getty, Skelly, their investment bankers, and D & M met to finalize the previously negotiated surface asset values, and to discuss subsurface asset problems. With the issues of the surface asset values then behind them, the parties focused on disputes regarding the dollar value of their respective reserves. At issue were the "imponderables" to be used by D & M in appraising the reserves, and it soon became apparent that the parties were at an impasse.

Thus, on October 27, 1976, Berg of Getty proposed that each side delegate to D & M the task of calculating the present fair market value of their respective reserves, given the obstacles presented by the projections and variables. Skelly concurred, and D & M accepted the task with the understanding that its methods would not be revealed to the parties. In addition, Getty, Skelly, and Mission agreed that D & M's valuation would be final and binding upon them. With this accord, D & M rendered its estimates on October 29, 1976.

On the morning of November 1, 1976, the parties and their investment bankers then met to determine a stock exchange ratio for the merger. * * * In particular, the parties sought to negotiate per share values for the asset, earnings, and market price factors, as well as the percentage weight to be assigned each element. Getty anticipated an exchange ratio of between .46 to .55 shares of its common stock for one share of Skelly common. Morgan, Skelly's spokesman, stressed the importance of earnings over assets and emphasized the market's undervaluation of Skelly stock. He therefore proposed .7 as the right figure.

There was testimony that this suggestion angered the Getty representatives, who viewed it as absurdly high. Kenneth Hill of Getty countered with a possible exchange ratio of .5. Thereafter, the parties discussed the elements of assets, earnings, and market price, including their subratios, and how they should be weighted under the Delaware Block method. While each side criticized the other, the negotiations slowly progressed. By the afternoon of November 1, Getty was offering a ratio of .57 and Skelly was proposing .61.

However, at this point the parties reached an impasse. Berg of Getty suggested terminating the discussion. Hays, a Getty director and its counsel, drafted a press release announcing the end of merger negotiations. As the meeting broke up, Hara of Skelly strongly urged Berg to continue the discussions. He persuaded Berg to consult with the Getty board of directors at its next meeting on November 5, 1976.

Berg did so, and at their meeting, Getty's directors concluded that .58 was the highest acceptable exchange ratio. Berg relayed this to Hara by telephone on the afternoon of November 5. Hara then suggested another meeting between Getty and Skelly on November 7 at the annual session of the American Petroleum Institute, a function which certain Getty and Skelly personnel would have attended anyway. Berg agreed.

At the November 7 meeting, Berg reiterated Getty's firm position that .58 was the highest acceptable exchange ratio. After discussion, the Skelly representatives left the room and met privately. At this point, a Skelly team member suggested that their company's earnings be adjusted to reflect a weighted average of only the last three years, rather than the past five years. It was noted that two of the last three years saw Skelly's highest historical earnings, and that Getty itself had used such a method in a prior transaction. Skelly presented this adjustment with a correlative new exchange ratio of .5875 to Getty. After a private caucus Getty agreed to the earnings revision and offered a ratio of .5875 Getty shares for one share of Skelly stock. Skelly accepted. Thus, as finally negotiated, the parties agreed to the following valuation:

	Ratio of value of Skelly Share to Getty Share	Percentage Weighting	Weighted Ratio of Skelly Share to Getty Share
Assets	.525	47.5%	.2494
Earnings	.667	47.5%	.3168
Market Price	.427	5.0%	.0213

	Ratio of value of Skelly Share to Getty Share	Percentage Weighting	Weighted Ratio of Skelly Share to Getty Share
Exchange Ratio			.5875

On November 13, 1976, the Skelly and Getty boards met to consider the merger. After a thorough review of the whole matter, Skelly's independent directors, and then its entire board, approved the agreement for submission to Skelly's shareholders. Similarly, Getty's board voted unanimously for the merger. On January 25, 1977, the shareholders of both companies assented to the transaction. Of Skelly's minority shares voted at the meeting, 89.4% favored the merger. In terms of all outstanding Skelly minority shares, this represented a vote of 58% in favor of the proposal. Skelly and Mission were merged into Getty on January 31, 1977.

* * *

The plaintiffs challenge the fairness of the transaction, including the exchange ratio and the propriety of delegating the final subsurface asset valuation to D & M.

* * *

Beginning with the burden of proof, we agree with the trial court that the plaintiffs' allegations were sufficient to challenge the fairness of the merger ratio. * * * Clearly, Getty, as majority shareholder of Skelly, stood on both sides of this transaction and bore the initial burden of establishing its entire fairness. However, approval of a merger, as here, by an informed vote of a majority of the minority shareholders, while not a legal prerequisite, shifts the burden of proving the unfairness of the merger entirely to the plaintiffs. Getty, nonetheless, retained the burden of showing complete disclosure of all material facts relevant to that vote.

On the basis of this record we are satisfied that Getty dealt fairly with Skelly throughout the transaction. Indeed, the adversarial nature of the negotiations completely supports a conclusion that they were conducted at arm's length. There is no credible evidence indicating that Getty, as the majority shareholder, dictated the terms of this merger. If anything, the facts are to the contrary. Thus, what we have here is more than the theoretical concept of what an independent board might do under like circumstances. * * *

Instead, it is clear that these contending parties to the merger in fact exerted their bargaining power against one another at arm's length. This is of considerable importance when addressing ultimate questions of fairness, since it may give rise to the proposition that the directors' actions are more appropriately measured by business judgment standards. * * *

Plaintiffs seek to compare this action to *Weinberger* by claiming that a memorandum, dated October 14, 1976, prepared by Robert J. Menzie, a Getty financial officer, was never disclosed to Skelly. In particular, plaintiffs liken this document, projecting a $52,165,000 after-tax decrease in Getty's 1976 earnings, in comparison to its 1975 earnings, to the Arledge and Chitiea report in *Weinberger,* which indicated that the majority shareholder, Signal, still considered the elimination of the minority an "outstanding investment opportunity" even at a price higher than that actually being offered. *See Weinberger,* 457 A.2d at 705, 708, 712. However, the two reports are factually and legally different. First, it is not clear that Skelly and its negotiators were unaware of Getty's projected earnings decrease. Morgan, one of Skelly's investment bankers and principal negotiators, testified on cross-examination:

> Mr. Morris, I unfortunately can't at this stage go back five years and remember exactly what numbers were given to me. In the normal course of business, you may be sure that when I went into the room on November 1st somebody in my group knew what the earnings projections of Getty were and had given me that information or had it there so, if the subject was necessary to be discussed, I could use it. And I do not recall at this time specifically what information it was, but I can assure you it was there.

Second, the Arledge–Chitiea report, used secretly by and exclusively for Signal, was prepared by two Signal directors, who were also UOP directors, using UOP information obtained solely in their capacities as UOP directors. *Weinberger,* 457 A.2d at 705. Here, the decreased earnings projection was prepared by a member of Getty's management for Getty's use as part of its annual reporting function. Moreover, there is not the slightest indication that its disclosure could have materially affected the exchange ratio negotiations. *See id.* at 709, 712. Third, the merger in *Weinberger* was expressly conditioned on approval of a majority of UOP's minority shareholders; here, there was no such condition. *See id.* at 707.

While it has been suggested that *Weinberger* stands for the proposition that a majority shareholder must under all circumstances disclose its top bid to the minority, that clearly is a misconception of what we said there. The sole basis for our conclusions in *Weinberger* regarding the non-disclosure of the Arledge–Chitiea report was because Signal appointed directors on UOP's board, who thus stood on both sides of the transaction, violated their undiminished duty of loyalty to UOP. It had nothing to do with Signal's duty, as the majority stockholder, to the other shareholders of UOP.

As to the approval of the merger proposal by the Getty and Skelly boards, the record shows that their action was taken on an informed basis. * * * At Skelly's board meeting, the directors were fully briefed by Smith Barney and by Blyth Eastman, on the basis of copies of valuation books prepared and distributed by the two investment banks. Skelly's directors had been given copies of the proxy statement prior to the meeting. Skelly's board received a legal opinion on the merger, as well as copies of D & M's final estimate. The directors also heard from the attorney representing Gruss, the Skelly shareholder who had been threatening suit since May 1976. The record also shows that certain

Skelly directors, including outside director Stuart, who controlled more stock than the plaintiff class, questioned Getty representatives Garber and Thompson, as well as Skelly management, on the fairness of the exchange ratio. Following this discussion, Copley, Jones, and Williams, who were Getty and Mission officers, as well as Skelly directors, were excused from the Skelly board meeting. Outside director Stuart moved to approve the proposed merger ratio. The resolution was unanimously adopted. Copley, Jones, and Williams returned and concurred with the resolution. At the Getty board meeting, Getty's directors were given a similar, in-depth briefing on the proposed merger, and voted to approve it.

* * *

After careful scrutiny of the methods employed by the parties, the process of information gathering, the negotiations, and all relevant economic and financial factors, we conclude that the Chancellor's findings regarding fairness of the price paid the Skelly minority shareholders were entirely correct.

* * *

Turning to the propriety of the delegation of the subsurface asset valuation to D & M, we note that this action too is subject to the entire fairness standard. However, plaintiffs' argument, as we understand it, is that this was an impermissible act in the sense that it was an abdication of directorial responsibility. * * *

Thus, unless it was a proper business decision in the first instance the ultimate question of fairness is moot.

An informed decision to delegate a task is as much an exercise of business judgment as any other. * * * The realities of modern corporate life are such that directors cannot be expected to manage the day-to-day activities of a company. This is recognized by the provisions of 8 *Del.C.* § 141(a) that the business and affairs of a Delaware corporation are managed "by or under the direction" of its board. In setting its agenda as to the matters in which it will be directly involved, and those it will delegate, a board's decisions in those areas are entitled to equal consideration as exercises of business judgment. * * * Moreover, the trial court found as a fact that D & M had an outstanding worldwide reputation as a petroleum engineering consultant. D & M has valued Getty's reserves since 1939, and has done similar work with Skelly for several years. However, there is no proof that D & M lacked independence or was in any way beholden to either party. The record fully supports a conclusion that D & M had the requisite reputation and experience to assist Getty and Skelly.

Second, it is important to note why the delegation was made, and what task was actually delegated. In late October 1976, Getty and Skelly were unable to agree on future price schedules of oil and natural gas. D & M was to apply the future price schedules to the reserves estimates and thereby calculate several economic analyses which the parties would then discuss. Given their disagreements, the parties turned to D & M to select prices, costs, and risk factors and then make a final estimate of asset value. * * * At this point the parties had their negotiated surface asset values, D & M's reserve estimates, their own reserve estimates, and the preliminary economic analyses used by D & M. Furthermore, evidence shows that Skelly personnel, who considered the use of D & M to be to their advantage, did in fact double-check D & M's results. However, the parties did not delegate the weighting task under the Delaware Block method, nor did they bind themselves to merge in the first instance. * * * Rather, the parties in effect selected an independent appraiser to value subsurface assets. Coupled with the fact that this was done in the course of arm's length negotiations, a conclusion which this record amply supports, it is clear that each party acted independently in delegating the task to D & M. Those actions meet the test of independence announced by us in *Aronson v. Lewis.*

* * *

COGGINS v. NEW ENGLAND PATRIOTS FOOTBALL CLUB, INC.

Supreme Judicial Court of Massachusetts, 1986.
397 Mass. 525, 492 N.E.2d 1112.

LIACOS, JUSTICE.

On November 18, 1959, William H. Sullivan, Jr. (Sullivan), purchased an American Football League (AFL) franchise for a professional football team. * * * For the franchise, Sullivan paid $25,000. Four months later, Sullivan organized a corporation, the American League Professional Football Team of Boston, Inc. Sullivan contributed his AFL franchise; nine other persons each contributed $25,000. In return, each of the ten investors received 10,000 shares of voting common stock in the corporation. Another four months later, in July, 1960, the corporation sold 120,000 shares of nonvoting common stock to the public at $5 a share.

* * *

In 1974 the other voting stockholders ousted him from the presidency and from operating control of the corporation. He then began the effort to regain control of the corporation—an effort which culminated in this and other law suits.

In November, 1975, Sullivan succeeded in obtaining ownership or control of all 100,000 of the voting shares, at a price of approximately $102 a share (adjusted cash value), of the corporation, by that time renamed the New England Patriots Football Club, Inc. (Old Patriots). "Upon completion of the purchase, he immediately used his 100% control to vote out the hostile directors, elect a friendly board and arrange his resumption of the presidency and the complete control of the Patriots. In order to finance this coup, Sullivan borrowed approximately $5,348,000 from the Rhode Island Hospital National Bank and the Lasalle National Bank of Chicago. As a condition of these loans, Sullivan was to use his best efforts to reorganize the Patriots so that the income of the corporation could be devoted to the payment of these personal loans and the assets of the corporation pledged to secure them. At this point they were secured by all of the voting shares held by Sullivan. In order to accomplish in effect the assumption by the corporation of Sullivan's personal obligations, it was necessary, as a matter of corporate law, to eliminate the interest of the nonvoting shares."

On October 20, 1976, Sullivan organized a new corporation called the New Patriots Football Club, Inc. (New Patriots). The board of directors of the Old Patriots and the board of directors of the New Patriots executed an agreement of merger of the two corporations providing that, after the merger, the voting stock of the Old Patriots would be extinguished, the nonvoting stock would be exchanged for cash at the rate of $15 a share, and the name of the New Patriots would be changed to the name formerly used by the Old Patriots. As part of this plan, Sullivan gave the New Patriots his 100,000 voting shares of the Old Patriots in return for 100% of the New Patriots stock.

General Laws c. 156B, § 78(c)(1)(iii), as amended through St.1976, c. 327, required approval of the merger agreement by a majority vote of each class of affected stock. Approval by the voting class, entirely controlled by Sullivan, was assured. The merger was approved by the class of nonvoting stockholders at a special meeting on December 8, 1976.[7] On January 31, 1977, the merger of the New Patriots and the Old Patriots was consummated.

David A. Coggins (Coggins) was the owner of ten shares of nonvoting stock in the Old Patriots. Coggins, a fan of the Patriots from the time of their formation, was serving in Vietnam in 1967 when he purchased the shares through his brother. Over the years, he followed the fortunes of the team, taking special pride in his status as an owner.[8] When he heard of the proposed merger, Coggins was upset that he could be forced to sell. Coggins voted against the merger and commenced this suit on behalf of those stockholders, who, like himself, believed the transaction to be unfair and illegal.

* * *

The defendants argue that judicial review of a merger cannot be invoked by disgruntled stockholders, absent illegal or fraudulent con-

---

7. On the date of the meeting, 139,800 shares of nonvoting stock were outstanding, held by approximately 2,400 stockholders. The Sullivan family owned 10,826 shares. Of the remaining 128,974, a total of 71,644 voted in favor of the merger, 22,795 did not vote, and 34,535 voted against. The plaintiffs in this case are stockholders of 2,291 of the 34,535 voting against the merger.

Prior to the 1976 amendment of G.L. c. 156B, § 78(c)(1)(iii), that section required a two-thirds vote of approval for a merger from each class of stock. The two-thirds requirement was reinstated in 1981 by St. 1981, c. 298, § 4.

8. It was, in part, the goal of the Old Patriots, in offering stock to the public, to generate loyal fans.

duct. They rely on G.L. c. 156B, § 98 (1984 ed.). In the defendants' view, "the Superior Court's finding of liability was premised solely on the claimed inadequacy of the offering price." Any dispute over offering price, they urge, must be resolved solely through the statutory remedy of appraisal.

We have held in regard to so called "close corporations" that the statute does not divest the courts of their equitable jurisdiction to assure that the conduct of controlling stockholders does not violate the fiduciary principles governing the relationship between majority and minority stockholders. * * *

The dangers of self-dealing and abuse of fiduciary duty are greatest in freeze-out situations like the Patriots merger, where a controlling stockholder and corporate director chooses to eliminate public ownership. It is in these cases that a judge should examine with closest scrutiny the motives and the behavior of the controlling stockholder. A showing of compliance with statutory procedures is an insufficient substitute for the inquiry of the courts when a minority stockholder claims that the corporate action "will be or is illegal or fraudulent as to him." G.L. c. 156B, § 98.

* * *

A controlling stockholder who is also a director standing on both sides of the transaction bears the burden of showing that the transaction does not violate fiduciary obligations. * * *

Judicial scrutiny should begin with recognition of the basic principle that the duty of a corporate director must be to further the legitimate goals of the corporation. The result of a freeze-out merger is the elimination of public ownership in the corporation. The controlling faction increases its equity from a majority to 100%, using corporate processes and corporate assets. The corporate directors who benefit from this transfer of ownership must demonstrate how the legitimate goals of the corporation are furthered. A director of a corporation violates his fiduciary duty when he uses the corporation for his or his family's personal benefit in a manner detrimental to the corporation. * * * Because the danger of abuse of fiduciary duty is especially great in a freeze-out merger, the court must be satisfied that the freeze-out was for the advancement of a legitimate corporate purpose. If satisfied that elimination of public ownership is in furtherance of a business purpose, the court should then proceed to determine if the transaction was fair by examining the totality of the circumstances.

The plaintiffs here adequately alleged that the merger of the Old Patriots and New Patriots was a freeze-out merger undertaken for no legitimate business purpose, but merely for the personal benefit of Sullivan. While we have recognized the right to "selfish ownership" in a corporation, such a right must be balanced against the concept of the majority stockholder's fiduciary obligation to the minority stockholders. * * * Consequently, the defendants bear the burden of proving, first, that the merger was for a legitimate business purpose, and, second, that, considering totality of circumstances, it was fair to the minority.

The decision of the Superior Court judge includes a finding that "the defendants have failed to demonstrate that the merger served any valid corporate objective unrelated to the personal interests of the majority shareholders. It thus appears that the sole reason for the merger was to effectuate a restructuring of the Patriots that would enable the repayment of the [personal] indebtedness incurred by Sullivan...." The trial judge considered the defendants' claims that the policy of the National Football League (NFL) requiring majority ownership by a single individual or family made it necessary to eliminate public ownership. He found that "the stock ownership of the Patriots as it existed just prior to the merger fully satisfied the rationale underlying the policy as expressed by NFL Commissioner Pete Rozelle. Having acquired 100% control of the voting common stock of the Patriots, Sullivan possessed unquestionable authority to act on behalf of the franchise at League meetings and effectively foreclosed the possible recurrence of the internal management disputes that had existed in 1974. Moreover, as the proxy statement itself notes, the Old Patriots were under no legal compulsion to eliminate public ownership." Likewise, the defendants did not succeed in showing a conflict between the interests of the league owners and the Old Patriots' stockholders. We perceive no error in these findings. They are fully supported by the evidence. Under the approach we set forth above, there is no need to consider further the elements of fairness of a transaction that is not related to a valid corporate purpose.

* * *

Questions

1. Can a firm be more valuable without minority shareholders than with minority shareholders? What costs are saved by 100 percent ownership? Should minority shareholders receive some of the cost savings? If so, how can the savings be allocated?

2. If a controlling shareholder executes a freeze-out to appropriate the benefit of new plans (or new opportunities) for the firm, should minority shareholders receive a portion of the value of the new plans? If so, how can the value be allocated? What if the new plans have a positive expected value ex ante but are very risky (large losses are possible as well as large gains)? Are your answers the same for minority shareholders who are frozen out in the second step of a two-stage takeover by another firm (the first step being a cash tender offer for 51 percent of the voting stock)?

3. How should a firm structure a freeze-out to comply with *Weinberger*? Can a parent firm avoid revealing its bottom-line or reservation price to the minority shareholders (e.g., the feasibility study in *Weinberger*) in the acquisition? If not, what is the effect of the disclosure?

4. Should the holdings in *Weinberger* or *Coggins* apply to issuer tender offers? To management buyouts? Do these acquisitions have similar conflict-of-interest problems?

Note
Fair Value in Squeeze–Out Mergers

If a court is asked to decide whether an acquisition price is fair under appraisal statutes or in a proceeding based on violations of fiduciary duty, what standards apply? We discussed this in an earlier chapter on appraisal proceedings, and those materials are relevant again here. See chapter 2.

In Sterling v. Mayflower Hotel Corp., 33 Del.Ch. 293, 93 A.2d 107 (1952), the court said: "Hilton as majority stockholder of Mayflower and the Hilton directors as its nominees occupy, in relation to the minority, a fiduciary position in dealing with Mayflower's property. Since they stand on both sides of the transaction, they bear the burden of establishing its entire fairness, and it must pass the test of careful scrutiny by the courts." The court added that "the test of fairness which we think [is] the correct one [is] that upon a merger the minority stockholder shall receive the substantial equivalent in value of what he had before." As we saw in *Weinberger v. UOP*, the court has relaxed this standard to allow judges to include some "nonspeculative" amount representing value generated by the merger itself. Is this development wise?

In a seminal article Professors Brudney and Chirelstein argue that the basic *Sterling* formula (termed the give-get test) is improper. They observe that when a parent corporation, P, absorbs its partially owned subsidiary, S,

> the fiduciary obligation may be envisioned in ... three possible forms. The first—which reflects the prevailing body of law—apparently assumes direct arm's-length dealings between P (the entity) and the individual shareholders of S. Such dealings are considered fair if the price paid for the minority shares is equal to their pre-merger value ... even though a gain results from the merger itself which is retained in full by P. The second alternative assumes that the dealings are between P and an uncontrolled S, with each entity being represented by an independent bargaining agent. On that assumption a wide range of outcomes is possible, and no single outcome seems to be dictated. If a fair bargain would entail an equal dollar division of the merger gain [between the two corporations], the S stockholders would receive ... the pre-merger value of their stock in S plus their share of half of the merger increment allocated to S. Finally, the third version of fiduciary duty ... entirely discards the idea of dealings between P and S or its stockholders. What is emphasized instead is the duty of management to treat all stockholders alike by giving each an equal return on his investment, whether that investment is in the shares of P or the shares of S. Under this formulation the allocation of values is fair if the S stockholders receive the pre-merger value of their shares [plus a proportional fraction of the] gain attributable to the merger.... This method provides a determinate or unique solution to the

sharing problem and avoids the difficulties inherent in the artificial assumption that dealing between P and S takes place at arm's-length.

Brudney & Chirelstein, *Fair Shares in Corporate Mergers and Takeovers*, 88 Harv.L.Rev. 297, 322–23 (1974). One example of the third alternative, where the gains attributable to the merger will increase the value of the survivor's common stock, is the allocation of that stock in proportion to the premerger values of the common stock of P and S. Id. at 311 n. 36. In a cash-out merger, the synergy value would have to be predicted, a difficult thing to do.

Professors Easterbrook and Fischel, on the other hand, embrace the give-get test of fairness. They object to the sharing of benefits as harmful to investors: "An investor with a reasonably diversified portfolio would be on the winning side of some transactions and the losing side of others.... [I]f shareholders of one corporation obtain little of the gain from a given merger, the shareholders of the other corporation obtain more." Because these transactions create value, investors will be better off if there are more of them than if there are fewer. More synergy-creating transactions will occur if those who execute them can keep the full benefits of what they spend time and money to create, so in the long run all diversified investors will be richer. Easterbrook & Fischel, *Corporate Control Transactions*, 91 Yale L.J. 698 (1982).

Chapter Six

THE REGISTRATION AND DISCLOSURE REQUIREMENTS OF THE FEDERAL SECURITIES ACT

SUBCHAPTER A. REGISTRATION UNDER THE FEDERAL SECURITIES ACT OF 1933: EXCHANGE TRANSACTIONS

Effect of the Act on Exchange Tender Offers

The Securities Act of 1933 protects the purchasers of securities, broadly defined to include both debt and equity investment securities, in public offerings. The classic scenario is a single firm raising capital to fund business expansion by selling stock to a large number of people who hope the stock will pay dividends, rise in value, or both. The act, however, applies to all major firm acquisitions in which the target shareholders receive securities in the bidder rather than cash.

If an acquisition takes the form of an exchange tender offer, that is, a public offer to exchange target stock for stock or debt in the buyer (or the buyer's parent), the offer is a distribution of securities by an issuer (the buyer) to the public (the holders of stock in the target) and is regulated under the Securities Act of 1933. Once the act applies, it imposes a detailed and costly regulatory apparatus.

The following is a brief summary: The buyer must register the distribution with the Securities and Exchange Commission unless the issuer can qualify under one of a limited number of exemptions. If the number of target shareholders is large (over thirty-five), these exemptions are of limited usefulness.[1] The registration statement must

---

1. The only major exemptions relevant to the acquisition of a publicly held company are section 3(a)(10), which exempts from registration securities issued in select exchange transactions where the terms of the issuance and exchange are approved after a hearing on the fairness by a court, official, or agency of the United States government, or any state banking or insurance commission, or other governmental authority expressly authorized to grant such approval, Rule 509, and regulation A, which exempts offerings of under $1.5 million as long as the issuer follows an abbreviated registration process.

The most important exemption for closely held targets is the so-called private-offering exemption in section 4(2) of the 1933

contain specified information about the security, the issuer, and the underwriters (investment bankers who place the security).

In filing a registration statement, a buyer may choose to use either form S–1 or a special form for acquisitions, form S–4. If using form S–4, the buyer must include information about the terms of the transaction (including pro forma financials for the projected combined firm), information about itself, and information about the target, which may be difficult to do if the acquisition is hostile. Moreover, under item 19(a) of form S–4, if the transaction is an exchange offer, the prospectus must provide a brief description of any material interest of the affiliates (controlling shareholders and managers, for example) in either company in the proposed transaction, information concerning voting securities and the principal holders of such securities in both companies, the vote, if any, required for approval, and information about executive compensation and certain relationships and related transactions involving the directors and executive officers of the surviving or acquiring company. The parties can use a form S–4 filing to satisfy both the buyer's schedule 14D–1 and the target's schedule 14D–9 filing requirements if the parties are careful to integrate any added informational requirements in the schedules into the S–4.

Similarly, when the buyer uses form S–1, it must provide, in addition to the information required in conventional public offerings of securities, the information required by item 9 (description of securities) and item 11 (information with respect to the registrant) as if the target were the issuer. The buyer must also include financial statements of the seller and pro forma financial statements for the combined firm. Regardless of the form the buyer uses, if the target firm's securities are registered pursuant to section 12 of the 1934 act, rule 432 also requires that the prospectus contain all the information required by rule 14d–6(e)(1) of the Williams Act, a provision detailing information to be included in a schedule 14d–1.

Before filing the registration statement, an issuer cannot offer the securities, nor make public statements anticipating the offer and warming up the market ("gun jumping"). Once the statement is filed, an issuer can offer, but not sell, the securities to the public. Only after the registration statement becomes "effective" can the issuer sell the secu-

act and in rules 505 and 506 of regulation D. Loosely stated, if the number of offerors is limited (usually under thirty-five) and the offerees have adequate information and the sophistication to understand the information, the transaction does not have to be registered with the SEC. Moreover, in calculating the number of offerees, some sophisticated purchasers ("accredited investors"), usually institutional investors, are excluded in rules 505 and 506 from the total count. The disadvantage of a private placement is that target shareholders cannot resell their shares without themselves registering or qualifying under an exemption. Rule 144 defines a very limited safe harbor for resales of stock reviewed in private placements. A new development however, is rule 144A, which provides unlimited resales of private placement stock for large institutional investors. Thus it is possible to exchange acquired stock for target stock held solely by large institutional investors in a private placement, free of resale restrictions. We have yet to see the influence of rule 144A on acquisitions, however.

rities, and then only if the issuer (or its underwriters) gives to each buyer a prospectus containing much of the information required in the registration statement.

It would seem consistent with the basic timing breakdown of the 1933 act to allow buyers to make an exchange tender offer on the same day they file a registration statement, receiving tenders before the effective date of the registration statement, so long as the shares are not accepted until after the registration statement becomes effective. In essence, the tender offeror would condition its offer on the effectiveness of the registration statement. Indeed, the SEC's Advisory Committee on Tender Offers recommended this procedure in July 1983. See Statement of Chairman Shad before Hearings of the House Subcommittee on Telecommunications, Consumer Protection, and Finance (March 28, 1984), reprinted in Fed.Sec.L.Rep. (CCH) ¶ 83,511. After initial agreement with the recommendation, id., the SEC later refused to sanction such a procedure, however. See SEC Release No. 6578 (April 23, 1985), reprinted in Fed.Sec.L.Rep. (CCH) ¶ 72,418. So, as it stands, an exchange tender offer can begin only after a registration statement has become effective.[2]

In 1982 the SEC adopted rule 415, which permits certain securities, including those to be offered in connection with business combinations, to be registered for offering on a delayed or continuous basis. Can a firm that has its securities "on the shelf" under such a registration engage in an exchange tender offer without further 1933 act filings? No. Attempts to circumvent the rule with a shelf registration of buyer securities under rule 415 have been specifically interdicted by the SEC's requirement that a buyer must file a posteffective amendment to its registration statement that includes specific information on an identified target. See form S-4, instruction H. Posteffective amendments become effective on the discretion of the director of the Division of Corporation Finance. 17 C.F.R. § 2000.30–1(a)(1). The only exception is for transactions that would be exempt from 1933 act filing requirements, typically because the number of target shareholders is very small. In such cases a prospectus supplement (sticker) is sufficient. If a posteffective amendment is required, it must contain a complete description of the transaction and the target and updated financial statements. Is rule 415 of any use then in acquisitions? Issuers with active acquisition programs using noncash consideration may still want to register a block of securities for the shelf and, at the time of each transaction, update the shelf prospectus as a way of saving the costs of preparing separate registration statements for each transaction.

A registration statement, according to the 1933 act, automatically becomes effective twenty days after filing unless the commission declares it effective sooner or takes action to toll the running of the

---

2. Apparently the SEC considers tenders by shareholders in response to a tender offer a "sale" under section 5 of the 1933 act even if the tender is subject to withdrawal rights or made contingent on the effectiveness of the registration statement.

period. In practice the SEC demands that all registrants waive the twenty-day period. See rule 473 (providing for a paragraph on the cover of a registration statement that effects a continuing amendment) and rule 461 (used by the SEC to condition acceleration on the issuer's filing a delaying amendment). The delaying amendment gives the SEC time to screen the registration statements and decide which ones to review thoroughly. The commission staff will not disclose its criteria for selection. If an issuer's statement is not reviewed, it receives notice five days after filing and may ask that the statement become effective anytime, on forty-eight hours' notice. If an issuer's statement is reviewed, the SEC, on the overwhelming majority of reviewed statements, requests additional information. This "letter of comment" appears, on average, for filings by repeat registrants twenty-eight days after filing. Once an issuer has satisfied the concerns in the letter, and this may take several weeks after the SEC sends its letter of comment, the SEC will declare the registration statement effective.

In passing on registration statements, the SEC does not approve or pass on the merits of a security. The sole task of the SEC is to ensure that the registration statement is, on its face, accurate and complete. The SEC is free to decide, after declaring a statement effective, that the statement was in fact misleading or false. The act and case law on the act provide for substantial civil and criminal liabilities against the issuer and its managers and others involved with the registration statement if there are material misstatements or omissions in the statement.

The act dramatically affects exchange tender offers by adding a layer of filings to the Williams Act filings.[3] This adds considerable expense and timing hurdles to the Williams Act timing regulations that a cash tender offer does not have to satisfy. The buyer must supply information about the target in the registration materials "if reasonably available." See SEC rule 409. The act also adds potential liability for acts (for "gun jumping" in the prefiling period and underwriter status in the posteffective period, for example) not at risk in cash tender offers and liability for filings not necessary in cash tender offers, all of which provide litigation fodder for recalcitrant targets. As discussed below, the buyer's stock held by the target's shareholders after the exchange is subject to resale restrictions.

In short, the 1933 act hinders the flexibility of exchange tender offers and encourages the use of cash tender offers. An exchange tender offer cannot be sprung on a target as a surprise, while a cash tender offer can. An exchange tender offer gives target managers more time to defend against the offer, and competing bidders have more time to enter the fray. An exchange tender offer is at a severe disadvantage against a cash tender offer in a bidding auction for a target; a cash tender offer can be made sooner and closed faster than an exchange

---

3. A third level of filings is required if the exchange tender offer stipulates that the right to vote the stock passes on tender. Such a tender offer may become a proxy solicitation and come under proxy solicitation requirements.

offer. Finally, an exchange tender offer costs more both in fees and in the present expected value of potential liability than a cash tender offer. It's no wonder that the financial markets have created sophisticated mechanisms for generating large amounts of cash for the use of buyers, and that cash is the preferred method of acquisition compensation, at least for the acquisition of the controlling block of stock.

Most laypeople assume that the target shareholders who have exchanged target shares for buyer securities in an exchange tender offer may immediately turn those securities into cash by selling them in the markets. This assumption is false. The SEC has developed a "presumptive underwriter" doctrine in a series of no-action letters that applies to target shareholders who receive a substantial amount (around 10 percent) of the block of buyer's stock used in the acquisition. If the doctrine applies, the shareholder must either file a full registration statement for the resale or qualify under rule 145(d) or rule 144, discussed in the next section. See SEC No–Action Letters on E.H. Crump Cos (avail. Oct. 18, 1979), MCI Communications (avail. Jan. 11, 1975), Barnett Banks of Fla., Inc. (avail. Dec. 13, 1976). Outside the safe harbor rules, the contours of the doctrine are hazy.

The facts of the following case are a rare example of a contested exchange tender offer.

PIPER v. CHRIS–CRAFT INDUSTRIES, INC.

Supreme Court of the United States, 1977.
430 U.S. 1, 97 S.Ct. 926, 51 L.Ed.2d 124.

* * *

Mr. Chief Justice Burger:

The three petitions present questions of first impression, arising out of a "sophisticated and hard fought contest" for control of Piper Aircraft Corp., a Pennsylvania-based manufacturer of light aircraft. Piper's management consisted principally of members of the Piper family, who owned 31% of Piper's outstanding stock. Chris–Craft Industries, Inc., a diversified manufacturer of recreational products, attempted to secure voting control of Piper through cash and exchange tender offers for Piper common stock. Chris–Craft's takeover attempt failed, and Bangor Punta Corp. (Bangor or Bangor Punta), with the support of the Piper family, obtained control of Piper in September 1969. Chris–Craft brought suit under § 14(e) of the Securities Exchange Act of 1934 and Rule 10b–6 alleging that Bangor Punta achieved control of the target corporation as a result of violations of the federal securities laws by the Piper family, Bangor Punta, and Bangor Punta's underwriter, First Boston Corp., who together had successfully repelled Chris–Craft's takeover attempt.

The struggle for control of Piper began in December 1968. At that time, Chris–Craft began making cash purchases of Piper common stock. By January 22, 1969, Chris–Craft had acquired 203,700 shares, or approximately 13% of Piper's 1,644,790 outstanding shares. On the next day, following unsuccessful preliminary overtures to Piper by Chris–Craft's president, Herbert Siegel, Chris–Craft publicly announced a cash tender offer for up to 300,000 Piper shares [1] at $65 per share, which was approximately $12 above the then-current market price. Responding promptly to Chris–Craft's bid, Piper's management met on the same day with the company's investment banker, First Boston, and other advisers. On January 24, the Piper family decided to oppose Chris–Craft's tender offer. As part of its resistance to Chris–Craft's takeover campaign, Piper management sent several letters to the company's stockholders during January 25–27, arguing against acceptance of Chris–Craft's offer. On January 27, a letter to shareholders from W.T. Piper, Jr., president of the company, stated that the Piper Board "has carefully studied this offer and is convinced that it is inadequate and not in the best interests of Piper's shareholders."

In addition to communicating with shareholders, Piper entered into an agreement with Grumman Aircraft Corp. on January 29, whereby Grumman agreed to purchase 300,000 authorized but unissued Piper shares at $65 per share. The agreement increased the amount of stock necessary for Chris–Craft to secure control and thus rendered Piper less vulnerable to Chris–Craft's attack. A Piper press release and letter to shareholders announced the Grumman transaction but failed to state either that Grumman had a "put" or option to sell the shares back to Piper at cost, plus interest, or that Piper was required to maintain the proceeds of the transaction in a separate fund free from liens.

Despite Piper's opposition, Chris–Craft succeeded in acquiring 304,606 shares by the time its cash tender offer expired on February 3. To obtain the additional 17% of Piper stock needed for control, Chris–Craft decided to make an exchange offer of Chris–Craft securities for Piper stock. Although Chris–Craft filed a registration statement and preliminary prospectus with the SEC in late February 1969, the exchange offer did not go into effect until May 15, 1969.

In the meantime, Chris–Craft made cash purchases of Piper stock on the open market until Mr. Siegel, the company's president, was expressly warned by SEC officials that such purchases, when made during the pendency of an exchange offer, violated SEC Rule 10b–6. At Mr. Siegel's direction, Chris–Craft immediately complied with the SEC's directive and canceled all outstanding orders for purchases of Piper stock.

While Chris–Craft's exchange offer was in registration, Piper in March 1969 terminated the agreement with Grumman and entered into negotiations with Bangor Punta. Bangor had initially been contacted by First Boston about the possibility of a Piper takeover in the wake of Chris–Craft's initial cash tender offer in January. With Grumman out of the picture, the Piper family agreed on May 8, 1969, to exchange

---

1. The cash tender offer indicated that Chris–Craft reserved the right to purchase shares in excess of the 300,000 specified amount.

their 31% stockholdings in Piper for Bangor Punta securities. Bangor also agreed to use its best efforts to achieve control of Piper by means of an exchange offer of Bangor securities for Piper common stock. A press release issued the same day announced the terms of the agreement, including a provision that the forthcoming exchange offer would involve Bangor securities to be valued, in the judgment of First Boston, "at not less than $80 per Piper share." [3]

While awaiting the effective date of its exchange offer, Bangor in mid–May 1969 purchased 120,200 shares of Piper stock in privately negotiated, off-exchange transactions from three large institutional investors. All three purchases were made after the SEC's issuance of a release on May 5 announcing proposed Rule 10b–13, a provision which, upon becoming effective in November 1969, would expressly prohibit a tender offeror from making purchases of the target company's stock during the pendency of an exchange offer. The SEC release stated that the proposed rule was "in effect, a codification of existing interpretations under Rule 10b–6," the provision invoked by SEC officials against Mr. Siegel of Chris–Craft a month earlier. Bangor officials, although aware of the release at the time of the three off-exchange purchases, made no attempt to secure an exemption for the transactions from the SEC, as provided by Rule 10b–6(f). The SEC, however, took no action concerning these purchases as it had with respect to Chris–Craft's open-market transactions.

With these three block purchases, amounting to 7% of Piper stock, Bangor Punta in mid-May took the lead in the takeover contest. The contest then centered upon the competing exchange offers. Chris–Craft's first exchange offer, which began in mid-May 1969, failed to produce tenders of the specified minimum number of Piper shares (80,000). Meanwhile, Bangor Punta's exchange offer, which had been announced on May 8, became effective on July 18. The registration materials which Bangor filed with the SEC in connection with the exchange offer included financial statements, reviewed by First Boston, representing that one of Bangor's subsidiaries, the Bangor & Aroostock Railroad (BAR), had a value of $18.4 million. This valuation was based upon a 1965 appraisal by investment bankers after a proposed sale of the BAR failed to materialize. The financial statements did not indicate that Bangor was considering the sale of the BAR or that an offer to purchase the railroad for $5 million had been received.[5]

In the final phase of the see-saw of competing offers, Chris–Craft modified the terms of its previously unsuccessful exchange offer to

---

3. Less than three weeks later, the SEC brought an action in Federal District Court charging that the Bangor press release violated "gun-jumping" provisions, 15 U.S.C. § 77e(c), and Rule 135, 17 CFR § 230.135 (1975), by stating a specific dollar valuation for unregistered securities. Without admitting any of the allegations, Bangor and Piper consented to a permanent injunction against similar releases before the effective date of Bangor's registration statement.

5. Shortly after the contest for control was completed, Bangor entered into an agreement to sell the BAR for $5 million, thereby resulting in a $13.8 million book loss.

make it more attractive. The revised offer succeeded in attracting 112,089 additional Piper shares, while Bangor's exchange offer, which terminated on July 29, resulted in the tendering of 110,802 shares. By August 4, 1969, at the conclusion of both offers, Bangor Punta owned a total of 44.5%, while Chris–Craft owned 40.6% of Piper stock. The remainder of Piper stock, 14.9%, remained in the hands of the public.

After completion of their respective exchange offers, both companies renewed market purchases of Piper stock,[6] but Chris–Craft, after purchasing 29,200 shares for cash in mid-August, withdrew from competition.[7] Bangor Punta continued making cash purchases until September 5, by which time it had acquired a majority interest in Piper. The final tally in the nine-month takeover battle showed that Bangor Punta held over 50% and Chris–Craft held 42% of Piper stock.

Effect of the Act on Statutory Mergers and Asset Sales

As we saw in chapter two, in statutory mergers and asset acquisitions the target shareholders, with few exceptions, have a right to vote on the transaction. If the target is publicly held, the proxy solicitation rules, see chapter two, pages 132–54, promulgated by the Securities and Exchange Commission under the authority of section 14(a) of the Securities Exchange Act of 1934, require the target to disclose fully the details of the transaction and regulate the form of the proxy and the disclosure statement. If the bidder uses its own stock in the merger or asset sale, the question becomes, Does the SEC add the requirements of the 1934 act to the proxy solicitation rules by construing the transactions to be a public offering of bidder securities? For an answer, please read SEC rule 145, preliminary note, (a), and (b), in your statutory supplement before you read the SEC supplementary releases below.

SECURITIES ACT RELEASE NO. 5316
(OCT. 6, 1972)

* * *

2. Rule 145(a)(2). Mergers or Consolidations

* * *

In certain instances, state law allows a merger of a parent and its 85 to 90 percent owned subsidiary to be consummated without shareholder approval. Because Rule 145(a) is couched in terms of offers arising in connection with a submission for the vote or consent of

---

6. Since the respective distributions of securities pursuant to the exchange offers had been completed at this point, the legality of these market purchases was unchallenged.

7. The reason for Chris–Craft's withdrawal from the contest is a matter in dispute. According to one view, espoused by Judge Mansfield at one stage in the ensuing litigation, Chris–Craft had " 'shot its bolt' in the financial sense by early February 1969.... It was in no position to purchase for cash any appreciable amount of Piper shares over and above the 304,606 tendered in response to its initial cash offer." 480 F.2d 341, 402 (CA2 1973).

security holders, short-form mergers not requiring such vote or consent are not within the scope of the Rule. However, if a security is to be issued in such short-form mergers, the Commission is of the opinion that the transaction involves an "offer", "offer to sell", "offer for sale", or "sale", within the meaning of Section 2(3) of the Act, and accordingly such transactions are subject to the registration provisions of the Act unless an exemption is available.

3. Rule 145(a)(3). Transfers of Assets

With regard to the third condition above, if the vote of the stockholders of the selling corporation is taken to authorize the sale, and the selling corporation thereafter decides to dissolve or distribute the securities within one year after the transaction, the sale of assets and the dissolution or distribution of the selling corporation are deemed to be portions of the same transaction and to involve a sale for value of the purchasing corporation's stock to the shareholders of the selling corporation. Accordingly, the transaction should be registered on Form S–14 [now form S–4] at the time the plan or agreement for the sale of assets is submitted to shareholders for their vote or consent if it is contemplated that the corporation receiving the securities will adopt resolution within one year for dissolution or distribution of the securities received. If the transaction is not registered at the time of submission of the plan or agreement for the vote or consent of security holders, but a resolution for dissolution or distribution of the securities received is adopted within one year, the issuer should file a registration statement covering the dissolution or distribution of securities on the appropriate form other than Form S–14, unless as exemption is available.

* * *

SECURITIES ACT OF 1933, SEC RELEASE NO. 5463
(Feb. 28, 1974)

Division of Corporation Finances's Interpretations of Rule 145 and Related Matters

* * *

Facts: The board of directors of X Company is considering an offer by Y Company whereby a significant portion (but not substantially all) of X Company's assets will be transferred to Y Company in return for shares of Y Company common stock which would be distributed to the stockholders of X Company on a pro-rata basis. Although not required to do so by state law or by X Company's certificate of incorporation or by-laws, X Company's board of directors will submit the matter to the stockholders of X Company for their authorization.

Question: Assuming that no statutory exemption is available, is Rule 145 applicable to this proposed transaction?

Interpretative Response: Yes. Rule 145(a)(3) states that:

(a) "sale" shall be deemed to be involved, within the meaning of Section 2(3) of the Act, so far as the security holders of a corporation ... are concerned where, pursuant to statutory provisions ... or similar controlling instruments, or otherwise, there is submitted for the vote or consent of such security holders a plan or agreement for ... transfers of assets.

Accordingly, inasmuch as the board of directors in its discretion has determined to submit the matter to stockholders, Rule 145 is applicable and the transaction may be registered on Form S–14 or S–1.

* * *

Facts: X Company and Y Company are about to sign an agreement in principle setting forth their understanding with respect to a proposed merger of the two companies which will be registered pursuant to Rule 145. One condition set forth in the agreement in principle requires that, prior to the consummation of the merger, Y Company divest itself of a significant subsidiary in order to avoid potential problems under the Federal anti-trust law. Although not set forth in the agreement in principle, it is clear from the preliminary negotiations that, subsequent to the merger, certain assets of Y Company will be liquidated because their book value is materially lower than their market value.

Question: Does Rule 145(b) prohibit the announcement of these facts prior to the filing of a registration statement?

Interpretative Response: No. Rule 145(b)(1) describes communications which will be deemed not to be a "prospectus" or "offer to sell" as defined in the Act. Inasmuch as the divestiture of a significant subsidiary is a material part of the transaction, and will have a material effect on the business of one party, it should be disclosed. To the extent that the assets to be liquidated are material to Y Company's operations, this plan should also be disclosed.

* * *

For statutory mergers and asset sales a form S–4 registration statement consists of the seller's proxy or information statement enclosed in the buyer's prospectus cover. In essence, the buyer adopts the seller's proxy as its prospectus, because the bulk of the information required by form S–4 is also required by regulation 14A, which governs the information required in a proxy statement. Indeed, the form S–4 serves also as a proxy statement for the target. If the buyer does not want to assume liability for the seller's representations in its proxy statement, then the buyer can register the transaction on a basic form S–1 instead of a form S–4, but S–1 does not permit liberal incorporation by reference to other 1934 act reports, as does form S–4, and thus is much more expensive to prepare and mail. If the target shareholders are already protected by the proxy solicitation rules of the 1934 act, why do we need the additional set of disclosure requirements that attach to a registration statement under the 1933 act?

The real effect of rule 145 comes in sections (c) and (d). Please read these sections in your statutory supplement. The main effects of these sections are, first, to make underwriters of the target firm and its controlling officers and shareholders (as underwriters they are liable for disclosure violations under section 11 of the 1933 act) and, second, to restrict the resale of securities obtained by target shareholders who "control" the target, so-called target affiliates (this group includes target managers as well as controlling shareholders). These resale requirements have a major impact on the willingness of target shareholders to vote for swap acquisitions, in which they take acquired securities for their target shares. Controlling target shareholders who are unwilling to hold securities in the acquired firm, and want to cash out immediately after the acquisition, will not agree to a swap.

Affiliates of the target can resell their securities only by registering the sale or by complying with the narrow resale restrictions in rule 145(d), which incorporates by reference parts of rule 144. Please read those sections of rule 144 in your statutory supplement. The affiliates who choose to register their resales can piggyback their registration on the buyer's form S–4. If the original form S–4 does not mention the resales, the target affiliates can file a posteffective amendment to the buyer's form containing the prospectus (offering document) that the affiliates intend to use in the sales and other information on the identity of the sellers, the underwriting and distribution arrangements for the resales, the closing of the acquisition in which the shares were issued, and any material developments with respect to the combined firm subsequent to the closing. The affiliates cannot send the prospectus to offerors until the amendment becomes effective. Because the shares to be resold by the affiliates can be registered only by the *acquired* firm, the target must bargain for a piggyback registration during the negotiations over the acquisition agreement and include registration rights in the agreement. Those rights normally include conditions on the length of time the buyer must keep the registration effective, the expiration of the registration right, the minimum number of shares to be registered, and the time of year at which registration may be requested.

You will note in reading rule 145(c) and (d) that people reselling securities registered under the 1934 act without use of a 1933 act registration statement in rule 145 transactions fall into four categories for the purposes of the safe harbor rules. First, if the target shareholder is not an affiliate of the target and not an affiliate of the buyer, rule 145(c) does not apply, and the resales are unrestricted. Second, if the target shareholder is an affiliate of the target and after the transaction is not an affiliate of the buyer, resales, to be protected, must comply with rule 145(d)(1), (2), or (3). Third, if the target shareholder is an affiliate of the target and an affiliate of the buyer after the transaction, resales are protected only if in compliance with rule 145(d)(1). And fourth, if the target shareholder is not an affiliate of the target and after the transaction becomes an affiliate of the buyer, rule 145(c) does not apply, but section 2(11) and rule 144 do, if no other exemption can be found.

Why is the SEC so concerned about resales by target affiliates? Remember that the SEC is intent on protecting the ultimate buyers in public offerings of securities by, among other things, requiring issuers to give buyers information about the firms (in prospectuses). If the SEC did not control resales of securities in statutory mergers, the parties could use statutory mergers to effect unregistered public distributions of securities. For example, a firm, anxious to avoid registration of a new public offering, could merge with a shell corporation wholly owned by a cooperating bank. The bank has placed in the shell a sizable amount of cash. The bank, which gets firm stock in the merger, then resells the stock to the public, recovering its outlay in the shell plus a small profit. In effect, the firm has sold its stock to the public for cash, and the purchasers have not received any issuer prospectuses. Without rule 145 the transaction would not require registration of the resales.

Problem

A large firm, Able, Inc., is negotiating to buy a smaller firm, Baker, Inc., which has three shareholders. One shareholder holds 51 percent of the stock and is on the board of directors; a second shareholder holds 30 percent of the stock and is the chief executive officer; a third shareholder holds 19 percent of the shares and is not involved in the firm's management. Able has no cash available for the merger, and Baker's shareholders do not want to hold stock or notes issued by Able. Able managers urge Baker to accept Able stock, arguing that the Baker shareholders can sell the Able stock for cash in a "very short period of time after the transaction." Moreover, Able offers to put the largest Baker shareholder on Able's board of directors if the transaction closes. The Baker shareholders come to you for advice. If they accept Able stock for their Baker stock, when can they resell their shares? Could the deal be restructured so they could resell earlier? What is the Securities and Exchange Commission trying to prevent by these restrictions?

The Effect of the Act on Exchange Reorganizations

The 1933 act contains a special exemption from registration for securities distributed in voluntary exchanges and recapitalizations. The exemption is contained in section 3(a)(9). Please read the section and Securities and Exchange Commission rules 149 and 150 in your statutory supplement.

Exchange transactions may occur in a wide variety of circumstances—for example a conversion of bonds to stock or preferred stock to common stock. The exemption is quite narrow. The issuer of both securities must be identical, no part of the offering may be made to anyone other than existing security holders, and there can be no paid consideration. The exemption is important for poison pill plans. Recall that popular poison pill plans consist of rights distributed as dividends on the common stock. A dividend is not a "sale" and does not require registration under the 1933 act. The right is triggered on a nonapproved stock acquisition and gives the holder the right to exchange, on generous terms, common stock in the target for stock in the buyer (flip-over) or stock in the target (flip-in). This exchange is exempted from registration under the act by section 3(a)(9). Poison pills are clever not only because they avoid the need for a ratifying shareholder vote but also because they avoid 1933 act registration requirements and, as we shall see later, are not taxed when issued.

SEC DIVISION OF CORP. FINANCE, NO ACTION LETTER, TIME, INC.

Fed.Sec.Law Rptr. (CCH) ¶ 82,095 (March 19, 1979).

This is in response to your letter of March 1, 1979 concerning the proposed solicitation by Time Incorporated ("Time") of proxies of holders of its Common Stock ("Common Stock"), Series A $1.575 Cumulative Convertible Preferred Stock ("Series A Preferred Stock") and Series B $1.575 Cumulative Convertible Preferred Stock ("Series B Preferred Stock"). The solicitation relates to a proposed amendment to Time's Restated Certificate of Incorporation by which each outstanding, reserved and unissued share of Series A Preferred Stock would be changed into a share of Series B Preferred Stock. Implementation of the amendment is proposed to be effectuated without compliance with the registration requirements of the Securities Act of 1933 (the "Act").

* * *

You state that as a result of the fact that more than 35% of the Series A Preferred Stock is closely held, there exists a relatively low trading volume for such shares. Accordingly, in view of the similarity of the two series, Time's management intends to submit for shareholder approval at Time's Annual Meeting a proposal to amend its Certificate of Incorporation to change each outstanding, reserved and unissued share of Series A Preferred Stock into one share of Series B Preferred Stock. As an integral part of the proposed amendment, the terms of the Series B Preferred Stock would also be changed to increase proportionately the number of shares of that series required to be redeemed annually pursuant to the sinking fund from 5% of the Series B shares originally issued to an amount reflecting an increase equal to approximately 5% of the Series A shares originally issued. You indicate that the vote of two-thirds of the outstanding shares of each series of Preferred Stock voting as a separate class and the vote of a majority of the outstanding shares of Common Stock and the two series of Preferred Stock, voting as a single class, will be required to authorize the amendment.

In connection with the solicitation, which you state will be accomplished in accordance with the requirements of Section 14(a) of the Securities Exchange Act of 1934, Time expects to retain the services of D.F. King & Co., Inc. ("D.F. King") to assist in the distribution of the proxy material. In this regard, with respect to the holders of Series A Preferred Stock, D.F. King would be expressly instructed not to make any recommendation, either directly or indirectly, regarding how such persons should vote on any question presented in the proxy material. However, as to the holders of Common and Series B shares, D.F. King may include a recommendation regarding how such persons should vote on questions presented in the proxy materials, including the proposed amendment. You point out that D.F. King would be expressly instructed to ascertain prior to making such recommendation whether a holder of Common Stock or Series B Preferred Stock is also a record holder or beneficial owner of any shares of Series A Preferred Stock. For its services, D.F. King will be compensated on a flat fee basis plus out-of-pocket disbursements, which fee will not be contingent upon either the number of affirmative proxies granted or the outcome of any proposal.

In addition, you state that officers and regular employees of Time may also contact stockholders, including Series A holders, and will be authorized to comment upon the merits of all such proposals, including the amendment and make recommendations thereon. No remuneration, other than regular salary and compensation, will be paid to such persons in connection with these activities.

It is your view that, insofar as the Common Stock and Series B Preferred Stock are concerned, the proposed amendment, including the change in the sinking fund terms of the Series B Preferred Stock, does not constitute the substitution of a new security under the Act or a "reclassification" within the meaning of Rule 145 thereunder and that, consequently, the solicitation of the votes of the holders of these shares may be made in the manner described in your letter without compliance with the registration provisions of the Act. Moreover, as to the exchange of Series A Preferred Stock for Series B Preferred Stock, you opine that the exemption afforded by Section 3(a)(9) of the Act is available.

On the basis of the facts presented, this Division will not recommend any enforcement action to the Commission if the proposed exchange of Series B Preferred Stock for Series A Preferred Stock is effectuated without compliance with the registration requirements of the Act in reliance upon your opinion as counsel that Section 3(a)(9) is applicable. This position is contingent upon the paid solicitor not making any recommendations to the Series A Preferred shareholders.

* * *

Questions

1. When a bidder triggers a "flip-in" poison pill plan and target shareholders exercise their stock rights under the plan to exchange one

share of target common stock for, say, two shares of target common stock, can the issuer use section 3(a)(9) to exempt the transaction from registration? Does it matter if the target firm pays a public relations firm to contact all the target's shareholders and encourage them to exercise their rights? Or if the target firm submits the adoption of its poison pill to a shareholder vote, by hiring a proxy solicitation expert to write and distribute the proxy?

If a poison pill plan that does not give target shareholders the right to exchange their stock for other stock, but instead gives them the right to buy more stock at below-market prices (exchange cash for new securities), is triggered, must the target register the new stock sold to the shareholders under the 1933 act?

2. Do reorganizations creating two classes of voting stock need to be registered under the 1933 act? Does it matter whether the reorganization plan is accomplished through an amendment of the charter or an issuer exchange tender offer?

SUBCHAPTER B. THE GENERAL ANTIFRAUD PROVISIONS OF THE FEDERAL SECURITIES LAWS AS THEY APPLY TO ACQUISITIONS

In previous chapters we covered the proxy solicitation regulations of the Securities Exchange Act of 1934, the tender offer regulations of the Williams Act, and in the previous subchapter we covered the public securities offering regulations of the Securities Act of 1933. The proxy solicitation material was relevant to our discussion of shareholder voting in statutory mergers and asset sales; the Williams Act controls the form and timing of tender offers, and the Securities Act regulates acquisitions in which the consideration for target assets or shares is bidder securities. Each of these regulatory systems has general sections or rules prohibiting the use of false or misleading statements in documents sent to the public or filed with the Securities and Exchange Commission.

The proxy regulations contain rule 14a–9; the tender offer regulations contain section 14(e) and SEC rules promulgated thereunder; the Securities Act of 1933 contains sections 11 and 17. Moreover, the SEC, pursuant to a general grant of authority under section 10 of the Exchange Act of 1934, promulgated the best known and most general antifraud provision of them all in rule 10b–5. The operative language of these sections is similar. Please read SEC rules 10b–5 and 14a–9 and section 14(e) in the Exchange Act in your statutory supplement. Finally, some of the individual forms and schedules that detail the disclosure requirement in tender offer statements can give rise to duties to avoid fraud (schedules 13E–4 and 14D–1, for example, each contain a requirement for disclosures of "material information"). Please read item 10(f) of schedule 14D–1 in your statutory supplement.

The provisions have two main purposes. First, they prohibit false statements in filings and public disclosure documents required by the securities laws or in voluntary public statements, such as press releases. Second, they prohibit incomplete statements that are misleading, even if the material presented is technically correct. This second function has grown to have a life of its own. The general antifraud provisions have themselves become vehicles for the SEC and the courts to fashion disclosure requirements that supplement and occasionally overshadow the detailed requirements of the statutes, rules, and schedules that are specific to certain events. The materials in this subchapter focus on the interpretations of the general disclosure requirements in these antifraud rules.

There is some question whether the more general provisions such as rule 10b–5 generate, by themselves, a third duty, that is, a duty to disclose that operates independently of a duty to be accurate and complete in required filings and voluntary statements to the public. The question is typically unimportant, however, because a firm in its normal operations has to make numerous routine disclosures to the SEC and the public and also, in its public relations with the capital markets, routinely chooses to make nonrequired disclosures to the markets. An allegation of a material nondisclosure can usually be attached to one or more of these public statements or filings. As we shall see, however, the argument is important in one case relevant to our inquiry, the disclosure of acquisition negotiations.

Finally, a note on what is not covered in these materials. The materials in this subchapter focus on the content of the substantive language of these antifraud provisions, that is, the nature of disclosures that courts and the SEC say do or do not meet the sections' requirements. The materials do not comprehensively cover the questions of who may sue for violations and do not cover the forms of relief available to plaintiffs that prevail. In general, the SEC is charged with primary enforcement responsibility, although the Department of Justice prosecutes any criminal accusations. As is well known, some of the antifraud sections, particularly rules 10b–5 and 14a–9, support litigation by private plaintiffs who can prove proper standing, materiality of the improper statements, causation, culpability of the defendant, and damages. Each of these elements is legally complex, and I defer to your course in securities regulation and the fine casebooks in that area for a fuller discussion of such causes. The materials make one important exception to this policy, however, and deal with the question of whether a frustrated bidder can sue a target under rule 10b–5.

SECTION 1. A FEDERAL COMMON LAW OF FIDUCIARY DUTY?

Federal court judges at both the district and the circuit court level, spurred on by academics, have flirted with using the antifraud regulations as a vehicle for developing a federal case law on fiduciary duty. Much of the impetus for this desire to federalize fiduciary duty comes from their disapproval of what the states have done in fashioning doctrine in these areas. The Supreme Court has refused to cooperate, however. As we shall see, the Supreme Court has had some difficulty reigning in the lower courts.

SANTA FE INDUSTRIES, INC. v. GREEN

Supreme Court of the United States, 1977.
430 U.S. 462, 97 S.Ct. 1292, 51 L.Ed.2d 480.

Mr. Justice White:

The issue in this case involves the reach and coverage of section 10(b) of the Securities Exchange Act of 1934 and Rule 10b–5 thereunder in the context of a Delaware short-form merger transaction used by the majority stockholder of a corporation to eliminate the minority interest.

In 1936, petitioner Santa Fe Industries, Inc. (Santa Fe), acquired control of 60% of the stock of Kirby Lumber Corp. (Kirby), a Delaware corporation. Through a series of purchases over the succeeding years, Santa Fe increased its control of Kirby's stock to 95%; the purchase prices during the period 1968–1973 ranged from $65 to $92.50 per share.[2] In 1974, wishing to acquire 100% ownership of Kirby, Santa Fe availed itself of § 253 of the Delaware Corporation Law, known as the "short-form merger" statute. Section 253 permits a parent corporation owning at least 90% of the stock of a subsidiary to merge with that subsidiary, upon approval by the parent's board of directors, and to make payment in cash for the shares of the minority stockholders. The statute does not require the consent of, or advance notice to, the minority stockholders. However, notice of the merger must be given within 10 days after its effective date, and any stockholder who is dissatisfied with the terms of the merger may petition the Delaware Court of Chancery for a decree ordering the surviving corporation to pay him the fair value of his shares, as determined by a court-appointed appraiser subject to review by the court. Del.Code Ann., Tit. 8, §§ 253, 262 (1975 ed. and Supp.1976).

Santa Fe obtained independent appraisals of the physical assets of Kirby—land, timber, buildings, and machinery—and of Kirby's oil, gas, and mineral interests. These appraisals, together with other financial information, were submitted to Morgan Stanley & Co. (Morgan Stanley), an investment banking firm retained to appraise the fair market value of Kirby stock. Kirby's physical assets were appraised at $320 million (amounting to $640 for each of the 500,000 shares); Kirby's stock was valued by Morgan Stanley at $125 per share. Under the terms of the merger, minority stockholders were offered $150 per share.

2. App. 33a (merger information statement, considered by parties and court below as part of the amended complaint). Santa Fe controlled Kirby through its wholly owned subsidiary, Santa Fe Natural

The provisions of the short-form merger statute were fully complied with.[3] The minority stockholders of Kirby were notified the day after the merger became effective and were advised of their right to obtain an appraisal in Delaware court if dissatisfied with the offer of $150 per share. They also received an information statement containing, in addition to the relevant financial data about Kirby, the appraisals of the value of Kirby's assets and the Morgan Stanley appraisal concluding that the fair market value of the stock was $125 per share.

Respondents, minority stockholders of Kirby, objected to the terms of the merger, but did not pursue their appraisal remedy in the Delaware Court of Chancery. Instead, they brought this action in federal court on behalf of the corporation and other minority stockholders, seeking to set aside the merger or to recover what they claimed to be the fair value of their shares. The amended complaint asserted that, based on the fair market value of Kirby's physical assets as revealed by the appraisal included in the information statement sent to minority shareholders, Kirby's stock was worth at least $772 per share.[5] The complaint alleged further that the merger took place without prior notice to minority stockholders; that the purpose of the merger was to appropriate the difference between the "conceded pro rata value of the physical assets," App. 103a, and the offer of $150 per share—to "freez[e] out the minority stockholders at a wholly inadequate price," *id.,* at 100a; and that Santa Fe, knowing the appraised value of the physical assets, obtained a "fraudulent appraisal" of the stock from Morgan Stanley and offered $25 above that appraisal "in order to lull the minority stockholders into erroneously believing that [Santa Fe was] generous." *Id.,* at 103a. This course of conduct was alleged to be "a violation of Rule 10b–5 because defendants employed a 'device, scheme, or artifice to defraud' and engaged in an 'act, practice or course of business which operates or would operate as a fraud or deceit upon any person, in connection with the purchase or sale of any security.'" *Ibid.* Morgan Stanley assertedly participated in the fraud as an accessory by submitting its appraisal of $125 per share although knowing the appraised value of the physical assets.

* * *

Resources, Inc., which owned the Kirby stock.

3. The merger became effective on July 31, 1974, and was accomplished in the following way. A new corporation, Forest Products, Inc., was organized as a Delaware corporation. The Kirby stock, together with cash, was transferred from Santa Fe's wholly owned subsidiary (see n. 2, supra) to Forest Products in exchange for all of the Forest Products stock. The new corporation was then merged into Kirby, with Kirby as the surviving corporation. The cash transferred to Forest Products was used to make the purchase offer for the Kirby shares not owned by the Santa Fe subsidiary.

5. The figure of $772 per share was calculated as follows:

"The difference of $311,000,000 ($622 per share) between the fair market value of Kirby's land and timber, alone, as per the defendants' own appraisal thereof at $320,000,000 and the $9,000,000 book value of said land and timber, added to the $150 per share, yields a pro rata share of the value of the physical assets of Kirby of at least $772 per share. The value of the stock was at least the pro rata value of the physical assets." App. 102a.

The language of § 10(b) gives no indication that Congress meant to prohibit any conduct not involving manipulation or deception. Nor have we been cited to any evidence in the legislative history that would support a departure from the language of the statute. "When a statute speaks so specifically in terms of manipulation and deception, ... and when its history reflects no more expansive intent, we are quite unwilling to extend the scope of the statute...." *Id.,* at 214. Thus the claim of fraud and fiduciary breach in this complaint states a cause of action under any part of Rule 10b–5 only if the conduct alleged can be fairly viewed as "manipulative or deceptive" within the meaning of the statute.

It is our judgment that the transaction, if carried out as alleged in the complaint, was neither deceptive nor manipulative and therefore did not violate either § 10(b) of the Act or Rule 10b–5.

As we have indicated, the case comes to us on the premise that the complaint failed to allege a material misrepresentation or material failure to disclose. The finding of the District Court, undisturbed by the Court of Appeals, was that there was no "omission" or "misstatement" in the information statement accompanying the notice of merger. On the basis of the information provided, minority shareholders could either accept the price offered or reject it and seek an appraisal in the Delaware Court of Chancery. Their choice was fairly presented, and they were furnished with all relevant information on which to base their decision.[14]

* * *

It is also readily apparent that the conduct alleged in the complaint was not "manipulative" within the meaning of the statute. "Manipulation" is "virtually a term of art when used in connection with securities markets."

The term refers generally to practices, such as wash sales, matched orders, or rigged prices, that are intended to mislead investors by artificially affecting market activity. * * * Section 10(b)'s general prohibition of practices deemed by the SEC to be "manipulative"—in this technical sense of artificially affecting market activity in order to mislead investors—is fully consistent with the fundamental purpose of the 1934 Act " 'to substitute a philosophy of full disclosure for the philosophy of *caveat emptor*....' " *Affilated Ute Citizens v. United*

---

14. In addition to their principal argument that the complaint alleges a fraud under clauses (a) and (c) of Rule 10b–5, respondents also argue that the complaint alleges nondisclosure and misrepresentation in violation of clause (b) of the Rule. Their major contention in this respect is that the majority stockholder's failure to give the minority advance notice of the merger was a material nondisclosure, even though the Delaware short-form merger statute does not require such notice. But respondents do not indicate how they might have acted differently had they had prior notice of the merger. Indeed, they accept the conclusion of both courts below that under Delaware law they could not have enjoined the merger because an appraisal proceeding is their sole remedy in the Delaware courts for any alleged unfairness in the terms of the merger. Thus, the failure to give advance notice was not a material nondisclosure within the meaning of the statute or the Rule.

States, 406 U.S. 128, 151 (1972), quoting *SEC v. Capital Gains Research Bureau,* 375 U.S. 180, 186 (1963). Indeed, nondisclosure is usually essential to the success of a manipulative scheme. No doubt Congress meant to prohibit the full range of ingenious devices that might be used to manipulate securities prices. But we do not think it would have chosen this "term of art" if it had meant to bring within the scope of § 10(b) instances of corporate mismanagement such as this, in which the essence of the complaint is that shareholders were treated unfairly by a fiduciary.

The language of the statute is, we think, "sufficiently clear in its context" to be dispositive here, *Ernst & Ernst, supra,* at 201; but even if it were not, there are additional considerations that weigh heavily against permitting a cause of action under Rule 10b–5 for the breach of corporate fiduciary duty alleged in this complaint. Congress did not expressly provide a private cause of action for violations of § 10(b). Although we have recognized an implied cause of action under that section in some circumstances, we have also recognized that a private cause of action under the antifraud provisions of the Securities Exchange Act should not be implied where it is "unnecessary to ensure the fulfillment of Congress' purposes" in adopting the Act. As we noted earlier, *supra,* this page, the Court repeatedly has described the "fundamental purpose" of the Act as implementing a "philosophy of full disclosure"; once full and fair disclosure has occurred, the fairness of the terms of the transaction is at most a tangential concern of the statute. As in *Cort v. Ash,* 422 U.S. 66, 80 (1975), we are reluctant to recognize a cause of action here to serve what is "at best a subsidiary purpose" of the federal legislation.

A second factor in determining whether Congress intended to create a federal cause of action in these circumstances is "whether 'the cause of action [is] one traditionally relegated to state law....'" *Piper v. Chris–Craft Industries, Inc., ante,* at 40, quoting *Cort v. Ash, supra,* at 78. The Delaware Legislature has supplied minority shareholders with a cause of action in the Delaware Court of Chancery to recover the fair value of shares allegedly undervalued in a short-form merger. Of course, the existence of a particular state-law remedy is not dispositive of the question whether Congress meant to provide a similar federal remedy, but as in *Cort* and *Piper,* we conclude that "it is entirely appropriate in this instance to relegate respondent and others in his situation to whatever remedy is created by state law."

The reasoning behind a holding that the complaint in this case alleged fraud under Rule 10b–5 could not be easily contained. It is difficult to imagine how a court could distinguish, for purposes of Rule 10b–5 fraud, between a majority stockholder's use of a short-form merger to eliminate the minority at an unfair price and the use of some other device, such as a long-form merger, tender offer, or liquidation, to achieve the same result; or indeed how a court could distinguish the alleged abuses in these going private transactions from other types of fiduciary self-dealing involving transactions in securities. The result would be to bring within the Rule a wide variety of corporate conduct traditionally left to state regulation. In addition to posing a "danger of vexatious litigation which could result from a widely expanded class of plaintiffs under Rule 10b–5," *Blue Chip Stamps v. Manor Drug Stores,* 421 U.S., at 740, this extension of the federal securities laws would overlap and quite possibly interfere with state corporate law. Federal courts applying a "federal fiduciary principle" under Rule 10b–5 could be expected to depart from state fiduciary standards at least to the extent necessary to ensure uniformity within the federal system.[16] Absent a clear indication of congressional intent, we are reluctant to federalize the substantial portion of the law of corporations that deals with transactions in securities, particularly where established state policies of corporate regulation would be overridden....

We thus adhere to the position that "Congress by § 10(b) did not seek to regulate transactions which constitute no more than internal corporate mismanagement." *Superintendent of Insurance v. Bankers Life & Cas. Co.,* 404 U.S., at 12. There may well be a need for uniform federal fiduciary standards to govern mergers such as that challenged in this complaint. But those standards should not be supplied by judicial extension of § 10(b) and Rule 10b–5 to "cover the corporate universe."[17]

The judgment of the Court of Appeals is reversed, and the case is remanded for further proceedings consistent with this opinion.

GOLDBERG v. MERIDOR

United States Court of Appeals, Second Circuit, 1977.
567 F.2d 209, cert. denied 434 U.S. 1069, 98 S.Ct. 1249, 55 L.Ed.2d 771 (1978).

FRIENDLY, CIRCUIT JUDGE:

In this derivative action in the District Court for the Southern District of New York, David Goldberg, a stockholder of Universal Gas &

---

16. For example, some States apparently require a "valid corporate purpose" for the elimination of the minority interest through a short-form merger, whereas other States do not. Compare *Bryan v. Brock & Blevins Co.,* 490 F.2d 563 (CA 5), cert. denied, 419 U.S. 844 (1974) (merger arranged by controlling stockholder for no business purpose except to eliminate 15% minority stockholder violated Georgia short-form merger statute) with *Stauffer v. Standard Brands, Inc.,* 41 Del.Ch. 7, 187 A.2d 78 (1962) (Delaware short-form merger statute allows majority stockholder to eliminate the minority interest without any corporate purpose and subject only to an appraisal remedy). Thus to the extent that Rule 10b–5 is interpreted to require a valid corporate purpose for elimination of minority shareholders as well as a fair price for their shares, it would impose a stricter standard of fiduciary duty than that required by the law of some States.

17. Cary, Federalism and Corporate Law: Reflections Upon Delaware, 83 Yale L.J. 663, 700 (1974) (footnote omitted). Professor Cary argues vigorously for comprehensive federal fiduciary standards, but urges a "frontal" attack by a new federal statute rather than an extension of Rule 10b–5. He writes: "It seems anomalous to jig-saw every kind of corporate dispute into the federal courts through the securities acts as they are presently written."

Oil Company, Inc. (UGO), a Panama corporation having its principal place of business in New York City, sought to recover damages and to obtain other relief against UGO's controlling parent, Maritimecor, S.A., also a Panama corporation.

* * *

With respect to transactions which culminated in an agreement providing for UGO's issuance to Maritimecor of up to 4,200,000 shares of UGO stock and its assumption of all of Maritimecor's liabilities (including a debt of $7,000,000 owed to UGO) in consideration of the transfer of all of Maritimecor's assets (except 2,800,000 UGO shares already held by Maritimecor). It suffices at this point to say that the complaint, filed February 3, 1976, alleged that the contract was grossly unfair to UGO and violated both § 10(b) of the Securities Exchange Act and the SEC's Rule 10b–5 and common law fiduciary duties.

* * *

* * * The "agreement and transfer was fraudulent and unfair in that the assets of Maritimecor were overpriced and of insufficient value, the liabilities of Maritimecor either exceeded the value of its assets or were so great that the net asset value was insufficient consideration, the liabilities included a $7,000,000 debt to UGO from Maritimecor, and the purpose and intent of said transaction was to cause the dissipation of the substantial assets of UGO for the benefit of defendants, Maritimecor and Maritime Fruit.

* * *

* * * In answer to defendants' argument "that deception and non-disclosure is a requirement for a 10b–5 case" which was disputed as a matter of law, plaintiff's counsel submitted an affidavit asserting that "insofar as plaintiff Goldberg, a minority shareholder is concerned, there has been no disclosure to him of the fraudulent nature of the transfer of Maritimecor assets and liabilities for stock of UGO". Counsel annexed two press releases dated August 1 and December 19, 1975, which described the agreement for and the consummation of the UGO–Maritimecor transaction. Counsel asserted that these press releases failed to disclose the facts noted in the margin [1] or "the conflicts of interest of the principals". * * * The August 1 press release held out an inviting picture that

> As a result of the transaction, UGO will replace Maritimecor as the principal operating subsidiary of MFC and, as such, will engage in a diversified line of shipping and shipping related activities including the sale of ships and ship-building contracts, the operation of reefers and

---

1. Maritimecor, as of the end of fiscal year 1974 had current liabilities of $42.5 million dollars, and in addition Maritimecor owed UGO about $7 million dollars which apparently was being forgiven in the transaction. The shareholders' net equity in Maritimecor was $40.4 million dollars or substantially less than its current liabilities. Further, included in the assets of Maritimecor are 2.8 million shares of UGO, the value of which are substantially decreased as a result of this transaction.

tankers, and upon their delivery, product carriers and oil drilling rigs, and underwriting marine insurance.

when allegedly the truth was that UGO had entered into a transaction that would ensure its doom.

* * *

* * * There is deception of the corporation (in effect, of its minority shareholders) when the corporation is influenced by its controlling shareholder to engage in a transaction adverse to the corporation's interests (in effect, the minority shareholders' interests) and there is nondisclosure or misleading disclosures as to the material facts of the transaction....[8]

* * *

Beyond this Goldberg and other minority shareholders would not have been without remedy if the alleged facts had been disclosed.

* * *

The availability of injunctive relief if the defendants had not lulled the minority stockholders of UGO into security by a deceptive disclosure, as they allegedly did, is in sharp contrast to Green, where the disclosure following the merger transaction was full and fair, and, as to the pre-merger period, respondents accepted "the conclusion of both courts below that under Delaware law they could not have enjoined the merger because an appraisal proceeding is their sole remedy in the Delaware courts for any alleged unfairness in the terms of the merger," fn. 14.[10]

* * *

MESKILL, CIRCUIT JUDGE, concurring in part and dissenting in part:

* * *

Under Panamanian law, no shareholder action was necessary to effect the UGO–Maritimecor merger. Accordingly, the burden is on the plaintiffs to demonstrate a substantial likelihood that they would have acted differently had full disclosure been made. * * * In order to prove materiality under this theory, Goldberg will have to demonstrate that he would, as a reasonable stockholder, have sought and obtained an injunction against the proposed action had the facts not been concealed.

8. We do not mean to suggest that § 10(b) or Rule 10b–5 requires insiders to characterize conflict of interest transactions with pejorative nouns or adjectives. However, if Maritimecor was in the parlous financial condition alleged in the opposing affidavit of plaintiff's counsel, a disclosure of the acquisition of Maritimecor that omitted these facts would be seriously misleading.

10. We need not now decide whether, as some commentators have suggested, in certain self-dealing situations disclosure of the fact that the transaction is to occur or has occurred is required by federal law— whether as an affirmative duty on the corporation in some circumstances to disclose under Rule 10b–5 even in the absence of its trading, * * * or as a requirement of applicable specific reporting provisions under the 1934 Act, see, e.g., * * * or as an obligation imposed by a national securities exchange.

* * *

* * *

The final suggested rationale of the majority is the "chastening effect" of full disclosure. The apparent theory is that those about to loot a corporation can be shamed into honesty through a requirment that they reveal their nefarious purposes.

* * *

Those who breach their fiduciary duties seldom disclose their intentions ahead of time. Yet under the majority's reasoning the failure to inform stockholders of a proposed defalcation gives rise to a cause of action under 10b–5. Thus, the majority has neatly undone the holdings of *Green, Piper* and *Cort* by creating a federal cause of action for a breach of fiduciary duty that will apply in all cases, save for those rare instances where the fiduciary denounces himself in advance.

* * *

Questions

1. Was the *Santa Fe* court successful in sending to state courts shareholder complaints about corporate mismanagement in mergers?

2. To satisfy the *Goldberg* standards, must the plaintiff show only that she had a cause of action to enjoin a merger under state law or that she would (or might) have succeeded in state court had she brought the action?

3. The Supreme Court has held that scienter is an element of a cause of action under rule 10b–5, but courts are split on whether scienter is an element of a cause of action under rule 14a–9. Compare Gould v. American–Hawaiian Steamship, Co., 535 F.2d 761 (3d Cir.1976), with Adams v. Standard Knitting Mills, Inc., 623 F.2d 422 (6th Cir.1980).

SCHREIBER v. BURLINGTON NORTHERN, INC.

Supreme Court of the United States, 1985.
472 U.S. 1, 105 S.Ct. 2458, 86 L.Ed.2d 1.

CHIEF JUSTICE BURGER:

We granted certiorari to resolve a conflict in the Circuits over whether misrepresentation or nondisclosure is a necessary element of a violation of § 14(e) of the Securities Exchange Act of 1934, 15 U.S.C. § 78n(e).

On December 21, 1982, Burlington Northern, Inc., made a hostile tender offer for El Paso Gas Co. Through a wholly owned subsidiary, Burlington proposed to purchase 25.1 million El Paso shares at $24 per share. Burlington reserved the right to terminate the offer if any of several specified events occurred. El Paso management initially opposed the takeover, but its shareholders responded favorably, fully subscribing the offer by the December 30, 1982, deadline.

Burlington did not accept those tendered shares; instead, after negotiations with El Paso management, Burlington announced on January 10, 1983, the terms of a new and friendly takeover agreement. Pursuant to the new agreement, Burlington undertook, *inter alia,* to (1) rescind the December tender offer, (2) purchase 4,166,667 shares from El Paso at $24 per share, (3) substitute a new tender offer for only 21 million shares at $24 per share, (4) provide procedural protections against a squeeze-out merger of the remaining El Paso shareholders, and (5) recognize "golden parachute" contracts between El Paso and four of its senior officers. By February 8, more than 40 million shares were tendered in response to Burlington's January offer, and the takeover was completed.

The rescission of the first tender caused a diminished payment to those shareholders who had tendered during the first offer. The January offer was greatly oversubscribed and consequently those shareholders who retendered were subject to substantial proration. Petitioner Barbara Schreiber filed suit on behalf of herself and similarly situated shareholders, alleging that Burlington, El Paso, and members of El Paso's board of directors violated § 14(e)'s prohibition of "fraudulent, deceptive, or manipulative acts or practices ... in connection with any tender offer." 15 U.S.C. § 78n(e). She claimed that Burlington's withdrawal of the December tender offer coupled with the substitution of the January tender offer was a "manipulative" distortion of the market for El Paso stock. Schreiber also alleged that Burlington violated § 14(e) by failing in the January offer to disclose the "golden parachutes" offered to four of El Paso's managers. She claims that this January nondisclosure was a deceptive act forbidden by § 14(e).

* * *

Petitioner relies on a construction of the phrase, "fraudulent, deceptive, or manipulative acts or practices." Petitioner reads the phrase "fraudulent, deceptive, or manipulative acts or practices" to include acts which, although fully disclosed, "artificially" affect the price of the takeover target's stock. Petitioner's interpretation relies on the belief that § 14(e) is directed at purposes broader than providing full and true information to investors.

Petitioner's reading of the term "manipulative" conflicts with the normal meaning of the term. * * * The meaning the Court has given the term "manipulative" is consistent with the use of the term at common law, and with its traditional dictionary definition.[5]

She argues, however, that the term "manipulative" takes on a meaning in § 14(e) that is different from the meaning it has in § 10(b). Petitioner claims that the use of the disjunctive "or" in § 14(e) implies that acts need not be deceptive or fraudulent to be manipulative. But Congress used the phrase "manipulative or deceptive" in § 10(b) as well, and we have interpreted "manipulative" in that context to require misrepresentation. Moreover, it is a " 'familiar principle of statutory

---

5. See Webster's Third New International Dictionary 1376 (1971) (Manipulation is "management with use of unfair, scheming, or underhanded methods").

construction that words grouped in a list should be given related meaning.'"

* * * All three species of misconduct, *i.e.,* "fraudulent, deceptive, or manipulative," listed by Congress are directed at failures to disclose. The use of the term "manipulative" provides emphasis and guidance to those who must determine which types of acts are reached by the statute; it does not suggest a deviation from the section's facial and primary concern with disclosure or congressional concern with disclosure which is the core of the Act.

Our conclusion that "manipulative" acts under § 14(e) require misrepresentation or nondisclosure is buttressed by the purpose and legislative history of the provision. Section 14(e) was originally added to the Securities Exchange Act as part of the Williams Act, 82 Stat. 457.

* * *

It is clear that Congress relied primarily on disclosure to implement the purpose of the Williams Act.

* * *

The expressed legislative intent was to preserve a neutral setting in which the contenders could fully present their arguments. * * * Nowhere in the legislative history is there the slightest suggestion that § 14(e) serves any purpose other than disclosure,[11] or that the term "manipulative" should be read as an invitation to the courts to oversee the substantive fairness of tender offers; the quality of any offer is a matter for the marketplace.

To adopt the reading of the term "manipulative" urged by petitioner would not only be unwarranted in light of the legislative purpose but would be at odds with it. Inviting judges to read the term "manipulative" with their own sense of what constitutes "unfair" or "artificial" conduct would inject uncertainty into the tender offer process. An essential piece of information—whether the court would deem the fully disclosed actions of one side or the other to be "manipulative"—would not be available until after the tender offer had closed. This uncertainty would directly contradict the expressed congressional desire to give investors full information.

Congress' consistent emphasis on disclosure persuades us that it intended takeover contests to be addressed to shareholders. In pursuit

11. The Act was amended in 1970, and Congress added to § 14(e) the sentence, "The Commission shall, for the purposes of this subsection, by rules and regulations define, and prescribe means reasonably designed to prevent, such acts and practices as are fraudulent, deceptive, or manipulative." Petitioner argues that this phrase would be pointless if § 14(e) was concerned with disclosure only.

We disagree. In adding the 1970 amendment, Congress simply provided a mechanism for defining and guarding against those acts and practices which involve material misrepresentation or nondisclosure. The amendment gives the Securities and Exchange Commission latitude to regulate nondeceptive activities as a "reasonably designed" means of preventing manipulative acts, without suggesting any change in the meaning of the term "manipulative" itself.

of this goal, Congress, consistent with the core mechanism of the Securities Exchange Act, created sweeping disclosure requirements and narrow substantive safeguards. The same Congress that placed such emphasis on shareholder choice would not at the same time have required judges to oversee tender offers for substantive fairness. It is even less likely that a Congress implementing that intention would express it only through the use of a single word placed in the middle of a provision otherwise devoted to disclosure.

We hold that the term "manipulative" as used in § 14(e) requires misrepresentation or nondisclosure....

Applying that definition to this case, we hold that the actions of respondents were not manipulative. The amended complaint fails to allege that the cancellation of the first tender offer was accompanied by any misrepresentation, nondisclosure, or deception.

* * *

Petitioner also alleges that El Paso management and Burlington entered into certain undisclosed and deceptive agreements during the making of the second tender offer. The substance of the allegations is that, in return for certain undisclosed benefits, El Paso managers agreed to support the second tender offer. But both courts noted that petitioner's complaint seeks only redress for injuries related to the cancellation of the first tender offer. Since the deceptive and misleading acts alleged by petitioner all occurred with reference to the making of the second tender offer—when the injuries suffered by petitioner had already been sustained—these acts bear no possible causal relationship to petitioner's alleged injuries.

* * *

After the loss in federal court, the stockholders of El Paso sought relief in the Delaware courts. The court held against the stockholders. Gilbert v. The El Paso Company, 575 A.2d 1131 (Del.1990). See pages 588–590, supra, for an excerpt of the opinion.

Questions

1. In *Schreiber* the plaintiff alleged deception in the disclosures relating to the second tender offer (the failure to disclose the "recognition" of fair golden parachutes). How does the court dismiss this claim? If the claim is accurate, doesn't the deception relate to the reasons for the withdrawal of the first tender offer? The plaintiffs also allege that a primary reason for the El Paso board's settlement was a desire of the El Paso insiders, who had *not* tendered into the first offer, to be able to tender into a second offer. If true, would this constitute manipulation?

2. If section 14(e) requires some form of deception, how can the Securities and Exchange Commission use the section to justify substantive

regulations such as rule 14e–1 (a tender offer must be open for twenty days)?

3. Does section 14(e), like rule 10b–5, require a showing of scienter?

4. Is there an analog in tender offers for a *Goldberg*-style action? That is, can a clever lawyer find a way to turn a fiduciary breach allegation against target directors? Consider the following case:

PANTER v. MARSHALL FIELD & CO.

United States Court of Appeals, Seventh Circuit, 1981.
646 F.2d 271, cert. denied 454 U.S. 1092, 102 S.Ct. 658, 70 L.Ed.2d 631 (1981).

PELL, CIRCUIT JUDGE:

[The plaintiffs were shareholders of Marshall Field and Company, which successfully resisted a takeover by Carter Hawley Hale. The full facts of the case are at pages 826–831, infra.]

* * *

The gravamen of the plaintiffs' 10b–5 claim is that Field's directors acted pursuant to a long-standing undisclosed policy of independence and resistance to all takeover attempts, designed to perpetuate the defendant directors' control of the corporation. The plaintiffs assert that the defendants' failure to disclose this policy was an omission of a material fact which made other statements and conduct of the defendants misleading. They also claim that the policy motivated the defendant directors to make other misrepresentations or omissions of material facts in relation to Field's prospects and plans.

As the Supreme Court noted in *Santa Fe Industries, Inc. v. Green*, 430 U.S. 462, 477–78, 97 S.Ct. 1292, 1302–03, 51 L.Ed.2d 480 (1977), the rule is a manifestation of the "philosophy of full disclosure," embodied in the Securities Exchange Act of 1934; it therefore requires proof of the element of deception, and does not provide a remedy for the breach of fiduciary duty a director owes his corporation and its shareholders under state law.

* * *

In the wake of *Santa Fe*, courts have consistently held that since a shareholder cannot recover under 10b–5 for a breach of fiduciary duty, neither can he "bootstrap" such a claim into a federal securities action by alleging that the disclosure philosophy of the statute obligates defendants to reveal either the culpability of their activities, or their impure motives for entering the allegedly improper transaction.

* * *

The plaintiffs' allegations that Field's directors rebuffed all acquisition attempts without regard to merit and failed to disclose the existence of an alleged policy so to act, are similarly insufficient to create a federal cause of action.

They simply state a claim for a breach of the fiduciary duty directors owe shareholders under state corporate law. This is precisely the type of claim the Supreme Court intended to bar from the federal forum when it announced the rule in *Santa Fe Industries*. It is therefore "entirely appropriate in this instance to relegate [plaintiffs] ... to whatever remedy is created by state law," *Santa Fe,* 430 U.S. at 478, 97 S.Ct. at 1303, to the extent their claims are based on the existence of or failure to disclose any putative policy of independence.

* * *

KRAMER v. TIME WARNER, INC.
United States District Court, Southern District of New York, 1990.
Fed.Sec.L.Rep. (CCH) ¶ 95,619.

Opinion of SAND, DISTRICT JUDGE.

This securities case arises out of the well-publicized merger of Time, Inc. ("Time") and Warner Communications, Inc. ("Warner"). Plaintiff, a former shareholder of Warner, seeks to represent a class consisting of former Warner shareholders who tendered their shares pursuant to Time's June 16, 1989 tender offer. The named defendants are Time Warner, Inc., Warner, and five individuals who formerly were directors and senior executives of Warner.

* * *

On March 3, 1989, Time and Warner entered into a stock for stock merger agreement. In late May, 1989, the two companies mailed a Joint Proxy Statement describing the merger to their shareholders, in anticipation of shareholder meetings to be held in late June. On June 7, 1989, Paramount Communications, Inc. launched an all cash tender offer for Time. On June 16, 1989, in response to the Paramount bid, the Boards of Directors of Time and Warner entered into an amended merger agreement which provided for a two-step acquisition plan consisting of a tender offer by Time for approximately 51% of Warner's outstanding common stock, to be followed later by a merger. The tender offer was announced the same day, and Time's Offer to Purchase was mailed to Warner shareholders a few days later. The tender offer was oversubscribed; as a result, shares were bought by Time from each tendering shareholder on a pro rata basis. The tender offer closed in late June, 1989, and the merger was completed in January, 1990.

The amended merger agreement executed by Time and Warner did not specify the exact consideration to be paid upon consummation of the merger for the 49% of shares not accepted by Time in the tender offer. However, the agreement did provide that the consideration would consist of some package of cash, debt or equity agreed to by Time and Warner, the value of which would be equal, as nearly as practicable, in the opinion of two investment banking firms, to the $70 per share paid in the tender offer.

On August 23, 1989, the Boards of Time and Warner agreed that the consideration paid on consummation of the merger for all remaining shares of Warner stock would consist of a package of three Time Warner, Inc. securities. Three investment banks issued opinions stating that the securities package, if issued on August 23rd, would have a value equal, as nearly as practicable, to $70 per share. However, when the securities package actually began trading on December 12, 1989, its market price was only approximately $61.75.

On December 13, 1989, plaintiff commenced the present action. Plaintiff's allegations center on certain compensation arrangements between Warner and its top management, including the individual defendants named in this case. The complaint states that in 1982, Warner's shareholders approved an Equity Unit Purchase Plan ("Equity Plan"). Pursuant to the Equity Plan, "plan shares" were sold to the individual defendants and other top Warner executives. These shares could be resold to Warner at a resale price based on Warner's book value. The Equity Plan gave the Executive Compensation Committee of Warner's Board the discretion to modify the resale price under certain circumstances. According to the complaint, Warner also issued stock options to some of its executives, including the named defendants herein, at various times.

The amended merger agreement executed by Time and Warner on June 16, 1989 discussed certain adjustments which were to be made to the Equity Plan and the stock option plan. The agreement provided that immediately prior to the consummation of the second step of the acquisition (the merger), the Executive Compensation Committee could adjust the resale price of the Equity Plan shares to equal $70 per share. The agreement also provided that on consummation of the merger, outstanding Warner stock options would be cancelled in exchange for an amount of cash equal to $70 per share less the stock option exercise price. The result of these provisions was that when the merger was consummated, Warner's top executives would be able to receive $70 in cash for each Equity Plan share and stock option share that they owned.

The gravamen of plaintiff's complaint is that he was treated unfairly because Warner's top management received a $70 value for their Equity Plan shares and stock options upon consummation of the merger, while plaintiff and his fellow Warner shareholders received only a $62 value for their common shares. Seeking redress, plaintiff filed the present complaint.

* * *

Plaintiff's first set of federal law claims centers on Time's Offer to Purchase dated June 16, 1989. Plaintiff makes three separate allegations regarding purported omissions or misrepresentations in the Offer to Purchase.

1. Alleged Misrepresentation as to Validity of
Adjustments to Equity Plan

Plaintiff alleges that the Offer to Purchase contained materially false statements regarding the adjustments to the Equity Plan that were to be made on consummation of the Time–Warner merger. As quoted in the complaint, the Offer to Purchase states:

> As contemplated by the Equity ... Plan, the committee administering such plan may adjust the 'Book Value Per Share' and the 'Resale price' to equal, effective immediately prior to consummation of the Merger, the Merger Value [i.e., $70 per plan share] ... and shall make such other changes as it deems appropriate to give effect to the Merger.

Complaint ¶ 31. Plaintiff claims that the Equity Plan in fact did not authorize the raising of the resale price in the event of a merger Complaint ¶ 31. Therefore, plaintiff asserts, the statement in the Offer to Purchase was materially false and misleading in violation of the antifraud provisions of the securities laws, specifically § 14(e) and § 10(b) of the Exchange Act.

* * *

In this case, plaintiff does not allege that the Offer to Purchase failed to disclose any material term of the proposed alterations to the Equity Plan. *See* Complaint ¶ 31. Rather, plaintiff argues that the statement in the Offer to Purchase was misleading because it impliedly represented that the alterations were authorized by the Plan when in fact, according to plaintiff, they were not. In essence, then, plaintiff's allegation is that defendants failed to characterize the alterations as unauthorized.

Under the federal securities laws, defendants were not required to characterize the alterations to the Equity Plan as being unauthorized. The disclosure required by the Exchange Act is not "a rite of confession". *Data Probe,* 722 F.2d at 5. As plaintiff concedes, defendants revealed the "objective factual matters," *id.* at 6, regarding the proposed alterations to the Equity Plan in the Offer to Purchase. Neither § 14(e) nor § 10(b) of the Exchange Act required them to do anything more.

* * *

2. Alleged Non-disclosure of Conflict of Interest

Plaintiff's second fraud allegation also focuses on the Equity Plan. Plaintiff alleges that upon consummation of the merger, the individual defendants and other top Warner executives received huge profits from the adjustments to the resale price of the Equity Plan shares. Complaint ¶¶ 21–22, 30–31. Plaintiff alleges that the lure of these profits created a conflict of interest for the individual defendants and others on the Warner Board because it colored their judgment in deciding whether to support the Time tender offer and recommend it to Warner's shareholders. Complaint ¶ 31. Plaintiff asserts that the Offer to Purchase was materially misleading in that it reported that the Warner Board approved of the Time tender offer but did not disclose adequately the Board's conflict of interest.

The failure to disclose a conflict of interest on the part of a member of management or the board of directors can constitute a violation of the federal securities laws. * * * However, the securities laws are not violated so long as the objective facts which create the conflict are disclosed. A corporation is not required to characterize those facts in a particular way, at least so long as the presentation of the facts is truly objective and does not create misleading impressions.

* * *

In this case, plaintiff's conflict of interest claim is foreclosed by *Data Probe*. As the complaint acknowledges, the Offer to Purchase fully disclosed the modifications that would be made to Warner's Equity Plan. Complaint ¶ 31. The Offer did not list the number of plan shares held by the individual defendants and the other members of Warner's board; however, as plaintiff admits in his Memorandum of Law, that information had been disclosed in the Joint Proxy Statement sent to Warner shareholders approximately three weeks before the Offer to purchase was mailed.... By examining the Joint Proxy Statement, any Warner shareholder capable of simple mathematics could have calculated the amounts that the Warner board members would receive as a result of the adjustment of the Equity Plan's resale price.

* * *

3. ALLEGED MISREPRESENTATION OF THE MERGER CONSIDERATION

Plaintiff's final allegation of fraud is that the Offer to Purchase misrepresented the consideration that would be paid upon consummation of the merger for all Warner shares not already owned by Time. As set forth in the complaint, the Offer to Purchase stated that the consideration would consist of "cash or debt or equity securities of Time," the precise form of which would be agreed to later by Time and Warner, and the value of which would equal to $70, "as nearly as practicable, in the opinion of two investment banking firms of national reputation." Plaintiff claims that this description of the consideration was defective in two respects. First, plaintiff asserts that the wording implies that at least part of the consideration would be in cash, when in fact the defendants knew that only securities would be provided. Second, plaintiff claims that the description was false because at the time the Offer to Purchase was promulgated, the defendants knew that the consideration ultimately delivered would be worth less than $70.

This Court holds that plaintiff's allegations regarding the description of the consideration in the Offer to Purchase fail to state a claim under federal law. With regard to plaintiff's claim that the wording of the Offer to Purchase implied that the consideration would be partly in cash, no claim is stated because plaintiff has failed to allege any misrepresentation. Here, there was no misrepresentation as to the form of consideration. The words used by the Offer to Purchase—"cash or debt or equity"—simply do not imply that any part of the consideration would be in cash. Thus, even if the defendants knew at the time the Offer to Purchase was promulgated that none of the consideration would be in cash, there was no misrepresentation.

As to plaintiff's allegation that defendants knew that the consideration would be worth less than $70, no claim is stated because plaintiff has not alleged sufficiently scienter on the part of the defendants. In order to be held liable for securities fraud, a defendant must possess the requisite intent....

In this case, plaintiff's complaint fails to allege facts from which a strong inference of fraud can be drawn. The complaint alleges scienter only in very conclusory terms. At oral argument, plaintiff maintained that two facts alleged in the complaint supported an inference of scienter: (1) that the individual defendants received cash and not securities pursuant to the adjustments in the Equity Plan and stock option plans; and (2) that the securities package turned out to be worth only $62 when it began trading in December, 1989. The fact that the individual defendants received cash raises no inference regarding their beliefs about the value of the securities package. Absent allegations showing that Warner's Board had reason to believe that the securities package would be worth less than $70, the choice of cash shows nothing about intent. That the package actually traded below $70 is similarly unenlightening as to the defendants' intent.... In essence, plaintiff's allegation is that defendants must have known that the securities package would trade at less than $70 because the package did, in fact, trade at less than $70.[5] This amounts to no more than "fraud by hindsight."

* * *

It is well-established that a plaintiff may not gain access to federal court by "bootstrapping" state corporate law claims into federal law claims. *See Santa Fe Indus., Inc. v. Green*, 430 U.S. 462, 477 (1977) ... In this case, as in *Santa Fe*, the gravamen of plaintiff's complaint is that the Directors of Warner treated him unfairly by taking a greater share of the spoils of the Time–Warner merger and leaving him less than he expected. It may be that plaintiff has stated valid claims under state corporate law, however, the present complaint fails to state any claim under the federal securities laws. Accordingly, defendants' motion to dismiss is granted.

The Frustrated Bidder's Standing to Sue Under Section 14(e)

PIPER v. CHRIS–CRAFT INDUSTRIES, INC.

Supreme Court of the United States, 1977.
430 U.S. 1, 97 S.Ct. 926, 51 L.Ed.2d 124.

[The facts of the case are contained in pages 732–735, supra.]

---

5. Defendants suggest that the reason for the low trading price was the widely-publicized collapse of the junk bond market in October, 1989. At oral argument, plaintiff's counsel conceded that a decline in the market had occurred.

* * *

On May 22, 1969, Chris–Craft filed suit seeking both damages and injunctive relief in the United States District Court for the Southern District of New York. Chris–Craft alleged that Bangor's block purchases of 120,200 Piper shares in mid-May violated Rule 10b–6 and that Bangor's May 8 press release, announcing an $80 valuation of Bangor securities to be offered in the forthcoming exchange offer, violated SEC "gun-jumping" provisions, 15 U.S.C. section 77e(c), and SEC Rule 135, 17 CFR section 230.135 (1976). Chris–Craft sought to enjoin Bangor from voting the Piper shares purchased in violation of Rule 10b–6 and from accepting any shares tendered by Piper stockholders pursuant to the exchange offer.

The threshold issue in these cases is whether tender offerors such as Chris–Craft, whose activities are regulated by the Williams Act, have a cause of action for damages against other regulated parties under the statute on a claim that antifraud violations by other parties have frustrated the bidder's efforts to obtain control of the target corporation. Without reading such a cause of action into the Act, none of the other issues need be reached.

Our analysis begins, of course, with the statute itself. Section 14(e), like § 10(b), makes no provision whatever for a private cause of action, such as those explicitly provided in other sections of the 1933 and 1934 Acts. This Court has nonetheless held that in some circumstances a private cause of action can be implied with respect to the 1934 Act's antifraud provisions, even though the relevant provisions are silent as to remedies. *J.I. Case Co. v. Borak,* 377 U.S. 426 (1964) (§ 14(a)); *Superintendent of Ins. v. Bankers Life & Cas. Co.,* 404 U.S. 6, 13 n. 9 (1971) (§ 10(b)).

The reasoning of these holdings is that, where congressional purposes are likely to be undermined absent private enforcement, private remedies may be implied in favor of the particular class intended to be protected by the statute.

* * *

The legislative history thus shows that Congress was intent upon regulating takeover bidders, theretofore operating covertly, in order to protect the shareholders of target companies. * * * Taken in their totality, these statements confirm that what Congress had in mind was the protection of shareholders, the "pawn[s] in a form of industrial warfare." The Senate Report expressed the purpose as "plac[ing] investors on an equal footing with the takeover bidder," Senate Report 4, without favoring either the tender offeror or existing management. This express policy of neutrality scarcely suggests an intent to confer highly important, new rights upon the class of participants whose activities prompted the legislation in the first instance.

* * *

It is clear, therefore, that Chris–Craft has not asserted standing under § 14(e) as a Piper shareholder. The reason is not hard to divine. As a tender offeror actively engaged in competing for Piper stock, Chris–Craft was not in the posture of a target shareholder confronted with the decision of whether to tender or retain its stock. Consequently, Chris–Craft could scarcely have alleged a need for the disclosures mandated by the Williams Act. In short, the fact that Chris–Craft necessarily acquired Piper stock as a means of taking over Piper adds nothing to its § 14(e) standing arguments. * * * As a disclosure mechanism aimed especially at protecting shareholders of target corporations, the Williams Act cannot consistently be interpreted as conferring a monetary remedy upon regulated parties, particularly where the award would not redound to the direct benefit of the protected class. Although it is correct to say that the $36 million damages award indirectly benefits those Piper shareholders who became Chris–Craft shareholders when they accepted Chris–Craft's exchange offer, it is equally true that the damages award injures those Piper shareholders who exchanged their shares for Bangor Punta's stock and who, as Bangor Punta shareholders, would necessarily bear a large part of the burden of any judgment against Bangor Punta. The class sought to be protected by the Williams Act are the shareholders of the *target* corporation; hence it can hardly be said that their interests as a class are served by a judgment in favor of Chris–Craft and against Bangor Punta. Moreover, the damages are awarded to the very party whose activities Congress intended to curb; Chris–Craft did not sue in the capacity of an injured Piper shareholder, but as a defeated tender offeror.

Nor can we agree that an ever-present threat of damages against a successful contestant in a battle for control will provide significant additional protection for shareholders in general. The deterrent value, if any, of such awards can never be ascertained with precision. More likely, however, is the prospect that shareholders may be prejudiced because some tender offers may never be made if there is a possibility of massive damages claims for what courts subsequently hold to be an actionable violation of § 14(e). Even a contestant who "wins the battle" for control may well wind up exposed to a costly "war" in a later and successful defense of its victory. Or at worst—on Chris–Craft's damages theory—the victorious tender offeror or the target corporation might be subject to a large substantive judgment, plus high costs of litigation.

In short, we conclude that shareholder protection, if enhanced at all by damages awards such as Chris–Craft contends for, can more directly be achieved with other, less drastic means more closely tailored to the precise congressional goal underlying the Williams Act. * * * as Judge Friendly observed in *Electronic Specialty Co. v. International Controls Corp.*, 409 F.2d 937, 947 (C.A.2 1969), in corporate control contests the stage of preliminary injunctive relief, rather than post-contest lawsuits, "is the time when relief can best be given." ... [28]

Apart from awarding damages, however, the Court of Appeals also ordered the District Court to enjoin Bangor Punta from voting the illegally acquired Piper shares for a period of five years. * * * As we previously indicated, Chris–Craft prior to the trial on liability expressly waived any claim to injunctive relief. The case was tried in the District Court, without a jury, exclusively as a suit for damages. * * * Under these circumstances, our holding that Chris–Craft does not have a cause of action for damages under § 14(e) renders that injunction inappropriate, premised as it was upon the impermissible award of damages.[33]

* * *

MOBIL CORP. v. MARATHON OIL CO.

United States Court of Appeals, Sixth District, 1981.
669 F.2d 366.

ENGEL, CIRCUIT JUDGE.

On October 30, 1981, Mobil Corporation ("Mobil") announced its intention to purchase up to 40 million outstanding common shares of stock in Marathon Oil Company ("Marathon") for $85 per share in cash. Mobil conditioned that purchase upon receipt of at least 30 million shares, just over one-half of the outstanding shares. It further stated its intention to acquire the balance of Marathon by merger following its purchase of those shares.

Marathon directors were concerned about the effects of a merger with Mobil, and they immediately held a board meeting. The directors determined that, together with consideration of other alternatives, they would seek a "white knight"—a more attractive candidate for merger. * * * United States Steel Corporation ("U.S. Steel") indicated its interest, and on November 18, 1981, offered what it termed a "final proposal" to be acted upon that day. By that proposal U.S. Steel offered $125 per share for 30 million shares of Marathon stock, with a plan for a follow-up merger with its subsidiary, U.S.S. Corporation ("USS").

The Marathon directors voted to recommend the U.S. Steel offer to the shareholders on November 18, 1981. Marathon, U.S. Steel and USS executed a formal merger agreement on that day. USS made its tender offer on November 19, 1981. Both USS and Marathon filed the appropriate documents with the Securities Exchange Commission.

---

28. Our holding is a limited one. Whether shareholder-offerees, the class protected by § 14(e), have an implied cause of action under § 14(e) is not before us, and we intimate no view on the matter. Nor is the target corporation's standing to sue in issue in this case. We hold only that a tender offeror, suing in its capacity as a takeover bidder, does not have standing to sue for damages under § 14(e).

33. We intimate no view upon whether as a general proposition a suit in equity for injunctive relief, as distinguished from an action for damages, would lie in favor of a tender offeror under either § 14(e) or Rule 10b–6.

The USS offer, and subsequently the merger agreement, had two significant conditions. First, they required a present, irrevocable option to purchase ten million authorized but unissued shares of Marathon common stock for $90 per share ("stock option"). These shares equalled approximately 17% of Marathon's outstanding shares. Next, they required an option to purchase Marathon's 48% interest in oil and mineral rights in the Yates Field for $2.8 billion. ("Yates Field option"). The latter option could be exercised only if USS's offer did not succeed and if a third party gained control of Marathon. Thus, in effect, a potential competing tender offeror could not acquire Yates Field upon a merger with Marathon.

The value of Yates Field to Marathon and to potential buyers is significant; Marathon has referred to the field as its "crown jewel."

* * *

Following this agreement, Mobil filed suit in the United States District Court for the Southern District of Ohio, seeking to enjoin the exercise of the options and any purchase of shares in accordance with the tender offer.

* * *

Although the issue has not been raised by either party, out of an abundance of caution we believe it necessary to determine whether Mobil has a private cause of action for injunctive relief under section 14(e) of the Williams Act. * * * This open question has not been resolved by the Supreme Court or by this circuit, although other courts faced with the issue have found that such a cause of action exists. After an examination of the *Piper* analysis, a consideration of the distinctions between damage actions and injunctive actions, and a recognition of the special problems associated with the dynamics of tender offer battles, we agree with these courts and hold that a tender offeror has an implied cause of action under the Williams Act to obtain timely injunctive relief for violations of section 14(e). * * * As a tender offeror, Mobil would not appear to be the intended beneficiary of the Act. We believe, however, that we can look to the practical realities of this type of action and determine that a cause of action is necessary to aid the shareholders of Marathon and to prevent violations of the Williams Act. A preliminary injunction against manipulative practices would be the only *means* of preserving the free, informed choice of shareholders that the Williams Act was designed to protect. In a tender offer battle, events occur with explosive speed and require immediate response by a party seeking to enjoin the unlawful conduct. Issues such as incomplete disclosure and manipulative practices can only be effectively spotted and argued by parties with complete knowledge of the target, its business, and others in the industry. The tender offeror has frequently made intensive investigations before deciding to commence its offer, and may often be the only party with enough knowledge and awareness to identify nondisclosure or manipulative practices in time to obtain a preliminary injunction.

* * *

* * * An injunctive action by a tender offeror has significantly different effects than a damage action. First, clear benefit is derived by the shareholders of the target. An injunction would protect the Marathon shareholders from making their decisions whether to sell without full information. As such, it furthers the purpose of the Williams Act. Second, an injunctive action does not tip the balance in favor of one tender offeror. This type of action serves merely to prevent the manipulative practices at which the Williams Act was aimed without deterring management or competing offerors from engaging in the battle. * * * Because of the unique ability of Mobil to act quickly while armed with information necessary to prove any section 14(e) violations, this injunctive action may often be the only means to provide adequate assurance that Marathon's shareholders have a fully informed, free choice. Moreover, because no monetary loss is threatened for one who inadvertently violates the Williams Act, an action for an injunction does not pose the danger of deterring future offers.

* * *

SECTION 2. SPECIFIC DISCLOSURE QUESTIONS

Subsection a. General Principles—Materiality and the Duty to Disclose

TSC INDUSTRIES, INC. v. NORTHWAY, INC.

Supreme Court of the United States, 1976.
426 U.S. 438, 96 S.Ct. 2126, 48 L.Ed.2d 757.

Mr. Justice Marshall:

The proxy rules promulgated by the Securities and Exchange Commission under the Securities Exchange Act of 1934 bar the use of proxy statements that are false or misleading with respect to the presentation or omission of material facts. We are called upon to consider the definition of a material fact under those rules, and the appropriateness of resolving the question of materiality by summary judgment in this case.

The dispute in this case centers on the acquisition of petitioner TSC Industries, Inc., by petitioner National Industries, Inc. In February 1969 National acquired 34% of TSC's voting securities by purchase from Charles E. Schmidt and his family. Schmidt, who had been TSC's founder and principal shareholder, promptly resigned along with his son from TSC's board of directors. Thereafter, five National nominees were placed on TSC's board; and Stanley R. Yarmuth, National's president and chief executive officer, became chairman of the TSC board, and Charles F. Simonelli, National's executive vice president, became chairman of the TSC executive committee. On October 16, 1969, the TSC board, with the attending National nominees abstaining, approved a proposal to liquidate and sell all of TSC's assets to National.

The proposal in substance provided for the exchange of TSC common and Series 1 preferred stock for National Series B preferred stock and warrants. On November 12, 1969, TSC and National issued a joint proxy statement to their shareholders, recommending approval of the proposal. The proxy solicitation was successful, TSC was placed in liquidation and dissolution, and the exchange of shares was effected.

This is an action brought by respondent Northway, a TSC shareholder, against TSC and National, claiming that their joint proxy statement was incomplete and materially misleading in violation of § 14(a) of the Securities Exchange Act of 1934, and Rules 14a–3 and 14a–9, promulgated thereunder. * * * The Rule 14a–9 claim, insofar as it concerns us, is that TSC and National omitted from the proxy statement material facts relating to the degree of National's control over TSC and the favorability of the terms of the proposal to TSC shareholders.

* * *

In a suit challenging the sufficiency under § 14(a) and Rule 14a–9 of a proxy statement soliciting votes in favor of a merger, we held that there was no need to demonstrate that the alleged defect in the proxy statement actually had a decisive effect on the voting. So long as the misstatement or omission was material, the causal relation between violation and injury is sufficiently established, we concluded, if "the proxy solicitation itself . . . was an essential link in the accomplishment of the transaction." 396 U.S., at 385.

* * *

The question of materiality, it is universally agreed, is an objective one, involving the significance of an omitted or misrepresented fact to a reasonable investor.

* * *

As an abstract proposition, the most desirable role for a court in a suit of this sort, coming after the consummation of the proposed transaction, would perhaps be to determine whether in fact the proposal would have been favored by the shareholders and consummated in the absence of any misstatement or omission. But as we recognized in *Mills*, such matters are not subject to determination with certainty. Doubts as to the critical nature of information misstated or omitted will be commonplace. And particularly in view of the prophylactic purpose of the Rule and the fact that the content of the proxy statement is within management's control, it is appropriate that these doubts be resolved in favor of those the statute is designed to protect.

We are aware, however, that the disclosure policy embodied in the proxy regulations is not without limit. Some information is of such dubious significance that insistence on its disclosure may accomplish more harm than good. The potential liability for a Rule 14a–9 violation can be great indeed, and if the standard of materiality is unnecessarily low, not only may the corporation and its management be subjected to liability for insignificant omissions or misstatements, but also management's fear of exposing itself to substantial liability may cause it simply to bury the shareholders in an avalanche of trivial information—a result that is hardly conducive to informed decision-making.

* * *

The general standard of materiality that we think best comports with the policies of Rule 14a–9 is as follows: An omitted fact is material if there is a substantial likelihood that a reasonable shareholder would consider it important in deciding how to vote. This standard is fully consistent with *Mills'* general description of materiality as a requirement that "the defect have a significant *propensity* to affect the voting process." It does not require proof of a substantial likelihood that disclosure of the omitted fact would have caused the reasonable investor to change his vote. What the standard does contemplate is a showing of a substantial likelihood that, under all the circumstances, the omitted fact would have assumed actual significance in the deliberations of the reasonable shareholder. Put another way, there must be a substantial likelihood that the disclosure of the omitted fact would have been viewed by the reasonable investor as having significantly altered the "total mix" of information made available.

* * *

National's Control of TSC

The Court of Appeals concluded that two omitted facts relating to National's potential influence, or control, over the management of TSC were material as a matter of law. First, the proxy statement failed to state that at the time the statement was issued, the chairman of the TSC board of directors was Stanley Yarmuth, National's president and chief executive officer, and the chairman of the TSC executive committee was Charles Simonelli, National's executive vice president. Second, the statement did not disclose that in filing reports required by the SEC, both TSC and National had indicated that National "may be deemed to be a 'parent' of TSC as that term is defined in the Rules and Regulations under the Securities Act of 1933." The Court of Appeals noted that TSC shareholders were relying on the TSC board of directors to negotiate on their behalf for the best possible rate of exchange with National. It then concluded that the omitted facts were material because they were "persuasive indicators that the TSC board was in fact under the control of National, and that National thus 'sat on both sides of the table' in setting the terms of the exchange."

We do not agree that the omission of these facts, when viewed against the disclosures contained in the proxy statement, warrants the entry of summary judgment against TSC and National on this record. Our conclusion is the same whether the omissions are considered separately or together.

The proxy statement prominently displayed the facts that National owned 34% of the outstanding shares in TSC, and that no other person owned more than 10%. It also prominently revealed that 5 out of 10 TSC directors were National nominees, and it recited the positions of those National nominees with National—indicating, among other things, that Stanley Yarmuth was president and a director of National, and that Charles Simonelli was executive vice president and a director of National. These disclosures clearly revealed the nature of National's relationship with TSC and alerted the reasonable shareholder to the fact that National exercised a degree of influence over TSC. In view of these disclosures, we certainly cannot say that the additional facts that Yarmuth was chairman of the TSC board of directors and Simonelli chairman of its executive committee were, on this record, so obviously important that reasonable minds could not differ on their materiality.

Nor can we say that it was materially misleading as a matter of law for TSC and National to have omitted reference to SEC filings indicating that National "may be deemed to be a parent of TSC." As we have already noted, both the District Court and the Court of Appeals concluded, in denying summary judgment on the Rule 14a–3 claim, that there was a genuine issue of fact as to whether National actually controlled TSC at the time of the proxy solicitation. We must assume for present purposes, then, that National did not control TSC. On that assumption, TSC and National obviously had no duty to state without qualification that control did exist. If the proxy statements were to disclose the conclusory statements in the SEC filings that National "may be deemed to be a parent of TSC," then it would have been appropriate, if not necessary, for the statement to have included a disclaimer of National control over TSC or a disclaimer of knowledge as to whether National controlled TSC. The net contribution of including the contents of the SEC filings accompanied by such disclaimers is not of such obvious significance, in view of the other facts contained in the proxy statement, that their exclusion renders the statement materially misleading as a matter of law.

Favorability of the Terms to TSC Shareholders

The Court of Appeals also found that the failure to disclose two sets of facts rendered the proxy statement materially deficient in its presentation of the favorability of the terms of the proposed transaction to TSC shareholders. The first omission was of information, described by the Court of Appeals as "bad news" for TSC shareholders, contained in a letter from an investment banking firm whose earlier favorable opinion of the fairness of the proposed transaction was reported in the proxy statement. The second omission related to purchases of National common stock by National and by Madison Fund, Inc., a large mutual fund, during the two years prior to the issuance of the proxy statement.

The proxy statement revealed that the investment banking firm of Hornblower & Weeks–Hemphill, Noyes had rendered a favorable opinion on the fairness to TSC shareholders of the terms for the exchange of TSC shares for National securities. In that opinion, the proxy statement explained, the firm had considered, "among other things, the current market prices of the securities of both corporations, the high redemption price of the National Series B preferred stock, the dividend and debt service requirements of both corporations, the substantial premium over current market values represented by the securities being offered to TSC stockholders, and the increased dividend income."

* * *

The closing price of the National warrants on November 7, 1969, was, as indicated in the proxy statement, $5.25. The TSC shareholders were misled, the Court of Appeals concluded, by the proxy statement's failure to disclose that in a communication two weeks after its favorable opinion letter, the Hornblower firm revealed that its determination of the fairness of the offer to TSC was based on the conclusion that the value of the warrants involved in the transaction would not be their current market price, but approximately $3.50. If the warrants were valued at $3.50 rather than $5.25, and the other securities valued at the November 7 closing price, the court figured, the apparent premium would be substantially reduced—from $3.23 (27%) to $1.48 (12%) in the case of the TSC preferred, and from $2.94 (22%) to $0.31 (2%) in the case of TSC common.

* * *

It would appear, however, that the subsequent communication from the Hornblower firm, which the Court of Appeals felt contained "bad news," contained nothing new at all. At the TSC board of directors meeting held on October 16, 1969, the date of the initial Hornblower opinion letter, Blancke Noyes, a TSC director and a partner in the Hornblower firm, had pointed out the likelihood of a decline in the market price of National warrants with the issuance of the additional warrants involved in the exchange, and reaffirmed his conclusion that the exchange offer was a fair one nevertheless. The subsequent Hornblower letter, signed by Mr. Noyes, purported merely to explain the basis of the calculations underlying the favorable opinion rendered in the October 16 letter. "In advising TSC as to the fairness of the offer from [National]," Mr. Noyes wrote, "we concluded that the warrants in question had a value of approximately $3.50." On its face, then, the subsequent letter from Hornblower does not appear to have contained anything to alter the favorable opinion rendered in the October 16 letter—including the conclusion that the securities being offered to TSC shareholders represented a "substantial premium over current market values."

The real question, though, is not whether the subsequent Hornblower letter contained anything that altered the Hornblower opinion in any way. It is, rather, whether the advice given at the October 16 meeting, and reduced to more precise terms in the subsequent Hornblower letter—that there might be a decline in the market price of the

National warrants—had to be disclosed in order to clarify the import of the proxy statement's reference to "the substantial premium over current market values represented by the securities being offered to TSC stockholders." We note initially that the proxy statement referred to the substantial premium as but one of several factors considered by Hornblower in rendering its favorable opinion of the terms of exchange. Still, we cannot assume that a TSC shareholder would focus only on the "bottom line" of the opinion to the exclusion of the considerations that produced it.

TSC and National insist that the reference to a substantial premium required no clarification or supplementation, for the reason that there was a substantial premium even if the National warrants are assumed to have been worth $3.50. In reaching the contrary conclusion, the Court of Appeals, they contend, ignored the rise in price of TSC securities between early October 1969, when the exchange ratio was set, and November 7, 1969—a rise in price that they suggest was a result of the favorable exchange ratio's becoming public knowledge. When the proxy statement was mailed, TSC and National contend, the market price of TSC securities already reflected a portion of the premium to which Hornblower had referred in rendering its favorable opinion of the terms of exchange. Thus, they note that Hornblower assessed the fairness of the proposed transaction by reference to early October market prices of TSC preferred, TSC common, and National preferred. On the basis of those prices and a $3.50 value for the National warrants involved in the exchange, TSC and National contend that the premium was substantial. Each share of TSC preferred, selling in early October at $11, would bring National preferred stock and warrants worth $13.10—for a premium of $2.10, or 19%. And each share of TSC common, selling in early October at $11.63, would bring National preferred stock and warrants worth $13.25—for a premium of $1.62, or 14%. We certainly cannot say as a matter of law that these premiums were not substantial. And if, as we must assume in considering the appropriateness of summary judgment, the increase in price of TSC's securities from early October to November 7 reflected in large part the market's reaction to the terms of the proposed exchange, it was not materially misleading as a matter of law for the proxy statement to refer to the existence of a substantial premium.

There remains the possibility, however, that although TSC and National may be correct in urging the existence of a substantial premium based upon a $3.50 value for the National warrants and the early October market prices of the other securities involved in the transaction, the proxy statement misled the TSC shareholder to calculate a premium substantially in excess of that premium. The premiums apparent from early October market prices and a $3.50 value for the National warrants—19% on TSC preferred and 14% on TSC common—are certainly less than those that would be derived through use of the November 7 closing prices listed in the proxy statement—27% on TSC preferred and 22% on TSC common. But we are unwilling to sustain a grant of summary judgment to Northway on that basis. To do so we would have to conclude as a matter of law, first, that the proxy statement would have misled the TSC shareholder to calculate his premium on the basis of November 7 market prices, and second, that the difference between that premium and that which would be apparent from early October prices and a $3.50 value for the National warrants was material. These are questions we think best left to the trier of fact.

The final omission that concerns us relates to purchases of National common stock by National and by Madison Fund, Inc., a mutual fund. Northway notes that National's board chairman was a director of Madison, and that Madison's president and chief executive, Edward Merkle, was employed by National pursuant to an agreement obligating him to provide at least one day per month for such duties as National might request.[19] Northway contends that the proxy statement, having called the TSC shareholders' attention to the market prices of the securities involved in the proposed transaction, should have revealed substantial purchases of National common stock made by National and Madison during the two years prior to the issuance of the proxy statement.[20] In particular, Northway contends that the TSC shareholders should, as a matter of law, have been informed that National and Madison purchases accounted for 8.5% of all reported transactions in National common stock during the period between National's acquisition of the Schmidt interests and the proxy solicitation. The theory behind Northway's contention is that disclosure of these purchases would have pointed to the existence, or at least the possible existence, of conspiratorial manipulation of the price of National common stock, which would have had an effect on the market price of the National preferred stock and warrants involved in the proposed transaction.

* * *

* * * In short, while the Court of Appeals viewed the purchases as significant only insofar as they suggested manipulation of the price of National securities, and acknowledged the existence of a genuine issue of fact as to whether there was any manipulation, the court nevertheless required disclosure to enable the shareholders to decide whether there was manipulation or not.

The Court of Appeals' approach would sanction the imposition of civil liability on a theory that undisclosed information may *suggest* the

---

19. Employed in 1967, Merkle initially received a salary of $2,500 per year (increased in 1968 to $12,000) and an option to purchase 10,000 shares of National common stock. App. 520, 522.

20. In a table entitled "Statements of Consolidated Stockholders' Equity," the proxy statement indicated that National acquired approximately 83,000 shares of its own common stock in 1968 and 1969, while it sold approximately 67,000 shares under stock option plans, employment agreements, and warrants. *Id.*, at 324, 330. The proxy statement did not disclose that Madison acquired approximately 170,000 shares of National common during the two-year period, or that approximately one year prior to the proxy solicitation Madison acquired $2 million in National debentures convertible to common.

existence of market manipulation, even if the responsible corporate officials knew that there was in fact no market manipulation. We do not agree that Rule 14a–9 requires such a result. Rule 14a–9 is concerned only with whether a proxy statement is misleading with respect to its presentation of material facts. If, as we must assume on a motion for summary judgment, there was no collusion or manipulation whatsoever in the National and Madison purchases—that is, if the purchases were made wholly independently for proper corporate and investment purposes, then by Northway's implicit acknowledgment they had no bearing on the soundness and reliability of the market prices listed in the proxy statement,[22] and it cannot have been materially misleading to fail to disclose them.[23]

That is not to say, of course, that the SEC could not enact a rule specifically requiring the disclosure of purchases such as were involved in this case, without regard to whether the purchases can be shown to have been collusive or manipulative. We simply hold that if liability is to be imposed in this case upon a theory that it was misleading to fail to disclose purchases suggestive of market manipulation, there must be some showing that there was in fact market manipulation.

In summary, none of the omissions claimed to have been in violation of Rule 14a–9 were, so far as the record reveals, materially misleading as a matter of law, and Northway was not entitled to partial summary judgment.

Questions

1. On the question of whether National was a parent of TSC, the plaintiff shareholders wanted more than a technical description of stock holdings. They wanted the proxy statement to include a characterization of the relationship that ordinary investors could understand. Do the facts that National owns 34 percent of the stock and no other shareholder owns more than 10 percent and that five of the ten directors are National nominees (because TSC directors resigned on the sale of the Schmidt family stock) convey the message that at the next annual shareholder meeting it is highly likely that all the TSC directors will be elected from a slate selected by National? On the other hand, is the court correct to resist requests for characterization using inherently hazy relational terms such as "influ-

---

22. There has been no suggestion that the purchases in question would have any significance if there was in fact no manipulation or collusion, although there may perhaps be such a claim in another case. Nor is there any indication that manipulation or collusion are matters as to whose existence National might have been left in doubt at the time the proxy statement was issued. Cf. n. 16, *supra*.

23. In holding that the failure to disclose the National and Madison purchases violated Rule 14a–9 as a matter of law, the Court of Appeals not only found it unnecessary to consider whether there was in fact any collusion or manipulation, but also found it unnecessary to consider whether the purchases had any significant effect on the price of National common stock or, more pertinently, the price of the National preferred stock and warrants involved in the proposed transaction. Since we find the existence of a genuine issue of fact with respect to whether there was manipulation sufficient to bar summary judgment, it is unnecessary to consider the remaining aspects of the Court of Appeals' decision.

ence," "control," "affiliate," "dominant," and "parent"? Note its statement that if the proxy statement includes an admission of control, then it must come with a disclaimer.

2. On the question of the fairness opinion issued by the investment banking firm to the TSC board, it was clear that the opinion was an important part of the proxy statement, justifying the exchange ratio. Yet the opinion was vague, not revealing the amount of the premium found to be "fair." This case is yet another example of the weasel language used by investment bankers to dress up a pitiful product; they say much less than they appear to say. Managers go along because they too are intent on "selling the deal" to shareholders. On the facts of the case, regardless of whether the investment banker's second letter, which was not disclosed to shareholders, qualified or just explained the earlier fairness opinion, which was disclosed, shouldn't shareholders of TSC have been told the amount of the exchange premium that the investment banker thought to be "substantial"? Is a 2 percent premium substantial? A 15 percent premium? A 25 percent premium? Note that this case was decided well before the advent of the high premiums paid in tender offers in the eighties. Did this have an impact on the decision? Could the court have concluded that the plaintiff shareholders simply ought not to complain about a TSC board decision to accept, based on 19 percent premium for the preferred and 14 percent for the common? ("After all, they did not lose money.")

Why were the October predictions, which were calculated using the $3.50 predicted value of the National warrants, since they were the basis for the TSC board's acceptance of the deal, not disclosed (along with the misleading November 7 prices)? What was the reason for the difference between the value of the warrants on November 7 ($5.25) and the value of the warrants after the transaction? Should not the dilution effect of the acquisition on the value of the warrants have been specifically disclosed and estimated?

Note the timing problems in the fairness opinion. When the investment bankers wrote the fairness opinion on the exchange ratio of the stock swap, they compared existing market prices (taking into account the dilution effects of the swap) of the two firms and found that TSC stockholders would receive a slight premium. Once the deal is announced, what happens to the market prices of the constituent firms? Should they continue to reflect a premium for TSC shareholders? The fairness opinion is important as a prediction of the relative market prices of the constituent firms on closing *assuming* that there was not preclosing public announcement of the deal (which of course is impossible). Is the best evidence of the premium the relative market prices before the first announcement of the deal? What risks are inherent in such an inference?

3. The most interesting part of the case is perhaps the court's treatment of the stock purchases by National itself and by Madison Mutual Fund. The proxy statement did detail the amount of National purchases but did not "call attention" to the purchases, presumably by stating the percentage of outstanding stock purchased. The proxy statement did not detail the Madison purchases at all. Can one separate the materiality of the two omissions on this basis?

More importantly, the court's handling of the issue is based on the requirements for prevailing on a summary judgment motion. The movant had to take the position that it should prevail even when admitting, for the sake of argument, that the purchases were not manipulative or collusive and had no effect on National stock prices. The court rejected the argument that voting shareholders had a right to judge, for themselves, the possibility of stock price manipulation. At the same time the court somewhat sheepishly admitted that the Securities and Exchange Commission could require such disclosures under its authority to pass rules detailing instances of fraud. This admission was a recognition by the court that stock dealings by insiders (here National's board chairman was a director of Madison) and the firm itself are often of substantial interest to investors. Do the stock trades, if not designed to affect National's price, suggest the possibility of insider trading? Must the shareholders make some showing of actual insider states before there is a rule 14a–9 violation for not disclosing the trades?

"Qualitative" Information

GAF CORP. v. HEYMAN

United States Court of Appeals, Second Circuit, 1983.
724 F.2d 727.

GEORGE C. PRATT, CIRCUIT JUDGE:

This is an expedited appeal from a judgment of the United States District Court for the Southern District of New York, entered after a bitter proxy contest in which shareholders of plaintiff GAF Corporation voted decisively to replace the corporation's incumbent board of directors with an insurgent slate headed by defendant Samuel J. Heyman. The district court ruled that the insurgents violated § 14(a) of the Securities Exchange Act of 1934, 15 U.S.C. § 78n(a) (1982), and Rule 14a–9(a) thereunder, 17 C.F.R. § 240.14a–9(a) (1983), by failing to disclose in their proxy materials any information concerning an action for breach of trust, brought by Heyman's sister against him and his mother a year before the 1983 campaign began, which GAF alleged cast doubt on Heyman's fitness to serve as a director. Although this family dispute among the Heymans did not involve GAF, the district court enjoined the entire insurgent slate from assuming the directorships to which they had been elected, set a new record date, and ordered a resolicitation of proxies and a new election. For the reasons below, we hold that non-disclosure of the Heyman family lawsuit was not a material omission in the context of this proxy contest. Accordingly, we reverse.

* * *

The positions of the parties regarding the central issue on appeal are fairly straightforward. Heyman contends that the Committee had no obligation to disclose in a GAF proxy fight either the contested, unproven, and unpursued allegations of a complaint filed in an unrelated intra-family dispute or the circumstances surrounding a family loan transaction not even mentioned in that complaint. In any event, Heyman argues, GAF's dissemination of the "breach of trust" allegations in its March 13 press release cured these omissions, since the "total mix" of information available to GAF shareholders would not have been significantly altered by fuller disclosure. On the other hand, GAF argues that the fact that a candidate for a position as a corporate fiduciary is a defendant in a pending lawsuit, charging him with improper self-dealing and other fiduciary misconduct, is necessarily important to stockholders called upon to decide who should be entrusted with the stewardship of their collective investment.

In considering these competing arguments, we are guided not only by the principles outlined above, but also by SEC Regulation S–K, 17 C.F.R. § 229.10 *et seq.* (1983). Regulation S–K, together with more general provisions such as Rule 14a–9, "states the requirements applicable to the content of * * * proxy and information statements under § 14 of the Exchange Act". The regulation provides the following instructions regarding involvement in legal proceedings that must be disclosed:

(f) *Involvement in certain legal proceedings.* Describe any of the following events that occurred during the past five years and that are material to an evaluation of the ability or integrity of any director, person nominated to become a director or executive officer of the registrant:

(1) A petition under the Federal bankruptcy laws or any state insolvency law was filed by or against, or a receiver, fiscal agent or similar officer was appointed by a court for the business or property of such person, or any partnership in which he was a general partner at or within two years before the time of such filing, or any corporation or business association of which he was an executive officer at or within two years before the time of such filing;

(2) Such person was convicted in a criminal proceeding or is a named subject of a pending criminal proceeding (excluding traffic violations and other minor offenses);

(3) Such person was the subject of any order, judgment, or decree, not subsequently reversed, suspended or vacated, of any court of competent jurisdiction, permanently or temporarily enjoining him from, or otherwise limiting, the following activities:

(i) Acting as an investment adviser, underwriter, broker or dealer in securities, or as an affiliated person, director or employee of any investment company, bank, savings and loan association or insurance company, or engaging in or continuing any conduct or practice in connection with such activity;

(ii) Engaging in any type of business practice; or

(iii) Engaging in any activity in connection with the purchase or sale of any security or in connection with any violation of Federal or State securities laws;

(4) Such person was the subject of any order, judgment or decree, not subsequently reversed, suspended or vacated, of any Federal or State authority barring, suspending or otherwise limiting for more than 60 days the right of such person to engage in any activity described in paragraph (f)(3)(i) of this Item, or to be associated with persons engaged in any such activity; or

(5) Such person was found by a court of competent jurisdiction in a civil action or by the Commission to have violated any Federal or State securities law, and the judgment in such civil action or finding by the Commission has not been subsequently reversed, suspended, or vacated.

17 C.F.R. § 229.401 (1983) (incorporated by reference in SEC Schedule 14A, Item 6, 17 C.F.R. § 240.14a–101 (1983)).

Nothing in this detailed regulation, which has been relegated to a footnote in GAF's brief, required Heyman to make any disclosure about the unproven allegations in the Connecticut action, much less the disputed loan transaction. While this court and others have indicated that compliance with Schedule 14A does not necessarily guarantee that a proxy statement satisfies Rule 14a–9(a), * * * the regulation does provide us with the Commission's expert view of the types of involvement in legal proceedings that are most likely to be matters of concern to shareholders in a proxy contest. See Exchange Act Release No. 15006, [1978 Transfer Binder] Fed.Sec.L.Rep. (CCH) ¶ 81,649 (July 28, 1978) ("The categories of information about officers' and directors' involvement in litigation [set forth above] are material to investors. They represent factual indicia of past management performance in areas of investor concern.")

In our view, the regulation's emphasis on orders, judgments, decrees, and findings in civil proceedings, in stark contrast to its express coverage of all pending criminal proceedings, strongly suggests that regardless of how serious they may appear on their face, unadjudicated allegations in a pending civil action against a director-nominee should not automatically be deemed material. In a society as litigious as ours, where plaintiffs are permitted great latitude in their pleadings, a reasonable shareholder would not place much stock in the bald, untested allegations in a civil complaint not involving the subject corporation without first examining, among other relevant factors, the relationship between the parties, the nature of the allegations, the circumstances out of which they arose, and the extent to which the action has been pursued. Whether that information would be considered important in deciding how to vote would then depend on the issues involved in the proxy contest itself.

Applying the first part of this approach to the unique circumstances present here, all of the relevant factual indicia militate against a finding of materiality. First, the Connecticut action was "pending" only in a technical sense. The action was stayed on consent only nine days after it was commenced, before Heyman even filed a responsive pleading. No formal discovery had been conducted. As the special master, who presided over the discovery proceedings and witnessed the deposition testimony in this action, observed:

> You are asking for everything because Abigail filed a lawsuit and then withdrew from filing a lawsuit. I gather there isn't any real discovery going on. The parties are working on some kind of settlement. Abigail is not a zealous litigant, or she certainly does not appear that way.

Second, the Connecticut action did not in any way involve GAF, * * * or for that matter any other public corporation, * * *. Nor did Abigail's complaint allege any violations of the securities laws of the type referred to in Regulation S–K, * * *. While we do not mean to suggest that pending litigation against a director-nominee based on state law and involving a family or other non-public business can never be material, actions of that nature are less likely to be matters of importance to public shareholders.

Third, the circumstances surrounding Abigail's allegations negate their materiality. All available evidence suggests that the action was nothing more than the outgrowth of a intra-family feud between Abigail and her new husband on one side and her mother and brother on the other. While Abigail's complaint did contain a myriad of allegations, both "serious" and petty, her apparent overriding objective was to separate her financial interests from the family business. Once her mother and brother agreed to pursue an amicable settlement, she in effect voluntarily withdrew the action. Furthermore, she subsequently swore that she supported her brother's slate in the proxy contest.

Thus, viewed in context, the three specific allegations in Abigail's complaint seized upon by GAF raise no serious question about Heyman's fitness to serve as a corporate director. Of even less significance is the $1,425,000 loan transaction, which was never specifically referred to in Abigail's complaint, but was the cornerstone of GAF's presentation below. While it may be true, as the district judge observed, that Abigail's general allegation as to diversion of assets was "broad enough to pertain to the loan" there is no basis for assuming that Abigail had any intention of asserting such a claim. Given that the "proxy rules simply do not require management to accuse itself of antisocial or illegal policies", * * * it would be fundamentally unfair to require Heyman to have anticipated and then disclosed the interpretation that GAF would place on the open-ended language of Abigail's complaint once the proxy contest was over.

* * *

Moreover, it is hardly surprising that Abigail's 28–page complaint never mentioned the loan transaction complained of by GAF. The loan was permitted by the elder Heyman's will and, as the district judge found, was "typical of many transactions engaged in by Heyman on behalf of the Heyman family entities" "except possibly in magnitude and duration". It would seem the "reasonable investor" would not have been influenced to change his proxy vote had the loan been disclosed.

The significance of the Connecticut action fades even further when its dormant allegations are compared with the issues that were raised in the proxy contest. Applying the literal language of Rule 14a–9(a), under which information omitted from a proxy statement is material if it is "necessary in order to make the statements therein not false or misleading", the district judge found that the Committee's proxy materials were defective because Heyman "presented himself to the shareholders as a man of considerable accomplishment and integrity" but "failed to hint at the serious allegations lodged against him or the transactions which are the basis of these claims." After reviewing the volumes of material that were generated during the proxy contest, however, we have found only a handful of excerpts that tend to support this view. For example, at the outset of the campaign, Heyman characterized himself and the Committee as "[h]aving all had extensive experience as responsible members of the corporate, business, and professional worlds". Similarly, after management pulled a complete reversal at the close of the contest and announced the proposed sale of the chemical business, the Committee inquired in a letter to shareholders, "Who can you rely upon to effectively distribute the proceeds?" But isolated excerpts of this nature cannot obscure the fact that the overwhelming weight of both sides' proxy literature and advertisements focused on fundamental economic issues of concern to shareholders: the record of management and the competing plans for realizing the asset values of GAF. Given the predominance of these economic issues, the district judge erred in holding that there was "a substantial likelihood" that a reasonable shareholder would have considered the Connecticut action "important in deciding how to vote." *TSC*, 426 U.S. at 449, 96 S.Ct. at 2132.

The court further erred by holding there was a "substantial likelihood" that disclosure of the action and its underlying facts "would have been viewed by the reasonable investor as having significantly altered the 'total mix' of information made available." *Id.* (footnote omitted). The fact that Heyman had been sued by his sister for "breach of trust" was disseminated by GAF more than six weeks before the annual meeting in its March 13 press release. The gist of the press release was also reported in the two Reuters news stories alluded to in GAF's complaint. Further, on the day of the election, a major story in the Wall Street Journal referred to GAF's attempt "to open the court papers in a suit brought against Mr. Heyman by his sister Abigail over family matters" as one of "a number of gambits that backfired or offended important stockholders."

GAF contends that "[n]o information whatever about the suit was ever included in direct communications to GAF shareholders." However, Heyman responds without contradiction "that GAF itself directly sent its press release to more than a dozen major institutions holding, or known to represent shareholders holding, a substantial number of GAF shares."

While there can be no doubt that the allegations and underlying facts of the Connecticut action were not "thoroughly aired", * * * we are convinced that this information "is of such dubious significance" that its disclosure may have "accomplish[ed] more harm than good". *TSC,* 426 U.S. at 448, 96 S.Ct. at 2131. In the "hurly-burly" of this contest, * * * particularly in its last few weeks when GAF announced deal after deal after deal, the shareholders had their hands full sorting out the proposed transactions and evaluating them in light of the combatants' competing programs. While GAF's incumbent management obviously would have preferred to shift attention away from these core economic issues, "bury[ing] the shareholders in an avalanche of trivial information", *TSC,* 426 U.S. at 448, 96 S.Ct. at 2131, would scarcely have served the interests of corporate democracy.

Moreover, the district court found that a reasonable person could conclude that Heyman had "acted with the best of motives, in good faith, in the best interests of Abigail, and for her benefit and protection." If resolicitation were required, Heyman would be free to characterize the facts underlying the Connecticut action in a similarly favorable fashion. In addition, he could state that Abigail, the supposed victim of his "breach of trust", supported his slate. It is therefore likely that the impact of GAF's press release would have been diminished rather than bolstered by any further disclosure.

Our conclusion that non-disclosure of the Connecticut action was not a material omission is reinforced by several additional factors. First, we consider it revealing that it was not until May 2, after the results of the election were apparent, that GAF asserted for the first time below that Heyman's failure to disclose the suit was material. GAF knew as early as March 13, when it issued its press release, that Abigail had sued Heyman for "breach of trust". Indeed, when it moved on March 11 to intervene in the Connecticut action, one of GAF's arguments was that the suit might implicate Heyman's integrity and fitness to serve as a director. Yet when it filed its complaint in this action on March 22, GAF advanced no such claim. Thus, there is a hollow ring to GAF's present argument that it was not until after this court issued the writ of mandamus that it could possibly have discovered the information necessary to support the theory upon which its whole case now rests.

Second, we cannot overlook that GAF is urging this court to hold Heyman to a stricter standard than GAF itself followed in deciding whether to disclose that a number of its incumbent directors had been defendants in various lawsuits alleging breach of fiduciary duty. Heyman claims, and GAF does not dispute, that (1) incumbent directors Sokol and Sommer were each alleged to have breached fiduciary duties as directors of American Cyanamid Company and Bristol–Meyers Company, respectively, and to have violated the securities laws, and that settlements in those actions resulted in tightening the control of the audit committee of each company; (2) incumbent director Berner was alleged to have breached fiduciary duties as president and chairman of the board of Curtiss–Wright Corporation by taking excessive compensation, and that settlement of the suits against him resulted in restricting his compensation and future rights to stock under Curtiss stock plans; (3) this court has previously determined that Berner committed a breach of trust and a violation of securities laws by unlawfully giving his brother-in-law confidential information which in turn was used to purchase stock at an unfair advantage; and (4) Berner and Werner were charged with breaching fiduciary duties *as directors of GAF,* by approving Werner's excessive compensation, and that settlement of this suit resulted in "measurable benefits to the Company."

At oral argument, GAF sought to distinguish these cases on the ground that they were all closed more than five years ago. But this at most establishes that GAF had complied with the "minimum" requirements of Schedule 14A. Applying to the incumbents the same sweeping standard that GAF would have us apply to Heyman, the integrity and fitness of these directors had been called into question to a sufficient extent to trigger a disclosure requirement under Rule 14a–9(a). If anything, the final decision or settlement agreement in a closed case involving management of a public corporation should be considered more important to voting stockholders than unadjudicated allegations in a pending family lawsuit.

This last point underscores the boundlessness of the disclosure requirement imposed by the district judge. Vast numbers of allegations arguably implicate a prospective director's "integrity and fitness". The ruling below, if left intact, would lead to a situation where proxy contestants, in order to minimize the risk of having an election set aside, would have to include in their solicitation materials descriptions, explanations, and denials regarding allegations in derivative actions, class actions, matrimonial disputes, and a host of other legal matters, all unrelated to the business of the subject corporation.

Furthermore, under the decision below, both sides in a proxy contest would have every incentive and legal right to pursue massive discovery to unearth facts which, it can later be claimed, amount to a breach of fiduciary duty that should have been alleged in a prior action against an opposing candidate. As this case graphically illustrates, the litigation ubiquitous in every proxy contest would thus become a forum for litigating, possibly relitigating, the issues in any pending or prior suit involving a director-nominee.

Finally, we think the district court was unduly influenced by what it perceived to be Heyman's bad faith in resisting GAF's efforts at discovery in the instant action. While we express no view on the wisdom of sealing the Connecticut action in the first place, the desire of the Heymans to keep their family dispute private is certainly understandable even in the absence of a proxy fight. This is not to say that the absence of an affirmative disclosure requirement is tantamount to a license to conceal. But the first three judicial officers who reviewed the sealing orders—Judge Daly, the special master, and Judge Knapp—all agreed with Heyman's interpretation that he could not properly discuss the sealed materials. That this court took a different view on the petition for mandamus does not mean, as the district court suggested, that Heyman was guilty of "suppression" or "obstruction".

UNITED STATES v. MATTHEWS
United States Court of Appeals, Second Circuit, 1986.
787 F.2d 38.

VAN GRAAFEILAND, CIRCUIT JUDGE:

Clark J. Matthews, II, appeals from a judgment of the United States District Court for the Eastern District of New York (Sifton, J.) convicting Matthews of violating section 14(a) of the Securities Exchange Act of 1934, 15 U.S.C. § 78n(a) and SEC's Implementing Rule 14a-9, 17 C.F.R. 240.-14a-9. This conviction was based on the second count of a two-count indictment. The first count charged that Matthews and S. Richmond Dole conspired with each other and with others to bribe members of the New York State Tax Commission in order to obtain favorable rulings on tax matters of interest to the defendants' employer, The Southland Corporation, and to file United States income tax returns for Southland which falsely listed the bribe payment as a legal fee. Both defendants were acquitted on this count.

The second count, which was against Matthews alone, charged in substance that Matthews' election to the Southland Board of Directors in 1981 was accomplished by means of a proxy statement which failed to disclose, among other things, that he was a member of the conspiracy alleged in Count I. For the reasons that follow, we reverse the judgment of conviction and remand to the district court with instructions to dismiss the indictment.

* * *

The Commission also has promulgated rules dealing specifically with proxy statements. *See* Schedule 14A, 17 C.F.R. § 240.14a-101. Item 6 of this section covers statements used in the election of directors and executive officers, and incorporates the disclosure requirements of Item 401 of Regulation S-K, 17 C.F.R. § 229.401. Item 401 provides that a candidate for director must disclose whether he has been "convicted in a criminal proceeding or is a named subject of a pending criminal proceeding (excluding traffic violations and other minor offenses)" providing that the incident in question occurred during the preceding five years and disclosure is material to an evaluation of the candidate's ability or integrity. 17 C.F.R. § 229.401(f).

In November 1980 attorneys at Arnold and Porter were informed that the federal prosecutor who had been presenting evidence to a grand jury during the preceding six months concerning possible criminal activities of Councilman Mastropieri now regarded Southland and DeFalco as targets of the investigation and Matthews and Dole as subjects.[3]

* * *

With full knowledge of Matthews' status as a "subject" of the grand jury's investigation, the Chairman of the Board nonetheless asked Matthews if he would run for election to the Board. Matthews inquired of Bleakley if, under the circumstances, he should run, and Bleakley told Matthews that there was no reason for him not to do so. Upon further inquiry by Matthews concerning disclosure, Bleakley told Matthews that Bleakley and his partners did not believe that the federal securities laws required Matthews to disclose that he was a subject of the investigation. Matthews ran and was elected.

* * *

The Proxy Statement upon which the Government's charges were based was for Southland's 1981 Annual Shareholders Meeting, at which eleven unopposed candidates for directorships, including Matthews, were elected. The Statement gave only basic information concerning each candidate. Insofar as Matthews was concerned, the Statement said that Matthews was forty-four years of age, that he served as Vice President and General Counsel from 1973 to 1979 and as Executive Vice President and Chief Financial Officer since 1979. The Statement also set forth Matthews' "Cash and cash-equivalent forms of remuneration" and the extent of his "Security Ownership." The Government contends that this simple recital was made false and misleading in violation of Rule 14a–9(a) because it (1) failed to disclose that Matthews had engaged in a conspiracy to bribe New York public officials and to defraud the United States by preventing the IRS from determining the true nature of the business expense deductions and (2) failed to disclose that Matthews had failed to disclose to the audit committee of the Board of Directors, Southland's independent auditors, outside tax counsel, the IRS, the SEC, the FBI and others that he was engaged in the conspiracy.

* * *

The issue with the most far-reaching implications in the field of federal securities law, however, is not what "true" facts Matthews should have disclosed, but whether section 14(a) of the Exchange Act and the SEC rules enacted pursuant thereto required Matthews to state to all the world that he was guilty of the uncharged crime of conspiracy. This query, we are satisfied, must be answered in the negative.

---

3. There is a clear distinction between the "subject" of a grand jury investigation and the "target" of such an investigation. One about whom a grand jury seeks information in an investigation of possible wrongdoing that not yet has focused on the individual involved is a "subject" of the investigation. The Department of Justice guidelines define a "target" as a "person as to whom the prosecutor or the grand jury has substantial evidence linking him/her to the commission of a crime and who, in the judgment of the prosecutor, is a putative defendant."

* * *

* * *

We deem it significant that those courts which have spoken in this area in the years following Matthews' asserted violations almost universally have rejected efforts to require that management make qualitative disclosures that were not at least implicit in the Commission's rules.

* * *

The Government has treated the instant case from the outset as one involving the withholding of qualitative rather than quantitative information. Government counsel conceded at oral argument that the Government had not proven that Matthews' actions had any adverse quantitative economic impact on Southland. Echoing the words of the district court, counsel contended that "[t]his was not a matter of dollars and cents, it was morality looked at through the eyeglasses of someone with economic interest." We are satisfied, however, that Matthews was not legally required to confess that he was guilty of an uncharged crime in order that Southland's shareholders could determine the morality of his conduct.

We hold that at least so long as uncharged criminal conduct is not required to be disclosed by any rule lawfully promulgated by the SEC, nondisclosure of such conduct cannot be the basis of a criminal prosecution. Our unwillingness to permit section 14(a) to be used as expansively as the Government has done in this case rests not only on the history of the Commission's approach to the problem of qualitative disclosures and the case law that has developed on this subject but also on the obvious due process implications that would arise from permitting a conviction to stand in the absence of clearer notice as to what disclosures are required in this uncertain area.

* * *

In the instant case, Matthews was charged with failing to disclose far more than just an "inherently suspect" activity. The district court instructed the jury that "[t]he essence of the crime alleged in Count Two is that in proxy materials the defendant Matthews omitted to inform the shareholders of the Southland Corporation of his alleged prior participation in the bribery and tax conspiracy charged in Count One of the indictment...." In view of the fact that a grand jury was actively investigating this very conspiracy when the proxy materials were issued, we do not understand the district court's holding that disclosure by Matthews of his participation in the conspiracy "[did] not pose a substantial possibility of incrimination", *United States v. Dole*, 601 F.Supp. 430, 433 (E.D.N.Y.1984).

* * *

Were we to face the issue directly, we are not certain we would find persuasive the argument that Matthews' self-incrimination privilege was not violated because he was not compelled to run for the office of director. Coercion associated with a person's livelihood, professional standing and reputation may, in some circumstances, be too powerful to ignore when Fifth Amendment rights are at issue.

* * *

Note
The Duty to Disclose

The cases suggest that the duty to disclose material information arises in three situations: (1) the firm or its insiders buy or sell the firm's own securities, (2) the firm voluntarily makes public announcements, and (3) the firm submits, in satisfaction of the requirements of federal securities law, reports to the Securities and Exchange Commission and the public. On the other hand, if a firm does not fit into one of the three classifications, it has no duty to disclose even if it is in possession of material nonpublic information. The number of cases that do not arguably fit in one of the three categories may be very small.

Once a firm makes statements in either category 2 or 3, it is obliged not to make an "untrue statement of material fact" or "omit to state a material fact necessary in order to make the statement made ... not misleading." Rule 10b–5(b). Since a firm routinely makes public announcements and submits required reports, how difficult is it to find a firm statement that is misleading in light of a concealed bombshell? For example, in the following case, if Alpha Industries had issued a press release announcing the successful negotiation of the subcontracts, would the press release be misleading because it did not contain details of the bribes paid to get the subcontracts? If, in Alpha's annual report, the firm expensed the bribes in the firm's income statement, would the report be misleading because it did not describe the nature of the expense?

ROEDER v. ALPHA INDUSTRIES, INC.
United States Court of Appeals, First Circuit, 1987.
814 F.2d 22.

BOWNES, CIRCUIT JUDGE.

Plaintiff-appellant Gilbert Roeder brought a class action suit on his own behalf and on behalf of others similarly situated against defendants-appellants Alpha Industries, Inc., a company in which he owned stock, and its officers and directors, * * * Roeder alleged defendants were liable for not publicly disclosing until indictment was imminent that Alpha had paid a bribe to obtain subcontracts.

* * *

Roeder bought 400 shares of Alpha's common stock at slightly more than $21 per share on December 30, 1983, which was after the alleged bribe was paid but before disclosure. He sold his shares on January 29, 1985, for a little more than $11 per share. He seeks to recover the loss in stock value attributable to what he alleges was an overdue announcement of Alpha's involvement with Adamsky.

* * *

The materiality of the information claimed not to have been disclosed, however, is not enough to make out a sustainable claim of securities fraud. Even if information is material, there is no liability under Rule 10b–5 unless there was a duty to disclose it.

A duty to disclose "does not arise from the mere possession of nonpublic market information." *Chiarella v. United States,* 445 U.S. 222, 235, 100 S.Ct. 1108, 1118, 63 L.Ed.2d 348 (1980). One situation in which there is a duty to disclose is when a corporate insider trades on confidential information. *Id.* at 228–29, 100 S.Ct. at 1114–15. Roeder's complaint, however, does not allege insider trading. When a corporation does make a disclosure—whether it be voluntary or required—there is a duty to make it complete and accurate. *SEC v. Texas Gulf Sulphur Co.,* 401 F.2d 833, 860–61 (2d Cir.1968), *cert. denied,* 394 U.S. 976, 89 S.Ct. 1454, 22 L.Ed.2d 756 (1969). "If ... a company chooses to reveal relevant, material information even though it had no duty to do so, it must disclose the whole truth." *Grossman v. Waste Management, Inc.,* 589 F.Supp. 395, 409 (N.D.Ill.1984). Roeder's complaint does not mention any required or voluntary disclosures Alpha made that were inaccurate, incomplete, or misleading.

Instead, Roeder claims that a corporation has an affirmative duty to disclose all material information even if there is no insider trading, no statute or regulation requiring disclosure, and no inaccurate, incomplete, or misleading prior disclosures. The prevailing view, however, is that there is no such affirmative duty of disclosure....[2]

* * *

In sum, Roeder's complaint does not allege facts that, if proved, would establish Alpha had a duty to disclose the alleged illegal payments. We affirm the dismissal of the securities fraud count because of

---

2. In *Issen v. GSC Enters., Inc.,* 538 F.Supp. 745 (N.D.Ill.1982), the court held that all material information had to be disclosed in annual reports "notwithstanding the absence of an explicit statutory or regulatory duty to do so." *Id.* at 750. The court said "it would seem clear that reasonable investors should be able to place their trust and confidence in the annual report issued by the corporation." *Id.* at 751 n. 0. Apparently, *Issen* stands alone in imposing a duty to include all material information in annual reports. *See* Block, Barton & Garfield, 40 Bus.Law. at 1249 n. 38. There are problems with using the annual report as a catchall depository for material information not required to be disclosed elsewhere. Certainly, literal compliance with reporting requirements does not absolve an issuer from liability if a material fact has been omitted that is "necessary in order to make the statements made, in the light of the circumstances under which they were made, not misleading." Rule 10b–5(b). The SEC, however, was "given complete discretion ... to require in corporate reports only such information as it deems necessary or appropriate in the public interest or to protect investors." S.Rep. No. 792, 73d Cong., 2d Sess. 10 (1934), *quoted in Natural Resources Defense Council, Inc. v. SEC,* 606 F.2d 1031, 1051 (D.C.Cir.1979). A general admonition to include "all material information" in annual reports preempts the promulgated regulations' instructions on what information to include and, because of the threat of civil liability, it would result in all sorts of information appearing in the reports that the SEC may prefer be left out. If the SEC wanted all possibly material information to be in the annual reports, we suspect that the regulations would have been amended to require it. The utility of such a regulation would be doubtful. In any case, Roeder's complaint did not even allege that Alpha's annual reports were at all misleading.

this deficiency. *See Roy v. City of Augusta, Maine,* 712 F.2d 1517, 1520 n. 3 (1st Cir.1983) (a dismissal can be affirmed on any valid ground).

* * *

State Law

Under general principles of fiduciary duty defined in the state court, a board has an obligation to make proper disclosures to its shareholders in anticipation of a shareholder vote. There are two issues: First, what standards do state courts apply in defining the obligation to disclose? Are they similar to the standards under federal securities law? And second, do the disclosure obligations that attach to shareholder communications in anticipation of a shareholder vote apply when a target board is responding to a tender offer?

ROBERTS v. GENERAL INSTRUMENT CORP.
Court of Chancery of Delaware, 1990.
Fed.Sec.L.Rep. (CCH) ¶ 95,465.

Opinion of ALLEN, CHANCELLOR.

Plaintiff, a holder of General Instrument Corporation common stock, seeks here to enjoin the closing of a tender offer to purchase for cash all outstanding shares of that company's common stock at $44.50 per share. The offer is extended by FLGI Acquisition Corp., a Delaware corporation formed by Forstmann Little & Co., a New York partnership ("Forstmann" or "Forstmann Little"). The offer is made pursuant to an agreement or merger negotiated with the board of directors of General Instrument and agreed upon on July 1, 1990."

* * *

Second, plaintiff asserts a series of points aimed at establishing (in the provisional way that on an application for preliminary injunction he is required to establish) that the disclosures contained in Forstmann's Offer to Purchase are materially incomplete. Thus, plaintiff claims that shareholders will make their decision to tender or not on inadequate information and will be presumptively injured.

* * *

With respect to disclosure the Forstmann defendants say that there is no basis to hold them responsible to meet the directors' state law duty of candor in their offering document and, more importantly, that the disclosures made were, in any case, full and complete.

* * *

The merger agreement provides for a two-step acquisition. The first step, a tender offer for all General Instrument stock was commenced on July 9, 1990 and is scheduled to expire, as it happens, on August 13, 1990. The tender offer closing is conditioned on at least a majority of the outstanding stock on a fully diluted basis being tendered and not withdrawn. Following closing of the offer and accomplishment of the corporate formalities, FLGI, the acquisition vehicle, will merge with General Instrument and any shares not purchased in the tender offer will be converted into cash at the tender offer price.

* * *

In addition to his claim that the directors have breached their duty of due care and fidelity, plaintiff asserts that all defendants have failed to make proper disclosure in connection with Forstmann Little's tender offer. A series of points are asserted. First, plaintiff attacks the omission of defendants to disclose financial projections for each of the company's separate businesses. Plaintiff acknowledges that defendants' disclosed consolidated projections for the entire company. Second, plaintiff objects to defendants' failure to disclose assumptions underlying the company projections that were disclosed and the divisional projections that were not disclosed. Third, plaintiff asserts that certain "hidden conflicts" were not adequately disclosed. These hidden conflicts are said to involve: (i) Lazard's role as financial advisor to the company and then to Forstmann Little, (ii) Merrill Lynch's representation of General Instrument prior to its work for the special committee, and (iii) management's purported covert arrangement to invest in the post-acquisition company.

The duty to disclose information to shareholders extends to all material information. Information is material under Delaware law if there is

> *a substantial likelihood* that, under all the circumstances, the omitted fact *would have assumed actual significance* in the deliberations of the reasonable shareholder. Put another way, there must be a substantial likelihood that the disclosure of the omitted fact would have been viewed by the reasonable investor as having *significantly altered the "total mix" of information made available.*

Rosenblatt v. Getty Oil Co., Del.Supr., 493 A.2d 929, 944 (1985), *quoting, TSC Indus., Inc. v. Northway, Inc.,* 426 U.S. 438 (1976) (emphasis added).

With respect to his claim that financial projections for various divisions of the company are required, plaintiff's argument chiefly is that both Forstmann and the Board's banker had and needed access to such data to properly evaluate the value of the company. How then, plaintiff asks, can that same breakdown not be material to shareholders asked to tender their stock?

To this Forstmann replies that its offer did include the consolidated projections for the company with which it had been furnished. This further level of detail is not material to shareholders it says and, in all events, it contains confidential information the disclosure of which would injure the company.

The last assertion is supported in this record. I make no judgment on its legal significance, however. Instead I rest my decision on this point, on the conclusion that plaintiff has not shown a reasonably likelihood that this level of detailed projection is material to a selling shareholder in this instance, even though it was presumably material to a buyer of the corporation.

Projections that are of interest to an acquiror seeking control of a company are not necessarily material to the decision of a minority shareholder to sell or hold stock.[5] A potential acquiror typically seeks great detail about the operations of a company. If it succeeds in its bid, it will have power over the organization and structure of the company's assets. It will have to determine which assets to sell, which to retain, and how to deploy those assets it retains. Indeed, acquirors often bid with such a plan in mind.

By contrast, a minority shareholder deciding whether to tender need not, and equally importantly will not as a practical matter, contemplate alternate management scenarios; will not consider alternative organizational plans for the company; will not consider which, if any, of the corporations assets should be sold or redeployed, or where in the organization expenses might be reduced, etc. The decision of a shareholder in a tender offer is more limited than the decision of a would-be acquiror (or lender) and the information material to her decision is different and not as extensive. It may in some instances be material to the shareholder's decision to know what the company's projections of earnings, etc. are, but the question of the necessity to disclose company projections is itself often not an easy one (*see Flynn v. Bass Brothers Enterprises, Inc.*, 744 F.2d 978 (3d Cir.1984)). It may even be material in some instances in which company projections are given to know how they break down into line of business projections. But what seems clear to me, for the reasons set forth above, is that a shareholder does not show such a breakdown is material to his decision simply by showing that a buyer of the corporation, a banker lending to the acquiror or one opining on the fairness of the price, required such a breakdown.

Subsection b. Preliminary Merger Negotiations

IN THE MATTER OF CARNATION COMPANY EXCHANGE ACT RELEASE NO. 22,214

(July 8, 1985).

In the view of the Commission, based upon the staff's investigation, certain public statements by Carnation Company ("Carnation") were materially false and misleading in violation of Section 10(b) of the

---

5. Plaintiff cites certain federal securities cases which suggest that hard (historical) information relied upon by an investor may be material to shareholders.

* * *

I do not disagree, if the emphasis is upon "may," for surely much information relied upon by a buyer will be important for the shareholder as well. But for the reason alluded to in text I do not think a clear and easy rule that everything material to a buyer of corporate control will be material to a seller of stock can be correct.

Securities Exchange Act of 1934 ("Exchange Act") and Rule 10b–5 thereunder. The statements concerned unusual market activity in Carnation stock and were made during a period in which Carnation was engaged in preliminary acquisition discussions with Nestle, S.A. ("Nestle"), a multinational corporation headquartered in Switzerland. The discussions led to an agreement pursuant to which Nestle would acquire all of Carnation's common stock in a cash tender offer at a premium over the market price of the stock prior to the announcement of the agreement.

* * *

Whenever an issuer makes a public statement or responds to an inquiry from a stock exchange official concerning rumors, unusual market activity, possible corporate developments or any other matter, the statement must be materially accurate and complete. If the issuer is aware of nonpublic information concerning acquisition discussions that are occurring at the time the statement is made, the issuer has an obligation to disclose sufficient information concerning the discussions to prevent the statements made from being materially misleading.[6] See Schlanger v. Four–Phase Systems, Inc., supra (issuer statement denying knowledge of any corporate development which would account for market activity in its stock at a time when the company was engaged in preliminary merger discussions could be materially misleading).

When an issuer makes a public statement, information concerning preliminary acquisition discussions is material and must be disclosed if the information assumes "actual significance in the deliberation of" and significantly alters "the total mix of information available [to]" the reasonable shareholder. TSC Industries, Inc. v. Northway, 426 U.S. 438 (1976). Thus, in the Commission's view, an issuer statement that there is no corporate development that would account for unusual market activity in its stock, made while the issuer is engaged in acquisition discussions, may be materially false and misleading.[8]

---

6. The Commission encourages public companies to respond promptly to market rumors concerning material corporate developments. See also New York Stock Exchange Listed Company Manual § 202.03 (1983) (Dealing with Rumors or Unusual Market Activity); American Stock Exchange Company Guide § 402(3) (1983) (Clarification or Confirmation of Rumors or Reports). However, an issuer that wants to prevent premature disclosure of nonpublic preliminary merger negotiations can, in appropriate circumstances, give a "no comment" response to press inquiries concerning rumors or unusual market activity. A "no comment" response would not be appropriate where, inter alia, the issuer has made a statement that has been rendered materially false or misleading as a result of subsequent events or market rumors are attributable to leaks from the issuer.

8. The Third Circuit has held that a statement by an issuer that it was aware of no reason that would explain that day's activity in its stock was not false, inaccurate or misleading because, although company management "clearly knew of information that might have accounted for the increase in trading, there was no indication that any of this privileged information had been leaked or that they knew of, or had, information that insiders were engaged in trading." Greenfield v. Heublein, Inc. 742 F.2d 751, 759 (3d Cir.1984), cert. denied, 105 S.Ct. 1189 (1985) (emphasis supplied). The Commission believes that Heublein was wrongly decided.

Applying these principles here, Carnation, in commenting publicly on takeover rumors and unusual market activity in its stock, was required to make statements which were truthful and not materially misleading. In the Commission's view, Carnation's public statements on August 7, 1984 and August 21, 1984 failed to satisfy these requirements in that the August 7 statement was materially misleading and the August 21 statement was materially false and misleading.

Carnation senior management on August 7 knew that one meeting and several telephone conversations between senior officers of Carnation and Nestle concerning Nestle's interest in a possible acquisition of Carnation had occurred and another such meeting was scheduled to occur in two days. Senior officers of Carnation had been told by D. Stuart, who owned or shared in the power to dispose of 19.9% of Carnation's outstanding common stock, that he had taken steps to attempt to arrange a sale of the company. Press reports of market rumors concerning Carnation had specifically referred to Nestle as a possible acquiror and to D. Stuart's efforts to arrange a sale of his Carnation stock. Under these circumstances, the Commission believes that the issuance of a statement by Carnation on August 7 stating that there was no news from the company and no corporate development that would account for that day's activity in its stock was materially misleading.

By the time the August 21 statement was made, senior officers of Carnation had already held two meetings with senior officers of Nestle and were in the process of holding a third in Switzerland. An acquisition price of $75 per share had been suggested (and rejected) and the possibility was raised that Nestle acquire the Stuart family's shares with an option to make a bid for the remainder of Carnation's common stock within a specified period of time. Carnation had asked its investment banker to opine on the fairness of a $90 per share price and had provided Nestle with nonpublic information concerning its operations and future prospects. Nestle had indicated to Carnation management that the company would be operated as a "stand-alone" enterprise in the event of a Nestle acquisition and had indicated that, in the event an offer was made, it might be forthcoming as early as August 24.

In the Commission's view, under these circumstances, the statements by Carnation on August 21 that Carnation knew of no corporate reason for the recent surge in its stock price and that Carnation was not negotiating with anyone were materially false and misleading. Further, the statement by Malone on August 21 that to the best of his knowledge, there was nothing to substantiate the rumor that Carnation was about to be acquired by Nestle was materially misleading, considering the facts known to Carnation executives other than Malone.

The omissions in the August 7 and August 21 statements, as well as the misstatements in the August 21 statement, in the Commission's view, were material because, if disclosed fully and accurately, they would have "assumed actual significance in the deliberations of," and would have "significantly altered the total mix of information made available [to]," the reasonable Carnation shareholder. TSC Industries, Inc. v. Northway, Inc., supra. Had Carnation disclosed in the August 7 and August 21 statements the contacts with Nestle and D. Stuart's actions, the reasonable Carnation shareholder would have considered that information to be significant in deciding whether to buy, sell or hold the stock.

* * *

BASIC INC. v. LEVINSON

Supreme Court of the United States, 1988.
485 U.S. 224, 108 S.Ct. 978, 99 L.Ed.2d 194.

JUSTICE BLACKMUM:

This case requires us to apply the materiality requirement of § 10(b) of the Securities Exchange Act of 1934, 48 Stat. 881, as amended, 15 U.S.C. § 78a *et seq.* (1934 Act), and the Securities and Exchange Commission's Rule 10b–5, promulgated thereunder, see 17 CFR § 240.10b–5 (1987), in the context of preliminary corporate merger discussions.

* * *

Prior to December 20, 1978, Basic Incorporated was a publicly traded company primarily engaged in the business of manufacturing chemical refractories for the steel industry. As early as 1965 or 1966, Combustion Engineering, Inc., a company producing mostly alumina-based refractories, expressed some interest in acquiring Basic, but was deterred from pursuing this inclination seriously because of antitrust concerns it then entertained. In 1976, however, regulatory action opened the way to a renewal of Combustion's interest. The "Strategic Plan," dated October 25, 1976, for Combustion's Industrial Products Group included the objective: "Acquire Basic Inc. $30 million."

Beginning in September 1976, Combustion representatives had meetings and telephone conversations with Basic officers and directors, including petitioners here, concerning the possibility of a merger.[3] During 1977 and 1978, Basic made three public statements denying that it was engaged in merger negotiations.[4] On December 18, 1978,

---

3. In light of our disposition of this case, any further characterization of these discussions must await application, on remand, of the materiality standard adopted today.

4. On October 21, 1977, after heavy trading and a new high in Basic stock, the following news item appeared in the Cleveland Plain Dealer:

"[Basic] President Max Muller said the company knew no reason for the stock's activity and that no negotiations were under way with any company for a merger.

He said Flintkote recently denied Wall Street rumors that it would make a tender offer of $25 a share for control of the Cleveland-based maker of refractories for the steel industry." App. 363.

On September 25, 1978, in reply to an inquiry from the New York Stock Exchange, Basic issued a release concerning increased activity in its stock and stated that

"management is unaware of any present or pending company development that would result in the abnormally heavy

Basic asked the New York Stock Exchange to suspend trading in its shares and issued a release stating that it had been "approached" by another company concerning a merger. *Id.,* at 413. On December 19, Basic's board endorsed Combustion's offer of $46 per share for its common stock, *id.,* at 335, 414–416, and on the following day publicly announced its approval of Combustion's tender offer for all outstanding shares.

Respondents are former Basic shareholders who sold their stock after Basic's first public statement of October 21, 1977, and before the suspension of trading in December 1978. Respondents brought a class action against Basic and its directors, asserting that the defendants issued three false or misleading public statements and thereby were in violation of § 10(b) of the 1934 Act and of Rule 10b–5. Respondents alleged that they were injured by selling Basic shares at artificially depressed prices in a market affected by petitioners' misleading statements and in reliance thereon.

* * *

The Court also explicitly has defined a standard of materiality under the securities laws, see *TSC Industries, Inc. v. Northway, Inc.,* 426 U.S. 438, 96 S.Ct. 2126, 48 L.Ed.2d 757 (1976), concluding in the proxy-solicitation context that "[a]n omitted fact is material if there is a substantial likelihood that a reasonable shareholder would consider it important in deciding how to vote." *Id.,* at 449, 96 S.Ct., at 2132.[7] * * * We now expressly adopt the *TSC Industries* standard of materiality for the § 10(b) and Rule 10b–5 context.

The application of this materiality standard to preliminary merger discussions is not self-evident. Where the impact of the corporate development on the target's fortune is certain and clear, the *TSC Industries* materiality definition admits straight-forward application. Where, on the other hand, the event is contingent or speculative in nature, it is difficult to ascertain whether the "reasonable investor" would have considered the omitted information significant at the time. Merger negotiations, because of the ever-present possibility that the contemplated transaction will not be effectuated, fall into the latter category.

Petitioners urge upon us a Third Circuit test for resolving this difficulty. * * * Under this approach, preliminary merger discussions do not become material until "agreement-in-principle" as to the price and structure of the transaction has been reached between the would-be merger partners. See *Greenfield v. Heublein, Inc.,* 742 F.2d 751, 757

---

trading activity and price fluctuation in company shares that have been experienced in the past few days." *Id.,* at 401.

On November 6, 1978, Basic issued to its shareholders a "Nine Months Report 1978." This Report stated:

"With regard to the stock market activity in the Company's shares we remain unaware of any present or pending developments which would account for the high volume of trading and price fluctuations in recent months." *Id.* at 403.

7. *TSC Industries* arose under § 14(a), as amended, of the 1934 Act, 15 U.S.C. § 78n(a), and Rule 14a–9, 17 CFR § 240.14a–9 (1975).

(CA3 1984), cert. denied, 469 U.S. 1215, 105 S.Ct. 1189, 84 L.Ed.2d 336 (1985). By definition, then, information concerning any negotiations not yet at the agreement-in-principle stage could be withheld or even misrepresented without a violation of Rule 10b–5.

Three rationales have been offered in support of the "agreement-in-principle" test. The first derives from the concern expressed in *TSC Industries* that an investor not be overwhelmed by excessively detailed and trivial information, and focuses on the substantial risk that preliminary merger discussions may collapse: because such discussions are inherently tentative, disclosure of their existence itself could mislead investors and foster false optimism. * * *

The other two justifications for the agreement-in-principle standard are based on management concerns: because the requirement of "agreement-in-principle" limits the scope of disclosure obligations, it helps preserve the confidentiality of merger discussions where earlier disclosure might prejudice the negotiations; and the test also provides a usable, bright-line rule for determining when disclosure must be made.

* * *

None of these policy-based rationales, however, purports to explain why drawing the line at agreement-in-principle reflects the significance of the information upon the investor's decision. The first rationale, and the only one connected to the concerns expressed in *TSC Industries,* stands soundly rejected, even by a Court of Appeals that otherwise has accepted the wisdom of the agreement-in-principle test. "It assumes that investors are nitwits, unable to appreciate—even when told—that mergers are risky propositions up until the closing." *Flamm v. Eberstadt,* 814 F.2d, at 1175. Disclosure, and not paternalistic withholding of accurate information, is the policy chosen and expressed by Congress. We have recognized time and again, a "fundamental purpose" of the various securities acts, "was to substitute a philosophy of full disclosure for the philosophy of *caveat emptor* and thus to achieve a high standard of business ethics in the securities industry."

* * *

The second rationale, the importance of secrecy during the early stages of merger discussions, also seems irrelevant to an assessment whether their existence is significant to the trading decision of a reasonable investor. To avoid a "bidding war" over its target, an acquiring firm often will insist that negotiations remain confidential, see, *e.g., In re Carnation Co.,* Exchange Act Release No. 22214, 33 SEC Docket 1025 (1985), and at least one Court of Appeals has stated that "silence pending settlement of the price and structure of a deal is beneficial to most investors, most of the time." *Flamm v. Eberstadt,* 814 F.2d, at 1177.

We need not ascertain, however, whether secrecy necessarily maximizes shareholder wealth—although we note that the proposition is at least disputed as a matter of theory and empirical research—for this case does not concern the *timing* of a disclosure; it concerns only its accuracy and completeness. We face here the narrow question whether information concerning the existence and status of preliminary merger discussions is significant to the reasonable investor's trading decision. Arguments based on the premise that some disclosure would be "premature" in a sense are more properly considered under the rubric of an issuer's duty to disclose. The "secrecy" rationale is simply inapposite to the definition of materiality.

The final justification offered in support of the agreement-in-principle test seems to be directed solely at the comfort of corporate managers. A bright-line rule indeed is easier to follow than a standard that requires the exercise of judgment in the light of all the circumstances. But ease of application alone is not an excuse for ignoring the purposes of the securities acts and Congress' policy decisions. Any approach that designates a single fact or occurrence as always determinative of an inherently fact-specific finding such as materiality, must necessarily be over- or underinclusive. In *TSC Industries* this Court explained: "The determination [of materiality] requires delicate assessments of the inferences a 'reasonable shareholder' would draw from a given set of facts and the significance of those inferences to him...." 426 U.S., at 450, 96 S.Ct., at 2133. After much study, the Advisory Committee on Corporate Disclosure cautioned the SEC against administratively confining materiality to a rigid formula. Courts also would do well to heed this advice.

We therefore find no valid justification for artificially excluding from the definition of materiality information concerning merger discussions, which would otherwise be considered significant to the trading decision of a reasonable investor, merely because agreement-in-principle as to price and structure has not yet been reached by the parties or their representatives.

* * *

Even before this Court's decision in *TSC Industries*, the Second Circuit had explained the role of the materiality requirement of Rule 10b–5, with respect to contingent or speculative information or events, in a manner that gave that term meaning that is independent of the other provisions of the Rule. Under such circumstances, materiality "will depend at any given time upon a balancing of both the indicated probability that the event will occur and the anticipated magnitude of the event in light of the totality of the company activity." *SEC v. Texas Gulf Sulphur Co.*, 401 F.2d, at 849.

* * *

In a subsequent decision, the late Judge Friendly, writing for a Second Circuit panel, applied the *Texas Gulf Sulphur* probability/magnitude approach in the specific context of preliminary merger negotiations. After acknowledging that materiality is something to be determined on the basis of the particular facts of each case, he stated:

"Since a merger in which it is bought out is the most important event that can occur in a small corporation's life, to wit, its death, we think that inside information, as regards a merger of this sort, can become material at an earlier stage than would be the case as regards lesser transactions—and this even though the mortality rate of mergers in such formative stages is doubtless high."

SEC v. Geon Industries, Inc., 531 F.2d 39, 47–48 (CA2 1976). We agree with that analysis.[16]

Whether merger discussions in any particular case are material therefore depends on the facts. Generally, in order to assess the probability that the event will occur, a factfinder will need to look to indicia of interest in the transaction at the highest corporate levels. Without attempting to catalog all such possible factors, we note by way of example that board resolutions, instructions to investment bankers, and actual negotiations between principals or their intermediaries may serve as indicia of interest. To assess the magnitude of the transaction to the issuer of the securities allegedly manipulated, a factfinder will need to consider such facts as the size of the two corporate entities and of the potential premiums over market value. No particular event or factor short of closing the transaction need be either necessary or sufficient by itself to render merger discussions material.[17]

As we clarify today, materiality depends on the significance the reasonable investor would place on the withheld or misrepresented information. The fact-specific inquiry we endorse here is consistent with the approach a number of courts have taken in assessing the materiality of merger negotiations. Because the standard of materiality we have adopted differs from that used by both courts below, we

---

16. The SEC in the present case endorses the highly fact-dependent probability/magnitude balancing approach of *Texas Gulf Sulphur*. It explains: "The *possibility* of a merger may have an immediate importance to investors in the company's securities even if no merger ultimately takes place." Brief for SEC as *Amicus Curiae* 10. The SEC's insights are helpful, and we accord them due deference. See *TSC Industries, Inc. v. Northway, Inc.*, 426 U.S., at 449, n. 10, 96 S.Ct., at 2132, n. 10.

17. To be actionable, of course, a statement must also be misleading. Silence, absent a duty to disclose, is not misleading under Rule 10b–5. "No comment" statements are generally the functional equivalent of silence. See *In re Carnation Co.*, supra. See also New York Stock Exchange Listed Company Manual § 202.01, reprinted in 3 CCH Fed.Sec.L.Rep. ¶ 23,515 (premature public announcement may properly be delayed for valid business purpose and where adequate security can be maintained); American Stock Exchange Company Guide §§ 401–405, reprinted in 3 CCH Fed.Sec.L.Rep. ¶¶ 23,124A–23,124E (similar provisions).

It has been suggested that given current market practices, a "no comment" statement is tantamount to an admission that merger discussions are underway. See *Flamm v. Eberstadt*, 814 F.2d, at 1178. That may well hold true to the extent that issuers adopt a policy of truthfully denying merger rumors when no discussions are underway, and of issuing "no comment" statements when they are in the midst of negotiations. There are, of course, other statement policies firms could adopt; we need not now advise issuers as to what kind of practice to follow, within the range permitted by law. Perhaps more importantly, we think that creating an exception to a regulatory scheme founded on a pro-disclosure legislative philosophy, because complying with the regulation might be "bad for business," is a role for Congress, not this Court. See also *id.*, at 1182 (opinion concurring in the judgment and concurring in part).

remand the case for reconsideration of the question whether a grant of summary judgment is appropriate on this record.[20]

* * *

TAYLOR v. FIRST UNION CORP.
United States Court of Appeals, Fourth Circuit, 1988.
857 F.2d 240.

* * *

WILKINSON, CIRCUIT JUDGE:

In February 1984, plaintiff Patricia Taylor and her husband, Bennie Taylor, sold their stock in Southern Bancorporation, Inc. to First Union Corporation for $18 a share. In September 1985, Southern and First Union entered into a merger agreement, and First Union offered to purchase all outstanding stock in Southern for $33 a share. Plaintiff filed suit against Southern and First Union alleging violations of § 10(b) of the Securities Exchange Act of 1934 and breach of fiduciary duty in connection with defendants' failure to disclose their merger discussions and their conduct surrounding the purchase of her stock.

* * *

Southern Bancorporation (Southern) was a South Carolina bank holding company that owned all of the common stock of Southern Bank & Trust Co. and World Acceptance Corp. Plaintiff, Patricia Taylor, and her husband, Bennie Taylor, owned 4.9% of the stock in Southern. In February 1984, Bennie Taylor was the Chief Executive Officer of World Acceptance and a member of the board of directors and executive committee of Southern. Bennie Taylor underwent surgery in March of 1983 which left him a paraplegic and resulted in serious emotional complications.

On January 11, 1984, representatives of First Union, a North Carolina bank holding company, met with representatives of Southern to discuss the possibility of the two companies developing a "relationship." Bennie Taylor was not present at this meeting. The evidence indicates that First Union raised the possibility of a merger with Southern in the event interstate banking became legal. First Union also expressed an interest in acquiring 4.99% of Southern's stock. Southern's board of directors met on January 31, 1984. Bennie Taylor was present at that meeting. After the board meeting, Southern's executive committee approved First Union's acquisition of Southern's stock. First Union then began acquiring stock on the market at the prevailing market price of $16 per share.

---

20. The Sixth Circuit rejected the District Court's narrow reading of Basic's "no developments" statement, see n. 4, supra, which focused on whether petitioners knew of any reason for the activity in Basic stock, that is, whether petitioners were aware of leaks concerning ongoing discussions.... We accept the Court of Appeals' reading of the statement as the more natural one, emphasizing management's knowledge of developments (as opposed to leaks) that would explain unusual trading activity.

On February 6, 1984, a special executive committee of Southern's board sought Bennie Taylor's resignation, allegedly because his deteriorating physical and mental condition made him unable to fulfill his responsibilities to the company, prompting the resignation of three senior officers and executives of World Acceptance. When Bennie Taylor refused to resign, he was terminated. Taylor apparently indicated at that time that he intended to sell his stock in Southern, and he subsequently retained an attorney to negotiate a sale. On February 8, 1984, Southern sent a letter to Taylor offering to pay his salary and benefits through December 31, 1984 if Taylor would agree to resign all offices and directorships at Southern and World Acceptance, to sell his stock in Southern to the company for fair market value, and to release Southern and World Acceptance from all claims arising from his employment and termination. The letter indicated that if Taylor did not accept the offer by February 19, 1984, his salary and all benefits would terminate on February 29, 1984.

Bennie Taylor subsequently offered to sell his stock to Southern for $18 per share, approximately $2 per share above market value. Southern declined to purchase the stock at that price and Taylor's attorney subsequently negotiated a sale of the stock to First Union for $18 per share. On February 28, 1984, Bennie Taylor executed a settlement memorandum prepared by Southern stating that he would sell all stock in Southern owned directly or indirectly by him to First Union for $18 per share. This agreement anticipated as well the sale of the stock owned by plaintiff, Patricia Taylor. Plaintiff was persuaded by Bennie Taylor and his attorney to sell her stock to First Union.

In June 1985, the Supreme Court, in *Northeast Bancorp, Inc. v. Board of Governors of the Federal Reserve System,* 472 U.S. 159, 105 S.Ct. 2545, 86 L.Ed.2d 112 (1985), held that interstate banking was constitutional. Subsequent state enabling legislation authorized the merger of North Carolina and South Carolina banks as of January 1, 1986. On September 15, 1985, Southern's president met with representatives of First Union to discuss a proposed merger. An agreement was negotiated authorizing First Union to purchase all of Southern's common stock for $33 per share. Southern's executive committee recommended acceptance of First Union's offer on September 20, 1985. The boards of Southern and First Union subsequently approved the merger and the merger took place, effective April 1, 1986.

* * *

We hold, as a matter of law, that plaintiff's allegations failed to state a claim under any prong of Rule 10b–5.

Plaintiff contends that First Union and Southern violated Rule 10b–5 by failing to disclose that, at their January 11, 1984 meeting, they agreed to establish a relationship, described as similar to "pinning" as that term was used socially thirty years ago, and agreed in principle to merge when interstate banking became permissible. We disagree. To be actionable under Rule 10b–5(b), a statement or omission must be both material and misleading....

Because their silence was neither material nor misleading, First Union and Southern were under no obligation to disclose to the Taylors their January 11, 1984 discussions of the possibility of a future merger.

The Supreme Court has recognized that "[s]ilence, absent a duty to disclose, is not misleading under Rule 10b–5." *Basic,* 108 S.Ct. at 987 n. 17.... Rule 10b–5 imposes such a duty to disclose only when silence would make other statements misleading or false.... Plaintiff has failed to identify any statement made misleading by the defendants' nondisclosure of their merger discussions. There is no allegation that defendants had previously denied the possibility of a merger at some future time. In fact, in its 1980 annual report, Southern was identified as a potential acquisition target should interstate banking become legal.

In addition to not being deceptive, the omission complained of here was not material.

* * *

In contrast to the circumstances of *Basic,* the evidence indicates that the discussions at issue here were preliminary, contingent, and speculative. At best, the merger discussions culminated in a vague "agreement" to establish a relationship. There was no agreement as to the price or structure of the deal. While, after *Basic,* this alone is not dispositive of the question of materiality, it is certainly not irrelevant to the totality of the circumstances test articulated in that case. Furthermore, neither the factual nor the legal predicates for a merger were in place. There is no evidence of board resolutions, actual negotiations, or instructions to investment bankers to facilitate a merger. *See Basic,* 108 S.Ct. at 987. A merger between First Union and Southern was contingent on events beyond the control of the parties. At the time First Union purchased plaintiff's stock, the Supreme Court had yet to rule on the constitutionality of interstate banking, and no merger could take place until enabling legislation was enacted both in North Carolina and South Carolina. The evidence also suggests that First Union sought unsuccessfully to acquire either of two other South Carolina banks, South Carolina National Bank and C & S of South Carolina, before merging with Southern.

In sum, any "pinning" relationship between First Union and Southern at the time of the purchase of plaintiff's stock was of a fickle and changeable character. Those in business routinely discuss and exchange information on matters which may or may not eventuate in some future agreement. Not every such business conversation gives rise to legal obligations. We recognize, of course, the unique significance of a merger in the life of a corporation and do not hold that the high mortality rate of proposed mergers absolves management of all duty to disclose.

* * *

The materiality of information concerning a proposed merger is directly related to the likelihood the merger will be accomplished; the more tentative the discussions the less useful such information will be to a reasonable investor in reaching a decision. Information of speculative and tentative discussions is of dubious and marginal significance to that decision. To hold otherwise would result in endless and bewildering guesses as to the need for disclosure, operate as a deterrent to the legitimate conduct of corporate operations, and threaten to "bury the shareholders in an avalanche of trivial information"; the very perils that the limit on disclosure imposed by the materiality requirement serves to avoid.

* * *

Note

More on the Duty to Disclose

The Carnation release and the *Basic* case both contained allegations that voluntary statements to the press violated rule 10b–5. Footnote 17 in *Basic* notes that "silence, absent a duty to disclose, is not misleading." The question becomes, When does a participant in preliminary merger discussion have a duty to disclose? The primary source of this duty comes from specific rules, forms, and schedules promulgated by the Securities and Exchange Commission. Some of the language in the regulations is very broad and could be read to impose a duty to disclose otherwise undisclosed preliminary merger negotiations. Consider, for example, item 303 of regulation S–K (please read the item in your statutory supplement), which is incorporated by reference into several disclosure statements. See item 11 of form S–1, proxy solicitations; item 13 of schedule 14A and annual and quarterly reports required by the Exchange Act of 1934; item 2 in form 10–Q; and item 8 in form 10–K. Does this mean that a firm engaged in preliminary merger negotiations must disclose them in its periodic reports, in any proxy solicitation (even if unrelated to the acquisition), or in any offering of securities (even if unrelated to the acquisition)? The SEC addressed some of these problems in the release that follows.

SEC RELEASE (MAY 18, 1989)—SECTION III F 4

SEA, 34 RELEASE No. 33–6835; 34–26831

* * *

4. PRELIMINARY MERGER NEGOTIATIONS

While Item 303 could be read to impose a duty to disclose otherwise nondisclosed preliminary merger negotiations, as known events or uncertainties reasonably likely to have material effects on future financial condition or results of operations, the Commission did not intend to apply, and has not applied, Item 303 in this manner. As reflected in the various disclosure requirements under the Securities Act and Exchange Act that specifically address merger transactions, the Commission historically has balanced the informational need of investors against the risk that premature disclosure of negotiations may jeopardize completion of the transaction.[50] In general, the Commission's recognition that registrants have an interest in preserving the confidentiality of such negotiations is clearest in the context of a registrant's continuous reporting obligations under the Exchange Act, where disclosure on Form 8–K of acquisitions or dispositions of assets not in the ordinary course of business is triggered by completion of the transaction.[51]

In contrast, where a registrant registers securities for sale under the Securities Act, the Commission requires disclosure of material probable acquisitions and dispositions of businesses, including the financial statements of the business to be acquired or sold.[52] Where the proceeds from the sale of the securities being registered are to be used to finance an acquisition of a business, the registration statement must disclose the intended use of proceeds. Again, accommodating the need for confidentiality of negotiations, registrants are specifically permitted not to disclose in registration statements the identity of the parties and the nature of the business sought if the acquisition is not yet probable and the board of directors determines that the acquisition would be jeopardized.[53]

The Commission's interpretation of Item 303, as applied to preliminary merger negotiations, incorporates the same policy determinations. Accordingly, where disclosure is not otherwise required, and has not otherwise been made, the MD & A need not contain a discussion of the impact of such negotiations where, in the registrant's view, inclusion of

---

50. *See, e.g.,* Securities Exchange Act Release No. 16384 (November 29, 1979) [44 FR 70326, 70336] (considering these conflicting interests in adopting Item 7 of Schedule 14D–9, 17 CFR 240.101, which requires that the subject company of a public tender offer provide two levels of disclosure: (a) a statement as to whether or not "any negotiation [which would result in certain transactions or fundamental changes] is being undertaken or is underway....

51. Item 2 of Form 8–K, 17 CFR 249.-308. *See also* Item 8 of Form 10–K, 17 CFR 249.310 (excluding pro forma financial information otherwise called for by Article 11 of Regulation S–X from the financial information required); Item 1 of Form 10–Q, 17 CFR 249.308a, and Rule 10–01 of Regulation S–X, 17 CFR 210.01. With respect to the disposal of a segment of a business, however, Accounting Principles Board Opinion 30 requires that results of operations of the segment be reclassified as discontinued operations, and any estimated loss on disposal be recorded, as of the data management commits itself to a formal plan to dispose of the segment (*i.e.,* the "measurement data"). Filings, including periodic reports under the Exchange Act that contain annual or interim financial statements are required to reflect the prescribed accounting treatment as of the measurement date.

52. Article 11 of Regulation S–X, 17 CFR 210.11–01 *et seq.* (generally requiring the provision of pro forma financial information where a significant acquisition or disposition "has occurred or is probable"). Entry into the continuous reporting system by registration under the Exchange Act also requires the provision of such pro forma financial information. Item 13 of Form 10, 17 CFR 249.210. *See also* Item 14 of Schedule 14A, 17 CFR 240.14a–101 (requiring Article 11 pro forma financial information and extensive other information about certain extraordinary transactions if shareholder action is to be taken wit respect to such a transaction).

53. Item 504 of Regulation S–K, 17 CFR 229.504, Instruction 6.

such information would jeopardize completion of the transaction. Where disclosure is otherwise required or has otherwise been made by or on behalf of the registrant, the interests in avoiding premature disclosure no longer exist. In such case, the negotiations would be subject to the same disclosure standards under Item 303 as any other known trend, demand, commitment, event or uncertainty. These policy determinations also would extend to preliminary negotiations for the acquisition or disposition of assets not in the ordinary course of business.

* * *

The release establishes a basic rule and notes exceptions for (1) registration statements filed for public offerings, (2) sales of a business segment, and (3) a schedule 14D-9 filed by a target responding to a tender offer. In setting out the exceptions, release 33-6830 specifically refers to, among other sections, two other SEC provisions of note, item 7 of schedule 14D-9, and item 504 of regulation S-K, instruction 6. The former is part of the filing a target must make when responding to a tender offer. The latter, part of regulation S-K specific to registration statements, is necessary when a firm is selling its securities to the public. Please read schedule 14D-9, item 7, and regulation S-K, item 504, instruction 6, in your statutory supplement.

IN RE REVLON
SEC Exchange Act Release No. 23,320.
(June 16, 1986) CCH ¶ 84,006

This administrative proceeding concerns the failure of Revlon to amend promptly a previously filed Schedule 14D-9 to disclose that Revlon had undertaken negotiations for a sale of the Revlon domestic beauty group and for a leveraged buyout of the remainder of Revlon.

* * *

On August 23, 1985, Pantry Pride offered to purchase any and all of Revlon's common stock at $47.50 per share and any and all its preferred stock at $26.67 per share (the "First Pantry Pride Offer"). In a Schedule 14D-9, dated August 27, 1985, Revlon disclosed its board of directors' rejection of the First Pantry Pride Offer as inadequate and further disclosed the adoption of certain defensive measures....

In response to the requirement of Item 7(a) to disclose "whether or not any negotiation is being undertaken or is underway" in response to the First Pantry Pride Offer, Revlon stated that it "may undertake negotiations which relate to or could result in: (i) an extraordinary transaction such as a merger or reorganization, involving the Company or any of its subsidiaries; (ii) a purchase, sale or transfer of a material amount of assets of the Company or any of its subsidiaries; (iii) a tender offer for or other acquisition of securities by or of the Company; (iv) a material change in the present capitalization or dividend policy of the Company." Revlon further stated at Item 7(a) that Revlon's management was working with its financial and legal advisers to explore other alternatives. Revlon added that "Currently, however, no negotiations have been undertaken with third parties."

Revlon's board also resolved, as permitted under the Instruction to Item 7(a), that disclosure of the terms or parties of any transaction or proposal under future consideration "might jeopardize the continuation of any discussions or negotiations that the Company may conduct." Accordingly, Revlon stated that it would not disclose the parties to, or possible terms of, any transaction among the various types listed above unless and until Revlon had reached an agreement in principle.

* * *

On September 13, Revlon announced the purchase of 10 million shares pursuant to its Exchange Offer. Pantry Pride withdrew its First Offer and announced in a press release, followed by the filing of a Tender Offer Statement on Schedule 14D–1 ("Schedule 14D–1") on September 16, a new Offer for all of Revlon's common stock at $42 per share, subject to 90% of the shares being tendered (the "Pantry Pride $42 Offer").

On September 18, Leonard Shaykin ("Shaykin") of Adler & Shaykin ("A & S") telephoned Revlon's special counsel Wachtell, Lipton, Rosen & Katz ("Wachtell Lipton") to express interest in a leveraged buyout ("LBO") for all of Revlon's assets. Wachtell Lipton arranged for Shaykin to meet with certain representatives of Lazard Freres & Co. ("Lazard"), Revlon's investment bankers, on September 19. At that meeting, Shaykin was informed that Revlon would only consider selling its domestic beauty group to A & S. Subsequently, Revlon began to provide A & S with financial information concerning Revlon.

Revlon and its financial and legal advisers, including representatives from Lazard, Wachtell Lipton, and Paul, Weiss Rifkind, Wharton & Garrison ("Paul Weiss"), met at Revlon on September 20 to discuss alternative strategies including the placement of preferred stock, a liquidation, and the sale of the Norcliff Thayer and Reheis Chemical divisions. At the end of that meeting the participants also briefly discussed the possibility of arranging an LBO for the rest of the company if A & S were to buy the domestic beauty group and authorized William Loomis ("Loomis") of Lazard to contact Forstmann Little & Co. ("Forstmann Little") to determine if that LBO firm had an interest in such a transaction. Without mentioning Revlon's name, Loomis called a limited partner of Forstmann Little on September 20 to arrange a telephone call on September 21.

During the resulting phone call on September 21, Loomis asked if Forstmann Little potentially was interested in acquiring Revlon without its cosmetics business. Theodore Forstmann ("Forstmann") later agreed to have Forstmann Little meet with Lazard subject to the clear understanding that Revlon would pay Forstmann Little a substantial cash sum as a "break-up" fee in the event Forstmann Little made an offer which Lazard opined to be fair to Revlon's shareholders, was accepted by Revlon, but was topped by another bid.

On September 22, Loomis went to Forstmann Little's offices to provide the firm with financial information regarding Revlon.[4] On September 23, Revlon's Chairman, Michael C. Bergerac ("Bergerac"), met with Shaykin in Revlon's offices. Bergerac recalls that by that time Revlon or its investment bankers had informed Adler & Shaykin that an appropriate price for Revlon's cosmetics business was $850 million plus the assumption of $100 million in foreign debt.

* * *

On September 24, Revlon's board met to evaluate the Pantry Pride $42 Offer and rejected it. In the Schedule 14D–9, dated September 24, 1985 (the "September 24 Schedule 14D–9"), Revlon recommended that shareholders not tender their shares in acceptance of the Pantry Pride $42 Offer. In Item 7(a) of its September 24 Schedule 14D–9 Revlon disclosed: (i) that it may undertake negotiations which related to or could result in extraordinary transactions such as a merger, reorganization, purchase, sale or transfer of a material amount of Revlon's assets, a tender offer for or other acquisition of securities by or of Revlon, or a material change in the present capitalization of Revlon, (ii) that its Board of Directors had determined that stockholders are entitled to maximize the value of their investment, and that, in this connection, Revlon's management had been working with financial and legal advisers to explore alternatives to the Pantry Pride Offer and had been directed to continue those efforts; and (iii) that the Board of Directors had determined that any disclosure with respect to the parties to, and the possible terms of, any transactions or proposals intended to maximize stockholder value might jeopardize the continuation of any such discussions or negotiations, and that no disclosure would be made until an agreement in principle had been reached.

* * *

By September 26, Forstmann Little had hired Goldman Sachs & Co. ("Goldman") to assist Forstmann Little in assessing the value of Revlon's noncosmetics businesses and had begun the process of securing financing for a transaction.

On September 26, Bergerac met Forstmann in New York for dinner.[5] At that dinner meeting, Bergerac and Forstmann discussed the subject of equity participation by Bergerac and other members of Revlon's management in a Forstmann Little LBO. Bergerac said that

---

4. During this period, Revlon also provided or made arrangements to provide confidential financial information to approximately twenty other companies in connection with Lazard's efforts to elicit interest in a sale of Revlon's Norcliff/Thayer and Rebeis Chemical divisions or a private placement of Revlon preferred stock.

5. Bergerac previously met Forstmann in 1984 when Revlon had briefly considered an LBO.

he thought the Revlon management group would be interested in purchasing, on the same basis as other investors, up to 25% of the available equity. Forstmann indicated that Forstmann Little historically offered between 10% and 20% to management.

On the evening of September 27, Bergerac and Revlon's chief financial officer attended a dinner meeting with members of Forstmann Little and representatives of Goldman and Fried Frank at a restaurant in New York. Forstmann arranged the meeting because he wanted Bergerac to meet with the senior Goldman Sachs people who would be evaluating Revlon's noncosmetics businesses. Forstmann Little spent September 28 and September 29 in conference with its lenders. Goldman interviewed Revlon personnel on September 28.

Bergerac met with Shaykin on September 28 at A & S' offices. Bergerac stated that he had "nothing" from Shaykin at this point. Bergerac advised Shaykin that unless Shaykin could arrange his financing in a very short time, nothing could be achieved. Shaykin then asked Bergerac to attend a meeting with A & S's lenders, scheduled for later that day, to explain the cosmetics business to them. After the second meeting with Shaykin and his lenders on Saturday, September 28, Bergerac was informed by Felix Rohatyn of Lazard ("Rohatyn") that Shaykin would present a firm offer on Sunday afternoon, September 29, at a meeting arranged by Loomis at Rohatyn's apartment. Bergerac informed Forstmann, and both of them met with Rohatyn, Loomis, and Shaykin the next day.

At that meeting on September 29, Shaykin presented a handwritten term sheet of A & S' proposed acquisition with a price term $802 million, plus the assumption of $30 million in foreign debt subject to certain adjustments. Shaykin admitted that he did not yet have firm financing commitments. The others present told Shaykin that his offer was too low because it would not support a per share price in the Forstmann Little LBO that was acceptable to Revlon. Shaykin suggested that the attorneys representing the parties should meet, nevertheless, to discuss the structure of the A & S proposal. The other parties agreed to such a meeting.

Later, in the evening of September 29, Shaykin and legal and other representatives of Revlon, A & S, Forstmann Little, and A & S's lenders attended a meeting at Fried Frank's offices. Prior to the meeting, counsel for Revlon, Forstmann Little, and A & S had conferred by telephone over the weekend concerning possible structures for the acquisition of Revlon by Forstmann Little and the sale of the domestic beauty group to A & S. At the Fried Frank meeting, A & S' counsel distributed photocopies of the handwritten term sheet which Shaykin had earlier that day shown to Bergerac, Forstmann, Loomis, and Rohatyn. A typed version was distributed later.

After the general meeting on September 29, counsel for Forstmann Little and Revlon met that night to explore possible LBO structures and Fried Frank delivered to Revlon's counsel copies of a draft acquisition agreement and joint tender offer. In addition, Fried Frank discussed with Revlon's counsel possible asset purchases or options.

* * *

At some time during the day on September 30, Fried Frank delivered a draft asset purchase agreement relating to Vision Care and National Health Laboratories to Revlon and its two outside law firms. By late in the day, A & S' counsel distributed a draft Beauty Group Purchase Agreement to Revlon and Forstmann Little and their respective counsel. On September 30, Forstmann Little, A & S and their respective lenders had two meetings with Revlon and its advisers to discuss the LBO and asset sale. The second meeting began at 5:00 p.m., and lasted until the early hours of Tuesday, October 1.

On October 1, Fried Frank distributed revised drafts of acquisition agreements to Revlon and its representatives, and A & S' counsel circulated a revised draft of the Beauty Group Purchase Agreement. Meetings were held that day at Wachtell Lipton with counsel to all the participants. Forstmann, Bergerac and Shaykin, together with other Forstmann Little and A & S representatives, conferred regarding the sale of the beauty group.

On October 2, Revlon filed Amendment No. 2 to its September 24 Schedule 14D–9 and issued a press release, attached thereto and sent out over the wire at 9:09 a.m., disclosing that its board had met the previous night and was considering several proposals, including an LBO with management participation for $54 per share, a new $53 Pantry Pride offer to the board,[6] the possible complete liquidation of Revlon, and a proposal by a major corporation to acquire Revlon (the "October 2 Amendment"). Revlon amended Item 7 of Schedule 14D–9 on October 3, 1985, to disclose a definitive merger agreement with Forstmann Little for $56 per share, an asset sale of the Domestic Beauty Group by Revlon to A & S for approximately $900 million and the sale by Forstmann Little of Revlon's Reheis Chemical and Norcliff/Thayer divisions to American Home Products Corp. after the merger.

* * *

The volume of trading in Revlon's common stock increased substantially on September 30 and October 1. The total trading volume[7] in the common stock increased from 426,500 shares on Thursday, September 26 to 1,587,100 shares on Monday, September 30 and to 2,389,600 shares on Tuesday, October 1.[8]

---

6. Pantry Pride had increased its $42 Offer to $50 per share on September 27, 1985 (the "Pantry Pride $50 Offer") and to $53 per share on October 1, 1985 (the "Pantry Pride $53 Offer").

7. Total trading volume includes trading, on a when-distributed basis, in the common shares which had been tendered but not accepted by Revlon pursuant to its Exchange Offer and which were to be returned upon the expiration of that offer on September 30. The prices, however, are stated solely for Revlon's common stock and not for shares trading on a "when-distributed" basis.

8. The New York Stock Exchange did not open on September 27 because of Hurricane Gloria.

During this period, the price of the common stock rose considerably while the price of the Exchange Offer Notes declined sharply. The closing price of the common stock increased from $42½ on September 26 to $46½ on September 30 and to $50⅜ on October 1, a twenty percent increase over two trading days. Because of an order imbalance, the NYSE delayed the opening of trading in Revlon common stock on October 1 until 10:23 A.M.

On October 2, after Revlon first disclosed that the company was considering an LBO at $54 per share, the price increased to $54⅜. The closing price of Revlon's Exchange Offer Notes, on the other hand, declined from $99 on September 30 to $92¾ on October 1, the date of the first public rumors of a possible Revlon LBO.

* * *

FINDINGS

The obligation to file an accurate Schedule 14D–9 arises under Section 14(d)(4) of the Exchange Act and Rule 14d–9 adopted thereunder. The reporting provisions of the Exchange Act are satisfied only by the filing of complete, accurate, and timely reports.

If any material change occurs in the information set forth in a Schedule 14D–9, then Rule 14d–9(b) requires that the subject company promptly disclose the change by filing an amendment on Schedule 14D–9 with the Commission; delivering a copy of the amendment to the bidder and providing notice to each national securities exchange upon which the subject company's securities are registered and listed for trading; and "disseminating such change in a manner reasonably designed to inform securityholders of such change."

An amendment must be filed promptly in view of "the market's sensitivity to the particular change of fact triggering the obligation to amend, and the effect on the market of the filing person's previous disclosures." *In the Matter of Cooper Laboratories, Inc.,* Exchange Act Rel. No. 22,171, 33 SEC 675, 683 (June 26, 1985) (Section 13(d)).

Rule 14d–9 and Item 7 of Schedule 14D–9 provide with respect to a solicitation or recommendation statement made pursuant to Section 14(d)(4) of the Exchange Act that the person filing the statement must disclose "Certain Negotiations and Transactions by the Subject Company." Item 7(a) requires disclosure of any negotiation which is underway or is being undertaken and which relates to, among other things, a tender offer or a transfer of a material amount of assets by the subject company. Item 7(b) requires disclosure of any transaction, board resolution, agreement in principle, or signed contract relating or made in response to a tender offer.[9]

The "Instruction" to Item 7(a) recognizes that negotiations can occur prior to an agreement in principle and allows target companies to

---

9. Item 7(a) requires a subject company to state "whether or not any negotiation is being undertaken or is underway by the subject company" in response to a tender offer.

withhold the "possible terms of any transaction or the parties thereto ... if in the opinion of the Board of Directors of the subject company such disclosure would jeopardize continuation of such negotiations." But Item 7(a) does not relieve the target company of the duty to disclose the fact of negotiations. The Instruction specifically requires that "[i]n such an event, disclosure that negotiations are being undertaken or are underway and are in the preliminary stages will be sufficient." Once those negotiations ripen into an agreement in principle, it becomes an event required to be disclosed under Item 7(b).

The Commission has emphasized the importance of the disclosures which Item 7 of Schedule 14D-9 requires to be made. In the release announcing the adoption of Rule 14d-9, the Commission stated that "the major developments referred to in Item 7 can be one of the most material items of information received by securityholders." Exchange Act Rel. No. 16,384, 18 SEC 1053, 1070 (November 29, 1979).

Revlon's disclosure pursuant to Item 7(a) of the September 24 Schedule 14D-9 stated that Revlon "may undertake" negotiations that relate to or could result in, among other things, a merger or a sale of substantial assets. The use of the auxiliary verb "may" implied in this context that no negotiations were then underway but that they might be undertaken in the future.[10]

The question as to when the discussions with Forstmann Little and A & S developed to the point of negotiations required to be disclosed pursuant to Item 7(a) depends upon the facts and circumstances of Revlon's dealings with Forstmann Little and A & S. The term "negotiations" should not be interpreted in a technical and restrictive manner. As used in Item 7(a), the term "negotiations" includes not only final price bargaining, but also applies to substantive discussions between the parties or their legal and financial advisers concerning a possible transaction.

The Commission concludes that the discussions between and among Revlon. A & S and Forstmann Little constituted negotiations as of the time period from the evening of September 26 to September 29. By that time, the parties had established contact, had begun and concluded their initial reviews of confidential financial information, had retained counsel to discuss between and among themselves the structure and timing of the acquisitions, and had discussed the percentage of equity to be offered Bergerac and the Revlon management group. Shaykin presented an offer to Revlon, Lazard and Forstmann Little on September 29 which, although rejected, became the basis upon which the parties negotiated, including discussions that night and the next day among counsel for the parties over the structure of the Shaykin proposal and the Forstmann Little LBO.

---

10. In item 7(a) of the Schedule 14D-9, Revlon did state that its board of directors had instructed its management to continue working with Revlon's financial and legal advisers to explore alternatives to Pantry Pride's Offer.

As set forth above, Revlon's September 24 Schedule 14D–9 stated that Revlon "may undertake" negotiations which could result in, among other things, a merger or sale of substantial assets and that Revlon's board had instructed its management to continue working with Revlon's financial and legal adviser to explore alternatives to the Pantry Pride Offer. However, given that Revlon's September 24 Schedule 14D–9 did not state that Revlon was then engaged in any negotiations of the type required to be disclosed under Item 7(a), the commencement of such negotiations constituted a "material change" in the information set forth in Revlon's September 24, 1985 Schedule 14D–9 and triggered the prompt amendment requirement of Rule 14d–9(b).

Consistent with the reasoning set forth in the Commission order in *Cooper Laboratories, supra,* the duty under Rule 14d–9(b) to amend "promptly" Revlon's Schedule 14D–9 was not discharged by its October 2 amendment. Compliance by Revlon with Rule 14d–9(b) required the filing of an amendment and the public dissemination of information disclosing the fact that negotiations were underway and were in preliminary stages (but not the terms of the possible transactions or the parties thereto) as soon as practicable after negotiations had commenced. Under the circumstances of this case, Revlon should have disseminated the information at least before the market opened on September 30 and simultaneously amended its Schedule 14D–9, previously filed with the Commission. Accordingly, Revlon violated Section 14(d)(4) of the Exchange Act and Rule 14d–9 thereunder by failing to amend promptly its Schedule 14D–9 as soon as practicable after negotiations had commenced.

* * *

IN RE KERN

Fed.Sec.L.Rep. (CCH) ¶ 84,342 (S.E.C.1988).

WARREN E. BLAIR, CHIEF ADMINISTRATIVE LAW JUDGE.

* * *

In substance the Division alleged that Allied failed to comply, and Kern caused Allied to fail to comply, with Section 14(d)(4) of the Exchange Act and Rule 14d–9 thereunder by failing to promptly amend a Schedule 14D–9 filed with the Commission on September 24, 1988. The alleged lack of compliance involved failure of Allied to disclose that in response to a tender offer (1) negotiations were under way with another party relating to or which would result in a sale of a material amount of Allied's assets and a material change in Allied's capitalization or result in an extraordinary transaction such as a merger or reorganization; (2) Allied and a third party reached an agreement in principle to a merger with the third party; and (3) Allied's Board of Directors adopted a resolution directing Allied's management to execute a merger agreement with a third party.

* * *

Kern is a partner in Sullivan & Cromwell, a large well-known New York City law firm, and head of the firm's mergers and acquisitions group. During the relevant period covered by the Division's allegations Sullivan & Cromwell, primarily through Kern, acted as Allied's principal outside counsel on the matters involved in these proceedings. Kern was also a member of Allied's Board of Directors during this time.

* * *

Allied was at all times relevant hereto a Delaware corporation with its principal executive offices located in New York City. Until December 31, 1986 Allied's common stock was registered pursuant to Section 12(b) of the Exchange Act and listed for trading on the New York Stock Exchange. On December 31, 1986 Allied became a wholly-owned subsidiary of Campeau Corporation ("Campeau"), a Canadian corporation. Since then, none of Allied's common stock has been publicly held. Allied is not now subject to the reporting requirements of Section 14(d) of the Exchange Act and Rule 14d–9 thereunder and its common stock is no longer registered with the Commission.

Campeau's efforts to acquire Allied were initiated on August 1, 1986 when Robert Campeau, Chairman and Chief Executive Officer of Campeau, met with Thomas M. Macioce ("Macioce"), his counterpart at Allied. About a month later, on September 4, Robert Campeau had a letter delivered to Macioce proposing that Campeau and Allied commence negotiations looking toward a merger at a price of $58 per share, with Allied shareholders to receive 80 percent in cash and the remainder in securities. Allied issued a press release the same day disclosing receipt of the merger proposal. On September 11, 1986 the Allied Board of Directors met and decided to reject Campeau's proposal. Allied issued a press release disclosing the Board's action. The next day, September 12, Campeau announced the commencement of a tender offer for approximately 60 per cent of Allied's shares at $58 per share. On September 23, 1986 Allied's Board of Directors met to consider the tender offer and determined to reject it. At the meeting the Board also passed a resolution authorizing Allied to continue to explore and investigate, with the assistance of Goldman, Sachs & Co. ("Goldman Sachs"), an investment banking firm, various alternatives to Campeau's tender offer. On September 24, 1986 Allied filed a Schedule 14D–9 disclosing the Board's recommended rejection of Campeau's tender offer and setting forth the following under Item 7(a):

> At its September 23, 1986 meeting, the Board considered and reviewed the feasibility and desirability of exploring and investigating certain types of possible transactions, including without limitation, a change in the present capitalization of the Company, the public or private sale of Shares or other securities of the Company to another company or person, the acquisition by the Company of Shares by tender offer or otherwise, the acquisition by the Company of all or part of the business of another company or person, and the acquisition of the Company or of one or more of its significant business segments or of certain of its assets or a portion of its Shares by another company or person. After

considerable discussion, the Board resolved that it was desirable and in the best interests of the Company and its stockholders to continue to explore and investigate, with the assistance and advice of Goldman Sachs, such transactions, although the Board noted that the initiation or continuation of such activities may be dependent upon future actions with respect to the Offer. There can be no assurance that these activities will result in any transaction being recommended to the Board or that any transaction which may be recommended will be authorized or consummated. The proposal or consummation of any transaction of the type referred to in this Item 7 may have an impact on the Offer.

At its September 23, 1986 meeting, the Board also adopted a resolution with respect to the need for confidentiality with respect to the parties to, and possible terms of, any transactions or proposals of the type referred to in the preceding portion of this Item 7 during negotiations with respect to any such transactions.

* * *

The Shopping Centers

The uninvited and unexpected interest of Campeau in Allied caused Macioce to look at the options available to forestall a Campeau takeover. During the first week of September, 1986 after receiving Robert Campeau's letter of September 4, Allied turned to Goldman Sachs for advice. Immediately representatives of Goldman Sachs began to meet with Macioce and other Allied senior officials and with lawyers from Sullivan & Cromwell. Additionally, Macioce arranged to have dinner on September 10 with Edward J. DeBartolo, Sr. ("DeBartolo"), a close business and social acquaintance of many years who was Chairman of the Board and Chief Executive Officer of Edward J. DeBartolo Corporation ("EJDC"), to discuss the Campeau offer and ascertain whether DeBartolo still had his previously indicated interest in Allied. Macioce told Kern prior to the Allied Board meeting of September 11 about his dinner with DeBartolo the night before.

After Campeau's announcement of its tender offer at $58 per share on September 12, Goldman Sachs reviewed possible defensive measures that Allied could pursue, with the primary focus being on a recapitalization of Allied. Key features of the recapitalization were a sale by Allied of six of its shopping centers and the securing of additional funds from banks to enable Allied to offer its stockholders a more attractive package than Campeau's. Various alternatives, including sale of Allied's shopping centers, were discussed at a meeting on September 17, 1986 attended by Kern and by representatives of Goldman Sachs and Allied. Kern and the Goldman Sachs people raised different possibilities for discussion. As the meeting progressed, some form of recapitalization of Allied became the central topic of consideration.

As part of a feasibility study of a recapitalization plan, Goldman Sachs, with Allied's authorization, approached several banks and advised them that Allied planned a sale of its shopping centers and certain of its operating divisions within a short time. Among the banks contacted as prospective lenders were Manufacturers Hanover Trust, Bankers Trust Company, Morgan Guarantee Bank, and Toronto–Dominion Bank.

On September 25, 1986, the day following the filing of Allied's Schedule 14D–9 disclosing the authorization of the Allied Board "to continue to explore and investigate" alternatives to the Campeau offer, Kern was at a meeting also attended by representatives of Allied and EJDC. The participants included a number of senior officers and legal advisers of the two companies as well as Kern, DeBartolo, and Macioce. The purpose of the meeting was to further discuss the possible sale of Allied's shopping centers to EJDC.

As a result of the negotiations in the lengthy morning and afternoon meetings that day, DeBartolo agreed to pay a price of $405 million dollars for the shopping centers, subject to a report on the quality of the malls based on a study to be completed within a few days, after which DeBartolo was to make a firm offer. Macioce was prepared by the end of his meetings with DeBartolo on September 25 to recommend to Allied's Board that the shopping centers be sold for $405 million and sometime that afternoon indicated to Kern that $405 million would be acceptable to Allied.

Macioce expected and understood that Kern would make legal decisions on disclosure questions without consulting officers of Allied except as Kern saw fit. Kern recognized his responsibility in this regard and gave thought to the need to amend Allied's Schedule 14D–9 filing to disclose the shopping center negotiations. He decided, without consultation with any officer or other director of Allied, that an amendment was not required. It is concluded that the failure of Allied to amend its Schedule 14D–9 filing was a violation of Section 14(d)(4) of the Exchange Act and Rule 14d–9 thereunder.

Allied was required by Rule 14d–9(b) under the Exchange Act to amend its Schedule 14D–9 to disclose promptly any material changes in the information set forth in its Schedule 14D–9. Allied's disclosure in Item 7(a) of its Schedule 14D–9 that Allied's Board had "resolved that it was desirable and in the best interests of the Company and its stockholders to continue to explore and investigate" certain types of transactions including acquisition by another company of one or more of Allied's business segments did not encompass what must be deemed negotiations for the shopping centers that took place on September 25. Those negotiations, which culminated in an understanding between DeBartolo and Macioce that $405 million dollars would be the price tag for the shopping centers and that a firm offer by DeBartolo might be forthcoming, constituted a "material change" in Allied's Schedule 14D–9 information. Consequently, Kern's decision not to amend Schedule 14D–9 to disclose promptly that material change caused Allied to violate Rule 14d–9(b), and Kern should have known that he was contributing to Allied's failure to comply with Section 14 of the Exchange Act.

Kern attempts to defend the failure to file a Schedule 14D–9 amendment disclosing the contemplated sale of Allied's six shopping centers by arguing that there was no agreement on price and terms on September 25 and that nothing occurred in the discussions that constituted a material change in Allied's initial disclosure. The record supports Kern's argument that no agreement between the parties on price and terms came into existence on September 25, but does not with respect to his assertion that a material change in the information set forth in Allied's September 24 disclosures under Item 7 had not taken place.

While no agreement in principle fixing the price and structure for the sale of the shopping centers had eventuated on September 25, the negotiations which Kern conceded were carried on that day were of a character and nature to give rise to a material change in the situation described under Item 7 of Allied's initial Schedule 14D–9. Kern's contention to the contrary cannot be accepted.

As of September 25 Allied stockholders and the investing public were aware by virtue of Allied's Item 7 disclosure that Allied's Board had reviewed "the feasibility and desirability of exploring and investigating certain types of possible transactions including without limitation, ... the acquisition of the Company [Allied] or of one or more of its significant business segments or of certain of its assets ... by another company or person," and that the Board resolved "that it was desirable and in the best interests of the Company and its stockholders to continue to explore and investigate, with the assistance and advice of Goldman Sachs, such transactions...." Kern's efforts to bring the shopping center negotiations within the ambit of the phrase "to continue to explore and investigate ... such transactions" are rejected. The disclosure in question cannot reasonably encompass the shopping center negotiations. The words "explore" and "investigate" imply efforts by Allied to locate transactions in keeping with the Board's resolution but do not suggest that a specific transaction of the magnitude of the sale of Allied's shopping centers would become the subject of on-going negotiations on September 25 and thereafter until aborted on September 29 by Campeau's raising its offer for Allied. Nor is it likely that a reasonable investor would construe Allied's disclosure to include such negotiations.

Having found that the shopping center negotiations were not covered in the information initially disclosed under Item 7, the next consideration is whether that change was material within the meaning of Rule 14d–9(b) so as to require the filing of an amendment to Allied's Schedule 14D–9. The controlling guidelines are found in *Basic Incorporated v. Levinson* in which the Supreme Court approved the use of the probability/magnitude formula enunciated in *SEC v. Texas Gulf Sulphur Co.*, and repeated the conclusion it reached in *TSC Industries, Inc.*

v. Northway, Inc. that "there must be a substantial likelihood that the disclosure of the omitted fact would have been viewed by the reasonable investor as having significantly altered the 'total mix' of information made available."

* * *

In defense of his judgment, Kern argues that the probability of a sale of the shopping centers was too remote to require further disclosure because a sale was contingent upon a recapitalization which was as yet highly speculative, that no offer had been made for the shopping centers, that there had been no agreement that there would be a sale of the shopping centers, and that there was considerable work to be done by EJDC before it would know whether it would offer to buy the centers. Kern was also concerned that the market not be misled as to the probability of a successful recapitalization.

Kern's arguments are not persuasive. Months before the September 25 meeting Macioce knew of DeBartolo's interest in acquiring Allied's shopping malls and the September 25 discussions were directed primarily at price, not whether the centers were on the market. The understanding of the top officials of Allied and EJDC that Allied would sell and EJDC would buy if a price could be agreed upon and Macioce's and DeBartolo's luncheon understanding that $405 million would be acceptable to both companies indicate that the probability of the shopping centers being sold was not as remote as Kern insists. Further, the amount of effort by the subordinate staff representatives of the two companies to gather the needed information to support the $405 million price points to a likely, not a remote, possibility that the sale would be consummated. Weighing all of the indicia in the record of the probability that the sale of the shopping centers would occur and the magnitude of that event, which Kern agreed would have been a material event, the balance lies heavily on the side of a finding of materiality and a need to disclose the negotiations that transpired on September 25. Moreover, where an initial Schedule 14D–9 does not, as was the situation here, state that the company was then engaged in any negotiations of the type required to be disclosed under Item 7(a), the commencement of such negotiations constitutes a "material change" in the information set forth in Schedule 14D–9 and "triggers the prompt amendment requirement of Rule 14d–9(b)."

Kern's expressed concern that an amendment to disclose the shopping center negotiations would have been misleading, particularly in light of the information filed by Allied the day before in its Schedule 14D–9, does not bolster his position. The shopping center negotiations represented a material change in the Schedule 14D–9 information and required disclosure. Any possibility that the market would be misled could have been readily dissipated by additional language calling attention to the contingencies involved.

THE MERGER NEGOTIATIONS

Allied's plans for sale of the shopping centers and recapitalization were disrupted on September 29, 1986 by Campeau's revising its tender offer to $66 per share for 80% of Allied's stock. Although the possibility of recapitalization was not then entirely abandoned, it became clear to Allied's senior management and Kern at that time that the sale of the shopping centers and recapitalization would not suffice to counter Campeau's offer. One alternative considered was the possibility of a "white knight" [10] merger with DeBartolo and a meeting with DeBartolo was arranged for the next day.

DeBartolo, Paul Bilzerian ("Bilzerian"), who was associated with EJDC in its efforts to acquire Allied,[11] and other representatives of EJDC met on September 30 in Macioce's office with Macioce, Kern, and other representatives of Allied. In the course of that meeting the Campeau offer was discussed and analyzed and consideration was given to the mechanics and timing of a competing offer by EJDC. Before the conclusion of the meeting DeBartolo and Bilzerian indicated to Macioce that they were going to make an all-cash offer for Allied stock at a price of $66 to $67 per share. They also said that they had been talking to investment counsel about the matter. Additionally, the need to be very careful to guard against leaks and to keep information confidential was brought up at the meeting as was the need for EJDC to have access to non-public information about Allied. After some hesitancy Allied agreed to allow the EJDC group to meet with Goldman Sachs and go through Goldman Sachs' materials on condition that EJDC sign a confidentiality agreement. The confidentiality agreement was signed and late that night or the next morning of October 1, 1986 EJDC began receiving the non-public information about Allied.

In a series of private meetings on October 1 and 2, Bilzerian continued negotiations on behalf of EJDC with Macioce. In the evening hours of October 2 Macioce accepted an offer by Bilzerian of $67 all-cash for all of Allied's shares and a break-up fee of a dollar a share plus expenses to be paid EJDC in the event a third party acquired Allied, subject only to Goldman Sachs convincing EJDC that Allied stock was worth $67 per share. Macioce assured Bilzerian that Goldman Sachs could do so, and they shook hands on the deal.

During the four-day period from Tuesday, September 30 until and including Friday, October 3, 1986 a series of meetings in which Kern also participated took place. In those meetings consideration was given by the Allied and EJDC representatives to the all-cash requirement,

---

10. In Wall St. parlance a "white knight" is a company that a take-over candidate hopes will thwart the plans of a hostile bidder and be a more friendly acquirer. Prior to September 29, 1986 Macioce had informed DeBartolo, in response to the latter's merger overtures, that Allied desired to remain independent.

11. ASC Acquisition Corp. ("ASC"), a Delaware corporation, was formed by EJDC for the purpose of making a tender offer for Allied. Bilzerian, a private investor, owned 10% of ASC.

coverage of the merger to all Allied outstanding shares, timing of the various steps in the proposed merger, maintenance of Allied's employee pension and profit-sharing plans, and payment of a break-up fee for EJDC if the deal collapsed. In that same period Sullivan & Cromwell and the law firm of Wilkie Farr and Gallagher, respectively outside counsel for Allied and EJDC, worked on drafting a merger agreement. By October 1 drafts of the agreement were available for review before a meeting of the parties on Thursday, October 2.

Separately from the negotiations on the terms of the merger, EJDC representatives went to work on September 30 with representatives of Goldman Sachs and Citibank to firm up financing for the prospective merger. EJDC felt that a meeting of the minds with Citibank relative to the financial arrangements had been reached by October 1, but because Citibank unexpectedly introduced an unacceptable provision for indemnification of Citibank, EJDC broke off the proposed financing through Citibank and turned to Chemical Bank which had earlier indicated an interest in participating in the financing. A meeting of the representatives of Chemical Bank and EJDC was arranged for the evening of October 2. The meeting, which extended into the morning hours of October 3, ended with a written commitment from Chemical and that commitment was immediately delivered to DeBartolo.

Continuing to exercise the legal discretion vested in him by Macioce, Kern, without consultation with any officer or other director of Allied, decided that no amendment to Allied's Schedule 14D–9 disclosing the merger negotiations with DeBartolo and Bilzerian during the period September 29 through October 3, 1986 would be filed. It appears from the record that Kern's decision not to file such amendment was erroneous and that as a result Allied failed to comply with Section 14(d)(4) of the Exchange Act and Rule 14d–9 thereunder. It also appears that Kern was a cause of Allied's failure to comply and knew or should have known that the omission to amend Allied's Schedule 14D–9 would contribute to the failure to comply.

Without attempting to pinpoint the precise moment when Allied's merger negotiations reached the stage where its disclosure in the Schedule 14D–9 of September 24 no longer sufficed to cover the material change in Allied's situation with respect to EJDC's proposed merger, it is clear that by the close of October 2, 1986 a material change in the information previously disclosed had occurred and that the new developments would have been of significant interest to Allied shareholders. That new information should have been made known to them by way of an amendment to Allied's Schedule 14D–9. Bearing in mind the Supreme Court's approval in its recent *Basic Inc. v. Levinson* decision of the concept expressed in *S.E.C. v. Texas Gulf Sulphur Co.* that materiality "will depend at any given time upon a balancing of both the indicated probability that the event will occur and the anticipated magnitude of the event in light of the totality of the company activity," there is little in the record to justify Kern's position that an amendment to disclose Allied's merger negotiations was not required. As the

Division points out, by October 2 Allied and EJDC negotiators had drafts of a merger agreement in their hands and Allied and EJDC negotiators had reached an agreement on price and other terms of the contemplated merger. Contrary to Kern's position, it is concluded that as of October 2 the probability of EJDC's competing tender offer going forward was strong and the probable effect of the negotiations was close to being of the first magnitude. Nor can there be any question that the emergence of a competing bid against Campeau's hostile tender offer was information defined as "material" within the terms of Rule 12b–2 under the Exchange Act. If disclosed fully and accurately the negotiations and the understandings of the parties would have undoubtedly "assumed actual significance in the deliberations of the reasonable shareholder," and there would have been "substantial likelihood that the disclosure of the omitted fact would have been viewed by the reasonable investor as having significantly altered the 'total mix' of information made available."

Kern argues that a critical aspect of the evidence concerning the events of September 30 to October 3 was that Allied and its advisors were pursuing and engaging in negotiations concerning two mutually exclusive alternatives. One was a recapitalization that would have left Allied independent and the alternative was a merger with DeBartolo. In his testimony at the hearing Kern characterized the merger discussions as "contingent negotiations" because negotiations were being carried on simultaneously with respect to each of the possibilities.

The record, however, reflects that with Campeau's revised tender offer of September 29, Kern and the Allied advisers had almost entirely discounted the feasibility of going forward with a recapitalization plan. Kern's investigative testimony was that when Campeau raised its offer "the recapitalization plan wouldn't work," and that "[w]e at least were not able to figure out a recapitalization mechanism that would produce to the stockholders the kind of return that Campo [sic] was then reportedly offering."

But even if Campeau's offer had not changed the picture regarding recapitalization, there appears to have been no reason to withhold information concerning the merger negotiations which by October 3 had reached a stage that completely overshadowed the alternate recapitalization plan. Under the circumstances, any "contingency negotiations" looking toward a recapitalization would have had a negligible effect upon the degree of probability that a merger with EJDC would occur, and reasonably should not have been a factor in determining whether an amendment to Allied's Schedule 14D–9 was required.

The second critical aspect of the negotiations which Kern relies upon in support of his decision not to amend Schedule 14D–9 to disclose the negotiations is that no merger agreement with DeBartolo would exist unless and until DeBartolo had firm financing commitments in hand. As Kern points out, DeBartolo did not have a firm commitment during the period of the discussions in question.

Kern's reliance upon the absence of firm financing to justify a decision not to amend is misplaced, for he is saying in effect that Allied was not required to amend unless and until there was certainty that a merger agreement would be executed. That is not a standard that can be accepted. The degree of probability, not certainty, is to be balanced against the anticipated magnitude of the event.[19] Here it is uncontroverted that the negotiations were being carried on at the highest corporate levels of Allied and EJDC, supplemented by private discussions between the head of Allied and an EJDC control person, and that investment bankers and advisers for both companies were busily engaged in the attempts of EJDC to obtain the necessary financing. The agreements reached during the discussions and the activities and status of the negotiators, when considered in the light of the magnitude of the corporate event under consideration and the potential premium of about $3 per share over existing market value that DeBartolo was willing to offer for Allied stock, are sufficient to dispel any doubt that the negotiations were material.[20]

The language of the Allied initial filing under Item 7(a) of Schedule 14D-9 that the Board had resolved "to continue to explore and investigate" certain types of possible transactions including the acquisition of Allied by another company cannot reasonably be construed to have conveyed to Allied stockholders or to public investors the information that Allied would agree to a merger at a price of $67 if the bidding "white knight" could secure financing.

There can be little doubt that within the meaning of Rule 14d-9 under the Exchange Act the negotiations of September 30 to October 3 resulted in a material change in the information set forth under Item 7(a) of Schedule 14D-9 and were required to be disclosed by the filing of an amendment to that item.

THE AGREEMENT IN PRINCIPLE AND BOARD RESOLUTION

Allied and EJDC reached an agreement in principle in the merger negotiations on October 3, 1986, with EJDC agreeing to offer $67 per share in cash for Allied stock and accepting a break-up fee of $1 per share plus expenses if the deal were not consummated. The only unresolved contingency was whether EJDC could raise the financing needed to carry out the tender offer. As of the morning of October 3 Kern assumed, on the basis of DeBartolo's assurances, that the necessary funds would become available.

The Allied Board meeting convened at 2:00 P.M. on October 3 and Kern acquainted the Board with DeBartolo's merger proposal. The minutes of that meeting reflect that:

> Mr. Kern, at Mr. Macioce's invitation, described the general framework and essential components of a proposal by The Edward J. DeBartolo Corporation ("DeBartolo") which would provide for the execution

---

[19]. See SEC v. Texas Gulf Sulphur, supra, at 849.

[20]. See Basic Inc. v. Levinson, supra, at 987.

of a merger agreement by the Corporation and two affiliates of DeBartolo (upon DeBartolo's securing of necessary financing commitments) calling for the making of an all-cash tender offer at a price of $67 per share for all the common stock of the Corporation, to be followed by a merger providing for an all-cash payment of an equal per share price for all shares not previously tendered. Mr. Kern noted that, as contrasted with the Campeau offer, there would be no conditions, other than standard ones, attached to the DeBartolo offer.

He also noted that the proposed merger agreement would make no provision for a "lock up" or special options or other deterrent to third parties from entering competing bids or to the Corporation from entertaining competing bids; would provide for retention of employee benefit plans and for the cashing out of outstanding options, restricted stock and phantom stock; would make no provision for any arrangement solely for the benefit of the management of the Corporation; would not give management any equity interest in the surviving corporation; would not prevent Allied from giving information to Campeau or anyone else in connection with a competing transaction; would provide for a break-up fee of $1 per share payable to, and reimbursement of expenses incurred by, the DeBartolo organization if the proposed transaction did not come to fruition either as a result of the Corporation's default or of a higher offer by a third party.

The minutes also reflect other presentations relating to efforts to maximize value for Allied stockholders, Macioce's recommendation of acceptance of the DeBartolo offer, and adoption of the following resolution:

> RESOLVED, that, considering this Corporation's business, financial condition and prospects, the terms and conditions of the proposed Agreement and Plan of Merger (the "Merger Agreement") among this Corporation, ASC Acquisition Corp., a Delaware corporation ("ASAC"), and a wholly owned subsidiary of ASAC and of an offer (the "ASAC Offer") by ASAC pursuant to the Merger Agreement for all Shares at a price of $67 per share payable in cash, and other matters, including presentations by this Corporation's legal and financial advisors at this meeting, this Board of Directors conclude, and it does hereby conclude, that the proposed terms of the Merger Agreement and the ASAC Offer are fair to and in the best interests of this Corporation and its stockholders and that, subject to ASAC's obtaining of the financial commitments contemplated by the Merger Agreement (the "Financing Condition"), it approve and recommend, and it does hereby approve and recommend, the ASAC Offer for acceptance by this Corporation's stockholders with the further recommendation that such stockholders tender all their Shares pursuant to the ASAC Offer, and that the proper officers of this Corporation be, and each of them hereby is, authorized to execute and deliver or make such filings, consents, documents or other instruments, including, without limitation, the filing of a Solicitation/Recommendation Statement on Schedule 14D–9 pursuant to the 1934 Act, and any supplements or amendments, in such form as the acting officer may approve, in response to the ASAC

Offer as may be necessary or appropriate to comply with applicable legal requirements, the approval of such acting officer and of this Board of Directors to be evidenced conclusively by such execution....

As of the evening of Friday, October 3, EJDC did not have the necessary financing to consummate a merger agreement and to commence a tender offer for Allied shares, but continued its efforts to obtain that financing during the weekend. Meetings involving EJDC and various banks were held Saturday and Sunday, October 4 and 5, 1986 and by the end of the weekend EJDC had a commitment letter from Citibank and a strong indication that Bankers Trust would act as co-lead in the financing of the tender offer. A final answer from Bankers Trust was to await the outcome of a meeting to be held at seven o'clock in the morning, Monday, October 6. Kern was told on Sunday that prior to the market opening the next day the bank commitments would be firm.

Kern was confident enough about the financing that on Monday, October 6 he requested the New York Stock Exchange to delay the opening of trading in Allied stock because he anticipated that an Allied announcement of the merger agreement with EJDC was in the immediate offing. Later that morning, after Allied learned that the financing had collapsed, trading in Allied stock opened with no news announcement being made by Allied.

Throughout October 8 and 7, 1986 EJDC had further discussions with certain banks which culminated in EJDC receiving financing commitments sufficient to enable it to enter into a merger agreement and commence a tender offer for Allied stock. During the evening of October 7 Allied entered into a merger agreement with two subsidiaries of EJDC and the execution of that agreement was publicly disclosed before the opening of the market on Wednesday, October 8, 1986. On October 8 Allied filed with the Commission Amendment No. 1 to its Schedule 14D-9 which described, pursuant to Item 7, the approval and execution of the merger agreement.

Allied's filing of Amendment No. 1 was days late to effect compliance with Rule 14d-9(b) which required Allied's prompt disclosure of any material change in the information set forth in its Schedule 14D-9. That failure to comply constituted a violation of Section 14(d)(4) of the Exchange Act and Rule 14d 9 thereunder. Kern was well aware of the developments leading up to and including the reaching of the agreement in principle between Allied and EJDC on the price and terms of their contemplated merger and of the passing of the Allied Board Resolution on October 3. Because he assumed sole responsibility for determining when an amendment to Allied's Schedule 14D-9 would be filed, Kern must be found to have caused Allied's violation. It must also be concluded that within the meaning of Section 15(c)(4) of the Exchange Act Kern knew or should have known that he was contributing to Allied's failure to comply.

Kern insists that Allied was under no obligation to file an amendment disclosing the "agreement in principle" or the merger resolution because he did not believe an "agreement in principle" was ever reached, and that by October 6 the Board Resolution of October 3 became a "non-event" when Allied learned that no financing was available. Those contentions are not persuasive.

The term "agreement in principle" does not lend itself to a precise legal definition but for purposes of Schedule 14D–9 the best approach to defining the term is that of the Third Circuit which indicated that "agreement in principle" is reached when would-be merger partners have agreed on the price and structure of the transaction.[21] Here, the top-level officers and representatives of the intended merger partner had reached agreement on the morning of October 3 not only upon price and structure but upon all substantive terms affecting the merger subject to EJDC obtaining financing. Kern steadfastly insists that there was no agreement on anything unless there was financing and that obtaining financing was a condition precedent before the terms agreed upon by the parties could come into existence. His position simply cannot bear up under scrutiny. If accepted, the entire concept of disclosure of an "agreement in principle" in a Schedule 14D–9 filing would be frustrated by the simple expedient of parties reaching agreement on each and every term of a merger and then evading disclosure requirements by subjecting the agreement to some condition precedent purporting to negate the existence of the agreement. The parties could thereby defer disclosure until such time as the "agreement in principle" became a fait accompli merger agreement which would then be disclosed. The latter is what happened here on October 8 when, by the filing of Allied's Amendment No. 1 to its Schedule 14D–1, the first public knowledge regarding the terms of the merger of Allied and EJDC came to light. Those terms which were embodied in the "agreement in principle" constituted material information and a material change in the information initially filed in Allied's Schedule 14D–9. That material change could and should have been disclosed by amendment on October 3 and, regardless of the availability of financing, no later than October 6. The condition precedent to the actual effectuation of a merger between Allied and EJDC could have been readily disclosed, satisfying both Kern's concern about possibly misleading the market and the requirements of the Commission's disclosure regulations.

Similarly, Kern cannot justify Allied's failure to file an amendment on Monday, October 6, disclosing the October 3 Board Resolution. That resolution approved an agreement, with the exception of the amount of the "break-up fee," subject to DeBartolo's obtaining the necessary financing commitments. The offer, with that exception and condition, for all Allied shares at $67 per share payable in cash did not, as suggested by Kern, become a "non-event" or relate to a "dead transac-

---

21. *See Greenfield v. Heublein, Inc.,* 742 F.2d 751, 757 (3d Cir.1984), *cert. denied* 469 U.S. 1215 (1985).

tion" by reason of DeBartolo's inability to find financing over the weekend. Kern knew on October 6 that EJDC was continuing its attempts to raise the necessary funds which the banks finally committed on October 7. Further proof of the viability of the October 3 resolution and its continuing efficacy need go no further than that Kern did not seek and the Allied Board did not adopt a further resolution approving a merger with EJDC before Allied entered into the merger agreement with EJDC's subsidiaries on the evening of October 7. Quite clearly the October 3 Board Resolution was a continuing one which constituted a material change in the information under Item 7 of Allied's Schedule 14D–9 and should have been promptly disclosed by an amendment. Again any concern that Kern might have had about misleading the market could have been dispelled by langauge alerting Allied shareholders and public investors to the problems encountered by EJDC in obtaining the necessary financing.

* * *

It appears from the record that during the relevant period Kern found himself in the center of a complex and fast-changing series of negotiations which required him to exercise his authority to have Allied comply with the disclosure requirements of Rule 14d–9. In the usual relationship of lawyer and client Kern would have had only the responsibility of giving legal advice to Macioce or other officers of Allied who in turn would have made the decisions whether amendments to Allied's Schedule 14D–9 were required. When Kern accepted discretionary authority to make those decisions he also accepted the responsibility the Allied officers had for compliance with Rule 14d–9 and cannot be heard now to complain that his legal judgments are being second-guessed in these proceedings. Were the law otherwise, corporate officials could find a safe harbor from accountability by giving discretionary authority to discharge their responsibility for compliance with disclosure requirements to a lawyer who in turn would be immune from action under Section 15(c)(4) unless his misconduct were so egregious as to also warrant disciplinary action under Rule 2(e) of the Commission's Rules of Practice. Delegation of authority by corporate officers to counsel to comply with Sections 12, 13, 14 or 15(d) of the Exchange Act would be encouraged, with Section 15(c)(4) becoming an ineffectual enforcement tool. Moreover, if a "cause" happens to be a person who is also counsel to the person out of compliance, adoption of Kern's approach to responsibility would create a two-tiered standard for enforcement of Section 15(c)(4), one for the "cause," who happens to be a lawyer, the other for a non-lawyer "cause." Such distinction would be at odds with the statutory language of Section 15(c)(4) which calls to account any person, not just a non-lawyer, who is a "cause."

* * *

If a firm is listed on the New York Stock Exchange, it is subject to the exchange rules on market rumors. A failure to comply with the rules will cause the exchange to stop trading in or even delist the firm's stock.

NEW YORK STOCK EXCHANGE MANUAL SECTIONS
202.01, 202.03, 202.04, and 202.05

* * *

202.01 Internal Handling of Confidential Corporate Matters

Unusual market activity or a substantial price change has on occasion occurred in a company's securities shortly before the announcement of an important corporate action or development. Such incidents are extremely embarrassing and damaging to both the company and the Exchange since the public may quickly conclude that someone acted on the basis of inside information.

Negotiations leading to mergers and acquisitions, stock splits, the making of arrangements preparatory to an exchange or tender offer, changes in dividend rates or earnings, calls for redemption, and new contracts, products, or discoveries are the type of developments where the risk of untimely and inadvertent disclosure of corporate plans are most likely to occur. Frequently, these matters require extensive discussion and study by corporate officials before final decisions can be made. Accordingly, extreme care must be used in order to keep the information on a confidential basis.

Where it is possible to confine formal or informal discussions to a small group of the top management of the company or companies involved, and their individual confidential advisors where adequate security can be maintained, premature public announcement may properly be avoided. In this regard, the market action of a company's securities should be closely watched at a time when consideration is being given to important corporate matters. If unusual market activity should arise, the company should be prepared to make an immediate public announcement of the matter.

At some point it usually becomes necessary to involve other persons to conduct preliminary studies or assist in other preparations for contemplated transactions, e.g., business appraisals, tentative financing arrangements, attitude of large outside holders, availability of major blocks of stock, engineering studies and market analyses and surveys. Experience has shown that maintaining security at this point is virtually impossible. Accordingly, fairness requires that the company make an immediate public announcement as soon as disclosures relating to such important matters are made to outsiders.

The extent of the disclosures will depend upon the stage of discussions, studies, or negotiations. So far as possible, public statements should be definite as to price, ratio, timing and/or any other pertinent information necessary to permit a reasonable evaluation of the matter. As a minimum, they should include those disclosures made to outsiders.

Where an initial announcement cannot be specific or complete, it will need to be supplemented from time to time as more definitive or different terms are discussed or determined.

Corporate employees, as well as directors and officers, should be regularly reminded as a matter of policy that they must not disclose confidential information they may receive in the course of their duties and must not attempt to take advantage of such information themselves.

In view of the importance of this matter and the potential difficulties involved, the Exchange suggests that a periodic review be made by each company of the manner in which confidential information is being handled within its own organization. A reminder notice of the company's policy to those in sensitive areas might also be helpful.

A sound corporate disclosure policy is essential to the maintenance of a fair and orderly securities market. It should minimize the occasions where the Exchange finds it necessary to temporarily halt trading in a security due to information leaks or rumors in connection with significant corporate transactions.

While the procedures are directed primarily at situations involving two or more companies, they are equally applicable to major corporate developments involving a single company.

* * *

202.03 Dealing With Rumors or Unusual Market Activity

The market activity of a company's securities should be closely watched at a time when consideration is being given to significant corporate matters. If rumors or unusual market activity indicate that information on impending developments has leaked out, a frank and explicit announcement is clearly required. If rumors are in fact false or inaccurate, they should be promptly denied or clarified. A statement to the effect that the company knows of no corporate developments to account for the unusual market activity can have a salutary effect. It is obvious that if such a public statement is contemplated, management should be checked prior to any public comment so as to avoid any embarrassment or potential criticism. If rumors are correct or there are developments, an immediate candid statement to the public as to the state of negotiations or of development of corporate plans in the rumored area must be made directly and openly. Such statements are essential despite the business inconvenience which may be caused and even though the matter may not as yet have been presented to the company's Board of Directors for consideration.

The Exchange recommends that its listed companies contact their Exchange representative if they become aware of rumors circulating about their company. Exchange Rule 435 provides that no member, member organization or allied member shall circulate in any manner rumors of a sensational character which might reasonably be expected to affect market conditions on the Exchange. Information provided concerning rumors will be promptly investigated.

202.04 Exchange Market Surveillance

The Exchange maintains a continuous market surveillance program through its Market Surveillance and Evaluation Division. An "on-line" computer system has been developed which monitors the price movement of every listed stock—on a trade-to-trade basis—throughout the trading session. The program is designed to closely review the markets in those securities in which unusual price and volume changes occur or where there is a large unexplained influx of buy or sell orders. If the price movement of a stock exceeds a predetermined guideline, it is immediately "flagged" and review of the situation is immediately undertaken to seek the causes of the exceptional activity. Under these circumstances, the company may be called by its Exchange representative to inquire about any company developments which have not been publicly announced but which could be responsible for unusual market activity. Where the market appears to reflect undisclosed information, the company will normally be requested to make the information public immediately. Occasionally it may be necessary to carry out a review of the trading after the fact, and the Exchange may request such information from the company as may be necessary to complete the inquiry.

The Listing Agreement provides that a company must furnish the Exchange with such information concerning the company as the Exchange may reasonably require.

Special Initial Margin and Capital Requirements—

Occasionally, a listed issue may be placed under special initial margin and capital requirements. Such a restriction in no way reflects upon the quality of corporate management, but, rather indicates a determination by the Floor Officials of the Exchange that the market in the issue has assumed a speculative tenor and has become volatile due to the influence of credit, which, if ignored, may lead to unfair and disorderly trading.

The determination to impose restrictions is based on a careful inspection of the trading for the latest one week period, defined as the previous Friday through subsequent Thursday, matched against various criteria. Other factors, such as the capitalization turnover, the ratio of last year's average weekly volume to the volume for the period considered, arbitrage, stop order bans, short position, earnings and recent corporate news are also reviewed.

The restriction itself is aimed primarily at eliminating the extension of credit to those who buy a security and sell it the same day seeking a short term profit. Such customers must have the full purchase value in the account prior to the entry of an order. Concomitantly, a broader requirement is usually imposed on all other margin customers in that they must put up the full purchase price within five business days, rather than only the percentage required by the Federal Reserve Board. Cash customers, of course, must in all instances put up 100% of the cost in seven days.

202.05 Timely Disclosure of Material News Developments

A listed company is expected to release quickly to the public any news or information which might reasonably be expected to materially affect the market for its securities. This is one of the most important and fundamental purposes of the listing agreement which the company enters into with the Exchange.

A listed company should also act promptly to dispel unfounded rumors which result in unusual market activity or price variations.

* * *

Questions

1. Assume a firm is engaged in preliminary merger negotiations with a second firm and has no legal duty to disclose the negotiations under the federal securities laws. If the firm wants the negotiations to remain confidential, how does it answer New York Stock Exchange inquiries about unusual trading in the firm's stock?

2. What steps ought a firm to take to increase its ability to keep desirable acquisition negotiations confidential for as long as possible?

Subsection c. Projections of Postacquisition Performance

It goes almost without saying that projections are an important part of all acquisitions. Participants negotiating an acquisition are necessarily projecting the postacquisition value of a combined firm and comparing this figure with projections of the value of the constituent firms standing alone. Once a deal is announced, shareholders who must vote or tender their shares or decide whether to sue want to know the projections made by the managers of both constituent firms. Moreover, consider the timing difficulties of any projections. A projection made to enable the chief executive officer to negotiate an agreement in principle will have assumptions about market value that will be stale when the board approves the acquisition agreement, to say nothing of when the proxy solicitation is mailed, when the shareholders vote, and when the deal is closed. If projections are disclosed, must they be continuously updated with the passage of time?

Legal standards aside, managers of the participants are ambivalent about revealing their projections to their shareholders. On the one hand, the managers want to "sell" the deal by using the projections to justify their decision; on the other hand, the managers are uncomfortable with putting themselves on record for criticizing, first, their negotiating skill in garnering a share of the anticipated gains from the acquisition and, second, their acceptance of projections that may turn out to have been wildly optimistic or pessimistic. The result of this conflict is a temptation for managers to establish "two sets of books," contracting for projections designed for circulation to their shareholders and, at the same time, using in-house or unwritten projections to help negotiate the deal.

This schizophrenia has infected the Securities and Exchange Commission as well. The SEC knows that shareholders view the projections as significant but fears that managers will misuse them and shareholders will misunderstand them (that is, overrate their importance). Moreover, the SEC is concerned that managers' misuse of projections would be difficult to police. A projection is only an opinion of future events, usually heavily qualified. When is a guarded opinion intentionally false or misleading? The SEC position on projections is hazy at best and continually changing as well. In general, however, the SEC has created three categories: predictions that are presumptively unlawful if publicized, predictions that can be made if reasonable (read "qualified") and in good faith, and predictions that must be made as part of required filings. The materials on proxy solicitations on pages 134–148 give some indication of how the agency defines these categories; you should review them here.[4]

As a result of the SEC's traditional suspicion of predictions, most lawyers advise their clients not to make predictions unless legally required to do so. Thus much of the litigation on projections in the reported case law in the past ten years deals with when managers ought to have disclosed projections in their public statements and filings. In *Basic Inc. v. Levinson,* supra, the Supreme Court was careful to point out in footnote 9 that its analysis was limited to preliminary merger discussions and it was not "address[ing] . . . any other kinds of contingent or speculative information, such as earnings forecasts or projections." The case law included in this subsection shows that the circuit courts have been all over the map on the matter. The recent reemphasis on proxy contests, however, has led solicitors in 1990 to brave the SEC rules in unprecedented numbers and to offer shareholders sophisticated business and financial analyses in proxy materials. The Corso and Silfen article at the conclusion of this subsection discusses this development.

PANTER v. MARSHALL FIELD & CO.

United States Court of Appeals, Seventh Circuit, 1981.
646 F.2d 271.

* * *

The plaintiffs, shareholders of Marshall Field & Company (Field's) sought to prove that the defendants, the company and its directors, had

---

4. Item 303 of regulation S–K is discussed in these materials. As noted in the previous subsection, this disclosure requirement is not only part of a proxy statement but also incorporated by reference in registration statements (form S–1, for example), annual and quarterly reports (forms 10–Q and 10–K), and tender offer statements (schedule 14D–1).

wrongfully deprived the plaintiffs of an opportunity to dispose of their shares at a substantial premium over market when the defendants successfully fended off a takeover attempt by Carter Hawley Hale (CHH), a national retail chain.

* * *

On December 10, Philip Hawley, the president and chief executive officer of CHH, called Arena and told him that unless Field's directors agreed to begin merger negotiations by the following Monday, December 12, he would make a public exchange proposal. He told Arena that CHH would propose beginning negotiations with an offer that for each share of Field's common stock CHH would exchange a number of its shares roughly equivalent to $36.00. Arena refused to enter such negotiations. Field's shares were trading on the market at around $22.00 per share on the Friday before Hawley delivered his ultimatum.

Arena construed Hawley's call as the beginning of an unfriendly takeover attempt by CHH. He contacted Flom, and arranged a meeting of key Field's directors, counsel, and investment bankers for the next day. At the meeting Arena reported the Kirkland & Ellis opinion. It was agreed to poll the absent directors for authorization to file a suit seeking resolution of the antitrust issues posed by the merger proposal. The group also determined to inform the New York Stock Exchange, and to call an emergency meeting of the Field's board for December 13.

On Monday, December 12, 1977, the CHH letter was received. Arena contacted all Field's directors but one by telephone, and they authorized the filing of the antitrust suit.

The special meeting of the board took place the next day with all members present. Also at the meeting were Field's attorneys and investment bankers. The lawyers, particularly Chaffetz, opined on the lack of legality of the merger, and the investment bankers evaluated the financial aspects of the merger. Field's management then made a report and projected that the company's future performance would be generally favorable. Many of the directors agreed with the investment bankers that a share of common stock would bring more than $36.00 in a sale of control of the company. After consideration of the above factors the directors voted unanimously to reject the proposal because in their judgment the merger as proposed would be "illegal, inadequate, and not in the best interests of Marshall Field & Company, its stockholders and the communities which it serves."

The directors also authorized issuance of a press release conveying their decision. On December 14, Field's issued the press release, which indicated that Field's directors and management had faith in the momentum of the company, and that "it would be in the best interests of our stockholders, customers and employees for us to take advantage of this momentum and continue to implement our growth plans as an independent company." Field's shares traded in the market in a range of $28.00 to $32.00 that day, and continued in approximately that range until January 31, 1978.

On December 20, 1977, Arena addressed a letter to Field's stockholders in which he spoke optimistically of the future and reviewed Field's immediate past performance. He pointed out that Field's had disposed of unprofitable ventures, and that "for the nine months ended October 31, income before ventures and taxes was up 24.4% and consolidated net income was up 13%." He referred to the CHH proposal for negotiation and to the advice of antitrust counsel "that a CHH–Marshall Field & Company merger would clearly violate the United States antitrust laws," and concluded that "[y]our Board of Directors believes the maximum benefits for Marshall Field & Company and its stockholders, employees, customers and the communities it serves will result from continuing to develop as an independent, publicly-owned Company."

On January 5, 1978, Field's issued another press release, announcing that it had amended its antitrust suit against CHH to include allegations of federal securities law violations. The release reiterated Field's confidence in its future, and stated "our management is continuing the implementation of our longstanding programs to further build and develop the business of Marshall Field & Company."

On January 19, 1978, Field's directors had their regular meeting. Two expansion proposals were on the agenda: one that the company expand into the Galleria, a Houston shopping mall where a planned Bonwit Teller store had failed to materialize, creating an attractive opening; the other that the company acquire a group of five Liberty House stores in the Pacific Northwest. The Galleria already contained a CHH Neiman–Marcus store. The board resolved to pursue both expansion programs. Field's executives and directors had long considered expansion into these two areas, and the company's interest in such expansion was well known to investment analysts in the department store field.

On February 1, CHH announced its intention to make an exchange offer of $42.00 in a combination of cash and CHH stock for each share of Field's stock tendered. The offer was conditioned on the fulfillment or non-occurrence of some twenty conditions. Appropriate documents for announcement of a tender offer were filed with the SEC. The market price of Field's stock rose to $34.00 per share, and stayed in the $30.00 to $34.00 range until February 22, 1978.

A special meeting of the Field's board was convened the next day to consider the new offer. The legal implications of the CHH filing were explained to the board by counsel, and Chaffetz brought the group up to date on the antitrust suit. There was no discussion of the adequacy of the offer in light of the board's determination that the proposed combination would clearly be illegal. The board also determined to go ahead with the Galleria plan, and approved the signing of a letter of agreement to enter the mall.

After the meeting Field's issued another press release reaffirming its opposition to the proposed merger. It concluded with a statement by Arena that "I assumed my position with Marshall Field & Company with the understanding that I would devote myself to making Marshall Field & Company a truly national retail business organization. We ... are determined not to be deterred from this course. Our recently announced agreement to acquire five Liberty House Stores in Tacoma, Washington and Portland, Oregon was one step in our program."

On February 8, another Field's press release announced that Field's had concluded negotiations for a department store to be opened in the Galleria. On February 22, CHH announced that it was withdrawing its proposed tender offer before it became effective, because "the expansion program announced by Marshall Field since February 1st has created sufficient doubt about Marshall Field's earning potential to make the offer no longer in the best interests of Carter Hawley Hale's shareholders." None of the events that conditioned CHH's tender offer had occurred since February 1. Following the announcement, the market price of Field's shares dropped to $19.00, lower than it had been on December 9, the last trading day prior to CHH's first proposed offer.

* * *

The plaintiffs also claim they were deceived by the "rosy" projections for future growth expressed by Field's management. Specifically they allege misrepresentations in press releases of December 14 and 15, 1977, which recounted how "confident about the future of the company" management was, and that momentum within the company was excellent. The plaintiffs allege that these misrepresentations culminated in a public letter dated December 20, 1977.[5] The plaintiffs claim that this letter, which cited a thirteen percent increase in consolidated net income before ventures and taxes, was fatally misleading in that it failed to disclose that the defendants' "five-year plan," a projective

---

5. The relevant portions of that letter stated:

A number of programs to improve our profitability and expand our profit base were initiated before I came here, and others have been started since I arrived. These include:

—Modernization and expansion of many of our stores

—Revitalization of our merchandising programs

—Analysis of further opportunities in new store locations and new market areas

—Disposition of unprofitable interests in real estate and hotel ventures

Even at this early date, these programs are having positive effect. For example, we have disposed of most of our interest in The Ritz–Carlton hotel. This has eliminated a significant drain on our earnings. The revitalized merchandising programs are generating increased sales.

—For the nine months ended October 31, income before ventures and taxes was up 24.4% and consolidated net income was up 13%.

—Sales showed a gain of 9.4%, virtually all from comparable stores open both years.

We limit our discussion to whether omission of the projections made the letter misleading because we find that no rational juror could find it deceptive on its face. The sentences immediately preceding those cited by the plaintiffs make it absolutely clear that Field's earnings would be adversely affected in that fiscal year by the unprofitable ventures. The thrust of the letter is that there is light at the end of the earnings tunnel, not that this will be a banner year for Field's earnings.

document generated for internal management use only, showed at that time an anticipated decline of seven percent in consolidated net income for the year.

While it is true that there is no duty upon management or directors to disclose financial projections, . . . it is also axiomatic that once a company undertakes partial disclosure of such information there is a duty to make the full disclosure of known facts necessary to avoid making such statements misleading.

* * *

However, projections, estimates, and other information must be reasonably certain before management may release them to the public.

* * *

The earnings projections the plaintiffs allege should have been disclosed were contained in a five-year plan which had been hastily updated only the very day of the board meeting to consider the CHH first proposal. It was one of a series of five-year plans which were continually updated and used internally by Field's management to explore planning and development. That the projections it contained were highly tentative seems the compelling inference from the evidence that Field's projections varied from those of its own investment bankers, were considered merely "valid to use for the present purpose," of evaluating the Carter Hawley offer, and that they ended up varying substantially from Field's performance as revealed by the actual year-end earnings which finally came in a full twenty-five percent down from the prior year. We therefore find that because the projections of the five-year plan were tentative estimates prepared for the enlightenment of management with no expectation that they be made public, there was no duty to reveal them. Indeed, in light of the degree by which they failed to project the extent of the decline in earnings, release of the seven percent estimate might have subjected the defendants to securities law liability.

* * *

CUDAHY, CIRCUIT JUDGE, concurring in part and dissenting in part:

* * *

Without attempting to analyze all the statements alleged in this case to be false or misleading, I address only the letter from Field's president to its shareholders dated December 20, 1977. In this letter the president reported consolidated net earnings for nine months ended October 21 to be up 13% without adverting in any way to his expectation (evidenced in a five-year plan just submitted to the Board) that consolidated net earnings for the year would decline by 6½%. Thus it was fully expected that there would be a *drop* in annual earnings from $2.01 to $1.86 per share. In fact, earnings for the year turned out to be $1.76 (down 25%). Having disseminated glowing generalities about the future, citing interim financial figures, defendants had the duty to disclose the anticipated, though unpleasant, immediate expectations of management. * * * The majority finds this very questionable communication to be so far from deceptive or misleading as not to require its submission to the jury.

By way of defending its conclusion, the majority argues that it was clear from the context of the letter that unprofitable ventures would turn the year-to-year comparison distinctly unfavorable. I think it just as rational to interpret the letter as saying that, but for the sour undertakings, the nine-month numbers would be even better. The majority also defends its conclusions by arguing that, since the internal estimates were not precise, it was better to leave the public with an upbeat nine-month impression than to suggest that the full year would be down, although no one knew exactly how much. But this defense ignores the fact that management's pitch to the shareholders was bolstered by three-quarter figures which the managers then believed to be unrepresentative of the full year. Whatever may have been management's (perhaps perennial) hope that "there [was] light at the end of the earnings' tunnel" (maj. op. *ante* at 291–292, note 5), this misleading use of the numbers created a serious question for the jury.

* * *

WALKER v. ACTION INDUSTRIES, INC.

United States Court of Appeals, Fourth Circuit, 1986.
802 F.2d 703, cert. denied 479 U.S. 1065, 107 S.Ct. 952, 93 L.Ed.2d 1000 (1987).

Ervin, Circuit Judge:

* * *

On July 16, 1982, Action made a tender offer to purchase 15% of its common stock at $4.00 per share until August 6. In connection with the tender offer, Action issued a tender offer statement pursuant to rule 13e–4, which contained financial information on the corporation. Action's fiscal year runs from July through June. The tender offer statement disclosed audited financial statements for fiscal years 1979, 1980 and 1981. These figures revealed a net loss of $2,306,900 in fiscal 1979, net earnings of $372,900 in fiscal 1980, and net earnings of $731,200 in fiscal 1981. Because the 1982 fiscal year had just ended, audited financial statements for that year were not available. Action did disclose, however, unaudited, interim financial statements for fiscal 1982 through March 27, 1982, the end of Action's third fiscal quarter. These figures indicated a net loss of $4,014,900 as compared with net earnings of $1,037,600 for the same period in the previous year. In § 14B of the tender offer statement, Action also made disclosures entitled "Events Subsequent to March 27, 1982," which stated in part:

> The Company's fiscal year ended on June 26, 1982. Although financial statements have not yet been prepared or audited, the Company expects results from continuing operations to reflect a sales increase compared with the prior year. However, earnings from continuing

operations are estimated to be somewhat lower than last year as a result of lower gross margins on sales and higher operating expenses.

In addition to financial statements, Action regularly prepared a number of other financial reports internally. On a weekly basis, Action prepared "work projections," which recorded actual orders and identified them as "firm" or "anticipated," depending on their likelihood of cancellation. Approximately monthly, Action prepared "gross sales forecasts." These reports projected monthly and quarterly sales based on the orders reflected in the weekly work projections. Action also tracked actual financial results in weekly "flash sales reports," which showed sales for the current week, month-to-date sales and quarter-to-date sales.

As early as May 1982, Action's internal financial reports indicated substantial increases in actual orders and projected sales for the first quarter of fiscal 1983 over the same period for fiscal 1982. As the July 16 tender offer grew nearer, and the first quarter of fiscal 1983 began, subsequent internal reports indicated even more substantial increases in actual orders and projected sales, as well as increases in actual sales over the prior year. Action, however, did not disclose the projected increases in sales or the increases in actual orders and sales in the tender offer statement, which was issued approximately twenty days into its first quarter of fiscal 1983.

At the time of the tender offer, Walker owned 2000 shares of Action which he had purchased in April 1982, at $3.25 per share. Walker learned of the July 16 tender offer from his broker, and based on that information, anticipated improved prospects for the company. Then, on July 21, without actually having received or read the tender offer statement, Walker purchased an additional 1500 shares of Action at $4.00 per share. Subsequently, Walker received and read the tender offer statement. The tender offer ended on August 6 without Walker having tendered or sold any of his shares.

On August 18, 1982, Action issued a press release regarding its year-end financial results for fiscal 1982. The press release and Action's audited financial statements, on which the press release was based, essentially confirmed the statements made in § 14B of the tender offer statement regarding the company's financial performance in fiscal 1982; sales were up but earnings were down. Between the time of the tender offer and the press release, Action's internal financial reports continued to indicate substantial increases in projected sales, and actual orders and sales, for the company's first quarter of fiscal 1983 and thereafter. As with the tender offer statement, however, Action refrained from disclosing such information in the press release. Walker read the press release and concluded that the company's prospects were not favorable. On September 21, he sold all of his Action shares on the open market at approximately $5.25 per share.

Action's stock traded as high as $7\frac{1}{8}$ per share on October 21. Then on October 28, Action issued a press release revealing its financial results for the first quarter of fiscal 1983 ending September 25, 1982. The release and accompanying unaudited, interim financial statements showed a 75% increase in sales, and net earnings of $1,467,600 compared with a net loss of $412,500, for the same period in the previous year. The following day, on October 29, Action stock traded as high as 9⅞. By November 12, the stock reached 15¾ per share.

Subsequently, Walker brought suit against Action and three of its directors. Walker pursued a claim under rule 10b–5 alleging that defendants had a duty to disclose financial projections and actual orders and sales for fiscal 1983 in the tender offer statement and the August 18 press release. Defendants' failure to make such disclosures, alleged Walker, constituted omissions of material facts in violation of rule 10b–5. * * * In this case, it is undisputed that defendants had a general duty to speak or disclose in connection with the tender offer and subsequent press release. Thus, Walker's claim presented a question of whether defendants had breached their duty to disclose, and thus violated rule 10b–5, through material omissions in the August 18 press release.

* * *

We turn first to Walker's argument that the district court should have instructed the jury that Action had a duty to disclose its financial projections. Historically, the Securities Exchange Commission (SEC) has discouraged the disclosure of financial projections and other "soft" information such as asset appraisals in proxy statements, tender offers and other disclosure documents on the ground that they were likely to mislead investors. * * * For example, in 1956 the SEC added a note to rule 14a–9 which listed "predictions as to specific future market values, earnings or dividends" as "examples of what, depending upon particular facts and circumstances, may be misleading" in proxy statements. SEC Sec.Exch.Act Rel. No. 5276 (Jan. 30, 1956), 21 Fed.Reg. 578 (1966).

The traditional SEC position, however, encountered substantial criticism in the early 1970s. * * * Then, in 1976, the SEC deleted earnings projections in the 14a–9 note from the list of potentially misleading disclosures. * * * In 1978, the SEC also adopted rule 175, which provides a "safe harbor" for "forward-looking statements" made in good faith. * * * Forward-looking statements are defined to include "a statement containing a projection of revenues, income (loss), earnings (loss) per share, capital expenditures, dividends, capital structure or other financial items." 17 C.F.R. § 230.175(1). Rule 175, however, does not require the disclosure of financial projections. * * * Thus, the SEC currently allows or permits disclosure of financial projections on a voluntary basis.

The circuits which have addressed whether there is a duty to disclose financial projections, and others of information such as asset appraisals, have reached varying results. These can be described as falling into three groups. First, the Seventh Circuit would appear to take the position that there is no duty to disclose financial projections.

See Panter v. Marshall Field & Co., 646 F.2d 271, 292 (7th Cir.) (no duty to disclose financial projections; rule 10b–5 and § 14(e) claim for material omissions in press release designed to thwart exchange offer by another company), *cert. denied*, 454 U.S. 1092, 102 S.Ct. 658, 70 L.Ed.2d 631 (1981). Although the Second Circuit has not considered whether there is a duty to disclose financial projections, it has declined to recognize a duty to disclose asset appraisals. *See Gerstle v. Gamble-Skogmo, Inc.*, 478 F.2d at 1294 (rule 14a–9 claim for material omissions in proxy statement). Thus, it appears that the Second Circuit also would not impose a duty to disclose financial projections.

* * *

Second, the Third Circuit has held that "[c]ourts should ascertain the duty to disclose asset valuations and other soft information on a case by case basis." *Flynn v. Bass Brothers Enterprises, Inc.*, 744 F.2d 978, 988 (3d Cir.1984) (rule 10b–5 and § 14(e) claim for material omissions in tender offer statement). ...

Whether there is duty to disclose soft information in a given case depends on a number of factors announced by the *Flynn* court.[9] In *Flynn*, however, the court declined to apply its newly announced standard retroactively.

Moreover, applying pre-*Flynn* standards, it found no duty to disclose the soft information at issue in that case.

A third approach has been adopted by the Sixth Circuit. It has ruled that there is no duty to disclose financial projections unless they are "substantially certain." *See Starkman v. Marathon Oil Company*, 772 F.2d at 241–42 (rule 10b–5 claim for material omissions in press release designed to thwart tender offer); *James v. Gerber Products Co.*, 587 F.2d 324, 327 (6th Cir.1978) (rule 10b–5 claim for failure to disclose in connection with shareholder's sale of stock back to issuing company); ... While the Sixth Circuit's "substantially certain" test appears similar to the "case by case" approach announced by the Third Circuit in *Flynn*, the Sixth Circuit has rejected *Flynn* as, among other things, "uncertain and unpredictable." *Starkman*, 772 F.2d at 242. It should also be noted that the Sixth Circuit in applying its "substantially certain" test, has yet to impose a duty to disclose financial projections in any case.

The Ninth Circuit appears properly categorized with the Sixth. In *Vaughn v. Teledyne, Inc.*, the Ninth Circuit found no duty to disclose financial projections where there was "no evidence ... that the estimates were made with ... reasonable certainty." 628 F.2d 1214, 1221

9. The factors a court must consider in making such a determination are: the facts upon which the information is based; the qualifications of those who prepared or compiled it; the purpose for which the information was originally intended; its relevance to the stockholders' impending decision; the degree of subjectivity or bias reflected in its preparation; the degree to which the information is unique; and the availability to the investor of other more reliable sources of information.

(9th Cir.1980) (rule 10b–5 and § 14(e) claim for material omissions in tender offer statement).

* * *

* * * We conclude that under the circumstances of this case Action had no duty to disclose its financial projections in the August 18 press release, for the reasons that follow.[11]

First, we note that Action made disclosures regarding its tender offer pursuant to rule 13e–4, which governs disclosures in the context of a corporation's tender offer for its own stock. Rule 13e–4 and its accompanying schedule 13E–4, 17 C.F.R. § 240.13e–101 (1985), require that certain information be disclosed. That information includes audited financial statements for the company's two most recent fiscal years and unaudited financial statements for the company's most recent quarter. *See id.* at Item 7(1) and (2). There is no requirement under these regulations that financial projections be disclosed. Thus, the SEC has declined to impose expressly a duty to disclose such information in the context of 13e–4 tender offer statements. It follows that there was a similar absence of any express duty to disclose financial projections in the subsequent press release.

Second, the SEC has not imposed a duty to disclose financial projections in disclosure documents generally. As already noted, financial projections were discouraged by the SEC for approximately twenty years. Now, such disclosures are allowed or permitted. The transition from nondisclosure to permissive disclosure was heralded primarily by the SEC's modification of its regulations such as the adoption of voluntary disclosure provisions in rule 175. We perceive the current SEC regulatory environment to be an experimental stage regarding financial projection disclosures. Respecting these evolutionary processes, we believe that a further transition, from permissive disclosure to required disclosure, should be occasioned by congressional or SEC adoption of more stringent disclosure requirements for financial projections, rather than by the courts.

Third, we are reluctant to recognize a duty to disclose financial projections in this case because of their uncertainty and their potential to mislead investors. Walker would have us impose a duty on Action to disclose its "gross sales forecasts," which projected monthly and quarterly sales. On May 20, 1982, the projections indicated a 30% increase in sales, based on firm orders, for the first quarter of fiscal 1983 compared with the previous year's first quarter. Projections dated June 17 indicated a 95% increase. On July 15 they indicated a 109% increase and on August 6, 129%. Clearly, the projections were changing constantly, with each new one rendering the last incorrect. A disclosure of the May or June projections would have grossly understated subsequent projections. Furthermore, the projections failed to reflect accurately actual sales. As the first quarter of fiscal 1983 pro-

11. We do not specifically adopt any of the various positions held by the other circuits regarding whether a duty exists to disclose financial projections.

gressed, Action's "flash sales reports" showed a quarter-to-date sales increase over the first quarter of fiscal 1982 of 166% on July 3. By July 17, that figure had dropped precipitously to 42%, but by August 7 it had jumped to 134%. Most importantly, the quarter ended with an actual sales increase of 75% compared with over 129% projected. Net income, however, increased tenfold, a performance hardly forewarned by the projections. Because of the evident uncertainty and misleading nature of the projections, we deem it unwise to require their disclosure. Indeed, in light of the disparity between actual and projected sales, we wonder whether Walker also would have sued had the disclosures been made, alleging that the projections were overly optimistic. *See Panter,* 646 F.2d at 291 (rule 10b–5 and § 14(e) claim for material omissions in press release which allegedly projected the company's prospects as too "rosy.")

Finally, we believe that the projection disclosures sought by Walker are impractical. Action made its "gross sales forecasts" at least monthly and sometimes more frequently. Also, as described above, each forecast was substantially different. Because of the frequency and volatility of these projections, the imposition of a duty to disclose them would have required virtually constant statements by Action in order not to mislead investors. Under these circumstances, we deem the projection disclosures urged by Walker to be impractical, if not unreasonable.

For all of these reasons, we conclude that defendants did not have a duty to disclose Action's financial projections.[12] * * * We also note that our holding is not intended to discourage disclosures of financial projections. Indeed, we fully support voluntary disclosure as contemplated by rule 175. Of course, it would appear prudent to release only those projections that are reasonably certain. ... Furthermore, if a company undertakes projection disclosures, it must make the full disclosures necessary to avoid making the statements misleading.

* * *

ISQUITH v. MIDDLE SOUTH UTILITIES, INC.

United States Court of Appeals, Fifth Circuit, 1988.
847 F.2d 186, cert. denied 488 U.S. 926, 109 S.Ct. 310, 102 L.Ed.2d 329 (1988).

KING, CIRCUIT JUDGE:

* * *

Courts in the past have consistently recognized that a defendant does not place itself beyond the reach of the securities laws merely by disclosing information that is predictive in nature. For example, when necessary, courts have readily conceded that predictions may be regarded as "facts" within the meaning of the anti-fraud provisions of the

---

12. Stated another way, as a matter of law, defendants' failure to disclose the financial projections was not an omission of material facts, which were necessary under the circumstances to make the statements made not misleading.

securities laws. Most often, whether liability is imposed depends on whether the predictive statement was "false" when it was made. The answer to this inquiry, however, does not turn on whether the prediction in fact proved to be wrong; instead, falsity is determined by examining the nature of the prediction—with the emphasis on whether the prediction suggested reliability, bespoke caution, was made in good faith, or had a sound factual or historical basis.[12] Because a clear body of law exists which recognizes those circumstances where liability can be imposed under the securities laws for disclosed predictions, the district court obviously erred in concluding that disclosed predictions are never actionable.

Undisclosed predictions, however, present a different problem. Until the early 1970's, the SEC prohibited companies from including most predictive information in the documents they filed with the SEC. * * * Courts generally recognized this policy and followed the SEC's lead by holding that the failure to disclose predictive information was not actionable under the securities laws. * * * In 1973, however, the SEC determined that "changes in its present policies with regard to the use of projections would assist in the protection of investors and would be in the public interest." Securities Act Release No. 5362 at 82,667. As the SEC explained: "Persons invest with the future in mind and the market value of a security reflects the judgments of investors about the future economic performance of the issuer. Thus projections are sought by all investors, whether institutional or individual." *Id.* In 1978, after taking a series of steps to implement this change of policy, the SEC issued a statement encouraging, although not requiring, disclo-

---

12. In 1979, the SEC acknowledged—by adopting safe harbor rules under both the 1933 Act and the 1934 Act—that a defendant can, under certain situations, be subject to liability under both Acts for including predictions in its SEC filings. * * * Essentially, the safe harbor rules the SEC adopted permit certain companies to make "forward-looking statements" in the documents they file with the SEC without incurring liability under the antifraud provisions of the securities laws. These rules specifically limit the definition of a "forward-looking statement" to:

(1) A statement containing a projection of revenues, income (loss), earnings (loss) per share, capital expenditures, dividends, capital structure or other financial items;

(2) A statement of management's plans and objectives for future operations;

(3) A statement of future economic performance contained in management's discussion and analysis of financial condition and results of operations included pursuant to Item 303 of Regulation S–K (§ 229.303 of this chapter) or Item 9 of Form 20–F or

(4) Disclosed statements of the assumptions underlying or relating to any of the statements described in paragraphs [(1), (2), and (3) above].

17 C.F.R. § 230.175(c) (1987); 17 C.F.R. § 240.3b–6(c) (1987). The safe harbor rules do not, however, offer protection for all forward-looking statements which fall within these four categories; forward-looking statements which are shown to have been "made or reaffirmed without a reasonable basis" or which were "disclosed other than in good faith" are still subject to the antifraud provisions. *Id.* As one author has noted, the SEC's standard for liability is "based essentially on the standard recognized in judicial decisions" prior to the SEC's adoption of these rules. * * * This standard for determining when a statement is false, according to the same author, makes sense because "the only truly factual elements involved in a projection are the implicit representations that the statements are made in good faith and with a reasonable basis."

sures of management projections both in filings with the SEC and in general. * * * The SEC's policy of encouraging the disclosure of projections is presently set forth in, among other places, its instructions for complying with Regulation S–K, see 17 C.F.R. ¶ 229.10(b) (1987), and certain safe harbor rules which it adopted in 1979, see supra note 12.[13]

Because of the SEC's change in policy, courts have begun to re-examine the position that a company's decision not to disclose predictive information is always immune from scrutiny under the securities laws. As a result of these re-examinations, courts have adopted a variety of approaches to dealing with the problem of undisclosed predictions. These approaches range from continuing a prior practice of never requiring that predictive information be disclosed to formulating new standards which recognize that sometimes disclosure will be required; the approaches vary significantly among the circuits and sometimes within a circuit depending on the type of predictive information at issue.

* * *

We make no attempt today either to examine in detail the several approaches which the various circuits have endorsed or to determine

---

13. Just as the SEC decided not to require disclosure of forward-looking statements, it also decided not to specifically require disclosure of the assumptions that underlie the forward-looking statements. See Safe Harbor Rule for Projections, Securities Act Release No. 6084, [1979 Transfer Binder] Fed.Sec.L.Rep. (CCH) ¶ 82,117 at 81,942 (July 5, 1979). In making the decision, however, the SEC re-emphasized its position on the significance of assumption disclosure:

> Under certain circumstances the disclosure of underlying assumptions may be material to an understanding of the projected results. The Commission also believes that the key assumptions underlying a forward looking statement are of such significance that their disclosure may be necessary in order for such statements to meet the reasonable basis and good faith standards embodied in the rule. Because of the potential importance of assumptions to investor understanding and in order to encourage their disclosure, the rule as adopted indicates specifically that disclosed assumptions also are within its scope.

Id. The SEC took a different position, however, with respect to the duty to correct information which has been previously disclosed:

> [T]he Commission remind[s] issuers of their responsibility to make full and prompt disclosure of material facts, both favorable and unfavorable, where management knows or has reason to know that its earlier statements no longer have a reasonable basis. With respect to forward-looking statements of material facts made in relation to specific transactions or events (such as proxy solicitations, tender offers, and purchases and sales of securities), there is an obligation to correct such statements prior to consummation of the transaction where they become false or misleading by reason of subsequent events which render material assumptions underlying such statements invalid. Similarly, there is a duty to correct where it is discovered prior to consummation of a transaction, that the underlying assumptions were false or misleading from the outset.

> Moreover, the Commission believes that, depending on the circumstances, there is a duty to correct statements made in any filing, whether or not the filing is related to a specified transaction or event, if the statements either have become inaccurate by virtue of subsequent events, or are later discovered to have been false and misleading from the outset, and the issuer knows or should know that persons are continuing to rely on all or any material portion of the statements.

> This duty will vary according to the facts and circumstances of individual cases.

Id. at 82,943.

when, or even if, predictive information must be disclosed in our circuit. Instead, we use these decisions from other circuits to make a point: that in each case, regardless of the particular approach the court finally followed, each court made its decision by recognizing the statutory policy interests both in requiring and not requiring disclosure, by focusing on the nature of the particular predictive information whose lack of disclosure was questioned, and by determining what the specific facts surrounding that predictive information indicated about the information's importance, reliability, or impact on the potential investor. What is required on remand, therefore, is the same kind of careful, sensitive inquiry in determining whether those predictions plaintiffs challenge that Middle South did make and those predictions plaintiffs challenge that Middle South did not make are actionable under either section 11 of the 1933 Act or Rule 10b–5. Such an inquiry is all the more appropriate in this case because of the central role that predictions have played in the history of Middle South.[15]

IN RE GENENTECH, INC.
Court of Chancery of Delaware, 1990.
Fed.Sec.L.Rptr. (CCH) ¶ 95,317 (June 6, 1990).

Before me is a motion, filed by purported stockholders of Genentech, Inc. ("Genentech" or the "company"), to preliminarily enjoin Genentech and its officers and directors, from allowing Genentech shareholders to vote on a transaction transferring control of the company from the public to Roche Holdings, Inc., a wholly-owned Delaware subsidiary of Roche Holdings, Ltd. (collectively "Roche") until disclosure of certain allegedly material information is made to the shareholders.

* * *

Genentech is a biotechnology company that employs recombinant DNA technology to develop, manufacture and market pharmaceutical products for use in human beings. Genentech was founded in 1976 by Robert A. Swanson and Dr. Herbert Boyer. Mr. Swanson and Dr. Boyer are each substantial stockholders of the company and serve as directors.

* * *

Genentech characterizes itself as an unusual company due to its ability and willingness to commit resources to long-term research and development. The company claims to be more like a "research insti-

---

15. In taking the position that a company's failure to disclose predictions is not actionable, the district court said it was afraid that negative predictions could become "self-fulfilling prophec[ies]." We are not convinced that such a fear is enough, by itself, to justify the nondisclosure, under all circumstances, of all predictions which portray companies in a negative light. Both section 11 of the 1933 Act and Rule 10b–5 are concerned with ensuring that material information has been properly disclosed to the investor. The district court should have concerned itself, therefore, with whether the information sought was material—not simply with whether that information was negative or positive, or would help or hurt Middle South.

tute" than an industrial firm because it fosters an environment in which scientific values are paramount. During the first six months of 1989, the company spent approximately 42% of its revenues on research and development. In furtherance of its goals, Genentech has attracted a high caliber group of research scientists. Indeed, the company's employees, as a whole, are highly educated—90% have a college degree and 50% have a postgraduate degree.

The challenged transaction stems from an analysis, conducted during the summer of 1989 by Genentech's management and board, of the status and prospects of the company's business and of the biotechnology and pharmaceutical industries. This analysis led the board to authorize a search for a strategic alliance between Genentech and another pharmaceutical company.

One of the board's primary considerations in its analysis was the company's ability to generate revenues and finance new product developments as an independent company. Currently, Genentech markets only two products—Activase (a clotting drug) and Protropin (a human growth hormone)—that generate revenue. These products, while highly successful in the past, have an uncertain future because they are both mature products. In addition, at the time of the analysis, Protropin's orphan drug status was threatened by legislative developments, and Activase's future sales potentially could have been negatively affected by then unknown results of a major clinical trial.

Genentech also had (and has) a large number of potential new products in different stages of its research and development "pipeline." These drugs include: CD4 and CD4–IgG (an AID's treatment), Actimmune (a dermatitis and infection treatment), DNASE (to treat cystic fibrosis) and Relaxin (a drug to help reduce Caesarean sections). The record indicates that each of these potential products involve significant uncertainty as to success and require substantial additional investment before they can be marketed. In other words, new revenue from these products, assuming successful development, will take several years and consume a great deal of money. Defendants assert that the average time for development of a new drug is at least seven-to-eight years with development costs of approximately $100 million to $150 million for each product. During this time Genentech was spending over 40% of its total product sales and license revenues on research and development. Defendants maintain that this rate of investment in R & D was not only the highest in the pharmaceutical industry, but fully three-to-four times the 10%–12% rate that is typical for such companies.

These factors put the company in a difficult position in regard to financing new product development as an independent company, with internally generated financial resources. One of the board's central concerns was that unless Genentech was able to introduce the products currently under development, on schedule, the company's earnings would be reduced to unacceptably low levels resulting in a substantially lower market price for Genentech's stock.

* * *

These factors lead the board to conclude that some form of strategic alliance with another pharmaceutical company was the best means for Genentech to obtain necessary long-term capital for its research and development and to meet future competitive challenges. A strategic alliance would help assure the survival of its unique science-driven culture. Genentech's financial advisors—Shearson Lehman Hutton, Inc. ("Shearson") and Wasserstein Perella—pursued, at the board's direction, such a transaction. Defendants maintain that Shearson and Wasserstein Perella were not limited to developing a specific type or form of transaction, but were given the mandate to obtain the best value for the shareholders.

* * *

In late December and in January, Roche and Genentech, through Shearson, developed the presently challenged proposal in which Roche will acquire the publicly held Genentech shares and purchase an additional 22 million shares (treasury stock) directly from Genentech—leaving Roche with a 60% equity interest in Genentech—and an option to obtain the remaining public equity. As part of this proposal, Roche allegedly insisted that it be able to cause redemption of the minority interest as a condition to its purchase of a 60% interest. Redemption prices were agreed to as part of the proposal. These agreed upon redemption prices effectively place a cap on the value of publicly held stock, for a set period of time. Defendants maintain that they tried to structure the proposal so that Genentech shareholders would receive "contingent value rights" ("CVR") which would not limit the upper end of the future market price of the stock. CVRs would, as I understand it, require Roche to pay specified amounts if the market price did not achieve certain price levels over a given time period. In effect public shareholders would be assured a minimum return (a floor) on the equity retained by them. Roche apparently insisted, through arm's-length negotiations, upon setting the redemption prices; it rejected outright the CVR concept.

The public shareholders, upon consummation of the transaction, are to receive $18 in cash and a one-half share of the new Genentech redeemable common stock.[4] Roche will provide the $1.6 billion in cash to be received by Genentech stockholders. The new redeemable common stock, upon approval by Genentech's shareholders, will be issued by Genentech. The stock will be redeemable, at the election of Roche, until June 30, 1995, at redemption prices increasing from $38 to $60 per share.[5] Roche can only cause the redemption of all the outstanding

---

4. It is uncontested that this new redeemable common stock is a unique form of equity security that has never before been introduced.

5. The redemption price increase from $38 per share before December 31, 1990, in

shares at the stipulated price. Roche will purchase additional equity in the form of newly issued stock for $491.5 million in cash. Genentech will continue to be a public company (with Roche as a 60% owner) listed on the New York Stock Exchange and managed by a 13-person board on which Roche will be limited (for five years) to two representatives.

On February 1–2, 1990, Genentech's board reviewed and approved the above described merger proposal. Mr. Frank of Shearson made the presentation on behalf of both financial advisors which included a binder with some 110 pages of financial analyses based on share price analyses, discounted cash flow analyses, purchase price ratio analyses and comparable company valuations. The figures on which these analyses were based were the long range plan projections—which were given to Roche and are contained in the proxy statement. As the proxy statement explains, these projections assume that all of the potential products in Genentech's product pipeline are commercially feasible, effective, safe and approved on schedule. These projections also reflect a 50% across-the-board discount that senior management and Genentech's financial advisors deemed appropriate in view of the risks inherent in all of the company's future product development. While the proxy statement does not list or describe the individual products in Genentech's pipeline, the products and their respective stages in the pipeline are listed in Genentech's annual statement that was mailed with the proxy statement.

It is uncontested that the proposed transaction was discussed in great detail. While the majority of these discussions are not presently at issue, a statement by Mr. Frank in response to a director's question has been made an issue by plaintiffs. It appears that in answer to a question about the expected market value of the new redeemable common stock, Mr. Frank expressed his view that the redeemable stock might have a trading price in the range of $23–$24 immediately following the merger, but that there could be no assurance of the reliability of this view.

Although, the proposed transaction was announced on February 2, 1990, no third party has expressed formal or informal interest in pursuing or discussing any alternative transaction with Genentech since the announcement. The merger agreement contains a provision limiting Genentech's ability to solicit alternative offers, but does not prevent it from entertaining an offer if one is made. Genentech's stock traded at $22 before the Roche agreement and now trades at around $26. The proxy statement [6] that is the subject of this motion was disseminated on or about May 2, 1990.

* * *

fixed increments of $1 per quarter to June 30, 1991. Thereafter, it increases by $1.25 per quarter until June 30, 1995, when it reaches $60 per share.

6. The proxy statement also serves as a prospectus for the new redeemable common stock. I will, however, merely refer to it as a proxy statement.

Plaintiffs' sole claim on the merits, in connection with this motion, is that defendants have breached their duty of complete candor. *See Lynch v. Vickers Energy Corp.*, Del.Supr., 383 A.2d 278 (1977). This attack is directed at alleged omissions and misstatements in the May 2, 1990, proxy statement. Defendants' fiduciary obligation to disclose all material facts in an atmosphere of complete candor is well established. *Sealy Mattress Co. of N.J. v. Sealy Inc.*, Del.Ch., 532 A.2d 1324, 1338 (1987) *citing Rosenblatt v. Getty Oil Co.*, Del.Supr., 493 A.2d 929, 944 (1985). As articulated in *Rosenblatt, supra,* the appropriate legal test requires disclosure of those material facts. A fact is material if there is a "substantial likelihood that the disclosure of the omitted fact would have been viewed by the reasonable investor as having significantly altered the 'total mix' of information made available." *Rosenblatt, supra, citing TSC Industries, Inc. v. Northway, Inc.*, 426 U.S. 438, 449 (1979).

* * *

THE "VALUE OF CONSIDERATION SHAREHOLDERS WILL RECEIVE" CLAIM

Plaintiffs subdivide their "value of consideration" claim into two parts. First they claim that the value of the consideration shareholders will receive has not been disclosed because there has been no disclosure of the value of the redeemable stock. Second they claim that the value of the consideration is additionally undisclosed because the proxy contains no statement that the value of the redemption price decreases over time. Both parts of plaintiffs' first claim are without merit for the following reasons.

In support of their contention that the value of the redeemable stock should have been disclosed, plaintiffs work from the assumption that such a value has and can be determined. Plaintiffs assert that Mr. Frank of Shearson told the board, when it approved the transaction, that the "blended value"[7] of the consideration the shareholders would receive in the transaction is $29 per share based on Mr. Frank's judgment as to the trading price of the redeemable stock after the merger. In other words, the trading value of the redeemable stock after the merger would be around $22 per share.

Defendants argue that Mr. Frank's statement was in the form of speculation and was not meant to carry, and was not given, the weight of an official valuation. Indeed, Mr. Frank clearly prefaced his statement to the board with the assertion that it was merely his opinion. Mr. Perkins, the chairman of the board, has testified that he understood Mr. Frank's statement as an expression of his personal views, and that such view was an estimate.

Defendants maintain that the board fully disclosed its position, in relation to the value of the redeemable common stock, when it stated in a letter to the shareholders: "The Board has not assigned a specific

7. The blended value is the sum of the $18 in cash and the one-half share of redeemable stock to be received in exchange for each share of common stock.

value to the Redeemable Common Stock to be received by stockholders in the Merger in respect of the other half of their shares." Defendants further maintain that the board reached this position because it is impossible to know the market price of a new equity security to be traded at a future date on the New York Stock Exchange.

In support of the board's position, defendants cite *Shamrock Holdings, Inc. v. Polaroid Corp.*, 709 F.Supp. 1311 (D.Del.1989). That case involved an effort to enjoin Polaroid's cash self-tender offer for part of its common stock. Shamrock argued that Polaroid should disclose the value of the remaining Polaroid equity security and the "blended value" of the consideration to be paid to Polaroid shareholders, *i.e.*, the weighted average of the cash paid in the self-tender and the future trading price of the remaining equity security. Polaroid was in possession of an estimate by a financial expert of the value of the security. Judge Wright found that such disclosures did not have to be made because of their speculative and potentially misleading nature, noting that the value of the securities "depend[ed] on market forces over which neither party has control." *Id.* 709 F.Supp. at 1324. Requiring disclosures of the predicted post-transaction market price of the remaining equity securities would force Polaroid "to engage in speculation as to how the market will react ... [and] might itself be misleading." *Id.*

Unlike the plaintiffs, I am convinced, for the very reasons stated by Judge Wright in *Polaroid*, that Genentech had no obligation to offer an opinion as to the post-transaction market price of the new, redeemable security. Market values of equity securities—especially unusual equity vehicles such as the proposed redeemable stock—are inherently unpredictable. This is especially so for an enterprise operating in a highly competitive industry subject to substantial economic risks. Plaintiffs insist, however, that the unique nature of the proposed redeemable stock is what distinguishes this case from *Polaroid*. *Polaroid* did not involve an exchange for a new type of security; stockholders in that case continued to hold a fraction of their original shares, along with the cash tender price. But this distinction, in my judgment, *supports* the application of the *Polaroid* rationale here. Contingencies affecting the potential trading price of a new and unorthodox equity vehicle must, as a practical matter, be far greater than is the case with conventional securities. Forcing Genentech to make such a disclosure would be to compel pure speculation on its part, with the likely charge later that its disclosure was misleading. Mr. Frank may be willing to hazard a guess in response to a board member's question, but it is another matter to convert an educated estimate into a required disclosure. In these circumstances and on this record, I cannot conclude that Mr. Frank's estimate of the trading price of the redeemable stock should be disclosed.

The second part of the first claim—that Genentech should disclose "that the value of the redemption price decreases over time"—is equally without merit. Exact redemption prices have been fully disclosed in the proxy statement. The concept of the time value of money—which is necessarily implicated—does not, in my opinion, require explanation. One may reasonably expect the investing public to understand that $60 in 1995 is not worth $60 today. It does not require a sophisticated investment banker to figure that out. As one court has stated, "corporations are not required to address their stockholders as if they were children in kindergarten." *Richland v. Crandall*, 262 F.Supp. 538, 554 (S.D.N.Y.1967). Because this Court finds that a reasonable Genentech stockholder would understand the time value of money, a specific disclosure that the value of the stock redemption price decreases over time is unnecessary information.

THE "MATERIAL OMISSIONS CONCERNING THE VALUE OF GENENTECH" CLAIM

Plaintiffs' second claim is again subdivided into two parts. First, plaintiffs contend that the proxy statement is materially misleading because it does not disclose financial analyses performed by Shearson and Wasserstein Perella of the values they calculated for the company or the transaction. Second, they claim that the proxy statement is additionally misleading for not disclosing certain information regarding the products in the Genentech research pipeline.

Plaintiffs first assert that those analyses produced by the financial advisors and given to the board must be given to the shareholders. Such a requirement is not, however, the law of Delaware. In Delaware only that information that is material must be disclosed. *Rosenblatt, supra*. Of the analyses in question, plaintiffs have only argued that certain "ranges of values" are material.

Defendants attack these ranges of values on several grounds. First, defendants allege that these analyses were relied upon by neither the investment bankers nor the board. Defendants further contend that the financial information relied upon by the board and the investment bankers—the long range plan projection,[8] or analyses based on those projections—were fully disclosed. In addition, defendants point out that none of the financial analyses in question undermine the fairness opinions. This is true, defendants argue, because the long range projections—that were fully disclosed—served as the basis for all of Shearson's calculations. The various ranges of values, in other words, are more mathematical extrapolations of the long range projections.

While it is clear that the underlying numbers (long range plan projections) were disclosed, the question before me is whether the numbers transformed into the ranges of values would affect the total mix of information made available to the shareholders. I find that the total mix of information would not be affected due to the breadth of the ranges of values and the underlying information on which they are

---

8. The so-called "long range projections" were prepared by Genentech management during the fall of 1989. The revenue and earnings projections start in 1990 and run until the year 2000. The projections are based on a host of assumptions which are inherently uncertain and involve numerous factors beyond Genentech's control. For this reason the projections are discounted by 50%.

based. As defendants point out, the ranges of values include numbers as low as $10 and as high as $47. Such ranges are of little or no help to a shareholder trying to determine the value of a company. The breadth of the ranges are not surprising when one examines the highly speculative information upon which they were calculated. The proxy statement goes to great length explaining the speculative nature of the information behind the long-term projections. This exercise would no doubt have to be repeated ad absurdum if I were to require disclosure of the ranges of values. Requiring such disclosure, of figures I find of marginal value, would only serve to weaken the proxy statement. *See TSC Industries, Inc. v. Northway, Inc.,* 426 U.S. at 449; *TCG Securities, Inc. v. Southern Union Co.,* Del.Ch., C.A. No. 11282, Chandler, V.C., slip op. at 22 (Jan. 31, 1990). This position is supported by the lack of evidence that the board or the investment bankers gave the ranges any serious consideration.

Next, plaintiffs argue that the value of the company has not been disclosed because certain information regarding the products in Genentech's research pipeline have not been disclosed. Plaintiffs contend that Genentech should be forced to disclose more detailed information about the products in its pipeline. It appears that plaintiffs seek disclosure of detailed ten-year product sales estimates for each product in the pipeline—such as those in the PA Report, commissioned for Shearson on behalf of Genentech.

Defendants answer that such information, as the disclaimer set forth at the beginning of the PA Report evidences, is highly speculative and potentially misleading. They also argue that disclosure of more specific product information—such as possible pricing strategies and estimates of timing of introduction of new products—would damage Genentech competitively. Finally, defendants assert that all material information concerning the products in Genentech's research pipeline have already been disclosed.

A quick review of what, concerning the products in the research pipeline, has been disclosed is necessary. Genentech's annual report, mailed with the proxy statement lists each drug in the research pipeline and indicates each drug's stage of development. The annual report does not contain the sales estimates for each product that are sought by plaintiffs. These figures are, however, factored into the long range projections fully disclosed and explained in the proxy statement. As disclosed, the projections assume that each product will make it to market and be successful. The figures sought by plaintiffs, the argument goes, have therefore been fully disclosed in a form Genentech's board thought would be most useful to its shareholders. The question therefore becomes: in light of the disclosures made, would the additional disclosure of sales and revenue projections for each individual drug in Genentech's pipeline affect the total mix of information presently before the shareholders? The answer is clearly no. Such information is of no use unless it has been combined and then properly discounted.

This has been done, and disclosed, in the form of the long range projections.

In addition, while such disclosures might be of marginal benefit, they are more likely to cause a great deal of harm due to their highly speculative and uncertain nature. *See Flynn v. Bass Brothers,* 744 F.2d 978, 988 (3d Cir.1984); *Weinberger v. Rio Grande Industries, Inc.,* Del.Ch., 519 A.2d 116, 129 (1986). To minimize such potential harm the figures sought by plaintiffs would necessarily have to be qualified [9] so heavily that their already marginal value would decrease. Genentech should not be forced to make such disclosures.

THE "VALUE OF ROCHE'S OPTION" CLAIM

Plaintiffs' fourth disclosure claim is that the value to Roche of its option to acquire the 40% of the company's equity retained by the public shareholders should be disclosed. They claim that Shearson calculated the value of the option utilizing the Black–Scholes methodology.[10] Plaintiffs have engaged an expert, William E. Ricks, to calculate the value of Roche's option using the Black–Scholes methodology. Defendants respond that the Black–Scholes calculation is conceivably of interest to Roche shareholders, but not to Genentech shareholders.

Defendants acknowledge that Shearson performed a very rough Black–Scholes calculation in order to understand the value to Roche of the option. Shearson evidently thought that if the option could be shown to have a high value, it could be used as a means to negotiate Roche to a higher offer. Apparently the calculation was not shown to or discussed with the Genentech board or with Roche. Nor was it included in the binder of material supporting the fairness opinion. Defendants further assert, through Mr. Frank's affidavit, that the Black–Scholes calculations were not presented to the board for any purpose because the calculations were viewed as unreliable and they had not played any role in the actual negotiations with Roche.

Reliability aside, plaintiffs have failed to offer any reason why Genentech's shareholders would find the value of the option, to Roche, at all meaningful or useful. At oral argument, plaintiffs' counsel insisted that the shareholders need to know how much the option is worth to Roche so they may determine the true worth of the proposed merger consideration. In other words, the overall consideration to be paid by Roche must be reduced by the value of the option to Roche, and from this figure the shareholders can accurately calculate the value of the transaction to them. This line of reasoning, it seems to me, is flawed. A Genentech stockholder is entitled to know what consideration he or she will receive for each share of Genentech stock, and that

---

9. Defendants have also argued that the information sought by plaintiffs could damage Genentech competitively. At oral argument, counsel for plaintiffs suggested that the information could somehow be "coded." This would, however, only compound the problem here discussed.

10. The methodology deals with several variables, consisting of the market price of the securities, the exercise price of the option, the term of the option and the price volatility of the underlying stock.

information is clearly disclosed in the proxy. But the theoretical value of the option to the buyer, Roche, does not alter, by even one rappen, the consideration flowing to a Genentech stockholder. An investor in Genentech will receive the consideration (subject to the redemption option) exactly as stated in the proxy, regardless of the option's value to Roche. As the Black–Scholes' calculations add nothing material to the total mix of information available to the stockholders, it need not be disclosed.

Subsection d. Backdoor Protection for Bondholders?

Recall the problems of bondholders presented in chapter 3. They have so far failed in asserting claims against leveraged buyouts based on breaches of fiduciary duty and of implicit covenants of good faith. Do the securities acts prove a successful avenue of attack?

McMAHAN & COMPANY v. WHEREHOUSE ENTERTAINMENT, INC.

United States Court of Appeals, Second Circuit, 1990.
900 F.2d 576.

Opinion of PRATT, CIRCUIT JUDGE.

Defendant Wherehouse Entertainment, Inc. offered 6¼% convertible subordinated debentures whose key selling feature was a right of holders to tender the debentures to Wherehouse in the case of certain triggering events which might endanger the value of the debentures. The tender right was to arise if:

> (a) A person or group * * * shall attain the beneficial ownership * * * of an equity interest representing at least 80% of the voting power * * * unless such attainment has been approved by a majority of the Independent Directors;
>
> (b) The Company * * * consolidates or merges * * * unless approved by a majority of the Independent Directors;
>
> (c) The Company * * * incurs * * * any Debt * * * excluding * * * Debt which is authorized or ratified by a majority of the Independent Directors, immediately after the incurrence of which the ratio of the Company's Consolidated Total Debt to its Consolidated Capitalization exceeds .65 to 1.0.

Indenture § 5.02, 11–12 (June 15, 1986) . . .

The offering materials defined an "Independent Director" as "a director of the Company" who was not a recent employee but who was a member of the board of directors on the date of the offering or who was subsequently elected to the board by the then-Independent Directors. Indenture, § 5.02, 12; Prospectus *Description of Debentures,* "Optional Debenture Tender", 26. The reason offered for this unusual right to tender was that it would be a protection against certain forms of take-over attempts, including leveraged buy-outs. Prospectus *Descrip-*

tion of Debentures, "Effect on Certain Takeovers", 27. At the heart of this appeal is the meaning of the limitation placed on the right to tender by the role of "Independent Directors".

Plaintiffs are financial institutions that purchased 34% of the convertible debentures. Eighteen months after the purchase, Wherehouse entered into a merger agreement with defendants WEI Holdings, Inc. and its subsidiary WEI Acquisition Corp. The practical effect of the merger, accomplished through a leveraged buy-out, left Wherehouse with a debt approaching 90% of its capitalization and left plaintiffs' debentures valued at only approximately 50% of par. Plaintiffs attempted to exercise their right to tender, but the company refused to redeem the debentures on the ground that the "board of directors" had approved the merger. Plaintiffs then commenced this suit for damages and an injunction to prevent the merger. Named as defendants were Wherehouse, various officers of Wherehouse, the underwriter of the debentures, WEI Holdings, Inc., WEI Acquisition Corp., and the bank that was financing the tender offer. Plaintiffs claimed that the descriptions of the debentures in the registration materials, as well as representations made during conversations, were materially misleading. Specifically, they claimed that, even though the defendants knew that the right to tender was illusory, their representations of the right as valuable and protected had misled investors into buying the debentures and therefore violated federal securities laws. * * * The district court held that defendants were not required to speculate about the likelihood of a waiver of debentureholders' right by the Independent Directors and that, even if the right were worthless, defendants were not required to use pejorative terms describing it as such. Moreover, it found the tender option was not illusory, because it (was possible that it) might provide a benefit to debentureholders in the case of a takeover hostile to shareholders which management chose to fight. Finally, according to the district court, the definition of "Independent Directors" was adequate because further description of their role, the extent of their discretion, their interests, or their intent would constitute mere legal conclusions, characterizations, or descriptions of underlying motives and were not required disclosures. Thus, the district court found that the descriptions of the right were not misstatements, and that the alleged omissions were not required to be disclosed under the securities laws.

We disagree with the district court's atomistic consideration of the presentation of the debentureholders' right to tender. The district court concluded that defendants had not misled plaintiffs because the information they included in the written and oral representations was "literally true". We think, however, that when read as a whole, the defendants' representations connoted a richer message than that conveyed by a literal reading of the statements. The central issue on all three claims is not whether the particular statements, taken separately, were literally true, but whether defendants' representations, taken together and in context, would have misled a reasonable investor about the nature of the debentures.

Some statements, although literally accurate, can become, through their context and manner of presentation, devices which mislead investors. For that reason, the disclosure required by the securities laws is measured not by literal truth, but by the ability of the material to accurately inform rather than mislead prospective buyers.

* * *

We hold that the district court erred in granting summary judgment to the defendants; because plaintiffs have raised a triable issue as to whether the written and oral representations about the right to tender these debentures were materially misleading to a reasonable investor in violation of § 11 and § 12 of the 1933 Securities Act and also of § 10(b) of the 1934 Securities Exchange Act.

* * *

Section 11 states that any signer, officer of the issuer, and underwriter may be held liable for a registration statement which "contained an untrue statement of a material fact or omitted to state a material fact * * * necessary to make the statements therein not mileading". Plaintiffs claim that these offering materials misstated the right to tender and omitted important information about it in violation of § 11. They argue that a reasonable investor would have believed that the right to tender was valuable because it was presented as a right to be exercised at the holder's option and as a protection against takeovers that might affect the security of the debentures. In truth, however, the right to tender was illusory, they argue, because it was designed to be exercised only at the option of management and therefore was intended to protect the interest of shareholders, not of debentureholders.

Plaintiffs are correct that the offering materials can reasonably be read to present the option to tender as a valuable right. The language used was invariably language of entitlement:

> *Holder's Right to Tender.* The Holder of any Security or Securities shall have *the right, at his option,* * * * *to tender* for redemption any such Security or Securities.

Indenture § 5.01, 10 (emphasis added). The prospectus summary provided that:

> "Each holder of Debentures has the *option to require* the Company to redeem the holder's Debentures."

"Optional Tender", 3 (emphasis added). And the prospectus itself stated:

> "Holders of the Debentures *will have the option* * * * *to require* the Company to redeem such Debentures."

Description of Debentures, "Optional Debentures Tender", 25 (emphasis added).

Further, a jury could reasonably view the presentation of the right to tender as a special feature to protect investors, for the offering materials stressed the purported value of the right in any takeover transaction which would threaten the value of the debentures.

> Since the events which give rise to such right of redemption could be expected to occur in connection with certain forms of takeover attempts, the optional tender provisions could deter takeovers where the person attempting the takeover views itself as unable to finance the redemption of the principal amount of Debentures which may be tendered * * * To the extent that Debentures may be tendered * * * the Company would be unable to use the financing provided by the sale of the Debentures offered hereby. In addition, the ability of the Company to obtain additional Senior Debt based on the existence of the Debentures would be similarly adversely affected.

Prospectus *Description of Debentures,* "Effect on Certain Takeovers", 27; *see also id.* "Optional Debenture Tender", 26.

Finally, the right was restricted only in that it was subject to action by "the Independent Directors". Similar language describing the restriction—the right to tender occurs upon a triggering event, "*unless* [the event is] approved by a majority of the Independent Directors" (emphasis added)—is found in the Indenture, § 5.02, 11–12; in the prospectus summary, "Optional Tender", 3; and again in the full prospectus, *Description of Debentures,* "Optional Debenture Tender", 25–26. A jury could reasonably find that this repeated use of the word "unless" encouraged the inference that exercise of the right would be the norm and that waiver would be the exception.

Although the offering materials explain that the Independent Directors would be chosen from the company's board of directors, the term "Independent Director" implies a special status, some distinction from an "ordinary" director. The term suggests that these directors would be "independent" of management and the normal obligations of board members to act in the interests of shareholders. Thus the restriction could reasonably be understood to mean that in the case of a triggering event, the right to tender would arise *unless* the Independent Directors find the event to be in the interests of the debentureholders. In short, as plaintiffs argue, a reasonable investor could have regarded the right to tender as a valuable right, protected by Independent Directors who would, in situations endangering the security of the debentures, consider debentureholders' interest before approving any waiver of their right.

By thus representing that in a takeover context the Independent Directors would be considering the interests of debentureholders, the defendants implied that the Independent Directors had a duty to protect the debentureholders' interests. Defendants, however, have shown nothing in their corporate charter or by-laws that would have permitted, much less required, these Independent Directors to favor debentureholders over shareholders. Moreover, at the time of the approval of this merger, the Independent Directors constituted all but one of the "ordinary" directors on the board. As ordinary directors, they had a fiduciary duty to protect the interest of shareholders in any takeover situation, regardless of debentureholders' interests or rights. It is inevitable, then, that the so-called Independent Directors had no independence; they would never protect the interest of debentureholders except by coincidence because, as ordinary directors, they were required by law to protect the interests of the shareholders. From this perspective, there is merit in plaintiffs' contentions that the right to tender was illusory and that the representations of it in the offering materials were misleading.

In sum, on a fair reading of the offering materials, despite their literal meaning, an investor could have reasonably believed that the tender option was presented as a valuable right for debentureholders; that it provided a special feature of protection for their interests; and that Independent Directors were to render independent votes on the right to tender based on the impact of a merger and on the interests of debentureholders. But if, as plaintiffs claim, the right to tender was illusory because the Independent Directors were tied to management, served its needs, protected shareholders' interests, and would inevitably waive the right in any merger beneficial to management regardless of debentureholders' interests, then the offering materials could be found by a rational trier of fact to be materially misleading in violation of § 11 of the Securities Act of 1933. Plaintiffs have therefore raised a genuine issue as to whether the written representations could have misled a reasonable investor, and summary judgment was therefore unwarranted.

Dissenting opinion of Sand, District Judge:

* * *

The question whether an anti-takeover provision provides a "special protection" to debentureholders cannot be answered in the negative merely because the "Independent Directors" decided to waive its provisions and approve a particular transaction. These directors were explicitly empowered to act in this fashion by virtue of the fully disclosed terms of the provision. A significant function of an anti-takeover provision is to serve as a deterrent to hostile takeovers, including takeovers which would be contrary to the interests of both shareholders and debentureholders. One cannot, I believe, fairly characterize such a provision as being "worthless" to the debentureholders, even though as a matter of Delaware law directors owe a fiduciary duty solely to shareholders. The anti-takeover provision was therefore a "special protection" to debentureholders, albeit a limited one.

Federal securities laws do not impose an obligation to advise investors of the fundamentals of corporate governance. The disclosure required by the federal securities laws is not a "rite of confession or exercise in common law pleading. What is required is the disclosure of material objective factual matters." *Data Probe Acquisition Corp. v.*

Data Lab, Inc., 722 F.2d 1, 5–6 (2d Cir.1983), *cert. denied,* 415 U.S. 1052 (1984). Especially is this so where, as here, the investor-complainants are sophisticated financial institutions making major investments. The role of the federal securities laws is not to remedy all perceived injustices in securities transactions. Rather, as invoked in this case, it proscribes only the making of false and misleading statements or material omissions.

CORSO AND SILFEN,* DISCLOSURE OF FINANCIAL INFORMATION IN CONTESTED PROXY SOLICITATIONS, M & A AND CORP. GOVERNANCE REP. 468
(Nov. 1990).

Recent Delaware court decisions and a diminished ability to finance unsolicited tender offer bids have frustrated the efforts of hostile suitors seeking to wrest corporate control from existing management. In increasing numbers, hostile suitors have redirected their efforts toward contested proxy solicitations, promising shareholders an opportunity to maximize value by electing a slate committed to implementing a particular value enhancing program. The result: proxy fights have evolved from "beauty contests," among slates with no discernible difference in platform, into debates over complex business and financial programs.

In seeking shareholder support, solicitors typically create the expectation for shareholders that electing their nominees will generate additional value. Usually, they analyze an issuer's financial performance over a period of time or in relation to certain benchmarks. Such solicitors also may propose an extraordinary transaction. To substantiate their claim that a particular platform will enable shareholders to realize greater value, solicitors (both management and insurgent groups alike) disseminate sophisticated business and financial analyses using complex financial comparisons, financial projections and valuation estimates. * * *

Participants in contested soliciations face the difficult task of ensuring that their economic arguments do not cross the regulatory line, established by Rule 14a–9, between acceptable contentious writing and materially misleading or false statements or material omissions. Other than the specific line-item requirements of Schedule 14A with respect to the proxy statement, there are few explicit standards controlling the content of soliciting materials. In the absence of any clearly-defined disclosure standards or specific judicial guidance with respect to the parameters of Rule 14a–9, solicitors are forced to balance their desire to argue most persuasively with the need to obey the limits prescribed by Rule 14a–9.

* Mr. Corso and Mr. Silfen are attorneys with the SEC, Division of Corporate Finance.

Contested solicitations, which debate economic issues, rely primarily upon the presentation of business and financial information that is easily susceptible to distortion. Such distortions may occur in a variety of ways, including citing projected financial information without disclosing the underlying assumptions, citing earnings trends without specifying the extent to which they are attributable to non-recurring items or discontinued operations, or describing an extraordinary transaction such as a restructuring without disclosing whether the solicitor has developed a specific plan to accomplish it, and if so, without delineating the details of such plan.

A distinct category of financial or business information—valuation claims—are particularly susceptible to distortion. The Commission addressed this issue in its 1980 Release in connection with proposals to liquidate all or part of an issuer. Such claims were found to be "only appropriate and consonant with Rule 14a–9 ... when made in good faith and on a reasonable basis and where accompanied by disclosure which facilitates shareholder understanding of the basis for and the limitations on the projected realizable value." Equally important, the 1980 Release states: "where valuations are so qualified and subject to material limitations and contingencies, inclusion in the proxy statement of specific realizable values may be unreasonable."

By analogy, the 1980 Release establishes the framework within which financial performance and other valuation information can be presented.[15] * * *

In questioning the effectiveness or competency of management, insurgents attempt to create the expectation of increased values in a redirected company. Also, by presenting an alternative plan for asset deployment, insurgents hope to convince shareholders of their ability to enhance the financial performance of the target company. By comparing statistics, such as financial performance trends or return on investment computations, an insurgent can present statistics which depict the failings of management. Further, by comparing the target company's actual performance to industry standards or market benchmarks, an insurgent can demonstrate the target's potential for improvement.
* * *

As discussed above, the principal argument proffered by insurgents is that the target's stock is undervalued. One way to illustrate a poor return on investment is to contrast the progression of the target's per share market price to some benchmark, such as to the Dow Jones Industrial Average (DOW) or to a Standard and Poor's Index (S & P). This type of comparison is similar to trend analysis; both involve comparisons over a fixed period of time, and thus, are useful in

---

15. Applying the standards formulated in the 1980 Release, the court in *Dynamics Corp. v. CTS Corp.*, 1986–87 Fed.Sec.L.Rep. (CCH) ¶ 392,765 (N.D.Ill.1986), found that a press release suggesting that the subject company could be sold at a specified price violated Rule 14a–9 because the disclosure failed to inform shareholders of the valuation methodologies employed and the projections used in deriving that price, as well as the likelihood of that value being realized.

identifying weak spots in management performance and in demonstrating potential for improvement. Unlike ordinary trendline comparisons, benchmark analyses compare a company's operating results, not against its prior performance, but against a financial composite that, by definition, cannot be reflected by any one company. Thus, benchmark comparisons, while always legitimate, frequently require qualification to make shareholders aware of the analyses' fundamental limitations.

A primary difficulty in using benchmark comparisons relates to the tendency to equate share price with return on investment. It is generally assumed that in valuing a security, the market assesses all relevant information, including the amount and frequency of dividends paid. In this regard, if a company always pays out all earnings as dividends, assuming other market conditions are constant, its per share price should not increase. However, if that same company retains all earnings, rather than the company achieving the same market price, the market must account for the need to purchase all unpaid dividends. Accordingly, solicitors frequently find it advisable to disclose dividend rates during each period covered by the benchmark comparison. Likewise, the manner in which the benchmark index accounts for dividends (e.g., fully reinvested or disregarded) may be material in certain circumstances.

Another potential problem in using benchmark comparisons arises since a company's performance does not necessarily reflect management's competence. Specifically, if the operating results of many companies in an industry group are affected by overall market conditions (e.g., the banking industry) it may be necessary to disclose that the company's inability to track the benchmark may relate directly to problems specific to its industry group, and only secondarily to management's performance. Moreover, the performance of comparable companies or comparable industry aggregates against the benchmark may be material. Similarly, if a comparison to a more relevant index (e.g., the transportation index) yields a materially different conclusion, the discussion may require qualifying or limiting disclosure. Whatever inferences are drawn from stock prices, at least some solicitors have believed it appropriate to caveat the presentation by clarifying that market prices are influenced by a number of factors.

As indicated above, the most prevalent form of benchmark comparisons is the graph of a target company's performance against the S & P 500 or the Dow. The Icahn Committee's use of this technique in its solicitation of USX shareholders is a typical comparison. It contrasted the USX's fifteen year relative stock performance to the S & P 500 Index. The graph demonstrated that after an overall decline during most of the 1980's, by 1990, USX had not quite equalled its 1975 base price; however, during the same period, the S & P 500 quadrupled. The Icahn Committee also decried: "The problem with USX can be summed up in two lines," charting the S & P 500 versus USX's stock price over the preceding eight years.

Although the most common form of benchmark analysis is a comparison to a market index, occasionally, as in the American General and USX contests, solicitors present more specific data. For example, in USX, the Icahn Committee sought to convince shareholders that by the conglomeration of steel and oil businesses, USX inhibited the ability of either business to perform on a par with its respective competitors. The Icahn Committee plotted, for the most recent two and a half year period, the percentage increase in USX's stock price against those of comparable steel companies in one graph and comparable oil companies in another. For each USX industry segment, the Icahn Committee then extrapolated a percentage increase, assuming that during the relevant period each respective USX segment had matched the performance of the comparable companies. The extrapolated rate, in both cases, was considerably higher than the rate achieved by USX.

In another variation, Torchmark presented "a standard against which to compare the performance of American General." To further its argument that American General should enter into a merger or asset sale (in which Torchmark pledged to make an acquisition proposal), Torchmark graphed its own results against those of American General over the last five years. The four categories compared were: growth in stock market price, growth in earnings per share, growth in dividends and return on equity. In each category, Torchmark's results greatly exceeded those of American General.

A number of solicitations this year involved platforms proposing that an issuer engage in an extraordinary transaction, such as a liquidation, spin-off, or a sale of portions of or the entire company. These proposals may discuss a specific transaction which the solicitor intends to implement or may express a desire to pursue a transaction on a best-efforts basis.

In describing such proposals, a solicitation should disclose the nature of the promise being made. Specifically, the disclosure should indicate whether the solicitor proposes a specific transaction or merely promises to exercise his best efforts in arranging a transaction, the feasibility of implementing the proposal, the basis for the insurgent's belief that the proposal can be consummated and the legal effect of shareholder action. If a participant undertakes to use his best efforts to structure a transaction, such disclosure may need to specify the substance of the solicitor's actions to date. For example, the materials should indicate whether the solicitor has identified a list of potential buyers, has contacted those potential buyers and if so, the nature of any response. Also, the status of any present discussions or indications of interest is particularly relevant. If the solicitor specifies a potentially realizable price or range of prices, compliance with the 1980 Release dictates that shareholders be informed of the assumptions used in calculating that range, including the prices ascribed to the various assets to be sold, the time period in which the value is expected to be realized and the amount of fees being assessed by the solicitor for initiating and structuring the transaction.

Both the Armstrong and NII solicitations assigned estimated realizable values to a liquidation of the issuer. In Armstrong, the Belzbergs described the values realizable under three different scenarios, involving a combination of a spin-off of certain assets, payment of a one time dividend and implementation of cost cutting measures. Materials sent to shareholders noted the lack of assurance that a transaction could be completed and included a letter from an investment banker, opining on the values achievable under the different scenarios. The opinion letter also described the material assumptions, qualifications and limitations underlying the restructuring plan.

Similarly, Centaur Partners' solicitation of NII shareholders ascribed an estimated range of realizable value, based upon a proposed restructuring plan involving, in the first phase, both a sale of certain assets, followed by a distribution of proceeds, and in the second phase, an acquisition of all shares in the restructured company in an all cash tender offer or merger. The analysis which resulted in the per share value figures, on an after-tax basis, was performed by one investment banker and confirmed by another. The description of the plan indicated the estimated time for completion, material assumptions and the limitations of the analysis, particularly the complete reliance upon publicly disclosed information about NII.

In a slightly different approach, Carl Icahn proposed that USX Corp. spin-off to shareholders a separate corporate entity containing at least 80 percent of the company's assets. Icahn argued that the combined value of these two entities would result in an aggregate per share value of $48 per share, which represented a 35 percent increase over the then closing price per share. In support of his proposal, Icahn discussed, in detail, the assumptions underlying the spin-off proposal's value. The proxy statement not only noted the estimated property values for oil and non-oil assets, but also specified the method by which the property values were calculated. Certain limitations in the analysis were highlighted, including that the analysis was based exclusively on publicly available information, assumed that the transaction would be tax free to USX and its stockholders and disclaimed any responsibility for the accuracy of the property estimates.

Shareholders reviewing the spin-off proposal also received the benefit of USX managements' assessment of the plan. In a series of advertisements, management disputed several elements of Icahn's analysis. In a particularly effective advertisement, management compared the results of applying certain per share multiples used in deriving the spin-off proposal to the pertinent financial information of comparable companies against the actual per share market price of those companies—the difference, which averaged 105 percent, was labeled the "Guesstimate Gap."

Additional disclosure considerations arise if an insurgent retains the right to bid for all or part of a target's assets. Typically, the procedural safeguards implemented to assuage concerns over potential conflicts of interest are described. In solicitations involving a slate committed to facilitate a specific transaction with an affiliate, the SEC staff will examine whether shareholders will be given another opportunity to vote on the transaction; the vote required to approve the transaction; and whether the proposal commenced a tender offer or involves a going-private transaction.

During its solicitation of Kollmorgen shareholders, Vernitron, seeking to elect a slate committed to facilitating its acquisition of Kollmorgen, disclosed Vernitron's intent to conduct a sixty day auction, establish a special committee, and retain an investment banking firm for the specific purpose of soliciting offers and assisting in the evaluation of competing acquisition proposals. Vernitron also identified the members of its proposed special committee, described the criteria to be used by the committee in evaluating competing offers, and declared its intent to provide potential third party bidders with access to Kollmorgen's books and records.

With increasing frequency, proxy contest participants rely upon third party valuation analyses rather than on their own independently performed analysis, apparently, believing that shareholders are likely to find such analyses more persuasive. Since Rule 14a–9 governs the appropriateness of using such reprints in soliciting material, solicitors should thoroughly examine the materials to independently assess their reasonableness. These materials are subject to the same scrutiny and the same standards of disclosure as any other proxy soliciting material. In republishing valuation information produced by third parties, a solicitor becomes responsible for its content and assumes liability for any inaccuracy in the material. A participant therefore must demonstrate the reasonableness of and the basis for the statements made, not merely support the fact that the statements were made.

Any investigation should include a review of the context and purpose of the original statement, as well as the currency and qualifications of the author who originally published the materials. In certain instances, the insurgent may need to contact the author to inform the author of the intended use of the materials and to determine whether the author knows of anything that would result in the material being false or misleading in the context of the soliciting material.

During the past proxy season, both management and insurgent groups effectively used third party analyses. Carl Icahn, in USX, featured an advertisement, entitled "Don't Just Take Our Word For It," with quotes from several "leading" analysts, affirming the validity of the spin-off analysis. By comparison, Armstrong's management urged shareholders to "[l]ook at Armstrong's recent performance through the eyes of three financial analysts," who agreed with management regarding the Company's favorable future prospects.

Subsection e. A Bidder's Public Promises

IN RE PHILLIPS PETROLEUM SECURITIES LITIGATION

United States Court of Appeals, Third Circuit, 1989.
881 F.2d 1236.

Opinion of SCIRICA, CIRCUIT JUDGE.

This is an appeal from a grant of summary judgment against a consolidated plaintiffs class, comprised of individuals who purchased stock in the Phillips Petroleum Company ("Phillips") from December 5, 1984 through December 21, 1984. The named defendants in the class action include Phillips and the Phillips Board of Directors (the "Phillips defendants"), the Mesa Partnership ("the Partnership") which attempted to acquire control of Phillips by a hostile takeover in December 1984, and individual members of the Partnership, including Mesa Petroleum Company ("Mesa") and Mesa's Chief Executive Officer, T. Boone Pickens, Jr. * * * After a settlement that removed the Phillips defendants from the litigation, plaintiffs moved for summary judgment on liability and the Mesa defendants cross-moved for summary judgment.

* * *

The Partnership began to purchase Phillips common stock on October 22, 1984. On December 4, 1984, the Partnership issued a press release stating it had acquired approximately 5.7% of Phillips's outstanding shares and that it was commencing a tender offer for 15 million shares of Phillips common stock at $60 per share. The press release stated explicitly that the Partnership would "not sell any Phillips shares owned by it back to Phillips except on an equal basis with all other shareholders."

The Partnership filed its Schedule 13–D on December 5, 1984, as required under Section 13(d) of the Williams Act, 15 U.S.C. § 78m(d)(1). The Schedule 13–D stated that the proposed tender offer was designed ultimately to obtain control of Phillips. Furthermore, the Schedule 13–D reiterated the statement from the previous day's press release that the Partnership did not intend to sell its shares to Phillips except on an equal basis with all shareholders.

The next day, December 6, 1984, T. Boone Pickens appeared on the nationally televised MacNeil/Lehrer News Hour representing the Partnership. In response to questioning by Mr. MacNeil, Pickens stated unequivocally that "[t]he only way we would consider selling back [to Phillips] is if they make the same offer to all shareholders."

Phillips responded to the Partnership's actions by attempting to block the takeover attempt in court.

* * *

At the same time the parties were jousting in court, however, Phillips was pursuing private negotiations with the Partnership. * * * From the inception of the tender offer through December 21, the Partnership had made no less than eight amendments to its Schedule 13–D; indeed, the Partnership made the eighth amendment on the afternoon of December 21. In none of those amendments had the Partnership changed its original statement that it would not sell any of its shares back to Phillips except on an equal basis with all other shareholders.

On the face of the record, it would appear that the Partnership should have had every reason to believe that the December 21 meeting would be to negotiate the terms for Phillips's concession to its offer. Instead, claim the defendants, Phillips presented the Partnership with its plans for a defensive recapitalization which all the defendants allege would have effectively blocked the takeover. Reduced to the barest terms, under the recapitalization plan Phillips proposed to exchange 29% of its common stock for debt securities valued at $60 per share (pro rata among all shareholders), and to sell 27.5 million newly issued shares to a new employee stock ownership plan at a market price assumed to be $50 per share while purchasing 27.5 million shares of its stock back in open market transactions. Additionally, the recapitalization included reductions in expenses and capital expenditures, as well as the sale of approximately $2 billion of Phillips's lower-earning assets.

The parties negotiated vigorously through the weekend, proposing and counter-proposing various plans. * * * On December 23, 1984, Phillips and the Partnership reached an agreement in which all shareholders were not treated on an equal basis. The final agreement provided, first, that Phillips would reclassify 38% of its common stock (pro rata for all shareholders) into preferred stock, which was then to be exchanged for debt in the principal amount of $60 per share. Second, Phillips would create an employee incentive stock ownership plan (an "EISOP"), to which it would sell no more than 32 million newly issued shares at market value. Finally, Phillips was required to purchase at least $1 billion of its common stock on the open market following the exchange. Investment bankers for Phillips placed the value of the blended package—debt securities plus Phillips stock—at $53 for shareholders.

The Partnership, however, received a different arrangement. If the recapitalization were approved by the shareholders, it would sell its shares back to Phillips for $53 per share in cash. In the event the shareholders did not approve the recapitalization, the Partnership was given several options: it was given a put whereby it could still sell its shares to Phillips for the same $53 cash per share; it could retain its Phillips shares, subject to a standstill agreement; or it could sell its Phillips shares to a third party. Additionally, Phillips agreed to pay the Partnership's certified expenses in waging the takeover battle, an amount of $25 million. Other shareholders were not compensated for their expenses.

The agreement was announced in a press release, issued on Sunday night, December 23. The following day, Monday, December 24, the Partnership amended its Schedule 13–D yet again, this time to say that the Partnership had agreed not to pursue its attempt to gain control of Phillips and that the Partnership would eventually dispose of its shares; the amendment, however, made no revision in the equal basis statement. The market reacted adversely to announcement of the agreement and, on that same Monday, the price of Phillips stock fell by more than nine points, closing at approximately $45 per share. The value of the blended package available to Phillips shareholders other than the Partnership, declined accordingly.

On March 3, 1985, the Phillips shareholders rejected the recapitalization plan. On March 6, the Partnership exercised its put under the December 23 agreement and sold its shares back to Phillips for $53 cash per share.

Subsequently, Phillips made another Exchange Offer to its shareholders, offering another blended package Phillips valued at slightly in excess of $52 per share. At no time were all Phillips shareholders offered the same $53 cash per share received by the Partnership.

* * *

Section 10(b) of the Securities Exchange Act of 1934, 15 U.S.C. § 78j(b), forbids "manipulative" or "deceptive" conduct "in connection with the purchase or sale of any security." *Santa Fe Industries, Inc. v. Green,* 430 U.S. 462, 473–74 (1977). Rule 10b–5, promulgated under § 10(b), prohibits the making of "any untrue statement of material fact" in connection with the purchase or sale of securities. 17 C.F.R. § 240.10b–5.

In order to establish a claim under § 10(b) and Rule 10b–5, a plaintiff must prove that the defendant i) made misstatements or omissions; ii) of material fact; iii) with scienter; iv) in connection with the purchase or sale of securities; v) upon which the plaintiff relied; and vi) that reliance proximately caused the plaintiff's injury. * * * The misrepresentations must touch upon the reasons for the investment's decline in value.

* * *

The district court ruled that nothing in the summary judgment record indicated the equal basis statements were considered untrue when made by the Partnership. Rather, the Partnership changed its intent to sell its shares back to Phillips only when faced with the defensive recapitalization. Consequently, said the district court, because statements in a Schedule 13–D need only be true when made, the plaintiffs failed to produce any evidence of scienter by the Partnership.

We believe the district court was correct that a statement of intent need only be true when made; a subsequent change of intention will not, by itself, give rise to a cause of action under Section 10(b) or Rule 10b–5. Similarly, we think it self-evident that a change from a party's initial statement of intent does not by itself prove that the initial statement was a misrepresentation.

* * *

Plaintiffs contend that, if the Partnership did change its intention only to sell its stock back to Phillips on a basis equal to all other stockholders—as opposed to the Partnership having always intended to sell back on an unequal basis—then they are liable under the federal securities laws nonetheless for failing to communicate that change of intention promptly. There can be no doubt that a duty exists to correct prior statements, if the prior statements were true when made but misleading if left unrevised.

* * *

The law has been less clear on what constitutes sufficiently prompt revision and dissemination of a statement of intent. With regard to amendment of a Schedule 13D, at least, the Securities and Exchange Commission itself has noted as much:

> No bright line test has been adopted in order to determine when an amendment to a Schedule 13D is "prompt." ... Strong policy considerations indicate that the "prompt" amendment requirement should be construed flexibly in order to comport with the circumstances of the particular case.

In the matter of Cooper Laboratories, Inc., Fed.Sec.L.Rep. (CCH) ¶ 83,788 at 87,526 (June 26, 1985). We believe, as other courts have recognized, that the question of whether an amendment is sufficiently prompt must be determined in each case based upon the particular facts and circumstances surrounding both prior disclosures by the acquirer and the material changes which trigger the obligation to amend.

* * *

Moreover, the same type of individual fact determination must be made with regard to amending other statements made outside a Schedule 13D, but still "in connection with" the purchase or sale of a security. An example of such a statement, in the case before us, would be Pickens's comments during the MacNeil/Lehrer News Hour.

On the record before us, however, the Partnership's delay in disseminating its change of intent could not have proximately caused the plaintiffs' injury. The plaintiff class is defined as purchasers of Phillips stock during the period from December 5, 1984 through December 21, 1984. Assuming that the equal basis statements were a true representation of the Partnership's intent when they were made, plaintiffs provide no evidence of a change of intent until after the stock market closed on Friday, December 21. But inasmuch as plaintiffs could not have sold their stock on the open market until it opened on Monday morning, December 24, the difference between announcing a change of intent Sunday night rather than Friday night would not have detrimentally altered plaintiffs' opportunities. Consequently, on this record a jury could not reasonably conclude that the Partnership was dilatory in announcing its change of intent. Because the plaintiff class does not include purchasers after December 21, 1984, assuming that the Partnership did change its intent over the weekend, it is difficult to understand how a delay in the announcement could have injured plaintiffs as they had already purchased the Phillips shares.

We arrive at a different conclusion with respect to a jury finding of recklessness by the Partnership. As we have noted, recklessness meets the scienter requirement of Section 10(b) and Rule 10b–5. Few markets shift as quickly and dramatically as the securities market, especially where a publicly traded company has been "put in play" by a hostile suitor. The equal basis statements were broad and unequivocal, providing no contingency for changing circumstances. Even though they needed only be true when made, such unequivocal statements presented an obvious danger of misleading the public—because they can fairly be read as a statement by the Partnership that, no matter what happened, it would not change its intentions. Indeed, the repetition of the equal basis statements as the takeover fight progressed would only serve to reinforce such a perception. A jury could, therefore, reasonably find making the statements to be an extreme departure from the standards of ordinary care.

* * *

Plaintiffs go even further, contending in the alternative that the Partnership did not change its intent in response to the defensive tactics of Phillips when it negotiated the buy-back agreement, but rather had no intention from the outset to honor the equal treatment statement. The record contains evidence to support this allegation as well. As we have noted, the decision by the Delaware Chancery Court on December 20, 1984, that the GAO Standstill Agreement was inapplicable left Phillips with no viable litigation defenses. The Partnership was free to pursue its tender offer and to buy Phillips stock in open market transactions. Both the district court's decision and the defendant's arguments, consequently, turn on the assumption that the defensive recapitalization proposed by Phillips on the night of December 21 was sufficiently impregnable on its face to cause the Partnership, after all of its efforts, to suddenly abandon its takeover fight.

While the record contains insufficient information about the recapitalization plan for a full understanding of all of the plan's subtleties, it contains more than enough details for a jury reasonably to conclude that it had only a chance for success or that the Partnership would not have been deterred by it. First, the plan required huge amounts of capital, at least $2 billion from the sale of Phillips assets and, perhaps, additional financing from lending institutions. A significant question of fact exists as to whether either of these sources could produce the necessary capital in time to stave off a hostile takeover by the Partnership. The Partnership in contrast, having already launched its tender offer, presumptively had financing in place. Second, because the recapitalization involved the exchange of debt securities for equity in the company pro rata among shareholders, the recapitalization as proposed to the Partnership on the night of December 21 "contemplate[d]" approval by the shareholders. Yet when an opportunity finally did occur more than two months later to present to the shareholders a recapitalization involving the same debt for equity exchange, the shareholders rejected the plan. Again, a significant issue of fact exists as to whether the Partnership actually believed the recapitalization could be implemented in time. Finally, and most notably, the success of the Phillips defensive recapitalization plan depended upon its ability to buy up 27.5 million shares of its own stock in the face of a competing tender offer by the Partnership. In sum, given all of these contingencies, the record contains sufficient circumstantial evidence from which a jury could reasonably conclude that the proposed recapitalization was an insufficient basis to cause the partnership to change its intent—but, rather, that the recapitalization was merely a reason given by the Partnership for following a course different from its stated intention.

Even if the defensive recapitalization did have a high probability of success, however, sufficient evidence exists in the record from which a jury could reasonably conclude the Partnership always intended to sell its shares back to Phillips on a different basis from that offered to other shareholders. When the tender offer was launched, it was foreseeable to the Partnership that it might at some point want to give up its takeover attempt and abandon its stake in Phillips. Indeed, it is exactly that contingency which the equal basis statements contemplate. It seems an unlikely possibility that the Partnership envisioned the board of Phillips Petroleum taking the corporation private, which would be the natural effect of a cash offer for all outstanding shares. The facts that some cash was not made available to other Phillips shareholders as part of the blended package, and that Phillips had to sell $2 billion of its assets to raise cash for the recapitalization, could provide the basis for a fair inference by a jury that a cash offer for all outstanding shares was not possible—and that, moreover, given the sophisticated valuation of Phillips that the Partnership would have had at its disposal, the Partnership would know such a global cash offer could not be made. Consequently, one could read the equal basis statements to imply that something other than cash would be given as at least part of the consideration in any buy-back arrangement.

Moreover, a reasonable jury could find the defendants' explanations as to why the Partnership did not take the same mixed package that was offered to the remainder of the shareholders to be insufficient to rebut the fair inferences that can be drawn from this record. Equal treatment for all shareholders was available, either by the Partnership accepting the same package of stock and debt securities ultimately offered to the other shareholders, or by the cash that was paid to the Partnership instead being offered pro rata to all shareholders instead of the debt securities. That the Phillips board would not allow the Partnership to maintain an interest in the company hardly strikes us as compelling. Nothing kept the Partnership simply from holding its stock in Phillips. Moreover, that the Partnership refused to take the same mixed package offered to the other shareholders—thereby both reducing the Partnership's position in the corporation to assuage the fears of the Phillips board, while simultaneously sharing the available cash pro rata with all of the Phillips shareholders—belies the defendants' contention that they believed all of the shareholders were getting equal value.

While a great deal of what the record contains amounts to no more than circumstantial evidence, we have previously observed that "[c]ircumstantial evidence may often be the principal, if not the only, means of proving bad faith." *McLean v. Alexander*, 599 F.2d at 1198. Given the contradiction between the Partnership's vigorous equal basis statements, plus the circumstances we have outlined, a jury could reasonably conclude that the Partnership either was reckless in making the equal basis statements given the foreseeability of what actually occurred, or that the Partnership intended from the outset of its tender offer to sell back to Phillips on an unequal basis. Consequently, the district court's entry of summary judgment on the security fraud claim for failure to adduce evidence of scienter was incorrect and we will vacate it.

* * *

Question

Assume the following facts: A bidder makes a hostile tender offer for $38 per share (the stock is trading at $29 per share), conditioned on the target board's redeeming a poison pill plan. The target board refuses, and the bidder starts a proxy contest to replace the board. In its proxy solicitation materials the bidder tells shareholders it is paving the way for its $38 a share takeover. After the proxy solicitation materials are mailed to shareholders and before the shareholder meeting is held, the stock of the target drops to $23 per share based on new public revelations of the deteriorating value of target assets. The target board reverses field and decides that the $38 a share offer is a very generous offer. The target board wants to force the bidder to buy the company at $38 a share. The target board worries, however, that if the bidder takes control of the board in the proxy contest, the bidder will redeem the poison pill and then lower its offer and execute a takeover at $31 per share. Can the target board make a credible threat to sue the bidder under rule 14a-9 if the bidder does not buy the firm at $38 a share?

SUBCHAPTER C. INSIDER TRADING IN ADVANCE OF ACQUISITIONS

SEC, REPORT FROM THE OFFICE OF CHIEF ECONOMIST, STOCK TRADING BEFORE THE ANNOUNCEMENT OF TENDER OFFERS: INSIDER TRADING OR MARKET ANTICIPATION?

(1989)

Recent insider trading actions by the SEC against Dennis Levine, Ivan Boesky, and others have raised several important questions about the effects of insider trading on pre-takeover bid increases in stock prices and surges in trading volumes.[1] These well-publicized cases involve illegal trading in takeover targets based on non-public information about impending bids. Press accounts reveal enormous profits to inside traders. In addition, press accounts suggest that pre-bid market activity in target stocks verifies the existence of widespread insider trading. In our research, however, we find that there are several readily identifiable factors influencing pre-bid trading and that pre-bid trading is not necessarily an accurate indicator of insider trading. While the ultimate source of pre-bid trading may be illegal information, trading in a stock once there is some indication that a firm is "in play" cannot necessarily be attributed to illegal trading.

It is apparent that stock prices and trading volumes of targets increase during the weeks immediately preceding public takeover bids. Several academic studies measure stock price activity preceding mergers and takeovers bids made between 1962 and 1980. They report that stock prices begin to move upwards in anticipation of bids as early as two weeks before formal announcement. They also show that about one-half of the total capital appreciation is accounted for by the close of trading the day before the formal bid. Although the researchers themselves do not generally ascribe these runups to widespread illegal activity, other commentators consider this to be direct evidence of insider trading.

Many argue that the opportunity to make large profits by conduct that is difficult to detect makes it sensible to attribute this pre-bid market activity to trading by insiders, tippees, and those who imitate their behavior. The SEC's enforcement actions against Boesky, Levine, and others, while dispelling the notion that insider trading prohibitions are unenforceable, have increased the discussion of the possibility of

---

1. In May 1986, the SEC charged Dennis Levine, an investment dealer at Drexel Burnham Lambert, with illegally trading in stocks and options of 54 companies. It alleged that Levine had made a profit of $12.6 million by trading on inside information related to actual or proposed tender offers, mergers and other business combinations.

Ivan Boesky agreed to pay $100 million and to plead guilty to one felony count to settle charges of insider trading. The settlement was announced by the SEC in November 1986. According to the SEC complaint, Levine passed on inside information to Boesky, resulting in at least $50 million profits to Boesky.

pervasive insider trading. Newspaper stories are replete with general condemnations of Wall Street's information arbitragers, reflecting a view that legitimate speculation based on sophisticated analyses of public information is overwhelmed by illegitimate trading on non-public information.

Our study attempts to shed additional light on how the market for information operates to anticipate tender offers. We examine pre-bid market activity (daily stock returns and trading volume) over 172 tender offers from 1981 to 1985, and present improved statistical measures of runup in stock prices and volume surges. In specific, we examine how several readily observable characteristics of the takeover bid affect pre-bid market activity. These characteristics include the amount of pre-bid speculation in the media, the foothold acquisition of the bidder and whether the bid is friendly or hostile. Presumably, illegal insider trading would not be dependent on these factors. If runup and volume surges were due primarily to illegal trading, then bid characteristics should not significantly influence pre-bid trading activity.

We summarize here our empirical results:

Based on 172 successful tender offers between 1981 and 1985, runup in stock prices is 38.8 percent of the total eventual control premium by the close of trading the day before the offer announcement. The runup index measures 27.6 percent as of two days before the announcement and 22.7 percent three days before the announcement.

Cumulative abnormal returns before the announcement are significantly different from zero as early as 17 trading days before the announcement.

About one-third of pre-bid market activity can be attributed to takeover speculation in the media. In bids with no rumors reported in the press, the runup index is only 32.7 percent one day before the announcement (19.1 percent two days before), as opposed to 50.3 percent (43.5 percent two days before) in those cases with reported rumors.

Foothold acquisitions by the bidder significantly affect pre-bid market activity. Runup as of day(–1) is 26.5 percent (10.2 percent on day(–2)) over 31 cases with average footholds of 2.56 percent, compared to 47.7 percent (40.2 percent on day(–2)) over the 32 cases with average footholds of 21.7 percent.

Friendly, negotiated takeovers have more pre-bid runup than hostile takeovers (47.1 percent versus 35.3 percent one day before the bid) when foothold acquisitions of the bidder are held constant at zero.

Average trading volume increases about 10 days before the announcement. Volume surges to almost 20 times normal daily volume on the announcement. On the day before the announcement, it is 5 times normal, on days(–2) and (–3), it is 3 times normal.

Illegal insider trading, as discussed here, refers to the restrictions imposed on insiders by Sections 10(b) and 14(e) of the Securities Exchange Act of 1934 and Rules 10b–5 and 14e–3 thereunder. Trading on inside information, in which the trader has material nonpublic information concerning some future event, is very different from legitimate anticipation of that event. Public policy does not condemn market speculation in anticipation of important corporate announcements, such as those concerning takeovers, mergers, or other corporate business. For specialists in the analysis of corporate and economic information, the private returns from predicting future corporate events exceed the private costs. Legitimate research gives some traders informational advantages and their earnings serve as compensation for their efforts.[4]

Basic economics guarantees that considerable resources will be devoted to information analysis with respect to potential corporate control transactions. The prospect of huge takeover premiums and the many kinds of clues legally available to skillful specialists assures us of an active market for information on prospective takeover targets.[5] This market should create the runups in stock price and volume surges we observe.[6] Because the market for information is not perfect, there may be cases in which the anticipatory market activity is not followed by a takeover. However, we consider here only those cases in which a tender offer was made.

Most economists defend legal investment analysis and believe that pre-bid market activity is inevitable. The trading is beneficial in that it makes capital markets more efficient. It aligns actual stock prices with their theoretically correct values, improving the allocation of scarce capital between competing uses. The actions of arbitragers, both before and after a takeover bid, provide considerable value to the market. In a recent *Wall Street Journal* article, Professor Michael Jensen of Harvard University and the University of Rochester noted some of the roles served by arbitragers after the bid is made:

4. When traders with better information (whether gained legally or not) profit from their investment positions, they presumably do so at the expense of less informed investors. The anonymous nature of most stock trading makes it difficult to determine who loses what the information specialist gains. Those selling into the market when the better-informed are buying probably would not have sold had they possessed the same valuable information. However, they still would have sold if the information specialist had refrained from buying, especially if the trading of the specialist did not affect significantly the stock price. This holds true whether the trading is based on insider information or on careful analysis and successful anticipation of the event.

5. Many studies have documented the large premiums paid to shareholders of takeover targets. The Office of the Chief Economist (OCE, 1985) reports that on average from 1981 through 1984, shareholders received a price 50 percent greater than the price at which the shares were trading prior to the offer.

6. Well-informed traders have strong incentives to minimize "leakage" of information that allows other traders to free-ride on their knowledge. Information specialists know that leakage is greater the larger the investment position and the more quickly it is assembled. Also differences in market conditions affect their ability to trade without information leakage. High variance in daily volume, perhaps caused by sporadic trading by institutional traders, and sophisticated techniques for masking the trader's identity can allow larger investment positions to be assembled with less leakage of information.

[Arbitragers] help direct resources to their highest-valued use. In doing so, the arbs provide three critically important services: 1) they help value alternative offers (including the plans of target management), 2) they provide risk-bearing services for investors who do not wish to bear the great uncertainty that occurs between the announcement and final outcome of a takeover bid or restructuring, and 3) they help resolve the collective action or free-rider problems of small, diffuse shareholders who cannot organize to negotiate directly with competing bidders for the target firm. (December 3, 1986, p. 26.)

INFORMATION SOURCES FOR LEGITIMATE TRADING

There are many sources of information on which trading in anticipation of a takeover may be based besides inside information. Particularly important is the Schedule 13D requirement of the Williams Act, which directs acquirers of more than five percent of a firm's equity to file a Schedule 13D reporting the acquisition within ten days of crossing this threshold.[7] This mandatory filing requires the purchaser to disclose the reasons for the purchase, specifically whether or not the purchaser intends to seek control. Once the original Schedule 13D has been filed, the acquirer is obliged to file an amendment to reveal any important changes in intent (say, a change from "passive investor" to "investor seeking control"). Several studies show that 13D filings cause significant increases in the target stock prices and surges in trading volume, particularly when the filer discloses takeover-type intentions.[8]

In addition to mandated disclosures, "street talk" can affect pre-bid market activity in takeover stocks. While some street talk might originate improperly from inside information, objective observers of the sleuthing done by professional traders, arbitragers, "shark watchers" and Wall Street reporters point to numerous sources of information:

[A]n army of traders, arbitragers and stock analysts is quick to spot unusual activity of corporate executives, the calling and canceling of meetings and other seemingly insignificant corporate developments that might give a clue to an upcoming major development.... Experts closely monitor such things as which brokerage firm is doing the heaviest buying and selling of a particular stock. Does the firm have a relationship with a known corporate raider? Is the buyer bidding up the price of a stock, indicating that he is anxious to get the shares in a hurry? (*New York Times*, August 12, 1986, p. D8.)

[I]t's not hard for all sorts of people to deduce that takeover action is about to occur in a stock. Computers are a big help here. Accumulation is instant news; so is unusual volume. Connected by a national network of direct phone lines, smart traders . . . talk to one another and to brokers constantly.... When investment bankers are hired,

---

7. The SEC recently recommended to Congress that they adopt legislation to close the gap for filing the Schedule 13D from ten days to two days after crossing the five percent ownership threshold.

8. * * * These studies report an average three to seven percent appreciation in share price (net of market) at the 13D Schedule filing date.

they frequently publish an internal memo that places their client corporation on a restricted list, to prevent conflicts of interest in trading and research recommendations. A company's name appearing on a restricted list often is all the information needed by shrewd investors. (*Forbes Magazine,* February 10, 1986, p. 33.)

[Arbitrager] Mulheren says his main sources are professional traders like himself, who make their living taking the pulse of the market and spotting unusual trading patterns. From the rim of [his] 10–person trading desk, Mulheren has access to about 170 trading wires that provide direct feeds into the major stock and commodity exchanges as well as a network of multinational brokers and securities firms. (*WSJ,* July 28, 1986, p. 1.)

Arbitragers use the knowledge that takeovers often come in "waves" with targets clustered somewhat by industry classification, as deregulation and other economic forces cause common adjustments in firms of common characteristics. Also, firm-specific knowledge, such as the impending demise of tight family control or internal disputes among managerial factions, often fuels legitimate takeover speculation. Finally, publicly available information disclosing large stock acquisitions and newspaper stories speculating on future takeovers can be important causes of pre-bid market activity, quite independent of illegal insider trading.

* * *

These statistics tell a story of an active market for information about impending takeover bids.

* * *

The statistical relations we measure between pre-bid activity and media speculations, footholds and friendly/hostile variables do not provide a complete response to contentions that insider trading is the dominant source of the information that spurs runup. We are unable to explain a great deal of the pre-bid trading. Also, it is possible, and logical to many, that illegal insider behavior could affect simultaneously runup and these other factors. Media speculation, for example, may usually emanate from "street talk," which could be ultimately fed by illegal disclosures.

On the other hand, a case can be made that the strong effects of foothold buying and media speculation on pre-bid market activity reflects a legitimate market for information. Systematic relationships between footholds or news stories and pre-bid market activity supports the existence of this market and suggests that significant pre-bid market activity is consistent with having little illegal insider trading. This conclusion implies that aggregate runup statistics are of little value as measures of illegal insider activity, although measures for individual stocks can still serve as very useful enforcement tools. Further research on the sources of information about impending takeovers is required to determine the ultimate source of pre-takeover bid trading in target stocks.

CHIARELLA v. UNITED STATES
Supreme Court of the United States, 1980.
445 U.S. 222, 100 S.Ct. 1108, 63 L.Ed.2d 348.

* * *

MR. JUSTICE POWELL:

The question in this case is whether a person who learns from the confidential documents of one corporation that it is planning an attempt to secure control of a second corporation violates § 10(b) of the Securities Exchange Act of 1934 if he fails to disclose the impending takeover before trading in the target company's securities.

Petitioner is a printer by trade. In 1975 and 1976, he worked as a "markup man" in the New York composing room of Pandick Press, a financial printer. Among documents that petitioner handled were five announcements of corporate takeover bids. When these documents were delivered to the printer, the identities of the acquiring and target corporations were concealed by blank spaces or false names. The true names were sent to the printer on the night of the final printing.

The petitioner, however, was able to deduce the names of the target companies before the final printing from other information contained in the documents. Without disclosing his knowledge, petitioner purchased stock in the target companies and sold the shares immediately after the takeover attempts were made public.[1] By this method, petitioner realized a gain of slightly more than $30,000 in the course of 14 months. Subsequently, the Securities and Exchange Commission (Commission or SEC) began an investigation of his trading activities. In May 1977, petitioner entered into a consent decree with the Commission in which he agreed to return his profits to the sellers of the shares. On the same day, he was discharged by Pandick Press.

In January 1978, petitioner was indicted on 17 counts of violating § 10(b) of the Securities Exchange Act of 1934 (1934 Act) and SEC Rule 10b–5.[3] After petitioner unsuccessfully moved to dismiss the indictment, he was brought to trial and convicted on all counts.

* * *

In *Cady, Roberts & Co.*, 40 S.E.C. 907 (1961), the Commission decided that a corporate insider must abstain from trading in the shares of his corporation unless he has first disclosed all material inside information known to him. The obligation to disclose or abstain derives from

"[a]n affirmative duty to disclose material information[, which] has been traditionally imposed on corporate 'insiders,' particularly officers,

---

1. Of the five transactions, four involved tender offers and one concerned a merger. 588 F.2d 1358, 1363, n. 2 (CA2 1978).

3. Section 32(a) of the 1934 Act sanctions criminal penalties against any person who willfully violates the Act. 15 U.S.C. § 78ff(a) (1976 ed., Supp. II). Petitioner was charged with 17 counts of violating the Act because he had received 17 letters confirming purchase of shares.

directors, or controlling stockholders. We, and the courts have consistently held that insiders must disclose material facts which are known to them by virtue of their position but which are not known to persons with whom they deal and which, if known, would affect their investment judgment." *Id.*, at 911.

The Commission emphasized that the duty arose from (i) the existence of a relationship affording access to inside information intended to be available only for a corporate purpose, and (ii) the unfairness of allowing a corporate insider to take advantage of that information by trading without disclosure. *Id.*, at 912, and n. 15.

That the relationship between a corporate insider and the stockholders of his corporation gives rise to a disclosure obligation is not a novel twist of the law. At common law, misrepresentation made for the purpose of inducing reliance upon the false statement is fraudulent. But one who fails to disclose material information prior to the consummation of a transaction commits fraud only when he is under a duty to do so. And the duty to disclose arises when one party has information "that the other [party] is entitled to know because of a fiduciary or other similar relation of trust and confidence between them." [9] In its *Cady, Roberts* decision, the Commission recognized a relationship of trust and confidence between the shareholders of a corporation and those insiders who have obtained confidential information by reason of their position with that corporation. This relationship gives rise to a duty to disclose because of the "necessity of preventing a corporate insider from . . . tak[ing] unfair advantage of the uninformed minority stockholders." *Speed v. Transamerica Corp.*, 99 F.Supp. 808, 829 (Del. 1951).

* * *

Thus, administrative and judicial interpretations have established that silence in connection with the purchase or sale of securities may operate as a fraud actionable under § 10(b) despite the absence of statutory language or legislative history specifically addressing the legality of nondisclosure. But such liability is premised upon a duty to disclose arising from a relationship of trust and confidence between parties to a transaction. Application of a duty to disclose prior to trading guarantees that corporate insiders, who have an obligation to place the shareholder's welfare before their own, will not benefit personally through fraudulent use of material, nonpublic information.

In this case, the petitioner was convicted of violating § 10(b) although he was not a corporate insider and he received no confidential information from the target company. Moreover, the "market information" upon which he relied did not concern the earning power or operations of the target company, but only the plans of the acquiring company. Petitioner's use of that information was not a fraud under § 10(b) unless he was subject to an affirmative duty to disclose it before trading. In this case, the jury instructions failed to specify any such

---

9. Restatement (Second) of Torts § 551(2)(a) (1976).

duty. In effect, the trial court instructed the jury that petitioner owed a duty to everyone; to all sellers, indeed, to the market as a whole. The jury simply was told to decide whether petitioner used material, nonpublic information at a time when "he knew other people trading in the securities market did not have access to the same information."

* * *

No duty could arise from petitioner's relationship with the sellers of the target company's securities, for petitioner had no prior dealings with them. He was not their agent, he was not a fiduciary, he was not a person in whom the sellers had placed their trust and confidence. He was, in fact, a complete stranger who dealt with the sellers only through impersonal market transactions.

* * *

In its brief to this Court, the United States offers an alternative theory to support petitioner's conviction. It argues that petitioner breached a duty to the acquiring corporation when he acted upon information that he obtained by virtue of his position as an employee of a printer employed by the corporation. The breach of this duty is said to support a conviction under § 10(b) for fraud perpetrated upon both the acquiring corporation and the sellers.

We need not decide whether this theory has merit for it was not submitted to the jury.

* * *

The jury instructions demonstrate that petitioner was convicted merely because of his failure to disclose material, non-public information to sellers from whom he bought the stock of target corporations. The jury was not instructed on the nature or elements of a duty owed by petitioner to anyone other than the sellers. Because we cannot affirm a criminal conviction on the basis of a theory not presented to the jury, * * * we will not speculate upon whether such a duty exists, whether it has been breached, or whether such a breach constitutes a violation of § 10(b).

* * *

MR. CHIEF JUSTICE BURGER, dissenting.

I believe that the jury instructions in this case properly charged a violation of § 10(b) and Rule 10b–5, and I would affirm the conviction.

As a general rule, neither party to an arm's-length business transaction has an obligation to disclose information to the other unless the parties stand in some confidential or fiduciary relation. See W. Prosser, Law of Torts § 106 (2d ed. 1955). This rule permits a businessman to capitalize on his experience and skill in securing and evaluating relevant information; it provides incentive for hard work, careful analysis, and astute forecasting. But the policies that underlie the rule also should limit its scope. In particular, the rule should give way when an informational advantage is obtained, not by superior experience, foresight, or industry, but by some unlawful means. * * * I would read § 10(b) and Rule 10b–5 to encompass and build on this principle: to mean that a person who has misappropriated nonpublic information has an absolute duty to disclose that information or to refrain from trading.

* * *

In sum, the evidence shows beyond all doubt that Chiarella, working literally in the shadows of the warning signs in the printshop, misappropriated—stole to put it bluntly—valuable nonpublic information entrusted to him in the utmost confidence. He then exploited his ill-gotten informational advantage by purchasing securities in the market. In my view, such conduct plainly violates § 10(b) and Rule 10b–5.

* * *

Please read Securities and Exchange Commission rule 14e–3 in your statutory supplement.

UNITED STATES OF AMERICA v. CHESTMAN
United States Court of Appeals, Second Circuit, 1990.
903 F.2d 75 (2nd Cir.1990), en banc pending

[On May 2, 1990, a three judge panel of the Second Circuit, on a vote of 2 to 1, reversed the conviction of a stockbroker for, among other things, violations of Rule 14e–3. One of the judges in the majority, Judge Mahoney, wrote that the SEC "exceeded its statutorily granted authority by promulgating rule 14e–3 without including any requirement of a breach of fiduciary duty." The second judge in the majority, Judge Carman, wrote that "there should be no conviction of a crime under rule 14e–3 unless there has been separate substantive proof of fraudulent, deceptive or manipulative acts." Since the trial judge failed to so instruct the jury, Judge Carman also voted to reverse the conviction. At the time of the writing of this book, the Second Circuit had voted to hear the case *en banc* and had held oral arguments and received briefs. Judge Mahoney's opinion on the power of the SEC to promulgate the rule, which may or may not be law when you read this, is potentially the most far reaching.]

MAHONEY, CIRCUIT JUDGE:

* * *

The rule plainly states that "it shall constitute a fraudulent, deceptive or manipulative act or practice within the meaning of section 14(e)" to trade on insider information in the tender offer context, absent prior public disclosure of the inside information and its source, *without more*. Specifically, there is no requirement that any fiduciary duty exist or be violated. I note in this connection that rule 14e–3 was promulgated by the Commission on September 12, 1980, see 45 Fed.Reg.

60,418 (1980), in the immediate aftermath of the Supreme Court's ruling on March 18, 1980 in *Chiarella v. United States,* 445 U.S. 222, 100 S.Ct. 1108, 63 L.Ed.2d 348 (1980), that a breach of fiduciary duty is essential to establish a violation of section 10(b) of the 1934 Act, 15 U.S.C. § 78j(b) (1988), and rule 10b–5 thereunder, 17 C.F.R. § 240.10b–5 (1989), *see Chiarella,* 445 U.S. at 229, 100 S.Ct. at 1115; and that "a duty to disclose under § 10(b) does not arise from the mere possession of nonpublic market information." * * *

As a general matter, principles developed under rule 10b–5 are applicable in determining whether section 14(e) violations have been committed. * * * As has been seen, Section 14(e) authorizes the Commission to prescribe rules which will "define ... such acts and practices as are fraudulent, deceptive or manipulative" in the tender offer context. This authorization, however, seems directed at the application of these legal concepts in a relatively novel area (especially in 1970, when section 14(e) was amended to add this language), *see Schreiber v. Burlington Northern, Inc.,* 472 U.S. 1, 11, 105 S.Ct. 2458, 2464, 86 L.Ed.2d 1 (1985) (section 14(e) requires disclosure "more explicitly addressed to the tender offer context than that required by § 10(b)"), rather than to constitute an authorization for the Commission to redefine the meaning of the terms "fraudulent, deceptive or manipulative" as established by authoritative Supreme Court interpretations of section 10(b) and rule 10b–5, upon which section 14(e) is concededly modeled. * * * In this connection, *Schreiber* explicitly states that the 1970 amendment to section 14(e) did not effect any change, or authorize the Commission to effect any change, in the basic meaning of the statutory term "manipulative." * * * I doubt that greater authority was provided to the Commission to redefine the statutory term "fraudulent."

* * *

CARPENTER v. UNITED STATES
Supreme Court of the United States, 1987.
484 U.S. 19, 108 S.Ct. 316, 98 L.Ed.2d 275.

JUSTICE WHITE delivered the opinion of the Court.

Petitioners Kenneth Felis and R. Foster Winans were convicted of violating section 10(b) of the Securities Exchange Act of 1934, 48 Stat. 891, 15 U.S.C. section 78j(b), and Rule 10b–5, 16 CFR section 240.10b–5 (1987). United States v. Winans, 612 F.Supp. 827 (SDNY 1985). * * *

In 1981, Winans became a reporter for the Wall Street Journal (the Journal) and in the summer of 1982 became one of the two writers of a daily column, "Heard on the Street." That column discussed selected stocks or groups of stocks, giving positive and negative information about those stocks and taking "a point of view with respect to investment in the stocks that it reviews." 612 F.Supp., at 830. Winans regularly interviewed corporate executives to put together interesting perspectives on the stocks that would be highlighted in upcoming columns, but, at least for the columns at issue here, none contained corporate inside information or any "hold for release" information. *Id.,* at 830, n. 2. Because of the "Heard" column's perceived quality and integrity, it had the potential of affecting the price of the stocks which it examined. The District Court concluded on the basis of testimony presented at trial that the "Heard" column "does have an impact on the market, difficult though it may be to quantify in any particular case." *Id.,* at 830.

The official policy and practice at the Journal was that prior to publication, the contents of the column were the Journal's confidential information. Despite the rule, with which Winans was familiar, he entered into a scheme in October 1983 with Peter Brant and petitioner Felis, both connected with the Kidder Peabody brokerage firm in New York City, to give them advance information as to the timing and contents of the "Heard" column. This permitted Brant and Felis and another conspirator, David Clark, a client of Brant, to buy or sell based on the probable impact of the column on the market. Profits were to be shared. The conspirators agreed that the scheme would not affect the journalistic purity of the "Heard" column, and the District Court did not find that the contents of any of the articles were altered to further the profit potential of petitioners' stock-trading scheme. *Id.,* at 832, 834–835. Over a four-month period, the brokers made prepublication trades on the basis of information given them by Winans about the contents of some 27 Heard columns. The net profits from these trades were about $690,000.

* * *

The District Court found, and the Court of Appeals agreed, that Winans had knowingly breached a duty of confidentiality by misappropriating prepublication information regarding the timing and contents of the "Heard" columns, information that had been gained in the course of his employment under the understanding that it would not be revealed in advance of publication and that if it were, he would report it to his employer. It was this appropriation of confidential information that underlay both the securities laws and mail and wire fraud counts. With respect to the § 10(b) charges, the courts below held that the deliberate breach of Winans' duty of confidentiality and concealment of the scheme was a fraud and deceit on the Journal. Although the victim of the fraud, the Journal, was not a buyer or seller of the stocks traded in or otherwise a market participant, the fraud was nevertheless considered to be "in connection with" a purchase or sale of securities within the meaning of the statute and the rule. The courts reasoned that the scheme's sole purpose was to buy and sell securities at a profit based on advance information of the column's contents. The courts below rejected petitioners' submission, which is one of the two questions presented here, that criminal liability could not be imposed on petitioners under Rule 10b–5 because "the newspaper is the only alleged victim of fraud and has no interest in the securities traded."

* * *

The Court is evenly divided with respect to the convictions under the securities laws and for that reason affirms the judgment below on those counts.

SUBCHAPTER D. THE SHORT SWING PROFITS PROHIBITION: A TRAP FOR THE UNWARY

KERN COUNTY LAND CO. v. OCCIDENTAL CORP.

Supreme Court of the United States, 1973.
411 U.S. 582, 93 S.Ct. 1736, 36 L.Ed.2d 503.

Mr. Justice White delivered the opinion of the Court.

Immediately upon the announcement of Occidental's tender offer, the Old Kern management undertook to frustrate Occidental's takeover attempt. A management letter to all stockholders cautioned against tender and indicated that Occidental's offer might not be the best available, since the management was engaged in merger discussions with several companies. When Occidental extended its tender offer, the president of Old Kern sent a telegram to all stockholders again advising against tender. In addition, Old Kern undertook merger discussions with Tenneco, Inc. (Tenneco), and, on May 19, 1967, the Board of Directors of Old Kern announced that it had approved a merger proposal advanced by Tenneco.[9] Under the terms of the merger, Tenneco would acquire the assets, property, and goodwill of Old Kern, subject to its liabilities, through "Kern County Land Co." (New Kern), a new corporation to be formed by Tenneco to receive the assets and carry on the business of Old Kern. The shareholders of Old Kern would receive a share of Tenneco cumulative convertible preference stock in exchange for each share of Old Kern common stock which they owned. On the same day, May 19, Occidental, in a quarterly report to stockholders, appraised the value of the new Tenneco stock at $105 per share.[11]

* * * Realizing that, if the Old Kern–Tenneco merger were approved and successfully closed, Occidental would have to exchange its Old Kern shares for Tenneco stock and would be locked into a minority

---

9. Although technically a sale of assets, the corporate combination has been consistently referred to by the parties as a "merger" and will be similarly denominated in this opinion. The only significance of the characterization is the fact that a sale of assets required, under California law, approval of only a majority of the Old Kern shareholders and provided no appraisal rights for dissenters.

11. The annual dividend of $5.50 per share on the new Tenneco stock would be more than double the current annual dividend of $2.60 per share on the Old Kern stock. Each share of the new Tenneco preference stock was convertible into 3.6 shares of Tenneco common stock. During 1967, Tenneco common stock had sold at a high of 32½ and a low of 20⅞. Moreover, in contrast to Occidental's cash offer, the Tenneco exchange was expected to be, and was ultimately approved by the Internal Revenue Service as, free of capital gains tax.

position in Tenneco, Occidental took other steps to protect itself. Between May 30 and June 2, it negotiated an arrangement with Tenneco whereby Occidental granted Tenneco Corp., a subsidiary of Tenneco, an option to purchase at $105 per share all of the Tenneco preference stock to which Occidental would be entitled in exchange for its Old Kern stock when and if the Old Kern–Tenneco merger was closed. The premium to secure the option, at $10 per share, totaled $8,866,230 and was to be paid immediately upon the signing of the option agreement.[14] If the option were exercised, the premium was to be applied to the purchase price. By the terms of the option agreement, the option could not be exercised prior to December 9, 1967, a date six months and one day after expiration of Occidental's tender offer. On June 2, 1967, within six months of the acquisition by Occidental of more than 10% ownership of Old Kern, Occidental and Tenneco Corp. executed the option.[15] Soon thereafter, Occidental announced that it would not oppose the Old Kern–Tenneco merger and dismissed its state court suits against Old Kern.[16]

The Old Kern–Tenneco merger plan was presented to and approved by Old Kern shareholders at their meeting on July 17, 1967. Occidental refrained from voting its Old Kern shares, but in a letter read at the meeting Occidental stated that it had determined prior to June 2 not to oppose the merger and that it did not consider the plan unfair or inequitable. Indeed, Occidental indicated that, had it been voting, it would have voted in favor of the merger.

* * *

The Old Kern–Tenneco merger transaction was closed on August 30. Old Kern shareholders thereupon became irrevocably entitled to receive Tenneco preference stock, share for share in exchange for their Old Kern stock. Old Kern was dissolved and all of its assets, including "all claims, demands, rights and choses in action accrued or to accrue under and by virtue of the Securities Exchange Act of 1934 ...," were transferred to New Kern.

The option granted by Occidental on June 2, 1967, was exercised on December 11, 1967. Occidental, not having previously availed itself of its right, exchanged certificates representing 887,549 shares of Old Kern stock for a certificate representing a like number of shares of Tenneco preference stock. The certificate was then endorsed over to the optionee-purchaser, and in return $84,229,185 was credited to Occidental's accounts at various banks. Adding to this amount the

---

14. An outside investment banking firm in New York had determined that between $9 and $12 per share was a fair premium on an option on the Old Kern stock.

15. On that date, and on the date of the exercise of the option, Old Kern common stock was selling at approximately $95 per share.

16. Seeking to prevent its acquisition of Tenneco shares pursuant to the merger from being matched with the sale of those shares upon exercise of the option for purposes of establishing § 16(b) liability, Occidental asked that the new Tenneco stock not be immediately registered pursuant to § 12 of the Securities Exchange Act of 1934, 15 U.S.C. § 78*l*.

$8,886,230 premium paid in June, Occidental received $93,905,415 for its Old Kern stock (including the 1,900 shares acquired prior to issuance of its tender offer). In addition, Occidental received dividends totaling $1,793,439.22. Occidental's total profit was $19,506,419.22 on the shares obtained through its tender offer.

On October 17, 1967, New Kern instituted a suit under § 16(b) against Occidental to recover the profits which Occidental had realized as a result of its dealings in Old Kern stock. * * *

In the present case, it is undisputed that Occidental became a "beneficial owner" within the terms of § 16(b) when, pursuant to its tender offer, it "purchased" more than 10% of the outstanding shares of Old Kern. We must decide, however, whether a "sale" within the ambit of the statute took place either when Occidental became irrevocably bound to exchange its shares of Old Kern for shares of Tenneco pursuant to the terms of the merger agreement between Old Kern and Tenneco or when Occidental gave an option to Tenneco to purchase from Occidental the Tenneco shares so acquired.[28]

On August 30, 1967, the Old Kern–Tenneco merger agreement was signed, and Occidental became irrevocably entitled to exchange its shares of Old Kern stock for shares of Tenneco preference stock. Concededly, the transaction must be viewed as though Occidental had made the exchange on that day. But, even so, did the exchange involve a "sale" of Old Kern shares within the meaning of § 16(b)? We agree with the Court of Appeals that it did not, for we think it totally unrealistic to assume or infer from the facts before us that Occidental either had or was likely to have access to inside information, by reason of its ownership of more than 10% of the outstanding shares of Old Kern, so as to afford it an opportunity to reap speculative, short-swing profits from its disposition within six months of its tender-offer purchases.

It cannot be contended that Occidental was an insider when, on May 8, 1967, it made an irrevocable offer to purchase 500,000 shares of Old Kern stock at a price substantially above market. At that time, it owned only 1,900 shares of Old Kern stock, far fewer than the 432,000 shares needed to constitute the 10% ownership required by the statute. There is no basis for finding that, at the time the tender offer was commenced, Occidental enjoyed an insider's opportunity to acquire information about Old Kern's affairs.

It is also wide of the mark to assert that Occidental, as a sophisticated corporation knowledgeable in matters of corporate affairs and finance, knew that its tender offer would either succeed or would be

---

28. Both events occurred within six months of Occidental's first acquisition of Old Kern shares pursuant to its tender offer. Although Occidental did not exchange its Old Kern shares until December 11, 1967, it is not contended that that date, rather than the date on which Occidental became irrevocably bound to do so, should control. Similarly, although the option was not exercised until December 11, 1967, no liability is asserted with respect to that event, because it occurred more than six months after Occidental's last acquisition of Old Kern stock.

met with a "defensive merger." If its takeover efforts failed, it is argued, Occidental knew it could sell its stock to the target company's merger partner at a substantial profit. Calculations of this sort, however, whether speculative or not and whether fair or unfair to other stockholders or to Old Kern, do not represent the kind of speculative abuse at which the statute is aimed, for they could not have been based on inside information obtained from substantial stockholdings that did not yet exist. Accepting both that Occidental made this very prediction and that it would recurringly be an accurate forecast in tender-offer situations, we nevertheless fail to perceive how the fruition of such anticipated events would require, or in any way depend upon, the receipt and use of inside information. If there are evils to be redressed by way of deterring those who would make tender offers, § 16(b) does not appear to us to have been designed for this task.

By May 10, 1967, Occidental had acquired more than 10% of the outstanding shares of Old Kern. It was thus a statutory insider when, on May 11, it extended its tender offer to include another 500,000 shares. We are quite unconvinced, however, that the situation had changed materially with respect to the possibilities of speculative abuse of inside information by Occidental. Perhaps Occidental anticipated that extending its offer would increase the likelihood of the ultimate success of its takeover attempt or the occurrence of a defensive merger. But, again, the expectation of such benefits was unrelated to the use of information unavailable to other stockholders or members of the public with sufficient funds and the intention to make the purchases Occidental had offered to make before June 8, 1967.

The possibility that Occidental had, or had the opportunity to have, any confidential information about Old Kern before or after May 11, 1967, seems extremely remote. Occidental was, after all, a tender offeror, threatening to seize control of Old Kern, displace its management, and use the company for its own ends. The Old Kern management vigorously and immediately opposed Occidental's efforts. Twice it communicated with its stockholders, advising against acceptance of Occidental's offer and indicating prior to May 11 and prior to Occidental's extension of its offer, that there was a possibility of an imminent merger and a more profitable exchange. Old Kern's management refused to discuss with Occidental officials the subject of an Old Kern–Occidental merger. Instead, it undertook negotiations with Tenneco and forthwith concluded an agreement, announcing the merger terms on May 19. Requests by Occidental for inspection of Old Kern records were sufficiently frustrated by Old Kern's management to force Occidental to litigate to secure the information it desired.

There is, therefore, nothing in connection with Occidental's acquisition of Old Kern stock pursuant to its tender offer to indicate either the possibility of inside information being available to Occidental by virtue of its stock ownership or the potential for speculative abuse of such inside information by Occidental. Much the same can be said of the events leading to the exchange of Occidental's Old Kern stock for

Tenneco preferred, which is one of the transactions that is sought to be classified a "sale" under § 16(b). The critical fact is that the exchange took place and was required pursuant to a merger between Old Kern and Tenneco. That merger was not engineered by Occidental but was sought by Old Kern to frustrate the attempts of Occidental to gain control of Old Kern. Occidental obviously did not participate in or control the negotiations or the agreement between Old Kern and Tenneco. Once agreement between those two companies crystallized, the course of subsequent events was out of Occidental's hands. Old Kern needed the consent of its stockholders, but as it turned out, Old Kern's management had the necessary votes without the affirmative vote of Occidental. The merger agreement was approved by a majority of the stockholders of Old Kern, excluding the votes to which Occidental was entitled by virtue of its ownership of Old Kern shares.

* * * Occidental, although registering its opinion that the merger would be beneficial to Old Kern shareholders, did not in fact vote at the stockholders' meeting at which merger approval was obtained. Under California law, its abstention was tantamount to a vote against approval of the merger. Moreover, at the time of stockholder ratification of the merger, Occidental's previous dealing in Old Kern stock was, as it had always been, fully disclosed.

Once the merger and exchange were approved, Occidental was left with no real choice with respect to the future of its shares of Old Kern. Occidental was in no position to prevent the issuance of a ruling by the Internal Revenue Service that the exchange of Old Kern stock for Tenneco preferred would be tax free; and, although various lawsuits were begun in state and federal courts seeking to postpone the merger closing beyond the statutory six-month period, those efforts were futile. The California Corporation Commissioner issued the necessary permits for the closing that took place on August 30, 1967. The merger left no right in dissenters to secure appraisal of their stock. Occidental could, of course, have disposed of its shares of Old Kern for cash before the merger was closed. Such an act would have been a § 16(b) sale and would have left Occidental with a prima facie § 16(b) liability. It was not, therefore, a realistic alternative for Occidental as long as it felt that it could successfully defend a suit like the present one.

* * *

We do not suggest that an exchange of stock pursuant to a merger may never result in § 16(b) liability. But the involuntary nature of Occidental's exchange, when coupled with the absence of the possibility of speculative abuse of inside information, convinces us that § 16(b) should not apply to transactions such as this one.

Petitioner also claims that the Occidental–Tenneco option agreement should itself be considered a sale, either because it was the kind of transaction the statute was designed to prevent or because the agreement was an option in form but a sale in fact. But the mere execution of an option to sell is not generally regarded as a "sale." * * * And we do not find in the execution of the Occidental–Tenneco option agreement a sufficient possibility for the speculative abuse of inside information with respect to Old Kern's affairs to warrant holding that the option agreement was itself a "sale" within the meaning of § 16(b). The mutual advantages of the arrangement appear quite clear. As the District Court found, Occidental wanted to avoid the position of a minority stockholder with a huge investment in a company over which it had no control and in which it had not chosen to invest. On the other hand, Tenneco did not want a potentially troublesome minority stockholder that had just been vanquished in a fight for the control of Old Kern. Motivations like these do not smack of insider trading; and it is not clear to us, as it was not to the Court of Appeals, how the negotiation and execution of the option agreement gave Occidental any possible opportunity to trade on inside information it might have obtained from its position as a major stockholder of Old Kern. Occidental wanted to get out, but only at a date more than six months thence. It was willing to get out at a price of $105 per share, a price at which it had publicly valued Tenneco preferred on May 19 when the Tenneco–Old Kern agreement was announced. In any event, Occidental was dealing with the putative new owners of Old Kern, who undoubtedly knew more about Old Kern and Tenneco's affairs than did Occidental. If Occidental had leverage in dealing with Tenneco, it is incredible that its source was inside information rather than the fact of its large stock ownership itself.

Neither does it appear that the option agreement, as drafted and executed by the parties, offered measurable possibilities for speculative abuse. What Occidental granted was a "call" option. Tenneco had the right to buy after six months, but Occidental could not force Tenneco to buy. The price was fixed at $105 for each share of Tenneco preferred. Occidental could not share in a rising market for the Tenneco stock. * * * If the stock fell more than $10 per share, the option might not be exercised, and Occidental might suffer a loss if the market further deteriorated to a point where Occidental was forced to sell. Thus, the option, by its very form, left Occidental with no choice but to sell if Tenneco exercised the option, which it was almost sure to do if the value of Tenneco stock remained relatively steady. On the other hand, it is difficult to perceive any speculative value to Occidental if the stock declined and Tenneco chose not to exercise its option.

* * *

The option, therefore, does not appear to have been an instrument with potential for speculative abuse, whether or not Occidental possessed inside information about the affairs of Old Kern. In addition, the option covered Tenneco preference stock, a stock as yet unissued, unregistered, and untraded. It was the value of this stock that underlay the option and that determined whether the option would be exercised, whether Occidental would be able to profit from the exercise, and whether there was any real likelihood of the exploitation of inside information. If Occidental had inside information when it negotiated and signed the option agreement, it was inside information with respect to Old Kern. Whatever it may have known or expected as to the future value of Old Kern stock, Occidental had no ownership position in Tenneco giving it any actual or presumed insights into the future value of Tenneco stock. That was the critical item of intelligence if Occidental was to use the option for purposes of speculation. Also, the date for exercise of the option was over six months in the future, a period that, under the statute itself, is assumed to dissipate whatever trading advantage might be imputed to a major stockholder with inside information.

* * *

By enshrining the statutory period into the option, Occidental also, at least if the statutory period is taken to accomplish its intended purpose, limited its speculative possibilities. Nor should it be forgotten that there was no absolute assurance that the merger, which was not controlled by Occidental, would be consummated. In the event the merger did not close, the option itself would become null and void.

Nor can we agree that we must reverse the Court of Appeals on the ground that the option agreement was in fact a sale because the premium paid was so large as to make the exercise of the option almost inevitable, particularly when coupled with Tenneco's desire to rid itself of a potentially troublesome stockholder. The argument has force, but resolution of the question is very much a matter of judgment, economic and otherwise, and the Court of Appeals rejected the argument. That court emphasized that the premium paid was what experts had said the option was worth, the possibility that the market might drop sufficiently in the six months following execution of the option to make exercise unlikely, and the fact that here, * * * the optionor did not surrender practically all emoluments of ownership by executing the option. Nor did any other special circumstances indicate that the parties understood and intended that the option was in fact a sale.[30] We see no satisfactory basis or reason for disagreeing with the judgment of the Court of Appeals in this respect.

* * *

---

30. In *Bershad v. McDonough*, 428 F.2d 693 (CA7 1970), the defendants were directors and greater-than-ten-percent stockholders of Cudahy Co. The defendants, within six months of their acquisition of beneficial ownership of Cudahy, granted an option to Smelting Refining & Mining Co. to purchase their Cudahy stock. The Seventh Circuit held that the grant of the option was a § 16(b) "sale" of the Cudahy stock. The Court of Appeals in the present case distinguished *Bershad* as follows:

"That case came before the court of appeals on a finding by the district court that, under the circumstances there presented, the stock had in fact been sold within the six months period, although the option was not formally exercised until later. The district court had relied on a number of circumstances, the most significant being that the optionor gave the optionee an irrevocable proxy to vote the shares and that the optionor and one of his associate directors resigned as directors within a few days after the grant of the option and were replaced by officers of the optionee. In other words, the district court found in effect that the 'option' was accompanied by a wink of the eye, and the court of appeals sustained this. Here there is no such finding, and no basis for one." 450 F.2d, at 165.

TEXAS INTERNATIONAL AIRLINES v. NATIONAL AIRLINES, INC.
United States Court of Appeals, Fifth Circuit, 1983.
714 F.2d 533, cert. denied 465 U.S. 1065, 104 S.Ct. 1326, 79 L.Ed.2d 721 (1984).

JOHNSON, CIRCUIT JUDGE:

Texas International (TI) appeals the grant of summary judgment for National Airlines (National) holding TI liable to National under section 16(b) of the Securities Exchange Act of 1934 (the Exchange Act) for the "short swing profits" made on the sale of 121,000 shares of National common stock.

* * *

On March 14, 1979, during an attempt by TI to gain control of National, TI purchased 121,000 shares of National common stock in open market brokerage transactions.[2] On March 14, the date of the purchase, TI was a beneficial owner of more than ten percent of National's common stock. On July 28, 1979, within six months of the March 14 purchase, TI and Pan American World Airways, Inc. (Pan Am) entered into a stock purchase agreement whereby TI agreed to sell 790,700 shares of National common stock to Pan Am at $50 per share.[3] The closing was held on July 30, 1979. Under the matching rules of section 16(b) the 790,700 shares sold by TI on July 28, 1979 are deemed to include the 121,000 shares purchased by TI in March.

On September 6, 1978, National and Pan Am had entered into a merger agreement which provided for the merger of National into Pan Am contingent upon certain conditions and, in connection with the merger, for the exchange by Pan Am of not less than $50 in cash for each share of National common stock, other than the shares held by Pan Am. On May 16, 1979, National stockholders approved the merger agreement dated September 6, 1978, as amended. TI, as a National stockholder, stood to receive $50 per share for its National stock if and when the merger closed. For whatever reason, TI decided not to wait until the merger went through to negotiate for the disposition of its holdings to Pan Am. It was not until after the July 28, 1979 sale by TI of its National stock to Pan Am that the National–Pan Am merger was effectuated.

* * *

TI urges this Court to create an exception to automatic section 16(b) liability in cases where a defendant can prove that, notwithstand-

---

[2]. These transactions were as follows: 11,000 shares at $40 per share; 10,000 shares at $40⅛ per share; 4,500 shares at $40⅜ per share; 95,500 shares at $40½ per share. The aggregate purchase price for the 121,000 shares was $4,890,687.50, including brokerage commissions of $9,680.00. At all relevant times, National's common stock was listed on the New York and Pacific Stock Exchanges and registered with the Securities and Exchange Commission pursuant to § 12(b) of the Exchange Act.

[3]. Pursuant to the agreement, Pan Am also agreed to pay TI the sum of $3,000,000 for an option to purchase the remaining 1,309,300 shares owned by TI. In November 1979, Pan Am exercised the option, which is not an issue on appeal.

ing its ownership of over ten percent of the stock of the issuer, the defendant had no access to inside information concerning the issuer. According to TI, the classic example of such a case is a sale of stock in the hostile takeover context. Application of section 16(b) in this type of case, argues TI, does not serve congressional goals—Congress intended short-swing profits to be disgorged only when the particular transaction serves as a vehicle for the realization of these profits based upon access to inside information.

TI's argument is unsupported by the legislative history of section 16(b). Although the abuse Congress sought to curb was speculation by stockholders with inside information, "the only method Congress deemed effective to curb the evils of insider trading was a *flat rule* taking the profits out of a *class of transactions* in which the possibility of abuse was believed to be intolerably great." *Kern County,* 93 S.Ct. at 1473 (emphasis added).

* * *

In *Kern County* the Supreme Court approved an extremely narrow exception to the objective standard of section 16(b). The Court held that when a transaction is "unorthodox" or "borderline," the courts should adopt a pragmatic approach in imposing section 16(b) liability which considers the opportunity for speculative abuse, i.e., whether the statutory "insider" had or was likely to have access to inside information.

TI engages in an analogy between the hostile and adversary situation that existed between the target company and the putative insider in *Kern County* and the adversary relationship between TI and National in the instant case. Even assuming the alleged parallelism between the adversary situations in the two cases and assuming that TI could prove that it neither had nor was likely to have access to inside information by virtue of its statutory "insider" status, no valid basis for an exception to section 16(b) liability on these facts is perceived. The Supreme Court in *Kern County* inquired into whether the transaction had the potential for abuse of inside information only because the transaction fell under the rubric of "unorthodox" or "borderline." [9] In *Kern County,* Occidental, a shareholder in Kern County Land Company (Old Kern) converted its shares in Old Kern into shares of the acquiring corporation pursuant to a merger. The Supreme Court clearly distinguished the unorthodox transaction—a conversion of securities—before it from the traditional cash-for-stock transaction in the instant case: "traditional cash-for-stock transactions ... are clearly within the purview of § 16(b)." *Kern County,* 93 S.Ct. at 1744.

TI lays frontal attack on the unorthodox transaction test as fundamentally flawed, principally because the form of consideration re-

---

9. The Court, in a nonexhaustive list, enumerated certain transactions which are unorthodox: stock conversions, exchanges pursuant to mergers and other corporate reorganizations, stock reclassifications, and dealings in options, rights, and warrants. *Kern County,* 93 S.Ct. at 1744 n. 24.

ceived—cash or stock—has nothing to do with whether inside information was or might have been used. What this attack fails to consider, however, is the significance of the factor of voluntariness in the Supreme Court's decision. The Court's sole concern was not that cash-for-stock sales present a greater opportunity for abuse of inside information than do stock-for-stock sales. Rather, language in the Supreme Court's opinion indicates that traditional cash-for-stock sales were excluded from the concept of unorthodox transactions because of their voluntary nature: * * * In the instant case, TI voluntarily entered into the stock purchase agreement with Pan Am before the National–Pan Am merger was effectuated. Despite the alleged lack of access to inside information and therefore the possibility of speculative abuse, the volitional character of the exchange is sufficient reason to trigger applicability of the language of section 16(b). For whatever reason, after the National–Pan Am merger had been approved, TI decided to take the initiative for the course of subsequent events into its own hands rather than wait for the merger to become accomplished. These circumstances do not warrant the creation of an exception to automatic section 16(b) liability.

* * *

GARZA, CIRCUIT JUDGE, dissenting:

* * *

Texas International (TI) correctly argues that there are many similarities between the present case and that presented to the Supreme Court in *Kern County*. The putative "insider" in both cases was a party seeking to institute a "hostile" takeover of the issuer. It is evident from the record in this case that in both cases the party seeking takeover had no "inside information" upon which it could obtain short swing profits. In both cases the statutory stockholder failed in its attempt to take over the target company. The Supreme Court recognized in *Kern County* that after the merger agreement was approved, Occidental had no choice but to take action to protect its own interest.

In this case TI moved to protect its own interest when it agreed to sell its stock to the takeover company, Pan American World Airways, Inc. (Pan Am), after it became apparent that TI had lost the takeover battle. Unfortunately for TI, the sale took place forty-eight days before the statutory period had run.

Admittedly, the forced merger present in *Kern County* distinguishes that case from the present one. However, the facts of this case present a scenario which favors extension of the "unorthodox" exception.

Like Occidental, no one can argue that TI actually made use of inside information to obtain any short swing profits. The reason for the existence of § 16(b) is in no way promoted by its application to the present transaction. Furthermore, TI's sale of stock was to the parent corporation for the purpose of protecting its own interests and cooperating in the merger transaction which Pan Am was attempting to effectuate.

The record clearly evidences that at the time of the sale by TI to Pan Am, no present or past shareholders of National Airlines had in any way been monetarily damaged by TI's purchase and sale of stock. In fact, it can be argued that the attempted takeover of National by TI helped to increase the value of National Airlines' stock. TI did not receive a higher price for the stock than any other shareholder. ALL shareholders of National Airlines received $50 per share.

Application of § 16(b) in this case serves only to permit Pan Am to avoid that portion of its contract with TI in which it agreed to pay $50 per share. The award in this case is nothing more than a "windfall" to Pan Am as the successor of National Airlines.

* * *

I agree that if Occidental in *Kern County* or TI in this case had sold its shares after the merger agreement to a third party, § 16(b) would have been clearly implicated. On the other hand, such is not the case if the sale was to the takeover company itself and the statutory insider, TI, received no more than any other shareholder of the issuer.

* * *

STERMAN v. FERRO CORP.
United States Court of Appeals, Sixth Circuit, 1986.
785 F.2d 162.

KRUPANSKY, CIRCUIT JUDGE.

Plaintiffs/appellants Harry Sterman and Etta K. Steiner (plaintiffs) appealed from the district court order granting a summary judgment in favor of the defendants, which dismissed plaintiffs' derivative claim.

The facts giving rise to this cause of action are basically undisputed. Between early 1981 and November 1982 defendant Crane Co. (Crane), through its chairman Thomas Evans (Evans), acquired 1,733,220 (or 22.4%) shares of Ferro Corporation (Ferro) common stock at prices ranging from $22 to $27 per share.[2]

* * *

In late spring of 1982, at the request of the board of directors, Milton Rosenthal (Rosenthal) (a Ferro director and acquaintance of Evans for more than twenty years) arranged a November 3, 1982 meeting between Evans, Posnick and Rosenthal at Evans' office in New York to discuss a possible repurchase of the Ferro stock held by Crane.

2. Of the entire block of 1,733,220 shares of Ferro stock accumulated by Crane, 1,568,200 shares, or over 90% had been acquired by Crane prior to the six month period ending November 8, 1982. Thus, only the remaining 10% could conceivably be subject to 16(b) liability.

During the scheduled meeting, Posnick offered to repurchase the Ferro shares at the then current market price. Evans demanded a higher price of $35 per share. Tentatively, the parties reached accord at a repurchase price of $30 per share plus a $.30 per share dividend payable on December 10, 1982 to all shareholders of record as of the close of business on November 15, 1982. The $30.30 repurchase price discussed by the parties was only tentative since Ferro's board of directors had not considered or acted upon the proposal.

Shortly after the November 3, 1982 meeting but prior to any action by Ferro's board of directors, Evans telephoned Rosenthal to advise him that, upon reconsideration, Crane could not agree to the discussed $30.30 per share price of Ferro Stock because of the short swing profit liability which would attach to the transaction. At that juncture of the negotiations Ferro was confronted with the dilemma of paying a higher price per share or terminating further negotiations. Exercising its business judgment, Ferro elected to continue the negotiations. Rosenthal advised Crane that Ferro would consider increasing the purchase price per share to permit Crane to net $30.30 per share after discharging its 16(b) liability. Evans responded favorably and the parties again reached a tentative agreement, subject to a final approval by the Ferro board of directors.

On November 8, 1982, the Ferro board of directors convened to consider the proposed offer of repurchase as negotiated by Rosenthal. The board of directors duly approved the offer of repurchase authorizing the payment of $31.03 per share of stock. The transaction resulted in an additional payment to Crane of $1,260,975, the precise amount of the short swing profit liability required to be paid to Ferro in satisfaction of the Section 16(b) liability that attached to the repurchase of the Ferro shares by Crane.[3]

The transaction was finalized on November 8, 1982 whereupon Ferro demanded a return of Crane's adjusted short swing profits. On November 11, 1982, Crane delivered a check to Ferro in the amount of $1,260,975, thereby discharging its 16(b) liability.

Plaintiffs brought suit against Ferro, ten individual directors of Ferro and Crane alleging that the transaction constituted an illegal waiver of short swing profits by the directors of Ferro because the November 3 agreement, contrary to the contentions of Crane and Ferro, was an irrevocable commitment between the parties fixing the repurchase price of Ferro stock at $30.30 per share; consequently, plaintiffs alleged, the difference between the $30.30 per share and the subse-

---

3. As previously noted, Crane acquired a total of 1,733,200 shares of Ferro stock. Of this total, however, only 165,000 shares were purchased within the six-month period ending on November 8, 1982, and were thus the only shares subject to section 16(b) liability. The aggregate cost to Crane of these 165,000 shares was $3,858,975, or an average price of $23.387727 per share. When the 165,000 shares were sold to Ferro for $31.03 per share on November 8, 1982, the average profit derived by Crane on each of the 165,000 shares was $7.642273, or an aggregate profit of $1,260,975. It was this amount which was to be paid to Ferro by Crane in discharge of its section 16(b) liability.

quently negotiated increased price per share of $31.31 arrived at on November 8 was an illegal payment to Crane approved by Ferro's Board of Directors and a breach of the Board's fiduciary duty to its stockholders.

* * *

A review of the record discloses compliance with the statute. It is apparent that the pricing of the transaction was structured in a manner to accommodate a Section 16(b) liability. The Section 16(b) liability was, in fact, discharged by an appropriate cash payment to Ferro at the close of the transaction. However, to be culpable under Section 16(b), there must have been an attempt to *avoid* payment of the short swing profits imposed thereby. Moreover, the Supreme Court has determined that a Section 16(b) violation does not necessarily attach where the parties have intentionally structured their transaction to accommodate the liability imposed by the statute:

> Liability cannot be imposed simply because the investor structured his transaction with the intent of avoiding liability under § 16(b). The question is, rather, whether the method used to "avoid" liability is one permitted by the statute.

Reliance Electric Co. v. Emerson Electric Co., 404 U.S. at 422, 92 S.Ct. at 599.

Accordingly, this court finds no violation of Section 16(b) of the Act.

Plaintiffs next charge Ferro with violating of Section 29(a) of the Securities and Exchange Act, 15 U.S.C. § 78cc(a), which reads in pertinent part as follows:

> Any condition, stipulation, or provision binding any person to waive compliance with any provision of this Chapter or of any rule or regulation thereunder, or of any rule of an exchange required thereby shall be void.

They urge that Ferro's board of directors illegally waived Crane's short swing profits liability. The gravamen of plaintiffs' contention is that since Ferro and Crane reached an "agreement in principle" to sell the stock at $30.30 per share, the subsequent agreement to sell the stock at $31.03 per share was tantamount to a waiver of Section 16(b) liability. Implicit in the plaintiff's argument is the erroneous hypothecation that the initial discussions between Ferro and Crane resulted in a valid contract between the parties fixing the repurchase price of the stock at $30.30 per share.

* * *

A review of this record discloses that the sale did not occur until November 8, 1982, the date upon which the Ferro board of directors convened and formally considered and approved the purchase of the Ferro stock at $31.03 per share. As the district court observed, there was no evidence that the parties considered and/or treated the $30.03 per share price discussed on November 3 as a firm and binding agreement.

*   *   *

Questions

1. What problems does section 16(b) pose for a firm considering a hostile bid? What problems does section 16(b) pose for a management buyout group that anticipates competition from a second bidder?

2. How can a firm structure greenmail payments to avoid section 16(b) liability if an unwanted shareholder bought 15 percent of the stock in the firm less than six months ago? (Note: In Foremost–McKesson, Inc. v. Provident Securities, Co., 423 U.S. 232, 96 S.Ct. 508, 46 L.Ed.2d 464 (1976), the Supreme Court held that the section excludes the purchase that makes a person a 10+ percent stockholder.)

3. If a bidder, holding over 15 percent of the shares of a target for less than six months, loses a tender offer contest to a second bidder, can the losing bidder tender its stock into the second bidder's offer without violating section 16(b)? Or must the losing bidder refuse to tender and wait for a back-end merger between the winning bidder and the target that eliminates all remaining target shareholders?

4. Can an arbitrageur buy 15 percent of the stock of a firm based on takeover rumors and then tender the stock into a tender offer that occurs within six months? Can a director who has acquired stock in the market tender the stock into a tender offer that occurs within six months of the purchases?

Chapter Seven

ACCOUNTING AND TAX ISSUES IN MERGERS AND ACQUISITIONS

Whenever two firms combine or one firm purchases a significant amount of stock in another, the transaction raises accounting and tax issues. How does the surviving or acquiring firm account for the transaction in its financial statements? Do the participants in the transaction (which includes both the constituent firms and their investors) recognize and realize taxable gain or loss under federal income tax statutes? The drafters of accounting and tax rules relevant to mergers and acquisitions have necessarily diverged from the path taken by states in drafting and interpreting their corporation codes. In chapter 2 we noted that state codes began with a tripartite division—mergers, sales of all a firm's assets, and stock sales—and states have refused (with the exception of California) to protect the integrity of the distinctions when clever lawyers designed asset and stock acquisitions to avoid the shareholder rights requirements of the classic merger provisions. Drafters of accounting rules and tax rules also begin with a basic classification system. Transactions in one category receive different accounting or tax treatment from transactions in another. Yet unlike state officials, these drafters have taken steps to preserve the integrity of the basic classifications.

Accounting and tax rules thus have two parts—a basic classification system and a series of rules designed to stop clever planners from avoiding the effect of the basic system. While the drafters aim to preserve the integrity of the basic distinction, accountants and lawyers aim to find crevices in the rules and statutes that may frustrate the basic distinctions and generate preferred outcomes for their clients. The drafters have the harder job, looking ahead to anticipate avoidance schemes, and the professional planners are often one step ahead of the drafters. To exacerbate the inequality, the drafters are on the public payroll, where pay and experience are often meager, and the planners are paid handsomely, attracting some of the country's finest minds. As a consequence, the drafters often look not ahead but behind, reacting to schemes. In a constantly evolving set of rules, yesterday's tricks produce today's rules, and today's tricks generate tomorrow's rules.

The effect on planners of accounting and tax rules is, of course, to integrate the costs and benefits provided by such rules into their overall choice of a form for an acquisition.

SUBCHAPTER A. ACCOUNTING FOR MERGERS AND ACQUISITIONS

INTRODUCTION TO FINANCIAL STATEMENTS

In the United States economic entities produce general-purpose financial statements that are intended to provide information on the financial condition of the entity. The financial statements include:

1. the earnings statement (income statement or profit and loss statement), which reflects operating performance of the entity for a specific period of time, generally one year;
2. the statement of financial position (balance sheet), which reflects the assets, liabilities, and owners' equity of the entity as of a specific moment in time; and
3. the statement of cash flows, which reflects the cash inflows and outflows of the entity for the period.

The statements, together often referred to as the financials, are prepared using accounting procedures, derived from the British system, that have evolved gradually.

The balance sheet is a snapshot description of the firm at a single point in time. It is divided into two sides: on the left are shown assets; on the right are shown liabilities and stockholders' equity (or net worth). Both sides are always in balance. In the asset column a firm lists all the goods and property owed as well as claims against others yet to be collected. Under liabilities the firm lists all debts due. Under the stockholders' equity the firm lists the amount the stockholders would divide if the firm were liquidated at its balance sheet, or "book," value.

The mistake a layperson can make is in equating the total equity or net worth figure in a balance sheet's lower right corner with a firm's actual value. Since assets are not carried at current market values, and there is no market value assigned to the firm's reputation or name, the net worth category cannot accurately reflect the market value of the firm. Profitable companies often show a very low net book value when compared to the market price of their shares, and manufacturing companies in declining industries, railroads and steel, for example, may show a very high book value per share. Insurance companies, banks, and investment companies, because their assets are largely liquid (cash, accounts receivable, and marketable securities), may show a book value that is a fair indication of market value.

The income statement is less a snapshot than a movie of a firm's activities; it shows the record of a firm's operation activities for a year. An income statement matches the amounts received from selling goods and services and other items of income (the sale of capital assets, for example) against all the costs and outlays incurred in order to operate the company. The result is a net profit or a net loss for the year. The costs incurred usually consist of the cost to the firm of goods sold; overhead expenses such as wages and salaries, rent, supplies, and depreciation; interest on money borrowed; and taxes owed. The mistake a layperson can make is in believing that the net income figure at the bottom of an income statement is, first, an accurate rendition of the past profitability of a firm relative to other firms and, second, an accurate predictor of how the company will do in the near future. The figures in an income statement reflect noncash outlays, nonrecurring events, and also several significant discretionary decisions of sophisticated accountants. A comparison of the health of two firms based on their income statements is a trained skill, going far beyond the simple comparison of two firms' net income figures.

The statement of cash flows (also known as the statement of changes in financial position and cash flow from operations, the sources and uses of funds statement, the statement of changes in financial position, and the funds statement) presents changes in a firm's financial position that are normally generated from operations and summarizes the financing and investing activities of the firm for the same period. The statement adds the cash balance at the beginning of the year, the cash generated from operations, the cash raised from the issuance of debt or capital stock, and the cash raised from the sale of fixed assets and subtracts the distributions of cash to shareholders in dividends, the cash paid in the redemption of debt or stock, and the cash acquisition price of fixed assets. The result is a cash balance at the end of the year. It is hoped that the firm is generating a positive cash flow. The mistake made by a layperson can be the assumption that a firm disclosing a net profit on its income statement is healthy. The statement of cash flows may indicate the contrary, and a history of negative cash flows is usually a precursor of trouble.

INTRODUCTION TO ACCOUNTING ISSUES IN INTERCOMPANY OWNERSHIP [3]

In this section we will examine the accounting procedures used to report various levels of ownership of another firm. We use a common set of hypothetical accounting statements to illustrate the reporting consequences of each alternative. The procedures are referenced to the professional literature. The companies are called Acquirer and Target, and the statements of financial position for the two companies are presented in table 1 as of 12/31/yr 0, assuming no preexisting interrelationship. In table 2 the hypothetical earnings statements of the two companies appear for the subsequent year (year 1), assuming that Acquirer has no interest in Target at any point during the year.

3. The material draws heavily on an unpublished Teaching Note on Accounting Issues in Intercompany Ownership, by Prof. John Elliot of the Johnson Graduate School of Management, May 1990.

TABLE 1

Hypothetical Statements of Financial Position
Independent Companies
as of 12/31/Yr 0

	Acquirer	Target
Current assets	$300	$ 50
Noncurrent assets	200	100
Total assets	$500	$150
Liabilities	$150	$ 25
Stated capital (common $1 par) [1]	75	40
Capital surplus	125	60
Retained earnings	150	25
Total equities	$500	$150

[1] Assume each company was originally capitalized by selling $1 par value common for $1.50. Thus each share of stock sold results in $1.00 of stated capital (shares outstanding times par for each share) and $0.50 of capital surplus. Acquirer has 75 shares outstanding, and Target has 40 shares outstanding.

TABLE 2

Hypothetical Earnings Statements
Independent Companies
for the Year Ending 12/31/Yr 1

	Acquirer	Target
Sales	$600	$200
Cost:		
Cost of goods sold	300	100
Expenses	100	40
Depreciation	80	30
Taxes	40	10
Total costs	520	180
Net earnings	$ 80	$ 20

The examples that follow necessarily simplify economic reality somewhat. In fact, whenever one company acquires any part of another, many economic relationships change. The buyer may finance the investment by borrowing, by issuing stock, by selling other assets of the firm, and so on. In each of the examples that follow, the assumption is that the acquiring firm issues new common stock sufficient to acquire the desired percentage of the target. We assume that the shares of the acquirer sell for $3 per share and the shares of the target sell for $3.75. These assumptions are arbitrary and consciously ignore many issues. For example, the very act of acquiring shares in another company may affect the value of both the acquirer's shares and the target's shares.

When Black and Decker recently purchased Emhardt, the announcement was associated with a significant decline in the price for Black and Decker shares and a significant increase in price for Emhardt shares. Indeed, when purchase of a whole company is observed, the per-share price paid by the acquiring company is typically 25 to 50 percent over the recent trading price. We ignore such issues in the examples below.

The three basic accounting methods are tied to the level of ownership achieved by the acquirer. They are the cost method for ownership of 20 percent or less, when no significant influence of investor over investee exists, the equity method for ownership of greater than 20 percent but less than 50 percent, when significant influence exists, and the consolidation method for ownership of greater than 50 percent.

SECTION 1. COST METHOD: ACQUISITIONS OF LESS THAN 20 PERCENT OF TARGET'S OUTSTANDING COMMON STOCK

Assume that Acquirer buys 10 percent (four shares) of Target at a cost of $15. To raise the $15, Acquirer sells five shares of its own stock in the open market. The shares of Target that Acquirer owns will be reflected as an asset in the statement of financial position and will initially be reported at cost, $15. Table 3 reflects the statement of financial position for Acquirer before and after this transaction.

TABLE 3

Cost Method
Acquirer Statements of Financial Position
Reflecting 10 Percent Interest in Target
as of 12/31/YR 0

	Before Buying 10% of Target	After Issuing Stock and Buying 10% of Target
Current assets	$300	$300
Investment in target		15
Noncurrent assets	200	200
	$500	$515
Liabilities	$150	$150
Stated capital	75	80
Capital surplus	125	135
Retained earnings	150	150
	$500	$515

As year 1 progresses, Acquirer generates the earnings reflected in table 2, as does Target. Because Acquirer now owns 10 percent of

Target, Target's profitability has favorable economic implications for Acquirer. However, Target's profitability will only affect Acquirer's financial statements to the extent that Target declares dividends. The declaration of a dividend on common shares is a voluntary act of Target's board of directors. Since Acquirer does not control Target, Acquirer cannot direct target to declare dividends, and therefore Acquirer's economic benefit from Target's earnings is uncertain until dividends are declared.[4] Once declared, the dividends become legal obligations of Target, and Acquirer may reflect them as income. Table 4 shows three earnings statements for Acquirer; before buying 10 percent of Target, after buying 10 percent but assuming no dividend is declared, and after buying 10 percent assuming a dividend of $0.50 per share is declared. Earnings in the first two cases are identical. Only in the latter case do net earnings change. While the dividend is $2.00, net earnings rise by less than $2.00, because the dividend is taxable.[5]

TABLE 4

Cost Method
Earnings Statements of Acquirer
Reflecting 10 Percent Interest in Target
for the Year Ending 12/31/YR 1

	Before Buying 10% of Target	After Buying 10% of Target — Target Does Not Declare Dividend	After Buying 10% of Target — Target Declares Dividend
Sales	$600	$600	$600
Dividend income	—	—	2
			$602
Costs:			
Cost of goods	$300	$300	$300
Expenses	100	100	100
Depreciation	80	80	80
Taxes	40	40	41
	$520	$520	$521
Net earnings	$ 80	$ 80	$ 81

Financial Accounting Standards Board Statement 12, "Accounting for Certain Marketable Securities," deals primarily with two issues:

4. In fact, dividends are theoretically income to the investor only to the extent Target has earnings after the investor purchases its ownership interest. The accounting and tax issues of this distinction are beyond the scope of this discussion.

5. In fact, dividends are taxed at special rates. In this series of examples details of taxation are ignored and tax is assumed at a constant 40 percent.

Should an investment be shown as a current asset or a long-lived asset, and how should declines in value be disclosed? Classification of investments as current or long-lived depends on the intent of the owner. If Acquirer purchased the 10 percent interest in Target with the intention of creating a long-term relationship, the investment should be classified as a long-lived (noncurrent) asset. But if the investment was a liquid investment undertaken for speculative purposes or as a temporary use for idle cash, it should be classified as a current asset. FASB Statement 12 requires that the current marketable securities be treated as a separate portfolio from the long-term marketable securities. Each separate portfolio is accounted for at the lower of (aggregate) cost or market. When the market value of the portfolio declines below cost, the lower market value is reported in the statement of financial position. The amount of the decline is reported differently for current and long-term portfolios. A decline below cost for a current portfolio is reported as a loss in the earnings statement. For a long-term portfolio the decline is reported as an adjustment to owners' equity with no effect on net earnings.

Increases and decreases in the value of the securities are not treated symmetrically. This practice is the *lower* of cost or market. Securities may either depreciate or appreciate in value; both unrealized gains and losses are possible. But unrealized gains are only reflected to the extent of previously recorded unrealized losses. In the Acquirer example, assume the target stock, which was purchased for $3.75 per share, rose to $5.00. Assume the investment is a current asset. Neither the earnings statement nor the asset-carrying value would change. If the value fell to $3.00 per share, a loss of $3.00 would be shown (4 shares × $.75) in the earnings statement in the year of the decline. Thereafter a recovery of value to $3.50 per share would produce a recovery of a previously reported loss in the earnings statement of $2.00 (4 shares × $.50).

The earnings statement is also affected by realized gains and losses on the sale of investment interests. Realization occurs when gain or loss is recognized in a completed transaction. Borrowing from tax concepts, the gain or loss is measured as the difference between the cost basis of the investment (its purchase price with modifications) and its sale price.

SECTION 2. EQUITY METHOD: ACQUISITIONS OF 20 PERCENT TO 50 PERCENT OF TARGET'S OUTSTANDING STOCK

The equity method is used to account for ownership interest of 20 percent to 50 percent ownership in another firm. The equity method is compared to the cost method in paragraph 6 of Accounting Principles Board Opinion 18:

    a. *The cost method.* An investor records an investment in the stock of an investee at cost, and recognizes as income dividends received that are distributed from net accumulated earnings of the investee since the date of acquisition by the investor. The net accumulated earnings of an investee subsequent to the date of investment are recognized by the investor only to the extent distributed by the investee as dividends. Dividends received in excess of earnings subsequent to the date of investment are considered a return of investment and are recorded as reductions of cost of the investment. A series of operating losses of an investee or other factors may indicate that a decrease in value of the investment has occurred which is other than temporary and should accordingly be recognized.

b. *The equity method.* An investor initially records an investment in the stock of an investee at cost, and adjusts the carrying amount of the investment to recognize the investor's share of the earnings or losses of the investee after the date of acquisition. The amount of the adjustment is included in the determination of net income by the investor, and such amount reflects adjustments similar to those made in preparing consolidated statements including adjustments to eliminate intercompany gains and losses, and to amortize, if appropriate, any difference between investor cost and underlying equity in net assets of the investee at the date of investment. The investment of an investor is also adjusted to reflect the investor's share of changes in the investee's capital. Dividends received from an investee reduce the carrying amount of the investment. A series of operating losses of an investee or other factors may indicate that a decrease in value of the investment has occurred which is other than temporary and which should be recognized even though the decrease in value is in excess of what would otherwise be recognized by application of the equity method.

As noted in paragraph 10 of APB Opinion 18, while the cost method recognizes earnings only on the receipt of dividends, the equity method links the investor's financial statements more directly to those of the investee:

10. Under the equity method, an investor recognizes its share of the earnings or losses of an investee in the periods for which they are reported by the investee in its financial statements rather than in the period in which an investee declares a dividend. An investor adjusts the carrying amount of an investment for its share of the earnings or losses of the investee subsequent to the date of investment and reports the recognized earnings or losses in income. Dividends received from an investee reduce the carrying amount of the investment. Thus, the equity method is an appropriate means of recognizing increases or decreases measured by generally accepted accounting principles in the economic resources underlying the investments. Furthermore, the equity method of accounting more closely meets the objectives of accrual

accounting than does the cost method since the investor recognizes its share of the earnings and losses of the investee in the periods in which they are reflected in the accounts of the investee.

The distinction between the two methods is generally tied to the percentage of the investee owned—the cost method below 20 percent and the equity method above 20 percent. But the real issue theoretically is control and influence by the investor, as discussed in paragraph 12 of APB Opinion 18:

12. The equity method tends to be most appropriate if an investment enables the investor to influence the operating and financial decisions of the investee. The investor then has a degree of responsibility for the return on its investment, and it is appropriate to include in the results of operations of the investor its share of the earnings or losses of the investee. Influence tends to be more effective as the investor's percent of ownership in the voting stock of the investee increases. Investments of relatively small percentages of voting stock of an investee tend to be passive in nature and enable the investor to have little or no influence on the operations of the investee.

Thus while the 20 percent cutoff is presumptive, cases can be found where circumstances lead to presumed control at lower levels of ownership or a lack of control at higher levels, though neither is common.

To illustrate the application of the equity method: Assume Acquirer purchased 30 percent (12 shares) of Target and financed the purchase ($45) by issuing 15 shares of Acquirer stock. Table 5 presents the year 0 statement of financial position, and table 6 presents the year 1 earnings statement.

TABLE 5

Equity Method
Acquirer Financials

Statement of Financial Position
as of 12/31/Yr 0

	Before Buying 30% of Target	After Buying 30% of Target
Current assets	$300	$300
Investment in target	—	45
Noncurrent assets	200	200
	$500	$545
Liabilities	$150	$150
Stated capital	75	90
Capital surplus	125	155
Retained earnings	150	150
	$500	$545

TABLE 6

Equity Method
Acquirer Financials

Earnings Statement
for Year Ending 12/31/Yr 1

	Before Buying 30% of Target	After Buying 30% of Target
Sales	$600	$600
Costs:		
Costs of goods	300	300
Expenses	100	100
Depreciation	80	80
Taxes	40	40
	$520	$520
Operating earnings	$ 80	$ 80
Equity in earnings of affiliate [1]	—	6
Net earnings	$ 80	$ 86

[1] The equity in earnings is 30 percent of Target's earnings, as disclosed in table 2. In this example the potential tax consequences are ignored.

Under the cost method, requiring that companies use the lower of cost or market accounting may lead to a carrying value below cost, but the carrying value never exceeds cost. In the equity method the carrying value may exceed cost. For Acquirer, the investment in Target at the end of year 1 would be increased by its $6 share in Target's earnings, to $51 on the balance sheet. Target's act of making a dividend payment would reduce Acquirer's carrying value of the investment in Target. A dividend payment of $3, for example, would reduce the $51 to $48 on the year 1 balance sheet, although Acquirer would add the $3 to its current assets column. Conceptually, when Target generates earnings, its economic resources are increased, and an increase in Acquirer's assets reflects that. When Target pays a dividend, it is distributing part of those resources.

SECTION 3. PURCHASE AND POOLING CONSOLIDATIONS: ONE COMPANY ACQUIRES OVER 50 PERCENT OF THE STOCK OF ANOTHER

When one company owns more than 50 percent of another, financial statements of the two companies are consolidated into one combined set of statements. Assuming an acquisition of over 50 percent of the stock in a target firm and, therefore, the need for consolidated financial statements, there are two methods of reporting. Accounting Principles Board Opinion 16 clarifies the use of two alternative bases of accounting for changes in corporate control, **purchase** accounting and **pooling of interests** accounting. A company is not allowed to choose the method to be used. The nature of the transaction that leads to common ownership of the two firms determines which of the two methods will be used. However, since there is a choice in how the acquisition is structured, the firms can negotiate an acquisition agreement that provides the desired accounting result. The financial statements of the acquirer will differ markedly, depending on whether the acquisition gets purchase or pooling treatment.

When **purchase** accounting is appropriate, the acquisition of one firm by another is treated as an arm's-length purchase and sale between disinterested parties. The transaction price is deemed to reflect, at minimum, the market value of the combination of assets and liabilities being acquired. That market value is allocated among all the assets and liabilities of the new firm, and a new basis of valuation arises for accounting in the future. The target's book values are not relevant. The assets are carried on the surviving entity's balance sheet at their current fair market values. The entire transaction is treated prospectively; that is, the assets are "stepped up" or "stepped down" to their fair market values. If the acquisition price exceeds a reasonable determination of the fair market cost of all target assets, the acquirer recognizes the excess as amortizable goodwill. Future results of the surviving company reflect the future operations of the acquired company, but no retroactive restatement occurs. For example, the consolidated acquirer statements for the year of purchase reflect only the *postacquisition* earnings of the target.

When **pooling** accounting is appropriate, the acquisition of one firm by another is treated as a combination of the separate interests. The predominant feature of a pooling is that the transaction involves an exchange of shares of stock rather than cash, and the prior shareholders of the separate companies continue as shareholders in the combined company. The combined firm is viewed as a merging of the previously separate firms. The owners of the combined firm are viewed as the union of the previously separate owners. Under this view the event is not interpreted as an arm's-length transaction, establishing market values that must be reflected in the combined financials, but rather as a change in the accounting entity. The accounting book values of the separate firms are retained as the relevant accounting values. The resulting financial statements are simply the combination of the separate financial statements of the previously separate firms, after giving effect to any intercompany transactions. No goodwill is created, since the book value of the target's assets carries over without change.[6] The only changes on the balance sheet would occur in the

---

6. Because the target's old accounting book values carry over without change, the costs of the acquisition (legal and accounting fees and expenses) are generally ex-

owners' capital section, where the capital stock and paid-in-capital accounts of the combined entity would have to reflect their actual outstanding shares after the combination. The financial statements of prior years would be restated as though the companies had always been together.

Paragraphs 16 to 41 of APB Opinion 16 consider the strengths and weaknesses of the two methods in detail. Two of these paragraphs are reproduced below:

> 21. Reporting economic substance. The purchase method adheres to traditional principles of accounting for the acquisition of assets. Those who support the purchase method of accounting for business combinations effected by issuing stock believe that an acquiring corporation accounts for the economic substance of the transaction by applying those principles and by recording:
>
>   a. All assets and liabilities which comprise the bargained cost of an acquired company, not merely those items previously shown in the financial statements of an acquired company.
>
>   b. The bargained costs of assets acquired less liabilities assumed, not the costs to a previous owner.
>
>   c. The fair value of the consideration received for stock issued, not the equity shown in the financial statements of an acquired company.
>
>   d. Retained earnings from its operations, not a fusion of its retained earnings and previous earnings of an acquired company.
>
>   e. Expenses and net income after an acquisition computed on the bargained cost of acquired assets less assumed liabilities, not on the costs to a previous owner.
>
> * * *
>
> 28. Validity of the concept. Those who support the pooling of interests method believe that a business combination effected by issuing common stock is different from a purchase in that no corporate assets are disbursed to stockholders and the net assets of the issuing corporation are enlarged by the net assets of the corporation whose stockholders accept common stock of the combined corporation. There is no newly invested capital nor have owners withdrawn assets from the group since the stock of a corporation is not one of its assets. Accordingly, the net assets of the constituents remain intact but combined; the stockholder groups remain intact but combined. Aggregate income is not changed since the total resources are not changed. Consequently, the historical costs and earnings of the separate corporations are appropriately combined. In a

pensed in the first combined postacquisition income statement.

business combination effected by exchanging stock, groups of stockholders combine their resources, talents, and risks to form a new entity to carry on in combination the previous businesses and to continue their earnings streams. The sharing of risks by the constituent stockholder groups is an important element in a business combination effected by exchanging stock. By pooling equity interests, each group continues to maintain risk elements of its former investment and they mutually exchange risks and benefits.

The APB's final conclusion is that each method is appropriate in certain circumstances.

42. The Board finds merit in both the purchase and pooling of interests methods of accounting for business combinations and accepts neither method to the exclusion of the other. The arguments in favor of the purchase method of accounting are more persuasive if cash or other assets are distributed or liabilities are incurred to effect a combination, but arguments in favor of the pooling of interests method of accounting are more persuasive if voting common stock is issued to effect a combination of common stock interests. Therefore, the Board concluded that some business combinations should be accounted for by the purchase method and other combinations should be accounted for by the pooling of interests method.

The remainder of APB Opinion 16 specifies under what conditions each is appropriate and how each is applied. In general, an acquirer can use the pooling method in stock swap acquisitions in which the target common shareholders receive, with very limited exceptions, solely common stock in the surviving firm. All other forms of acquisition must use the purchase method. This is true regardless of the mechanics of the acquisition. It does not matter if the combination is a statutory merger (the target merges into the acquirer or a subsidiary of the acquirer or the acquirer merges into the target), an acquisition of the target's assets by the acquirer or one of its subsidiaries, or an acquisition of the target's stock by the acquirer or one of its subsidiaries. The transaction is a pooling if the consideration received by the target shareholders is common stock in the surviving entity; if not, it is a purchase.

In the materials that follow, we investigate the details of the two different accounting approaches for business combinations, summarize the accounting consequences of each approach, and detail when a transaction qualifies for the pooling method. At the conclusion of these materials we investigate a hybrid of the two approaches used in accounting for leveraged buyouts.

While the examples of pooling and purchasing that follow appear side by side in some cases, it is important to remember that the actual steps differ. To dramatize the accounting consequences, the comparisons contemplate similar changes in ownership for both scenarios. In the **pooling** case think of the transaction as the issuance of new shares by the acquirer, which exchanges the new shares directly with the shareholders of the target. In the **purchase** case the acquirer sells new shares in the open market for cash and immediately exchanges the cash proceeds for target company stock. The similarities for pooling and purchase accounting and their differences are best illustrated by starting from a basic example in which the two treatments appear substantially identical and moving, by relaxing our assumptions, to cases in which the two treatments are very different.

Table 7 presents a simple case of a consolidation. Assume first that Acquirer buys Target for $125 and raises the money by selling 50 new shares of Acquirer stock to members of the public, a purchase transaction. Assume that the book value of the assets and liabilities exactly equals the market value.[7] The simplifying assumptions produce the results presented in table 7. The earnings statement of the consolidated firm is prepared by simply adding across. This is also the method used for all the entries in the statement of financial position except the owners' equity section. In the owners' equity section, the total consolidated sum of common stock and paid-in-capital and retained earnings ($125 + $200 + $150 = $475) for the combined entity is actually set before the acquisition by the stock sale and does not change with the acquisition. After the stock sale but before the acquisition, the acquirer's equity section equals the sum of the pre-stock sale figures ($75 + $125 + $150 = $350) and the allocated proceeds of the sale ($50 + $75 + $0 = $125). The acquisition itself results in an elimination of the $125 cash account reflecting the proceeds of the stock sale and the addition of accounts containing the assets and liabilities of Target, which net $125.

Assume Acquirer exchanges 50 new shares for all the outstanding Target shares. In the owners' equity section the par value of the new outstanding stock held by the Target shareholders, $50, is added to the stated capital account, and the excess of the Target shareholders' capital contribution over this amount, $40 plus $35 minus $50, or $25, is added to the paid-in-capital account, for an entry of $150 in the consolidated statement. The retained earnings accounts are summed, resulting in an entry of $200 in the consolidated balance sheet. Moreover, the identity of the postacquisition shareholders in the survivor of the combination is changed. If Acquirer **purchased** Target by using cash from a new sale of stock, Target owners' equity does not survive the consolidation. The Target owners are cashed out. If the Acquirer shareholders **pooled** their equity with the Target shareholders, the Target shareholders take stock in the Acquirer, which survives the combination.

We will add sophistication to our understanding of accounting for business consolidations by gradually relaxing the assumptions in our

---

7. Moreover, this example assumes that Acquirer purchases 100 percent of Target and that Acquirer and Target do not do business with each other. Neither is a customer of the other, and no liabilities exist between them.

basic example in table 7. In table 8 we will add the concept of goodwill; in tables 9 and 10 we will add assets whose purchase price exceeds their book value; and in table 11 we will add intercompany obligations that predate the acquisition.

TABLE 7

Financial Statements Given 100 Percent Ownership

Panel A
Statement of Financial Position
as of 12/31/Yr 0

	Precombination Acquirer	Target	Consolidated Purchase	Pooling
Current assets	$300	$ 50	$350	$350
Noncurrent assets	200	100	300	300
	$500	$150	$650	$650
Liabilities	$150	$ 25	$175	$175
Stated capital				
($1 par common)	75[a]	40	125[b]	125[b]
Surplus capital	125[c]	35	200	150
Retained earnings	150	50	150	200
	$500	$150	$650	$650

[a] Stated capital is the par times the shares outstanding. Here there are 75 shares outstanding.
[b] There are now 125 shares outstanding.
[c] Surplus capital is the excess of the price of the stock over its par value minus shareholder distributions. Here, for example, the stock may have sold initially for $1.66 a share.

Panel B
Earnings Statement
for the Year Ending 12/31/Yr 1

	Precombination Acquirer	Target	Consolidated
Sales	$600	$200	$800
Costs:			
Cost of goods	300	100	400
Expenses	100	40	140
Depreciation	80	30	110
Taxes	40	10	50
	520	180	700
Net earnings	$ 80	$ 20	$100

First, we relax our basic assumption that the acquirer pays book value for the target. In table 8 assume that the acquirer issues capital stock with a par value of $50 and a market value of $150 in completing its acquisition of the subsidiary. This example differs from the case in table 7 because the price for the target shares is $150 rather than $125. The difference is assumed to be goodwill or going-concern value. Thus the book value of individual assets is still assumed to be their market value in the transaction.

TABLE 8

Financial Statements Given 100 Percent Ownership $150 Acquisition Price

	Before Combination		Postcombination Combined Firm	
	Acquirer	Target	Pooling	Purchase
Current assets	$300	$ 50	$350[a]	$350[a]
Noncurrent assets	200	100	300[a]	300[a]
Goodwill				25
Total assets	$500	$150	$650	$675
Liabilities	$150	$ 25	$175	$175
Stated capital	75	40	125[b]	125[b]
Surplus capital	125	35	150[c]	225[c]
Retained earnings	150	50	200	150
Total	$500	$150	$650	$675

[a] Purchase equal pooling only because we assumed equal book values and fair market values of individual assets.

[b] Purchase equals pooling in all cases because we account for the par value of the acquirer stock only, which includes the newly issued stock.

[c] Surplus capital is a residual figure. In the pooling case it is Acquirer's surplus capital ($125) plus Target's contributed capital ($40 + $35 = $75) less the par value of new Acquirer stock ($50). In the purchase case it is Acquirer's surplus capital ($125) plus the excess of new Acquirer stock at market ($150) over its par value ($50).

Note in table 8, first, that goodwill is recognized in a purchase but is not recognized in a pooling of interests and, second, that the purchase method eliminates retained earnings of the target before acquisition, while the pooling incorporates preacquisition retained earnings into the combined firm. The recognition of goodwill is a substantial handicap, because goodwill must be depreciated like any other asset, typically using the straight-line method over forty years (one-fortieth of the amount is deducted each year after the acquisition for forty years). The required amortization of goodwill in purchase accounting reduces the net earnings of the acquirer, as compared with a transaction that uses the pooling method of accounting. The yearly amount amortized is a deduction from net income on the income statement and reduces earnings per share. As the amount of goodwill that is required to be amortized goes up, the earnings per share of a firm will go down. Yet, goodwill is not deductible against earnings on the firm's tax calculations.

Accounting for goodwill has recently made the news with a recent proposal by the British Accounting Standards Committee (ASC). Currently some United States business leaders claim that British firms enjoy a competitive edge over United States firms in contested auctions for identified targets. A successful American acquirer must amortize the goodwill premium over forty years, while the British have a choice; they can amortize goodwill, or they can charge it against shareholder equity, avoiding a reduction in their earnings. The benefit does have a cost; a reduction in shareholder equity increases a firm's debt-to-equity ration, which could reduce a firm's borrowing power. The ASC proposal is to require British firms to amortize goodwill as United States firms currently do, although over a twenty-year rather than a forty-year period. The proposal is part of an international effort to standardize accounting methods. Is the complaint valid? Do the accounting methods have any impact on the substantive value of the target to the acquirer?

To add a third level of sophistication to our example, we must relax a second assumption. In table 7 the target was acquired for $150, although the market value and book value of its assets were equal, at a net $125, and we assumed the difference was goodwill. The assumption that the purchase price (or market value) of the identifiable assets and liabilities equaled book value is more often false than true. Table 9 reflects situations where the excess of the purchase price over the book value of the acquired firm is not solely a reflection of goodwill, but the excess can be tied directly to identifiable assets and liabilities. Purchases above the book value of the identifiable assets are only important from an accounting perspective using purchase accounting. The details of the example are characterized in the notes to table 9.

TABLE 9

Purchase Accounting
Assets with Market Values in Excess of Book

	Before Combination			Consolidated
	Acquirer	Target		
		Book	Market	
Cash and accounts receivable	$ 75	$ 10	$ 10	$ 85
Inventories	100	20	35 [a]	135
Notes receivable	125	20	25 [b]	150
Noncurrent assets	200	100	105 [c]	305
Goodwill			15 [d]	15 [d]
Total assets	$500	$150	$190	$690
Liabilities	$150	$ 25	$ 25	$175
Stated capital	75	40	165 [e]	125 [f]

	Before Combination			Consolidated
	Acquirer	Target Book	Market	
Surplus capital	$125	$ 35		$240
Retained earnings	150	50		150
Totals	$500	$150	$190	$690

Note: The initial values shown for the acquirer are the values before the actual acquisition occurs. Thus they do not reflect the issuance of the $150 in common stock for cash or the use of the $150 to acquire the shares of the target.

[a] Inventory values are in excess of book value because of inflation (or the target uses LIFO).

[b] Notes receivable valued at market exceed book because of a decrease in interest rates.

[c] Noncurrent assets are in excess of market because depreciation patterns have not perfectly matched rates of decline in market value.

[d] The goodwill reflects the target company's ability to earn above-normal returns due, for example, to the skill and training of employees, established business relations, reputation, etc. The monetary measure of goodwill is the residual after all assets and liabilities are stated at market.

[e] In the market valuation of the target, the notion of allocating the value between par value, surplus capital, and retained earnings is not useful. These items have no separable values. Collectively they represent the total value of the firm.

[f] The combined firm will reflect the actual number of shares outstanding after the combination.

To add a fourth and final level of sophistication, we relax our basic assumption that there are no intercompany dealings between the acquirer and the target before the acquisition. This assumption allowed us to stipulate in table 8 that the consolidated earnings were the sum of the individual earnings of the two constituent entities. In table 10 we consider a much more common case, in which the acquisition of control is preceeded by dealings between the acquirer and the target. Because of intercompany transactions, goodwill, and step-ups in asset bases, consolidated earnings are less than the sum of the separate earnings of the firms. Moreover, the earnings in a purchase consolidation are less than the earnings in a pooling consolidation. This is the normal case. The detailed assumptions behind the statements are presented in the notes to the table.

TABLE 10

Income Statement Effects
Acquired Assets Having Market Values in Excess of Book

	Acquirer	Target	Consolidated Pooling	Consolidated Purchase
Sales	$600	$200	$780 [a]	$780 [a]
Costs:				
Cost of goods	300	100	390 [a]	405 [a]

	Acquirer	Target	Consolidated Pooling	Purchase
Expenses	$100	$40	$140 [b]	$140
Depreciation	80	30	110 [c]	111
Taxes	40	10	46 [d]	41
Goodwill	0	0	0 [e]	1
Total costs	520	180	686	698
Net earnings	$80	$20	$94 [f]	$82

[a] The acquirer and the target are assumed to conduct some business with each other. To eliminate that intercompany business, the combined sales are reduced by $20. There is a corresponding decrease in the cost of sales of $10 in the pooling case. In the purchase case the reduction in the cost of goods due to intercompany transactions is more than offset by the consequences of writing the acquired inventory up to market value.
[b] Expenses are assumed unchanged in the combination and constant under pooling and purchase. In fact many business combinations involve some synergy, with the result that some expenses can be eliminated as a result of cuts in staffing.
[c] In pooling, the depreciation is the sum of the parts. Under purchase it is higher because the acquired assets have been written up to market value and have a higher depreciable basis.
[d] In combining the firms, taxes are reduced because intercompany sales are not recognized as taxable income. In the purchase case, taxes are further reduced as a result of higher depreciation and cost of goods sold. A tax rate of 33 percent is assumed.
[e] Goodwill is recorded and amortized against income only in the purchase case.
[f] The comparison of total earnings is significantly affected by the specific assumptions made, but the compelling fact is that net earnings are typically less under purchase accounting than under pooling.

The Accounting Rules in Practice

In general, the nature of the transaction and the nature (size) of the ownership interest determine the accounting treatment for an investment in another company. Many investors hold 19 percent of another company to avoid the accounting difficulties associated with the equity method. For start-up companies that will generate accounting losses for a few years, investors can avoid reporting a share of those losses by owning less than 20 percent. On the other hand, an investor may prefer to own over 20 percent of a non-dividend-paying profitable corporation.

Similar concerns arise in the neighborhood of 50 percent ownership. Many companies own exactly 50 percent of joint ventures and accordingly use the equity method. This may reflect the economic reality of shared ownership and decision making, but it may also reflect a desire not to consolidate the investee's debt. Effectively the equity method allows "off-balance-sheet financing" because the one line "investment in equity companies" reflects only the adjusted cost basis of the investment. Table 11 shows the potential impact of this off-balance-sheet financing. Note that debt to total assets is 33 percent ($5,000/$15,000) for the investor and 67 percent ($40,000/$60,000) for the investee. In consolidation, the effect of the heavy indebtedness at the investee level is reflected by a debt to total assets of 69 percent (if minority interest is treated as equity).

TABLE 11

Off–Balance–Sheet Financing
The Equity Method v. Consolidation

	Investor	Equity Investee	Consolidated
Current assets	$ 1,000	$20,000	$21,000
Noncurrent assets	4,000	40,000	44,000
Equity in investee	10,000		
	15,000	60,000	65,000
Current liabilities	5,000	20,000	25,000
Noncurrent liabilities	0	20,000	20,000
Minority interest			10,000
Owner's equity	10,000	20,000	10,000
	15,000	60,000	

Are investors misled by off-balance-sheet financing? This remains an open question. Some investors use computer screening programs to select companies with certain attributes, and under the equity method the investor would show low debt-to-equity ratios and high profitability (earnings/sales), since the earnings statement reflects only the investee profit, not sales. On the other hand, the footnotes to the financials and other disclosures of the investor would assist an analyst in developing a more complete picture. In addition, the real question might be whether the investor is liable for the investee debt. That depends on the explicit contracts between the parties. But even if the investor is not liable for the debt, if the investee becomes bankrupt, the investor ends up with a worthless investment in the equity investee—so the financial risk of the investee debt is real, even if one step removed.

Table 12 summarizes the accounting consequences of pooling versus purchase accounting. In general, in a purchase, the assets of the combined entity will be higher and the net earnings lower, which means that earnings per share (EPS) will also be lower. Only in a purchase is goodwill recognized. The recognition of goodwill has the effect of continuing to reduce earnings until it is fully amortized. Thus if management is concerned about maximizing earnings as reported on future income statements, it will have a preference for pooling when goodwill is large or when the carrying value of the acquired assets is well below market value. But higher book earnings in a pooling may be associated with undesirable tax consequences. With asset-carrying value reported below market value, postacquisition taxes may be more under the pooling method because both taxable earnings will be higher. If there is no goodwill in the transaction, a purchase has the advantage of adding in the target's earnings only after the acquisition, which typically causes favorable year-to-year earnings comparisons.

More important, perhaps, is that as we shall see in subchapter B, an acquirer's decision to use pooling or purchase accounting is also

Ch. 7 MERGERS AND ACQUISITIONS 911

related to its decision to seek tax-free status for the exchange. An acquisition using the pooling method of accounting is usually a tax-free exchange, and an acquisition using the purchase method of accounting is often (but not always) a taxable exchange. The tax and accounting rules are not coterminous, however. Thus a tax-free acquisition does occasionally fail the pooling requirements, and a rare taxable acquisition may constitute a pooling. In a tax-free exchange the acquirer has a carryover tax basis in the acquired assets. In taxable exchanges the acquirer has a step up in the tax basis of the acquired assets equal to the purchase price.

TABLE 12

Summary of Purchase and Pooling

Item	Pooling of Interests	Purchase
1. Measuring and recording at date of acquisition by the parent company.	Acquisition is accomplished by exchanging shares of stock. A purchase/sale transaction is not assumed; therefore, the cost principle is not applied. The investment account is debited for the book value of the subsidiary stock acquired.	Acquisition usually is accomplished by purchasing the shares with cash and/or debt. A purchase/sale transaction is assumed; therefore, the cost principle is applied. On acquisition date, the investment account is debited for the market value of the resources acquired.
2. Goodwill.	Goodwill is not recognized by the parent company.	Goodwill is recognized by the parent company to the extent that the purchase price exceeds the sum of acquisition market values of the assets (less the liabilities) of the subsidiary.
3. Method of aggregating or combining by the parent company to derive	Assets and liabilities (less any eliminations) of the subsidiary are added, at	Assets and liabilities (less any eliminations) of the subsidiary are

Item	Pooling of Interests	Purchase
the consolidated balance sheet.	book value, to the book values of the parent.	added, at their acquisition market values, to the book values of the assets and liabilities of the parent.
4. Method of aggregating or combining by the parent company to derive the consolidated income statement.	Revenues and expenses as reported by each company, less any eliminations, are aggregated.	Revenues as reported, less any eliminations, are aggregated. Expenses, plus additional depreciation and amortization of goodwill, less any eliminations, are aggregated.
5. Eliminations.	Eliminate all intercompany debts, revenues, and expenses. Eliminate investment account on parent's books and owners' equity of the subsidiary, excluding retained earnings.	Eliminate all intercompany debts, revenues, and expenses. Eliminate the investment account on parent's books and common stock and retained earnings of the subsidiary.
6. Usual comparative effects on the consolidated financial statements.	Expenses—lower Net income—higher EPS—higher Noncash assets—lower Liabilities—same Capital stock—higher Retained earnings—higher	Expenses—higher Net income—lower EPS—lower Noncash assets—higher Liabilities—same Capital stock—lower Retained earnings—lower

D. Short & G. Welsch, Fundamentals of Financial Accounting 683 (6th ed. 1990)

The Test for Pooling

Since, given a choice, participants in an acquisition would prefer to use the pooling method of accounting, the Financial Accounting Standards Board had to anticipate the ingenuity of planners' attempts to take an acquisition that, without complications, would use the purchase method of accounting and transform it into an acquisition that, at least in part, could use the pooling method of accounting. For example, pooling requires that the target shareholders, after the acquisition, hold stock in the surviving firm. Can a firm that wants to cash out target shareholders but use pooling accounting execute a statutory merger in which the target shareholders are given callable common stock in the surviving firm and then, after the merger is closed, call the stock? Accounting Principles Board Opinion 16 is designed to prohibit such end runs. It distinguishes the conditions that must be met for pooling of interests accounting to be used. These are summarized in the excerpt below. The intent of APB Opinion 16 is that the essence of the transaction should represent the long-term combination at both the shareholder and the firm level of two separate companies. Thus much of the opinion is spent on disqualifying multistep transactions that would avoid a full pooling of the shareholder interest. The criteria tend therefore to be expressed in the negative; if certain conditions exist, pooling cannot be used. Table 13 gives you only a taste of the requirements. The APB opinion spends several pages discussing these issues, and in the twenty years since the promulgation of the opinion, the FASB has issued hundreds of supplementing interpretations.

M. GINSBURG & J. LEVIN, MERGERS, ACQUISITIONS AND LEVERAGED BUYOUTS

582–84 (1990).

In order to qualify for pooling accounting treatment, an acquisition must meet, *inter alia*, all of the following requirements:

(1) T's voting common shareholders must all be offered and receive only P voting common stock in exchange for their T voting common stock, except as set forth below.

   (a) If P has multiple classes of common stock outstanding, T's voting common shareholders must receive P common stock with rights identical to those of the majority of P's outstanding voting common stock (i.e., the class of voting common stock which controls P).

   (b) A holder of a T warrant, option or convertible which is exercisable/convertible into T voting common stock and which is sufficiently in the money is treated as holding equivalent T voting common stock (and generally a warrant or option holder will more readily be so treated than a convertible holder). Thus, such a T security holder must receive *either* (i) P voting common stock with rights identical to those of the majority of P's outstanding voting common stock *or* (ii) a P security equivalent to his T security (i.e., a P warrant, option or convertible which is exercisable/convertible into P voting common stock with rights identical to those of the majority of P's outstanding voting common stock).

(c) There is an *important exception to this requirement that P voting common stock be the sole consideration to T's voting common shareholders (and equivalents)*: P may pay cash or other consideration for less than 10 percent of T's voting common stock (or equivalents), so long as such consideration is used only (i) to pay for fractional shares or (ii) to purchase *all* of the voting common stock (and equivalents) held by one or more T shareholders who do not wish to receive P stock. Thus, P voting common stock must be the principal consideration issued for T's voting common stock (and equivalents) in a pooling; and cash, P debentures, P preferred stock (whether or not convertible), and other P securities (e.g., nonvoting P common or P common with voting rights different than the controlling class) can be issued in exchange for only a small fraction of T's voting common stock (and equivalents) in a pooling.

(d) The less–than–10–percent–cash–and–other–consideration basket (the "10 percent basket") described in (c) above is *reduced* to the extent (i) either P or T holds "tainted treasury stock" (as described in (3) below), (ii) either P or T holds any intercompany investment in the other (as described in (7) below), and/or (iii) any T voting common stock remains outstanding as a minority interest (as described in (e) immediately below).

(e) It is permissible for a few T voting common shareholders to remain outstanding as minority interests, so long as these minority interests plus the other items described in (c) and (d) immediately above do not exceed the 10 percent basket.

(f) A holder of T *nonvoting* common stock (which is not convertible into T *voting* common stock and is not otherwise treated as a T *voting* common stock equivalent) can apparently receive cash or other consideration without disrupting pooling accounting.

(g) A holder of T preferred stock, warrants, debentures, and the like (which is not treated as a T voting common stock equivalent) can receive cash or other consideration without disrupting pooling accounting.

(2) Neither P nor T can have been a subsidiary or division of another corporation within two years before initiation of the plan of combination.

This rule is *not* violated where P's subsidiary ("S") acquires T voting common stock for *P* voting common stock. In this case *P* is viewed as the "acquiring" company, and so long as P has not been a subsidiary or division of another company ("Bigco") for at least two years (and meets all the other pooling requirements), P can acquire T (through S) in a pooling.

However, this rule *is* violated (and hence pooling is precluded) where:

   (a) P is currently a Bigco subsidiary and acquires T in exchange for *P* stock (rather than *Bigco* stock).

   (b) P is not a Bigco subsidiary, but P was formerly a Bigco subsidiary (or division), Bigco had sold P's stock to the public or P's stock or assets to a third party or group less than two years before, and P is acquiring T in exchange for P stock.

   (c) At the time P acquires T for P stock, T is a subsidiary or division of Bigco.

   (d) At the time P acquires T, T is not a subsidiary or division of Bigco, but T was formerly a Bigco subsidiary or division and Bigco had sold T's stock to the public or T's assets or stock to a third party or group less than two years before.

(3) Neither P nor T can have reacquired shares of its voting common stock within two years before initiation of the P–T plan of combination or between the initiation date and consummation (i.e., "tainted treasury stock"). There are several narrow exceptions to this rule, including the use of all or a portion of the 10 percent basket described in * * * (1)(c) and (d) to cover a small amount of tainted T treasury stock, purging tainted T treasury stock by certain types of reissuances, and purchases of T treasury stock pursuant to a regular systematic plan.

(4) Neither P nor T can have made certain other types of changes in its voting common stock equity interests during such period (e.g., a spin-off or other abnormal distribution or an issuance of new stock). Changes of this type can not be covered by the 10 percent basket described in * * * (1)(c) and (d).

(5) The consideration must be completely resolved at the consummation of the transaction, i.e., there can be no earn-out, whether structured as contingent or escrowed stock, and only limited liability of T or its shareholders to P for breaches of contractual representations and warranties.

   (a) Pooling is not prevented where T or its shareholders put in escrow (i) not more than 10 percent of the P stock received for a period not exceeding one year (or, if shorter, until completion of the first post-acquisition audit) to secure their liability to P for breach of general representations and warranties in the acquisition agreement relating to pre-acquisition facts and claims (but not to predictions of future earnings or other future events) and/or (ii) a reasonable amount of P stock to secure P against specifically identified T contingencies (e.g., a tax dispute, lawsuit or other claim existing at the consummation of the acquisition), but not relating to predictions of future earnings or other future events, for a period which is reasonable in light of the specific contingencies so identified.

(b) Pooling is precluded where the acquisition agreement makes T's shareholders (i) liable to P for money damages if a contractual representation or warranty is breached (e.g., there is an undisclosed T liability) *or* (ii) liable to deliver any property to P for breach of such a contractual representation or warranty, other than as permitted by (a) above.

(6) P's and T's affiliates (generally their officers, directors, 10 percent shareholders, and any other members of their control groups) generally may not dispose of any P or T voting common stock (or their equivalents) for a period beginning 30 days before consummation of the P-T acquisition and lasting until public issuance of financial results covering at least 30 days of post-acquisition P-T combined operations.

(7) Prior to the combination, intercorporate investments between P and T can not exceed 10 percent of outstanding voting common stock, and any such intercorporate investments reduce the 10 percent basket described in * * * (1)(c) and (d).

(8) P may not agree to re-acquire any of the common stock issued to T's former shareholders nor may P enter into other financial arrangements for the benefit of T's former shareholders.

(9) P must not intend to dispose of any significant portion of P's or T's assets within two years, other than in the ordinary course of business or to eliminate duplicate facilities or excess capacity.

(10) A number of other highly technical and arbitrary rules, including retroactive invalidation of pooling where, shortly after a pooling acquisition, P takes an action that would have precluded pooling if undertaken before the acquisition. * * *

Minimizing Goodwill in Purchase Transactions

The overall effect of Accounting Principles Board Opinion 16, however, was to severely limit the use of pooling accounting in the complex and often contested acquisitions of the late eighties. This generated acquisitions that recognized large amounts of goodwill, much to the dismay of managers of acquiring firms. The following article illustrates the extent to which planners will go to avoid goodwill when pooling treatment is impossible.

HERZ & ABAHOONIE, INNOVATIONS TO MINIMIZE ACQUISITION GOODWILL
Mergers & Acquisitions 35, 36, 38 (March/April 1990)

* * *

In the successful deal, Dow Chemical Co. acquired control of Marion Laboratories Inc. in a two-step process involving a tender offer for 39 percent of Marion's shares, coupled with voting proxies on an additional 13 percent of the stock of Marion, followed by a contribution of the stock of Dow's Merrell Dow Pharmaceuticals Inc. subsidiary into Marion. A significant kicker was a brand new security, the Contingent Value Right (CVR), that was issued to Marion's remaining public shareholders. It entitles them to receive additional cash payments if the share price of the newly formed company, Marion Merrell Dow Inc., doesn't reach targeted levels in the early 1990s. This transaction minimized goodwill by taking advantage of the accounting treatment for transfers among companies under common control. * * *

The lengths to which these deals went reflect the overarching desire of acquirers to avoid goodwill so they can minimize or prevent earnings-per-share dilution and compete effectively with foreign buyers that write off goodwill immediately against shareholders' equity. They also suggest that it is often impossible to meet all of the rules required for the pooling-of-interests transaction that has been the traditional method for avoiding goodwill. * * *

Because Dow effectively gained control of Marion after Step I, the transfer of Merrell Dow to Marion was treated as a transfer among companies under common control. Under generally accepted accounting principles, that type of transfer is recorded at book value. Consequently, the combination of Marion and Merrell Dow resulted in "prospective pooling accounting" at the Marion Merrell Dow level.

While Marion Merrell Dow will have goodwill on its balance sheet, it will only be to the extent of the $126 million of existing goodwill on Merrell Dow's balance sheet prior to the merger. Dow will reflect fair value step-ups (including goodwill) on its balance sheet to the extent that the amount of cash paid plus 33 percent of the book value of the assets surrendered (Merrell Dow Pharmaceuticals) plus the fair value of the CVRs exceeds 67 percent of the book value of Marion. However, the amount of goodwill will be far less than the amount that would have been recorded if the transaction had not been structured in this manner.

* * *

Note

Accounting for LBOs

Leveraged buyouts typically consist of a holding company with no substantive operations taking over a functioning firm. The holding company raises funds primarily through debt and purchases all the outstanding voting equity of the target entity. The holding company then merges with the target to form a consolidated firm and attach the acquisition debt to the target's assets. At issue is how the consolidated firm ought to record the assets of the target firm. The two traditional choices are the fair market value at the time of the acquisition, purchase accounting, or the value used by the operating firm in its financials before the acquisition (a carryover basis), similar to pooling accounting. If accountants use fair value, the consolidated balance sheet has a larger equity account (to offset the stepped-up basis of the assets) and larger depreciation charges for its income statement. If accountants use a carryover basis, the funds distributed to selling shareholders are accounted for as charges to equity, and the consolidated fund may show a deficit in its opening equity accounts. In other words, should accountants treat leveraged buyouts as an honest acquisition between independent parties or as a single-firm recapitalization involving a dispersal of equity to existing shareholders?

Leveraged buyout participants prfer the stepped-up basis because it gives them financing flexibility. With positive equity accounts they could, for example, place additional debt or declare dividends without violating legal capital requirements or preexisting debt covenants. The higher depreciation charges reduce taxable income. Moreover, a negative net worth may trigger liability for violations of fraudulent conveyance statutes or pretransaction debt covenants with target-firm creditors.

The Financial Accounting Standards Board's Emerging Issues Task Force (EITF) reached a consensus on how to treat LBOs at its May 1989 meeting. EITF, Basis in Leveraged Buyout Transactions, Issue No. 88–16 (May 1989). The proposal is excessively complicated and still the subject of much debate. In essence it does the following: First, it establishes criteria for a control change based on shareholder composition. Second, it stipulates that if there is no control change, the transaction is treated as a recapitalization, and the consolidated firm must use a carryover basis. Third, it stipulates that if there is a control change, the consolidated firm uses a hybrid basis, a weighted average of the operating firm carryover basis and the fair market value of its assets. The weighted average for 100 percent acquisitions depends on two calculations—the proportion of the continuing shareholders that are included in the new control group and the percentage of equity securities included in the payment package for target shareholders. For the proportion of continuing shareholders that are not in the control group, the consolidated firm takes a fair value basis; for the proportion of continuing shareholders that are in the control group, the firm takes a carryover basis. If the target shareholders receive more than 20 percent of the total consideration in equity securities (the remainder is in cash, notes, or debtlike preferred stock), only the portion of the assets equal to the percentage of nonequity consideration receives purchase accounting treatment, and the remainder receives a carryover basis.

GORMAN, HOW ACCOUNTING RULES SHOOK UP LBO DEAL MAKING

Mergers & Acquisitions 45, 46, 48, 50 (July/Aug. 1990)

* * *

Assume Lola Co., with 1,000 shares outstanding, is owned 10–percent by management and 90–percent by the public. Each share is trading at $20, making the fair value of the company $20,000. Let us further assume that the book value of the company was $4,000 and the premium above book value was attributable to depreciable assets with an average remaining useful life of five years. A leveraged buyout is undertaken on June 30, 1989, whereby management acquires the 90 percent of the company it does not own by borrowing $18,000, at 10–percent interest and secured by Lola Co.'s assets, to buy the 900 publicly held shares.

The following discussion emphasizes the impact that the accounting basis question has on the financial position and reported results of operations of the post-LBO entity. It is important to note, under the new LBO accounting rules, that the way in which the LBO transaction is corporately structured will also influence the accounting. Whether a holding company (NEWCO) is formed to execute the buyout or the buyout proceeds without the use of a holding company will make a difference as to how the post-LBO entity is presented in its financial statements. This is rather unique as most phases of the accounting literature rely on the substance of transactions, rather than their form, to determine how the transaction is to be recorded.

* * *

The next step is to calculate the effects on Lola Co.'s post-LBO balance sheet (see Table 1) and profit and loss statement (see Table 2) from three different types of transaction formats and the required differences in their accounting treatments. In each case, the fact pattern of the Lola Co. LBO was applied to the historical pre-LBO accounting records and the only substantive differences were in the structuring. The three treatments are:

- A recapitalization of Lola, i.e., a new holding is not formed to execute the transaction.
- Lola is acquired by a NEWCO, a newly formed holding company, with 100–percent fair valuation applied to Lola's net assets.
- Use of the LBO accounting principles required by the new consensus.

Notice the pronounced differences in shareholders' equity and in operating income.

In the recapitalization, Lola Co. itself was management's vehicle for acquiring the public's stock for $18,000, and a new holding company was not formed. Lola emerges with a shareholders' equity deficit of $14,000, in place of pre-transaction equity of $4,000, because equity was charged with the $18,000 cost of the treasury stock acquisition.

However, Lola posts a pretax profit of $1,200 and the recapitalization approach is the only one that allows the company to remain in the black for p & l purposes. That is because depreciation was the same as before the LBO.

* * *

In the Fair Value Acquisition approach, it is assumed that all of the premium above the book value at which Lola is being valued by the market is attributable to its fixed assets. A holding company has been formed to execute the LBO. If full fair valuation is permitted, the adjusted fixed assets would be recorded at $18,800. That amount is calculated, since all the premium over book value of Lola Co. is attributable to the company's fixed assets, by adding the $2,800 book value of the fixed assets and the $20,000 fair value of the company and subtracting the $4,000 historical total book value.

As with the recapitalization, the $18,000 in borrowings to buy the public's shares are added to liabilities. But the increase in the adjusted value of the fixed assets has produced an increase in the value of total assets. As a result, Lola winds up with post-LBO shareholders' equity of $2,000, half of the pre-transaction equity but still on the positive side.

The trade-off is that the profit and loss statement does not fare as well. The pretax loss is $2,000, largely because of an increase in depreciation which reflects the $1,000 historical depreciation plus depreciation of the step-up in basis.

* * *

Table 1: Balance Sheet of Lola Co.

	Historical Basis of Accounting (Pre–LBO)	Holding Company is not formed to execute the transaction — Recapitalization Accounting (Post–LBO)	Fair–Value Acquisition Accounting	Holding Company is formed to execute the transaction — LBO Accounting Required by EITF Consensus No. 88–16
Current assets	$1,500	$1,500	$1,500	$1,500
Fixed assets, net	2,800	2,800	18,800	17,200
Total assets	**$4,300**	**$4,300**	**$20,300**	**$18,700**
Current liabilities	$300	$300	$300	$300
Long-term debt	—	18,000	18,000	18,000
Shareholder's equity (deficit)	4,000	(14,000)	2,000	400
Total Liabilities	**$4,300**	**$4,300**	**$20,300**	**$18,700**

* * *

Table 2: Statement of Pretax Income (Loss) of Lola Co.

	Historical Basis of Accounting (Assuming no LBO Occurred)	Holding Company is not formed to execute the transaction — Recapitalization Accounting (Post–LBO)	Fair–Value Acquisition Accounting	Holding Company is formed to execute the transaction — LBO Accounting Required by EITF Consensus No. 88–16
Sales	$10,000	$10,000	$10,000	$10,000
Cost of sales, excl. depreciation	(4,000)	(4,000)	(4,000)	(4,000)

General and administrative costs	(2,000)	(2,000)	(2,000)	(2,000)
Depreciation	(1,000)	(1,000)	(4,200)	(3,880)
Operating income	$3,000	$3,000	$(200)	$120
Interest expense	—	1,800	1,800	1,800
Pretax income (loss)	$3,000	$1,200	$(2,000)	$(1,680)

SUBCHAPTER B. TAX TREATMENT OF MERGERS, ACQUISITIONS, AND REORGANIZATIONS

Introduction

The federal income tax code taxes gains and losses on held property only when they are "gains derived from dealings in property." I.R.C. § 61(a)(3). The basic calculation of gain or loss is contained in section 1001(a):

> The gain from the sale or other disposition of property shall be the excess of the amount realized therefrom over the adjusted basis provided in section 1011 for determining gain, and the loss shall be the excess of the adjusted basis provided in such section for determining loss over the amount realized.

Not all exchanges are taxable events, however. For example, assume a taxpayer buys a share of convertible preferred stock for $100. The conversion right gives the taxpayer the option of exchanging her share of preferred stock for one share of the firm's common stock. Exercising the conversion right, even if the value of the common received at the time of conversion is $200, is not a taxable "sale or disposition" of the preferred stock. See Rev.Rule 57–535, 1957–2 C.B. 513. The conversion is not a "realization event" because there is not a sufficient change in the form of ownership. Moreover, even if there is a sufficient change in the form of ownership to realize gain, the tax code may expressly exempt the gain from taxation; the realized gain is not "recognized." The tax-free status of most acquisitive reorganizations comes from an exemption from recognition for realized gains in the transaction.

An adjusted basis is the taxpayer's original basis with adjustments downward for depreciation and similar tax allowances and adjustments upward to reflect improvements or other capital outlays. An original basis is often the cost of the property when first acquired by the taxpayer, but it can be a "substituted basis" if the property is acquired in an exchange that is either not a taxable "sale or disposition" (the gain is not realized) or in which the realized gains from an otherwise taxable event are, by statutory exception, not recognized. In our earlier example of the convertible security, the taxpayer takes a substituted basis in the new common stock equal to her old adjusted basis in the preferred stock—$100 (not $200, the value of the common at the time of conversion). Not realizing a tax on the $100 gain is not a tax waiver but rather a tax deferral; the Internal Revenue Service will collect the tax on the $100 appreciation when the common stock is sold later in a taxable transaction.

In mergers, acquisitions, and reorganizations shareholders of constituent corporations often exchange one investment instrument for another. A target shareholder can exchange target shares for shares in the acquirer or for cash, for example. Each of these events is taxable under section 1001(a) unless we can find an applicable statutory exception that allows for nonrecognition of the gain realized. Moreover in these acquisitive transactions firms may exchange one form of investment for another. A target firm may exchange its assets for cash, and an acquirer may exchange its cash for the assets of a target firm. Since we tax corporations as well as individuals, each of the events is also taxable to the firm under 1001(a) unless we can qualify it under a statutory exception. Sections 354(a)(1) and 361, incorporating the definitions in section 368, contain the statutory exception for selected transactions.

SECTION 1. TAX-FREE REORGANIZATIONS

Section 354(a)(1) provides, with some limitations, for the tax-free treatment of investors who exchange stock or securities of one corporation for stock or securities of another corporation if both corporations are "parties" to a reorganization as defined in section 368. Section 361 provides, with some exceptions, for the tax-free treatment of a transferor corporation in a statutory reorganization defined in section 368. Thus if the detailed provisions of 368 are met by a transaction, the participants avoid a tax at both the corporate and the shareholder level. The unifying theme of the section is "continuity of interest"; that is, Congress provides tax-free treatment to corporate reorganizations only if, after the transaction, participating shareholders in both constituent firms can be said to continue to hold their investments in the surviving firm in a form materially similar to the form of their pretransaction investments. The ostensible rationale for nonrecognition treatment of qualifying reorganizations is that the transaction does not change the position of the participants enough to warrant an immediate imposition of a tax.

The reorganizations covered by section 368 are commonly divided into four groups: (1) acquisitive or amalgamating reorganizations in which two or more corporations are combined, (2) divisive reorganizations in which a single corporation subdivides, (3) single-party reorganizations in which a firm changes its capital structure or its place of incorporation, and (4) bankruptcy reorganizations. The amalgamating reorganizations can qualify under subsections (a)(1)(A) through (C) and in some cases (D); the divisive reorganizations include the remainder of the (D) reorganizations (and some that are covered in section 355 as well); the single-party reorganizations qualify under (E) and (F); and the bankruptcy reorganizations qualify under (G). Special rules for triangular mergers are contained in (a)(2)(D) and (E).

Section 368 is provided in full below along with interpretive regulations issued by the United States Treasury Department relevant to the section.

I.R.C. SECTION 368
(1986).

Sec. 308

(a) REORGANIZATION—

(1) IN GENERAL.—For purposes of parts I and II and this part, the term "reorganization" means—

(A) a statutory merger or consolidation;

(B) the acquisition by one corporation, in exchange solely for all or a part of its voting stock (or in exchange solely for all or a part of the voting stock of a corporation which is in control of the acquiring corporation) of stock of another corporation if, immediately after the acquisition, the acquiring corporation has control of such other corporation (whether or not such acquiring corporation had control immediately before the acquisition);

(C) the acquisition by one corporation, in exchange solely for all or a part of its voting stock (or in exchange solely for all or a part of the voting stock of a corporation which is in control of the acquiring corporation), of substantially all of the properties of another corporation, but in determining whether the exchange is solely for stock the assumption by the acquiring corporation of a liability of the other, or the fact that property acquired is subject to a liability, shall be disregarded;

(D) a transfer by a corporation of all or a part of its assets to another corporation if immediately after the transfer the transferor, or one or more of its shareholders (including persons who were shareholders immediately before the transfer), or any combination thereof, is in control of the corporation to which the assets are transferred; but only if, in pursuance of the plan, stock or securities of the corporation to which the assets are transferred are distributed in a transaction which qualifies under section 354, 355, or 356;

(E) a recapitalization;

(F) a mere change in identity, form, or place of organization of one corporation, however effected; or

(G) a transfer by a corporation of all or part of its assets to another corporation in a title 11 or similar case, but only if, in pursuance of the plan, stock or securities of the corporation to which the assets are transferred are distributed in a transaction which qualifies under section 354, 355, or 356.

(2) SPECIAL RULES RELATING TO PARAGRAPH (1).—

(A) REORGANIZATIONS DESCRIBED IN BOTH PARAGRAPH (1)(C) AND PARAGRAPH (1)(D).—If a transaction is described in both paragraph (1)(C) and paragraph (1)(D), then, for purposes of this subchapter (other than for purposes of subparagraph (C)), such transaction shall be treated as described only in paragraph (1)(D).

(B) ADDITIONAL CONSIDERATION IN CERTAIN PARAGRAPH (1)(C) CASES—If—

(i) one corporation acquires substantially all of the properties of another corporation.

(ii) the acquisition would qualify under paragraph (1)(C) but for the fact that the acquiring corporation exchanges money or other property in addition to voting stock, and

(iii) the acquiring corporation acquires, solely for voting stock described in paragraph (1)(C), property of the other corporation having a fair market value which is at least 80 percent of the fair market value of all of the property of the other corporation.

then such acquisition shall (subject to subparagraph (A) of this paragraph) be treated as qualifying under paragraph (1)(C). Solely for the purpose of determining whether clause (iii) of the preceding sentence applies, the amount of any liability assumed by the acquiring corporation, and the amount of any liability to which any property acquired by the acquiring corporation is subject, shall be treated as money paid for the property.

(C) TRANSFERS OF ASSETS OR STOCK TO SUBSIDIARIES IN CERTAIN PARAGRAPH (1)(A), (1)(B), (1)(C), AND (1)(G) CASES.—A transaction otherwise qualifying under paragraph (1)(A), (1)(B), or (1)(C) shall not be disqualified by reason of the fact that part or all of the assets or stock which were acquired in the transaction are transferred to a corporation controlled by the corporation acquiring such assets or stock. A similar rule shall apply to a transaction otherwise qualifying under paragraph (1)(G) where the requirements of subparagraphs (A) and (B) of section 354(b)(1) are met with respect to the acquisition of the assets.

(D) USE OF STOCK OF CONTROLLING CORPORATION IN PARAGRAPH (1)(A) AND (1)(G) CASES.—The acquisition by one corporation, in exchange for stock of a corporation (referred to in this subparagraph as "controlling corporation") which is in control of the acquiring corporation, of substantially all of the properties of another corporation shall not disqualify a transaction under paragraph (1)(A) or (1)(G) if—

(i) no stock of the acquiring corporation is used in the transaction, and

(ii) in the case of a transaction under paragraph (1)(A), such transaction would have qualified under paragraph (1)(A) had the merger been into the controlling corporation.

(E) STATUTORY MERGER USING VOTING STOCK OF CORPORATION CONTROLLING MERGED CORPORATION.—A transaction otherwise qualifying under paragraph (1)(A) shall not be disqualified by reason of the fact that stock of a corporation (referred to in this subparagraph as the "controlling corporation") which before the merger was in control of the merged corporation is used in the transaction, if—

(i) after the transaction, the corporation surviving the merger holds substantially all of its properties and of the properties of the merged corporation (other than stock of the controlling corporation distributed in the transaction); and

(ii) in the transaction, former shareholders of the surviving corporation exchanged, for an amount of voting stock of the controlling corporation, an amount of stock in the surviving corporation which constitutes control of such corporation.

* * *

(G) DISTRIBUTION REQUIREMENT FOR PARAGRAPH (1)(C)—

(i) IN GENERAL.—A transaction shall fail to meet the requirements of paragraph (1)(C) unless the acquired corporation distributes the stock, securities, and other properties it receives, as well as its other properties, in pursuance of the plan of reorganization. For purposes of the preceding sentence, if the acquired corporation is liquidated pursuant to the plan of reorganization, any distribution to its creditors in connection with such liquidation shall be treated as pursuant to the plan of reorganization.

(ii) Exception.—The Secretary may waive the application of clause (i) to any transaction subject to any conditions the Secretary may prescribe.

* * *

(b) PARTY TO A REORGANIZATION.—For purposes of this part, the term "a party to a reorganization" includes—

(1) a corporation resulting from a reorganization, and

(2) both corporations, in the case of a reorganization resulting from the acquisition by one corporation of stock or properties of another.

In the case of a reorganization qualifying under paragraph (1)(B) or (1)(C) of subsection (a), if the stock exchanged for the stock or properties is stock of a corporation which is in control of the acquiring corporation, the term "a party to a reorganization" includes the corporation so controlling the acquiring corporation. In the case of a reorganization qualifying under paragraph (1)(A), (1)(B), (1)(C), or (1)(G) of subsection (a) by reason of paragraph (2)(C) of subsection (a), the term "a party to a reorganization" includes the corporation controlling the corporation to which the acquired assets or stock are transferred. In the case of a reorganization qualifying under paragraph (1)(A) or (1)(G) of subsection (a) by reason of paragraph (2)(D) of that subsection, the term "a party to a reorganization" includes the controlling corporation referred to in such paragraph (2)(D). In the case of a reorganization qualifying under subsection (a)(1)(A) by reason of subsection (a)(2)(E), the term "party to a reorganization" includes the controlling corporation referred to in subsection (a)(2)(E).

(c) CONTROL DEFINED.—For purposes of part I (other than section 304), part II, this part, and part V, the term "control" means the ownership of stock possessing at least 80 percent of the total combined voting power of all classes of stock entitled to vote and at least 80 percent of the total number of shares of all other classes of stock of the corporation.

TREAS. REG. § 1.368–1

(1980)

Regulations

§ 1.368–1. Purpose and scope of exception of reorganization exchanges.

* * *

(b) *Purpose.* Under the general rule, upon the exchange of property, gain or loss must be accounted for if the new property differs in a material particular, either in kind or in extent, from the old property. The purpose of the reorganization provisions of the Code is to except from the general rule certain specifically described exchanges incident to such readjustments of corporate structures made in one of the particular ways specified in the Code, as are required by business exigencies and which effect only a readjustment of continuing interest in property under modified corporate forms. Requisite to a reorganization under the Code are a continuity of the business enterprise under the modified corporate form, and (except as provided in section 368(a)(1)(D)) a continuity of interest therein on the part of those persons who, directly or indirectly, were the owners of the enterprise prior to the reorganization. The continuity of business enterprise requirement is described in paragraph (d) of this section. The Code recognizes as a reorganization the amalgamation (occurring in a specified way) of two corporate enterprises under a single corporate structure if there exists among the holders of the stock and securities of either of the old corporations the requisite continuity of interest in the new corporation, but there is not a reorganization if the holders of the stock and securities of the old corporation are merely the holders of short-term notes in the new corporation. * * * A plan of reorganization must contemplate the bona fide execution of one of the transactions specifically described as a reorganization in section 368(a) and for the bona fide consummation of each of the requisite acts under which nonrecognition of gain is claimed. Such transaction and such acts must be an ordinary and necessary incident of the conduct of the enterprise and must provide for a continuation of the enterprise. A scheme, which involves an abrupt departure from normal reorganization procedure in connection with a transaction on which the imposition of tax is imminent, such as a mere device that puts on the form of a corporate reorganization as a disguise for concealing its real character, and the object and accomplishment of which is the consummation of a preconceived plan having no business or corporate purpose, is not a plan of reorganization.

(d) *Continuity of business enterprise*

* * *

(2) *General rule.* Continuity of business enterprise requires that the acquiring corporation (*P*) either (i) continue the acquired corporation's (*T*'s) historic business or (ii) use a significant portion of *T*'s historic business assets in a business. The application of this general rule to certain transactions, such as mergers of holding companies, will depend on all facts and circumstances. The policy underlying this general rule, which is to ensure that reorganizations are limited to readjustments of continuing interests in property under modified corporate form, provides the guidance necessary to make these facts and circumstances determinations.

* * *

Example (4). *T* manufactures children's toys and *P* distributes steel and allied products. On January 1, 1981, *T* sells all of its assets to a third party for $100,000 cash and $900,000 in notes. On March 1, 1981, *T* merges into *P*. Continuity of business enterprise is lacking. The use of the sales proceeds in *P*'s business is not sufficient.

Example (5). *T* manufactures farm machinery and *P* operates a lumber mill. *T* merges into *P*. *P* disposes of *T*'s assets immediately after the merger as part of the plan of reorganization. *P* does not continue *T*'s farm machinery manufacturing business. Continuity of business enterprise is lacking. * * *

TREAS. REG. § 1.368-2
(1980).

§ **1.368-2. Definition of terms.**—(a) The application of the term "reorganization" is to be strictly limited to the specific transactions set forth in section 368(a). The term does not embrace the mere purchase by one corporation of the properties of another corporation, for it imports a continuity of interest on the part of the transferor or its shareholders in the properties transferred. If the properties are transferred for cash and deferred payment obligations of the transferee evidenced by short-term notes, the transaction is a sale and not an exchange in which gain or loss is not recognized.

(b)(1) In order to qualify as a reorganization under section 368(a)(1)(A) the transaction must be a merger or consolidation effected pursuant to the corporation laws of the United States or a State or Territory or the District of Columbia.

(2) In order for the transaction to qualify under section 368(a)(1)(A) by reason of the application of section 368(a)(2)(D), one corporation (the acquiring corporation) must acquire substantially all of the properties of another corporation (the acquired corporation) partly or entirely in exchange for stock of a corporation which is in control of the acquiring corporation (the controlling corporation), provided that (i) the transaction would have qualified under section 368(a)(1)(A) if the merger had been into the controlling corporation, and (ii) no stock of the acquiring corporation is used in the transaction. The foregoing test of whether the transaction would have qualified under section 368(a)(1)(A) if the merger had been into the controlling corporation means that the general requirements of a reorganization under section 368(a)(1)(A) (such as a business purpose, continuity of business enterprise, and continuity of interest) must be met in addition to the special requirements of section 368(a)(2)(D). Under this test, it is not relevant whether the merger into the controlling corporation could have been effected pursuant to State or Federal corporation law. The term "substantially all" has the same meaning as it has in section 368(a)(1)(C). Although no stock of the acquiring corporation can be used in the transaction, there is no prohibition (other than the continuity of interest requirement) against using other property, such as cash or securities, of either the acquiring corporation or the parent or both. In addition, the controlling corporation may assume liabilities of the acquired corporation without disqualifying the transaction under section 368(a)(2)(D), and for purposes of section 357(a) the controlling corporation is considered a party to the exchange. For example, if the controlling corporation agrees to substitute its stock for stock of the acquired corporation under an outstanding employee stock option agreement, this assumption of liability will not prevent the transaction from qualifying as a reorganization under section 368(a)(2)(D) and the assumption of liability is not treated as money or other property for purposes of section 361(b). Section 368(a)(2)(D) applies whether or not the controlling corporation (or the acquiring corporation) is formed immediately before the merger, in anticipation of the merger, or after preliminary steps have been taken to merge directly into the controlling corporation. Section 368(a)(2)(D) applies only to statutory mergers occurring after October 22, 1968.

* * *

(c) In order to qualify as a "reorganization" under section 368(a)(1)(B), the acquisition by the acquiring corporation of stock of another corporation must be in exchange solely for all or a part of the voting stock of the acquiring corporation (or, in the case of transactions occurring after December 31, 1963, solely for all or a part of the voting stock of a corporation which is in control of the acquiring corporation), and the acquiring corporation must be in control of the other corporation immediately after the transaction. If, for example, corporation X in one transaction exchanges nonvoting preferred stock or bonds in addition to all or a part of its voting stock in the acquisition of stock of corporation Y, the transaction is not a reorganization under section 368(a)(1)(B). Nor is a transaction a reorganization described in section 368(a)(1)(B) if stock is acquired in exchange for voting stock both of the acquiring corporation and of a corporation which is in control of the acquiring corporation. The acquisition of the stock of another corporation by the acquiring corporation solely for its voting stock (or solely for voting stock of a corporation which is in control of the acquiring corporation) is permitted tax free even though the acquiring corporation already owns some of the stock of the other corporation. Such an acquisition is permitted tax free in a single transaction or in a series of transactions taking place over a relatively short period of time such as 12 months. For example, corporation A purchased 30 percent of the common stock of corporation W (the only class of stock outstanding) for cash in 1939. On March 1, 1955, corporation A offers to exchange its own voting stock for all the stock of corporation W tendered within 6 months from the date of the offer. Within the 6 months' period corporation A acquires an additional 60 percent of stock of corporation W solely for its own voting stock, so that it owns 90 percent of the stock of corporation W. No gain or loss is recognized with respect to the exchanges of stock of corporation A for stock of corporation W. For this purpose, it is immaterial whether such exchanges occurred before corporation A acquired control (80 percent) of corporation W or after such control was acquired. If corporation A had acquired 80 percent of the stock of corporation W for cash in 1939, it could likewise acquire some or all of the remainder of such stock solely in exchange for its own voting stock without recognition of gain or loss.

(d) In order to qualify as a reorganization under section 368(a)(1)(C), the transaction must be one described in subparagraph (1) or (2) of this paragraph:

> (1) One corporation must acquire substantially all the properties of another corporation solely in exchange for all or a part of its own voting stock, or solely in exchange for all or a part of the voting stock of a corporation which is in control of the acquiring corporation. For example, Corporation P owns all the stock of Corporation A. All the properties of Corporation W are transferred to Corporation A either solely in exchange for voting stock of Corporation P or solely in exchange for less than 80 percent of the

voting stock of Corporation A. Either of such transactions constitutes a reorganization under section 368(a)(1)(C). However, if the properties of Corporation W are acquired in exchange for voting stock of both Corporation P and Corporation A, the transaction will not constitute a reorganization under section 368(a)(1)(C). In determining whether the exchange meets the requirement of "solely for voting stock", the assumption by the acquiring corporation of liabilities of the transferor corporation, or the fact that property acquired from the transferor corporation is subject to a liability, shall be disregarded. Though such an assumption does not prevent an exchange from being solely for voting stock for the purposes of the definition of a reorganization contained in section 368(a)(1)(C), it may in some cases, however, so alter the character of the transaction as to place the transaction outside the purposes and assumptions of the reorganization provisions. Section 368(a)(1)(C) does not prevent consideration of the effect of an assumption of liabilities on the general character of the transaction but merely provides that the requirement that the exchange be solely for voting stock is satisfied if the only additional consideration is an assumption of liabilities.

(2) One corporation—

(i) Must acquire substantially all of the properties of another corporation in such manner that the acquisition would qualify under (1) above, but for the fact that the acquiring corporation exchanges money, or other property in addition to such voting stock, and

(ii) Must acquire solely for voting stock (either of the acquiring corporation or of a corporation which is in control of the acquiring corporation) properties of the other corporation having a fair market value which is at least 80 percent of the fair market value of all the properties of the other corporation.

(3) For the purposes of subparagraph (2)(ii) only, a liability assumed or to which the properties are subject is considered money paid for the properties. For example, Corporation A has properties with a fair market value of $100,000 and liabilities of $10,000. In exchange for these properties, Corporation Y transfers its own voting stock, assumes the $10,000 liabilities, and pays $8,000 in cash. The transaction is a reorganization even though a part of the properties of Corporation A is acquired for cash. On the other hand, if the properties of Corporation A worth $100,000, were subject to $50,000 in liabilities, an acquisition of all the properties, subject to the liabilities, for any consideration other than solely voting stock would not qualify as a reorganization under this section since the liabilities alone are in excess of 20 percent of the fair market value of the properties. If the transaction would qualify under either subparagraph (1) or (2) of this paragraph and

also under section 368(a)(1)(D), such transaction shall not be treated as a reorganization under section 368(a)(1)(C).

(e) A "recapitalization", and therefore a reorganization, takes place if, for example:

(1) A corporation with $200,000 par value of bonds outstanding, instead of paying them off in cash, discharges them by issuing preferred shares to the bondholders;

(2) There is surrendered to a corporation for cancellation 25 percent of its preferred stock in exchange for no par value common stock;

(3) A corporation issues preferred stock, previously authorized but unissued, for outstanding common stock;

(4) An exchange is made of a corporation's outstanding preferred stock, having certain priorities with reference to the amount and time of payment of dividends and the distribution of the corporate assets upon liquidation, for a new issue of such corporation's common stock having no such rights;

(5) An exchange is made of an amount of a corporation's outstanding preferred stock with dividends in arrears for other stock of the corporation. However, if pursuant to such an exchange there is an increase in the proportionate interest of the preferred shareholders in the assets or earnings and profits of the corporation, then under § 1.305–7(c)(2), an amount equal to the lesser of (i) the amount by which the fair market value or liquidation preference, whichever is greater, of the stock received in the exchange (determined immediately following the recapitalization) exceeds the issue price of the preferred stock surrendered, or (ii) the amount of the dividends in arrears, shall be treated under section 305(c) as a deemed distribution to which sections 305(b)(4) and 301 apply.

* * *

Questions

1. Treasury Regulation section 1.368–1(b) imposes a continuity of *business* enterprise requirement on top of the statutory definitions. The requirement is satisfied if the buyer either continues the historic business of the seller or uses in its business a significant portion of the seller's historic assets. Why should tax collectors care whether the buyer continues the seller's business? The Department of Treasury provided an answer in the following release. Is it persuasive?

T.D. 7745, 1981–1 C.B. 134

* * *

Overall Policy Considerations

A number of taxpayers submitting comments argued that the proposed regulation is inconsistent with the underlying policy of the reorganization provisions since it requires *T*'s shareholders to recognize gain even though the shareholders continue their investment in corporate solution. They suggest that the appropriate time to tax *T*'s shareholders is when they "cash in" their investment through a sale or other taxable disposition of the *P* stock received in the transaction. Similarly, they argue that it is inappropriate to require gain recognition at the shareholder level merely because of a change in asset composition at the corporate level.

* * *

An exception to the general rule of gain or loss recognition is contained in the reorganization provisions—sections 354 through 368—of the Code. As stated in § 1.1002–1(c), the underlying assumption of any tax-free exchange "is that the new property is substantially a continuation of the old investment still unliquidated" and, with respect to corporate reorganizations, nonrecognition results because "the new enterprise, the new corporate structure, and the new property are substantially continuations of the old still unliquidated." * * *

The courts have long recognized that a tax-free reorganization presupposes that *T*'s shareholders retain a material proprietary interest in *P* (continuity of interest). * * *

A necessary corollary to this continuity of interest requirement is that the interest retained represent a link to *T*'s business or its business assets. The continuity of business enterprise requirement ensures that tax-free reorganizations effect only a readjustment of the *T* shareholders' continuing interest in *T*'s property under a modified corporate form. *See* § 1.368–1(b). Absent such a link between *T*'s shareholders and *T*'s business or assets there would be no reason to require *T*'s shareholders to retain a continuing stock interest in *P*. If the shareholders' link to *T*'s business or its assets is broken by, for example, a sale of *T*'s business to an unrelated party as part of the overall plan of reorganization, the interest received in *P* is no different than an interest in any corporation. An exchange of stock without a link to the underlying business or business assets resembles any stock for stock exchange and, as such, is a taxable event. Thus, it is not enough that the shareholders' investment remains in corporate solution.

* * *

2. The tax code also imposes a continuity of *shareholder* interest requirement. The requirement affects the form of consideration that the buyer can offer the shareholders of the seller in the acquisition. In B and C reorganizations the form of consideration is restricted by statute. Can the acquiring corporation escrow some of the stock used as consideration to assure that the selling firm has complied with the terms of the acquisition agreement? In A reorganizations the continuity of shareholder interest is established in the case law and in Treasury revenue proclamations.

REV.PROC. 77-37, § 3.02

The "continuity of interest requirement of section 1.368–1(b) of the Income Tax Regulations is satisfied if there is continuing interest through stock ownership in the acquiring or transferee corporation (or a corporation in "control" thereof within the meaning of section 368(c) of the Code) on the part of the former shareholders of the acquired or transferor corporation which is equal in value, as of the effective date of the reorganization, to at least 50 percent of the value of all of the formerly outstanding stock of the acquired or transferor corporation as of the same date. It is not necessary that each shareholder of the acquired or transferor corporation receive in the exchange stock of the acquiring or transferee corporation, or a corporation in "control" thereof, which is equal in value to at least 50 percent of the value of his former stock interest in the acquired or transferor corporation, so long as one or more of the shareholders of the acquired or transferor corporation have a continuing interest through stock ownership in the acquiring or transferee corporation (or a corporation in "control" thereof) which is, in the aggregate, equal in value to at least 50 percent of the value of all of the formerly outstanding stock of the acquired or transferor corporation. Sales, redemptions, and other dispositions of stock occurring prior or subsequent to the exchange which are part of the plan of reorganization will be considered in determining whether there is a 50 percent continuing interest through stock ownership as of the effective date of the reorganization.

* * *

Assume the acquired to be a corporation that has assets valued at $1 million and liabilities of $150,000. What is the maximum amount of cash or debt that a buyer can use as consideration in lieu of its voting stock in an A, B, or C reorganization? Why are the requirements different among the three types of reorganizations?

3. In a B reorganization can the buyer who has acquired all the voting stock of the seller exchange its stock with the bondholders of the seller as well? See Rev.Rule 70-1 Cum.Bull. 77.

4. In a C reorganization, as detailed in the following revenue proclamation, why is the meaning of "substantially all" much stricter than it is in state corporation codes?

REV.PROC. 77-37, § 3.01

The "substantially all" requirement * * * is satisfied if there is a transfer * * * of assets representing at least 90 percent of the fair market value of the net assets and at least 70 percent of the fair market value of the gross assets held by the corporation immediately prior to the transfer. All payments to dissenters and all redemptions and distributions (except for regular, normal distributions) made by the corporation immediately preceding the transfer and which are part of the plan of reorganization will be considered as assets held by the corporation immediately prior to the transfer.

5. In a B or C reorganization, if shareholders seek their appraisal rights and demand cash instead of stock, does it destroy the tax-free status

of the reorganization? Can the problem be avoided if the selling firm pays off the shareholders before the closing? See Rev.Rule 68–285. 1968–1 C.B. 147; Rev. 68–562, 1968–2 C.B. 157.

6. Can straight triangular acquisitions, in which the buyer's subsidiary acquires the selling firm, be tax-free reorganizations? See § 368(a)(2)(D).

Can reverse triangular acquisitions, in which the buyer's subsidiary merges into the selling firm, be tax-free reorganizations? See § 368(a)(2)(E). In a reverse triangular merger are the rules for consideration as flexible as in a straight triangular merger? Can the acquirer use anything other than its own voting stock to acquire control of the target? Once an acquirer has control, can it use any type of consideration to purchase the remainder of the target stock?

7. What are the significant uses of D, E, and F reorganizations? Can an acquisitive transaction take the form of a D reorganization? Does the following transaction qualify? Target transfers all its assets to Acquirer for a controlling block of Acquirer stock, and Target liquidates. What is the major difference between a nondivisive D reorganization and a C reorganization? If a transaction qualifies as both a C and a D, how is it treated? See § 368(a)(2)(A). Note that the definition of control in D reorganizations is relaxed. See § 368(a)(2)(H).

8. Why is the classification system used in the federal tax code different from the classification system used in state corporate codes and the classification system used in accounting practice?

AMERICAN LAW INSTITUTE, PROPOSALS ON CORPORATE ACQUISITIONS AND DISPOSITIONS

30–33 (1982)

Corporate acquisitions are classified and differently treated for purposes of financial accounting, corporate law, and securities regulation, as well as income taxation, and classification for tax purposes is often criticized for being in conflict with the classification for these other purposes.

One kind of conflict is simply a matter of different criteria for making apparently analogous classifications. The most obvious conflict of this kind is between the criteria for reorganization treatment under the tax law and those for pooling-of-interest treatment for financial accounting purposes. The requirements for pooling-of-interest accounting are generally much more restrictive.

It is not clear, however, that this kind of conflict is very serious or that there is any feasible way to eliminate it. The purposes and uses of financial reporting are quite different from those of tax accounting, and while different criteria may produce administrative complications, there is no reason to assume they could be eliminated while responding adequately to those different purposes.

For financial reporting purposes, even a simple stock purchase is accounted for by allocating the stock purchase price among assets of the acquired company, so that consolidated financial income of the acquiring corporate group will be essentially the same as if there had been an asset purchase. For tax purposes, on the other hand, computation of income from a corporation whose stock has been purchased will be generally unaffected by the purchase price paid for the stock, even if taxable income is thereafter reported and taxed on a consolidated return of the acquiring corporation. The inconsistency between financial and tax accounting in this case is essentially the same as after a reorganization acquisition that does not qualify for pooling-of-interest accounting, though it does not seem to have been so widely criticized as involving an undesirable conflict.

A more serious kind of conflict arises because tax classification depends on taking particular corporate procedural steps, which may sometimes be impossible or inconvenient for nontax reasons. The tax law offers a different set of tax consequences, for example, for a stock purchase than for an asset purchase, but in a particular situation it may be inconvenient or impossible to deal individually with shareholders for the purchase of their shares, or to have a corporate sale of assets, and a conflict then may emerge between what is convenient and feasible as a matter of corporate procedure and what is most desirable from a tax standpoint. Corporation P might wish to acquire X, for example, on a carryover basis, by purchasing its stock, in order to avoid immediate taxes on depreciation recapture. But an asset acquisition might be more convenient than a stock purchase because the latter requires direct dealing with a multitude of individual shareholders.

* * *

* * * The main explicit distinction in the classification of acquisitions under existing law is between reorganizations and purchases. But from a functional standpoint, focusing on the computation of corporate taxable income, a more fundamental differentiation exists between all acquisitions in which basis and other tax attributes carry over in the acquisition transaction so that the computation of taxable income from conduct of the acquired business is uninterrupted by the acquisition, and others in which tax attributes do not carry over and there is a fresh start in computing taxable income from the acquired business on the basis of cost in the acquisition transaction itself. It is convenient to call the former "carryover-basis" acquisitions and the latter "cost-basis" acquisitions. Reorganizations fall in the category of carryover-basis acquisitions.

* * *

There are affirmative reasons for preserving both cost-basis and carryover-basis modes of treatment of potential corporate income tax liabilities in an acquisition transaction, and for preserving effective taxpayer choice between them for a substantial number of kinds of transactions.

First, cost-basis treatment makes sense because it enables a corporate purchaser of assets to buy those assets without entanglement in the tax history of the prior owner, just as corporate law makes it possible, generally, to purchase assets without assuming financial and continuing business obligations of the seller. Furthermore, cost-basis treatment enables a purchaser to buy from a prior corporate owner on just the same terms, so far as its own taxes are concerned, as from an unincorporated seller or from a larger corporation for which the assets are not substantially all its assets, or from several different sellers.

Moreover, it seems perfectly feasible, as a condition to cost-basis treatment, to insist on an adequate accounting for previously unrealized corporate tax liabilities by the old corporate owner. Present law shows the way to do that in the case of depreciation recapture. Present law fails to require an adequate accounting for some other sorts of gains, such as inventory appreciation, and so cost-basis acquisitions now provide a way of causing those gains to escape corporate income tax altogether. But the remedy for these abuses is to require a more adequate accounting by the transferor, not to ban cost-basis acquisitions. * * *

Second, carryover-basis treatment makes sense because it provides a way to preserve the flow of corporate tax revenues without imposing a barrier against economically desirable changes in ownership. A corporation may have very substantial unrealized gains, but a shortage of cash with which to pay any current tax on them. A purchaser may also be without cash to provide for payment of such taxes. Just as corporate law and procedure provide for the acquisition of assets subject to financial and business obligations, so that an acquisition will not necessarily require the raising of funds to pay them off, so carryover-basis tax treatment makes it possible in effect to conduct an acquisition subject to ongoing corporate income tax liabilities.

Moreover, the possibility of carryover-basis treatment does not seem to entail compromise of any important government interest. Carryover of losses and deferral of tax on gain are the advantages that taxpayers, may secure from carryover-basis treatment. But neither of these imposes a cost on the government that warrants prohibition of carryover treatment.

Carryover of losses is subject to special limitations, under existing law, applicable to both reorganizations and stock purchases. Sections 269, 382. Those limitations are imperfect in some respects, and the policies underlying them are debatable. * * * But the strategy of dealing specially with carryover of losses is essentially sound; any general restriction on carryover treatment would be both unnecessary and insufficient to deal with the special problems of loss carryovers.

If net undeducted losses are subjected to special limitations, then the primary issue in allowing carryover treatment is one of deferral or acceleration of tax on net unrealized gains. If one takes the view that previously unrealized gains should always be taxed as soon as possible whenever any kind of transaction presents a feasible occasion for taxation, then carryover-basis treatment of a corporate acquisition will appear as unjustified deferral. But one may start from the observation that the corporate income tax is generally imposed on profits realized from corporate operations, not on the excess over basis of value that reflects expectations of future profits. This is the general case even when individual shareholders realize their shares of that value by selling their stock. Carryover-basis treatment of a corporate stock acquisition is just an extension of that general pattern to cases in which all or a major part of the shares of a corporation are sold to a corporate transferee. Carryover treatment of asset acquisitions involves a further extension to cases in which essentially the same result is achieved by a corporate asset transfer. In such cases the corporate transferor will only avoid tax if it makes distributions that subject its shareholders to whatever taxes they would have incurred on a direct sale or exchange of their shares. Against this background, any attempt to insist on cost-basis treatment of acquisition transactions would represent an unjustified acceleration of corporate income-tax liabilities, not elimination of unjustified deferral.

Third, the reasons for preserving both carryover and cost-basis treatment also support the notion of taxpayer choice between them. The reasons have to do with either treatment being adequate—or being able to be made adequate—from the government's standpoint, and each being able to meet certain different needs of taxpayers in particular situations. Since the taxpayer parties to an acquisition will be best able to determine the relative magnitude of those needs, it makes sense to give them a choice in determining the mode of tax treatment.

* * *

The trouble with present law is not that tax classification of acquisitions is effectively elective, but that the election is tied unnecessarily to matters of corporate procedure. The solution to the trouble is to make tax classification explicitly elective and as independent as possible of corporate procedural considerations. While the reasons for electivity in tax classification are analogous to some of the reasons for electivity in matters of corporate procedure, there is no compelling reason to tie the two together. Indeed any such tie-in has the effect of arbitrarily limiting free electivity in cases in which tax and corporate procedural considerations conflict. Simple and explicit procedures should be provided, therefore, whereby any acquisition that would otherwise be a cost-basis acquisition can be classified as a carryover-basis acquisition, and vice versa, if all affected corporate parties consent to that change in classification.

* * *

The Mechanics of Tax-Free Treatment

D. KAHN & P. GANN, CORPORATE TAXATION
(3d ed. 1989) pp. 674–75.

10–2 Corporation X has 100 shares of stock outstanding, all of which are owned by Jones. Each share has a fair market value of $1,800 and an adjusted basis of $100. X owns assets with a combined fair market value of $200,000 and a combined adjusted basis of $150,000, and has outstanding $20,000 in liabilities. Payment by X of these liabilities would not be a deductible expenditure. Corporation Y is a publicly held corporation that has more than 100,000 shares of common voting stock outstanding. Y is going to acquire X in a reorganization, the consideration for which will be 180 shares of Y common voting stock, each with a value of $1,000. The following paragraphs discuss the applicable nonrecognition and basis provisions to Corporations X and Y and to Jones if the reorganization is accomplished as either an A, B, or C reorganization.

A Reorganization. Corporation X is merged into Corporation Y under state statutory merger provisions. Accordingly, Y becomes the owner of all the assets and liabilities previously owned by X, and X ceases to exist as an entity. Jones' stock in X is cancelled, and Y issues 180 shares of Y common voting stock to Jones having a fair market value of $180,000. Jones realizes a gain of $170,000 on the exchange of his X stock for Y stock; but under § 354(a), none of that gain is recognized. Jones' basis in the 180 shares of Y stock is $10,000, the same as his basis in his cancelled X stock. § 358(a).

If instead of issuing 180 shares of common stock, Y issues 150 shares of common voting stock plus a bond with a fair market value and principal amount of $30,000, the $30,000 bond will constitute boot, and Jones will recognize $30,000 of his $170,000 realized gain. §§ 354(a) and 356(a). * * * Jones' basis in the 150 shares of Y stock is his basis in the cancelled X stock ($10,000), less the fair market value of the boot received in the exchange ($30,000), plus the gain he recognized on the exchange ($30,000). § 358(a)(1). Thus, Jones' basis in the 150 shares of Y stock is $10,000. His basis in the $30,000 bond is its fair market value of $30,000. § 358(a)(2).

Y recognizes no income by virtue of acquiring the assets of X. § 1032. Y's basis in the acquired assets is $150,000, the same as X's basis in the property. § 362(b). X recognizes no gain because of the transfer of its property to Y or because Y assumed X's $20,000 in liabilities. §§ 357(a), 361(a).

B Reorganization. Jones exchanges his 100 shares of X for 180 shares of common voting stock of Y. After the exchange, Jones owns 180 shares of Y, and Y owns all 100 shares of X. Jones realizes a gain of $170,000 on the exchange; but under § 354(a), none of that gain is recognized. Jones' basis in the 180 shares of Y stock is $10,000, the same as his basis in the X stock. § 358(a). Y recognizes no income when it acquires the X stock. § 1032. Y's basis in the 100 shares of X stock is $10,000, the same as the basis of Jones in that stock. § 362(b).

C Reorganization. X transfers all of its assets and liabilities to Y in exchange for 180 shares of Y common voting stock, and shortly thereafter, pursuant to the plan of reorganization, X is liquidated. X realizes a gain of $50,000 on the exchange of assets for Y stock plus the assumption by Y of X's liabilities; but under § 361(a), none of that gain is recognized. X also does not recognize any gain because Y assumed X's $20,000 in liabilities. §§ 357(a), 361(a). X's basis in the 180 shares of Y stock is its basis in the assets transferred ($150,000), less the amount of liabilities assumed ($20,000), or $130,000. § 358(a), (d). Since X was promptly liquidated, however, its basis in the Y stock will have no tax significance. Y recognizes no gain on the exchange of its common stock for X's assets. § 1032. Y's basis in the acquired assets is $150,000, the same as X's basis in the property. § 362(b). Since X did not recognize a gain on the exchange, Y obtains no increase over X's basis in the transferred assets. Since X is liquidated as part of the plan of reorganization, the 180 shares of Y will be distributed to Jones. X will not recognize a gain on distributing those 180 shares of Y stock to X's shareholders. § 361(c). Jones will realize a gain of $170,000 because of the liquidation of X, but that gain will not be recognized. § 354(a). Jones' basis in the 180 shares of Y stock will be $10,000, the same as his basis in the X stock cancelled on the liquidation of X. § 358(a).

Instead of these facts, assume that X transfers all of its assets and liabilities to Y in exchange for 170 shares of Y common voting stock plus $10,000 cash, and X promptly distributes those properties to its shareholder, Jones, in liquidation. Again, X realizes a gain of $50,000 on the exchange of assets for Y stock. Even though X received $10,000 cash, it will not recognize any of its gain. § 361(b)(1). Since X's basis in the 170 shares of Y stock is equal to its own basis in the assets transferred ($150,000), less the cash it received ($10,000) and the amount of liabilities assumed ($20,000), plus any gain (zero) that it recognized on the exchange. § 358(a), (d). Since X's gain on the exchange is zero, its basis in the Y stock is $120,000. However, because X was promptly liquidated, that basis is not significant. Y's basis in the assets transferred from X is $150,000, the same as X's basis in the assets. § 362(b). Jones realizes a gain of $170,000 when X is liquidated. This gain is recognized to the extent of the $10,000 boot received. §§ 354(a) and 356(a). Jones's basis in the 170 shares of Y stock that he received on X's liquidation is equal to his basis in the X stock that he surrendered ($10,000), plus the gain he recognized on the exchange ($10,000), less the amount of money he received ($10,000). § 358(a)(1). Thus, Jones' basis in the 170 shares of Y stock is $10,000.

* * *

Tax Attribute Provisions

Section 381, subject to the limitations of sections 269, 382, 383, and 384 (these limitations are discussed in subsection a of the next section), provides for the carryover of net operating losses, earnings and profits, capital losses, and other tax attributes to the transferee or successor corporation in a reorganization. The carryover of tax attributes is a significant characteristic of a reorganization. The relative desirability or undesirability of the acquired corporations' tax attributes is an important factor (albeit often not a dispositive one) in determining whether to qualify an acquisition as a reorganization or a taxable transaction.

A Taxable Exchange Compared

Assume the same basic facts as are contained in the Kahn and Gahn extract, pp. 938–39.

Instead of a B reorganization, Jones exchanges his X Corporation stock for $180,000 in cash from Y Corporation. Jones is fully taxable on any gain or loss realized on the sale of the X shares. Y's basis in the X shares purchased is equal to the purchase price paid by Y for the shares plus the expenses of the acquisition. (In a tax-free reorganization the costs of the acquisition may be deductible as an ordinary business expense, however.) X's basis in its assets, however, does not change as a result of Y's purchase of the X stock (unless Y makes a so-called section 338 election, a matter we will leave for your corporate tax course). X's ability to use thereafter its net operating loss, capital loss, and tax credit carryforwards may be limited by code sections 269, 383, and 384, and perhaps by the separate return limitation year (SRLY) rules of the consolidated return regulations. X's other tax attributes are not affected by the purchase of X's stock.

If Jones receives $180,000 of notes for his X shares, he generally reports (absent a contrary election under section 453(f)) gain on the installment method, so long as neither the notes received nor the X stock traded is readily tradable and subject to penalty provision imposed by new code section 453A on large installment sales. In general this means that Jones will report a proportionate part of his total gain on the sale each time he collects a part of the purchase price for his stock (represented by payments on the notes). The installment method does not apply if Jones's stock is traded on an "established securities market." Moreover new section 453A imposes an annual interest charge on Jones's tax liability deferred by the installment method to the extent that the face amount of his receivables exceeds $5 million. The new section also triggers immediate gain recognition on any installment receivable (in sales of over $150,000) to the extent that Jones uses the receivable as direct security for his own debts.

Assume, instead of an A or C reorganization, Y Corporation purchases all of X Corporation's assets for $180,000 in cash. The transaction is accomplished either by a traditional asset sale or in a statutory forward merger of X into Y in which Jones receives $180,000 in cash for his canceled X stock. Y takes a basis in X's assets equal to the purchase price (plus any X liabilities transferred to Y and Y's expenses of the transaction). X is taxed on its full gain or loss in its assets (including goodwill), whether it promptly liquidates or not (with X's gain or loss on each asset being ordinary or capital in character, depending on the nature of each asset sold). If T liquidates, Jones is fully taxable on any gain or loss realized on the disposition of his X shares—the excess of the cash and fair market value of property received over his basis in X stock.

The benefit to Y of any step-up in basis in X's assets will depend on the extent to which the step-up can be allocated to inventory and depreciable or amortizable assets (tangible or intangible) rather than to nonamortizable goodwill (tax treatment of goodwill does not correspond with accounting treatment of goodwill). Y may also benefit if part of the consideration that it pays in an acquisition is allocated to deductible items such as salary and convenants not to compete for Jones rather than to the purchase price of the acquired assets.

To the extent that X receives Y notes (so long as such notes are not readily tradable and meet other requirements for using the installment method) and X does not liquidate or otherwise dispose of the notes, X can generally postpone taxation of its gain on certain of its assets (not including, for example, inventory or marketable securities) under the installment method. If X distributes Y notes to Jones in a prompt liquidation, Jones may report the gain on the installment method, so long as the Y notes are not readily tradable and the notes otherwise meet the requirements of the installment method.

Question

When would the parties favor, solely for tax purposes, a taxable transaction? Assume, for example, the target has assets with an aggregate basis exceeded by their aggregate fair market value. Assume, on the other hand, the target's aggregate basis is less than the assets' fair market value but the target has net operating loss carryforwards that are about to expire.

SECTION 2. ARE ACQUISITIONS DRIVEN BY TAXES?

Introduction

If the tax obligations of two independent firms are reduced when the firms combine, the parties can divide the gains created by the savings in an acquisition. If Congress does not intend the tax code to encourage mergers, which it does not, the United States Treasury suffers the loss whenever tax-driven acquisitions occur. In many ways the problem is similar to the problems of opportunistic behavior we studied in chapter 3, with the United States Treasury in the position of preexisting creditors, employees, and tort claimants. As clever planners discover new methods of minimizing taxes through acquisitions, Congress responds by amending the tax code. From 1986 to 1990, for example, Congress amended the code each year to stop perceived loopholes in tax law applicable to acquisitions. There are two significant issues in the debate. First, should tax attributes, particularly net operating loss carrybacks and carryforwards, survive in an acquisition? Second, does the tax code encourage highly leveraged acquisitions because a firm can deduct interest payments on its debt securities but not dividend payments on its stock? Each issue is examined below.

Subsection a. Survival of Tax Attributes in an Acquisition

The tax code operates on an artificial one-year accounting system. If a corporation is profitable one year, making $10 million, and loses $5 million the next, without special averaging rules it must pay tax on $10 million in one year and no tax in the next. A firm making the same profits in the two-year period, $2.5 million each year, will pay taxes on only a total of $5 million dollars. Congress has designed, in section 172, a net operation loss (NOL) carryover provision that allows a corporation to average its losses with its profits in both the three prior years and the fifteen years subsequent. The carryover provisions have generated two controversies with respect to acquisitions.

First, can a losing firm sell its NOLs? A struggling corporation showing net losses on its income statement for some time will generate net operating losses that it cannot use. It has no profits in prior years and is unlikely to generate profits in subsequent years. Can it combine with a firm that is profitable and use its NOLs to offset the taxable income of the profitable firm? Congress's answer is contained in the Tax Reform Act of 1986 Congress, which includes section 382. The conference committee report explaining the provision, and supplementary provisions, is presented below.

Second, can NOLs help fund a leveraged acquisition? A leveraged buyout group borrows funds to buy an otherwise profitable firm. After the acquisition the buyout group releverages the firm to refinance the buyout debt, causing the firm to show large losses. Can the firm carry back these losses to prior years, when the firm was showing a profit, and claim a refund of the taxes the firm paid in those years? Section 172(b)(1)(M), newly amended to section 172 in the Revenue Reconciliation Act of 1989, is Congress's answer. The House committee report on the section follows the conference committee report on section 382 below.

TAX REFORM ACT OF 1986

Conference Report No. 99–841 (Sept. 18, 1986), 99th Cong., 2d Sess. reprinted in 73, No. 41 Stand.Fed.Tax Rpt. (CCH) II–170, II–172–173, II–185, II–187, II–189, II–194 (Sept. 21, 1986).

Overview

The Act alters the character of the special limitations on the use of NOL carryforwards. After an ownership change, as described below, the taxable income of a loss corporation available for offset by pre-acquisition NOL carryforwards is limited annually to a prescribed rate times the value of the loss corporation's stock immediately before the ownership change. In addition, NOL carryforwards are disallowed entirely unless the loss corporation satisfies continuity-of-business enterprise requirements for the two-year period following any ownership change. The Act also expands the scope of the special limitations to include built-in losses and allows loss corporations to take into account built-in gains. The Act includes numerous technical changes and several anti-avoidance rules. Finally, the Act applies similar rules to carryforwards other than NOLs, such as net capital losses and excess foreign tax credits.

Ownership Change

The special limitations apply after any ownership change. An ownership change occurs, in general, if the percentage of stock of the new loss corporation owned by any one or more 5–percent shareholders * * * has increased by more than 50 percentage points relative to the lowest percentage of stock of the old loss corporation owned by those 5–percent shareholders at any time during the testing period (generally a three-year period) (new sec. 382(g)(1)). The determination of whether an ownership change has occurred is made by aggregating the increases in percentage ownership for each 5–percent shareholder whose percentage ownership has increased during the testing period. * * * The determination of whether an ownership change has occurred is made after any owner shift involving a 5–percent shareholder or any equity structure shift. * * *

An equity structure shift is defined as any tax-free reorganization within the meaning of section 368, other than a divisive "D" or "G" reorganization or an "F" reorganization (new sec. 382(g)(3)(A)). In addition, to the extent provided in regulations, the term equity structure shift may include other transactions, such as public offerings not involving a 5–percent shareholder or taxable reorganization-type transactions (*e.g.,* mergers or other reorganization-type transactions that do not qualify for tax-free treatment due to the nature of the consideration or the failure to satisfy any of the other requirements for a tax-free transaction) (new secs. 382(g)(3)(B), (g)(4), and (m)(5)). * * *

Effect of Ownership Change

Section 382 limitation

For any taxable year ending after the change date (*i.e.,* the date on which an owner shift resulting in an ownership change occurs or the date of the reorganization in the case of an equity structure shift resulting in an ownership change), the amount of a loss corporation's (or a successor corporation's) taxable income that can be offset by a pre-change loss * * * cannot exceed the section 382 limitation for such year (new sec. 382(a)). The section 382 limitation for any taxable year is generally the amount equal to the value of the loss corporation immediately before the ownership change multiplied by the long-term tax-exempt rate (described below) (new sec. 382(b)(1)).

The value of a loss corporation is generally the fair market value of the corporation's stock (including preferred stock described in section 1504(a)(4)) immediately before the ownership change (new sec. 382(e)(1)).
* * *

The long-term tax-exempt rate is defined as the highest of the Federal long-term rates determined under section 1274(d), as adjusted to reflect differences between rates on long-term taxable and tax-exempt obligations, in effect for the month in which the change date occurs or the two prior months (new sec. 382(f)). The Treasury Department will publish the long-term tax-exempt rate by revenue ruling within 30 days after the date of enactment and monthly thereafter. The long-term tax-exempt rate will be computed as the yield on a diversified pool of prime, general obligation tax-exempt bonds with remaining periods to maturity of more than nine years.

The use of a rate lower than the long-term Federal rate is necessary to ensure that the value of NOL carryforwards to the buying corporation is not more than their value to the loss corporation. Otherwise there would be a tax incentive to acquire loss corporations. If the loss corporation were to sell its assets and invest in long-term Treasury obligations, it could absorb its NOL carryforwards at a rate equal to the yield on long-term government obligations. Since the price paid by the buyer is larger than the value of the loss company's assets (because the value of NOL carryforwards are taken into account), applying the long-term Treasury rate to the purchase price would result in faster utilization of NOL carryforwards by the buying corporation. The long-term tax-exempt rate normally will fall between 66 (1 minus the maximum corporate tax rate of 34 percent) and 100 percent of the long-term Federal rate.

* * *

Following an ownership change, a loss corporation's NOL carryforwards * * * are subject to complete disallowance * * * unless the loss corporation's business enterprise is continued at all times during the two-year period following the ownership change. If a loss corporation fails to satisfy the continuity of business enterprise requirements, no NOL carryforwards would be allowed to the new loss corporation for any post-change year. This continuity of business enterprise requirement is the same requirement that must be satisfied to qualify a transaction as a tax-free reorganization under section 368. * * *

The Act does not alter the continuing application of section 269, relating to acquisitions made to evade or avoid taxes, as under prior law. Similarly, the SRLY and CRCO principles under the regulations governing the filing of consolidated returns will continue to apply.
* * *

ACQUISITIONS TO EVADE OR AVOID INCOME TAX

The Secretary of the Treasury was authorized to disallow deductions, credits, or other allowances following an acquisition of control of a corporation or a tax-free acquisition of a corporation's assets if the principal purpose of the acquisition was tax avoidance (sec. 269). This provision applied in the following cases:

(1) where any person or persons acquired (by purchase or in a tax-free transaction) at least 50 percent of a corporation's voting stock, or stock representing 50 percent of the value of the corporation's outstanding stock;

(2) where a corporation acquired property from a previously unrelated corporation and the acquiring corporation's basis for the property was determined by reference to the transferor's basis.

* * *

Treasury regulations under section 269 provided that the acquisition of assets with an aggregate basis that is materially greater than their value (i.e., assets with built-in losses), coupled with the utilization of the basis to create tax-reducing losses, is indicative of a tax-avoidance motive. * * *

CONSOLIDATED RETURN REGULATIONS

To the extent that NOL carryforwards were not limited by the application of section 382 or section 269, after an acquisition, the use of such losses might be limited under the consolidated return regulations. In general, if an acquired corporation joined the acquiring corporation in the filing of a consolidated tax return by an affiliated group of corporations, the use of the acquired corporation's pre-acquisition NOL carryforwards against income generated by other members of the group was limited by the "separate return limitation year" ("SRLY") rules.
* * * An acquired corporation was permitted to use pre-acquisition NOLs only up to the amount of its own contribution to the consolidated group's taxable income. * * *

Applicable Treasury regulations provided rules to prevent taxpayers from circumventing the SRLY rules by structuring a transaction as a "reverse acquisition" (defined in regulations as an acquisition where the "acquired" corporation's shareholders end up owning more than 50 percent of the value of the "acquiring" corporation). * * *

REVENUE RECONCILIATION ACT OF 1989

House Ways and Means Comm. Rep. No. ___, reprinted in 76, No. 50 Stand.Fed. Tax Rpts. (CCH) ¶ 10,165 at 421 (Nov. 27, 1989).

Corporate equity reduction transaction.—A corporate equity reduction transaction ("CERT") means either a major stock acquisition or an excess distribution. A major stock acquisition is an acquisition by a corporation (or any group of persons acting in concert with such corporation) of at least 50 percent of the vote or value of the stock of another corporation. * * *

An excess distribution is the excess of the aggregate distributions and redemptions made by a corporation during the taxable year with respect to its stock (other than stock described in section 1504(a)(4)), over 150 percent of the average of such distributions and redemptions for the preceding 3 taxable years. * * * Notwithstanding the above, a distribution or redemption (or series thereof) is not treated as an excess distribution if it does not exceed 10 percent of the value of the corporation's outstanding stock (other than stock described in section 1504(a)(4)) measured at the beginning of the corporation's taxable year.

Limitation of net operating loss carryback.—If a C corporation has an NOL in the taxable year in which it is involved in a CERT or in the following 2 taxable years, the corporation may be limited in its ability to carry back some portion of the loss. A C corporation is treated as being involved in a CERT if it is either the acquired or acquiring corporation, or successor thereto (in the case of a major stock acquisition) or the distributing or redeeming corporation, or successor thereto (in the case of an excess distribution). Any portion of an NOL that cannot be carried back due to the operation of this provision may be carried forward to the corporation's future taxable years, as otherwise provided under present law.

The portion of the corporation's NOL carryback that is limited is the lesser of (1) the corporation's interest expense that is allocable to the CERT, or (2) the excess of the corporation's interest expense in the loss limitation year over the average of the corporation's interest expense for the 3 taxable years prior to the taxable year in which the CERT occurred. If the lesser of these two amounts is less than $1 million, the provision does not apply. * * *

(1) Profitable corporation P, a calendar year C corporation, is capitalized with $150 million of debt and $50 million of equity. P's annual interest expense has been $15 million for the past 3 years. P has paid a 1% annual dividend to its shareholders, or an average of $.5 million, for each of the past 3 years. On January 1, 1990, P borrows $50 million and distributes the proceeds to its shareholders. Due to increased interest deductions of $5 million, P incurs an NOL in 1990 of $4 million.

P was involved in a CERT in 1990 because P made an excess distribution to its shareholders (i.e., the $50 million distribution exceeds 150% of the average $.5 million dividend). The portion of P's $4 million NOL that is limited under the provision is the lesser of (1) P's interest expense that is allocable to the CERT ($5 million), or (2) the excess of P's interest expense in 1990 ($20 million) over P's average interest expense for the past 3 years ($15 million), or $5 million. Thus, P would not be able to carry back the $4 million NOL to any taxable year prior to 1990.

* * *

Subsection b. Leverage and the Corporate Tax System

STAFF REPORT, FEDERAL INCOME TAX ASPECTS OF CORPORATE FINANCIAL STRUCTURES.

Joint Comm. on Taxation, 5–7, 15–17, 53–59 (Jan. 18, 1989).

I. BACKGROUND

The United States is still in the midst of a period of rapid merger activity which began several years ago. As this boom in merger activity has accelerated, correspondingly major, though less well publicized, changes in the role of debt, equity and corporate distributions have occurred which has resulted in an increasing use of debt by the corporate sector. The shift away from equity toward debt finance is not solely due to leveraged buyouts nor is it a product of short-term trading of securities by market participants. Since the tax treatment of corporate debt has not changed recently, there is little evidence that the tax bias of debt over equity has led to increased takeover activity or changes in corporate financial structure. Many factors other than taxes affect financing activities and acquisitions. There are indications, however, that the tax system influences corporate merger and financing decisions and may serve as an additional incentive for debt finance.

The parallel shifts in corporate financing and merger activity have created concern for those with interests in monetary policy, the regulation of financial institutions and security markets, and antitrust and competitive policy, as well as tax policy. Some argue that the time and expense involved in corporate acquisitions divert resources and managerial energy from productive investment toward short-term goals; others claim this acquisition activity serves to redeploy corporate assets in a more efficient pattern and focuses management attention on the long-term goals of production and profitability. The changes in financing behavior cause some people to conclude that the U.S. economic system may now be more vulnerable to economic downturns and that the risk to private investors, the U.S. government, and the nation as a whole has increased. While the tax system may not be the cause for the recent changes in merger and corporate financial behavior, because the tax system does influence these decisions, it is important to identify the public policy goals that should determine the Federal government's response and the role that tax policy plays in achieving these goals. In addition, since over $94 billion in tax revenue was raised by the corporate income tax in fiscal year 1988, trends which reduce the corporate income tax base require careful scrutiny.

A. Corporate Restructurings that Affect Debt and Equity

There are a variety of transactions that affect the level of debt and equity in the corporate sector. Many of these transactions involve mergers and acquisitions, others do not; they all share the common trait that they may serve to reduce equity or increase debt in the corporate sector. What follows is a brief description of a few transactions and financing methods that may be of particular interest from a tax policy perspective.

Acquisitions.—Acquisitions for which the target shareholders receive cash in exchange for their shares, and in which the funding for the acquisition is provided by new debt issues or retained earnings of the acquiror, serve to reduce the level of corporate equity and generally to increase the level of debt relative to equity in the corporate sector. The acquisition process may take many forms, hostile or friendly, and may be relatively simple or involve any of the more complex maneuverings that have generated so much publicity.

Leveraged buyouts.—Leveraged buyouts are a particular form of debt-financed acquisition in which the acquiring group finances the acquisition of an existing target corporation, or a division or subsidiary of an existing company, primarily with debt secured by the assets or stock of the target corporation. Such an acquisition often produces unusually high debt to equity ratios (sometimes greater than ten to one) in the resulting company. The management of the target corporation frequently obtains a significant portion of the equity in the resulting company. The acquired corporation sometimes is taken private and, therefore, is no longer subject to the reporting requirements that apply to public corporations. It is common, however, sometimes after major asset sales or restructurings by the leveraged company, for the private company eventually to go public again, sometimes with a new infusion of equity.

Leveraged ESOPs.—An employee stock ownership plan (ESOP) is a type of tax-qualified pension plan that is designed to invest primarily in the securities of the employer maintaining the plan and that can be used as a technique of corporate finance. An ESOP that borrows to acquire employer securities is referred to as a leveraged ESOP. ESOPs may be used to effect a takeover and to defend against a hostile takeover. The Code contains numerous tax incentives designed to encourage the use and establishment of ESOPs and to facilitate the acquisition of employer securities by ESOPs through leveraging. Because of these tax benefits, use of an ESOP can result in a lower cost of borrowing than would be the case if traditional debt or equity financing were used. Despite the tax advantages, ESOPs may not be attractive in all cases because the rules relating to leveraged ESOPs require that some transfer of ownership to employees occur and may place limitations on the terms of the leveraging transaction. To the extent that ESOPs make leveraging more attractive, they may increase the degree of leverage in the economy.

Debt-for-equity swaps.—A corporation may exchange new debt for existing equity in the company. This transaction increases the degree of leverage of the corporation.

Redemptions of stock.—It has become increasingly common, particularly for large public corporations, to buy back their own shares. These repurchases of shares by the corporation will reduce outstanding equity and, particularly if financed by issues of debt, increase leverage.

Extraordinary distributions.—The quarterly or annual dividend has long been the prototypical method for distributing corporate earnings to equity investors. Sometimes a distribution amounting to a very large percentage of the value of the firm will be made to shareholders. This extraordinary distribution may be financed by debt and often is used in defensive restructurings in an attempt to avoid a takeover. The resulting corporate financial structure may be highly leveraged.

* * *

II. Present Law Tax Rules

A. Treatment of Corporations and Their Investors

Under present law, corporations and their investors are generally separate taxable entities.[14a] The tax treatment of the corporation and the investor may vary depending upon whether the investor's interest in the corporation is considered debt or equity.

1. Treatment of debt versus equity at the corporate level

If a corporation earns a return on its assets and distributes that return to investors, the tax treatment of the corporation will depend on the characterization of the investors' interests in the corporation as debt or equity. Returns from corporate assets that are paid to debtholders are not taxed at the corporate level because interest payments generally are deductible for purposes of computing taxable income. Conversely, returns from corporate assets that are paid out as distributions with respect to stock (e.g., dividend distributions) are subject to corporate-level tax because distributions with respect to stock generally are not deductible by a corporation.

The characterization of an investor's investment as debt or equity also affects the tax treatment of the issuing corporation if the interest is retired either at a premium or at a discount. A premium paid by a corporation to redeem stock is not deductible, whereas a premium paid to retire debt is deductible. If stock is redeemed for a price less than the issue price, the issuing corporation recognizes no income, whereas if debt is retired at a discount, the corporation recognizes income from the discharge of indebtedness.

2. Treatment of debt versus equity at the investor level

a. U.S. individuals

[14a]. Corporations which are taxed at the corporate level are frequently referred to as "C corporations." The tax treatment of such corporations is governed by Subchapter C of the Code.

Individual shareholders are, in general, taxed on the return from corporate assets only when amounts are distributed with respect to their stock (e.g., dividend distributions) or when gain is realized from a sale or other disposition of their shares. Thus, individual-level tax generally is deferred to the extent management of the corporation chooses to invest earnings rather than distribute them. At present, individual shareholders are taxed at a maximum rate of 28 percent on both dividend distributions and on gains from the sale or other disposition of stock.

The full amount of a dividend distribution is subject to the individual-level tax.[16a] Distributions with respect to stock that exceed corporate earnings and profits, and thus are not dividends, are treated as a tax-free return of capital that reduces the shareholder's basis in the stock. Distributions in excess of corporate earnings and profits that exceed a shareholder's basis in the stock are treated as amounts received in exchange for the stock and, accordingly, are taxed to the shareholder as capital gain (currently taxed at the same rate as ordinary income). In the case of a sale or other disposition of stock, a shareholder recovers basis in the stock tax-free and is subject to tax only on gain (i.e., the excess of the amount received over basis). If an individual shareholder retains stock until death, any appreciation that occurred before death will permanently escape investor-level income tax.[17]

Individual debtholders are, in general, taxed on interest received periodically as paid, on original issue discount as accrued, and on market discount upon the sale or disposition of the debt instrument. Such interest income is currently taxed at a maximum rate of 28 percent. Individual debtholders are also subject to tax at a 28-percent maximum rate on gain from the sale or other disposition of debt (i.e., the excess of the amount received over basis). If an individual debtholder retains debt until death, the appreciation that occurred before death generally will permanently escape investor-level income tax.

b. *U.S. corporations*

Corporate shareholders, like individual shareholders, are, in general, taxed on the return from the assets of the corporation in which they

---

16a. A distribution is treated as a dividend to the extent it does not exceed the current or accumulated earnings and profits of the distributing corporation.

17. Such appreciation might give rise to Federal estate and gift tax. In many instances, however, opportunities for deferral and the rate structure under the Federal estate and gift tax may result in significantly less tax than would be imposed under the income tax. The value of stock held at death would be included in the decedent's gross estate and, if not passing to a surviving spouse or to charity, the decedent's taxable estate as well.

The extent to which such inclusion gives rive to Federal estate and gift tax depends on the value of the decedent's taxable transfers. The Federal estate and gift tax rates begin at 18 percent on the first $10,000 of taxable transfers and reach 55 percent (50 percent for decedents dying afte 1992) on taxable transfers over $3 million. A unified credit in effect exempts the first $600,000 from estate and gift tax. The graduated rates and unified credit are phased out for estates in excess of $10 million.

own stock only when amounts are distributed with respect to their stock (e.g., dividend distributions) or when gain is realized from a sale or other disposition of their shares. Thus, tax generally is deferred to the extent management of the distributing corporation chooses to invest earnings rather than distribute them.

If corporate income is distributed as a dividend, corporate shareholders are entitled to a dividends received deduction based on the ownership of the distributing corporation by the corporate shareholder. Under present law, corporations owning less than the portfolio threshold of 20 percent of the stock of a distributing corporation (by vote and value) are entitled to a deduction equal to 70 percent of the dividends received from a domestic corporation. Corporations owning at least 20 percent of the payor's stock are entitled to an 80–percent deduction and corporations owning 80 percent or more may be entitled to a 100–percent deduction. Because the maximum rate of tax on income received by a corporation is 34 percent, the maximum rate of tax on dividends received by a corporation is generally 10.2 percent (30 percent of the amount of the dividend times 34 percent).[21]

At present, corporate shareholders are taxed at a maximum rate of 34 percent on gains from the sale or other disposition of stock (i.e., the excess of the amount realized over basis).

Corporate debtholders are, in general, taxed on interest received periodically as such interest is paid or accrued, on original issue discount as accrued, and on market discount upon the sale or disposition of the debt instrument. Such interest income is currently taxed at a maximum rate of 34 percent. Corporate debtholders are also subject to tax at a 34–percent maximum rate on gains from the sale or other disposition of the debt (i.e., the excess of the amount realized over basis).

* * *

IV. Policy Issues

The recent wave of debt-financed mergers and acquisitions, both friendly and hostile, and the significant changes in patterns of corporate financing and distributions raise a number of public policy issues, including: (1) does the tax system encourage corporate debt financing relative to equity financing; (2) do leveraged buyouts increase economic efficiency or do they merely transfer wealth, (3) does the growth in corporate debt finance threaten macroeconomic stability; (4) does in-

---

21. In the case of certain "extraordinary dividends," the effective rate of tax may be as high as the maximum corporate rate of 34 percent, imposed at the time of the sale or disposition of the underlying stock (sec. 1059).

As with individual shareholders, distributions with respect to stock that exceed the distributing corporations's earnings and profits, and thus are not dividends, are treated as a tax-free return of capital that reduces the shareholder's basis in the stock. Distributions in excess of the distributing corporation's earnings and profits that exceed a shareholder's basis in the stock are treated as amounts received in exchange for the stock and accordingly are taxed to the shareholder as capital gain (currently taxed at the same rate as ordinary income).

creasing leverage place additional demands on Federal guarantees of the financial system; and (5) does the role of ESOPs and tax-exempt institutions in these transactions reflect sound social policy?

A. Tax Advantage of Debt Versus Equity

The total effect of the tax system on the incentives for corporations to use debt or equity depends on the interaction between the tax treatment at the shareholder and corporate levels.

The case of no income taxes.—In a simple world without taxes or additional costs in times of financial distress, economic theory suggests that the value of a corporation, as measured by the total value of the outstanding debt and equity, would be unchanged by the degree of leverage of the firm.[88] This conclusion explicitly recognizes that debt issued by the corporation represents an ownership right to future income of the corporation in a fashion similar to that of equity. In this simple world there would be no advantage to debt or to equity and the debt-equity ratio of the firm would not affect the cost of financing investment.

Effect of corporate income tax

Tax advantages

Taxes greatly complicate this analysis. Since the interest expense on debt is deductible for computing the corporate income tax while the return to equity is not, the tax at the corporate level provides a strong incentive for debt rather than equity finance.

The advantages of debt financing can be illustrated by comparing two corporations with $1,000 of assets that are identical except for financial structure: the first is entirely equity financed; while the second is 50-percent debt financed. Both corporations earn $150 of operating income. The all-equity corporation pays $51 in corporate tax and retains or distributes $99 of after-tax income ($150 less $51). Thus, as shown in Table IV-A, the return on equity is 9.9 percent ($99 divided by $1,000).

Table IV-A.—Effect of Debt Financing on Returns to Equity Investment

Item	All-equity corporation	50–percent debt-financed corporation
Beginning Balance Sheet:		
Total assets....................	$1,000	$1,000
Debt	0	500

---

88. Franco Modigliani and Merton Miller, "The Cost of Capital, Corporation Finance, and the Theory of Investment," American Economic Review, June 1958, pp. 261–297. Updated versions of this argument require only that market prices adjust so that there remain no available, unexploited arbitrage profits. See Stephen Ross, "Comment on the Modigliani–Miller Propositions," Journal of Economic Perspectives, Fall 1988, pp. 127–133, for a nontechnical discussion of this point.

Item	All-equity corporation	50–percent debt-financed corporation
Shareholders' equity	$1,000	$ 500
Income Statement:		
Operating income	150	150
Interest expense	0	50
Taxable income	150	100
Income tax	51	34
Income after corporate tax	99	66
Return on Equity [1] (percent)	9.9	13.2

[1] Return on equity is computed as income after corporate tax divided by beginning shareholders' equity.

The leveraged corporation is financed by $500 of debt and $500 of stock. If the interest rate is 10 percent, then interest expense is $50 (10 percent times $500). Taxable income is $100 after deducting interest expense. The leveraged corporation is liable for $34 in corporate tax (34 percent times $100) and distributes or retains $66 of after-tax income ($100 less $34). Consequently, the return on equity is 13.2 percent ($66 divided by $500). Thus, as shown in Table IV-A, increasing the debt ratio from zero to 50 percent increases the rate of return on equity from 9.9 to 13.2 percent.

This arithmetic demonstrates that a leveraged corporation can generate a higher return on equity (net of corporate income tax) than an unleveraged company or, equivalently, that an unleveraged company needs to earn a higher profit before corporate tax to provide investors the same return net of corporate tax as could be obtained with an unleveraged company. More generally, the return on equity rises with increasing debt capitalization so long as the interest rate is less than the pre-tax rate of return on corporate assets. This suggests that the Code creates an incentive to raise the debt-equity ratio to the point where the corporate income tax (or outstanding equity) is eliminated.

Costs of financial distress

With higher levels of debt the possibility of financial distress increases, as do the expected costs to the firm which occur with such distress. These additional costs include such items as the increase in the costs of debt funds; constraints on credit, expenditure or operating decisions; and the direct costs of being in bankruptcy. These expected costs of financial distress may, at sufficiently high debt-equity ratios, offset the corporate tax advantage to additional debt finance.

Effect of shareholder income tax

The above analysis focuses solely on the effect of interest deductibility at the corporate level. Shareholder-level income taxation may offset to some degree the corporate tax incentive for corporate debt relative to equity.

Shareholder treatment of debt and equity

The conclusion that debt is tax favored relative to equity remains unchanged if interest on corporate debt and returns on equity are taxed at the same effective rate to investors. In this case, the returns to investors on both debt and equity are reduced proportionately by the income tax; the advantage to debt presented by corporate tax deductibility remains. One noteworthy exception exists if the marginal investments on both debt and equity are effectively tax-exempt.[89] Given the previously documented importance of tax-exempt pension funds in the bond and equity markets, this case may be of some importance (See Part I.B. of this pamphlet).

Shareholder level tax treatment of equity

In general, returns to shareholders and debtholders are not taxed the same. Although dividends, like interest income, are taxed currently, equity income in other forms may reduce the effective investor-level tax on equity below that on debt. First, the firm may retain earnings and not pay dividends currently. In general, the accumulation of earnings by the firm will cause the value of the firm's shares to rise.[90] Rather than being taxed currently on corporate earnings, a shareholder will be able to defer the taxation on the value of the retained earnings reflected in the price of the stock until the shareholder sells the stock. Thus, even though the tax rates on interest, dividends, and capital gains are the same, the ability to defer the tax on returns from equity reduces the effective rate of individual tax on equity investment below that on income from interest on corporate debt.[91]

Other aspects of capital gain taxation serve to reduce further the individual income tax on equity. Since tax on capital gain is normally triggered after a voluntary recognition event (e.g., the sale of stock), the taxpayer can time the realization of capital gain income when the effective rate of tax is low. The rate of tax could be low if the taxpayer is in a low or zero tax bracket because other income is abnormally low, if other capital losses shelter the capital gain, or if changes in the tax law cause the statutory rate on capital gains to be low. Perhaps most important, the step up in the adjusted tax basis of the stock upon the

---

89. Merton Miller and Myron Scholes ("Dividends and Taxes," Journal of Financial Economics, 1978, pp. 333–364) suggest that certain nuances of the Tax Code may render otherwise taxable investors untaxed on the margin between interest and equity. For example, if a taxpayer has investment interest expense that cannot be deducted because it exceeds current investment income to the taxpayer, any additional dividends is effectively sheltered from tax by additional interest deductions. Daniel Feenberg ("Does the Investment Interest Limitation Explain the Existence of Dividends?" Journal of Financial Economics, 1981) presents evidence that this argument was unlikely to be important for most individual investors. However, the reduction in the deductibility of consumer interest by the 1986 Act may increase the plausibility of this argument.

90. Alan Auerbach ("Wealth Maximization and the Cost of Capital." Quarterly Journal of Economics, 1979, pp. 488–500) argues that, for mature firms, that a dollar of retained earnings will cause the value of the firm to increase by less than a dollar.

91. Before the 1986 Act, the 60–percent capital gain exclusion caused a further reduction in the effective rate of tax on equity investment.

death of the shareholder may permit the shareholder's heirs to avoid tax completely on capital gains. For all these reasons, the effective rate of tax on undistributed earnings may be already quite low.

Corporations can distribute their earnings to owners of equity in forms that generally result in less tax to shareholders than do dividend distributions. Share repurchases have become an important method of distributing corporate earnings to equity holders. When employed by large publicly traded firms, repurchases of the corporation's own shares permit the shareholders to treat the distribution as a sale of stock (i.e., to obtain capital gain treatment, and recover the basis in the stock without tax).[92] The remaining shareholders may benefit because they have rights to a larger fraction of the firm and may see a corresponding increase in the value of their shares.[93] Thus, less individual tax will generally be imposed on a $100 repurchase of stock than on $100 of dividends. In addition, share repurchases allow shareholders to choose whether to receive corporate distributions by choosing whether to sell or retain shares, so as to minimize tax liability.[94]

Acquisitions of the stock of one corporation for cash or property of another corporation provides a similar method for distributing corporate earnings out of corporate solution with less shareholder tax than through a dividend. The target shareholders generally treat the acquisition as a sale and recover their basis free of tax. For purposes of analyzing the individual tax effect of corporate earnings disbursements, this transaction can be thought of as equivalent to a stock merger of the target with the acquiror followed by the repurchase of the target shareholders' shares by the resulting merged firm. The result is similar to the case of a share repurchase in that cash is distributed to shareholders with less than the full dividend tax, except that two firms are involved instead of one.

Since dividends typically are subject to more tax than other methods for providing returns to shareholders, the puzzle of why firms pay dividends remains. Because dividends are paid at the discretion of the firm, it appears that firms cause their shareholders to pay more tax on equity income than is strictly necessary.[95] Until a better under-

---

92. Sec. 302 governs the treatment of stock redemptions and may cause some repurchases to be treated as dividends.

93. If a dollar of repurchases by the firm reduces the value of the equity by one dollar, the remaining shareholders are no worse off; if the repurchase reduces the value by less than a dollar (perhaps because the normally higher shareholder tax on dividends is avoided) the remaining shareholders are made better off. See, Auerbach, supra.

94. Some have proposed that the taxation of share repurchases follow the taxation of dividend distributions at the investor level. One method by which this could be done is to treat the repurchase as a pro rata dividend to all shareholders followed by a pro rata sale of shares of the selling shareholders to the remaining shareholders. See, Chirelstein, "Optional Redemptions and Optional Dividends: Taxing the Repurchase of Common Shares," 78 Yale Law Journal 739 (1969).

95. The trends outlined in Part I.A demonstrate that corporations are shifting away from dividends as the predominant method for distributing income.

standing of corporate distribution policy exists, the role of dividend taxation on equity financing decisions remains uncertain.

To summarize, although the current taxation of dividends to investors is clearly significant, there are numerous reasons why the overall individual tax on equity investments may be less than that on interest income from debt. Since the effective shareholder tax on returns from equity may be less than that on debt holdings, the shareholder tax may offset some or all of the advantage to debt at the corporate level.

Interaction of corporate and shareholder taxation

With shareholders in different income tax brackets, high tax rate taxpayers will tend to concentrate their wealth in the form of equity and low tax rate taxpayers will tend to concentrate their wealth in the form of debt. The distribution of wealth among investors with different marginal tax rates affects the demand for investments in the form of debt or equity. The interaction between the demand of investors, and the supply provided by corporations, determines the aggregate amount of corporate debt and equity in the economy.

At some aggregate mix between debt and equity, the difference in the investor-level tax on income from equity and debt may be sufficient to offset completely, at the margin, the apparent advantage of debt at the corporate level. Even if the difference in investor tax treatment of debt and equity is not sufficient to offset completely the corporate tax advantage, the advantage to debt may be less than the corporate-level tax treatment alone would provide.

Some believe that, because the top personal tax rate was reduced below the top corporate tax rate in the 1986 Act and because the share of wealth held by tax-exempt entities is substantial, the tax advantage of debt at the corporate level outweighs its disadvantages to investors.[96] They would argue that changes in tax law have provided the motive force in the drive toward higher leverage. However, given that the observed changes in corporate financial behavior began well before 1986, the changes due to the 1986 Act may be of relatively little importance in determining changes in leverage and acquisition behavior. The individual rate reductions in the Economic Recovery Tax Act of 1981, some respond, started the shift toward more debt in corporate structures and the 1986 Act merely provided another push in that direction.

Implications for policy

The analysis above suggests that any policy change designed to reduce the tax incentive for debt must consider the interaction of both corporate and shareholder taxes. For example, proposals to change the income tax rates for individuals or corporations will change the incen-

---

[96]. Merton Miller, "The Modigliani–Miller Propositions After Thirty years," Journal of Economic Perspectives, Fall 1988, pp. 99–120. Also see the discussion of corporate integration in part V.A.1 of this pamphlet, infra, for a numerical analysis of various possible total tax effects and the effect of the Tax Reform Act of 1986.

tive for corporate debt. Likewise, proposals to change the tax treatment of tax-exempt entities may alter the aggregate mix and distribution of debt and equity.

In addition, proposals to reduce the bias toward debt over equity, for example, by reducing the total tax on dividends, must confront the somewhat voluntary nature of the dividend tax. Since the payment of dividends by corporations generally is discretionary and other means exist for providing value to shareholders with less tax, corporations can affect the level of shareholder level tax incurred. Until a better understanding of the determinants of corporate distribution behavior exists, the total impact of policies designed to reduce the bias between debt and equity are uncertain.

The tax rules are not totally silent on the deduction of interest payments incurred in acquisition financing. As we have already seen, under section 172 net operating losses generated by increased interest deductions as the result of leveraged acquisition may not be carried back against income generated by the target in prior profitable years. Moreover, if parties to an acquisition attempt to use debt instruments that for all practical purposes are equity instruments, the Internal Revenue Service may disallow the interest deductions. Congress, in section 385, gave the secretary of treasury the power to pass regulations classifying equity and debt instruments, but the IRS, after several aborted attempts, has apparently suspended any efforts to promulgate regulations under the section. Congress, apparently impatient with the IRS, amended section 163 in 1989 and 1990 to reclassify original issue discount instruments (OIDS), often used in acquisition financing. Finally, section 279 of the code "expressly limits" the interest deductions allowable for acquisition debt, but the section has proven to be largely toothless for modern acquisitions. The readings below deal with these sections.

The Debt–Equity Distinction: Section 385

In highly leveraged acquisitions such as the RJR Nabisco buyout, the acquisition group pays target shareholders in investment instruments that are subordinated to all other debt and that have time-dependent repayment obligations. The instruments are either below-investment-grade debt (junk bonds) or a special form of preferred stock. The distinction between debt and preferred stock financing in a heavily leveraged acquisition has important tax consequences for both the issuer and the recipient. An acquirer can deduct interest payments on debt but not dividend payments on preferred stock. Dividends received by a corporate holder of preferred stock are subject to the 80 percent dividends-received deduction, but interest received by a corporate holder of a debt instrument is fully taxable. Repayment of debt principal is tax-free to the recipient, but redemption of preferred stock may be taxable to the recipient as a dividend. Finally, a firm may amortize the expenses of issuing debt (reducing its taxable earnings) but may amortize only certain organization expenses of issuing stock.

Code section 385 authorizes the Treasury to issue regulations to determine whether an interest in a corporation should be treated as stock or debt for tax purposes. The section also provides a nonexclusive list of factors that the regulations may take into account in making the determination: (1) whether there is an unconditional promise to pay on demand or on a specified date a certain sum and to pay a fixed rate of interest, (2) whether the instrument is subordinated or preferred to any other corporate debt, (3) the issuer's debt-equity ratio, (4) whether the instrument is convertible into equity, and (5) the relationship between the issuer's stock and the instrument. In 1980 the Treasury released the first of three drafts of the section 385 regulations. They were withdrawn before they took effect, because of embarrassment over the treatment of hybrid instruments. In 1989 Congress amended the section to permit future regulations to treat an instrument as a hybrid, part stock and part equity, for tax purposes. The Treasury has yet to take the bait, however.

Although the Internal Revenue Service has often successfully taken the position that a purported debt instrument should be treated as equity for tax purposes, it has rarely argued that stock should be treated as debt. The reason is not hard to fathom; equity characterization usually produces more revenue, with the denial of interest deductions for the issuer and the potential dividend taxation of the holder. With the withdrawal of the regulations the courts have returned to a general use of a list of factors that weigh in favor of debt treatment for a given instrument: (1) a fixed maturity date not too far removed, (2) an unconditional obligation to pay, (3) a fixed rate of interest, (4) rights in the holder, such as acceleration, that accrue on default, (5) the absence of convertibility into equity, of voting power or other forms of voice in management, and of any participation in distributions of capital surplus, (6) the ability of the issuer at the time of issuance to meet anticipated repayment obligations, (7) a reasonable debt-equity upon issuance, (8) the subordination of other debt instruments to it, and (9) the holder's acting like a creditor by taking steps to protect his rights.

Problem

A leveraged buyout group, holding $100,000 in cash, borrows another $1 million from a commercial bank. The bank also takes a 49 percent equity position in the acquisition vehicle. The group uses all its cash to buy all the shares of, and then merge into, a target firm. Repayment of the principal on the loan is in fifty years, and interest on the loan is at 3 percent (below market), payable yearly. After the acquisition there is a substantial risk that the target firm will not have the cash flow to service the debt. In fact, the firm does not make any interest payments on the loan, and the bank takes no action on the defaults. Is the loan debt or equity?

Original Issue Discount Instruments: Section 163(e)(5) and (i)

In 1989 Congress took steps to recharacterize the tax treatment of two special debt instruments used in leveraged acquisition financing: "zero coupon" debentures and "pay-in-kind" (PIK) debentures. Recall that traditional debt instruments are issued at a price approximately equal to its final redemption price, with the return to the holder taking the form of periodic interest payments. Zero coupon debentures are original issue discount instruments (OIDs) that eliminate periodic interest payments. They are issued at prices well below their final redemption price, and the return to a holder is the appreciation at the time of redemption. A PIK debenture requires the issuer to pay periodic interest in the form of additional debt ("bunny" debentures) or equity instruments of the issuer. Issuers use both instruments to finance leveraged acquisitions when the cash flow position of the surviving firm will, for a time, be very tight.

Before 1989 OID and bunny debentures were generally treated as interest income to the holder and were deductible by the issuer in equal installments over the life of the instrument (on a constant-yield basis). If the PIK payments were in stock, the fair market value of the stock was treated as interest currently paid, giving the issuer a deduction and the holder income for that amount. Section 163(e)(5) and (i), enacted in December 1989, limits interest deductions for high-yield zero coupon debentures and PIK debentures. If either instrument qualifies as a high-yield discount obligation (AHYDI), then the issuer's interest deductions are deferred until cash is actually paid and are in some cases partially eliminated (explained in the conference report below). The interest is nevertheless reported by the holder as income as it accrues under the regular OID rules. A debenture is an AHYDO if it is issued by a corporation with a maturity date more than five years from issuance, has a yield to maturity of at least five percentage points over the application federal rate (AFR)[8] in effect for the month in which the debenture is issued, and has a "significant original issue discount" (using a series of complex measurements). Section 163(i) treats PIK debenture interest in the same fashion as OID. If a PIK debenture pays interest in the form of bunny debentures, for example, the interest is treated as paid at the maturity date of the bunny debentures.

REVENUE RECONCILIATION ACT OF 1989

Conference Committee Report No. (Nov. 22, 1989), reprinted in 76, No. 50
Std.Fed.Tax Rpts, (CCH) 406 (Nov. 27, 1989).

The conferees believe that a portion of the return on certain high-yield OID obligations is similar to a distribution of corporate

---

8. The AFR is determined by the Treasury. For example, the AFR for February 1990 was 7.90 percent for obligations with a term of three to nine years, with interest compounded semiannually.

earnings with respect to equity. Thus, the conference agreement bifurcates the yield on applicable instruments, creating an interest element that is deductible when paid and a return on equity element for which no deduction is granted and for which the dividends received deduction may be allowed.

* * *

A portion of the OID ("the disqualified portion") on an applicable instrument is afforded special treatment. The issuer is allowed no deduction with respect to the disqualified portion. The holder, however, is allowed a dividends received deduction for that part of the disqualified portion that would have been treated as a dividend had it been distributed by the issuing corporation with respect to stock.

In general, the disqualified portion of OID is the portion of the total return on the obligation that bears the same ratio to the total return as the disqualified yield bears to the total yield to maturity on the instrument. The term "disqualified yield" means that portion of the yield that exceeds the applicable Federal rate for the month in which the obligation is issued (the "AFR") plus six percentage points. If the yield to maturity on the obligation determined by disregarding the OID exceeds the AFR plus six percentage points, then the disqualified portion is the entire amount of the OID. * * * The remainder of the OID on the instrument (the portion other than the disqualified portion) is not deductible until paid in property other than stock or obligations of the issuer.

General Limits on Acquisition Indebtedness: Section 279

In October 1969 Congress attempted to impose, through code section 279, a general interest deduction ceiling on acquisition financing. Congress designed the section to catch financing peculiar to the conglomerate merger wave of the late sixties, which made heavy use of convertible subordinated debt instruments. The wave had largely passed by the time the section became effective, and modern leveraged acquisitions use much more imaginative financing techniques. The section is thus easily avoided by modern planners, and Congress has yet to pass proposals that would remedy the section's many loopholes. The proposals demonstrate the potential breadth of such an approach, however. A 1987 House bill proposed a $5–million–per–year ceiling on the interest deduction for debt arising in any acquisition of 50 percent or more of a target firm's stock, regardless of whether the debt was subordinated or issued with conversion privileges. See Revenue Act of 1987, Conference Committee Report (Dec. 22, 1987), reprinted in Vol. 74, No. 54 Std.Fed.Tax Rpts. (CCH) A–31 (Dec. 23, 1987). The provision would have applied to normal bank financing incurred without an equity kicker. A second proposal imposed interest deductions for debt used to finance hostile asset and stock acquisitions. Id. at A–38.

The section as is prevents debtors from deducting interest paid or incurred on qualifying debt in a given year to the extent that the interest exceeds $5 million less any interest paid on nonqualifying acquisition debt. Debt is subject to the disallowance only if it is (1) issued as consideration in an acquisition of stock or two-thirds of the assets of another firm, (2) subordinated to trade creditors or any substantial amount of other unsecured debt, (3) convertible (directly or indirectly) into stock of the issuer, *and* (4) issued when the debtor is thinly capitalized (its debt-to-equity ratio exceeding two to one or its average earnings not exceeding three times the annual interest to be paid). There are several common methods of avoiding the provision. The debtor issues nonconvertible debt, issues combined units of its subordinated debt and its common stock, issues debt subordinated only to secured debt, uses a holding company to issue debt implicitly subordinated by law to a subsidiary's unsecured debt, or has the target firm adopt the debt (causing the transaction to be treated as a redemption).

State Tax Law

FABER, NEW YORK STATE ANTITAKEOVER BILL: FIRST STEP DOWN A ROCKY ROAD

Tax Notes 1263–72 (June 5, 1989).

New York has become the first state to pass its own legislation aimed at reducing the tax benefits from corporate takeovers.

* * *

Impetus for the bill came from the need to raise additional revenue to balance the state's budget and a sense among many legislators that corporate takeovers were to be discouraged. The proponents of the bill estimate that it will raise about $30,000,000 in taxes each year, although that figure has been questioned.

Several of the bill's provisions operate only if there is a substantial increase in the extent to which the acquiring corporation and the target rely on debt. These provisions do not require that the specific acquisition be financed by debt; they come into play if there is an acquisition and if the overall debt burden of the corporate parties increases. Apparently, the theory is that debt and money are fungible. If there is an increase in the debt burden of the corporate parties to an acquisition, a portion of the interest deductions that would otherwise be available to the corporate parties is disallowed, net operating loss carryovers of the target corporation are extinguished, and previous investment tax credits are recaptured.

Other provisions of the bill apply regardless of whether there is an increase in leverage. If there is an acquisition, whether or not it is accompanied by an increase in leverage, carryovers of unused investment tax credits are destroyed and certain sales of target stock or assets in "bust-up" takeovers are taxable, despite the normal New York state rule that gains from the sale of stock of subsidiaries are exempt from tax.

* * *

New York is the first state to adopt its own antitakeover tax legislation. It will undoubtedly not be the last. Politicians in other states are likely, as were those in New York, to see corporate acquisitions as being easy fiscal targets. The constituencies for corporate acquisitions lack political power in the state legislatures and legislators looking for additional revenues are likely to follow New York's lead and set their sights on corporate acquisitions. The New York statute is likely to serve as a model for legislation in other states and it bears careful study.

The Policy Debate

WARREN, RECENT CORPORATE RESTRUCTURING AND THE CORPORATE TAX SYSTEM

42 Tax Notes 715–20 (Feb. 6, 1989).

* * *

POSSIBLE LEGISLATIVE SOLUTIONS

A. Reducing the Tax Advantage of Debt

1. Proposals. Perhaps because the most publicized of the transactions under discussion, such as leveraged buyouts, have involved the substitution of corporate debt for equity, the most widely discussed legislative proposals have mandated additional restrictions on the deductibility of interest, in order to reduce the tax advantages of corporate debt over equity. Thus, it has been suggested that all corporate interest deductions be eliminated, that deductibility of acquisition-related interest be disallowed when corporate gain is not realized, that interest deductions related to "excessive debt" (defined on an industry-wide basis) be disallowed in acquisition and related transactions, that interest deductions be limited to cash payments, that no deduction be allowed for interest on debt incurred to displace outstanding equity, and that deductible corporate interest be limited to a rate defined in relation to an applicable Federal rate. These limitations, which are but a few of the those that have been suggested, have quite different, and sometimes conflicting, policy goals.[16]

2. Advantages. Proposals along these lines have the advantage of responding to the most acutely perceived part of the problem—acquisitions and other transactions involving the substitution of debt for equity. Such proposals also build on familiar tax concepts, including the distinction between debt and equity, as well as existing, but not

---

16. These goals include: distinguishing debt from equity; protecting the current corporate tax base; assuring that all corporate income is taxed twice (once at the corporate and once at the investor level); offsetting the failure to realize corporate gain on the transfer of shares; and adjusting the interest deduction for inflation.

very effective, limitations on deductibility of interest on acquisition indebtedness.

3. Disadvantages. There are, nonetheless, at least five significant disadvantages to simply enacting additional restrictions on interest deductibility as a targeted response to the transactions under discussion.

First, such restrictions raise significant implementation issues at their boundaries. Given the general description of the problem above, any limitation that applied only to acquisition transactions would be only a partial solution, leaving in place opportunities to eliminate future corporate taxes in nonacquisition transactions. Extending the limitation to all debt-financed distributions would still be a partial solution on the view that nontaxable distributions are the central tax-system problem, because such a limitation would not apply to nondebt-financed transactions.

Even if the distributions view of the problem is rejected, a limitation on interest related to debt-financed distributions would create significant implementation issues at the boundaries. For example, would the limitation apply to an acquiring corporation which used borrowed funds to purchase the assets of a target company that independently liquidated at some later date? Similarly, would a liquidation-reincorporation doctrine be necessary to deal with tax-free liquidations followed by the return of assets to corporate solution in exchange for debt? These questions would be avoided by a limitation on all corporate interest deductions, but such a broad limitation would increase the cost of debt capital for all corporations, including those which have not taken advantage of the possibility of eliminating corporate taxes by making distributions to shareholders. By itself, a general limitation on all corporate interest deductions would thus be an overly broad reaction to the problem under discussion and should be considered only in the context of general corporate tax reform.

Second, the very tax concepts on which interest limitation proposals build, most notably the distinction between debt and equity, are themselves among the most problematic and least satisfactory aspects of current corporate tax law. Nondeductibility of interest would, for example, eliminate the need to distinguish nondeductible dividends, but create the need to distinguish deductible rent.

Third, the additional categories required by such proposals (such as "excessive" versus "nonexcessive" debt in a particular "industry") are likely to be extremely complicated to implement or, alternatively, simple but arbitrary in their application.

Fourth, applying new limitations to U.S. corporations might provide a relative advantage to acquisition of American companies by foreign corporations, if foreign jurisdictions did not impose similar restrictions.

Fifth, restrictions on corporate interest deductions could dramatically adversely affect stock prices; that, at least, was the assertion of some observers after the House of Representatives passed legislation along these lines in 1987.

B. ADDITIONAL TAXATION OF DISTRIBUTIONS

The second potential legislative response to elimination of corporate taxes through shareholder distributions focuses on shareholder taxation of those distributions, rather than on deductibility of corporate interest payments.

1. The ALI Draft Proposal. The Federal Income Tax Project of the American Law Institute is considering a proposal that would directly address the distributions version of the problem discussed above. Distributions other than ordinary dividends would be subject to a minimum tax, which would be paid by the distributing corporation and creditable by the receiving shareholder against shareholder taxes otherwise due on the distribution. Thus, dividend and nondividend distributions of existing corporate assets would generally be subject to either a shareholder or corporate withholding tax. Certain returns of shareholder capital would be exempted. Portfolio investments in corporate stock by corporate shareholders would bear a correlative burden through denial of the intercorporate dividend deduction.

A related, but separable, proposal would permit the deduction of dividends, up to a specified amount, paid on newly contributed equity, so that returns on future corporate financing would be treated equivalently, whether the financing took the form of debt or equity.

a. Advantages. The ALI draft proposal directly addresses the problem described above if distribution taxation is considered the central issue. Corporate taxes could no longer be eliminated through nontaxable corporate distributions, because the distribution would be taxable, whether or not financed with debt, and whether or not part of an acquisition transaction. Windfall gains would be prevented, and nondividend distributions to otherwise nontaxable shareholders would bear a tax by virtue of the nonrefundable corporate minimum tax on distributions.

b. Disadvantages. For some observers, the ALI draft proposal for a minimum tax on distributions has the defect of appearing to add a third tier of tax to the corporate tax system, which already includes corporate and shareholder income taxes. The shareholder credit and a sufficiently broad exemption for return of capital should help alleviate this concern. For other observers, the ALI draft proposal goes too far because they see no need to preserve or capture a future corporate tax if distributed corporate assets are not returned to corporate solution through debt finance.

* * *

2. Other Proposals for Taxing Distributions. Because of the importance to the issue under discussion of shareholders who are nontaxable on certain corporate distributions, another approach would be to reduce existing opportunities for less than full taxation of shareholders. Examples would include expanding the scope of the unrelated business income tax as applied to charitable institutions, taxing certain investment income of pension funds, eliminating the step-up in basis of assets at death, and strengthening U.S. taxation of foreign shareholders and debtholders of U.S. corporations. Similarly, the importance of the rate relationships discussed above indicates that pressures for corporate distributions would be reduced if the shareholder tax rate were again higher than the corporate rate.

* * *

C. Reducing the Tax Disadvantage of Equity

1. Integration Proposals. The third principal means of eliminating the problem identified above is to reduce the tax disadvantage of new equity finance by integrating the individual and corporate income taxes. In very general terms, such integration could be accomplished by allowing either a corporate deduction for dividends or a shareholder credit for corporate taxes paid with respect to distributed earnings. The House of Representatives' version of the Tax Reform Act of 1986 included a phased-in partial deduction for dividends. Under either dividend deduction or shareholder credit integration, the corporate income tax would become a withholding tax on distributions to suppliers of corporate capital, functioning as an adjunct to shareholder or debtholder income taxation.

2. Advantages. Integration is a massive subject that has long been on the agenda of the congressional tax-writing committees and various Administrations. Adoption of an integrated system would eliminate many of the defects in our corporate tax system, including the one under discussion, primarily because debt would no longer be treated significantly differently from equity. The ability to avoid future corporate taxes by making nontaxed nondividend distributions would be eliminated to the extent such distributions were subject to the shareholder credit mechanism.

Integration also would subject U.S. companies to a tax regime that was similar to that of many other industrialized nations, a number of which have implemented partial integration systems in recent years. Finally, integration, particularly of the shareholder credit variety, would permit explicit congressional decisions about the appropriate treatment of distributees who might not otherwise be taxable. If, for example, it were decided that corporate income distributed to charitable institutions, pension funds, and foreign shareholders should not go completely untaxed, the shareholder credit could be made nonrefundable. In short, integration is the most ideal long-run solution to both the particular problem posed by recent corporate restructurings and the urgent need to reform the corporate tax system more generally.

3. Disadvantages. Like many long-run solutions, integration has certain short-run disadvantages. For example, immediate, full enactment of a dividend deduction would undoubtedly generate significant revenue losses. Such an enactment also might allow current shareholders to reap the full benefit of any windfall gains due to capitalization of taxes. But, there is no need to enact integration in one fell swoop. It could easily be phased in, as was the 1985 House legislation. And the possibility of positive windfall gains in the stock markets might well give Congress more flexibility to consider adopting limitations on interest deductions, which could have the opposite effect on share prices if enacted by themselves.

* * *

It would probably be easiest to accomplish these results, as well as equivalent treatment of debt and equity, in a shareholder credit system that also required withholding on corporate interest payments, together with a nonrefundable credit for nontaxable debtholders.[23] To the extent of integration, *the result would be that all income earned on corporate assets, however financed, would always be taxed once,* a result that is certainly not achieved today. Such a regime might well not have the negative revenue implications generally associated with integration. There would, of course, be important design issues to be resolved in treating debt and equity equivalently, including the appropriate taxation of financial intermediaries.

* * *

JENSEN, KAPLAN, EFFECTS OF LBOs ON TAX REVENUES OF THE U.S. TREASURY

42 Tax Notes 727–733 (Feb. 6, 1989).

We examine the tax effects of leveraged buyouts (LBOs) in which a group of investors (including managers) take a company private, a topic that is receiving increasing attention from legislators, the business community, and the press. In examining the tax implications of these transactions, many observers have focused on the interest deductibility of the debt used to finance them. It has been noted that LBO firms' increased debt payments generate sufficient tax deductions to ensure that many of them do not pay income taxes in the period immediately following the LBO. Some argue these transactions are being subsidized by the Federal taxpayer in the sense that they cause net losses of tax revenues to the U.S. Treasury. Our analysis, based on current tax law and data from buyouts in the period 1979 through 1985, indicates these arguments are incorrect; Treasury revenues from LBO firms increase on average by about 61 percent over the prebuyout payments. Our estimates indicate that at a total dollar volume of LBO transactions of $75 billion per year, the Treasury gains about $9 billion in the first year and about $16.5 billion per year in present value of future net tax receipts.

---

23. Shareholder credit integration has exactly the same effect as a dividend or interest deduction, coupled with withholding.

What often has been overlooked is the fact that there are five ways in which LBOs can generate incremental revenues to the U.S. Treasury. First, because they create substantial realized capital gains for shareholders, LBOs give rise to increased capital gains taxes. Second, LBO firms realize significant increases in operating income, which are also taxable. Third, many of the creditors who finance LBOs are taxed on the interest income from LBO debt payments. Fourth, LBO firms contribute to tax revenues by using capital more efficiently. Finally, many LBO firms sell off assets, triggering additional corporate taxes on the capital gains. Offsetting these incremental revenue gains are increased interest deductions on the large debt commonly incurred, and lower tax revenues on dividends, because LBOs generally do not pay dividends on common equity.

* * *

Because the RJR–Nabisco LBO by Kohlberg, Kravis and Roberts is so large, and involved such heated bidding, it has attracted much attention and controversy. Along with this have come accusations that the gains to shareholders are at the expense of Treasury.[8] Table 3 contains our estimates of the implications of the transaction for the U.S. Treasury, which indicate Treasury is highly likely to gain rather than lose tax revenues. In prevent value terms, the increased revenue for Treasury is $3.76 billion, $3.28 billion of which it will likely gain in the year following the buyout. These payments are more than eight times higher than the approximately $370 million in Federal taxes paid by RJR–Nabisco in 1987.[9] Indeed, at a rate of $370 million per year, the total present value of RJR–Nabisco's tax payments into perpetuity is only $3.7 billion, just slightly higher than the first year's tax revenues induced by the buyout.

To obtain these estimates of the RJR tax revenues after the buyout, we assume that 60 percent of the increased debt is permanent, but none is retired in the first year, that 35 percent of the interest is received *by taxable* investors, that 60 percent of the prebuyout stock is owned by taxable investors, that 30 percent of the stock at the postbuyout sale is owned by taxable investors, that operating income rises by 25 percent, that capital expenditures decrease by 20 percent, and that 25 percent of the assets are sold in the first year with a tax basis of 73 percent of the prebuyout market value of equity. The 82–percent premium to the pre-buyout shareholders in this case (assuming the cash value of the offer is $100, not the stated $109) was exceptionally high, perhaps because of the intense bidding. We have conservatively assumed that the total value increase in the LBO will be equal to the sample average of 109 percent in the period 1979 through 1985, implying a $15 per share gain for the buyout investors.

8. *Time* magazine, for example, in its cover story of December 5, 1988, "A Game of Greed," claims the U.S. taxpayers will lose between $2 and $5 billion in the long run, p. 69.

9. Total taxes paid by RJR–Nabisco in 1987 were $682 million, but $313 million of this were "foreign and other" taxes.

The typical LBO is more beneficial to the U.S. Treasury than many observers realize. Increased interest deductions and foregone dividend payments clearly have the potential to reduce tax revenues. However, the large capital gains that result from LBOs, increases in their operating income and capital efficiency, enhanced creditor income, and taxes on asset sales have the potential to increase tax revenues. The net effect of these tax changes varies across transactions; some LBOs may result in tax revenue reductions, while others may generate new tax revenues. As the examples in our tables show, however, the preponderance of evidence indicates that in the aggregate, these transactions generate revenue gains for Treasury.

Based on the data from transactions over $50 million in the period 1979 through 1985, on average, LBO transactions increase tax revenues to the U.S. Treasury by $110 million on a present value basis, and by $59.4 million in the year after the buyout. The present value of gains translates to a permanent equivalent annual increase of approximately $11 million on average, or a 61-percent increase in taxes per buyout firm. Our conservative assumptions in Table 2, which we believe understate Treasury revenues, indicate that even in those circumstances, Treasury is likely to break even. Our application of the analysis to the RJR–Nabisco transaction indicates contrary to popular views, that the transaction will enrich Treasury by over $3 billion, whether viewed from a short- or long-term perspective.

Policies that restrict LBO transactions likely will reduce future tax revenues received by Treasury. At a total volume of $75 billion per year, LBO transactions are generating about $16.5 billion in present value of tax revenues for the Treasury per year, and on a current account basis, they generate approximately $9 billion per year. It appears that from a narrow tax policy perspective, great care should be taken in adopting policies that discourage LBO transactions.

* * *

SECTION 3. MISCELLANEOUS TAX PROVISIONS RELEVANT TO ACQUISITIONS: GOLDEN PARACHUTES, GREENMAIL, POISON PILLS, AND ACQUISITION EXPENSES

Congress is slowly accumulating a series of provisions tucked in various places in the tax code that affect defensive tactics in acquisitions. Two such provisions, on golden parachutes and greenmail, are noted below. Moreover, the Internal Revenue Service has an important role to play in various defenses. Its position on the taxability of the novel option instruments, known collectively as poison pill plans, issued as dividends on stock has been a significant boon to those plans. Finally, the IRS has taken a tough stance on deductibility of acquisition fees and expenses.

Golden Parachutes: Sections 280G and 4999

In the Tax Reform Act of 1984 Congress imposed tax penalties for excess golden parachutes, payments to executives connected to changes in control. Minor amendments in the Tax Reform Act of 1986 and the Technical and Miscellaneous Revenue Act of 1988 and Treasury regulations proposed in May 1989 complete the present picture. Section 280G disallows a deduction to the firm for, and section 4999 imposes a 20 percent nondeductible excise tax on the recipient of, any "excess parachute payment."

IRS PROPOSED REGULATIONS (PS–217–84)

Fed.Reg. (May 5, 1989); reprinted Fed.Tax Law Rptr. (CCH) ¶ 49,235 (Adv.Sheets 1990).

* * *

OVERVIEW OF STATUTORY PROVISIONS

In applying the golden parachute provisions, the first step is to identify payments that constitute "parachute payments." Section 280G(b)(2)(A) defines a "parachute payment" as any payment that meets all of the following four conditions: (a) the payment is in the nature of compensation; (b) the payment is to, or for the benefit of, a disqualified individual; (c) the payment is contingent on a change in the ownership of a corporation, the effective control of a corporation, or the ownership of a substantial portion of the assets of a corporation ("change in ownership or control"); and (d) the payment has (together with other payments described above in (a), (b), and (c) with respect to the same individual) an aggregate present value of at least 3 times the individual's base amount.

For this purpose, an individual's base amount is, in general, the individual's average annualized includible compensation for the most recent 5 taxable years ending before the change in ownership or control.

Section 280G(b)(2)(B) provides that the term "parachute payment" also includes any payment in the nature of compensation to, or for the benefit of, a disqualified individual if the payment is pursuant to an agreement that violates any generally enforced securities laws or regulations ("securities violation parachute payment").

Once payments are identified as "parachute payments", the next step is to determine any "excess" portion of the payments. Section 280G(b)(1) defines the term "excess parachute payment" as an amount equal to the excess of any parachute payment over the portion of the disqualified individual's base amount that is allocated to such payment. For this purpose, the portion of the base amount allocated to a parachute payment is the amount that bears the same ratio to the base amount as the present value of the parachute payment bears to the aggregate present value of all such payments to the same disqualified individual.

Generally, excess parachute payments may be reduced by certain amounts of reasonable compensation. Section 280G(b)(4)(B) provides that except in the case of securities violation parachute payments, the amount of an excess parachute payment is reduced by any portion of the payment that the taxpayer establishes by clear and convincing evidence is reasonable compensation for personal services actually rendered by the disqualified individual before the date of change in ownership or control. Such reasonable compensation is first offset against the portion of the base amount allocated to the payment.

EXEMPT PAYMENTS

* * *

Section 280G(b)(5) provides an exemption for payments with respect to certain corporations. Pursuant to that section, the term "parachute payment" does not include any payment made to a disqualified individual with respect to a corporation which, immediately before the change in ownership or control, was a small business corporation (as defined in section 1361(b) but without regard to paragraph (1)(C) thereof). In addition, the term "parachute payment" does not include any payment made with respect to a corporation if, immediately before the change in ownership or control, no stock in the corporation was readily tradable on an established securities market (or otherwise) and certain shareholder approval requirements are met with respect to the payment. For this purpose, stock that is described in section 1504(a)(4) is not treated as being readily tradable on an established securities market if the payment does not adversely affect the shareholder's redemption and liquidation rights. The proposed regulations provide guidance on applying the exemptions contained in section 280G(b)(5).

Section 280G(b)(6) exempts certain payments under a qualified plan. Pursuant to that section, the term "parachute payment" does not include any payment to or from: (a) a plan described in section 401(a) which includes a trust exempt from tax under section 501(a); (b) an annuity plan described in section 403(a); or (c) a simplified employee pension as defined in section 408(k).

Finally, section 280G(b)(4)(A) exempts certain payments of reasonable compensation. Pursuant to that section, except in the case of securities violation parachute payments, the term "parachute payment" does not include the portion of any payment which the taxpayer establishes by clear and convincing evidence is reasonable compensation for personal services to be rendered on or after the date of the change in ownership or control. The proposed regulations provide guidance for determining amounts of reasonable compensation.

DISQUALIFIED INDIVIDUALS

To be a parachute payment, a payment must be made to (or for the benefit of) a "disqualified individual." Section 280G(c) defines the term "disqualified individual" to include any individual who (a) is an employee or independent contractor who performs personal services for a corporation, and (b) is an officer, shareholder, or highly-compensated individual. The proposed regulations provide guidance on who will be treated as an "officer," a "shareholder," and a "highly-compensated individual" for this purpose.

Section 280G(c) provides that a "highly-compensated individual" with respect to a corporation only includes an individual who is (or would be if the individual were an employee) a member of the group consisting of the highest paid 1 percent of the employees of the corporation or, if less, the 250 highest paid employees of the corporation. The proposed regulations provide rules for applying this definition. In addition, the proposed regulations provide that no individual whose annual compensation is less than $75,000 will be treated as a highly compensated individual. The proposed regulations also provide an exception to the definition of "highly-compensated individual" to prevent fees earned by independent service providers (such as independent brokers, attorneys, and investment bankers) from becoming subject to section 280G when they perform services in connection with a change in ownership or control.

With respect to who will be treated as a "shareholder" for purposes of section 280G(c), the proposed regulations provide a *de minimis* rule. Pursuant to this rule, only an individual who owns stock of a corporation having a value that exceeds the lesser of $1 million, or 1 percent of the total value of the outstanding shares of all classes of the corporation's stock, is treated as a disqualified individual with respect to the corporation by reason of stock ownership. For purposes of determining the amount of the stock owned by an individual, the constructive ownership rules of section 318(a) shall apply.

The proposed regulations also limit the number of employees who will be treated as disqualified individuals with respect to a corporation by reason of being "officers" of the corporation. The proposed regulations provide that no more than 50 employees (or, if less, the greater of 3 employees or 10 percent of the employees of the corporation) will be treated as disqualified individuals with respect to a corporation by reason of being an officer of the corporation. In the case of an affiliated group treated as one corporation, the previous sentence will be applied to each member of such group.

* * *

Popularity of Golden and Tin Parachutes

The surge of corporate takeovers throughout the 1980s has led many employers to provide protection for employees in the form of parachute payments, according to a Hewitt Associates survey of 250 major employers. Hewitt Associates, *Competitive Practices in Change in Control Arrangements* (1990). More than half of the surveyed employers have adopted change-in-control arrangements for selected executives. The prevalence of executive change-in-control arrangements has increased significantly, from 39 percent in 1987 to 51 percent in 1990.

Golden parachutes are agreements between corporations and their key personnel under which the corporation agrees to pay the employees certain amounts in the event that control of the corporation changes. The survey found that the median base salary for executives receiving golden parachute payments is $112,000.

Most golden parachutes require a "double trigger" to activate payments: a change in control must occur, and the executive must be terminated. The vast majority of companies define termination as involuntary or "constructive"—for example, a reduction in pay or a demotion. Typically, golden parachute agreements prescribe a maximum time period of two years between the date on which a change in control occurs and the termination of the executive, for purposes of triggering payments. More than half of the arrangements do not cap parachute payments to the legislated ceiling of three times a "base amount." When payments are greater, the excess over the base amount is nondeductible by the corporation and is subject to an excise tax payable by the executive. About 33 percent of companies gross up executives for any excise taxes due on parachute payments, up from 27 percent in 1988. These results suggest that companies are placing less emphasis on tax consequences when designing change-in-control arrangements.

The survey found that tin parachutes, severance payments made to rank-and-file employees who have lost their jobs as the result of a hostile corporate takeover, were less common than golden parachutes, although their use is increasing. In a 1988 survey 6 percent of employers offered tin parachutes, as compared with 19 percent in 1990.

Usually tin parachute arrangements cover all exempt and nonexempt employees, with the exception of executives covered under golden parachute agreements. Like golden parachutes, tin parachutes typically require a double trigger. The survey found that more than half of the tin parachutes provide for a continuation of health and life insurance benefits after termination.

Greenmail: Section 5881

REVENUE ACT OF 1987

Conference Comm.Rep. (Dec. 22, 1987), reprinted in 75, No. 1 Stand.Fed.Tax Rpts. (CCH) ¶ 2044 at 300 (Dec. 28, 1987).

* * *

[*Greenmail excise tax*] [T]he bill [House] provides that a person who receives "greenmail" is subject to a non-deductible 50–percent excise tax on any gain realized on such receipt. Greenmail is defined as any consideration paid by a corporation in redemption of its stock if such stock has been held by the shareholder for less than two years and the shareholder (or any related person or person acting in concert with the shareholder) made or threatened a public tender offer for stock in the corporation during that period.

The conference agreement adopts ... the House bill provision imposing an excise tax on greenmail, with certain modifications; ...

The greenmail excise tax does not apply if, prior to the redemption, the redeeming corporation offered to purchase the stock of other shareholders for the same consideration and on the same terms that it redeemed the stock of the taxpayer. The provision is intended to apply where a taxpayer otherwise subject to the provision sells his stock to an entity related to the issuing corporation (e.g., a controlled subsidiary).

* * *

Poison Pill Plans

IRS REV.RUL. 90–11
1990–1 C.B. 10.

Issue

What are the federal income tax consequences, if any, of a corporation's adoption of a plan, * * * commonly referred to as a "poison pill" plan, which provides the corporation's shareholders with the right to purchase additional shares of stock upon the occurrence of certain events?

Facts

X is a publicly held domestic corporation. X's board of directors adopted a plan (the "Plan") that provides the common shareholders of X with "poison pill" rights (the "Rights"). The adoption of the Plan constituted the distribution of a dividend under state law. The principal purpose of the adoption of the Plan was to establish a mechanism by which the corporation could, in the future, provide shareholders with rights to purchase stock at substantially less than fair market value as a means of responding to unsolicited offers to acquire X. * * *

At the time X's board of directors adopted the Plan, the likelihood that the Rights would, at any time, be exercised was both remote and speculative.

Holding

The adoption of the Plan by X's board of directors does not constitute the distribution of stock or property by X to its shareholders, an exchange of property or stock (either taxable or nontaxable), or any other event giving rise to the realization of gross income by any taxpayer. This revenue ruling does not address the federal income tax consequences of any redemption of Rights, or of any transaction involving Rights subsequent to a triggering event. * * *

Deductibility of Acquisition Fees and Expenses

NATIONAL STARCH & CHEMICAL CORP. v. C.I.R.
United States Court of Appeals, Third Circuit, 1990.
918 F.2d 426.

Sloviter, Circuit Judge:

This is an appeal by National Starch and Chemical Corporation (National Starch) from a decision of the Tax Court affirming the disallowance by the Internal Revenue Service (IRS) of the investment banking fee, legal fees and related expenses incurred by National Starch's Board of Directors in deciding whether to acquiesce in a takeover by Unilever United States, Inc. National Starch contends that these were ordinary and necessary business expenses deductible under section 162(a) of the Internal Revenue Code. The Tax Court agreed with the Commissioner of Internal Revenue that all of the fees were nondeductible capital expenditures. * * *

In 1977, Unilever approached National Starch, one of Unilever's suppliers, to gauge its interest in being the target of a friendly takeover. All of the stock of Unilever United States, Inc. is owned by Unilever N.V. (jointly referred to as Unilever), a publicly held Netherlands Corporation. Unilever was interested in increasing its United States revenues relative to its overall revenues. * * * When it appeared likely that a favorable ruling would be forthcoming from the IRS, National Starch engaged Morgan Stanley & Co. (Morgan Stanley) to do a preliminary analysis, review National Starch's alternatives, make a valuation judgment after studying National Starch, render a fairness opinion, and coordinate the technical details of the merger.

Morgan Stanley prepared and delivered a report to the Board on the fairness of the offer. Unilever had originally proposed a price of $65 to $70 for each share of National Starch, which Morgan Stanley concluded was fair. Unilever thereafter offered $70 a share. National Starch's management suggested a price of $80 a share, which Morgan Stanley relayed to Unilever on the Board's behalf. Morgan Stanley thereafter reported back a Unilever offer of $73.50 a share, the price ultimately agreed upon.

After the sale of the stock, National Starch retained its former management, and it did not materially increase the sale of its products to Unilever. The management at National Starch viewed the transaction as "swapping approximately 3500 shareholders for one." App. at 141. As a matter of administrative convenience, it changed its charter to eliminate its authorized and unissued preferred stock and decreased its authorized common stock to 1,000 shares.

National Starch's tax return for the year that ended August 15, 1978 (the date of acquisition) treated the $2,225,586 Morgan Stanley fee as a deduction for an ordinary and necessary business expense under section 162(a) of the Internal Revenue Code. * * *

The issue before us is whether National Starch's expenditures for investment banking and legal fees can be deducted under section 162(a) of the Internal Revenue Code as ordinary and necessary business expenses or whether they must be capitalized under section 263. Section 162 provides: "[t]here shall be allowed as a deduction all the ordinary and necessary expenses paid or incurred during the taxable year in carrying on any trade or business...." 26 U.S.C. § 162(a)

(1988). This provision must be interpreted in tandem with section 263, which prohibits deductions for "[a]ny amount paid out for new buildings or for permanent improvements or betterments made to increase the value of any property or estate." 26 U.S.C. § 263(a)(1) (1988).

The Supreme Court has enumerated five separate requirements for deductibility under section 162(a). The item must (1) be paid or incurred during the taxable year (2) for carrying on any trade or business, and (3) be an expense (4) that is "necessary" and (5) "ordinary." *Commissioner v. Lincoln Savings & Loan Ass'n* [71–1 USTC ¶ 9476], 403 U.S. 345, 352 (1971). Only the "ordinary expense" requirement is in dispute here. The Court has stated, in somewhat circular fashion, that the principal function of the term "ordinary" is to distinguish between expenses currently deductible and capital expenditures which, if deductible at all, must be amortized over the useful life of the asset.

* * *

Tax deductions are a matter of legislative grace. * * * Thus, the burden is on the taxpayer to show that the expenses are deductible. * * *

Notwithstanding National Starch's protestations to the contrary, the common characteristic of expenses that have been found to be capital, in fact the *sine qua non* of capitalization, is the presence of a not insignificant future benefit that is more than merely incidental. * * *

In this case, the Tax Court held that the expenditures were not deductible in light of its determination that National Starch's directors concluded that it would be in the corporation's "long-term interest to shift ownership of the corporate stock to Unilever." [CCH Dec. 45,851] 93 T.C. at 75. The Tax Court found that the transaction provided at least two inherently permanent benefits to National Starch: (1) the availability of Unilever's enormous resources, and (2) the opportunity for synergy created by Unilever's affiliation with National Starch. *Id.* at 76. These are factual findings of the Tax Court which we may not overturn unless clearly erroneous. * * *

In its discussion of the long-term benefits to National Starch as a result of the affiliation with Unilever, the Tax Court stated that "the very availability of the resources of Unilever was an immediate, as well as a long-term, benefit because it broadened [National Starch's] opportunities." [CCH Dec. 45,851], 93 T.C. at 76–77. There is ample support in the record for this finding. National Starch had assets in 1976, the year before Unilever's approach, which were in excess of $241 million, App. at 373, and its operating income was $48 million. App. at 372. Unilever was gargantuan in comparison. It had combined assets in 1976 worth close to five and a half billion dollars, App. at 667, and its operating profit was in excess of one billion dollars. App. at 665.

National Starch recognized that Unilever's sheer wealth provided it with a significant benefit. National Starch's 1978 Annual Progress Report stated that, "We will benefit greatly from the availability of Unilever's enormous resources, especially in the area of basic technology." App. at 391. Although this was written after the takeover, there is no reason why it did not equally represent the view of the Board of Directors in agreeing to the takeover.

Of additional significance to the finding of long-term benefit was the Tax Court's subsidiary finding that even though there is no evidence of an immediate benefit from the affiliation, it created the opportunity for synergy. [CCH Dec. 45,851], 93 T.C. at 76. National Starch primarily produces specialty starches, adhesives and related chemical products sold to a large number of industrial users for use in manufacturing a wide variety of consumer products and product packaging. App. at 608–14. Unilever describes itself as "one of the dozen largest businesses in the world by turnover—and the largest in consumer goods." App. at 415. The larger part of Unilever is in branded and packaged consumer goods: mainly foods, detergents, and toilet preparations. Significantly, Unilever listed other "important" activities as including chemicals, paper, plastics and packaging. *Id.*

It was undisputed that prior to the affiliation National Starch sold its products to Unilever and has continued to do so thereafter. App. at 142. National Starch emphasizes that there has been no material increase in the volume of such sales, but the Tax Court noted that "[t]he lack of benefits in the short term does not imply their absence in the long term, especially given the time it takes to plan and implement significant changes in a corporation's operations." [CCH Dec. 45,851], 93 T.C. at 76.

* * *

As an additional reason for nondeductibility, the Commissioner proposes that we adopt the rule that "[*a*]*ny* transaction in which a corporate taxpayer is transformed from a publicly-held corporation to a one-shareholder corporation involves an effective change in the taxpayer's corporate structure that will benefit future operations," and therefore expenses incurred with respect to such an ownership shift are capital expenditures. Appellee's Brief at 21–22 (emphasis in original). The Tax Court did not reach this issue. There is some plausibility in the Commissioner's argument that the elimination of the risk of proxy fights and shareholders' derivative suits, as well as of the costs of annual filings with the SEC and the solicitation of proxies, are long-term benefits arising from the radical change in the corporate enterprise which will last for the indefinite future. However, we need not decide whether to accept the absolute rule sought by the Commissioner. In this case, more than a mere change in corporate ownership was effected. Because the transaction entailed the affiliation of National Starch with Unilever which, as we have held above, sufficed to create the requisite long-term benefit, we will leave for another case consideration whether the benefits of restructuring ownership alone would be sufficient to require capitalization of the fees pertinent thereto.

On the other hand, it is important to note that the Board of Directors was motivated, at least in part, by concern for the future development of National Starch in the event of the death of the Greenwalls, the company's largest stockholders, who were ages 79 and 81 at that time. Oscar M. Reubhausen, Chairman of the Board of National Starch at the time of this litigation, testified that he told Morgan Stanley that the "estates problems" concerning the Greenwalls were "overhanging the market" and represented a "question mark— 'for National Starch Corporation for the future.'" App. at 203. He thus viewed the Unilever offer as a "particular opportunity put before National Starch." App. at 203–204.

Indeed, Morgan Stanley referred to that very concern in a letter to the Board summarizing its assignment. It stated that, "We understand that National Starch is interested in having Morgan Stanley review its strategic alternatives within the context both of the longer term situation of a 15% equity ownership in National Starch which at some point will be transferred from its present individual 'founding' owners and of an evaluation of an immediate proposed business combination involving Unilever." App. at 597. It is thus evident from the record that the National Starch directors viewed the Unilever offer as a transaction that would promote the long-term betterment of the corporation.

In addition, the fact that the Tax Court rejected the Commissioner's argument that the transaction was essentially a reorganization under section 368(a)(1)(B), for which expenditures must be capitalized, does not preclude consideration of the general rationale behind requiring capitalization of expenses for restructuring. As explained by Justice Blackmun, writing as a circuit judge (who, coincidentally, also authored *Lincoln Savings*), reorganization expenses are treated as capital because they relate to the corporation's operations and betterment into the indefinite future, as distinguished from income production or other current needs.

* * *

If capital expenditures were immediately deductible, the taxpayer's income would be distorted both in the current year and in later years when the benefits are in fact received.

* * *

Although National Starch notes correctly that the fees and expenses at issue are not susceptible to depreciation or amortization because the benefit to the company has no ascertainable useful life, other courts have also concluded that section 263 requires denial of immediate deductibility in comparable situations. * * * In this respect, the expenses are analogous to the treatment of goodwill which is neither deductible nor depreciable until the business is sold, even though the benefits (increased profits) are obtained throughout the life of the business. * * *

Finally, we consider whether the expenditures are deductible merely because they may have been necessary under Delaware law for the Board members to satisfy their fiduciary obligation to the shareholders. Precedent suggests otherwise. The Court in *Lincoln Savings* held that additional premium payments must be capitalized even though the governing statute required their payment by the taxpayer. [71–1 USTC ¶ 9476], 403 U.S. at 359. * * *

Chapter Eight

PROTECTING CONSUMER AND NATIONAL SECURITY INTERESTS IN MERGERS AND ACQUISITIONS

As we saw in chapter 3, acquisitions can impose costs on members of the public that may not be internalized by the parties to the transaction. Indeed the parties to a transaction not only may be indifferent to the public interest but may profit from public injury. Thus an argument that a merger creates value simply because the stock price of the combined firm (plus the value of any nonstock consideration) is greater than the combined stock prices of the constituent firms before the deal is announced is incomplete without an investigation of the effect of the merger on other public interests (the externalities). In earlier chapters we covered laws that regulate acquisitions to promote various aspects of the public interest—laws that relate to the health of our capital trading markets, to the collection of public taxes, to the preservation of a clean environment, to the goal of full employment, and to the compensation of tort victims. We have yet to cover, however, laws that protect consumers and laws that protect national security interests by limiting foreign ownership.

Subchapter A focuses on laws that protect consumers by facilitating competition among producers in our product markets. Subchapter B deals with laws that restrict international acquisitions of domestic companies that are essential to our national security.

SUBCHAPTER A. CONSUMER PROTECTION: ANTITRUST LAWS

Consumer protection in acquisitions has been a central part of the American legal landscape since the late 1800s. Industrial combinations after the Civil War demonstrated one form of opportunistic behavior in acquisitions: Two competing firms combine, creating a single firm that has enough market power to engage in noncompetitive pricing, or enough size to collude with other major firms to fix prices through express or tacit agreements. The surviving firm in such a combination may be more profitable than the two constituent firms standing separately, but at the expense of their consumers. The firms, in bargaining over the merger price, simply split the expected gains created by monopolistic or oligopolistic pricing behavior. A federal antitrust statute known as the Clayton Act, and state antitrust statutes modeled after the Clayton Act, are designed to deter such acquisitions.

SECTION 1. THE CLAYTON ACT

THE CLAYTON ACT, § 7
15 U.S.C.A. § 18.

§ 18. Acquisition by one corporation of stock of another

No person engaged in commerce or in any activity affecting commerce shall acquire, directly or indirectly, the whole or any part of the stock or other share capital and no person subject to the jurisdiction of the Federal Trade Commission shall acquire the whole or any part of the assets of another person engaged also in commerce or in any activity affecting commerce, where in any line of commerce or in any activity affecting commerce in any section of the country, the effect of such acquisition may be substantially to lessen competition, or to tend to create a monopoly.

No person shall acquire, directly or indirectly, the whole or any part of the stock or other share capital and no person subject to the jurisdiction of the Federal Trade Commission shall acquire the whole or any part of the assets of one or more persons engaged in commerce or in any activity affecting commerce, where in any line of commerce or in any activity affecting commerce in any section of the country, the effect of such acquisition, of such stocks or assets, or of the use of such stock by the voting or granting of proxies or otherwise, may be substantially to lessen competition, or to tend to create a monopoly.

This section shall not apply to persons purchasing such stock solely for investment and not using the same by voting or otherwise to bring about, or in attempting to bring about, the substantial lessening of competition. Nor shall anything contained in this section prevent a corporation engaged in commerce or in any activity affecting commerce from causing the formation of subsidiary corporations for the actual carrying on of their immediate lawful business, or the natural and legitimate branches or extensions thereof, or from owning and holding all or a part of the stock of such subsidiary corporations, when the effect of such formation is not to substantially lessen competition.

* * *

The responsibility for prosecuting violations of the Clayton Act is vested in both the United States Department of Justice and the Federal Trade Commission. The Department of Justice has issued guidelines for when it will prosecute violations of the act:

U.S. DEPT. OF JUSTICE 1987 MERGER GUIDELINES
52 Anti-trust & Trade Reg. Rptr. (BNA) Special Supplement (1987).

These Guidelines state in outline form the present enforcement policy of the U.S. Department of Justice ("Department") concerning acquisitions and mergers ("mergers") subject to section 7 of the Clayton Act or to section 1 of the Sherman Act. They describe the general principles and specific standards normally used by the Department in analyzing mergers. By stating its policy as simply and clearly as possible, the Department hopes to reduce the uncertainty associated with enforcement of the antitrust laws in this area.

* * *

The Guidelines are designed primarily to indicate when the Department is likely to challenge mergers, not how it will conduct the litigation of cases that it decides to bring.

* * *

The unifying theme of the Guidelines is that mergers should not be permitted to create or enhance "market power" or to facilitate its exercise. A sole seller (a "monopolist") of a product with no good substitutes can maintain a selling price that is above the level that would prevail if the market were competitive. Where only a few firms account for most of the sales of a product, those firms can in some circumstances either explicitly or implicitly coordinate their actions in order to approximate the performance of a monopolist. This ability of one or more firms profitably to maintain prices above competitive levels for a significant period of time is termed "market power." Sellers with market power also may eliminate rivalry on variables other than price. In either case, the result is a transfer of wealth from buyers to sellers and a misallocation of resources.

"Market power" also encompasses the ability of a single buyer or group of buyers to depress the price paid for a product to a level that is below the competitive price. The exercise of market power by buyers has wealth transfer and resource misallocation effects analogous to those associated with the exercise of market power by sellers.

Although they sometimes harm competition, mergers generally play an important role in a free enterprise economy. They can penalize ineffective management and facilitate the efficient flow of investment capital and the redeployment of existing productive assets. While challenging competitively harmful mergers, the Department seeks to avoid unnecessary interference with that larger universe of mergers that are either competitively beneficial or neutral. In attempting to mediate between these dual concerns, however, the Guidelines reflect the congressional intent that merger enforcement should interdict competitive problems in their incipiency.

2. MARKET DEFINITION AND MEASUREMENT

2.0 Using the standards stated below, the Department will define and measure the market for each product or service (hereinafter "product") of each of the merging firms. The standards in the Guidelines are designed to ensure that the Department analyzes the likely competitive impact of a merger within economically meaningful markets—i.e., markets that could be subject to the exercise of market power. Accordingly, for each product of each merging firm, the Department seeks to define a market in which firms could effectively exercise market power if they were able to coordinate their actions. Formally, a market is defined as a product or group of products and a geographic area in which it is sold such that a hypothetical, profit-maximizing firm, not subject to price regulation, that was the only present and future seller of those products in that area would impose a "small but significant and nontransitory" increase in price above prevailing or likely future levels. The group of products and geographic area that comprise a market will be referred to respectively as the "product market" and the "geographic market."

In determining whether one or more firms would be in a position to exercise market power, it is necessary to evaluate both the probable demand responses of consumers and the probable supply responses of other firms. A price increase could be made unprofitable by any of four types of demand or supply responses: 1) consumers switching to other products; 2) consumers switching to the same product produced by firms in other areas; 3) producers of other products switching existing facilities to the production of the product; or 4) producers entering into the production of the product by substantially modifying existing facilities or by constructing new facilities. Each type of response is considered under the Guidelines.

* * *

3. Horizontal Mergers

3.0 Where the merging firms are in the same product and geographic market, the merger is horizontal. In such cases, the Department will focus first on the post-merger concentration of the market and the increase in concentration caused by the merger. For mergers that result in low market concentration or a relatively slight increase in concentration, the Department will be able to determine without a detailed examination of other factors that the merger poses no significant threat to competition. In other cases, however, the Department will proceed to examine a variety of other factors relevant to that question.

3.1 Concentration and Market Shares

Market concentration is a function of the number of firms in a market and their respective market shares.[13] Other things being equal, concentration affects the likelihood that one firm, or a small group of

---

13. Markets can range from atomistic, where very large numbers of firms that are small relative to the overall size of the market compete with one another, to monopolistic, where one firm controls the entire market. Far more common, and more difficult analytically, is the large middle range of instances where a relatively small number of firms accounts for most of the sales in the market.

firms, could successfully exercise market power. The smaller the percentage of total supply that a firm controls, the more severely it must restrict its own output in order to produce a given price increase, and the less likely it is that an output restriction will be profitable. If collective action is necessary, an additional constraint applies. As the number of firms necessary to control a given percentage of total supply increases, the difficulties and costs of reaching and enforcing consensus with respect to the control of that supply also increase.

As an aid to the interpretation of market data, the Department will use the Herfindahl–Hirschman Index ("HHI") of market concentration. The HHI is calculated by summing the squares of the individual market shares of all the firms included in the market under the standards in Section 2 of these Guidelines.[14] Unlike the traditional four-firm concentration ratio, the HHI reflects both the distribution of the market shares of the top four firms and the composition of the market outside the top four firms. It also gives proportionately greater weight to the market shares of the larger firms, which probably accords with their relative importance in any collusive interaction.

The Department divides the spectrum of market concentration as measured by the HHI into three regions that can be broadly characterized as unconcentrated (HHI below 1000), moderately concentrated (HHI between 1000 and 1800), and highly concentrated (HHI above 1800). An empirical study by the Department of the size dispersion of firms within markets indicates that the critical HHI thresholds at 1000 and 1800 correspond roughly to four-firm concentration ratios of 50 percent and 70 percent, respectively. Although the resulting regions provide a useful format for merger analysis, the numerical divisions suggest greater precision than is possible with the available economic tools and information. Other things being equal, cases falling just above and just below a threshold present comparable competitive concerns. Moreover, because concentration and market share data present a historical picture of the market, the Department must interpret such data in light of the relevant circumstances and the forward-looking objective of the Guidelines—to determine likely future effects of a given merger.

3.11 General Standards

In evaluating horizontal mergers, the Department will consider both the post-merger market concentration and the increase in concentration resulting from the merger.[15] The link between concentration

14. For example, a market consisting of four firms with market shares of 30 percent, 30 percent, 20 percent and 20 percent has an HHI of 2600 ($30^2 + 30^2 + 20^2 + 20^2 = 2600$). The HHI ranges from 10,000 (in the case of a pure monopoly) to a number approaching zero (in the case of an atomistic market). Although it is desirable to include all firms in the calculation, lack of information about small fringe firms is not critical because such firms do not affect the HHI significantly.

15. The increase in concentration as measured by the HHI can be calculated independently of the overall market concentration by doubling the product of the market shares of the merging firms. For example, the merger of firms with shares of 5 percent and 10 percent of the market

and market power is explained above. The increase in concentration is relevant to several key issues. Although mergers among small firms increase concentration, they are less likely to have anticompetitive consequences. Moreover, even in concentrated markets, it is desirable to allow firms some scope for merger activity in order to achieve economies of scale and to permit exit from the market. However, market share and concentration data provide only the starting point for analyzing the competitive impact of a merger. Before determining whether to challenge a merger, the Department will consider all other relevant factors that pertain to its competitive impact.

The general standards for horizontal mergers are as follows:

a) Post–Merger HHI Below 1000. Markets in this region generally would be considered to be unconcentrated. Because implicit coordination among firms is likely to be difficult and because the prohibitions of section 1 of the Sherman Act are usually an adequate response to any explicit collusion that might occur, the Department will not challenge mergers falling in this region, except in extraordinary circumstances.

b) Post–Merger HHI Between 1000 and 1800. Because this region extends from the point at which the competitive concerns associated with concentration are raised to the point at which they become quite serious, generalization is particularly difficult. The Department, however, is unlikely to challenge a merger producing an increase in the HHI of less than 100 points.[16] The Department is likely to challenge mergers in this region that produce an increase in the HHI of more than 100 points, unless the Department concludes, on the basis of the post-merger HHI, the increase in the HHI, and the presence or absence of the factors discussed in Sections 3.2, 3.3, 3.4, and 3.5 that the merger is not likely substantially to lessen competition.

c) Post–Merger HHI Above 1800. Markets in this region generally are considered to be highly concentrated. Additional concentration resulting from mergers is a matter of significant competitive concern. The Department is unlikely, however, to challenge mergers producing an increase in the HHI of less than 50 points.[17] The Department is likely to challenge mergers in this region that produce an increase in the HHI of more than 50 points, unless the Department concludes, on the basis of the post-merger HHI, the increase in the HHI, and the presence or absence of the factors discussed in Sections 3.2, 3.3, 3.4, and

would increase the HHI by 100 ($5 \times 10 \times 2 = 100$). The explanation for this technique is as follows: In calculating the HHI before the merger, the market shares of the merging firms are squared individually: $(a)^2 + (b)^2$. After the merger, the sum of those shares would be squared: $(a + b)^2$, which equals $a^2 + 2ab + b^2$. The increase in the HHI therefore is represented by $2ab$.

16. Mergers producing increases in concentration close to the 100 point threshold include those between firms with market shares of 25 percent and 2 percent, 16 percent and 3 percent, 12 percent and 4 percent, 10 percent and 5 percent, 8 percent and 6 percent, and 7 percent and 7 percent.

17. Mergers producing increases in concentration close to the 50 point threshold include those between firms with market shares of 12 percent and 2 percent, 8 percent and 3 percent, 6 percent and 4 percent, and 5 percent and 5 percent.

3.5 that the merger is not likely substantially to lessen competition. However, if the increase in the HHI exceeds 100 and the post-merger HHI substantially exceeds 1800, only in extraordinary cases will such factors establish that the merger is not likely substantially to lessen competition.

3.12 Leading Firm Proviso

In some cases, typically where one of the merging firms is small, mergers that may create or enhance the market power of a single dominant firm could pass scrutiny under the standards stated in Section 3.11. Notwithstanding those standards, the Department is likely to challenge the merger of any firm with a market share of at least one percent with the leading firm in the market, provided the leading firm has a market share that is at least 35 percent. Because the ease and profitability of collusion are of little relevance to the ability of a single dominant firm to exercise market power, the Department will not consider the presence or absence of the factors discussed in Section 3.4 because they relate to the likelihood of collusion. The Department will consider, however, the factors in Sections 3.2, 3.3, and 3.5 because they are relevant to the competitive concerns associated with a leading-firm merger.

3.2 Factors Affecting the Significance of Market Shares and Concentration

In a variety of situations, market share and market concentration data may either understate or overstate the likely future competitive significance of a firm or firms in the market. The following are examples of such situations.

3.21 Changing Market Conditions

Market concentration and market share data of necessity are based on historical evidence. However, recent or on-going changes in the market may indicate that the current market share of a particular firm either understates or overstates the firm's future competitive significance. For example, if a new technology that is important to long-term competitive viability is not available to a particular firm, the Department may conclude that the historical market share of the firm overstates the firm's future competitive significance. The Department will consider reasonably predictable effects of recent or on-going changes in market conditions in interpreting market concentration and market share data.

3.22 Financial Condition of Firms in the Relevant Market

The Department will consider the financial condition of a merging firm or any firm in the relevant market, to the extent that it is relevant to an analysis of the firm's likely future competitive significance.[18] If the financial difficulties of a firm cannot be explained as

---

18. This factor is distinguished from the failing company doctrine, which is an affirmative defense to an otherwise unlaw-

phenomena of, for example, the business cycle but clearly reflect an underlying structural weakness of the firm, the firm's current market share may overstate its likely future competitive significance. For example, a firm's current market share may overstate its future competitive significance if that firm has chronic financial difficulties resulting from obsolete productive facilities in a market experiencing a long-term decline in demand.

3.3 Ease of Entry

If entry into a market is so easy that existing competitors could not succeed in raising price for any significant period of time, the Department is unlikely to challenge mergers in that market. Under the standards in Section 2.21, firms that do not currently sell the relevant product, but that could easily and economically sell it using existing facilities, are included in the market and are assigned a market share. This section considers the additional competitive effects of 1) production substitution requiring significant modifications of existing facilities and 2) entry through the construction of new facilities.[20]

In assessing the ease of entry into a market, the Department will consider the likelihood and probable magnitude of entry in response to a "small but significant and nontransitory" increase in price.[21] Both the price to be increased and what constitutes a "small but significant and nontransitory" increase in price will be determined as they are in product market definition, except that a two-year time period generally will be used.[22] The more difficult entry into the market is, the more likely the Department is to challenge the merger.

* * *

* * *

3.5 Efficiencies

The primary benefit of mergers to the economy is their efficiency-enhancing potential, which can increase the competitiveness of firms ful merger and which, as noted in Section 5.1, the Department will construe strictly.

* * *

20. "Entry" may occur as firms outside the market enter for the first time or as fringe firms currently in the market greatly expand their current capacity.

21. In general, entry is more likely to occur when the additional assets necessary to produce the relevant product are short-lived or widely used outside the particular market. Conversely, entry is less likely to occur when those assets are long-lived and highly specialized to the particular application. Entry is generally facilitated by the growth of the market and hindered by its stagnation or decline. Entry also is hindered by the need for scarce special skills or resources or the need to achieve a substantial market share in order to realize important economies of scale. See also Section 4.212 (Increased Difficulty of Simultaneous Entry to Both Markets).

22. Although this type of supply response may take longer to materialize than those considered under Section 2.21, its prospect may have a greater deterrent effect on the exercise of market power by present sellers. Where new entry involves the dedication of long-lived assets to a market, the resulting capacity and its adverse effects on profitability will be present in the market until those assets are economically depreciated.

* * *

and result in lower prices to consumers. Because the antitrust laws, and thus the standards of the Guidelines, are designed to proscribe only mergers that present a significant danger to competition, they do not present an obstacle to most mergers. As a consequence, in the majority of cases, the Guidelines will allow firms to achieve available efficiencies through mergers without interference from the Department.

Some mergers that the Department otherwise might challenge may be reasonably necessary to achieve significant net efficiencies. If the parties to the merger establish by clear and convincing evidence that a merger will achieve such efficiencies, the Department will consider those efficiencies in deciding whether to challenge the merger. Cognizable efficiencies include, but are not limited to, achieving economies of scale, better integration of production facilities, plant specialization, lower transportation costs, and similar efficiencies relating to specific manufacturing, servicing, or distribution operations of the merging firms. The Department may also consider claimed efficiencies resulting from reductions in general selling, administrative, and overhead expenses, or that otherwise do not relate to specific manufacturing, servicing, or distribution operations of the merging firms, although, as a practical matter, these types of efficiencies may be difficult to demonstrate. In addition, the Department will reject claims of efficiencies if equivalent or comparable savings can reasonably be achieved by the parties through other means. The parties must establish a greater level of expected net efficiencies the more significant are the competitive risks identified in Section 3.

5. DEFENSES

5.1 Failing Firm

The "failing firm defense" is a long-established, but ambiguous, doctrine under which an anticompetitive merger may be allowed because one of the merging firms is "failing." Because the defense can immunize significantly anticompetitive mergers, the Department will construe its elements strictly.

The Department is unlikely to challenge an anti-competitive merger in which one of the merging firms is allegedly failing when: 1) the allegedly failing firm probably would be unable to meet its financial obligations in the near future; 2) it probably would not be able to reorganize successfully under Chapter 11 of the Bankruptcy Act; and 3) it has made unsuccessful good faith efforts to elicit reasonable alternative offers of acquisition of the failing firm that would both keep it in the market and pose a less severe danger to competition than does the proposed merger.

* * *

NANNI,[*] MERGER ENFORCEMENT AT THE ANTITRUST DIVISION
58 Antitrust L.J. 329, 338–42 (1989)

* * *

The second subject I want to talk about briefly is the role of the Merger Guidelines. * * * If you read them one way, they look like a very detailed prescription; if you read them another way, you can see that they are filled with qualifications and balances and intangible compromises.

The numerical computations, the HHI figures, which purport to have a low level, a medium level, and a high level where you are in a lot of trouble, are reasonably reliable in one direction. If the concentration levels are very low, it is usually going to be very hard for anybody to figure out how market power could be exercised. But, as they get higher, the reverse is not true; it remains possible to try to prove rationally, under the Guidelines, that, even at high levels of concentration, other factors which are explicitly identified in the Guidelines mean that a company cannot ultimately exercise market power.

The aim, after all, of the Guidelines is not to figure out whether an industry is concentrated. The aim is to figure out whether the companies in it can exercise market power, either at present or after the merger. In that sense, the Guidelines seem to be best viewed as a kind of framework for people to think intelligently about answering that question: "Will these two companies, when merged, be able to exercise themselves, or facilitate the exercise in the industry, of market power, the power to raise price over cost?"

At that point, it seems to me, you can view the initial cut in trying to define a product market, a geographic market, and calculate shares as answering one major question you would want to know about the industry: Is there a significant prospect that, all other things being equal and not knowing anything else, market power can be exercised? If prospects are very low, the answer is almost certain to be no. If they are higher, then you face that possibility.

But at that point, you have to go on and ask the questions which the Guidelines pose very explicitly about the ability to collude in the particular industry, assuming you're not dealing with a company so dominant that it can exercise market power itself; and, even if you think the prospects for collusion are there, you have to ask yourself about the possibility that other companies can enter or switch production facilities to the product in question and frustrate any price increase.

Once you recognize that those two other questions have to be asked, there isn't any way to use any mathematical formula in the Guidelines to answer the question. What you have is a typical advo-

---

[*] Anthony Nanni, at the time of the reported discussion, was chief of the Litigation Section of the Antitrust Division of the U.S. Department of Justice.

cate's problem, of mustering evidence on three or four different points —concentration, entry, ability to collude—even before you come to [the] defenses.

Finally, let me say a word briefly about the defenses, ... I'm referring primarily to a claim that the merger may be anticompetitive, but it is overcome, it is alleged, by very substantial efficiencies and/or that the merger involves a failing company.

* * *

In the case of a failing company, that is fairly obvious. Its downward trend, its prospects for the future, may just reflect the fact that its past market share doesn't reflect its future power, so you can make an argument on market power based on the failure.

In the case of efficiencies, it's a slightly more complicated connection. I think my argument would usually be—and I think this is a reasonable argument—that, whether or not all of the purported tests on efficiencies have been satisfied, the very fact that you can demonstrate some efficiencies may provide an explanation for why the merger is occurring that will help rebut suspicions that the main reason is to exercise market power. It doesn't rule it out; you can be doing it for both reasons. Nevertheless, ultimately it can work its way back into a market power analysis.

* * *

I think one reason is that the problems have not been fully worked out, particularly with efficiencies, whose role has changed, at least in the last decade. Partly, they represent that there is a more difficult problem. Not only hasn't it been worked out, but it is more difficult to solve, because you have finally reached a policy trade-off. Unlike the first three-quarters of the Guidelines addressed to the single question, "Is there market power or will there be market power facilitated by the merger?", here you have the question, at least in some people's view, of whether, even if there is market power, at some point the adverse consequences of having the company fail, the loss of efficiencies, ought to outweigh it. So you have a buried policy decision which, I think, has not really been completely resolved. And then, finally, if all else fails, the fact remains that the Guidelines don't address them very clearly; therefore, you have more maneuvering room.

What are these open issues? I suppose one open issue is, in the case of efficiencies, just how clearly you have to prove that the efficiencies will be passed along to consumers. After all, if you try to work out in your mind a case in which you assume a company will be able to exercise a significant amount of power, and then nevertheless assume there will be efficiencies, those conditions don't sound especially right for proving that consumers are going to benefit from the efficiencies. I suppose you could argue on one side that it shouldn't matter; you can argue on the other side that unless the pass-along will occur, the efficiencies shouldn't be considered at all. All I want to say about it is that there is a considerable amount of maneuvering room and nothing very explicit in the Guidelines.

On the failing company, a similar unanswered question is: "What happens if a company is failing?" And the question then posed is: "Is there a less anticompetitive purchaser?" Well, yes there is, but the less anticompetitive purchaser isn't willing to pay very much for the company. At what point do you begin to say, "It's less anticompetitive, but there's a limit to how much of a bath you can expect the company to take," and at what point do you say instead, "Look, we're enforcing the antitrust laws, our aim is to protect competition, and as long as it's a dollar over the next-best alternative, we're just going to take a tough line"? The Guidelines don't answer that either.

So, happily for people who want to be advocates, there is plenty of room left, at least on a number of issues, even for policy arguments and, on the basic market power question, a tremendous amount of room for mustering evidence.

* * *

UNITED STATES v. WASTE MANAGEMENT, INC.

United States Court of Appeals, Second Circuit, 1984.
743 F.2d 976.

WINTER, CIRCUIT JUDGE:

* * *

WMI is in the solid waste disposal business. It provides services in twenty-seven states and had revenues of approximately $442 million in 1980. At the time of the acquisition, EMW was a diversified holding company that owned a subsidiary by the name of Waste Resources, which was in the waste disposal business in ten states and had revenues of $54 million in 1980.

WMI and Waste Resources each had subsidiaries that operated in or near Dallas. WMI has one subsidiary, American Container Service ("ACS") in Dallas, and another, Texas Waste Management, in the Dallas suburb of Lewisville. Waste Resources had a Dallas subsidiary called Texas Industrial Disposal, Inc. ("TIDI"). WMI now operates TIDI as a WMI sub.

Waste collection involves several different types of equipment and serves the needs of various types of customers. For present purposes, it is important to distinguish between "non-containerized" and "containerized" equipment. "Non-containerized" refers to trucks with compactors into which trash cans and bags are loaded by hand. "Containerized" equipment consists of two types of receptacles, "dumpsters" and "roll off," each emptied by different kinds of trucks. Dumpsters typically have a volume of one to eight cubic yards and are emptied by "front-load" trucks that pick the dumpsters up with clamps and empty them into a hopper. Roll-off containers range up to 50 cubic yards in volume and are carried to a dump, emptied and then returned. Trucks that transport roll-off containers are known, not surprisingly, as roll-off trucks. If the customer desires containerized service, the waste hauler provides the dumpster or roll-off container.

There are various relevant classes of customers: (i) single or multiple dwelling residential customers; (ii) apartment complexes of varying size, (iii) "business" customers—stores, restaurants, etc., and (iv) "industrial" customers—construction sites, factories, etc. Customers choose among the kinds of services according to their individual needs, the quantity of trash produced being a critical factor.

The parties strenuously disagree over the proper definition of the relevant product and geographic markets. The government contended in the district court that the product market should be defined in terms of equipment type and that front-load and roll-off waste collection service each constitutes a separate product market. WMI argued that the market includes all forms of waste collection.

* * *

A. Market Definition and Determination of Market Share

In determining the relevant product and geographic market, Judge Griesa considered only firms that presently collect waste in competition with WMI's subs TIDI and ACS. He thus did not consider the effect of potential competition by new entrants upon the market power of the merged firm but rather treated this as part of the rebuttal to the *prima facie* case. Although potential competition resulting from easy entry can as logically be appraised as part of market definition, *see* R. Posner, Antitrust Law 132–33 (1976), we will utilize the traditional analysis of defining the market in terms of existing competitors.

We thus begin by determining which firms presently collect waste in actual competition with WMI (a term we use henceforth to include TIDI and ACS). WMI provides waste disposal services to business and industrial customers as do a number of other private haulers. Neither WMI nor these other haulers provides substantial services to residential customers since residential waste is generally collected by private or municipal haulers who provide only limited services to business/industrial customers. Residential and business/industrial customers are thus served largely by different firms.

One reason for the distinction between residential and business/industrial collection is found in customer preferences for collection by particular equipment at existing prices. Thus, residential customers largely prefer non-containerized service while business/industrial customers usually opt for containerized hauling. There is of course overlap, and the district court therefore did not define the market solely in terms of equipment distinctions. Some large apartment complexes prefer containerized service (and were included by Judge Griesa as customers in the relevant market), and some businesses make do with hand collection (also included as customers in the relevant market).

Another reason for the distinction (as modified by the overlaps) between residential and business/industrial collection is that most private haulers provide only containerized service and most municipalities provide only non-containerized service. The largest municipality, the City of Dallas, provides no containerized service. Moreover, the few municipalities that do provide containerized service to business/industrial customers were included as sellers in the relevant product market.

At bottom, however, the distinction between residential and business/industrial service rests on two facts, one economic and the other political. First, customers with large amounts of trash have a greater need for containerized service than do customers with smaller quantities; the former tend to be business/industrial and the latter residential. Second, the latter customers are, for political reasons, served by hand collection provided at low prices by municipalities. At the fringe, of course, some business/industrial customers have sufficiently little trash to be able to choose hand collection at existing prices while some residential customers, such as large apartment complexes, prefer containerized service. Some business/industrial customers haul their trash themselves, although the record indicates that is not a feasible alternative for many at existing prices.

Customer preferences for service, therefore, turn largely on the quantity of trash produced, and different kinds of equipment are most useful for different quantities of trash. It might be that in a market without municipal haulers the larger private haulers would offer a full line of services, and the relevant product market would be all trash collection. However, the decision of the City of Dallas and other municipalities to provide non-containerized service has narrowed the market available to private haulers. The fact that only a small fringe of customers have a meaningful choice at existing prices between hand collection, containerized service, or self-hauling demonstrates that the bulk of business/industrial customers will view the alternatives as economically feasible only when confronted with substantial increases in the cost of containerized service. We regard this as legally sufficient to support Judge Griesa's view of which existing firms presently compete with WMI.

Nor is there support for WMI's claim that the power of Dallas or other municipalities to provide containerized service is a constraint on the prices charged by private firms serving the market so defined. Such an expansion of services would be essentially political since the City of Dallas is not a profit-seeking entrepreneur, and there is no evidence that such a decision is likely absent very substantial price increases by private haulers.

Indeed, for all of the smoke blown by WMI over Judge Griesa's market definition, internal TIDI documents fully support his findings. In October, 1980, TIDI completed a "Budget Questionnaire" that had been sent by Waste Resources. This required TIDI to list its major competitors by name, percentage of market, and kinds of equipment. TIDI listed only private haulers as competitors, and these provided almost exclusively containerized service. The major competitors included therein were five private firms with 83 trucks suitable for containerized service and two trucks suitable for hand collection. This questionnaire amply documents Judge Griesa's conclusions as to the product market as defined in terms of existing competitors.

The district court found the relevant geographic market to be Dallas County, plus a small fringe, but not Tarrant County, of which the city of Fort Worth is part. WMI argued below, and continues to argue here, that the relevant geographic market consists of the entire Dallas–Fort Worth metropolitan area. We disagree. Dallas and Fort Worth constitute a Single Standard Metropolitan Statistical Area based on the Office of Management and Budget's judgments regarding economic and social integration. Nevertheless, the bulk of existing Dallas and Fort Worth haulers presently operate exclusively in their respective cities. Only a few, situated near the border between Dallas and Tarrant Counties, do business in both. The area between the two cities is not heavily urbanized and some of the towns between them have granted long term exclusive franchises to waste collectors. Since the travel times between the more heavily populated cities is 45 to 50 minutes, daily service between both areas by the same trucks would be costly. Existing firms that presently compete with WMI are thus found for the most part only in Dallas County, a finding consistent with the TIDI Budget Questionnaire.

The district court found that TIDI's and ACS's combined share of the market so defined was 48.8%. This finding was based on a comparison of revenues of the various haulers within this market, and it is to that evidence that we now turn.

In the pre-acquisition Budget Questionnaire filled out by TIDI, it listed its major competitors and gave their approximate market shares. TIDI's responses and Judge Griesa's findings are compared as follows:

Name	TIDI's Estimate of Approximate % of Market	Judge Griesa's Finding of % of Market
ACS	26	22.5
Moore Ind.	15	11.1
BFI	10	7.2
AIDS	5	3.4
S.C.A.	4	2.5

TIDI calculated its own market share as 40–45%, as compared with the 26.3% found by Judge Griesa. The difference between the TIDI estimates and Judge Griesa's findings are accounted for by Judge Griesa's inclusion of municipal revenues from business/industrial waste disposal.

B. WMI's REBUTTAL

A post-merger market share of 48.8% is sufficient to establish *prima facie* illegality under *United States v. Philadelphia National Bank,* 374 U.S. 321, 83 S.Ct. 1715, 10 L.Ed.2d 915 (1963), and its progeny. That decision held that large market shares are a convenient proxy for appraising the danger of monopoly power resulting from a horizontal merger. *Id.* at 362–63, 83 S.Ct. at 1740–41. Under its rationale, a merger resulting in a large market share is presumptively illegal, rebuttable only by a demonstration that the merger will not have anticompetitive effects. *Id.* at 363, 83 S.Ct. at 1741. Thus in *United States v. General Dynamics Corp.,* 415 U.S. 486, 94 S.Ct. 1186, 39 L.Ed.2d 530 (1974), the Court upheld a merger of two leading coal producers because substantially all of the production of one firm was tied up in long-term contracts and its reserves were insubstantial. Since that firm's future ability to compete was negligible, the Court reasoned that its disappearance as an independent competitor could not affect the market.

WMI does not claim that 48.8% is too small a share to trigger the *Philadelphia National Bank* presumption. Rather, it argues that the presumption is rebutted by the fact that competitors can enter the Dallas waste hauling market with such ease that the finding of a 48.8% market share does not accurately reflect market power. WMI argues that it is unable to raise prices over the competitive level because new firms would quickly enter the market and undercut them.

* * *

* * *

The Supreme Court has never directly held that ease of entry may rebut a showing of *prima facie* illegality under *Philadelphia National Bank.* However, on several occasions it has held that appraisal of the impact of a proposed merger upon competition must take into account potential competition from firms not presently active in the relevant product and geographic markets.

* * *

Finally, the *Merger Guidelines* issued by the government itself not only recognize the economic principle that ease of entry is relevant to appraising the impact upon competition of a merger but also state that it may override all other factors. Where entry is "so easy that existing competitors could not succeed in raising prices for any significant period of time," the government has announced that it will usually not challenge a merger. *United States Department of Justice 1984 Merger Guidelines,* 46 Antitrust & Trade Reg.Rep. (BNA) No. 1169 Spec.Supp. § 3.3, at S–6. If the Department of Justice routinely considers ease of entry as relevant to determining the competitive impact of a merger, it may not argue to a court addressing the same issue that ease of entry is irrelevant. We conclude, therefore, that entry by potential competitors may be considered in appraising whether a merger will "substantially lessen competition."

Turning to the evidence in this case, we believe that entry into the relevant product and geographic market by new firms or by existing firms in the Fort Worth area is so easy that any anti-competitive impact of the merger before us would be eliminated more quickly by such competition than by litigation. See R. Bork, The Antitrust Paradox 222 (1978). Judge Griesa specifically found that individuals operating out of their homes can acquire trucks and some containers and compete successfully "with any other company." The government's response to this factual finding is largely to the effect that economies of scale are more important than Judge Griesa believed. As with his other findings of fact, however, this one is not clearly erroneous, as there are examples in the record of such entrepreneurs entering and prospering.

In any event, entry by larger companies is also relatively easy. At existing prices most Fort Worth and Dallas haulers operate within their own cities, but it is clear from the record that Fort Worth haulers could easily establish themselves in Dallas if the price of trash collection rose above the competitive level. Although it may be true that daily travel from Fort Worth to Dallas and back is costly, there is no barrier to Fort Worth haulers' acquiring garage facilities in Dallas permitting them to station some of their trucks there permanently or for portions of each week. The risks of such a strategy are low since substantial business can be assured through bidding on contracts even before such garage facilities are acquired, as one Fort Worth firm demonstrated by winning such a contract and then opening a facility in a Dallas suburb. That example can hardly be ignored by WMI or other Dallas haulers (not to mention their customers) in arriving at contract bids. The existence of haulers in Fort Worth, therefore, constrains prices charged by Dallas haulers, much as Falstaff constrained pricing by northeast breweries.

The fact that such entry has not happened more frequently reflects only the existence of competitive, entry-forestalling prices, as contemplated in *Falstaff*. 410 U.S. at 532–537, 93 S.Ct. at 1100–1103. We have no doubt that, if WMI were now to seek to acquire a major hauler in Fort Worth, the *Falstaff* decision would compel us to treat the Fort Worth hauler as a potential competitor of WMI. We perceive no reason why Fort Worth haulers should be treated as potential competitors in those circumstances but not in the present case.

Judge Griesa's conclusion that "there is no showing of any circumstances, related to ease of entry or the trend of the business, which promises in and of itself to materially erode the competitive strength of TIDI and ACS" is consistent with our decision. TIDI and ACS may well retain their present market share. However, in view of the findings as to ease of entry, that share can be retained only by competitive pricing. Ease of entry constrains not only WMI, but every firm in the market. Should WMI attempt to exercise market power by raising prices, none of its smaller competitors would be able to follow the price increases because of the ease with which new competitors would appear. WMI would then face lower prices charged by all existing competitors as well as entry by new ones, a condition fatal to its economic prospects if not rectified.

The government argues that consumers may prefer WMI's services, even at a higher price, over those of a new entrant because of its "proven track record." We fail to see how the existence of good will achieved through effective service is an impediment to, rather than the natural result of, competition. The government also argues that existing contracts bind most customers to a particular hauler and thereby prevent new entrants from acquiring business. If so, they also prevent the price increases until new entrants can submit competitive bids.

Given Judge Griesa's factual findings, we conclude that the 48.8% market share attributed to WMI does not accurately reflect future market power. Since that power is in fact insubstantial, the merger does not, therefore, substantially lessen competition in the relevant market and does not violate Section 7.

Reversed.

Questions

1. Most mergers that are on the borderline of legality under the Clayton Act simultaneously enlarge pricing power and create substantial operating efficiencies. The former is socially harmful, and the latter are socially beneficial. How does the Department of Justice attempt to balance the two factors in assessing the legality of a merger?

2. What steps must an expert take to measure market share for the Herfendehl–Herschman Index calculation? How accurate are such numbers? The most frequent dispute in applying the HHI calculation lies in the definition of the relevant market. A market defined narrowly will give merging firms with similar product lines the appearance of market power, while a broadly defined market will give the opposite appearance. What factors should an expert use to decide whether products compete? Should potential future product extensions, which might have become competing products, be considered? If so, how will this weigh into the HHI calculation? Do considerations such as these indicate that the seemingly logical and mathematical HHI really only covers a subjective determination with a mathematical facade?

3. Should antitrust law concern itself with mergers that create monopsonies? (A monopsony is the mirror image of monopoly—it exists when a buyer has enough market power to force suppliers of goods and labor to sell to it at less than competitive prices.) For example, should we be concerned if the only three major employers in a small town merge and extract extra tax concessions from the municipality (on threats of closing) that the constituent firms acting alone could not extract?

4. How can a target firm use the antitrust prohibitions to defend against a hostile bidder? Can a target firm buy a third firm that competes with the bidder in a particular merger to create antitrust problems? How can a bidder nullify the effects of a defensive acquisition?

SECTION 2. PREMERGER NOTIFICATION: THE HART-SCOTT-RODINO ANTITRUST IMPROVEMENTS ACT OF 1976

In 1976 Congress added section 7A to the Clayton Act to give antitrust agencies an opportunity to determine whether a *proposed* acquisition might violate the Clayton Act. The act, called the Hart-Scott-Rodino Antitrust Improvements Act of 1976, has a very low notification threshold and significantly affects the timing of acquisitions by imposing a waiting period before any qualifying merger can be consummated. The Hart-Scott-Rodino (HSR) notice also may tip off a target firm to an unwanted bid long before notice may be required under the federal securities acts.

15 U.S.C.A. § 7A

(a) Filing

Except as exempted pursuant to subsection (c) of this section, no person shall acquire, directly or indirectly, any voting securities or assets of any other person, unless both persons (or in the case of a tender offer, the acquiring person) file notification pursuant to rules under subsection (d)(1) of this section and the waiting period described in subsection (b)(1) of this section has expired, if—

> (1) the acquiring person, or the person whose voting securities or assets are being acquired, is engaged in commerce or in any activity affecting commerce;
>
> (2)(A) any voting securities or assets of a person engaged in manufacturing which has annual net sales or total assets of $10,000,000 or more are being acquired by any person which has total assets or annual net sales of $100,000,000 or more;
>
> (B) any voting securities or assets of a person not engaged in manufacturing which has total assets of $10,000,000 or more are being acquired by any person which has total assets or annual net sales of $100,000,000 or more; or
>
> (C) any voting securities or assets of a person with annual net sales or total assets of $100,000,000 or more are being acquired by any person with total assets or annual net sales of $10,000,000 or more; and
>
> (3) as a result of such acquisition, the acquiring person would hold—

(A) 15 per centum or more of the voting securities or assets of the acquired person, or

(B) an aggregate total amount of the voting securities and assets of the acquired person in excess of $15,000,000.

In the case of a tender offer, the person whose voting securities are sought to be acquired by a person required to file notification under this subsection shall file notification pursuant to rules under subsection (d) of this section.

(b) Waiting period; publication; voting securities

(1) The waiting period required under subsection (a) of this section shall—

(A) begin on the date of the receipt by the Federal Trade Commission and the Assistant Attorney General in charge of the Antitrust Division of the Department of Justice (hereinafter referred to in this section as the "Assistant Attorney General") of—

(i) the completed notification required under subsection (a) of this section, or

(ii) if such notification is not completed, the notification to the extent completed and a statement of the reasons for such noncompliance,

from both persons, or, in the case of a tender offer, the acquiring person; and

(B) end on the thirtieth day after the date of such receipt (or in the case of a cash tender offer, the fifteenth day), or on such later date as may be set under subsection (e)(2) or (g)(2) of this section.

(2) The Federal Trade Commission and the Assistant Attorney General may, in individual cases, terminate the waiting period specified in paragraph (1) and allow any person to proceed with any acquisition subject to this section, and promptly shall cause to be published in the Federal Register a notice that neither intends to take any action within such period with respect to such acquisition.

(3) As used in this section—

(A) The term "voting securities" means any securities which at present or upon conversion entitle the owner or holder thereof to vote for the election of directors of the issuer or, with respect to unincorporated issuers, persons exercising similar functions.

(B) The amount or percentage of voting securities or assets of a person which are acquired or held by another person shall be determined by aggregating the amount or percentage of such voting securities or assets held or acquired by such other person and each affiliate thereof.

(c) Exempt transactions

The following classes of transactions are exempt from the requirements of this section—

(1) acquisitions of goods or realty transferred in the ordinary course of business;

(2) acquisitions of bonds, mortgages, deeds of trust, or other obligations which are not voting securities;

(3) acquisitions of voting securities of an issuer at least 50 per centum of the voting securities of which are owned by the acquiring person prior to such acquisition;

* * *

(9) acquisitions, solely for the purpose of investment, of voting securities, if, as a result of such acquisition, the securities acquired or held do not exceed 10 per centum of the outstanding voting securities of the issuer;

(10) acquisitions of voting securities, if, as a result of such acquisition, the voting securities acquired do not increase, directly or indirectly, the acquiring person's per centum share of outstanding voting securities of the issuer;

* * *

(h) Disclosure exemption

Any information or documentary material filed with the Assistant Attorney General or the Federal Trade Commission pursuant to this section shall be exempt from disclosure under section 552 of Title 5, and no such information or documentary material may be made public, except as may be relevant to any administrative or judicial action or proceeding. Nothing in this section is intended to prevent disclosure to either body of Congress or to any duly authorized committee or subcommittee of the Congress.

* * *

The Federal Trade Commission promulgated rules to deal with, among other issues, five perceived problems in the statute. First, can an acquirer split up one transaction into many to avoid the requirements of the rule? The Federal Trade Commission, as the drafters of accounting rules and tax rules, had to formulate standards for integrating separate transactions. See rule 801.13. Second, what are the reporting obligations of an acquirer that initially purchases, and reports on, a toehold acquisition in a target and later follows up with a more substantial acquisition? Note the interplay of rules 801.1(h) and 801.20. Third, must an acquirer report $1,500 million asset or stock purchases? The statute sets itself a very low threshold for 15 percent stock or asset acquisitions. Compare section 7A(a)(3)(A) with rule 802.20. Fourth, how does the "size of person" test apply to a partnership formed solely for the purpose of making the acquisition? See rules 801.1(b) and 801.11(c). Fifth, how does an acquirer calculate the most significant aspect of the act, the waiting period? See rules 801.30 and 803.10.

RULES, REGULATIONS, STATEMENTS AND INTERPRETATIONS UNDER THE HART–SCOTT–RODINO ANTITRUST IMPROVEMENTS ACT OF 1976

16 C.F.R. §§ 801.1(b)(h), 801.11(d) & (e), 801.13, 801.30, 802.20 and 803.10 (1990).

§ 801.1 Definitions.

When used in the act and these rules—

* * *

(b) *Control.* The term "control" (as used in the terms "control(s)," "controlling," "controlled by" and "under common control with") means:

(1) *Either.* (i) Holding 50 percent or more of the outstanding voting securities of an issuer or

(ii) In the case of an entity that has no outstanding voting securities, having the right to 50 percent or more of the profits of the entity, or having the right in the event of dissolution to 50 percent or more of the assets of the entity; or

(2) Having the contractual power presently to designate 50 percent or more of the directors of a corporation, or in the case of unincorporated entities, of individuals exercising similar functions.

* * *

(h) *Notification threshold.* The term "notification threshold" means:

(1) Fifteen percent of the outstanding voting securities of an issuer, or an aggregate total amount of voting securities and assets of the acquired person valued in excess of $15 million;

(2) Fifteen percent of the outstanding voting securities of an issuer, if valued in excess of $15 million;

(3) Twenty-five percent of the outstanding voting securities of an issuer; or

(4) Fifty percent of the outstanding voting securities of an issuer.

* * *

§ 801.11 Annual net sales and total assets.

* * *

(d) No assets of any natural person or of any estate of a deceased natural person, other than investment assets, voting securities and other income-producing property, shall be included in determining the total assets of a person.

(e) Subject to the limitations of paragraph (d) of this section, the total assets of:

(1) An acquiring person that does not have the regularly prepared balance sheet described in paragraph (c)(2) of this section shall be, for acquisitions of each acquired person:

(i) All assets held by the acquiring person at the time of the acquisition,

(ii) Less all cash that will be used by the acquiring person as consideration in an acquisition of assets from, or in an acquisition of voting securities issued by, that acquired person (or an entity within that acquired person) and less all cash that will be used for expenses incidental to the acquisition, and less all securities of the acquired person (or an entity within that acquired person)

* * *

Examples: [A]ssume that A is a newly-formed company which is not controlled by any other entity. Assume also that A has no sales and does not have the balance sheet described in paragraph (c)(2) of this section.

1. A will borrow $105 million in cash and will purchase assets from B for $100 million. In order to establish whether A's acquisition of B's assets is reportable, A's total assets are determined by subtracting the $100 million that it will use to acquire B's assets from the $105 million that A will have at the time of the acquisition. Therefore, A has total assets of $5 million and does not meet the size-of-person test of section 7A(a)(2).

* * *

§ 801.13 Voting securities or assets to be held as a result of acquisition.

(a) *Voting securities.* (1) Subject to the provisions of § 801.15, and paragraph (a)(3) of this section, all voting securities of the issuer which will be held by the acquiring person after the consummation of an acquisition shall be deemed voting securities held as a result of the acquisition. The value of such voting securities shall be the sum of the value of the voting securities to be acquired, determined in accordance with § 801.10(a), and the value of the voting securities held by the acquiring person prior to the acquisition, determined in accordance with paragraph (a)(2) of this section.

(2) The value of voting securities of an issuer held prior to an acquisition shall be—

(i) If the security is traded on a national securities exchange or is authorized to be quoted in an interdealer quotation system of a national securities association registered with the United States Securities and Exchange Commission, the market price calculated in accordance with § 801.10(c)(1); or

(ii) If paragraph (a)(2)(i) of this section is not applicable, the fair market value determined in accordance with § 801.10(c)(3).

Examples: 1. Assume that acquiring person "A" holds $19 million of the voting securities of X, and is to acquire another $1 million of the same voting securities. Since under paragraph (a) of this rule all voting securities "A" will hold after the acquisition are held "as a result of" the acquisition, "A" will hold $20 million of the voting securities of X as a result of the acquisition. "A" must therefore observe the requirements of the act before making the acquisition, unless the present acquisition is exempt under section 7A(c), § 802.21 or any other rule.

(3) Voting securities held by the acquiring person prior to an acquisition shall not be deemed voting securities held as a result of that subsequent acquisition if:

(i) The acquiring person is, in the subsequent acquisition, acquiring only assets; and

(ii) The acquisition of the previously acquired voting securities was subject to the filing and waiting requirements of the act (and such requirements were observed) or was exempt pursuant to § 802.21.

(b) *Assets.* (1) All assets to be acquired from the acquired person shall be assets held as a result of the acquisition. The value of such assets shall be determined in accordance with § 801.10(b).

(2)(i) If the acquiring person has signed a letter of intent or entered into a contract or agreement in principle to acquire assets from the acquired person, and

(ii) Subject to the provisions of § 801.15, if the acquiring person has acquired from the acquired person within the 180 calendar days preceding the signing of such agreement any assets which are presently held by the acquiring person, and the acquisition of which was not previously subject to the requirements of the act or the acquisition of which was subject to the requirements of the act but they were not observed, then only for purposes of section 7A(a)(3)(B) and § 801.1(h)(1), both the acquiring and the acquired persons shall treat such assets as though they had not previously been acquired and are being acquired as part of the present acquisition. The value of any assets previously acquired which are subject to this paragraph shall be determined in accordance with § 801.10(b) as of the time of their prior acquisition.

Example: Acquiring person "A" proposes to make two acquisitions of assets from acquired person "B," 90 days apart, and wishes to determine whether notification is necessary prior to the second acquisition. For purposes of the percentage test of section 7A(a)(3)(A), "A" would hold only the assets it acquired in the second acquisition. For purposes of the $15 million test of section 7A(a)(3)(B), however, "A" must aggregate both of its acquisitions and must value each as of the time of its occurrence.

* * *

§ 801.20 Acquisitions subsequent to exceeding threshold.

Acquisitions meeting the criteria of section 7A(a), and not otherwise exempted by section 7A(c) or § 802.21 or any other of these rules, are subject to the requirements of the act even though:

(a) Earlier acquisitions of assets or voting securities may have been subject to the requirements of the act;

(b) The acquiring person's holdings initially may have met or exceeded a notification threshold before the effective date of these rules; or

(c) The acquiring person's holdings initially may have met or exceeded a notification threshold by reason of increases in market values or events other than acquisitions.

* * *

§ 801.30 Tender offers and acquisitions of voting securities from third parties.

(a) This section applies to:

(1) Acquisitions on a national securities exchange or through an interdealer quotation system registered with the United States Securities and Exchange Commission;

* * *

(3) Tender offers:

* * *

(5) All acquisitions (other than mergers and consolidations) in which voting securities are to be acquired from a holder or holders other than the issuer or an entity included within the same person as the issuer;

(6) Conversions; and

(7) Acquisitions of voting securities resulting from the exercise of options or warrants which are—

(i) Issued by the issuer whose voting securities are to be acquired (or by any entity included within the same person as the issuer); and

(ii) The subject of a currently effective registration statement filed with the United States Securities and Exchange Commission under the Securities Act of 1933.

(b) For acquisitions described by paragraph (a) of this section:

(1) The waiting period required under the act shall commence upon the filing of notification by the acquiring person as provided in § 803.10(a); and

(2) The acquired person shall file the notification required by the act, in accordance with these rules, no later than 5 p.m. eastern time on the 15th (or, in the case of cash tender offers, the 10th) calendar day following the date of receipt, as defined by § 803.10(a), by the Federal Trade Commission and Assistant Attorney General of the notification filed by the acquiring person. Should the 15th (or, in the case of cash tender offers, the 10th) calendar day fall on a weekend day or federal holiday, the notification shall be filed no later than 10 a.m. eastern time on the next following business day.

* * *

§ 802.20 Minimum dollar value

An acquisition which would be subject to the requirements of the act and which satisfies section 7A(a)(3)(A), but which does not satisfy section 7A(a)(3)(B), shall be exempt from the requirements of the act if as a result of the acquisition the acquiring person would not hold:

(a) Assets of the acquired person valued at more than $15 million; or

(b) Voting securities which confer control of an issuer which, together with all entities which it controls, has annual net sales or total assets of $25 million or more.

§ 803.10 Running of time.

(a) *Beginning of waiting period.* The waiting period required by the act shall begin on the date of receipt of the notification required by the act, in the manner provided by these rules (or, if such notification is not completed, the notification to the extent completed and a statement of the reasons for such noncompliance in accordance with § 803.3) from:

(1) In the case of acquisitions to which § 801.30 applies, the acquiring person;

(2) In the case of the formation of a joint venture or other corporation covered by § 801.40, all persons contributing to the formation of the joint venture or other corporation that are required by the act and these rules to file notification;

(3) In the case of all other acquisitions, all persons required by the act and these rules to file notification.

(b) *Expiration of waiting period.* (1) For purposes of section 7A(b)(1)(B), the waiting period shall expire at 11:59 p.m. Eastern Time on the 30th (or in the case of a cash tender offer, the 15th) calendar day (or if § 802.23 applies, such other day as that section may provide) following the beginning of the waiting period as determined under paragraph (a) of this section, unless extended pursuant to section 7A(e) and § 803.20, or section 7A(g)(2), or unless terminated pursuant to section 7A(b)(2) and § 803.11.

(2) Unless further extended pursuant to section 7A(g)(2), or terminated pursuant to section 7A(b)(2) and § 803.11, any waiting period which has been extended pursuant to section 7A(e)92) and § 803.20 shall expire at 11:59 p.m. Eastern Time—

(i) On the 20th (or, in the case of a cash tender offer, the 10th) day following the date of receipt of all additional information or documentary material requested from all persons to whom such requests have been directed (or, if a request is not fully complied with, the information and documentary material submitted and a statement of the reasons for such non-compliance in accordance with § 803.3), by the Federal Trade Commission or Assistant Attorney General, whichever requested additional information or documentary material, at the office designated in paragraph (c) of this section, or

(ii) As provided in paragraph (b)(1) of this section, whichever is later.

* * *

The HSR Waiting Period and the Confidentiality of HSR Filings

The most significant aspect of the Hart–Scott–Rodino Antitrust Improvements Act is the waiting period. If delay is a major concern of an acquiring party, the act can effect significant burdens. Once the Federal Trade Commission and the Department of Justice receive complete filings, the initial waiting period begins to run—fifteen days for cash tender offers and thirty days for all others. See § 7A(b)(1) and (e). If, upon a review of the completed filings of the constituent parties, the reviewing agencies determine that the proposed transaction has no anticompetitive effects, they must grant an early termination of the waiting period, if the parties so request. See Heublein, Inc. v. FTC, 539 F.Supp. 123 (D.Conn.1982). If an agency grants early termination, the names of the filing parties and the target are published, but the contents of the filing are not. See § 7A(b)(2). For most transactions the agencies complete their antitrust review within two weeks and terminate the waiting period soon thereafter.

Before the expiration of the waiting period the FTC or the DOJ may request additional documents or information (the "second request"), which automatically extends the initial waiting period until the requesting agency obtains "substantial compliance" with the request. § 7A(e)(1); rule 803.20(a)(1). Upon receipt of the additional information, an additional waiting period begins to run and expires at the end of the tenth day for cash tender offers, and the twentieth day for all others. See § 7A(1). The act thus favors cash tender offers in contested acquisitions. A person making a cash tender offer may be free to purchase shares fifteen to twenty-five days in advance of a person making an exchange tender offer. This bias in favor of cash stock acquisitions, and in favor of three-step transactions that use cash tender offers in the second stage, is substantial.

The initial Hart–Scott–Rodino filing and any second request filings are confidential. § 7A(h). Thus the premerger data are exempt from the Freedom of Information Act. However, under the section, information may be made public in an administrative or judicial proceeding, or disclosed to Congress or to a duly authorized committee or subcommittee of Congress. The FTC and DOJ staffs have agreed that parties will receive ten days' advance notice of such disclosures when possible or, at minimum, time to seek a protective order. See FTC, Formal Interpretation of the Premerger Notification Rules Establishing Policy with Regard to Disclosure of Premerger Notification Materials in Certain Subsequent Actions or Proceedings, 45 Fed.Reg. 21,215 (1980). The Hart–Scott–Rodino filings are not, without a protective order, exempt from discovery requests in litigation. There is nothing that limits the rights of a party in a private action challenging the proposed acquisition to gain access to the filing and accompanying documents through civil discovery proceedings. Two federal circuit courts of appeal have held, however, that state attorneys general, as members of the public, cannot obtain the materials. See, e.g., Lieberman v. FTC, 771 F.2d 32 (2d Cir.1985).

The act creates significant disincentives for hostile acquisitions. First, the act eliminates surprise in tender offers. Although the waiting period for hostile tender offers (an acquisition covered in rule 801.30) begins when the acquirer files its report (for all other acquisitions *both* parties to the transaction must file reports to start the waiting period), rule 801.30(b)(2) requires a *target* to file a report within ten days of a cash tender offer and within fifteen days of an exchange tender offer. Section 803.5 requires that the acquirer's filing in an 801.30 transaction include an affidavit that the acquirer has notified the target of the transaction. *In all hostile tender offers the target must receive advance notice of an acquisition so it can make its required filings.* This gives the target more time to defend against unwanted acquisitions and the option to disclose prematurely the bidder's intentions to the public or to other potential bidders. Second, the act's thirty-day waiting period significantly burdens street sweeps. See chapter 4, supra at 00. The waiting period, with notice to the target, stops the otherwise lightning-quick character of the technique.

Parties intent on avoiding early disclosure under the Hart–Scott–Rodino Act have attempted, with limited success, to use a variety of techniques to avoid making a Hart–Scott–Rodino filing until they must otherwise file under section 13(d) of the Williams Act. See chapter 4, supra at pages 335–352.

First, some acquirers have attempted to avoid buying the stock. For example, the selling shareholder agrees to a "lockup" option; that is, she agrees to sell her holdings at a fixed price after the waiting period expires. A broker agrees to reciprocal put and call options with the bidder in which the bidder gains the right to buy shares at a fixed price after the waiting period expires, and the broker gains the right to sell shares to the bidder after the waiting period expires. The FTC takes the position that these options are not legitimate methods of delaying a Hart–Scott–Rodino filing.

Second, acquirers have claimed exemptions under the act for acquisitions of up to 10 percent of their targets' securities for "investment only." § 7A(c)(9). At issue is how serious a bidder must be about a takeover before it loses the investment exception. Can an invester buy up to 10 percent under the exemption with an intent to "test the waters" for a possible takeover attempt? On the other hand, a bidder could take the opposite approach, filing Hart–Scott–Rodino notices on many targets in the hopes of disguising its intention to buy any one of them. Some bidders, for example, have filed well in advance of any firm intention to move on any particular target by (1) identifying several possible targets and filing on each (it must have a "good faith intention" to pass the reporting threshold on each), (2) waiting for the market effects of its announcement to dissipate (a filing is good for one year), and then (3) announcing a tender offer for one target.

The third method of avoidance is the formation of a partnership acquisition vehicle in which two partners hold 49 percent of the equity and a third partner holds 2 percent of the equity. Under the present act and rules the size-of-person test of a partnership is applied only to partners who "control" the partnership by having the right to over 50 percent of the profits. If the partnership is newly formed and has no controlling partner, it can make an acquisition without reporting if the total assets of the partnership are less than $10 million, after netting out the assets to be used in the acquisition. Rule 801.11(e). After the acquisition one of the partners buys out the others; this second acquisition of all of a partnership is not itself reportable. See 52 Fed.Reg. 20,058, 20,061 (May 29, 1987). The FTC has attacked such partnerships on the grounds that the nominal partner was not independent or that there was no reason for the structure other than avoidance of filing obligations. E.g., United States v. Tengelmann Warehandelsgesellschaft, 1989–1 Trade Cas. (CCH) ¶ 68,623 (D.C.1989).

Fourth, the acquirer just refuses to file the required Hart–Scott–Rodino Act notice, filing when it also files its Williams Act material and absorbing the Hart–Scott–Rodino Act penalties as a cost of the acquisition. Noncompliance may subject the violator to up to $10,000 in penalties for each day in violation of the act. § 7A(g)(1). Civil penalties have ranged from $200,000 to $750,000. E.g., United States v. Trump, 1988–1 Trade Cas. (CCH) ¶ 67,968 (D.D.C.1988) ($750,000 in civil penalties).

The FTC has proposed a number of recent rules changes to address some of these problems. In 53 Fed.Reg. 36,831–69 (Sept. 22, 1988) the FTC proposed a blanket exemption for all acquisitions that would result in the acquiring person holding 10 percent or less of an issuer's voting securities. In the alternative the FTC proposed to permit purchases under an escrow arrangement, pending review, or to free the acquirer from notifying the target for all purchases under 10 percent. More recently the FTC has proposed, in 54 Fed.Reg. 7960–64 (Feb. 14, 1989), several changes designed to require reports of acquisitions by newly formed partnerships without controlling partners.

The most startling aspect of the act is the poor correlation of its provisions with its ostensible purpose. Very few of the Hart–Scott–Rodino filings result in action by the FTC or the DOJ. See Clark, below. Moreover, when one of the government agencies does take corrective action, modifying the terms of a proposed merger to comport with the Clayton Act, the settlement does not preclude future suits. The government reserves the right to sue if it should change its mind, and in the *California v. American Stores Co.* case below the Supreme Court held that negotiated settlements between the government and constituent parties to a merger prompted by a Hart–Scott–Rodino Act filing do not divest private plaintiffs from suing to set aside a merger.

Clark,* Merger Enforcement at the Antitrust Division
58 Antitrust L.J. 329, 330–33 (1989).

* * *

First, a very brief statistical report about our merger activity last year. There were some 2,300 Hart–Scott–Rodino filings last year, which overstates somewhat the number of transactions, because, in some cases, there are more than one filing. There are always two notification forms filed, and sometimes four or more, depending upon how the transaction is structured.

The Division investigated and conducted formal investigations of approximately sixty transactions. The Federal Trade Commission conducted more than that; I don't have a specific number, but it was a larger number.

We issued about twenty-five second requests under Hart–Scott–Rodino of those sixty. In calendar year 1988, we challenged some twelve transactions as violations of Section 7. That includes mergers in which we announced publicly that we would challenge, but after which the parties withdrew from their agreement, so there was never an actual filing. By my count, the Federal Trade Commission challenged fourteen in the same way.

* * *

Most of the cases that we file are not litigated; the parties either withdraw from their transaction or we agree on a settlement of some

* John Clark was, at the time of the discussion, deputy director of operations, Antitrust Division, U.S. Dept. of Justice.

kind, perhaps a partial divestiture, that would satisfy the problems that we have. There were, however, four cases litigated last year, that is, Antitrust Division cases, in the district courts, two involving mergers of non-profit hospitals that present some very interesting issues, including a jurisdictional one involving the application of Section 7 to non-profit institutions. Those cases also involved, for one of the first times, litigation of the efficiencies issue. I think we may well see both cases appealed. The results were split, one in favor of the government, one in favor of defendants.

* * *

Question

Does the act give the government more advance warning than it could otherwise glean from normal press releases, news reports, stock exchange inquiries into stock price irregularities, and other Securities and Exchange Commission public filings or announcements?

CALIFORNIA v. AMERICAN STORES CO.

Supreme Court of the United States, 1990.
__ U.S. __, 110 S.Ct. 1853, 109 L.Ed.2d 240.

JUSTICE STEVENS delivered the opinion of the Court.

By merging with a major competitor, American Stores Co. (American) more than doubled the number of supermarkets that it owns in California. The State sued, claiming that the merger violates the federal antitrust laws and will harm consumers in 62 California cities. The complaint prayed for a preliminary injunction requiring American to operate the acquired stores separately until the case is decided, and then to divest itself of all of the acquired assets located in California.

* * *

American operates over 1,500 retail grocery stores in 40 States. Prior to the merger, its 252 stores in California made it the fourth largest supermarket chain in that State. Lucky Stores, Inc. (Lucky), which operated in seven Western and Midwestern States, was the largest, with 340 stores. The second and third largest, Von's Companies and Safeway Stores, were merged in December 1987.

On March 21, 1988, American notified the Federal Trade Commission (FTC) that it intended to acquire all of Lucky's outstanding stock for a price of $2.5 billion. The FTC conducted an investigation and negotiated a settlement with American. On May 31, it simultaneously filed both a complaint alleging that the merger violated § 7 of the Clayton Act and a proposed consent order disposing of the § 7 charges subject to certain conditions. Among those conditions was a requirement that American comply with a "Hold Separate Agreement" preventing it from integrating the two companies' assets and operations until after it had divested itself of several designated supermarkets.[2] American accepted the terms of the FTC's consent order. In early June, it acquired and paid for Lucky's stock and consummated a Delaware "short form merger."

Thus, as a matter of legal form American and Lucky were merged into a single corporate entity on June 9, 1988, but as a matter of practical fact their business operations have not yet been combined.

On August 31, 1988, the FTC gave its final approval to the merger. The next day California filed this action in the United States District Court for the Central District of California.

* * *

If we assume that the merger violated the antitrust laws, and if we agree with the District Court's finding that the conduct of the merged enterprise threatens economic harm to California consumers, the literal text of § 16 is plainly sufficient to authorize injunctive relief, including an order of divestiture, that will prohibit that conduct from causing that harm.

* * *

Our conclusion that a district court has the power to order divestiture in appropriate cases brought under § 16 of the Clayton Act does not, of course, mean that such power should be exercised in every situation in which the Government would be entitled to such relief under § 15. In a Government case the proof of the violation of law may itself establish sufficient public injury to warrant relief.

* * *

A private litigant, however, must have standing—in the words of § 16, he must prove "threatened loss or damage" to his own interests in order to obtain relief. Moreover, equitable defenses such as laches, or perhaps "unclean hands," may protect consummated transactions from belated attacks by private parties when it would not be too late for the Government to vindicate the public interest.

* * *

JUSTICE KENNEDY, concurring.

In agreement with our holding that § 16 of the Clayton Act does authorize divestiture as a remedy for violations of § 7 of the Clayton Act, I join the Court's opinion. I write further to note that both the respondents and various interested labor unions, the latter as *amici curiae,* have argued for a different result on the basis of the Hart–

---

2. Among other requirements, the Hold Separate Agreement obligated Alpha Beta to maintain separate books and records for the acquisition; to prevent any waste or deterioration of the acquired company's California operation; to refrain from replacing the company's executives; to assure that it is maintained as a viable competitor in California; to refrain from selling or otherwise disposing of the acquired company's warehouse, distribution or manufacturing facilities or any retail grocery stores in California; and to preserve separate purchasing for its retail grocery sales. 697 F.Supp. 1125, 1134 (C.D.Cal.1988).

Scott–Rodino Antitrust Improvements Act of 1976 (Clayton Act § 7A, as added and amended), 15 U.S.C. § 18a. See Brief for Respondents 47–48; Brief for United Food and Commercial International Union *et al.* as *Amici Curiae* 7–15. Although I do not believe that § 7A is controlling as an interpretation of the earlier enacted § 16, it may be of vital relevance in determining whether to order divestiture in a particular case.

Section 7A enables the Federal Government to review certain transactions that might violate § 7 before they occur. The provision, in brief, requires those contemplating an acquisition within its coverage to provide the Federal Trade Commission (FTC) with the information necessary for determining "whether such acquisition may, if consummated, violate the antitrust laws." 15 U.S.C. § 18a(d)(1). During the mandatory waiting period that follows the submission of this information, see § 18a(b)(1), the agency may decide, as it did in this case, to negotiate a settlement intended to eliminate potential violations.

The procedure may resolve antitrust disputes in a manner making it easier for businesses and unions to predict the consequences of mergers and to conform their economic strategies in accordance with the probable outcome.

The respondents, and the unions in their brief as *amici,* argue that a State or private person should not have the power to sue for divestiture under § 16 following a settlement approved by the FTC. They maintain that the possibility of such actions will reduce the Federal Government's negotiating strength and destroy the predictability that Congress sought to provide when it enacted § 7A. It is plausible, in my view, that allowing suits under § 16 may have these effects in certain instances. But the respondents and unions have identified nothing in § 7A that contradicts the Court's interpretation of § 7 and § 16. Section 7A, indeed, may itself contain language contrary to their position. See, *e.g.,* 15 U.S.C. § 18a(i)(1). Although Congress might desire at some point to enact a strict rule prohibiting divestiture after a negotiated settlement with the FTC, it has not done so yet.

The Court's opinion, however, does not render compliance with the Hart–Scott Rodino Antitrust Improvements Act irrelevant to divestiture actions under § 16. The Act, for instance, may bear upon the issue of laches. By establishing a time period for review of merger proposals by the FTC, § 7A may lend a degree of objectivity to the laches determination. Here the State received the respondents' § 7A filings in mid-April 1988, and so had formal notice of the parties' intentions well before completion of the merger or the settlement with the FTC. It elected not to act at that time, but now seeks a divestiture which, the facts suggest, would upset labor agreements and other matters influenced in important ways by the FTC proceeding. These considerations should bear upon the ultimate disposition of the case. As the Ninth Circuit stated:

"California could have sued several months earlier and attempted to enjoin the merger before the stock sale was completed. The Attorney General chose not to do so. California must accept the consequences of his choice." 872 F.2d 837, 846 (1989).

With the understanding that these consequences may include the bar of laches, I join the Court's decision.

Questions

1. Does the case balkanize antitrust enforcement? How does the case affect the incentive of parties to a combination to negotiate a settlement with the Federal Trade Commission or the Department of Justice? Must merger practitioners now get transactions cleared by both federal and state agencies? Or can practitioners effectively put state agencies and private parties on notice of an ongoing review by a federal agency to create a laches defense? If the FTC refuses to seek an injunction against a merger, what effect will the FTC action have on a federal court interpreting the Clayton Act in a private action? On a state court interpreting a state version of the Clayton Act in a private action?

The Supreme Court, in Cargill Inc. v. Monfort of Colorado, Inc., 479 U.S. 104, 107 S.Ct. 484, 93 L.Ed.2d 427 (1986), held that competitors could sue to challenge a merger only if they established "antitrust injury," which most competitors, who are not consumers, are unable to establish. Given the increased legal obstacles facing a competitor and the fact that a customer, whose standing is acknowledged, is unlikely to shoulder the significant expense of an antitrust challenge, nonfederal enforcement of the Clayton Act in the context of a friendly acquisition is ceded largely to the states. States' attorneys general have taken an increasingly aggressive position on the matter, due in large part to a reaction to the permissive enforcement policies of the Reagan administration. See City of Pittsburgh v. May Dept. Stores Co., 1986–2 Trade Cas. (CCH) ¶ 67,304 (1986) (the state forced divestitures in a transaction cleared by the federal authorities).

2. Could states pass their own Hart–Scott–Rodino acts as the next wave of antitakeover legislation? See *Edgar v. Mite* and *CTS Corp. v. Dynamics,* supra. What is the difference between a state HSR act and the Illinois statute in *Mite*?

SECTION 3. COLLUSION BETWEEN BIDDERS IN TENDER OFFERS

FINNEGAN v. CAMPEAU CORP.

United States Court of Appeals, Second Circuit, 1990.
915 F.2d 824.

CARDAMONE, CIR. J.:

* * * In March 1988 Federated was "put into play," that is, offered for sale to the highest bidder and a battle for its control between Macy's and Campeau began. At first the rival bidders pushed up the price of Federated stock with each submitting a bid one step higher than the other. In April 1988 it dawned on the contestants that constantly raising the price of the target company was economically disadvantageous for them. Consequently, they allegedly reached an understanding under which Macy's agreed to withdraw its latest bid and allow Campeau to acquire Federated. In exchange, Campeau agreed to permit Macy's to purchase two Federated divisions—I. Magnin and Bullock's Wilshire—and to pay Macy's $60 million to cover its legal and investment banking expenses. The difference between the $73.50 a share ultimately paid by Campeau to acquire Federated and Macy's withdrawn bid of $75.51 amounted to about $172 million. Whether Campeau's purchase was worth the price it had to pay is questionable in light of Campeau's present insolvent condition and Federated's Chapter 11 petition filed in the United States Bankruptcy Court in Cincinnati, Ohio.

* * *

In his complaint Finnegan charges that the agreement between Macy's and Campeau constitutes a conspiracy in violation of § 1 of the Sherman Act (Act), 15 U.S.C. § 1 (1988). Specifically, he asserts that Macy's and Campeau conspired to "refrain[ ] from bidding against each other for the purchase of the shares of common stock of Federated in order to supress [sic], . . . and eliminate competition in the market for Federated common stock and to cause the sale of said shares at a price lower than a competitive price."

* * *

Nevertheless, the doctrine of implied revocation provides a firm foundation for the district court's dismissal. Although the Williams Act, 82 Stat. 454, *codified* at 15 U.S.C. §§ 78m(d)–(e) & 78n(d)–(f) (1988), does not foreclose all antitrust claims arising in the context of market manipulation, we hold that the Sherman Act is implicitly repealed in the circumstances of the case at bar.

The three seminal Supreme Court cases, *Silver v. New York Stock Exchange*, 373 U.S. 341 (1963), *Gordon v. New York Stock Exchange*, 422 U.S. 659 (1975), and *United States v. National Association of Securities Dealers*, 422 U.S. 694 (1975), establish the rules for implied revocation of the antitrust laws in the field of securities regulation. To begin with, repeal "by implication is not favored and not casually to be allowed. Only where there is a 'plain repugnancy between the antitrust and regulatory provisions' will repeal be implied." *Gordon*, 422 U.S. at 682 (quoting *Philadelphia Nat'l Bank*, 374 U.S. at 350–51). The holdings in *Silver* and *Gordon* teach that antitrust laws do not come into play when they would prohibit an action that a regulatory scheme permits. *Strobl*, 768 F.2d at 27.

In *Silver*, the New York Stock Exchange denied its members' request for direct telephone connections to nonmembers located in Texas. Because the Securities and Exchange Commission (SEC) lacked authority to supervise the Stock Exchange's rules on direct telephone connections the antitrust laws were not revoked by implication. The holding in *Silver* was expressly limited to cases involving Stock Exchange rules and orders that lay outside the jurisdiction of the SEC, leaving open the possibility of implied revocation in other contexts. See 373 U.S. at 358 n. 12, 360. In *Gordon,* the Court examined the other context expressly left open in *Silver.* There the New York Stock Exchange ruling in dispute—establishing a system of fixed commission rates—was subject to regulation and approval by the SEC under § 19(b)(9) of the Securities Exchange Act of 1934 (1934 Act), 15 U.S.C. § 78s(b) (1988). 422 U.S. at 685. In *Gordon* the elements of implied repeal were met because allowing the antitrust laws to play a role in the area of commission rates would unduly interfere with the operation of the securities law.

Further, in *National Association of Securities Dealers,* implicit revocation with respect to certain sales and distribution restrictions used in marketing securities of mutual funds was found. The Supreme Court held that because the SEC had the power to authorize such restrictions on sales and distributions under § 22(f) of the Investment Company Act of 1940, 15 U.S.C. § 80a–22(f) (1988), and because there was "no way to reconcile the Commission's power to authorize these restrictions with the competing mandate of the antitrust laws," there was an implied repeal of the latter laws. 422 U.S. at 722. By way of contrast, in *Strobl* we found there was no inconsistency between the Commodity Exchange Act and the Sherman Act because price manipulation—a practice forbidden by the Sherman Act—was also forbidden by the Commodity Exchange Act. 768 F.2d at 27. As a consequence of the above decisions, repeal by implication may only be found where there is a conflict between the provisions of the antitrust and securities laws.

* * *

Section 14(d) of the statute grants to the SEC the authority to prescribe substantive rules and regulations setting forth information necessary to protect shareholders of target companies. Under § 14(d), a bidder for a public company whose shares are registered with the SEC under the 1934 Act must file a Schedule 14D–1 with the SEC on the date of the commencement of the tender offer. The disclosure requirements of Schedule 14D–1 and the language of the Williams Act contemplate agreements between bidders. Item 7 of Schedule 14D–1 reads:

> *Contracts, Arrangements, Understandings or Relationships with Respect to the Subject Company's Securities.* Describe any contract, arrangement, understanding or relationship ... between the bidder ... and any person with respect to any securities of the subject company (including ... joint ventures ...), naming the persons with whom such contracts, arrangements, understandings or relationships have been entered into....

17 C.F.R. § 240.14d–100 (1989).

Further, § 14(d)(2) of the 1934 Act, 15 U.S.C. § 78n(d)(2) (1988), reads:

When two or more persons act as a partnership, limited partnership, syndicate, or other group for the purpose of acquiring, holding, or disposing of securities of an issuer, such syndicate or group shall be deemed a "person" for purposes of this subsection.

Because disclosure is the means by which Congress sought to protect target shareholders, the prior provisions make clear that once information regarding an agreement between rival bidders has been revealed in a filing, the target company's shareholders have received the protection Congress and the SEC designed for them and there has been compliance with the Williams Act.

Recognizing the logical implication of the word "group" as anticipating the sort of bid made by Macy's and Campeau, appellant contends that these provisions authorize only those agreements made by bidders prior to engaging in a contest for control of a target company, not agreements made by rival bidders during the bidding process such as was the case here. We are unable to agree with this view because neither the Williams Act nor the SEC regulations make a distinction between joint bids made by parties prior to entering a battle for control of the target and those made by parties who are rival bidders at the outset. We would think the SEC justified in deeming an agreement such as that alleged here to be a joint bid and to require the parties to file amendments to their existing filings under Schedule 14D–1, see 17 C.F.R. § 240.14d–3(b) (1990). Further, joint bids are not that uncommon. For example, in 1984 Reliance Financial Services Corporation and Fisher Brothers jointly offered to purchase Walt Disney Productions, and Waste Management, Inc. and Genstar made a joint offer for SCA Services, Inc.

* * *

Congress drafted the Williams Act with language allowing joint bids for target companies and the SEC promulgated a regulation—Regulation 14D–1, 17 C.F.R. §§ 240.14d–1 through 240.14d–101 (1990)—that requires disclosure of agreements between bidders. In order for § 14(d) and the accompanying SEC regulation to function as intended, such agreements cannot be subject to suit under the antitrust laws; to permit such a suit would foster a direct conflict between the securities and antitrust laws. * * * We cannot presume that Congress has allowed competing bidders to make a joint bid under the Williams Act and the SEC's regulations and taken that right away by authorizing suit against such joint bidders under the antitrust laws.

The SEC also has the power to regulate tender offers under the antifraud provision of the same statute. Among the sections added to the 1934 Act by the Williams Act was § 14(e), 15 U.S.C. § 78n(e) (1988), which made it "unlawful for any person ... to engage in any fraudulent, deceptive, or manipulative acts or practices, in connection with any tender offer...."

* * *

The SEC is able to regulate agreements between bidders by virtue of its authority to define fraudulent, deceptive or manipulative practices and to prescribe means to prevent such practices. 15 U.S.C. § 78n(e). Through its power to prohibit fraudulent activity, the SEC has supervisory authority over the submission of joint bids or other agreements in the corporate auction contest. *Cf. National Ass'n of Sec. Dealers,* 422 U.S. at 726–28 (SEC election not to initiate restrictive regulations constituted administrative oversight). Although such agreements are not defined as deceptive practices under the regulations, the fact that they must be disclosed under Regulation 14D-1 clearly implies that the SEC contemplated their existence. That the SEC has chosen not to prohibit agreements between rival bidders as fraudulent or manipulative practices once shareholders are properly informed of them, does not reduce the SEC's supervisory authority over such agreements.

Consequently, because the SEC has the power to regulate bidders' agreements under § 14(e), * * *, and has implicitly authorized them by requiring their disclosure under Schedule 14D-1 as part of a takeover battle, * * * to permit an antitrust suit to lie against joint takeover bidders would conflict with the proper functioning of the securities laws.

* * *

A further though lesser conflict may also be seen between the antitrust laws and the Williams Act. It surfaces in the legislative policy of maintaining neutrality among bidders, shareholders and target company management. Congress realized "that takeover bids should not be discouraged because they serve a useful purpose in providing a check on entrenched but inefficient management." S.Rep. No. 550, 90th Cong., 1st Sess. 3–4 (1967). If the antitrust laws were applied to prohibit agreements between rival bidders, it would discourage potential bidders from making a tender offer. Once more than one bidder entered the fray for control of a target company, the shareholders of that company could use the antitrust laws to force a fight to the last ditch, notwithstanding that the bidders could agree on terms more advantageous to themselves. Certainly this would discourage takeover activity—an end Congress sought to avoid in enacting the Williams Act. * * *

Here, the application of the antitrust laws would upset the balance among incumbent management, target shareholders and bidders which Congress sought to achieve through the Williams Act. Allowing antitrust suits to rule out agreements between rival bidders would give target shareholders undue advantage in the takeover context and discourage such activity. Fewer takeover attempts ultimately favor incumbent management whose entrenched position is thereby less subject to challenge. * * *

Question

As a policy question, should antitrust statutes apply to contestants in an ongoing auction for a target? To potential bidders who meet to discuss a future acquisition of a target? Who are the "victims" of such collusion? Are the victims better or worse off with a prohibition on collusion between bidders?

SUBCHAPTER B. FOREIGN ACQUISITIONS OF UNITED STATES CORPORATIONS THAT "IMPAIR NATIONAL SECURITY"—THE EXON–FLORIO AMENDMENT

OMNIBUS TRADE AND COMPETITIVENESS ACT OF 1988

50 U.S.C.A. § 2170.

§ 2170. Authority to review certain mergers, acquisitions, and takeovers

(a) Investigations

The President or the President's designee may make an investigation to determine the effects on national security of mergers, acquisitions, and takeovers proposed or pending on or after August 23, 1988 by or with foreign persons which could result in foreign control of persons engaged in interstate commerce in the United States. If it is determined that an investigation should be undertaken, it shall commence no later than 30 days after receipt by the President or the President's designee of written notification of the proposed or pending merger, acquisition, or takeover as prescribed by regulations promulgated pursuant to this section. Such investigation shall be completed no later than 45 days after such determination.

(b) Confidentiality of information

Any information or documentary material filed with the President or the President's designee pursuant to this section shall be exempt from disclosure under section 552 of Title 5 and no such information or documentary material may be made public, except as may be relevant to any administrative or judicial action or proceeding. Nothing in this subsection shall be construed to prevent disclosure to either House of Congress or to any duly authorized committee or subcommittee of the Congress.

(c) Action by the President

Subject to subsection (d) of this section, the President may take such action for such time as the President considers appropriate to suspend or prohibit any acquisition, merger, or takeover, of a person engaged in interstate commerce in the United States proposed or pending on or after August 23, 1988 by or with foreign persons so that such control will not threaten to impair the national security. The

President shall announce the decision to take action pursuant to this subsection not later than 15 days after the investigation described in subsection (a) of this section is completed. The President may direct the Attorney General to seek appropriate relief, including divestment relief, in the district courts of the United States in order to implement and enforce this section.

(d) Findings of the President

The President may exercise the authority conferred by subsection (c) of this section only if the President finds that—

(1) there is credible evidence that leads the President to believe that the foreign interest exercising control might take action that threatens to impair the national security, and

(2) provisions of law, other than this section and the International Emergency Economic Powers Act (50 U.S.C. 1701–1706), do not in the President's judgment provide adequate and appropriate authority for the President to protect the national security in the matter before the President.

The provisions of subsection (d) of this section shall not be subject to judicial review.

(e) Factors to be considered

For purposes of this section, the President or the President's designee may, taking into account the requirements of national security, consider among other factors—

(1) domestic production needed for projected national defense requiremements,

(2) the capability and capacity of domestic industries to meet national defense requirements, including the availability of human resources, products, technology, materials, and other supplies and services, and

(3) the control of domestic industries and commercial activity by foreign citizens as it affects the capability and capacity of the United States to meet the requirements of national security.

(f) Report to the Congress

If the President determines to take action under subsection (c) of this section, the President shall immediately transmit to the Secretary of the Senate and the Clerk of the House of Representatives a written report of the action which the President intends to take, including a detailed explanation of the findings made under subsection (d) of this section.

In December 1988 the president delegated his authority under section 5021 to investigate and ultimately block foreign acquisitions that threaten to impair national security to the interagency Committee on Foreign Investment in the United States (CFIUS). CFIUS, created earlier by a 1975 executive order, is chaired by the Secretary of the Treasury and is composed of representatives of the Departments of Treasury, State, Defense, Commerce, and Justice, the Office of the U.S. Trade Representative, the Office of Management and Budget, and the Council of Economic Advisors. See Regulations Pertaining to Mergers, Acquisitions, and Takeovers by Foreign Persons, 54 Fed.Reg. 29,744 (1989). Regulations implementing section 5021 were proposed by the Department of Treasury on July 11, 1989. Id. The proposed regulations adopt a function approach to the question of foreign control: Control is defined as the power (actual or potential) to formulate, direct, or decide matters affecting United States business, regardless of the percentage of shares owned or controlled by the foreign entity.

SPIEGEL & BERG, THE NATIONAL SECURITY TEST FOR FOREIGN ACQUISITIONS, MERGERS AND ACQUISITIONS

32, 34, 36–37 (Nov./Dec. 1989).

* * *

Transactions that are potentially subject to notice under the proposed regulations are those resulting in the transfer of actual or potential control of a "U.S. person" to a "foreign person." A "U.S. person" includes any entity that engages in an ongoing business activity in U.S. interstate commerce, irrespective of the nationality of the individuals controlling it. A "foreign person" is defined as any foreign national or any entity over which control is or could be exercised by a foreign interest.

* * *

Transactions that do not qualify as reviewable acquisitions under the proposals include:

- Purchases of securities of a U.S. person solely for investment, if the foreign person holds 10 percent or less of the outstanding securities;
- Purchases made directly by a financial entity in the ordinary course of business for its own account, provided that a significant portion of that business does not involve the acquisition of entities;
- Acquisitions of assets such as inventory, real estate, or equipment; and
- Acquisitions of voting securities by a securities underwriter.

Despite the publication of the guidelines in the proposed regulations, the key term "national security" remains undefined. The commentary to the proposed regulations adopts the interpretation found in the congressional Conference Report to the Omnibus Trade and Competitiveness Act, which states simply that the "term 'national security' is intended to be interpreted broadly without limitation to particular industries," allowing the president or his designee to review transactions on a case-by-case basis.

The only guidance offered regarding the interpretation of "national security" appears in the commentary to the proposed regulations. It states that the "intent of the regulations is to indicate that notice, while voluntary, (is) clearly appropriate when, for example, a company is being acquired that provides products or key technologies essential to the U.S. defense industrial base." The commentary also states that the proposed regulations do not require that notices be submitted "in cases where the entire output of a company to be acquired consists of products and/or services that clearly have no special relation to national security."

* * *

Strategic considerations are central to the Exon–Florio process, regardless of whether the transaction is friendly or hostile. From the bidder's perspective, it is absolutely critical to consider Exon–Florio well in advance of commencing a hostile tender offer. * * * The following commentary identifies several strategic considerations from the bidder's perspective, but it must be emphasized that, in practice, every case will be highly fact-specific.

At one extreme, a bidder might decide not to contact or file notice with CFIUS at any time. The advantages are maintaining secrecy before launching the bid and not unnecessarily bringing the transaction to the attention of a government agency. Obviously, this strategy would be pursued only if the bidder were highly confident that, if investigated, the transaction would survive scrutiny under Exon–Florio. If the bidder miscalculates, it risks an investigation while the tender offer is underway and an order either prohibiting consummation of the transaction or requiring divestiture. A particularly troublesome disadvantage of this strategy is the ability of CFIUS, or the President, to investigate the deal at any future time.

At the other extreme, a bidder could file with CFIUS before launching the offer. The obvious disadvantage is a lack of secrecy. Indeed, CFIUS' own regulations permit the committee to request information from the "non-notifying party," i.e., the target company, and there is reason to believe that CFIUS will, in fact, contact the "non-notifying party" in every instance. Moreover, upon learning of the filing, the target may have obligations under the securities laws to disclose the information, if material, to the public. Although an early filing would eliminate the risks of giving notice (i.e., unexpected investigation or an order prohibiting the transaction), only in a rare case would it be worth the risks in the context of the hostile bid.

A middle-of-the-road strategy that might be employed in many routine cases would be to commence the tender offer and file with CFIUS before closing the transaction. Additionally, the bidder could structure the transaction so that the offer is conditional upon no investigation by CFIUS and/or no prohibitive action by the President. This option would preserve secrecy and, at the same time, avoid the problem of being contractually committed to purchase securities from shareholders while legally prevented from doing so. It also would foreclose an investigation and divestiture order in the future, eliminating the possibility that the bidder will have to divest later, possibly at unfavorable prices.

On the other hand, the bidder could make a post-commencement, preclosing filing with the offer not conditioned on any particular result under Exon–Florio. This strategy might be useful if only certain limited assets or business segments are implicated by the statute, especially where they are not central to the acquisition as a whole and can be divested easily, if necessary.

* * *

A related strategy would be to commence the tender offer and file the CFIUS notice only after closing. A favorable determination on the basis of this filing would foreclose the possibility of review at a future date, possibly by a less hospitable administration.

Target companies in hostile bids have a number of strategic issues to consider. A target has a strong incentive to file a notice under the Exon–Florio provision as a delay tactic in a hostile bid. While the pendency of Exon–Florio filing would not, in itself, legally prevent consummation of the transaction, it could, as a practical matter, lead to modification or withdrawal of the proposal, due to market exposure on the part of the bidder, or uncertainty among arbitrage holders who must tender in order for the offer to succeed.

In most cases, a target would want to file a notice with CFIUS as soon as possible. The proposed regulations provide that either party may submit notice of a "proposed or completed acquisition." Since the proposed regulations do not specify what event triggers a "proposed acquisition," a target might file a notice as soon as it has credible evidence of a contemplated takeover attempt. On the other hand, if the nature of the "national security" assets in question make Exon Florio review a potential "showstopper," the target may want to delay initiation of the review until the most opportune time. As far as antitakeover planning is concerned, many companies undoubtedly will consider the Exon–Florio defense as part of their overall defense arsenals. For example, a potential target could purchase, as part of its inventory of assets, certain assets that raise national security implications. Similar defensive techniques have been employed through the purchase of insurance companies and radio or television stations, where government approval of such acquisitions is a prerequisite to the completion of a tender offer. The difficulty in identifying iron-clad "national security" assets that will fit this defense strategy creates some degree of uncertainty, however.

Another consideration in a potential target's anti-takeover planning is its relationships with members of Congress and with member agencies of CFIUS. As noted, unless the CFIUS decision to approve a transaction is unanimous, the committee must submit a report to the President setting forth the differing views. Thus, a target with a valid Exon–Florio defense should consider contacting CFIUS member agencies and key members of Congress to ensure that its case receives appropriate attention.

This is important because CFIUS, although chaired by the Department of Treasury, is made up of eight separate agencies, each with its own perspective. A CFIUS consensus is reached by hammering out the differences, both political and substantive, between agencies that harbor views as diverse as the Office of Management and Budget and the Department of Defense. It should be kept in mind that each of these agencies has its own constituencies, both in the Congress and among the groups whose interests the agency oversees. A successful strategy within the CFIUS Exon–Florio process depends largely upon the identification of arguments of central importance to an agency's mission and contact with appropriate staff and officials to ensure that these arguments are fully understood and become part of the interagency deliberation.

* * *

Even in a friendly deal, the parties should be aware that a third-party business competitor, while lacking standing to file a notice itself, could appeal to members of Congress to put pressure on member agencies to trigger a review of a transaction, whether completed or proposed.

* * *

Questions

1. How broad is the concept of "national security"? Does it include, among other things, the competitive position of domestic industries, or is it limited to the maintenance of a facility for effective national defense? Neither the act nor the proposed regulations attempt to define the concept, and the legislative history makes it clear that Congress intended the terms to be applied broadly. In its commentary accompanying the proposed regulations the Treasury Department identified only toys and games, food products, hotels and restaurants, and legal services as products unrelated to national security.

2. How easily can the act be misused by protectionists in this country to stop foreign investment in American industry? Or by target managers defending against an unwanted takeover? Statistics reveal that CFIUS is more likely to conduct a formal investigation if the attempted takeover is hostile than if it is friendly. Conway & Savarino, Defense Strategies to Protect against Foreign Investment, Nat.L.J. at S11 (Sept. 25, 1989).

The act has added a new term to the takeover defense arsenal—the "Pentagon ploy." In a Pentagon ploy, the target board lobbies the Department of Defense for support in the firm's push for a formal CFIUS investigation. The Department of Defense has representatives on CFIUS who will vote on whether to conduct a formal investigation and, ultimately, whether to recommend to the President that the attempted takeover should be stopped. Moreover, the Defense Department can block an acquisition on its own by revoking a defense contractor's security clearance, significantly devaluing the firm by diminishing its earning potential. If a firm cannot use the Pentagon ploy because it does not have a division engaged in defense industry contracting (a "black program" division), can the firm acquire a defense contractor just to defeat a foreign takeover?

In a related ploy a firm can use the United States export control laws and regulations that prevent the transfer of technical data from a defense contractor to a foreigner. E.g., Arms Export Control Act of 1976, 22 U.S.C.A. § 2751 et seq. The Export Administration Regulation and the International Traffic in Arms Regulations, enforced by the secretary of state and the secretary of commerce, respectively, treat the acquisition of a United States corporation by a non-United States corporation as an export of the technology of the United States to the nation of the acquirer. E.g., Export Administration Regulations, 15 C.F.R. § 768 (1989); International Traffic in Arms Regulations, 22 C.F.R. § 121 (1988).

3. How should foreign companies with substantial capital investment in the United States be treated? What of companies with significant investments in many countries, or United States corporations with most of their operations in foreign countries? Should the act focus on place of incorporation, locus of decision making, or bulk of operations? How do your answers to these questions affect your answer to question 1? Can a foreign acquirer pass muster by erecting a "blind trust" to insulate a defense subsidiary from parental control?

Congressional Inadvertence?

The Exon–Florio provision, which was a part of the Defense Production Act, lapsed in 1990 because Congress failed to reauthorize the act. The Treasury announced that the Committee on Foreign Investment in the United States "will continue to receive voluntary notices" of acquisitions subject to Exon–Florio and that "persons wishing to file notices with CFIUS should continue to be guided by the proposed regulations." 5 Corp. Counsel Weekly (BNA) 6 (Nov. 14, 1990).

Chapter Nine

DELEVERAGING: WORKOUTS AND BANKRUPTCY REORGANIZATIONS

Introduction

In the 1980s many of our largest corporations replaced significant amounts of their outstanding equity with debt. See Staff Report, supra at page 947. The methods of equity replacement varied: In a leveraged buyout an acquiring corporation purchases stock of a target corporation in either a hostile or a friendly takeover; in a debt-financed asset acquisition an acquiring corporation purchases the assets of a target corporation (which liquidates); in a debt-financed share repurchase a publicly held corporation borrows funds and uses the proceeds to purchase its own stock; in a debt-financed extraordinary dividend a publicly held corporation borrows funds and uses the proceeds to pay dividends to shareholders in excess of current earnings on equity.

As the eighties progressed, the financing became more and more extreme. In the early eighties a leveraged buyout had debt coverage of 2:1 (roughly, projected earnings were twice interest obligations on debt). Financial theorists changed the relevant source of debt coverage from earnings (which reflect noncash payments such as depreciation) to various measures of pure cash flow. The new theories significantly diluted the basic coverage ratio of 2:1, and by the mid-eighties the required coverage ratio itself drifted downward to 1:1. Finally, by the late eighties investment bankers jettisoned the requirement that debt instruments pay interest currently and in cash. If the leverage in a deal was too great to permit interest to be paid, investors allowed issuers to defer paying interest for several years. Original issue discount, zero coupon, deferred coupon and pay-in-kind became the lexicon of a pay-later generation of debt instruments. Please review the securities issued in the RJR Nabisco buyout, supra at pages 592–604. See also chapter 7, supra at pages 966–68.

Slight errors in the projections of business cash flow meant severe financial distress. In 1988 Federated Stores Inc. bought Campeau Corporation, and later in 1990 Federated filed a Chapter 11 bankruptcy petition. Several other leveraged firms are also in bankruptcy—Revco,

D.S., Inc., Fruehauf, Dart Drugs, LTV, and Resorts International, among others. Numerous other debt-laden companies are scrambling to deleverage in order to avoid Chapter 11. At the heart of their efforts is a renegotiation with their debt holders. Successful renegotiations are known as workouts. In workout negotiations no term of outstanding debt is exempt; principal amount, interest rate, and maturity are all on the table. An issuer offers cash or a swap of new securities for outstanding debt in order to reduce its overall debt service requirements. Restrictive covenants in trust indentures are the subject of consent solicitations in which issuers seek permission to eliminate the covenants.

Workouts are negotiated in the context of the threat of bankruptcy proceedings. Insolvent businesses that choose bankruptcy have the fundamental choice of a liquidation under Chapter 7 of the federal Bankruptcy Code or a reorganization under Chapter 11 of the code. Chapter 11 is favored because it preserves the value of an ongoing business that has stable cash flow potential. An understanding of the effect of these sections on all the parties to a corporation teetering on the edge of insolvency is therefore necessary to an understanding of the nature of any workouts that occur outside bankruptcy. The first part of this chapter focuses on the rights of creditors outside bankruptcy, and the second part focuses on Chapter 11 proceedings.

J. ANDERSON, CHAPTER 11 REORGANIZATIONS 1-1 TO 1-3
(1983)

Reorganization law deals with the rehabilitation of financially troubled business enterprises. Such enterprises are normally owned by *debtors*, i.e., corporations, partnerships, individuals, or any other entities eligible to file for relief under the Bankruptcy Code. The reorganization system seeks to address and resolve three problem areas facing any distressed entity: (1) what financial decisions and actions must be made to make the troubled debtor economically sound; (2) what readjustments of the rights between creditors and stockholders must be achieved to make the rehabilitation fair to all parties; and (3) if revival of the business is impossible so that it cannot continue to operate, how must the liquidation of the debtor's assets proceed so that it will be orderly and achieve a maximum recovery for all interested parties? In essence, reorganizations are the processes by which financial decisions are implemented through legal mechanisms in attempts to produce stable, rejuvenated businesses.

When a company cannot pay its debts as they mature, what alternatives are available to stablize and then rehabilitate its finances? Obviously, the debtor can approach its creditors and negotiate a *workout*. Generally, a workout is an agreement between a debtor and its creditors to gain an extension of time within which to make payments, or to reduce (compromise) the amounts owed, or both. If the workout is unsuccessful, the debtor always has the alternatives to begin selling assets to gain liquidity or to sell the business as a whole. Of course, if a workout is unavailable, and if the sale of assets is impossible or impractical, the debtor must normally seek relief under the Bankruptcy Code. Then, the available choices are a liquidation under Chapter 7 or a reorganization (or a more orderly liquidation) under Chapter 11.

Generally, where the business has substantial assets or is capable of generating substantial profits from future operations, liquidation under Chapter 7 is not the most palatable alternative. Even if a liquidation proves to be the only ultimate alternative, most businesses of a substantial size will benefit more by a slow and orderly liquidation via Chapter 11 under the supervision of the debtor or creditors' committee than by a rapid liquidation under Chapter 7. Those having a stake in the business are generally more knowledgeable about the assets to be sold and have more incentive to enhance recovery through Chapter 11. Thus, if a liquidation is the debtor's only alternative, an orderly liquidating reorganization may be preferable to a forced liquidation under the provisions of Chapter 7, especially since a trustee is normally appointed under Chapter 7. A trustee may not have requisite experience with the debtor's assets to ably market them, nor the greatest desire to gain the maximum recovery from them.

Moreover, the assets of the business may be worth far more through continued operations as compared to what the assets will realize at a quick sale. Further, intangible benefits such as goodwill, tax losses which may be carried forward, key personnel, and beneficial executory contracts may be lost through a forced liquidation under Chapter 7, whereas the same intangible benefits may be preserved through a reorganization for the benefit of both the debtor and its creditors.

Where reorganization before the bankruptcy court is the soundest financial alternative, certain principles emerge. First, the normal *race of diligence* amongst creditors to obtain payments from the debtor or foreclose on the debtor's property must be halted in order to maintain the status quo.[7] The decision to reorganize and the form which the reorganization must take cannot be made until there has been a reasonable opportunity to determine the restructuring which will be most fair and advantageous to all parties. To preserve the debtor's business as a going concern, while readjusting the rights of all stakeholders, the judicial exercise of certain power and authority is usually required to maintain the economic nucleus of the debtor's business. Such powers are conferred by law upon the bankruptcy court and include the power:

---

7. An automatic stay is provided under § 362 of the Bankruptcy Code, which prohibits the commencement or continuation of any acts against the debtor or the property of his or her estate, and especially those acts to collect from the debtor, foreclose upon property, obtain possession of property, seize property, or generally take any detrimental action against the debtor and his or her property. *See* 11 USC § 362.

1. To restrain secured creditors, taxing authorities, landlords, and others from seizing property or cancelling beneficial contracts

2. To allow the debtor to borrow money and secure the borrowings by liens on the debtor's assets equal or superior to the liens of existing creditors

3. To permit the debtor to propose in the plan various means of recapitalization, including extensions, moratoria, compositions, exchanges of debt for equity, and such other financial readjustments as may be necessary to return the debtor to the business world in a stable and profitable condition

4. To conform and bind any dissenting creditors to reorganization plans acceptable and beneficial to a majority of creditors, after full disclosure of pertinent facts and after a voting process in which creditors may have a substantial voice in the ultimate plan that gains judicial approval

These judicial powers must be invoked where necessary, and especially where the parties to the reorganization cannot agree fully among themselves on all financial and legal decisions. To further enhance the debtor's ability to readjust the rights of stakeholders, a final reorganization principle governs the valuation of the distressed businesses and their assets. If market value is applied to value a debtor's business and its assets in determining their disposition, the recovery and rights of junior interests such as junior lienholders, unsecured creditors, and equity security holders may be eroded. Forced sales during unfavorable market conditions may preclude recovery by junior interests, and the reorganization laws foster protection from forced sales in recessionary economic climates. To fulfill the spirit of the statutory reorganization provisions, reorganization values must generally be used as substitutes for traditional market values.

* * *

SUBCHAPTER A. WORKOUTS

The Participants in the Renegotiation

CIERI, HEIMAN, HENZE, JENKS, KIRSCHNER, RILEY, & SULLIVAN, AN INTRODUCTION TO LEGAL AND PRACTICAL CONSIDERATIONS IN THE RESTRUCTURING OF TROUBLED LEVERAGED BUYOUTS

45 Bus. Lawyer 333, 337–47 (Nov.1989).

THE CAPITAL STRUCTURE OF AN LBO COMPANY

As the name suggests, the capital structure of an LBO company is leveraged. In most LBOs, the total equity investment is typically ten to fifteen percent of the company's capitalization, with the balance being a combination of senior and subordinated debt. In the Revco LBO, for example, the total purchase price was $1.3 billion, of which approximately $1.1 billion was debt. In the $6.5 billion LBO of Beatrice in 1986, new equity investment was $600 million, or approximately nine percent of the purchase price. As was reflected by the balance sheets of Revco and Beatrice immediately subsequent to their respective LBOs, the debt-to-equity ratio of an LBO company is significantly greater than the ratio historically considered appropriate.

The capital structure of an LBO typically consists of three levels: senior indebtedness, which is secured debt that provides a majority of the financing; equity, which typically means only common stock; and mezzanine financing, which encompasses everything between the senior debt and the equity, usually a variety of junk bonds or one or more classes of preferred stock.

Senior Debt

In an LBO, the secured senior debt may take a variety of forms and, depending on the transaction, represents approximately fifty percent to sixty percent of the financing. The usual sources of senior debt are banks, insurance companies, and employee stock ownership plans.[28] Typically, senior debt is fully collateralized by the assets of the LBO company and may be structured as a long-term note or a short-term revolving line of credit that is tied to the value of the assets, decreasing or increasing as the value of the assets fluctuates. It may also include a receivables facility. Senior debt holders have often been encouraged to obtain unsecured debt as part of a financing "package" or "strip." In addition, senior debt holders are often given an equity position in the company, through common stock with warrants or some other type of contingent interest as an equity kicker, with the intent that they will be able to share in some of the rewards of the LBO if it is successful, but with the risk that, if the LBO fails, their equity interests will be valueless and their debt positions subject to challenge.[30]

Since the purchase price should be, at least in theory, the current fair market value of the LBO company's assets, including good will, the amount of the senior debt should not exceed a certain percentage of the fair market value of the LBO company's assets. Senior debt is also frequently protected by interest rate caps, swaps, or fixed rates on subordinated debt, as well as dividend limitations.[31] Furthermore,

28. An employee stock ownership plan ("ESOP") is often a participant because of the tax benefits other lenders obtain by funnelling funds through the ESOP. . . .

30. The claims of senior lenders could be challenged on several grounds, including as fraudulent conveyances, as claims that should be equitably subordinated, or as preferences. . . .

31. Interest rate caps are becoming increasingly popular as the participants in an LBO attempt to hedge against significant increases in rates. Typically, the borrower purchases an interest rate cap by paying a fee to a bank in exchange for a promise by the bank to pay to the borrower enough to cover the "excess" interest in the event rates exceed a certain level. The bank will protect itself by investing in the Eurodollar futures market and the Treasury securities market, where rising interest rates would generate enough of a profit to pay the "excess" interest. In the RJR–Nabisco LBO, KKR purchased interest rate caps for approximately $6 billion of its senior debt, thereby assuring that its interest rate would not rise more than two percent. The reported price for the caps was approximately $500,000 per $100 mil-

senior lenders tend to utilize strict underwriting standards for determining which LBOs to fund.

Recent transactions, however, have revealed some problems with historical assumptions regarding the safety of senior LBO debt. First, bidding competition has lifted prices, placing upward pressure on loan-to-value ratios. Second, when valuing a target company's assets, senior lenders have not always adjusted asset values to reflect potential economic downturns or depressed prices in the event of foreclosure. Third, senior lenders may not have considered the consequences of an inability to complete a planned, and possibly necessary, divestiture of a portion of the LBO company. Fourth, some senior lenders may not have carefully considered their vulnerability to sharp, prolonged increases in interest rates. Finally, but most importantly, it appears that some senior lenders may, like the other participants in LBOs, have become overly optimistic regarding a company's ability to generate sufficient cash flow to service significantly greater debt.

Federal Reserve Chairman Alan Greenspan has expressed concern about lending to LBOs generally, and loans by banks in particular. According to Mr. Greenspan, lenders—including senior lenders—have not carefully considered the risks associated with LBOs and "should make certain that they examine the prospects for LBO loans under a range of economic and financial circumstances." The Federal Reserve Board has issued guidelines mandating closer scrutiny of highly leveraged borrowers, which the guidelines define to include borrowers whose debt is more than three times equity.[36] The obvious concern is that, just as optimism in the oil and gas industry led to risky loans and bank failures once those loans soured, prolonged interest rate increases, cash flow shortfalls, inability to complete asset divestitures, or an economic downturn could individually or together cause some LBOs to crumble.

Equity

Typically, ten percent to fifteen percent of the capital base of an LBO is common stock, warrants, or other forms of equity. The amount and composition of the equity in a particular LBO is determined by several factors, including the size of the company to be acquired. The larger the target company the greater the need for cash and the less likely it is that management or an LBO firm alone can provide all of the equity. An additional factor is the creditworthiness of the target company, which dictates the amount that lenders are willing to provide. The less there is to borrow, the greater the demand for equity. A final factor is the equity participants' preference: does management or the

---

lion of debt. N.Y. Times, Feb. 16, 1989, at D2, col. 1.

36. The guidelines, which codify the Board's existing procedural recommendations, provide that banks should (i) evaluate a borrower's current and future cash flow under varying economic scenarios, including the possibility of an economic decline, (ii) set in-house limits on lending for leveraged transactions, (iii) maintain internal controls to monitor compliance with the in-house limits; and (iv) avoid compromising sound banking practices in an effort to broaden market share or realize substantial fees. Wall St.J., Feb. 23, 1989, at A4, col. 1. . . .

LBO firm want to include other participants or lenders as equity participants through equity kickers?

Equity investors in an LBO may include: (i) former shareholders of the LBO company, who are cashed out of a large portion of their interests but may retain a small ownership interest or "equity stub" in the new company; (ii) management of the LBO company, who may be initiators of the LBO and intend to be the new owners of the LBO company, or who may be given an equity interest and retained by an acquirer in recognition of their experience and knowledge (which the LBO company may need subsequent to the LBO); (iii) venture capital investors or LBO firms, who may be passive investors content to allow management to run the LBO company or who may in fact become new management; and (iv) the holders of senior debt or "mezzanine financing," who may receive an equity interest as part of a financing package.

Mezzanine Financing

The critical component of any LBO is the layer of financing that makes up the difference between the cost of the LBO company and the amount of equity and senior debt available. Mezzanine financing can take a variety of forms, although it is most frequently preferred stock or junk bonds.[40] The relatively high yields on junk bonds and other LBO–related indebtedness, combined with low default rates, have attracted many individual and institutional investors.

Junk bonds, developed to provide a source of financing for companies without investment grade ratings (including roughly twenty-five percent of the Fortune 500), have themselves taken a variety of forms in the LBO market. Junk bonds can be convertible bonds, debentures, payment-in-kind ("PIK") notes, or zero-coupon bonds. The combination of instruments used turns on the expected cash flow of the LBO company, whether from operations alone or from a combination of operations and expected divestitures. If it is expected that the LBO company will experience, initially, cash flow shortages, zero-coupon bonds will offer relief through interest deferral. If cash flow problems are likely to persist, PIK notes, which require no cash outlays for extended periods, will be preferred.

The usual purchasers of junk bonds include risk-oriented outside investors, insurance companies, and senior debt holders (in combination with their secured loans). Their purchase decisions typically are justified by the historically low default rate of junk bond debt in LBOs. The relatively recent utilization of PIK notes and zero-coupon bonds makes it difficult to determine, however, whether the default rate will remain as low as it has been in the past. PIK notes and zero-coupon bonds have allowed many LBO companies to avoid making any interest payments; consequently, few LBO companies have defaulted. As the

---

40. A junk bond has been defined as "a debt security which has not been rated as 'investment quality.'"

day of reckoning approaches—and actual cash outlays are required—default rates may increase.

The actual default rate for junk bonds is itself the subject of some considerable controversy. Until recently, the almost unchallenged belief was that the default rate for junk bonds was never greater than 2.1%. An unpublished report by several Harvard University researchers, however, indicates that the default rate is significantly higher. For example, junk bonds issued during 1977 and 1978 have a current default rate of over thirty-four percent, while junk bonds issued from 1979 through 1983 have a default rate between nineteen percent and twenty-six percent, and junk bonds issued between 1984 and 1986 have a default rate of up to nine percent. The implication is that the default rate for junk bonds increases as the bonds grow older and that the great number of junk bonds issued recently will produce a corresponding increase in default rates in the future.

In addition to junk bonds and other sources of subordinated debt, one or more investment banking firms may provide, initially, all or most of the senior or subordinated debt through a bridge loan, which is then paid down and replaced upon the sale of junk bonds. Bridge loans are becoming increasingly necessary as market pressures force buyers to negotiate a buyout with financing already committed. Between June 1987 and June 1988, bridge loans accounted for twelve percent of all financing for major corporate takeovers. The provision of bridge loans by investment banks has raised concerns on the part of some commentators that investment banks, with substantially less capital than commercial banks, are risking large portions of their capital, and that, by participating in a transaction, investment bankers are abandoning their independent advisory position and creating potential conflicts of interest.

* * *

The participants in an LBO or an LBO restructuring can be as diverse as the initial form and structure of an LBO. Nevertheless, several categories exist into one of which most, if not all, participants can be placed and within which certain characteristics and interests are common. The following categories, while not meant to be exclusive, provide a useful framework for analyzing LBO participants and their interests.

Management

The management of an LBO company may be the executives who have historically run the business or businesses of the LBO company, members or representatives of an LBO firm, or a combination thereof. As previously discussed, some LBO firms are strictly passive investors, while others participate, to some degree, in the daily affairs of the companies they acquire.

To the extent that "management" means the executives who have historically run the business, as contrasted with representatives of an

LBO firm, they may have interests which conflict with the interests of other participants, simply by virtue of the fact that the economic stakes of the two differ. In most LBOs, the senior executives have a substantial equity stake, but that is not the exclusive source of their economic return. Their current return is their compensation. While they may view their equity stake as a long-term investment, executives may also be motivated by non-economic factors, such as corporate loyalty, employee welfare, or the development or enhancement of their reputation as effective, enlightened managers. An LBO firm or other financial investor may not take these factors into account. As a result of these different financial stakes in the LBO company and different economic and non-economic performance rewards, there may be tension between management and the LBO company's new owners.

This conflict has been described as "trench warfare," reflecting the tension that exists as the new investors seek immediate cash returns, while management attempts to pursue long-term goals. The distinction between pre–LBO management and other equity investors, and the respective roles of each, assumes critical importance if an LBO company should falter. Pre–LBO management may wish to take steps, the end result of which would be improved operating results, even if it means that the equity is diluted or otherwise adversely affected. Other equity investors, however, will oppose any proposal that would affect negatively (that is, dilute) the LBO company's equity.

Moreover, as the LBO company falters, numerous decisions will be required that will cause friction between the new equity holders and management. For example, when the LBO company is unable to service all of its debt, one alternative to forestall default or foreclosure is to offer the holders of the debt an equity position in the company. Such an alternative would be particularly attractive to the management of an otherwise healthy company experiencing short-term cash flow problems. Individual members of management would possibly be willing to dilute their investment in exchange for breathing room for the company and job security for themselves. The remaining equity holders may not be so willing to dilute their interests.

A second source of friction may result from the differing views regarding the business direction of the company. Notwithstanding negative covenants and their restriction on expansion, pre–LBO management may be growth-oriented, while other equity participants will want to utilize all available cash flow to reduce the LBO company's debt. Management can be expected to want to retain valuable divisions or assets, while the other equity participants will be more willing to sell divisions, units, or assets, close plants and facilities, scale back research and development, and reduce employment.

In summary, assuming that the LBO company is otherwise operationally healthy, management's real interest will be in effecting a prompt recapitalization based on its view of the realistic prospects of the company. Management will likely desire to accomplish this in one effort rather than incrementally, in order to minimize the time drain. In this regard, management's interest will be contrary to that of almost all other participants. Management will want to avoid temporary fixes such as deferrals in principal payments or small reductions; preferring, instead, a recapitalization that solves all of the LBO company's problems and enables the management to return its attention to managing the LBO company.

Lenders

As discussed previously, the lenders to an LBO may be broken into two broad categories: secured and unsecured. Secured, or senior, lenders usually provide approximately sixty percent of the financing for an LBO and obtain security interests in most, if not all, of the company's assets. This financing is typically in the form of a term loan with a five- or ten-year amortization period or a revolving credit facility. Unsecured lenders, the usual form of the mezzanine level of LBO financing, provide the balance of the funds for the LBO and assume most of the risk. While unsecured or mezzanine financing may be subordinated debt with equity kickers or preferred stock, it typically takes the form of junk bonds.

Should an LBO falter, the conflicts that may arise between an LBO company and its lenders, and between lender groups, will obviously stem primarily from the company's inability to service its debt and its desire to restructure that debt. The company will seek immediate and permanent, or at least long-term, relief that translates into debt reduction. Lenders will generally prefer granting only interim relief, more in the way of deferrals and extensions rather than reductions. Senior lenders holding a secured position can be expected to take the firmest stand, granting minimal relief and using the threat of foreclosure as their strongest bargaining chip. Junk bond holders and other unsecured creditors may be slightly more accommodating since their bargaining position is not as strong.

The conflict between the company and its lenders may reach the point that it begins to resemble a "game of chicken." Revco, for example, sought a stand-still agreement with the holders of a $400 million issue of its junk bonds. The discussions broke down when a holder of $100 million of the issue informed the company that it was about to accelerate interest payments because of Revco's default. Revco perceived that it had no choice but to file a voluntary bankruptcy petition.

This new-found assertiveness of debtholders has also surfaced in other bankruptcy cases, such as Coleco Industries, Inc. and Public Service of New Hampshire, neither of which involved an LBO, but both of which demonstrate a militancy in bondholders. In both cases, the companies sought to restructure their debt, but upon terms that were perceived to be decidedly unfair to certain bondholders. These bondholders were willing to risk bankruptcy rather than accept what they perceived as an unfair dilution of their interests.

In any attempt to restructure the debt of an LBO, it will be important for the LBO company to convince all of its lenders that bankruptcy is a real, if somewhat unpleasant, possibility. Senior secured lenders may (and should) be less concerned about bankruptcy because of the security interests they hold. Generally, however, the prospect of a foreclosure of their security interests is very unattractive to senior lenders, not only because of the concern over the delay in achieving foreclosure and the risk of losing some of the value of those assets, but also because of the obvious practical considerations involved in taking control of some or all of the LBO company's assets. Holders of unsecured debt may be more willing to compromise their positions upon the threat of bankruptcy if the company can show that they will receive less in bankruptcy than through an out-of-court restructuring because of the fees and expenses resulting from the bankruptcy and the delays inherent in the bankruptcy process.

New Investors

For an LBO company experiencing financial difficulty, one option is for the company to seek new investors to provide an influx of cash to the LBO company. Alternatively, holders of the LBO company's debt may be willing to refinance or restructure the debt in exchange for an equity position. In either case, the LBO company obtains needed cash, but its investors are likely to see their holdings diluted.

Regulatory factors to which particular investors are subject may require, upon the infusion of new cash, some balancing of equity ownership through different classes of stock to achieve the desired dollar amount of capital without exceeding regulatory limitations on ownership. Banks, for example, are limited with respect to the equity interest they may have in a particular company. Options and warrants can be used to solve these problems and as alternative means of inducing particular new investors to participate through a combination of debt and equity investments.

If the LBO company is able to locate new investors, those investors will seek to identify quickly the company's problem, whether it is a poorly conceived capital structure or poor operations, and will seek control appropriate to correct the problem. New investors will likely prefer LBO companies with profitable operations or, at least, operations that are not significant cash drains. Moreover, they will likely demand a position senior to existing equity and, to the extent they can demand and obtain it, a position senior to unsecured debt. It is almost impossible, however, outside of bankruptcy, for new investors to obtain a position ahead of (or even on a parity with) existing secured creditors.

While the new investors may be familiar with investing in turnaround situations and, therefore, will be patient and realistic about the illiquidity of their investment, in no case will they be foolish. In addition to negotiating for improved rights relative to other equity and debt holders, they will seek indemnification from some of the participants in the LBO. Indemnification and higher status may be too much for the other participants and could, therefore, prevent the infusion of fresh cash. A troubled LBO may be the source of possibly endless litigation, especially if a bankruptcy petition is filed.

The participants outlined in this section are the more significant participants, from a business standpoint, in an LBO and an LBO restructuring. Other participants worthy of mention are former shareholders, former creditors and professional advisors, including investment bankers, appraisers, auditors, and lawyers. Professionals are not really participants except as advisors or counselors. They generate significant fees from the LBO and the divestitures that result, but normally act simply as advisors, without risk for failed LBOs. Nevertheless, if an LBO fails and the various participants are looking for targets for lawsuits, professionals may be a source of recovery for claims based upon bad projections. Former shareholders who have been cashed out want to keep the money they received by avoiding fraudulent conveyance liability; similarly, former creditors, the usual petitioners in a fraudulent conveyance action, want to be paid and do not want to be LBO victims holding debt that is subordinated, actually or effectively, to all other interests.

Contract Rights

VLAHAKIS, DELEVERAGING: A SEARCH FOR RULES IN A FINANCIAL FREE-FOR-ALL
5 M & A and Corp. Gov. Law Rep. 290 (1990).

An analysis of the relationship between a corporation and the holders of its debt requires recourse, at least in the first instance, to the terms of the contract. Aside from certain minimal protective provisions which must be found in every indenture governing publicly issued debt under the Trust Indenture Act, the terms are subject to negotiation between the parties. Principal, interest rate and maturity are the key pricing terms. Other terms—such as optional and mandatory redemption provisions, sinking fund requirements, conversion rights, and prepayment provisions—also directly affect the pricing of a security. Finally, a wide variety of affirmative and negative covenants are available to restrict an issuer's ability to impair the creditworthiness of its debt and have some impact, albeit less direct, on price.

The Trust Indenture Act provides that indentures for public debt must require the unanimous consent of debtholders to change the three key financial terms, namely the principal amount, interest rate, and date of maturity. Other terms of the indenture can typically be changed by a less than unanimous vote of the debtholders, often by as little as a majority.

As a purely contractual matter, issuers seeking to restructure their publicly held debt have two different techniques available. A tender offer may be used to buy in outstanding debt, either for cash, or for newly issued debt or equity securities. A cash tender offer at a discount to face amount would reduce the total debt outstanding. An exchange offer where new debt and/or equity securities are exchanged for the outstanding debt at a discount to face amount can not only reduce the total debt outstanding but also, in effect, lower the average interest rate and extend the average maturity on the outstanding debt by issuing new securities which extend, defer or eliminate altogether the debt service requirement. Nontendering debtholders, of course, are not affected by the fact that others have tendered—they retain debt with its original principal amount, interest rate and maturity.

In lieu of, or in conjunction with, a tender offer, an issuer can solicit consents of the debtholders to amend the terms of the outstanding debt. Since unanimous consent is required to amend the principal amount, interest rate and maturity, a consent solicitation is used instead to remove restrictive covenants which limit the issuer's flexibility in restructuring. In this case, provided that the required majority or supermajority consent is obtained, non-consenting debtholders are affected by the conduct of those granting consent—since the required majority has the power to change the terms of the entire issue. Moreover, the very holders granting the consent—if simultaneously tendering their debt—will not have to live with the effects of having agreed to remove one or more covenants. Hence, the term "exit" consents.

If the issuer is combining a tender offer with a consent solicitation, an additional matter must be taken into account. Since most indentures disable the issuer from voting any of its debt held in its treasury, the receipt and exercise of the associated consents from debtholders must be a condition precedent to the purchase of the debt by the corporation in order for the votes to "count". The transaction must be characterized as a two-step process in which the consents are granted before the debt is actually acquired. The same issue may arise in a tender offer made by an "affiliate" of the issuer, as this term is defined in the relevant provision of the trust indenture, since the restriction on voting rights which applies to the issuer often applies to its affiliates as well.

The realities of the marketplace, combined with the phenomenon of the prisoners' dilemma, have permitted financially distressed companies to create quite powerful incentives for debtholders to participate in a restructuring. The public debt of a troubled company trades at a steep discount to its face amount, to the extent it trades at all. Issuers can reduce their outstanding debt by offering to buy it in at prices of $.40 to $.50 on the dollar, or lower—a "premium" to the market price. In order to insure a sufficient reduction in the level of debt outstanding, an issuer can impose a condition that 70%, 80% or 90% of the outstanding principal amount be tendered before any debt will be purchased. The issuer may require that debtholders seeking to tender also consent to remove some or all of the restrictive covenants from the indenture, as a condition to the acceptance of their debt in the offer.

Or, the issuer can simultaneously solicit such consents, and can pay separately for them.

The prospect of salvaging some portion of their loss on the debt via the "premium" offered by the issuer, along with the possible receipt of cash for a consent, present an irresistible "carrot" when compared to the "stick" of non-tendered debt which will be covenant-less and, in all likelihood, will trade at prices even less than the pre-tender offer all-time lows. Ironically, the very debtholders who are protected under the indenture by not having to reduce principal amount or interest, or extend maturities, without their individual consent may be forced to do just that in order to avoid the worse fate of the non-tendering debtholder.

Techniques beyond the carrot and stick of a "premium" to market and the threat to the post-tender offer value of the nontendered debt have developed. Thus, an issuer can offer new debt secured by specific assets, still at a discount to the face amount of existing debt, but effectively leaving non-tendering debtholders in a junior position in the event of a subsequent bankruptcy. To the extent that existing debt has a negative pledge clause (which would prohibit the granting of security in new debt), such a covenant can be eliminated via exit consents solicited from tendering debtholders. Similarly, if debt of a holding company is to be restructured, and if the holding company has few assets other than the stock of an operating subsidiary, new debt of the operating subsidiary can be offered in exchange for holding company debt thereby placing tendering debtholders "closer" to the meaningful assets than non-tendering holders.

* * *

Off Contract Rights
State Law

Bondholders have claims for a breach of specific contract provisions. If there are no specific contract provisions, bondholders have argued, first, for a breach of fiduciary duty, and, second, for a breach of implied covenants of good faith and fair dealing. We covered these largely unsuccessful theories in chapter 3, supra at pages 183–192.

Debtholders are advancing a third theory of recovery, a variant on their claim for a breach of fiduciary duty. Even if there is no general fiduciary obligation to creditors, creditors argue that a fiduciary duty ought to attach in their favor when the firm is effectively insolvent. In formal insolvency proceedings, courts recognize a shift of the relative rights and duties of managers to stakeholders. Creditors or trustees of firms in insolvency can sue managers on behalf of the firm for damages caused by a breach of their fiduciary duty to the corporation. See, e.g., Pepper v. Litton, 308 U.S. 295, 60 S.Ct. 238, 84 L.Ed. 281 (1939); Meyers v. Moody, 693 F.2d 1196 (5th Cir.1982). Directors of an insolvent company are trustees of corporate property for creditors first, shareholders second. Bank Leumi–Le–Israel, B.M. v. Sunbelt Industries,

Inc., 485 F.Supp. 556 (S.D.Ga.1980). Should courts extend fiduciary duties to debt holders when a firm is insolvent but not yet formally in insolvency or bankruptcy proceedings? How could a court determine precisely when a board's duties to stockholders ends in favor of a duty to creditors and when a board ought to be held liable for its failure to shift its allegiances?

Federal Securities Law

Congress and the Securities and Exchange Commission have largely overlooked debt restructurings. The Williams Act has limited application to debt tender offers. Please reread the Coffee extract, supra at ___. Sections 13(e) and 14(d) apply only to equity securities. Only section 14(e) and the SEC regulations promulgated under the section, which apply to all tender offers, affect tender offers for debt instruments. Review the sections and rules in your statutory supplement. What protections are lost and what remain for debt tender offers?

Moreover, the SEC has historically waived the application of even the minimal twenty-day timing protections of rule 14e–1 if the offer satisfies certain conditions. The SEC staff has stated, for example, in no-action letters that it would waive the twenty-day minimum offering period for an any-and-all self-tender offer for nonconvertible debt securities if the offer (1) were open to all holders, (2) were designed to afford a holder a reasonable opportunity to tender, (3) included expedited dissemination of the details of the offer if open for less than ten days, and (4) were not made in anticipation of, or in response to, another tender offer. See, e.g., SEC No–Action Letter, Merrill Lynch, Pierce, Fenner & Smith, Inc., (avail. July 2, 1986).

If the self-tender offer is an exchange offer, the newly issued securities must be registered under the Securities Act of 1933, unless they qualify for an exemption under section 3(a)(9). The exemption is available if (1) the security being offered and the security being tendered are of the same issuer, (2) no part of the offering is made to non-security holders, (3) security holders are not asked for anything other than their old securities, and (4) there is no compensation to anyone who solicits tender. The fourth requirement is the most problematic. Review the material in chapter 6, supra at pages 739–742.

SEC NO–ACTION LETTER, SEAMAN FURNITURE
(avail. Oct. 10, 1989).

On behalf of our client, Seaman Furniture Company, Inc. (the "Company"), we request the advice of the Staff that it will not recommend any enforcement action to the Securities and Exchange Commission (the "SEC") if the Company effects the exchange offer described below (the "Exchange Offer") in reliance on the exemption from registration contained in Section 3(a)(9) ("Section 3(a)(9)") of the Securities Act of 1933, as amended (the "Act"). . . .

On December 15, 1987, SFC Acquisition Corp., a Delaware corporation ("Acquisition") and a wholly owned subsidiary of SFC Holdings, Inc., a Delaware corporation ("Holdings"), purchased approximately 77% of the outstanding shares of common stock of the Company pursuant to a cash tender offer (the "Tender Offer") commenced in accordance with a merger agreement among Holdings, Acquisition and the Company. On February 25, 1988, Acquisition was merged into the Company (the "Merger"), the shares of common stock of the Company which were not purchased pursuant to the Tender Offer were converted into the right to receive 15% Junior Subordinated Debentures due 1999 of Acquisition (the "Existing Sub Debt"), and the Company became a wholly owned subsidiary of Holdings and assumed the Existing Sub Debt. Over 98% of the outstanding shares of common stock of the Company were tendered into the cash tender offer and received cash on a pro rata basis. Approximately 80% of the common stock of Holdings outstanding on a fully diluted basis is beneficially owned by limited partnerships of which KKR Associates, L.P., a New York limited partnership ("KKR"), is the sole general partner. Approximately 17% and 3%, respectively, of the common stock of Holdings outstanding on a fully diluted basis is beneficially owned by Mr. Morton Seaman, the chief executive officer of the Company, and other members of management of the Company, respectively. As of today, two members of the Seaman family, four representatives of KKR and the executive vice president of the Company constitute the Board of Directors of Holdings and the Company.

The Existing Sub Debt issued to the Company's public stockholders in connection with the Merger was covered by a Registration Statement on Form S–4 (No. 33–19882). Following the Merger, the Company continued to file periodic reports (including its Annual Report on Form 10–K for the fiscal year during which the Registration Statement on Form S–4 became effective) under the Securities Exchange Act of 1934, as amended (the "Exchange Act"), until the Existing Sub Debt was deregistered in December, 1988 because it was held of record by less than 300 holders.

* * *

In the last half of its fiscal year ended April 30, 1989 the Company experienced sluggish sales which it believes were indicative of the economic climate prevalent in the marketplace in which it operates. As these trends continued into the 1990 fiscal year, the Company became convinced that it would have to attempt to restructure its outstanding indebtedness.

In July, 1989 formal negotiations with officers of Manufacturers Hanover Trust Company, the agent bank under the Company's bank credit agreement, were commenced to discuss the company's weakened financial condition. Discussions with a steering committee of the Company's 26 bank lenders (all of which are large commercial banking institutions) continued through early September, at which time a proposed restructuring of the Company's bank debt was agreed to in principle.

During July, 1989 the Company hired investment bankers from Merrill Lynch Capital Markets to act as its financial advisors in connection with a possible restructuring of the Company's debt. On August 23, 1989, following the distribution by the Company to its securityholders of the Company's audited financial statements for the year ended April 30, 1989 and a letter to the holders of Existing Sub Debt stating, among other things, that the Company would no longer be able to service its bank debt, a meeting was arranged with institutional investors which were believed to hold a substantial percentage of the Existing Sub Debt. Also attending this meeting were officers and directors of the Company, the Existing Sub Debt trustee and its counsel, counsel to various of the investors, and the Company's legal and financial advisors. At the meeting, officers and directors of the Company advised the holders of Existing Sub Debt that, among other things, the Company would be formulating a proposal to restructure the Company. The trustee and seven of the holders of Existing Sub Debt which attended the meeting subsequently formed a committee (the "Committee"). At the request of the Committee, the Company subsequently agreed to pay the fees and expenses of legal counsel and financial advisors selected by the Committee to represent the Committee.

In early September, the Company submitted a restructuring proposal to the financial advisors and legal counsel for the Committee. Active discussions and negotiations with the Committee's legal and financial advisors took place from September 12, 1989 through September 20, 1989. By September 22, 1989, the seven holders of Existing Sub Debt which constituted the Committee executed and delivered to the Company the form of letter attached hereto as Exhibit A, and on September 25, 1989 the Company issued the press release attached hereto as Exhibit B. The Company understands that all of such members of the Committee are sophisticated institutional investors, and these investors have represented to the company that they own approximately 42% in principal amount of the Existing Sub Debt. The Company also has been advised that the high yield debt trading unit of Merrill Lynch Capital Markets (the "ML Trading Unit") owns, for the ML Trading Unit's own account, approximately 16% in principal amount of the Existing Sub Debt, which the Company believes is the largest position that any holder has in these securities. The ML Trading Unit attended the meeting on August 23, 1989 referred to above, but it is not a member of the Committee. At the request of the Company, the ML Trading Unit has executed and delivered to the Company the form of letter attached hereto as Exhibit A in its capacity as a holder of Existing Sub Debt. The investment bankers from Merrill Lynch Capital Markets who have acted as the Company's financial advisors have advised the Company that they have no responsibility for the Existing Sub Debt owned by the ML Trading Unit, have no involvement in the management of such investment and, as a result of the "Chinese wall" between their department and the ML Trading Unit, have had no substantive contact with the persons responsible for the management of the ML Trading Unit's investment in Existing Sub Debt concerning the management of such investment, the Company's various restructuring proposals or the Exchange Offer. It is the company's belief that the ML Trading Unit and most, if not all, of the members of the Committee acquired Existing Sub Debt following the Merger in the ordinary course of their business as entities which are regularly engaged in the business of investing in securities.

The restructuring proposal can be summarized as follows: (1) pursuant to the Exchange Offer, the Company will exchange $20.8 million in principal amount of its new junior subordinated debentures (the "New Sub Debt") and approximately 8% of its common stock (subject to dilution) for approximately $83 million in principal amount (90%) of the Existing Sub Debt, (2) the principal amount of the Company's senior bank debt will be reduced from approximately $270 million to $150 million and the Company will issue to the banks $25 million in principal amount of its senior subordinated notes and approximately 44.5% of its common stock (subject to dilution), (3) Mr. Seaman and KKR and its affiliates will purchase for cash $42 million in principal amount of the Company's senior subordinated debt and (4) Mr. Seaman, KKR and the banks will participate in a new $15 million revolving letter of credit facility for the Company. ... The parties to the restructuring also have agreed to grant each other releases from potential litigation claims with respect to Existing Sub Debt which is exchanged pursuant to the Exchange Offer (as opposed to the Existing Sub Debt which is expected to remain outstanding) to the extent such claims arise out of the Tender Offer and the Merger. In addition, holders of Existing Sub Debt will waive accrued interest on Existing Sub Debt exchanged pursuant to the Exchange Offer. As contemplated by the term sheets, the Company will attempt to register the New Sub Debt under the Exchange Act and resume filing periodic reports after the Exchange Offer is consummated. The Company's obligations under the Existing Sub Debt are not, and the Company's obligations under the New Sub Debt will not be, guaranteed by Holdings.

The Company's independent public accountants have qualified their opinion with respect to the audited financial statements of the Company for the fiscal year ended April 30, 1989 and unfavorable publicity concerning the Company's financial condition has adversely affected the Company. The negotiation of the proposed restructuring among the banks, the Committee's financial and legal advisors, and the Company was more difficult and time consuming than originally expected. The viability of the Company is dependent upon the willingness of its suppliers to provide it with furniture to sell. Understandably, the Company's trade creditors will remain very concerned about the Company's creditworthiness until the restructuring is consummated. Likewise, the restructuring proposal provides for, and is dependent upon, an additional investment of $42 million by existing shareholders of the Company. If it takes a great deal of time to effectuate the restructuring, changed circumstances could conceivably put this investment at risk. Accordingly, it is imperative that the Company consummate the proposed restructuring quickly in order, among other things, to: (a) fully restore the confidence of the Company's trade creditors; (b) receive the infusions of cash to be made upon the closing of the restructuring; and (c) reduce interest expense. Definitive documentation for the restructuring of the Company's senior bank debt is presently being prepared and should be finalized in the next few weeks. Clearly, the most time consuming aspect of the restructuring will be the Exchange Offer. It is our belief that the most expeditious manner to effectuate the Exchange Offer would be in reliance upon the exemption from registration under the Act contained in Section 3(a)(9), which, as discussed below, we believe should be available to the Company.

* * *

Since their engagement by the Company in July, 1989, the investment bankers from Merrill Lynch Capital Markets who have acted as the Company's financial advisors have performed the following services for the Company: (1) performed financial analyses; (2) assisted the Company in formulating a restructuring proposal; (3) advised the Company with respect to the terms of the new securities to be issued in connection with the restructuring and the new capital structure of the Company; (4) participated in meetings between representatives of the Company, on the one hand, and the banks, on the other hand; (5) participated in meetings between representatives of the Company, on the one hand, and the legal and financial advisors to the Committee, on the other hand; and (6) conversed by telephone with representatives of the banks and the legal and financial advisors to the Committee. Merrill Lynch Capital Markets will not: (1) be named as a dealer manager of the Exchange Offer; (2) deliver a fairness opinion with respect to the Exchange Offer; or (3) communicate directly with any holder of Existing Sub Debt with respect to substantive matters relating to the restructuring or the Exchange Offer. The Company understands that during the aforementioned telephone conversations and meetings its financial advisors have: (1) outlined the current status of negotiations between the Company and the other creditors of the Company; (2) discussed the Company's financial statements and projections; (3) presented the Company's current proposals with respect to the terms of the Exchange Offer and the restructuring to the banks and the legal and financial advisors to the Committee; and (4) received and discussed the counterproposals of the banks and the legal and financial advisors to the Committee and relayed such counterproposals to the Company. We understand that the Company's financial advisors have not (1) expressed to the banks or the legal or financial advisors to the Committee their views as to (a) the fairness of the proposed restructuring or the Exchange Offer or (b) the value of the securities to be issued in connection with the Exchange Offer or (2) made any recommendation to the banks or the legal and financial advisors to the Committee with respect to the restructuring or the Exchange Offer.

Merrill Lynch will be paid a fixed fee prior to or upon the commencement of the Exchange Offer. The compensation of Merrill Lynch is not contingent upon the success of the Exchange Offer.

* * *

Based on the facts presented, the Division will not recommend enforcement action to the Commission if the Company, in reliance on your opinion as counsel that the exemption provided by section 3(a)(9) of the Securities Act of 1933 ("Securities Act") is available, proceeds with the described Exchange Offer without registration under the Securities Act.

* * *

For solicitations aimed at gaining enough bondholder votes to waive protective trust indenture covenants, section 14(a) of the Securities Exchange Act of 1934, governing the solicitation of proxies and written consents, may apply. See chapter 2, supra at page 133. The section applies to any security, debt or equity, registered under section 12 of the act, but many debt securities are not so registered. Even so, although an issuer making a self-tender offer or soliciting consents on nonregistered debt securities has no disclosure obligations under section 5 of the 1933 act and sections 13(e) and 14(a) of the 1934 act, disclosure of material nonpublic information may be required under the general antifraud provisions of sections 10(b) and 14(e) of the 1934 act. The SEC and the courts applying these open-ended provisions may look for guidance to the more specific provisions of schedule 14A.

Other problems under the federal securities laws for a debtor seeking to convince creditors to tender their debt instruments or mail in proxies or consents are common to all issuers experiencing a material deterioration in their financial condition.

First, when and how must an issuer disclose its poor financial condition to the secondary trading markets? Most financially distressed issuers are reluctant to issue negative information before it is absolutely required. Nervous suppliers, customers, and employees, if fully informed, may defect and worsen existing problems. Between periodic filings under the 1934 act an issuer with a materially deteriorating financial condition must determine whether to make interim disclosures or wait for the new periodic filing. Form 8–K is required only in the event of an actual bankruptcy or receivership. A policy of not disclosing difficulties outside periodic reports can work only if managers do not voluntarily make public statements that may be misleading absent a full disclosure of the firm's problems. See the materials in chapter 6, supra at pages 784, 799. At some point, if a duty to disclose attaches, the internal formulation of a financial restructuring plan must itself be disclosed under the materiality standards in *Basic Inc. v. Levinson,* supra at 791. Is the development of a reorganization plan material? A firm's discussions with debt holders under the plan? A firm's agreement with representative debt holders?

Second, an issuer in need of restructuring will normally hire an investment banker to develop an array of projections and, perhaps, negotiate on behalf of the firm with the larger holders of the outstanding public debt issue. The problem is that good investment bankers may also make a market in the traded debt securities of the issuer and may also themselves hold in their investment portfolios various amounts of the issuer's stock or debt. The federal securities laws regulate the activities of multiservice firms. Section 15(f), for example, of the 1934 act requires an investment bank to establish, maintain, and enforce policies and procedures designed to prevent the misuse of material nonpublic information by trading on the information for its own account. In short, an investment bank must maintain an effective "Chinese wall" between its consulting and trading departments.

SUBCHAPTER B: CHAPTER 11 REORGANIZATIONS

Chapter 7, providing for a liquidation of an insolvent entity, offers the management and equity holders of a business very little; once the business is liquidated, managers are out of work, and equity holders usually receive nothing in the final distribution.

The major disadvantage of a Chapter 7 to creditors, however, is that they may receive less from a liquidation than they could receive if the business were reorganized to survive, with its debt obligations extended and reduced. Thus if the ongoing value of the firm is greater than its liquidation value, the creditors could reduce their losses by helping the company survive rather than liquidating it. When an operating company does produce goods or services at a profit and has a valuable consumer reputation (goodwill), the usual case in leveraged transactions, it is usually in the interests of the creditors to agree to a reorganization rather than force a liquidation. As a consequence, most, if not all, large-scale bankruptcy reorganizations are Chapter 11 proceedings.

There is an automatic stay on the collection of any debts, protecting each creditor from the aggressive collection efforts of the other creditors. A court assembles the debtor's property under the control of a trustee in bankruptcy (TIB), with whom a creditor can negotiate for priority. The TIB has special powers to void transfers already made and to void unperfected security interests, offering the possibility that the TIB may enlarge the amount of assets available to all creditors.

A Chapter 11 petition is an invitation to a negotiation among all the investors in a firm. A debtor files a Chapter 11 petition, which imposes an automatic stay on debt collections, and the business continues to operate in the "ordinary course," § 363(c) [all references in this text are to Title 11 of the United States Code, which contains the federal bankruptcy code], under the control of the debtor in possession (DIP). The DIP is ordinarily the same management team as was in control before the petition. After the petition the DIP uses the breathing room provided by the automatic stay to sell losing divisions, trim excess staff, cut back on unnecessary expenses, and so on. The DIP may also obtain additional financing with court approval. § 364(b) to (d).

Once some operating stability is achieved, the debtor negotiates a plan with its major creditors. A creditors' committee is appointed, § 1102, to monitor and negotiate with the DIP. The debtor proposes a plan of reorganization in which it promises to pay each class of creditors a certain percentage of their claims over a stated period of time. The plan and an explanatory disclosure statement are distributed to all creditors who have filed claims. If the plan is approved by a specified vote of the creditors in each class, it is confirmed by a court. §§ 1126(c) & 1129. Every dissenting creditor who has not accepted the plan must get at least as much as that creditor would have received in a Chapter 7 liquidation. § 1129(a)(7). If a plan does not receive the requisite votes of a class of creditors, a court may still confirm the plan if it finds the class is "unimpaired" by the plan or if the plan is "fair and equitable to the class." The latter procedure is a "confirmation by cram-down." Upon confirmation of a plan, the debtor is discharged from all its prepetition debts except as provided in the plan. § 1141(d).

All Chapter 11 negotiations are held in the shadow of Chapter 7. The debtor can convert a Chapter 11 proceeding into a Chapter 7 proceeding, § 1112(a), and the creditors can apply to the court to do the same on a proper showing. § 1112(b). Moreover, if the creditors do not approve the plan of reorganization, the proceeding becomes a Chapter 7 liquidation proceeding. § 1112(b). All parties must assess their positions and the positions of each other under Chapter 7 (a "liquidation analysis") and negotiate accordingly. Workouts are two steps away from a Chapter 7; they are negotiated in the shadow of a Chapter 11 proceeding and with an awareness of the ultimate possibility of a Chapter 7 proceeding. An understanding of workouts and Chapter 11 is far more important than their obvious application to distressed firms, however. When investors are deciding to engage in leveraged transactions in the first instance, they must have some sense of the effect and cost of workouts and Chapter 11 proceedings to price their new investment instruments. An LBO investor tempted to buy newly offered LBO securities is well advised to understand the effect of workouts or Chapter 11 proceedings on the securities in order to discount the price appropriately for the risk of the firm's insolvency.

These materials leave the many legal details of Chapters 11 and 7 to your bankruptcy or debtor and creditor course. Our focus is on the parts of Chapter 11 that most directly affect the general decisions of managers and equity stakeholders to engage in highly leveraged takeovers or to seek a restructuring in lieu of, or under, Chapter 11. At the core of these materials is the question of how Chapter 11 affects the worst-case scenario of various takeover investors. First, can managers and equity holders plan on coming out of a Chapter 11 bankruptcy with their jobs or some of their equity intact? Or will a court appoint a trustee to replace existing managers? Section 1 deals with who manages a firm in and after a Chapter 11 proceeding. Second, can equity holders of an insolvent firm emerge from a Chapter 11 with some value for their shares? Section 2 deals with the position of equity stakeholders in a Chapter 11 proceeding, focusing on the absolute priority rule of section 1129(b). Third, does a Chapter 11 proceeding avoid the requirements of otherwise burdensome federal and state regulations on reorganizations? Section 3 contains materials on the applicability of state corporation law and federal securities law to a firm's operations in Chapter 11. Section 4 breaks the pattern of the first three sections and focuses on "vulture acquisitions"—acquisitions of firms in Chapter 11 proceedings.

CIERI, HEIMAN, HENZE, JENKS, KIRSCHNER, RILEY & SULLIVAN, AN INTRODUCTION TO LEGAL AND PRACTICAL CONSIDERATIONS IN THE RESTRUCTURING OF TROUBLED LEVERAGED BUYOUTS
45 Bus.Lawyer 333, 385–389 (Nov. 1989)

BENEFITS OF BANKRUPTCY

Because a troubled LBO company usually needs breathing room and time to accumulate cash, the nature of a chapter 11 reorganization is particularly well-suited for a faltering LBO company. First, upon filing a bankruptcy petition, the LBO company, now a debtor or debtor-in-possession, achieves indirectly what it could not achieve directly during its attempt to restructure—a temporary suspension of its debt service and a suspension of attempts by creditors to foreclose upon or assert liens against any of its properties. The automatic stay of section 362 of the Bankruptcy Code effectively freezes all actions against the company and prevents all holders of claims against the company from enforcing those claims. The holders of the LBO company's debt may not declare the debt in default nor may they attempt to levy upon assets of the company.

A second aspect of bankruptcy that is particularly beneficial to an LBO company is that the LBO company is under no obligation to pay any pre-petition claims. In fact, it is generally prevented from paying such claims. Moreover, interest accumulation on the unsecured debt is effectively suspended during the bankruptcy proceeding, while the accumulation of interest on secured debt during bankruptcy will depend upon whether the value of the collateral securing such indebtedness exceeds the amount of the indebtedness.

For the LBO company in bankruptcy, obtaining credit to assure continued business operations will be critical. The company may obtain unsecured credit in the ordinary course of business without bankruptcy court approval. The claims of creditors supplying ordinary-course credit, such as trade creditors or suppliers, will have the priority of an administrative expense, which assures the creditor payment ahead of pre-petition creditors.

Small amounts of unsecured credit typically will not be sufficient for the LBO company in bankruptcy. To obtain more significant credit outside the ordinary course of business, whether that credit is secured or unsecured, requires bankruptcy court authorization, after notice and a hearing. Since the extension of large amounts of post-petition credit, which could have administrative priority, could devalue their claims, pre-petition unsecured creditors of a bankrupt LBO company are considered parties in interest entitled to notice of the LBO company's motion to obtain credit and grant an administrative priority.

If the bankrupt LBO company is unable to obtain unsecured credit sufficient to meet its needs, the Bankruptcy Code provides for obtaining credit upon a secured or super-priority basis. The bankruptcy court may, upon a debtor's request and after notice and hearing, authorize borrowing with (i) a super priority over any and all administrative expenses or (ii) security in the form of a lien on free assets or in the form of a junior lien on encumbered assets. The granting of the super-priority administrative position or the security interest may be authorized only if the LBO company is unable to obtain unsecured credit and if the liens of prior secured creditors are not adversely affected.

If an LBO company is unable to obtain unsecured credit and if there are no unencumbered assets to secure further secured credit, the Bankruptcy Code authorizes the bankruptcy court to allow the LBO company to borrow money on a secured basis and grant a lien that is senior or equal to existing liens. This extraordinary relief is authorized only if the holders of the prior liens are given adequate protection for their interest and if there is no other available source of money.

In the case of a bankrupt LBO company, most, if not all, of its assets will likely be pledged, mortgaged, or otherwise encumbered, leaving it no alternative but to attempt to grant a super-priority lien. A super-priority lien pursuant to section 364 is, therefore, a particularly useful tool for an LBO company in bankruptcy. Outside of bankruptcy, it would be almost impossible for the company to obtain financing since existing secured lenders would likely not agree to a new lien that is equal to, or superior to, their interests.

Finally, unlike out-of-court work-outs in which one recalcitrant creditor may prevent a restructuring, when a plan of reorganization is ultimately proposed and confirmed, the plan will bind all of the company's creditors, even those that oppose it. Moreover, during the initial phase of the case, and often for the entire proceeding, the LBO company would have the exclusive right to propose a plan of reorganization.

Burdens of Bankruptcy

While the filing of a bankruptcy petition has some benefits for the LBO company, it does require changes that management and equity holders may find unpleasant. Bankruptcy entails some risk for the LBO company and for its management. The Bankruptcy Code allows the removal of management and the appointment of a trustee to run the company under certain circumstances. While removal of management is not common, management is, nevertheless, stripped of a good deal of its autonomy and authority in a Chapter 11 proceeding. In addition, the filing of a petition in bankruptcy introduces a level of scrutiny by the bankruptcy court and the creditors' committee that most companies find difficult; this may prove especially difficult for post–LBO management that took the company private to avoid the scrutiny and demands of shareholders. For example, sales of assets, unless in the ordinary course of business, must be approved by the bankruptcy court and may be challenged by creditors. Even pre-petition agreements to sell assets are not binding, absent court approval.

Another significant change resulting from bankruptcy is that, once bankruptcy is filed, the company and its assets exist for the benefit of creditors. Management is saddled with fiduciary duties to the company's creditors which may require actions that conflict with management's investment interests. In addition, management now must oversee a company in which its interest has been significantly diluted or may even be eliminated. It is likely that such dilution or elimination will be reflected in any plan of reorganization ultimately confirmed by the court. Moreover, to the extent management or other equity holders may also hold secured or unsecured debt claims, those claims may be subordinated because of their role in the failed LBO.

Another result of a bankruptcy filing is that, because management is obligated to run the company for the benefit of creditors, management of the company will theoretically be charged with the duty of filing and pursuing any lawsuits that the company may have. These potential lawsuits include lawsuits against lenders, whether secured or unsecured, against current equity holders, whether an LBO firm or management, and, possibly, against the former shareholders. In other words, management may find itself not only holding a worthless position in an insolvent company but also be faced with suing the participants in the LBO. Reluctance on the part of management to pursue such remedies often results in the creditors' committee assuming the role. * * *

LEVIN, CLEANING UP THE MESS: THE NEED FOR BANKRUPTCY REFORM
Inv. Dealers' Digest 18 (April 16, 1990)

For many of the smaller companies among that number, Chapter 11 of the Bankruptcy Code may be perfectly adequate to their needs of either reorganization or orderly liquidation. Others, not so fortunate, are being sucked down by the ever-mounting expenses of lawyers, appraisers, financial advisers, and accountants.

But for big, highly leveraged companies that land in Chapter 11 reorganizations, their complicated debt structures raise a whole new set of issues that breed delay, contention and astronomically high legal and related expenses.

For example, in the bankruptcy of LTV Corp., the third largest U.S. steel company, there were about 55 public debt issues and about 10 different classes of creditors. The cost of balancing unsecured creditor rights and settling claims often generates multi-million dollar legal fees, like the $100 million incurred by Manville Corp., the asbestos maker.

* * *

In the opinion of many experts who advise failing companies, the law is patently ill-equipped to steer big-name bankruptcies through reorganizations. The issues raised by the financial realities of failing mega-deals range from the trading of debt claims to pension obligations to the rights of bondholders and stockholders through to fiendishly complex tax and accounting questions.

* * *

The experts say the rise in big-business bankruptcies will create more confusion and spur more litigation to sift through issues that the bankruptcy law fails to address. "Today, we see a lot of non-traditional bankruptcy problems being solved in the bankruptcy courts," says Harry Dixon, chairman of the American Bankruptcy Institute.

"The bankruptcy courts of the United States handle more money than all of the other courts in the country combined," adds Dixon, a chief architect of the 1978 reform act. "They are really misnamed. Today, they should not be called bankruptcy courts. They should be called commercial courts because the laws of commerce in the U.S. are largely being re-made today in the courts of bankruptcy."

* * *

SECTION 1. WHO RUNS A FIRM IN CHAPTER 11?

Chapter 11 establishes the presumption that existing management should remain in possession absent strong reasons for appointment of a substitute trustee. This is enormously important for managers responsible for choosing whether a troubled firm ought to use bankruptcy reorganization. If managers can stay in control during the reorganization, it is likely that they will also be left in control when the firm emerges from the reorganization. When creditors complain that management is not running the business in a way to enhance its chances of success, sympathetic courts first appoint an examiner to investigate the debtor's affairs and monitor the debtor's activities.

§ 1104(b). In extreme cases the court can replace the management with a trustee. § 1104. The following cases illustrate the standards used by the bankruptcy court in replacing a DIP.

IN RE SHARON STEEL CORP.

United States Court of Appeals, Third Circuit, 1989.
871 F.2d 1217.

GIBBONS, CHIEF JUDGE:

DWG Corporation and Victor Posner appeal from a district court decision affirming a bankruptcy court order appointing a trustee-in-bankruptcy for debtor Sharon Steel ("the debtor" or "Sharon") pursuant to 11 U.S.C. § 1104. DWG and Posner contend that the bankruptcy court should have denied the committee of unsecured creditors' ("the committee") petition for a trustee because the request violated contractual obligations between the committee and the debtor-in-possession.

* * *

Sharon Steel Corporation manufactures steel in a facility located near Sharon, Pennsylvania. The Sharon facility includes two blast furnaces. By April, 1987, only one of these—number 3—was operational. Sharon's most efficient blast furnace, number 2, was shut down pending $18 million in repairs. Furthermore, furnace number 3, which was three years overdue for relining, faced imminent shutdown. On April 17, 1987, confronted with $742 million in liabilities, only $478 million in assets, and pressing creditors, Sharon filed a voluntary petition for reorganization under Chapter 11 of the Bankruptcy Code. 11 U.S.C. §§ 1100–1174 (1982 & Supp. IV 1986).

Sharon management remained in control of the corporation's operations as debtor-in-possession. At all times relevant to this case, appellant Victor Posner served as Sharon's chairman, president, and chief executive officer. Appellant DWG, under common control with Sharon, provided financial management services to Sharon and other Posner-controlled companies. It operated out of a Miami office building owned by Posner and provided 13,000 square feet of office space to Sharon to house its executive offices, charging Sharon $24 per square foot.

Some five months after Sharon filed for reorganization, the committee, dissatisfied with the progress—or lack thereof—made by Sharon's management, petitioned the bankruptcy court for appointment of a trustee pursuant to 11 U.S.C. § 1104. On the following day, September 29, 1987, the court approved an $18 million loan package to enable the debtor to reline blast furnace number 2.

* * *

The bankruptcy court's Opinion on Appointment of a Trustee, dated May 2, 1988, 86 B.R. 455, sets forth its reasons for granting the motion for appointment of a trustee and denying the motion to vacate that order and approve the stipulation. It relied on 11 U.S.C. § 1104, which provides:

> (a) At any time after the commencement of the case but before confirmation of a plan, on request of a party in interest ..., and after notice and a hearing, the court shall order the appointment of a trustee—
>
> (1) for cause, including fraud, dishonesty, incompetence, or gross mismanagement of the affairs of the debtor by current management, either before or after the commencement of the case, or similar cause, but not including the number of holders of securities of the debtor or the amount of assets or liabilities of the debtor; or
>
> (2) if such appointment is in the interests of creditors, any equity security holders, and other interests of the estate, without regard to the number of holders of securities of the debtor or the amount of assets or liabilities of the debtor.

11 U.S.C. § 1104 (1982 & Supp. IV 1986) (footnote added). The facts before the court, it found, satisfied both subparts. It cited numerous prepetition transfers of Sharon assets that amounted at best to voidable preferences and at worst to fraudulent conveyances, none of which had been questioned by the debtor-in-possession.[9] Not only had Sharon

---

9. These either preferential transfers or fraudulent conveyances include a $3.7 million wire transfer made by Sharon to DWG on April 16, 1986 apparently in payment of a $3.58 million annual charge including $122,433.21 rent for the chairman's office, $74,465.53 for use of a yacht that Sharon owned, $170,483.26 for airplane usage (although the plane also was owned by Sharon), $230,422.28 for use of the guest apartments in Miami, and $100,833.21 for accommodations in the Waldorf–Astoria; a December 1986 transfer by Sharon to NPC Leasing Company, under common control with Sharon, of title to a yacht and airplane, each minimally valued at $750,000; a March 16, 1987 transfer of 141,000 common shares in Chesapeake Financial Corporation, valued by the trustee at $24 million, to Insurance and Risk Management, also connected to Sharon by interlocking directors, in satisfaction of an antecedent debt of $1,512,493.75; and approximately $16 million in compensation paid to Victor Posner between 1983 and September 1987, including $4.4 million paid by Sharon for his defense in a criminal action for individual tax evasion and conspiracy, and approximately $1.8 in compensation paid to Stephen Posner. App. 2107–08, 2112, 2114.

In its conclusions of law, the bankruptcy court held the transfers of the $3.7 million to DWG, the yacht and plane to NPC Leasing, and the 141,000 shares of Chesapeake Financial Corporation to Insurance and Risk Management constituted prima facie voidable preferences. It also held that the 1985 through March 1987 transfers of $9.8 million to Victor Posner and $940,000 to Stephen Posner "were not shown to be for an adequate consideration, and prima facia [sic] constitute fraudulent conveyances." App. 2124. The bankruptcy court also credited expert testimony that valued the Miami office space at $12.50 per square foot and noted that DWG charged Sharon $24. App. 2112.

The trustee has instituted several actions to recover various of these assets for the estate. He has sued Posner in United States district court for reimbursement of the criminal defense costs, excessive compensation paid to him, and damages caused by his mismanagement of the debtor. Civil Action No. 88–1850 (originally filed in the bankruptcy court on July 12, 1988 as Adversary No. 88–0042). The trustee also has brought two actions in the bankruptcy court: on August 19, 1988, Adversary No. 88–0052 to obtain books, records and financial information from DWG, Posner, and others; and on March 11, 1988, Adversary No. 88–0019 to recover the 141,000 shares of Chesapeake Financial Corporation stock from Insurance and Risk Management.

failed to sue for recovery of these transfers, but the bankruptcy court questioned the current management's ability to fulfill its fiduciary duty to pursue these claims since Sharon shares common management with the recipients of the transfers, who also owe conflicting fiduciary duties to the recipients. Disclosure of the transfers did not cure the preferential or fraudulent transfers.

The bankruptcy court also faulted Sharon's day-to-day management of the estate. Sharon, which continued to rely on DWG for financial services, had not yet closed out its books for the period preceding reorganization. Thus, not only was the debtor continuing to hemorrhage money at an estimated $2 million per month at a time when steel prices were rising, but the debtor could not even measure the precise size of these losses since it had no postpetition profit and loss statements.

Similarly, the court also criticized Sharon's failure to renegotiate its $30 million working capital loan from the 28% to 30% interest rate originally agreed to to a reasonable 14% to 15%—an action that would save Sharon $4 million a year. It also impugned the wisdom (and the propriety) of Sharon's repayment during 1985 and 1986 of $294 million in secured bank loans "in order to facilitate new loans from those banks to other Posner companies." App. 2113. Given Sharon's blast furnace crisis and the fact that the payments left Sharon so cash-poor that it was forced to enter into the $30 million, high-interest working capital loan, it concluded such actions amounted to gross mismanagement. *Id.*

Last, the bankruptcy court raised an even more fundamental issue when it questioned the $279,872.50 in attorneys' fees expended during the last quarter of 1987 to fight the appointment of the trustee:

> While the equity owners are entitled to representation and to assert their rights, one must speculate whether the expenditure of such resources was appropriate, and whether Sharon's counsel in doing so was fulfilling its fiduciary duty to the debtor's estate, or was defending the private position of the equity owners. The funds expended come from the estate, and in view of the admitted insolvency, will likely be borne chiefly by creditors.

App. 2118. The bankruptcy court determined that the sum of the above behavior amounted to cause under section 1104(a)(1). It also demonstrated the necessity of new management just to keep Sharon operating, therefore implicating the interests of the creditors and equity holders alike specified for appointment of a trustee under subsection (b).

* * *

Posner and DWG assert that the proper standard under which to review the bankruptcy court's decision to appoint a trustee is a plenary

---

The trustee also filed suit against Posner in the bankruptcy court on June 3, 1988 for the return of 14 original Norman Rockwell oil paintings that belonged to Sharon. Adversary No. 88–0030. In October 1988, the bankruptcy court approved without prejudice a stipulation requiring Posner to return the paintings.

one. Once again, the trustee and the committee argue for a clearly erroneous standard. While support clearly exists for their position, ... we agree with Posner and DWG that such a standard is inappropriate. We do not agree with Posner and DWG, however, that we exercise plenary review over appointment of a trustee. Instead, we join the Fourth Circuit in adopting an abuse of discretion standard. *See Committee of Dalkon Shield Claimants v. A.H. Robins Co., Inc.*, 828 F.2d 239, 242 (4th Cir.1987). Such a standard best comports with the language, structure, and purpose of section 1104(a).

It is settled that appointment of a trustee should be the exception, rather than the rule.

* * *

While 11 U.S.C. § 1104(a) mandates appointment of a trustee when the bankruptcy court finds cause—seemingly requiring plenary review, "a determination of cause ... is within the discretion of the court," *Committee of Dalkon Shield Claimants,* 828 F.2d at 242.

Subsection (a)(2) also creates a flexible standard, instructing the court to appoint a trustee when doing so addresses "the interests of the creditors, equity security holders, and other interests of the estate." 11 U.S.C. § 1104(a)(2) (1982 & Supp. IV 1986); * * * Subsection (a)(2) allows appointment of a trustee even when no "cause" exists. * * * Because subsection (a)(2) envisions a flexible standard, an abuse of discretion standard offers the most appropriate type of review for this subsection as well.

For the reasons already discussed, section 1104(a) decisions must be made on a case-by-case basis. Subsection (a)(1) requires the bankruptcy court, upon motion, to appoint a trustee when the movant has proved "cause," which the statute defines to include incompetence and gross mismanagement. Subsection (a)(2) emphasizes the court's discretion, allowing it to appoint a trustee when to do so would serve the parties' and estate's interests.

The movant, in this case the committee, must prove the need for a trustee by clear and convincing evidence.

* * *

The bankruptcy court found that the committee satisfied its burden under both subsections, and we cannot say that it abused its discretion in so concluding.

The bankruptcy court opinion conveys the image of a titanic industrial vessel foundering on the shoals of bankruptcy, steered there by at best careless management practices. These practices include payment of $294 million to secured creditors and $9.8 million and $970,000 without consideration to Victor and Stephen Posner respectively during a period when Sharon was so cash-poor that it could not afford to reline the vital number 2 blast furnace—so cash-poor that to continue operations on a daily basis it borrowed $30 million at 28% to 30% interest.

Other questionable management actions cited by the court include the petition-eve payment of $3.7 million to DWG, transfer of Sharon's yacht and plane to NPC, and transfer of the 141,000 shares of Chesapeake Financial Corporation stock to Insurance and Risk Management. At no time did Sharon's postpetition management try to recover any part of these transfers (or any part of the sums paid to Victor and Stephen Posner).

DWG and Posner claim that the court's November 1988 authorization for the committee to sue for recovery of these transfers cures its failure and eliminates any management conflicts of interest, rendering the court's determination erroneous. In fact, they claim that all of the alleged prepetition incidents of gross mismanagement have been corrected, forcing the court to rely on postpetition mismanagement, which they claim falls short of providing clear and convincing proof that a trustee is required. Specifically, they point to the appointment of Walter Sieckman as chief operating officer, and the court-acknowledged management improvements he had wrought since coming aboard. They also claim that Sharon's by-laws, in compliance with Pennsylvania law, authorized payment of Posner's $4.4 million in legal fees. According to Posner and DWG, these factors make the court's reliance upon the prepetition management problems improper.

* * *

Believing that they had cleared the prepetition gross mismanagement determinations, Posner and DWG hoped to sail past the trustee appointment by arguing that the court's remaining determinations of postpetition gross mismanagement do not satisfy the heavy burden of proof imposed on the movants. The court concluded that current management's failure to negotiate a reduction in the interest rate on the $30 million operating loan, to obtain up-to-date, comprehensive postpetition financial statements from DWG, and to cut or eliminate the estimated $2 million lost monthly despite the protection of the bankruptcy laws satisfied both subsections of section 1104(a). Furthermore, it held "[t]he ongoing problem of fair allocation of costs of the Miami offices among Sharon and other Posner-owned businesses is exacerbated by the conflicts of interest, and only an independent trustee can make a proper investigation and determination of the best interests of Sharon."

Once again, we cannot say that the bankruptcy court abused its discretion. Under the discretionary determination of cause required by 11 U.S.C. § 1104(a)(1) and the flexible standard embodied in (a)(2), the court acted within its discretion in concluding that the totality of the circumstances signaled the need for a trustee. Despite improvements instituted by Walter Sieckman, too many major problems remained— problems symptomatic of potential bankruptcy despite the calm harbor provided by Chapter 11. Failure to force closure of the prepetition books and production of current financial statements nine months after filing, combined with continued losses exacerbated by the failure to cut a major expense like the approximately $4 million in added interest on the operating loan, signaled the court that as captain, the debtor-in-possession had continued to steer Sharon toward bankruptcy rather than to turn her about toward solvency. Corrective measures that are too few too late cannot defeat a change in command. The bankruptcy court's opinion clearly indicates it felt appointment necessary to save Sharon from bankruptcy. We agree.

* * *

COMMITTEE OF DALKON SHIELD CLAIMANTS v. A.H. ROBINS CO., INC.

United States Court of Appeals, Fourth Circuit, 1987.
828 F.2d 239.

DONALD RUSSELL, CIRCUIT JUDGE:

This is an appeal by the Dalkon Shield Claimants' Committee from the district court's order denying the Committee's motion pursuant to 11 U.S.C. § 1104 (1987) for the appointment of a United States trustee for A.H. Robins Company. The issue before us is whether the court was obligated to appoint a trustee to manage Robins after the court found Robins in civil contempt of its Order barring Robins from selectively paying off pre-petition debts without prior court approval.

On August 23, 1985 the district court entered a Consent Order providing in part that Robins could not pay pre-petition debts without prior court approval. Subsequently, and without court approval or knowledge, Robins made payments on pre-petition claims including: (a) payments under a benefit plan to present and past executives of Robins, (b) payments through its subsidiaries on certain pre-petition debts, (c) payments under executory contracts which had not been assumed and (d) payments to settle a pre-petition lawsuit brought by an employee of Robins. Moreover, Robins used certain of its subsidiaries to make prohibited charitable contributions and to make certain investments.

The Committee moved for the appointment of a trustee pursuant to Section 1104(a) to protect creditors from further abuses by Robins. Following the hearing on the appellants' motion, the district court ruled that Robins was in civil contempt and that sanctions would be imposed at a later date. The court found that the debtor had not only "knowingly, unknowingly, or because of failure to comprehend the Court's order violated a court order, but also [had] taken certain actions prohibited by both the spirit and the letter of the bankruptcy laws." The court, however, declined to appoint a trustee to run Robins' business as requested by the Committee, deciding instead to appoint an examiner pursuant to Section 1104(b).

* * *

We find that a careful reading of the court's opinion reveals that the court did not find cause to appoint a trustee within the meaning of Section 1104(a)(1). The court noted specifically that it had not found fraud or mismanagement. Further, it stated that the concepts of incompetence and dishonesty cover a wide spectrum of conduct and that the court has broad discretion in applying such concepts to show cause. The court examined the entire situation, including the consequences of appointing a trustee, and determined that the debtor had not given the court cause to appoint a trustee. The Committee misconstrues the court's statement regarding its discretion, given in a finding of cause, to appoint a trustee. We believe that the court's statement can only be construed to be a general assertion by the court of its discretionary authority in the event, not present here, that it were to find cause.

The Committee, however, also argues that the facts of this case compel a finding of cause. It asserts that Robins' lack of candor and preferential treatment of certain pre-petition creditors were dishonest and otherwise constituted cause. Like the district court, we recognize that Robins' conduct was improper and warranted a civil contempt sanction. But a policy of flexibility pervades the bankruptcy code with the ultimate aim of protecting creditors. A determination of cause, therefore, is within the discretion of the court and due consideration must be given to the various interests involved in the bankruptcy proceeding. "[T]he concepts of incompetence, dishonesty, gross mismanagement and even fraud all cover a wide range of conduct.... Implicit in a finding of incompetence, dishonesty, etc., for purposes of section 1104(a)(1), is whether the conduct shown rises to a level sufficient to warrant the appointment of a trustee." *General Oil*, 42 B.R. at 409. Obviously, to require the appointment of a trustee, regardless of the consequences, in the event of an act of dishonesty by the debtor, however slight or immaterial, could frustrate the purpose of the Bankruptcy Act. Section 1104(a)(1), therefore, must be construed, if possible, to make it harmonious with the Act in its entirety. Such a construction requires that the courts be given discretionary authority to determine whether conduct rises to the level of "cause."

Given the court's discretion and the careful consideration that it gave to the interests involved, we find that the court did not err in declining to find cause. The court's decision not to appoint a trustee was also within its discretionary authority and it is clear that the court did not abuse this authority. Since we hold that the court did not abuse its discretion in determining that cause did not exist, we need not reach the question concerning the statutory consequences of a finding of cause.

Question

When an LBO fails and a company must file for reorganization under Chapter 11, the managers are also typically the residual claimants, the equity holders, who stand to lose the total value of their equity interest. Is the managers' temptation to find other ways to pull money out of a firm in reorganization too strong to justify current legal doctrine? Should there be a different standard for cases where management holds a substantial equity position?

SECTION 2. THE BARGAINING POSITION OF EQUITY HOLDERS IN CHAPTER 11 PROCEEDINGS

A plan of reorganization represents a negotiation among the firm's various investors (equity holders), as well as debt holders. An important part of the confirmation hearing is the acceptance of the plan by all creditors or equity holders whose claims or interests are impaired. § 1129(a)(7). A class of creditors accepts a plan by a vote of a simple majority in number of creditors, and of two-thirds in amount of debt of those who actually vote. § 1126(c). A class of equity holders accepts a plan by a two-thirds vote. § 1126(d). If a plan is not accepted by all classes, a court can confirm the plan only under its "cram-down" powers. § 1129(b). The code permits cram-down of the rejecting class only if the plan does not discriminate unfairly between classes and is "fair and equitable." The minimum requirements for "fair and equitable" are divided into three categories governing the rights of secured creditors, unsecured creditors, and stockholders. § 1129(b)(2). As a general matter, liens of secured creditors must be preserved by the plan, and the creditors must be paid the "present value" of their allowed secured claims. Unsecured creditors and preferred stockholders must be paid in full, or the plan must provide that any parties "junior" to them will get nothing. This is often called the absolute priority rule. The definition of "paid in full" for equity securities is the greater of the market value of their interest, fixed liquidation preference, and redemption price due. § 1129(b)(2)(C).

As you might expect, holders of common stock in a firm that is insolvent—that is, the firm's debts exceed its assets—have no incentive to vote for a plan that gives them nothing. In such cases, the court often will have to exercise its cram-down powers to approve such a plan over their objection. The bargaining power of the common shares is limited to their ability to cause trouble and expense if they are not given something to induce them to vote in favor of any proposed plan. Moreover, on occasion the holders of common stock attempt to get a court to confirm a plan that they favor over the objections of senior claims or interests. In the cases that follow, equity holders have attempted to emerge from Chapter 11 with some of their equity interests intact. The first case is an instance of clever desperation; the second two cases represent the shareholders' best chance for success—a claim of new capital investment.

IN RE GENESEE CEMENT, INC.
United States Bankruptcy Court, Eastern District of Michigan, 1983.
31 B.R. 442.

BERNSTEIN, BANKRUPTCY JUDGE.

The debtor has filed an amended plan of reorganization which provides that the claims of unsecured creditors will be impaired and the equity security holder, the 100 percent shareholder, will retain its interest. Must the disclosure statement explain that unless the impaired class of holders of unsecured claims accepts the plan, the debtor's plan cannot be confirmed under 11 U.S.C. § 1129(b)(2)(B)(ii) because it would violate the "fair and equitable" test?

The amended disclosure statement explains that the debtor, a Michigan corporation, was formed in 1957 and is a wholly-owned subsidiary of the Palmer Corporation. The debtor owns and presently operates a cement block plant. Prior to the filing of its Chapter 11 petition, the debtor also operated a redi-mix cement plant as a lessee from its parent corporation. During the Chapter 11 case, the Court approved a sale by the parent corporation (and a termination of the lease) of the redi-mix concrete division.

The economic performance of the debtor during the Chapter 11 has been positive although marginal. Its net income from the petition date, April 22, 1982, through March of 1983 is approximately $40,000. This is a significant improvement over the pre-petition losses of $220,762 in 1982 and $409,907 in 1981. The debtor has, moreover, paid its secured debt as well as post-petition taxes and trade payables on a current basis.

The pre-petition obligations include a Michigan single business tax liability of $4,025.00, allowed unsecured claims of $93,058.48, and unpaid fees to the debtor's counsel of approximately $6,000, subject to approval by the Court.

The plan proposes to pay the pre-petition tax over six years from the date of assessment, a 10 percent dividend to unsecured creditors, and allowed [post-petition] debts in full upon confirmation. The debtor has also disclosed an estimated tax loss carry-forward of $405,312 to shelter future taxable income.

Finally, under the plan, the parent corporation as the sole equity security holder is to retain its interest.

The amended disclosure statement also sets forth a detailed liquidation analysis, including appraisals of assets and projection of sales.

The rub in this amended disclosure statement is the debtor's contention, explicitly set forth in that statement, that because the reorganized corporation will have a negative net worth—the secured debt exceeds the forced sale value of the collateral, the value of the interest of the equity security is zero; therefore, the equity security holder "will have recovered nothing under the plan." For this reason the debtor argues that a cram-down against the nonaccepting impaired class of unsecured creditors will not offend the "fair and equitable" test of 11 U.S.C. § 1129(b)(2)(B)(ii).

This Court disagrees with the debtor's disingenuous construction of 11 U.S.C. § 1129(b)(2)(B)(ii). First a literal reading of 11 U.S.C.

§ 1129(b)(2)(B)(ii) is absolute on its face: the equity security holder cannot *"receive or retain"* any property on account of its interest under the plan of reorganization if the impaired class of unsecured creditors does not accept the plan. This is simply a matter of equity and public policy; the equity security holder, as proponent of the plan, cannot both discount and discharge prior claims and also retain its ownership interest in the reorganized company unless the unsecured creditors affirmatively accept that treatment. Otherwise the holder of a junior interest would succeed in subordinating a legal claim entitled to priority as a matter of state law. It is too basic a maxim to bear repetition that an equity security holder's interest can only be retained if trade creditors' claims are fully paid.

Secondly, this Court is very skeptical that the present discounted value of the interest of the equity security holder is zero. To reach that result, the debtor relies upon a forced sale, rather than fair market value, of the corporation's tangible assets. That has the practical effect of deflating the value of the interest of the equity security holder. More importantly, the very large tax loss carry-forward should be taken into consideration. The expected profits of the company will be sheltered, as the debtor candidly admits. For these reasons the liquidation analysis as it reflects on the value of the equity security holder's interest is seriously misleading.

Thirdly, the retained interest of the equity security holders has a value measured in terms other than net worth. As noted in *Boyd*, [228 U.S. 482 (1913),] there is "value" in the retention by the equity security holder of *control* of the reorganized company.

In light of the foregoing, the Court cannot approve the amended disclosure statement in its present form. The Court is, however, disposed to approving a second amended disclosure statement, without further hearing or notice to creditors, provided that 11 U.S.C. § 1129(b)(2)(B)(ii) is properly explained, and the alternatives facing the unsecured creditors, including the consequences of denial of confirmation, are also properly explained. The Court is cognizant of the fact that this opinion requires the debtor to waive a red cape at the impaired unsecured creditors. Full disclosure providing adequate information so that unsecured creditors can make an informed choice is always painful and risky If the debtor expects to persuade the unsecured creditors to waive 90 percent of their allowed claims, it must bite that bullet.

The debtor's application for approval of its amended disclosure statement is denied.

* * *

IN RE FUTURE ENERGY CORP.
United States Bankruptcy Court, Southern District of Ohio, 1988.
83 B.R. 470.

R. Guy Cole, Jr., Bankruptcy Judge.

This matter is before the Court following a hearing held to consider confirmation of the Third Amended Plan of Reorganization ("Plan") filed in this Chapter 11 case. The Plan has been jointly proposed by Future Energy Corporation (hereinafter "Future" or "debtor" or "debtor-in-possession"), Krutex Energy Corporation ("Krutex") and Canyon Development Corporation ("Canyon")—(hereinafter referred to as the "Proponents"). Objections to confirmation have been lodged by Columbia Gas Transmission Corp. ("TCO"), the holder of an unsecured claim, and Pattison Petroleum Corporation ("Pattison"), the holder of both a secured and an unsecured claim against Future.

* * * On January 14, 1987, following extensive negotiations, Krutex acquired 100% of the outstanding common shares of Future. Hence, Future became a wholly-owned subsidiary of Krutex prior to filing for relief in this Court. * * * Future filed its Chapter 11 petition on February 10, 1987.

* * *

Subsequent to the filing of Future's Chapter 11 petition, Krutex, through Decker and its counsel, continued to negotiate with various creditors of Future in an attempt to obtain assignments of their claims.

* * *

Because Canyon also was acquiring the claims of Future's creditors, it became apparent by the early summer of 1987 that a "bidding war" had developed between Krutex and Canyon over the control of Future's assets. Krutex determined that the time and expense involved in attempting to successfully reorganize Future would be increased unnecessarily if the competition between Krutex and Canyon continued. Accordingly, Krutex and Canyon commenced a series of negotiations which culminated on August 19, 1987, in the sale by Krutex to Canyon of 80% of the outstanding common shares of Future. Pursuant to the terms of this agreement, Canyon assumed responsibility for Future's actual day-to-day operations. Under the agreement, although Krutex relinquished control of Future's operations to Canyon, it retained a percentage share of Future's oil and gas working and royalty interests.

* * *

1) *Consideration Received by Krutex From Canyon*

(a) Krutex received a cash payment of $66,400 from Canyon.

2) *Consideration Received by Canyon From Krutex*

(a) Canyon received 80% of the outstanding common shares of Future;

(b) Canyon received an assignment of Krutex's claim against Future in the amount of $66,400, which arose from the loan made by Krutex to Future on February 6, 1987, as well as an assignment of the security interests collateralizing its $66,400 loan to Future; and

(c) Krutex arranged for the assignment by Foreland to Canyon of a 25% working interest in the oil and gas properties of Future and a 25% interest in Future's gas transmission revenues.

* * *

The Plan provides for the cancellation of all the existing shares of Future's stock. Upon confirmation, however, 100% of the stock of the newly-reorganized Future would be issued to Canyon. In return, Canyon proposes to make a capital contribution consisting of the following:

(1) To the extent that the post-confirmation revenues of Future are insufficient to pay the five percent dividend to unsecured creditors contemplated by the Plan, Canyon will fund the distribution to unsecured creditors. Approximately $35,000 will be required to provide for unsecured creditors under the Plan;

(2) Canyon will release Future from all liability on the secured claims of Halliburton and Ohio Steel, in the face amounts of $231,578.95 and $91,310.01, respectively, which were purchased by Canyon for $105,000 and $17,000, respectively; and

(3) Canyon will pay the attorney fees it incurred in connection with the formation and proposal of the Plan and will not seek to recover such fees from the estate.

* * *

The Bankruptcy Code provides two means by which a Chapter 11 plan may be confirmed. The first way, which has been referred to as the "consent" or "acceptance" method, is to meet all eleven requirements of § 1129(a), including subsection (a)(8), which provides that all impaired classes of claims or interests must accept the plan. The second way to achieve confirmation of a plan of reorganization is pursuant to the so-called cram-down provisions of § 1129(b). Section 1129(b) provides that, if a plan meets all of the applicable requirements of § 1129(a), except paragraph (8), the Court, upon request by the proponent of the plan, shall confirm the plan if it does not discriminate unfairly and is fair and equitable with respect to each class of claims or interests that is impaired under and has not accepted the plan. Confirmation under § 1129(b) is referred to as a cram-down because the plan is permitted to go into effect over the objections of one or more impaired classes of creditors.

* * *

The Proponents invoke the cram-down provisions of § 1129(b) in an attempt to gain confirmation of the Plan over the objections of TCO and Pattison. The Proponents concede that both Classes C–1 (working interest holders whose claims are secured by production proceeds) and C–2 (unrecorded working interest holders whose claims are unsecured as a matter of state law) have rejected the Plan. Pattison is a member of both of these dissenting classes.

* * *

Section 1129(b)(2)(B) provides that, with respect to a class of dissenting unsecured creditors, a plan will be deemed to be fair and equitable if one of two tests is met. First, the plan may provide that each unsecured creditor in the class receive or retain property having a value, as of the effective date of the plan, equal to the allowed amount of its claim. 11 U.S.C. § 1129(b)(2)(B)(i). Here, the Plan does not provide the unsecured creditors in Classes C–2 and D–1 with property equal to the amount of their allowed claims. Hence, the Plan does not meet the fair and equitable standard of § 1129(b)(2)(B)(i).

Alternatively, a plan of reorganization may provide any treatment for a class of unsecured creditors, including no participation at all, so long as no junior claims or interests participate in the plan or retain an interest in the debtor's property. 11 U.S.C. § 1129(b)(2)(B)(ii). Essentially, § 1129(b)(2)(B)(ii) applies a modified version of the traditional absolute priority rule, which was initially established in *National Pacific Railway Co. v. Boyd*, 228 U.S. 482, 33 S.Ct. 554, 57 L.Ed. 931 (1913). Simply stated, the absolute priority rule provides that a dissenting class of unsecured creditors must be provided for in full before any junior class can receive or retain any property under the plan.

* * *

[A]n exception to the absolute priority rule has been established by the decisional law. This exception provides that a holder of a claim or interest may receive a distribution or retain an interest in the reorganized debtor, even though all senior classes of creditors are not to be paid in full under the plan, if the holder of the claim or interest makes a contribution of new capital in the form of money or money's worth that is reasonably equivalent in value to the interest retained or the distribution received.

* * *

The Proponents assert that Canyon has made a substantial contribution of new capital to the debtor. Hence, they submit that the absolute priority rule has been satisfied and the Plan may be crammed down over the objection of the dissenting unsecured classes. This contention will be examined below.

Canyon asserts that its new capital contribution, which justifies retention of a 100% ownership interest in Future, consists of the following: (1) Canyon's release of Future from all liability on the secured claims of Halliburton and Ohio Steel; (2) Canyon's payment of its own attorney fees attributable to the formulation and presentation of the Plan; and (3) Canyon's commitment to fund the five percent distribution to unsecured creditors (in the approximate amount of $35,000) in the event Future cannot fund such a distribution. TCO and Pattison argue that Canyon's release of claims does not constitute a capital contribution. Alternatively, the objectors submit that, if Canyon's release of the Halliburton and Ohio Steel claims is deemed to be a capital contribution, it is not such a substantial capital contribution as would allow Canyon's retention of an ownership interest in Future.

TCO and Pattison urge the Court to rule that Canyon's release of Future from liability on the Halliburton and Ohio Steel claims does not constitute a capital contribution. The Proponents, on the other hand, submit that Canyon's proposed release should be deemed to be a capital contribution which is sufficient to satisfy the exception to the absolute priority rule established in *Case*. In support of this proposition, the Proponents cite *United States v. Cole*, 90 F.Supp. 147 (S.D.Cal.1950) and *Crow v. Newspaper Dealer Supply, Inc.*, 603 F.Supp. 847 (E.D.Mo.1985). Each of these cases is clearly inapposite. Neither *Cole* (a criminal income tax evasion case) nor *Crow* (action to recover on a promissory note which was brought in federal court due to diversity of citizenship) deal with bankruptcy law, much less the present issue. These decisions provide absolutely no support for the Proponents' argument. Instead, these cases merely state, in *dicta*, that under state law (in California and Missouri, respectively) shares of stock may be issued by a corporation in return for foregiveness of debt.

The Court's review of the case law has revealed no decision which squarely addresses the issue before it: Should Canyon's release of claims be deemed to be a capital contribution? In the vast majority of the reported decisions reviewed by the Court, the party seeking to retain an ownership interest in the reorganized debtor made a capital contribution in the form of cash or property. Two recent decisions have dealt with an analogous question: Whether a shareholder's guarantee of the debt of the reorganized debtor constitutes a capital contribution? In both *In re Potter Material Service, Inc.*, supra, and *In re Sawmill Hydraulics, Inc.*, 72 B.R. 454 (Bankr.C.D.Ill.1987), it was held that a shareholder's guarantee of the debt of the reorganized debtor should be deemed to be a capital contribution. The principle which may be derived from these decisions is that, if the transaction in question both benefits the debtor and places the shareholder in a position of economic risk, a capital contribution within the meaning of *Case* and its progeny shall be deemed to have been made.[42] *In re Sawmill Hydraulics, Inc.*, 72 B.R. at 457.

Applying the principles postulated by the courts in *Potter Material Service* and *Sawmill Hydraulics* to the present case, the Court concludes that Canyon's release of claims may be deemed to be a form of

---

42. Essentially, the Court must determine whether Canyon's release of secured claims constitutes a contribution in "money's worth." *See, Case v. Los Angeles Lumber Products Co.*, 308 U.S. at 122, 60 S.Ct. at 10. The most expansive interpretation of the phrase "money's worth" was given by the Eighth Circuit in *In re Ahlers*, 794 F.2d 388 (8th Cir.1986). In *Ahlers*, the court held that a debtor's contribution of labor and expertise to his farming operation was a capital contribution in money's worth within the meaning of *Case*. *Id.*, at 402. The oft-criticized *Ahlers* decision is presently on appeal to the Supreme Court, *see, Norwest Bank Worthington v. Ahlers*, ___ U.S. ___, 107 S.Ct. 3227, 97 L.Ed.2d 733 (1987) (granting certiorari).

capital contribution. The release of two fairly substantial secured claims is of obvious benefit to the debtor. Moreover, the economic risk criterion also is clearly satisfied. Indeed, if Canyon executes a release of the Halliburton and Ohio Steel claims and Future then fails to comply with the terms of its confirmed plan, Canyon will certainly sustain a very real economic loss. Accordingly, the Court concludes that Canyon has assumed an economic risk in releasing Future from liability on the Halliburton and Ohio Steel claims and, hence, this transaction shall be viewed as a capital contribution. * * * But, on the record made at hearing, the Court is unable to ascertain the value of Canyon's capital contribution.

* * *

Canyon also submits that its capital contribution consists of its payment of the attorney fees which were expended in connection with the formulation and presentation of the Plan. Payment of professional fees of a debtor that is seeking confirmation of a Chapter 11 plan has been deemed to be an element of a capital contribution for purposes of satisfying the absolute priority rule. * * * Review of the record reveals, however, that no testimony regarding the amount of attorney fees incurred by Canyon in formulating and presenting the Plan was offered. Accordingly, the Court is left again with insufficient evidence to ascertain the total amount of Canyon's capital contribution.

Finally, the Court notes that it has not considered Canyon's promise to fund the proposed five percent distribution to unsecured creditors (in the event Future is unable to do so from post-petition operating revenues) as a component of Canyon's capital contribution. It is well-established that a new capital investment must be a present contribution, not a contribution promised in the future. * * * Thus, Canyon's promise of a future contribution is not properly included as an element of its proposed capital contribution.

Under the *Case* decision, the Court is required to make a comparison between the value of the shareholder's retained interest in the reorganized debtor and such shareholder's new capital investment in order to determine whether the new investment equals or exceeds the retained interest in the corporation. 308 U.S. at 121, 60 S.Ct. at 10. * * * As the foregoing discussion indicates, the Court is unable to ascertain the value of Canyon's proposed capital contribution due to glaring deficiencies in the record. * * * The incomplete record made by the Proponents at hearing likewise precludes the Court from determining a value for Canyon's retained interest in the reorganized debtor.

* * *

Questions

1. Did Canyon pay $66,400 in cash for equity in Future or for assignments of Krutex's claims in Future?

2. How has Canyon put "new money" into Future? Why has he chosen to do so?

3. What problems does this new development in Chapter 11 proceedings (equity holders putting new funds into the firm to keep their equity position) pose for bankruptcy courts?

NORWEST BANK WORTHINGTON v. AHLERS
Supreme Court of the United States, 1988.
485 U.S. 197, 108 S.Ct. 963, 99 L.Ed.2d 169.

* * *

As the Court of Appeals stated, the absolute priority rule "provides that a dissenting class of unsecured creditors must be provided for in full before any junior class can receive or retain any property [under a reorganization] plan." *Id.*, at 401. The rule had its genesis in judicial construction of the undefined requirement of the early bankruptcy statute that reorganization plans be "fair and equitable."

... The rule has since gained express statutory force, and was incorporated into Chapter 11 of the Bankruptcy Code adopted in 1978. See 11 U.S.C. § 1129(b)(2)(B)(ii) (1982 ed., Supp. IV). Under current law, no Chapter 11 reorganization plan can be confirmed over the creditors' legitimate objections (absent certain conditions not relevant here) if it fails to comply with the absolute priority rule.

There is little doubt that a reorganization plan in which respondents retain an equity interest in the farm is contrary to the absolute priority rule. The Court of Appeals did not suggest otherwise in ruling for respondents, but found that such a plan could be confirmed over petitioners' objections because of an "exception" or "modification" to the absolute priority rule recognized in this Court's cases.

The Court of Appeals relied on the following dicta in *Case v. Los Angeles Lumber Products Co., supra,* 308 U.S., at 121–122, 60 S.Ct., at 10:

> "It is, of course, clear that there are circumstances under which stockholders may participate in a plan of reorganization of an insolvent debtor...
>
> "[W]e believe that to accord 'the creditor of his full right of priority against the corporate assets' where the debtor is insolvent, the stockholder's participation must be based on a contribution in money or money's worth, reasonably equivalent in view of all the circumstances to the participation of the stockholder."

The Court of Appeals found this language applicable to this case, concluding that respondents' future contributions of "labor, experience, and expertise" in running the farm—because they have "value" and are "measurable"—are "money or money's worth" within the meaning of *Los Angeles Lumber.* 794 F.2d, at 402. We disagree.[3]

---

3. The United States, as *amicus curiae,* urges us to reverse the Court of Appeals'

Los Angeles Lumber itself rejected an analogous proposition, finding that the promise of the existing shareholders to pledge their "financial standing and influence in the community" and their "continuity of management" to the reorganized enterprise was "[in]adequate consideration" that could not possibly be deemed "money's worth." *Los Angeles Lumber,* 308 U.S., at 122, 60 S.Ct., at 10. No doubt, the efforts promised by the *Los Angeles Lumber* equity-holders—like those of respondents—had "value" and would have been of some benefit to any reorganized enterprise. But ultimately, as the Court said in *Los Angeles Lumber,* "They reflect merely vague hopes or possibilities." *Id.,* at 122–123, 60 S.Ct., at 11. The same is true of respondents' pledge of future labor and management skills.

Viewed from the time of approval of the plan, respondents' promise of future services is intangible, inalienable, and, in all likelihood, unenforceable. It "has no place in the asset column of the balance sheet of the new [entity]." *Los Angeles Lumber, supra,* at 122–123, 60 S.Ct., at 11. Unlike "money or money's worth," a promise of future services cannot be exchanged in any market for something of value to the creditors *today.* In fact, no decision of this Court or any Court of Appeals, other than the decision below, has ever found a promise to contribute future labor, management, or expertise sufficient to qualify for the *Los Angeles Lumber* exception to the absolute priority rule. In short, there is no way to distinguish between the promises respondents proffer here and those of the shareholders in *Los Angeles Lumber;* neither is an adequate contribution to escape the absolute priority rule.

Respondents suggest that, even if their proposed contributions to the reorganized farm do not fit within the *Los Angeles Lumber* dicta, they do satisfy some broader exception to the absolute priority rule. Brief for Respondents 23–24. But no such broader exception exists. Even if Congress meant to retain the *Los Angeles Lumber* exception to the absolute priority rule when it codified the rule in Chapter 11—a proposition that can be debated, see n. 3, *supra*—it is clear that Congress had no intention to expand that exception any further. When considering adoption of the current Code, Congress received a proposal

ruling and hold that codification of the absolute priority rule has eliminated any "exception" to that rule suggested by *Los Angeles Lumber,* 308 U.S. 106, 60 S.Ct. 1, 84 L.Ed. 110 (1939). See Brief for United States as *Amicus Curiae* 17–23. Relying on the statutory language and the legislative history, the Solicitor General argues that the 1978 Bankruptcy Code "dropped the infusion-of-new-capital exception to the absolute priority rule." *Id.,* at 22.

We need not reach this question to resolve the instant dispute. As we discuss *infra,* at —, we think it clear that even if the *Los Angeles Lumber* exception to the absolute priority rule has survived enactment of the Bankruptcy Code, this excep-

tion does not encompass respondents' promise to contribute their "labor, experience, and expertise" to the reorganized enterprise.

Thus, our decision today should not be taken as any comment on the continuing vitality of the *Los Angeles Lumber* exception—a question which has divided the lower courts since passage of the Code in 1978.... (Bkrtcy.Ct.SDNY 1982). Rather, we simply conclude that even if an "infusion-of-'money-or-money's-worth'" exception to the absolute priority rule has survived the enactment of § 1129(b), respondents' proposed contribution to the reorganization plan is inadequate to gain the benefit of this exception.

by the Bankruptcy Commission to modify the absolute priority rule to permit equity-holders to participate in a reorganized enterprise based on their contribution of "continued management ... essential to the business" or other participation beyond "money or money's worth." See H.R.Doc. No. 93–137, pt. 1, pp. 258–259 (1973). This proposal—quite similar to the Court of Appeals' holding in this case—prompted adverse reactions from numerous sources. Congress ultimately rejected the proposed liberalization of the absolute priority rule and adopted the codification of the rule now found in 11 U.S.C. § 1129(b)(2)(B) (1982 ed. and Supp. IV). "This [section] codifies the absolute priority rule from the dissenting class on down." See H.R.Rep. No. 95–595, p. 413 (1977), U.S.Code Cong. & Admin.News 1978, pp. 5787, 6369. We think the statutory language and the legislative history of § 1129(b) clearly bar any expansion of any exception to the absolute priority rule beyond that recognized in our cases at the time Congress enacted the 1978 Bankruptcy Code.

* * *

SECTION 3. THE APPLICATION OF STATE CORPORATE CODES AND FEDERAL SECURITIES LAWS IN A BANKRUPTCY PROCEEDING

The Bankruptcy Code expressly allows a firm in Chapter 11 proceedings to exchange debt for equity and issue other new securities, § 1123(a)(J), sell assets, § 1123(a)(5)(B) & (D), and engage in consolidations and mergers. § 1123(a)(3). As we saw in earlier chapters, state corporate codes and federal securities laws affect the rights of shareholders in each of these instances. What becomes of these protections in bankruptcy proceedings?

Subsection a. State Corporation Laws

Please read Delaware General Corporation Law section 363 in your statutory supplement. What state corporate code procedures are not followed in the following case?

IN RE WHITE MOTOR CREDIT CORP.
United States Bankruptcy Court, Northern District of Ohio, 1981.
14 B.R. 584.

MARK SCHLACHET, BANKRUPTCY JUDGE.

This matter arises upon (a) the application of certain debtors (sometimes referred to as a "debtor") for a hearing to consider a sale of substantially all of the operating assets of White Motor Corporation ("White" or "White Motor") and Gemini Manufacturing Co. ("Gemini"), and (b) the application relating to such sale filed by the Official Creditors' Committee of Gemini.

* * *

On September 4, 1980, White Motor and certain of its affiliates, including subsidiaries Gemini and White Motor Credit Corporation ("White Credit"), each filed with the Court a petition under Chapter 11 of Title 11 of the United States Code (the "Bankruptcy Code").

* * *

As indicated above, White Motor has incurred significant losses in excess of $33 million since the filing date and management forecasts that such losses will continue.

On June 9, 1981, White Motor, Gemini and White Motor International, Inc. entered into an agreement with AB Volvo for the sale of substantially all those debtors' truck manufacturing operations to a subsidiary of AB Volvo. The conditions precedent to the obligations of AB Volvo under this purchase agreement include (a) the entry of an order which unconditionally approves the agreement and the transaction contemplated by it and (b) consummation of the sale no later than August 31, 1981. Accordingly, unless the Volvo transaction is approved by the Court at a time which will permit the closing to take place by August 31, 1981, AB Volvo may withdraw its offer to purchase the truck manufacturing operations of White Motor and its affiliates.

* * *

The contemplated sale constitutes a reorganization of White Motor, transforming the manufacturing debtors into what subordinated debt's representative has called a "pot of cash." Debtors seek to accomplish this reorganization under the administrative power of section 363 of the Bankruptcy Code, which section simply permits a sale other than in the ordinary course of business after notice and opportunity for hearing. Such a procedure side-steps the procedural and substantive provisions of Chapter 11 itself, including the disclosure statement (§ 1125), vote (§ 1126) and confirmation standards (§ 1129). There is no acknowledgement or recognition of the sale of all or substantially all of the property of a Chapter 11 debtor outside the provisions of Chapter 11 itself. *See, e.g.,* 11 U.S.C. §§ 1123(a)(5) and (b)(4), 1141(d)(3). ... Indeed, under the Bankruptcy Act there existed an outright conflict among the circuits.

* * *

The more restrictive Act authority, *i.e., Solar,* would require an actual emergency, defined perhaps as virtual or near catastrophe. Such emergency would not be found in mere deadlines or eleventh hour pressure imposed by the parties. The liberal view embraced by the Fifth, Seventh and Ninth Circuits permitted such sales in the best interests of the estate merely to avoid erosion of the assets, although in most cases findings of fact indicated severe diminution should the sale not be approved.

* * *

As a matter of legislative intent, to endow section 363 with the purpose of or a potential for a total reorganization would nullify, at debtor's option, the major protections and standards of chapter 11 of the Code. For example, while section 1129 requires a confirmation hearing as to every liquidating (or other) reorganization plan, section 363 taken together with section 102 requires mere opportunity for hearing. In the instant case, therefore, the Volvo transaction could proceed without any hearing or court order whatever. So manifestly unacceptable a possibility renders further investigation of statutory thrust unnecessary.

It is clear, and the Court holds accordingly, that in a chapter 11 reorganization under the Bankruptcy Code, section 363(b) does not authorize sale of all or substantially all assets of the estate.

THE EMERGENCY EXCEPTION

There is an emergency, or at least a crisis, in this case—but one of the debtor's own making. The situation is not one of imminent loss of all assets, but rather, a substantial likelihood of a comparative loss approaching $40 million, according to the debtor's Liquidation Analysis (July 17, 1981), should the sale not proceed. The crisis might have been avoided by firmer Court control and supervision of debtor's activities, or by empowering the examiner with additional functions pursuant to 11 U.S.C. § 1104(c). In any event, it would appear that Congress left the "emergency" exception in tact and its application is appropriate in this case. 11 U.S.C. § 105.

There are, moreover, other considerations which warrant exceptional treatment of the proposed sale to Volvo. First, White is and has been a first rate if not the leading truck manufacturer in its class VIII classification. Its engineering tradition is second to none. It has, however, suffered over a long period of time from a lack of strong management. While its current chief executive, Wallace Askins, cannot be praised too highly, one man may not be able to, in short order, reinstill the will to survive and accomplish the necessary infusion of dealer confidence.

White's chronic management problems indicate a significant likelihood—particularly under current market conditions over which it has no control—of a less advantageous liquidation should the Volvo agreement not gain approval. In other words, there exists no viable and acceptable alternative to Volvo at this time. No major constituency in this case can cite a strong probability of position enhancement should the Court not consider Volvo prior to August 31st. The potential and probable diminution of assets might well (to those with even a negotiating position) more than offset the anticipated benefits in a stand-alone scenario.

The lack of disclosure and vote cannot at this time be overcome. Nevertheless, it should be noted that the representation enjoyed by employees, pensioners, shareholders and other constituencies herein has been significant if not decisive. Committees have been appointed to represent all substantial interests. These committees have retained professionals, *e.g.* the equity security holders committee is receiving the assistance of a financial consultant in an effort to identify and assess alternatives to Volvo. All Court appointees have been encouraged to co-operate with various interested parties. The SEC and UAW have actively participated in most proceedings and the examiner has proved invaluable as a source of sunshine and enlightenment. Thus, the Volvo transaction has not emerged without the most thorough opportunities for analysis and assessment by all concerned.

Conditional notice of the Volvo proposal has been afforded all creditors, shareholders and other parties in interest. They may appear and be heard.

Thus, while counsel has erroneously disregarded the Court's candid remarks concerning the propriety of a plan format, there has in fact been no purposeful effort by the debtor's management to evade the disclosure requirements of the Code. Indeed, the impact of Volvo on the fate of White Credit (a major subsidiary with a potential dividend to White Motor of $100 million or more) is perhaps the principal justification for the failure to propose a plan in the Motor case. Moreover, based on the present record, the investment banker appears to have performed his tasks well and true; and the examiner has reported that good faith efforts to negotiate a Motor and White Credit plan have been diligently proposed by the debtors and most parties in interest.

The Gemini Problem

The proposed sale of Gemini assets (*i.e.*, the sole source of and manufacturer of cabs for White trucks) presents its own unique problems. Here we have a distinct corporate entity whose assets are commandeered in order to make the Volvo transaction possible. Creditors of Gemini are not told how much Volvo is paying for the assets or what they are worth. Thus, our worst fears emanating from the absence of a reorganization plan are realized.

Specifically, Gemini's creditors are vendors and employees. The lending-institution overlap, which is characteristic of the Motor/Credit relationship, does not exist among Gemini creditors. Hence, a principal justification or reason for failure to file a liquidating plan does not exist. Gemini has other-than-Motor customers. Although Volvo is indifferent as to any allocation to Gemini from gross proceeds, Motor and its creditors have taken no steps to assuage the fears of Gemini creditors emanating from a perceived de facto consolidation of the two firms for purposes of the Volvo transaction.

Thus, a conflict has developed between the two debtors as evidenced by their opposing positions on the sale. While this aspect of the problem should not, in itself, disqualify the transaction, special procedures may be appropriate to assure a fair and expeditious disposition in the Gemini matter. Such procedures must originate with its creditors' committee.

* * *

Accordingly, the Court orders as follows:

1. A hearing to consider the proposed sale to Volvo will be held on August 20, 1981, notwithstanding the absence of a plan of reorganization.

2. Upon approval, if any, of the said transaction, Gemini and/or White shall segregate for the benefit of the Gemini estate the sum of $3,500,000, subject to further Order of this Court.

3. In the absence of a plan or plans of reorganization being filed for White Motor, White Credit, Gemini or other affiliates on or before August 31, 1981, the Court may be required to either (a) terminate the exclusive period as to one or more debtors or (b) further empower the examiner(s) to execute the duties contained in 11 U.S.C. § 1106(a)(5).

Question

1. Do the shareholders of White or Gemini get to vote on the sale of substantially all the assets of each firm? Do they get appraisal rights? What protections do shareholders have in such sales? What justifies the waiver of the state code sections on asset sales?

2. What is the difference between a sale of substantially all the assets under Delaware section 363 and a sale of substantially all the assets after confirmation of a plan of reorganization? In which type of sale do creditors and stockholders have more protections?

IN RE JOHNS–MANVILLE CORP.

United States Court of Appeals, Second Circuit, 1986.
801 F.2d 60.

MAHONEY, CIRCUIT JUDGE:

This action, one segment in a long-running Chapter 11 reorganization proceeding, arose in consequence of the competing interests of creditors, stockholders, and the board of directors in the development of rehabilitation plans for appellee, the Manville Corporation ("Manville"), formerly Johns–Manville Corporation. Appellants are the Equity Security Holders Committee and individual members of that committee (collectively the "Equity Committee"), appointed by the bankruptcy court to represent the interests of stockholders in Manville's reorganization. ... Manville is aligned for purposes of this appeal with the Committee of Asbestos Health Related Claimants and/or Creditors (the "Asbestos Health Committee"), which represents the interests of the victims of diseases resulting from exposure to asbestos who have presently existing claims in tort against Manville, and with the Legal Representative, who represents the interests of future claimants who have not yet manifested such diseases.

The instant conflict arises in part because each of the committees representing the various interests in Manville must depend upon the Manville board of directors to advance those interests in the bankruptcy court at this stage of the rehabilitation proceedings. As debtor, Manville had the exclusive right under the Bankruptcy Code to file rehabilitation plans for the first 120 days of reorganization, and the bankruptcy court in these proceedings has granted Manville several extensions prolonging its exclusive filing period. *See* 11 U.S.C. § 1121(b), (d) (1982 & Supp. III 1985). Therefore, although in theory each of the committees may one day have the opportunity to submit a rehabilitation plan to the bankruptcy court if Manville's own proposals are rejected or if a trustee is appointed to replace the Manville board, *see id.* § 1121(c), Manville has for three or four years enjoyed the exclusive right, after negotiating with the committees, to file proposed plans. And although any of the committees may decline to accept a plan submitted to the bankruptcy court for confirmation, the power to formulate such plans in the first instance or at least to exercise a voice in their formulation is clearly a desideratum under the program laid down by the Bankruptcy Code, because the bankruptcy court may confirm a plan with or without the acquiescence of all classes of claims. If any impaired class [3] rejects Manville's proposed plan, the court will nevertheless confirm it, upon Manville's request, so long as at least one impaired class has accepted the plan and so long as the court determines that the plan "does not discriminate unfairly" and is "fair and equitable" to each impaired class that has not accepted it. 11 U.S.C. § 1129(b)(1) (1982 & Supp. III 1985).

In order to channel negotiations toward acceptable plans, the various factions interested in Manville's rehabilitation have formed *ad hoc* alliances when the occasion has called for them. The challenge all the committees have faced is to fashion a plan that will preserve Manville's capacity to generate enough revenue to pay existing creditors, to cover its liabilities to present and future tort claimants where liability is certain though its precise extent is unknown, and to satisfy Manville's shareholders. The seemingly strange bedfellows in the instant litigation, Manville and the committees representing present and future tort claimants, have long struggled to devise a reorganization plan acceptable to each.

* * *

To their credit, Manville and the Legal Representative finally came to terms in August of 1985, formulating a plan that would earmark billions of dollars for payment to present and future asbestosis victims as well as to others damaged by the asbestos products that Manville once manufactured and sold. They have now received the blessing of the Asbestos Health Committee and apparently of the other creditor committees. Having reconciled their differences, however, they en-

---

3. With certain exceptions, impairment of claims or interests, defined at 11 U.S.C. § 1124 (1982 & Supp. II 1984), occurs when a plan alters the legal, equitable, or contractual rights of the claim or interest holder.

countered opposition from the Equity Committee immediately following their breakthrough, on the eve of their submission of the plan to the bankruptcy court for confirmation. Under protest, the Equity Committee had been cut out of the negotiations that led to their plan, and if the product of Manville's new understanding with the tort claimants and other creditors is confirmed, equity may be diluted by 90% or more. *In re Johns–Manville Corp.,* 60 B.R. 842, 846 (S.D.N.Y.1986). Displeased with that prospect, which the Equity Committee views as evidence of the Manville board's abdication of its responsibilities to the shareholders, the Equity Committee brought an action in Delaware state court seeking to compel Manville to hold a shareholders' meeting, pursuant to section 211(c) of Delaware's General Corporation Law.[4] The Equity Committee's avowed purpose was to replace Manville directors, so that new directors might reconsider submitting the proposed plan.

* * *

Turning, then, to the decision to enjoin, we first encounter the well-settled rule that the right to compel a shareholders' meeting for the purpose of electing a new board subsists during reorganization proceedings.

* * *

As a consequence of the shareholders' right to govern their corporation, a prerogative ordinarily uncompromised by reorganization, "a bankruptcy court should not lightly employ its equitable power to block an election of a new board of directors." ... In accordance with this rule, the parties and the lower courts agree that the Equity Committee's right to call a meeting may be impaired only if the Equity Committee is guilty of "clear abuse" in attempting to call one. ... we cannot agree that the Equity Committee's professed desire to arrogate more bargaining power in the negotiation of a plan—in contrast to some secret desire to destroy all prospects for reorganization—may in itself constitute clear abuse. The law of this circuit directs that the shareholders' natural wish to participate in this matter of corporate governance be respected. ... the shareholders' mere intention to exercise bargaining power—whether by actually replacing the directors or by "bargaining away" their chip without replacing the board, as the district court suggests they may have wished to do—cannot without more constitute clear abuse. Unless the Equity Committee were to bargain in bad faith—*e.g.,* to demonstrate a willingness to risk rehabilitation altogether in order to win a larger share for equity—its desire to negotiate for a larger share is protected. Moreover, if rehabilitation is placed at risk as a result of the other committees' intransigent unwillingness to negotiate with the Equity Committee, as opposed to their real inability, within some reasonable amount of time, to formulate any

---

4. Del.Code Ann. tit. 8, § 211(c) (1983) provides that upon "a failure to hold the annual meeting ... for a period of 13 months ... after its last annual meeting, the Court of Chancery may summarily order a meeting to be held upon the application of any stockholder or director."

confirmable plan more satisfactory to equity, the Equity Committee should not alone bear the consequences of a stalemate by being deemed guilty of clear abuse.[6] ... Surely if the Equity Committee is permitted to elect new directors in order to redirect or alter the course of a reorganization—and the district court here explicitly recognized that the committee is permitted to do that, ... the Equity Committee should be permitted, in the district court's words of disapproval, to "use the threat of a new board as a lever vis-a-vis other interested constituencies and vis-a-vis the current Manville board." ... The Equity Committee denies that there is evidence tending to show that it meant to use any "threat" as a "lever," but if there is any such evidence, it would suggest only that the Equity Committee might be willing to back away from replacing the directors if it were to find the board more responsive to its interests. For related reasons, we are not persuaded that the Equity Committee's failure to call for a meeting at an earlier stage in the negotiations places its desire for leverage in a different light. If dissatisfaction with the board's representation of shareholders is a legitimate ground for calling a meeting, the Equity Committee did not waive the right to call a meeting by waiting until it became dissatisfied.[7]

Finally, we reject appellees' suggestion that the availability to the Equity Committee of other means with which to oppose Manville's plan robs the Equity Committee of its chosen means. It is true that the Equity Committee could have sought the appointment of a trustee to displace Manville as the sole author of proposed plans and that it may later object to the confirmation of any plan Manville submits to the bankruptcy court. But those correctives provide only imperfect substitutes for a voice in the original formulation of a plan. More to the present point, perhaps, those avenues to shareholder satisfaction cannot be said to be exclusive in light of this circuit's legitimation of the shareholders' right to elect new directors for the frank purpose of advancing a plan they prefer.

---

6. We note that if Manville were determined to be insolvent, so that the shareholders lacked equity in the corporation, denial of the right to call a meeting would likely be proper, because the shareholders would no longer be real parties in interest. Although the bankruptcy court discussed the possibility of Manville's insolvency in connection with its treatment of the Equity Committee's request for retention of special counsel and reimbursement of expenses, see In re Johns–Manville Corp., 52 B.R. at 885, an issue that is not a subject of this appeal, the district court did not uphold the determination of clear abuse on that basis, and the parties have not briefed that issue.

7. We do not suggest, of course, that an Equity Committee's delay in calling a shareholders' meeting may never contribute to a finding of clear abuse. As the Securities and Exchange Commission pointed out in its brief, an attempt to call a shareholders' meeting after a plan has been submitted to the bankruptcy court and after confirmation hearings have begun would usually be more disruptive to the proceedings than an earlier attempt would be. Such an attempt might also indicate bad faith and a willingness to risk jeopardy to rehabilitation. On the other hand, a rule that required a call before dissatisfaction had crystallized would only encourage preemptive efforts that might otherwise be avoided by negotiation. In this case, the Equity Committee apparently acted promptly upon learning of Manville's proposed plan and is certainly not accountable for any movement toward confirmation that may have occurred thereafter over its objections.

In this connection, we must reject Manville's argument that a full inquiry into "clear abuse" would duplicate the confirmation proceedings that will follow submission of its present plan or any other. Unlike the analysis to determine clear abuse, the object of the confirmation proceedings will be to weigh Manville's proposed plan against other possible plans, taking into account the interests of impaired classes that object to Manville's proposals. In contrast, the determination whether the Equity Committee is guilty of clear abuse turns on whether rehabilitation will be seriously threatened, rather than merely delayed, if Manville's present plan is not submitted for confirmation now.... Quite apart from its right to contest confirmation, the Equity Committee has the right to a fair hearing on the latter question and to a decision that recognizes its right to influence its own board.

We now reach the district court's alternative ground for affirming the grant of summary judgment. The bankruptcy court's finding that the proposed stockholders' meeting might jeopardize the reorganization process, "or at least ... delay or halt plan negotiations," a finding reflected in the district court's view that the Equity Committee might have intended to "torpedo" the reorganization, poses an issue more difficult than the question of the stockholders' desire for a voice in negotiations. While delay to rehabilitation would not by itself provide a ground for overriding the shareholders' right to govern Manville—delay being a concomitant of the right to change boards—real jeopardy to reorganization prospects would provide such a ground.

* * *

The Equity Committee persuasively calls into question whether the bankruptcy court had any basis for concluding here that an election would jeopardize the reorganization process, particularly since the bankruptcy court's articulated basis appears to have been colored by an unsubstantiated suspicion that the Equity Committee affirmatively wished to jeopardize reorganization. Perhaps Potter was willing to embark on a suicide mission, "sounding the 'death knell' to ... himself" along with the debtor. But as the Equity Committee argues, the lower courts in this case pointed to no evidence to support any finding that it wished to "torpedo" the reorganization, which the Equity Committee contends would be an irrational goal from its perspective.

* * *

Whether the Equity Committee's call for a shareholders' meeting constitutes clear abuse and whether such a meeting would cause irreparable harm to Manville's reorganization are triable issues of fact. The summary judgment award to Manville is therefore reversed.

Question

If stockholders in bankruptcy proceedings lose the right to vote on asset sales and mergers, why should they retain the right to remove the board of directors? How carefully have the drafters of bankruptcy legislation thought about the effect of bankruptcy proceedings in normal corporate governance questions?

Subsection b. Federal Securities Laws

Securities are often issued in a Chapter 11 reorganization proceeding pursuant to the plan of reorganization to rehabilitate a failing company. Creditors and equity holders are often asked to exchange their claims and interests for new securities issued under the plan. Section 1145(a) of the Bankruptcy Code provides an exception from the registration requirements under the Securities Act of 1933 for securities issued under a plan of reorganization. Moreover, section 1145(b) permits more-liberal resales by the recipients of reorganization securities than does the 1933 act.

There is also a significant safe harbor provision in section 1125. In section 1125 the proponent of a plan is required to file a disclosure statement containing "adequate information" and have it approved by the court as a precondition to soliciting acceptances by class vote of a plan of reorganization. The *In re Genesee* opinion, supra at 1057, is an example of a petition for approval of a disclosure statement. The compilation, preparation, and formulation of the disclosure statement is not governed by the disclosure provisions of the 1933 act. Moreover, parties soliciting support for plans of reorganization do not have to comply with the proxy solicitation regulations under the Securities Exchange Act of 1934. E.g., Public Service Co. of New Hampshire v. Consolidated Utilities and Communications, Inc., 846 F.2d 803 (1st Cir.1988).

The Securities and Exchange Commission may appear before a bankruptcy court and be heard on any issue, § 1109(a), but section 1125(d) provides that a determination of whether the disclosure statement contains adequate information is a finding of fact to be made exclusively by the bankruptcy court, and no securities agency may appeal an order approving the disclosure statement. Moreover, investment bankers, large creditors, and managers oppose an active SEC in Chapter 11 proceedings. These participants believe the proceeding is already excessively complex. Section 1125(e) provides that a person who solicits and participates in good faith and in compliance with the provisions of the code in any securities offering under a plan of reorganization will not be liable for any violations of securities laws.

SEC RULING ON SEC ROLE IN BANKRUPTCY REORGANIZATION
Fed.Sec.L.Rep. (CCH) ¶ 84,502 (Oct. 18, 1989).

* * *

The Bankruptcy Code, which became effective October 1, 1979, consolidated the various reorganization provisions of the old Bankruptcy Act, including Chapters X and XI, into Chapter 11. Chapter 11 encourages negotiation of a consensual plan of reorganization between a debtor and those creditors and stockholders whose claims and interests are to be compromised. Unlike the procedure under old Chapter X, where an independent trustee was appointed to be the focal point of the reorganization, in new Chapter 11 the debtor (*i.e.*, existing management) typically remains in possession during the pendency of the reorganization proceeding and is granted a period of time during which it exclusively may propose a plan. Interested parties negotiate with the debtor through official committees. Once a plan is proposed, approval is solicited through a "disclosure statement," which substitutes in effect for a Securities Act registration statement and Exchange Act proxy statement if securities are issued under the plan.[6] Under Chapter 11, a plan need not be "fair" in the absolute priority sense, if each class affected (or "impaired") by the plan votes to approve it.[7] According to Congress, the premise underlying the Chapter 11 standard for confirmation is "the same as the premise of the federal securities law:" that once parties are given adequate disclosure of all relevant information they should be able to make an informed decision as to whether to accept a proposed reorganization plan.

One of the major changes effected by the Bankruptcy Code was the advent of official committees, whose expenses and professional fees are paid as an administrative expense of the estate, to represent the various constituent interests. The Code mandates the appointment of an official committee to represent the interests of unsecured creditors; other committees may, in the discretion of the court, be appointed to represent the interests of equity holders or other constituencies. Representation by an official committee was deemed essential to participation in the formulation of a plan in light of the emphasis on the formulation of a consensual plan in lieu of adherence to the absolute priority standard.

The Bankruptcy Code abolished the requirement that the court submit reorganization plans to the Commission for examination and an advisory report in order to expedite the reorganization process. ...

1. INVESTOR COMMITTEES

As noted, one of the major changes under the Bankruptcy Code was the creation of the official committee system. An official committee for unsecured creditors is mandated in all Chapter 11 cases, and additional committees may be appointed to represent other constituencies, such as bondholders or shareholders. The U.S. Trustee is granted authority to appoint additional committees. In cases in which the U.S. Trustee determines not to appoint an additional committee, the bankruptcy

---

6. 11 U.S.C. §§ 1125(d), 1145. Where the solicitation involves bad faith or fraud, the anti-fraud provisions of the securities laws would be applicable.

7. A "fairness" concept, similar to the "fair and equitable" rule of Chapter X, is preserved under the present statute only in those situations where at least one class has voted to accept the plan and another class rejects it. In that instance, the plan proponent may invoke the so-called "cramdown" provision (Section 1129(b)) to seek court approval of the plan notwithstanding the objection of the rejecting class.

court has authority to direct the U.S. Trustee to do so. Actual committee membership is left to the discretion of the U.S. Trustee.

According to the drafters of the Code, committees are to serve as "the primary negotiating bodies for the formulation of the plan of reorganization." Congress intended that committees represent and protect the interests of the various classes of creditors and equity security holders from which they are selected and provide supervision of the debtor in possession.

The Commission's observations of investor committee practices do not provide clear evidence of whether the committee structure is effective in protecting the interests of public securities holders. In some cases, it appears that committees are not formed or are unable, either because of internal conflicts or delays in organizing or for other reasons, to deal appropriately with critical issues.

* * *

In certain cases in which it appears to the Commission staff that shareholders may have an economic interest in the reorganization, no one has sought appointment of an equity committee. The Commission wishes to explore the reason why committees are not formed in some cases where certain evidence suggests that equity holders may have a meaningful economic stake in the debtor. Are investors generally aware of their right to seek formation of an official committee to represent their interests? The Commission staff has informed the Commission that frequently there is an absence of publicly available financial information about corporations undergoing reorganization. Does this lack of current financial information deter persons from seeking formation of a committee, or are other factors predominately responsible for that decision? Alternatively, investors may have determined that the costs of seeking committee formation and participating in committee activities are not justified by the likely rewards. Does the failure of investors to seek a committee represent an informed decision of this nature?

As pointed out above, the Commission has moved or supported motions for the appointment of investor committees in about 12% of the cases where it has appeared. But the Commission has not sought a committee in every case meeting its criteria for appointment.[15]

15. Since January 1984, the Commission sought or supported the appointment of investor committees in 33 cases, or about 12% of the cases in which the Commission filed a notice of appearance. The Commission does not seek the appointment of an investor committee in every case involving a public company. Generally, the Commission takes the position that separate stockholder representation is not appropriate in cases in which the debtor is so hopelessly insolvent that liquidation appears likely or where the assets of the debtor are completely pledged and investor interests are likely to be extinguished. Among the factors that the Commission considers in determining whether to seek the appointment of an official committee are the value of the equity as publicly reported by the issuer, the going concern or inherent value (if realistically higher), the likelihood of reorganization, the extent of management holdings of common stock, the degree to which incumbent management can be relied on to represent ade-

Are the Commission's general standards for determining whether to seek the appointment of additional investor committees appropriate?

* * *

The Commission staff reports that in some cases, even when an investor committee is authorized early in the case, there are significant delays in the actual appointment of the committee's members, thus delaying the functioning of the committee in the case. The Commission solicits comments on the reasons for this phenomenon and what steps, if any, the Commission should take to remedy this problem. Is the delay in part caused by a difficulty in finding investors willing to serve on a committee or a reluctance by investors to serve on committees? Should the U.S. Trustee, or the Commission, take some action to speed the process of committee formation? The staff has observed in some cases that investors refrain from accepting membership of a committee because of a concern that such membership would result in access to nonpublic information which, in turn, would inhibit the investors' ability to trade in the debtor's securities. Are potential securities trading restrictions for committee members considered a significant impediment to accepting membership on an official committee? To what extent, if any, can or should the Commission change its own rules or procedures to address those concerns?

2. Management (the Debtor in Possession)

Unlike prior Chapter X, under which a trustee was appointed automatically in all large cases, Chapter 11 leaves debtor's current management in control of the proceedings with an initial exclusive right to file a reorganization plan.[22] One commentator has noted that the Code has made stockholders much more dependent on management to negotiate a plan that protects their interests, because a Chapter 11 plan can modify, dilute or even cancel their interests without their consent. The staff has observed that in some cases management is more likely to look after the interests of shareholders when management owns a substantial amount of the outstanding common stock. On the other hand, the staff has found that employment may have a potential conflict of interest in that it may also seek to negotiate for its own continued services after reorganization. Under what circumstances can shareholders rely on management to represent their interests? Of course, levels of management equity ownership vary widely among public companies. Should the percentage of equity owned by management influence the Commission in determining whether to participate in a particular proceeding? If so, how and why?[24]

quately investor interests, and the asset size of the debtor.

22. Section 1121 of the Bankruptcy Code grants the debtor in possession an initial 120–day period of exclusivity, but bankruptcy courts, especially in cases in-volving large public companies, routinely grant extensions of the period of exclusivity. *See* 5 *Collier on Bankruptcy* ¶ 1121.04 at 1121–13 (15th ed. 1989).

24. Recently, in a number of cases, shareholders, dissatisfied with manage-

* * *

6. FUNDS SPECIALIZING IN SECURITIES OF DISTRESSED COMPANIES

It has been reported that, in the past year, funds specializing in securities of distressed companies, generally known as "recovery" or "vulture" funds, have raised from $300 million to $500 million to invest primarily in debt but also to a limited extent in equity securities of corporations undergoing reorganization. One commentator has referred to a $3 billion "pool" available for investment in securities of companies in bankruptcy. The evolution of funds that specialize in the securities of distressed enterprises has attracted supporters and critics. Supporters claim that, with substantial funds now available for the purchase of distressed securities, the discount from face value has narrowed substantially, resulting in a more efficient market with higher stock and bond prices. If so, the small public investor may benefit from the participation of these funds because their presence helps support the price of securities issued by debtor firms. Critics complain, however, that, if the bankruptcy process were more effective in representing the interests of public security holders to begin with, the price of securities might not decline as steeply in the wake of bankruptcy and that the profit opportunities for funds specializing in distressed enterprises would not be as great. They complain that it is the small investor who typically sells his securities early in the bankruptcy process and who loses money as a result of the steep decline in the price of the securities.

The Commission is interested in learning about the impact of these funds on the reorganization process. How do the recovery funds affect the interests of public securityholders?

* * *

SECTION 4. CHAPTER 11 ACQUISITIONS: "VULTURE TAKEOVERS"

FRAUMAN & BLAUNER, BANKRUPT ENTITIES TARGETED: TRADING CLAIMS CAN SERVE AS THE BASIS OF A TAKEOVER
N.Y. Law J. p. 5, col. 2 (June 2, 1990).

As a growing number of investors and corporate raiders are discovering, bankruptcy is developing into one of the hot spots for mergers and acquisitions in the 1990s.

Dozens of different entities, from investment banks and money managers to pension funds and universities, have gathered close to $1.5

---

ment's efforts to negotiate a favorable reorganization plan, have sought, through state-law procedure, to replace management by compelling an annual meeting for the election of directors; courts have long recognized the right of shareholders to do so unless the exercise of such function is likely to threaten the reorganization. See *In re Johns–Manville Corp.*, 52 B.R. 879 (Bankr.S.D.N.Y.1985), aff'd, 60 B.R. 842 (S.D.N.Y.1986), rev'd and remanded, 801 F.2d 60 (2d Cir.1986).

billion to invest in troubled companies and are raising more. Their targets are large, medium and small bankrupt companies, both publicly and privately owned. While the most significant portion of these funds is intended only for passive investments in securities of companies in Chapter 11, another part will be used to purchase or trade claims against bankruptcy debtors primarily as a takeover technique.

Trading claims can serve as the basis of a takeover of a Chapter 11 company or its trophy assets in a variety of different ways. Earlier this year, for example, Japonica Partners, a New York-based investment partnership, purchased nearly $70 million of bank claims against Allegheny International and became Allegheny's largest creditor. It subsequently voted against Allegheny's reorganization plan and initiated a hostile takeover of the company itself.

Approximately 18 months ago, a subsidiary of The Horsham Corp., a publicly held Canadian company purchased $545 million of bank claims against the Apex Oil Co., at that time one of the largest privately owned businesses in America. The Horsham subsidiary then used those claims at their full face value as "currency" to acquire Apex's major assets, including the oil refining, distribution and marketing operations owned by Clark Oil & Refining Corp., an Apex affiliate.

A couple of years ago, Leucadia International was able to acquire through an intermediary most of the claims against the Baldwin–United Co. that were to be exchanged for equity as part of Baldwin–United's plan of reorganization. As a result, after Leucadia purchased some additional equity, it gained control of the reorganized company and of one of Baldwin–United's major assets—a very large net operating tax loss carryforward.

Investors have long sought to acquire claims against bankrupt companies, and creditors who feared a small or no payout from bankruptcy were happy to oblige. As far back as the 1920s and 1930s, investors purchased defaulted railroad bonds and debentures.

The most common bankruptcy securities traded by investors have been debt securities. Shareholders are entitled to control the operations of a company in Chapter 11 through its board of directors as they would under general corporate law so long as no trustee has been appointed by the bankruptcy court, and recent court decisions have affirmed their ability to hold a shareholders' meeting while the company in which they own stock is in Chapter 11. Obviously, though, equity interests in a bankrupt and insolvent company generally have less power than debt holders.

Traditionally, an investor's role in a bankruptcy proceeding was rather passive. After buying securities at a low price, most investors would wait and try to sell the securities when their values had recovered, thereby profiting from the spread.

On occasion, investors would not merely await a rise in the value of their claims to sell out or the conclusion of a bankruptcy case for a payout but would use their position as holders of claims to participate in the negotiation of a plan of reorganization for the debtor company, seeking to increase the amount their class of claims would receive from the company after bankruptcy. That, in fact, has become more common recently.

The newest role investors have taken in the bankruptcy claims trading area is the aggressive trading of claims as has occurred in the Allegheny, Apex and Baldwin–United bankruptcy proceedings to facilitate a takeover of a bankrupt business or the acquisition of its major assets.

A company in Chapter 11 may be forced to sell some or all of its assets at "distress sale" prices because it does not have sufficient capital to operate those assets in Chapter 11. Sometimes, a company may be able to exit Chapter 11 only by selling assets and using the sale proceeds to fund a plan of reorganization.

* * *

The rules of bankruptcy procedure and court decisions impose certain requirements upon investors before they can act on the claims that they have purchased.

An investor must file a proof of claim against the debtor after it acquires the claim if no proof of claim has been filed previously. For claims (other than claims based on a bond or debenture) that are acquired after the debtor has entered bankruptcy, the proof of claim must be supported by a statement of the transferring creditor that acknowledges the transfer and states the consideration therefor. If no such statement is available, the investor must explain why and must set forth the consideration for the transfer itself.

In situations where an investor acquires a claim after a creditor has filed a proof of claim against the debtor, the situation is somewhat different.

In that case, the investor must provide the court with the terms of the transfer of the claim. Once that happens, and it must be within a "reasonable time" following the transfer or the assignment risks being barred, the bankruptcy court clerk will notify the original claimant that it has 20 days to object to the transfer. If the court finds that the claim has been unconditionally transferred, "it shall enter an order substituting the transferee for the original claimant."

Despite the apparently limited role that bankruptcy judges are authorized to play in connection with assignments of claims and despite the virtually non-existent regulation of claims trading in the Bankruptcy Code, some judges have imposed a duty of disclosure on investors.

In one case, an investor sought to acquire claims against Revere Copper & Brass Inc. for 20 percent of their face value although a plan of reorganization was being considered that would pay almost 65 percent to those claimants.

The bankruptcy court, noting that "one of the evils attendant upon a solicitation of claims for a cash payment ... is that solicited creditors may be unaware of their rights and options and fall prey to the belief that the bankruptcy inevitably will result in their receiving the proverbial ten cents on the dollar," ruled that it would not approve a transfer of any claim unless the investor could show that the transferors had been given "sufficient information" to make an "informed judgment" on the offer. Barring that, the transferors would be allowed 30 days to revoke the transfers.[7]

A similar decision was issued in the LTV Corp. bankruptcy proceeding. There, the court ruled that a creditor is entitled to make an "informed judgment" about the value of its claim before an investor can purchase it and that the investor must supply the creditor with information to meet that requirement.[8] In this case, an entity purchased more than 400 claims against an LTV affiliate at a large discount from face value but did not disclose that it was essentially a wholly owned subsidiary of Regal International or that Regal intended to acquire the LTV affiliate. Nor did it disclose that Regal expected to propose a plan of reorganization for that debtor that provided for full payment to its creditors.

A somewhat different course was taken by the bankruptcy judge in the Allegheny bankruptcy proceeding, before Japonica Partners became involved. There, the court ordered investors to notify Allegheny in advance of any agreement to transfer claims so that Allegheny could estimate the value of those claims and inform the original claimants.[9]

BRODSKY & ZWEIBEL, CHAPTER 11 ACQUISITIONS: PAYOFFS FOR PATIENCE

Mergers and Acquisitions 47 (Sept/Oct 1990).

* * *

There are legal advantages to acquiring companies in Chapter 11—notably, the ability to resolve uncertainties regarding the target, the opportunity to shape the reorganized target, and the chance to overcome some traditional obstacles to hostile acquisitions (as well as certain tax benefits, not discussed in this article). But there are legal problems to be coped with, including the cumbersome bankruptcy process, a structure that facilitates bidding competition, difficulties in acquiring a strategic stake in the target, and a de facto "shark repellent" that can block a deal.

* * *

---

[7]. In re Revere Copper & Brass Inc., 58 B.R. 1 (Bankr.S.D.N.Y.1985).

[8]. In re Chateaugay, 86 B 11270/334, 402 and 464, slip op. (S.D.N.Y. March 11, 1988).

[9]. In re Allegheny International Inc., 100 B.R. 941 (Bankr.W.D.Pa.1988).

First, the Chapter 11 process is very beneficial in defining pre-petition liabilities—liabilities incurred before the commencement of the Chapter 11 case. The operative term in bankruptcy parlance is "claim," which is very broadly defined in the Bankruptcy Code to mean any right to payment—even contingent rights.

At the commencement of a Chapter 11 case, the debtor is required to schedule all claims as well as interests (i.e., equity interests). A party whose claim or interest is not listed (or is incorrectly listed) on these schedules, or, in the case of a claim, is listed as disputed, contingent, or unliquidated, must file a proof of claim or interest by a fixed date, as a condition to the claim or interest being recognized ("allowed").

The ultimate objective of Chapter 11 is, of course, to provide a comprehensive resolution of the debtor's claims and interests. Subject to very limited exceptions, all pre-petition claims and interests—even those for which no proof of claim or interest has been filed—are discharged by the plan of reorganization.

Second, even post-petition liabilities are reasonably well-defined by the Chapter 11 process. Post-petition claims are categorized as "administrative claims" and must be paid in full upon consummation of the plan of reorganization, ahead of all pre-petition unsecured claims. Furthermore, court approval is required for transactions outside of the ordinary course of the debtor's business, and the company is subject to continual scrutiny by the official creditors' committee and other interested parties.

Third, the debtor's assets can be sold free and clear of all claims—regardless of whether the sale occurs as part of the plan of reorganization or beforehand, during the case. This eliminates the risk of unwanted liabilities following the purchased assets.

Fourth, the Chapter 11 process affords greater certainty concerning the target's assets. The debtor's title to property can be adjudicated as part of the Chapter 11 case. Further, the legal effectiveness of the debtor's contractual rights (including the status of setoffs and counterclaims) can be adjudicated in the case.

Finally, Chapter 11 can add certainty concerning whether the transfer that the buyer and seller have agreed upon is effective. Outside of the Bankruptcy Code, an asset transfer is subject to requirements of third-party consents, regulatory restrictions, and questions about effectiveness of the transfer as against third parties. By contrast, in Chapter 11:

- Executory contracts and unexpired leases can generally be assigned without third-party consents. Any contract that the debtor assumes may be assigned, if the assignee provides adequate assurance of future performance.
- Non-bankruptcy legal restrictions on transfer are overridden in the case of transfer pursuant to a plan of reorganization.

• Sales can be made free of interests of third parties, relying on the same provisions which, as noted above, allow sales to be free of the debtor's liabilities.

The Chapter 11 proceeding also allows an acquirer great opportunity to alter or assume the capital structure and contracts of the target company. This can enhance the value of the acquisition to the buyer and also facilitate the mechanics of the acquisition.

* * *

Chapter 11 allows an entire capital structure to be assumed and/or reshaped. In a Chapter 11 plan, advantageous debt issues can be "reinstated"—i.e., continued in existence on a nonaccelerated basis—provided that all defaults are cured. In bankruptcy parlance, such debt is "unimpaired." The holders of unimpaired debt are conclusively deemed to have accepted the plan. Attractive debt can be reinstated even if unattractive debt, including more-junior debt, is replaced with new, higher-rate debt.

Debt that is disadvantageous, or that needs to be compromised as part of the reorganization process, can be modified in Chapter 11. A Chapter 11 plan can modify principal amounts, interest rates, payment schedules, covenants, and subordination provisions. Prohibitions on, or prepayments triggered by, the buyer's acquisition can be overridden. Debt can be changed into equity.

Such changes obviously impair the affected debt, thereby entitling the debt holders to vote on the plan. For a class of creditors to accept a plan, approving holders must represent two-thirds in dollar amount and more than 50 percent of the number of holders in that class, in each case expressed as a portion of holders who actually vote.

Even with this voting requirement, it may be much easier to modify debts in Chapter 11 than outside of it. First and foremost, the Chapter 11 voting requirement overrides more stringent (as well as less stringent) contractual procedures for amendments. For example, in accordance with the Trust Indenture Act, indentures for publicly held debt require unanimity for most modifications of payment terms. Second, the possibility of a "cramdown"—a confirmation of the plan over the objections of a given class (discussed later)—may moderate any dissent. Third, including a given debt issue within a larger class may permit the requisite majority to be reached even if the holders of that particular issue generally oppose the plan.

The flexibility afforded by Chapter 11 permits the acquirer to use the debtor's existing indebtedness, rather than raise new capital for the acquisition. This saves issuance expense and may reduce the pressure on the buyer to agree to covenants that might otherwise be necessitated in the marketplace.

The Bankruptcy Code also affords the debtor, and hence the buyer, flexibility in maintaining, terminating, and assigning executory contracts and unexpired leases.

In the normal acquisition, executory contracts and unexpired leases of the target are static. If the buyer finds these contracts advantageous, the contracts may prohibit assignment.

Conversely, if the buyer finds the target's contracts disadvantageous, the buyer nonetheless may inherit them. In a stock purchase or merger, this occurs by operation of law. In an asset purchase, the seller may be unwilling to retain the contracts, and may be unable to perform them after the acquisition.

Chapter 11 generally allows the debtor to reinstate (in bankruptcy parlance, "assume") or assign executory contracts and unexpired leases, provided that defaults are cured, the creditor is compensated for any "actual pecuniary loss" resulting from the default, and there is adequate assurance of future performance. Certain bankruptcy-related defaults may be disregarded for this purpose.

While advantageous contracts and leases generally can be assumed or assigned, disadvantageous ones can be "rejected"—i.e., terminated—in the Chapter 11 proceedings. Rejection results in a claim for damages for breach of contract. However, in a reorganization that compromises claims, the benefit from terminating the contract will only be partly off-set by the corresponding distribution on account of this damage claim. Furthermore, some damage claims—those for real estate leases and employment contracts—will be less in Chapter 11 than under standard contract law. There are also special provisions that constrain, but do not preclude, rejection of real estate leases, intellectual property licenses, labor contracts, and retiree benefit plans.

Outside of Chapter 11, asset dispositions and most mergers generally require approval by the board of directors. Although hostile bidders can attempt to gain control of the board by acquiring a majority of the stock in a tender offer, management retains considerable power to resist these efforts.

In Chapter 11, the situation is quite different. First, management is under continual scrutiny of the court and creditors. Indications that management is being less than capable and fair-minded can undermine its credibility and its influence in the proceedings.

Second, non-management parties may appeal directly to voting constituencies by proposing and soliciting acceptances of a competing plan of reorganization. This is exactly what occurred in the *Public Service Co. of New Hampshire* case. At one point, three bidders had filed plans competing with management's own non-acquisition plan and were negotiating with creditor and stockholder representatives to obtain their support.

The Bankruptcy Code affords the debtor the exclusive right to file a plan of reorganization during the first 120 days of the case. The court may, and generally does, extend this "exclusivity period." But once the exclusivity period lapses, bidders can—directly if the court allows, or through a stockholder or creditor—submit competing plans of reorganization.

Courts appear to be showing decreasing patience with debtors' requests for repeated extensions of these "exclusivity periods." For example, in the *Texaco Inc.* case, the court granted a second extension of the exclusivity period to allow Texaco to appeal the judgment in favor of Pennzoil Co., which had precipitated the bankruptcy. However, the court left one exception—if the creditors' and stockholders' committees could reach a settlement with Pennzoil, they could file a competing plan immediately. Within a few weeks after that decision, Texaco itself reached a settlement with Pennzoil that provided the basis for Texaco's reorganization.

Third, management's powers can be overridden or diluted by the appointment of a trustee or examiner. The "estate" of the Chapter 11 debtor is typically operated by the debtor itself, as debtor-in-possession. The bankruptcy court may, however, appoint a trustee to operate the estate. In practical terms, the trustee supplants the debtor's board of directors and chief executive officer.

The bankruptcy court can appoint a trustee because of, among other things, "gross mismanagement" by current management or because the appointment is in the interests of creditors or stockholders. Although trustees generally are not appointed in Chapter 11 cases, the threat of one may influence management to be more responsive. In the *Eastern Air Lines* case, the airline's union sought the appointment of a trustee at the commencement of the case, alleging both mismanagement by existing management and improper dealings between the debtor and its affiliates. At Eastern's suggestion, the court initially appointed an examiner rather than a trustee, although later naming a trustee in a separate action.

An examiner's statutory role is to investigate the debtor's affairs but not, as with a trustee, to run the business. Beyond their statutory role, examiners are also used to facilitate negotiations over the plan and related issues (e.g., Public Service Co. of New Hampshire and Eastern Air Lines) and to seek out potential acquirers (e.g., Eastern Air Lines).

Examiners are being appointed with greater frequency in major cases—to allow the court to play a more activist, expediting role in the case. An examiner can devote full time to a case and may bring business expertise that the court does not have. For example, a former head of the New York Public Service Commission was appointed as an examiner in the *Public Service Co. of New Hampshire* case, in part because of the arcane but critical utility rate-making issues.

A business disposition that would require shareholder vote under corporate law will usually require a shareholder vote in Chapter 11. The biggest exception to this is a Chapter 11 procedure colloquially referred to as "cramdown"—which allows a plan to be confirmed over the objections of one or more impaired classes.

The bankruptcy court can cram down a plan with respect to a given class if all of the following are satisfied:

- At least one impaired class has accepted the plan;
- The plan does not "discriminate unfairly" against the rejecting class; and
- The plan is "fair and equitable" with respect to the rejecting class.

For a plan to be regarded as fair and equitable with respect to a class of stockholders, either of the following must occur:

- The value of the property retained by or distributed to that class is not less than the value of the stockholders' interest immediately before giving effect to the plan (or, if greater, the applicable liquidation preference or redemption price); or
- Any class junior to this class does not retain or receive any equity interest.

The "fair and equitable" test—which is the "absolute priority" rule that governed Chapter X reorganizations under the old Bankruptcy Act—essentially says to the rejecting class, "You are not entitled to insist on a plan that improves your position; but if the plan leaves you with less than your entitlement, no one more junior than you should receive anything."

The court is unlikely to cram down a plan if there is a reasonable alternative that would offer a higher enterprise value with a concomitant benefit to the dissenting class. On the other hand, the price that a third party is willing to pay for the debtor in an open bidding environment is an important indication of enterprise value.

When a shareholder vote is required, corporate statutes typically require approval by a majority of the votes cast, provided that a quorum of shareholders, typically a majority of all outstanding shares, is present. If an acquisition is sought by a major shareholder, something more than a simple majority may be required by the charter documents or statute.

In Chapter 11, the majority for shareholder acceptance of a plan is two-thirds of shares voted, with no quorum requirement. However, at least one class of impaired claims or interests must accept the plan without counting the vote of "insiders." "Shark repellents" provided in charter documents and corporate statutes are overridden by the voting provisions of the Bankruptcy Code.

Appraisal rights under state corporate laws are inapplicable to dispositions in Chapter 11. These are statutory rights of dissenting shareholders in certain transactions to receive cash payment for the fair value of their shares in lieu of the consideration given accepting shareholders.

On the negative side, a Chapter 11 acquisition entails an inherently more cumbersome process than the usual acquisition.

The process is pervasively judicial. The bankruptcy court must approve any significant sale occurring outside of the plan of reorganization. If the sale is to occur as part of the plan, the court must confirm the plan. In either case, any party in interest may speak to the issue before the court. This judicial role may be less disruptive than in many hostile acquisitions, but it is a significant element of any Chapter 11 acquisition.

There are more constituencies to deal with in a Chapter 11 acquisition. As noted earlier, management is less able to block a hostile acquisition. The flip side is that it is not enough for a buyer to reach an agreement only with management. Any party in interest, including creditors, may seek to block the acquisition judicially. In the case of an acquisition as part of a plan, other parties may propose a competing plan, and all impaired classes must, subject to the cramdown process, accept the plan. This leads to a much more diffused power structure in which the buyer often must appeal separately to various constituencies and in which a deal struck with one constituency is subject to holdup or renegotiation by another.

A Chapter 11 acquisition may become hostage to internecine warfare among classes. If the acquisition is pursuant to a plan, that plan must provide for the treatment of all classes. The buyer will care about the reorganized target's capital structure but otherwise will be indifferent to the comparative treatment of existing creditors and stockholders. Even if the acquisition occurs outside of a plan, the positions taken by the various constituencies may be informed by their ambitions and strategies for the "end game."

Chapter 11 offers a procedural context that promotes competition. It is impossible for any bid to be pursued in secrecy. The bidder must deal not only with management but also with the official committees and often other constituencies. Any resulting understanding must be filed with the court. The court will want to be satisfied that the disposition optimizes the recovery for creditors and stockholders. This necessarily imposes on the proponent of the transaction the onus of demonstrating that this disposition is better than other available alternatives, and that other alternatives have been sought. Until the court acts, the bidder is exposed to the possibility of a better, competing offer. If an efficient bidding process has not already occurred, court approval of acquisition agreements is generally subject to no "higher and better offer" being received within a specified time after announcement of the proposed transaction.

Finally, the debtor cannot bind itself to an acquisition agreement until either the court approves the sale, in the case of a sale during the case, or the plan of reorganization featuring the transaction takes effect. That process will entail preparation and filing of the plan and the disclosure statement (the solicitation document), a court hearing on the disclosure statement, solicitation of acceptance of the plan, and the confirmation hearing following the voting period.

An early bidder thus runs the risk of being an uncompensated stalking horse.

Hostile acquirers often purchase a significant block of the target's stock before starting the bidding process, as a means of enhancing the likelihood of success of reaping profits if they are beaten out. Hostile acquisitions of publicly held companies generally are effected through a tender offer followed by a back-end merger.

A like strategy with respect to a Chapter 11 debtor would entail purchasing claims against or interests in the debtor. Chapter 11 poses a few obstacles to this strategy.

A significant portion of the impaired claims may be unsecuritized— e.g., bank loans and trade claims. This precludes a liquid market in which to purchase these claims. Also, a purchaser of such claims is not protected by the "bona fide purchaser" doctrine applicable to securities. The debtor is free to assert against the purchaser any defenses or set-off rights applicable to the original creditor.

While non-bankruptcy laws allow a potential bidder to purchase securities of the target without disclosing the intended bid until it is necessary to file a 13D form, a small number of recent cases suggests a contrary result with a purchaser of claims during a Chapter 11 case. These cases have involved purchases of non-securitized claims, the transfer of which requires bankruptcy court approval. Some courts have blocked transfers when the buyer did not advise the seller of the anticipated terms of a plan of reorganization that was going to be filed.

Since there may be multiple, undefined voting classes and each class impaired by the plan is entitled to vote, the bidder might need to purchase claims or interests from numerous classes—not just those entitled to vote under non-bankruptcy law.

The Bankruptcy Code contains a "shark repellent" inherent in the majority required for a class of claims to accept a plan. As noted earlier, that majority is two-thirds in dollar amount and a straight majority in number of holders actually voting. To give an extreme example, if a bidder acquired the claims of all creditors but one, the bidder would not constitute a majority, because the bidder would only be 50 percent in number of creditors. Indeed, it could be that the more claims the bidder buys, the harder it is to obtain a majority, since those who refuse to sell may also be the most likely to reject the bidder's plan. It is generally accepted that the bidder cannot circumvent this problem by allocating its holdings among various persons acting in concert.

Question

When does an acquirer negotiate with a distressed target to put the firm in Chapter 11 before the agreed acquisition closes (a so-called "packaged bankruptcy")?

Index

References are to Pages

ACCOUNTING
Generally, 891–895
Cost method accounting for intercompany ownership, 895–897
Equity method accounting for intercompany ownership, 897–900
Financial statements, 892–893
Goodwill, 916–917
Leveraged buyouts, 917–921
Pooling requirements, 912–916
Purchase v. pooling consolidations, 900–913
    Comparison-table, 911–912
    Considerations-economic and business, 909–911
    Purchase v. pooling, 900–909

ACQUISITION AGREEMENTS
Generally, 668–669, 678–679
Breach by parties, 675–678
Shareholder approval, 669–678
Third party interference, 679–686

ACQUISITIONS AND REORGANIZATIONS
Classification systems, 35–40
    Accounting principles, 35
    Antitrust laws, 37
    Securities laws, 37
    State corporate codes, 36–37
    Tax law, 36
Contract rights, effect on, See Successor Liability
Definitions, 38–40
    Acquisition, 38–39
    Merger, 38
    Recapitalization, 39–40
Employee rights, See Employee Rights
Opportunistic behavior, 155–162

ANTITAKEOVER DEVICES
See also Defensive Reorganizations, Golden Parachutes, Greenmail, Poison Pill Plans, Shark Repellent Amendments
Generally, 462–465
Collective bargaining agreements, 233–239
Employee stock ownership plans, 620–636
Firm value, effect on, 465–469
Golden parachutes, See Golden Parachutes
Greenmail, 662–671, 972–973

ANTITAKEOVER DEVICES—Cont'd
Tin parachutes, 242–243

ANTITAKEOVER LEGISLATION
Generally, 43, 414–423, 455–458
Business combination acts, 439, 443–446
Constituency statutes, 658
Control share acts, 423, 425–434
Delaware § 203, 43
Disgorgement statutes, 458
Fair price statutes, 424
Moratorium statutes, 447–455
Nonshareholders, protection for, 435–438
Redemption statutes, 446
Stock prices, effect on, 459–460
Taxation, 968–973

ANTITRUST LAWS
Generally, 979–980
Clayton Act § 7, 980
Collusion between bidders, 1012–1017
Enforcement, 990–996
Hart–Scott–Rodino Antitrust Improvements Act, See Hart–Scott–Rodino Antitrust Improvements Act
Merger guidelines, 981–990

ASSET SALES
De facto merger doctrine, 86–92
State Corporate Codes, 42–43, 109–110
Successor liability, See Successor Liability
Tax, C reorganizations, 923

BANK OF NEW YORK CO. v. IRVING BANK CORP.
Bank of New York acquisition, 515

BANKRUPTCY
See also Chapter 11 Reorganizations, Workouts
Deleveraging from the 1980's, 1024–1025
Policy of reorganizations, 1025–1027

BIDDER
See also Stock Acquisitions
Definition of, 379–385
Standing to sue for target's breach to its shareholders, 657–658, 660
Standing to sue under § 14(e), 760–765

INDEX

References are to Pages

BOARDS OF DIRECTORS
See also Fiduciary Duty, Independent Directors
Generally, 461–462
Defensive Reorganizations, See Defensive Reorganizations
Selling the firm-standard of review, 529–604
    Business judgement rule, 529–545, 583–590
    Fair auction test, 545–553
    Intrinsic fairness test, 553–573
    Leveraged buyout, 591–604
    Management buyout, 578–583
Shareholder resolutions, 527–529
Waiver of liability by corporation, 606

BONDHOLDERS
See also Bulk Sales Act, Fraudulent Conveyance Laws
Corporate code protections, 197–200
Disclosure, corporation's duty of, 848–853
Fiduciary duty to in leveraged transactions, 183–197

BULK SALES ACT
Generally, 217–222

BUYBACKS
Generally, 392–393, 404–408
Debt repurchases, 408–414
Disclosure obligations, 401–403
Going private, 396–399
Transferable put rights, 394–396

CHAPTER 11 REORGANIZATIONS
Generally, 1044–1046
Bankruptcy benefits, 1046–1048
Bankruptcy drawbacks, 1048–1049
Debtor-in-possession, 1049–1056
    Management, 1049–1050
    Trustee (replacement with), 1050–1056
Equity holders role in the proceedings, "the fair and equitable test", 1057–1067
Federal securities law requirements, 1076–1080
State corporate code requirements, 1067–1075
Vulture takeovers, 1080–1090
    Benefits to investors, 1083–1090
    Trading claims, 1080–1083

COLLECTIVE BARGAINING AGREEMENTS
Generally, 223–224
Antitakeover device, use as, 233–239
Control change clauses, 224–232
Successorship in acquisitions, 243–258

CONTROL SHARES
Corporate opportunity, misappropriation of, through sale of control shares, 700–702
Looter, sale to, 687–693
Office, sale of an, 693–698

CONTROL SHARES—Cont'd
Proceeds, division of, 699

CORPORATE GOVERNANCE
Generally, 121–126
Shareholders voting as management control, 126–127

CREDITORS
See also Bondholders, Bulk Sales Acts, Fraudulent Conveyance Laws
Post–LBO creditors, 216–217
Shareholder resolutions, 527–529
Shareholder voting, 126–127
State corporate codes, 128–132

DEFENSIVE REORGANIZATIONS
Generally, 612–634
Standard of review, 646–655

DELAWARE CORPORATE CODE
Generally, 41–42
Acquisitions, 42
Antitakeover statute, 43
Asset sales, 42–43
Dissolved corps, 282
EE protection in acquisitions, 259
Mergers, 42
Reorganizations, 50
Shareholder appraisal rights, 52, 58

DISCLOSURE
Affirmative disclosure, 765–772, 784–788, 799–801
Bidder disclosure requirements, 352
Bidder's public promises, liability under rule 10b–5, 859–865
Bondholders, protection for, 848–853
Disclosure of 5 percent ownership, 335–347
Materiality under the Federal Securities Laws, 765–774
Merger Negotiations, See Merger Negotiations, Disclosure Projections, See Projections, Disclosure of Proxy Statements, See Proxy Statements
Qualitative information, 774–784
Remedies for violations of the securities laws, 347–351
Target disclosure obligations in self-tender offer, 386–392
Target disclosure obligations in third-party tender offer, 385

EMPLOYEE RIGHTS
Civil Rights (Discrimination) Claims, 298–303
Collective bargaining agreements, See Collective Bargaining Agreements
Employee statutory protections, 259–264
Lobbying by union, 263–264
    Federal plant closing laws, 260–263
    State legislation, 259–260
Pension plans, See Pension Plans

EMPLOYEE STOCK OWNERSHIP PLANS
Antitakeover device, use as, 620–634

INDEX

References are to Pages

EMPLOYEE STOCK OWNERSHIP PLANS
—Cont'd
Fiduciary Duty of ESOP Trustee, 636–638
Tax advantages, 634–636

FEDERAL SECURITIES LAWS
See also Proxy Regulations
Generally, 335, 737–739
Antifraud provisions, 742–743
Asset sales, 736–737
Chapter 11 reorganizations, 1076–1080
Disclosure, See Disclosure
Exchange reorganizations, 739–741
Fiduciary duty (common law), 743–765
    Rule 10b–5, 744–751, 755–756
    Section 14(e), 751–754, 756–760
Insider trading, See Insider Trading
Merger negotiations, 801–821
Proxy regulations, See Proxy Regulations
Section 14(e), bidder's standing to sue, 760–765
Statutory mergers, 735–736
Tender offers, effect on, 728–732
Williams Act, See Williams Act
Workouts, 1038–1044

FIDUCIARY DUTY
See also Independent Directors
Bondholders, in leveraged transactions, 183–197
ESOP trustee in tender offer, 636–638
Pension plan trustee in a tender offer, 636–646
Shareholders (acquiror's), boards duty to, 702–705
Shareholders (target's), boards duty to, 705–727
    Fair value in squeeze out mergers, 726–727
    Frozen-in minority, 706–708
    Frozen-out minority, 708–725
Standing to sue-bidder for target's breach, 657–658

FOREIGN ACQUISITIONS (Exon–Florio provision)
Generally, 1017–1019, 1023
National security test, 1019–1022

FRAUDULENT CONVEYANCE LAWS
See also Bulk Sales Act
Fraudulent Conveyance Acts, 201
Leveraged buyouts, application to, 201–207, 209–215

GOING PRIVATE TRANSACTIONS
Generally, 396–399

GOLDEN PARACHUTES
See also Antitakeover Devices, Tin Parachutes
Tax legislation, 969–972

GREENMAIL
Generally, 660–668
Tax legislation, 972–973

HART–SCOTT–RODINO ANTITRUST IMPROVEMENTS ACT
Generally, 997, 999–1000, 1004–1005
Confidentiality of filings, 1006–1008
Enforcement, 1008–1012
Interpretative rules, 1000–1005
Notification of proposed acquisition, 997–999
Waiting period, 1005–1006

INDEPENDENT DIRECTORS
Personal liability, 529–545
Management buyouts, evaluation of, 573–590, 591–604
Selling the firm, standard of review, 545–577
Waiver of liability by corporation, 606

INSIDER TRADING
Generally, 871–874
Misappropriation of information, 874–877
Short swing profits, 877–890
Tender offers, effect on pre-bid stock prices, 866–871

LEVERAGE
See also Leveraged Buyouts
Taxation, effect on beverage, 947–957

LEVERAGED BUYOUTS
See also Management Buyouts
Generally, 591–605, 1024–1025
Accounting for leveraged buyouts, 917–921
Bankruptcy benefits, 1046–1048
Fraudulent conveyance laws, impact on LBOs, 201–207, 209–215
History in the 1980's, 12–28
Investment banker liability, 607–612
Post LBO creditors, rights of, 216–217
Reverse leveraged buyouts, 408–414
RJR Nabisco Inc., In re- the high water mark of LBOs, 591–605
Successor liability, 322–323
Tax revenues, effect on, 966–968
Workouts, 1027–1035

MANAGEMENT BUYOUTS
See also Leveraged Buyouts
Generally, 401
Disclosure obligations, 401–403
Independent directors, evaluation by, 573–590, 591–604
Standard of review, 574–578

MERGER NEGOTIATIONS, DISCLOSURE
Generally, 788–791, 799
Disclosure, duty of, 796–799, 801
Federal Securities Laws, 801–821
Materiality, 791–796
New York Stock Exchange listing rules, 821–825
Securities and Exchange Commission releases, 788–791, 799–801

MERGERS
See also Triangular Mergers

INDEX

References are to Pages

MERGERS—Cont'd
Generally, 1
Circumvention of statutory rights, 102–109, 110–111
Employee rights, See Employee Rights
Squeeze-out mergers, 705–706, 708–725
Statutory mergers, State Corporate Codes, 162–163
Tax, A reorganizations, 923

METROMEDIA
Metromedia buyout, 612

MILLS ACQUISITION CO. v. MACMILLAN INC.
MacMillan acquisition, 553–573

MODEL BUSINESS CORPORATION ACT
Generally, 42, 45–46
Dissolved corps, 282
Dividend & Redemption Restrictions, 200
Shareholder Appraisal Rights, 53, 57–58

NEW YORK STOCK EXCHANGE
Merger negotiation rules, 821–825
Shareholder voting requirements, 114–117
Shark repellent amendment restrictions, 478–479

PARAMOUNT COMMUNICATIONS, INC., v. TIME, INC.
Time–Warner merger, 646–655

PENSION PLANS
Generally, 264–265
Buyer's liability, 265–267
Employee's Retirement Income Security Act, 266–269
Overfunded plans, 269–270
Seller's liability, 267–269, 271–276
Trustee's fiduciary liability in a tender offer, 636–646

POISON PILL PLANS
Generally, 485–493, 498–509
Boards of directors, restrictions on powers of, 515–518
Discriminating plans, 510–513
Proxy consent solicitations, unapproved, 519–523
Supervoting plans, 523–526
Tax legislation, 973
Topology, 493–497
Call plans, 494–497
Put plans, 497

PROJECTIONS, DISCLOSURE OF
Generally, 825–826, 836–839
Candor, duty of, 839–848
Disclosure, duty of, 820–836

PROXY REGULATIONS
See also Shareholder Voting
Generally, 132
Disclosure by corporation, 138–154
Adequate, 138–148
Mandatory disclosure debate, 148–154

PROXY REGULATIONS—Cont'd
Future corporate performance, 134–137
Statutory requirements, 133–134

PROXY STATEMENTS
See also Disclosure
Amend, duty to, 801–808
Antifraud liability, 765–772
Proxy contests, disclosure in, 853–859

RJR NABISCO, INC., IN RE
RJR buyout, 591–605

REVLON, INC. v. MAC ANDREWS & FORBES HOLDINGS, INC.
Pantry Pride hostile takeover attempt, 545–553

RULE 10b–5
Bidder's public promises, 859–865
Fiduciary duties (federal common law), 744–751, 755–756

SHAMROCK HOLDINGS, INC. v. POLAROID CORP.
Polaroid reorganization, 620–634

SHAREHOLDER APPRAISAL RIGHTS
Generally, 52–54
Exclusivity of the remedy, 75–85
Delaware, 75–83
Other jurisdictions, 83–85
Fair value, 59–74
Interpretation of fair value, 59–71
Valuation approaches, 71–74
Procedure, 57–58
Purposes of the remedy, 55–57
Squeeze out mergers, 726–727
Stock market exception, 54

SHAREHOLDER VOTING
Generally, 126–127
Circumvention of statutory rights, 86–111
Asset sales, 86–92
Long-term supply contracts, 110–111
Mergers, 102–109
Partnerships, 109–110
Tender offers, 92–94
Triangular mergers, 94–102
Class voting, 46–49
De facto merger doctrine, 86–92
New York Stock Exchange listing requirements—relevance to shareholder voting, 114–117
Shareholder resolutions, 527–529
Voting not to vote, 117–121, 128–131

SHARK REPELLENT AMENDMENTS
Generally, 469–478
Corporate code requirements, 469–472
New York Stock Exchange restrictions on, 478–479
SEC restrictions on, 479–484

SHORT SWING PROFITS, 877–890

SMITH v. VAN GORKOM
Trans Union takeover, 529–545

STANDSTILL AGREEMENTS
Successor firm, extension of agreement to, 169–175

STATE CORPORATE CODES
See also Delaware Corporate Code, Model Business Corporation Act
Generally, 41–42
Chapter 11 reorganizations, 1067–1075
Constituency statutes, 658
Disclosure, 786
Dividend and redemption restrictions, 197–200
Equivalent transactions treated alike, 111–116
    California Corporations Code, 111–112
    Public policy, 112–113
    Stock exchange listing requirements, 114–116
Extraterritorial effects, 49–50
Model Business Corporation Act, 42, 45–46
Purposes, 42
Race to laxity debate, 117

STOCK ACQUISITIONS
See also Tender Offers
Buybacks, See Buybacks
State corp. code, 92–94
Statutory exchange offers, 739–741
Street sweeps, 374–379
Tax, B reorganizations, 923

STOCK EXCHANGES
See also New York Stock Exchange
Listing requirements, 114–116
Mandatory disclosure, 116–117

STREET SWEEPS, 374–379

SUCCESSOR LIABILITY
Generally, 155–162, 276–277
Asset acquisitions, 277–281
Bargaining theory, 160–162
Bondholders, fiduciary duty to in leveraged transactions, 183–200
Collective bargaining agreements, See Collective Bargaining Agreements
Dissolved corporations, 282–287
Employee discrimination, 298–303
Employee statutory protections, See Employee Rights
Environmental torts, 304–317
Lender liability, 329–334
Parent liability for subsidiary, 318–329
Pension plans, See Pension Plans
Preexisting contract rights, acquisition effect on, 163–183
    Asset acquisitions, 175
    Debt obligations, 175–180
    Intellectual property rights, 163–168
    Leases, 181–183
    Standstill agreements, 169–175
Preexisting obligations, statutory merger effect on, 162–163

SUCCESSOR LIABILITY—Cont'd
Products liability, 287–298

TAKEOVERS
Economic analysis of takeovers in the 1980's, 1–10
Future in the 1990's, 28–29
Public policies, 10–11, 29–33

TAXATION
Generally, 921–922, 941–942
Antitakeover tax legislation, 968–973
Application to mergers and acquisitions, 921–922
Debt-equity distinction, 957–958
Debt limitations, 960–961
Deductibility of acquisition expenses, 973–978
Leveraged buyouts, effect on tax revenues, 966–968
Leverage, effect of taxation on, 947–957
Original issue discount instruments, 959–960
State tax law, 961–962
Taxable exchange v. tax-free reorganization, 940–941
Tax attributes, 940, 942–947
Tax-free reorganizations, See Tax–Free Reorganizations
Tax law, proposals to reform, 962–966

TAX–FREE REORGANIZATIONS
Generally, 922–923
Classification conflicts, 934–938
Internal revenue code sections, 923–926
Mechanics, 938–939
Policy considerations, 931–934
Taxable exchange—comparison to, 940–941
Tax attributes, 940
Treasury regulations, 926–931

TENDER OFFERS
See also Buybacks, Stock Acquisitions
Generally, 92–94
Bidder, definition of, 379–385
Conditional offers, 354–357
Contested exchange tender offer, 732–735
Definition of tender offer, 361–374
Disclosure obligations of target, 385–392
    Bidder's tender offer, 386–392
    Third-party tender offer, 385
Securities laws effect on tender offers, 357–358, 728–732
Self tender offers, 393
Shareholders, equal treatment for, 358–361
Standing to sue—bidder for target's breach, 657–658
Third-party offers, 351–352, 385

TRIANGULAR MERGERS
State corporate codes, 94–102
Tax, D reorganizations, 923

TRIANGULAR MERGERS—Cont'd
Ual buyout, 239–242

WILLIAMS ACT
Effect on tender offers, 357–358
Issuer Buybacks v. Leveraged Buyouts, 401–403
Section 13(d) Disclosure of 5 percent ownership, 335–351
    Effect of section 13(d) on takeovers, 338–339
    Proposed rule, 335–336

WILLIAMS ACT—Cont'd
Section 13(d) Disclosure of 5 percent ownership—Cont'd
    Remedies for violators, 339–351
Section 13(e) self tender offering, 393
Section 14(d) Third-party tender offers, 351–352, 385

WORKOUTS
Federal securities laws, 1038–1044
Participants, 1027–1035
Preexisting contracts, 1035–1037
State law rights, 1037–1038

†